China Law Deskbook

A Legal Guide for Foreign-Invested Enterprises

Second Edition

中国法律手册

James M. Zimmerman, Esq.

吉莫曼

ABA Section of International Law
Your Gateway to International Practice

ABA
Defending Liberty
Pursuing Justice

China Law Deskbook
A Legal Guide for Foreign-Invested Enterprises
Second Edition

James M. Zimmerman, Esq.
Beijing, People s Republic of China

吉莫曼

Cover design by Grey Cat Design.
Interior design by Lachina Publishing Services.

The materials contained herein represent the opinions and views of the authors and/or the editors, and should not be construed to be the views or opinions of the law firms or companies with whom such persons are in partnership with, associated with, or employed by, nor of the American Bar Association or the Section of International Law, unless adopted pursuant to the bylaws of the Association.

Nothing contained in this book is to be considered as the rendering of legal advice, either generally or in connection with any specific issue or case. Nor do these materials purport to explain or interpret any specific bond or policy, or any provisions thereof, issued by any particular insurance company, or to render insurance or other professional advice. Readers are responsible for obtaining advice from their own lawyer or other professional. This book and any forms and agreements herein are intended for educational and informational purposes only.

08 07 06 05 04 5 4 3 2 1

Zimmerman, James M., 1958–
China law deskbook : a legal guide for foreign-invested enterprises / James M. Zimmerman.— 2nd ed.
p. cm.
Includes bibliographical references and index.
ISBN 1-59031-364-X
1. Business law—China. 2. Business enterprises, Foreign—Law and legislation—China. 3. Investments, Foreign—Law and legislation—China. I. Title
KNQ 78.BB7Z56 2004
346.5107—dc22
2004011191
CIP

Discounts are available for books ordered in bulk. Special consideration is given to state bars, CLE programs, and other bar-related organizations. Inquire at Book Publishing, ABA Publishing, American Bar Association, 321 N. Clark, Chicago, Illinois 60610.

www.abanet.org

Summary of Contents

Contents

Foreword

China is going through remarkable times, and the ongoing judicial and legislative reforms are something that China has much to be proud about. It has developed, and continues to develop, a legal system from scratch in just over twenty years. But the ongoing developments make China a business environment that is perceived by many to be complex, uncertain, and, in short, a work in progress. Having lived and worked permanently in China since 1998, I have had the unique and rewarding opportunity of witnessing the extraordinary development of China's legal and economic systems, and have come to appreciate the trends, tribulations, and victories that are evident in a country that is on a quest to elevate itself to a position as a respected member of the international community.

Recognizing the complexities and uncertainty created by the ongoing legal developments, I wrote the original *China Law Deskbook* in the mid-1990s, and it was published in 1999. Today, much has happened in China since the original *Deskbook* was published, and keeping up with all of the changes to the law has been a challenge. My objective in writing the second edition, as with the original edition, is to create a research tool that, in simple language and backed by supporting research materials, highlights the key laws and regulations that may be of interest to foreign investors, corporate lawyers, and private practitioners involved or interested in China on behalf of their clients. A premier value of the *Deskbook* is its reference to the actual laws and regulations, and information that is accessible online through the Internet or fee-based services. The goal of the *Deskbook* is to be one tool in the China law repertoire of resources that can ease the research needs of practitioners.

I am grateful to many people I have worked with over the years—partners, associates, legal assistants, colleagues in the legal community, and clients—who have supported this writing project, and there are too many individuals to include everyone by name. I am also grateful to the members of the Chinese bar who have offered encouragement with respect to the *Deskbook,* as well as those who have played vital roles in law exchanges between the foreign bar in China and the Chinese bar. These legal exchanges have done much to improve and enhance the relationship between Chinese and American lawyers, and they will continue to help us improve upon our respective legal systems.

I welcome the comments, insights, and thoughts of my colleagues in the business and legal communities. If you have questions concerning the *Deskbook,* or wish to view updates and new materials, please visit http://www.chinalawdeskbook.com.

James M. Zimmerman
Beijing, China
September 2004

About the Author

James M. Zimmerman is a partner with the law firm of Squire, Sanders & Dempsey L.L.P., and is the Chief Representative for the firm's Beijing, People's Republic of China, office. Mr. Zimmerman is recognized as one of Asia's leading business lawyers in the categories of Chinese Law and Dispute Resolution in the *AsiaLaw Leading Lawyers Survey 2002 and 2003* (published by Euromoney Publications). He is the author of numerous publications, including the original 1999 version of the *China Law Deskbook: A Legal Guide for Foreign-Invested Enterprises,* a publication of the American Bar Association. Mr. Zimmerman is also the author of *Extraterritorial Employment Standards of the United States: The Regulation of the Overseas Workplace* (Quorum/Greenwood Press 1992). Mr. Zimmerman has written a number articles and chapters on China law and international trade topics which are published in several national and international journals, including *The China Business Review, Cornell International Law Journal, International Labor Review, Hastings International and Comparative Law Review,* and *Boston College Environmental Affairs Law Review.* Mr. Zimmerman served as the Chair of the China Law Committee of the American Bar Association's Section on International Law & Practice from 1999 to 2003, and the Chair of the Legal Committee for the American Chamber of Commerce, People's Republic of China from 2002 to 2004. He received an MBA from the University of California, Irvine, in 1982, and a JD from the University of San Diego in 1987. Mr. Zimmerman is licensed in the State of California and has been a registered foreign lawyer in China since 1998. Mr. Zimmerman resides in Beijing with his wife, Ellen, and three daughters.

谨以此献给我的家人

List of Abbreviations

AMC	Asset Management Company
BOT	Build, operate, and transfer
CCP	Chinese Communist Party
CEPA	Closer Economic Partnership Arrangement
CIETAC	China International Economic and Trade Arbitration Commission
CIF	Cost, insurance, and freight
CBRC	China Banking Regulatory Commission
CIRC	China Insurance Regulatory Commission
COFTEC	Commission of Foreign Trade and Economic Cooperation (local branch of MOFCOM and sometimes referred to as COFCOM)
CSRC	China Securities Regulatory Commission
CJV	Contractual joint venture
EJV	Equity joint venture
FDI	Foreign Direct Investment
FEC	Foreign economic contract
FERC	Foreign exchange registration certificate
FESCO	Foreign Enterprise Service Corporation
FICLS	Foreign-Invested Company Limited by Shares
FIE	Foreign-invested enterprise or foreign investment enterprise
FOREX	Foreign exchange
GAC	General Administration of Customs (China Customs)
GATT	General Agreement on Trade and Tariff
GDP	Gross Domestic Product
HKSAR	Hong Kong Special Administrative Region
HTS	Harmonized Tariff Schedule
IAMC	Insurance Asset Management Company
LLC	Limited liability company
MFN	Most Favored Nation
MOC	Ministry of Construction
MOCT	Ministry of Culture
MOF	Ministry of Finance
MOFCOM	Ministry of Commerce
MOFTEC	Ministry of Foreign Trade and Economic Cooperation (currently merged into MOFCOM)

MOJ	Ministry of Justice
MOLSS	Ministry of Labor and Social Security
MOST	Ministry of Science and Technology
MPS	Ministry of Public Security (or Public Security Bureau)
NAO	National Audit Office
NPC	National People's Congress
OLA	Office of Legislative Affairs
PBOC	People's Bank of China
PRC	People's Republic of China
QFII	Qualified Foreign Institutional Investor
RMB	Renminbi
RO	Representative Office
SAFE	State Administration of Foreign Exchange
SAIC	State Administration of Industry and Commerce
SAQIEE	State Administration for Quarantine and Inspection of Exit/Entrance
SARFT	State Administration of Radio, Film, and Television
SASAC	State Asset Supervision and Administration Commission
SAT	State Administration of Taxation
SEPA	State Environmental Protection Administration
SEZ	Special Economic Zone
SFDA	State Food and Drug Administration (formerly the State Drug Administration)
SIPO	State Intellectual Property Office
SOE	State-owned enterprise
SRDC	State Reform and Development Commission (formerly the State Development Planning Commission)
VAT	Value-added tax
WFOE	Wholly foreign-owned enterprise
WTO	World Trade Organization

Chapter 1

Introduction: Trade, Politics, and Development of the Law in China

Twenty years ago, China was one of the world's poorest countries, with 80 percent of its population having a daily income of less than one dollar per day and an adult literacy rate of one-third.[1] Under Maoist China, the system was based upon communist ideology—totalitarian, egalitarian, and poor. Relatively speaking, China in the late 1970s had virtually no legal system and few laws and regulations in comparison with developed countries at that time. Commencing with its economic reforms in 1978, the country's average annual growth rate has been approximately 8 to 10 percent per year, and in several peak years, the economy grew by 13 percent.[2]

When Deng Xiaoping came to power in 1978, he set into motion reforms to privatize agriculture and industry, welcomed foreign investors on a restricted basis, and attempted to decentralize economic and political decision making. Today, illiteracy has dropped to below 10 percent, consumption has more than doubled, and the poverty rate has declined by 60 percent.

China's growth has been fueled by foreign direct investment (FDI), which continues to increase annually. FDI in China has increased at a rate of 18 percent each year for the past sixteen years. FDI topped at $2 billion in 1986, $52.7 billion in 2002, and over $57 billion in 2003. By the end of 2003, China had approved almost 400,000 foreign-invested enterprises

---

1. The People's Republic of China has the highest population of any country in the world. As reported in 2000, China has over 1.26 billion people, which represents one-fifth of the entire world population. China Statistical Press, China Statistical Yearbook 2000, at 96.

2. Z. Hu & M. Khan, *Why Is China Growing So Fast?*, International Monetary Fund, Economic Issues No. 8 (1997), available on the IMF Web site at http://www.imf.org/external/pubs/ft/Issues8.

(FIEs) with a contractual value of over $750 billion from 180 countries, including FIEs from 400 of the world's 500 largest multinational enterprises.[3] The value of new contracts in 2003 rose only 7.3 percent per year compared to 2002, but the number of contracts has increased by 23.3 percent, which indicates that projects are smaller in value than in previous years.

U.S. exports to China have also risen significantly in the past few years, particularly with respect to telecommunications, power generation, oil and gas exploration, chemicals, aircraft, fertilizer, wheat/cereal products, and construction machinery.[4] China's airport infrastructure construction is anticipated to reach an estimated sum of $8.4 billion, and aircraft sales are estimated at $10–15 billion over the next ten years.[5] U.S. firms are pursuing a number of untapped markets in China, including pharmaceuticals, automotive components, automotive production machinery, medical equipment and devices, and transportation.

In addition to relaxing the standards for FDI, the government is encouraging the growth of the private sector and has taken steps to reform its state sector. In December 2003, the PRC government unveiled an anticipated proposed constitutional amendment that provides that the "lawful private assets" of citizens are "inviolable."[6] Under the amendment, the government

---

3. Many foreign companies are expanding their operations in China, including an increase in research and development investments. A few examples in 2003 include the following investments: Dupont China Holdings Ltd. announced that it would invest up to $100 million in an R&D operation in Shanghai; Honeywell committed an initial $18 million for an R&D center in China; Lucent Technologies committed to invest $50 million to an R&D facility to develop CDMA2000 standards; and Motorola announced a $500 million research facility investment in Beijing. *See* The U.S.-China Business Council, China Operations 2003, Analysis: Foreign Investment in China, First Half 2003, at 21.

4. DOC China Commercial Guide, at 1.

5. DOC China Commercial Guide, at 3, 15.

6. *See generally* C. Hutzler, *China to Protect Private Property in Constitution,* Wall St. J. (Dec. 22, 2003); *China Legislature Proposes Amendment For Pvt Ppty Rights,* Dow Jones Newswires (Dec. 22, 2003). The official Chinese news agency, Xinhua, states that the proposed amendment would put private property "on an equal footing with public property." The amendments were adopted at the March 2004 NPC meeting. Another amendment proposed would enshrine in the constitution the Three Represents theories of Jiang Zemin, which provides that the party must represent the interests of the business community and entrepreneurs, as well as the working class. Jiang's theory is accepted as official party policy. *See generally Constitution to Embrace "Three Represents" and Private Property,* Xinhua News Agency (Dec. 22, 2003), available online at http://www.xinhuanet.com; *Constitutional Amendments to Have Far-Reaching Influence,* Xinhua News Agency (Dec. 28, 2003), available online at http://www.xinhuanet.com; *Amended Constitution Published,* available on the Web site of the Supreme People's Court at http://www.chinacourt.org (March 16, 2004). The 2004 amendments to the constitution also confirm state support for human rights; provide that compensation shall be paid to property owners for any expropriation of land by the state; change the references to "martial law" to "state of emergency"; and recognize that delegates to the NPC from special administrative regions (i.e., HKSAR, Macao SAR) may be elected. *NPC Concludes: Enacts 14 Amendments, Approves Work Report,* China Market Intelligence, The U.S.-China Business Council (March 18, 2004). Article 13 of the Constitution was amended to provide that the "lawful private property of citizens shall not be violated. The state shall protect private property rights and inheritance rights of citizens in accordance with the law. The state may, in the public interest, expropriate or requisition private property of citizens in accordance with the law and shall provide compensation therefore." Under Article 33, the following clause was added: "The state respects and preserves human rights."

would be committed to protecting both private wealth and inheritance rights. While the amendment will grant the government the right of expropriation of private property rights, the amendment also requires that compensation be provided to private property owners. In contrast, the current version of the Constitution emphasizes that public property is not only inviolable but "sacred." The amendment is designed to provide legal basis for the protection of private property for the first time in China since the commencement of the Communist era in 1949. The protection of private property is considered essential to continuing to push forward with China's economic reforms. Such changes are meant to bring China's legal framework in line with its increasingly capitalist economy and in response to its WTO obligations. Entrepreneurs who are playing an increasingly critical role in job growth have been lobbying for the constitutional protection. However, the amendment does not elevate the status of private property to the same status as state-owned property, which will continue to maintain a dominant role in the economy.

China continues to dismantle its cradle-to-grave system that has financially stifled the state sector for years. In this regard, the government issued a joint opinion in April 2002 designed to improve the competitiveness and financial standing of state-owned enterprises (SOEs) by reducing their social service obligations.[7] The basic national policy continues to concentrate on economic reform so as to raise the living standard of the Chinese people.[8] As a result of economic reforms, large Chinese companies have expanded aggressively in the global markets.[9]

7. Opinions on Advancing Separation of Social Service Functions from State Owned Enterprises, promulgated April 2002 jointly by the State Economic and Trade Commission, Ministry of Finance, Ministry of Education, Ministry of Health, Ministry of Labor and Social Security, and Ministry of Construction. The order applies only to SOEs owned by governments at the provincial level or below, and not to the larger SOEs, which are under the direct supervision of the central government. The central government plans to devise a separate set of rules for larger SOEs. The order emphasizes that existing subsidies for housing, medical care, and other services are required to be reflected in workers' salaries. The order requires that within three years of promulgation, the social service organizations (i.e., schools, hospitals, housing, and other service departments) owned and operated by provincial SOEs to be separated from the parent enterprises. Social service organizations owned and operated by SOEs in less-developed areas are granted a five-year time period to separate from the parent enterprises. The order does not set deadlines for SOEs located in rural areas. Educational facilities separated from their parent SOEs are to be transferred to local governments. Former parent companies and local governments are required to provide operating funds to separated institutions for the first three to five years. After five years, local governments will provide all funds. SOE hospitals may either operate independently, merge with other existing facilities, or close. Other SOE service departments, such as housing and utility maintenance services, must form for-profit companies providing services to the public after separating from their parent companies. Though this plan to reform SOEs is a step forward, it will be difficult to implement. Hundreds of thousands of SOE employees will face reassignment, and many of them will lose their jobs. And the plan will not succeed without massive amounts of funding.

8. *See News Conference with Xie Feng, Chinese Embassy Spokesperson*, FEDERAL NEWS SERVICE, July 22, 2002, available on Lexis, News Library. In 2002, the GDP per capita of China was $800, which is one-fourth of Japan's.

9. Outbound investment by leading Chinese companies continued to increase in 2003 including the following examples: Sinopec Corp. and the State Oil Company of Azerbaijan Republic agreed to

In November 2001, the 140 member countries of the World Trade Organization (WTO) agreed to a set of documents that outline the terms pursuant to which China would be admitted as a member of the WTO (the "China/WTO Agreement"). China accepted the WTO's membership invitation by filing its Notice of Accession on November 11, 2001, and formally became a WTO member on December 11, 2001.[10]

China's WTO membership confirms China's policy of ongoing economic reform and is indicative that China has no intention of returning to the once planned economy that dragged the country to economic stagnation. The China/WTO Agreement, which subjects China to the WTO's rule-based system of international trade and commercial dealings, is the result of over twenty years of economic and legal reform that commenced in 1979.

Membership in the WTO is a reciprocal arrangement. While China must grant national treatment and nondiscrimination to foreign suppliers of goods, WTO member countries like the United States are prohibited from placing an embargo on Chinese goods, discriminating with regard to tariff rates, or imposing unilateral sanctions. Thus, a foreign investor in China need not fear the impact of the annual ups and downs of political relations between China and the United States.[11]

After World War II, China, by and through the Nationalist Government, was an original party to the 1947 General Agreement on Tariffs and Trade (GATT). When the Communist Government in China came to power in 1949 (after the Nationalist Government fell and sought refuge in Taiwan), it withdrew from GATT because it was no longer willing to honor the tariff concessions and open trade obligations of the trade agreement. In 1986, the People's Republic of China applied to reactivate its membership. In 1995, after being informed that it could not resume its membership, China notified the WTO that it would apply for accession to World Trade Organization under Article XII of the Marrakesh Agreement Establishing the WTO and,

---

a $140 million transaction for the rehabilitation of an onshore oilfield in Azerbaijan; PetroChina Co., Ltd., and the government of Sudan agreed to invest approximately $1 billion to expand Sudan's largest refinery and oil pipeline. *See* THE U.S.-CHINA BUSINESS COUNCIL, CHINA OPERATIONS 2003, ANALYSIS: FOREIGN INVESTMENT IN CHINA, FIRST HALF 2003, at 21.

10. *See generally* M. Dudek & A. Wang, *China's Long WTO March*, CHINA L. & PRAC. (April 2001).

11. Prior to membership in the WTO, China's most favored nation (MFN) status with the United States was subject to annual review and renewal by the U.S. government. The annual review process was a source of tension between the pro-China business lobby and those opposed to open trade with China as a result of several sensitive issues such as weapon sales, human rights violations, aggression toward Taiwan, trade imbalances, and other reasons. The Congressional-Executive Commission on China (CECC) has released a number of reports critical of China's human rights practices and security-related issues. For copies of the reports, testimony, and other materials, *see* http://www.cecc.gov.

as a result, China was required to go through the time-consuming process applicable to new WTO members.

The WTO entry process first required that China prepare and submit a memorandum covering all WTO-related criteria of its trade and economic policies. From 1995 to 2001, China provided the WTO with detailed information concerning its policies, which was submitted to a Working Party of WTO member country representatives.[12]

The purpose of the WTO Accession Working Party (hereinafter the "Working Party") was to draft and negotiate a Protocol of Accession (POA), which includes the binding terms and conditions applicable to China's accession to the trade organization.[13] The Protocol of Accession contains commitments and clarifications as to matters that may be covered by WTO Agreements. The Protocol of Accession also includes a *Report of the Working Party* in which the Working Party addresses how China's laws and regulations and rules conform to the WTO agreements and obligations. The *Report of the Working Party* includes specific "commitment paragraphs," which are concessions made by China to gain admission to the WTO and *Market Access Schedules* for agricultural goods, manufacturers, and services sector.[14]

The Market Access Schedules, which comprise a comprehensive set of schedules setting forth timetables for market entry, are based upon the bilaterally negotiated agreements between China and various WTO members. If one country negotiates favorable terms, such terms apply to all member countries and, in the event of a conflict, the most favorable concession terms apply to all members. The key bilateral agreements include the November 15, 1999, U.S./China Agreement[15] between the United States and China and the

12. In 1987, the Working Party for China was first formed to evaluate China's request to resume its GATT membership. In 1995, the original Working Party was converted to a WTO Accession Working Party when China applied for membership under Article XII of the WTO Agreement.

13. The Protocol requires that China is subject to all WTO Agreements on accession (December 11, 2001), unless otherwise noted in the Agreement. Most of the exceptions are outlined in the Annexes attached to the Protocol.

14. In contrast to the Protocol of Accession, which is relatively short and describes how the WTO Agreements will be applied to China, the *Report of the Working Party* is a detailed examination and evaluation of China's trade and foreign investment system. The *Report* outlines the questions of the Working Party Member country representatives and China's responses thereto, which explains how China's existing legal system conforms to WTO Agreement obligations. In some situations, China provided information and evidence that its current laws and regulations already conformed to WTO requirements, while in other instances China recognizes the need to change its laws and outlines its formal commitments as to how the system will be amended.

15. The United States played a critical role in negotiating China's accession to the WTO and was the first country to execute a bilateral agreement with China. The U.S./China WTO Agreement covered all agricultural products, industrial goods, and services sectors. The EU/China WTO Agreement covers those specific areas and products that were of key significance to the European Union.

WTO Agreements

Protocol of Accession

Report of the Working Party

Market Access Schedules

WTO China Annexes

Annex 1A:	Information to be Provided by China in the Context of the Transitional Review Mechanism
Annex 1B:	Issues to be addressed by the General Council in Accordance with Section 18.2 of China's Protocol of Accession
Annex 2A1:	Products Subject to State Trading (Import)
Annex 2A2:	Products Subject to State Trading (Export)
Annex 2B:	Products Subject to Designated Trading
Annex 3:	Non-Tariff Measures Subject to Phase Elimination
Annex 4:	Products and Services Subject to Price Controls
Annex 5A:	Notification pursuant to Article XXV of the Agreement on Subsidies and Countervailing Measures [i.e., List of Subsidies]
Annex 5B:	Subsidies to be Phased Out
Annex 6:	Products Subject to Export Duty
Annex 7:	Reservations by WTO Members
Annex 8:	Schedule of Concession and Commitments on Goods
Annex 9:	Schedule of Specific Commitments on Services

May 19, 2000, EU/China Agreement between the European Union and China.[16] The various bilateral agreements have been compiled into two schedules: China's Schedule of Concessions and Commitments on Goods[17] and China's Schedule of Specific Commitments on Services.[18]

16. The agreement with Mexico was the final bilateral agreement reached with China. In this regard, China agreed to allow Mexico to extend its current countervailing duties on 1,300 Chinese products for six years. A number of the Working Party Member countries were not willing to grant China full WTO rights. These reservations, from countries like Mexico, the Czech Republic, Poland, and the EU, are listed in Annex 8, together with timetables for the phasing out of these restrictions.

17. Document WT/ACC/CHN49/Add.1. See the Web site of the World Trade Organization at http://www.wto.org for copies of all WTO documents.

18. Document WT/ACC/CHN/49/Add.2.

A. China/WTO Agreements

In addition to being a Geneva-based international organization, the WTO is a compilation of over sixty separate trade agreements, protocols, and understandings that bind the member countries which, in general, set forth a rule-based system for international trade, intellectual property protection, and foreign direct investment. Of most critical importance are the General Agreement on Tariffs and Trade (GATT), the General Agreement on Trade in Services (GATS), and the Agreement on Trade-Related Aspects of Intellectual Property Rights (TRIPS).[19]

China's accession to the WTO requires that it adhere to all of these agreements in force on the date of accession (December 11, 2001), each of which constitutes a legally binding international obligation and supersedes any conflicting domestic (national or local) legislation. The Protocol further states that the China/WTO Agreements are to be registered under the provisions of Article 102 of the Charter of the United Nations, which represents its binding nature as an international obligation of all member countries.

The China/WTO Agreements set forth three types of commitments required for China's membership to the WTO including specific tariff reductions, market access for services, and commitments outlining the steps China will take to comply with its treaty obligations.

1. China's Commitment: Tariff Reductions

The *tariff reduction* commitments are set forth in China's Schedule of Concessions and Commitments on Goods.[20] As agreed upon in the China/WTO Agreements, industrial tariffs will decrease from an overall average of 24.6 percent in 1997 to an overall average of 9.4 percent by 2006. For industrial products, tariffs will decrease to 7.1 percent with the majority of tariff cuts fully implemented by 2004. For agricultural products, tariffs will be reduced from an overall average of 31.5 percent to 14.5 percent by January 2004. With a reduction of tariffs, foreign goods manufacturers will be able to import goods into China more cost-effectively.

2. China's Commitment: Market Access for Services

With respect to *market access for services*, China agreed to open various services sectors based upon a timetable of commitments. Under the Marrakesh

19. The Patent Law, Copyright Law, and Trademark Law have been amended prior to China's accession to WTO, and generally conform to TRIPS. Much work still needs to be done in the enforcement of China's intellectual property laws.

20. Document WT/ACC/CHN49/Add.1. *See generally China Begins Cutting Average Tariff Rate to 10.4%*, Xinhua News Agency (Jan. 2, 2004), available online at http://www.xinhuanet.com.

Tariff Reductions: Industrial Commodities

Commodity	*Pre-WTO Tariff*	*Tariff after Accession*
• Aerospace	10.5%	7.5%
• Agriculture	31%	14%
• Automobiles	80–100%	25% by 2006
• Chemicals	Up to 35%	0%, 5.5%, or 6.5%
• Elec/IT Products	Up to 35%	0% (select)
• Films/Videos	9–15%	5–10%
• Steel	7.5% average	6%
• Wood and paper	12–18% wood	5–7.5%
	15–25% paper	5–7.5%

Tariff Reductions: Agricultural Products

Commodity	*Pre-WTO Tariff*	*Tariff after Accession*
Beef	45%	12%
Grapes	40%	13%
Wine	65%	20%
Cheese	50%	12%
Poultry	20%	10%
Pork	20%	12%

Agreement of 1994, WTO member countries are required to commit to gradual opening of services through negotiations every five years under the General Agreement on Services (GATS). The negotiations between the member states and China in regard to market access to the services industry were contentious. While most developed countries, including the U.S. and EU countries, demanded greater access to China's services industry, China's negotiators had requested developing country status, which would have allowed China to keep its services industry effectively closed to foreign participation.[21] After years of debate, member countries conditioned their respective bilateral agreements

21. During negotiations, China requested that it be treated as a developing country, rather than a developed country. The difference would have allowed China to be given greater flexibility if considered a developing country. Although the per capita income of its people justified treatment as a developing country, it was the view of the U.S. and EU that China's strong GDP, foreign trade (over $350 billion

upon specific commitments from China to open its telecommunications, insurance, banking, securities, audio-visual, and professional services sectors.[22]

China's Schedule of Specific Commitments on Services in Annex 9, Part II of the Working Party Report ("Access Schedule") contains specific commitments in regard to the opening of various services sectors and outlines the phase-in period with regard to how and when the sector will be opened. The following briefly outlines the market-access commitments made by China:

a. Automobiles and Automotive Industry

All restrictions on the types and models of cars produced locally will be lifted two years after accession. Motor vehicle joint ventures will be able to have provincial level approvals if under $60 million after one year, $90 million after two years, and $150 million after four years from accession. China agreed to allow nonbank, foreign financial institutions to be able to provide financing for all forms of motor vehicles. Upon accession, the 50-percent maximum foreign ownership for engine joint ventures will be lifted and allows wholly foreign-owned production of engines.[23]

b. Banking and Financial Institutions

China committed to imposing only "prudential" measures in regard to the licensing of foreign-invested banks; namely, that there will be no economic needs test or quantitative limits on licenses. Within five years of accession, all nonprudential measures restricting ownership and operation of foreign financial institutions will be phased out. Upon accession to WTO, China agreed to eliminate all geographic or customer restrictions for foreign currency business, and that the local RMB currency business will be phased in on a regional basis, and will be free from all geographic restrictions five years after accession. Foreign operators will be permitted to provide local

---

in 2000), and successful foreign investment program did not justify treatment as a developing country. The Working Party granted China a measure of developing country status (such as in agriculture and the phase-in of its full WTO compliance), but in most areas, the Working Party asked and expected full compliance as required of developed countries.

22. GATS requires members to open their services sectors, but GATS participation by WTO member countries is not mandatory. As a consequence, many WTO members have not taken the liberty to open their services industries to foreign participation.

23. *See generally* W. Yi, *China's WTO Compliance and Foreign Investment in the Auto Industry,* China L. & Prac. (Feb. 2003). For a discussion of the automobile finance rules, *see* Chapter 11, Financial Regulation, § D.3.

currency services to Chinese enterprises two years after accession, and to all Chinese customers five years after accession (2006).[24]

c. Construction and Engineering

China has agreed to allow for majority foreign-owned joint ventures in the construction industry upon accession, and wholly foreign-owned construction enterprises after three years (December 2004).[25]

d. Distribution, Trading Rights, and Retail Services

Prior to entry into WTO, China jealously guarded trading rights issued to state-run import/export companies, which stifled competition for imports, as well as reduced domestic companies' access to export markets. In recent years, trading rights have gradually been extended to a much wider range of companies, including Chinese domestic companies, as part of China's market reforms. But the law currently prohibits individuals from undertaking foreign trade (i.e., import and export activities). Under the amendment to the Foreign Trade Law adopted in 2004, all individuals, legal entities, and organizations may participate in foreign trade.[26]

Within one year after accession (December 2002) foreign investors will be allowed to establish joint ventures with minority interests to engage in the wholesale business of most imported and domestically produced goods (with the exception of certain commodities listed in Annex 2 such as books, newspapers, magazines, pharmaceuticals, pesticides, chemical fertilizers, processed oil, and crude oil). Two years after accession (December 2003) foreign majority ownership of joint ventures with trading rights will be allowed, and wholly foreign-owned enterprises will be allowed three years after accession (December 2004). After five years (December 2006), foreign enterprises may begin to distribute certain restricted products such as chemical fertilizers, processed oil, and crude oil.

In June of 2003, the Ministry of Commerce and General Administration of Customs jointly issued a notice allowing free-trade zones (FTZs) in Shanghai (Waigaoqiao), Shenzhen (Futian, Shatoujiao, and Yantian), Tianjin, and Xiamen (Xiangyu) to grant trading rights to enterprises in those

24. *See generally* C. Wei, M. De Sombre, and H. Zhang, *China Post-WTO Reforms in Financial Services: Achievements and Challenges*, CHINA L. & PRAC. (March 2003).

25. For a discussion of the laws and regulations concerning the construction industry, *see* Chapter 5, Foreign Investment Guidelines and Industry-Specific Regulations, § B.5; Chapter 7, Contract Law, § B.7; and Chapter 8, Tender Law and Government Procurement.

26. For an analysis of the foreign trade law, *see* Chapter 5, Foreign Investment Guidelines and Industry-Specific Regulations, § B.12.

zones.[27] Under the FTZ Trading Rights Notice, enterprises in the four FTZs are authorized to enjoy the same treatment as the non-FTZ enterprises in the same regions with respect to the right to freely import and export goods. The provisions are designed to provide FTZ enterprises with more freedom to trade goods with non-FTZ entities and to dispense with the need to use a trade agent for transactions with domestic companies outside the zones.

Effective June 1, 2004, the Ministry of Commerce (MOFCOM) promulgated regulations addressing the activities of FIEs in the commercial and distribution sector.[28] The FIE Commercial Sector Regulations specify the standards by which foreign-invested commercial enterprises may conduct retail, wholesale, franchise, or commission agency business.

e. Health Care: Medical and Dental Services

Upon accession in December 2001, China agreed to allow qualified foreign operators the right to provide medical and dental services through foreign majority-owned joint venture hospitals or clinics "with quantitative limitations in line with China's needs." However, China provides that the majority of medical personnel of JV hospitals or clinics be Chinese nationals, although foreign doctors are permitted to provide "short-term medical services" after obtaining authorization from the relevant government authorities.[29]

f. Insurance Services

China's WTO obligations provide that China will allow foreign insurers selling nonlife insurance to establish joint ventures with 51-percent ownership upon accession, and, after two years (December 2003), they will be allowed to establish wholly foreign-owned branches with "no form of establishment restrictions." Foreign life insurance companies are permitted to establish joint ventures with 50-percent ownership upon accession.

Foreign insurance brokerage firms of large-scale commercial risks (including reinsurance and international marine, aviation, and transport insurance and reinsurance) are allowed to establish joint ventures with

---

27. Notice on Trial Work Granting Import and Export Rights to the Enterprises in the Four FTZs (issued by MOFCOM and GAC in June 2003) (hereinafter the "FTZ Trading Rights Notice"). *See generally* W. Fu, *Establishment & Operation of WFOEs in Free Trade Zones,* China L. & Prac. (June 2003).

28. Regulations for the Administration of Foreign Invested Enterprises in the Commercial Sector (issued on April 16, 2004, by the Ministry of Commerce) (hereinafter the "FIE Commercial Sector Regulations").

29. The Access Schedule defines "short-term service" as six months with the possibility of another six-month extension. For an analysis of the regulations of foreign investments in hospitals and clinics, *see* Chapter 5, Foreign Investment Guidelines and Industry-Specific Regulations, § B.15.

foreign equity to a maximum of 50 percent upon accession; 51 percent after three years; and after five years, wholly owned subsidiaries will be authorized. China has further committed to seven new insurance licenses, five for life insurance and two for nonlife insurance companies, and an additional two foreign insurance companies will be allowed to establish in a second city.[30]

g. Foreign-Produced Films

Pursuant to its WTO commitments, China will increase the quota on imports of foreign films to forty films per year (up from ten per year in 2001). In three years after accession (December 2004), China will further raise the import quota to fifty films per year, of which twenty will be on a revenue-sharing basis.[31]

h. Pharmaceuticals

Foreign investors will be allowed to engage in the wholesale distribution and retail sales of pharmaceutical products within three years of China's accession to WTO (December 2004). However, China has reserved the right to exercise price controls over certain imported and domestically produced pharmaceuticals.[32]

i. Professional Services: Law Firms and Accounting Firms

Upon accession to WTO, foreign-owned accounting firms are authorized to provide taxation and management consulting services, and are no longer required to have a local Chinese partner. Foreign-owned law firms are allowed to provide expanded legal services and to establish a presence in multiple cities.[33]

j. Telecommunications Services

Pursuant to the Access Schedule, foreign investors may hold a maximum 25 percent share in mobile voice and data services communications upon

30. For information concerning China's WTO commitments in the insurance industry, see the Web site of the China Insurance Regulatory Commission at http://www.circ.gov.cn. On December 18, 2002, CIRC issued a press release that outlines the progress made to date concerning market access in the insurance industry. For a discussion of China's insurance laws and regulations, see Chapter 12, Insurance Law and Regulation.

31. For an analysis of the entertainment industry and opportunities for Sino-foreign film production, *see* Chapter 5, Foreign Investment Guidelines and Industry-Specific Regulations, § B.10.

32. For a discussion of the pharmaceutical industry and drug regulations in China, *see* Chapter 13, Consumer Protection, § G.

33. For a discussion of the rules governing foreign law firms and accountants in China, *see* Chapter 5, Foreign Investment Guidelines and Industry-Specific Regulations, §§ B.1, B.18.

accession, 35 percent stake after one year, and 49 percent after three years. With respect to value-added services such as Internet, paging, and other services, foreign operators may hold 30 percent ownership in companies located in Beijing, Shanghai, and Guangzhou upon accession. Two years after accession, geographic restrictions are lifted and foreign ownership interest may be up to 50 percent. Foreign operators in fixed line and long distance services can hold a 25 percent stake after three years and 49 percent after six years.[34]

3. China's Commitments: Treaty Obligations

In addition to China's agreement with respect to *tariff reductions* and *market access for services*, the China/WTO Agreement also addresses China's treaty obligations of WTO membership. The WTO treaty obligations, which consist of sixty separate treaties, agreements, and understandings that create a rule-based system of trade law developed over fifty years since the original negotiations, became applicable to China upon accession. The following are the most important agreements under WTO:

a. Agreements on Trade in Goods

The agreements on trade in goods are numerous and address a variety of trade-related matters including, but not limited to, the following: (a) that WTO member states convert nontariff barriers concerning agricultural commodities to tariffs only (i.e., Agreement on Agriculture); (b) that laws governing food safety, animal or plant health, and similar regulations be based upon objective and scientific data (i.e., Agreement on the Application of Sanitary and Phytosanitary Measures); and (c) that laws governing direct foreign investment afford national treatment and be transparent within two years of accession unless there is a recognized exception (i.e., Agreement on Trade-Related Investment Measures, or TRIMs).

b. Agreements on Trade Facilitation

The agreements on trade facilitation clarify the scope of the General Agreement on Tariffs and Trade and include (a) the Agreement on

34. *See also* Telecommunications Business Catalogue (issued on February 21, 2003, by the Ministry of Information Industries, and effective April 1, 2003). The Telecom Business Catalogue amends the standards for various telecom-related business and clarifies terms used in prior regulations to be consistent with WTO. See also Chapter 6, Information Technology, Telecommunications, and Software Development.

Implementation of Article VII of the GATT (Customs Valuation);[35] and (b) the Agreement on Import Licensing Procedures.[36]

c. Protocol of Accession: Matters Specific to China

The Protocol of Accession includes the binding terms and conditions applicable to China's accession to the trade body and clarifications as to matters that may be covered by WTO Agreements. Several issues raised in the Protocol include the following commitments:

(1) Administration of the Trade Regime. Upon accession, China agreed to apply a uniform administration of its trade regime throughout the entire country, including the Special Economic Zones border trade regions, minority autonomous areas, and other special zones.[37] China agreed to apply or

35. The Customs Valuation Agreement sets forth rules to unify the standards and procedures for customs valuation and recognizes in hierarchical order the five WTO-approved methods to determine the customs value of imported goods. The first method of valuation is the transaction value, and thereafter followed by several other valuation methods such as the identical goods transactions method, similar goods transactions method, the deductive method, and the computed method. To meet its commitments to abide by the Customs Valuation Agreement, China adopted the Measures of the Customs of the People's Republic of China for the Examination and Approval of the Dutiable Value of Import and Export Goods, promulgated and effective on January 1, 2002, by the General Customs Administration (hereinafter the "Customs Valuation Measures"). The Customs Valuation Measures recognize that the dutiable value of imported goods shall be examined and determined by Customs on the basis of the transaction price of the goods and shall include the freight, relevant expenses, and insurance incurred before the unloading of the goods at the port of discharge in the PRC. Also, the transaction price of the import goods shall mean the price actually paid or payable by the buyer for purchasing the goods and have been adjusted according to the following Articles 4 and 5 of the measures. The measures also specify proper methods for the calculation of freight, relevant expenses, and insurance in the dutiable value of import and export goods, and they also discuss legal liabilities and certain supplementary provisions. The Customs Valuation Measures supersede the "Measures of the Customs of People's Republic of China for the Examination and Approval of Dutiable Value of Import and Export Goods" implemented as from September 1, 1992, and the "Measures of the Customs of People's Republic of China for the Examination and Approval of Dutiable Value of the Goods Imported for Processing Trade" implemented as from October 1, 1999. For a discussion of customs rules and regulations, *see* Chapter 15, Customs and Trade Regulations.

36. The Agreement on Import Licensing is designed to simplify import licensing procedures by providing for transparency of regulatory standards and procedures, application submission timetables, and standards for the protection of confidential information. Member countries may elect to have either automatic or non-automatic licensing.

37. The licensing organizations and the licensing procedures for services industry participants are required to be published in an official publication. The policy of allowing an application only after an applicant is notified that it may apply will terminate. Fees charged to issue licenses will be based on administrative costs of providing the license, and not the value of the license itself. Applicants will be provided with written notice of the reasons for a rejection of their application, and reapplication will be allowed. Upon approval of a license, the applicant may commence business operations upon registration with the State Administration of Industry and Commerce and the effective date of a business license may not be postponed without justification. In August 2003, the Standing Committee of the 10th NPC adopted the Administrative Licensing Law, which comes into effect on July 1, 2004. The law is consistent with international practice and addresses the concerns of transparency in the licensing process and the elimination of administrative barriers to trade. *See generally New Licensing Law Cuts Through Gov't Red Tape,* CHINA DAILY ONLINE (Nov. 7, 2003), available online at http://www.chinadaily.com.cn. An unofficial translation of the Licensing Law is available on the Web site of the THE U.S.-CHINA BUSINESS COUNCIL at http://www.uschina.org.

administer its trade laws in a uniform, impartial, and reasonable manner, and local and provincial authorities will be bound by WTO obligations. China also agreed to establish a mechanism under which individuals and enterprises can bring to the attention of the government instances of "non-uniform application of the trade regime." China further agreed that only published laws, regulations, and other measures will be enforceable against WTO member countries and that China agreed to establish designated judicial tribunals that are empowered to make a prompt and impartial review of administrative actions affecting trade in goods and services.[38]

(2) Nondiscrimination. China agreed that foreign individuals, foreign enterprises, and foreign investment enterprises (FIEs) in China shall receive treatment that is "no less favorable" than domestic individuals and enterprises. The principle is referred to as "national treatment" and prohibits discrimination between foreign products/services and domestic products/services. WTO also prohibits discrimination between trading partners. This principle is also known as most favored nation treatment and applies with respect to (a) the procurement of inputs, goods, and services; and (b) prices and availability of transportation, energy, telecommunications, and utility resources.[39]

(3) Non-Tariff Barriers. Non-tariff barriers to trade have been a problem for importers for many years and significantly impact trade. The most prevalent form of such barriers is the import licensing system, quota allocations, and specific tendering requirements. After accession to WTO, China commits to phase out these requirements before or no later than the end of 2006. Annex 3 lists all products subject to licensing, quota, or tendering requirements and lists the timetable for when such barriers will be eliminated. China further agreed to report annually to the WTO's Committee on Import Licensing those commodities that continue to require import licenses, and agreed to justify why such licensing remains necessary.[40] Additionally, China agreed that,

38. Upon accession, China committed to provide translations to member countries into one or more of the official languages of the WTO of all laws, regulations, and other measures pertaining to trade in goods, services, TRIPs, or foreign exchange.

39. With respect to the "no less favorable" language, the WTO Agreements do not require that foreign and domestic enterprises be treated the same. China is only required to treat foreign enterprises "no less favorably" than domestic enterprises. As a result, it is permissible to allow China to provide preferential tax treatment for an FIE, although it would not be permissible to provide a domestic enterprise with a tax break without granting the same treatment to FIEs.

40. *See* Catalogue of Commodities Subject to Import License Administration (issued by the Ministry of Commerce and the General Administration of Customs effective January 1, 2004), available at http://www.mofcom.gov.cn.

in accordance with TRIMs, several requirements imposed on FIEs would be eliminated, including all foreign exchange balancing obligations, local content rules, and export performance requirements.[41]

(4) Price Controls. Upon accession, China agreed to eliminate most price controls and to continue to implement a system of market pricing, except for those products listed in Annex 4 of the Protocol. Price controls will continue to apply to certain state-controlled commodities such as tobacco, natural gas, and pharmaceuticals. Guidance price controls, whereby the government adopts a suggested or reference price and allows enterprises to price their products within 5 to 15 percent of the guidance price, will continue to apply to certain specified commodities such as grain, vegetable oil, sugar, processed oil, fertilizers, silkworm cocoons, and cotton. Under WTO, China is allowed to continue to use guidance pricing for some services sectors such as transport, commission agents (trademark, advertising, tax, and bidding), financial services, residential housing, and medical services.

(5) Subsidies. Under the Agreement on Subsidies and Countervailing Measures (SCM Agreement), China is required to notify the WTO of all subsidies granted by the government. Annex 5A of the Protocol of Accession acts as China's formal notification under the SCM Agreement and describes the subsidies granted by the PRC government to domestic producers. Annex 5B (Subsidies to be Phased Out) describes the subsidies which will be eliminated and the timetable.[42]

(6) Taxes on Imports and Exports. Upon accession, China agrees that all export taxes other than those listed in Annex 6 of the Protocol of Accession will be abolished. Annex 6 lists products subject to an export tax at the average rate of 20 percent. By agreement, foreign-invested enterprises will eventually be granted the right to receive a rebate on export VAT in a similar fashion as domestic enterprises.[43]

---

41. *See generally* N. Leigh, *Local Content Requirements After China's WTO Entry,* CHINA L. & PRAC. (January 2002).

42. China reserves the right to subsidize certain enterprises, while gradually eliminating the subsidies. China has listed its subsidies in Annex 5A of the Agreement, and they vary from elevation of poverty programs to the encouragement of high-technology projects.

43. Adjustment of the Rates of Export Tax Rebate Circular (promulgated jointly by the Ministry of Finance and the State Administration of Taxation on Oct. 13, 2003). *See generally* Supplementary Notice of the State Administration of Taxation Concerning the Management of Tax Refunds and Exemptions for Export Goods According to Enterprise Classification (issued on August 2, 2001, by the SAT), *reprinted in* CHINA LAWS FOR FOREIGN BUSINESS (CCH), Taxation ¶ 31-813.

(7) Technical Barriers to Trade. As part of its WTO commitments, China agreed to publish all technical barriers to trade including all formal or informal technical regulations, standards, or conformity assessment procedures applied to imported goods. Upon accession, China is required to bring these standards into compliance with the Agreement on Technical Barriers to Trade.[44] The technical standards apply to both foreign and domestic products, and all producers are subject to a single inspection organization.

(8) Right to Trade. Prior to 2001, only a limited number of domestic companies had the right to import and export goods. These companies were divided by industry sector, which bars trading companies in particular industry sectors from importing goods outside their approved industries. With the exception of certain commodities, over a three-year period after accession, such trading rights will be extended to all enterprises in China, allowing them to trade in all goods.[45]

B. China's WTO Compliance Record

There are many governments and organizations, such as the U.S.-China Business Council and the American Chamber of Commerce China, that are actively monitoring China's compliance with its WTO obligations. In early 2004, after two full years of WTO membership, most observers state that China has made good efforts but still has a long way to go to implement its obligations. In mid-2003, the USCBC reported that the PRC government has been "slow to implement its most significant commitments" and in certain situations appears to have "stalled" in the implementation.[46] Specific

44. *See generally* Z. Huanxin, *Technical Standards Updated to Suit WTO,* China Daily (April 2, 2004) (quotes Li Zhonghai, director of China's Standardization Administration, who states that "[a]ny Chinese national compulsory standards that fail to conform with the legitimate objectives stated in the WTO/TBT will be either abolished or revised."). The Standardization Administration maintains its own Web site and solicits comments for national standards. *See* http://www.sac.gov.cn.

45. The exceptions to the right to trade are outlined in Annex 2, where China reserves the right to control imports of grain, vegetable oil, tobacco, crude and processed oil, and chemical fertilizers and the export of tea, rice, corn, tungsten, processed oil, silk, cotton yarn, and antimony. During the three-year transition period of 2001–2004, certain products may be traded only by approved import/export companies, including commodities such as natural rubber, timber, acrylics, and steel. Crude and processed oil will be liberalized so that 15 percent per year over current levels of imports are added to quotas and assigned to independent enterprises. For a discussion of trading rights, *see* Chapter 5, Foreign Investment Guidelines and Industry-Specific Regulations, §§ B.13.

46. *See* China Operations 2003, China's WTO Membership in the Second Year, Written Testimony by the U.S.-China Business Council, September 10, 2003, Submitted in Response to the Office of the USTR's Request for Comments and Notice of Hearing Concerning China's Compliance with World Trade Organization (WTO) Commitments, at 67. *See generally* R. Murphy, *Filling the Glass Half Full: The WTO and Structural Reform in China,* China L. & Prac. (Oct. 2003); J.Walton, *WTO: China Enters Year Three,* China Bus. Rev. (January 2004).

problem areas in China's first two years of membership include complicated import licensing procedures for agricultural products; cumbersome quota allocation procedures; adoption of new sanitary and phytosanitary measures that target imports of soybeans; high registered capital requirements for foreign services firms (i.e., banking, insurance, logistics, and telecom services) to establish a presence or branch offices; late promulgation of the automobile finance regulations; continued preferential treatment of border trade and domestically produced integrated circuits; failure to enforce intellectual property rights, lack of transparency in enforcement proceedings, and inadequacy of penalties imposed on infringing parties; and problems with China Customs concerning valuation and new emphasis on revenue collection that is precipitated by tariff reductions under WTO.[47] However, the government has taken steps to ensure that import laws and regulations be distributed to the public for comment. As an example, MOFCOM issued regulations on November 25, 2003, which provide that any MOFCOM-issued regulation or administrative policy is required to be distributed to the public for comment prior to promulgation if the proposed regulation is important to the interests of citizens, legal persons, and other organizations. With the exception of regulations deemed to be confidential under state secrecy standards, MOFCOM is required to publish the draft regulatory proposals through three channels, namely, the MOFCOM official Web site, the MOFCOM *Gazette*, and the *International Business Daily*, which is affiliated with MOFCOM. MOFCOM is also the first PRC government agency to use the Internet for public debate concerning law and policy issues in China.[48] More effort must me made to eliminate inefficient bureaucratic procedures and improve transparency in government.[49] Furthermore, while the government

47. *See* China Operations 2003, China's WTO Membership in the Second Year, Written Testimony by the U.S.-China Business Council, September 10, 2003, Submitted in Response to the Office of the USTR's Request for Comments and Notice of Hearing Concerning China's Compliance with World Trade Organization (WTO) Commitments, at 63–65. For a discussion concerning the ongoing problems with counterfeiting in China and lack of effective remedies to stop infringement of IP rights, *see* E. Iritani, *Bootleggers Raise Stakes in China's Piracy Fight, Los Angeles Times* (July 20, 2003), available online at http://www.latimes.com. The U.S. Government initiated the case against China at the WTO on March 18, 2004, alleging that China's value-added tax (VAT) refund policy unfairly discriminates against imported semiconductors and integrated circuits. For a press release and copy of the WTO petition, see the Web site of the USTR at http://www.ustr.gov.

48. *See Meet MOFCOM Officials Online,* China Market Intelligence, The U.S.-China Business Council (March 3, 2004). For a schedule and transcript of the question sessions, *see* http://www.mofcom.gov.cn.

49. In an interesting development concerning transparency, the Ministry of Public Security ordered police officials to issue press releases and to hold frequent news conferences with the media to "promote transparency in police affairs." Traditionally, police officials would ignore the media, and especially the foreign media. The new rule is effective in January 2004, and police are required to issue their first press release before January 22, 2004, the first day of the Chinese New Year. *See generally Chinese Police to Open up to Media Questions,* Xinhua News Agency (January 2, 2004), and *China Orders Police to Issue News*

has adopted or amended many laws to meet its WTO obligations, the leadership must take steps to actually implement and enforce the laws and regulations that are promulgated.

The obstacles to full implementation of WTO obligations are protectionism, lack of understanding of obligations, and lack of resources. If China does not move quickly enough, it is likely that foreign governments will contemplate taking unilateral action against China to safeguard their commercial interests.[50] It is left for observation as to whether China will deliver on its important outstanding WTO commitments.[51]

C. U.S./China Trade and Political Relations

The relationship between the U.S. and China has, since at least 1989, been characterized as difficult at best, and many issues remain ongoing concerns and potential flashpoints in the relationship. Continued tension is created by China's rhetoric threatening to attack Taiwan if the country moves closer to declaring independence, and the lack of restraint is met with consternation by the U.S. government, notwithstanding the U.S. policy agreeing to the "one China" principle.[52] Proliferation of weapons and weapons-related technology is an ongoing concern, and various U.S. agencies have sanctioned Chinese companies for violations of a range of proliferation activities. Human rights issues have also been a concern, primarily with respect to arbitrary detentions, crackdown on use of the Internet for benign political dissension, and

Releases, Talk to Media, Dow Jones Newswires (January 2, 2004). Another interesting example of transparency is the announcement by the Beijing Municipal People's Congress seeking public comments with respect to its legislation proposals for 2003. The announcement listed 58 municipal regulations on a broad range of topics including, but not limited to, regulations concerning labor disputes, rules for management of franchise operations, enterprise liquidation standards, etc. Information concerning the announcement is available on the Web site of the Beijing Municipal People's Congress at http://www.bjrd.gov.cn.

50. The U.S.-China Bilateral Agreement with respect to China's entry into the WTO provides as a protective measure that if imports from China surge at any time for a particular product, there are mechanisms for trade consultations to resolve the issue and, if negotiations are unsuccessful, the U.S. may impose restrictions on importation of the product to prevent market disruption.

51. China maintains that it has complied with its obligations under WTO. In August 2002, the Chinese government claimed that it had finished review of 2,300 laws and regulations of which 830 laws were abolished and 325 were amended. The government also claimed that it was in compliance with its tariff reduction obligations and that the average tariff was approximately 12 percent, and that Customs had reduced tariffs for 5,332 items. The government also noted that it had established the WTO Notification & Enquiry Center, which has received over 350 inquiries in its first six months of operation and has sent out over 200 notices in response to the inquiries on various trade-related issues. *Chinese Embassy Spokesperson Xie Feng,* July 22, 2002.

52. As the threatening rhetoric increases, so does the ongoing economic integration between Taiwan and the Mainland. In 2002, the bilateral trade exceeded $30 billion and a cumulative investment from Taiwan to China exceeded $50 billion. It is also estimated that over 70,000 Taiwanese are living in China (including management personnel, workers, and retirees). It is left for observation as to whether the increased economic linkages will ease the political stalemate.

constraints on religious freedom under the guise of quashing cult activities or terrorism. At the same time, China has played a constructive role in mediating the conflict on the Korean peninsula by hosting trilateral and six-party talks with the U.S., China, North Korea, and other players in Asia.

On the economic front, the trade deficit with China and the value of Chinese currency continue to be a source of tension and debate between the U.S. and China. A few comments on the renminbi value and trade deficit issues are instructive.

1. Valuation of the Renminbi: Chinese Currency Issue

The value of Chinese currency (the Yuan, renminbi, or RMB) is a contentious political issue between the United States and China, especially in 2003/2004. As background, since the mid-1990s China has set the value of the RMB within a narrow range to the dollar which, in effect, acts as a fixed exchange rate (8.3 to 1). For various reasons, the RMB exchange rate has declined against major foreign currencies. PRC policy is to hold the RMB exchange rate steady, which has resulted in large foreign exchange reserves. Many critics believe that China is purposefully undervaluing the RMB to bolster the already competitive position of low-price Chinese goods, and thus to make them even cheaper in overseas markets. Critics in the U.S. believe that an undervalued RMB is a subsidy to Chinese goods exported to the U.S. and are urging China to adjust the exchange rate to push the RMB value higher.[53]

China has maintained the same monetary policy since 1995 and wants to deter speculators and avoid deflation as experienced in Japan and Hong Kong. China fears (based upon the experience of other Asian economies during the financial crisis of the past) that a floating exchange rate could be manipulated by speculation and international currency fluctuations and lead to a financial crisis. A revaluation of the RMB may also accelerate deflation, which has been a historical problem. Moreover, China's banking system is weak and immature and is unprepared to manage a financial crisis that could possibly spiral out of control, with a bad loan portfolio

53. The currency issue has led to the introduction of a series of legislation in the U.S. Congress designed to counter the impact of the RMB value. Two proposals would require that the U.S. unilaterally assess an across-the-board tariff against Chinese products unless China floats or revalues the RMB to an acceptable level (H.R. 3058 (Rep. English); S. 1586 (Sen. Schumer)). A third proposal would require the U.S. to negotiate an end to currency manipulations by various Asian countries, including China. If negotiations failed, the U.S. would be required to initiate unilateral or multilateral trade remedies (S.1592 (Sen. Lieberman)).

of 35 to 50 percent of the GDP. The China Banking Regulatory Commission was only formed in early 2003 and is still trying to gain the experience as a regulatory agency and to develop the tools to better supervise China's banking system.[54]

Consumers in the U.S. buy Chinese-made goods because they are low-cost to begin with, and not because of the decline in currency value. The RMB value is really not determined by trade, but by the inflow and retention of foreign capital. What China needs to do is to encourage the use of its foreign exchange reserves.

PRC officials, including both the heads of the People's Bank of China (PBOC) and the Ministry of Finance (MOF), have promised greater flexibility for valuing the RMB for years, and realize that there are advantages to flexibility. However, it is unlikely that they will take any real action other than to encourage more Chinese citizens to spend money overseas (which will have insignificant impact), or possibly either to increase the band around which the RMB fluctuates and allow it to settle within a slightly higher range, or even perform a small one-time revaluation. If the band around the RMB is widened (or a "managed floating rate"), the end result may be an exchange rate of around RMB8.10 to the dollar. But the true value of the RMB is subject to conjecture and cannot be estimated.

As one solution, the PRC government reduced the VAT rebates offered to exporters, which will make the exports more expensive and thereafter increase the competitiveness of U.S. goods. To this effect, the MOF and the State Administration of Taxation (SAT) issued a joint order on October 13, 2003, which lowered the average export rebate by three percent, to 12.11 percent, effective as of January 1, 2004.[55] The reduction of export rebates is supposed to make exports more expensive, but this is really not the case because the rebate program is unworkable given that the government in late 2003 had a backlog of some $24 billion in unpaid export tax rebates. Further reform of the VAT rebate system is expected.

To counter the critics, what China needs to do is to provide real market access, and ahead of the WTO timetables agreed upon for accession.

---

54. For a discussion of China's banking system and the role of the China Banking Regulatory Commission, *see* Chapter 11, Financial Regulation.

55. Adjustment of the Rates of Export Tax Rebate Circular (promulgated jointly by the Ministry of Finance and the State Administration of Taxation on Oct. 13, 2003). *See generally PRC Government Cuts Export Tax Rebate*, CHINA MARKET INTELLIGENCE, THE U.S.-CHINA BUSINESS COUNCIL (October 13, 2003), available online to members at http://uschina.org; S. Xiangman and M. Roos, *Export Tax Rebates: China's Approach to Reforming the System*, CHINA L. & PRAC. (Dec. 2003).

Observers are hopeful that the Chinese government will liberalize trade in services and rapidly grant full trading rights for foreign investors and without unreasonable minimum capital requirements. This would indeed open the markets to the sale of U.S. goods and services and level the playing field to some degree.[56]

2. U.S./China Trade Deficit

The issue of China's trade deficit with the U.S. is a complicated statistical concept that is equally misunderstood, misinterpreted, and used for political purposes.[57] While the deficit with China actually increased in 2003, it also declined for other Asian economies such as South Korea and Taiwan. This is because a significant amount of manufacturing has shifted from these countries to China, and the U.S. trade deficit equation is likely to change again as Japan, Singapore, Taiwan, and South Korea continue to shift their production to the Mainland. More and more cars, semiconductors, appliances, etc., are being produced in China at the expense of other former production centers in Asia.

Since 1990, China is one of the fastest-growing export markets for U.S. goods. Annual exports to China from the U.S. have quadrupled since 1990, and stand at $22.1 billion in 2002. The principal exports from the U.S. include aircraft, medical equipment, electrical machinery, and power generation equipment. In addition, while the U.S. has a trade deficit with China for goods, the U.S. has a trade surplus in trade in services (and has for much of the past decade). The trade surplus in services was approximately $2.2 billion in 2001, and is likely to increase as China meets its market access commitments for services.[58]

Moreover, most imported merchandise from China (90 percent) is substitutes from other low-wage countries such as Mexico, Malaysia, Vietnam, Indonesia, etc. The imports from China include low-tech electrical machinery, toys, apparel, and footwear. Less than 10 percent of imports from China

---

56. WFOEs allowed full trading rights in December 2004 and JVs with majority ownership allowed full trading rights in December 2003. The chief concern is that, although China will open the market based upon the WTO timetable, the government will also impose registration and capital barriers that are counterproductive.

57. In 2002, the U.S. Department of Commerce reported that the trade deficit between the U.S. and China was $103.1 billion. This figure is based upon FAS (free-alongside ship) value and U.S. imports' General Customs Value. The USCBC reports that a more accurate figure is $88.5 billion. *See* The U.S.-China Business Council, China Operations 2003, Understanding the U.S.-China Balance of Trade, at 39.

58. Services account for 78.8 percent of the U.S. economy.

compete directly with U.S.-produced goods. The end result is that U.S. consumers benefit from the ability to purchase low-cost low-tech goods from China.

The only way that China will increase its "imports" from the U.S. is to continue to liberalize trade in goods and services pursuant to, if not before, WTO timetables.

D. Political Reform, Participatory Government, and Law Reform

Many observers believe that as China continues its ongoing economic and legal reform, political or democratic reform must naturally follow. The growing middle class and increase in international communications has placed pressure on the government to be more responsive to the attention of citizens' concerns. While modest in form, there are recent examples of democratic reform in China, such as permitting village elections and establishing a professional staff within the National People's Congress, which are designed to make the government more accountable and representative of the people and not solely the party. At the Chinese Communist Party study session on September 29, 2003, President Hu Jintao stated that China must strengthen "the socialist democratic system" and continue to move toward the rule of law in China.[59] Hu's statement is indicative that the survival of the CCP in the long term will depend on whether the system provides for greater citizen participation and a voice in government policy than in the past. In time, the government will need to take steps to allow further citizen participation in government, or risk being alienated from the populace.

China will continue to be an attractive destination of FDI but, in order to bolster the confidence of investors, it must continue to move quickly to make progress with respect to the following challenges:

- Make progress with respect to the recognition of the rule of law in which property rights are fully respected
- Promote and enforce corporate governance standards to ensure that company practices are transparent and responsive to investors' interests
- Take aggressive steps to halt corruption and economic crimes

59. THE U.S.-CHINA BUSINESS COUNCIL, CHINA OPERATIONS 2003, CHINA ANALYSIS: CHINESE POLITICS UPDATE, at 44.

Practice Tips: Rules on China's Ongoing Legal, Economic, and Political Reform

- Some things relevant in the 80s and 90s may not be relevant today—many of the laws and practices of the past are out of sync with China's new economy, and investors should be prepared to *adjust from prior arrangements and understandings*
- Some things that are relevant today may not be relevant in the future—many of the laws and practices in the future will be affected by China's ongoing reform, and it's critical to *anticipate and plan for change*
- Some things will always be relevant in doing business in China—such as
  - The drive of China's people to be accepted as respected members of the international community
  - A strong desire to do things in China's own way (or with Chinese characteristics) given the sensitivities stemming from past foreign intervention and a history of unequal treaties and extraterritorial treatment
  - The "rule of law" is a concept that the Chinese people are cautiously embracing in light of cultural acceptance for the "rule by man" that takes its genesis from the autocratic-based systems of Confucianism, feudalism, warlordism, foreign subjugation, and Communism that historically has controlled Chinese society in the past

- Continue to reform China's banking regulatory system and decrease the high volume of its nonperforming loan portfolio, while moving toward a more flexible policy on the convertibility of the RMB
- Continue to meet and adhere to full compliance with WTO market access and other trade obligations, and to do so on a uniform basis nationwide

Since 1979, and specifically post-WTO, China has engaged in prolific legislative and regulatory activity and has enacted new laws, and issued regulations, orders, rules, and explanatory circulars that impact a foreign party's operations, including laws affecting foreign investment, securities and corporate governance, financial reform, labor relations, foreign exchange control, and customs and taxation. The PRC leadership is repeatedly promulgating and amending laws and regulations on a reactive basis

Practice Tip

There are many new laws or amendments to existing laws in the pipeline. In December 2003, the Standing Committee of the 10th National People's Congress (NPC) released its five-year legislative plan that describes the 76 laws to be promulgated or amended. Business- and trade-related laws listed in the five-year legislative plan include:

Proposed New Laws

Property Rights Law

Futures Transaction Law

Taxation Basic Law

Fiscal Transfer Payment Law

Western Development Promotion Law

Right Infringement Liability Law

Commercial Registration Law

Enterprise Bankruptcy Law

State-Owned Asset Law

Foreign Exchange Law

Antitrust Law

Antidumping and Antisubsidy Law

Enterprise Income Tax Law

Banking Industry Supervision and Administration Law

Labor Contract Law

Proposed Amended Laws

PRC Company Law

Partnership Enterprise Law

Securities Law

Individual Income Tax Law

Audit Law

Foreign Trade Law

Civil Litigation Law

Arbitration Law

Source: *NPC Sets Legislative Five-Year Plan,* China Market Intelligence, The U.S.-China Business Council, December 17, 2003.

that leads to compliance questions, regulatory turf wars, and inconsistent application. In addition, many laws and regulatory measures are based upon underlying policy statements that reflect the government's priorities, objectives, and attitudes toward foreign investment and economic development. The continuing legal reform in China adds to the unpredictability of operating in the PRC, and the best protection is to monitor the legal and political environments.

The purpose of the *China Law Deskbook* is to provide practitioners, corporate counsel, academics, and government attorneys involved in China with a current and concise guide concerning the laws issued by the National People's Congress (NPC) of the People's Republic of China, the NPC's Standing Committee, the State Council, and the various Chinese government ministries that promulgate administrative measures affecting the China operations of foreign investors. The *China Law Deskbook* is organized by broad topic categories and provides a summary of the critical legal issues for foreign-invested enterprises (FIE), including corporate organizational structure, industry-specific regulatory matters, tax issues, labor and employment, financial regulation, contracts, liquidation and bankruptcy, customs and the importation process, intellectual property protection, land-use, the protection of the environment and natural resources, mediation and arbitration, litigation, and special rules for zones and administrative regions.

Chapter 2 addresses the historical development of China's contemporary legal system. It starts with an analysis of the philosophical influences from Classical China, including Confucian tradition, Daoism, and Legalism. This chapter then analyzes the role the Western powers had on the development of China's legal system. Finally, Chapter 2 explores the impact of political theories of Marxism-Leninism and Mao Zedong Thought on China's legal system.

Chapter 3 is a summary of Chinese legislative and regulatory institutions and their functions, including a discussion of recent institutional reorganization initiated by the Chinese government. Chapter 3 also provides an overview of the Chinese judicial system, as well as a discussion concerning the role and status of the legal profession in the PRC. This chapter concludes with a discussion of the "rule of law" in China and the forces affecting China's ability to develop a legal system that is consistent, precise, and independent from political interference.

Chapter 4 addresses the various organizational structures available to FIEs for establishing a presence in China. It describes the laws and regulations governing representative offices, branch offices, equity joint ventures, cooperative enterprises, wholly foreign-owned enterprises, joint venture trading companies, holding or investment companies, a company limited by shares, a limited liability company, BOTs, service centers, and partnership arrangements. This chapter also summarizes the procedures for establishing an FIE in China, and the proper format for articles of association and feasibility studies.

Chapter 5 addresses the regulatory environment for industry-specific sectors, including services and manufacturing.

Chapter 6 is a summary of the laws and regulations pertaining to the information technology, telecommunications, and software development industries.

Chapter 7 is a summary of the laws and regulations governing contractual relationships in China. It addresses a number of key laws that affect the rights and obligations of contracting parties, including the Civil Law, the Secured Interests Law, and the Contract Law, effective October 1, 1999, which supersedes the Economic Contract Law, the Foreign Economic Contract Law, and the Technology Contract Law. This chapter also analyzes the requirements for specialized contracts including sales of goods contracts, loan contracts, lease agreements, construction contracts, contracts for works of hire, agency contracts, and technology contracts such as technology development contracts, technology transfers, and technical service contracts.

Chapter 8 is a review of China's new tender and procurement systems, which impact foreign contractors and suppliers of goods under government contracts. This chapter analyzes the Tender Law, which governs the public and private bidding process, and the Procurement Law, which governs how government agencies are permitted to purchase goods and services.

The taxation of FIEs in China is covered in Chapter 9. This chapter addresses the rules governing foreign enterprise income tax and turnover taxes such as the business, consumption, and value-added taxes imposed by the Chinese government. Chapter 9 also briefly discusses the enforcement efforts of China's taxation authorities.

China's Labor Law and personnel management rules are addressed in Chapter 10. This chapter addresses the rights and obligations of employers and employees, the wage and hour rules, registration requirements for expatriate employees, worker rights protection, and dispute resolution in the labor context.

Chapter 11 discusses a broad range of issues affecting the regulation of domestic and foreign-funded financial institutions. This chapter analyzes the rules governing the use and control of foreign exchange, including the registration requirements to hold and exchange foreign currency. Chapter 11 further addresses the accounting requirements for FIEs, as well as the auditing laws and joint annual review procedures imposed upon foreign-funded operations. Chapter 12 follows up by addressing the laws and regulations of China's insurance industry.

Chapter 13, entitled "Consumer Protection," is a summary of the laws concerning product quality, consumer protection, advertising, pricing, and unfair competition. The chapter also addresses the regulatory environment for the food, pharmaceutical, and medical device industries. The chapter describes the administrative sanctions and penalties that may be imposed if a business operator fails to comply with China's consumer protection laws.

Chapter 14 provides an analysis of China's intellectual property laws, including the laws and regulatory measures concerning the protection of copyrights, trademarks, and patents. Chapter 14 also analyzes the enforcement mechanisms and remedies available to the owners of intellectual property, including customs protection against infringing imports and exports.

Chapter 15 provides an analysis of China's customs laws, including classification, valuation, import licenses, inspection and entry, bonded areas and warehouses, and customs enforcement. This chapter also summarizes the standards and administrative procedures under China's trade remedies laws, such as regulations on anti-dumping, anti-subsidy, and import safeguard measures.

Chapter 16 addresses the rules concerning the regulation of securities trading, public offerings, and the control of securities markets. This chapter analyzes the mechanisms and agencies responsible for supervising the Chinese stock market, including the regulations governing domestic (A-shares) and foreign capital shares (B-shares).

Chapter 17 summarizes the laws and regulations governing land-use, commercial land development, and natural resources.

Chapter 18 addresses the environmental protection laws of China, including the laws on the control of solid waste, water, and air pollution; regulations concerning the requirement of environmental impact assessment reporting; and standards for clean production. As China undergoes considerable infrastructure development fueled by foreign investment, the government has adopted standards to control the exploitation of its resources and to minimize the impact on the environment.

Chapter 19 addresses mergers, acquisitions, and divisions, including an explanation of anti-monopoly and competition law issues in Chinese M&A.

Chapter 20 covers China's bankruptcy law, including creditors' remedies and procedural steps for petitioners. This chapter also addresses the liquidation standards for FIEs that terminate and dissolve prior to the expiration of their stipulated term.

Chapter 21 concerns the mediation and arbitration of business disputes in China. This chapter analyzes the procedural rules concerning arbitration before the China International Economic and Trade Arbitration Commission (CIETAC) and the procedures for the enforcement of CIETAC arbitral awards in China and the United States.

Chapter 22 addresses the rules and procedures for litigation in the people's courts in China.

Chapter 23 discusses the criminal liability for officers and directors of FIEs under China's Criminal Law, including crimes involving FIE registration, stock transactions, intellectual property rights, environmental damage, and industrial accidents. This chapter also briefly discusses the prohibitions and penalties under the U.S. Foreign Corrupt Practices Act (FCPA) and China's criminal laws for illegal payment activities in China. Chapter 23 also addresses the standards for the detention of foreigners in criminal and civil matters.

Chapter 24 describes the laws establishing the special economic zones, open cities, and coastal areas, including foreign investment incentives and preferential treatment for FIEs. This chapter also analyzes the Joint Declaration between the PRC and Great Britain and the Basic Law of the Hong Kong Special Administrative Region (HKSAR).

In Appendix A, the *Deskbook* provides a number of sample contracts and other sample documents for FIEs. Appendix B is entitled the "Bibliography and Electronic Research Guide" and sets forth a selective list of publications, as well as a comprehensive list of current and active Web sites that provide a wide range of information concerning China. Finally, Appendix C outlines contact information for U.S. and Chinese government resources, bar associations, international organizations, and other resources that maintain information concerning China's legal and business environment. For consistency and authority, the *China Law Deskbook* primarily cites the laws and regulations translated and *reprinted in* the China Laws for Foreign Business series published by CCH International or the China Law & Practice series published by Euromoney Publications.

The China Law Deskbook *is intended to be a general overview of the laws of the People's Republic of China and is not designed as a comprehensive analysis of China's legal system. The* Deskbook, *including the sample contracts and information in the appendices, is provided to readers as a general guide and cannot and should not be construed as legal advice. Further, the laws and regulations cited throughout the* Deskbook *are not intended to be an exhaustive list of the laws, regulations, and rules affecting foreign business in China. Readers are advised to consult with legal counsel, tax advisors, and other professionals with respect to China-related transactions. The dynamics of China's legal system require constant monitoring in order to ensure that the laws, regulations, and the practice are current.*

Chapter 2

Development of the Chinese Legal System

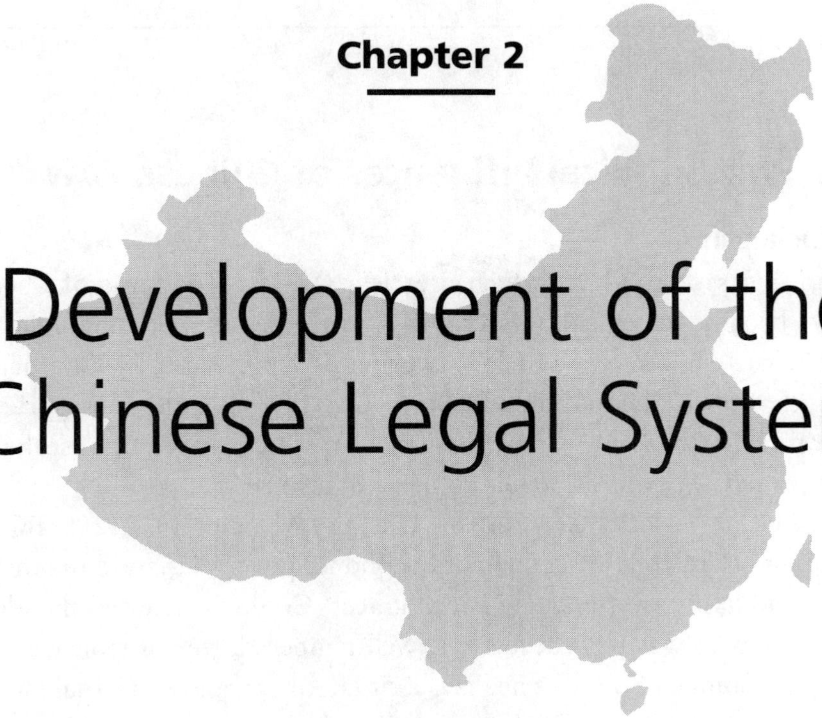

In order to develop an understanding of contemporary Chinese law, it is imperative to appreciate the social, cultural, political, and historical aspects of Chinese legal tradition. China's current legal system reflects a number of influences including the deeply-rooted philosophies and culture of classical China such as Confucianism, Daoism, and Legalism. China's legal system is also influenced by external forces such as the extraterritorial privileges exerted under the Treaty System between China and the Western powers which, in effect, forced China to adopt Western legal principles such as the codes of continental European countries. After the Communist Party took control in 1949, Chinese law was influenced heavily by the political philosophies of Marxism-Leninism and Mao Zedong Thought, and the Soviet legal system. In the last twenty years, China has adopted a number of laws and regulations, especially in the area of commerce, foreign investment, and securities regulations, from various international sources. As China continues to reform its economy, at the behest of the international community, it has been quick to tap into the legal standards of its trading partners to hasten its development efforts, to build the confidence of foreign investors, and to accommodate the entrepreneurial capitalism sweeping the country. This chapter addresses the internal and external factors that have influenced the development of China's contemporary legal system.

A. Philosophical Influences of Chinese Law

1. Confucianism

Confucian codes of conduct, which are clearly defined patterns of obedience, have become inextricably intertwined in Chinese society and culture. The traditional Chinese view of law is primarily influenced by Confucian teachings that an individual should be guided by *li* (virtue or propriety) rather than by *fa* (the law).[1] Confucianism is an ethical system that seeks to teach the proper way for all people to behave in society.

Confucius (551–479 BCE) and his disciple, Mencius (372–289 BCE), developed an entire code of gentlemanly conduct governing good manners, demeanor and gestures, dress, and social grace.[2] Confucius viewed the ideal person as one who was poised, fearless, well-tempered, free of violence and vulgarity, and competent. If one neglects a ritual, or engages in a ritual incorrectly, he demonstrates moral anarchy or disorder in an egregious manner.

Confucianism emphasized that *li* represented positive measures for preventing crime and maintaining social order, while *fa* served as a measure of punishment that only encouraged people to evade the law rather than to do what is right. Confucianism emphasized the duties and obligations of people rather than their individual rights. The focus is more on the interests and harmony of the family, clan, or community rather than the rights of a single person.[3] Confucius taught that most of the ills of society happened because people forgot their stations in life and rulers failed to practice virtue.

The rationale of Confucianism is that society is organized in a hierarchy of superior-inferior relationships: the rulers to the subjects, parents to children, men to women. Filial piety (*xiao*), or respect for elders, is a cornerstone of Confucianism. If every person performed his or her role, stability and social order would be sustained. Confucius emphasized complete obedience and loyalty of the inferior to the superior and, at the same time, the benevolence of the superior to the inferior.

Under Confucianism, there has never been a rigid code of law given that good conduct had to come within the person and could not be enforced by

1. J. Zhang, A Survey of Legal History (*Fa Shi Jian Lue*), Mass Publishing House, Beijing, China (1987) at 65; Zhiping, *Explicating "Law": A Comparative Perspective of Chinese and Western Legal Culture,* 3 J. Chinese L. 55 (1989) (discusses the differences between China's concepts of law and other legal systems); V. Li, Law Without Lawyers: A Comparative View of Law in China and the United States 13–15, 25–26 (1977) (author discusses the "rule of law" under Confucian philosophy).

2. Confucius is a Latinized form of the title *Kongfuzi* (Master Kong), and Mencius is a Latinized form of the title *Mengfuzi* (Master Meng).

3. A. Chen, An Introduction to the Legal System of the People's Republic of China 38 (1992).

some organization.[4] On the civil side, taking legal action against your neighbor also meant an incapacity to work things out in negotiation.[5] If a person chose to have the rulers decide a civil dispute, the result was arbitrary justice by those that held power.

Confucius was born around the year 551 BCE in what is today the Shandong Province. Although he held only insignificant government positions, he preached a philosophy to the existing rulers on how to improve their governing but died without seeing his ideas reduced to practice. Confucius was not a religious leader, nor did he claim any special divine status. Confucius's popularity eventually took hold after his death in about 479 BCE and became the dominant philosophy of the administrative classes. Confucianism influenced every aspect of Chinese life, including its governmental systems, politics, and the law. Confucianism developed during a time of moral chaos, in which common values were widely rejected, crime was rampant, warlordism was the norm, and government was corrupt and distrusted by the people. Before Confucius, China was a feudal society on the verge of collapse due to increased population and ongoing war. During the Han Dynasty (206 BCE–220 CE), Confucianism was employed as an ideological reference point to allow the Han emperors to run China with a reasonable degree of efficiency. Since that time, and up to the end of the Qing Dynasty in 1911, Confucius's teachings were a mainstay of curriculum for government officials.[6] A familiarity with Confucian canons was the principal requirement for civil service examinations.

Confucius believed that people could live together peacefully if they lived by certain traditions that maintained tranquility and social order. He believed that there existed a period of time of quiet peace and prosperity in China, and advocated for a return to these traditions. Confucius established the Chinese past as an infallible model for the present.

---

4. One sinologist noted that "[s]ince the ruler swayed people by his virtuous conduct and moral example, not by law, it was felt that enlightened and civilized persons would be guided by such an example and by the norms of proper conduct without need of regulations." J. FAIRBANK, THE UNITED STATES AND CHINA at 106 (1972). *See also* Ma, *The Chinese Concept of the Individual and the Reception of Foreign Law,* 9 J. CHINESE L. 207 (1995) (discusses the role of the individual in traditional Chinese law and the difficulty of adopting foreign law in the PRC).

5. For all human intercourse in China society, the concept of "losing face," which has its roots in Confucianism, takes on an important role. The concept of face is akin to status, and a person will go to great lengths to avoid "losing face." To be proven wrong or incompetent is a profound humiliation. To let down the family, unit, or group is a great shame to the Chinese. Foreigners involved in negotiating with the Chinese need to appreciate this concept. *See generally* R. KING & S. SCHATZKY, COPING WITH CHINA 112–13 (1991).

6. One course of study is *xiu shen,* or culturation of the self. *Xiu shen* came to mean self-discipline or self-abnegation, and was invoked to make the young conscious of their lowly place in life and responsive to authority and deference to superiors. *See generally,* C. HUCKER, CHINA'S IMPERIAL PAST (1973); J. FAIRBANK, CHINA'S IMPERIAL PAST (1975); J. GERNET, A HISTORY OF CHINESE CIVILIZATION (1982).

Confucian bureaucrats kept the empire intact for two thousand years, developing in isolation from the rest of the world. Although the dynasties were replaced by the Republic from 1912 to 1949 and by the Communist regime thereafter, the ethos of Confucius remains alive and in practice in modern Chinese society. Although governments and ruling parties have changed over time, and each has attempted to abandon the influence of Confucianism, the people continue to revert back to the conservative values of Confucianism's respect for authority, pursuit of privilege, and social grace.

Mencius, like Confucius, believed that rulers received a mandate from heaven justifying their positions in order to guarantee peace and order among the people they rule. Unlike Confucius, Mencius believed that if a ruler failed to be virtuous, then the people would be absolved of all loyalty to the ruler and could revolt against the ruler. This concept served as a basis for numerous revolutions in China and a succession of new rulers.

Although Confucianism has repeatedly been under attack by the successive governments in this century, the values of the family and the clan have been given greater importance in the past twenty years as China experiments with entrepreneurial capitalism.

2. Daoism

Daoism (Taoism), a school of thought developed by philosophers Lao Zi (5th century BCE) and Zhuang Zi (4th century BCE), maintains that a person follow the *Dao*, the way, without interference of desires. Daoists, also known as Quietists, advocated inaction (*wuwei*), political passivity, and spontaneity without human interference. Daoism opposes institutions and organizations, moral laws, and governments as human artifices that obstruct the *Dao*. In practicing *wuwei*, a person accepts without struggle the experiences of life. The purpose of human life, then, is to live a life according to the *Dao*, which requires passivity, individuality, naturalness, calm, simplicity, a free-and-easy approach to life, non-striving, humility, and lack of planning (for a plan is to go counter to the *Dao*). Daoism taught the art of living and surviving by conforming to the natural way of things.

Daoists advocated that the best way to govern the world is not to govern it. Daoism encourages avoiding public duty in order to search for a vision of the transcendental world of the spirit. Daoism viewed that a proper government would be one that would not wage war, would not be complex, would not interfere in people's lives, would not emphasize luxury, ritual, and wealth, and, if practical, would be inactive. The inactivity envisioned would be a government that is merely a guide and not one that governs. Daoists believed that the order and harmony in nature were far more stable, unified, and enduring than either the power of the state or the civilized institutions constructed by humans.

During its history, Daoism has been referred to as the "other way" given that it coexisted with Confucianism. Daoism, while not radically different, offered a range of alternatives to the Confucian way of life. While Confucianism inspired a religion of ethics and social behavior, Daoism inspired mysticism. Where Confucianism was the school for the elite, Daoism flourished among the common people. Confucianism denounced the principle of *wuwei* and believed in a more active form of government and rigid social control. Daoism sought to promote the inner peace of individuals and harmony with their environment.

Although Daoism may be different from Confucianism, it is not contradictory. Many individuals were both Daoist and Confucianist; each philosophy appealed to different sides of a person's character. A typical Daoist was someone that was an artisan who depended upon inner spiritual concentration to perfect his or her creativity and skills. Daoists emphasized physical well-being, healthy diets, gymnastics and massage, and herbal medicine. The Daoist was also someone weary of social activism.

Daoists believe in a system of moral retribution. The Daoist gods in heaven and hell would exact strict punishments for wrongdoing. Such a system of moral retribution made it unnecessary for government to develop laws to control behavior. This belief reinforced the values of society and kept the people in check.

3. Legalism

A third school of thought that significantly influenced the current Chinese legal system is Legalism (*fajia*), which has its roots in the teachings of Shang Yang (d. 338 BCE), the advisor to Shi Huang Di, the First Emperor of China. Shi Huang Di was regarded as abusive and a tyrant by Confucianists, although he succeeded in unifying the nation and put an end to warlordism.

The Legalist advocated rewards and punishments by which to keep all people in order. To the Legalist, man was basically evil and selfish, and required a draconian set of laws that would make the continent easier to control and to avoid social disruption. The Legalist philosophy advocated dismantling feudal privileges, strict accountability for actions, and the standardization of individual duties in a manner whereby everyone is bound equally to the same standard. Legalism emphasized that the standards do not favor the nobles over the common people.

The Legalist saw the law as a means to secure institutional continuity by means of a strict, clear, and public legal code.[7] The Legalist argued that a ruler could not govern effectively without a set of laws.[8] The Legalist doctrine aimed at enforcing the law to strengthen the state over the rule of the family or clan. Group responsibility was ordered within the family and among units of families, and all people were under an honor system to report crime or face collective punishment. The constant threat of punishment led to distrust of all forms of government.

Confucianism, Daoism, and Legalism each played a role in developing the legal system of China, both classical and contemporary.[9] Confucianism, as opposed to Legalism, maintains that the ruling class was controlled by virtue rather than the law. Legalism called for the suppression of dissent. However, both Confucianism and Legalism sought the reunification of a then divided China, but took different approaches. Although the Legalists reject the Daoist principle of inaction, Legalism attempts to achieve the ideal world of Daoism by the promulgation and enforcement of positive laws that regulate behavior. Overall, the Rule of Law (*fazhi*) in ancient China is characterized as a Rule of Man (*renzhi*) whereby the law was designed for the benefit of those governing, rather than as an instrument of divine sanction or supreme authority.[10] To the Legalists, the ruler was above the law. To the Confucianist, legal institutions were secondary to the judgment of moral men. In classical China, the law was a tool of suppression. In contemporary China, legal scholars view the *renzhi* as a part of China's feudal past. An appreciation of these philosophies gives the outsider a better understanding of how the Chinese people view the role of law in Chinese society and the legal institutions that develop, implement, and enforce the law in China.

---

7. *See* B. SCHWARTZ, THE WORLD OF THOUGHT IN ANCIENT CHINA 321–43 (1985). *See also* Johnson, *Status and Liability for Punishment in the Tang Code,* 71 CHI.-KENT L. REV. 217, 218–19 (1995) (discussion of the differences between Legalist and Confucian philosophies).

8. One scholar viewed the law of the Legalist was "intended to serve the despot, not to limit him." V. RUBIN, INDIVIDUAL AND STATE IN ANCIENT CHINA: ESSAYS ON FOUR CHINESE PHILOSOPHERS 70 (1976).

9. *See* Li, *Philosophical Influences on Contemporary Chinese Law,* 6 IND. INT'L & COMP. L. REV. 327, 321–35 (1996) (comparison of Confucianism, Daoism, and Legalism and the impact on China's legal system). Buddhism also had an impact on Chinese society, but did not play a significant role in the development of the Chinese legal system. Buddhism, based on the teachings of the Indian Prince Siddhartha (563–483 BCE), is a religious belief that advocates the use of meditation to achieve a state of nirvana and to find relief for human suffering. Buddhism blended with Confucianism and Daoism during its introduction to China. Approximately 68 million Chinese consider themselves Buddhists.

10. For an analysis of the ideal of a rule of law in ancient China, *See* Turner, *Rule of Law Ideals in Early China?,* 6 J. CHINESE L. 1 (1992).

B. External Influences on the Development of Contemporary Chinese Law

In addition to the purely internal philosophies, the development of China's contemporary legal system was strongly influenced by a number of external factors including the demands placed on China to reform its legal system as a condition to abolish extraterritorial judicial privileges, and the political philosophy of Marxist-Leninist thought that took hold in China after years of war, foreign interference, and abject poverty.

1. Extraterritorial Privileges and Foreign Demands for Legal Reform

For centuries, China flourished in isolation from the rest of the world. Codification of the law in ancient China, which was primarily penal in nature, was undertaken during the Qin (221–206 BCE), Tang (618–907 CE),[11] Song (960–1279 CE), Ming (1368–1644 CE), and Qing (1644–1912 CE) dynasties.[12] However, the Chinese courts rarely had occasion to exercise jurisdiction over purely commercial disputes given that civil matters, as a matter of tradition, were settled through either mediation or arbitration. The avoidance of the court process to resolve civil disputes is a result of the distrust over legal institutions, where the decision making was arbitrary, and of the Confucianist emphasis on resolving matters in a virtuous manner.[13]

During the Qing Dynasty (1644–1912), the Western world approached the Manchu rulers for strategic purposes and to open trade. China, at least initially, was ambivalent toward the foreigners and believed that it had no need for relations with Europe and the United States. As traders set up posts in China's coastal areas, the Manchus allowed the foreigners to govern their own affairs but gradually asserted jurisdiction, especially in matters involving crimes against Chinese citizens.

After China was weakened by its defeat during the Opium War, the Western powers, including Great Britain, Germany, France, and the United States, imposed upon China a number of unilateral treaties granting land

---

11. *See generally* Johnson, *supra* note 7, at 217 (1995) (the Tang code is regarded as the basis for subsequent criminal laws developed throughout Asia). The Tang code placed an emphasis on the use of interrogation and confession, and less reliance on lawyers in the representation of an accused. The Tang code is the product of over a thousand years of legal development.

12. For a discussion of the different dynasties, *See* J. FAIRBANKS, CHINA: A NEW HISTORY (1994); Z. JIFAN, CHINESE LEGAL HISTORY (1982). Because of the low literacy rate in Classical China, it is likely that only a few people were aware of the written legal codes. *See* Johnson, *supra* note 7, at 220.

13. The extensive use of personal connections (*guanxi*) to, among other things, circumvent the law or to gain leniency seriously undermines the public's confidence in the law. *See infra* Chapter 3, Legislating, the Judiciary, and Lawyers in China, § B.4.

and trading concessions in various parts of China, and thereby effectively dismembered China and parceled her off into spheres of influence.[14]

The unequal treaties—as they are referred to by the Chinese—established a system of extraterritorial privileges under which foreign subjects were exempt from local jurisdiction, and, instead, were subject to their own national authorities for conduct while physically present in China. Extraterritorial privileges include an exemption from jurisdiction of local courts; freedom from arrest by local officials; and the right to a criminal or civil trial by consular or national courts.[15] Prior to the establishment of extraterritorial privileges, China asserted jurisdiction over foreigners and subjected them to local Chinese law.[16]

The United States, for example, secured its extraterritorial privilege in its treaty with China, concluded on July 3, 1844. The China Treaty of 1844 provides that "citizens of the United States who may commit any crime in China shall be subject to be tried and punished only by the consul, or other public functionary of the United States, thereto authorized, according to the laws of the United States" [and that] "all questions in regard to rights, whether of property or person, arising between citizens of the United States in China, shall be subject to the jurisdiction of and regulated by the authorities of their own Government."[17] At one time, the United States, as well as several European governments, had extraterritorial privileges in many African and Middle and Far East countries.[18]

---

14. In some sense, the Qing welcomed the Western powers to assist the ailing government in quashing rebellions, such as the Boxer Rebellion in 1900 by foreign troops (primarily U.S. Marines).

15. E. BORCHARD, DIPLOMATIC PROTECTION OF CITIZENS ABROAD 433 (1915); E. DICKINSON, THE EQUALITY OF STATES IN INTERNATIONAL LAW 224–25 (1920); *See also* S. LIU, EXTRATERRITORIALITY: ITS RISE AND ITS DECLINE 23 (1925); G. KEETON, THE DEVELOPMENT OF EXTRATERRITORIALITY IN CHINA 157 (1925).

16. Section 34 of the Chinese Penal Code provided that "all foreigners who come to submit themselves to the government of the Empire, shall, when guilty of offences, be tried and sentenced according to established laws." G. Staunton, *Penal Code of China* 36 (1810), *reprinted in* S. LIU, *supra* note 15, at 81–82.

17. China-United States Treaty of 1844, arts. 21, 24. This treaty is also referred to as the Treaty of Wanghia after the small village in Southern China where it was signed. For a discussion of the Treaty of Wanghia, *See* 5 J. Moore, INTERNATIONAL LAW DIGEST 416–26 (1906). This treaty followed the Treaty of Nanjing between Great Britain and China concluded on August 29, 1842, and which ended the Opium War. For a Chinese view of the treaty system, *See* AN OUTLINE HISTORY OF CHINA, Foreign Language Press, Beijing (ed. Bai Shouyi 1982) pgs. 431–36. *See also* J. SPENCE, THE SEARCH FOR MODERN CHINA 158–64 (1990); J. FAIRBANKS, *supra* note 12, at 199–205 (1994). Extraterritorial jurisdiction in China was secured by nineteen countries including, in chronological order: Russia, Great Britain, the United States, France, Sweden, Norway, German Customs Union, Denmark, The Netherlands, Spain, Belgium, Italy, Austria-Hungary, Peru, Brazil, Portugal, Japan, Mexico, and Switzerland. *See also* Quigley, *Extraterritoriality in China,* 20 AM. J. INT'L L. 46, 51 n. 21 (1926).

18. *See* H.R. Doc. No. 326, 59th Cong., 2d Sess. 216–46 (report contains treaties, statutes, and regulations relating to extraterritorial jurisdiction of the United States); *See generally* G. Keeton, *supra* note 15; S. Liu, *supra* note 15; Quigley, *supra* note 17.

This peculiar institution is explained by one jurist as follows: "Owing to diversities of law, custom, and social habits, the citizens and subjects of nations possessing European civilization enjoy in countries of non-European civilization, chiefly in the East, an extensive exemption from the operation of the local law. This exemption is termed 'extraterritoriality.'"[19]

The Western powers imposed the system of extraterritoriality based upon the perceived imperfections in the Chinese legal system. The primary objections to China's legal system concerned the claims that the use of penalties was too severe, torture was employed to obtain confessions of guilt, and the courts were corrupt.[20] One British diplomat and proponent of extraterritoriality, Sir George Staunton, claimed that "[t]he Chinese laws, as specially applied, and endeavored to be enforced, in cases of homicide, committed by foreigners, are not only unjust, but absolutely intolerable. The demand for blood, in all cases, without reference to circumstances, whether palliative or even justifying, is undoubtedly an intolerable grievance."[21] Prior to the unequal treaties providing for extraterritorial privileges, there were several reported cases involving homicide either as a result of self-defense or through gross negligence where the accused was sentenced to death by local Chinese authorities without consideration of whether the conduct was intentional, accidental, or justified under the circumstances.[22]

In the first case concerning U.S. interests, the American vessel *Emily* in 1821 was forced to hand over a crew member to local authorities who was convicted and executed for causing the death of a woman when he dropped an earthenware pitcher from the vessel onto the woman who fell and drowned in the Pearl River near Canton (Guangzhou). The crewmember, Terranova, was handed over to the Chinese authorities after the Qing government threatened the cessation of all U.S. trade in the Canton region. The captain of the *Emily* wavered and turned over Terranova on the fear that his vessel, loaded with illegal opium, would be confiscated. At the trial, there were no Western observers allowed present in the courtroom, and, after a one-day trial, Terranova was sentenced to death by strangulation. The sentencing of the sailor violated the Qing government's own procedures in cases

19. 2 J.B. MOORE, A DIGEST OF INTERNATIONAL LAW 593 (1906).

20. W. KOO, STATUS OF ALIENS IN CHINA 123–26 (1912).

21. Remarks on the British Relations with China and the Proposed Plans for Improving Them (2nd ed., London, 1836), *reprinted in* S. LIU, *supra* note 15, at 85. Several Chinese jurists disputed the claims that China's legal system was defective and found that such claims were exaggerated for the purpose of preserving foreign control over Chinese territory. *See* S. LIU, *supra* note 15, at 88 n. 1. One noted historian argues that China's penal system, although harsh, had a standard of law and order that was comparable to that prevalent in Europe or the United States at the time. *See* J. SPENCE, *supra* note 17, at 126.

22. *See* 2 J. MOORE, INTERNATIONAL LAW DIGEST 644–45 (1906). *See also* J. SPENCE, *supra* note 17, at 127 (discussion concerning the *Terranova* case).

of accidental homicide. Cases such as the *Terranova* matter led to the general feeling that the administration of justice in China was capricious, and that individuals guilty of accidental homicide would receive the same punishment as those guilty of murder. The *Terranova* case is cited as a major justification for the establishment of the United States extraterritorial system in China.[23]

In response to treaty authorization, foreign governments established a multiplicity of courts located physically in China. At one time, there were almost one hundred consular courts throughout China with the largest number established by Japan (44), Great Britain (25), the United States (18), and France (16).[24] Each consular court applied the law of its own state and prescribed penalties which that state determined to be proper. The four sources of law of the U.S. consular courts and the United States Court for China included acts of Congress, common law, special decrees and regulations, and Chinese law.[25] Each court had exclusive jurisdiction over its own citizens, regardless of the crime or civil claim. For example, a claim against an American citizen, thus, was required to be made before the U.S. consular court having jurisdiction over the defendant.

In addition to the consular court systems, the United States and Great Britain established their own judicial court systems in China for major civil and criminal cases. The U.S., for example, in 1906 established the United States Court for China, which had exclusive jurisdiction in criminal cases except "where the punishment of the offense charged cannot exceed by law one hundred dollars' fine or sixty days' imprisonment or both," and in civil disputes except where "the sum or value of the property involved in the controversy does not exceed five hundred dollars United States money."[26] In all other matters, the U.S. consular court had jurisdiction. A litigant had the right to appeal a decision of the United States Court for China to the Ninth Circuit Court of Appeals.

On the other hand, claims or charges made against a Chinese citizen by a foreign party were heard by the Chinese Mixed Courts, in which, in addition to the Chinese magistrate, the foreign claimant was allowed to have an assessor present. In contrast, a Chinese claimant was not allowed to have a representative present in the foreign consular courts. In theory, the "Mixed

23. *See* J. Moore, *supra* note 22, at 644–45.
24. The other countries with consular or national courts in China included Portugal (8), Belgium (6), Italy (5), Denmark (1), The Netherlands (1), Spain (1), and Switzerland (1).
25. W. Willoughby, Foreign Rights and Interests in China 44–51 (1920).
26. *See* Quigley, *supra* note 17, at 54–55.

Courts" were Chinese courts having jurisdiction over Chinese defendants and administering Chinese law. By treaty, however, a foreign party was allowed to have an "assessor" attend the proceedings "in the interests of justice," to "examine and to cross-examine witnesses," and "to protest against [the proceedings] in detail."[27] The result was that the foreign governments, and in particular Great Britain, the U.S., and France, were allowed to control the proceedings. An American lawyer who practiced law in Shanghai from 1903 to 1905 made the following observation concerning the Mixed Court system in Shanghai:

> Whether from indifference, or because of tacit understanding that their presence was not required, Chinese officials have seldom, if ever, attended the proceedings of foreign tribunals when the interests of their countrymen were involved in suits against foreigners. But foreign representatives have always asserted and exercised the right of attending the trial of cases against Chinese when the interests of their nationals were involved. This has led to one of the gravest abuses connected with foreign intercourse in China. Little by little these representatives have arrogated to themselves the right to sit in judgment on mixed cases, and by threats of intimidation to bring the Chinese magistrate who, theoretically, has the sole decision, to the view of the controversy that they favor. Justice under such circumstances is impossible, for to the weakness and native dishonesty of the magistrate is added the aggressive partiality of the foreign representative, who, in the majority of cases does not profess to be a judge at all, but an active advocate on the bench of the cause of its nationals.[28]

In earlier periods, the Chinese found extraterritorial privileges to be acceptable since the imperial governments preferred that foreign communities police their own ranks.[29] It was also a system that works for a small population and where the foreigners and the local citizenry did not mix. As one

27. *Id.* at 55–56.

28. Ohlinger, *Extraterritorial Jurisdiction in China,* 4 MICH. L. REV. 341, 345–46 (1906). A British barrister noted that the Mixed Court usually adjourned without deciding a case since the assessor and the Chinese Magistrate could never agree on the outcome. *See* Latter, *The Government of Foreigners in China,* 75 L. QUARTERLY REV. 316, 321 (1903) ("Too often do proceedings in this court develop into a mere wrangle between the assessor and magistrate, each advocating the cause of his own sovereign's subject.") The use of assessors in other civil-law countries is common, but they usually respect and defer to the authority and decisions of the judge.

29. One writer noted that: "The truth is, China wanted as little intercourse as possible with foreigners, and seeing that it was very difficult to keep them out of her territory, she was willing to let them manage their own household affairs, as best suited to themselves, when they took up their abode therein." T. JERNIGAN, CHINA IN LAW AND COMMERCE 194 (1905).

writer noted that "the Chinese, when they found that the foreign devils were not to be kept out of their dominions, accepted the inevitable but prayed on all accounts to be excused from the task of governing and administering justice to these barbarians."[30] As populations swelled, the system became cumbersome and subject to abuse.

Understandably, the system of extraterritorial privileges, a by-product of the colonial era, was condemned by China as an affront to its sovereignty and its right to maintain judicial autonomy free of foreign influence and interference. Clearly, the extraterritorial system placed the foreign party in a far better position than the local citizenry. Foreigners, under the cloak of extraterritoriality, were immune from local taxes that the Chinese themselves had to pay.

The system was also criticized by foreign lawyers as severely flawed in its ability to effectively administer justice[31] and as a means to skirt the law. One commentator, a former American assessor of the Mixed Court in Shanghai, noted:

> The strongest plea for the abolition of extraterritoriality lies in the abuse of this privilege on the part of subjects of foreign powers who use it as a cloak for illegal acts. The continued smuggling of opium and morphine into China is but a single example, although the most striking, of the wrong that is being done to China under the cloak of a foreign extraterritorial jurisdiction.[32]

The use of consuls to decide cases has been criticized given that members of the consular service may not have been trained lawyers or judges. Most importantly, the first duty of a consul was to protect the interest of the state's nationals, and was, by definition, biased against the foreign party seeking redress. In addition, the foreign courts were able to exercise jurisdiction only over its own citizens. The courts had no power to punish a noncitizen plaintiff who commits perjury. The courts were also limited in that they could not entertain a counterclaim against a noncitizen plaintiff.

The extraterritorial system also resulted in the general populace's distrust for its own government, which it saw as being inept in handling foreigners. One writer noted that "[b]y making the foreigner immune to Chinese legal control, extraterritoriality put the Chinese ruling class into a situation

30. Latter, *supra* note 28, at 316.

31. For a discussion of the flaws and weaknesses of the extraterritorial court system, *See* Latter, *supra* note 28, at 316.

32. Bishop, *Extraterritoriality in China,* 5 Chinese Social & Pol. Sci. Rev. 175, 177 (1920).

reminiscent of earlier times, obliged to govern China under a degree of alien hegemony."[33]

After the practice existed for over 60 years, and on the demand of the Chinese government, Great Britain and the United States promised to abolish the extraterritorial system on the condition that China establish a legal system consistent with international norms.[34] Article 15 of the commercial treaty between the United States and China of 1903 provides as follows:

> The Government of China having expressed a strong desire to reform its judicial system and to bring it into accord with that of Western nations, the United States agrees to give every assistance to such reform and will also be prepared to relinquish extra-territorial rights when satisfied that the state of the Chinese laws, the arrangements for their administration, and other considerations warrant it in so doing.

In response, the Chinese government took steps to reform its legal system, including the establishment of an independent judiciary and codification of its laws. In 1902, the Emperor Guangxu issued an order to reform China's legal system and established a law reform commission headed by jurist Shen Jiaben.[35] The Qing Dynasty established China's new Supreme Court in 1906 and encouraged the establishment of courts throughout the provinces. The Qing, as well as the Republic (1912–1949), took steps to promulgate criminal and commercial laws. The Republic also took steps to

---

33. J. Fairbanks, *supra* note 12, at 204.

34. 1 J. MacMurray, Treaties & Agreements Concerning China 351 (1921). 1 Malloy, Treaties 269. Article 12, of the treaty between China and Great Britain dated September 5, 1902, provides as follows:

> China having expressed a strong desire to reform her judicial system and to bring it into accord with that of Western nations, Great Britain agrees to give every assistance to such reform, and she will also be prepared to relinquish her extra-territorial rights when she is satisfied that the state of Chinese laws, the arrangement for their administration, and other considerations warrant her in so doing.

Several other countries agreed to relinquish their extraterritorial privileges on the condition that China reform its judicial system including Sweden and Switzerland. *Id.* at 745 (Sweden); 2 J. MacMurray, Treaties & Agreements Concerning China 1430 (1921) (Switzerland). The Western powers agreed to relinquish their extraterritorial rights in Japan after comprehensive reforms were carried out by the Japanese government including the adoption and enforcement of a code of laws based upon Continental European codes. *See* G. Keeton, *supra* note 15, at 170.

35. Shen Jiaben played a key role in the development of China's legal system. Shen organized a group of scholars to translate into Chinese the law books of Western countries including books from Germany, Italy, the United States, Russia, Britain, France, and the Netherlands. In 1906, Shen established the first government-run law school. For a discussion of Shen Jiaben's achievements, *See* Gao, *Shen Jiaben—"Matchmaker" Between Chinese and Western Laws in the Later Years of the Qing Dynasty,* 11 China L. Q. Jun. 30, 1997, at 96.

reform China's penal system including the improvement of sanitary conditions at prisons, the construction of modern prison facilities, and the establishment of programs for reeducation of prisoners. The Qing abolished deportation, torture, and the use of the cangue—a square wooden yoke confining the neck and hands and used to publicly humiliate minor criminals.[36]

Despite undertaking numerous reforms in the first two decades of the 20th century, the foreign powers failed to relinquish their extraterritorial privileges. The Chinese government, in several international fora, repeatedly demanded an end to extraterritoriality.[37] At the Paris Peace Conference in 1919, China made an attempt to secure the abolition of the extraterritorial system based upon the adoption of a number of laws and a constitution consistent with Western legal standards.[38] In a statement to the Conference, the Chinese delegation demanded that extraterritoriality be abandoned by the Western powers:

> While we do not claim that the Chinese laws and their administration have reached such a state as has been attained by the most advanced nations, we do feel confident to assert that China has made very considerable progress in the administration of justice and in all matters pertaining thereto since the signing of the [various] Commercial Treaties.[39]

No action was taken at the Paris Peace Conference, and the system of extraterritoriality continued. Indeed, the Western powers reneged on their promise to return to China the German concessions in the Shandong Province and, insultingly, the Treaty of Versailles granted Japan the leaseholds formerly held by Germany.[40]

36. For a discussion of the legal reforms and legal administration during the early part of the 20th century, *see* Quigley, *supra* note 17, at 61–67.

37. The Chinese Government, in declaring war upon Germany and Austria-Hungary in 1917, abrogated the extraterritorial rights of those countries. Germany formally surrendered its extraterritorial privileges in the Sino-German agreement of May 30, 1921. In 1920, the Soviet government announced its intention to surrender its extraterritorial privileges and other rights in China. Quigley, *supra* note 17, at 51–52.

38. At the time of the Paris Peace Conference, China had adopted a National Constitution; developed civil, criminal, commercial, and procedural codes; established new court systems; improved legal training; and reformed the prison and police systems. These codes are based upon the codes of several Continental European countries including France, Germany, and Switzerland. S. Liu, *supra* at note 15, at 219–20.

39. Questions for Readjustment Submitted by China to the Paris Peace Conference (Paris, 1919), 14–18.

40. The Versailles Treaty called for the handing over of Germany's former leased territories in China to Japan. The treatment of China at Versailles led to mass protests in Tiananmen Square on May 4, 1919, thereby launching what is known as the May Fourth Movement, which is characterized as the first true nationalist movement in China. Thousands of students took to the streets in Beijing in the largest and most violent demonstration yet seen in the capitol. The demonstrators were incensed by the hypocrisy of the

The Chinese government also made a plea to end the extraterritorial system during the Conference on the Limitation of Armament in November of 1921, which was held in Washington, D.C.[41] During the LOA Conference, the Chinese delegation emphasized that the system of extraterritoriality was "in derogation of China's sovereign rights, and is regarded by the Chinese people as a national humiliation."[42] At the LOA Conference, Dr. Chung Hui Wang, the Chief Justice of China, argued that his country had made considerable progress in modernizing its judicial system. He stated:

> A law codification mission for the compilation and revision of law has been sitting since 1904. Five codes have been prepared, some of which have already been put into force. . . . These codes have been prepared with the assistance of foreign experts, and are based on the principles of modern jurisprudence. . . . Then there is a new system of law courts established in 1910. The judges are all modern, trained lawyers, and no one could be appointed a judge unless he had attained the requisite legal training.[43]

Although the LOA Conference did not result in an end to the system, the participants adopted a resolution that resulted in the first serious review of extraterritoriality, which provides, in pertinent part:

> [T]he Governments . . . shall establish a Commission . . . to inquire into the present practice of extraterritorial jurisdiction in China, and into the laws and judicial system and methods of judicial administration in China, and to assist and further the efforts of the Chinese Government to effect such legislation and judicial reforms as would warrant the several Powers in relinquishing, either progressively or otherwise, their respective rights of extraterritoriality.[44]

China, despite years of civil war and protracted discussions with the foreign powers to abolish the extraterritorial system, continued to reform its

---

Western powers, which raised China's hopes that the "unequal treaties would be abolished and Chinese sovereignty restored." The protests in Beijing led to nationwide demonstrations throughout China and reshaped intellectual thought in China over the next decades. The May Fourth Movement inspired Chinese activists of all types of ideologies. J. SPENCE, *supra* note 17, at 293–94, 310–19.

41. For a discussion of the arguments made by the Chinese delegation at the Conference on the Limitation of Armament (hereinafter "LOA Conference"), *see* S. LIU, *supra* note 15, at 223–25. *See also* Quigley, *supra* note 17, at 46 (discussion of LOA Conference and resolutions).

42. S. LIU, *supra* note 15, at 223.

43. CONFERENCE ON THE LIMITATION OF ARMAMENT, 932–36 (Washington, 1922).

44. CONFERENCE ON THE LIMITATION OF ARMAMENT, 932–36, 1010 (Washington, 1922).

legal system. Unfortunately, the West resisted in relinquishing its extraterritorial privileges for uncertain reasons. One view was that China was a battlefield of military factions incapable of developing and enforcing a predictable rule of law. Others claimed that Chinese embryonic legal institutions could not be trusted, and the horrors of Chinese prisons, torture, and punishment were too vivid to ignore. The real issue, however, was that foreign powers could not envision a loss of the extensive settlements and concessions, nor would they unilaterally relinquish their privileges until their international enemies—and specifically the Japanese—either renounced their interests in the Mainland or were evicted from China altogether. In January of 1943, the Western powers formally abandoned the system of extraterritoriality. China was thereafter allowed to subject foreigners to Chinese laws and court system.[45] In 1949, the Chinese Communist Party (CCP) abolished all laws and the legal system set up by the Republic.

Extraterritorial privileges, forced upon successive Chinese regimes, left the victorious Communists bitter and hostile toward the West in general. Such privileges, as well as economic coercion, semi-colonialism, and foreign aggression, led the CCP to isolate the country from the rest of the world, which included a total abandonment of the improvements made to its legal system. The lesson that China learned from extraterritoriality is that the legal system was a vital element of control over individuals and property, foreign trade, and economic development, and that it could never afford to lose control of its judicial functions in the future. The reform of the legal system would either come from within, or with the assistance of foreign legal experts at the express invitation of domestic sources and not by external force or threat.

2. Marxism-Leninism and Mao Zedong Thought and the Development of Chinese Law

In February of 1949, the CCP forcefully removed the Guomingdang government, including its judiciary and the entire body of laws. The CCP issued a directive abolishing the Guomingdang's six codes, all modeled after European legal codes, including the Constitution, Commercial Law, Civil Law, Civil Code of Procedure, and Criminal Code.[46] In September of 1949,

45. Under China's current Constitution, all foreign enterprises and individuals are bound by China's laws. CONSTITUTION OF THE PEOPLE'S REPUBLIC OF CHINA, arts. 18 & 32.

46. The CCP order is referred to as the *Directive Regarding the Abolition of the Guomingdang's Complete Book of Six Codes and the Affirmation of the Legal Principles in the Liberated Areas. See* Li, *Philosophical Influences on Contemporary Chinese Law,* 6 IND. INT'L & COMP. L. REV. 327 (1996).

the CCP issued the *Common Program of the Chinese People's Consultative Conference*, which became the temporary basic law of China until 1954.

The CCP pursued a program based upon the concept of historical determinism, which provides that the party is the primary means of transforming China from a feudalistic society into a Communist utopian society. In order to perfect its unique historical role, the CCP pursued a policy of class struggle that involved the destruction of "class enemies." The hope of utopia appealed to the people after years of war resulted in impoverishment.

Mao borrowed heavily from Confucianism while at the same time denouncing the feudalistic ethos of the ancient philosophy. Mao sought to create a proletarian culture to supplant all feudal, imperialistic, and bourgeois culture. The collective responsibility system of the Communists had its roots in Confucian thought. The Confucianist theory of loyalty to the family was redirected into loyalty to the CCP and the State. The Confucian ideal of virtue under Maoist thought was simply the unequivocal support and practice of the CCP's current political program. The virtuous in Maoist China was a person who followed the party line. Further, both Maoism and Confucianism eschewed written law entirely in favor of general principles and left it up to the "experts"—cadres in the former and the mandarins in the latter—to apply the principles to specific cases, and oftentimes with punitive results. The recognition of general principles, as opposed to the rule of law, is why China, in stark contrast to developed countries, had virtually no written law in the late 1970s.

Mao also drew heavily on legalism and, like the government of Shi Huang Di, the Communist used legalism to mobilize the masses to action and to crush opponents. Both Maoism and legalism share the belief that the state is the sole determinant of right and wrong (to the exclusion of other standards of personal morality such as religion). Legalism and communism are both systems that maintain social control and order implemented through a system of rewards and punishments, and through the institution of an honor system that promotes espionage among the family and work units.

Prior to 1949, approximately 60,000 lawyers practiced in China. In 1957, at the time of liberalization period known as the Hundred Flowers Movement,[47] there were approximately 800 "legal advisor's" offices nationwide. Those offices were staffed by 2,500 full-time and 300 part-time lawyers. During this period, Soviet legal scholars taught students in China, and

47. *See* J. SPENCE, *supra* note 17, at 569–73.

Chinese students studied in the Soviet Union. China developed a legal framework that includes the first PRC Constitution in 1954 and a set of organic laws designed to administer the court and prosecutorial systems. Soviet laws and principles were readily adopted as models until a shift in politics led to the Soviet Union falling into disfavor with Beijing in 1957.[48]

In May of 1957, Mao Zedong encouraged the "blooming of a hundred flowers and the contending of a hundred schools of thought." Mao called on intellectuals of China to speak out against the abuses in the CCP. After a period of five weeks, the program was terminated and resulted in an "anti-rightist" campaign against those that spoke out. The legal profession and the judicial system were affected. Ideological repression was followed by a purge of the government and the CCP. The anti-rightist movement was followed by an abandonment of the Ministry of Justice (MOJ) in 1959 along with its organizational structure for the legal profession.

From 1958 to 1965, the country focused its attention on developing policy to rapidly transform the country into a world power. During this time period, Mao launched the Great Leap Forward movement, which was intended to heighten economic productivity and self-reliance in China through collectivization of people's communes and decentralization of industrial production.[49] The Great Leap Forward resulted in fundamental changes to the family and clan structure by pooling families into communes to participate in massive irrigation and construction projects. The Great Leap Forward is regarded as a failure since the government overstated the production and agricultural results, which led to widespread famine. The Great Leap Forward set the stage for the next round of revolutionary excesses of the Cultural Revolution. Development of the law and legal institutions took on secondary importance to Mao's goal of mass mobilization to achieve self-reliance.

The environment for the legal profession did not improve during the late 1960s. The Cultural Revolution (1966–1976), which began as a political struggle between Mao Zedong and other CCP leaders for dominance of the party, led to the abandonment of China's fledgling legal system. The excesses of the Cultural Revolution prohibited the development of either a Western- or Soviet-styled legal system. During the Cultural Revolution, the few open law schools were closed and the law faculty sent to labor camps. The law

48. After the Soviet Union fell into disfavor with the PRC, many Chinese jurists and scholars urged the government to modernize China's legal system by employing Western legal principles. The reformers were later condemned as rightist intellectuals with anti-socialist views. *See* Li, *supra* note 46, at 328.

49. *See generally* J. Spence, *supra* note 17, at 578–84.

libraries and books were destroyed by the Red Guard.[50] The legal profession disappeared overnight and almost no laws were enacted and no law books published during the Cultural Revolution.

With the near abolition of the legal profession during the 1960s, civil disputes were resolved by local mediators, and criminal matters were handled in the political arena by the Ministry of Public Security, party committee structure, or the state courts that remained open.

3. Influence of Foreign Investment Post-1978

The Cultural Revolution ended in 1976 with the death of Mao and the arrest of the "Gang of Four."[51] After ten years of lawlessness during the Cultural Revolution, the Chinese government took steps to slowly open China to the rest of the world. In 1978, the government instituted the Four Modernizations, a program designed to develop and modernize China's agriculture, industry, national defense, and science and technology. Incumbent in this bold plan was the building of a modern legal system as a key element to ensure the institutionalization of economic reform, and to gain the confidence of the global community. The Chinese government also emphasized that the excesses of the Cultural Revolution occurred as a result of certain officials taking advantage of China's incomplete legal system to seize power. To guard China from returning to a similar situation, the NPC stressed the need to develop a legal system that ensures the stability and continuity of the laws; guarantees the equality of all the people before the laws and to deny anyone the privilege of being above the law; and that the law may be revised only through legal procedures and not at the personal whim of a particular leader.[52]

In the interim, the United States officially recognized the People's Republic of China on January 1, 1979, and several months later the two governments established formal diplomatic relations with the opening of

---

50. Mao invoked the energy of the youthful Red Guard against their elders. The Red Guard, at the encouragement of the Cultural Revolution leaders, destroyed historical buildings, temples, and art objects, and attacked—using physical and emotional tactics—teachers, school administrators, party leaders, and parents. *See* J. SPENCE, *supra* note 17, at 602–17. Mao is quoted as instructing the Red Guard to "[d]epend on the rule of man, not the rule of law." *See* Capener, *Law and Lawyers in China: An Update,* 13 UTAH B.J. 35–36 (1985).

51. The "Gang of Four," which included Jiang Qing, the wife of Mao, had tremendous power during the Cultural Revolution and were blamed for many of the excesses of the period. *See generally* J. SPENCE, *supra* note 17, at 603–17; YAN JIA QI, THE TEN YEAR HISTORY OF CULTURAL REVOLUTION IN CHINA (1987); R. WITKE, COMRADE CHIANG CH'ING 295–356 (1977) (biography of Jiang Qing and her role in the Cultural Revolution).

52. Chiu, *Certain Problems in Recent Law Reform in the People's Republic of China,* 3 COMP. L. Y. B. 1, 12 (1979).

respective embassies in Beijing and Washington, D.C.[53] At this time, the United States recognized the PRC as the sole legal government of China and terminated diplomatic ties with Taiwan, the Republic of China. However, the United States continued its commercial and unofficial diplomatic ties with Taiwan pursuant to the Taiwan Relations Act.[54]

The reforms led to China's experiment with entrepreneurial capitalism, or "market socialism." The economic liberalization policies of the 1980s gave rise to consumer expectations, personal ambition and initiative, and wealth. The Chinese government, in response, has used the law to harness the entrepreneurial values and to preserve the party's existence and legitimacy. At the same time, the Chinese government has been, and continues to be, under pressure from its trading partners to strengthen its laws, improve the enforcement of its laws, and allow for greater transparency and access to its laws and regulations in order to facilitate market access and stability in its business environment. Although the CCP has not formally abandoned the doctrine of historical determinism, it has replaced the purely Communist utopian ideal with a more realistic market-driven vision for China's future.

53. In 1972, the United States and the PRC opened trade with the signing of the Shanghai Communiqué. Since that time, the US and the PRC have executed a number of important bilateral agreements.

54. 22 U.S.C. chap. 48.

Chapter 3

Legislating, the Judiciary, and Lawyers in China

The development of the law-making process in the People's Republic of China has gone through a number of stages since its inception in 1949. During the period 1949–1957, the government established the groundwork for the new socialist legal system and borrowed heavily from the Soviet legal system. During the period 1966–1976, the Cultural Revolution led to a virtual destruction of the legal system, and virtually no new laws were adopted. In July 1979, after China made a commitment to reform its legal system to encourage economic development, the National People's Congress (NPC) promulgated a number of organic laws (*zuzhi fa*) that outlined the status, internal structure, and legislative drafting procedures for the government's administrative and legislative entities.[1] The NPC also developed *zuzhi fa* for the administration of the court system and prosecutorial functions of the state. At the same time, the NPC also promulgated the Criminal Law and Criminal Procedure Law of the People's Republic of China.[2] A revised Constitution was adopted on December 4, 1982, by the 5th Session of the 5th National People's Congress.[3]

---

1. On July 1, 1979, the NPC adopted the Organic Law of the Local People's Congresses and Local People's Governments, the Electoral Law for the National People's Congress and Local People's Congresses of All Levels, the Organic Law of the People's Court, and the Organic Law of the People's Procuratorates. The NPC also adopted a resolution declaring that all laws enacted since the founding of the PRC were to remain in effect as long as they did not conflict with the Constitution and more recently enacted legislation. In reality, most of the laws from the Mao era have either been replaced or are no longer in force. Capener, *An American in Beijing: Perspectives on the Rule of Law in China*, 1988 B.Y.U. L. Rev. 567, 573; Li, *Philosophical Influences on Contemporary Chinese Law*, 6 IND. INT'L & COMP. L. REV. 327, 331 (1996).
2. *See infra* Chapter 23, Criminal Liability for FIE Activities.
3. The 1982 version of the Constitution was amended by the NPC in 1988, 1993, 1999, and 2004. *See* CONSTITUTION OF THE PEOPLE'S REPUBLIC OF CHINA (adopted on December 4, 1982, by the 5th Sess. of

Since the early 1980s, the PRC leadership has consistently called for improvements to China's legal system to further the economic development plans of the government. Deng Xiaoping stated in 1984 that China's "legal system is not perfect, and therefore we shall have to formulate a number of laws, decrees and regulations to have our democracy systemized and governed by law."[4] In October 1987, CCP General Secretary Zhao Ziyang, in a report to the 13th Party Congress, emphasized the need to "further perfect legislation governing business dealings with foreign firms."[5]

This chapter reviews the administrative framework for law-making institutions in China, the role of the CCP in the legislative process, the Chinese judiciary, and the burgeoning legal profession in the PRC.

A. Legislative Institutions

1. National People's Congress

The NPC is the "highest organ of state power" and is constitutionally charged with the legislative power of the state.[6] Under China's Constitution, "[a]ll citizens of the People's Republic of China are equal before the law" and "[a]ll power in the People's Republic belongs to the people."[7] The NPC is a single-chamber body and is composed of approximately 3,000 delegates elected by the various provinces, autonomous regions, and municipalities directly under the supervision of the central government (i.e., Beijing, Shanghai, and Tianjin), and by the armed forces.[8] Under the NPC's control are the State Council (the Central People's Government), the Supreme People's Court, the Supreme People's Procuratorate, and the Central Military Commission.

The NPC meets in session once a year for a two- or three-week period of time, and primarily evaluates and approves the law-making activities of the NPC's Standing Committee, the members of which are appointed by the NPC.[9] The NPC's legislative functions include the power to amend and

the National People's Congress and amended) *reprinted in* CHINA LAWS FOR FOREIGN BUSINESS (CCH), Business Regulation ¶ 4-500.

4. SELECTED WORKS OF DENG XIAOPING, 219, 318–19 (Chinese ed. 1984).

5. U.S.-CHINA BUSINESS COUNCIL, THE CHINA MARKET INTELLIGENCE, Nov. 1987, at 2.

6. CONSTITUTION OF THE PEOPLE'S REPUBLIC OF CHINA, arts. 57, 58 (hereinafter "CONST."). In theory, no law or administrative or local rules and regulations are allowed to contravene the constitution, and all state organizations, the armed forces, and political parties are bound by the terms of the Constitution. No organization or individual is above the Constitution or the law. CONST., art. 5.

7. CONST., arts. 2, 33.

8. CONST., art. 59.

9. CONST., art. 67. The NPC has the right to select members of the Standing Committee of the NPC; to elect the President and the Vice-President of the PRC; to decide on the choice of the Premier, Vice-Premiers, State Councilors, and ministers in charge of the various ministries and commissions; elect the President of the Supreme Court; and other functions. CONST., art. 67 (9)–(13).

implement the Constitution, and to enact the basic law (*jiben falu*).[10] In addition to the power of appointment, the NPC has the right to: examine and approve the Standing Committee's report on implementing the plan for national economic and social development; examine and approve the state budget and the report on its implementation; approve the establishment of provinces, autonomous regions, and municipalities under the supervision of the central government; decide on the establishment of special administrative regions and the systems to be instituted therein; and declare war and mobilize the armed services.[11]

The NPC's Standing Committee, which consists of approximately 150–200 individuals appointed by the NPC, is responsible for the interpretation and implementation of the Constitution,[12] and the enactment, interpretation, and amendment of the laws.[13] In theory, the NPC's Standing Committee is empowered to enact laws other than basic laws, and to amend basic laws in a manner consistent with the original legislation. Since 1979, the Standing Committee has enacted over 300 laws.[14] Any deputy/delegate of the NPC, and any member of the Standing Committee, may introduce legislative proposals for consideration.[15] The legislative procedures of the PRC do not provide for public debate or participation, nor do they provide for formal publication and distribution of draft laws.[16]

10. The "basic law" is referred to as national legislation that has a significant impact on fundamental rights and obligations. The importance of "basic law" is unclear given that other bodies including the NPC's Standing Committee and the State Council have taken the lead in developing laws and regulations that significantly impact fundamental rights and obligations. From a practical point of view, the role of NPC law making is delegated to the NPC Standing Committee given that the NPC meets infrequently.

11. CONST., art. 67 (1)–(8), (14)–(21).

12. Unlike the U.S. legal system, the courts in China do not have the power to interpret the Constitution. Only the NPC and the Standing Committee share this role.

13. CONST., arts. 65, 66, 67.

14. The standing committees of the local people's congresses in the various provinces have enacted over 3,000 local rules and regulations.

15. CONST., art. 72. The NPC's legislative procedures mandate that a proposal for a law requires the support of 38 NPC delegates in order to be submitted for consideration. Upon submission, the proposal is tendered to a special committee with jurisdiction to review the proposal (*see infra* note 20 and accompanying text) for evaluation. The special committee will in turn report its assessment to the Legal Committee of the NPC's Standing Committee and the NPC's Commission of Legal Affairs. The Commission, which consists of approximately 100 legal experts, is responsible for evaluating the legislative proposal and reports to the Legal Committee. The Legal Committee finalizes the draft for submission to the NPC. The NPC's legislative procedures are set forth in the *Rules of Procedure of the National People's Congress of the People's Republic of China (1989)*. For an analysis of the Rules, *see* Leung, *Chinese Law-Making: A Case of Legislative Disorder,* 8 CHINA LAW NEWS 1, 2 (Feb. 27, 1998). *See generally* LEGISLATIVE DRAFTING FOR MARKET REFORM: SOME LESSONS FROM CHINA (A. Seidman & R. Seidman, eds. 1997).

16. *See infra* footnote 40 and accompanying text (discussion of Legislation Law). *See generally* Leung, *supra* note 15, at 5 (author proposes that the NPC provide for a procedure to review law proposals and to require that the proponents prepare a legislative "impact statement" that evaluates the impact and need for the proposed law). On April 29, 1998, Li Peng, the Chairman of the Standing Committee of the NPC, stated that the NPC needs to make the legislating process more open to public opinion. The proposal

To ensure that its legislative efforts are implemented, the NPC Standing Committee has carried out multiple forms of supervision over the performance of the government, the courts, and the People's Procuratorate. In 1993, the NPC, recognizing that implementation lags behind the promulgation of legislation, adopted the *Regulations of the NPC Standing Committee on the Inspection and Supervision of Law Enforcement* (the "Supervision Regulations").[17] The Supervision Regulations established a framework for systematic inspection and supervision of law enforcement to ensure that the laws are accepted, applied, and enforced. Between 1994 and 1996, the NPC established a total of 46 supervision task forces to evaluate the implementation and enforcement of 13 laws, including the Labor Law[18] and the Environmental Protection Law.[19]

A number of special committees are under the supervision of the Standing Committee, including the Nationalities Committee, the Law Committee, the Financial and Economics Committee, the Education, Science, Culture, and Public Health Committee, the Foreign Affairs Committee, the Overseas Chinese Committee, the Committee for Internal and Judicial Affairs, and the Committee on Environmental and Resource Protection.[20] These committees evaluate and develop legislation concerning their respective areas of expertise.

The CCP does not have the constitutional authority to initiate and control the legislative process, or to draft and lobby for particular legislation.[21] However, the CCP's own Constitution provides that the party has the authority to supervise the legislative, judicial, and administrative organizations of the state.[22] In addition, party membership has traditionally been an

---

received the unanimous support of the 140 members of the Second Session of the 9th NPC's Standing Committee meeting. In response, the NPC published a draft of the revised land administration law. *See also* Sun, *Legislation Needs Democracy,* CHINA DAILY (Apr. 30, 1998), available on Lexis, News Library, or on the Web site of the CHINA DAILY at http://www.chinadaily.com.cn. Thereafter, the NPC published a number of draft laws, including the draft Marriage Law and draft Contract Law, and solicited the input of individuals, enterprises, and foreign parties affected by the legislative proposals. *See* Guo, *Draft Marriage Clause Draws Controversy,* CHINA DAILY (Oct. 16, 1998), available on Lexis, News Library, or on the Web site of the CHINA DAILY at http://www.chinadaily.com.cn; *Democratic Legislation to Produce Better Laws,* CHINA DAILY (Sept. 28, 1998), available on Lexis, News Library, or on the Web site of CHINA DAILY at http://www.chinadaily.com.cn (The CHINA DAILY states that "[t]he top legislature recently published the draft of the contract law to solicit public advice. This shows the country welcomes public participation in the legal system.").

17. Jin, *New Approaches of People's Congresses in China to Supervise Law Enforcement,* 10 CHINA L. Q. (Mar. 15, 1997) at 53.

18. *See infra* Chapter 10, Labor and Employment Law.

19. *See infra* Chapter 18, Environmental Protection. For an analysis of the report issued by the NPC concerning the implementation of the Law on Environmental Protection, *See* Jin, *supra* note 17, at 55–56.

20. CONST., art. 70. All of the committees mentioned, except for the last two, are permanent committees.

21. China has eight political parties in addition to the CCP. These parties have a small membership and play an inconsequential role. Observers, however, believe that political reform will develop over time. *See generally* Chen, *China to Test Waters of Political Reform,* WALL ST. J., July 27, 1998, A11, col. 1.

22. CONSTITUTION OF THE COMMUNIST PARTY OF CHINA (1982), translated in BEIJING REVIEW, 1982, No. 38: 8.

essential requirement for a leadership position and party politics play a crucial role in advancement and achievement in government. Critics claim that the NPC is not a true legislative organization that encourages debate; rather, it is a rubber-stamping body that unquestioningly follows the party line and the annual meetings and media coverage are intended to create the illusion of democracy.

2. President of the PRC

The President of the PRC is elected by the NPC and is the chief executive officer of the government. The President has the power to promulgate the statutes adopted by the NPC; appoint and remove members of the State Council; issue orders of pardons; proclaim martial law; declare a state of war and issue orders of mobilization; accept diplomatic credentials offered by foreign representatives; appoint and recall China's diplomatic envoys stationed abroad; and ratify and abrogate treaties and important agreements signed with foreign governments.[23] The Constitution provides that any citizen who has reached the age of 45 and is eligible to vote may be a candidate for the presidency; however, he or she must be nominated and elected by the NPC.[24] There is no limitation on the President's term of office.[25]

3. State Council

The State Council, also referred to as the Central People's Government, is similar in function to the cabinet of the U.S. Executive Branch and is empowered to enact administrative rules and regulations.[26] The State Council is the highest organ of State administration, and supervises the various ministries, bureaus, commissions, and local governments.[27] Some of the more important ministries and commissions under the State Council include Ministry of Foreign Affairs, Ministry of Commerce, Ministry of Public Security, Ministry of Justice, and Ministry of Finance. The State Council and its ministries and commission are authorized to issue orders, directives, and administrative regulations (*xingzheng fagui*) within the jurisdiction of its respective departments.[28] Such administrative regulations have the power of law in that they

23. CONST., art. 80. China is currently studying reforming its political system to allow for the presidency to be elected rather than appointed by the NPC. The position is largely a ceremonial post at the current time. *See* Chen, *supra* note 21, at A11.

24. CONST., § II, preamble.

25. CONST., art. 83.

26. CONST., art. 89. The State Council's legislative powers are not clearly defined, which allows the Council to control both the executive and legislative functions through administrative fiat.

27. *See generally,* I. Derbyshire, Politics in China: From Mao to the Post-Deng Era, 174–75 (1991).

28. CONST., art. 90.

are only subordinate to the Constitution and the basic and national laws. State Council administrative regulations are also controlling over local and provincial laws and regulations. Since 1979, the State Council has issued over 700 administrative laws and regulations concerning its various ministries and commissions.

The division of the State Council responsible for legislative matters is the Office of Legislative Affairs (OLA), also referred to as the Legal Bureau. The OLA was originally established in 1954 and abolished in 1959, and was later reestablished in 1986. The principal functions of the OLA are to develop legislative plans; to draft, edit, and publish national legislation; and to evaluate the implementation of legislation. The OLA solicits the opinions of legal scholars and other experts in the law drafting process. After a draft law is prepared, the OLA will submit the draft to the Legislative Affairs Commission, which is a ministry-level organization and working committee of the NPC's Standing Committee. The Legislative Affairs Commission has several departments, including the Economic Law Department, Civil Law Department, and the State Law Department. The Legislative Affairs Commission is responsible for reviewing and revising laws submitted by the OLA, and will thereafter submit the bills to the NPC Standing Committee or directly to the NPC. If adopted, a legislative proposal will be promulgated into law by the President.

In 1998 and 2003, the NPC announced institutional reorganization of the various ministries and, among other things, reduced the total number from 40 to 29.[29] The NPC retained 27 of the original ministries and added two new ministries. The purpose of the reforms is to improve efficiency, streamline the massive government bureaucracy, separate the government from economic enterprise administration, reduce the scope of corruption, and reduce the civil service.[30] Those ministries most affected by the 1998 reforms are those focused on industry-specific areas such as coal, internal trade, and chemicals. The 1998 reform plan also calls for privatization of certain ministry-owned enterprises. The State Council is responsible for carrying out

29. *See generally,* Harpole, *New Governmental Structure Emerges from Ninth National People's Congress Session,* 9 CHINA LAW NEWS 1 (Mar. 26, 1998); *Restructuring China's Government: Reins of Reform,* EIU Business Asia (April 6, 1998), available on Lexis, News Library. For a chart outlining the government reorganization, *see* China Information Services LLC's Web site "China OnLine" at http://www.chinaonline.com.

30. Since 1979, the number of civil servants in China had grown by 82.3 percent, while the size of the population only increased by 27.1 percent. The reforms call for eliminating approximately 4 million government jobs. *See Domestic News Economic Plans,* CHINA ECONOMIC REV. (April 23, 1998), available on Lexis, News Library.

the reorganization plan. The most significant changes in 1998 and 2003 include the following:

a. Ministry of Commerce

The 1998 institutional reform plan broadened the power of the State Economic and Trade Commission (SETC), which was responsible for developing and implementing national economic policy.[31] The SETC assumed regulatory control over five different ministries including the Ministry of Coal Industry, Ministry of Machine Building Industry, Ministry of Metallurgical Industry, Ministry of Internal Trade, and the Ministry of Chemical Industry. These industry-specific ministries became bureaus under the auspices of the SETC. The Ministry of Chemical Industry was replaced by the SETC-controlled Petrochemical Industry Bureau and assumed regulatory functions over the China Petroleum and Natural Gas Corporation and the China Petroleum and Chemical Industry Corporation.[32]

In 2003, the SETC was later merged with the Ministry of Foreign Trade and Economic Cooperation (MOFTEC) to form the Ministry of Commerce (MOFCOM). MOFCOM assumed (1) all of MOFTEC's foreign investment and other authority, (2) certain responsibilities from the State Economic & Trade Commission ("SETC"), including overall domestic and foreign trade and economic policy and administration, and administration of industrial product and raw material import and export, and (3) the responsibility from the State Development Planning Commission ("SDPC") to administer agriculture trade. The SETC thereafter ceased to exist.

b. Ministry of Information Industry

The Ministry of Information Industry (MII) replaced and assumed the functions of the Ministry of Posts and Telecommunications (MPT), the Ministry of Electronics Industry, and the Ministry of Radio, Film, and Television, the China Aerospace Industry Corporation, and the China Aviation Industry Corporation.[33]

---

31. *See An Introduction to the Institutional Reform of the State Economic and Trade Commission,* 135 China International Business (MOFTEC) 3 (1998).

32. *See generally Emergence of Two Big Companies in Oil Industrial Regrouping,* China Chemical Reporter (May 6, 1998), available on Lexis, News Library; Young & Wood, *State to Create Two New Petrochemicals Giants,* Chemical Week (April 22, 1998), available on Lexis, News Library.

33. For a chart outlining the telecommunications industry in China, *see* China Information Services LLC's Web site "China OnLine" at http://www.chinaonline.com. *See Brief Introduction to the Departments of the Ministry of Information Industry,* 134 China International Business (MOFTEC) 37 (1998) (discusses the different departments of the MII).

c. Ministry of Labor and Social Security

The Ministry of Labor and Social Security replaces the Ministry of Labor, the Ministry of Personnel, Ministry of Civil Affairs, and the medical insurance functions of the Ministry of Health.

d. Ministry of Education/Ministry of Science and Technology

The Ministry of Education replaces the State Education Commission. The Ministry of Science and Technology replaces the State Science and Technology Commission.

e. Ministry of Land and Natural Resources

The Ministry of Land and Natural Resources assumed the functions of the State Land Administration, the Ministry of Geology and Mineral Resources, the State Oceanography Bureau, and the State Bureau of Surveying and Cartography.

f. State Environmental Protection Administration

The PRC's Environmental Protection Bureau was given a new title and promoted from subministry to a ministry-level entity. The new entity is known as the State Environmental Protection Administration and has greater powers over environmental protection enforcement issues. The bureau formerly was under the supervision of the Ministry of Construction. The new title and elevation to a higher level reflects the NPC's great concern with environmental affairs and public expectation of environmental protection.[34]

g. State Development Planning Commission

In 1998, the State Development Planning Commission replaced the State Planning Commission (SPC), an entity that held a key role in China's planned economy. As China moves from a planned economy to a market economy, the role of the Commission will diminish. In 2003, the SDPC was renamed the State Reform and Development Committee (SRDC) and has been restructured to assume (1) most of the SDPC's responsibilities, (2) the duties of the State Economic System Restructuring Office (SESRC), which was abolished, and (3) certain responsibilities of the former SETC such as the administration of investments in technology by domestic enterprises, industry planning, and planning for trade of key industrial products and raw materials.

34. *See China Agency Given Greater Powers,* CHINA DAILY (Apr. 1, 1998), available on Lexis, News Library, or on the Web site of the CHINA DAILY at http://www.chinadaily.com.cn.

h. State Drug Administration

The 1998 reform provided that the State Drug Administration replaces the State Pharmaceutical Administration, the State Administration of Traditional Chinese Medicines, and the pharmaceutical department of the Ministry of Health. In 2003, the SDA's role was expanded to supervise food, health products, and cosmetics, and was renamed the State Food and Drug Administration (SFDA). Some of the food- and cosmetic-related functions of the Ministry of Health were transferred to the SFDA. The SFDA is the primary regulatory agency responsible for supervising the pharmaceutical, medical device, food, cosmetics, and health foods industries.

i. State Asset Regulatory Commission

In 2003, the government formed the State Asset Regulatory Commission (SARC), which is responsible for all duties of the Central Enterprise Working Committee of the PRC Communist Party, the duties of the SETC, and the Ministry of Finance with respect to the reform and supervision of state-owned enterprises and state-owned assets.

j. China Banking Regulatory Commission

As part of the 2003 reform, the China Banking Regulatory Commission was formed to regulate and supervise the banking industry in China, and assumes these functions that were previously under the control of the People's Bank of China (PBOC), which will continue to function as a central bank and not a regulatory agency.

k. Ministries/Commissions Reduced in Status

The State Forestry Bureau replaces the Ministry of Forestry and will come under the direct supervision of the State Council. The State Physical Culture & Sports Commission is replaced by the Council of Physical Culture & Sports. The State Administration of Radio, Film, & Television (SARFT) replaces the Ministry of Radio, Film, and Television. In addition, the State Commission for Restructuring the Economic System is reorganized as a research institution under the control of the State Council.

4. Local People's Congresses

In China, there are 23 provinces (including Taiwan), three municipalities directly under the central government (i.e. Beijing, Shanghai, and Tianjin), five autonomous regions inhabited primarily by minority groups (non-Han), and the Hong Kong Special Administrative Region.[35] The people's congresses of the provinces, regions, and municipalities, and their respective standing committees, may adopt regulations that govern local activities. The local congresses are required to report their legislative activities to the NPC's Standing Committee for approval. Although the organizational structure of the local congresses mirrors the NPC structure, it is unclear as to whether the provincial governments will adopt the reforms initiated by the NPC.

The local people's congresses have adopted over 5,000 local laws since 1979, ranging from traffic rules and foreign investment incentives to domestic relations laws.[36] In addition to enacting laws that regulate purely local activities, local people's congresses have also been authorized to enact foreign investment laws for the four special economic zones, the designated coastal cities and Hainan Island, and technological and special development zones. For example, the cities of Shenzhen and Shanghai have been authorized to enact laws on an experimental basis to allow authorities to observe their function and effects prior to nationwide application. Local law may not be in conflict with the Constitution or with national laws or administrative regulations. As a result, a foreign investor must take into consideration a wide range of laws that may affect a particular operation, including laws developed on a national, provincial, or local level, and those developed by zone authorities.

5. Language and the Hierarchy of the Law

Chinese written laws use a number of terms to define the scope of application and the level of authority of enactment. Terms include laws (*fa*), regulations or provisions (*tiaoli*), rules (*guize*), detailed rules (*xize*), methods or measures (*banfa*), decisions (*jueding*), resolutions (*jueyi, guiding*), and orders (*mingling*). A law (*fa*) is a statute that has been enacted by the NPC or its Standing Committee.[37] Regulations (*tiaoli*), also translated as "provisions" or "measures," are administrative rules designed to implement a law or policy and are usually issued by the State Council. In contrast, a regulation (*guiding*) is issued by a lower-level agency and addresses a narrower question.

35. The Hong Kong SAR is discussed separately. *See* Chapter 24, Special Zones of the PRC, § B.

36. Although the legislative power of the NPC is paramount over local authorities, local legislation sometimes conflicts with national legislation concerning certain issues. For example, in 1986 the central government issued regulations setting a national standard for usury. This rule was disputed by some local authorities given that interest rates on private loans differed depending upon the development level of a particular region. *See* Ping, *Drafting the Contract Law in China,* 10 COLUM. J. ASIAN LAW, 245, 247 (1996).

37. For example, the Labor Law of the People's Republic of China is a basic law adopted by the NPC. The term *fa* is used in a number of compounds such as *fadian* (i.e., a systematic body of law), and *falinghuibian* (i.e., a collective body of laws and regulations).

A set of rules (*guize*) or detailed rules (*xize*) is usually issued by a ministry, and often includes specific rules of interpretation or explanation of a law or regulation. Methods or measures (*banfa*) are rules or regulations that are more detailed and seek to address a narrow issue. A judicial or administrative decision (*jueding*) is for explanatory purposes.

State organizations, political parties, and social organizations adopt resolutions (*jueyi*), which have little prescriptive legislative value but record common concerns and opinions expressed at a particular meeting or forum. An order (*mingling*) refers to a proclamation issued by a state organization that is intended to prescribe legal standards.

The use of the various terms generally reflects the governmental level of enactment or promulgation. Although the government is careful to avoid the conflicting use of the above terms, in the mid-1980s the State Council realized that the overlapping use of the terms made it "difficult to determine the extent of [the law's] effectiveness, the nature of the authority which promulgated it, or the scope of its applications."[38] The State Council has taken steps to emphasize that the terms be used properly to reflect the level of authority and the scope of enactment.

In countries with more well-developed legal systems, primary and secondary legal resources are generally available for legal practitioners. In China, however, the publication of laws and regulations has become standard only since the mid-1980s. Prior to the Open Door policy, publication of China's laws was irregular. Even today, many laws are not published until long after they have been promulgated, and China has no public reporter system of judicial opinions or decisions. It is anticipated that Chinese laws will become more accessible, however, with the introduction of electronic publishing.

6. Review of the Legislative Process

Although China must be complimented for its extraordinary efforts to rebuild its legal system, the legislative process has been characterized as lacking in transparency, and has resulted in the development of laws and regulations that favor the interests of government rather than individuals and private enterprise.[39] The language of Chinese law is also often purposefully

38. *Report of the State Council Working Group for Reorganizing Laws and Regulations of Various Departments of the State Council and Future Work,* June 10, 1985, *reprinted in* STATE COUNCIL BULLETIN, 1985, No. 20, at 745.

39. *See* Corne, *Legal System Reforms Promise Substantive—but Limited—Improvement,* 11 CHINA L. & PRAC. 29 (June 1997).

ambiguous and vague in order to leave open several possible interpretations. Such vagueness allows administrative agencies broad powers to promulgate regulations, rules, and explanatory circulars that interpret the law in a manner that best fits the agency's view with little oversight and supervision of the administrative rulemaking process.

Any discussion of the law in China would not be complete without mention of the unpublished internal (*neibu*) rules and regulations issued by the various ministries and commissions. *Neibu* are usually internal policy directives concerning the implementation and interpretation of codified laws which, until promulgated, are confidential and may not be disclosed to foreign parties. *Neibu* may involve internal policies concerning the use of foreign currency accounts, employment issues, production scheduling, or any other unwritten requirement passed down from the top to the lower-level officials in a government organization. Now that China is a member of the WTO, it has an obligation to publish any law or regulation that applies to foreign investors.

In an attempt to address the deficiencies in the system, the NPC in 2000 adopted the Legislation Law, which outlines the scope of lawmaking and rulemaking authority of legislative and administrative organs and also formalizes the legislative process and specifically with respect to the laws promulgated by the NPC and its standing committee.[40] The Legislation Law outlines standards for the drafting, revision, and repeal of laws, administrative regulations, local regulations, and special enactments, including the formulation, revision, and repeal of the rules and regulations by the State Council departments and local governments. The Legislation Law also lists the matters for which the NPC has exclusive jurisdiction for lawmaking, including matters involving the deprivation of citizens' political rights, criminal punishments or compulsive measures and punishments limiting personal freedom, expropriation of private or non-State-owned property, the basic laws regulating the economic system (such as foreign trade, tax, finance, banking, and customs), and litigation and arbitration systems.[41]

The Legislation Law details the national-level legislative process, including the authority and jurisdiction of the NPC Standing Committee to issue interpretations and clarifications of the law. In situations where clarification of a law is required or new circumstances require clarification of the implementation of

40. Legislation Law (promulgated on March 15, 2000, by the State Council). For an analysis of the Legislation Law, *see* P. Corne, *The New PRC Legislation Law: The Emperor's New Clothes?,* 14 China L. & Prac., pg. 30 May 2000. *See also* M. Dudek & A. Wang, *Lifting the Veil: Transparency in China,* 16 China L. & Prac., pg. 64 June 2002.

41. Legislation Law, art. 8.

a law, the NPC Standing Committee is authorized to interpret the law.[42] The Legislation Law also provides that the State Council, the Central Military Commission, the Supreme People's Court, the Supreme People's Procuratorate, and provincial level people's congresses may request the NPC Standing Committee to interpret a law in question.[43]

In addition to the Legislation Law, the State Council has issued a number of regulations concerning the legislative process specifically to meet China's obligations of transparency under WTO. These regulations include the Regulations on Administrative Regulation Formulation Procedures, the Regulations on Legal Code Formulation Procedures, and the Regulations on Recordal of Regulations and Legal Codes. These regulations provide that all new and amended administrative regulations and codes must be published in the Gazette of the State Council (or similar publication of the applicable local government) 30 days before implementation. The regulations also allow, but do not require, administrative agencies to solicit draft regulations and rules for comment by affected individuals or enterprises, or to hold public hearings concerning proposals.

The Regulations on Recordal of Regulations and Legal Codes require the administrative authorities to register all promulgated regulations and rules with the Office of Legal Affairs (OLA) of the State Council. In addition, and most importantly, the Recordal Regulations establish a review process whereby interested persons may request that the OLA review a regulation or rule to determine consistency with the basic laws or national legislation. The Recordal Regulations provide a mechanism for legislative consistency and a potential avenue of review to counter any activist legislation at the provincial or municipal level that is inconsistent with a law of the central government.

Although the Legislation Law and various State Council regulations on the law and rulemaking process are a step in the right direction to institutionalize legislative review, the judiciary is still barred from invalidating a law or regulation, although the courts may refuse to apply a regulation that conflicts with a higher law, regulation, or the Constitution. The absence of independent judicial oversight of the rulemaking process, a mainstay of the doctrine of separation of powers, has not been advanced under China's legal system.

42. Legislation Law, Chap. 4. Traditionally, the Supreme People's Court has assumed the unofficial position of interpreter of the national law by publishing interpretations in the SPC's Gazette. *See* N. Liu, Judicial Interpretation in China (1997).

43. Legislation Law, arts. 42, 43.

B. Judicial System

1. Supreme People's Court

The Supreme People's Court is the highest judicial organ in the PRC and is specifically authorized by the Constitution.[44] The Supreme People's Court supervises the administration of justice by the local people's courts. Although the Supreme People's Court issues directives for the purpose of guiding China's lower courts in applying a particular law or with respect to judicial administration, there is no formal system of judicial precedent.[45] The court does not have the powers to interpret the law even though it has, in recent years, assumed the role of interpreting the law by issuing explanatory memoranda with respect to particular laws or legal issues and especially at the behest of the lower courts. The authority to interpret is vested with the legislative bodies such as the government ministries. The people's courts are empowered to adjudicate only individual cases, and are not allowed to set precedent for other courts or cases. This system ensures that no individual judge or group of judges can make the law and allows the NPC to retain control and authority over the law-making process.[46] Statutory law plays a prominent role in China's legal system while judicial precedent plays a supplementary role. Nevertheless, the Supreme People's Court has issued thousands of written judicial interpretations that provide the lower courts with guidance on a broad range of substantive and procedural topics.

The Chinese court system is divided into four levels: (1) the Supreme People's Court at the national level; (2) the higher people's court at the provincial level; (3) the intermediate people's court at the municipal level; and (4) the basic people's court at the county level. In general, each court consists of criminal, civil, economic, and administrative divisions. In addition, specialized courts have been established within the court systems in every major city in China. For example, Intellectual Property Tribunals have

---

44. CONST., art. 127. The Supreme People's Court traces its roots back to the first Supreme Court established in China in 1931. The term "people's court" was adopted in 1948.

45. *See* Liu, *"Legal Precedents" with Chinese Characteristics: Published Cases in the Gazette of the Supreme People's Court,* 5 J. CHINESE L. 107 (1991) (discussing the role of published decisions in China and the development of the law). The majority of the decisions published by the Supreme People's Court (since commencing in 1985) have focused on providing guidance to the lower courts for purposes of uniformity in sentencing standards in criminal cases. *Id.* at 128–29. *See also* A. CHEN, AN INTRODUCTION TO THE LEGAL SYSTEM OF THE PEOPLE'S REPUBLIC OF CHINA (1992). Chen states: "The typical judgment of a Chinese court is short and does not set out lines or steps of legal reasoning and logical analysis in a way as detailed as in the judgments in common law courts. Relevant statutory provisions may be referred to, but the precise relationship between them in their application to the case will not usually be discussed at length. As there is no established doctrine of precedent, case law will seldom be referred to in the judgment. Lawyers' submissions are not usually responded to in the judgment. Dissenting judgments are not allowed." *Id.* at 114.

46. *See* Baker, *Forgotten Legal China,* 17 HOUSTON J. INT'L L. 363, 367–68 (1995).

been established by the Beijing Municipal Intermediate People's Court and the Beijing Municipal Higher People's Court. There are also special courts established as separate branches, such as the Maritime Court, Military Court, and Railway Transport Court, which are under the supervision of the Supreme People's Court.[47]

In theory, all courts in China exercise judicial autonomy, and are not subject to interference by state administrative organs, public organizations, or individuals.[48] However, the Supreme People's Court, and the judicial system in general, is subject to the supervision of the NPC and the NPC Standing Committee with respect to administrative issues, the political direction of judicial policy, and the general application of the law.[49]

The NPC has adopted a Code of Civil Procedure governing the court process in civil actions.[50] Prior to 1910, China had no formal civil procedure law and developed such a law only after the Western Powers pressured China to modify and improve its legal system as an incentive to relinquish extraterritorial privileges.[51] In contrast, there is evidence of criminal codes as far back as the Qin Dynasty (221–206 BCE).[52] The 1991 Civil Procedure Code is a by-product of the ongoing legal reform resulting from China's Open Door policy.

A foreign national or foreign entity initiating or responding to legal action in the people's court has the same litigation rights and obligations as Chinese citizens.[53] The 1991 Civil Procedure Code has a specific section designed for actions involving foreign parties. Whenever this section does not contain a specific provision dealing with a foreign party, all other provisions are deemed to apply.

---

47. There are 54 military courts, 73 railway courts, and 10 maritime courts in cities throughout China including Guangzhou, Shanghai, Qingdao, Tianjin, Wuhan, Dalian, Haikou, Ningbo, Beihai, and Xiamen.

48. CONST., arts. 126, 128; *See also* Code of Civil Procedure of the People's Republic of China, art. 6 (adopted April 9, 1991, by the 4th Session of the Standing Committee of the 7th National People's Congress), *reprinted in* CHINA LAWS FOR FOREIGN BUSINESS (CCH), Business Regulation ¶ 19-201 (hereinafter "Civil Procedure Code"). One writer noted that the independence of the judiciary "represents a great breakthrough in Chinese legal history, which is replete with examples of court decisions resulting from personal influence." Sang, *China's Civil Procedure Law: A New Guide for Dispute Resolution in China,* 26 INT'L LAW. 413, 416 (1992). A survey of lawyers and judges found that 80 percent believed that "judicial independence" means freedom from interference from administrative organs and not the CCP. P. Corne, *Foreign Investment in China: The Administrative Legal System* 252, fn. 33 (1997).

49. CONST., art. 128. The people's courts, including the Supreme People's Court, are not allowed to interpret the Constitution. Only the NPC and its Standing Committee have the power.

50. The Civil Procedure Code replaced the former civil procedure law, which was adopted in 1982. For an analysis of the Civil Procedure Code, *see* Sang, *supra* note 48, at 413.

51. A civil procedure law was developed by Shen Jianben, a jurist appointed by Emperor Guangxu in 1902. *See supra* Chapter 2, Development of the Chinese Legal System, § B, fn. 35 and accompanying text. The Nationalist Government enacted a civil procedure law in 1936, which was abolished when the CCP took power. In the 1950s, the NPC drafted a civil procedure law which was never promulgated. Sang, *supra* note 48, at 414.

52. Sang, *supra* note 48, at 414.

53. Civil Procedure Code, art. 5. One qualification to this rule of equal rights is if the foreign party's country imposes restrictions on Chinese citizens. In such a case, the people's court will exercise reciprocity

2. People's Procuratorates

As in other civil law systems, China has a procuracy system that parallels the court system but is independent from both the courts and the Ministry of Justice, and is responsible for supervision of the judicial system.[54] During the Cultural Revolution the procuratorial organs were dissolved but were later revived in 1979. In July of 1979, the NPC adopted a revised Organic Law of the People's Procuratorates that provides that the procurators are entrusted with supervision of the courts and administrative tribunals; investigation and prosecution of illegal conduct committed by government officials and judicial officers including acts of embezzlement, bribery, and other forms of corruption; and investigation and prosecution of activities deemed to be a threat to public security.[55]

The procuratorates act independently and are not subject to interference by government agencies or individuals.[56] The procuracy may intervene on behalf of the State before any tribunal. The Supreme People's Procuratorate answers directly to the NPC and its Standing Committee, and is responsible for supervising the local and special procuratorates.[57]

3. Legal Profession

In ancient China, lawyers were not trained in schools but usually by a teacher as an apprentice, or father to son. The Chinese bar, until recently, was essentially nonexistent. Traditionally, the Chinese people have never supported the use of lawyers in society. An attorney's worthiness of hire is

---

and place the same restrictions on the foreign litigant. In addition, foreign party actions will not be decided within any specific period of time. In contrast, in purely domestic actions, the court is required to render a decision within six months of filing. *Id.* at 135, 250. Diplomatic corps may assert immunity under principles of international law. *Id.* at art. 239. Of particular concern for foreigners is the court's right to issue an injunction prohibiting a foreigner from leaving the country in unresolved civil cases. *See* Law of the People's Republic of China on the Control of Foreigners Entering and Leaving the Country (adopted on November 22, 1985, at the 13th Sess. of the Standing Comm. of the NPC) art. 23 (2), *reprinted in* CHINA LAWS FOR FOREIGN BUSINESS (CCH), Business Regulation ¶ 19-510.

54. CONST., art. 129; Public Procurators law of the People's Republic of China (promulgated on July 1, 1995, by the National People's Congress) (outlines the qualifications, appointment process, removal, training and education, and penalties for procurators). For a discussion of the Supreme People's Procuratorate, *see* P. Corne, *supra* note 48, at 261–62. Information concerning the Supreme People's Procuratorate is available on the Web site of the Supreme People's Court at http://www.chinacourt.org.

55. CONST., art. 129; Civil Procedure Code, art. 14.

56. CONST., art. 131. *See China Procurators Emphasizing Procedural Awareness,* CHINA DAILY (June 4, 1998), available on Lexis, News Library, or on the Web site of the CHINA DAILY at http://www.chinadaily.com.cn. The Supreme People's Procuratorate requires more transparency in the procuratorial system. Effective October 26, 1998, procuratorates are required to provide witnesses, suspects, and victims in criminal cases with a written card outlining their basic legal rights. *See* Shaw, *A Historic First: Rights Listed on Cards,* CHINA DAILY (Oct. 27, 1998), available on Lexis, News Library, or on the Web site of the CHINA DAILY at http://www.chinadaily.com.cn.

57. CONST., art. 133.

still not fully accepted because the role of the advocate oftentimes conflicts with the Chinese preference for conciliation and mediation.

As China's legal system becomes more and more complex and the government continues its support of law school education, the legal profession gains more respect and prominence. With the reopening of the MOJ in 1978, legal education began anew with approximately 2,000 students enrolled in the study of law the first year.[58] Today, there are now several institutions that offer legal training to students, including law schools under the direction of the MOJ and major Chinese national and provincial universities.[59]

On August 26, 1980, the MOJ issued regulations that govern the legal profession in China.[60] In order to qualify as a lawyer, the 1980 Lawyer's Regulations requires that a person receive a certificate from the MOJ and be "patriotic" and "support the socialist system." Qualifications for a certificate included legal training, internships, and the taking of a bar examination.

To further encourage the development of the legal profession, the NPC's Standing Committee initiated a five-year public education program on China's laws and legal education system in November of 1985.[61] The public education program resulted in the publication of numerous newspaper articles explaining the new system, interviews and lectures were held on television and radio, and public trials were used as educational tools.[62]

In 1997, the NPC's first comprehensive law governing the legal profession became effective.[63] Prior to January 1, 1997, PRC lawyers were considered "functionaries of the State" and their duties were "to ensure the proper implementation of the law and the protection of the interests of the

58. In 1979, there were only 79 government-supported law firms and 212 lawyers nationwide. In 1998, there were over 8,300 law firms with over 100,000 lawyers. In 2002, there were over 110,000 lawyers and 10,000 law firms or offices nationwide. The passage rate for the lawyers examination is only 10% for first-time takers. Zong, *Legal System Puts Its Achievements on Record,* CHINA DAILY (June 17, 1998); *Number of Lawyers in China Rising Rapidly—Trade Group*, WALL ST. J. (July 7, 2002).

59. Li, *supra* note 1, at 329. *See also* Guo, *Lawyers' Job Appealing to Young, Educated,* CHINA DAILY (Oct. 12, 1998), available on Lexis, News Library, or on the Web site of the CHINA DAILY at http://www.chinadaily.com.cn.

60. Provisional Regulations of the People's Republic of China on Lawyers (adopted 26 August 1980 by the 15th Sess. of the Standing Committee of the 5th NPC), art. 1, *reprinted in* CHINA LAWS FOR FOREIGN BUSINESS (CCH), Business Regulation ¶ 19-450 (hereinafter "1980 Lawyer's Regulations"). For a discussion of the 1980 Lawyer's Regulations, *see* Cohen, *China's New Lawyer's Law,* 66 A.B.A.J. 1533 (1980).

61. *Legal Studies: A Nationwide Assignment*, BEIJING REVIEW, December 23, 1989.

62. Li, *supra* note 1, at 328–29.

63. Law of the People's Republic of China on Lawyers (adopted May 15, 1996, by the 19th Sess. of the Standing Committee of the 8th NPC), art. 1 (hereinafter "the 1997 PRC Lawyer's Law"), *reprinted in* CHINA LAWS FOR FOREIGN BUSINESS (CCH), Business Regulation ¶ 16-650. *See also* Rules of the Shenzhen SEZ on Lawyers (adopted on February 24, 1995, by the 28th Sess. of the Standing Comm. of the 1st Shenzhen Municipal People's Congress and amended on April 9, 1997, by the Standing Comm. of the Shenzhen People's Congress), *reprinted in* CHINA LAWS FOR FOREIGN BUSINESS, Special Zones & Cities ¶ 71-225. The MOJ has also developed regulations for law partnerships which sets forth the

State and collectives."[64] Law firms were considered public institutions under the leadership and supervision of the MOJ.[65] In contrast, the 1997 PRC Lawyer's Law drops the "functionaries" language and provides that lawyers are required to "protect the legal rights and interests of the parties concerned."[66] Nevertheless, the Chinese legal profession is still not wholly independent from the government because the MOJ is required to supervise lawyers, law firms, and lawyer's associations.[67] The MOJ is responsible for administering qualifying exams and licensing,[68] and disciplining attorneys for misconduct.[69] The 1997 PRC Lawyer's Law provides that a lawyer and his or her firm is liable for compensation as a result of malpractice.[70]

The independence of Chinese lawyers remains in question. In a 1993 survey of Chinese lawyers, 94 percent of the 127 interviewed reported that their legal work was interfered with by the government, the CCP, or by social contacts involving litigants.[71] Such interference has led many lawyers

---

requirements for minimum capital, minimum number of partners (3), and a written partnership agreement. The partnership law also sets forth grounds for termination of the partnership, liquidation, liability issues, and professional ethics. *See* Administrative Measures on Partnership Law Firms (promulgated on October 25, 1996, by the MOJ), *reprinted in* CHINA LAWS FOR FOREIGN BUSINESS (CCH), Business Regulation ¶ 13-355. Establishment, Amendment and Cancellation of Registation of Partnership Law Firms Procedures (issued on January 20, 2003, by the Judicial Bureau of the Beijing Municipality). At least 30 percent of China's lawyers are university graduates with bachelor's degrees and 54.7 percent are junior college graduates. In addition, more than 3,000 are holders of advanced degrees or are foreign trained. *See Record of Events (October–December 1996),* CHINA LAW 101 (1996); Wang & Shao, *Vital for Market Economy: Lawyer's Education Advancing,* CHINA DAILY (June 24, 1998), available on Lexis, News Library, or on the Web site of the CHINA DAILY at http://www.chinadaily.com.cn; *China Sets Standards for Legal Profession,* THE LAWYER (Jan. 14, 1997), available on Lexis, News Library.

64. 1980 Lawyer's Regulations, art. 1.

65. 1980 Lawyer's Regulations, art. 13.

66. 1997 PRC Lawyer's Law, art. 1.

67. 1997 PRC Lawyer's Law, art. 4. In August of 1988, the American Bar Association agreed to assist the All-China Lawyers Association in developing an independent bar. *See U.S. Lawyers to Help China Organize Independent Bar,* CHINA DAILY (Aug. 11, 1998), available on Lexis, News Library, or on the Web site of the CHINA DAILY at http://www.chinadaily.com.cn.

68. 1997 PRC Lawyer's Law, arts. 5–14. The National Lawyer Qualification Examination is administered annually and usually during the month of October. In 1998, 15,102 individuals, or 12 percent of the candidates, passed the examination. Over 120,000 people, a record, participated in 1998's examination. The MOJ found that 82 percent of the candidates who passed the exam in 1998 were under the age of 30. Shao, *Exam Tests Abilities of Lawyers,* CHINA DAILY (Dec. 8, 1998), available on Lexis, News Library, or on the Web site of CHINA DAILY at http://www.chinadaily.com.cn.

69. 1997 PRC Lawyer's Law, art. 44.

70. 1997 PRC Lawyer's Law, art. 49.

71. GONG XIANG RUI, FU ZHU BIAN, ZHANG SHU YI AND JIANG MING AN, THE IDEAL AND REALITY OF THE RULE OF LAW (FAZHI DE LIXIANG YU XIANSHI), Beijing: China University of Politics and Law Press, p. 34, tables 3-3-3 and 3-3-4 (1993). *See also* P. Corne, *supra* note 48, at 244–255. In July of 1998, the All-China Lawyer's Association (ACLA) established the National Committee for the Protection of Lawyer's Rights and Interests, an organization designed to protect the rights of the legal profession in China. The Committee provides legal assistance to attorneys whose "life and property are infringed upon in the conduct of their legitimate practice." *See China Lawyers Need to be Defended Too,* CHINA DAILY (Aug. 11, 1998), available on Lexis, News Library, or on the Web site of the CHINA DAILY at http://www.chinadaily.com.cn. For a discussion concerning the problems confronting the legal profession in China, *see Lawyers in China: Obstacles to Independence and the Defense of Rights* (Lawyers Committee for Human Rights, New York: 1998), available via the Web site of the LCHR at http://www.lchr.org.

to take a more conciliatory approach when representing foreign parties. Although many Chinese lawyers are slowly becoming more zealous advocates of their clients' interests, Chinese attorneys traditionally will not aggressively represent their clients in either court proceedings or in contract negotiations because they risk damaging their careers. Moreover, under the 1997 PRC Lawyer's Law, a lawyer may be disbarred or disciplined if he or she reveals "state secrets" or conceals important facts during an investigation or trial.[72] A lawyer thus risks disbarment if he or she offers evidence that is exculpatory but represents "state secrets" or refuses to advise the prosecution of evidence that is incriminating.

Foreign law firms were formally allowed to practice in China on a limited basis in 1992. The MOJ's approval process has historically been on a trial basis and the waiting list for licensing has been extensive. Post-WTO, the government is allowed to provide greater access to foreign law firms in China, and in 2003 there were 115 foreign law firms approved to open representative offices.[73] Foreign law firms are prohibited from representing clients in Chinese courts or in matters involving purely domestic legal issues.[74] Overseas firms may represent their foreign clients in China and throughout Asia from China, and represent Chinese-funded companies registered overseas.

China is also taking steps to ensure that its judges and court officials are properly trained and supervised.[75] Many judges were appointed based upon

---

72. 1997 PRC Lawyer's Law, art. 45. The disclosure of "state secrets" is prohibited by law, and the relevant regulations define the terms secret information and illegal disclosure in broad terms. "State Secrets" are defined as "matters that affect the security and interests of the state" and are illustrated by broad categories of information relating to national defense, "import policy decisions on state affairs," "economic and social development," "science and technology development," "criminal investigations," and "other state secrets that by decision of the state departments on protecting state secrets should be safeguarded." Law on Safeguarding State Security of the People's Republic of China (promulgated by the State Council in 1993); Detailed Rules for the Implementation of the Law on Safeguarding State Security of the People's Republic of China (promulgated by the State Council in 1994).

73. Ministry of Justice Announcement No. 19 (115 representative offices of foreign law firms approved) (issued on October 8, 2003, by the MOJ); *see* Chapter 5, Foreign Investment Guidelines and Industry-Specific Regulations § B. 18.

74. Civil Procedure Code, art. 241. *See generally* Bangsberg, *China Eyeing Legal Sector: Foreign Law Firms May Get More Latitude,* J. OF COMMERCE (Aug. 18, 1998), available on Lexis, News Library, or at the Web site for the JOURNAL OF COMMERCE at http://www.joc.com. *See also* Interim Provisions of the Ministry of Justice and the State Administration of Industry and Commerce on the Setting Up of the Office of Foreign Law Firms in China (issued on May 26, 1992, by the MOJ and the SAIC). *See also* Administrative Measures on Resident Representative Offices in Mainland China of Law Firms from Hong Kong and Macao Special Administrative Regions (Order No. 70 of the Ministry of Justice and Promulgated on March 13, 2002), *reprinted in* CHINA LAWS FOR FOREIGN BUSINESS (CCH), Business Regulation ¶ 7-610 (outlining procedures for the establishment, management, and termination of rep office law firms from Hong Kong and Macao); Implementing Rules Regarding Foreign Law Firms (issued by on June 4, 2002, by the Ministry of Justice). *See generally* R. Guo, *Time to Honor China's WTO Commitments: MOJ Issues Implementing Rules Regarding Foreign Law Firms,* CHINA L. & PRAC. (Oct. 2002).

75. Decision on Amendments to the Law of Judges of the People's Republic of China (promulgated on June 30, 2001, by the Standing Committee. of the 9th NPC). The Amended Judges Law enhances the qualifications and training for judges. In order to qualify, a candidate for a judge position is required to

party activities or military background, and may not have received any formal legal training. In response, China has established the Academy of Judges, based in Beijing, which is designed to provide continuing legal education for judges and to train attorneys that aspire to be judges. The president of the Supreme People's Court, Ren Jianxin, is the newly appointed chancellor of the Academy, which will ultimately have 100 teachers and accommodate 400 students.

4. Rule of Law in China

China has recently made progress in developing a legal system that reflects, and in some respects is consistent with, international norms. Prolific legislative activity and increased emphasis on implementation and enforcement are positive steps and indicative that China is serious about the establishment of a genuine legal system based upon the rule of law.[76] Nevertheless, the legacy

(1) hold a bachelor of laws degree or non-law degree with relevant legal expertise, and have worked in the legal field for at least two years; or (2) obtain a master of laws degree or a non-law master's degree with one year of work experience. To sit on the Supreme People's Court or upper-level courts the qualifications are higher. Candidates for judge positions are required to pass the Uniform Judiciary Examination. The Supreme People's Court established a telephone hotline for persons to complain about any judge or judicial officer that engages in embezzlement, bribery, or other corrupt activities such as an abuse of power, concealing or forging evidence, leaking secrets, or unlawful coercion. *See Reporting Center,* China Daily (May 12, 1998), available on Lexis, News Library, or on the Web site of the China Daily at http://www.chinadaily.com.cn. The courts have also convicted prosecutors that abuse their positions of authority. On March 17, 1998, the Intermediate Court of Fuzhou, Fujian Province, sentenced three procurators for torturing a suspect into confessing a crime to 15-year jail terms. *Procurators in Jail,* China Daily (March 27, 1998), available on Lexis, News Library, or on the Web site of the China Daily at http://www.chinadaily.com.cn. For a discussion on the PRC's reform of judicial administration and recently developed standards for judicial officers, *see* R. Brown, Understanding Chinese Courts and Legal Process: Law with Chinese Characteristics (1997). The MOJ encourages legal exchanges between Chinese practitioners and judges with their foreign counterparts. *See generally* Wang & Shao, *China, U.S. Discuss Legal Traditions,* China Daily (Feb. 3, 1999), available on Lexis, News Library, or on the Web site of China Daily at http://www.chinadaily.com.cn (article discusses visit to China by U.S. Supreme Court Justice Anthony Kennedy)*;* Shao, *A Trial Look at Trial Law System,* China Daily (Oct. 30, 1998), available on Lexis, News Library, or on the Web site of China Daily at http://www.chinadaily.com.cn (article discusses mock trials designed to improve the quality of China's judges co-sponsored by the American Bar Association, the Berlin Judges Association, the Ford Foundation, and the State Judges College in Beijing). The number of female judges in China has increased. The Supreme People's Court notes that there are approximately 28,000 female judges in China, or 16.8 percent of the total number of judges in China. *See* Hu, *Women Judges Respectable,* China Daily (Sept. 16, 1998), available on Lexis, News Library, or at the Web site of China Daily at http://www.chinadaily.com.cn. The Supreme People's Court issued a directive in 1999 allowing for the appointment of judges in a competitive manner and based upon qualifications, rather than politics, favoritism, or *guanxi. See Judgeships Now Open to Competition,* China Daily (April 9, 1999), available on Lexis, News Library, or at the Web site of China Daily at http://www.chinadaily.com.cn. Since 2000, the courts have clamped down on misconduct by judicial officers. *See 1517 Court Staff Found Violating Law, Discipline*, People's Daily (Jan. 7, 2001); *Supreme Court Tightens Internal Discipline Through Inspection*, People's Daily (Oct. 8, 2002); *China Punishes 972 Court Staff for Violating Discipline Law*, People's Daily (Dec. 16, 2003), available online at http://www.peopledaily.com.cn.

76. The "rule of law" has been defined as the "supremacy of the law" and provides that decisions should be made by the application of known principles or laws without the intervention of discretion in

of the past and persistent political intermeddling raise questions as to whether a true rule of law exists, or will ever exist, in China.[77] Until there is assurance that Chinese courts will follow the written law without regard to politics, confidence in the legal system will remain an open issue.[78]

Moreover, the extensive use of personal connections (*guanxi*) to circumvent the law or to gain leniency seriously undermines the public's confidence in the judicial system. The institution of *guanxi*, or connections, has its roots in the hierarchical social order of Confucianism and plays an important role in contemporary Chinese society. As a result of a constant shortage of services and goods, people are compelled to use networking to overcome the Chinese bureaucracy. Those who have such connections are able to improve their job and personal situations, obtain a superior apartment, or may "go through the back door" (*zou hou men*) to secure government approval.[79]

A by-product of *guanxi* is the institution of nepotism in China, which has allowed senior cadres and their children (*gaoganzidi*) to monopolize key businesses and to hold substantial real property interests in Hong Kong and

---

their application. BLACK'S LAW DICTIONARY 1196 (5th ed. 1979). *See generally* Capener, *An American in Beijing: Perspectives on the Rule of Law in China,* 1988 B.Y.U. L. REV. 567 (1988); Turner, *Rule of Law Ideals in Early China?,* 6 J. CHINESE L. 1 (1992). *See also* Hong, *Members See Need for Society of More Law,* CHINA DAILY (Mar. 5, 1998), available on Lexis, News Library, or on the Web site of the CHINA DAILY at http://www.chinadaily.com.cn (NPC members call for improving the legal system to strengthen enforcement, improving the skills and training of law enforcement personnel, and changing trial methods to increase the openness of judicial system). In April 1998, MOJ Minister Gao Changli stated that the "rule of law" will be the guiding principle of China's judicial departments during the upcoming years. Chen, *Minister: Promoting "Rule of Law,"* CHINA DAILY (Apr. 27, 1998), available on Lexis, News Library, or on the Web site of the CHINA DAILY at http://www.chinadaily.com.cn; Hong, *Governing by Law Key to State,* CHINA DAILY (March 13, 1998), available on Lexis, News Library, or on the Web site of the CHINA DAILY at http://www.chinadaily.com.cn. During its 1999 session, the NPC amended the Constitution to affirmatively assert the country's adherence to the rule of law. The amendment includes the following language added to Article 5 of the Constitution: "The People's Republic of China should implement the principle of ruling the country by law, governing the country according to law, and making it a socialist country ruled by law." The NPC Standing Committee maintains that this constitutional amendment is designed to ensure that China will "no longer change its ruling styles with the change of leaders." Xu, *Amendments Wait for NPC Approval,* CHINA DAILY (Feb. 1, 1999), available on Lexis, News Library, or on the Web site of CHINA DAILY at http://www.chinadaily.com.cn.

77. As is evident in the enforcement of its criminal laws after Tiananmen Square in 1989, the Chinese government still views the law and policy as a tool of social control. The CCP also has its own set of rules to impose party discipline on errant members which it does so independent of the criminal law. *See Legal System & Human Rights Under the Absolute Leadership of the Party,* INSIDE CHINA MAINLAND (May 1, 1998), available on Lexis, News Library; *China Publishes Guide to Communist Discipline,* REUTERS WORLD SERVICE (Mar. 7, 1997), available on Lexis, News Library.

78. On May 21, 1998, the president of the Supreme People's Court, Xiao Yang, invited members of the National People's Congress to criticize the Court's work. Interestingly, Xiao stressed that sound supervision of the Court by the NPC was necessary to ensure the impartiality of the Court. Xiao's statements appear to further welcome political interference in the Court's work. *See Supervision Sought,* CHINA DAILY (March 23, 1998), available on Lexis, News Library, or on the Web site of the CHINA DAILY at http://www.chinadaily.com.cn.

79. There is no English equivalent to the term *guanxi,* but it usually is translated as "personal connections." The Chinese term actually has a negative connotation and implies the misuse of a personal relationship with a government official. *See generally* J. Cohen, *Dispute Resolution in China: Putting the House in Order,* CHINA L. & PRAC. (Jan. 2002).

throughout the mainland.[80] To the majority of the Chinese people, they view such favoritism as a remnant of feudal times. Consequently, the common people and foreign investors demanding certainty cannot be expected to develop confidence in China's legal system until more progress is made concerning the adoption and recognition of the rule of law.[81]

Practice Tip: The Relevance of Political Clout

Guanxi, roughly translated as "connections," is less relevant in today's China, and will probably further diminish in value over the next decade. The practice of *guanxi* has its roots in two things: (1) Confucian principles required that people respect their elders and officials, and (2) a method of allocating scarce resources to people in Chinese society. True *guanxi* may result in misuse and corruption. In the past, the Chinese government (and low-paid government officials) were empowered to authorize or approve the grant or use of land and resources, access to energy, access to business opportunities and government procurement projects, issuance of permits/licenses or concessions, etc. Officials would dole out resources and opportunities to those who paid homage or gave something in return. Today, while the government is still the source of power and allocation of these items, there are laws and established procedures in place to regulate the allocation and procurement processes, and laws to counter the corruption that oftentimes goes hand in hand with the personal power that may be abused as a result of the practice of *guanxi*. There are several reasons why *guanxi* is diminishing as a business tool: (1) the government's emphasis on the rule of law (as opposed to the rule of man evident in Maoist China); (2) the procedural safeguards available for administrative abuses of power, such as under the Administrative Litigation Law and the new Licensing Law (which, in theory, are intended to provide administrative and judicial avenues to complain or appeal adverse decisions of bureaucrats); and (3) the crackdown on corruption. In prior years, there was a lack of transparency in the permit process, which required having the relationships/connections to get what one needed or risk wasting time or the inability to secure the needed license or opportunity. The *guanxi* of the past almost invariably meant that some form of compensation was required. Today, having *guanxi* is not necessarily the same as making payoffs to

(Continued)

80. The *gaoganzidi* have exploited their top-level connections in Beijing for gifts of property and money provided by Hong Kong business leaders eager to court Beijing for their own financial betterment. *See* P. Corne, *supra* note 48, at 232–33.

81. Some observers believe that *guanxi* will never be supplanted by the rule of law. *See* P. Corne, *supra* note 48, at 230–31. Corne believes that "it is unlikely that administrators or the regulated will change their behavior to make law their principal reference." *Id.* at 231.

(*Continued from previous page*)

government officials. Any foreign party with the right product and right strategy can develop relationships/connections to help them succeed in China. No payoffs are required. Similarly, if a foreign investor follows the law, it should be allowed to secure the permit/licenses to operate. Again, no payoffs are necessary. If a foreign investor finds itself making payoffs, then it may eventually find itself in a trap of unlawful activity. The best practice for foreign investors that intend to produce and sell in China is to develop and nurture relationships with distributors, suppliers, customers, government, media, etc., that will help meet a company's objective in raising its profile and sales in China.

Chapter 4

FIE Organizational Structure and Approval Procedures

A foreign party interested in tapping the China market, or interested in utilizing China's vast natural resources and low-cost labor resources, is required to analyze the various types of investment vehicles available under Chinese law to determine the best entry strategy to meet its objectives. This analysis requires an evaluation of, among other things, such issues as the anticipated scope of investment in China, the need for a Chinese "partner," the identification of a suitable Chinese "partner," and the market for the foreign party's products/services in China or restrictions thereto.

This chapter addresses the laws and regulations pertaining to the organizational structures and methods of investment available to foreign-invested enterprises (FIEs) including a processing trade arrangement, joint venture (equity and contractual), holding company, a company limited by shares, partnership arrangement, service center arrangement, wholly foreign-owned enterprise, representative office, and branch organization. This chapter also discusses the approval procedures that an FIE will typically follow for registration, and the approval procedures for the assignment of a joint venture interest or an amendment to the registered capital of a joint venture.

A. Operations without Partners

In general, there are two investment vehicles under Chinese law which allow for a foreign party to establish an operation in China without the need of a Chinese party. The laws and regulations governing representative offices and wholly foreign-owned enterprises are restricted but allow the foreign party some flexibility in managing market entry and without the influence or involvement of a Chinese partner.

1. Representative Office

The State Council has promulgated regulations for the establishment of representative offices (ROs).[1] An RO may perform a limited number of activities including data collection, market research, assistance with negotiations of contracts, the hosting of delegations of company representatives from the RO's overseas offices, management of warranty and after-sale service, technical support, and research and development. An RO may not engage in profit-making activity and may not receive fees for services, sign contracts, or directly generate income.[2] A business license is required to exhibit signage and logs depicting company names and trademarks, distribute advertisements, or to use the company's name on stationery, business cards, or brochures that idenfity the company's presence in China. A business license

1. Provisional Regulations of the State Council of the People's Republic of China for the Control of Resident Representative Offices of Foreign Enterprises (promulgated October 30, 1980, by the State Council), *reprinted in* CHINA LAWS FOR FOREIGN BUSINESS (CCH), Business Regulations ¶ 7-500 (hereinafter the "Representative Office Regulations"). *See* Procedures of the State Administration for Industry and Commerce of the People's Republic of China for the Registration and Administration of Resident Representative Offices of Foreign Enterprises (promulgated March 5, 1983, by the State Council), *reprinted in* CHINA LAWS FOR FOREIGN BUSINESS (CCH), Business Regulation ¶ 7-560 (hereinafter the "Representative Office Procedures"). *See also* Detailed Rules of the Ministry of Foreign Trade and Economic Cooperation (MOFTEC) for the Implementation of the Provisional Regulations Governing the Examination, Approval and Administration of Representative Offices of Foreign Enterprises (promulgated February 13, 1995, by the Ministry of Foreign Trade and Economic Cooperation), *reprinted in* CHINA LAWS FOR FOREIGN BUSINESS (CCH), Business Regulation ¶ 7-590 (hereinafter the "Representative Office Rules"). The representative offices of foreign financial institutions, including commercial banks, investment banks, securities companies, insurance companies, insurance brokerage and agency firms, insurance adjusters, funds management companies, foreign exchange companies, credit card companies, and financial leasing companies, are required to follow special registration and supervision procedures. The approval and regulatory agency of these types of representative offices is the People's Bank of China. *See* Administrative Measures on Representative Offices in China of Foreign Financial Institutions (promulgated on April 29, 1996, by the People's Bank of China and revised and re-promulgated by Order No. 8 on June 13, 2002, by the People's Bank of China), *reprinted in* CHINA LAWS FOR FOREIGN BUSINESS (CCH), Business Regulation ¶ 7-540. For a copy of the applications for establishing a representative office, *see* the Web site of the China Council for the Promotion of International Trade (CCPIT) and the Tianjin Chamber of International Commerce at http://www.chinainfornet.com/ccpit. For a bullet point analysis of the laws and regulations involving the establishment of a representative office, *see* Fact Sheet: Representative Office, THE U.S.-CHINA BUSINESS COUNCIL (last updated July 2, 2003), available online for members at http://www.uschina.org.

2. Representative Office Rules, art. 4; Representative Office Procedures, arts. 3, 15. On March 17, 2003, the State Administration of Industry and Commerce released for public comment a draft of the Measures on the Administration of the Registration of Foreign Resident Representative Offices. These measures reaffirm the general principle that foreign representative offices are limited to liaison activities and may not engage in direct profit-making business. Nevertheless, the draft measures also recognize exceptions to the general rule pursuant to China's WTO obligations for representative offices that engage in law, accountancy, tax services, and management consulting. These measures also abolish the annual renewal requirement for representative offices and retain the three-year extension requirement as the sole renewal and extension procedure.

is also required to sign a long-term office lease; import company materials, office equipment, and supplies; to import the household items of foreign employees; to hire Chinese citizens; to open bank accounts; or to secure telecommunications services. The RO is not allowed to start business activities before approval is granted and the registration procedure completed. A failure to obtain a certificate (business license) or renewal may result in penalties. In practice, many commercial landlords, including hotels and office buildings, allow a foreign party to lease space for a period of up to one year before it obtains its RO registration certificate. The RO, however, is prohibited from opening a bank account until it receives approval. As an interim measure, the banks usually allow the chief representative to open a personal account to allow for the payment of expenses pending approval of the operation.[3]

A Chinese enterprise is required to act as the foreign party's sponsor and will approach the Ministry of Commerce (MOFCOM) or MOFCOM branch on its behalf to obtain approval for the establishment of an RO. There are several Chinese organizations, such as the Foreign Enterprise Service Corporation (FESCO), which are in the business of helping foreign parties obtain "sponsors" or that act as sponsors for foreign parties. Although approval from MOFCOM is still required, the sponsorship requirement does not have the same weight as in the past.

The RO application procedures require that a foreign party submit an application letter, a notarized copy of the foreign party's business license, certified articles of incorporation or other documents demonstrating legal existence and standing of the foreign party, documents concerning the financial standing of the applicant including a letter of creditworthiness from the foreign party's financial institution,[4] personal resumes of the proposed resident representative, and a notarized letter of appointment of the resident representative by the company's CEO.[5] An application for a representative office may be rejected if the applicant fails to provide the documents required by law, or in the form required by law (i.e., notarization). In some jurisdictions, the approval authorities require a minimum registered capital requirement of $10,000 to establish a representative office.

In order to ensure that an RO maintains its tax-exempt status, a foreign party's application should state that the scope of the RO is to engage in

3. This practice appears to violate Article 48 of the Commercial Bank Law. For a discussion on the Commercial Bank Law, *see* Chapter 11, Financial Regulation § A.2.

4. A sample letter of creditworthiness is *reprinted* at Appendix A.9.

5. Representative Office Regulations, art. 3.

"authorized activities," and that the objective of the RO is to service customers and to exchange information with interested persons. Many foreign companies make the mistake of stating in their application that the purpose of their RO is to engage in sales and other revenue-generating activities. Such statements may expose a firm to tax liability or scrutiny by the tax authorities.

A chief representative of a China operation must be selected and approved in order to obtain a business license. The chief representative is usually an individual who has supervisory control over the China operation. Although the chief representative is legally responsible for the RO, this person is not required to be present in China on a full-time basis.

MOFCOM or its local branch has thirty days to approve an RO application.[6] Within thirty days of receipt of the letter of approval, a foreign party is required to file its application for registration with the local branch of the State Administration of Industry and Commerce (SAIC). The SAIC generally takes approximately thirty to sixty days to approve the application and issue the business license. After a business license is approved, an RO is required to register with the taxation authorities to address tax issues, such as tax exemption, within thirty days and to contact China Customs to resolve entry procedures for any office equipment imported for the RO.[7] The SAIC or its local branch has the authority to oversee the business activities of representative offices and is empowered to demand and inspect the records of an RO.[8]

2. Wholly Foreign-Owned Enterprise

a. General Principles

Chinese law allows for the establishment of an entity referred to as a wholly foreign-owned enterprise.[9] Originally, approval for a WFOE was difficult to

---

6. Representative Office Rules, art. 9.

7. Representative Office Rules, art. 15. *See also* Regulations Concerning Import and Export of Articles by Resident Offices and Their Staff of Foreign Enterprises and Press in China (promulgated on May 1, 1984, by the Customs General Administration of the PRC), *reprinted in* CHINA LAWS FOR FOREIGN BUSINESS (CCH), Customs ¶ 50-620.

8. Representative Office Rules, art. 23. *See also* Notice of the State Administration of Taxation on Issues Concerning Taxation Inspections of Foreign Enterprise Resident Representative Offices (promulgated on June 12, 1996, by the SAT), *reprinted in* CHINA LAWS FOR FOREIGN BUSINESS (CCH), Taxation ¶ 32-669 (outlining the procedures for tax audits for ROs). An RO that fails to contact the tax authorities (national and local) within the thirty-day period of time may penalized and/or lose their right to operate tax exempt. The tax authorities often require documentation concerning the foreign party's intellectual property and foreign operations, in addition to documentation to demonstrate the purpose of the RO. Although tax-exempt status is negotiable, the authorities usually will require the payment of income tax based on the RO's office expenses (cost-plus basis) or based on actual revenues. *See* Tax Administration Issues Relevant to Resident Representative Offices of Foreign Enterprises Circular (issued on March 12, 2003, by the State Administration of Taxation). *See* also Chapter 9, Taxation Law § B.

9. Law of the People's Republic of China on Wholly Foreign-Owned Enterprises (adopted April 12, 1986, at the 4th Sess. of the 6th NPC), *reprinted in* CHINA LAWS FOR FOREIGN BUSINESS (CCH), Business

obtain since 100% foreign-owned ventures in China were looked upon with suspicion and contrary to the practice of requiring foreign investors to work alongside Chinese partners. Post-WTO, foreign parties have greater flexibility in establishing a WFOE and, today, the WFOE structure is the preferred choice of entity used by foreign investors. This preference for WFOEs (and away from joint ventures) is based on the understanding that foreign investors have more confidence in their ability to operate a company in China without a partner, and also because of control and management issues, cultural differences, and other difficulties that arise in the joint venture context. Joint ventures are still required in situations where 100% foreign ownership is not allowed or where the market requires that a foreign investor team up with a local partner.

A WFOE is required to take the form of a limited liability company, and the foreign party's liability is limited to the subscribed investment.[10] The WFOE Law provides that a WFOE must be supportive of China's national economy and the law encourages the use of advanced technology and equipment or to market all or most of its products outside of China.[11] The law provides that foreign investors are prohibited from doing anything to "harm the social order or public interest of China."[12] In addition, prior to 2001, the WFOE Rules provided that a WFOE must "achieve significant economic results" and were required to comply with at least one of the following conditions for establishment:

(1) adopt advanced technology and equipment, engage in the development of new products, economize on the use of energy and

Regulation ¶ 13-506 (hereinafter the "WFOE Law"), and as amended on October 31, 2000. *See also* Detailed Rules for the Implementation of the Law of the People's Republic of China on Foreign Investment Enterprises (approved October 28, 1990, by the State Council), *reprinted in* CHINA LAWS FOR FOREIGN BUSINESS (CCH), Business Regulation ¶ 13-507 (hereinafter the "WFOE Rules"), and as revised on April 12, 2001; An Explanation of Several Terms Used in the Detailed Rules for the Implementation of the Law of the People's Republic of China on Sole Foreign Investment Enterprises (issued December 6, 1991, by the Ministry of Foreign Economic Relations and Trade), *reprinted in* CHINA LAWS FOR FOREIGN BUSINESS (CCH), Business Regulation ¶ 13-505. The revised WFOE Rules explicitly state that the Contract Law, effective October 1, 1999, now applies to contracts that WFOEs enter into, thus alleviating any confusion over contracts concluded under the former contract rules. WFOEs may now also reduce their registered capital due to changes in their total investment and scale of business operation subject to examination and approval. This is in accordance with the SAIC and MOFTEC's 1994 notice permitting the reduction of registered capital in FIEs. Prior to this, only CJVs were permitted under the Implementation Rules of the CJV Law to reduce their registered capital, while EJVs and WFOEs were still forbidden from doing so under their respective implementation rules.

10. WFOE Law, art. 8; WFOE Rules, art. 19. A WFOE may also take the corporate form of other "liability" structures subject to government approval.

11. WFOE Law, art. 3.

12. WFOE Law, art. 4.

raw materials, achieve product upgrading, or produce import substitutes

(2) have annual exports amounting to at least 50 percent of the value of its total product output for the year and achieve a foreign exchange balance or surplus.

Although originally the law restricts the establishment of WFOEs to export-oriented or technologically advanced enterprises, these restrictions starting in the late 1990s were not strictly enforced and have formally been abandoned now that China is a member of the WTO.[13] However, WFOEs are still *prohibited* in certain industries (although joint ventures may be allowed), and a foreign investor must consult with current government-issued catalogues on permissible foreign investment to determine if a WFOE will be approved.[14]

MOFCOM has the discretion to reject an application for a WFOE in the following circumstances:

(1) if the establishment of the WFOE would be detrimental to China's sovereignty or the social public interest
(2) if the establishment of the WFOE would endanger the national security of China
(3) if the establishment of the WFOE would violate China's laws and regulations
(4) if the establishment of the WFOE fails to conform with the requirements for developing China's national economy
(5) if the proposed WFOE is likely to endanger the environment[15]

The foreign party must specify the term or duration of the WFOE at the time of the initial application, and an application for extension may be

13. On October 31, 2000, the WFOE Law was amended and, in general, provides that WFOEs are encouraged, but no longer required to use advanced technology or to export the majority of their products. WFOEs are also no longer obligated to report their production and operation plans to government authorities, nor do WFOEs have to maintain a balanced ratio between their foreign exchange incomes and expenditures.

14. WFOE Rules, art. 4. For a reference to the types of technology encouraged by the government, *see* the *Catalogue of Encouraged Foreign Investment in High and New Technology Products (2003)* (issued on July 18, 2003, by the Ministry of Commerce and the Ministry of Science and Technology). The 2003 catalogue furthers the Chinese government's policy of encouraging foreign investment in underdeveloped industries and groups 196 product types into 11 principal categories: electronic information; software; space and aviation; optical-mechanical-electrical integration; biomedicines and medical treatment instruments; new materials; new energies and high-efficiency energies; environmental protection; earth, air, and sea; nuclear application technologies; and modern agriculture.

15. WFOE Rules, art. 5.

Practice Tip

In the 1980s, regulatory limitations restricted the growth of WFOEs and promoted the EJVs and CJVs as the dominant form of foreign direct investment (FDI). Today, with relaxed standards for WFOEs and with local governments much more desperate to expand their tax base and produce more jobs for the large number of unemployed former SOE workers, the WFOE has become the predominant foreign investment vehicle in China. Practitioners are also noticing that localities are much more willing to bend the restrictive approval requirements (set by Beijing) for WFOEs. It is important to determine the practice at the local level, but at the same time practitioners are warned that local authorities may grant concessions or issue a business license outside the scope of their authority. The exercise of caution is recommended when dealing with local branches of the ministry of commerce.

submitted six months prior to the expiration of the term.[16] The foreign party must obtain the approval of the government with respect to any merger, acquisition, equity transfer, or other major corporate restructuring.[17]

b. Application Procedures for WFOEs

Prior to submitting an application for approval of a WFOE, the foreign party is required to submit a preliminary proposal to the local people's government that outlines the purpose and objectives of the enterprise, its scope and scale of operations, products to be manufactured, technology and equipment to be used, domestic and overseas markets for the products, land-use issues, and the public utility needs for the operation.[18] A preliminary proposal must be accepted or rejected within thirty days of submission.

The application for establishment of a WFOE is filed with a local branch of MOFCOM, which has three months from the date of receipt to approve or deny an application.[19] To obtain approval for a WFOE, the foreign party is required to submit the following:

(1) an application to establish a WFOE[20]
(2) a feasibility study report

16. WFOE Law, art. 20; WFOE Rules, arts. 70, 71.

17. WFOE Law, art. 10; WFOE Rules, art. 17. The foreign party is also required to employ an accountant registered in China to examine the details concerning a transfer or merger, and is required to issue a capital inspection report concerning the corporate restructuring.

18. WFOE Rules, art. 9.

19. WFOE Law, art. 6; WFOE Rules, art. 10. If the application is incomplete, the examining officer usually returns the application and grants the applicant a fixed period of time to provide supplemental information or documentation.

20. An application for a WFOE is required to include the following information: (1) name, title, address of the foreign party, and name, nationality, and position of its legal representative; (2) name and

(3) articles of association of the WFOE[21]
(4) documentation concerning the legal representatives of the WFOE[22]
(5) documentation demonstrating the legal existence of the foreign party and a letter from the foreign party's financial institution concerning the credit standing of the company
(6) approval certificate concerning the WFOE's preliminary proposal submitted to the local people's government
(7) a detailed list of the goods and materials the WFOE intends to import for the operation
(8) other documents that may be required by MOFCOM[23]

Upon approval, the WFOE is required to apply to the SAIC for a business license. The date of issuance of the business license is the date of establishment of the enterprise.[24]

address of the proposed WFOE; (3) scope of operation, products, and production scale; (4) total amount of investment in the proposed enterprise, registered capital, source of capital, method of investment and term of investment; (5) organizational format and structure of the WFOE; (6) information concerning the production technology to be employed, sophistication level of technology, and ownership of technology; (7) product marketing, sales territory and channels, and ratio of domestic versus overseas markets; (8) foreign exchange procedures; (9) personnel policies and procedures, arrangements for employee recruitment, training, wages, welfare benefits, and insurance; (10) anticipated level of environmental pollution and remedial procedures; (11) site selection and facilities to be used; (12) construction capital, resources, and raw materials required for production and operations and supply sources; (13) progress timeline for project implementation; and (14) anticipated term of duration of the proposed enterprise. WFOE Rules, art. 14.

21. The articles of association are required to include (1) name and address of WFOE; (2) purpose and scope of operations; (3) total amount of investment, registered capital, and investment term; (4) organizational framework; (5) internal management body such as a board of directors, its powers of office and rules of procedure, legal representative, and the duties and jurisdiction of the general manager, chief engineer, and chief financial officer; (6) principles governing finance, accounting, and auditing and related systems; (7) labor management and personnel policies; (8) duration of operations, termination, and liquidation; and (9) procedures for amendment of the articles of association. WFOE Rules, art. 15. The articles of association become valid at the time of approval by the government. WFOE Rules, art. 16.

22. The legal representative of a WFOE shall be responsible for exercising the powers and functions of the enterprise pursuant to the provisions of the articles of association. If a legal representative is unable to exercise its powers and functions, it shall commission in writing an agent to exercise the powers of office on its behalf. WFOE Rules, art. 24. *See* Reply to Questions on Amending the Registration of the Legal Representative of Foreign-Invested Enterprises (promulgated on June 6, 2003, by the State Administration of Industry and Commerce). The SAIC Reply provides that if a quorum of the board of directors of an FIE is not possible because of the legal representative's failure to cooperate, a majority of the board, the largest shareholder, or the shareholder with the most voting shares may convene a board meeting and, upon a majority vote, replace the legal representative. If the articles of association outline a method for the appointment and removal of the legal representative by either shareholder appointment or according to a pre-existing shareholder agreement, a meeting of the board of directors is not necessary to remove a legal representative.

23. WFOE Rules, art. 10. If two or more foreign parties apply jointly to establish a WFOE, they are required to submit the contract between the parties.

24. WFOE Law, art. 7; WFOE Rules, art. 12.

WFOE: Checklist of Issues

The following is a checklist of issues for purposes of preparing the necessary documentation for the establishment of a WFOE:

1. Office Location of WFOE: A decision must be made as to the location of the WFOE given that there are many different approval authorities in the various cities and development zones, and each with its own administration.
2. Registered Capital and Total Investment: The applicant is required to enumerate the registered capital and total investment of the enterprise. The registered capital includes all cash, technology, machinery, etc. contributed by the foreign company to the operation. The cash contribution can be the cash provided by the foreign party as the working capital of the enterprise. The total investment includes the registered capital and loans to the WFOE.
3. Business Scope: In most instances, the best practice is to apply for a broad business scope to allow the applicant the flexibility in the operation and to prepare for any changes in the future. A sample business scope to be included in the Application and the Articles of Association of the WFOE is as follows: The business scope of the Enterprise includes manufacturing, marketing, sales, production, research and development, engineering, integration, installation, training services, technical support, after-sales services, warranty services, and the sale of spare parts with regard to _____ processing systems and technology in or outside of China.
4. Documentation: The following documents to submit with the application and supporting materials include:
   a. Articles of Incorporation, Corporate Charter, or Business License of foreign company (preferably a certified copy) (this document should, of course, reflect the jurisdiction of incorporation and the date of incorporation)

(Continued)

c. Investment Contributions for WFOEs

The registered capital of a WFOE is referred to as the total amount of capital registered with the SAIC for the establishment of the enterprise, namely, the total amount of investment subscribed by the foreign investor. The amount of registered capital of a WFOE shall be sufficient to support its scale of operations and the ratio of registered capital and total investment shall comply with China's relevant regulations.[25] The regulations prohibit a

25. WFOE Rules, art. 20.

(Continued from previous page)

b. Financial statements of foreign party for three years
c. Bank Letter of Creditworthiness: This should be prepared by the foreign investor's financial institution and on the bank's original stationery. An original should be submitted with the application to COFTEC/MOFCOM.
d. Lease Agreement for WFOE premises
e. Appointment Letter of Chairman of the Board of WFOE: This should be signed by the corporate secretary or CEO and on company stationery. The original is required to be submitted.
f. Feasibility Study Report: The current practice is to provide a short and concise feasibility study report. In the past, these documents were voluminous and comprehensive.
g. Articles of Association
h. Application

5. Information Needed for the Application includes the following:
   a. Name and nationality of the Legal Representative of the foreign investor
   b. Name and nationality of the Legal Representative of the WFOE who is usually the chairman of the board of directors. Oftentimes, COFTEC will require the legal rep's CV and a photocopy of his/her passport photo page.
   c. Board of Directors of the WFOE. A three (3) member board (chairman plus 2 others) is recommended.
   d. General manager of the WFOE. A CV and a photocopy of his/her passport photo page is required.
   e. Name of contact person for the company in China (if other than general manager or legal rep)
   f. WFOE's address, telephone number, facsimile number
   g. Number of employees of the WFOE: foreign staff, local staff
   h. Registered capital and total investment (as noted above)

Practice Tip: Feasibility Study Report

In general, the feasibility study report of today is not the comprehensive behemoth document of yesterday. The new rule is simplicity and conciseness for most general WFOEs and JVs. Expect to elaborate on issues for FIEs that are holding companies, FIEs in new types of investment areas (e.g., foreign-funded venture capital enterprises, foreign-funded securities FIEs, etc.), or where substantial state-owned assets are involved. Knowing what a particular COFTEC will require for content will save you the trouble of spending the funds and resources in preparing a feasibility study that goes beyond what is truly necessary.

WFOE from reducing its registered capital during the duration of its operations.[26] A foreign party is required to obtain the approval of the government to increase, assign, or mortgage its registered capital.[27]

The investment contributed by the foreign party to establish a WFOE may include convertible foreign currency, machinery and equipment, industrial property rights, or proprietary technology. Subject to government approval, a foreign investor may also invest RMB dividends obtained from other sole foreign investment enterprises that it operates in China.[28] If the applicant intends to use machinery or equipment as its investment, the machinery or equipment must be essential for use in production by the enterprise and unavailable for purchase within China. The capitalized value of the machinery or equipment cannot exceed the fair market price for the same or similar type of equipment available on the international market.[29] The applicant is required to submit a detailed list of all equipment and machinery that it intends to use as its investment contribution. Machinery and equipment that are imported for a WFOE are required to undergo inspection by the commodity inspection authorities prior to clearance from China Customs. If the machinery and equipment fail to meet the details provided by the foreign applicant in its submitted list, the SAIC has the authority to demand that the foreign party correct the deficiency.[30]

If a foreign investor proposes to use industrial property rights or proprietary technology as its investment, the foreign investor has title to the rights or technology. The value of the industrial property rights or proprietary technology shall not exceed 20 percent of the enterprise's registered capital.[31] The applicant is required to provide detailed information concerning the technology, including a copy of the certificate of title, technical specifications, practical value of the technology, and information concerning the calculation of value and methods of valuation.[32] The government has the right to inspect the industrial property rights and proprietary technology, as well as to reject any technology that fails to meet the applicant's representations.[33]

The time limit for the payment of cash contributions shall be stipulated in the WFOE application and the articles of association. A foreign investor may tender its investment in installments, but the final payment is required

26. WFOE Rules, art. 21.
27. WFOE Rules, arts. 22, 23.
28. WFOE Rules, art. 25.
29. WFOE Rules, art. 26.
30. WFOE Rules, art. 29.
31. WFOE Rules, art. 27.
32. WFOE Rules, art. 27.
33. WFOE Rules, art. 29.

to be contributed within three (3) years of the date of issue of the business license. The initial installment payment is required to be no less than 15 percent of the amount of investment to be subscribed by the foreign investor, and is required to be tendered within three months of the date of issue of the enterprise's business license. If a foreign investor is unable to pay the initial installment within the period prescribed above, the issued approval certificate is automatically invalid.[34]

d. WFOE Operational Issues

The WFOE Law provides that the "investments, profits, and other legitimate rights and interests" of the foreign party are protected under Chinese law and that the government will "not nationalize or expropriate enterprises with sole foreign investment."[35] A WFOE has the right to manage its operation "free of interference" so long as the business is operated in accordance with its articles of association.[36] The government may oversee the "investment status" to ensure that the required capital, technology, and equipment are timely contributed in accordance with the approved application and articles of association of the WFOE.[37] A WFOE is allowed to purchase raw materials, equipment, consumables, and other items needed for the company's operation from inside or outside of China. The law does require that the company give preference to Chinese sources for its materials needs.[38] The WFOE, however, must comply with the requirements for export licenses, export quotas, import procedures, and all other customs laws and regulations.[39]

A WFOE is required to establish its financial records in China and to prepare and submit its accounting records in accordance with the applicable financial and tax laws and regulations.[40] A WFOE is subject to the tax laws

34. WFOE Rules, art. 30. If any installment payments are not paid on schedule, the government has the power to invalidate a business license if the payment is more than a month in arrears. However, a party may request an extension of time with the SAIC. *Id.* art. 31. After the payment of each installment, the WFOE is required to retain a registered accountant to examine the payments and issue a certificate of verification of investment. *Id.* art. 32.

35. WFOE Law, arts. 4, 5. Only in "special circumstances" can the government nationalize or expropriate the property of a WFOE. A foreign investor may remit abroad its profits earned from the WFOE, including all income and funds obtained after liquidation of the enterprise. *Id.* art. 19. If the WFOE goes through a liquidation process, it is required to follow the liquidation laws and regulations. *Id.* arts. 21, 22; WFOE Rules, art. 73–79. For a discussion concerning the liquidation process, *see* Chapter 20, Enterprise Liquidation, Reorganization, and Bankruptcy § A. The wages of foreign staff may be remitted abroad after payment of all individual income tax. *Id.*

36. WFOE Law, art. 11; WFOE Rules, art. 6.

37. WFOE Law, art. 9.

38. WFOE Law, art. 15.

39. WFOE Rules, art. 8.

40. WFOE Law, art. 14; WFOE Rules, arts. 48–51 (tax matters), 56–63 (accounting issues). A failure to maintain records in China may result in the imposition of penalties by the SAIC, including monetary fines or revocation of the company's business license.

Comparison of Representative Office with WFOE

Issue	Representative Office	WFOE
1. Legal Capacity	Limited to marketing, research, and liaison activities	Granted a specific business scope that would allow actual business activities (Note: WFOE scope of business will be limited to a paragraph of enumerated activities that must be approved by MOFCOM/ COFTEC.)
2. Limited Liability	No—Constitutes part of foreign legal entity that registered the office	Yes—Separate legal entity that signs contracts in its own name
3. Registered Capital	None required	Depends on jurisdiction; minimum for Beijing in 2003 approximately $105,000
4. Management Structure	Generally controlled by Chief Representative	Operates like a corporation; requires board of directors and officers
5. Ongoing Costs	Both forms incur similar expenses relating to the maintenance of books and records (audits, financials, tax returns) and de minimis fees for periodic renewal of registration documents. Assuming the same level of activity, the Representative Office would be less expensive in this regard because its records are less complex and extensive in contrast to a WFOE. In addition, the WFOE is required to create statutory reserves out of operating profit for a staff bonus and public welfare fund and a reserve fund.	

(Continued)

(*Continued from previous page*)

Issue	Representative Office	WFOE
6. Labor	Must engage an authorized PRC labor bureau (e.g., FESCO) to indirectly hire PRC employees	May sign employment contracts directly with PRC employees or use FESCO (If direct employment used, a labor union may impose fees of up to 2 percent of Chinese employees' compensation.)
7. Income/ Foreign Exchange	May not generate income	May generate income including local currency and foreign exchange (e.g., from exports) and may purchase and remit foreign exchange
8. Corporate Tax	Usually pays corporate tax and business tax on a cost plus basis (may qualify for an exemption)	Pays corporate tax and business tax on an actual revenue and expense basis (may qualify for a tax holiday/reduction)
9. Repatriation of Profit	May neither generate nor remit profits	May freely declare dividends (temporarily not subject to withholding)
10. Ease of Approval	Approval granted with ease and within 30 days	Approval is a multiple step process and may take 30 to 60 days to complete (more if business activities or industry is controversial)
11. Overall Advantage	Ease of Approval	Greater control/autonomy
12. Overall Disadvantage	No right to engage in income generation	Regulatory hurdles and possible demands for unnecessarily high registered capital by MOFCOM/COFTEC authorities

and regulations applicable to all foreign enterprises, and an enterprise that reinvests after-tax profits in China is entitled to preferential treatment.[41] As with all enterprises, a WFOE is required to adhere to the foreign exchange rules and regulations.[42]

If a WFOE employs Chinese nationals, it is required to abide by the labor laws and regulations and shall provide its employees with labor contracts that include provisions outlining such matters as dismissal, compensation, benefits, and medical insurance.[43] The WFOE Law further provides that the company is required to allow the employees the right to establish a trade union organization and shall provide the necessary facilities for the activities of the trade union.[44]

B. Operations Involving Chinese Partners

Many foreign companies have found that a successful market entry strategy requires the involvement of a Chinese "partner" such as a joint venture partner (equity and contractual), representative, or distributor. A local partner can assist in developing an operational base and access to distributors if the domestic market is targeted. A Chinese partner may also assist the joint venture company in securing resources required for production such as raw materials, components, consumables, energy and utilities, and transportation. A local Chinese partner may be able to use its *guanxi* ("connections") to assist in securing government approval, concessions, and opportunities. Yet, as other investment vehicles have become available such as WFOEs and

41. WFOE Law, art. 17; WFOE Rules, arts. 50–51. For a discussion of the tax laws affecting WFOEs, *see infra* Chapter 9, Taxation Law. A WFOE is required to register with the tax authorities within 30 days of receiving its business license. WFOE Rules, art. 12. *See also* Notice on Issues Relating to Enterprise Income Tax Refunds for Reinvestment by Foreign Investors (issued on July 17, 2002, by the SAT), *reprinted in* China Laws for Foreign Business (CCH), Taxation ¶ 32-621 (procedures for handling tax refunds and preferential treatment for profits reinvested by FIEs); Notice of the State Bureau of Taxation Concerning Several Questions on Tax Refunds for Funds Reinvested by Foreign Investors in Foreign Investment Enterprises (issued on June 15, 1993, by the SAT), *reprinted in* China Laws for Foreign Business (CCH), Taxation ¶ 32-702.

42. WFOE Law, art. 18; WFOE Rules, arts. 52–55. *See* Foreign Debt Administration Tentative Procedures (promulgated on March 1, 2003, by the State Administration of Foreign Exchange [SAFE]) (provides certain new and tighter foreign debt registration standards for foreign-invested enterprises including the requirement that an FIE's foreign debt agreements will not be effective until they have been registered with SAFE and require that the balance of existing short-term foreign debts be aggregated with existing medium-term and long-term foreign debts for the purpose of applying the borrowing limit to new foreign debt).

43. WFOE Law, art. 12.

44. WFOE Law, art. 13; WFOE Rules, arts. 66–69. For a discussion concerning trade unions, *see* Chapter 10, Labor and Employment Law § A.1.

equity participation, the JV is slowly falling out of favor with foreign companies doing business in China.[45]

1. Joint Venture Enterprises (JV)

China has adopted laws and regulations addressing the principal type of joint venture enterprises: contractual (or cooperative) joint ventures (CJV)[46] and equity joint ventures (EJV).[47] An EJV is established as a limited liability company in the PRC.[48] A CJV may be established as a limited liability company, or take the form similar to a partnership where each party is liable for the acts of the venture.[49] The liability for the parties to joint venture losses is based on the ratio of capital contribution in an EJV[50] or on the contractual terms in a CJV.[51] The EJV and CJV laws and regulations

45. *See China Economy: MNCs Trade JVs for Wholly Owned Ventures,* EIU VIEWSWIRE (June 16, 1998), available on Lexis, News Library. *See generally* S. NG, STRUCTURING FOR SUCCESS IN CHINA (1996).

46. Law of the People's Republic of China on Chinese-Foreign Contractual Joint Ventures (adopted April 16, 1988, at the 1st Sess. of the 7th NPC, revised on October 31, 2000, at the 18th Meeting of the Standing Comm. of the NPC), *reprinted in* CHINA LAWS FOR FOREIGN BUSINESS (CCH), Business Regulation ¶ 6-100 (hereinafter the "CJV Law"). *See also* Detailed Rules for the Implementation of the Law of the People's Republic of China on Chinese-Foreign Contractual Joint Ventures (promulgated September 4, 1995, by MOFTEC), *reprinted in* CHINA LAWS FOR FOREIGN BUSINESS (CCH), Business Regulation ¶ 6-105 (hereinafter the "CJV Rules"), and as amended on October 31, 2000. The CJV Law was amended in preparation for China's WTO obligations. Under the amended rules, CJVs are no longer required to favor domestic suppliers during the purchase of raw materials, fuels, and other materials for production. CJVs will also no longer be required to maintain a balanced ratio between its foreign exchange income and expenditures. *See also* Interpretation of the Implementation of Certain Articles of the Detailed Rules for the Implementation of the Law of the PRC on Sino-Foreign Cooperative Enterprises (promulgated on October 22, 1996, by MOFTEC), *reprinted in* CHINA LAWS FOR FOREIGN BUSINESS (CCH), Business Regulation ¶ 6-110. The rules interpreting the CJV Rules are available on the Web site of MOFCOM at http://www.mofcom.gov.cn. CJVs are also governed by the Contract Law. *See* Chapter 7, Contract Law §§ A and D. For a bullet point analysis of the CJV Law and Regulations, *see* Fact Sheet: Contractual Joint Venture, The U.S.-CHINA BUSINESS COUNCIL (last updated June 27, 2003), available online for members at http://www.uschina.org.

47. Law of the People's Republic of China on Chinese-Foreign EJVs (adopted July 1, 1979, at the 2nd Sess. of the 5th NPC, amended April 4, 1990, at the 3rd Sess. of the 7th NPC, revised on March 15, 2001, at the 4th Sess. of the 9th NPC), *reprinted in* CHINA LAWS FOR FOREIGN BUSINESS (CCH), Business Regulation ¶ 6-500 (hereinafter the "EJV Law"). *See also* Regulations for the Implementation of the Law of the People's Republic of China on Chinese-Foreign EJVs (promulgated September 20, 1983, by the State Council, amended on January 15, 1986, by the State Council, and revised on July 21, 2001, by the State Council), *reprinted in* CHINA LAWS FOR FOREIGN BUSINESS (CCH), Business Regulation ¶ 6-550 (hereinafter the "EVJ Regulations"). The State Council revised the *Implementation Regulations for the Law of the People's Republic of China on Sino-Foreign Equity Joint Ventures* in 2001. The revisions represent further efforts to achieve legislative and regulatory uniformity and conformity with domestic law and regulations as well as international commitments. The previous implementation regulations were in conflict with MFN treatment as well as other fundamental WTO rules. Specifically, two provisions regarding domestic substitution and export-orientated investment requirements for FIEs have been rescinded. For a sample equity joint venture contract, *see* Appendix A. EJVs are also governed by the Contract Law. *See* Chapter 7, Contract Law § A. For a bullet point analysis of the EJV Law and Regulations, *see* Fact Sheet: Equity Joint Venture, The U.S.-China Business Council (last updated June 27, 2003), available online for members at http://www.uschina.org.

48. EJV Law, art. 4; EJV Regulations, art. 19.

49. CJV Law, art. 2; CJV Regulations, art. 14.

50. EJV Law, art. 4.

51. CJV Law, arts. 2, 22.

encourage a joint venture operation be high technology-oriented or export-oriented.[52]

a. Profit Distribution

The parties to an EJV share the profits of the enterprise based upon their respective equity interest.[53] The parties to a CJV have the discretion to determine, by contract, how the enterprise will apportion its profits.[54] It is possible for a contractual joint venture to be structured so that the respective parties are entitled to different distribution ratios in different years. For example, in some cooperative joint ventures nearly all of the capital is provided by the foreign party while the Chinese party's contribution is solely in the form of terms of cooperation. In such cases, the parties may agree in the joint venture contract that the foreign party will receive a higher percentage of the profits or dividends of the joint venture for a stated period of time (for example, the first five years of the joint venture) for the purpose of recovering its capital contribution and a lower percentage of the profits after the expiration of such period. It is also possible for a CJV to distribute profits in-kind, such as by distribution of the products produced by the joint venture. With approval from the tax authorities, the foreign party to a CJV may recover its investment prior to the payment of income tax by the operation. The CJV law provides that the foreign party has the right to recover its capital investment prior to the distribution of profits but, in such situations, the Chinese party has the statutory right to ownership of the CJV's assets at the conclusion of the contract term of the venture.[55]

b. Management Structure

The parties to a CJV may determine management structure per negotiation.[56] The management structure of an EJV operation must follow provisions of the EJV law and regulations and, as a general rule, the proportionate share of

52. EJV Law, art. 4. This rule is narrowly construed, but high-technology products are encouraged. For a reference to the types of technology encouraged by the government, *see* the *Catalogue of Encouraged Foreign Investment in High and New Technology Products (2003)* (issued on July 18, 2003, by the Ministry of Commerce and the Ministry of Science and Technology). The 2003 catalogue furthers the Chinese government's policy of encouraging foreign investment in underdeveloped industries and groups 196 product types into 11 principal categories: electronic information; software; space and aviation; optical-mechanical-electrical integration; biomedicines and medical treatment instruments; new materials; new energies and high-efficiency energies; environmental protection; earth, air and sea; nuclear application technologies; and modern agriculture.

53. EJV Law, art. 4.

54. CJV Law, arts. 2, 22.

55. CJV Law, art. 22; CJV Regulations, art. 44.

56. CJV Law, art. 11.

Practice Tip

JV versus a WFOE (Is a partner necessary?): Foreign investors prefer the wholly owned foreign enterprise ("WFOE") to the joint venture investment vehicle for a number of reasons, including control of the operation, the requirement of always having to consult with a Chinese partner in a JV arrangement, the poor financial conditions of state-owned enterprises, and stringent PRC technology transfer regulations. The CJV and EJV are more beneficial for the growth of Chinese firms in terms of access to capital, technology, export markets, and international management techniques. If a Chinese partner is required by law or by necessity, the foreign investor should carefully evaluate, among other things, the following:

- ✔ the assets, capabilities, resources, and expertise of the Chinese partner
- ✔ the financial obligations including loans, encumbrances, accounts payable, etc., of the Chinese partner
- ✔ the social and welfare obligations, labor relations, and human resources and obligations of the Chinese partner
- ✔ the Chinese partner's relationship with customers, government officials, and other foreign investors
- ✔ the corporate documents of the Chinese partner to determine whether they operate within their approved business scope and/or have approval to engage in the proposed business

equity participation usually dictates the scope of a party's ability to manage the joint venture company.[57] The joint venture contract should set forth the management structure for the operation, including which party is entitled to appoint the general manager and other key management personnel. If the foreign party plans to use expatriates as officers of the joint venture company, the joint venture contract should acknowledge that such expatriate staff will be compensated at international standards. The Chinese party should also agree to assist expatriate staff in obtaining visas, work permits, and other necessary documents, as well as housing, medical care, and other necessities.

(1) Unanimous Approval Items. The joint venture contract should set forth a list of matters requiring unanimous approval by the Board of Directors of the joint venture company in order to be effective. Some of the types of matters for which unanimous approval is often required (either by

57. EJV Law, art. 6.

the foreign party or the Chinese party, depending on which holds the minority interest) include the following:

(1) amendments to the joint venture contract
(2) liquidation or dissolution of the joint venture company[58]
(3) increase of the registered capital of the joint venture company, or transfer of any interest of a party to the joint venture company[59]
(4) merger of the joint venture company with any other economic organization or any sale or other disposition of a significant portion of the assets of the joint venture company[60]
(5) pledge, encumbrance, or mortgage of the assets of the joint venture company[61]
(6) significant loans or investments by the joint venture company
(7) annual and interim production or operating plans, the annual and interim financial budget and operating budget, including anticipated operating costs and expenses, and the annual and interim financial statements of the joint venture company and any significant change in any of the foregoing
(8) appointment and change of the joint venture company's independent auditor and the determination or any significant modification to the joint venture company's accounting principles
(9) significant changes to the business scope and scale of production stipulated in the joint venture contract
(10) determination of the salary and benefits for the general manager and other senior management personnel of the joint venture company and any changes thereto
(11) appointment and removal of the general manager and other senior management staff of the joint venture company
(12) determination of the scale of wages, benefits, and allowances of the workers and staff of the joint venture company
(13) approval and amendment of (i) any contract, commitment, or expenditure that exceeds an agreed-upon amount or (ii) any financial commitment by the joint venture company that would result in total debt of the joint venture company exceeding an agreed-upon amount

58. *See* Chapter 20, Enterprise Liquidation, Reorganization, and Bankruptcy; *see also infra* § 4, Termination Events.
59. *See infra* § F, Assignment of Investor Interests and Modification to Capital Contribution.
60. *Id.*
61. *Id.*

(14) settlement of any claim, arbitration, or litigation initiated against the joint venture company
(15) commencement of any claim, arbitration, or litigation by the joint venture company against a third party

The items listed at numbers (1), (2), (3), and (4) above are required by law for EJVs, while the items listed at numbers (1), (2), (3), (4), and (5) above are required by law for CJVs. All other items are negotiable and depend upon the circumstances.

(2) Deadlock Resolution. The joint venture contract should provide that a termination event will occur if agreement cannot be reached by the Board of Directors within a reasonable period of time on a matter that is material to the joint venture company (including matters requiring unanimous consent). Such termination event should be limited, however, to situations in which neither party has referred the matter to arbitration. As an alternative, the joint venture agreement may provide for a sale of the joint venture to a third party in the event of a board deadlock on a material issue. Such sale would be subject to approval by the Chinese approval authority.

c. Contributions

The contributions of the parties to a CJV may include industrial property rights, intellectual property rights, technology, buildings, and production facilities and equipment.[62] Capital contributions to a CJV may also be in made in the form of cash or property. In addition, the parties to a CJV may also make certain contributions as "terms of cooperation" for which no specific value is assigned. For example, the Chinese party may contribute land to a contractual joint venture as a "term of cooperation" without having the value of the land-use rights assessed or specified as part of the registered capital of a CJV. However, if the terms of cooperation involve state-owned assets, the CJV Rules require that the assets be valued in accordance with relevant laws and regulations. Another example includes an arrangement by a party of a guarantee to assist in financing the joint venture company.

The CJV Rules require that the terms of cooperation be limited to property rights. This requirement does not adequately reflect the practice, where the Chinese party's terms of cooperation might include, for example, such items as the completion of the government approval process or obtaining

62. CJV Law, art. 8; CJV Regulations, art. 18.

special approvals or licenses. The legal status of joint ventures containing these types of terms of cooperation is somewhat unclear.

Capital contributions to the registered capital of an EJV company may be in the form of cash, equipment, industrial property rights (including patent rights, trademarks, copyrights), or nonpatented technology. In-kind capital contributions to an EJV must be valued in accordance with Chinese law, and such noncash contributions are required to be "indispensable to production" or capable of making "notable savings" in raw materials or energy resources.[63]

(1) Valuation of Capital Contributions. In most joint ventures, the capital contributions of the parties will determine each party's interest in the joint venture company. There are a number of issues that commonly arise concerning capital contributions, including the valuation of noncash contributions and the timing of the contributions. To the extent that the Chinese party is a state-owned enterprise and is making in-kind contributions to the registered capital of the joint venture company, the contribution is subject to valuation by a Chinese accounting firm. As a result, it is advisable that the foreign party take steps to manage, as much as possible, the asset evaluation process to avoid unrealistically high valuations of assets contributed by the Chinese party. One method of managing this process is for the parties to reach an agreement as to the value of any in-kind capital contribution and, in writing, explain the basis of such valuation to the appraisal firm prior to the commencement of the formal valuation process.

The foreign party will also want to ensure that the valuation is based upon international approval procedures and standards. The foreign party may also require, as a condition precedent to making its capital contribution to the joint venture company, the receipt and approval by the foreign party of the valuation report and approval documents issued by the relevant government authorities.

If the foreign party contributes machinery to the joint venture, a valuation of the machinery is required to be undertaken by the State Import and Export Commodities Inspection Bureau. This valuation may be conducted at the time the machinery enters China, and after the joint venture agreement has been executed and approved. As a result, it is possible that the valuation reached by the Commodities Inspection Bureau will differ from that contained in the joint venture contract. Again, it is important that the foreign

63. EJV Law, art. 5; EJV Regulations, chap. IV.

party manage the valuation process, including securing an agreement with the Chinese party concerning the value of the foreign party's contribution.

After the valuation report of the Chinese or foreign party's respective contributions have been approved by the relevant authority, it is difficult to obtain an amendment to the valuation report. If the valuation differs from the value placed on the assets by the parties, it may result in a different economic outcome, which may lead the parties to restructure their transaction. In some cases, the difference in valuation could reduce the percentage of the capital ownership of the foreign party, and change the party holding the majority equity interest from the foreign party to the Chinese party. A change in equity ownership may have serious implications for the management of the joint venture and the profits to be shared by the foreign party, and may be unacceptable to the foreign party. In order to avoid a shift in the equity position, the foreign party may need to make a larger capital contribution to offset the lower valuation report. If the problem results from a higher-than-expected valuation of the Chinese party's contribution, the amount of additional capital that must be contributed by the foreign party can be reduced by having the joint venture use the additional capital contributed by the foreign party to purchase part of the assets to be contributed by the Chinese party as an in-kind capital contribution. This would lower the amount of the Chinese party's capital contribution, and therefore its equity interest, so that less cash could be contributed by the foreign party in order to retain its majority interest.

Another solution to counter the effects of lower-than-expected valuation reports is to structure the transaction as a cash contribution by the foreign party. The cash would be used by the joint venture to purchase the machinery from the foreign party or supplier. Alternatively, the joint venture contract could provide that a termination event will occur if the valuation of the foreign party's contribution falls below a certain level. Such a clause may be useful as a source of leverage in renegotiating the joint venture contract, since it may be difficult as a practical matter to retrieve the foreign party's machinery from China if the joint venture is terminated.

(2) Timing of Capital Contributions. The joint venture contract should set forth a schedule for each party's capital contributions. Under Chinese law, if the foreign party's contribution is to be made in a single payment, the payment must be made within six months of the date on which the joint venture company's business license is issued. If the contributions are to be made on an installment basis, the first installment must be made within three months of the date of issuance and be for at least fifteen percent (15%) of the total

capital to be contributed by the foreign party. Chinese law also stipulates the maximum allowable period in which all capital contribution installments must be made. For example, for joint venture companies with a total investment of $3 million to $10 million, the maximum time period is three years.

An additional consideration with respect to capital contributions is whether the foreign party desires to have conditions precedent to its capital contribution obligations. Some conditions to be considered include the receipt by the joint venture company of a valid land-use certificate, or the entering into by the joint venture of certain contracts that have been agreed upon in the joint venture contract, such as trademark or technology licensing agreements with the foreign party or service contracts with the Chinese or foreign party. Given that such contracts must be signed by the joint venture company, and the joint venture company is not in existence at the time the joint venture contract is executed, the inclusion of conditions precedent in the joint venture contract is a way to ensure that such contracts are ultimately signed before the joint venture commences operations. In order to strengthen any conditions contained in the joint venture contract, the contract should provide that the failure to meet any of the conditions will act as a termination event.

(3) Loans. The joint venture company is permitted under law to incur domestic or overseas loans. If the joint venture is expected to borrow in order to meet its funding needs, language should be included in the joint venture contract authorizing the board of directors to approve such borrowing. Any foreign borrowing must be reported to and registered with the State Administration of Foreign Exchange (SAFE) in accordance with procedures set forth in the relevant Chinese regulations.[64] With respect to loans procured by the Chinese party, the parties should note that while the joint venture is entitled to borrow domestically, Chinese partners to the joint venture will not be allowed under Chinese law to make loans unless they are financial institutions (such as banks, trust and investment companies) recognized under Chinese law, and therefore will not be able to provide any their capital in the form of a shareholder loan to the joint venture. Thus, borrowings will have to come from Chinese banks and other financial

64. For a discussion concerning foreign exchange regulation, *see* Chapter 11, Financial Regulation § B. *See* Foreign Debt Administration Tentative Procedures (promulgated on March 1, 2003, by the State Administration of Foreign Exchange) (provides certain new and tighter foreign debt registration standards for foreign-invested enterprises, including the requirement that an FIE's foreign debt agreements will not be effective until they have been registered with SAFE and that the balance of existing short-term foreign debts will be aggregated with existing medium-term and long-term foreign debts for the purpose of applying the borrowing limit to new foreign debt).

institutions or from overseas sources (including the foreign partner to the joint venture). Similarly, the Chinese party will most likely be prohibited under Chinese law from providing a foreign currency guarantee to the joint venture, the foreign partner, or their respective creditors. As a practical matter, only a very limited number of PRC entities (such as financial institutions) are authorized to provide guarantees, and as each of the guarantees is subject to the approval of and registration with the SAFE, they are very difficult in practice to secure.[65]

d. Technology Transfer

The foreign party to a JV may provide technology to a joint venture company as either a contribution to the joint venture, in which case the joint venture will own the technology, or it can license the technology to the joint venture.[66] If the technology is used as a capital contribution, it cannot constitute more than twenty percent (20 percent) of the joint venture company's registered capital. If the technology is licensed, the joint venture company is required to pay a royalty to the foreign party. The license or technology transfer agreement is subject to the approval of the Chinese government. The approval is usually granted at the same time that the joint venture contract is approved, and the agreed-upon draft form of technology license or transfer contract should be included with the application for approval of the JV in order to facilitate the approval process.

There are no limits on the amount of the royalty payments, although there are government guidelines to assist the Chinese party and the approval authorities in evaluating the appropriateness of the royalty amount. If the foreign party chooses to license the technology, the joint venture will need to obtain sufficient foreign exchange to make the royalty payments. A technology license or transfer agreement may be governed by foreign law and subject to dispute resolution outside of China.[67]

e. Land-Use Rights

The status of land and real estate to be used by a joint venture in China is always an important issue and the subject of many disputes between foreign and Chinese parties.[68] In most JV negotiations, the Chinese party offers to

65. For a discussion concerning guarantees, *see* Chapter 7, Contract Law § C.1.

66. *See generally* Chapter 7, Contract Law § B.9. A sample technology transfer/license contract is set forth in Appendix A.

67. For a discussion of choice of forum provisions under the Contract Law, *see* Chapter 7, Contract Law § A.7 and *infra* at p. 102.

68. For a discussion of land-use rights, *see* Chapter 17, Land-Use, Real Estate Development, and Natural Resources § A.

transfer land and facilities that it uses for existing operations to a joint venture company as part of its capital contribution. Oftentimes, the reality is that the Chinese enterprise does not own transferable land-use rights that it occupies and uses, although it may claim and guarantee that it "owns" such rights. As a result, a transfer of land-use rights will be effective only if the Chinese party owns transferable land-use rights to the site in question, or the Chinese party is required to reach an agreement with the local land administration with authority to grant land-use rights.

If the Chinese party does not currently have transferable land-use rights, the parties may adopt one of several strategies to address land-use issues:

(1) Purchase of Transferable Land-Use Rights. The joint venture company may purchase transferable land-use rights to the site for up to a fifty-year period (for industrial joint ventures) from the local land administration bureau by entering into a Land-Use Rights Grant Contract with the bureau and paying the applicable land premium. The joint venture company is allowed to transfer or mortgage the land-use rights to a third party, subject to certain conditions in a land-use contract.

(2) Lease Arrangement. The joint venture company may enter into a lease with the local land administration bureau to lease the site for the duration of the joint venture company. A lease, however, does not result in the joint venture company's obtaining any ownership interest in the land and therefore the land-use rights obtained under the lease will not be transferable or eligible to be used as security and may not be encumbered. Under a lease, land-use fees are determined in accordance with local regulations and are payable by the joint venture company to the local land administration bureau. Land-use fees for leases are subject to adjustment after the first five years.

(3) Nontransferable Land-Use Rights. The Chinese party may contribute nontransferable land-use rights to the joint venture company as part of its capital contribution. The joint venture company would have the right to use the land for the duration of the joint venture, but such rights would not be transferable or eligible to be used as collateral security, which use may be necessary in order to obtain financing for any required construction. Any contribution of nontransferable land-use rights is subject to the approval of the land administration bureau, and the Chinese side is usually required to pay annual land-use fees for the duration of the joint venture.

In a contractual joint venture the Chinese party (subject to the approval of the local land administration bureau) could simply permit the joint venture company to use the land as part of the terms of cooperation of the joint venture arrangement. Under these circumstances, the joint venture company would not own the land-use rights.

f. Special Issues in Contract Negotiations

A foreign party and its legal counsel should evaluate, and take into consideration during the negotiation and preparation of a joint venture contract, a number of issues that often occur throughout the life of a venture, including the following:

(1) Buy-Out Provisions. Under Chinese law, a party to a joint venture company has the right of first refusal on the transfer of equity interests in the joint venture by the other party. When drafting the joint venture contract, Chinese parties often prefer to include only a general provision concerning the right of first refusal, leaving the details to be negotiated at the time a transfer is proposed. Foreign parties may object to the lack of specificity, particularly in multiparty joint ventures in which the right of first refusal may accrue to more than one party. As a result, foreign parties sometimes propose the inclusion of an "offer" and "acceptance" mechanism similar to those found in U.S. shareholders' buy-out agreements. Under this mechanism, the equity interest to be transferred is first offered to the other equity holders at the proposed sale price to the third party, before any transfer to a third party can be made.

(2) Relationship with Chinese Party. The Chinese party may provide a portion of its factory for use by the joint venture, in which case the joint venture may be dependent upon the Chinese party for access to its premises, electricity and water supply, and other basic utilities. Often, the Chinese party favors its own operations over those of the joint venture company. The joint venture contract should contain provisions that require the Chinese party to treat the joint venture on the same basis as the Chinese party's own operations.

The foreign party should also carefully evaluate its Chinese partner's strengths and weaknesses. China's rapid shift from a centrally planned to a market or quasi-market economy, however, has made it particularly difficult to locate business partners with a proven track record or even reliable information. Many Chinese enterprises are burdened with debt, continue to employ redundant personnel, have obsolete equipment, facilities, and products, and have poor or nonexistent distribution networks. A foreign party should conduct a thorough due diligence of its proposed partners prior to and during JV contractual negotiations, including, but not limited to, a mutual exchange of financial information, credit references, customer references, and resumes of key personnel. A careful assessment of a proposed partner may reveal whether the Chinese party is capable of performing its obligations.

(3) Obligations of the Parties. The joint venture agreement should set forth the administrative responsibilities and duties of the parties. For example, the Chinese party will usually be responsible for securing land-use rights for the joint venture; obtaining any Chinese government approvals necessary; obtaining supplies of water, electricity, and other utilities; obtaining import and export licenses; and clearing all imported materials and equipment through customs. The foreign party will usually be responsible for overseas matters affecting the joint venture, including assisting in export sales, international marketing, U.S. customs matters, and other issues. Both parties usually will be jointly responsible for operational matters, such as ensuring proper management and arranging for the joint venture to keep proper books and records. The delegation of duties between the parties should be given careful consideration, and should be based upon the expertise and resources of the respective parties.

(4) Termination Events. The parties to a joint venture contract usually negotiate a number of events that may result in termination of the JV company. Termination events may include the filing for bankruptcy protection, insolvency, significant and continuous losses sustained by the JV company, force majeure, failure to obtain or maintain government approvals including JV registration, business licenses, tax exemptions and other preferential treatment, or export licenses from host country governments (e.g., U.S. Bureau of Export Administration), material breach, failure to obtain financing, failure to obtain patent rights or other rights to technology, or other significant events that justify the termination of the relationship. The termination event usually triggers the liquidation of the JV company. In some situations, however, such as where one party commits a material breach, the nonbreaching party may have the right to purchase the other party's interest in the JV company rather than proceeding to dissolve and liquidate the company. The purchase price may be based upon the value of the joint venture as agreed upon by the parties (i.e., annually), as appraised by an independent accounting firm at or before the occurrence of the termination event, or calculated on some other method expressed in the parties' agreement. The downside to the purchase option is that government approval is required to transform the joint venture into a wholly foreign-owned enterprise. The rights to purchase increase in complexity when the JV company consists of three or more partners.

(5) Choice of Law and Dispute Resolution. Although joint venture contracts in China must be governed by Chinese law, dispute resolution under such contracts may be conducted before arbitration institutions outside of China. A dispute resolution provision may also require that the arbitration proceedings be conducted in English or other language. Many U.S./China joint venture contracts provide for arbitration before such institutions as the International Court of Arbitration for the International Chamber of Commerce, the Arbitration Institute of the Stockholm Chamber of Commerce, the Court of Arbitration of the Zurich Chamber of Commerce, the London Court of International Arbitration, the Hong Kong International Arbitration Center, and the Singapore International Arbitration Center. A party to a contract is strongly advised to evaluate the current procedural rules and fee structure for an arbitration institution, and prior to choosing the institution as a forum. Because China is a party to the New York Convention on Recognition and Enforcement of Foreign Arbitral Awards ("New York Convention"), arbitral awards made by overseas tribunals generally are enforceable in China.[69]

g. Use of Form JV Contracts

In the early 1980s, MOFTEC (now MOFCOM) published a suggested joint venture contract form that has been widely used in China. Frequently, the Chinese party to a joint venture will suggest using the MOFCOM form for the joint venture contract or a version thereof. There is no legal requirement that the MOFCOM form be used, although as a practical matter MOFCOM or its authorized local agent will expect the general format of joint venture contracts to be consistent with the form. Because of the age of the MOFCOM form, it does not address the many developments that have taken place in Chinese law over the past ten years and may not be suitable for complex transactions. Consequently, the MOFCOM form should never be used in its entirety "as is," although many of the individual clauses, especially those that simply recite provisions of the relevant laws, may be appropriate. Provided that the general format of the form is followed, any changes or amendments to the form should not result in a denial of approval or cause a delay in the approval process.[70]

69. For a discussion of China's arbitration system, *see* Chapter 21, Mediation and Arbitration. *See also* sample arbitration provision, Appendix A.

70. For a sample joint venture contract, *see* Appendix A.

2. Equity Joint Venture Trading Company

In 1996, MOFTEC (now MOFCOM) promulgated regulations for the trial establishment of Sino-foreign joint equity foreign trade companies, which were later amended in 2003.[71] The 2003 amendments significantly relaxed the financial requirements, geographical restrictions, and registered capital requirements. Under the JV Trading Company Regulations, foreign and Chinese enterprises may form an equity joint venture that specializes in import and export trade.[72] Prior to 2003, the regulations provided that the trial areas for the establishment of a joint equity foreign trade company shall be limited to the Shanghai Pudong New Area and the Shenzhen Special Economic Zone; however, the geographical limitations have since been dropped.[73] The JV Trading Company Regulations provide that, in accordance with the law, a JV Trading Company may engage in import and export of goods, technology, and related services on its own behalf or as an agent within the scope of business and products for which it has been approved, and may engage in the wholesaling of its imported goods in China.[74]

The JV Trading Company Regulations provide that a joint equity foreign trade company must be established as a limited liability company.[75] The proportion of the registered capital of a JV Trading Company contributed by the foreign party shall be at least 25 percent, and the foreign party may own a controlling interest in the company. In contrast, prior to 2003, the Chinese partner to a joint equity foreign trade company was required to hold no less than 51 percent of the registered capital of the company and that the Chinese partner had the right and duty to appoint the legal representative of the company.[76] The control requirements have been relaxed to

71. Provisional Measures on the Trial Establishment of Sino-Foreign Joint Equity Foreign Trade Companies (promulgated September 30, 1996, by the Ministry of Foreign Trade and Economic Cooperation and re-promulgated on January 31, 2003), *reprinted in* CHINA LAWS FOR FOREIGN BUSINESS (CCH), Business Regulation ¶ 6-615 (hereinafter the "JV Trading Company Regulations"). A translation of the Sino-Foreign Joint Venture Trading Company Rules is available on the Web site of MOFCOM at http://www.mofcom.gov.cn. See China Issues New Regulations on Foreign Trade, ASIAN ECON. NEWS (Oct. 7, 1996), available on Lexis, News Library. For examples of companies that have established joint venture trading companies, *see* Gersten, *U.S. Agribusiness Is Growing in China,* J. OF COMM. 5D (Oct. 1, 1997) (Continental Grain Co.); *First Joint Venture Trading Company Set up by Dow Chemical in China,* Chemical Bus. NEWSBASE (Aug. 1, 1997) (Dow); *China's First Joint Venture Foreign Trade Company Set Up,* AGENCE FRANCE (July 11, 1997) (Mitsubishi, Daewoo); all available on Lexis, News Library. For an analysis of the 2003 amendments to the JV Trading Company Regulations, *see* S. Feng, *Gaining Access to China's Foreign Trade Industry,* CHINA L. & PRAC. (April 2003).

72. JV Trading Company Regulations, art. 2.

73. JV Trading Company Regulations, art. 16.

74. JV Trading Company Regulations, art. 8. Engaging in other areas of business outside the approved business scope is prohibited.

75. JV Trading Company Regulations, art. 3.

76. JV Trading Company Regulations, art. 3. The regulations also provide that applications for JV trading companies with foreign ownership greater than 51 percent will not be accepted prior to December 11, 2003. JV Trading Company Regulations, art. 16.

meet WTO market access obligations. However, WFOE trading companies are still not allowed under the current version of the regulations.

The foreign party to a joint equity foreign trade company must have an average annual trade volume with China of more than $30 million for the three years prior to application or more than $20 million for the three years prior to the application if the company's place of registration is in the central or western regions of the country.[77] The Chinese party to a joint equity foreign trade company must meet the following requirements: (1) have the right to engage in foreign trading activities; and (2) have an average annual import and export volume of more than $30 million for the three years prior to the application, or $20 million if the place of registration is in the central or western region of the country.[78]

The regulations maintain that a joint equity foreign trade company must meet the following requirements:

(1) Registered capital of at least RMB50 million ($6 million), or RMB30 million if the place of registration is in the central or western region of the country
(2) Name and organizational structure
(3) Business premises, professional staff, and other necessary physical requirements appropriate to its foreign trade operations[79]

The Chinese partner to a joint equity foreign trade company is required to submit the following documents at the time of filing its application for approval to MOFCOM:

(1) Project proposal, feasibility study report, joint equity foreign trade company contract, and articles of association
(2) Registration certificates and certificates of creditworthiness
(3) Documentation concerning the legal representative of both parties
(4) Approval documents for enterprises owned and operated by the foreign party in China, including the business license and capital verification report

77. JV Trading Company Regulations, art. 4, § 1. Prior to 2003, the regulations required that the foreign party have a total business volume of more than $5 billion for the year prior to the application, and to have maintained a representative office in China for at least three years or have invested at least $30 million in China. These financial requirements have been dropped.

78. JV Trading Company Regulations, art. 4, § 2. Prior to 2003, the Chinese party to a JV trading company was required to have an average annual import and export volume of more than $200 million for the three years prior to the application, with an export volume of no less than $100 million.

79. JV Trading Company Regulations, art. 4, § 3. Under prior rules, the minimum capital requirements were RMB100 million ($12 million).

(5) Registration certificates for company branch offices or joint equity enterprises established overseas by the Chinese partner
(6) Financial balance sheets of both parties for the previous three years and audit verification certificates issued by an auditing organization
(7) Information concerning the business and product scope of the proposed joint equity foreign trade company
(8) Other documents required by MOFCOM[80]

The regulations provide that the applicants will be issued a certificate of approval by MOFCOM if the joint equity foreign trade company meets the statutory requirements. After MOFCOM approves the application, the Chinese party is required to apply to the SAIC for a business license within thirty days.[81] The contribution of the foreign partner to the registered capital of a joint equity foreign trade company is required to be in the form of convertible currency.[82] The contribution of the Chinese partner to the registered capital may be in the form of renminbi, in-kind, intangible assets, or other property rights.[83] The parties to a joint equity foreign trade company are required to tender their respective capital contributions within one month of the date of issue of the business license.

The regulations provide that a joint equity foreign trade company is required to conduct foreign exchange settlement, and sales and payments of foreign exchange, in accordance with the application laws and regulations applicable to foreign exchange.[84] A joint equity foreign trade company is required to pay its taxes and follow customs procedures in accordance with the applicable laws and regulations.[85] A joint equity foreign trade company is required to submit financial, accounting, and statistical reports to the various government agencies as may be required by law.[86] The regulations further provide that a joint equity foreign trade company is "subject to the

80. JV Trading Company Regulations, art. 5.
81. JV Trading Company Regulations, art. 6.
82. JV Trading Company Regulations, art. 7.
83. JV Trading Company Regulations, art. 7.
84. JV Trading Company Regulations, art. 10.
85. JV Trading Company Regulations, art. 9, 11. The government grants a tax refund for exports to joint equity foreign trade companies in a manner consistent with the rules applicable to state-owned trading companies. A joint equity foreign trade company is required to apply for all quotes and licenses in accordance with the Customs Law and regulations.
86. JV Trading Company Regulations, art. 12. In addition to being subject to the jurisdiction of Chinese law, the JV Trading Company Regulations provide that a joint equity foreign trade company may join an import-export chamber of commerce or foreign investment enterprise association and agrees to "abide by the coordinating control of this chamber of commerce or association." *Id.* art. 14. Under the prior rules, membership was mandatory.

jurisdiction of Chinese laws and statutes . . . [and] [i]ts legal rights and interests will receive the protection of Chinese laws and statutes."[87]

On December 7, 2003, MOFCOM issued regulations that permit service providers from the special administrative regions of Hong Kong and Macao to establish joint venture trading enterprises or wholly foreign-owned trading enterprises on the Mainland.[88] The regulations were adopted pursuant to China's treaty obligations under the Closer Economic Partnership Arrangement (CEPA). The CEPA Trading Company Measures require that the foreign investor maintain, on average, $10 million in annual trade with the Mainland for three years, and the minimum registered capital required is RMB20 million ($240,000).

3. Partnership Enterprise

The NPC adopted the first national partnership law in 1997, which is intended to govern the relationship between two or more individuals involved as business partners.[89] The Partnership Law allows for the creation of a business operation under a partnership contract between two or more parties that have the capability to assume unlimited legal liability.[90] Under the law, the partners are jointly liable for the obligations of the partnership enterprise.

87. JV Trading Company Regulations, art. 15. The regulations provide that the law also applies to companies and enterprises from Hong Kong, Macao, and Taiwan.

88. Supplementary Provisions on the Interim Measures on the Establishment of Sino-Foreign Equity Joint Venture Trading Companies (promulgated on December 7, 2003, by the Ministry of Commerce) (hereinafter the "CEPA Trading Company Measures").

89. Partnership Law of the People's Republic of China (adopted February 23, 1997, at the 24th Sess. of the Standing Comm. of the 8th NPC), *reprinted in* CHINA LAWS FOR FOREIGN BUSINESS (CCH), Business Regulation ¶ 13–350 (hereinafter the "Partnership Law"). The Civil Law also briefly addresses partnership law issues. *See* General Principles of Civil Law of the People's Republic of China (adopted April 12, 1986, by the 4th Sess. of the 6th NPC), arts. 30–35, *reprinted in* CHINA LAWS FOR FOREIGN BUSINESS (CCH), Business Regulation ¶ 19-150 (hereinafter the "Civil Law"). The Shenzhen SEZ adopted a partnership law in 1994. *See* Rules of the Shenzhen SEZ on Partnership (adopted on March 1, 1994, by the 21st Sess. of the Standing Comm. of the 1st Shenzhen Municipal People's Congress). The Guangdong province adopted a partnership law in 1995, which is the experimental forerunner of the national law. *See* Rules of Guangdong Province on Partnership Business Operations (promulgated on May 9, 1995, by the Guangdong Provincial People's Government), *reprinted in* CHINA LAWS FOR FOREIGN BUSINESS (CCH), Special Zones & Cities ¶ 270-010. *See generally* Clark, Howson & Gangliang, *China's New Partnership Law,* 4 CHINA BUSINESS REV. 30 (July 17, 1997), available on Lexis, News Library. *See also* Administrative Measures of the People's Republic of China on the Registration of Partnership Enterprises (promulgated on November 19, 1997, by the State Council), *reprinted in* CHINA LAWS FOR FOREIGN BUSINESS (CCH), Business Regulation ¶ 13-357 (hereinafter the "Registration of Partnership Enterprises Regulations"); Notice on Relevant Issues Concerning the Implementation of the Administrative Measures of the People's Republic of China on the Registration of Partnership Enterprises (promulgated on February 19, 1998, by the SAIC), *reprinted in* CHINA LAWS FOR FOREIGN BUSINESS (CCH), Business Regulation ¶ 23-351 (hereinafter "Registration of Partnership Enterprises").

90. Partnership Law, art. 2.

The partners are required to have sufficient assets to engage in the partnership business, a partnership name, and business premises.[91] The Partnership Law precludes social institutions such as schools, hospitals, and other nonprofit organizations from entering into a partnership arrangement.[92] Since a partnership business and its partners cannot insulate themselves from personal liability, or operate as a limited liability company or limited liability partnership, the business entity is prohibited from using language such as "limited liability," "Ltd.," or "limited" in the partnership name.[93]

The law does not specifically apply to foreign persons or entities and, in practice, the SAIC and the tax authorities maintain that arrangements with foreign "partners" are subject to the CJV law and regulations and not the Partnership Law.[94] However, as China continues its legal reform, and specifically with respect to the recognition of principles concerning freedom of contract, it is anticipated that foreign individuals and entities will be allowed to enter into partnership relationships with Chinese or other foreign parties in the PRC.

a. Partnership Contract and Approval Procedures

To register the establishment of a partnership enterprise, the applicants are required to submit to the SAIC a registration application, the partnership contract, and identification documentation of the partners.[95] The Partnership Law requires that the parties enter into a contract which must be filed with, and approved by, the SAIC[96] and is required to contain a number of key provisions, including the following:

(1) Name of the partnership enterprise and address of its main business premises

---

91. Partnership Law, art. 8.

92. Partnership Law, art. 10.

93. Partnership Law, arts. 5, 66. The SAIC may impose a fine of up to RMB2,000 for improperly using the language "limited" or "limited liability" in the business name. *Id.* art. 66.

94. The CJV Law is viewed as a partnership law between foreign and domestic parties. The Partnership Law allows for domestic entities to enter into cooperative arrangements in a similar fashion as the CJV rules. Arguably, joint venture enterprises, which are considered domestic entities, may enter into partnership arrangements with Chinese-owned enterprises. Whether the CJV standards are abandoned in the future for the more detailed and flexible Business Partnership Law is left for observation. For a discussion of the CJV structure, *see infra* footnote 47 and accompanying text. The SAIC maintains that only domestic investment enterprises may operate as partnerships. *See* Provisioins Concerning Enterprise Registration Classifications (promulgated on August 28, 1998, by the State Bureau of Statistics and the SAIC), *reprinted in* China Laws for Foreign Business (CCH), Business Regulation ¶ 13-589.

95. Partnership Law, art. 15; Registration of Partnership Enterprises Regulations, arts. 7, 8. The applicant is required to submit to the SAIC the following documents: (1) an application to register the establishment of the enterprise; (2) proof of identity of all of the partners; (3) the letter of appointment for the managing partner; (4) the partnership contract; (5) proof of equity ownership of contributed property; (6) proof of business premises such as a lease or land-use contract; and (7) other documents that may be required by the SAIC.

96. Partnership Law, arts. 15, 17. The State Administration of Industry and Commerce promulgated regulations effective November 19, 1997, concerning registration procedures for partnership enterprises

(2) Object of the partnership enterprise and business scope
(3) Names and address of the partners
(4) Contribution methods, the amounts of capital contributions of each partner, and contribution deadlines
(5) Measures on profit distribution and the sharing of responsibility for losses
(6) Procedures for handling the general affairs of the partnership enterprise
(7) Entry into the partnership and retirement therefrom[97]
(8) Dissolution and liquidation of the partnership enterprise
(9) Liability for breach of the partnership contract[98]

The partnership contract may also provide for dispute resolution procedures and the term of the partnership enterprise.[99] A partnership contract is valid at the time the parties enter into the agreement. A partnership contract may only be revised or amended subject to the unanimous consent of the partners.[100]

The SAIC is required to approve or deny an application within thirty days of receiving the application.[101] An application that complies with the basic conditions of the Partnership Law is approved and a business license is issued. If an application is rejected, the SAIC is required to provide written notice to the applicants.[102] The date of issuance of a business license of a partnership enterprise is the date of establishment. The partners are prohibited by law from engaging in business activities in the name of the partnership enterprise before the SAIC issues a business license.[103]

b. Partnership Property and Partner Contribution

A partner may use cash, goods, land-use rights, intellectual property rights, or other property rights as its capital contribution.[104] If a partner intends to

---

including the information and documentation required to receive a business license. The registration regulations provide that partnership enterprises are required to undergo annual joint review as required of other enterprises. *See* Registration of Partnership Enterprises, arts. 21–25. *See also* Harpole, *New Developments: Partnership Registration,* 6 CHINA L. NEWS 10 (Dec. 1997). Registration of Partnership Enterprises Regulations, arts. 17–20.

97. Articles 44–56 of the Partnership Law provide in detail the requirements for entry into and retirement from a partnership enterprise.

98. Partnership Law, art. 13.

99. Partnership Law, arts. 13, 76.

100. Partnership Law, art. 14. The partnership is required to file an application for amendments to its registration. Registration of Partnership Enterprises Regulations, arts. 11–13.

101. Partnership Law, art. 16; Registration of Partnership Enterprises Regulations, art. 9.

102. Partnership Law, art. 16.

103. Partnership Law, art. 17; Registration of Partnership Enterprises Regulations, art. 10.

104. Partnership Law, art. 11.

make a noncash contribution to the partnership business, the parties may agree on the value of the contribution or commission an authorized appraisal firm to set the valuation. A partner may also provide labor as its capital contribution, subject to the unanimous consent of all partners. The Partnership Law provides that partners are required to tender their capital contributions in accordance with contribution methods as set forth in the partnership contract.[105] The partners may increase the amount of their capital contributions to the partnership enterprise in accordance with the terms of the partnership contract. The increased capital may be used only to expand the enterprise's scope of operations or to compensate for losses.[106]

Capital contributed by the parties, and all earnings obtained in the name of the partnership enterprise, is regarded as property of the enterprise.[107] The partners to a partnership enterprise are entitled to profits and responsible for losses in the proportions stipulated in the partnership contract. If the parties have not agreed upon a proportion with respect to the allocation of profits and losses, all partners shall share profits and losses equally.[108]

The property of the enterprise is required to be jointly administered and used by all partners for partnership business in accordance with the law and the parties' contract.[109] The assets and property of the partnership business are owned by the partnership and cannot be removed, withdrawn, encumbered, or sold unilaterally.[110] The partners are therefore prohibited from encumbering partnership assets without the consent of all partners, assigning or transferring an interest in the partnership to third parties, and assigning or transferring the assets of the partnership to third parties.[111] If any partner sustains damages as a result of an unlawful transfer, assignment, or encumbrance of partnership property, the breaching partner is liable for compensation.[112] A partner that intends to assign all or a portion of its share of the partnership enterprise property to a third party is required to obtain the consent of the other partners.[113] The Partnership Law provides that all

105. Partnership Law, art. 12.
106. Partnership Law, art. 33.
107. Partnership Law, arts. 19, 27.
108. Partnership Law, art. 32. The Partnership Law provides that the parties' contract cannot apportion all of the profits and/or all of the losses to one particular partner. The Partnership Law provides that the parties may distribute profits in accordance with the contract or by stipulation. *Id.* art. 34. The law further provides that any partner who pays more than his or her share for partnership losses has a claim for indemnification against the other partners. *Id.* art. 40.
109. Partnership Law, art. 19.
110. Partnership Law, art. 21, 22, 23.
111. Partnership Law, art. 21, 23. The Partnership Law provides that all partners are liable to creditors for the improper disposal or transfer of the assets of the partnership. *Id.* art. 20.
112. Partnership Law, art. 24.
113. Partnership Law, art. 21. All intended transfers or assignments require that all partners be notified.

partners have a right of first refusal to purchase the interest of a partner that intends to sell, transfer, or assign its interests in partnership property.[114]

c. Management of Partnership Affairs

The Partnership Law provides that all partners in a partnership enterprise shall equal rights with respect to the general affairs of the enterprise. In the alternative, the management of a partnership business may be delegated to a managing partner under the terms and conditions of the partnership agreement.[115] The managing partner appointed by the partners is required to conduct the business of the enterprise within the authorized scope of operations.[116] The Partnership Law provides that the managing partner has the right to manage the affairs of the operation without the interference of the other partners.[117] However, the delegating partners have the right to provide overall supervision and control over the partnership business pursuant to the terms of the partnership agreement and as provided by law.[118]

The parties to a partnership agreement have a fiduciary relationship to the business operation and other partners.[119] The Partnership Law provides that a partner is prohibited from operating a business, individually or in cooperation with another party, that directly competes with the partnership enterprise. The Partnership Law sets forth a general obligation that a partner "is prohibited from engaging in activities which harm the interests of the partnership enterprise."[120]

A partnership enterprise is required to obtain the unanimous approval of all partners with respect to the following matters:

(1) Disposal of real property of the partnership enterprise
(2) Amendment of the name of the partnership enterprise

---

114. Partnership Law, art. 22.

115. Partnership Law, art. 25. The partners also can jointly manage the business pursuant to agreed-upon terms and conditions. The partnership agreement should contain specific terms to address issues of deadlocks in order to ensure that any dispute can be resolved without disrupting the business operation of the partnership.

116. Partnership Law, art. 35. A managing partner that acts outside the scope of operations is liable for payment of compensation to the partners if they sustain losses. A partnership enterprise is required to establish financial and accounting systems in accordance with the law and is required to fulfill its obligations to the tax authorities. *Id.* arts. 36, 37.

117. Partnership Law, art. 26. A partner who does not participate in management has the right to supervise the work of the managing partner. The managing partner is obligated to report to the other partners the operational and financial affairs of the enterprise. *Id.* at art. 27.

118. Partnership Law, art. 26.

119. Partnership Law, art. 30.

120. Partnership Law, art. 30. If a managing partner fails to meet the requirements of the parties, he or she may be removed by the partners in accordance with the parties' contract. *Id.* art. 29.

(3) Assignment or disposal of the intellectual property rights and other property rights of the partnership enterprise
(4) Application to the SAIC for amendment to the partnership registration
(5) Providing security to another party in the name of the partnership enterprise
(6) Delegation of management duties to third parties
(7) Other matters stipulated in the partnership contract[121]

The Partnership Law sets forth the provisions for dissolution and liquidation of the partnership enterprise, including the standards for dissolution, liquidation procedures and notice requirements to creditors, remedies to the people's court with respect to the liquidation process, standards for priority payments during liquidation, and standards for the liquidation report. The Partnership Law further outlines the civil and criminal liability involving partnership activities, including misappropriation of partnership assets, violations of noncompetition standards, violations of liquidators, and remedies for creditors.[122] The law also outlines the requirements for record keeping and the rights of partners to access and inspect partnership records, including financial and operations-related documentation, and partnership property.[123]

C. Special Function Operations

Chinese law permits the establishment of operations that have a limited scope such as manufacturing operations designed for exports, maintenance and technical service, branch offices of existing enterprises, holding companies, foreign-funded venture capital enterprises, and research and development centers.[124]

1. Processing Trade Contract

A foreign party and a Chinese enterprise may enter into a processing trade contract[125] by which the foreign party provides all or a portion of the equipment, materials, and components to a Chinese enterprise to manufacture

121. Partnership Law, art. 31.
122. Partnership Law, arts. 57–64, 73–75.
123. Partnership Law, art. 28.
124. For clarification, this section generally categorizes and evaluates those special function operations that are applicable to all industries. The rules unique to industry-specific operations are addressed by subject matter in Chapter 5, Foreign Investment Guidelines and Industry-Specific Regulations.
125. Processing trade arrangements may also be referred to as "contract factories" or "OEM Services."

merchandise in accordance with contractual specifications.[126] The imported equipment, materials, and components used in the processing trade arrangement are exempt from import or export license requirements. However, the finished goods are required to be exported and, if sold domestically, the parties are required to follow Customs procedures.[127] A processing trade contract does not require that the foreign party establish a presence in China.

The Chinese party to a processing trade contract usually provides the factory facilities and equipment, energy resources and other utilities, labor resources, and consumables. The factory receives compensation in accordance with the parties' processing trade or manufacturing contract. A well-written contract should include provisions outlining the manufacturing process, production schedule, subcontracting issues, packaging, materials to be used, warehousing and security, pricing terms, contract duration and termination, warranties of manufacturer, the protection and use of proprietary information and intellectual property, indemnification and insurance, governing law, and dispute resolution.[128]

2. Maintenance and Technical Service Operations

Under previous practice, the Chinese government permited the establishment of special maintenance and technical service operations to allow foreign companies to provide post-sale warranty service and repairs, and accessibility to spare parts and other items to support equipment, machinery, and other items purchased by Chinese enterprises.[129] Today, after-sales service or warranty service operations are usually set up as WFOEs by the foreign party or by contract with qualified Chinese companies.

---

126. *See* Measures of Guangdong Province to Encourage the Development of Processing, Assembling, and Compensation Trade Projects with Foreign Parties (promulgated on March 2, 1988, by the Guangdong Provincial People's Government), *reprinted in* China Laws for Foreign Business (CCH), Special Zones ¶ 70-881; *Stipulation on Issues Relating to the Import of Equipment for the Processing Trade,* 135 China International Business (MOFTEC) 48 (1998). For a sample manufacturing agreement, *see* Appendix A. *See also* Notice on Several Issues concerning the Import of Equipment for the Processing Trade (promulgated on July 1, 1998, by MOFTEC and China Customs), *reprinted in* China Laws for Foreign Business (CCH), Taxation & Customs ¶ 31-807 (outlines exemption standards for imported equipment for processing trade).

127. For a discussion of the rules governing customs procedures for the processing trade, *see* Chapter 15, Customs and Trade Regulation § B.3.

128. For a sample processing trade and manufacturing contract, *see* Appendix A. A processing trade contract is governed by the Contract Law. *See* Chapter 7, Contract Law § B.6.

129. *See* Regulations for Developing Maintenance and Technical Service Operations and Consignment Sales of Spare Parts and Accessories for Imported Mechanical and Electrical Products and Instruments (promulgated on November 22, 1986, by the State Council), *reprinted in* China Laws for Foreign Business (CCH), Customs ¶ 50-690 (hereinafter "Maintenance and Technical Service Operations Regulations"). Maintenance and Technical Service Operations Contracts are governed by the Contract Law. *See* Chapter 7, Contract Law § B.9.c.

3. Branch Offices

An enterprise, under the Company Law, [130] may establish branch offices "within the territory of China to engage in production and business operations."[131] While the term "business operations" is not defined in the Company Law, in practice, the rules apply to any business activities, including production, marketing, and sales.

An FIE is required to file an application with MOFCOM in order to establish a branch office. The application for registration of a branch office is required to include the FIE's articles of association, company registration certificate, and information concerning the location, scope, and objective of the branch office.[132] If approval is received to open a branch office from MOFCOM, the SAIC or its local affiliate will issue a business license.[133] A company is required to appoint a representative responsible for the branch, and to provide adequate funding and other resources to operate the branch office. Under the Company Law, the State Council has the authority to require "a minimum amount of operational funds" for branch offices.[134]

An FIE may establish more than one branch office in China.[135] Pre-existing and approved joint ventures, WFOEs, and other entities with operations in China have been allowed to set up branch offices. The principal disadvantage of a branch office is that it may not exist independently of the parent company and the parent assumes all liability for the activities of the branch. As a result, a branch office may not operate as a separate subsidiary with limited liability.[136] A foreign company that intends to close a branch office is required to liquidate the operation pursuant to the liquidation procedures provided by law. The Company Law provides that the assets of the branch office "shall not be permitted to be moved out of China before the settlement

---

130. Company Law of the People's Republic of China (adopted December 29, 1993, by the 5th Sess. of the Standing Comm. of the 8th NPC, revised and repromulgated on December 25, 1999, by the 13th Sess. of the Standing Comm. of the 9th NPC), *reprinted in* CHINA LAWS FOR FOREIGN BUSINESS (CCH), Business Regulation ¶ 13-518 (hereinafter the "Company Law"). On February 19, 2003, the SAIC issued a preliminary draft of the *Measures for the Administration of the Registration of Branches and Sub-Branches of Foreign-Invested Enterprises,* which addresses establishment, amendment, and deregistration of branch companies and sub-branch companies. Under the draft measures, previously unregistered branch entities will be required to register within thirty days after official promulgation of these measures.

131. Company Law, chap. IX. Depending upon the business activities, other laws may provide more stringent requirements for branch offices such as in banking and insurance. *See* Chapter 11, Financial Regulation § A.2.; Chapter 12, Insurance Law and Regulation § A.1.

132. Company Law, art. 200.

133. Company Law, art. 200.

134. Company Law, art. 201.

135. Company Law, art. 199. In contrast, many foreign firms are precluded from opening more than one representative office in China.

136. Company Law, art. 203.

of its debts."[137] The lack of limited liability protection limits the application of the branch office rules.

The SAIC approved the *Notice on Relevant Issues for Foreign-Invested Enterprise Branches Established Outside of Free-Trade Zones (SAIC Decree No. 363 [2001]),* which lifts restrictions that prevented foreign-invested enterprises (FIEs) in free-trade zones (FTZs) from establishing offices outside the zones. The notice also allows an FIE in an FTZ to establish offices outside the FTZ to perform liaison work under the parent FIE's business scope. The new rules took effect on the date of approval, December 17, 2001.

4. Holding Company

In mid-2003, there were over 300 foreign-invested holding companies operating in China since the adoption of regulations in 1995.[138] The government amended the Holding Company Regulations in 2003 and 2004 to conform to existing practices. The Holding Company Regulations define an "investment company" as an entity established in China by a solely foreign-funded business or by companies that are jointly funded by Chinese and foreign investors for the purpose of engaging in direct investment.[139] A holding company is required to be established as a limited liability company (LLC) and may consist of foreign investment alone or in conjunction with Chinese partners. The principal function of a holding company is to provide the enterprises funded by the company with support for sales, management, financial and subsidiary investment, research and development, manufacturing, services, marketing, and procurement activities.

A proposed holding company is required to have registered capital of not less than $30 million, which may be paid in renminbi from profits obtained in China.[140] The FIE Holding Company Regulations provide that

---

137. Company Law, art. 205. For a discussion concerning the liquidation procedures recognized by Chinese law, *see* Chapter 20, Enterprise Liquidation, Reorganization, and Bankruptcy § A.

138. Provisional Regulations Governing the Establishment of Investment-Type Companies by Foreign Business Investment (promulgated on April 4, 1995, by MOFTEC and re-promulgated and amended on March 1, 2003, and February 13, 2004, by the Ministry of Commerce), *reprinted in* CHINA LAWS FOR FOREIGN BUSINESS (CCH), Business Regulation (CCH) ¶ 13-400 (hereinafter the "Holding Company Regulations"). *See also* Mollard & Tiang, *Explanation on Holding Company Rules Marks a First Step to Standardization,* 11 CHINA L. & PRAC. 44 (May 1997) (analysis of explanatory circular which elaborates on the holding company regulations). For a bullet point analysis of the Holding Company Regulations, *see* Fact Sheet: Holding Company, The U.S.-CHINA BUSINESS COUNCIL (last updated June 27, 2003), available online for members at http://www.uschina.org. *See generally* P. Corne, *MOFTEC'S Swansong: Easing Restrictions on PRC Holding Companies,* CHINA L. & PRAC. (May 2003).

139. Holding Company Regulations, art. 1.

140. Holding Company Regulations, art. 2, § 3.

a foreign party that desires to establish a holding company must meet the following requirements:

(1) Be creditworthy and maintain sufficient economic resources to establish an investment company
(2) Have existing foreign-funded enterprises in China in which the investor's capital contribution exceeds $10 million
(3) Have more than three proposed investment projects that have been approved in China
(4) Have total worldwide assets of $400 million or more the year prior to the holding company application[141]

In the alternative, a foreign investor may qualify to establish a holding company if it has established more than ten foreign-funded enterprises in which the investor's capital contribution is in excess of $30 million.[142] In situations where there are multiple foreign investors to a holding company, at least one of the principal foreign parties is required to meet the basic requirements of the Holding Company Regulations. Subsidiary operations of parent companies that meet the minimum requirements are qualified to apply for approval to establish a holding company.

The Holding Company Regulations require that a Chinese investor in a jointly funded investment company is required to be creditworthy, maintain sufficient economic resources for the establishment of an investment company, and have total assets of not less than RMB100 million ($12 million).[143]

An applicant for a holding company is required to submit the following documents to MOFCOM for approval:

(1) Project proposals for the establishment of the jointly funded investment company, feasibility study report, contract, and articles of association, if applicable
(2) A project proposal for the establishment of a solely foreign-funded investment company signed by the foreign investor, application of foreign enterprise concerned, feasibility study report, and articles of association of the proposed company
(3) Documentation certifying the investor's creditworthiness, certificates of registration, and certification for the legal representatives of the enterprise

141. Holding Company Regulations, art. 2, § 1 (1).

142. Holding Company Regulations, art. 2, § 1 (2). Prior to February 2004, the regulations required that the ten FIEs be "manufacturing or infrastructure construction" enterprises. This requirement was dropped.

143. Holding Company Regulations, art. 2, § 2.

(4) Documents of approval for the enterprises in which the foreign investor has already invested, business licenses, and capital verification reports issued by certified public accountants registered in China
(5) Balance sheets and other financial records of the investor for the past three years
(6) Other documents as required by MOFCOM[144]

The applicants are required to contribute their registered capital within a period of two years after the issuance of a business license. A foreign party is required to contribute its share of registered capital in the form of freely convertible currency, or in RMB income generated in China from dividend distributions, stock transfers, or liquidation proceeds.[145] A Chinese investor may contribute its share of registered capital in RMB.[146] The procedures for application of a holding company are consistent with the procedures for establishing a foreign-invested enterprise.[147]

Upon approval, a holding company may engage in the following activities:

(1) Invest in areas permitted and encouraged by the government[148]
(2) Provide the following services to enterprises funded by the investment company where there has been written authorization from that enterprise (with unanimous approval of the board of directors):
    (i) assist or represent an enterprise funded by the investment company to purchase for its own use, domestically or overseas, machinery and equipment, office equipment and raw materials required for production, components and spare parts; to sell products manufactured by those enterprises; and to provide after-sales service;

144. Holding Company Regulations, art. 3. The regulations require that the legal representative of the investors sign the documents. If the legal representative does not sign the documents, the application is required to include a power of attorney for the person that executed the subject documents.

145. Prior to 2003, foreign investors under the old regulations could only contribute the registered capital of a holding company in freely convertible foreign currency. Under the 2003 amendments, however, foreign investors may pay the contributions in RMB profits obtained in the PRC, or RMB proceeds legally obtained from various activities including transfer of equity interest or liquidation. If the foreign investor pays the registered capital in RMB, it has to submit substantiation of origin as well as tax payment receipts.

146. Holding Company Regulations, art. 4.

147. Holding Company Regulations, art. 9.

148. Under the 2003 amendments to the Holding Company Regulations, the scope of investments that holding companies are permitted to make have been expanded. Previously, investments were limited to areas of industry, agriculture, infrastructure, and energy that were permitted or encouraged by the State. Today, the scope of investment has been expanded to any area permitted by the State. In addition, holding companies may now be used by investors that operate purely in service industries, such as fund management or securities.

(ii) subject to the approval of the SAFE, balance foreign exchange between those enterprises funded by the investment company;
(iii) provide technical support, staff training, enterprise personnel management, and other services; and
(iv) assist an enterprise in seeking loans and credit guarantees.

(3) Provide investors with consultant services
(4) Establish centers or departments that engage in research and development of new technologies or high-tech products and offer other relevant technical services
(5) Provide market information, investment policies, and other consulting services to the invested companies of the holding companies
(6) Serve as a subcontractor for services outsourced by its parent company and affiliated companies.[149]

With special approval from MOFCOM, a holding company may also engage in the following activities:

(1) Act as a distributor for the products of the invested companies in the domestic and international markets
(2) Provide transportation, warehousing, and other general services to invested companies
(3) Export products of the invested companies and handle VAT rebates on exports
(4) Provide systems integration and resell the integrated systems in the domestic and international markets[150]
(5) Provide technical training services to domestic agents and distributors of the invested company products
(6) Import products from the overseas parent, which are similar to the products of the invested companies, for purposes of market development prior to full production by the invested companies[151]
(7) Lease equipment to invested companies under an operating lease contract, or establish for-profit leasing companies

149. Holding Company Regulations, art. 5. An investment company may, with the approval of the CBRC, provide the enterprises under its management and control with financial support. *Id.* art. 7.

150. In situations where a holding company's invested companies do not produce sufficient products for system integration, the holding company may procure supporting products domestically or internationally when the value of such procurement does not exceed 50 percent of the total value of products required for system integration.

151. The regulations limit the amount of imports of supporting products for market development to no more than 35 percent of the registered capital that is contributed by the foreign party in foreign currency. The payment for market development imports must be paid in foreign currency, foreign currency profits, or foreign currency loans obtained overseas.

(8) Provide after-sales service to the holding company's parent company
(9) Participate in offshore construction projects[152]

A holding company, with approval and after its registered capital has been fully contributed, may establish branch offices in any location where the invested companies' operations are located or where product sales are concentrated.

A foreign-funded investment company is required to own a 25-percent interest in the total registered capital of an enterprise under its control and management.[153] A holding company may hold unlisted shares in a company limited by shares, and may do so with or without the 25 percent minimum foreign shareholding requirement. The 2003 Amendments confirm the existing practice that allows a holding company to be a promoter of a joint stock company, or hold unlisted shares in both foreign-invested and domestic joint stock companies. However, holding companies cannot hold listed shares or list the shares that they hold. A holding company is also required to guarantee that the enterprises under its control and management will contribute capital and transfer technology in the time required by contract or by law.[154] A holding company's activities are not restricted to the place of registration.[155]

The Holding Company Regulations limit the loans of a holding company (i.e., the mid- to long-term debt) that may be procured by a holding company to a maximum of four times its registered capital. Under the 2003 Amendments to the Holding Company Regulations, if a holding company's registered capital is more than $100 million, the maximum debt service of the holding company may be six times its registered capital.

A holding company is required to abide by the tax laws and regulations, and is entitled to preferential tax treatment afforded to foreign-funded enterprises if it contributes more than 25 percent of the registered capital of the enterprises under its management and control.[156] A holding company is

152. These additional business activities are subject to special approval by MOFCOM, which will require that the minimum registered capital of $30 million be paid in full.

153. Holding Company Regulations, art. 6. *See also* Supplementary Rules (II) to "Tentative Provisions for the Establishment of Investment-type Companies by Foreign Investors" (promulgated on May 31, 2001, by MOFTEC).

154. Holding Company Regulations, art. 12.

155. Holding Company Regulations, art. 13. An investment company may establish branch offices if it meets the requirements for such offices as outlined in the Company Law. For a discussion concerning the rules governing branch offices, *see infra* footnote 89 and accompanying text.

156. Holding Company Regulations, arts. 10, 14, 17. *See also* Notice of the Ministry of Finance and the State Administration of Taxation on Certain Taxation Issues Concerning Foreign Investment Enterprises Engaging in Investment Business (promulgated on January 13, 1995, by the MOF and the SAT), *reprinted in* CHINA LAWS FOR FOREIGN BUSINESS (CCH), Taxation ¶ 32-742 (addresses tax rules for

subject to a 30 percent national income tax and a 3 percent local tax, and is ineligible for preferential tax treatment afforded to production enterprises. Dividends received by the holding company from its invested companies are exempt from income tax, and there is no withholding obligation on dividends paid by the holding company to its foreign investor. The law also allows for a 40 percent refund for dividend income reinvested in a holding company's invested companies, and a 100 percent rebate on income generated by approved export-oriented or technologically advanced FIEs. With respect to VAT, a holding company is eligible for a rebate when it exports products produced by subsidiaries or exports products purchased in China that comply with the holding company's business scope in accordance with the law. A holding company is required to submit an annual report of its activities to MOFCOM before the end of the first quarter of the following year.[157] The Holding Company Regulations apply to all foreign-funded investment companies including investors from Taiwan, Hong Kong, or Macao.[158]

The February 2004 amendments to the Holding Company Regulations outline the standards for the establishment of a holding company as a regional headquarters.[159] Specifically, a regional headquarters holding company must have a minimum registered capital of $100 million, or the amount of registered capital that has been actually paid is not lower than $50 million, and the total amount of assets of the enterprise that is invested by the holding company one year before the application is not lower than RMB3 billion ($362.3 million) and the total profit amount shall not be lower than RMB100 million ($12.1 million). A holding company set up as a regional headquarters is entitled to certain benefits and expanded scope of business including the right to engage in logistics and distribution services, financial services for subsidiary operations, project contracting services, and other activities.[160]

investment companies and tax preferential treatment). A holding company is required to obtain the approval of the SAFE if it intends to transfer its foreign exchange funds for purposing of investing in China. *See* Notice on Several Issues on the Handling of Relevant Tax Issues Related to the Provision of Services by a Foreign-Invested Holding Company to its Subsidiary Companies (issued by the State Administration of Taxation and effective as of January 1, 2003). The Holding Company Tax Notice requires holding companies to treat subsidiaries as third parties when providing services, and that holding companies are required to sign service contracts with their subsidiaries outlining the fees and costs. The Holding Company Tax Notice also provides that if the same service is provided to several subsidiaries or affiliates, the holding company may spread the total cost among the subsidiaries according to a set of parameters as reported to and approved by the tax authorities.

157. Holding Company Regulations, art. 15.
158. Holding Company Regulations, art. 18.
159. Holding Company Regulations, art. 21.
160. Holding Company Regulations, art. 21 (II).

5. Foreign-Invested Venture Capital Investment Enterprises (FIVCE)

On August 18, 2001, MOFCOM (then MOFTEC), the Ministry of Science and Technology (MOST), and SAIC issued the Provisional Regulations of the Establishment of Foreign-Invested Venture Capital Investment Enterprises (FIVCE Regulations),[161] which formally opens the venture capital business to foreign investors in China. Foreign entities can establish venture capital enterprises (private equity funds) either as a foreign-invested limited liability company or as a Sino-foreign joint venture without legal person status in China. The FIVCE Regulations also provide detailed requirements concerning capital contributions, establishment conditions for withdrawing stock from invested companies, and required business scope of the FIVCE.

The FIVCE Regulations were adopted in order to encourage foreign companies, enterprises, and other economic organizations and individuals (hereinafter referred to as "foreign investors") to invest in high and new technologies in China, and to formally establish and perfect the mechanism of venture capital investment.[162] Under the regulations, foreign investors are allowed to establish, independently or with Chinese investors, limited liability foreign investment companies ("Corporate FIVCE") or nonlegal person Sino-foreign cooperative enterprises ("Non-Legal Person FIVCE") which have *venture investment* as their business activity.[163]

161. Provisional Regulations on the Establishment of Foreign-Invested Venture Capital Investment Enterprises (issued on August 18, 2001, by MOFTEC, Ministry of Science and Technology, State Administration of Taxation, and State Administration of Industry and Commerce, effective on September 1, 2001, and as amended on March 1, 2003); Regulations of the Administration of Foreign-Invested Venture Capital Enterprises (issued on January 30, 2003, by MOFTEC, SAIC, MOST, SAT, and SAFE) (the FIVCE Administration Regulations cover the creation, operation, and dissolution of FIVCEs). *See also* Venture Capital Investment Regulations (promulgated on February 27, 2003, by the Shenzhen Municipal People's Congress); Promotion of the Development of Venture Capital Investment Tentative Provisions (issued on February 14, 2003, by the Guangdong Provincial Development and Planning Commission). *See generally* M. Burke, *Venture Capital Options Expand—A Bit,* THE CHINA BUSINESS REVIEW (July–August 2003); *China's Foreign Venture Capital Law: How Far from Customary International Fund Practice?,* CHINA L. & PRAC. (Oct. 2001). Pursuant to the FIVCE Regulations, several new VC funds were created in 2003. For example, KLM Capital, Ascendas Pte, Ltd., and Beijing Tsinghua Science Park created a $50 million fund for investments in high-growth or late-stage companies in materials, energy, and environmental technologies; JP Morgan Fleming, a subsidiary of JP Morgan Chase & Co., announced that it would take a 33-percent interest ($5.9 million) in a fund with Shanghai International Trust and Investment Co., Ltd.; ABN-AMRO Holding NV formed a $300 million fund with Xiangcai Hefeng Fund Management. *See* THE U.S.-CHINA BUSINESS COUNCIL, CHINA OPERATIONS 2003, ANALYSIS: FOREIGN INVESTMENT IN CHINA, FIRST HALF 2003, p. 20. *See also* P. Wonacott, *Private Equity Funds Launch Oversight Association in China,* WALL ST. J. (June 17, 2002) (author notes that the China Venture Capital Association was established for lobbying on key policy issues with the Chinese government).

162. FIVCE Regulations, art. 1. The definition of "foreign investors" also includes investors from Hong Kong SAR, Macao SAR, and Taiwan. FIVCE Regulations, art. 29.

163. The term "venture investment" used in the FIVCE Regulations refers to the form of investment in which equity investment is made mainly in high- and new-technology enterprises that have not been

In order to establish an FIVCE, the following conditions must be met:

(1) The FIVCE has at least two but not more than 50 investors, and shall have at least one principal investor (general partner) that meets the qualifications of the regulations
(2) The minimum amount of the total capital contribution subscribed for from all investors shall be \$10 million for each Non-Legal Person FIVCE and \$5 million for each Corporate FIVCE[164]
(3) The FIVCE has an established organizational structure and an investment strategy
(4) Except for situations where an FIVCE has contracted with a venture capital investment management company to manage its activities, each FIVCE shall have at least three professional personnel with venture capital investment experience[165]

The principal investor (general partner) to an FIVCE is required to meet the following conditions and qualifications:

(1) Venture capital investment is the main line of business for the principal investor
(2) In the three years before the application the principal investor has had cumulative capital under its management of not less than \$100 million, of which at least \$50 million has been used for venture capital investments; and in the case of the principal investor being a Chinese Investor, the cumulative capital shall be RMB100 million, of which at least RMB50 million has been used for venture capital investments
(3) The principal investor has at least three professional management personnel with at least three years' experience in the venture capital investment area
(4) The principal investor is not prohibited by law from engaging in venture capital investment or investment consultancy business or subject to penalty for commitment of fraud by the judicial authority or any relevant regulatory authority in its home country[166]

---

listed yet (hereinafter referred to as "invested enterprises"), and where venture management services are provided, so as to obtain benefits from an increase in capital value. FIVCE Regulations, art. 3.

164. With the exception of the principal investor(s), each other investor's minimum capital contribution shall not be less than \$1 million. Foreign Investors are required to contribute their capital contributions in freely convertible currencies and Chinese Investors in renminbi.

165. FIVCE Regulations, art. 6.

166. FIVCE Regulations, art. 7.

For a Non-Legal Person FIVCE, at least 1 percent of the total capital contribution subscribed for by all investors to the FIVCE and at least 1 percent of the total actual capital contribution from all investors to the FIVCE shall be made by its principal investor(s) and such principal investor(s) shall be jointly and severally liable for the debts of the FIVCE entity. For a Corporate FIVCE, at least 30 percent of the total capital contribution subscribed for by all investors to the FIVCE and at least 30 percent of the total actual capital contribution from all investors to the FIVCE shall be made by the principal investor(s).[167]

An application for approval of an FIVCE must be filed with the Ministry of Commerce or local branch office.[168] An application will be reviewed by MOFCOM in cooperation with the Ministry of Science and Technology. The FIVCE Regulations provide that the applicants are required to submit various materials in support of their application including the contract of the FIVCE or articles of association, declaration of qualification by the principal investor, legal opinion regarding the existence of the principal investor, written descriptions of the principal investor's business activities, proof of creditworthiness, and other supporting materials.[169] All approved FIVCEs are required to contain the language "Venture Capital Investment" in their company names, and no other foreign-invested enterprises may contain this language without government approval.[170]

The capital contributions for a Corporate FIVCE are to be made pursuant to existing FIE regulations.[171] The capital contributions by investors of a Non-Legal Person FIVCE may, within a maximum period of five years, make their capital contributions in installments based on the progress of the venture capital investments made by the FIVCE. The amount of the capital contribution to be made in each installment shall be determined independently by the FIVCE in accordance with the contract of the FIVCE and the agreements it signed with its investor members. During the existence of an FIVCE, the investors generally may not reduce the amount of the agreed-upon capital contributions. However, the investors may reduce the amount of their subscribed capital if such reduction is agreed by the investors collectively as representing more than 50 percent of the total contributed

167. FIVCE Regulations, art. 7. Any investor may also apply to become a principal investor if its affiliated entity satisfies the requirements set forth above under Article 7. An "affiliated entity" means an entity that controls, is controlled by, or is under common control with the investor concerned and a party is "controlled" by another party if the controlling party owns more than 50-percent voting power of the controlled party. FIVCE Regulations, art. 7 (4).

168. FIVCE Regulations, art. 8.

169. FIVCE Regulations, arts. 9, 11.

170. FIVCE Regulations, art. 10.

171. FIVCE Regulations, art. 16.

capital to the FIVCE and the principal investor(s), will not result in a breach of minimum capital requirements, and is further approved by the relevant authorities. During the existence of an FIVCE, no principal investor may withdraw from such FIVCE. If a principal investor is required to withdraw in special circumstances, such principal investor shall first obtain the consent of other investors collectively representing more than 50 percent of the total contributed capital to the FIVCE and shall transfer its interests to a substitute principal investor that meets the statutory requirements. After an FIVCE has been established, additional investors may be admitted if such admission is consistent with the law, the FIVCE contract, and with the consent of the principal investor(s). Of the income derived by an FIVCE from sale or other disposition of its equity investment, the amount equal to such FIVCE's original amount of capital contribution may be distributed directly to the investors. Such distribution will constitute a reduction by the investors of the amount of their contributed capital.[172]

With respect to management organization, a Non-Legal Person FIVCE is required to form a joint management committee and a Corporate FIVCE shall establish a board of directors. The joint management committee or the board of directors shall exist and operate pursuant to either the investors contract or the articles of association of the FIVCE and shall manage the FIVCE on behalf of the investors.[173] The management committee or board of directors may either delegate the day-to-day management affairs to a general manager or a separate venture capital management enterprise.[174] The management and operating personnel shall periodically report to the board of directors (or the joint management committee) on the following matters: (1) authorized major investment activities; (2) interim and annual operating performance reports and financial reports; (3) other matters required by laws and regulations; and (4) other matters provided in the investors' contract or the articles of association of the FIVCE.[175]

A venture capital management enterprise may take the form of a company or partnership, and may be engaged to manage more than one FIVCE.[176] The venture capital investment management enterprise engaged to manage an FIVCE is required to be principally in the business of venture

172. FIVCE Regulations, art. 13. Capital contributions are required to be verified and registered with the approval authorities. FIVCE Regulations, art. 15.
173. FIVCE Regulations, art. 17.
174. FIVCE Regulations, arts. 17–22.
175. FIVCE Regulations, art. 20.
176. FIVCE Regulations, arts. 24, 25.

capital management, employ qualified personnel, have registered capital of not less that RMB1 million or its equivalent in foreign exchange, and have an internal control system.[177] A venture capital management enterprise is required to apply for government approval and, upon approval, can use the language "Venture Capital Management" in its company name.[178]

The regulations require that the investments in the FIVCE be used primarily for equity investment in invested enterprises. An FIVCE may invest all or a portion of its capital in high and new technology sectors in which foreign investment is encouraged and permitted by the State. An FIVCE may also provide venture investment consultation and advice to invested enterprises.[179] An FIVCE is not allowed to engage in the following activities: (1) invest in industry sectors in which foreign investment is prohibited by the State; (2) invest, directly or indirectly, in securities, options, futures, or any other activities derived from financial business, but this does not include shares held by or allocated to a foreign investment venture enterprise after the invested enterprise has been listed; (3) invest, directly or indirectly, in real estate that is not for the use of the FIVCE; (4) borrowing to make investments; (5) using the funds of persons other than investors to make investment; (6) extending loans or guarantees; or (6) other activities prohibited by laws and regulations.[180]

Where an FIVCE invests in an invested enterprise, the ratio of investment of the FIVCE or the ratio of investment of the foreign investors jointly shall be, in general, no less than 25 percent of the registered capital of the invested enterprise. Upon approval, the invested enterprise shall enjoy the preferential treatment provided to FIEs, and be issued an FIE certificate of approval and enterprise business license.[181] Investors in an FIVCE in the form of a cooperative enterprise may agree on the mechanism of the internal distribution of profits and to do so in accordance with international practice. Investors in a cooperative FIVCE shall bear joint and several liability for the foreign venture investment enterprise, and may also agree in the cooperative contract that at least one investor bears joint and several liability for the foreign investment venture enterprise, and that other investors are liable for

177. FIVCE Regulations, art. 23.
178. FIVCE Regulations, arts. 27–30.
179. FIVCE Regulations, arts. 3, 31. Investment activities by FIVCEs within China shall be handled with reference to the provisions of the *Guiding the Direction of Foreign Investment Provisions* and the *Foreign Investment Industrial Guidance Catalogue*. FIVCE Regulations, art. 39. The FIVCE Regulations set forth provisions on the approval process for investments in the restricted and permitted categories of the investment catalogues, and also with respect to services sectors. FIVCE Regulations, arts. 40, 41, 42.
180. FIVCE Regulations, art. 32.
181. FIVCE Regulations, art. 46.

the amount of investment they have subscribed or bear liability in accordance with agreements as stipulated in the cooperative contract.[182]

An FIVCE is allowed to remit profits overseas so long as all tax obligations of the FIVCE and the investors are properly handled.[183] The term of an FIVCE shall be set forth in the investors' contract or articles of association, which may not exceed twelve years but can be extended upon approval of the authorities.[184] In the event of termination or liquidation of the FIVCE, liquidation and license cancellation procedures must be followed.[185]

6. BOT: Build, Operate, and Transfer

The Chinese government supports the use of the build, operate, and transfer organizational structure to encourage long-term financing and large foreign investment in capital-intensive infrastructure projects. A BOT may take the form of an EJV, CJV, or WFOE and is required to obtain government approval. In order to encourage BOT investors, the government agencies responsible for the project may make limited guarantees including an extended term of operation of a project to provide the investors with an opportunity to recoup their investment. The government, however, is barred from providing a guarantee to investors for a fixed return on investment and is prohibited from providing any security for the project financing. The BOT structure has not been used very often in China and application is limited to energy projects.[186]

7. FIE Research and Development (R&D) Centers

Research and development centers established by foreign investors is an activity encouraged by the PRC government under the Catalogue for the Guidance of Industries for Foreign Investment.[187] The FIE R&D Regulations

182. FIVCE Regulations, arts. 15, 16.

183. FIVCE Regulations, arts. 35, 36. *See also* Tax Issues Relevant to Paying of Enterprise Income Tax by Foreign-Invested Capital Investment Enterprises Circular (issued on June 4, 2003, by the State Administration of Taxation) (provides that venture capital investment enterprises that engage in equity investment or provide consultancy services are not production-type enterprises and therefore are not entitled to preferential treatment).

184. FIVCE Regulations, art. 37.

185. FIVCE Regulations, arts. 37, 38.

186. For a discussion of the standards for BOT projects and organizational structure, *see* Chen, *BOT in China: Opportunities and Uncertainties,* 14 CHINA LAW NEWS 1 (Aug. 28, 1998); Wang, Tiong, Ting & Ashley, *Risk Management Framework for BOT Power Projects in China,* 4 J. PROJECT FIN. 56 (Winter 1999), available on Lexis, News Library (discusses legal issues and risk management issues concerning BOT projects); *China Sets Regulations on BOT Investment,* ASIA PULSE (Dec. 28, 1998), available on Lexis, News Library (discusses procedures for establishment and approval of BOT projects); Rong, *Build-Operate-Transfer (BOT): The Rules,* 136 CHINA INTERNATIONAL BUSINESS (MOFTEC) 56 (1998).

187. Circular on Questions Relating to Foreign Investment in, and the Establishment of, Research & Development Centers (issued by MOFTEC on April 18, 2000), *reprinted in* CHINA LAWS FOR FOREIGN

provide a framework that enables technology-intensive foreign investors, particularly in industries with evolving technologies, to establish specialized R&D centers in a variety of ways, namely, that R&D enterprises with foreign investment may take the form of (a) an FIE (i.e., an equity joint venture, a cooperative joint venture, or a WFOE); (b) independent departments of FIEs; or (c) branch offices of an FIE.[188]

A foreign-invested R&D enterprise may be involved with product application research, high-technology research, and public service research. However, R&D activities that may be restricted or prohibited under the Catalogue for the Guidance of Industries for Foreign Investment are not allowed. Foreign-invested R&D enterprises must engage in research and development and experimental development (including pilot testing) in the areas of natural sciences and their related scientific and technical fields.[189] A foreign-invested R&D enterprise may not engage in: (a) technology trading other than that involving the technological achievements of its own research and development, or (b) production activities other than pilot testing in support of the research and development. In that regard, it would appear that the "products" of an FIE R&D center would include physical products such as prototypes and software as well as intangible products and related services.

BUSINESS (CCH), Business Regulation ¶ 6-630 (hereinafter referred to as the "FIE R&D Enterprise Regulations"); Catalogue of Encouraged Foreign Investment in High and New Technology Products (issued on July 18, 2003, by MOFCOM and MOST). For an analysis of the FIE R&D Enterprise Regulations, *see Why FIEs Should Set Up an R&D Center,* CHINA L. & PRAC. (June 2000); T. Zhengyu, *Structuring Companies in China: Software Enterprises or R&D Centers,* CHINA L. & PRAC. (Dec. 2003); FACT SHEET: RESEARCH AND DEVELOPMENT CENTERS, THE U.S.-CHINA BUSINESS COUNCIL (July 18, 2003), available online for members at http://www.uschina.org. A number of foreign companies are increasing their R&D investments in China. A few examples in 2003 include the following investments: Dupont China Holdings Ltd. announced that it would invest up to $100 million in an R&D operation in Shanghai; Honeywell committed an initial $18 million for an R&D center in China; Lucent Technologies committed to invest $50 million to an R&D facility to develop CDMA2000 standards; and Motorola announced a $500 million research facility investment in Beijing. *See* CHINA OPERATIONS 2003, ANALYSIS: FOREIGN INVESTMENT IN CHINA, FIRST HALF 2003, THE U.S.-CHINA BUSINESS COUNCIL, 21. Certain municipal jurisdictions have adopted their own measures to encourage R&D operations. *See generally* New Law Digest, Encouraging the Development of Incubators for Science and Technology Enterprises (issued by the Shenzhen Municipal Government on April 10, 2003), CHINA L. & PRAC. (June 2003); New Law Digest, Encouraging Foreign Investors to Invest in the Establishment of Research and Development Organizations. Several Opinions, issued by the Shanghai Municipal Government on September 15, 2003, CHINA L. & PRAC. (Oct. 2003).

188. FIE R&D Regulations, art. 1 (1). *See also* Provisional Measures on the Establishment of Sino-Foreign Equity Joint Research and Development Institutions and Sino-Foreign Cooperative Joint Research and Development Institutions (promulgated on September 10, 1997, by the State Science and Technology Commission), *reprinted in* CHINA LAWS FOR FOREIGN BUSINESS (CCH), Business Regulation ¶ 6-628 (outlines procedures for establishment, amendment, and termination of JV research institutions, obligations of the parties, and preferential treatment).

189. FIE R&D Regulations, art. 1 (2). The term "R&D centers" does not include training centers. The investment in an R&D center established by a foreign investment enterprise of Restricted Category A in the form of an independent department or a branch may not exceed 50% of the enterprise's total amount of investment.

Foreign-invested R&D enterprises may assign technological achievements resulting from their research and development, and may engage in cooperative research and development with domestic (Chinese) scientific research institutes by means of either (a) entrustment (it is not clear if the center would be the entrustor or the entrustee), or (b) joint development. The R&D center must have a defined research and development field and specific research and development projects, fixed premises, and apparatus and equipment required for scientific research and other conditions designed for scientific research.[190] The R&D center's investment in research and development may not be less than $2 million. Such funding is for research and development purposes only. Although the regulations state that the minimum funding is required to be US$2 million, in practice the government has treated this figure as a minimum "total investment" and therefore requires a minimum registered capital of US$1.4 million, or 70 percent of the total investment. The balance of $600,000 may be in the form of loans to the R&D enterprise.[191] The regulations require that the R&D operation have a dedicated management and scientific research personnel. Personnel directly engaged in R&D must hold the equivalent of an undergraduate degree or higher, and must account for at least 80% of the operation's total number of personnel.[192]

An application for an R&D operation is subject to examination and approval by provincial-level MOFCOM authorities.[193] Where an independent R&D department is proposed to be established within an existing FIE that has an authorized scope of business (namely, includes the language "research" or "development"), the FIE must file details of the proposed department with the approval authority that previously approved the FIE. If the business scope of the FIE does not include research and/or development, it may file an application for approval to amend its articles of association to include R&D activities.[194] An R&D operation is required to report to MOFCOM or its branch on an annual basis.[195]

190. FIE R&D Regulations, art. 2 (1).
191. FIE R&D Regulations, art. 2 (1).
192. FIE R&D Regulations, art. 2 (2).
193. FIE R&D Regulations, art. 3 (1). An application for approval of an FIE R&D operation is required to include the following: (a) a description of the R&D plan and implementation; (b) details of the site, personnel, and scientific research conditions; (c) the source, specific application and amount of the funds required for research and development, and a budget report; (d) a list of the equipment for own use, and its corresponding technology, fittings and spares, which are to be imported within the total amount of investment or with self-owned funds, and the prototypes and chemical agents involved in the research and development process; and (e) a description of the advanced nature of the research and development and a statement as to the ownership of the research and development achievements. FIE R&D Regulations, art. 2 (b) (3).
194. FIE R&D Regulations, art. 3 (2) (b).
195. FIE R&D Regulations, art. 4 (4).

With approval, an FIE R&D operation may import equipment and related technology duty-free and import VAT tax-free. The duty exemption does not apply to any goods listed in the Catalogue of Imported Goods Not Exempt from Taxation for Foreign Investment Projects. Revenue generated from the license of commercialized technology developed by an R&D operation is exempt from business tax and subject to state/local income taxation; however, an R&D operation, with government approval, may be granted a reduced income tax rate normally granted to high technology operations. Subject to the approval of the tax authorities, certain technology development expenses may be deducted from the current year's taxable income.[196]

D. Equity Investments

When the People's Republic of China first opened its doors to foreign investment in the late 1970s, the joint venture enterprise, which, in essence, is a closely held limited liability company, was the type of investment vehicle best suited under China's then-current system given that the Chinese parties to joint ventures were primarily State-owned enterprises without shareholders. During the 1980s and early 1990s, China, on a selective basis, allowed for the adoption of rules that provided for other forms of investment vehicles to be established, such as limited liability companies and joint stock companies, also referred to as companies limited by shares. These "company laws," developed in order to encourage domestic and foreign investors to participate in more investment opportunities, were originally local in application and limited to the special economic zones and coastal ports.[197]

---

196. FIE R&D Regulations, Annex. In situations where technology development expenses increased by 10% or more as compared to those of the preceding year, a further 50% of the technology development expenses actually incurred may be deducted from the current year's taxable income, subject to the approval of the tax authorities.

197. *See* Provisional Regulations of Shenzhen Municipality on Companies Limited by Shares (issued March 18, 1992, by the Shenzhen Municipal People's Government), *reprinted in* China Laws for Foreign Business (CCH), Special Zones & Cities ¶ 73-571; Rules of Shenzhen Special Economic Zone on Limited Liability Companies (adopted on April 26, 1993, by the 5th Sess. of the 1st Shenzhen People's Congress), *reprinted in* China Laws for Foreign Business (CCH), Special Zones & Cities ¶ 71-035; Rules of the Guangdong Province on Companies (adopted on May 14, 1993, by the 2nd Sess. of the Standing Comm. of the 8th Guangdong People's Congress), *reprinted in* China Laws for Foreign Business (CCH), Special Zones & Cities ¶ 70-920; Provisional Regulations of Shanghai Municipality on Companies Limited by Shares (promulgated on May 18, 1992, by the Shanghai Municipal People's Government), *reprinted in* China Laws for Foreign Business (CCH), Special Zones & Cities ¶ 91-090. The Shanghai municipal government has adopted rules allowing for the establishment of employee-owned "cooperative share-formulated" enterprises. Persons that are not employees of the company may purchase up to thirty-nine percent of the total investment in the enterprise. *See* Provisional Measures of Shanghai Municipality on Cooperative Share-Formulated Enterprises (promulgated on May 17, 1997, by the Shanghai Municipal People's Government), *reprinted in* China Laws for Foreign Business (CCH), Special Zones & Cities ¶ 240-085.

1. Company Law

In 1994, China created a national framework for the establishment of independent market-oriented entities with the promulgation of the Company Law.[198] The Company Law provides for the establishment of a limited liability company and a company limited by shares. These corporate forms are similar to those of Continental European civil law countries and both enjoy limited liability protection. Both entities have shareholders and must hold shareholders' meetings, maintain shareholder lists, and issue stock certificates to shareholders.[199] Under the Company Law, the decision-making authority of both companies is empowered to a board of directors.[200] The Company Law also sets forth the process for transforming state enterprises into the two forms of corporate entities.[201]

a. Limited Liability Company

A limited liability company (LLC) under the Company Law is similar to the form allowed for joint ventures and other FIEs.[202] An LLC is defined in the Company Law as an enterprise with legal person status with the liability of each shareholder limited to its respective capital contribution.[203] An LLC can be formed between 2 to 50 shareholders, and there is no limitation on foreign investment. The Company Law does, however, have certain

---

198. Company Law of the PRC (adopted December 29, 1993, by the 5th Sess. of the Standing Comm. of the 8th NPC, revised and repromulgated on December 25, 1999, by the 13th Sess. of the Standing Comm. of the 9th NPC), *reprinted in* CHINA LAWS FOR FOREIGN BUSINESS (CCH), Business Regulation ¶ 13-518 (hereinafter referred to as the "Company Law"). For an analysis of the Company Law, *See* Torbert, *Broadening the Scope of Investment: China's New Company Law Codifies Investor Protection,* CHINA BUSINESS REVIEW 48 (May-June 1994); Han, *China's Company Law: Practicing Capitalism in a Transitional Economy,* 5 PAC. RIM L. & POL'Y 457 (1996).

199. For a detailed discussion of the Company Law, *see* Chapter 16, Securities Regulations § B.

200. Under the Company Law, a supervisory committee composed of representatives of employees and shareholders has a right to oversee and evaluate the activities of a company limited by shares. The Company Law further provides that a company is required to consider the opinions of trade unions or employees and to consult with them before the company makes any major decisions regarding compensation, benefits, health and safety, and other issues affecting the workforce. Company Law, arts. 55, 121. In addition, the Company Law requires management to obtain the opinions of employees and trade unions when making decisions on major issues concerning production or operations. Company Law, art. 56, 122. It is unclear as to whether the unions and employees have any remedy if the company chooses to forgo any suggestions made by the workforce. However, some state enterprises use the employee representative committees to evaluate the performance of enterprise management. *Executives Sacked After Appraisal,* CHINA DAILY (June 1, 1998), available on Lexis, News Library, or on the Web site of the CHINA DAILY at http://www.chinadaily.com.cn (notes that 2,300 managers in the Liaoning Province were dismissed because of poor performance appraisals from workers).

201. Company Law, art. 21.

202. Company Law, chap. II. These provisions have no impact on FIEs already organized and existing as limited liability companies.

203. Company Law, art. 3.

minimum registered capital requirements depending upon the type of business engaged by the company, including the following:

(1) RMB500,000: Production and manufacturing operations
(2) RMB500,000: Commercial wholesalers
(3) RMB300,000: Retailers
(4) RMB100,000: Scientific and technological development and consulting services

The transfer of interests in an LLC from a shareholder to a nonshareholder requires the consent of a majority of the owners of the LLC. However, if the nonconsenting shareholders refuse to purchase the shares of the selling shareholder, the proposed transfer is deemed to be approved.[204]

b. Company Limited by Shares

A company limited by shares is a corporate entity with limited liability status. The shareholders are liable for corporate debts up to the amount of their investment. Under the Company Law, all shares must be of equal value and the minimum registered capital is RMB10,000,000.[205] The stock of companies limited by shares is issued in the form of share certificates carrying equal rights and benefits for each class of stock, and at or above the par value.[206] A foreign company or individual may invest in a Chinese company limited by shares in several ways including the purchase of what are known as B-Shares, or shares denominated by renminbi but quoted in foreign exchange and held only by foreigners. A foreign party may also purchase a Chinese company's foreign capital shares that are listed overseas in Hong Kong (H-Shares) or New York (N-Shares).

The benefit of investing in an existing Chinese company allows a foreign party to participate in the market without committing personnel, physical assets, or significant cash resources. An equity investment in a Chinese company is an alternative to participating in a joint venture enterprise, which can be an expensive and time-consuming operation requiring constant consultation with the Chinese party.

204. Company Law, art. 35.
205. Company Law, art. 78.
206. Company Law, arts. 129–32. For a detailed discussion on the issuance and listing of shares in China, *see* Chapter 16, Securities Regulations § C.

Chinese law also permits an FIE to be established as a company limited by shares.[207] An FIE limited by shares refers to an enterprise consisting of both Chinese and foreign shareholders with corporate status established with total capital that is equivalent to the value of the stock. In such a company, the shareholders assume an amount of liability equal to the percentage of shares purchased. An existing FIE may convert to a company limited by shares but must demonstrate a record of profitability for a period of three years.[208] The FIE Limited by Shares Regulations requires that the parties submit an application and supporting documents to MOFCOM for approval.[209] An FIE will not lose its tax deductions and exemptions by converting to an FIE limited by shares, but the laws and policies of China concerning foreign investment continue to apply even after conversion.[210]

The regulations also permit state-owned enterprises (SOE) to convert to an FIE limited by shares. In such a situation, the Chinese SOE and foreign shareholders act as promoters and enter into a promoter's agreement and articles of association for the new enterprise.[211] In order for an SOE to convert to an FIE limited by shares, the SOE is required to have been operating for a minimum period of five years and have a profit for the preceding three years. The shares of the FIE limited by shares must be purchased by the foreign shareholders in freely convertible foreign currency and constitute at least 25 percent of the FIE's registered capital. The scope and purpose of the FIE limited by shares must be consistent with state policy concerning foreign investment enterprises. The objective of this rule is to encourage foreign investors to assist SOEs in becoming independent and profitable enterprises.

2. Equity Investment in an SOE

The traditional method of establishing a joint venture is for the parties to contribute, among other things, capital, equipment, and technology, and to

---

207. Provisional Regulations on Several Issues Concerning the Establishment of Foreign Investment Companies Limited by Shares (promulgated on January 10, 1995, by MOFTEC), *reprinted in* China Laws for Foreign Business (CCH), Business Regulation ¶ 13-405 (hereinafter "FIE Limited by Shares Regulations"). *See* Chapter 16, Securities Regulations, § C. On February 19, 2003, the SAIC circulated for public comment a draft of the proposed *Interim Measures on the Administration of the Registration of Foreign-Invested Companies Limited by Shares.* Under the proposed rules, a Foreign-Invested Companies Limited by Shares (FICLS) is a company with registered capital divided into shares of equal value and a foreign investor may hold at least 25 percent of the shares. An FICLS may be established by the "promoter method," where at least five promoters purchase all of the initial shares, or by the "share float method," where the promoters purchase a portion of the initial shares and the balance of the shares is made available to the public. The measures specify procedures for the registration, amendment of registration and deregistration of FICLSs, and related administrative requirements.

208. FIE Limited by Shares Regulations, art. 15.

209. FIE Limited by Shares Regulations, art. 9.

210. FIE Limited by Shares Regulations, arts. 3 & 4.

211. FIE Limited by Shares Regulations, art. 18.

establish a new joint venture entity. In contrast, the Chinese government allows for the formation of a joint venture in situations where a foreign investor purchases an equity interest in a state-owned enterprise (SOE).[212] By agreement, the foreign party tenders purchase funds and the SOE is converted to a joint venture enterprise rather than setting up a new entity. The purpose of the rule is consistent with government policy to better use state-owned assets and to encourage foreign investors to invest in underperforming enterprises that have potential with the infusion of capital.

A PRC valuation expert must appraise the assets of the SOE, and the results are to be confirmed by the State Assets Regulatory Commission. The purchase price, also referred to as the equity assignment fee, is based upon the valuation results. The parties are required to enter into an equity assignment contract, and the SAIC or local branch is required to approve the contract, feasibility study, and project proposal. For larger projects, or those subject to the approval of the central government, the SAIC and MOFCOM must be consulted. The foreign party is required to tender the purchase funds within thirty days of issuance of the business license and does not have rights as an equity holder or managerial control until the funds are paid.[213]

The foreign party should carefully analyze any decision to purchase an equity interest in an SOE. Many SOEs are burdened with debt, have obsolete equipment and facilities, and employ redundant employees. A due diligence process should analyze the target SOE's financial obligations, including guarantees or mutual debts with other state-owned enterprises, pension obligations, and other financial matters that could pose problems for the operation once it is converted to a joint venture. The foreign party should also analyze the target SOE's personnel practices to determine if there are unnecessary personnel and require, as a condition of the equity assignment, that the SOE reassign, transfer, or terminate certain personnel prior to the tender of funds. In addition, the foreign party should also stipulate, with the approval of the government, that the purchase funds be used to retire problem debt, pay for certain land-use rights, or other issues that may affect the JV operation.

212. *See* Cheng, *New Method of Setting Up a Sino-Foreign Joint Venture,* 11 China L. & Prac. 52 (July/Aug 1997). For a sample equity transfer agreement, *see* Appendix A. In April 1998, Kodak employed a unique strategy to purchase the assets of three state-owned film producers. Kodak established a "joint share" company to purchase the SOEs and merged them together into a holding company structure. For a discussion concerning Kodak's strategy, *see China: Out of the Strait-Jacket,* EIU Business China (April 27, 1998), available on Lexis, News Library.

213. Supplementary Regulations on the Certain Regulations on the Subscription of Capital by the Parties to Sino-Foreign EJVs (promulgated on September 29, 1997, by MOFTEC and the SAIC), *reprinted in* China Laws for Foreign Business (CCH), Business Regulation ¶ 6-600. For a discussion of the rules concerning the acquisition of domestic enterprises by foreign investors, *see* Chapter 19, Mergers, Acquisitions and Divisions § A.

E. Procedures for Establishment of a Foreign-Invested Enterprise

The approval procedure for an FIE is a two-step process. In contrast to most Western countries—which, in general, will allow a party to set up a corporate entity upon the filing of articles of incorpation or corporate charter—the Chinese government requires a foreign investor to file an application to obtain a certificate of approval by the ministry responsible for foreign trade and commerce, namely, MOFCOM or the local branch (COFCOM or COFTEC). After a certificate of approval is received by MOFCOM, the applicant files an application to the SAIC (or branch) to obtain a business license. Prior to filing an application, a foreign investor must consult with the Industrial Catalogue Guiding Foreign Investment to determine whether the intended investment is encouraged, permitted, restricted, or prohibited. This analysis requires that the applicant determine whether there are limitations on the business activities for a foreign investor (which would impact how broad the language would be in the business scope as set forth in the business license). Also included in this analysis is whether the government requires a minimum registered capital (which, if too high, may effectively bar a foreign investor from establishing the operation) and the total investment of the foreign party.[214]

The business license is a document that is issued by the SAIC or branch and states the enterprise's legal name, company structure (i.e., WFOE, joint venture, share company, etc.), business scope, legal representative, legal address, and registered capital. Without a valid business license, a company in China does not exist and is not legally authorized to engage in business. In contrast to corporations established in the United States, the operation of an enterprise is limited by the defined and approved "business scope," which

214. Registered capital—or the shareholders contributed equity capital—includes cash, technology, and equipment. The total investment of an FIE includes the registered capital and capital funded by debt obligations. In general, the registered capital of an FIE may be paid in installments, with usually 15% paid within 90 days of issuance of the business license. The balance of registered capital must be injected into the operation based on the following formula: less than $500,000 payable in 1 year; less than $1 million payable in 18 months; less than $3 million but more than $1 million payable in 2 years; less than $10 million but more than $3 million payable in 3 years; and more than $10 million is subject to negotiation. Local rules may have application with respect to the timing of contributing registered capital. The ratio of registered capital to the total investment is based on the following formula: total investment of less than $3 million requires that the registered capital be 70% of total investment; total investment of between $3 million and $10 million requires that the registered capital be 50% of total investment; total investment of between $10 million and $30 million requires that the registered capital be 40% of total investment; and total investment of over $30 million requires that the registered capital be 33% of total investment. Registered capital may only be reduced during the life of an FIE by amending the entity's articles of association and obtaining the approval of MOFCOM or local COFTEC. The limitation on the reduction of registered capital may result in capital being tied up in an FIE until dissolution and liquidation, or by government approval.

is usually narrowly defined. While most applicants endeavor to obtain a broad business scope, the usual practice of the SAIC is to provide a business scope for a relatively narrow band of activities.

The branches of MOFCOM in the provincial capitals, open cities, and Special Economic Zones (SEZs) have the authority to approve FIE projects valued at up to $30 million, and most other cities and regions have the authority to approve projects valued at less than $10 million.[215] Projects that are valued in excess of $30 million require the approval of MOFCOM, and FIE projects valued in excess of $100 million must obtain the approval of the State Council. Regardless of the amount at issue, MOFCOM has jurisdiction to review any FIE project. The key issues for MOFCOM continue to be whether the proposed project meets the State Council's foreign investment guidelines, promotes export sales, encourages economic development in regions earmarked for investment, and involves the introduction of high technology or essential resources needed in China.[216] If a proposed FIE

215. *See* Notice of the State Administration of Industry and Commerce on the Circulation of an Opinion on Relevant Issues Concerning the Implementation of Administrative Laws and Regulations on Company Registration Applicable to Foreign Investment Enterprises (promulgated on July 18, 1995, by the SAIC), *reprinted in* CHINA LAWS FOR FOREIGN BUSINESS (CCH), Business Regulation ¶ 13-588; Notice of MOFTEC and the State Administration for Industry and Commerce on Relevant Regulations and Procedures for Adjustment of Aggregate Investment and Registered Capital by Foreign Investment Enterprises (issued on May 25, 1995, by MOFTEC and the SAIC), *reprinted in* CHINA LAWS FOR FOREIGN BUSINESS (CCH), Business Regulation ¶ 13-592; Principles and Main Points of the Ministry of Foreign Economic Relations and Trade Concerning the Examination and Approval of Contracts and Articles of Association of Foreign Investment Enterprises (promulgated on October 5, 1993, by MOFTEC), *reprinted in* CHINA LAWS FOR FOREIGN BUSINESS (CCH), Business Regulation ¶ 13-557 (sets forth basic principles for the approval of FIE contracts and articles of association); Administrative Measures of the State Administration of Industry and Commerce Authorizing the Registration of Foreign Investment Enterprises (promulgated on December 10, 2002, by the SAIC), *reprinted in* CHINA LAWS FOR FOREIGN BUSINESS (CCH), Business Regulation ¶ 13-560; Administrative Rules of the People's Republic of China Governing the Registration of Companies (promulgated on June 24, 1994, by the State Council of the PRC), *reprinted in* CHINA LAWS FOR FOREIGN BUSINESS (CCH), Business Regulation ¶ 13-568; Notice on Certain Issues Concerning the Further Strengthening of the Administration of Examination, Approval and Registration of Foreign Investment Enterprises (promulgated on November 3, 1994, by the SAIC and MOFTEC), *reprinted in* CHINA LAWS FOR FOREIGN BUSINESS (CCH), Business Regulation ¶ 13-524; State Council Notice on Strengthening Examination and Approval Procedures for Large-Scale Foreign Investment Enterprises (issued on March 13, 1991, by the State Council), *reprinted in* CHINA LAWS FOR FOREIGN BUSINESS (CCH), Business Regulation ¶ 13-508; Administrative Regulations of the People's Republic of China Governing the Registration of Legal Corporations (promulgated on June 3, 1988, by the State Council), *reprinted in* CHINA LAWS FOR FOREIGN BUSINESS (CCH), Business Regulation ¶ 13-542; Notice of the Ministry of Foreign Economic Relations and Trade Concerning Questions on the Use of the New Edition "Approval Certificate of the People's Republic of China for Foreign Investment Enterprises" (promulgated on October 5, 1993, by MOFTEC), *reprinted in* CHINA LAWS FOR FOREIGN BUSINESS (CCH), Business Regulation ¶ 13-543. *See also* Administrative Measures of Shanghai Municipality on Examination and Approval Procedures for Foreign Investment Enterprises (promulgated on August 23, 1996, by the Standing Comm. of Shanghai Municipal People's Congress), *reprinted in* CHINA LAWS FOR FOREIGN BUSINESS (CCH), Special Zones & Cities ¶ 240-055.

216. For a reference to the types of technology encouraged by the government, *see* the *Catalogue of Encouraged Foreign Investment in High and New Technology Products (2003)* (issued on July 18, 2003, by the Ministry of Commerce and the Ministry of Science and Technology). The 2003 catalogue furthers the Chinese government's policy of encouraging foreign investment in underdeveloped industries and

project includes terms that are unfair to the Chinese party, or if the foreign party is from a country with strained relations with the PRC, the Chinese government is likely to look on the proposal with disfavor.

The application for approval is required to include, if applicable, the joint venture contract, articles of association, application form, feasibility study, and letter of creditworthiness from the foreign party's financial institution. In general, within 45 days of submission of the application and supporting documents, MOFCOM is required to respond, in writing, to the applicant. Upon receipt of the approval certificate from MOFCOM, the applicant is required to apply to the SAIC to obtain a business license.[217] The date of establishment of the FIE is the date of issuance of the business license. In general, and subject to extensions, the FIE is required to register with the tax authorities within 30 days of issuance of the business license.

After a company is established, it is required to obtain several sets of "chops" or "seals," which are issued by an engraving entity approved by the Ministry of Public Security (MPS) or local branch thereof. The usual practice is for a company to obtain separate chops for purposes of customs, banking, receipts (for issuance of tax receipts), and general business correspondence. The company will also be issued an "enterprise" seal, which is usually held by a legal representative and is used for executing contracts and other obligations. Given that a chop imprint—and especially the imprint of the enterprise seal—is a substitute for a signature, due care must be exercised to ensure that the chops are maintained in a safe location and are not subject to misuse by persons without authority.

An FIE with less than 25% foreign equity is not eligible for any preferential tax treatment, and the approval certificate and business license of an FIE with less than 25% foreign equity shall specify that it has "less than 25% foreign equity."[218] If an FIE in the form of a company limited by shares falls below the 25% threshold, it may retain tax benefits. A foreign investor investing in a new "regular" FIE has a grace period to make an actual investment, generally more than one year after the FIE receives its business license.

---

groups 196 product types into 11 principal categories: electronic information; software; space and aviation; optical-mechanical-electrical integration; biomedicines and medical treatment instruments; new materials; new energies and high-efficiency energies; environmental protection; earth, air and sea; nuclear application technologies; and modern agriculture.

217. Administrative Regulations of the People's Republic of China Governing the Registration of Legal Corporations (promulgated June 3, 1988, by the State Council), *reprinted in* China Laws for Foreign Business (CCH), Business Regulation ¶ 13-542. These regulations outline the rules affecting the issuance and revocation of a registration certificate and business license.

218. Issues Relevant to Strengthening the Administration of the Examination, Approval, Registration, Foreign Exchange Issues and Taxation of Foreign-Invested Enterprises Circular (promulgated on December 30, 2002, by MOFTEC, SAT, SAIC, and SAFE).

For a "special" FIE, which has less than 25% foreign equity, the law provides that the investor has three months to inject its cash investment and six months for investment in kind. If a foreign investor acquires an equity stake in a domestic company, the company may thereafter be converted into an FIE through the FIE examination and approval process. For investments in established and operating enterprises, the law requires that a foreign investor inject its full investment within three months after the FIE receives its revised business license. Before a foreign investor makes full payment of the purchase price for the acquisition, it is prohibited from taking control of the FIE's management or consolidating its financial reports with the FIE until payment is made.

1. Articles of Association

The law requires that an EJV, WFOE, joint venture trading company, limited liability company, company limited by shares, holding company, and other investment vehicles are required to submit articles of association for approval. The articles are similar to bylaws for an American-styled corporation and outline the operational procedures for the organization. The articles of association for a single-owner WFOE are usually much shorter than those of a joint venture, which requires that the relationship between the parties be well documented. As a general rule, the greater the number of parties to a venture and the larger the investment, the more detail is required in the articles. A well-drafted set of articles should contain, at a minimum, provisions outlining the following:

(1) Purpose and scope of the business
(2) Shares and registered capital, reduction of capital and buy-back of shares, and share certificates and share ledger (if applicable)
(3) Rights and obligations of the parties or shareholders
(4) Power of shareholders' meetings, corporate resolutions, and procedures (if applicable)
(5) Power and duties of the board of directors
(6) Obligations and job duties of the company manager
(7) Power and procedures concerning supervisory committees (if applicable)
(8) Qualifications of company directors, supervisors, managers, and other senior management personnel
(9) Financial and accounting system and distribution of profits
(10) Procedures for the appointment of an accounting firm
(11) Company merger and division
(12) Company dissolution and liquidation

(13) Personnel issues
(14) Procedures for amendment of articles of association
(15) Resolution of disputes
(16) Description of advanced technology for production

Depending upon the circumstances, the government may demand that provisions be added or deleted to the articles of association.[219]

2. Feasibility Study

The government requires the submission of a feasibility study for purposes of FIE approval. The feasibility study is required to evaluate a number of financial and operational issues including, but not limited to, the following:

(1) Amount of investment to be contributed by the parties
(2) Technology, industrial rights, and machinery to be contributed by the parties
(3) Products to be produced, if any, and the scope of production
(4) Market research concerning the company's products, its competitors, and the industry sector in general
(5) The anticipated percentage of exports and domestic sales
(6) Proposed prices for the products or services
(7) Personnel matters
(8) Energy and materials requirements
(9) Physical facilities required for production

The feasibility study should not be perceived as an unnecessary bureaucratic burden, but rather as one aspect of the foreign party's due diligence assessment of its Chinese partner, and, in general, an analysis of its business plan for market entry into China. A foreign party to a proposed joint venture should use the feasibility study preparation period as a means to obtain information concerning the limitations and resources of the Chinese party. Oftentimes, the Chinese party volunteers to prepare and submit the feasibility study for approval. Such unilateral preparation does the foreign party no service given that the foreign party shares civil and criminal liability for any false or misleading statements included in a feasibility study submitted in

219. Companies that are listed overseas are required to adopt a standard set of articles of association approved by the PRC government. A company is allowed to modify the language so long as the objectives of the essential clauses are maintained. Authorization is required to alter or delete the content of the clauses. Notice on the Implementation of Essential Clauses in Articles of Association of Companies Listed Overseas (promulgated on August 27, 1994, by the SCSC), *reprinted in* CHINA LAWS FOR FOREIGN BUSINESS (CCH), Business Regulation ¶ 13-410 (hereinafter the "SCSC Notice, Essential Clauses"). *See* Chapter 16, Securities Regulations § C.

support of an FIE application.[220] The importance of joint preparation of the feasibility study cannot be understated.

Feasibility studies prepared for operations involving a single foreign investor that do not involve a Chinese partner (i.e., WFOE, holding company, R&D cetner, etc.), are focused more on the foreign investors' products or services, past and present investment activities in China, and future plans for their proposed operaiton.

F. Assignment of Investor Interests and Modification to Capital Contributions

An FIE is required to follow administrative rules if an assignment of an investor's interest is made, or if the parties modify the capital contributions of the enterprise.

1. Assignment and Transfer

Under the EVJ law, an assignment or transfer of a party's share in the registered capital of the venture requires the consent of the other party and the approval of the original examining authorities.[221] This requirement, however, focused on assignment of a party's interest to a third party rather than to the venture's co-partners. The EJV Law and the regulations failed to provide standards for the government's approval or disapproval of assignments. In the absence of standards, the SAIC was free to make assignment approval decisions in an arbitrary manner. As a result, approvals differed from city to city, and many assignments, especially between the parties, were conducted surreptitiously and without the approval of the government.

Under regulations issued in May of 1997, MOFCOM and the SAIC affirm the requirement that assignments are invalid unless approval is obtained.[222] Approval is required where there is a "change" to the investors' or shareholders' rights to the foreign investment enterprise including under the following circumstances:

(1) The parties agree to transfer or assign an investor's rights to third persons

(2) The parties agree to transfer or assign an investor's rights to the parties' affiliated organization or subsidiary

(3) The parties agree to adjust the registered capital of the enterprise, which leads to a change in the percentage of ownership in the enterprise

220. *See* Chapter 23, Criminal Liability for FIE Activities § A.1.

221. EVJ Law, art. 4; EVJ Regulations, art. 23.

222. Certain Regulations on Changes to Shareholders' Rights in Foreign Investment Enterprises (promulgated on May 28, 1997, by MOFTEC and the SAIC), art. 3, *reprinted in* China Laws for Foreign Business (CCH), Business Regulation ¶ 13-512 (hereinafter "FIE Assignment Regulations").

(4) The parties intend to pledge their interest in an enterprise to a creditor
(5) An enterprise investor is bankrupt, dissolved, cancelled, revoked, or deceased, and its successor, creditor, or other beneficiary acquires the investor's rights in accordance with the law
(6) An enterprise investor merges or divides and its postmerger or division successor carries on the investor's rights of the original investor
(7) An enterprise investor fails to perform the capital contribution obligations stipulated in the enterprise contract or articles of association and the investor is replaced or investor's rights are transferred or assigned subject to the approval of the original examining and approval authority[223]

The FIE Assignment Regulations provide a detailed list of the documentation required for obtaining approval from MOFCOM and the SAIC. In general, the assignment application must include the parties' original FIE contract and articles of association; approval certificates and business license of the FIE; resolutions of the board of directors concerning the proposed change; and the assignment or transfer agreement.[224] The FIE Assignment Regulations require that an agreement to transfer an investor's interest in an FIE must include provisions with respect to the following items:

(1) The names and addresses of the transferor and transferee and the names, titles, and nationality of their legal representatives
(2) The percentage or ratio of an investor's interest to be assigned or transferred
(3) The method and time of delivery of the assignment or transfer of the investor's interest
(4) A description of the rights and obligations borne by the transferee in accordance with the FIE contract and the articles of association
(5) The liability for a breach of the assignment agreement
(6) The applicable law and mechanisms for dispute resolution
(7) The date of commencement and termination of the assignment agreement[225]

The examining authority is required to approve or disapprove an assignment or transfer within thirty days of the filing of the application.

A change in investors' interests cannot result in a foreign party having a controlling interest in an enterprise that, by law, requires the Chinese party to maintain control.[226] In addition, a change in ownership may not reduce

223. FIE Assignment Regulations, art. 2.
224. FIE Assignment Regulations, art. 9.
225. FIE Assignment Regulations, art. 10.
226. FIE Assignment Regulations, art. 4.

the foreign party's investment ratio to less than 25 percent of the registered capital of the enterprise.[227]

The FIE Assignment Regulations provide that a change in ownership cannot violate the foreign investment rules. In situations in which the foreign party assigns its interest in a joint venture to the Chinese party, the entity no longer is entitled to beneficial treatment as a foreign investment enterprise. It becomes, in reality, a wholly Chinese-owned enterprise and is required to have its FIE registration cancelled.

A foreign party to an FIE may pledge its interest in its capital contribution to a venture with the approval of the SAIC and with the consent of its partners.[228] A party is not allowed to pledge any portion of its capital contribution that has not been paid, nor can it pledge the interest of the other parties to the venture without their express consent. A pledgee is prohibited from transferring the pledged investor's rights without the consent of the pledgor-investor and the other investors in the enterprise. The pledgor-investor is not permitted to transfer or re-pledge the pledged investor's rights without the consent of the pledgee. A pledge agreement must be prepared and registered in conformance with the Secured Interests Law.[229]

In order to obtain approval for a pledge of an investor's rights, the FIE is required to submit to the approval authorities a resolution of the board of directors of the FIE demonstrating the consent of the parties to the pledge. The assignment application must also include a capital contribution certificate of the pledgor-investor demonstrating that all capital requirements have been met by the parties to the FIE.[230]

2. Adjustments to Capital Contributions

If an FIE determines that it is necessary to adjust its aggregate investment or registered capital, it must apply to the original approval authorities to effectuate the change. An enterprise can only modify its capital contribution by unanimous consent of the investors.[231] An enterprise is prohibited from requesting an amendment to its total investment or registered capital in a number of circumstances, including the following:

(1) If the law requires a minimum investment for the type of operation in question

227. FIE Assignment Regulations, art. 5.
228. FIE Assignment Regulations, art. 6.
229. FIE Assignment Regulations, art. 6. *See* Chapter 7, Contract Law § C.3.b.
230. FIE Assignment Regulations, art. 12.
231. Capital Contribution Adjustment Regulations, art. 2, § 1.

(2) If the enterprise is involved in a financial dispute that is the subject of an arbitration or judicial proceeding
(3) If the enterprises contract or articles provide for a minimum production amount that cannot be met if the investment is reduced
(4) If the contract provides that the foreign party is allowed to recover its investment prior to the issuance of profits and the foreign party has recovered its total amount of investment[232]

An application for adjustment must include a resolution of the board of directors, statement of the reasons for the adjustment, certified financial statements, an inventory statement outlining the property of the enterprise, a list of creditors, and a copy of the business license.[233] If the adjustment receives preliminary approval, the enterprise is required to advise its creditors within ten days of receipt of approval from the examining authorities. The enterprise is also required, within thirty days of receiving approval, to publish notice of the adjustments in a newspaper of provincial level.[234] By law, a creditor has the right to demand payment or a guarantee from an FIE that obtains approval to adjust its capital contributions. Final approval of the adjustment will be granted only if the enterprise demonstrates that notice to creditors was provided, and debt repayment or guarantees were made with the enterprise's creditors.[235]

G. Special Rules for Headquarter Operations

Various city and provincial jurisdictions provide special benefits to foreign investors that establish regional headquarters, which are required to be operations that conduct business in China and another Asian country.[236]

---

232. Notice of MOFTEC and the SAIC on Relevant Regulations and Procedures for Adjustment of Aggregate Investment and Registered Capital by Foreign Investment Enterprises (issued on May 25, 1995, by MOFTEC and the SAIC), art. 1, *reprinted in* China Laws for Foreign Business (CCH), Business Regulation ¶ 13-592 (the "Capital Contribution Adjustment Regulations").

233. Capital Contribution Adjustment Regulations, art. 2, § 1.

234. Capital Contribution Adjustment Regulations, art. 2, § 2.

235. Capital Contribution Adjustment Regulations, art. 2, § 3.

236. Several Regulations Regarding Encouraging Multinational Companies to Establish Regional Head Offices in Beijing (promulgated January 29, 1999, by Beijing Municipal Government); Temporary Regulations to Encourage the Establishment of Regional Head Offices in Shanghai by Multinationals (issued on July 20, 2002, by the Shanghai Municipal Government). The Shanghai HQ FIE Provisions provide certain benefits for FIEs that establish their regional headquarters in Shanghai. "Regional headquarters" is defined as a Shanghai-based investment or management FIE with investment from a multinational company that manages that multinational company's subsidiaries in the region. A regional headquarters is to be set up as an investment company or management company and the parent company's assets exceed $400 million. The provisions also require that the multinational company have an investment in China greater than $30 million, that it invest in or manage more than three FIEs, and that it have a registered capital of more than $2 million. The Shanghai HQ FIE Provisions also provide that those multinational companies that do not satisfy all of the conditions listed but have made

In general, these regulations provide various forms of preferential treatments including (a) an exemption from local income taxes; (b) refund of income taxes associated with reinvestment; (c) facilitating the establishment of Sino-foreign trading joint ventures, Sino-foreign wholesale joint ventures, financing companies, and distribution companies; (d) permitting the establishment of more than one foreign exchange account subject to the approval of the administrative authorities on foreign exchange; (e) approving a wider business scope for holding companies; (f) permitting the establishment of bonded warehouses and bonded manufacturing plants subject to customs approval; (g) facilitating the establishment of research and development institutions, training institutions, and technology support centers; and (h) lower registered capital requirements. Foreign enterprises are required to apply to the Beijing or Shanghai Municipal Commission on Foreign Economic Relations and Trade for approval to receive the benefits of establishing a regional headquarters office.

Key Laws and Regulations

Representative Offices

Provisional Regulations of the State Council of the People's Republic of China for the Control of Resident Representative Offices of Foreign Enterprises (promulgated October 30, 1980, by the State Council)

Procedures of the State Administration for Industry and Commerce of the People's Republic of China for the Registration and Administration of Resident Representative Offices of Foreign Enterprises (promulgated March 5, 1983, by the State Council)

(Continued)

extraordinary contributions to the region's economy also be deemed regional headquarters. A Shanghai regional headquarters operation may provide the following management and services to its subsidiaries: investment and operational decision making; marketing and sales services; capital and financial management; technical support, research and development; information support and services; employee training and management; and other operational, management and service activities as permitted by law. In addition, a research and development–focused regional headquarters may enjoy preferential treatments as a high-tech enterprise. Regional headquarters set up in Pudong will enjoy preferential tax treatments. Foreign employees assigned to work at a regional headquarters may be able to obtain work permits and visas from one to five years. Regional headquarters established to engage in purchase and distribution may be granted import and export rights, and exported goods are authorized to obtain VAT rebates. *See generally* Y. Wang, *Establishing a Regional Headquarters in Shanghai,* China L. & Prac. (June 2003) (author describes the permitted business scope and procedures for establishing a regional headquarters in Shanghai); *Shanghai Bound: New Regulations Seek to Attract Regional HQs,* China L. & Prac. (Sept. 2002); W. Zhao & L. Li, *Issues in Shanghai's Regional HQ's Legislation,* China L. & Prac. (Sept. 2003).

(Continued from previous page)

Detailed Rules of the Ministry of Foreign Trade and Economic Cooperation (MOFTEC) for the Implementation of the Provisional Regulations Governing the Examination, Approval, and Administration of Representative Offices of Foreign Enterprises (promulgated February 13, 1995, by the Ministry of Foreign Trade and Economic Cooperation)

Regulations Concerning Import and Export of Articles by Resident Offices and Their Staff of Foreign Enterprises and Press in China (promulgated on May 1, 1984, by the Customs General Administration of the PRC)

Notice of the State Administration of Taxation on Issues Concerning Taxation Inspections of Foreign Enterprise Resident Representative Offices (promulgated on June 12, 1996, by the SAT)

Tax Administration Issues Relevant to Resident Representative Offices of Foreign Enterprises Circular (issued on March 12, 2003, by the State Administration of Taxation)

Wholly Foreign-Owned Enterprises

Law of the People's Republic of China on Wholly Foreign-Owned Enterprises (adopted April 12, 1986, at the 4th Sess. of the 6th National People's Congress and as amended on October 31, 2000)

Detailed Rules for the Implementation of the Law of the People's Republic of China on Foreign Investment Enterprises (approved October 28, 1990, by the State Council and as revised on April 12, 2001)

Explanation of Several Terms Used in the Detailed Rules for the Implementation of the Law of the People's Republic of China on Sole Foreign Investment Enterprises (issued December 6, 1991, by the Ministry of Foreign Economic Relations and Trade)

Notice on Issues Relating to Enterprise Income Tax Refunds for Reinvestment by Foreign Investors (issued on July 17, 2002, by the SAT)

Notice of the State Bureau of Taxation Concerning Several Questions on Tax Refunds for Funds Reinvested by Foreign Investors in Foreign Investment Enterprises (issued on June 15, 1993, by the SAT)

Contractual Joint Ventures

Law of the People's Republic of China on Chinese-Foreign Contractual Joint Ventures (adopted April 16, 1988, at the 1st Sess. of the 7th National People's Congress, revised on October 31, 2000 at the 18th Meeting of the Standing Comm. of the National People's Congress)

Detailed Rules for the Implementation of the Law of the People's Republic of China on Chinese-Foreign Contractual Joint Ventures (promulgated September 4, 1995, by the MOFTEC)

(Continued)

(*Continued from previous page*)

Interpretation of the Implementation of Certain Articles of the Detailed Rules for the Implementation of the Law of the PRC on Sino-Foreign Cooperative Enterprises (promulgated on October 22, 1996, by the MOFTEC)

Equity Joint Ventures

Law of the People's Republic of China on Chinese-Foreign EJVs (adopted July 1, 1979, at the 2nd Sess. of the 5th National People's Congress, amended April 4, 1990, at the 3rd Sess. of the 7th National People's Congress, revised on March 15, 2001, at the 4th Sess. of the 9th National People's Congress)

Regulations for the Implementation of the Law of the People's Republic of China on Chinese-Foreign EJVs (promulgated September 20, 1983, by the State Council, amended on January 15, 1986, by the State Council, and revised on July 21, 2001, by the State Council)

Joint Venture Trading Companies

Provisional Measures on the Trial Establishment of Sino-Foreign Joint Equity Foreign Trade Companies (promulgated September 30, 1996, by the Ministry of Foreign Trade and Economic Cooperation, and re-promulgated on January 31, 2003)

Supplementary Provisions on the Interim Measures on the Establishment of Sino-Foreign Equity Joint Venture Trading Companies (promulgated on December 7, 2003, by the Ministry of Commerce)

Partnerships

Partnership Law of the People's Republic of China (adopted February 23, 1997, at the 24th Sess. of the Standing Comm. of the 8th National People's Congress)

Rules of the Shenzhen SEZ on Partnership (adopted on March 1, 1994, by the 21st Sess. of the Standing Comm. of the 1st Shenzhen Municipal People's Congress)

Rules of Guangdong Province on Partnership Business Operations (promulgated on May 9, 1995, by the Guangdong Provincial People's Government)

Administrative Measures of the People's Republic of China on the Registration of Partnership Enterprises (promulgated on November 19, 1997, by the State Council)

Notice on Relevant Issues Concerning the Implementation of the Administrative Measures of the People's Republic of China on the Registration of Partnership Enterprises (promulgated on February 19, 1998, by the SAIC)

Holding Company

Provisional Regulations Governing the Establishment of Investment-Type Companies by Foreign Business Investment (promulgated on April 4, 1995, by

(*Continued*)

(Continued from previous page)

MOFTEC, and repromulgated and amended on March 1, 2003, and February 13, 2004, by the Ministry of Commerce)

Supplementary Rules (II) to "Tentative Provisions for the Establishment of Investment-Type Companies by Foreign Investors" (promulgated on May 31, 2001, by the Ministry of Foreign Trade and Economic Cooperation)

Notice of the Ministry of Finance and the State Administration of Taxation on Certain Taxation Issues Concerning Foreign Investment Enterprises Engaging in Investment Business (promulgated on January 13, 1995, by the MOF and the SAT)

Notice on Several Issues on the Handling of Relevant Tax Issues Related to the Provision of Services by a Foreign Invested Holding Company to its Subsidiary Companies (issued by the State Administration of Taxation and effective as of January 1, 2003)

Foreign-Invested Venture Capital Enterprises

Provisional Regulations on the Establishment of Foreign-Invested Venture Capital Investment Enterprises (issued on August 18, 2001, by MOFTEC, Ministry of Science and Technology, State Administration of Taxation, and State Administration of Industry and Commerce, effective on September 1, 2001, and as amended on March 1, 2003)

Regulation on the Administration of Foreign-Invested Venture Capital Enterprises (issued on January 30, 2003 by MOFTEC, SAIC, Ministry of Science and Technology (MOST), State Administration of Taxation (SAT), and State Administration of Foreign Exchange)

Venture Capital Investment Regulations (promulgated on February 27, 2003, by the Shenzhen Municipal People's Congress)

Promotion of the Development of Venture Capital Investment Tentative Provisions (issued on February 14, 2003, by the Guangdong Provincial Development and Planning Commission)

Tax Issues Relevant to Paying of Enterprise Income Tax by Foreign-Invested Capital Investment Enterprises Circular (issued on June 4, 2003, by the State Administration of Taxation)

FIE Research & Development Operations

Circular on Questions Relating to Foreign Investment in, and the Establishment of, Research & Development Centers (issued by the Ministry of Foreign Trade and Economic Cooperation on April 18, 2000)

Encouraging the Development of Incubators for Science and Technology Enterprises (issued by the Shenzhen Municipal Government on April 10, 2003)

(Continued)

(*Continued from previous page*)

Encouraging Foreign Investors to Invest in the Establishment of Research and Development Organizations Several Opinions, issued by the Shanghai Municipal Government on September 15, 2003)

Provisional Measures on the Establishment of Sino-Foreign Equity Joint Research and Development Institutions and Sino-Foreign Cooperative Joint Research and Development Institutions (promulgated on September 10, 1997, by the State Science and Technology Commission)

Companies Limited by Shares

Provisional Regulations of Shenzhen Municipality on Companies Limited by Shares (issued March 18, 1992, by the Shenzhen Municipal People's Government)

Rules of Shenzhen Special Economic Zone on Limited Liability Companies (adopted on April 26, 1993, by the 5th Sess. of the 1st Shenzhen People's Congress)

Rules of the Guangdong Province on Companies (adopted on May 14, 1993, by the 2nd Sess. of the Standing Comm. of the 8th Guangdong People's Congress)

Provisional Regulations of Shanghai Municipality on Companies Limited by Shares (promulgated on May 18, 1992, by the Shanghai Municipal People's Government)

Provisional Measures of Shanghai Municipality on Cooperative Share-Formulated Enterprises (promulgated on May 17, 1997, by the Shanghai Municipal People's Government)

Company Law of the PRC (adopted December 29, 1993, by the 5th Sess. of the Standing Comm. of the 8th National People's Congress, revised and re-promulgated on December 25, 1999, by the 13th Sess of the Standing Comm. Of the 9th National People's Congress)

Provisional Regulations on Several Issues Concerning the Establishment of Foreign Investment Companies Limited by Shares (promulgated on January 10, 1995, by the MOFTEC)

Supplementary Regulations on the Certain Regulations on the Subscription of Capital by the Parties to Sino-Foreign EJVs (promulgated on September 29, 1997, by the MOFTEC and the SAIC)

Enterprise Registration Procedures

Notice of the State Administration of Industry and Commerce on the Circulation of an Opinion on Relevant Issues Concerning the Implementation of Administrative Laws and Regulations on Company Registration Applicable to Foreign Investment Enterprises, (promulgated on July 18, 1995, by the SAIC)

(*Continued*)

(Continued from previous page)

Notice of MOFTEC and the State Administration for Industry and Commerce on Relevant Regulations and Procedures for Adjustment of Aggregate Investment and Registered Capital by Foreign Investment Enterprises (issued on May 25, 1995, by the MOFTEC and SAIC)

Principles and Main Points of the Ministry of Foreign Economic Relations and Trade Concerning the Examination and Approval of Contracts and Articles of Association of Foreign Investment Enterprises (promulgated on October 5, 1993, by the MOFTEC)

Administrative Measures of the State Administration of Industry and Commerce Authorizing the Registration of Foreign Investment Enterprises (promulgated on December 10, 2002, by the SAIC)

Administrative Rules of the People's Republic of China Governing the Registration of Companies (promulgated on June 24, 1994, by the State Council of the PRC)

Notice on Certain Issues Concerning the Further Strengthening of the Administration of Examination, Approval and Registration of Foreign Investment Enterprises (promulgated on November 3, 1994, by the SAIC and MOFTEC)

State Council Notice on Strengthening Examination and Approval Procedures for Large Scale Foreign Investment Enterprises (issued on March 13, 1991, by the State Council)

Administrative Regulations of the People's Republic of China Governing the Registration of Legal Corporations (promulgated on June 3, 1988, by the State Council)

Notice of the Ministry of Foreign Economic Relations and Trade Concerning Questions on the Use of the New Edition "Approval Certificate of the People's Republic of China for Foreign Investment Enterprises" (promulgated on October 5, 1993, by the MOFTEC)

Administrative Measures of Shanghai Municipality on Examination and Approval Procedures for Foreign Investment Enterprises (promulgated on August 23, 1996, by the Standing Comm. of Shanghai Municipal People's Congress)

Administrative Regulations of the People's Republic of China Governing the Registration of Legal Corporations (promulgated June 3, 1988, by the State Council)

Issues Relevant to Strengthening the Administration of the Examination, Approval, Registration, Foreign Exchange Issues and Taxation of Foreign-Invested Enterprises Circular (promulgated on December 30, 2002, by the Ministry of Foreign Trade and Economic Cooperation, State Administration of Taxation, State Administration of Industry and Commerce, and the State Administration of Foreign Exchange)

(Continued)

(*Continued from previous page*)

Notice on the Implementation of Essential Clauses in Articles of Association of Companies Listed Overseas (promulgated on August 27, 1994, by the SCSC)

Notice of the MOFTEC and the SAIC on Relevant Regulations and Procedures for Adjustment of Aggregate Investment and Registered Capital by Foreign Investment Enterprises (issued on May 25, 1995, by MOFTEC and the SAIC)

Rules Concerning Headquarter Operations

Several Regulations Regarding Encouraging Multinational Companies to Establish Regional Head Offices in Beijing (promulgated January 29, 1999 by Beijing Municipal Government)

Temporary Regulations to Encourage the Establishment of Regional Head Offices in Shanghai by Multinationals (issued on July 20, 2002, by the Shanghai Municipal Government)

Chapter 5

Foreign Investment Guidelines and Industry-Specific Regulations

Foreign investment in certain industry and services sectors may be subject to restrictions, special registration, and approval procedures, as well as product standards and certification. A starting place for any analysis of the potential restrictions with respect to foreign investment in a particular industry or service sector is to review the foreign investment catalogue issued by the government. There are various laws, regulations, rules, or circulars issued by government agencies that outline the requirements for specific industries. This chapter analyzes the foreign investment guidelines, as well as the laws and regulations that regulate specific industry sectors.

A. Catalogue Guiding Foreign Investment

In March 2002, the Chinese government released the revised Catalogue Guiding Foreign Investment in Industry and the revised Regulation on Guiding Foreign Investment Direction.[1] The revised Catalogue Guiding Foreign Investment in Industry and the revised Regulation on Guiding Foreign

1. Catalogue Guiding Foreign Investment in Industry (Joint Order [2002] No. 21), promulgated on March 13, 2002, by the State Development and Planning Commission (SDPC), State Economic and Trade Commission (SETC), and Ministry of Foreign Trade and Economic Cooperation (MOFTEC). For an English and Chinese version of the Catalogue, see the Web site of the China Council for the Promotion of International Trade at http://www.ccpit.org. *See generally* H. Liu, *The Revised Foreign Investment Catalogue: Grounds for Optimism?*, China L. & Prac. (April 2002). *See also* Issuing of Guidelines of Shanghai Municipality for Foreign Investment in Industry Circular (promulgated by the Shanghai Development and Reform Commission, the Shanghai Foreign Economic Relations and Trade Commission, and the Shanghai Economic Commission on and effective as of September 15, 2003). For a reference to the types of technology encouraged by the government, *see* the *Catalogue of Encouraged Foreign Investment in High and New Technology Products (2003)* (issued on July 18, 2003, by MOFCOM and the Ministry

Investment Direction maintain the previous catalogues' division of investment projects into encouraged, restricted, and prohibited categories. Investment sectors omitted from the catalogue and otherwise not restricted by other PRC regulations are categorized as permitted investments. The encouraged category contains 262 investment areas, up from 186 in the previous version. The prohibited category covers 33 areas. The restricted category contains 92 investment areas and is a consolidation of the two previous restricted categories (A and B).

In the 1998 catalogue, foreign investment in the restricted B category required central-level approval regardless of project value. In the new catalogue, all primary, secondary, and tertiary industry projects above $30 million and listed in the restricted category require central-level Ministry of Commerce (MOFCOM) approval. Primary and secondary industry projects between $10 million and $30 million and tertiary industry projects between $5 million and $30 million that are included in the restricted category require provincial-level MOFCOM approval. Restricted projects below $10 million in primary and secondary industries, and below $5 million in tertiary industries, require municipal-level MOFCOM approval.

The investment scope outlined in the revised catalogue appears to conform to China's first-year World Trade Organization (WTO) commitments.[2] The catalogue does not, however, detail China's business scope, geographic, or quantitative commitments.

---

of Science and Technology [MOST]). The 2003 catalogue furthers the Chinese government's policy of encouraging foreign investment in underdeveloped industries and groups 196 product types into 11 principal categories: electronic information; software; space and aviation; optical-mechanical-electrical integration; biomedicines and medical treatment instruments; new materials; new energies and high-efficiency energies; environmental protection; earth, air and sea; nuclear application technologies; and modern agriculture.

2. Consistent with the 2002 Catalogue Guiding Foreign Investment, the Beijing municipal government adopted guidelines on foreign investment in the services industry, which are effective April 1, 2002. Zhou He, vice-director with the Beijing Foreign Trade and Economic Co-operation Commission, issued a statement providing that "[t]he new policy is based on the Chinese Foreign Investment Guidelines issued by the central government this month and designed to face the challenges and opportunities brought by China's accession to the World Trade Organization and Beijing's successful bid for the 2008 Olympic Games." The new guidelines are designed to open up the services industry sectors with respect to commerce, construction, education, environmental protection, finance, logistics, telecommunications, tourism, and transport. Foreigners are allowed to set up wholly foreign-owned enterprises, as long as they are engaged in architecture technology consultancy, investment management, public relations, personnel training, restaurant business, real-estate development, and management. Foreign commercial and logistics enterprises are encouraged to take part in the operation of modern logistics, chain stores, and supermarkets, as well as e-business. The municipal government is attempting to strengthen the competitive edge of its telecom companies by promoting Sino-foreign cooperation and assets reorganization. "For the tourism sector, the existing joint ventures should further expand their scale of operations and enhance their efficiency and service quality in a short period of time," Zhou said. Meanwhile, the Beijing municipal government will spare no effort to attract more international tourism organizations and foreign business associations to set up regional headquarters and representative institutes in the city and encourage foreign investors to take part in the construction and renovation of large-scale traveling facilities and visiting sites. See *Beijing Issues Guidelines on Foreign Investment in Service Industry,* CHINA DAILY, March 27, 2002, available on Lexis, News Library or the Web site of the CHINA DAILY at http://www.chinadaily.com.cn.

2002 Catalogue: Industry Sectors from Prohibited to Restricted Category

Distribution services

Telecommunication services

Construction/management of public utilities

2002 Catalogue: Industry Sectors from Restricted to Encouraged Category

Automobile production

Manufacture of MRI devices

Shipbuilding and related equipment construction

Operation of airfreight companies

Production of satellite navigation equipment

B. Regulation of the Services Sector

China has also adopted laws, regulations, and rules governing the activities of a broad range of services sectors.[3] Most of these standards have been revised in recent years to be consistent with China's WTO obligations.

1. Accountants and Accounting Firms

Accountants and accounting firms are subject to the Certified Public Accountants Law of the PRC.[4] The State Administration of Taxation has

3. As noted below in text and footnotes, the government has adopted specific rules for the finance industry, domestic and internal commerce, tourism, transportation, legal services, accounting services, engineering and design, medical and health-related services, freight forwarding, etc. *See generally, Current Status and Prospect of the Opening of China's Service Industry,* 134 CHINA INTERNATIONAL BUSINESS (MOFTEC) 24 (1998); *Approval Procedures for Establishment of Service Trade Enterprises,* 134 CHINA INTERNATIONAL BUSINESS (MOFTEC) 27 (1998); Xiao, *How to Open Up Service Trade,* 134 CHINA INTERNATIONAL BUSINESS (MOFTEC) 31 (1998).

4. Certified Public Accountants Law of the PRC (promulgated on October 31, 1993, by the 4th Sess. of the Standing Comm. of the 8th NPC), *reprinted in* CHINA LAWS FOR FOREIGN BUSINESS (CCH), Business Regulations ¶ 16-645; Examination and Approval of the Registration of China Registered Foreign Accountants (Tentative Procedures) (issued on Sept. 28, 1998, by the Ministry of Finance), *reprinted in* CHINA LAWS FOR FOREIGN BUSINESS (CCH), Taxation ¶ 35-847 (outlines application procedures for foreign accountants in China and criteria of approval such as a minimum of two years' experience); Administration of the Examination and Approval of Accounting Firm Branches Tentative Procedures (issued by the Ministry of Finance in 2000); Matters Relevant to the Administration of Registration for Cross-Province Established Branches of Accounting Firms (issued on May 24, 2001, by the Ministry of Finance) (outlines standards for establishing branch offices in China, including requirement that the firm

also developed a set of rules governing tax specialists retained by a taxpayer to handle taxation matters including tax registration, purchase of invoices, preparation and filing of declarations or withholding statements, payment of tax or application for refunds, establishment of a tax accounting system, tax consultation, and application for administrative review and tax litigation.[5] The Ministry of Finance has developed its own set of guidelines and standards for auditing and accounting practices.[6] The Chinese Institute of Certified Public Accountants also issues a number of informational circulars and practice guidelines to the industry on a broad range of topics such as professional rules of conduct, factors to consider to indicate the risk of fraud, and audit techniques and reports.[7]

---

employ adequate personnel and registered accountants, standards for registration and approval post-merger, penalties for failure to register, etc.). Various provincial governments have adopted their own standards. *See, e.g.,* Administrative Rules of the Shenzhen Special Economic Zone on Certified Public Accountants (promulgated on March 16, 1995, by the Standing Comm. of the Shenzhen Municipal People's Congress), *reprinted in* CHINA LAWS FOR FOREIGN BUSINESS (CCH), Special Zones & Cities ¶ 120-020; Qualification Requirements for Senior Accountants (issued on Feb. 14, 2000, by the Guangdong Provincial People's Congress). The government has changed the standards for the accounting profession. *See* Foley, *Accounting Adjustments: Planned Changes in China's Accounting Profession,* 4 CHINA BUSINESS REVIEW (July 17, 1998). *See* Relevant Examination and Approval Policies, Principles, and Procedures Governing Foreign Investment in the Establishment of Accounting Firms, *reprinted in* 135 CHINA INTERNATIONAL BUSINESS (MOFTEC) 51 (1998). *See also* Notice of the Ministry of Finance and the China Securities Supervision and Management Committee on the Regulations Governing Certain Issues Concerning the Practice of Auditing Operations for Chinese Enterprises Listed Overseas by Sino-Foreign Cooperative Accounting Firms and Overseas Accounting Firms (promulgated on March 2, 1994, by the Ministry of Finance and the China Securities Supervision and Management Committee), *reprinted in* CHINA LAWS FOR FOREIGN BUSINESS (CCH), Taxation ¶ 35-840.

5. *See also* Trial Measures on Tax Agency (promulgated on October 19, 1994, by the State Administration of Taxation), *reprinted in* CHINA LAWS FOR FOREIGN BUSINESS (CCH), Taxation ¶ 39-630.

6. Specific Independent Audit Guideline No. 25—Accounting Estimates (issued on January 21, 2001, by the Ministry of Finance) (outline standards for auditing of the accounting statements of listed companies by registered accountants and provide that a registered accountant shall comply with the principles of independent auditing, and obtain sufficient and appropriate audit evidence to determine whether the accounting estimates of the entity are reasonable and whether their disclosure is appropriate, outline standards that provide that the auditor may review and test the process for deriving the accounting estimates, or compare such estimates with independent estimates, or review the estimates in light of post-period facts, and provide that at the end of the auditing procedures, the auditor shall make a final determination as to the reasonableness of the estimates); Specific Independent Audit Guideline No. 19: Other Information Disclosed with Audited Accounts (issued on Feb. 4, 1999, by the Ministry of Finance); Independent Audit Guideline No. 21: Understanding the Work Unit Being Audited (issued on Feb. 4, 1999, by the Ministry of Finance) (outlines requirements that auditors should thoroughly investigate an enterprise under audit, and states what the registered accountant uses to determine the enterprise's economic situation, such as interest rates, capital supply, production technology, and environmental protection problems, etc.); Independent Audit Guideline No. 22: Consideration of Internal Audit Work (issued on Feb. 4, 1999, by the Ministry of Finance); Administration of the Licenses for Registered Accountants to Engage in Business Relevant to Securities and Futures Provisions (issued on June 10, 2000, by the Ministry of Finance).

7. Professional Ethical Code of Chinese Certified Public Accountants Guiding Opinion (issued on June 25, 2002, by the Chinese Institute of Certified Public Accountants). The guidelines include

2. Advertising Agencies

The NPC adopted the Advertising Law of the PRC, which outlines the registration procedures, obligations, and legal liability for advertising agencies and advertisers.[8] Pursuant to its WTO obligations, China is required to permit foreign majority ownership in advertising firms on or before December 11, 2003, and WFOEs on or before December 11, 2005. On March 2, 2004, the MOFCOM and State Administration of Industry and Commerce (SAIC) jointly issued rules that outline the requirements for FIE advertising companies.[9] To establish a Chinese-foreign joint advertising enterprise, the parties to the venture are required to have engaged in the advertising business and have been in operation for a minimum of two years.[10] The FIE Advertising Company Rules provide for majority ownership of up to 70% in cooperative or equity advertising joint ventures. Approved FIE advertising companies may engage in design, production, publishing, and advertising agency business activities for domestic and international customers. The rules further provide that FIE advertising companies may not be established as WFOEs until December 11, 2005.[11] FIE advertising companies may establish branch operations if they have annual sales of not less than RMB20 million and all registered capital is paid in full.[12]

3. Asset Appraisal Enterprises

MOFTEC (now MOFCOM) adopted regulations in 1997 that provide that an asset appraisal enterprise may be set up as a joint venture but not as a

standards concerning independence, professional competence, confidentiality obligations, fees and commissions, audit engagement from predecessor accountant, advertising, soliciting, and promotion. The guidelines also address issues concerning actions that may impair the independence and judgment of an accountant (Arts. 9 to 14), obligations of confidentiality (Art. 22), prohibitions on contingent fee arrangements (Art. 31), rules on conflicts of interest (Arts. 36, 37), and advertising and solicitation activities (Arts. 46–48)); Audit Technique Reminder No. 1: Financial Fraud Risks (issued on July 31, 2002, by the Chinese Institute of Certified Public Accountants) (outlines factors to consider in determining fraud risks); Chinese Certified Public Accountants Practice Standard Guidelines No. 5: Audit Reports (Trial Implementation) (issued on May 13, 2003, by the Chinese Institute of Certified Public Accountants) (outlines standards for audit reports and opinions may be issued).

8. See Chapter 13, Consumer Protection § C; Advertising Law of the People's Republic of China (adopted October 27, 1994, by the 10th Sess. of the Standing Comm. of the 8th NPC), *reprinted in* China Laws for Foreign Business (CCH), Business Regulation ¶ 16-495 (hereinafter "the Advertising Law"). *See Relevant Examination and Approval Procedures Governing Foreign Investment in the Advertising Sector,* 135 China International Business (MOFTEC) 50 (1998).

9. Administration of Foreign-Invested Advertising Companies Provisions (issued on March 2, 2004, by MOFCOM and SAIC) (hereinafter the "Advertising FIE Provisions").

10. Advertising FIE Provisions, art. 10.

11. Advertising FIE Provisions, art. 23. Under CEPA, Hong Kong and Macao advertising services providers are allowed to set up a WFOE commencing January 1, 2004.

12. Advertising FIE Provisions, art. 11.

WFOE.[13] The regulations outline a number of other conditions and requirements for approval.

4. Chambers of Commerce and International Foundations

Foreign trade associations and chambers of commerce that intend to establish offices in China are required to follow special rules formulated by the State Council. The association is required to submit an application to the China International Board of Commerce and Ministry of Civil Affairs for approval.[14]

China has also adopted regulations outlining the standards and procedures to allow overseas groups and individuals to establish foundations in China. Effective June 1, 2004, the Ministry of Civil Affairs will allow overseas foundations to engage in activities in China in a similar fashion as domestic foundations so long as they are consistent with China's public welfare regulations.[15]

---

13. *See* Certain Provisional Regulations on the Establishment of Foreign-Funded Asset Assessment Institutions (promulgated on April 7, 1997, by the State Administration of State-Owned Assets and the MOFTEC), *reprinted in* CHINA LAWS FOR FOREIGN BUSINESS (CCH), Business Regulation ¶ 6-620; Provisional Regulations on Foreign Asset Assessment Institutions Which Conduct Asset Assessment Business within Chinese Territory (promulgated on May 19, 1997, by the State Administration of State-Owned Assets), *reprinted in* CHINA LAWS FOR FOREIGN BUSINESS (CCH), Business Regulation ¶ 6-624. *See also* Administrative Rules of Guangdong Province on Asset Assessment (promulgated on January 10, 1998, as Announcement No. 188 of the 8th Sess. of the Standing Comm. of the Guangdong Provincial People's Congress), *reprinted in* CHINA LAWS FOR FOREIGN BUSINESS (CCH), Special Zones & Cities ¶ 270-050. The State Administration for Quarantine and Inspection of Exit Entrance (SAQIEE) issued the *Management Measures on the Certification of Offshore Valuation Institutions,* which became effective on October 1, 2000. Pursuant to the Measures, a certified offshore valuation institution may engage in the valuation of foreign investment assets and foreign compensation trade assets when such assets involve any form of FIE capital contribution or assets that an FIE has entrusted its foreign investor to purchase. Under the Measures, an offshore valuation institution must meet the following requirements and conditions for certification: (1) available technical support for engaging in such valuation; (2) a good reputation in the industry; and (3) at least $500,000 in registered capital. Upon successful SAQIEE examination, the certified offshore valuation institution will be issued a five-year certificate. *See also* Attention by Certified Asset Appraisers Toward the Legal Ownership of Appraised Objects Guiding Opinion (issued on Jan. 28, 2003, by the Chinese Institute of Certified Public Accountants) (outlines the standards for appraisal services in the valuation of property, such as to provide documentation of the ownership of the appraised object, as well as proof of the truthfulness, legality, and completeness of the documentation; outlines requirement that certified appraisers disclose to their clients that confirmation of ownership or opinions on ownership is beyond the scope of appraisal services; etc.).

14. *See* Provisional Regulations on Control of Foreign Boards of Commerce (adopted on April 28, 1989, at the 39th Executive Meeting of the State Council), *reprinted in* CHINA LAWS FOR FOREIGN BUSINESS (CCH), Business Regulation ¶ 16-595. With respect to the employment of foreign personnel, foreign chambers of commerce are required to follow the procedures set forth in the Notice Concerning the Employment of Foreign Nationals by Foreign Chambers of Commerce in China (issued on January 20, 1999, by the Ministry of Civil Affairs, Division of Administration of Civilian Organizations) and the Administrative Regulations on the Employment of Foreigners in China (jointly issued on January 22, 1996, by the MOL, MPS, and MOFTEC), *reprinted* in CHINA LAWS FOR FOREIGN BUSINESS (CCH), Business Regulation ¶ 12-630.

15. *See* Regulations on the Establishment of Overseas Foundations (issued on March 19, 2004, by the Ministry of Civil Affairs). *See generally Ministry Releases Rules on Nonprofits,* China Market Intelligence, U.S.-CHINA BUSINESS COUNCIL (March 24, 2004).

5. Construction Industry

The NPC has adopted the Construction Law designed to improve the supervision and administration of construction activities, to promote the construction industry, and to ensure that construction projects are undertaken in a safe manner. The Construction Law outlines the qualifications for contractors, construction project building permits, construction contracts, tender process, construction project supervision, construction work safety management, construction project quality control, and legal liability. The Construction Law is effective March 1, 1998, and applies to all parties engaged in construction activities in China, including the construction of the various types of structures and their auxiliary facilities, as well as the installation activities involving related wiring circuits, pipelines, and equipment.[16]

Effective December 1, 2002, the PRC government adopted regulations that apply to foreign enterprises involved in construction, engineering, or construction design in China.[17] The prior restriction on foreign investors

---

16. *See* Construction Law of the People's Republic of China (adopted on November 1, 1997, by the 28th Sess. of the Standing Comm. of the 8th NPC), *reprinted in* CHINA LAWS FOR FOREIGN BUSINESS (CCH), Business Regulation ¶ 19-565 (outlines the qualifications for contractors, construction project building permits, construction contracts, tender process, construction project supervision, construction work safety management, construction project quality control, and legal liability). The Shanghai city government has also developed a set of guidelines for the construction industry, which are effective December 1, 1997. The Shanghai rules outline the qualifications for persons engaged in building activities, general contractor and subcontract activities, role of supervisory agencies, project contracts and building cost calculations, project quality and safety, and penalties and legal liability). *See* Administrative Rules of the Shanghai Municipality on the Construction Market (adopted on October 21, 1997, by the 39th Sess. of the Standing Comm. of the 10th Shanghai Municipal People's Congress, and amended on October 31, 1999), *reprinted in* CHINA LAWS FOR FOREIGN BUSINESS (CCH), Special Zones & Cities ¶ 240-100. A foreign contractor involved with road construction is subject to the Highway Law of the PRC, which outlines the standards for road planning, road construction, road maintenance and administration, toll roads, and legal liability. The government is allowing greater participation in China's construction and engineering services market to foreign companies. *See* Highway Law of the People's Republic of China (promulgated on July 3, 1997, by the 26th Sess. of the Standing Comm. of the 8th NPC of the People's Republic of China), *reprinted in* CHINA LAWS FOR FOREIGN BUSINESS (CCH), Business Regulation ¶ 19-628 (outlines the standards for road planning, road construction, road maintenance and administration, toll roads, and legal liability); Electric Power Law of the PRC (adopted and promulgated on December 28, 1995, by the 17th Sess. of the Standing Comm. of the 8th NPC), *reprinted* in CHINA LAWS FOR FOREIGN BUSINESS (CCH), Business Regulation ¶ 19-604 (outlines the standards, *inter alia,* concerning the construction of power generation facilities). The government is allowing greater participation in China's construction and engineering services market to foreign companies. *See,* Zhao, *Nation to Further Open Construction Market,* CHINA DAILY (Oct. 27, 1998), available on Lexis, News Library, or on the Web site of the CHINA DAILY at http://www.chinadaily.com.cn; *See* Development Plan and Policies of China's Construction and Engineering Sectors, 137 CHINA INTERNATIONAL BUSINESS (MOFTEC) 34 (1998); *Development Plan and Policies of China's Residential Housing Sector,* 137 CHINA INTERNATIONAL BUSINESS (MOFTEC) 38 (1998). In September 2004, the Ministry of Construction released a draft revised version of the Construction Law for public comment. *See* http://www.cin.gov.cn.

17. Administration of Foreign-Invested Construction Enterprises Provisions (promulgated on Sept. 27, 2002, by the Ministry of Construction and the Ministry of Foreign Trade and Economic Cooperation) (hereinafter the "FIE Construction Regulations"); Relevant Administration of Qualifications in the Administration of Foreign-Invested Construction Enterprises Provisions Implementing Procedures (issued by the Ministry of Construction on April 8, 2003) (hereinafter the "FIE Construction Implementing Regulations"). *See generally* L. Luo, *Foreign-Invested Construction Rules in the PRC: Building the Future?,* CHINA L. & PRAC. (December 2002); T. Mahony, *Foreign-Invested Construction Enterprises: The Next Legal Step,* CHINA L. & PRAC. (June 2003).

establishing a wholly foreign-owned (WFOE) construction or construction design enterprise in China has been removed in line with China's WTO obligations.[18] As a result, foreign construction or construction design companies can establish wholly foreign-owned enterprises, equity joint venture, or contractual joint venture enterprises. Foreign investors may also establish an FIE construction company through reinvestment by an existing FIE or by purchasing an equity stake in another construction company. The FIE Construction Implementing Regulations provide that "construction activities" are defined to include "new construction, expansion and reconstruction activities in the fields of civil engineering, construction engineering, lines, pipelines and equipment installation, and refurbishment."[19]

Under prior rules, foreign investors were allowed to participate in construction projects only on a project basis and to obtain a "foreign contractor qualification certificate" and business license.[20] Under the FIE Construction Regulations, foreign investors that are approved for work in China may engage in multiple projects simultaneously and are not limited to a single contract or project.

The approval procedures under the FIE Construction Regulations require that a foreign contractor obtain approval from the Ministry of Commerce, and then obtain approval from the Ministry of Construction.[21] The total

18. FIE Construction Regulations, art. 2. Pursuant to the WTO Market Accession Schedule regarding a foreign service supplier's entry in China's architectural services, China is obligated to allow foreign involvement in China's architectural and engineering services in the form of commercial presence (*i.e.*, a joint venture) upon China's accession to WTO. However, upon accession foreign investors may only be allowed to participate in the form of an equity joint venture or cooperative joint venture. Nevertheless, foreign majority ownership is permitted. Within five years after China's accession to WTO (i.e., December 2006), foreign investors will be allowed to set up WFOEs that engage in construction and engineering services. However, the schedule specified that the foreign partner shall be registered architects or engineers or enterprises in architectural or engineers in its home country.

19. FIE Construction Implementing Regulations, art. 2. *See also* Administration of Foreign-Invested Urban Planning Services Enterprises Provisions (promulgated on February 13, 2003, and effective on May 1, 2003, by the Ministry of Construction and the Ministry of Foreign Trade and Economic Cooperation) (provides that FIEs are permissible to provide "urban planning services" and similar consultancy activities with regard to urban planning); Notice on Matters Related to Foreign-Invested Enterprises Obtaining Qualification Certificates for Urban Planning Services (promulgated on May 5, 2003, by the Ministry of Construction [MOC]) provides guidance as to the materials to be included with an application for certification as a foreign-invested urban planning service enterprise, and provides that local or provincial planning bureaus forward completed applications to the MOC within 30 days and compels the MOC to issue a Foreign-Invested Enterprise Urban Planning Service Qualification Certificate or a rejection notice within an additional 30 days. *See generally* S. Silverman, *Pushing Ahead with Foreign-Invested Urban Planning Enterprises,* China L. & Prac. (May 2003).

20. FIE Construction Regulations, art. 3.

21. FIE Construction Regulations, arts. 6–14. The materials to be submitted in support of an application to MOFCOM include a feasibility study, articles of association, bank creditworthiness and proof of corporate existence, financial statements, and documents concerning FIE personnel. FIE Construction Regulations, art. 10. The materials to be submitted to the Ministry of Construction include FIE construction enterprise qualification application, approval certificate from MOFCOM, and various other documents. FIE Construction Regulations, art. 11. All documents are required to be submitted in

amount of capital contributed by the Chinese party to a Sino-foreign construction JV shall not be less than 25 percent of the enterprise's registered capital and, as a result, a foreign party may hold up to 75 percent of an equity stake in a JV construction company.[22] With respect to WFOE construction enterprises, the FIE Construction Regulations limit the scope of activities to foreign/international-funded projects, or projects in which the technical needs of a project make it difficult for Chinese contractors to complete.[23] After an enterprise is established, the company is required to apply for a *construction enterprise qualification certificate* from the Ministry of Construction or branch office, and is required to abide by the laws and construction standards adopted by the PRC.[24]

6. Convention and Exhibition Companies

MOFCOM has issued regulations outlining the standards and procedures for the establishment of convention and exhibition (CEC) enterprises as either joint venture operations or wholly foreign-owned enterprises.[25] Applicants for the establishment of a CEC enterprise must have significant experience with respect to hosting international expositions, professional exhibitions, or international conventions. Approved CEC enterprises will be allowed to provide convention and exhibition services inside China and overseas.

Chinese, and companies established prior to the effective date of the regulations are required to renew their applications. FIE Construction Regulations, arts. 13, 14. Because of the dual application process and consultation between MOFCOM and the MOC, an application may take as long as 100 days to be approved. FIE Construction Regulations, art. 7.

22. FIE Construction Regulations, art. 12. Interestingly, a WFOE is permitted or a 75/25 percent JV is permitted, but for any Chinese partner their stake cannot be less that 25 percent.

23. FIE Construction Regulations, art. 15. The business scope of WFOE construction companies is limited to the following: (1) projects funded by foreign investment, with foreign donations or with foreign investment and foreign donations; (2) projects funded by international financial institutions that are, pursuant to the loan terms, granted through international invitations of bids; (3) Sino-foreign joint construction projects in which the foreign investment accounts for 50 percent or more of the total; and Sino-foreign joint construction projects approved by the government in which the foreign investment accounts for less than 50 percent of the total but due to technical difficulties cannot be implemented solely by Chinese construction enterprises; or (4) Chinese-invested construction projects approved by the government that due to technical difficulties cannot be implemented solely by Chinese construction enterprises may be jointly contracted for by Chinese and foreign construction enterprises. If an FIE violates the provisions of Article 15 by contracting a project beyond its business scope, it may be fined between 2 and 4 percent of the contract value, have its income confiscated, be ordered to suspend operations, or lose its business license. FIE Construction Regulations, art. 20.

24. *See* Construction Law; Administration of the Quality of Construction Works Regulations (issued by the Ministry of Construction on Jan. 20, 2000); Administration of Construction Survey and Design Regulations (issued by the Ministry of Construction on Sept. 25, 2000).

25. Provisional Rules on Establishing Foreign-Invested Convention and Exhibition Companies (promulgated on February 13, 2004, by the Ministry of Commerce and effective on April 12, 2004) (hereinafter the "CEC Regulations"). The regulations go beyond the scope of China's WTO obligations, which only required the establishment of CEC enterprises as majority foreign-owned joint ventures. Applications for CEC enterprises are required to include, among other things, evidence of the foreign investor's financial credibility and experience in the convention and exhibition industry.

7. Direct Marketing Operations

The Direct Marketing Procedures prohibit foreign persons from engaging in direct marketing activities in the PRC.[26] Local enterprises that engage in direct marketing are required to sell only products produced within China and certified for quality. The procedures also govern the manner in which direct sales may take place. In April 1998, Chinese authorities began cracking down on direct sales companies that were unapproved by the government.[27] In June 1998, the government issued an order instructing direct marketing organizations to convert to store operations, and set forth requirements, conversion procedures, and standards for sales personnel. In response, some foreign companies, such as Avon, restructured their operations as retailers/wholesalers.[28]

8. Educational Institutions and Certification Organizations

Foreign persons interested in establishing a Chinese-foreign educational institution are required to meet certain requirements and undergo an application process as required by regulations adopted by the State Council in 2003.[29]

---

26. *See* Notice of the State Council on the Prohibition of Direct-Sale Business Activities (Guofa 1998 Document No. 10) and the Notice on Relevant Issues Concerning the Conversion of Sales Methods Used by Foreign Investment Direct-Sale Enterprises (promulgated on June 18, 1998, by MOFTEC, SAIC, and SAT), *reprinted in* China Laws for Foreign Business CCH, Business Regulation ¶ 13-562. The law on direct marketing activities are set to change in 2004. *See* D. Yan, *Draft Direct Selling Law Set for September*, CHINA DAILY (May 14, 2004).

27. Administration of Direct Marketing Procedures (adopted on January 20, 1997, by the State Administration of Industry and Commerce), *reprinted in* 11 CHINA L. & PRAC. 15 (June 1997). *See* Notice Concerning the Change of Sales Method by Foreign-Invested Chuanxiao ("Pyramid" or "Direct Sales") Enterprises (issued on June 18, 1998, by the Ministry of Foreign Trade and Economic Cooperation, State Administration of Industry and Commerce, and the State Bureau of Internal Trade), *reprinted in* CHINA LAWS FOR FOREIGN BUSINESS (CCH), Business Regulation ¶ 13-562. *See also* Opinion on Furthering the Development of the Strike Hard Campaign Against Chuanxiao and Disguised Chuanxiao (issued on March 11, 2003, by the State Administration of Industry and Commerce) (standards for cracking down on "chuanxiao" operations, which are direct sales or chain selling operations). To meet their WTO commitments, MOFCOM and SAIC intend to adopt rules governing the direct sales industry in 2004. The draft rules, however, have been criticized as not allowing domestic firms to engage in direct sales. *See* D. Yan, *Equality in Direct Selling Sector Urged,* CHINA DAILY (April 2, 2004).

28. Zhang, *Avon Plans to Resume Operations in China,* CHINA DAILY (June 9, 1998), available on Lexis, News Library, or on the Web site of the CHINA DAILY at http://www.chinadaily.com.cn.

29. PRC Sino-Foreign Cooperation in Running Schools Regulations (promulgated on March 1, 2003, and effective September 1, 2003, by the State Council) (outlines standards for foreign educational institutions, registration procedures, establishment and preparatory stages, prohibitions on foreign-based religious schools from setting up in China, procedures for operations and curricula, procedures for school closure, and other standards); Provisional Regulations for Sino-Foreign Cooperation in the Running Schools (promulgated on January 26, 1995, by the State Education Commission), *reprinted in* CHINA LAWS FOR FOREIGN BUSINESS (CCH), Business Regulation ¶ 19-600. In 1998, the State Education Commission was elevated to a ministry level agency. *See generally* Y. Wu, *Sino-Foreign Education Gets a Boost with New Regulations,* CHINA L. & PRAC. (June 2003) (author discusses standards and practices concerning new regulations for joint schools including capital contributions, institutional structure, management and teaching quality, enrollment quotas and awards of degrees/certificates, fees and compensation, rights to assets, and legal liability); B. Dolven & T. Saywell, *China Goes for Private Lessons: Schools Are Big Business as Families Pay for Children's Head Start,* WALL ST. J. (Jan. 6, 2004), available online at http://www.awsj.com.

The government has also adopted standards for the regulatory approval of certification organizations, certification training organizations, and certification consultancies.[30] In addition to meeting the specified requirements for ordinary certification bodies, training organizations, and consultancies, foreign-invested certification bodies, training organizations, and consultancies must also meet the following conditions: (1) the organization must have registered capital of at least $350,000; (2) the foreign investors must have obtained state accreditation qualifications or recognition in their own countries; and (3) the foreign investors must have had at least three years' relevant service experience. The examination and approval of applications to establish certification bodies, certification training organizations, and certification consultancies in which foreign investors are to hold a controlling interest is not permitted before December 11, 2003. Examination and approval of applications to establish wholly foreign-owned certification bodies, certification training organizations, and certification consultancies will not be permitted before December 11, 2005. The Measures also contain rules governing the establishment of representative offices of foreign certification bodies, training organizations, and consultancies.

On May 31, 2000, the State Administration for Exit/Entry Inspection and Quarantine issued the *Management Measures for Application Agents for Safety and Quality Licenses for Import Goods*. The Measures outline the standards and registration procedures for enterprises that operate as Import Safety/Quality Agents, which may be any domestic or foreign enterprise entrusted by foreign exporters or their representatives to handle issues such as applying for safety and quality licenses for import goods or obtaining a safety/quality authentication mark in the name of the foreign exporter. These enterprises must be registered with the State Administration for

30. *See* Measures for the Examination, Approval, Registration, Supervision and Administration of Certification Bodies, Certification Training Organizations and Certification Consultancies (jointly issued on April 2, 2002, by the State Certification and Accreditation Administration, SAIC, the State Administration of Quality Supervision, Inspection and Quarantine, and MOFTEC). The 2002 rules appear to conflict with regulations adopted in September 2003 by the State Council. In September 2003, the State Council issued regulations to develop a uniform set of catalogues, technical standards, marks, and fees used in the certification and authentication of important domestic and imported products, services, and management systems to ensure overall public and consumer safety. *See* Regulations of the People's Republic of China on Certification and Authentication (promulgated on September 3, 2003, by the State Council and effective on November 1, 2003). The 2003 Certification Regulations implement a licensing system for certification institutions, a qualifications recognition system for testing laboratories and institutions, and a two-track system of product certification (i.e., voluntary certification and compulsory certification for products). Foreign-invested certification enterprises may be established in China; however, by law a foreign certification institution may only establish a representative office and is prohibited from engaging in certification activities in China.

Exit/Entry Inspection and Quarantine before they can become Import Safety/Quality Agents.

9. Employment Agencies

The Ministry of Labor and Social Security and SAIC jointly issued regulations that allow foreign employment agencies to enter the Chinese employment agency business by establishing either an equity or contractual joint venture with qualified Chinese partners.[31] The registered capital requirement for JV employment agencies is $300,000, and the agency is required to have more than three full-time employees that are qualified in employment agency services.[32] However, Chinese law prohibits the establishment of wholly foreign-owned employment agencies, and only JV operations will be approved. In addition, the representative offices of foreign employment agency firms are prohibited from engaging in employment agency services and must do so through a properly approved JV operation.[33] The Measures outline the permitted business scope, the requirements of the foreign and Chinese investors, and the application procedures for the establishment of such employment agencies.

10. Entertainment: Films, Radio, and Television

As in many aspects of life in China, the film industry experienced a rebirth with the end of the Cultural Revolution in 1976. In the early 1980s, Chinese films began to move away from purely state-sanctioned propaganda designed to educate and control the thinking of the masses, to address a broader range of topics that are both experimental and entertaining to the public.

31. Interim Measures on the Administration of the Establishment of Employment Agencies in Sino-Foreign Equity Joint Ventures and Contractual Joint Ventures (issued on October 9, 2001, by the Ministry of Labor and Social Security and SAIC, effective on December 1, 2001) (hereinafter the "JV Employment Agency Measures"); Sino-Foreign Equity Joint Skilled Personnel Agencies Tentative Provisions (promulgated on Sept. 4, 2003, by the Ministry of Personnel, Ministry of Commerce, and State Administration of Industry and Commerce). *See also* Administration of Employment Agencies for Skilled Personnel Market Procedures (promulgated on Sept. 11, 1998, by the Beijing Municipal People's Government); Administration of Employment Agencies Regulations (promulgated on Sept. 1, 1998, by the Chongqing Municipal People's Government); Promotion of the Establishment of Sino-Foreign Joint Venture Human Resources Agencies Tentative Provisions (promulgated on June 27, 2002, by the Beijing Municipal People's Government); Administration of the Establishment of Sino-Foreign Equity and Cooperative Joint Venture Employment Agencies Tentative Provisions (promulgated on April 23, 2002, by the Shanghai Municipal People's Government). The Ministry of Labor and Social Security also adopted regulations for overseas employment agencies that recruit Chinese citizens for employment abroad. *See* Overseas Employment Agency Provisions (promulgated on May 14, 2002, by the Ministry of Labor and Social Security, Ministry of Public Security, and the State Administration of Industry and Commerce) (outlines the permit process and permissible recruitment activities for overseas employment agencies in China).

32. JV Employment Agency Measures, art. 6.

33. JV Employment Agency Measures, art. 3.

In the 1990s, the government loosened its tight reins on the industry to encourage profitability and economic independence as a result of China's move toward a more market-based economy. In general, China's economic reforms elevated more of its citizens to middle-class status, increased overall consumer spending, and sparked interest in all forms of entertainment, and especially foreign film and music.

Today, China encourages joint production between foreign and domestic studios and, under WTO commitments, will allow the showing of more foreign-produced films in the domestic market. Yet, despite the incremental opportunities created by WTO, China will continue to exercise control over the industry to meet its two key objectives: (1) to encourage and preserve the domestic industry; and (2) to continue to exercise some level of control over content and subject matter.

The film industry in the People's Republic of China is regulated by the State Administration of Radio, Film and Television (SARFT).[34]

a. Film Co-Production

In 2001, the film production companies and film distribution companies in China went through a restructuring process designed to better improve financial performance in the industry.[35] Under SARFT, there are three film production groups (i.e., China Film Group, Southern Film Group, and Shanghai Film Group) and four film distribution groups (i.e., China Film Distribution Group, Southern Film Distribution Group, Shanghai Film Distribution Group, and Beijing Film Distribution Group). Thirty domestic companies in China are currently approved for film production in China. Effective February 2002, Chinese private companies and investors may apply to independently produce films. China lifted its restrictions on film production funding effective February 1, 2002, and thus for the first time allowing private investment in filmmaking.[36] Any Chinese individual or business enterprise is authorized,

34. Prior to March of 1998, SARFT was a ministry-level agency but was downgraded to an independent "administration" during the institutional restructuring in the mid-1990s. The original intention of the restructuring process was to loosen the regulatory grip that has had a positive impact on the domestic television and film industries; however, the practical effect of this so-called downgrade on matters involving foreign investors is negligible given the continued high degree of regulatory control. *See* Opinions on Boosting Development of Broadcasting, Film, and TV Industry (issued by the State Administration of Radio, Film, and Television in January 2004) (outlines SARFT development plans for the entertainment industry).

35. In 2004 SARFT intends to issue regulations to better improve competition in the film industry. *See generally New Rule Issued to Bolster Movie Industry,* People's Daily Online (March 29, 2004).

36. Administration of Films Regulations (promulgated by the State Council on Dec. 25, 2001, and effective on Feb. 1, 2002); Administration of Sino-Foreign Cooperation in Production of Films Provisions (promulgated on Oct. 8, 2003, and effective on Dec. 1, 2003, by SARFT); Interim Provisions for Admission

upon receiving a single film license, to produce films, and it is no longer necessary to "buy" a quota number from a studio.

Foreign companies are not allowed to wholly own a production company in China. Nor are foreign parties allowed to independently produce a film in China. However, the law allows a foreign investor to link up with a local production company to jointly produce a film with approval from SARFT.[37] In the past, foreign parties were only allowed to work with the China Film Joint Production Company. Today, all licensed production studios are authorized to work with foreign companies. The key benefits of working with a qualified and well-connected Chinese production company are that they will usually handle all applications and permits, resolve censorship issues, assist with scouting for locations and facilities, and assist with local labor issues for actors, extras, and crew.

The average budget for a feature film produced in China in 2002 was approximately $100,000 to $300,000. The low amount generally reflects the low labor costs in China, as well as the relatively cheaper expense of scene construction and lack of expensive special effects, stunts, and pyrotechnics that have yet to play a major part in China's film industry. The one uncertainty for films in China is the government approval process, which, although standards have relaxed, still poses a hurdle for producers. A script must first be approved by censors from the Propaganda Bureau, which focuses on political issues and sexual content, and the less of each of these topics in a script, the faster the film will receive approval.[38] A film must pass through the approval process once again after the film is shot and edited.

Approved Chinese film producers may produce films in cooperation with foreign film producers. Local production studios may absorb overseas investment to jointly produce films and TV shows. Over fifteen co-production projects were completed in 2002, up from ten in 2001. Co-production projects in recent years originated from such countries and regions as the HKSAR, Taiwan, Australia, France, Korea, Czech Republic, and the United States.[39]

Qualifications of Operating Film Production, Distribution, and Film Showing Business (promulgated on Oct. 29, 2003, by SARFT and effective on Dec. 1, 2003) (outline application requirements for industry companies). *See generally More Foreign Investment Allowed in PRC Film Industry,* CHINA MARKET INTELLIGENCE, THE U.S.-CHINA BUSINESS COUNCIL (Nov. 26, 2003). For a Chinese version of the regulations, *see* the Web site of SARFT at http://www.sarft.gov.cn.

37. Administration of Film Regulations, arts. 18, 19.

38. Administration of Film Regulations, art. 24.

39. More foreign companies view China as a cheap, politically stable production location. Quentin Tarantino's Miramax action film "Kill Bill," which stars Uma Thurman, was partially filmed in China. Tarantino is the first big-name director to use China as a low-cost production base dressed up to look like somewhere else (i.e., Japan). Miramax's "The Great Raid," about WWII in the Philippines, was filmed in China. The Philippines, post-9/11, is considered to be too politically unstable for production.

b. Importing/Distributing Foreign Films

Starting in 2002 as a result of China's entry into the WTO, the number of foreign films authorized for screening in China's theaters increases from ten per year to twenty. Within five years, the quota will be increased to thirty per year; however, the allocation of screen time of Chinese-produced films cannot be less than two-thirds of the total screen time of all films.

Notwithstanding WTO, China Film Distribution Group remains the only government agent authorized to import foreign films.[40]

c. Foreign Investment in Theater Construction/Management

In 1990, there were 14,000 authorized theaters in China. In 1999, that number dropped down to 4,000 with the decrease attributed to the closing of antiquated facilities. Average annual box office receipts in China are $100 million and growing annually.

The real problem in developing the film industry in China is the lack of big-screen cinemas and need for investment in modern theaters. Given the present poor condition of most theaters and the inefficiencies of the film distribution system, it is difficult to imagine how China can accommodate a large number of films from abroad and still maintain a domestic film industry. There is need for a modern distribution system and comfortable multiplex theaters.[41]

In response to the decline in theaters, the SARFT and the Ministry of Foreign Trade and Economic Cooperation (MOFTEC) jointly issued regulations in 2000 to encourage foreign investment in cinema construction and management.[42] The FIE Theater Regulations provide that (i) the term of foreign-invested theaters will extend no more than 30 years; (ii) the form of

---

Chinese authorities are increasingly comfortable with co-productions. State-owned film studios, with whom foreign filmmakers are required to form partnerships, offer attractive terms, such as allowing foreign partners to hire their own crews. And Chinese crews, who have no independent unions, are accustomed to long working days and low pay. *Hollywood Meets Beijing in Tarantino Flick*, CHINA DAILY (September 23, 2002).

40. Administration of Film Regulations, art. 30. SARFT has formed a new company to break the monopoly on film distribution. At the present time, the state-owned China Film Distribution Group has the sole rights to import and distribute foreign films. While they will retain a monopoly on imports, SARFT is setting up a competing firm to distribute films in competition with the China Film Group. (The Chinese way of breaking up a monopoly is to create a duopoly, which has the same effect. More change is anticipated.)

41. H. Yueming, *Old Cinemas Face a Hard Time*, CHINA DAILY (July 25, 2001). In addition to the poor cinema facilities, the availability of cheap DVD players and knock-off DVDs has led most Chinese consumers to avoid the cinemas and view films at home. The urban Chinese are no strangers to foreign films, and especially Hong Kong and American films that are widely available for sale throughout China in pirated format. With the advent of DVDs, more than 90 percent of the Chinese market for home viewing is controlled by counterfeiters. For example, a Harry Potter film was for sale on Beijing streets three days after its premiere in Los Angeles. In spite of the ongoing government crackdowns, piracy is still thriving in the unofficial economy. On the positive side, the flood of pirated movies has ignited consumer demand for foreign films that will be very hard to quash (at least at the home viewing level).

42. Provisional Regulations of Foreign-Invested Theaters (adopted on October 25, 2000, by MOFTEC and SARFT) (hereinafter the "FIE Theater Regulations").

foreign-invested theaters may be set up as either an equity joint venture (EJV) or contractual joint venture (CJV); (iii) the registered capital shall be no less than RMB10 million ($1.2 million); and (iv) the Chinese party(ies) will have a share no less than 51 percent in the EJVs or the main management rights in the CJVs. The FIE Theater Regulations also provide the procedures for application and approval.

On the positive side, the FIE Theater Regulations permit the parties to contractually agree upon profit allocation and timing for return on investment, notwithstanding the requirement that the Chinese party(ies) control the operation. In addition, the regulations provide that it is not necessary for one Chinese party to control the 51 percent interest required by law. Hence, several Chinese enterprises may make up the 51 percent domestic interest and, depending upon the specific enterprises involved, a diverse group of Chinese partners may effectively limit their overall power since voting blocks may form within the JV that are not limited to foreign versus Chinese interests.

At the same time, the government has also expressed a policy that it would not approve any plans for new theater construction over the next three years (2002–2005). The stated objective of this rule is to encourage renovation of currently existing theaters before capital is invested in new cinema construction. While this rule appears to be wholly counterproductive in light of the government's interest in promoting the domestic film industry, whether this rule will be applied or ignored is left for observation.[43]

d. Production/Importation of Audio-Visual Products

Foreign investors and private individuals may set up joint ventures to produce, manufacture, and distribute audio visual products (DVDs, VCDs, CDs, tapes) in China.[44] The capital contribution of the foreign party may not exceed 49 percent, and the foreign party must have an established presence in China (i.e., rep office) for more than three years without any record of copyright infringement. Foreign and private JVs may enter into all aspects

---

43. *See generally Warner Bros. Launches Multiplexes as China Opens Film Industry,* CHINA DAILY (January 19, 2004); *Warner Buys into China Cinema,* http://www.CNN.com (July 4, 2002).

44. The State Council amended the *Administrative Regulations on Films* ("Film Regulations") and the *Administrative Regulations on Audio and Video Products* ("Audio Regulations") on December 25, 2001, and both of them will be effective as of February 1, 2002. The Audio Regulations provide that contractual joint ventures (CJVs) engaging in the distribution of audiovisual products will be allowed. The Ministry of Culture (MOCT) and the Ministry of Foreign Trade and Economic Cooperation (MOFTEC) issued the *Administrative Measures of Sino-Foreign Cooperative Audiovisual Products Distribution Enterprises* ("Audio Measures") on December 10, 2001, which is effective as of January 10, 2002. The Audio Measures provide the requirements of investors and the application and approval procedures. Among others, the Audio Measures provide that the share held by Chinese parties will be no less than 51 percent, and the cooperation term should extend no more than fifteen years.

of wholesale, retail, and rental distribution. The term of the joint venture enterprise may not exceed fifteen years but is renewable upon approval. The importation of audiovisual products is subject to an import licensing process as governed by applicable rules adopted by the Ministry of Culture and General Administration of Customs.[45]

e. Broadcasting and Television

Although China's WTO commitments do not include broadcasting and television, China is aware of the forthcoming impact of foreign media and entertainment spurred on by China's general liberalization. The government has, therefore, restructured local stations and companies into groups to defend their status. For example, local TV stations have now absorbed cable TV stations, and news broadcast and TV groups have emerged in Beijing, Shanghai, Hunan, Tianjing, and Guangdong. In December 2001, a national group also emerged that consists of China Central Television (CCTV), Central National Radio, China Radio International, China Films Group Corp., China Broadcast, Film & TV Transmission Networks Co. Ltd., and China Broadcast Television Internet Corp., as well as other entities.

Under regulations adopted in February 2002, foreign satellite television channels may broadcast to agreed-upon areas such as guesthouses, three star hotels (or above) catering to foreign guests, and buildings exclusively for office and residential use by expatriates.[46] Under the Foreign Satellite Television Procedures, operators of foreign satellite television channels are

---

45. Administration of Import of Audio and Video Products Procedures (issued on June 1, 2002, by the Ministry of Culture (MOCT) and General Administration of Customs) (hereinafter the "Audio-Visual Products Import Procedures"). The Audio-Visual Products Import Procedures cover the importation of finished audiovisual goods, including audiotapes, videotapes, phonograph records, compact discs, and video compact discs with recorded content (Audio-Visual Products). Importation of certain types of content, such as content that opposes the basic principles of the Chinese Constitution and is viewed as harmful to the sovereignty of the State or its territorial integrity is prohibited. The Audio-Visual Products Import Procedures create an import licensing system to be carried out by MOCT or branch entities, and prohibits any person from publishing, duplicating, or distributing by means of wholesale or retail, renting, screening for commercial purposes, or disseminating through an information network any Audio-Visual Products that are not approved. Approval is also required for products to be given away at corporate events or exhibitions. In order to obtain an import license, the importer is required to submit the product to the MOCT for content examination. The application is to include the text of the content in Chinese and the relevant foreign language and the import agreement. If the product is imported for publishing purposes, the license agreement (in both Chinese and the relevant foreign language), the original copyright certificate, the copyright authorization certificate, and the registration and certification documents must also be included. MOCT has 30 days from the date of receipt of the application materials to evaluate and approve or reject the application. Approval is provided on a single import shipment basis only.

46. Administration of the Examination and Approval of the Landing of Foreign Satellite Television Channels Tentative Procedures (promulgated on February 1, 2002, by the State Administration of Radio, Film and Television) (hereinafter the "Foreign Satellite Television Procedures"). *See generally* N. Leigh, *New Procedures to Control Satellite Television in China,* China L. & Prac. (May 2002). *SARFT Revised Rules on Foreign Satellite TV Channels in China*, China Market Intelligence, U.S.-China Business Council (December 17, 2003).

required to appoint an exclusive agent, which is an enterprise designated by SARFT, and meet certain conditions in order to secure landing rights. Foreign broadcasters are also required to abide by PRC content requirements and pay fees for transmission rights. The procedures are unclear on whether a foreign broadcaster is allowed to secure approval for more than one channel. The requirements for approval of landing rights include the following:

(1) The programming content of the television channel must not violate Chinese laws, regulations, or related rules
(2) The channel is rated among the top three television media in its home country (region) in terms of overall ranking and audience rating
(3) The foreign broadcaster has the resources to engage in "reciprocal" cooperation with China and undertakes to land, and actively assists in landing, Chinese radio and television programs abroad[47]
(4) The foreign broadcaster has friendly relations with China and actively encourages friendly exchanges and cooperation between Chinese and foreign radio and television broadcasters
(5) The foreign broadcaster agrees to centralize the transmission of its programs via the agent and undertakes not to land such program in China by any other means[48]

The Foreign Satellite Television Procedures outline the application procedures to secure landing rights, and applications are accepted and approved once a year between the months of July and September. An application is required to be submitted by a SARFT-approved agent, along with supporting documentation and examples of reception devices such as decoders. Upon approval, the foreign broadcaster is required to execute a contract with the SARFT agent within 90 days.[49]

In general, the Foreign Satellite Television Procedures prohibit content that is in violation of the law including, for example, information that opposes the PRC Constitution, compromises state security, incites racial hatred, disturbs social order, broadcasts obscenity, or infringes the lawful

47. SARFT includes "reciprocal" cooperation as a new requirement for cooperation and indicates that a condition of landing rights in China is that foreign broadcasters must actively assist and/or offer reciprocal arrangements to broadcast programs from the state-owned China Central Television (CCTV). Several examples demonstrate the importance of reciprocal cooperation. For example, AOL Time Warner commenced broadcasting China Entertainment Television (CETV) via Guangdong Cable TV Networks' (GCTV) cable system beginning January 2002. Another deal has approved to allow Star TV (News Corp.) to launch a Chinese-language entertainment channel in Guangdong province. Both arrangements require that CCTV 9 will be aired through News Corp's Fox Network and Time Warner cable systems.

48. Foreign Satellite Television Procedures, art. 5. Rule is designed to prevent companies from illegally transmitting, or transmitting "by other means," into China.

49. Foreign Satellite Television Procedures, arts. 6–10, 12.

rights and interests of a third party. If any content contravenes Chinese law or results in "negative consequences," the broadcaster is required to take steps to immediately correct the situation and must suspend broadcasting any inappropriate content. The law does not define the term "negative consequences," which is left purposefully vague to allow the authorities the maximum amount of discretion in application. The Foreign Satellite Television Procedures provide that a foreign broadcaster may have its landing rights revoked if its content violates Chinese laws or regulations three or more times in one year. Thereafter, the foreign broadcaster cannot reapply for landing rights for three years.[50]

11. Express Mail and Package Delivery Companies

In 1998, China Customs adopted regulations which outline the conditions for establishment of mail and package delivery companies, obligations, and registration procedures.[51] In response, several express mail and package delivery companies established a presence in China. In December 2001, the State Postal Bureau (China Post) and its supervising agency (the Ministry of Information Industries) issued an announcement that requires all express delivery services to apply to the provincial postal authorities for certification. The certification process was purportedly designed to enhance security and prevent chemical and biological attacks through the mail system post-9/11. In February 2002, China Post issued a second announcement that limits the type of mail that express companies may deliver. These rules have created a number of uncertainties for foreign investors.[52]

12. Financial Institutions

Foreign-funded financial institutions, including banks, financial leasing companies, and trust investment companies, are governed by a number of different laws, rules, and regulations. The People's Bank of China (PBOC)

---

50. Foreign Satellite Television Procedures, arts. 13–15.

51. *See* Methods of the People's Republic of China on the Supervision and Regulation of Entry and Exit Express Delivery (issued on April 1, 1998, by the Customs General Administration), *reprinted in* 132 China International Business (MOFTEC) 57 (1998). *See generally* The Integrated Express Industry in China: A Catalyst for Investment and Growth, The U.S.-China Business Council (September 2003), available online to members at http://www.uschina.org. *See also* Rules on Supervision of Cross-Border Express Mail (issued on November 18, 2003, by the General Administration of Customs) (outlines rules for express mail operator, clearance procedures, capital requirements for operators, and other standards).

52. China Post's express mail service, EMS, was not subject to the certification requirements, but other Chinese express mail companies (such as Sinotrans, which is owned by MOFTEC/MOFCOM) and foreign joint ventures were required to apply for certification. MOFTEC publicly rebuked China Post for improperly regulating companies under MOFTEC's supervision. For more information on this dispute, *see* http://www.uschina.org/members/postal-controversy.html.

and the China Banking Regulatory Commission (CBRO) have adopted rules specifically addressing the application process, capital requirements, appointment of personnel, reporting requirements, and other rules specifically applicable to foreign-funded financial institutions.[53]

13. Franchise, Retail, Wholesale, and Commission-Based Agency Operations

The Ministry of Internal Trade issued administrative measures concerning commercial franchise operations on November 14, 1997, which regulate the activities of franchises. The regulations apply to all commercial operators, including food and service industries. The regulations require that a franchise contract include certain mandatory language, contain standards for franchise operations, and set forth the rights and liabilities of franchisees and franchisors.[54] The government has adopted specific rules for certain types of franchise operations.[55]

---

53. For a discussion on China's banking regulations, *see* Chapter 11, Financial Regulation § A.3.

54. Administration of Commercial Franchise Procedures (Trial Implementation) (promulgated on Nov. 14, 1997, by the Ministry of Internal Trade). Both MOFTEC and the SETC (which are also both the predecessors of the Ministry of Commerce) maintain that the 1997 Franchise Measures apply only to domestic franchise operators and not cross-border franchise operations. *See* Harpole, *New Developments: Trial Franchise Law,* 7 CHINA LAW NEWS 11 (Jan. 1998); Harpole, *New Trial Law Establishes Legal Framework for Franchise Operations,* 9 CHINA LAW NEWS 5 (Mar. 1998); J. Chan, *Franchising in China,* CHINA L. & PRAC. (June 1999); *Franchising: Who Is Responsible for What?,* CHINA L. & PRAC. (Oct. 1999).

55. The SETC adopted regulations concerning the franchising of gas stations in China. *See* Regulating Petrol Station Franchise Several Opinions (promulgated on Aug. 26, 2002, by the State Economic and Trade Commission) (hereinafter the "Petrol Station Franchise Regulations"). The Petrol Station Franchise Regulations provide that a "Petrol station franchise" refers to the retail of oil products and the provision of related services by a petrol station in a uniform system of operation under a franchise contract between the franchiser and the franchisee whereby the franchisee is authorized to use the trade name, registered trademark, proprietary technology, operation mode, operation technique, and service standards. Under the regulations, only specified Chinese companies may act as franchisors; namely, PetroChina Company Limited (PetroChina), China Petroleum and Chemicals Corporation (Sinopec), and their authorized subsidiaries. The regulations provide that franchisees shall comply with local petrol station development plans and meet State standards with respect to environmental protection, fire prevention, and construction safety. Franchisees are also required to have a two-year record of regulatory compliance. The franchisor is required to provide operation manuals, technical guidance, training, and other services to the franchisees. The franchisee shall not sell third-party oil products, conduct its own promotion, assign the franchise to other parties, or disclose the trade secrets of the franchiser. The franchiser may charge an initial franchise fee, royalties, and other agreed fees. *See also* Strengthening the Administration of Chain Operation of Internet Access Services Providers Circular (promulgated on April 22, 2003, by the Ministry of Culture) (outlines procedures for establishment and management of franchise chain operations of Internet access services). On June 5, 2003, the Ministry of Culture announced a ban on new nationwide Internet cafe franchises licenses. Up to that date, the Ministry of Culture had issued ten such licenses to domestic companies for purposes of centralizing the industry sector. The Circular requires that licensed operators to open at least 20 Internet cafe outlets in at least two provinces or municipalities. The Circular was issued in response to a fire in a Beijing Internet cafe that killed 24 people in 2002, and the government has accordingly focused its efforts on supervising the operations and safety of Internet cafes. *See China Stops Issuing Nationwide Internet Cafe Franchise Licenses,* CHINA MARKET INTELLIGENCE, THE U.S.-CHINA BUSINESS COUNCIL (June 18, 2003), available online to members at http://www.uschina.org.

According to the 1997 Franchise Measures, there are currently two basic forms of franchising, namely, direct franchising and sub-franchising. Direct franchising means that the franchisor directly grants the franchising rights to the franchisee and the franchisee operates its business pursuant to the parties' agreement and may not transfer the franchised rights to any third party. Sub-franchising means that the franchisor grants to a master franchisee the sole franchised rights within certain territory and the franchise may operate the business itself or transfer the franchised rights to a third party based upon the terms and conditions in the master franchise agreement.

The 1997 Franchise Measures outline the qualifications and requirements for franchisees and franchisors. To start, the Measures require that the franchisor be an independent legal person while the franchisee has the discretion to be an individual or legal entity. Franchisors are also obligated to disclose material information to prospective franchisees before the execution of the franchise agreement including, but not limited to, basic information about the franchisor, the operational results of the franchisor and its existing franchisees, the financial statements of existing outlets, fees and payment obligations, and any payment terms for the sales of goods and services by the franchisor to the franchisee. Domestic franchisors are also required to register with the China Chain Store and Franchise Association (CCFA). Franchisors' statutory obligations to franchisees also include:

(1) Provide a reasonable amount of assistance to franchisees to establish and operate the franchise business
(2) Provide the franchisee with an operating manual and other materials that contain details of the operation of the franchise business, and to ensure that the manual be revised or amended to include up-to-date improvements with respect to the operation of the business
(3) Provide training to the franchisee with respect to the operation of the business (e.g., retailing and management techniques)

Under the regulations, franchisees have the obligation to manage and control the intellectual property rights of the franchisor and to manage the operation in a manner that preserves the goodwill of the franchise operation. The franchisee is also obligated to inform the franchisor of any potential violations of the IP rights of the franchisor by third parties, and to operate the business in a manner consistent with the franchise agreement. The regulations provide that franchisees are required to pay for all fees due under the franchise agreement such as the advanced membership fee, fee for use of franchise rights, service fees, and any performance guarantee fee.

In July 2001, the SETC floated a draft set of revised Franchise Regulations, which have been under development for several years and supposedly, in late 2003, under review by the State Council.[56] In the interim, and given that the 1997 Franchise Measures have been interpreted as to not apply to cross-border franchise operations, foreign franchisors have had to establish a presence in China using other organizational structures (i.e., joint ventures, WFOEs, etc.) or commercial arrangements (i.e., equity investments, cross-border licensing, master franchising outside of China, etc.) or combination thereof, and under the limitations of foreign investment guidelines and restrictions. However, traditional franchising or the sale of franchises to Chinese individuals or entities has, until further legislation is fully implemented, been severely limited in application. Under China's WTO commitments, foreign investors are allowed to engage in franchising within three years after China's accession to the WTO (or on or before December 11, 2004).

As with the franchising sector, retailing must be open to foreign investors on or before December 11, 2004. At present, retailing and other types of commercial trading activities are classified as a restricted industry for foreign investment. As such, foreign investment in restricted industries must go through a time-consuming and cumbersome approval process, or to be set up in a manner that evades, in whole or in part, the limitations imposed by the law or in practice.

Under various provisions adopted by the State Council and State Internal Trade Bureau (SITB), formerly known as the Ministry of Internal Trade (MIT) and currently part of MOFCOM, a foreigner cannot own more than 49 percent of the shares of an enterprise in the retail sector, which must be established in Beijing or Shanghai. The length of cooperation for an FIE in the retail sector is also limited to a maximum of thirty years.[57] The SITB has developed standards for the classification of retail outlets to standardize market practices. According to a circular issued by the SITB, retail outlets are categorized into eight types: department stores, supermarkets, large-scale

56. *See generally Slow Train Coming: New Draft Regulations on Franchising,* CHINA L. & PRAC. (Oct. 2001). The Draft Franchise Regulations state that direct investment by foreign franchisors must comply with applicable foreign investment laws. Cross-border franchises without direct investment in China are not mentioned in the draft regulations.

57. *See also* Certain Regulations of Shanghai Municipality on Commercial Chain Enterprises (promulgated on November 25, 1997, by the Shanghai Municipal People's Government), *reprinted in* CHINA LAWS FOR FOREIGN BUSINESS (CCH), Special Zones & Cities ¶ 240-105 (outlining the registration requirements, operational standards for chain store operations, and requirements for chain store and franchise agreements). Foreign firms can also retain approved enterprises as agents, representatives, distributors, or marketers. For a sample distribution and marketing agreement, *see* Appendix A. *See generally* SETTING UP SHOP: RETAILING IN CHINA (F&T Tax, ed. 1996) (may be ordered through the following Web site: http://www.expertlegal.com).

comprehensive supermarkets, convenience shops, warehouse stores, shops for special products, boutiques, and shopping centers.[58]

Effective June 1, 2004, MOFCOM promulgated regulations addressing the activities of FIEs in the commercial sector.[59] The FIE Commercial Sector Regulations specify the standards by which foreign-invested commercial

58. *See* National Chain Store Business Development Plan (issued by on June 26, 1995, by the Ministry of Internal Trade); Standardization of the Operation and Management of Chain Stores Opinion (promulgated on March 27, 1997, by the Ministry of Internal Trade); Directing of the Examination and Approval of Foreign Investment Opinion (promulgated on Nov. 5, 1996, by the Ministry of Foreign Trade and Economic Cooperation); Certain Questions Concerning the Administration of Registration of Chain Stores Circular (issued on May 30, 1997, by the Ministry of Internal Trade); Questions Concerning the Financial Management of Chain Store Enterprise Businesses Tentative Provisions (promulgated on Sept. 29, 1997, by the Ministry of Finance); Questions Concerning the Screening and Rectifying of Foreign Investment Commercial Enterprises in Non-Trial Locations Circular (issued on Aug. 5, 1997, by the State Council); Promoting the Development of Chain Business Several Opinions (issued on Aug. 12, 2002, by the State Council Office for Restructuring Economic System and SETC). The Ministry of Finance and State Administration of Taxation issued the Notice Regarding Chain Store Taxes on February 27, 2003, which allows chain store operations to centralize VAT and income tax payments at their company headquarters. The tax rules are designed to encourage the growth of the chain store industry, as well as to counter tax avoidance by chain stores and ease tax collection by requiring that chain stores centralize record-keeping in a single corporate database to allow greater access and transparency of records to the tax authorities. *See generally SETC Tightens Chain Store Administration,* China Market Intelligence, The U.S.-China Business Council (February 19, 2003); *NBS Reports on China's Wholesale and Retail Markets,* China Market Intelligence, The U.S.-China Business Council (April 24, 2002).

59. Regulations for the Administration of Foreign-Invested Enterprises in the Commercial Sector (issued on April 16, 2004, by the Ministry of Commerce) (hereinafter the "FIE Commercial Sector Regulations"). In November 2003, MOFCOM released a draft retail law for review in the community entitled the Provisional Administrative Measures on Foreign-Invested Commercial Enterprises. *See generally* Foreign Retail Giants to Be Regulated, China Daily (Nov. 11, 2003); R. Buckman, China May Restrict Retailers: Beijing Considers Rules That Would Limit Growth of Foreign Companies, Wall St. J. (December 10, 2003), available online at http://www.wsj.com; *MOFCOM Floats Draft Distribution Rules,* China Market Intelligence, The U.S.-China Business Council (December 3, 2003). Under the draft FIE Commercial Enterprise Measures, the government intended to categorize commercial enterprises into three classes: Class A (enterprises that have never violated the law or policy of China); Class B (enterprises that have been investigated for violations of the law); and Class C (enterprises that continue to violate the law and policy of China). MOFCOM intended to exercise its discretion in determining which retailers fall within the three classes. Before setting up a new operation, Class B retailers would be required to wait for one year after an investigation and be required to submit documentation that demonstrates that they have corrected any violations of the law. Class C retailers would lose all rights to expand or invest in new commercial operations or branch stores. Only Class A retailers would be allowed to invest or expand in new operations in China. In March 2004, MOFCOM announced that it would withdraw the retailer ranking system that had been criticized by the foreign business community in China. *See MOFCOM Strikes Controversial Retailer Ranking System From Upcoming Regulations,* China Market Intelligence, The U.S.-China Business Council (March 10, 2004). Under the draft FIE Commercial Enterprise Measures, a foreign investor is required to invest RMB30 million ($3.63 million) as registered capital for an operation with more than 8,000 square meters. For retail operations between 3000–8000 square meters, the registered capital requirements are RMB5 million ($602,410). For stores of less than 3000 square meters, the foreign investor is required to put up 30% of the total required investment to open and operate the venture. For stores of less than 3000 square meters, foreign investors may not open more than 300 such retail operations. Under the draft FIE Commercial Enterprise Measures, foreign retail investors are obligated to acquire the land-use rights for the retail business in accordance with the land administration regulations, and the location and construction of retail stores must conform with local urban commercial development plans. The measures prohibit a foreign retailer from securing approval to open new stores if it has more than three operations that have been approved and are not open for business.

enterprises may conduct retail, wholesale, franchise, or commission agency business. The Regulations provide that MOFCOM exercises supervision and control over the market entry of FIE Commercial Enterprises.[60]

The FIE Commercial Sector Regulations define the following categories of foreign-invested commercial enterprises: Wholesale companies sell goods and affiliated services to retailers, industrial/commercial/institutional users, or other wholesalers; retail companies sell goods and affiliated services to individuals and institutional consumers in fixed locations, or through TV, telephone, mail, Internet, and vending machines; franchise companies make profits or franchise royalties by authorizing others to use the franchise's trademarks, brands, and business models; and commission agencies consist of an agent, broker, auctioneer, or goods wholesaler who charges fees to sell goods and affiliated services on behalf of other parties on a contract basis.[61] The regulations provide that foreign companies, enterprises, and other economic organizations and individuals must establish an FIE in China in order to engage in wholesaling, retailing, franchising, or commission-based activities.[62]

The FIE Commercial Sector Regulations do not specify the level of registered capital required for companies engaged in wholesaling, retailing, franchising, or commission-based activities. However, the regulations do require that the applicants meet the minimum registered capital requirements set forth in the Company Law.[63] The term of operation of an FIE commercial enterprise shall not exceed 30 years, or 40 years in the western region of the country.[64] The regulations list the application documents and materials required for approval of new and established operations.[65] The land-use rights of an operation are required to be for commercial use and acquired by tender, auction, or

60. FIE Commercial Sector Regulations, art. 5. Provincial departments of MOFCOM may approve a foreign-invested distribution enterprise to establish stores with an area of less than 3,000 square meters if the company has no more than three stores in the province and no more than 30 in China and stores with less than 300 square meters with at most 30 stores in the province, and at most 300 similar stores in China. If a company exceeds these limits, the enterprise needs to obtain approval from MOFCOM. MOFCOM is required to complete the application process within four months. FIE Commercial Sector Regulations, art. 10.

61. FIE Commercial Sector Regulations, art. 3.

62. FIE Commercial Sector Regulations, art. 3.

63. FIE Commercial Sector Regulations, art. 7. The approved regulations differ from the draft that circulated for comments in late 2003, namely, the approved and issued version has removed minimum registered capital requirements and instead requires the minimum registered capital for foreign-invested commercial enterprises to comply with relevant stipulations in the PRC Company Law.

64. FIE Commercial Sector Regulations, art. 7.

65. FIE Commercial Sector Regulations, arts. 12, 13, 14. The documents required include an application letter, articles of association, feasibility study report, letters of creditworthiness, valuation reports of state-owned assets, list of merchandise to be imported/exported, list of FIE directors, name pre-registration certificate, copies of land-use rights document and/or lease, and power of attorney for representative handling the application. If applicable, trademark license, tech transfer, service contracts, etc., should also be submitted.

listed in accordance with the law.[66] Commercial enterprises involving merchandise or commodities that are subject to quotas or licensing can only be sold or imported/exported in conformance with applicable regulations.[67]

The FIE Commercial Sector Regulations allow foreign-invested retailing enterprises to engage in the retail sales of merchandise, to import merchandise for the enterprise's own sales, to engage in procurement activities of domestic products for export, and other ancillary business activities.[68] Retailing enterprises set up as WFOEs are permitted after December 11, 2004. Prior to December 11, 2004, retailing FIE commercial enterprises and stores may be established only in provincial capitals, SEZs, or directly administered cities such as Beijing, Shanghai, and Tianjin. After December 11, 2004, there are no geographical restrictions.[69]

The FIE Commercial Sector Regulations also allow foreign-invested wholesale enterprises to engage in merchandise wholesaling, to act as commission-based agencies (except for auction-related activities), and to engage in import and export activities.[70] An enterprise may also engage in franchising activities with approval, and the regulations require that the class of merchandise or services to be provided must be set forth in the business scope and articles of association of the enterprise.[71] Wholesaling FIE commercial enterprises are permitted in all China from June 1, 2004.

The FIE Commercial Sector Regulations provide that foreign-invested distribution companies that sell books, periodicals, and newspapers, processed oil, pharmaceuticals, and automobiles follow regulations that MOFCOM will issue separately.[72] Foreign investors from Hong Kong and Macao are subject

66. FIE Commercial Sector Regulations, art. 15. The regulations provide that new stores opened by FIE companies must be consistent with municipal urban development plans where the store will be located and must present local government documentation to that effect when submitting an application to MOFCOM. It is foreseeable that the land-use and urban planning requirement may be used as a market entry barrier to restrict the number of FIE commercial operations in a given city.

67. FIE Commercial Sector Regulations, art. 16.

68. FIE Commercial Sector Regulations, art. 9. Retail operations that engage in television, telephone, mail order, Internet, or vending machine sales will not be approved. FIE Commercial Sector Regulations, art. 10 (3).

69. FIE Commercial Sector Regulations, art. 21.

70. FIE Commercial Sector Regulations, art. 9. An FIE commercial enterprise that engages in auction-related activities must comply with the Auction Law and the Cultural Relics Law and is subject to other separate regulations. FIE Commercial Sector Regulations, art. 20.

71. FIE Commercial Sector Regulations, art. 9.

72. FIE Commercial Sector Regulations, art. 17. Wholesaling enterprises may not engage in pharmaceuticals, pesticides, or mulching film before December 11, 2004, and are not permitted to engage in sales of chemical fertilizer, processed oil, or crude oil before December 11, 2006. They may not engage in sales of salt or tobacco. Retail enterprises may not engage in sales of drugs, pesticides, mulching film, or processed oil before December 11, 2004, and are not permitted to engage in chemical fertilizer sales before December 11, 2006. They are not permitted to engage in the sale of tobacco products. Until the WTO timetables are effective, a foreign investor may not hold more than a 49% interest in an FIE commercial enterprise in the restrictive sectors noted herein.

to preferential treatment under CEPA, and CEPA-qualified services providers are allowed to set up WFOEs from January 1, 2004.[73]

14. Freight Transport Agencies, Logistics Enterprises, Ocean Shipping, and Railway Cargo Transportation

(a) Freight Transport Agencies and Logistics Enterprises

The government has adopted regulations concerning the establishment of joint ventures engaged in freight forwarding services.[74] The FIE Freight Forwarding Agency Regulations provide that foreign investors may establish FIE International Forwarding Agencies in the form of equity joint ventures, cooperative joint ventures, or wholly foreign-owned enterprises. In situations in which a foreign investor establishes a Sino-foreign equity or cooperative international forwarding joint venture enterprise, the Chinese party's capital contribution must not be less than 25 percent.[75] Although authorized by the regulations, WFOE applications will be accepted only in line with the market access requirements of WTO.[76] The FIE Freight Forwarding Agency Regulations further provide that foreign investors may acquire or merge with established international forwarding agencies in China by means of acquisition of an equity stake, but the shareholder ratio and investor qualifications are required to be in conformance with applicable laws

73. FIE Commercial Sector Regulations, art. 25. CEPA-qualified services providers may set up in local cities throughout China and at the county-level cities in the Guangdong Province. For a discussion of the market access provisions of CEPA (the Closer Economic Partnership Arrangement), *see* Chapter 24, Special Zones of the PRC § B.3.

74. Administration of Foreign-Invested International Freight Forwarding Agencies Procedures (Promulgated by the Ministry of Foreign Trade and Economic Cooperation on December 11, 2002, and effective thirty days from the date of promulgation) (hereinafter the "FIE Freight Forwarding Agency Regulations"). The New Provisions became effective on January 10, 2003, and repeal the Order No. 31—Administration of Foreign-Invested International Freight Forwarding Agencies Provisions (the 2001 Freight Forwarding Provisions), which were issued by MOFTEC and effective from January 1, 2002. *See generally* D. Ryan, *MOFTEC Delivers: Foreign Majority Ownership Permitted in International Freight Forwarding Companies,* CHINA L. & PRAC. (Feb. 2003). *See also* Supplementary Provisions to the Measures for the Administration of Foreign-Invested International Freight Agencies (promulgated on December 7, 2003, by the Ministry of Commerce) (provide that a freight agency be established as a limited liability company or company limited by shares); and Detailed Rules on the Provisions for the Administration of International Freight Agencies (promulgated on January 1, 2004, by the Ministry of Commerce) (provide that freight agencies may only establish affiliates or branch companies after one year of operation by the parent, and provide the procedures for examination and approval, registration, and annual review of the agencies).

75. Foreign investors can apply to establish a 75-percent stake in a new international freight-forwarding joint venture, which is an increase from the 49-percent stake that foreign investors were previously allowed in freight-forwarding joint ventures. The FIE Freight Forwarding Agency Regulations expressly provide that foreign parties in existing international freight-forwarding joint ventures can apply to increase their equity interests to 75 percent.

76. FIE Freight Forwarding Agency Regulations, art. 4. China's WTO commitments require that WFOEs be permitted four years after accession, December 11, 2005. Given that WFOEs will eventually be permitted, the current provisions requiring a JV arrangement have limited value.

and regulations, including the standards applicable to the acquisition of state-owned assets. An investor is required to file an application for approval with MOFCOM.[77]

The regulations require that the largest of the Chinese and/or foreign investors of an FIE Freight Forwarding Agency be engaged in the international forwarding agency business, export and import operation, or related transport or storage business. The regulations also require that the applicants have a three-year history of full compliance with the standards of the industry.[78] The law requires that a foreign investor operate for two years in China before investing in a second international freight-forwarding agency.[79]

The FIE Freight Forwarding Agency Regulations provide that an agency established under these rules is required to meet the following conditions:

(1) A minimum registered capital of $1 million
(2) At least five personnel who have been engaged in international forwarding agency business for at least three years or with appropriate qualification certificates
(3) Permanent business premises
(4) Necessary business facilities and premises such as communications, transportation, loading and unloading, and packing facilities[80]

The permitted business activities include warehousing, freight forwarding, loading and unloading of freight, international courier services, and customhouse brokerage services. Upon approval, an agency may engage in all or a part of the following freight-forwarding activities:

(1) Booking (i.e., leasing of vessels, and chartering of airplanes and shipping space), consignment, warehouse storage, and packing
(2) Supervising loading and unloading, container grouping and unpacking, allocating goods, providing transit as well as related short-distance transport services
(3) Arranging customs declarations, customs examination and inspection, and insurance

77. FIE Freight Forwarding Agency Regulations, art. 3. An application is required to be accompanied by various supporting documents and materials including the articles of association, feasibility study, proof of corporate existence, creditworthiness letters, documents and information concerning the qualifications of principal personnel of the operation, and proof of business premises/facilities. FIE Freight Forwarding Agency Regulations, art. 9.

78. FIE Freight Forwarding Agency Regulations, art. 5.

79. FIE Freight Forwarding Agency Regulations, art. 6.

80. FIE Freight Forwarding Agency Regulations, art. 7.

(4) Preparing documents, payment of transportation fees, settlement of accounts and miscellaneous freight charges
(5) Agency business of international exhibits, personal items, and transportation of transit cargoes
(6) Arranging international transportation, container transport (including the packing of containers)
(7) International express delivery (excluding personal mail and postal services for official documents of provincial or higher branches of the party, government, or military)[81]
(8) Consultation and other international forwarding agency business[82]

The term of operation for an FIE Freight Forwarding Agency may not exceed twenty years.[83] After one year of operation, an agency may establish branch offices with a business scope that is consistent with the head office operation, and for each additional branch office, an agency is required to increase its registered capital by $120,000.[84]

On June 20, 2002, MOFTEC issued a *Notice on Relevant Issues Regarding the Experimental Establishment of Foreign-Invested Logistics Enterprises.*[85] The Logistics FIE Notice provides that a foreign-invested logistics company *"shall, according to actual requirements, be able to provide clients with multi-functional integrated supply-chain services of storage, loading and unloading, processing, packaging, delivery, information-handling, import and export, or other fields in a complete network for unified commodity shipment."* The Logistics FIE Notice permits two general types of foreign-invested logistics operations in China: (a) International Logistics and (b) Third-Party Logistics. An International Logistics FIE[86] will be permitted to undertake import and export trading and ancillary services, including self-operated or agency commodity import and export operations, and the receipt of entrustment to provide agency import and export operations, for exporting processing enterprises; and to provide international

81. The transport of mail and postal items requires approval from the Ministry of Post and obtaining a Postal Entrustment Certificate in order to engage in the transport of mail and postal articles. The transport of personal letters and most types of government-related documents is prohibited.
82. FIE Freight Forwarding Agency Regulations, art. 8.
83. FIE Freight Forwarding Agency Regulations, art. 10.
84. FIE Freight Forwarding Agency Regulations, art. 11. The application procedures and documentary requirements for establishing a branch office are outlined in Article 11 of the regulations. In particular, an applicant is required to submit verification that all registered capital has been contributed.
85. *Notice on Relevant Issues Regarding the Experimental Establishment of Foreign-Invested Logistics Enterprises* (promulgated by the MOFTEC, and effective as of July 19, 2002). *See generally* M. Dudek, A. Hotung, and C. Zhang, *Market Access Report: Logistics,* China L. & Prac. (April 2003); *A New Platform for Foreign Logistics Services Providers in China,* China L. & Prac. (Sept. 2002).
86. Logistics FIE Notice, art. 1.

freight forwarding business in relation to the imported/exported goods by sea, by air, or by land.[87]

A Third-Party Logistics FIE is permitted to engage in the transportation, warehousing, loading and unloading, processing, packaging, and distribution of regular goods by road, domestic cargo transportation agency (domestic freight forwarding), as well as information processing and related logistics services utilizing computer networks for management and shipping work.[88] A Logistics FIE is only permitted to take the form of an Equity Joint Venture or a Cooperative Joint Venture, and is not permitted to establish a wholly foreign-owned enterprise. Further, the equity ownership of the foreign investor(s) in an International Logistics FIE may not exceed 50 percent.[89]

For a Third-Party Logistics FIE, at least one investor must have achieved "*outstanding achievement and shipping experience in shipping transport or distribution services*"—that investor must be the largest shareholder among either the Chinese or foreign investors. Prima facie, this would indicate that it is possible for foreign investor(s) to hold a 99.9 percent shareholding in the Third-Party Logistics FIE. However, in practice, in circumstances in which a wholly foreign-owned enterprise is not permitted, MOFCOM is unlikely to permit a foreign-investor equity shareholding in excess of 75 percent.

The Logistics FIE Notice imposes a number of restrictions on the qualifications of the investing parties including as follows: For an International Logistics FIE, at least one investor (foreign or Chinese) must possess "*outstanding achievement and shipping experience in international trade, international commodities shipping, or international commodities shipping agency operations.*" The investor satisfying the above requirements must be the largest investor.

The minimum registered capital of a Logistics FIE may not be less than $5,000,000.[90] Existing FIEs seeking to expand their business scope to include logistics apparently qualify if they have existing investments of at least $5 million, and do not need to add $5 million to their existing investments. The term of a Logistics FIE may not exceed twenty years, but extension(s) may be permitted upon application to the approval authority.[91] Presently, Logistics

87. Logistics FIE Notice, art. 5 (1).
88. Logistics FIE Notice, art. 5 (2).
89. Logistics FIE Notice, art. 4 (2).
90. Logistics FIE Notice, art. 4 (1).
91. Logistics FIE Notice, art. 9.

FIEs are permitted on a trial basis only in Beijing, Tianjin, Shanghai, Chongqing, Zhejiang, Jiangsu, Guangdong, and Shenzhen.[92] These geographic restrictions did not appear in China's WTO commitments.

An application for the establishment of a Logistics FIE is processed through MOFCOM's sub-offices at the provincial level, but the operation is subject to the final approval of MOFCOM.[93] Additionally, Logistics FIEs may establish branch offices in accordance with the applicable laws and regulations governing the establishment of branch companies.[94]

The Logistics FIE Notice permits two types of logistics companies—the main difference between the two being that one possesses trading rights and one does not. But given the trading rights phase-in (with minority foreign-owned third-party logistics companies being granted trading rights from December 11, 2002), the difference between the Logistics FIE Notice's two types of logistics companies is unclear.[95]

(b) Ocean Shipping

The Ocean Shipping Regulations apply to enterprises engaged in international transportation and berth in Chinese ports, ocean shipping carriers, non-vessel operation common carriers (NVOCC), and those carriers offering specified auxiliary activities relating to ocean shipping such as ship agency, ship management, stevedoring, warehousing, and container loading business.[96]

92. Logistics FIE Notice, art. 12.

93. Logistics FIE Notice, art. 7. The documents required to be submitted for the government's review include (i) Application; (ii) Feasibility Study Report; (iii) Qualification certification of the investing parties, as well as explanatory information; (iv) Legal certification and credit standing certification of the investors; (v) Joint Venture Contract and Articles of Association; (vi) Name list and resumes of the directors and the chief executive personnel; (vii) Notification of the Preapproved Enterprise's Name issued by the administration of industry and commerce; (viii) Certification for the business location of the enterprise; and (ix) Other materials required by the approval authority.

94. Logistics FIE Notice, art. 10.

95. China's WTO commitments require the gradual phase-in of trading rights for all FIEs, beginning with FIEs with minority foreign investment from December 11, 2002, and thereafter expanding to include WFOEs by December 11, 2004.

96. International Sea Transportation Regulations (issued on December 11, 2002, by the State Council) (hereinafter "Ocean Shipping Regulations"). *See also* Provisions on Administration of Foreign Investment in International Maritime Transportation (issued on March 2, 2004, by the Ministry of Communications and the Ministry of Commerce). *See generally China Releases Rules on Foreign-Invested International Maritime Shipping,* CHINA MARKET INTELLIGENCE, THE U.S.-CHINA BUSINESS COUNCIL (May 5, 2004). The FIE Maritime Transport Provisions, effective June 1, 2004, allow for equity and contractual joint ventures in international shipping services, international shipping agency services, international ship management services, loading and unloading of international shipments and international maritime container freight stations, and container yard services. Enterprises offering international maritime cargo warehousing services and routine services for vessels owned or operated directly by the foreign investor may be set up as a WFOE or JV. Under the FIE Maritime Transport Provisions, an international shipping FIE is

Shipping companies must comply with certain conditions specified in the Regulations, such as: (i) the companies must own "suitable" vessels, including a number of Chinese-flagged ships; (ii) vessels must comply with ocean traffic safety and technology criteria; (iii) the companies must be capable of processing bills of lading, passenger tickets, and multimodal transport documents; and (iv) the vessels must have experienced business managers who have obtained employment and educational qualifications as designated by the Ministry of Communication (MOCM), the regulatory agency responsible for commercial issues related to China's inland waters and territorial sea.[97] The Ocean Shipping Regulations provide that ocean shipping businesses and auxiliary businesses are under MOCM supervision and freight-forwarding businesses are under MOFCOM supervision.

The Ocean Shipping Regulations prohibit foreign shipping companies' representative offices from establishing subsidiary companies to engage in commercial activities. Upon MOCM approval, foreign investors may invest in and incorporate a Sino-foreign equity or cooperative joint venture to operate an international shipping service, ship agency, ship management, stevedoring, warehousing, container station or container yard business, and incorporate a WFOE to engage in warehousing for ocean cargo. For joint venture enterprises, the foreign investor's equity interest and capital

---

required to have a fleet of PRC-registered vessels. The PRC party to an international shipping FIE must have both a controlling interest and management control over the operation (i.e., the foreign-invested interest must be 49% or less; and the chairman of the board of directors and the general manager are required to be appointed by the Chinese party). The PRC party to an international shipping agency FIE must have a controlling stake in the operation, and the enterprise must have electronic data interchange capabilities and at least two PRC senior executives with at least three years of experience in international maritime transportation business operations. The FIE Maritime Transport Provisions define "senior executives" as PRC citizens with secondary or higher technical or academic titles who serve as department managers or higher. The FIE Maritime Transport Provisions set out procedures for companies that wish to apply, change, or expand their scope of business; establish branches; or modify investment contributions, structure of shares, or articles of association.

97. To obtain approval to offer international liner services, shipping companies must submit an application to the MOCM that includes: (i) general company information, such as name and major shareholders; (ii) identification of the primary managers; (iii) particulars of ships involved; (iv) details of proposed routes, sailing schedules, and calling ports; and (v) tariff information. The MOCM is required to complete its examination of the application materials and to notify the applicant within 30 days after receipt of the submissions. The Ocean Shipping Regulations provide that business operators of international ship agency services must have (i) at least two senior business managers with more than three years of relevant experience, and (ii) a fixed place of business and necessary operating equipment. The Regulations provide that operators of international ship management businesses must have the following: (i) two senior managers with more than three years of relevant experience; (ii) employees who have certificates of captain and chief officer for the types of ships and sea areas; and (iii) necessary equipment and facilities. For shipping business, non-vessel carriage business, and ship agency business, applications are to be made to the central MOCM. International ship management businesses and auxiliary businesses relating to ocean shipping should apply to the local-level MOCM branch.

contributions may not exceed forty-nine percent (49%). The Regulations further provide that the Chinese investors in an Ocean Shipping JV are required to appoint the joint venture's chairman of the board of the directors and the general manager. The Ocean Shipping Regulations stipulate that if any country or territory adopts prohibitive, restrictive, or other similar measures in a discriminatory manner against PRC ocean transport operators, ships, or crew, the PRC government may adopt reciprocal measures.

The Ocean Shipping Regulations outline a tariff rate reporting policy, which requires that liner business operators and non-vessel carriage business operator (NVCBO) report their "published freight rates" and "contract price" to the MOCM.[98] Such rates and prices are effective for 30 days and 24 hours, respectively, after the MOCM accepts the report.[99] Ocean shipping companies engaged in international liner service are required to execute freight and tariff agreements with Chinese ports, and to provide MOCM with a copy of such agreements within 15 days of execution. The regulations require international ocean carriers and the NVCBOs to provide sample copies of bills of lading, passenger tickets, and multimodal transport documents to the MOCM.[100]

(c) Railway Cargo Transportation

The government permits foreign investment in the form of a joint venture to engage in railway cargo transportation activities. Foreign equity stake in such a joint venture may not be more than 49%, and the registered capital of the operation must be at least $25 million. The maximum term of operation of a rail transportation joint venture shall not exceed 20 years and the Chinese partner must be a railway transport enterprise with over 10 years of

98. The regulations define "non-vessel carriage business" as the non-vessel carriage business operator (NVCBO) or company that accepts a shipment as a carrier, issuing a bill of lading or other transport documents, imposing freight, completing the international ocean transportation, and undertaking international shipping business within the responsibilities of a carrier but without actually owning a vessel. To be approved as an NVCBO, the company must be a Chinese enterprise legal person, register its bill of lading, and pay a cash deposit to the MOCM of RMB800,000, plus an additional RMB200,000 for each branch office. Prior to signing an agreement with an NVCBO, an ocean carrier must confirm that the NVCBO has complied with the bill of lading filing requirement and has posted the required security.

99. International shipping carriers and NVCBOs may not (i) provide services at a secret discount; (ii) engage in anticompetitive activity such as discriminatory pricing; or (iii) otherwise harm their competitors or the international ocean shipping market.

100. Enterprises that have not registered a bill of lading are prohibited from engaging in a non-vessel carriage business.

experience in the railway cargo transportation sector.[101] Investments in the rail passenger transportation sector is currently not open to foreign investment.

15. Hospitals and Clinics

The government has adopted regulations pertaining to the establishment of foreign-funded hospitals and clinics.[102] The regulations provide that joint venture hospitals can be established with a total investment value of not less than RMB20 million ($2.5 million) and the equity share of the Chinese party of no less than thirty percent (30 percent). The term of the FIE JV hospital may not exceed twenty years, and wholly foreign-owned hospitals are not allowed.

16. Insurance

The China Insurance Regulatory Commission (CIRC) is the approval authority for FIE-related insurance business. Applicants are required to go through stringent approval procedures with approval taking several years to obtain. The law requires that insurers maintain certain capital requirements, deposit guarantee funds with the CIRC, and allocate reserve funds to cover claims. The law also regulates premium rates and sets forth reporting requirements.[103]

17. Journalists and Foreign News Agencies

A foreign news agency is required to apply for approval to dispatch a journalist to China or to establish a News agency office.[104] The current

101. Interim Measures on the Examination, Approval and Administration of Foreign Investment in the Railway Cargo Transportation Sector (promulgated on August 29, 2000, by the Ministry of Foreign Trade & Economic Cooperation and the Ministry of Railways). *See generally China to Allow Foreign Investment in Rail,* China Market Intelligence, The U.S.-China Business Council (November 30, 2001) (provides that there will be no limits on foreign equity ownership in such JVs after 2006).

102. Provisional Measures for the Administration of Sino-Foreign Equity Joint Venture and Cooperative Joint Venture Medical Institutions (promulgated on July 1, 2000, by the Ministry of Health and the Ministry of Foreign Trade and Economic Cooperation) *reprinted in* China Laws for Foreign Business (CCH), Business Regulation ¶ 6-635 (outlines the procedures and conditions for establishing JV medical institutions, application process, amendments and termination of operations, medical practice standards, supervision standards, etc.) (hereinafter the "FIE JV Hospital Regulations"). These measures supersede the Regulations on the Operation of Hospitals and Clinics for Foreigners and Overseas Chinese and the Practice of Medicine in China by Foreign Doctors (promulgated on February 10, 1989, by the Ministry of Public Health and the Ministry of Foreign Economic Relations and Trade) and the Relevant Examination and Approval Procedures Governing Foreign Investment in Establishment of Medical Institutions *reprinted in* 135 China International Business (MOFTEC) 50 (1998). *See generally Shanghai Seeks Foreign Capital for Medical Services*, China Daily (March 15, 2004).

103. For a discussion concerning the regulatory system for China's insurance industry, *see* Chapter 12, Insurance Law and Regulation § A.

104. *See* Administrative Regulations Governing Foreign Journalists and Resident Foreign News Agencies (promulgated on January 19, 1990, by the State Council), *reprinted in* China Laws for Foreign Business (CCH), Business Regulation ¶ 19-560; Measures of Beijing Municipality for Implementation of the Administrative Regulations Governing Foreign Journalists and Resident Foreign News Agencies

regulations were adopted after the Tiananmen Square incident in Beijing on June 4, 1989. Reporters must also abide by the confidentiality standards of the PRC. Online news service networks are required to be approved by the Chinese government's Xinhua News Agency under the 1996 Administrative Measures for the Dissemination of Economic Information Inside China by Foreign News Agencies and their Subscriber News Organizations. The users of online News service networks are required to register as well.[105]

In addition, foreigners are prohibited from investing in radio and television stations in China. In addition to a prohibition on foreign investments, the Radio and Television Rules set forth the requirements for radio and television stations, standards for programming, standards for advertisements, and standards for copyrights.[106] The rules also set forth the approval procedures for broadcasting foreign films or programs, and penalties for unauthorized broadcasting of foreign programs.

18. Lawyers and Law Firms

The State Council has adopted regulations governing the representative offices of foreign law firms in China, which are effective January 1, 2002.[107]

(promulgated on March 19, 1990, by the Beijing Municipal People's Government), *reprinted in* China Laws for Foreign Business (CCH), Business Regulation ¶ 19-562. *See* Regulations on Confidentiality in Publishing and the Media (jointly promulgated on August 3, 1992, by the State Administration of Media and Publications, the State Confidentiality Bureau, the Ministry of Broadcasting, Film and Television, and the Central Foreign Propaganda Group), *reprinted in* China Laws for Foreign Business (CCH), Business Regulation ¶ 19-578.

China also restricts the access of filmmakers and photographers to its cultural properties and cultural relics. The State Bureau of Cultural Relics plans to revise its 1984 regulations to allow for greater access to entertainment firms to boost international recognition for China's historical sites. *See* Shao, *Access to Cultural Properties for Filming to Be Eased,* China Daily (Sept. 11, 1998), available on Lexis, News Library, or on the Web site of the China Daily at http://www.chinadaily.com.cn.

105. *See generally China Regulations: Intranet Restrictions Create Waves,* EIU Views Wire (Nov. 30, 1998), available on Lexis, News Library.

106. *See* Administrative Rules on Radio and Television (promulgated on August 11, 1997, by the State Council), art. 10, *reprinted in* China Laws for Foreign Business (CCH), Business Regulation ¶ 19-632 (hereinafter the "Radio and Television Rules").

107. Administration Regulations of Representative Offices of Foreign Law Firms in China (promulgated by the State Council on December 22, 2001, and effective as of January 1, 2002) (hereinafter the "Foreign Law Firm Regulations"); Implementing Regulations of the Administration of Representative Law Firms in China Regulations (issued on July 1, 2002, and effective on September 1, 2002) (hereinafter the "Foreign Law Firm Implementing Regulations"). *See generally* Ministry of Justice Announcement No. 19 (115 China Representative Offices of Foreign Law Firms Approved to Practice in China) (issued on Oct. 8, 2003, by the Ministry of Justice); Ministry of Justice Announcement No. 20 (35 Mainland Representative Offices of Hong Kong Law Firms Approved to Practice on the Mainland) (issued on Oct. 8, 2003, by the Ministry of Justice). *See supra* Chapter 3, Legislating, the Judiciary, and Lawyers in China § B.1.3. *See also* Administrative Measures on Resident Representative Offices in Mainland China of Law Firms from Hong Kong and Macao Special Administrative Regions (promulgated as Order No. 70 of the Ministry of Justice of the People's Republic of China on March 13, 2002), *reprinted in* China Laws for Foreign Business (CCH), Business Regulation ¶ 7-610 (outlines the procedures and standards for establishing an office of a Hong Kong or Macao law firm on the Mainland, the business scope of rules of practice, supervision, and administration, and legal liability).

The Foreign Law Firm Regulations apply to foreign law firms that establish representative offices in China to engage in legal services, and provide that representative offices of foreign law firms and their representatives shall comply with professional ethics and practice disciplines of China and shall not harm China's national security and public interest.[108] Both law firms and their resident representatives are required to apply for approval and register with the lawyer supervision bureaus of the Ministry of Justice, and are required to have a record without disciplinary action by the home country of the law firm.[109] The MOJ may take up to six months to approve or reject an application for a practicing permit.[110] Upon receipt of a practicing permit, a representative office is required to complete all visa, labor, and taxation approvals in thirty days.[111] A representative office is not allowed to commence business operations until all application formalities are completed.[112]

108. Foreign Law Firm Regulations, arts. 2, 3. The Foreign Law Firm Implementing Regulations provide that a "foreign law firm" means an entity of foreign practicing lawyers established outside the PRC to provide non-PRC legal services with all or some of its members assuming joint and several civil liability. Foreign law firms do not include any association of two or more foreign lawyers or law firms who do not share profits and risks. Foreign Law Firm Implementing Regulations, art. 2. A "foreign practicing lawyer" means a person who has duly obtained legal practice qualifications and is licensed to practice law in the country where he/she obtains the legal practice qualifications. Foreign Law Firm Implementing Regulations, art. 3.

109. Foreign Law Firm Regulations, arts. 6–10. A foreign law firm's need to establish a representative office in China shall be based upon certain factors such as the social economic development and the legal service development of the proposed office location and the main practice areas and expertise of the foreign law firm. Foreign Law Firm Implementing Regulations, art. 4. To apply for establishment of an additional office, the foreign law firm shall have had a PRC representative office for at least three consecutive years and good compliance record in the PRC. Foreign Law Firm Implementing Regulations, art. 10. An applicant law firm is required to submit the following documents to the judicial administrative department of the city or province where the proposed Representative Office is to be established: (1) an application letter signed by the person principally in charge of the foreign law firm to set up the Representative Office and to assign a resident representative; (2) documents evidencing that the foreign law firm has been lawfully established in its home country; (3) a partnership agreement or Articles of Association of the foreign law firm and a list of responsible persons and partners; (4) authorizations from the foreign law firm to each of the proposed representatives of the Representative Office and the Confirmation Letter indicating that the proposed chief representative is a partner of, or holds an equivalent position in, the foreign law firm; (5) documents evidencing the qualifications of the proposed representatives to practice law, and evidencing that the proposed chief representative has practiced law outside China for no less than three years and that the other proposed representatives have practiced law outside China for no less than two years; (6) documents from the bar association in the country where the foreign law firm is established confirming the membership of each of the proposed representatives; and (7) documents from the judicial administrative institution in the country of the foreign law firm confirming that the foreign law firm and the proposed representative(s) have not been penalized for criminal offences or violations of professional ethics. The documents listed above shall be notarized by a notary public in the applicant's home country and certified by the foreign affairs authority or an organization authorized by the foreign affairs authority of the applicant's country, and shall further be certified by the embassy or consulate of China in the applicant's home country. Foreign law firms shall submit the documents in triplicate with Chinese translations attached for any document that is written in a foreign language. Foreign Law Firm Regulations, art. 8.

110. Foreign Law Firm Implementing Regulations, art. 13.

111. Foreign Law Firm Implementing Regulations, arts. 14, 15.

112. Foreign Law Firm Implementing Regulations, art. 16.

The MOJ restricts the type of work for which a foreign lawyer resident in China can be engaged. The Foreign Law Firm Regulations provide that registered representative offices and their resident representatives shall limit their services to:

(1) Advising on the laws of the countries where their lawyers are permitted to practice law and on international treaties and practices
(2) Handling, when instructed by clients or Chinese law firms, legal affairs of the countries where their lawyers are permitted to practice law
(3) Instructing, on behalf of their foreign clients, Chinese law firms to deal with Chinese legal affairs
(4) Entering into contracts to maintain long-term relations with Chinese law firms for legal affairs
(5) Advising on the impact of China's legal environment[113]

Representative offices of foreign law firms are prohibited from employing Chinese registered lawyers.[114] In addition, a foreign law firm and its parent law firm are forbidden to: (1) invest directly or indirectly in a PRC law firm; (2) form a profit-sharing or risk-sharing practicing arrangement with a PRC law firm or a PRC lawyer; (3) set up joint office with, or station its personnel in, a PRC law firm to provide legal services; or (4) manage, operate, control, or possess equity interest in a PRC law firm.[115] The Representative Offices may charge their clients for the provision of legal services set out in these Regulations and such fees must be settled within China.[116] The Foreign

113. Foreign Law Firm Regulations, art. 15. For the purpose of Article 15 of the Foreign Law Firm Regulations, the Implementing Regulations provide that a representative office (or its representative) will be deemed to be providing PRC legal services if it (1) participates in litigation in the PRC; (2) provides opinion or certifying statements on specific questions of written documents (including contracts, agreements, and articles of association) to which the PRC law shall apply; (3) provides opinion or certifying statements on acts or events to which the PRC law shall apply; (4) provides opinion or comments in the capacity of attorney in arbitration on the application of the PRC law and on facts which involve the PRC law; or (5) represents a client to handle registration, change, application, filing, and other procedures with the PRC government or other organizations authorized by law or regulations to exercise administrative functions. Foreign Law Firm Implementing Regulations, art. 32.

114. Foreign Law Firm Regulations, art. 16. Article 40 of the Foreign Law Firm Implementing Regulations provides that the following activities are deemed to be employing PRC-admitted lawyers: (1) to reach employment or labor agreement(s) with PRC-admitted lawyers; (2) to establish *de facto* employment or labor relationships with PRC-admitted lawyers; (3) to reach an agreement with a PRC-admitted lawyer on sharing profits or risks or participating in management; (4) to pay any remuneration, fees, or business dividends to PRC-admitted lawyers; or (5) to employ PRC-admitted lawyers to engage in external business activities on behalf of the representative office or the law firm to which the representative office is affiliated.

115. Foreign Law Firm Implementing Regulations, art. 39.

116. Foreign Law Firm Regulations, art. 20.

Law Firm Regulations outline various penalties, including monetary penalties and suspension of licenses, for violation of the Regulations.[117]

19. Leasing Companies

On August 14, 2001, MOFTEC issued the *Provisional Administrative Measures Regarding Examination and Approval of Foreign-Invested Leasing Companies*.[118] These Measures apply to foreign-invested leasing companies (FILC) that are established in China as Sino-foreign equity joint ventures or cooperative joint ventures. Under the FILC Measures, FILCs may be established as limited liability leasing companies to engage in finance leasing or other leasing businesses. The FILC Measures set forth the requirements for FILCs such as the term of operation, personnel qualifications, registered capital, business scope, and other issues. The FILC Measures outline the standards for qualifications of Chinese and foreign investors in such leasing companies as well as the required examination and approval process.

The FILC Measures address the requirements for two types of leasing joint ventures: the Financial Leasing Company (FLC), JVs involved with financial leasing business; and the Other Leasing Company (OLC), JVs engaging in any other type of leasing service.[119] The key difference between the two leasing vehicles is based upon whether ownership of the leased asset is transferred at the end of the lease term. Under the terms of a finance lease, the ownership of the leased property is transferred from lessor to lessee at the end of the lease term. In this case, the lessor's taxable income on the lease is the net value calculated by deducting the real cost of the leased asset from the total lease payments. If the lease JV is an OLC, no transfer of ownership takes place and as a result, the total lease payments constitute the lessor's taxable income.[120]

The FILC Measures require that the parties to a financial leasing company be financially strong. In this regard, the rules require that the Chinese investor to an FLC have total assets of not less than RMB400 million in the

117. Foreign Law Firm Regulations, arts. 24–33.

118. Provisional Administrative Measures regarding Examination and Approval of Foreign-Invested Leasing Companies (issued on August 14, 2001, by MOFTEC, effective on September 1, 2001), *reprinted in* China Laws for Foreign Business (CCH), Business Regulation ¶ 13-606 (hereinafter the "FLJV Measures"). *See also* Measures on the Management of Financial Leasing Companies (promulgated on June 30, 2000, as order No. 4 [2000] of the People's Bank of China), *reprinted in* China Laws for Foreign Business (CCH), Business Regulation ¶ 8-370.

119. FLJV Measures, art. 7.

120. FLJV Measures, arts. 12, 13. Leasing companies may engage in a broad range of leasing activities and goods. A leasing company must follow the law with respect to the importation of goods subject to quotas and licenses. FLJV Measures, art. 15.

year prior to the application and the foreign investor have total assets of not less than $400 million in the year prior to the application and at least five years' experience in the operation of a financial leasing business.[121] With respect to an OLC, the Chinese investor must have total assets of not less than RMB100 million in the year prior to the application, and the foreign investor must have total assets of not less than $50 million in the year prior to the application and have at least three years experience in the operation of a leasing business.[122]

The FILC Measures specify the qualifications for proposed FLCs and OLCs. A proposed FLC must meet the following conditions: (1) registered capital of at least $20 million; (2) the capital contribution of the Chinese party must be at least 20 percent of the registered capital; (3) the term of operation does not exceed thirty (30) years; and (4) the FLC has appropriate management personnel and the senior management personnel must have professional qualifications and at least three years of experience in the business.[123] JVs seeking to establish OLCs must meet the following requirements: (1) registered capital of at least $5 million; (2) the capital contribution of the Chinese Party must be at least 20 percent of the total registered capital of the joint venture; (3) the term of operation does not exceed twenty years; and (4) the OLC has appropriate management personnel and the senior management personnel must have professional qualifications and at least three years of experience in the industry.[124]

The FILC Measures require the investors to file an application for approval to MOFCOM. In addition to the application, the investors are required to submit a feasibility study, the parties' contract and articles of association, proof of corporate existence of the parties, letters of creditworthiness issued by the parties' banks, financial statements, list of the proposed board members, information substantiating the qualifications of management personnel, and other supporting documents.[125] Upon receipt of an approval certificate from MOFCOM, the applicant is required to register with SAIC to obtain a business license.[126]

121. FLJV Measures, art. 6.
122. FLJV Measures, art. 8.
123. FLJV Measures, art. 7.
124. FLJV Measures, art. 9.
125. FLJV Measures, art. 10.
126. FLJV Measures, art. 11.

20. Procurement Centers

The PRC government has adopted regulations governing the establishment of FIE export procurement centers, which permit a foreign investor to set up an operation for the purpose of procuring and exporting goods from China.[127] The FIE Procurement Center Provisions provide that foreign investors are permitted to establish a procurement center operation as either a joint venture or a WFOE with a minimum registered capital of RMB30 million ($3.63 million). The business scope of such an operation includes the following activities: (1) procuring domestic merchandise for export, and providing storage, information consulting, and technical services related to export; (2) importing raw and auxiliary materials, consigning them to other companies for processing, and exporting the processed materials; and (3) importing sample goods needed for export operations.[128] A foreign investor can establish an export procurement center through a China-based holding company or independently.[129] Upon submission of the application for approval, MOFCOM is required to approve or reject the application within 30 days.[130]

21. Securities Brokerage and Underwriting

The government, led by the China Securities Regulatory Commission (CSRC), has developed rules and regulations for securities brokerage and underwriting firms doing business in China.[131]

22. Travel Agencies and Tour Operators

China has adopted a set of rules governing travel agencies to allow foreign-invested travel agencies to conduct inbound and domestic tours within

127. Provisions on the Administration of Establishing Foreign-Invested Export Procurement Centers (promulgated on November 17, 2003, by the Ministry of Commerce, General Administration of Customs, State Administration of Taxation, and the State Administration of Foreign Exchange) (hereinafter the "FIE Procurement Center Provisions"). *See generally* Y. Xun, *Export Procurement Centres as a New Foreign-Invested Trading Vehicle,* CHINA L. & PRAC. (February 2004).

128. FIE Procurement Center Provisions, art. 7.

129. FIE Procurement Center Provisions, art. 5.

130. FIE Procurement Center Provisions, art. 6. The application materials include an application letter, documents substantiating corporate existence of the investor(s), feasibility study report, information concerning the members of the company's board of directors, and a pre-approval notice from the SAIC.

131. See Chapter 16, Securities Regulations § C.5. The China Securities Regulatory Commission (CSRC), in line with the Measures on Establishment of Foreign-Invested Securities Firms, released application forms and related documents on July 1. The documents on the CSRC Web site (http://www.csrc.gov.cn/) consist of three forms: the Application Form to Establish a Foreign-Invested Securities Firm; the Application Form for Transformation of a Domestic Securities Firm into a Foreign-Invested Securities Firm; and the Application Form for Qualifications of a Securities Firm's Overseas Employees holding Senior Management Posts.

China.[132] The Management Regulations on Administration of Travel Agencies and their implementing regulations were adopted on January 1, 2002, and require joint ventures to have at least RMB4 million ($484,000) in registered capital. The foreign partner must have no record of illegal activities for the last three years, have an annual income from tourism of more than $40 million, and be a member of its national tourism association. In order to be approved as a WFOE travel agency, the government requires annual sales of the foreign investor to be a minimum of $500 million.[133] The rules indicate that foreign-invested companies should apply directly to the China National Tourism Administration and the Ministry of Foreign Trade and Economic Cooperation for approval.

The FIE Travel Agency Regulations and WFOE Travel Agency Provisions correspond to the commitments made in China's WTO accession agreement. FIE Travel Agencies are not subject to limits on the services they may provide for travelers holding foreign passports. But when conducting business with mainland Chinese travelers, such companies may arrange only inbound tours and are prohibited from arranging outbound tours, including those to Hong Kong Special Administrative Region (SAR), Macao SAR, and Taiwan. The FIE Travel Agency Regulations do not specifically mention any geographic scope or limitations; however, the WFOE Travel Agency Provisions and China's WTO commitments indicate that travel agencies would be limited to providing service only in the cities of Beijing, Shanghai, Guangzhou, and Xian.[134] Although branch offices are not allowed, within six years after accession, the restrictions on establishment of branches as well as all geographic limitations will be eliminated, and at which time FIEs will be subject to the same rules as Chinese travel companies. Foreign partners will

---

132. Management Regulations on Administration of Travel Agencies (promulgated as State Council Order No. 334, adopted on December 11, 2001, and effective January 1, 2002); Implementing Regulations for Management Regulations on Administration of Travel Agencies (promulgated by the State Tourism Bureau Order No. 16, signed and effective Dec. 26, 2001). *See also* Establishment of Foreign-Controlled and Wholly Foreign-Owned Travel Agencies Tentative Provisions (promulgated by the China National Tourism Administration and the Ministry of Commerce on June 12, 2003) (hereinafter "WFOE Travel Agency Provisions"). *See also* Administration of Travel Agencies Procedures (promulgated on December 6, 1999, by the Shanghai Municipal Commission for the Administration of Tourism) (outlines procedures for licensing and regulating travel agencies that operate in Shanghai and states that foreign travel agencies may set up resident offices in Shanghai if they satisfy certain specified requirements and conditions, provides that the establishment of Sino-foreign joint venture travel agencies is subject to the relevant provisions of the administrative department in charge of tourism and the administrative department in charge of foreign trade and economic cooperation, and provides guidelines for various aspects of the relationship between a travel agency and a consumer, including travel contracts, insurance, safety, advertising, promotion methods, dispute resolution, and compensation). *See generally* M. Dudek & L. Zhu, *Market Access Report: Travel and Tourism*, CHINA L. & PRAC. (Oct. 2002); D. Yu, *New Provisions on Foreign Investment in the Tourism Industry*, CHINA L. & PRAC. (July 2003).

133. WFOE Travel Agency Provisions, art. 4.

134. WFOE Travel Agency Provisions, art. 7.

be allowed to take a majority stake in 2003, and wholly foreign-owned travel agencies will be permitted beginning in 2005.

C. Regulation of Technology, Industrial, and Manufacturing Sectors

In general, a foreign investment enterprise involved with production or operational activities is required to register with MOFCOM or a local branch and obtain a business license from the SAIC.[135]

1. Automotive Industry

Foreign investment in the automotive sector continues to increase annually, and notwithstanding a May 2003 report issued by the National Development and Reform Commission that outlines certain protectionist policies that target projected overcapacity in the industry.[136]

China also agreed to allow non-bank, foreign financial institutions to be able to provide financing for all forms of motor vehicles. With respect to foreign investment, provincial authorities are allowed to approve investments of up to $150 million (raised from $30 million), and China's joint-venture requirement has been revoked, which allows wholly foreign-owned production of engines.

2. Aviation and Airport Infrastructure Development

Effective August 1, 2002, foreign investors are allowed to take a noncontrolling interest in Chinese civil airlines and civil airports as well as in air tourism, aircraft maintenance, aviation fuels, and industrial service general

135. Administrative Measures on the Registration of Enterprises of Foreign Countries (Regions) Engaging in Production and Operational Activities within the Territory of China (promulgated August 15, 1992, by the SAIC), *reprinted in* China Laws for Foreign Business (CCH), Business Regulation ¶ 13-584 (hereinafter the "Production and Operational Activities Regulations").

136. The U.S.-China Business Council, China Operations 2003, Analysis: Foreign Investment in China, First Half 2003. (Report notes that several large investments were made in the auto sector in 2003, including an additional $218 million investment by Beijing Automotive Industry Holding Co. and DaimlerChrysler AG; $193.4 million project to produce heavy-duty trucks in Jinan by Volvo Truck Corporation and China National Heavy Duty Truck Corporation; $2 billion investment in trucks and cars by Dong Feng Motor Co. and Nissan Motor Co. Ltd.; and $944 million investment by Volkswagen into its existing operations in China.) In December 2003, various agencies launched a campaign to resolve problems in the auto industry. Pursuant to the Notice on the Campaign to Rectify the Auto Market, the government intends to examine and abolish local rules and laws that protect sales of locally made automobiles and discriminate against vehicles manufactured in other locations, and to crack down on the used auto market, on sales of counterfeit auto parts, and on substandard and fraudulent auto repair facilities. *See* Notice on the Campaign to Rectify the Auto Market (issued on December 11, 2003, by the Inter-Ministerial Coordinating Group), available in Chinese on the Web site of the Ministry of Commerce at http://www.mofcom.gov.cn.

aviation enterprises pursuant to regulations issued by the General Administration of Civil Aviation of China (CAAC).[137] The Regulation on Foreign Investment in the Civil Aviation Industry (Order No. 110), which was jointly issued by CAAC, the Ministry of Foreign Trade and Economic Cooperation, and the State Development Planning Commission, limits foreign participation by any one foreign investor and its subsidiaries to 25 percent in civil airlines and caps total foreign investment at 49 percent per project, prohibits investment in air traffic control systems, and limits all joint venture contracts to a maximum of thirty years.[138]

The Aviation Investment Regulations also promote foreign participation in aviation-related sectors such as ground services, airline food service and catering, freight storage, and airport parking. With respect to investments in aviation in the rural areas of China, the Aviation Investment Regulations provide that investment limits are open to negotiation between prospective partners. The new regulation does not require that board chairs and general managers be Chinese, and allows foreign investors to buy aviation company stocks listed domestically or overseas, which will encourage future aviation sector listings.

In September of 2003, the State Council issued an order shifting the ownership of 93 regional and local airports (excluding the airports in Beijing and Lhasa) from CAAC to local government authorities effective at the end of 2003. As a result of this restructuring process, the central government shifted the management and financial burden of maintaining China's airports to the local governments. In addition to shifting ownership to the local governments, the State Council encouraged local authorities to increase

137. Regulation on Foreign Investment in the Civil Aviation Industry (Order No. 110) (jointly issued on December 10, 2001, by the General Administration of Civil Aviation of China, the Ministry of Foreign Trade and Economic Cooperation, and the State Development Planning Commission, and promulgated by the State Council on June 21, 2002), *reprinted in* China Laws for Foreign Business (CCH), Business Regulation ¶ 13-615 (hereinafter the Aviation Investment Regulations). For the Chinese text of the regulation, see the Web site of CAAC at http://www.caacjournal.com. *See generally* Coleman, *Airlines Keep Plugging Away at Promising Chinese Market,* Wall Street Journal Online, July 10, 2002; *Chinese Aviation Opens Wider to Foreign Investors,* People's Daily Online, July 4, 2002; A. Lockhart & H. Lau, *Flying High: China's Aviation Industry Looks to the Future,* China L. & Prac. (Nov. 2003); *Mainland Airports Transferred to Local Governments; Foreign Investors May Benefit,* China Market Intelligence, The U.S.-China Business Council (October 22, 2003). *See also* Notice of the State Administration of Taxation on Questions Concerning the Application of Preferential Tax Treatment for Foreign Investment Enterprises Which Engage in Special Investment Projects Such as Harbors and Wharves (promulgated on August 4, 1995, by the SAT), *reprinted in* China Laws for Foreign Business (CCH), Taxation ¶ 32-634 (an FIE that engages in infrastructure projects such as harbor, wharf, airport, railroad, highway, power generation, mining, water conservation, communications, or agriculture development operation may enjoy preferential treatment).

138. The regulations supersede a 1994 CAAC notice that provided that foreign investors were allowed up to a 35-percent stake in airlines and a 49-percent stake in airport construction enterprises.

private investment in airport facilities, including investments by foreign parties under the guidance of the Aviation Investment Regulations.

3. Energy and Power Generation

In 1996, the NPC adopted the first electricity law that addresses the establishment of power generation facilities, preferential policies, liability, and the production, supply, and consumption of electric power. The law provides a general legal framework for foreign investors interested in the domestic energy production market.[139]

4. Mineral Resources Exploration and Exploitation

The Mineral Resources Law outlines the registration requirements for mining operations, obligations and restrictions on exploration rights, exploration and extraction methods, liability issues, and administrative penalties for violations. The law and implementing regulations provide detailed

139. Electric Power Law of the PRC (adopted and promulgated on December 28, 1995, by the 17th Sess. of the Standing Comm. of the 8th NPC), *reprinted in* CHINA LAWS FOR FOREIGN BUSINESS (CCH), Business Regulation ¶ 19-604; Operation of the Power Markets Basic Rules (Trial Implementation) (issued by the State Electricity Regulatory Commission on July 31, 2003) (outlines the procedures for governing the power market operations, and sets forth terms standards and terms for market operators, power generation enterprises, standards for power market transactions, standards for power transmission services, standards for electricity metering and payment settlement, procedures for power system safety, and standards for the release and dissemination of date and information concerning the power markets); Accelerating the Marketization of the Urban Utilities Industry Opinion (issued on December 27, 2002, by the Ministry of Construction) (the opinion outlines the views of the Ministry of Construction on the ongoing trend toward privatization of public utilities, sets forth the general administrative legal basis for privatization, and states that foreign investment in the form of JVs or WFOEs is encouraged for the construction of urban utility facilities). The Foreign Investment Industrial Guidance Catalogue provides that the construction and operation of gas, thermal energy, and water supply networks in large and medium-sized cities are encouraged. *See generally* A. Kearney, *Private Investment in Urban Utilities,* CHINA L. & PRAC. (February 2003), M. Arruda & K. Li, *China's Energy Sector: Development, Structure and Future*, CHINA L. & PRAC. (November 2003); Zheng, *New Power Projects to Be Bid Out Publicly,* CHINA DAILY, July 13, 1998, available on Lexis, News Library, or on the Web site of the CHINA DAILY at http://www.chinadaily.com.cn. *See also* Provisions on Electric Power Projects Invested by Foreign Investors (issued on March 20, 1997, by the Ministry of Power Industry), *reprinted in* 127 CHINA INTERNATIONAL BUSINESS (MOFTEC) 46 (1998) (addresses the scope of foreign investment in power projects, approval procedures, requirements for equipment purchases, pricing of electricity, requirements for contract provisions, and applicable law and dispute resolution); Interim Provisions for Submission and Approval Procedure on Electric Power Project Invested Directly by Foreigners (issued on December 9, 1997, by the Ministry of Power Industry), *reprinted in* 127 CHINA INTERNATIONAL BUSINESS (MOFTEC) 46 (1998) (outlines detailed procedures for approval procedures, including the required content of the feasibility study and project proposal). For a general discussion concerning foreign investment with regard to natural gas–related energy projects, *see* C. Pan, *Gas: A New Direction in Power Generation,* CHINA L. & PRAC. (December 1999); C. Pan, *Gas Revisited: New Policies and Incentives for Foreign Investment,* CHINA L. & PRAC. (September 2000). For the standards for tax treatment for energy infrastructure projects, *see* Notice of the State Administration of Taxation on Questions Concerning the Application of Preferential Tax Treatment for Foreign Investment Enterprises Which Engage in Special Investment Projects Such as Harbors and Wharves (promulgated on August 4, 1995, by the SAT), *reprinted in* CHINA LAWS FOR FOREIGN BUSINESS (CCH), Taxation ¶ 32-634 (an FIE that engages in infrastructure projects such as harbor, wharf, airport, railroad, highway, power generation, mining, water conservation, communications, or agriculture development operation may enjoy preferential treatment).

requirements for applications and registration of mining operations, rights and obligations of holders of exploration rights, reporting requirements, fees, and dispute resolution.[140] The Ministry of Land and Natural Resources has adopted regulations with respect to the methods for obtaining mineral exploration and mining rights.[141]

5. Petroleum Exploration and Exploitation

The oil and gas industry in China has its own set of regulations concerning conditions for approval of exploration operations and registration requirements.[142]

140. *See* Mineral Resources Law of the People's Republic of China (originally adopted on March 19, 1986, and amended on August 29, 1996, by the 21st Sess. of the Standing Comm. of the 8th NPC), *reprinted in* CHINA LAWS FOR FOREIGN BUSINESS (CCH), Business Regulation ¶ 14-711; Detailed Rules for the Implementation of the Mineral Resources Law of the People's Republic of China (promulgated on March 26, 1994, by the State Council), *reprinted in* CHINA LAWS FOR FOREIGN BUSINESS (CCH), Business Regulation ¶ 14-700; Administrative Regulations Governing Collection of Mineral Resource Royalty Fees (promulgated on February 27, 1994, by the State Council), *reprinted in* CHINA LAWS FOR FOREIGN BUSINESS (CCH), Business Regulation ¶ 14-703 (outlines rules for royalty computation for mining operations); Certain Suggestions on Further Encouraging Foreign Investment in the Exploration and Mining of Non-Petroleum Non-Gas Resources (issued by the Ministry of State Land and Natural Resources, State Planning Commission, State Economic and Trade Commission, Ministry of Finance, Ministry of Foreign Trade and Economic Cooperation, and State Administration of Industry and Commerce on September 28, 2000), *reprinted in* CHINA LAWS FOR FOREIGN BUSINESS (CCH), Business Regulation ¶ 14-561. *See* Provisional Management Rules on Foreign Investment in Rare Earth Industry (issued on August 1, 2002, by the State Development Planning Commission) (Rules limit foreign investment in the rare earth industry—metallic compounds used in high-tech or military applications—to abstraction/ore dressing, processing facilities, and applications development, and WFOEs are disallowed).

141. Administration of Invitation for Bids, Auction and Listing of Exploration Rights and Mining Rights Procedures (Trial Implementation) (issued by the Ministry of Land and Natural Resources on June 11, 2003, and effective on August 1, 2003) (outlining the procedures for bid, auction, and listing of mining rights); Administration of Registration of Mineral Resource Exploration Blocks Procedures (issued by the Ministry of Land and Natural Resources on February 12, 1998); Administration of Registration for Exploitation of Mineral Resources Procedures (issued by the Ministry of Land and Natural Resources on February 12, 1998). *See generally* M. Ward & C. Izzard, *Obtaining a Right to Mine in the PRC: Impediments and Opportunities,* CHINA L. & PRAC. (July 2003); *Unearthing Mine Rights in the PRC,* CHINA L. & PRAC. (May 2001).

142. *See* Provisional Measures Governing Control of Registration of Oil and Natural Gas Exploration and Exploitation (approved on December 16, 1987, by the State Council and promulgated on December 24, 1987, by the Ministry of Petroleum Industry), *reprinted* in CHINA LAWS FOR FOREIGN BUSINESS (CCH), Business Regulation ¶ 14-661 (outlining registration requirements for exploration/exploitation operations); Regulations of the People's Republic of China on the Exploitation of Offshore Petroleum Resources in Cooperation with Foreign Enterprises (adopted on January 30, 1982, by the State Council, and revised and re-promulgated on Sept. 23, 2001, by the State Council), *reprinted* in CHINA LAWS FOR FOREIGN BUSINESS (CCH), Business Regulation ¶ 14-560 (regulations outlining the requirement of exploration/exploitation contracts, operational issues, and obligations of the parties to an offshore petroleum contract); Regulations on the Payment of Royalties for the Exploitation of Offshore Petroleum Resources (promulgated on January 1, 1989, by the Ministry of Finance), *reprinted* in CHINA LAWS FOR FOREIGN BUSINESS (CCH), Business Regulation ¶ 14-565 (outlining rules for royalty payments for offshore operations); Regulations Regarding the Exploitation of Onshore Oil Resources in Cooperation with Foreign Parties (promulgated on September 23, 2001, by the State Council) (outlines the standards for cooperative onshore exploration projects, rights of foreign contractors, standards for petroleum operations, legal liability, and settlement of disputes); Provisional Regulations on the Payment of Sino-Foreign Co-Operative Ventures of Royalties for the Exploitation of Onshore Oil Resources (promulgated and issued by the Ministry of Finance and approved by the State Council on January 13, 1990), *reprinted* in CHINA LAWS FOR FOREIGN BUSINESS (CCH), Business Regulation ¶ 14-640 (outlining royalty payments

6. Port Administration and Infrastructure Development

The government has adopted a law establishing a basic framework for port administration, operations, and development.[143] The Port Administration Law covers three principal areas including port planning and construction, operation and management, and safety and inspection administration.[144] The law mandates that the Ministry of Communication is the responsible agency for overall port planning and supervision; however, the daily operations of ports may be delegated to local authorities and enterprises. The Port Administration Law encourages both domestic and foreign investment in the construction of ports and provides that the State shall protect the lawful rights of investors in port-related projects. Under the law, port operators are required to apply to the Ministry of Communication or delegated port authority for an operating license prior to commencing operations.[145] Port-related activities subject to licensing include dock and port installation activities, tourist transportation services, loading and unloading activities, warehousing activities, and port hauling activities. Port operators must meet certain standards under the law, such as having fixed premises, sufficient equipment, and qualified personnel.[146] The Port Administration Law specifically requires that port administrators issue operating licenses in a transparent and fair manner, and

for onshore and inland oil exploration operations). China has also adopted special environmental protection rules for offshore oil producers that require the preparation of a marine environmental impact report. *See* Regulations of the People's Republic of China Concerning Environmental Protection in Offshore Oil Exploration and Exploitation (promulgated on December 29, 1983, by the State Council), *reprinted* in CHINA LAWS FOR FOREIGN BUSINESS (CCH), Business Regulation ¶ 14-660. For a discussion concerning the impact of institutional reform on the petroleum regulatory environment, *see For China's Oil Industry: What Has Reorganization Achieved?*, 135 CHINA INTERNATIONAL BUSINESS (MOFTEC) 25 (1998).

143. Port Administration Law (promulgated on June 28, 2003, by the Standing Committee of the NPC) (hereinafter the "Port Administration Law"). The law is effective on January 1, 2004. *See also* Ports Law (adopted at the 3rd Session of the Standing Committee of the 10th NPC, promulgated on June 28, 2003, and effective as of January 1, 2004). *See generally* L. Qiang, *Foreign Investment in the Yangshan Deep-sea Port,* CHINA L. & PRAC. (October 2003). *See also* Notice of the State Administration of Taxation on Questions Concerning the Application of Preferential Tax Treatment for Foreign Investment Enterprises Which Engage in Special Investment Projects Such as Harbors and Wharves (promulgated on August 4, 1995, by the SAT), *reprinted in* CHINA LAWS FOR FOREIGN BUSINESS (CCH), Taxation ¶ 32-634 (an FIE that engages in infrastructure projects such as harbor, wharf, airport, railroad, highway, power generation, mining, water conservation, communications, or agriculture development operation may enjoy preferential treatment).

144. During the process of formulating port plans, debates among relevant experts shall be organized, and an environmental impact assessment shall be conducted according to law. Port Administration Law, arts. 7, 15.

145. Port Administration Law, art. 22. The port administrative department is required to make decisions according to whether or not to grant port operating licenses within 30 days after its receipt of the written application. If a license is granted, a certificate of license for port operations shall be issued. If an application for license is denied, the applicant shall be notified in writing of the reasons for such denial. Port Administration Law, art. 24.

146. Port Administration Law, art. 23.

port operators are prohibited from engaging in monopolistic activities or acts of unfair competition.[147]

7. Production and Manufacturing Activities

FIEs involved with production and manufacturing activities are required to obtain the approval of MOFCOM to engage in production-type activities.[148]

8. Publishing

The State Council has adopted regulations that apply to publishing activities in China, which include publication, printing, reproduction, import, and distribution of publications.[149] Pursuant to the Publishing Administration Regulations, the establishment of any publishing operation, publication distributor, or trading company engaged in the importation of publications is required to be approved by the State Council's General Administration of Press and Publishing.[150] With government approval, a printing or reproduction enterprise may accept printing or reproduction business from foreign parties with the stipulation that the publication's contents to be printed or reproduced shall be subject to review by the authorities and upon completion of the work exported from China.[151] The regulations further provide that the importation of newspapers and periodicals shall be facilitated by certain trading companies authorized by the General Administration of Press and Publishing.[152] The GAPP and its provincial-level branches have the authority to review and prohibit the importation of any publications

147. Port Administration Law, art. 29.

148. Administrative Measures on the Registration of Enterprises of Foreign Countries (Regions) Engaging in Production and Operational Activities within the Territory of China (promulgated August 15, 1992, by the SAIC), *reprinted in* CHINA LAWS FOR FOREIGN BUSINESS (CCH), Business Regulation ¶ 13-584 (hereinafter the "Production and Operational Activities Regulations").

149. Administration of Publishing Regulations (promulgated on December 25, 2001, by the State Council, and effective on February 1, 2002), *reprinted in* CHINA LAWS FOR FOREIGN BUSINESS (CCH), Business Regulation ¶ 19-613 (hereinafter referred to as the "Publishing Administration Regulations"). The regulations repealed the previous Administration of Publishing Regulations adopted on January 2, 1997. For a discussion of the publishing regulations prior to 2001, *see Distributing Publications in China: Foreigners Kept Out,* CHINA L. & PRAC. (May 2000). *See also* Regulations of the Printing Industry (Order No. 315 of the State Council, promulgated on August 2, 2001), *reprinted in* CHINA LAWS FOR FOREIGN BUSINESS (CCH), Business Regulation ¶ 19-616 (outlining the standards for establishing a printing business, rules for printing of publications and packaging, legal liability, etc.).

150. Publishing Administration Regulations, art. 12, 36, 43. Publishing operations that are limited in geographic scope are to be approved at the provincial level. *Id.* at 32.

151. Publishing Administration Regulations, art. 34.

152. Publishing Administration Regulations, art. 41.

intended for import.[153] The Publishing Administration Regulations specifically provide that foreign investment in a publication distribution business is permitted; however, the approval of FIEs is governed by a separate set of regulations.[154]

The GAPP has issued a set of regulations governing the distribution of foreign-invested publications.[155] Under the FIE Publications Procedures, the term "distribution business" means the retail and wholesaling of books, newspapers, and periodicals. The procedures also define "foreign-invested books, newspapers and periodicals distributors" to refer to joint venture or WFOE distributors of books, newspapers, and periodicals.[156] The FIE Publications Procedures also specifically apply to the establishment and supervision of books, newspapers, and periodicals distributors by investors from Hong Kong, Macao, and Taiwan.[157]

The FIE Publications Procedures provide that foreign investors may purchase shares of or merge with domestic publications distributors for the purpose of establishing a foreign-invested books, newspapers, and periodicals distributor.[158] FIE publications distributors may be set up as limited liability companies or companies limited by shares, and are required to have minimum registered capital of RMB30 million (distributors) and RMB5 million (retailers).[159] The maximum term of operation of an FIE publications operation is thirty years.[160] The FIE Publications Procedures set forth in detail the application procedures for establishment of a foreign-invested books, newspapers, and periodicals distributor.[161] The procedures outline the standards and approval process for FIE distributors that wish to engage in online sales, chain store operations, or book clubs.[162]

---

153. Publishing Administration Regulations, art. 44.
154. Publishing Administration Regulations, art. 39.
155. Administration of Foreign-Invested Books, Newspapers, and Periodicals Distributors Procedures (issued on March 17, 2003, by the General Administration of Publishing and Publications, and effective on May 1, 2003, or December 1, 2004, for wholly foreign-owned enterprises) (hereinafter the "FIE Publications Procedures"). *See generally* P. Qu & A. Zichterman, *Filling the Gap: Foreign Acquisitions in the Publishing Distribution Sector*, China L. & Prac. (February 2004).
156. FIE Publications Procedures, art. 2.
157. FIE Publications Procedures, art. 21.
158. FIE Publications Procedures, art. 2.
159. FIE Publications Procedures, art. 3.
160. FIE Publications Procedures, arts. 7, 8.
161. FIE Publications Procedures, arts. 9–14.
162. FIE Publications Procedures, arts. 7–14.

Key Laws and Regulations

Catalogue Guiding Foreign Investment in Industry (Joint Order [2002] No. 21), promulgated on March 13, 2002, by the State Development and Planning Commission (SDPC), State Economic and Trade Commission (SETC), and Ministry of Foreign Trade and Economic Cooperation (MOFTEC)

Issuing of Guidelines of Shanghai Municipality for Foreign Investment in Industry Circular (promulgated by the Shanghai Development and Reform Commission, the Shanghai Foreign Economic Relations and Trade Commission, and the Shanghai Economic Commission on and effective as of September 15, 2003)

Catalogue of Encouraged Foreign Investment in High and New Technology Products (2003) (issued on July 18, 2003, by the Ministry of Commerce and the Ministry of Science and Technology)

Chapter 6

Information Technology, Telecommunications, and Software Development

The information technology market in China presents unique opportunities for foreign investors.[1] Over the years, China's IT market has evolved considerably as various government agencies were created and/or merged to enhance the regulatory environment for IT, telecommunications, E-commerce, and related sectors.

The creation of the Ministry of Information Industry (MII) in 1998 offered little encouragement for foreign investors as a result of the MII's policies toward foreign investors, domestic competition, and its efforts to preserve the competitive position of China Telecom at the expense of consumers, local competitors, and foreign investors. The MII is basically an agency that is comprised of former MPT officials that favor the MPT-created China Telecom over all other players, including the former Ministry of Electronics Industry-created China Unicom. China Telecom has been resistant to foreign investors and has taken steps to quash efforts by local enterprises that attempt to compete, including China Unicom.[2] After years of debate, the MII has divided

1. *See generally* ExportIT China, International Trade Administration, U.S. Department of Commerce (2003), available online at http://www.ita.doc.gov. The ExportIT China report addresses the market opportunities and challenges for U.S. exporters of IT-related products and services.

2. As an example, the MII, at the behest of China Telecom, placed a ban on the so-called "Chinese-Chinese-Foreign" (CCF) telecom joint ventures that China Unicom created with close to 45 different foreign companies. The CCF JVs were structured as a means to circumvent the regulations on the ban against foreign investment in telecom services companies. A CCF venture is one in which the foreign company forms a JV with a Chinese company thereby creating a Chinese entity. The new Chinese entity in

China Telecom into three distinct businesses (fixed line phone services, mobile communications, and paging services) and claims that the restructuring process will lead to more competition. Since the three business groups will not be in competition with one another, it is unlikely that the restructuring process will lead to competition in the marketplace. Only by allowing other parties to compete with the three groups will there be true competition that will benefit the consumer (and foreign parties that wish to participate in the market).[3] Now that China is a member of the WTO, the door is opened to a limited

---

turn forms a joint venture with a Chinese telecommunications operator. The MII claims that the ban is nothing more than the enforcement of preexisting rules. The policies of the MII (and China Telecom) are anticompetitive as they relate to the efforts of even local Chinese companies that attempt to compete. As an example, China Telecom initiated a criminal prosecution against a local company that attempted to provide international telecom services. Even though the government lost the case, they still took steps to quash the competition. In January 1999, the Fuzhou Intermediate People's Court in Fujian Province ruled that an Internet Protocol (IP) telephone service is not subject to China's State telecom monopoly. In what appears to be a landmark case involving the Internet's use in China, the appellate court overruled a lower court's ruling and found that a State Council circular issued in 1993 did not grant a monopoly to China Telecom for all Internet telephone business. The lower court convicted the two defendant brothers of violating Article 250 of China's Criminal Law, which outlaws any unlicensed operation in monopolized businesses. The lower court agreed with the Public Security Bureau—which was encouraged by China Telecom—that the defendants illegally operated an international long-distance calling service, which is a State monopoly in China, and that the PSB was simply enforcing the criminal laws. Based on the opinions of Internet experts, the Intermediate People's Court ruled that international calls using the Internet are technologically different from conventional international telephone calls. Following the court ruling, the Ministry of Information Industry (MII) publicly stated that it is illegal for unauthorized companies to operate IP phone service in China. The MII maintains that only China Telecom and China Unicom are authorized by the State Council to provide basic telecom services in China, and China Telecom is the only authorized entity to operate international telecom service. The MII further stated that they will encourage the crackdown on companies illegally providing domestic long distance and international IP phone services. IP phone service providers in Henan, Guangdong, and Shanghai have been raided and had their equipment confiscated. The MII contends that IP phone service providers use the government-built Internet infrastructure to run their IP phone businesses without paying the conventional transmission fee and argues that the MII's position is supported by Article 250 of China's Criminal Law and MII's Notice No. 573 of September 18, 1998, that states that only Internet information services are permitted. The Chief Judge at the Fuzhou Intermediate People's Court, Qu Feng, responded to the comments of the MII by stating that "in adherence to the principle of non-retroactivity, the court can make its determination based on the 1993 Circular issued by the State Council, but not on the 1998 Notice by MII." Qu further stated that "the rule of law was stressed at the 15th Communist Party Congress [and] one of the important features of a country under the rule of law is that the whole society must abide by the principle of 'No crime without a law.' " See *China-Internet Users Ruled Innocent,* CHINA DAILY (Jan. 21, 1999), available on Lexis, News Library, or on the Web site of the CHINA DAILY at http://www.chinadaily.com.cn; *China to Ban Illegal Telecom Business,* XINHUA NEWS AGENCY (Feb. 5, 1999), available on Lexis, News Library; *China—Contradictions on Internet Telephony,* INTERNATIONAL MARKET INSIGHT REPORTS (Feb. 8, 1999), available on Lexis, News Library. In another Internet case, a court in Shanghai convicted a Web site builder in December 1998 under Article 105 of the Criminal Law for sending 30,000 e-mail addresses to a Chinese dissident magazine in Washington, D.C. Although the defendant provided the addresses to the magazine to bolster his own business, the dissidents used the addresses for political pamphleteering. The court found the act of handing out the e-mails to be subversive. Vines, *China Fires the First Shot in Internet War,* THE INDEPENDENT (London) 15 (Dec. 4, 1998), available on Lexis, News Library; Goodale, *China's Great Internet Trial,* NEW YORK LAW JOURNAL 3 (Feb. 5, 1999), available on Lexis, News Library.

3. In order to meet the government's 8-percent growth objectives, China has taken steps to stimulate the domestic economy by investing in infrastructure construction including telecom. As a result, China is spending a significant amount of money on fiber-optic cable and microwave transmission equipment. For example, in July 1998 China Telecom signed fourteen contracts with various foreign companies, including Lucent, NEC, Alcatel, Nortel, Siemens, and Fujitsu worth $110 million for fiber-optic cable and

degree over the first three years since accession.[4] At present, there are six large basic telecom operators, including China Telecom, China Mobile, China Netcom, China Unicom, China Satellite, and China Railcom, and more than 4,000 value-added telecom operators nationwide.

In September 2000, the State Council adopted a set of regulations that regulate the telecommunications industry.[5] The Telecom Regulations address various matters concerning the telecom infrastructure, standards for operators, foreign participation, security issues, and other matters concerning the industry. The Telecom Regulations apply to any telecommunication activity or activity relevant to telecommunications undertaken within the territory of the People's Republic of China. For the purposes of the Telecom Regulations, "telecommunications" refers to the conveyance, transmission, or reception of voice, text, data, images, or any other form of information through wired or wireless electromagnetic or optic-electric systems.[6]

The Ministry of Information Industries (MII), and its local branch administrations, is the regulatory agency responsible for enforcing the Telecom Regulations and managing the nationwide telecommunication industry.[7] The Telecom Regulations mandate that the MII follow the principles of separating

---

microwave transmission equipment. The cable is earmarked for the twelve fiber-optic cable trunks in the country and involves dense wavelength division multiplexing technology. The microwave technology uses synchronous digital hierarchy technology. Both technologies are supposed to significantly increase in-line transmission capacity and will add 3 million transmission lines to China's national trunk line network. Although there is tremendous opportunity to assist China in developing its telecom infrastructure—including both the fixed-line and mobile markets—the trend with respect to the opportunities for mobile equipment appears to be moving away from U.S. companies such as Qualcomm (with its CDMA technology) and more toward the European-developed technology (GSM). This trend, however, may change with the right influence on the regulators. As a result, the China market is likely to become a battleground for the foreign sellers of mobile equipment over the next six months. *See* Arnold, *China Suspends Plans to Adopt Phone Standard,* ASIAN WALL STREET JOURNAL 7 (Feb. 24, 1999), available on Lexis, News Library.

4. China's participation in the WTO Agreement on Basic Telecommunications Services (BTA) commits China to the gradual opening of its telecom services sector to foreign participation. Among other things, the BTA sets forth provisions that provide safeguard against anticompetitive practices, and promotes competition for interconnection rights, cost-based pricing, transparency, and the creation of an independent regulatory authority that operates without commercial interests in the telecom sector. Under WTO, China is required to open its market as follows: (1) Mobile Voice and Data Services under the following schedule: Upon Accession, 25 percent, in Shanghai, Guangzhou, and Beijing; One Year after Accession, 35 percent, Another 14 Cities; Three Years after Accession, 49 percent, No Geographic Restrictions; (2) Domestic Services and International Services: Three Years after Accession, 25 percent, in Shanghai, Guangzhou, and Beijing; Five Years after Accession, 35 percent, Another 14 Cities; Six Years after Accession, 49 percent, No Geographic Restrictions.

5. Telecommunication Regulations of the People's Republic of China, Order No. 291 of the State Council of the People's Republic of China Promulgated 25 September 2000 and effective on promulgation, *reprinted in* CHINA LAWS FOR FOREIGN BUSINESS (CCH), Business Regulation ¶ 19-520 (hereinafter the "Telecom Regulations"). *See generally* A. Subrahmanyan, *Looking Ahead: Issues in China's Telecommunications Law*, CHINA L. & PRAC. (March 2004).

6. Telecom Regulations, art. 2.

7. Telecom Regulations, art. 3. The Telecom Regulations mandate that the security of the telecommunication network and of information shall be protected by law, and that no government organization or individual shall be allowed to exploit the telecommunication network in any way that endangers national security, public interest, or the lawful rights or interests of another party. Art. 6.

government administration from enterprise management, eliminating monopolies, encouraging competition, promoting development, and practicing transparency.[8]

A. Telecommunications and Internet

1. Permit Procedures for Telecommunication Services

The Telecom Regulations provide for the implementation of a permit system for telecommunication service operations according to the classification of the telecommunication services. To operate a telecommunication service, a service provider must first obtain a permit from the MII or the telecommunication administration authority of the province, autonomous region, or centrally administered municipality in accordance with the Telecom Regulations.[9]

---

8. Telecom Regulations, art. 4. *See also* Notice on Several Issues Concerning Domestic Joint Ventures Engaging in Telecoms Services Established by Telecoms Operators, issued by the MII on July 26, 2001 (Reiterating that companies providing telecom services must obtain operation permits. Joint Ventures, in which telecoms operators hold 51 percent more, should file with the MII or its local counterparts and apply for operation permits. Other Joint Ventures, in which telecoms operators have held less than 51 percent, should apply for operation permits as new entities, a process that could take a long time.); Notice on Opening Operation Market of Users' Local Networks on a Trial basis, issued by the MII on June 1, 2001 (provides that the MII has chosen thirteen cities where the operation market of users' local networks will be open. Such networks are a part of basic telecoms services; however, the MII will administrate it as if it were a value-added telecoms service. This means that the last mile access networks are open to telecoms operators to compete with each other.); Notice on Further Strengthening the Administration of the Satellite Communications Market, issued by the MII on June 6, 2001 (provides that domestic companies that lease satellite transponders or VSAT services in China should have the relevant licenses issued by the MII. Foreign satellite companies that lease satellite transponders must do so by leasing domestic satellite companies that have already obtained the relevant licenses or, upon the approval of the MII, directly lease to the entities that will use these transponders); Provisional Procedures for the Supervision and Administration of Quality in Telecommunications Services (Telecom Procedures), issued by the MII on January 11, 2001 (provide specifically for (1) relational terms for telecom operators, administrative authorities, and users; (2) the duties and methods administrative authorities will bring to supervision of the industry; and (3) the rights and responsibilities of operators. An index of user satisfaction will be the primary standard in evaluating operator service quality. Standards designed by operators on the basis of existing law and regulations define the rights and obligations of both operators and users and are filed with governmental authorities. Operators will be required to make public their contact information to facilitate user complaints. The Telecom Procedures further provide that governmental authorities inspect operators. These provisions are intended to be applicable to all operators within China. Any foreign-invested operators approved under new legislation will be governed by the same standards.); Telecommunications Services Standards (Trial), issued by the MII on May 24, 2003 (This regulation sets out telecommunications services standards in detail. Telecommunications operators should provide services based on these requirements.)

9. Telecom Regulations, art. 7. An operator must also secure a business license from the applicable administration of industry and commerce (AIC). Art. 16. *See also* Measures on the Administration of Licenses for Operation of Telecommunications Services, promulgated on December 26, 2001, by the Ministry of Information Industry (sets forth standards for the administration of operator's licenses, application procedures, and documentation requirements) (hereinafter the "Telecom License Application Measures"). A license holder is required to go through an annual examination by the MII. Telecom License Application Measures, arts. 31–33.

Telecommunication services are categorized into basic telecommunication services and value-added services. "Basic telecommunication services" refers to those services that provide basic public network facilities, public data transmission, and basic voice communication service.[10] "Value-added telecommunication services" refers to those services that provide a telecommunication and information service by using basic public network facilities.[11] The specific categories of the telecommunication service classification are listed in the supplementary Telecommunication Service Classification Catalogue attached to the Telecom Regulations. The MII has the discretion to revise any of the telecommunication service classifications listed in the catalogue to meet the actual market circumstances and technological advances.[12]

An operator of basic telecommunication services is required to apply to the MII to obtain a Basic Telecommunication Service Operation Permit. The Telecom Regulations also provide that such permits are to be issued by means of public tenders.[13] The operation of a basic telecommunication service must meet the following requirements:

(1) The operator must be a lawfully established company *exclusively* involved in basic telecommunication service, and at least 51 percent

10. Basic services include domestic telephone service, international telephone service, mobile voice and data services, paging services, satellite telecom and satellite mobile telecom, Internet and other public data transmission (backbone infrastructure), leasing or sales of broadband, wavelength, optical fiber, optical cable, conduit and other network elements, backhaul network (carrier's carrier), access/connect, network outsourcing, and resale of basic telecom services. *See also* Notice on the Adjustment of the Telecom Business Catalogue, issued by the MII on June 11, 2001. This Notice provides more detail and expands on the definitions of basic telecom business and value-added telecom business. For example, the basic telecom business includes nine different definitions comprised of 23 items, replacing the nine original definitions in the old catalogue. In addition, the value-added telecom business includes five definitions comprised of 17 items, which replaced the nine original definitions in the old catalogue. On February 21, 2003, the MII issued a revised *Catalogue of Telecommunications Services* (*Telecom Catalogue*), effective April 1, 2003, which amends the 2001 catalogue. The 2003 Telecom Catalogue reconfirms MII's distinction between basic telecom services (BTS) and value-added telecom services (VATS). BTS is divided into two broad categories based on such criteria as the security of the national telecom backbone and the allocation of network resources. Foreign investment is currently permitted in the area of VATS; however, BTS is still dominated by domestic network operators. The Telecom Catalogue divides VATS into two categories: (i) data and transaction processing, teleconferencing, video-conferencing, and net-conferencing, virtual private networks, and data hosting; and (ii) communications storage and re-transmission, call centers, Internet access, and general information services.

11. Value-added Services include electronic mail, voice mail, online information and database retrieval, electronic data interchange, enhanced/value-added facsimile services (mass fax distribution services), code and protocol conversion, data processing, ICP, ISP, and video conferencing.

12. Telecom Regulations, art. 8.

13. Telecom Regulations, art. 12. *See also* Answers to Several Questions Regarding Applications for Telecom Business Operation Licenses (the "Answers"), issued by the MII on July 19, 2001. The Answers resolve questions concerning the application procedures and qualifications for obtaining telecom business operation licenses. The Answers complement the Telecom Regulations issued by the State Council last year, and focus on the cross-provinces value-added telecom operations, because these are under the control and administration of the MII and the degree to which they will open is broader than basic telecom operations. Additionally, the Answers establish an agency to accept application materials and conduct pre-examination of such applications.

of the share rights or stock shares of the company must be owned by the State
(2) Feasibility study reports and technology plans for network establishment must be provided
(3) The operator must have sufficient capital and professional/technical personnel who are suited to engage in telecom operational activities
(4) The operator must have infrastructure and the appropriate resources for the operation
(5) The operator must have credible reputation or capacity to provide users with a long-term service
(6) Any other requirements prescribed by the State[14]

An operator of value-added telecommunication service is also required to obtain permits from the MII. If the planned service is limited to a single administrative area of one province, autonomous region, or centrally administered municipality, the operator is required to apply for and obtain a Value-added Telecommunication Service Operation Permit, and a Trans-Regional Value-added Telecommunication Service Operation Permit where the service covers two or more provinces, autonomous regions, or centrally administered municipalities.[15] An operator of a value-added telecommunication service is required to meet the following conditions and standards:

(1) The operator must be a lawfully established company
(2) The operator must have funding and specialist personnel who are suited to engaging in operational activities
(3) The operator must have credible reputation or capacity to provide users with a long-term service
(4) Any other requirements prescribed by the State[16]

---

14. Telecom Regulations, arts. 9, 10. To apply to operate a basic telecommunication service, an application must be filed with the MII. The MII is required to complete its review of the application in 180 days from the date of filing. If an application is rejected, the MII must provide the applicant with an explanation of grounds for rejection. Art. 11. The standards for application review require that the MII take into consideration factors such as national security, the security of the telecommunication network, the sustained use of telecommunication resources, environmental protection, the state of competition in the telecommunication market, and other factors. Art. 12. The minimum capital requirement for basic telecom services is RMB250 million if the operation is in a single jurisdiction and RMB2 billion for multi-jurisdiction enterprises. Telecom License Application Measures, art. 5. Article 7 of the Telecom License Application Measures outlines in detail the information and documents to submit with the application for a basic telecom license.

15. Telecom Regulations, art. 9.

16. Telecom Regulations, art. 13. An application for value-added service must be reviewed and approved/rejected by the MII within 60 days of filing. The MII is required to provide written explanation of any rejected application. Art. 14. In contrast to the requirements for basic telecom operators, the requirements for value-added service providers are more relaxed in the Telecom Regulations. For value-added operations, the operator does not need to be exclusively in the telecom industry; there is no

An operator is required to file an application of approval to change the scope of the services, to cease operations, or to change the principal operator.[17]

2. Telecommunication Internetwork Connection

The law requires that telecommunication networks cooperate with one another and specifically prohibits a principal telecommunication service operator from denying a request for interconnection or intercommunication by any other telecommunication service operator or special telecommunication network unit.[18] Principal telecommunication services operators are also required to develop nondiscriminatory and transparent interconnection procedures with the approval of the MII.[19] Parties to an interconnection arrangement are required to enter into an interconnection agreement, which must be filed with the MII.[20] Both parties are required to fulfill their obligations under an

---

Chinese majority-ownership requirement (however, WTO market-access agreements limit the ownership interests); there is no requirement that a feasibility and technical report be submitted to the MII, and no requirement that the licenses be issued by tender (which suggests unlimited value-added licenses). However, the Telecom License Application Measures require a feasibility study report, business operations, and other requirements. In addition, an operator of value-added telecom services is required to have registered capital of RMB1 million for single-jurisdiction operations and RMB10 million for multiple jurisdiction operations. Telecom License Application Measures, art. 6. Article 8 of the Telecom License Application Measures outlines in detail the information and documents to submit with the application for a value-added telecom license.

17. Telecom Regulations, art. 15.

18. The term "principal telecommunication service operator" as used in this article refers to those operators who control the vital basic telecommunication facilities, own a relatively large share in the telecommunication service market, and are able to exert a substantial influence over other telecommunication service operators entering the telecommunication service market. Principal telecommunication service operators shall be determined by the responsible department for the information industry under the State Council. Telecom Regulations, art. 17.

19. Telecom Regulations, art. 18. *See also* Administrative Measures on the Interconnection of Public Telecommunications Networks (the "Measures"), issued by the MII on May 10, 2001. In conformity with the Telecommunications Regulations, the MII promulgated the new Measures to replace the regulations that were issued on September 7, 1999. The Measures apply to the interconnection among basic telecommunications networks, including IP phone networks. Operators shall establish authorities in charge of such work to keep channels continually open among operators. Requirements or principles are provided on interconnection arrangements, project construction, methods for sharing cost burden, time limitations to finish interconnection work, network management after interconnection, and coordination or settlement of dispute with respect to interconnection. Specifically, operators at the provincial level or higher shall sign the interconnection agreements, which reduce the burden on their lower-level branches. The MII or provincial communications administration bureaus will supervise relevant issues, conduct administrative coordination, and make administrative decisions. Parties to disputes may apply for administrative review or action if they are not satisfied with the decisions.

20. Telecom Regulations, art. 19. If the parties negotiating an interconnection agreement are unable to agree on the terms, either party may seek mediation assistance from the MII in order to expedite negotiations. The requesting party may not request mediation for 60 days after its request for interconnection. If, within 45 days of one or both parties applying for mediation on internetwork connection, an agreement has not yet been reached, the mediating authority may set a hearing with the assistance of technological specialists to encourage or force an interconnection agreement between the parties. Telecom Regulations, art. 20. *See also* Measures on the Disposal of the Disputes over the Interconnection of the Telecommunication Network, promulgated on November 19, 2001, by the Ministry of Information Industry (sets forth the procedures, standards, and application forms for interconnection disputes); Administrative Rules on Experts' Review for Telecommunication Equipment's Entry into Network,

interconnection agreement and neither party may suspend interconnection without approval from the MII. If any dispute arises between the parties to an interconnection agreement, the parties are required to mediate their dispute before the MII's mediating authority. The quality of the telecommunication of the internetwork connection must conform to the state standards and, in situations in which a principal telecommunication service operator provides an interconnection to another service operator, the quality of the service may not be below that of a similar service from the same network, nor of a similar service provided to its subsidiaries or subdivisions.[21]

3. Fees for Telecom Services

The Telecom Regulations provide that fees for telecom services are classified by market-regulated prices, government guidance prices, and government-determined prices. Based thereon, the fees for basic telecommunication services may conform to either government-determined prices, government guidance prices, or market-regulated prices. Value-added telecommunication service fees may reflect market-regulated prices or government guidance prices. For services in which full market competition is evident, the telecommunication fees may be determined by market-regulated prices. The MII has published a catalogue that classifies the telecommunication fees used for all three categories of services. The MII also sets the service fee standards for government-determined prices and the government guidance prices, and is required to hold hearings and receive comments from telecom service operators.[22]

---

promulgated on August 29, 2001, by the Ministry of Information Industry (outlines rules and procedures for the use of technical experts in interconnection issues) *See generally Fixed-Line Operators Agree on Network Interconnection*, China Market Intelligence, The U.S.-China Business Council (June 4, 2003), available online to members at http://www.uschina.org.

21. Telecom Regulations, art. 21.

22. Telecom Regulations, arts. 23–26. *See also* Notice on Abolishment of Initial Installation Fee on Local Telephone, Posts and Telecoms Surcharge, and Other Governmental Fund Items, issued by the MII and the Ministry of Finance on July 1, 2001 (provides that the initial installation fee on local telephone, posts, and telecoms surcharge is abolished); Notice on Structural Adjustments to the Telecommunications Tariffs, issued by the MII, the State Development Planning Commission, and the Ministry of Finance on December 25, 2000. Among other things, the provisions provide that Internet telephony phone services can use "market-adjusting-prices," i.e., operators have the right to set the prices of the Internet telephony phone services. However, the means of settlement of international phone services from abroad is decided by the MII. *See also* Interim Provisions on Market Prices for Telecommunications Services, promulgated on May 28, 2002, by the Ministry of Information Industry and effective on August 1, 2002 (outlines standards for pricing of telecom services). *See also* Notice on Implementation of Market Price Adjustment for Certain Telecommunications Services (issued on September 11, 2002, by the MII and State Development and Planning Commission) (provides that fees for services such as voice mail, paging services, IP phones, and satellite telephones are liberalized based on market forces, but any price adjustments must be registered with the MII); Provisional Regulation on Telecom Service Price Approval and Filing Process (issued on August 29, 2002, by the MII and State Development and Planning Commission) (provides that telecom companies must supply detailed financial information substantiating the calculation of fees and the impact any fee change will have on the market, and further provides that the government will continue to set the rates for basic telecom services for local calls made on mobile phones, fixed lines, or public phones).

4. Telecommunication Resources and User Fees

The Telecom Regulations provide that telecommunications resources, which are defined as the limited resources of radio frequency, satellite orbital position, telecommunication network code numbering, and other resources that are used to operate telecommunication networks, are to be distributed by means of allocation or auction.[23] Any telecom service operator who owns or uses telecommunication resources is required to pay a user fee, which is set and collected by the MII.[24] Operators that are granted the right to use telecommunication resources must commence the use of allocated resources within the prescribed time limit and achieve the minimum capacity of use as may be required. The Telecom Regulations prohibit any unauthorized use, transfer, or renting out of a telecommunication resources or alteration to the use of the telecommunication resources without approval by the MII.[25]

5. Standards for Telecom Service Operators and Users

The Telecom Regulations set forth various standards for service operators and the services they provide.[26] Specifically, service operators are required to publicly announce the type, scope, fee standards, and time limit of the services provided. Operators are also required to guarantee installation and connection of equipment requested by telecommunication users and to repair or reconnect any obstruction reported within 48 hours in the urban areas and 72 hours in the rural areas.[27] The Telecom Regulations also provide that operators are required to provide users with a detailed list of charges for domestic long-distance communications, international communications, mobile communications, information services, and other services provided.[28]

23. Telecom Regulations, arts. 27, 29.
24. Telecom Regulations, art. 28.
25. Telecom Regulations, art. 29.
26. Telecom Regulations, art. 32. The operators of local telephone services and mobile telephone services must provide free of charge calls made for fire alarms, burglar alarms, emergency medical treatment, traffic accident reports, and other telecommunication services in the interests of public welfare, and ensure that the communication lines are accessible. Art. 37.
27. Telecom Regulations, art. 32. A failure to connect a user in the time required exposes the operator to a fine equal to one (1) percent of the amount of the installation fee, reinstallation fee, or any other fee, which shall be paid each day to the telecommunication user. A user may be exempt from monthly rental fees during any period of obstruction to service or during project construction. Arts. 33, 36. An operator is also required to provide notice of any construction or installation work that will disrupt service. A failure to provide such notice exposes the operator to a claim for compensation if the user sustains losses. Art. 36.
28. Telecom Regulations, art. 34. Operators also have a duty to notify users if expenses are excessive, which is defined as five or more times greater than the average telecommunication cost of the user for the preceding three months. Art. 34.

The Telecom Regulations prohibit service operators from engaging in the following activities:

(1) Requiring the telecommunication user to purchase its designated service
(2) Restricting the telecommunication user's purchase to specific equipment, or denying the telecommunication user the use of self-purchased telecommunication equipment that has been granted a permit to enter the network
(3) Improperly altering fee standards
(4) Refusing, delaying, or suspending service to a telecommunication user without justification
(5) Failing to fulfill promises made to telecommunication users, or engaging in false advertisement
(6) Engaging in acts of retaliation against telecommunications users that have filed complaints against the operator[29]

A user that is unsatisfied with a telecom service operator has a right to file a complaint with the MII or its branch office. The MII is required to respond to consumer complaints within 30 days of receipt.[30]

The Telecom Regulations provide that users are required to pay for the telecommunications services provided and, in situations in which a user fails to pay the operator on time and in full, the operator may demand a daily noncompliance fee of three-tenths (0.3) percent of the cost due and unpaid. The operator may suspend service to any user who fails to pay for charges that remain unpaid after 30 days. If payment is not received after 60 days of date of suspension of services, the operator may terminate service to the user and demand both its charges and noncompliance fees that have accrued to

29. Telecom Regulations, arts. 41, 42. The MII supervises the compliance of the operators and may conduct investigations or on-site inspections of operator's premises. Art. 43.

30. Telecom Regulations, arts. 39, 40. *See also* Provisional Procedures for the Supervision and Administration of Quality in Telecommunications Services, issued by the MII on January 11, 2001. The Procedures provide specifically for (1) relational terms for telecom operators, administrative authorities, and users; (2) the duties and methods administrative authorities will use to supervise the industry; and (3) the rights and responsibilities of operators. An index of user satisfaction will be the primary standard in evaluating operator service quality. Standards designed by operators on the basis of existing law and regulations will define the rights and obligations of both operators and users and be filed with governmental authorities. Operators will be required to make public their contact information to facilitate user complaints, and reply promptly to any such made. The Procedures further provide that governmental authorities can make occasional spot checks of operators, the latter make periodic self-checks, and users evaluate the quality of operator services through the National Telecom Users Committee or User Complaints Processing Centers. These provisions are intended to be applicable to all operators within China. Any foreign-invested operators approved under legislation will be governed by the same standards.

date. Operators are required to resume suspended services within 48 hours if a user pays its bill in full.[31]

6. Telecommunication Construction

The Telecom Regulations provide that the construction of public telecommunication networks, special telecommunication networks, and radio and television transmission networks are required to comply with government planning policies and be approved prior to the commencement of construction. Any party involved in constructing roads, bridges, tunnels, railroads, and other large projects is required to consult with the local telecommunication authorities before commencing construction, and to avoid any disruption of existing telecom cables, lines, or facilities.[32]

---

31. Telecom Regulations, art. 35.

32. Telecom Regulations, arts. 45, 46, 48, 49, 50, 51. *See* Measures for the Administration of Telecommunication Construction, promulgated on January 4, 2002, by the Ministry of Information Industry and the State Development Planning Commission (outlines standards for planning, examination, and approval of telecom construction projects, administration of telecom construction industry, and penalties). The Telecom Construction Procedures require MII approval prior to building telecommunications or cable television networks, and apply to new construction, reconstruction and expansion of public telecom networks, dedicated telecom networks, and radio and television transmission networks within the PRC. The Telecom Construction Procedures stipulate that the construction of international transmission networks and international communications channels are subject to central planning and approval. As part of the application and approval process, the applicant is required to draft a five-year plan addressing a number of planning considerations such as the capabilities of the current network and strategies for development during the five-year period. Financial projections must also be disclosed, including information on the funds required to finish construction and any fund-raising strategies, and the plan is required to include route maps, current and projected service demand, development targets, transmission capacity, and the level of investment. Under the Telecom Construction Procedures, enterprises are to compile ongoing plans or interim reports on an annual basis, to be submitted to the MII before the end of January each year. Contents of an annual report must include the current status of the construction projects and how the funds have been utilized during the course of the year. The MII or the local telecom bureau will evaluate the ongoing plans and may invite the input of specialists in the industry. Review and approval of such plans is to be finished within 45 days of the receipt of the plan. *See also* Administration of the Construction of International Communications Facilities Provisions (issued by the MII and effective as of August 1, 2002). The MII International Communications Facilities Provisions confirm that all international telecommunications offered in the PRC are required to pass through an MII-authorized gateway. Facilities linking the PRC to Hong Kong, Macao, or Taiwan are deemed international communication facilities. An international communications facility includes: (i) all forms of communications infrastructure, including fixed line, radio, and satellite channels linking international communications channel gateways in Mainland China to areas outside of China, and (ii) the service transfer point between domestic and international telecom transmission channels. *See also* Administration of International Communications Gateway Exchanges Procedures (issued by the Ministry of Information Industry and effective on October 1, 2002) (hereinafter the "MII Gateway Procedures"). Pursuant to the MII Gateway Procedures, only a state-owned telecom service provider may create, operate, or maintain an international communications facility. These regulations retain MII's overall supervisory responsibility for international communications facilities, with local supervision delegated to local-level MII branches. MII reviews and approves applications to construct an international communications facility. If the applicable investment limits (RMB50,000,000) exceed an approved project, the applicant is required to obtain approval. Only the MII is authorized to provide approval to an international communications facility project. *See also* Notice on the Rectification of Illegal Optical Network Construction Projects, Restoring Order to the Construction of Long Distance Optical Networks, issued by the MII and the State Development and Planning Commission (SDPC) on March 27, 2001. According to this Notice, illegal construction has caused extensive network overlap in China's optical networks, endangering

Basic telecommunication service operators may attach overhead telecommunication lines, or install small antennas, mobile communication base stations, or other public telecommunication facilities to public buildings. However, the service operator intending to install equipment must first notify the building property rights holder or user and pay a usage fee to the property rights holder in accordance with the law.[33] No organization or individual may prevent or hinder basic telecommunication service operators from lawfully engaging in telecommunication facility construction or in providing telecommunication users with telecommunication services. However, prohibited or restricted areas as provided by state regulations are excepted. Telecommunication vehicles conducting special communications, emergency telecommunications, emergency repairs, or other emergency missions, with the approval of the public security and traffic control authority and under the proviso that traffic safety and accessibility shall be safeguarded, may be exempt from restrictions of any kind in relation to "no motor vehicle access" signs.[34]

7. Permits for Telecommunication Terminal Equipment

Pursuant to the Telecom Regulations, the MII has implemented a permit system for telecommunication terminal equipment, radio telecommunication equipment, and other equipment related to internetwork connection. All telecommunication terminal equipment, radio telecommunication equipment, or other equipment that is to be connected to a public telecommunication network must comply with the standards prescribed by the State, and obtain a network connection permit. An application for a permit must include a product quality certificate from an authorized examination organization. Upon receipt of an application, the MII will review the materials and, within 60 days, either approve the network connection permit or

national communication security and creating potential chaos of related construction projects nationwide. The Notice thus requires all projects lacking approval from the SDPC, the MII, or other empowered authorities to cease construction immediately. Projects invested in locally must be reported to the SDPC and the MII; those involving Army participation should be reported to the Communication Department of General Staff Headquarters. In addition, all entities without licenses to provide basic telecommunications services must report within 30 days all optical network resources in their possession. The Notice then reiterates the pre-WTO prohibition against overseas investment and participation in telecommunications operations in China. In boosting orderly competition, the MII will issue licenses for the lease or sale of network elements, including bandwidth, wavelength, optical fiber, and optical cable. Other basic telecommunications service operators can purchase or lease networks resources from operators holding a "license for the sale or lease of network elements," or construct any approved optical networks themselves. Companies failing to obey these provisions are forbidden to conduct business through their network resources, and those that persist in conducting illegal business operations may incur penalties including the confiscation of those networks.

33. Telecom Regulations, art. 47.

34. Telecom Regulations, arts. 52, 53.

explain the basis for rejection.[35] Equipment manufacturers are required to affix the permit number on the telecommunications equipment sold to the public and must guarantee the quality of the equipment.[36]

8. Telecommunication Security Standards

As required under the Telecom Regulations, operators are required to establish an internal security protection system in accordance with the relevant state telecommunication security provisions. Operators are also required to meet national security and telecommunication network security standards in the design, construction, and operation of telecommunication networks.[37]

The regulations provide that freedom and communication confidentiality of telecom users who are lawfully using telecommunications shall be respected and protected by law. With the exception of criminal or national security investigations, no party may investigate, examine, or transmit the telecommunication content of another person.[38] However, the Telecom

35. Telecom Regulations, arts. 54, 55. *See also* Provisional Administrative Measures on Inspection and Measure of the Anti-seismic Capability of Telecoms Equipment, issued by the Ministry of Information Industry June 15, 2001, and effective as of January 1, 2002 (providing that telecoms equipment to be installed in special areas should first pass the inspection and measures of anti-seismic capability); Administrative Measures on Network Access for Telecommunications Equipment, issued by the MII on May 10, 2001 (MII updated the regulations with the adoption of the Telecommunications Regulations, and outlines that the license administration system covers only three kinds of equipment: telecommunications terminal equipment, wireless telecommunications equipment, and telecommunications network equipment involving the mutual connection of networks, definitions of which appear in the regulations. The selling of telecom equipment in China is prohibited without license from the MII. The Telecommunications Administration Bureau and the Communications Administration Bureaus at the provincial level are responsible for the regulation and inspection of issued licenses.); Notice Concerning the Names of Telecoms Equipment Subject to the Network Access Licensing System, issued by the MII on June 25, 2001 (provides detailed names of telecoms equipment subject to the network access licensing system); Measures on Examination and Approval of Production Quality Assurance for Telecoms Equipment for Accessing Networks, issued by the MII on August 29, 2001 (provide detailed procedures for inspection of production quality of manufacturers that apply for permits for accessing networks for their equipment); Administrative Regulations on Specialists' Appraisal and Inspection of Equipment for Accessing Networks, issued by the MII on August 29, 2001 (provide the detailed procedures for appraisal and inspection of equipment for accessing networks); Administrative Regulations on Remodeling Telecoms Terminal Equipment for Accessing Networks, issued by the MII on August 29, 2001 (provide the procedures for inspection of telecoms terminal equipment for accessing networks); Regulations on the Trial of Mobile Telephone Sets, issued by the MII on August 29, 2001 (provide the appraisal procedures on new kinds of mobile telephone sets); Interim Measures on the Administration of Vibration Proof Performance of Telecommunication Equipment, promulgated on August 1, 2001, by the Ministry of Information Industry (outlines standards for vibration-proof performance of telecom equipment). *See also* Notice on Further Strengthening the Administration of Network Access for Mobile Phones (issued on April 4, 2003, by the Ministry of Information Industry). The Notice outlines certification procedures for testing and network access approval of new mobile telecommunications products. Mobile telephone manufacturers are required to submit a standardized application form to the MII's Telecommunications Equipment Authentication Center, which details the design and production parameters and the sales prospects of any new mobile phone units. Manufacturers are required to guarantee the normal use, design, and functioning of the product. The MII is authorized to conduct post-certification inspections of factory facilities to ensure that manufacturers adhere to quality standards.

36. Telecom Regulations, art. 56.

37. Telecom Regulations, arts. 60, 61.

38. Telecom Regulations, art. 66.

Regulations place strict restrictions on the use and dissemination of prohibited content via the telecommunications network. In this regard, Article 57 of the Regulations provides that no individual or organization may use a telecommunication network to produce, reproduce, publish, or disseminate any information with the following content:

(1) Opposing the basic principles defined in the Constitution
(2) Endangering national security, divulging state secrets, subverting state political power, or undermining national unity
(3) Damaging the honor or interests of the State
(4) Inciting hatred or discrimination against ethnic minorities, or undermining the unity of nationalities
(5) Undermining state religious policies, or propagating cults or feudalistic superstitions
(6) Disseminating rumors, disrupting public order, or undermining social stability
(7) Propagating obscenity, pornography, gambling, violence, homicide, or terrorism, or instigating criminal activity
(8) Humiliating or libeling another party, or encroaching on the lawful rights or interests of another party
(9) Any other content prohibited by the law or administrative regulations[39]

The Telecom Regulations further provide that if a telecommunication service operator discovers that the content of information being transmitted over the network is in violation of Article 57 of these Regulations, the operator is

39. Telecom Regulations, art. 57. These standards are identical to Article 15 of the Internet Information Services Rules. A violation of Article 57 is grounds for criminal sanctions. Telecom Regulations, art. 67. The law provides that telecommunication users are responsible for the content and the consequences of any information transmitted via use of a telecommunication network. Where a telecommunication user wishes to use a telecommunication network to transmit information that is considered secret state information, measures must be taken to maintain secrecy in accordance with the provisions of the law to safeguard such state secrets. Telecom Regulations, art. 63. The disclosure of "state secrets" is prohibited by law, and the relevant regulations define the terms secret information and illegal disclosure in broad terms. "State Secrets" are defined as "matters that affect the security and interests of the state," and are illustrated by broad categories of information relating to national defense, "import policy decisions on state affairs," "economic and social development," "science and technology development," "criminal investigations," and "other state secrets that by decision of the state departments on protecting state secrets should be safeguarded." Law on Safeguarding State Security of the People's Republic of China (promulgated by the State Council in 1993); Detailed Rules for the Implementation of the Law on Safeguarding State Security of the People's Republic of China (promulgated by the State Council in 1994). Many of these prohibitions are already being ignored when the commercial interests of the State take priority. As an example, the prohibition on pornography has been ignored with the approval of commercial enterprises that promote phone sex. See Levy, *China Lets a Thousand Love Chats Take Bloom; Officials Justify Phone Sex Industry,* Chicago Tribune, Mar. 28, 2002, available via Lexis or the Web site of the Chicago Tribune at http://www.chicagotribune.com.

required to immediately terminate the transmission. Furthermore, the operator has an affirmative duty to maintain any records of the illegal transmission and to file a report with the MII and the Ministry of Public Security.[40]

The Telecom Regulations provide that no individual or organization may endanger telecommunication network security or information security by engaging in any of the following acts:

(1) Deleting or modifying any function; stored, processed, or transmitted data; or application process of a telecommunication network
(2) Exploiting a telecommunication network in order to steal or undermine the information of another party, or to undermine the lawful rights or interests of another party
(3) Deliberately producing, reproducing, or spreading computer viruses, or in any other way attacking the telecommunication network or other telecommunication facility of another party
(4) In any other way endangering telecommunication network security or information security[41]

The regulations further provide that no individual or organization may engage in activities that disrupt the telecommunication market order, including the following:

(1) Hiring special international telecommunication lines, or illegally installing transfer and reception equipment, or taking other measures to illegally operate a telecommunication service internationally or in the Hong Kong Special Administrative Region, Macao Special Administrative Region, or Taiwan region[42]
(2) Illegally connecting to the telecommunication lines of another party, reproducing the telecommunication code number of another party, or using telecommunication equipment or code numbers that are known to be of stolen connections or reproductions
(3) Forging or altering telephone cards or any other valuable telecommunication service vouchers
(4) Using a fake or falsely used identification card to carry out network connection procedures to use a mobile telephone

40. Telecom Regulations, art. 62. This rule is identical to Article 16 of the Internet Information Services Rules issued by the State Council in September 2000.

41. Telecom Regulations, art. 58. A violation of Article 58 is grounds for criminal and civil sanctions. Telecom Regulations, art. 68. A fine may be imposed of three to five times the illegal income received; and if no income is received, a fine of RMB10,000 to RMB100,000 may be imposed.

42. All international communication services, including service to Hong Kong, Macao, and Taiwan, must be conducted through the International Communication Exchange Administration. Telecom Regulations, art. 65.

9. Penalties

The Telecom Regulations set forth a number of provisions that outline the penalties for violations of the regulations including the imposition of monetary penalties, confiscation of profits (if any), revocation of permits and licenses, and suspension of operation or forced reorganization. Potential violations include, but are not limited to, the following:

(1) Violations of content restrictions under Article 57
(2) False use or improper transfer of telecommunication service operation permits or telecom equipment permits, or the counterfeit use of network connection permit numbers on telecom equipment
(3) Selling any telecom terminal equipment without a network connection permit, or selling a product that is of lower quality subsequent to receiving a network connection permit
(4) Illegal operation of a telecommunication service under Article 59 (1) or Article 7
(5) Establishing an international communication exchange to communicate internationally without approval
(6) Illegally using, transferring, or renting telecommunication resources, or altering the application of telecommunication resources
(7) Illegally suspending internetwork connections or reception services
(8) Refusing the obligation to provide universal service as required under Article 44
(9) Charging excessive fees
(10) Failing to take effective measures to eliminate obstructions to network communications
(11) Illegally providing another party with the content of information transmitted via use of a telecommunication network by a user
(12) Refusing to pay a usage fee for telecommunication resources
(13) Engaging in unfair competition in violation of Article 42
(14) Refusing the request of another telecommunication service operator or the MII for interconnection
(15) Providing substandard internetwork connection service to other telecommunication network operators
(16) Refusing to provide free of charge a detailed list of charges for domestic long-distance communications, international communications, mobile communications, information services, and other services, or refusing to provide evidence, free of charge, of the payment of local telephone fees at the request of a telecommunication user

(17) Engaging in any action in violation of Article 41 concerning the fair treatment of telecommunication users
(18) Interfering with telecommunication service operators who are providing public telecommunication service to users
(19) Illegally altering or removing telecommunication lines or facilities[43]

The Telecom Regulations further provide that criminal and civil penalties may be imposed if any telecom regulatory authority abuses its power, neglects its duties, or practices favoritism.[44]

10. FIE Telecom Regulations

The MII issued regulations for foreign-invested telecom enterprises (FIE Telecom Enterprises) that were effective January 1, 2002.[45] The FIE Telecom Regulations provide that an FIE Telecom Enterprise refers to a telecommunications business established in the People's Republic of China with investments from foreign and Chinese investors in the form of Sino-foreign joint

---

43. Telecom Regulations, arts. 67–78. The Supreme People's Court has also issued an interpretation of the law with respect to penalties that may be imposed for violations of the Telecom Regulations. *See* Interpretation on the Specific Applicable Laws Governing Cases Relating to the Disturbance of Administrative Order in the Telecommunications Market, issued by the Supreme People's Court, effective as of May 24, 2000. The SPC Interpretation provides that individuals or organizations that illegally operate international telecommunications services or telecommunications services relating to Hong Kong, Macao, and/or Taiwan, for profit by leasing specific international lines, setting up "transferring and connecting equipment," or by any other means, shall be charged with operating an illegal business enterprise under the Criminal Law and punished accordingly. The Interpretation states the specific situations that will be considered as serious. Secondly, the Interpretation provides that whoever establishes or uses a wireless radio station, occupies frequency, or illegally operates international telecommunications services or telecommunications services relating to Hong Kong, Macao, and/or Taiwan for profit without authorization, shall be charged with illegal business operation and disruption of the normal operation of wireless communications. Thirdly, the Interpretation provides that workers of state-owned telecoms companies or enterprises that contribute to the bankruptcy or serious loss of their companies or enterprises due to the flagrant neglect of duty or abuse of their office shall be charged with impairing the orderly administration of companies and enterprises according to Article 168 of the Criminal Law. In addition, the Interpretation also provides for regulation of recent illegal activities commonly found in the telecommunications market, such as secretly using someone else's username and password to log onto the public information network, or use of identification certificates of another person (or disguised use) to access networks and use mobile phones.

44. Telecom Regulations, art. 79.

45. Pursuant to Article 80 of the Telecom Regulations, the MII issued the FIE Telecom Regulations. *See* Regulations for Managing FIE Telecom Enterprise, promulgated on December 11, 2001, as Order No. 333 of the State Council, *reprinted in* CHINA LAWS FOR FOREIGN BUSINESS (CCH), Business Regulation ¶ 6-637, also *reprinted in China Issues Regulations for Telecom Business with Foreign Investment*, Xinhua News Agency, Beijing, December 20, 2001, available online at http://www.xinhua.com.cn. The regulations superseded two prior sets of rules that barred foreign investment in domestic telecom companies. The two regulations include the Provisional Regulations on the Administration of Examining and Approving Telecommunications Businesses issued on September 11, 1993, and the Provisional Regulations on the Administration of the Telecommunications Market enacted on November 10, 1995, banning overseas investment in China's telecom carriers. *See generally* N. Leigh, *Telecom Permits: Improving Procedures and Transparency,* CHINA L. & PRAC. (July 2003) (author addresses the operators' permit process appplicable to FIEs); *Blueprint for China's Post-WTO Telecom Competition Framework;* CHINA L. & PRAC. (January 2002).

venture.[46] An FIE Telecom Enterprise is required to comply with the Telecom Regulations and other relevant laws and administrative regulations concerning the telecommunications industry. Under the regulations, an FIE Telecom Enterprise may provide basic telecommunications services and value-added telecommunications services; and its specific services may be categorized according to the rules in the Telecom Regulations.[47]

The registered capital of an FIE Telecom Enterprise shall meet the following requirements:

(1) An FIE Telecom Enterprise that provides nationwide telecommunications services, or services in areas that straddle provinces, autonomous regions, and municipalities under the Central Government's direct jurisdiction, shall have a minimum registered capital of RMB2 billion; and a business that provides value-added services shall have a minimum registered capital of RMB10 million
(2) An FIE Telecom Enterprise that provides basic telecommunications services within a province, autonomous region, or municipality under the Central Government's direct jurisdiction shall have a minimum registered capital of RMB200 million; and a business that provides value-added telecommunications services shall have a minimum registered capital of RMB10 million[48]

The foreign party's total investment in the FIE Telecom Enterprise, with the exception of paging services, may not exceed 49 percent of the registered capital of the enterprise. The foreign party's total investment in an FIE Telecom Enterprise involving value-added services, including paging services, shall not exceed 50 percent of the registered capital of the enterprise.[49]

The principal Chinese investor of an FIE Telecom Enterprise that provides basic telecommunications services shall meet the following requirements:

(1) Legally established company
(2) Sufficient capital and professional/technical personnel to conduct the business

46. FIE Telecom Regulations, art. 2. The provision mentions only a joint venture, as the permissible investment method specifically fails to mention a wholly foreign-owned enterprise. The FIE Telecom Regulations apply to all foreign parties, including companies based in the Hong Kong Special Administrative Region, the Macao Special Administrative Region, and Taiwan. Art. 24.

47. FIE Telecom Regulations, arts. 3, 4.

48. FIE Telecom Regulations, art. 5.

49. FIE Telecom Regulations, art. 6. The MII has the ultimate discretion to decide the proportionate share of Chinese and foreign interests; however, such determination must be consistent with China's WTO obligations.

(3) Meets the requirements that the State Council department in charge of information industry has set for special trades

The "principal Chinese investor" of the FIE Telecom Enterprise refers to the promoter whose capital subscription is the highest among all the other Chinese investors, and whose capital subscription accounts for 30 percent or more of the investors' total capital subscription.[50]

The principal foreign investor of an FIE Telecom Enterprise that provides basic telecommunications services must meet the following requirements:

(1) Legally established business
(2) Has a license for providing basic telecommunications services in the country or region in which it is registered
(3) Has the capital and professional personnel commensurate with its business[51]
(4) Has a record of good business performance and experiences with respect to providing basic telecommunications services

The "principal foreign investor" of an FIE Telecom Enterprise refers to the promoter whose capital subscription is the highest among all the other foreign investors, and whose capital subscription accounts for 30 percent or more of the investors' total capital subscription.[52] The requirements for the foreign party to an FIE Telecom Enterprise engaged in value-added services are more relaxed than those providing basic services. In this regard, a principal foreign investor who invests in operating an FIE Telecom Enterprise that provides value-added telecommunications services shall only need to demonstrate a record of good business performance and experiences in providing value-added services.[53]

The FIE Telecom Enterprise that provides basic telecommunications services, or that provides value-added telecommunications services in areas that involve multiple jurisdictions, are required to submit an application to the

50. FIE Telecom Regulations, art. 8.

51. The current FIE Telecom Regulations do not include specific financial and performance requirements for the foreign party. In contrast, under prior drafts of the regulations, the foreign party for a basic telecom services enterprise was required to have average annual telecom operations revenue of $10 billion over the prior two years and a representative office in China for three years. The prior draft also required the foreign party in a value-added services enterprise to have annual business revenue of $500,000 and assets of $1 million. The Chinese partner had similar performance requirements. However, these performance requirements were not included in the final adopted version of the regulations.

52. FIE Telecom Regulations, art. 9.

53. FIE Telecom Regulations, art. 10.

MII by and through the principal Chinese investor. The applicant is required to submit the following documents to secure approval from the MII:

(1) Project proposal
(2) Feasibility study report
(3) Investor credentials and background information

For applications concerning enterprises involved with basic telecom services, the MII is require to review the application and to render a decision within 180 days to approve or reject the application. If the application involves an enterprise that intends to provide value-added services, the MII is required to review the application and to render a decision within 90 days to approve or reject the application. If the application is approved, the MII will issue an "Opinion on Examining the FIE Telecom Enterprise." If it is rejected, the MII will notify the applicant and sponsoring Chinese party of the reasons for rejection.[54]

An FIE Telecom Enterprise that applies to provide value-added telecommunications services to a single jurisdiction is required to submit its application by and through its Chinese partner to the MII's local branch office. The applicant must file an application, a feasibility study, information concerning the foreign party's credentials, and documentation concerning the value-added services to be provided. The application must be reviewed and approved/rejected in 60 days. If approved at the local level, the matter is referred to the MII for further review. The MII then has 30 days to approve or reject an application. If the MII approves the application, it will issue the "Opinion on Examining the FIE Telecom Enterprise," and if the application is rejected, the MII is required to notify the applicant of the reasons for rejection in writing.[55] The Ministry of Commerce (MOFCOM) is also required to review the application and to issue a "Certificate of Approval for Business with Foreign Investment."[56] Thereafter, the investors file an application with the Administration of Industry and Commerce to secure a business license.

54. FIE Telecom Regulations, art. 11. The project proposal of the FIE Telecom Enterprise shall include the following information and materials: the names of business partners and background information concerning the partners, the total amount of money to be invested in the business, the registered capital, the percentage of money to be contributed by different partners, the type of services to be provided, and the term of operation of the joint venture. The feasibility study report of the FIE Telecom Enterprise shall include the following information and materials: the basic situation of the business planned to be established, and its kinds of services, business forecast, development plan, analysis of investment returns, and projected time of operations. Art. 14.

55. FIE Telecom Regulations, art. 13. For projects that require the review of the State Council or the State Development and Planning Commission, the regulations provide that the review period is extended by an additional 30 days. Art. 15.

56. FIE Telecom Regulations, art. 16.

The FIE Telecom Enterprise wishing to operate a trans-regional telecommunications business must have the approval of the MII and must operate the business through an international telecommunications bureau established with authorization of the MII.[57] Prior approval of the MII is required if an FIE Telecom Enterprise desires to become a publicly listed company overseas.[58]

A violation of the FIE Telecom Regulations is grounds for civil and criminal penalties. If the parties to an FIE Telecom Enterprise violate the terms of Article 6, which sets the maximum amount of foreign ownership, the MII may impose a monetary penalty between RMB100,000 and RMB500,000 or revoke the license of the enterprise.[59] If any FIE Telecom Enterprise violates Article 18 of these regulations, which requires approval for operating in multiple jurisdictions, the MII may impose a monetary fine between RMB200,000 and RMB1 million or revoke the license of the enterprise.[60] The use of false or misleading information in a party's application is grounds for penalties between RMB200,000 and RMB1 million and/or revocation of a license.[61]

11. Regulation of the Intranet

All users of foreign computer information networks are required to register with the Ministry of Information Industry, formerly the Ministry of Posts and Telecommunications.[62] The government also regulates the use of intranets by international corporations, which are used primarily for internal communications. In March 1998, the MII adopted the Implementing Measures for the Provisional Rules on the Administration of Computer Information Network International Link-ups, which provide that multinationals using internal international networks are required to limit the use of intranets to internal communications within the corporation.[63] The rules appear to prohibit users from linking up to the Internet from a corporate intranet, or from sending or receiving E-mails from external addresses.

57. FIE Telecom Regulations, art. 18.
58. FIE Telecom Regulations, art. 23.
59. FIE Telecom Regulations, art. 19.
60. FIE Telecom Regulations, art. 20.
61. FIE Telecom Regulations, art. 21.
62. *See* Provisional Administrative Regulations of the People's Republic of China on International Connections to Computer Information Networks (promulgated on February 1, 1996, by the State Council and amended on May 20, 1997, by the State Council), *reprinted in* CHINA LAWS FOR FOREIGN BUSINESS (CCH), Business Regulation ¶ 19-610.
63. *China Regulations: Intranet Restrictions Create Waves,* EIU VIEWS WIRE (Nov. 30, 1998), available on Lexis, News Library; Wei, *New Internet Business Permit System,* 2 CHINA LAW UPDATE 15–16 (Feb. 1999).

These rules are confusing at best and, if the rules are strictly enforced, practically all users of intranets would be found in violation of the standards. It is anticipated that the MII will use the intranet standards at an opportunity and in a manner that fits the government's agenda.

12. Regulation of Internet Operations

a. Internet Information Services

In September 2000, the State Council adopted rules governing Internet information services that are under the regulatory oversight of the MII.[64] The stated purpose of the Internet Information Services Rules is to regulate activities of Internet information services and to promote the healthy and orderly development of the Internet information services industry. The Rules provide that the term "Internet information services" refers to service activities that provide information to online users through the Internet.[65] In addition to the MII, the Ministry of Culture asserts jurisdiction over the approval of Internet service providers.[66]

64. Administrative Measures Governing Internet Information Services, Decree No. 292 of the State Council of the People's Republic of China, Promulgated 25 September 2000, reprinted in CHINA LAWS FOR FOREIGN BUSINESS (CCH), Business Regulation ¶ 16-670 (hereinafter the "Internet Information Services Rules"). The jurisdictions of Beijing and Shanghai have adopted their own measures to support Decree No. 292 of the State Council. *See* Notice of the Shanghai Municipal Communications Administration Bureau, issued on November 25, 2000. The Shanghai Notice was issued in order to implement the provisions of the Internet Information Services Administrative Measures ("Measures"), Decree No. 292 of the State Council, to regulate Internet content provision ("ICP") activities in Shanghai, and to promote the healthy and orderly development of ICPs. Any company carrying out commercial or noncommercial ICP activities in Shanghai is required to apply with the Municipal Communications Administration Bureau for a Value-added Telecommunication Business Operating Permit for Internet Information Service ("Operating Permit") or for filing procedures. Entities carrying out ICP services in connection with news, publication, education, health care, pharmacy, and medical instruments, etc., will be approved by relevant administrative departments in accordance with the law before applying for the Operating Permit or carrying out filing procedures. Those entities carrying out ICP services with the intention of carrying out Bulletin Board Services shall, in accordance with the Measures and Internet Bulletin Board Services Administrative Provisions, Decree No. 3 of the MII, shall file a special application with the Municipal Communications Administration Bureau. After obtaining the Operating Permit, commercial institutions shall carry out relevant formalities with enterprise registration authorities. Applicants holding the Operating Permit or proof of filing can then engage Internet service providers (ISPs). ISPs shall not provide any institutions without the Operating Permit or proof of filing with the means for carrying out ICP services. In the case of institutions that have already been carrying out Internet information services but fail to obtain the Operating Permit or proof of filing before January 31, 2001, the ISPs are obliged to cease services. Those that violate these Measures or provide ISP services without the Operating Permit or proof of filing shall be subject to administrative penalties and possible criminal liability. The measures do not clarify the position of foreign investment enterprises which provide ICP services or engage in ICP activities. *See also* Notice on Issues Concerning the Administration of the Operation Permits and Filing in relation to Internet Information Service Business, issued by the Beijing Municipal Communications Administration Bureau on November 3, 2000.

65. Internet Information Services Rules, art. 2.

66. *See* Notice on Strengthening the Administration of Chain Providers of Internet Access Services (issued on April 22, 2003, by the Ministry of Culture) (provides that the Ministry of Culture has

Internet information services are divided into commercial and noncommercial services. Commercial Internet information services refer to paid services that provide information to or create Web pages for online users through the Internet. Noncommercial Internet information services refer to services that are provided through the Internet free to the general public.[67] Pursuant to the Internet Information Services Rules, the MII has implemented a license system for Internet information services of a commercial nature, and implemented a filing-for-record system for Internet information services of a noncommercial nature. The Rules prohibit any party from engaging in Internet information services without first obtaining a license or having completed the filing-for-record procedures.[68] The Rules further provide that in service industries that require approval of the competent department in charge of the relevant industry, such as in the areas of media, publishing, education, health care, and pharmaceuticals and medical devices, the party must receive such approval before filing an application with the MII for a license or undergoing the filing-for-record formalities.[69]

---

jurisdiction as the examination and approval authority for nationwide and interprovincial Internet access service providers; that each provincial authority may approve no more than three operators, while the central authority may, in principle, approve no more than 10 nationwide interprovincial Internet access chains; and that the establishment of new, independently operated Internet access service providers is prohibited under the Notice).

67. Internet Information Services Rules, art. 3.

68. Internet Information Services Rules, art. 4.

69. Internet Information Services Rules, arts. 5, 18. Various government agencies have adopted regulations to control Internet-related activities in their specific industry sectors. *See* Notice on Questions Concerning E-commerce Activities Relating to Audio and Video Products on the Internet, issued by the Ministry of Culture on March 17, 2000 (provides that an entity must obtain permits from the Ministry of Culture to perform such activities, and restrictions are placed on the sale of foreign-made products online); Notice on Enhancing Administration of the Online Release of Film or Television Program through Information Networks to the Public, issued by the State Administration of Radio, Film and Television (SARFT) in October 1999 (provides that SARFT has the power to approve entities to release radio, film, or television programs through various information networks, including the Internet); Provisional Administrative Measures on Online Securities Brokerages, issued by CSRC, effective on March 30, 2000 (provides that an entity must obtain a permit from CSRC to perform securities brokerage services online); Provisional Regulations on Publication Market, issued by the State Press and Publication Administration (SPPA) effective as of November 8, 1999 (provides that entities other than distributors of publications shall not be permitted to open "online-bookstores," or engage in sales and purchase of publications through the Internet); Administrative Measures on Medical and Health Information Services on Internet, issued by the Ministry of Health on January 8, 2001 (prohibit the provision of online diagnosis and treatment); Provisional Administrative Regulations on Internet Drugs Information Services, issued by the State Drug Administration on January 11, 2001, which has been effective as of February 1, 2001 (opens a door for e-commerce in the area of medicine and requires application for approval); Notice on Enhancing Administration of Educational Web sites and Online Schools, issued by the Ministry of Education and effective as of April 20, 2000, and Provisional Administrative Procedures on Educational Web sites and Online Schools, issued by the Ministry of Education on July 5, 2000 (govern issues concerning educational Web sites and online schools in China); Provisional Administrative Measures on Online Banking Services, issued by the People's Bank of China (PBOC) on June 29, 2001 (provide that online banking services are now permitted and set forth the market access standards for online banking services); Provisional Regulations for the Administration of Internet Sites That Engage in the Business of News Publication, issued by Press Office of the State Council (POSC) and MII on November 7, 2000 (The POSC Regulations provide strict limitation on the provision of online news; these regulations, for the

Operators that provide commercial Internet information services are required to apply to the Communications Administration Bureau of the MII for a license to operate value-added telecommunications services in Internet information services. An operator shall, in addition to compliance with requirements as prescribed by the Telecom Regulations, meet the following conditions:

(1) Maintain a business development plan
(2) Maintain network and information security procedures, including security measures for Web site safety, management systems for maintaining information security and confidentiality, and management systems for safeguarding users' information
(3) Obtain approval documents from the competent authorities in charge of the relevant industry, where the services fall within the scope of Article 5 of these Internet Information Services Rules[70]

---

first time, regulate Internet sites that engage in the Chinese news publication business, and stipulate that the phrase "news publication" refers to the release and reprinting of news on the Internet. The POSC will be in charge of the nationwide administration of such business. Web sites engaging in the business of news publication are categorized into two types based on the nature of their sponsors. "News Web sites" are those Web sites that may lawfully engage in the news publication business, that is, those established by central press units, press units under the departments of central or state authorities, press units directly subordinate to a province, autonomous region, municipality directly under the central government, or municipality in which the people's government of the province or autonomous region is located. "General-interest Non-press Web sites" are those Web sites lawfully established by general-interest Internet sites with approval from the POSC. Other Web sites may not engage in such activities. Detailed information must be provided by entities that may apply to establish such Web sites or news Web pages. Only the POSC has the authority to approve such Web sites. The POSC's provincial-level counterparts can approve the establishment of news Web pages only by certain press entities. Special approval is needed to link news Web sites to similar Web sites outside China. After obtaining approval from the POSC, such Web sites have to further apply to MII for the issue of a License of Internet Information Service for Value-added Telecoms Business. Without specific approval, no Web sites are allowed to link to foreign news Web sites, or to disseminate news issued by foreign news media or Internet sites.)

70. Internet Information Services Rules, arts. 6, 7. The MII is required to approve or reject an application within 60 days of receipt. Upon approval, the operator is required to obtain a business license from the relevant administration of industry and commerce. *See also* Administration of Internet Electronic Messaging Services Provisions, issued by the Ministry of Information Industry on October 27, 2000. These provisions stipulate that it is necessary to apply for a specific approval for the provision of Internet electronic messaging services in China. These Provisions were issued by the MII in accordance with Article 9 of the Administrative Procedures on Internet Information Services. The aim of these Provisions is to strengthen Article 9, otherwise known as the Electronic Messaging System (EMS) Provision. EMS refers to acts enabling online subscribers to publish information on the Internet in an interactive form, such as bulletin boards, whiteboards, discussion forums, chat rooms, message boards, etc. As the definition of EMS is very broad and technical, the term "interactive form" may embrace a wide range of the possibilities that future technology will bring to the Internet. MII and its local counterparts at the provincial levels are the authorities in charge. The Provisions stipulate that no unit or individual may engage in EMS provision without having obtained. There are a number of obligations for EMS providers. For example, they must post their operating permit numbers or record numbers and their EMS rules in a prominent place on their EMS systems and remind online subscribers of their legal liability for the publication of information. They may not provide services beyond what has been approved. They must maintain the confidentiality of the personal information concerning the online subscribers and may not disclose this information to third parties without the subscribers' consent unless the law provides otherwise. If they discover information in their EMS system that is clearly prohibited content, the EMS provider must immediately delete such information, save any pertinent records, and report the incident to the relevant state authority.

An operator that intends to engage in noncommercial Internet information services shall submit to the MII or local telecommunications authorities the following materials for purposes of the filing-for-record requirement:

(1) The general situation of the host unit and the person(s) in charge of Web sites
(2) The addresses of the Web sites and the items of services
(3) The approval documents of the relevant competent departments, where the service items fall within the scope of Article 5 of the Internet Information Services Rules[71]

Materials submitted for filing-for-record are required to be recorded and numbered by the MII and local telecommunication authorities.

The MII publishes a list of names of the Internet information services providers who have obtained the operation licenses or have completed the filing-for-record procedures. The Internet Information Services Rules provide that an information services operator is required to deliver its services in compliance with the items as stipulated in the license or in the record filed, and is prohibited from providing services outside the scope of its license or beyond the materials submitted for the file. A noncommercial Internet information services provider, for example, shall not engage in revenue-generating activities. In addition, an Internet information services provider who intends to amend or alter its service scope or change its Web site address, is required to file an application at least 30 days prior to changing the scope of its services or Web site address. An Internet information services provider is required to post its operation license number or filing-for-record number on its Web site.[72]

In addition to the restrictions on content set forth in Article 57 of the Telecom Regulations (which are identical to Article 15 of the Internet Information Services Rules), an Internet information services provider is required to ensure that the content of all information provided on the site is lawful.[73]

71. Internet Information Services Rules, art. 8.

72. Internet Information Services Rules, arts. 9–12.

73. Internet Information Services Rules, arts. 13–15. *See also* Provisional Measures for the Administration of Network Advertisements in Beijing Municipality (the "Measures"), issued by Beijing Administration of Industry and Commerce (Beijing AIC) in April 2001 and effective as of May 1, 2001. Though merely local in scope, the Measures represent the first attempt to specifically regulate network advertisements in China. "Network advertisement" is defined therein to include all advertisements issued by providers of Internet information services through such means as flags, buttons, text links, and electronic mail. The Beijing AIC administrative center will administer and supervise all network advertisements within its jurisdiction. The Measures provide material requirements for service providers applying for advertising business licenses, procedures for the administration of network advertisements, and several requirements on special goods or services, including pharmaceuticals and agricultural products. Finally, the Measures require that Internet information service providers with foreign investments comply with all relevant

Operators are also required to keep records for a period of 60 days of all content included in their Web sites, the time of subscriber access to the Internet, the account numbers of the subscribers, and other information and to submit such records for inspection to the relevant government authorities.[74] As required under Article 62 of the Telecom Regulations, an Internet information services provider is required to cease circulation of any materials that it discovers are in violation of Article 15 of the Internet Information Services Rules and Article 57 of the Telecom Regulations, and to maintain records of the violations and file a report with the MII and Ministry of Public Security.

FIE establishment regulations before they may obtain a license for network advertising. *See generally Online Consumer Protection,* CHINA L. & PRAC. (October 2000). *See also* Protection of the Lawful Rights and Interests of Consumers in Online Economic Activities Notice (promulgated on July 7, 2000, by the Beijing Municipal Government); Administration of Internet Online Business Tentative Procedures (promulgated on May 22, 2000, by the Fujian Provincial Administration for Industry and Commerce) (list the Internet online business activities that require registration and outlines registration procedures; lists prohibited acts when advertising over the Internet; outline procedures for online auctions, etc.). Various provincial governments have adopted rules governing transaction on the Internet and policies encouraging electronic commerce. *See* Electronic Transactions Regulations (issued on February 1, 2003, by the Guangdong Provincial People's Congress) (these are the first measures in China to regulate electronic transactions, to encourage the use of a "safe electronic signature," and to provide that electronic signatures will be viewed as legally binding to the same effect as handwritten signatures); Supervision and Administration of Electronic Commerce Tentative Procedures (issued and effective from August 1, 2002, by the Beijing Municipal Administration for Industry and Commerce) (hereinafter the "Beijing E-Commerce Procedures"). The Beijing E-Commerce Procedures apply to all business-to-business and business-to-consumer activities within the jurisdiction of Beijing. The Procedures define "E-commerce" as any trading of a commodity and distribution of trade information between two parties in a commercial transaction via the Internet. An "operator" is defined as the owner of a Web site, or the contractor who uses the Web site to engage in online transactions. Operators in Beijing must hold an Internet Information Services and Value-added Telecommunication Business Permit from the Beijing Municipal Telecommunications Administration and be registered with the BAIC in order to conduct business activities. The Beijing E-Commerce Procedures outline a number of consumer protection standards, including the requirement that online merchants sell goods at the price agreed to online. The Procedures create a transaction confirmation process, which requires that the operator close its communications with the buyer by sending a confirmation notice that states the quantity of the goods, payment, after-tax price, delivery charges, and returns information. The law allows buyers to rescind their purchase within twelve hours of receipt of the confirmation notice, or within another agreed-upon time period. In certain situations, such as where goods are defective, the law provides that buyers may return the goods within seven days of receipt. The return rule does not apply to custom-made items, perishable items, or software. The Beijing E-Commerce Procedures require that operators maintain transaction records for two years, subject to BAIC inspection. The Procedures also provide that operators must ensure that their Web sites are not allowed to be used for illegal activity, hacking, or the use of false e-mail addresses. The NPC has adopted an electronic signature law. *See China Drafts Electronic Signature Law,* CHINA DAILY (April 3, 2004).

74. Internet Information Services Rules, arts. 13–15. *See also* Decision on Ensuring the Security of the Internet, issued by the Standing Committee of the National People's Congress on December 28, 2000. This Decision is issued by the NPC's Standing Committee and outlines the penalties for activities that violate the Criminal Law through use of the Internet. Article 1 of the Decision provides the general objective of protecting the security of the Internet, including computer networks and communication networks. *See also* Regulations on the Administration of Secrecy Maintenance for Internet Computer Information Systems, issued by the State Secrecy Bureau on January 1, 2000. The State Secrecy Bureau is an agency with substantial regulatory power. The general principle of the regulations is that whoever posts information on the Internet is responsible for the consequences of unlawful disclosure.

If a commercial Internet information services provider applies for public listing in China or overseas, or for the establishment of an equity joint venture or joint cooperation with foreign investors, it shall apply, in advance, to the MII for approval. In such cases, the ratio of the foreign investor's interest in the investment is required to comply with provisions of relevant laws and administrative regulations.[75]

The Internet Information Services Rules provide that the regulatory authorities are empowered to pursue various penalties, including fines, revocation of license, suspension of operations, and criminal penalties to address violations of the Rules. Penalties may be pursued in situations wherein an operator engages in commercial Internet information services without a license or outside the permissible scope of its license; publishes or disseminates information in violation of the content restrictions of the Rules and the Telecom Regulations or promptly fails to cease circulating offending materials; fails to keep proper records of content on its Web sites as required by Article 14; fails to post the operation license number on its Web site; or violates other industry-specific laws and regulations for specialized information providers.[76]

b. Internet Publishing

In addition to the Internet Information Services Rules adopted by the MII, the General Administration of Press and Publishing (GAPP) has adopted a separate set of regulations controlling the publication of content via the Internet.[77] The Internet Publishing Regulations provide that Internet publishing activities are required "to comply with the Constitution and relevant laws and regulations, conform with the policy of serving the people and the

75. Internet Information Services Rules, art. 17.

76. Internet Information Services Rules, arts. 19–24. The breach of any duty by government authorities responsible for regulatory oversight is grounds for civil and criminal penalties. Art. 25. The issue of privacy rights is something that is underdeveloped in China, especially in respect to the Internet. Although there are no specific laws on privacy rights, such rights can be inferred from the PRC Constitution (*see* Article 38 on "fundamental rights") and the PRC Civil Law ("right of reputation"). *See generally* S. Huang, & R. Ji, *Privacy Protection in China's Cyberspace,* CHINA L. & PRAC. (February 2003).

77. Administration of Internet Publishing Tentative Procedures (promulgated by the GAPP and the MII on June 27, 2002, and effective as of August 1, 2002) (hereinafter the "Internet Publishing Procedures"). *See also* Provisional Regulations on Management of Cultural Products on the Internet (issued by the Ministry of Culture on May 10, 2003). (The Regulations provide that "cultural products" include products produced, distributed, and circulated over the Internet, including audio and video products, games, plays, arts, and animated cartoons. They require that companies dealing with cultural products on the Internet obtain approval from the Ministry of Culture. The Regulations also contain a broad list of prohibited content. They are effective July 1, 2003, and all companies subject to the Regulations are required to apply for approval by September 1, 2003.) *See generally Internet Publishing: China Pushes for Increased Supervision and Self-Discipline in the Industry*, CHINA L. & PRAC. (September 2002).

socialist cause, disseminate and aggregate all thought, ethics and scientific, technological and cultural knowledge that are beneficial in improving the qualities of the nation, driving economic development and promoting social progress, and enrich the spiritual life of the people."[78] The principal regulatory authority responsible for Internet publishing is the GAPP.[79]

Under the Internet Publishing Regulations, the term "Internet publishing" means an act of online dissemination whereby Internet information service providers select, edit, and process works created by themselves or others and subsequently post the same on the Internet or transmit the work to the user's end via the Internet for browsing, reading, or downloading by the public. The works of service providers include (1) content of such types of publications as books, newspapers, periodicals, audio and video products, electronic publications, etc. that have been formerly published, or works that have been made public in other media; or (2) edited and processed works of literature, art, natural science, social science, engineering technology, etc. For the purposes of these Regulations, the term "Internet publishers" means Internet information service providers that engage in Internet publishing business with the approval of the GAPP and the MII.[80] The Internet Publishing Regulations provide that approval by the GAPP is required to engage in any Internet publishing activities.[81]

Upon approval, an Internet publisher is required to display its approval number on its Web site.[82] If an Internet publisher fails to commence Internet publishing activities within 180 days after its registration date, the

78. Internet Publishing Procedures, arts. 2, 17.

79. The GAPP is in charge of the supervision and administration of Internet publishing throughout China. Its primary duties and responsibilities include (1) formulating, and organizing the implementation of, national Internet publishing plans; (2) formulating principles, policies, rules, and regulations on the administration of Internet publishing; (3) formulating, and organizing the implementation of, national plans on the total number, structure, and distribution of Internet publishers; (4) submitting Internet publishers to advance examination and approval; and (5) overseeing published online content in accordance with relevant laws, rules, and regulations and punishing violations of State laws and regulations on publishing. Internet Publishing Regulations, art. 4.

80. Internet Publishing Regulations, art. 5.

81. Internet Publishing Regulations, art. 8. After approval by the GAPP, the publisher is required to obtain the approval of the MII. Internet Publishing Regulations, art. 11. If a company goes through any name change or merger/acquisition, or termination/dissolution of operations, GAPP approval is required. Internet Publishing Regulations, arts. 13, 14. If publishing activities are engaged in without approval, the press and publication authorities may suspend a company's operation, confiscate the equipment used to engage in the illegal publishing activities, and confiscate any illegal income. In addition, if the illegal turnover is RMB10,000 or more, MII may impose a fine of not less than five times and not more than 10 times the illegal turnover; if the illegal turnover was less than RMB10,000, MII may impose a fine of not less than RMB10,000 and not more than RMB50,000. Internet Publishing Regulations, art. 24.

82. Internet Publishing Regulations, art. 12. If a party violates Article 12, the press and publication executive authorities may issue a warning and impose a fine of not less than RMB5,000 and not more than RMB50,000. Internet Publishing Regulations, art. 25.

publishers registration may be cancelled.[83] A publisher is required to report to the GAPP if any of its published materials involves "significant topics" such as State security or social stability, and a failure to report such topics is grounds for penalties.[84] Under the GAPP standards, an Internet publisher may not publish materials that

(1) contradict the basic principles determined in the Constitution
(2) compromise national unity, sovereignty, or territorial integrity
(3) disclose State secrets, compromise State security, or harm the reputation or interests of the State
(4) incite ethnic hatred or ethnic discrimination, damage inter-ethnic unity, or violate the customs and habits of ethnic groups
(5) propagate evil cults or superstitions
(6) disseminate rumors, disturb the social order, or aim to destabilize society
(7) propagate obscenity, gambling, or violence, or incite the commission of crimes
(8) insult or slander a third party or infringe upon the lawful rights and interests of a third party
(9) compromise public morality or refined indigenous culture and traditions or
(10) are otherwise content prohibited by laws, administrative regulations, or State rules[85]

In addition to the above, material published over the Internet that targets minors may not include content that induces minors to imitate acts that are contrary to public morality, are illegal or criminal, or are of a "horrific, cruel or other such nature that is harmful to the physical and psychological health of minors."[86]

---

83. Internet Publishing Regulations, art. 15.

84. Internet Publishing Regulations, art. 16. For violations of Article 16, the authorities may issue an order to cease the posting or transmission of the work on the significant topic, issue a warning, or impose a fine of not less than RMB10,000 and not more than RMB50,000. If the circumstances are "serious," the government may suspend or revoke a party's approval. Internet Publishing Regulations, art. 26.

85. Internet Publishing Regulations, art. 17.

86. Internet Publishing Regulations, art. 18. If an Internet publisher discovers that posted materials contain information in violation of Articles 17 and 18, the publisher is immediately required to cease the posting or transmission thereof, maintain a record of the publication, and submit a report to the local press and publication authorities and the GAPP. Internet Publishing Regulations, art. 20. If an Internet publisher posts or transmits any of the prohibited content specified in Articles 17 and 18 hereof, the authorities may confiscate any illegal income, impose a fine of not less than five times and not more than 10 times the illegal turnover (if in excess of RMB10,000); if the illegal turnover was less than RMB10,000, GAPP will impose a fine of not less than RMB10,000 and not more than RMB50,000. If the circumstances are "serious," the authorities may order that an operation be suspended or approval be revoked. Internet Publishing Regulations, art. 27.

Internet publishers are required to set up an editorial responsibility system that includes the use of qualified and trained editorial staff obligated to examine content to ensure the lawfulness of the material to be published.[87] Internet publishers are required by law to maintain a record of the contents of the published materials, as well as information concerning the times of posting or transmission and the URLs or domain names. Copies of such records shall be kept for 60 days and shall be provided to the government authorities upon request.[88] Internet publishers are expressly required to comply with all copyright laws and regulations.[89] An Internet publisher is liable if any published material is false or unfair and thereby infringes on the lawful interests of any citizen or legal person.[90]

In addition, the State Administration of Radio, Film and Television (SARFT) asserts jurisdiction over the transmission of news, film and television, entertainment, and professional audio-video programs over all types of networks, including the Internet and networks using cable or wireless technologies.[91] Any party transmitting audio-video programs must obtain SARFT approval and be licensed. Parties that operate Web sites in China are prohibited from providing connection services for the purchase or transmission of audio-video programs to unlicensed operators of Web sites inside or outside China.

c. Regulation of Internet Cafés

The government regulates the establishment and operation of Internet cafés, and notably in response to a tragic fire at an overcrowded Beijing Internet café in 2002.[92] The Internet Café Regulations cover all business operations that

87. Internet Publishing Regulations, art. 21.
88. Internet Publishing Regulations, art. 22.
89. Internet Publishing Regulations, art. 23.
90. Internet Publishing Regulations, art. 19.
91. Measures for Administration of the Transmission of Audio-Video Programs Over the Internet and Other Information Networks (issued on February 10, 2003, by the State Administration of Radio, Film and Television).
92. *See* Regulation on Administration of Business Establishments that Provide Internet Services (promulgated on November 15, 2002, by the State Council). *See also* Administrative Measures on Places of Business for Internet Login Services (the "Measures"), issued by the MII, the Ministry of Public Security (MPS), the Ministry of Culture (MOCT), and the State Administration of Industry and Commerce (SAIC), on April 3, 2001. The Measures were issued to accompany a notice from the State Council strengthening the administration of places of business for Internet access services. The Measures provide details for the administration of Internet log-in services nationwide, including so-called "Internet bars" or "Internet cafes." With the Measures, information industry authorities of all governmental levels have been given charge of approving service licenses for log-in service operators. Public security authorities are to regulate network security and punish activities that constitute a breach of network security regulations. Cultural authorities will serve to control their content, and Administrations of Industry and Commerce (from the SAIC down) will approve business licenses and punish illegal business activities. The Measures also provide application procedures and requirements for the operation of an Internet log-in service location, as well as details on the obligations of operators. After the effective date of these Measures, all operators of Internet log-in services will be required to obtain approvals from the MPS and the

provide Internet services to the public through computers or other electronic devices, such as Internet cafés or computer rooms. Educational institutions and libraries are exempt from the regulations. An Internet café must be operated by an enterprise, not by an individual. Prior to the commencement of operations, an application must be filed with the MOCT or approved branch office. Upon approval by the MOCT, an application is further examined by the public security bureau with jurisdiction over the business. The public security bureau is required to inspect the business premises for information network safety and fire safety. With the public security authority's approval, the MOCT entity will perform a final review before issuing a Network Culture Business License. Upon receipt of the Network Culture Business License, the enterprise may apply to the relevant SAIC office for a business license.

The Internet Café Regulations prohibit certain activities. Specifically, the business operator and customers are prohibited from producing, downloading, or disseminating prohibited or sensitive content. The regulations further prohibit business operators and users from using an Internet café to intentionally produce and distribute computer viruses. The Internet connection used by the operator must be obtained from a licensed Internet connection service provider, and the on-site computers are to connect to the Internet via a local network and not directly link to the Internet. The business operator is to register a customer's identification and keep a record of Internet use for at least 60 days and is subject to inspection by the public security bureau or MOCT officials. The Internet Café Regulations outline administrative fines for noncompliance from RMB5,000 to RMB50,000, and criminal liabilities may be incurred in severe circumstances.

d. Anti-Spam Standards

The Internet Society of China (ISC), a government-sanctioned industry group, issued standards that are intended to prohibit or restrict unsolicited commercial e-mail transmission (also referred to as spam). The ISC defines spam to include unsolicited promotional e-mail, e-mail the recipient cannot refuse to receive, e-mail that fails to contain the sender's identity or contact information, and e-mail that contains false information concerning the sender.[93] The standards also require ISC members to share information and work together to curb the dissemination of spam.

MOCT, service licenses from the MII, and business licenses from the SAIC to operate legally. They must then sign a letter of responsibility for information security with the ISP providing their access service.

93. Anti-Spam Standards (issued on February 25, 2003, by the Internet Society of China). *See generally* M. Fong, *The Spam-China Link*, WALL ST. J. (March 24, 2004) (article states that eight of ten U.S.-based spam operators use servers in China to host the Web sites that spam recipients are referred to, and states that the efforts of the Internet Society of China are insufficient to stop the spamming activities in China).

13. Domain Name Registration in China

The Ministry of Information Industry and the China Internet Network Information Center (CNNIC) have issued a number of rules governing the registration and use of Chinese language domain names. The various rules set forth the standards for registration[94] and dispute resolution procedures for conflicting claims over domain names.[95] The Supreme People's Court has issued a set of regulations outlining the management of cases involving domain name disputes.[96] The Beijing Higher People's Court has adopted its

94. *See* Administration of China Internet Domain Names Procedures (issued on September 30, 2002, by the MII, and superseding rules adopted in 2000). The MII Domain Name Procedures create a first-in-time system for domain names—the first applicant for a domain name applicant has priority over other applicants. No domain name reservations are allowed, except for reservations for certain words related to the original application. There are exceptions to the priority rule: (i) if the domain name infringes on an existing name, logo, or mark, (ii) if the applicant does not have any rights underlying the domain name or portion thereof; and (iii) if the applicant registers or uses the domain name in bad faith. A party that is the owner of a well-known trademark recognized by the Trademark Office has priority in applying for second-level .cn domain names. Under the Supreme People's Court rules, a court may cancel a domain name registration if (i) the domain name is identical or substantially similar to a well-known mark, or (ii) if the domain name is unused after registration and there is no intent to use the domain name. The new regulations also create a new regime for Chinese-character and .cn domain names, including third-level .cn English domain names, second-level .cn English domain names, and Chinese-character third-level domain names. In addition, foreign businesses are allowed to register .cn domain names. The MII Domain Name Procedures prohibit certain items from being part of a domain name, including (i) activities in opposition to the PRC Constitution or national security; (ii) exposure of state secrets; (iii) defaming another person; and (iv) pornography, violence, or gambling. The China Internet Network Information Center (CNNIC) will not provide registration services but will remain the official administrator and Registry operator of Chinese-character third-level domain names and .cn domains. In its regulatory role, CNNIC drafted new measures to regulate domain name registration service providers. Chinese Domain Name registrations can only be obtained through CNNIC-accredited registrars, such as NeuStar, the exclusive gateway for registrars outside of China.

95. *See* Measures for the Settlement of Disputes Arising from Chinese Domain Names Registration (Trial), issued by CNNIC on November 1, 2000, and effective as of December 1, 2000. The CNNIC Dispute Resolution Procedures list the organizations designated to handle Chinese domain name disputes. Also set out are the principles behind the handling of Chinese domain name disputes, the validity of judgments on such disputes, the conditions for filing a complaint of Chinese domain name dispute, and several examples that demonstrate the "malicious registration of other's domain names." These Measures apply only to the settlement of disputes relating to Chinese domain names registered with CNNIC and trademarks protected under PRC laws. The China International Economic and Trade Arbitration Committee (CIETAC) has been designated by CNNIC as the dispute resolution organization to handle Chinese domain name disputes. CIETAC began accepting cases as of January 1, 2001. *See also* Resolution of Domain Name Disputes Procedures (issued on September 30, 2002, by the China Internet Network Information Center [CNNIC]); Policies for Resolution of Domain Name Disputes Procedural Rules (issued on September 30, 2002, by the [CNNIC]). Domain name disputes may also be heard through the Hong Kong International Arbitration Center under these regulations. Parties may agree to submit their disputes to an arbitral body of their choice or to file an action in a people's court having the jurisdiction over the district in which CNNIC is located (for domestic disputes) or in the First Intermediate People's Court of Beijing Municipality (for foreign disputes).

96. *See* Interpretation on the Specific Applicable Laws Governing Civil Disputes Cases relating to Computer Network Domain Names, issued by the Supreme People's Court on July 17, 2001, and effective as of July 24, 2001 (provides the regulations on civil disputes concerning registration and using of domain names and the criteria for claims of infringement or unfair competition). The SPC has also adopted interpretation of the law concerning the management of copyright infringement cases involving computer networks. *See* Interpretation on the Specific Applicable Laws Governing Cases of Copyright Disputes relating to Computer Networks, issued by the Supreme People's Court as Fa Shi (2000) No. 48, effective as of December 21, 2000, and amended January 2004, *reprinted in* China Laws for Foreign Business (CCH), Business Regulation ¶ 11-720. *See generally* J. Deng, *The Supreme People's Courts Take on*

own order with respect to the management of cases involving domain name disputes.[97] The MII also regulates companies that are in the business of providing domain name registration services.[98]

B. Software Enterprises and Software Products

1. Policies to Encourage Software Enterprises

The Chinese government has adopted a number of policies and regulations to encourage the development of the domestic and foreign-funded software industry.[99] The Software and Integrated Circuit Policies set forth provisions concerning investment and financing policies, tax policies, policies concerning research and development objectives, policies encouraging the export of software products, policies for income distribution and incentives,

---

Copyright Liabilities for ISPs, CHINA L. & PRAC. (April 2004). The SPC Computer Copyright Infringement Interpretation provides for jurisdiction relating to copyright disputes concerning computer networks, the nature of the digital form of products, the usage of such copyrights, the torts that network services providers (NSPs) are liable for, and related penalties. The Interpretation specifically provides a method to determine the jurisdiction of courts on such copyright disputes. It makes tort lawsuits possible by providing that even if it is difficult to determine the place where the tort is committed or where the defendant has his domicile, the location of the computer terminal used by the plaintiff to find the content that causes a tort can be deemed as the place where the tort is committed. In addition, the Interpretation provides that the digital format is one form of works or products listed and protected by copyright regulations in China. Therefore, if a product with literary, artistic, or scientific value is original and can be duplicated, the people's courts shall protect the copyright. The Interpretation further provides that the usage of copyright shall comply with the copyright law and copyright owners have the right of an author based on law. This represents the first time clear and specific standards to judge the tort activities of NSPs have been provided. The principle of determination of liability adopted in the Interpretation is the doctrine of liability for wrongs. NSPs will be responsible for torts in which they are liable. In order to warn an NSP of an online tort or request the registration information regarding an NSP's users, a copyright owner shall display the identification card, the certificate of ownership, and the evidence of tort activities. It shall be deemed that no warning or requirement has been given if the owner does not provide one of these items. The Interpretation provides the standards for compensation, which will generally range from RMB500 to RMB300,000. The maximum compensation must be less than RMB500,000.

97. *See* Several Guidance Opinions on the Handling of Intellectual Property Civil Dispute Cases Involving the Registration and Use of Domain Names by the Beijing High People's Court on August 15, 2000. The Beijing High People's Court has recently issued the Opinions for use in Beijing. The Opinions list "malicious" practices regarding the false registration of domain names that are well-known or registered trademarks names that violate business ethics and constitute noncompetitive business activities. If a defendant is found guilty of "malicious" behavior, the court can order the defendant to cease using the domain name and to pay damages to the rightful owner of the name.

98. *See* Circular on Strengthening the Administration of Internet Domain Names in China (issued on July 31, 2003, by the MII) (requires all entities that provide domain name registration services within China, including entities that register domain names with non-Chinese suffixes, to comply with the requirements provided in the domain name administration measures and to file an application with the MII). *See also* Circular on the Interpretation of Applicable Laws on the Qualifications of Providers of Domain Name Registration Services (issued on November 20, 2003, by the MII) (requires that an applicant for the provision of domain name registration services be qualified to provide "information services (ICP) business").

99. Policies Encouraging the Development of the Software and Integrated Circuit Industries, promulgated by the State Council on June 24, 2000, reprinted in CHINA L. & PRAC., September 2000 (hereinafter the "Software and Integrated Circuit Policies").

educational policies, policies for the supervision of the software industry, and policies concerning intellectual property rights.

The Software and Integrated Circuit Policies provide certain tax relief for software enterprises, including rebates on VAT tax in excess of 3 percent paid, to be used for expanding the enterprise or research and development activities.[100] The Policies also provide that newly established software enterprises are eligible for an exemption from import duty and import VAT for production equipment and production software.[101]

The Policies further provide that newly established software enterprises are eligible for two years of tax exemption and three years of half-rate on income tax from the year that the enterprise becomes profitable.[102] Software enterprises may also categorize their personnel and training expenses as before-tax expense for purposes of calculating enterprise income tax.[103] Under Article 7 of the Software and Integrated Circuit Policies, a qualified software enterprise is an entity to be taxed at a reduced income tax rate of 10 percent.[104]

---

100. Software and Integrated Circuit Policies, art. 5. *See also* Circular on Tax Policies for Further Encouraging Development of Software Industry and IC Industry (adopted by the Ministry of Finance and the State Administration of Taxation, effective from January 1, 2002, to December 31, 2010), *reprinted in* CHINA LAWS FOR FOREIGN BUSINESS (CCH), Taxation ¶ 31-860. Manufacturers of integrated circuits who have paid VAT will receive a rebate for all but 3% of the VAT paid. The rules require that the rebated funds be applied back into the business and specifically for the use in the manufacturing, research, and development of integrated circuit products. The rules exempt from corporate income tax for two years domestic manufacturers of integrated circuits that produce chips with a line width below 0.8 microns, and such enterprises are entitled to further exemption of 50% of corporate income tax for three years starting from the first profitable year. Foreign investment companies producing integrated circuits are already entitled to the 50% tax break, and the rule brings domestic manufacturers in parity with FIEs. Domestic and FIE chip manufacturers who invest profits in new or existing integrated circuit companies and promise to operate for at least five years, are eligible for a 40% rebate on income tax paid. Manufacturers who reinvest their after-tax profits in western China and promise to operate for at least five years receive an 80% rebate on income tax paid. *See also* Notice on Relevant Issues Concerning the Implementation of Preferential Income Tax Policies for Software Enterprises and High-Technology Enterprises (issued on May 29, 2003, by the State Administration of Taxation, and effective January 1, 2003) (provides that software production enterprises established after July 1, 2000, will be considered "newly established software production enterprises" entitled to preferential tax treatment; provides a definition of "first profit-making year"; outlines the method for determining eligibility of a software enterprise for tax reductions and exemptions; and sets forth the applicable tax rate for newly established software production enterprises and high-technology enterprises to be 15%); Reply on the Enjoyment of Preferential Enterprise Income Tax Policies for Technologically Advanced Enterprises by Foreign-Invested Enterprises with Investment in Installments (issued on July 9, 2003, by the State Administration of Taxation) (provides that FIEs established pursuant to an approved contract that requires the contribution of capital in installments are eligible for tax preferences, and may enjoy a 50% reduction of enterprise income tax for an additional three years beyond the initial five-year tax holiday).

101. Software and Integrated Circuit Policies, arts. 6, 8, 14, 15.

102. Software and Integrated Circuit Policies, arts. 6, 8.

103. Software and Integrated Circuit Policies, art. 9.

104. Software and Integrated Circuit Policies, art. 7. *See also* Administrative Measures on Recognition of Key Software Enterprises under the State Planning Scheme (Trial Implementation), Jigaoji (2001), No. 1351, adopted on July 24, 2001, by the State Development and Planning Commission, Ministry of Information, MOFTEC, State Administration of Taxation, reprinted in CHINA LAWS FOR FOREIGN BUSINESS (CCH), Business Regulation ¶ 16-661.

In addition to preferential tax treatment, software enterprises may be entitled to preferential interest rates on loans issued by the Import and Export Bank of China and preferred rates on export credit insurance.[105] Software enterprises with annual exports exceeding $1 million have the right to export their own software and do not need to work with an approved trading company.[106]

The Software and Integrated Circuit Policies also provide that software enterprises have the autonomy to set salary and compensation levels based upon performance and technical accomplishments. The Policies further provide that an enterprise may accept patents and other technology as capital contributions and in return provide corresponding shares in the enterprise to the inventors or contributors.[107] In order to encourage export sales, senior managers of such enterprises are entitled to go through simplified entry and exit approval procedures to facilitate foreign travel.[108] The Software and Integrated Circuit Policies outline additional policies of the government such as the emphasis on education to improve software talent,[109] government procurement policies aimed at providing preference to domestic software producers,[110] and protection of intellectual property rights.[111]

2. Standards for Key Software Enterprises

A qualified software enterprise must satisfy one of the following conditions:

(1) Annual revenue from software-related sales in excess of RMB100 million

(2) Annual export volume in excess of US$500,000, with the volume of software exports constituting 50 percent or more of the annual revenue of the enterprise; or a software export volume constituting 70 percent or more of the annual revenue of the enterprise

(3) In accordance with the requirements of the software industry development plan of the State, and in compliance with the State's guidelines for investment in the software industry, the software sales volume in certain major fields ranking among the top five[112]

105. Software and Integrated Circuit Policies, art. 12.
106. Software and Integrated Circuit Policies, art. 13.
107. Software and Integrated Circuit Policies, arts. 18–20. The use of stock options as compensation for employees is encouraged but must be in compliance with applicable securities regulations. Art. 21.
108. Software and Integrated Circuit Policies, arts. 14, 15.
109. Software and Integrated Circuit Policies, arts. 22–24.
110. Software and Integrated Circuit Policies, arts. 25–27.
111. Software and Integrated Circuit Policies, arts. 32–24.
112. Key Software Enterprise Measures, art. 2.

The criteria for an enterprise qualified as a Key Software Enterprise is as follows:

(1) The enterprise is a legal person that is established within the territory of China in accordance with the law
(2) The enterprise engages in the business of, and has its main business income derived from, computer software development and production, system integration and application services, and other related technical services
(3) The enterprise developed or owns the intellectual property rights to software products; or the enterprise has provided qualified technical services such as computer information system integration
(4) The enterprise employs technical personnel, engaged in software product development and technical services, consisting of at least half of the company's employees
(5) The enterprise has technological facilities and business premises that are necessary for the development of software and the technical services of the enterprise
(6) The enterprise has the ability to ensure the quality of its software products and technical services
(7) The enterprise invests at least 8 percent of its annual software-related income in software technology and product research and development
(8) The annual software sales revenue of the enterprise constitutes more than 35 percent of the total annual revenue of the enterprise, among which income derived from self-produced software constitutes more than 50 percent of the software sales revenue
(9) The ownership of the enterprise and its property is undisputed, and the enterprise is in compliance with all applicable laws and regulations[113]

The China Software Industry Association is responsible for the preliminary examination and annual inspection of Key Software Enterprises, and has the following functions and responsibilities:

(1) To accept applications for recognition for Key Software Enterprises under the State planning policies
(2) To organize the appraisal and examination of Key Software Enterprises under the State planning policies and the annual inspection

113. Measures on Administration of Software Enterprises, art. 12.

(3) To produce a list of enterprises which have passed the preliminary examination as Key Software Enterprises under the State planning policies and the annual inspection, and to submit it to the competent departments of the State for examination and approval[114]

When applying for recognition as a Key Software Enterprise, the following documents shall be submitted by the applicant:

(1) The certificate of recognition as a software enterprise from the China Software Industry Association
(2) An application form for recognition as a Key Software Enterprise under the State planning policies, including a statement of assets and liabilities, a statement of profit and loss, a statement of cash flow, enterprise income tax returns, the structure of the workforce and the educational backgrounds of the personnel, the environment for software development, the situation of the enterprise's operations, and other relevant information
(3) The total volume of the enterprise's software to be exported in the current year
(4) Other documents as required by the competent governmental departments[115]

---

114. Software and Integrated Circuit Policies, art. 30; Key Software Enterprise Measures, art. 3. The competent departments of the State refers to the State Development and Planning Commission, the Ministry of Information Industry, the Ministry of Commerce, and the State Administration of Taxation. *See also* Criteria for Confirmation and Measures on Administration of Software Enterprises (Trial Implementation), promulgated on October 16, 2000, by the Ministry of Information Industry, Ministry of Education, Ministry of Science and Technology, and State Administration of Taxation, *reprinted in* CHINA LAWS FOR FOREIGN BUSINESS (CCH), Business Regulation ¶ 16-660 (outlining the standards for the China Software Industry Association, procedures for confirming key software enterprises, procedures for annual inspections) (hereinafter the "Measures on Administration of Software Enterprises"). The Measures on Administration of Software Enterprises have been characterized in the press as ambiguous given that the tax authorities in Beijing interpret the Measures to exclude developers of customized software. *See China: Muddy Tax Policies Present Problems for Software Manufacturers, Officials,* CHINA ONLINE, May 18, 2001.

115. Key Software Enterprise Measures, art. 4. An applicant that submits false information may be debarred from involvement in the program for three years. Art. 9. *See also* Measures on Administration of Software Enterprises, Article 13, which provides that a software enterprise applying for confirmation shall submit to the government the following documents: (1) the software enterprise confirmation application form, including balance sheet, statement of assets and liabilities, cash flow table, and situations of the enterprise such as personnel arrangement and the composition of their educational backgrounds, software development environment, business operations, and other relevant matters; (2) the duplicate and copies of the business license of the enterprise legal person; (3) a list of software products that are developed, produced, or operated by the enterprise, including software products developed by the enterprise and products sold by the enterprise as an agent; (4) materials proving that the enterprise has developed the software products or holds intellectual property rights over the software products, including software product registration certificate, software copyright registration certificate, or patent certificate, etc; (5) a system integration enterprise shall submit materials such as the qualification grading certificate issued by the Ministry of Information Industry; and (6) other documents as required by the Ministry of Information Industry.

The China Software Industry Association shall conduct an annual inspection of Key Software Enterprises and report the results of the annual inspection to the competent departments of the government for approval. When an enterprise is approved as having passed the annual inspection, the China Software Industry Association shall affix the seal of "satisfactory annual inspection" on the certificate of recognition of a Key Software Enterprise and thereafter be entitled to ongoing preferential tax treatment. An enterprise that fails to pass the annual inspection shall not be able to enjoy the preferential policy of 10 percent income tax in that year.[116]

3. Software Product Standards and Regulation

The MII has adopted regulations concerning the development, manufacture, sale, and registration of software products in China.[117] The Software Product Measures apply to activities of business operation and administration of software products (including domestically produced software and imported software) within the territory of the People's Republic of China. The Software Product Measures do not apply to software developed and used by individuals or organizations for individual or internal use. The Software Product Measures provide that the development, manufacture, sale, importation, and exportation of software products and other related activities are required to comply with all relevant laws, regulations, and standards of China, and prohibit any individual or enterprise from engaging in the development, manufacture, sale, importation, and exportation of the following software products that:

(1) Infringe intellectual property rights of others[118]
(2) Contain computer viruses
(3) May endanger the security of computer systems
(4) Contain any material that is prohibited by the State from circulation
(5) Fail to comply with the State's standards on software[119]

116. Software and Integrated Circuit Policies, art. 29; Key Software Enterprise Measures, arts. 6, 7. A party that has been denied approval as a Key Software Enterprise or fails its annual inspection may apply for reconsideration. Art. 8. *See also* Measures on Administration of Software Enterprises, art. 18.

117. Software and Integrated Circuit Policies, art. 31; Measures on the Administration of Software Products, promulgated on October 27, 2000, as Decree No. 5 (2000) of the Ministry of Information Industry, reprinted in CHINA LAWS FOR FOREIGN BUSINESS (CCH), Business Regulation ¶ 16-665 (hereinafter the "Software Products Measures"). *China Issues Rules Governing Software,* Xinhua News Agency, November 9, 2000, available on Lexis, News Library or at the Xinhua Web site at http://www.xinhua.com.cn.

118. Software and Integrated Circuit Policies, arts. 32–34.

119. Software Product Measures, art. 4.

The Ministry of Information Industry or its local branch is the government agency responsible for regulatory oversight and, in regard to software products, has the following duties and responsibilities:

(1) Formulating and publishing standards and norms for testing software products
(2) Filing for the records of domestically produced software products that have been registered in various provinces, autonomous regions, and directly administered municipalities
(3) Instructing, supervising, and inspecting the administration of software products in various regions across the country
(4) Authorizing software product test organizations to carry out tests in accordance with standards and norms for software products and standards and norms for software product tests
(5) Formulating a uniform software registration number system nationwide, and producing software product registration certificates
(6) Issuing public notices on registered software products[120]

a. Registration of Software Products

All software products are required to be registered, and products that have not been registered cannot be distributed or sold in China. Only software products that are registered and that satisfy the standards in the Software Product Measures may receive applicable preferential treatment.[121] Although imported software is required to be registered, only domestically produced software is entitled to preferential treatment. Upon approval and verification of the registration materials submitted to the MII, a domestic applicant receives a registration number. For imported software, the China Software Association is responsible for review of applications for registration of imported software products and, upon examination and approval, the Association will issue a product registration certificate.[122] A software product

120. Software Product Measures, arts. 5, 6.

121. Software Product Measures, arts. 7–9. The manufacturer of domestically produced software is required to register its products with the China Software Association. The following documents must be submitted with the registration: (1) the application form for software product registration; (2) a copy of the applicant's business license; (3) a sample of the software product to be registered; (4) proof of intellectual property rights; (5) product test certificates produced by the software testing agency authorized by the Ministry of Information Industry; and (6) other documents as may be required. Art. 8.

122. Software Product Measures, arts. 9–10. For registration and filing for the record of imported software products, the enterprise responsible for the importation shall submit the following documents: (1) the application form for software product registration; (2) a copy of the applicant's business license; (3) a sample of the software products; (4) proof of intellectual property rights; (5) the test results produced by an authorized software test organization; and (6) proof and other necessary documents establishing that the software product complies with software importation policies and provisions of the State.

registration certificate is valid for a period of five years, and subsequent extensions may be granted.[123]

b. Manufacture of Software Products

All software products manufactured in China must comply with the laws and applicable technical standards. Developers and manufacturers of software products are required to be authorized to engage in software development, have the technical and infrastructure resources to manufacture software, and be capable of guaranteeing a quality software product.[124] A software manufacturer may produce only software in which it has a copyright interest or that it has been licensed to manufacture by the original copyright owner.[125]

The packaging of software products supplied to users must indicate the name and version of the software, the copyright owner of the software, software registration number, software manufacturing unit (or importing unit) and its address, and date of manufacture. Software products (including imported or foreign software products manufactured in China) supplied to users shall include a sufficiently detailed user manual, instructions, or other explanatory documents concerning the application and use of the software product. Such manuals or instructions are required to be in Chinese. The contact responsible for technical support and warranty service must be included in the user manual, instructions, or the software product itself. A software manufacturer and those that produce software product carriers (such as compact disks and floppy disk drives) are prohibited from manufacturing software products that have not been registered.[126]

c. Sale of Software Products

The Software Product Measures provide that software developers and manufacturers are authorized to directly market and sell their software products. In situations in which manufacturers use distributors or agents to market their products, the Measures require that a written agency agreement be executed between the agency and the developer/manufacturer. An agency agreement shall state the scope and limitations of agency, geographical coverage, term of the agency relationship, technical support, and other matters that may be required by the Ministry of Information Industry.[127] For software

123. Software Product Measures, art. 12.
124. Software Product Measures, arts. 13, 14, 17.
125. Software Product Measures, art. 15. The Measures specifically prohibit a manufacturer from producing or selling pirated software. Arts. 21, 26.
126. Software Product Measures, arts. 18–20.
127. Software Product Measures, arts. 22–23.

products subject to a license to use, the licensor is required to advise the user of the license terms and conditions. The software seller is required to inform the users of the technical support contacts as well as fees for such services. If the technical support contact is not specified, the software products seller shall be deemed as the unit that will provide technical support. If there is no indication of service fee and its amount, such technical support service fee shall be deemed to have been included in the price of the software products. Only registered software may be distributed and/or sold in China. Counterfeit software may not be sold or given away for free.[128]

d. Encryption and Security Product Regulations

Certain types of software products may be subject to regulations that apply to encryption-related or security-related products. According to regulations issued by the State Council in 1999, encryption products from foreign countries are prohibited from being sold in China.[129] If a domestic entity (such as a research institute) intends to import encryption products for its own use, the imported products containing encryption technology must be approved by the State Encryption Administration. However, the import of encryption products for sale in the Chinese market would not be approved, as this would violate the provision that no foreign encryption products are allowed to be sold in China.

The foreign business community in China reacted negatively to the adoption of the Encryption Regulations given the ambiguous and potentially sweeping application, which could prohibit many electronic devices, such as mobile telephones, that contain some encryption technology. Subsequently, the State Encryption Administration announced in March 2000 (without issuing any official document) that the term "encryption products and equipment containing encryption technology" is limited to "special purpose hardware and software with encryption and decryption as the core function" and does not include "other devices such as wireless phones, Windows software, Internet browser software, etc." However, the State Encryption Administration failed to specify the standards to determine whether a device is "special purpose" or has encryption as its core function. It is left for observation as to how the State Encryption Administration will interpret the law.

According to regulations issued by the State Council in 1994, a sales permit is required for any "computer information system security product"

128. Software Product Measures, arts. 24, 25, 26.

129. Commercial Encryption Administrative Regulations, promulgated by the State Council in 1999 (the "Encryption Regulations").

("security product") in China. Prior to the issuance of the sales permit, samples of the security product in question must be submitted to an appraisal institution designated by the Ministry of Public Security for testing.[130] The Measures define "security product" as "special purpose hardware and software used for protecting the safety of computer information systems."

For domestically produced security products, the domestic manufacturer is required to submit the product samples for testing. For security products manufactured in a foreign country and imported for sale in China, the foreign manufacturer must designate a Chinese entity with legal person status for testing of the sample products.

The appraisal institution designated by the Ministry of Public Security for testing security products is the "Ministry of Public Security Computer Information System Security Products Quality Supervision and Testing Center" (the "Center"). At a minimum, the following must be submitted to the Center for testing of a security product:

(1) Two pieces of the sample product
(2) Business license of the applicant and, for foreign products, the business license of the Chinese entity designated by the foreign manufacturer
(3) Description of the functions and capabilities of the product in Chinese
(4) Installation instruction for the software product
(5) User's guidebook
(6) Approval from the relevant encryption administration, if the security product uses encryption technology
(7) Power of attorney issued by the foreign manufacturer to the applicant (*Note:* the applicant should be the master distributor of the foreign manufacturer in China)
(8) Reference letter for the person who is responsible for delivering the application and receiving the testing report

The testing process normally takes 30 days to complete. Pursuant to the Measures, subsequent to the completion of the testing of the security product, application may be made to the Ministry of Public Security for a sales permit. At a minimum, the following must be submitted to the Ministry of Public Security:

(1) Completed application form
(2) Business license

130. PRC Computer Information System Security Regulations, promulgated by the State Council in 1994; Administrative Measures for the Examination and Sales Licensing of Computer Information System Security Products, promulgated by the Ministry of Public Security in 1997 (the "Measures").

(3) Appraisal report
(4) Filing with the Ministry of Public Security if the product is a virus protection product
(5) Power of attorney issued by the foreign manufacturer to the applicant
(6) Approval from the relevant encryption administration, if the security product uses encryption technology
(7) Technical guidebook for the product

The Ministry of Public Security normally completes the examination process in 30 days and thereafter will issue a sales permit.

Following the adoption of the 1999 encryption rules, the government adopted a new encryption policy for wireless local area networks (LANs) in November 2003.[131] The Wireless LAN Encryption Standards Announcement provides that, effective December 1, 2003, Chinese and overseas computer manufacturers are required to use and include Chinese encryption standards (i.e., standards numbered GB15629.11-2003; GB15629.1102-2003) in terminal equipment employed in wireless local area networks. The terminal equipment at issue is commonly used in providing high-speed wireless Internet access services (e.g., Wi-Fi services) in public areas such as cafés, airport terminals, and hotel and office lobbies. After the effective date, the standards prohibit the importation, manufacture, and sale in China of any equipment used in wireless LANs that fails to comply with the designated encryption standards. Equipment currently in use is apparently not subject to the designated encryption standards. In addition, the Announcement provides that the restrictions do not apply to products that have been manufactured and imported into China before December 1, 2003, or products that are the subject of sales contracts executed before the effective date.[132] The Announcement further states that the encryption standards do not apply to LAN equipment reprocessed or manufactured in China for the export market. Although the standards are purportedly adopted to increase security, they also enhance government control and regulation

131. Announcement Regarding Implementation of Mandatory National Standards for Wireless LAN (jointly issued on November 26, 2003, by the General Administration of Quality Supervision, Inspection & Quarantine and the Standardization Administration of China) (hereinafter the "Wireless LAN Encryption Standards"). *See generally New Wireless Encryption Standards Raise Obstacles*. CHINA MARKET INTELLIGENCE U.S.-CHINA BUSINESS COUNCIL (December 17, 2003).

132. For products the subject of a sales executed prior to the effective date, the goods must be imported and sold in China prior to June 1, 2004; thereafter, the goods would be automatically subject to the new encryption standards.

over the Internet sector. It is left for observation as to the application of the encryption standards.

C. Integrated Circuits Industry

The government has also adopted measures encouraging the development of the integrated circuits industry.[133] The Software and Integrated Circuits Policies provide that both domestic and foreign enterprises are encouraged to establish equity joint ventures or wholly foreign-owned integrated circuit production enterprises in China.[134] Under the Policies, an enterprise is entitled to a tax refund amounting to in excess of 6 percent of the VAT taxes paid by the enterprise, which funds must be used by the enterprise for research and development or to expand production.[135] Integrated circuit producers that have investments exceeding RMB8 billion or involve the production of integrated circuits with a line width of less than 0.25 microns are eligible for additional preferential tax treatment such as an exemption from customs duties and import VAT on the import of raw materials and consumables for use in production, and may also reinvest their after-tax profits. The Policies further provide that the depreciation period on integrated circuit production equipment may be as short as three years.[136] For circuits that cannot be produced in China, the producer may be allowed, with government approval, to import overseas-produced goods at a preferential duty rate.[137] The Policies further provide that integrated circuit designs are treated as software products for purposes of intellectual property protection.[138]

133. Policies Encouraging the Development of the Software and Integrated Circuit Industries, promulgated by the State Council on June 24, 2000, reprinted in CHINA L. & PRAC., September 2000, arts. 40–51. Foreign investment in China's semiconductor in 2001 was just under $2 billion. China is attracting foreign investment because of the low labor costs, land resources, and booming market demand. Seventy percent of the foreign investment was going to Shanghai/Suzhou. *See e.g., China: Shanghai Chip Investment to Grow $2 Billion*, CHINA ONLINE, June 21, 2002, available on Lexis, News Library; *Semiconductor Investment in Shanghai to Increase by 30%*, China IT & Telecom Report, June 21, 2002, available on Lexis, News Library.

134. Software and Integrated Circuit Policies, art. 40.

135. Software and Integrated Circuit Policies, art. 41.

136. Software and Integrated Circuit Policies, arts. 42–47.

137. Software and Integrated Circuit Policies, art. 48.

138. Software and Integrated Circuit Policies, art. 50. *See also* Regulations for the Protection of the Layout Design of Integrated Circuits, adopted on March 28, 2001, by the State Council, *reprinted in* CHINA LAWS FOR FOREIGN BUSINESS (CCH), Business Regulation ¶ 11-730 (outlines the standards for proprietary rights in semiconductor integrated circuits, registration procedures for protection, legal liabilities); Detailed Implementation Rules for the Regulations for the Protection of the Layout Design of Integrated Circuits, promulgated on September 18, 2001, as Order No. 11 of the State Office for Intellectual Property, *reprinted in* CHINA LAWS FOR FOREIGN BUSINESS (CCH), Business Regulation ¶ 11-731 (provides details of application and examination procedures, use of samples in application process, confidentiality of submissions, protection granted, fees, administrative procedures, and appeals).

Key Laws and Regulations

Telecommunications

Telecommunication Regulations of the People's Republic of China (promulgated on September 25, 2000, by the State Council of the People's Republic of China)

Notice on Several Issues Concerning Domestic Joint Ventures Engaging in Telecoms Services Established by Telecoms Operators (issued on July 26, 2001, by the Ministry of Information Industry)

Notice on Opening Operation Market of Users' Local Networks on a Trial Basis (issued on June 1, 2001, by the Ministry of Information Industry)

Notice on Further Strengthening the Administration of the Satellite Communications Market (issued on June 6, 2001, by the Ministry of Information Industry)

Provisional Procedures for the Supervision and Administration of Quality in Telecommunications Services (issued on January 11, 2001, by the Ministry of Information Industry)

Measures on the Administration of Licenses for Operation of Telecommunications Services (promulgated on December 26, 2001, by the Ministry of Information Industry)

Notice on the Adjustment of the Telecom Business Catalogue (issued on June 11, 2001, by the Ministry of Information Industry)

Catalogue of Telecommunications Services (issued on February 21, 2003, by the Ministry of Information Industry)

Answers to Several Questions Regarding Applications for Telecom Business Operation Licenses (issued on July 19, 2001, by the Ministry of Information Industry)

Administrative Measures on the Interconnection of Public Telecommunications Networks (issued on May 10, 2001, by the Ministry of Information Industry)

Measures on the Disposal of the Disputes over the Interconnection of the Telecommunication Network (promulgated on November 19, 2001, by the Ministry of Information Industry)

Administrative Rules on Experts' Review for Telecommunication Equipment's Entry into Network (promulgated on August 29, 2001, by the Ministry of Information Industry)

Notice on Abolishment of Initial Installation Fee on Local Telephone, Posts and Telecoms Surcharge, and Other Governmental Fund Items (issued on July 1, 2001, by the Ministry of Information Industry and the Ministry of Finance)

Notice on Structural Adjustments to the Telecommunications Tariffs (issued on December 25, 2000, by the Ministry of Information Industry, the State Development Planning Commission and the Ministry of Finance)

(*Continued*)

(Continued from previous page)

Interim Provisions on Marking Prices for Telecommunications Services (promulgated on May 28, 2002 by the Ministry of Information Industry)

Notice on Implementation of Market Price Adjustment for Certain Telecommunications Services (issued on September 11, 2002 by the Ministry of Information Industry and State Development and Planning Commission)

Provisional Regulation on Telecom Service Price Approval and Filing Process (issued on August 29, 2002, by the Ministry of Information Industry and State Development and Planning Commission)

Provisional Procedures for the Supervision and Administration of Quality in Telecommunications Services (issued on January 11, 2001, by the Ministry of Information Industry)

Measures for the Administration of Telecommunication Construction (promulgated on January 4, 2002, by the Ministry of Information Industry and the State Development Planning Commission)

Administration of the Construction of International Communications Facilities Provisions (issued on August 1, 2002, by the Ministry of Information Industry)

Administration of International Communications Gateway Exchanges Procedures (issued on October 1, 2002, by the Ministry of Information Industry)

Notice on the Rectification of Illegal Optical Network Construction Projects, Restoring Order to the Construction of Long Distance Optical Networks (issued on March 27, 2001, by the Ministry of Information Industry and the State Development and Planning Commission)

Provisional Administrative Measures on Inspection and Measure of the Anti-Seismic Capability of Telecoms Equipment (issued on January 1, 2002, by the Ministry of Information Industry)

Administrative Measures on Network Access for Telecommunications Equipment (issued on May 10, 2001, by the Ministry of Information Industry)

Notice Concerning the Names of Telecoms Equipment Subject to the Network Access Licensing System (issued on June 25, 2001, by the Ministry of Information Industry)

Measures on Examination and Approval of Production Quality Assurance for Telecoms Equipment for Accessing Networks (issued on August 29, 2001, by the Ministry of Information Industry)

Administrative Regulations on Specialists' Appraisal and Inspection of Equipment for Accessing Networks (issued on August 29, 2001, by the Ministry of Information Industry)

Administrative Regulations on Remodeling Telecoms Terminal Equipment for Accessing Networks (issued on August 29, 2001, by the Ministry of Information Industry)

(Continued)

(Continued from previous page)

Regulations on the Trial of Mobile Telephone Sets (issued on August 29, 2001, by the Ministry of Information Industry)

Interim Measures on the Administration of Vibration Proof Performance of Telecommunication Equipment (promulgated on August 1, 2001, by the Ministry of Information Industry)

Notice on Further Strengthening the Administration of Network Access for Mobile Phones (issued on April 4, 2003, by the Ministry of Information Industry)

State Secrecy and Security Standards

State Security Law of the People's Republic of China (promulgated on February 22, 1993, by the Standing Committee of the National People's Congress)

Detailed Rules for the Implementation of the Law on Safeguarding State Security of the People's Republic of China (promulgated in 1994 by the State Council)

Interpretation on the Specific Applicable Laws Governing Cases relating to the Disturbance of Administrative Order in the Telecommunications Market (issued on May 24, 2000, by the Supreme People's Court)

Internet and E-Commerce Regulations

Administrative Measures Governing Internet Information Services (promulgated on September 25, 2000, by the State Council)

Notice on Issues Concerning the Administration of the Operation Permits and Filing in relation to Internet Information Service Business (issued on November 3, 2000, by the Beijing Municipal Communications Administration Bureau)

Notice on Strengthening the Administration of Chain Providers of Internet Access Services (issued on April 22, 2003, by the Ministry of Culture)

Notice on Questions Concerning E-Commerce Activities Relating to Audio and Video Products on the Internet (issued on March 17, 2000, by the Ministry of Culture)

Notice on Enhancing Administration of the Online Release of Film or Television Program through Information Networks to the Public (issued by the State Administration of Radio, Film and Television in October 1999)

Provisional Administrative Measures on Online Securities Brokerages (issued on March 30, 2000, by China Securities Regulatory Commission)

Provisional Regulations on Publication Market (issued on November 8, 1999, by the State Press and Publication Administration)

Administrative Measures on Medical and Health Information Services on Internet (issued on January 8, 2001, by the Ministry of Health)

(Continued)

(*Continued from previous page*)

Provisional Administrative Regulations on Internet Drugs Information Services, issued on January 11, 2001, by the State Drug Administration)

Notice on Enhancing Administration of Educational Web sites and Online Schools, issued on April 20, 2000, by the Ministry of Education)

Provisional Administrative Procedures on Educational Websites and Online Schools (issued on July 5, 2000, by the Ministry of Education)

Provisional Administrative Measures on Online Banking Services (issued on June 29, 2001, by the People's Bank of China)

Provisional Regulations for the Administration of Internet Sites That Engage in the Business of News Publication (issued on November 7, 2000, by Press Office of the State Council ("POSC") and Ministry of Information Industry)

Administration of Internet Electronic Messaging Services Provisions (issued on October 27, 2000, by the Ministry of Information Industry)

Provisional Measures for the Administration of Network Advertisements in Beijing Municipality (issued on May 1, 2001, by Beijing Administration of Industry and Commerce)

Protection of the Lawful Rights and Interests of Consumers in Online Economic Activities Notice (promulgated on July 7, 2000, by the Beijing Municipal Government)

Administration of Internet Online Business Tentative Procedures (promulgated on May 22, 2000, by the Fujian Provincial Administration for Industry and Commerce)

Electronic Transactions Regulations (issued on February 1, 2003, by the Guangdong Provincial People's Congress)

Supervision and Administration of Electronic Commerce Tentative Procedures (issued and effective from August 1, 2002, by the Beijing Municipal Administration for Industry and Commerce)

Decision on Ensuring the Security of the Internet (issued on December 28, 2000, by the Standing Committee of the National People's Congress)

Regulations on the Administration of Secrecy Maintenance for Internet Computer Information Systems (issued on January 1, 2000, by the State Secrecy Bureau)

Administration of Internet Publishing Tentative Procedures (promulgated on June 27, 2002, by the General Administration of Press and Publishing and the Ministry of Information Industry)

Provisional Regulation on Management of Cultural Products on the Internet (issued on May 10, 2003, by the Ministry of Culture)

Measures for Administration of the Transmission of Audio-Video Programs Over the Internet and Other Information Networks (issued on February 10, 2003, by the State Administration of Radio, Film and Television)

(*Continued*)

(*Continued from previous page*)

Regulation on Administration of Business Establishments that Provide Internet Services (promulgated on November 15, 2002, by the State Council)

Administrative Measures on Places of Business for Internet Login Services (issued on April 3, 2001, by the Ministry of Information Industry, the Ministry of Public Security, the Ministry of Culture, and the State Administration of Industry and Commerce)

Anti-Spam Standards (issued on February 25, 2003, by the Internet Society of China)

Domain Name Procedures

Administration of China Internet Domain Names Procedures (issued on September 30, 2002, by the Ministry of Information Industry)

Measures for the Settlement of Disputes Arising from Chinese Domain Names Registration (Trial issued on November 1, 2000, by China National Network Information Center)

Interpretation on the Specific Applicable Laws Governing Civil Disputes Cases relating to Computer Network Domain Names (issued on July 17, 2001, by the Supreme People's Court)

Interpretation on the Specific Applicable Laws Governing Cases of Copyright Disputes relating to Computer Networks (issued on December 21, 2000 and amended in January 2004, by the Supreme People's Court)

Circular on Strengthening the Administration of Internet Domain Names in China (issued on July 31, 2003, by the Ministry of Information Industry)

Circular on the Interpretation of Applicable Laws on the Qualifications of Providers of Domain Name Registration Services (issued on November 20, 2003, by the Ministry of Information Industry)

Policies for Software/IC Industries

Policies Encouraging the Development of the Software and Integrated Circuit Industries (promulgated on June 24, 2000, by the State Council)

Circular on Tax Policies for Further Encouraging Development of Software Industry and IC Industry (adopted on January 1, 2002, by the Ministry of Finance and the State Administration of Taxation)

Notice on Relevant Issues Concerning the Implementation of Preferential Income Tax Policies for Software Enterprises and High-Technology Enterprises (issued on May 29, 2003, by the State Administration of Taxation)

Reply on the Enjoyment of Preferential Enterprise Income Tax Policies for Technologically Advanced Enterprises by Foreign-Invested Enterprises with Investment in Installments (issued on July 9, 2003, by the State Administration of Taxation)

(*Continued*)

(*Continued from previous page*)

Administrative Measures on Recognition of Key Software Enterprises under the State Planning Scheme (adopted on July 24, 2001 by the State Development and Planning Commission, Ministry of Information, MOFTEC, State Administration of Taxation)

Criteria for Confirmation and Measures on Administration of Software Enterprises (promulgated on October 16, 2000, by the Ministry of Information Industry, Ministry of Education, Ministry of Science and Technology, and State Administration of Taxation)

Chapter 7

Contract Law

China's laws and regulations governing contractual relations, as developed over the past twenty years, have been overlapping and redundant in their application. A particular law was applied based not so much on the type of contract involved but rather the citizenship of the parties to the contract (i.e., Chinese citizens versus foreigners). Chinese contract law in has evolved from a more paternalistic approach—registration and approval of contracts—to the recognition of freedom of contract to allow parties to enter into commercial relationships. However, the Chinese government still maintains that certain contractual relations with foreign parties require close supervision. The key laws governing commercial contracts include the Civil Law,[1] the Secured Interests Law,[2] and the

1. General Principles of Civil Law of the People's Republic of China (adopted April 12, 1986, by the 4th Sess. of the 6th NPC), *reprinted in* CHINA LAWS FOR FOREIGN BUSINESS (CCH), Business Regulation ¶ 19-150 (hereinafter the "Civil Law").

2. Secured Interests Law of the People's Republic of China (adopted June 30, 1995, by the 14th Sess. of the Standing Comm. of the 8th NPC), *reprinted in* CHINA LAWS FOR FOREIGN BUSINESS (CCH), Business Regulation ¶ 5-605 (hereinafter the "Secured Interests Law"). *See generally* Creating & Enforcing Security in the PRC, ASIA LAW & PRACTICE (1997). An English translation of the Secured Interests Law is also available on the Web site (Law Digest link) of the PRC Ministry of Commerce at http://www.mofcom.gov.cn. *See also* Several Issues Concerning the Application of the PRC Secured Interests Law Interpretations (promulgated by the Supreme People's Court on December 8, 2000, and effective as of December 13, 2000), *reprinted in* CHINA L. & PRAC., Feb. 2001 (hereinafter the "SPC Secured Interests Law Interpretation"). *See* A. Godwin & Z. Lili, *Judicial Interpretation on the PRC Security Law,* CHINA L. & PRAC., Feb. 2001; D. Wang, *Developments and Prospects in China's Security Law,* CHINA L. & PRAC. (April 2003). *See also* Administration of the Provision of Security to Foreign Entities by Domestic Institutions Inside China Procedures (promulgated by the People's Bank of China, effective as of October 1, 1996), and Implementing Rules (issued by SAFE effective January 1, 1998).

Contract Law,[3] adopted in March 1999, which supersedes the Economic Contract Law,[4] the Foreign Economic Contract Law,[5] the Technology Contract Law,[6] and the Technology Import Contract

3. Contract Law (adopted at the 2nd Session of the 9th National People's Congress on March 15, 1999) *reprinted in* CHINA LAWS FOR FOREIGN BUSINESS (CCH), Business Regulation ¶ 5-650. *See also* First Interpretation of the Supreme People's Court on Certain Issues in Relation to the Application of the Contract Law of the People's Republic of China (adopted by the 1,090th Sess. of the Judicial Comm. of the Supreme People's Court on December 1, 1999, and effective on December 29, 1999, Fa Shi [1999] No. 19) (hereinafter "SPC Contract Law Interpretation"). An English translation of the Contract Law and SPC Contract Law Interpretation are available on the Web site (Law Digest link) of the PRC Ministry of Commerce at http://www.mofcom.gov.cn. *See generally* Ping, *Drafting the Contract Law in China,* 10 COLUM. J. ASIAN LAW 245 (1996) (discussion of distinctions between the Economic Contract Law and the Foreign Economic Contract Law and need for uniformity); Zhang & McLean, *China's Foreign Economic Contract Law: Its Significance and Analysis,* 8 J. INT'L L. BUS. 120 (1987) (analysis of the FEC law); MacNeil, *Contract in China: Law, Practice, and Dispute Resolution,* 38 STAN. L. REV. 303 (1986); Rubenstein, *Legal and Institutional Uncertainties in the Domestic Contract Law of the People's Republic of China,* 42 MCGILL L. J. 495 (1997). *See* Karlen, *New Contract Law Nearer in China,* NAT'L L.J. A14 (Sept. 7, 1998); Scogin & Braude, *New Contract Basics,* CHINA BUSINESS REVIEW 36 (Jan./Feb. 1999) (describing the September 1998 draft of the Contract Law); *China Amends Draft Contract Law,* ASIA PULSE (Dec. 24, 1998), available on Lexis, News Library; *Parliamentary Chairman Studies Contract Law Legislation,* Xinhua News Agency (Jan. 13, 1999), available on Lexis, News Library; *Experts Discussing Contract Law,* CHINA DAILY (Feb. 4, 1999), available on Lexis, News Library, or on the Web site of CHINA DAILY at http://www.chinadaily.com.cn; Harpole, *Proposed New Contract Law,* CHINA LAW UPDATE 3 (December 1998). The Law Committee of the NPC requested and received assistance and input from the public concerning the preparation of the Contract Law. In addition to various Chinese law professors and organizations, the Legal Committee for the American Chamber of Commerce in the People's Republic of China, Beijing, provided substantive feedback, which the NPC accepted in preparing revised drafts. The author has communications and memoranda in his files concerning the efforts of the AmCham Legal Committee to participate in China's legislation drafting process. Article 428 of the Contract Law provides that the Economic Contract Law, the FEC Law, and the Technology Contract Law are repealed effective October 1, 1999.

4. Economic Contract Law of the People's Republic of China (adopted December 13, 1981, by the 4th Sess. of the NPC, amended September 2, 1993, at the 3rd Sess. of the Standing Comm. of the 8th NPC), *reprinted in* CHINA LAWS FOR FOREIGN BUSINESS (CCH), Business Regulation ¶ 5-500 (hereinafter the "Economic Contract Law"). The Economic Contract Law has since been repealed by the Contract Law.

5. Foreign Economic Contract Law of the People's Republic of China (adopted March 21, 1985, at the 10th Sess. of the Standing Comm. of the 6th NPC), *reprinted in* CHINA LAWS FOR FOREIGN BUSINESS (CCH), Business Regulation ¶ 5-550 (hereinafter the "FEC Law"). The FEC Law has since been repealed by the Contract Law. In 1984, the Guangdong Provincial Government developed a similar law for the Shenzhen SEZ. *See* Regulations of Shenzhen Special Economic Zone on Economic Contracts Involving Foreigners (promulgated on February 7, 1984, by the Guangdong Provincial People's Government), *reprinted in* CHINA LAWS FOR FOREIGN BUSINESS (CCH), Special Zones & Cities ¶ 73-505 (hereinafter the "Shenzhen FEC Law"). The Shenzhen FEC Law differs in some respects to the FEC Law and, in particular, with respect to the limitations period for contract actions. *Id.* at art. 38. The SPC clarified that the courts are required to disregard local contract law and to follow and enforce the national Contract Law. Article 4 of the SPC Contract Law Interpretation provides as follows: "Upon effectiveness of the Contract Law, a people's court shall rely on the laws formulated by the National People's Congress and its Standing Committee, and the regulations formulated by the State Council, but not any local regulations or rules, in finding whether a contract is valid." *See generally* Lewis, *Contract Law in the People's Republic of China—Rule or Tool?: Can the PRC's Foreign Economic Contract Law Be Administered According to the Rule of Law?,* 30 V AND. J. TRANSN'L L. 495 (1997); Grow, *Resolving Commercial Disputes in China: Foreign Firms and the Role of Contract Law,* 14 J. INT'L L. BUS. 161 (1993); Dernelle, *Direct Foreign Investment and Contractual Relations in the People's Republic of China,* 6 DEPAUL L.J. 331 (1994).

6. Law of the People's Republic of China on Technology Contracts (adopted June 23, 1987, by the 21st Sess. of the Standing Comm. of the 6th NPC), *reprinted in* CHINA LAWS FOR FOREIGN BUSINESS (CCH), Business Regulation ¶ 5-577 (hereinafter the "Technology Contract Law"). *See also* Administrative Measures of Beijing Municipality on Authentication and Registration of Technology Contracts (issued December 1, 1990, by the Beijing Municipal People's Government), *reprinted in* CHINA LAWS FOR FOREIGN BUSINESS (CCH), Business Regulation ¶ 5-579.

Regulations.[7] This chapter addresses China's contract laws and specifically the application of the rules for contractual arrangements that impact foreign-invested enterprises and foreign parties engaged in trade with Chinese parties.

A discussion of China's contract laws begins with the Contract Law, which was promulgated in March 1999 with an effective date of October 1, 1999. While the Contract Law expressly repeals the Economic Contract Law, the Foreign Economic Contract Law, and the Technology Contract Law, there is less certainty as to whether the law applies retroactively to contracts entered into pursuant to the laws existing at the time the contract was entered into.[8]

A. Contract Law

The Contract Law addresses general contractual principles such as formation, validity of contract, performance, modification, assignment, termination, and liability for breach. The Contract Law provides that a contract "is an agreement among individuals, legal persons and/or other organizations as equal parties for the establishment, modification or termination of a relationship."[9] The law recognizes that the mutual assent of the parties is fundamental in contract formation and that the parties observe the principles of

7. Regulations on Administration of Technology Import Contracts of the People's Republic of China (promulgated on May 24, 1985, by the State Council), *reprinted in* CHINA LAWS FOR FOREIGN BUSINESS (CCH), Business Regulation ¶ 5-570 (the "Technology Import Contract Regulations"). The Technology Import Contract Regulations are available on the Web site of MOFCOM at http://www.mofcom.gov.cn. *See* Detailed Rules for the Implementation of the Administrative Regulations of the People's Republic of China on Technology Import Contracts (approved December 30, 1987, by the State Council), *reprinted in* CHINA LAWS FOR FOREIGN BUSINESS (CCH), Business Regulation ¶ 5-573 (the "Technology Import Contract Detailed Rules"). *See also* Provisional Regulations of Shenzhen Special Economic Zone Governing the Import of Technology (promulgated on February 8, 1984, by the Guangdong Provincial People's Government), *reprinted in* CHINA LAWS FOR FOREIGN BUSINESS (CCH), Special Zones & Cities ¶ 73-510.

8. The SPC attempted to resolve this issue by stating that "[a]ny proceeding instituted with a people's court in respect of disputes which arise out of a contract formed after the effectiveness of the Contract Law, shall be governed by the Contract Law. Except for anything otherwise under this Interpretation, any proceeding instituted with a people's court in respect of disputes which had arisen out of a contract formed prior to the effectiveness of the Contract Law, the laws for the time being shall apply, provided that relevant provisions of the Contract Law may apply to the extent that such laws for the time being are silent on the relevant issue." SPC Contract Law Interpretation, art. 1. The SPC further clarified that "[w]here a contract was formed prior to the effectiveness of the Contract Law while its term extends beyond the date of effectiveness of the Contract or falls after the effectiveness of Contract Law, relevant provisions of Chapter IV of the Contract Law shall apply to disputes arising out of the performance of the contract." SPC Contract Law Interpretation, art. 2. Article 3 of the SPC Contract Law Interpretation provides: "In deciding whether a contract formed prior to the effectiveness of the Contract Law is valid, the people's court shall apply the Contract Law to the extent such contract may become void under the laws for the time being but is valid under the Contract Law." Article 5 of the SPC Contract Law Interpretation provides: "The Contract Law shall not be applied in any retrial by a people's court of a case in respect of which a final verdict had been rendered prior to the effectiveness of the Contract Law."

9. Contract Law, art. 2. The Contract Law specifically does not apply to agreements concerning personal relationships such as marriage, adoption, and guardianship. *See* Civil Law, arts. 16–19 (guardianship rules).

fairness, honesty, and good faith.[10] The Contract Law further provides that "in forming and performing a contract, the parties shall follow the laws and administrative regulations and respect social public morals, and shall not disturb social and economic order or damage social and public interests."[11] A contract formed under the law shall be legally binding on the parties, each of which must perform its own obligations as agreed upon in the contract, and no party shall unilaterally alter or rescind the contract.[12]

1. Contract Formation

The Contract Law recognizes oral contracts but on the condition that they are performed immediately.[13] Otherwise, all contracts must be "in writing," which can include "a written contract, letter, electronic data text (including telegram, telex, facsimile, electronic data interchange and electronic mail), etc. that can tangibly express the content contained therein."[14] In general, only a limited number of contracts require notarization—namely, real property transfers, mortgage rights, gift contracts, or contracts or documents related to inheritance.

The former Economic Contract Law required that contracts contain certain mandatory language.[15] In contrast, the Contract Law provides that a

10. Contract Law, arts. 3, 4, 5, 6, 13, 60, 92. The Contract Law holds the parties to a standard of good faith and fair dealing during contract negotiations. Specifically, a party is liable for damages if the other party sustains losses as a result of bad faith and dishonesty during contract negotiations. In addition, the law provides that a party to contract negotiations shall not reveal to third persons or misuse commercial secrets that are disclosed during contract negotiations. If a party reveals or misuses another party's commercial secrets and the owner of such secrets sustains losses as a result thereof, the party in violation is liable for damages. Contract Law, arts. 43. The Contract Law does not further elaborate on the "fairness" requirement of Article 5. Article 59 of the Civil Law defines "unfairness" as "taking advantage of the other party's lack of experience, thereby creating a situation where the parties' rights and obligations are not in conformity with the principles of fairness and compensation with equal value."

11. Contract Law, art. 7.

12. Contract Law, art. 8.

13. Contract Law, art. 10. The recognition of oral contracts is a major change of policy from the rules under the Economic Contract Law and the Foreign Economic Contract Law, which require that all contracts be in writing. *See* Economic Contract Law, art. 7; FEC Law, art. 7. In earlier drafts of the Contract Law, the drafters required that "foreign related" contracts be in writing. After receiving input from the foreign legal community in Beijing, the drafters deleted the requirement that foreign-related contracts be in writing.

14. Contract Law, art. 11. If a contract is concluded by the parties in the form of a letter or electronic data text, one party may, prior to the formation of the contract, require entry into a written confirmation. *Id.* art. 32. The use and acceptance of "electronic signatures" is becoming recognized in China. In this regard, various provincial governments have adopted rules governing transactions on the Internet and policies encouraging the use of electronic signatures. *See* Electronic Transactions Regulations (issued on February 1, 2003, by the Guangdong Provincial People's Congress) (these are the first measures in China to regulate electronic transactions, and they encourage the use of a "safe electronic signature" and provide that electronic signatures will be viewed as legally binding to the same effect as handwritten signatures). The NPC adopted an electronic signature law. *See China Drafts Electronic Signature Law*, China Daily (April 3, 2004).

15. Economic Contract Law, art. 12.

> **Practice Tip**
>
> The Contract Law recognizes the enforceability of an oral contract except in situations where the law or regulations require that the contract be in writing (e.g., joint venture contracts and insurance contracts must be in writing). From a practical point of view, it would be difficult to enforce an oral agreement of any kind unless the written communications exchanged between the parties, actions and activities of the parties, and other events clearly indicate the terms of the parties' contractual relationship and expectations. The Courts and arbitration institutions have limited experience with oral agreements and, most commercial obligations involving foreign parties, are required to be documented in some manner.

contract "shall generally include" the following terms and conditions:

(1) Name and domicile of each party
(2) Subject matter
(3) Quantity
(4) Quality
(5) Price or remuneration
(6) Term for performance
(7) Place and method of performance
(8) Liability for breach of contract
(9) Dispute resolution procedures[16]

The law further provides that the parties "may refer to model texts of various contracts" in the preparation of a contract. The Contract Law, however, does not make reference to any particular "model" contracts that are either preferred or approved under Chinese law. Further, the law provides no guidance on how the courts or arbitration tribunals will treat the use of model contracts, especially if a "model" contract is untested in practice.[17]

---

16. Contract Law, art. 12.

17. Contract Law, art. 12. The Contract Law places the burden on a party providing "standardized clauses" to "remind the other party to pay attention to any clauses which release or limit its liabilities" and "shall explain the clauses if requested by the other party." Contract Law, art. 39. The definition of "standardized clauses" is "clauses which have been drafted in advance by a party for repeated use." The Contract Law also provides that attempts to release a party from its obligations or designed to deny the other party certain critical rights are invalid. If a dispute arises concerning the understanding of a standardized clause, the Contract Law provides that the clause will be interpreted against the party that provided the contractual language. In the event of a discrepancy between a standardized clause and a nonstandardized clause, the nonstandardized clause shall prevail. *Id.* arts. 41–42, 53. This rule is recognized in the Insurance Law concerning the interpretation of standard insurance contracts. *See* Insurance Law, art. 30. The Contract Law provides that a provision that seeks to exempt a party from liability as a result

In the absence of provisions in a contract addressing quality, compensation, and place of performance, the parties may enter into a supplemental agreement.[18] For any terms that remain ambiguous, the Contract Law outlines the following rules of interpretation:

(1) *Quality and Quantity:* In the event that the requirement of quality and quantity requested is ambiguous, the performance shall be made in accordance with national standards. In the event a national standard does not exist, the performance shall be made in accordance with customary standard.

(2) *Pricing Terms:* In the event that the price is ambiguous, the payment shall be made in accordance with the market price in the place of performance at the time when the contract is executed. In the event that the price is fixed by the government pursuant to the law, the payment shall be made according to the price fixed by the government.[19]

(3) *Place of Performance:* In the event that the place of performance is ambiguous, the performance shall be made at the location of the recipient of the currency if a currency is to be delivered, or at the location of the real property if a real property is to be delivered. With respect to other subject matter, performance shall occur at the location of the party who is to perform the obligation.

(4) *Time for Performance:* In the event that the time period for performance is ambiguous, the obligor may perform at any time and the obligee may also demand the performance at any time, provided that the necessary preparation time shall be given to the other party.

(5) *Manner of Performance:* In the event the manner of performance is ambiguous, the performance shall be made in such a manner that facilitates the realization of the objective of the contract.

(6) *Performance-Related Expenses:* In the event that the parties fail to specify the obligations for performance-related expenses, such costs shall be borne by the party who performs the obligation.[20]

---

of intentional misconduct or gross negligence, which results in loss of property or bodily injury to the other party, is invalid. Contract Law, art. 53. The Consumer Protection Law has similar restrictions on manufacturers and sellers. Consumer Protection Law, art. 24. *See generally,* Chapter 13, Consumer Protection § B.1.

18. Contract Law, art. 61.

19. In the event that the official price is used, the price shall be the price at the time of delivery, if the official price is adjusted within the delivery term as provided for in the contract. In the event that the delivery of goods is delayed, the original price shall be adopted if the price rises, and the new price shall be adopted if the price falls. In the event that the delivery is accepted or the payment is made after the expiration of the term, the new price shall be adopted if the price rises, and the original price shall be adopted if the price falls. Contract Law, art. 63.

20. Contract Law, art. 62. This rule is consistent with Civil Law, art. 88. The Contract Law also provides that in the event of a dispute in the construction and interpretation of a contract term, the

The Contract Law recognizes the principles of offer and acceptance in the formation of a contract.[21] An "offer" is defined as "the expression of an intent to enter into a contract with another party."[22] An expression of intent is required to satisfy the following conditions:

(1) The contents are specific and definite
(2) When the offeree has indicated acceptance, the offeror shall be bound by the expression of intention[23]

The Contract Law provides that an offer is effective at the time it is received by the offeree.[24] An offer may be withdrawn provided that the recipient receives notice of withdrawal prior to or at the same time as the offer reaches the offeree.[25] In addition, an offer is revocable at any time prior to acceptance.[26] An offer is irrevocable if:

(1) The offer stipulates a time limit for acceptance
(2) The irrevocability of the offer is expressly stated in the contract
(3) The offeree has grounds to believe that the offer is irrevocable and has already performed under the contract[27]

The Contract Law provides that an offer is void under the following circumstances:

(1) If rejected by the offeree and the offeror receives notice of the rejection
(2) The offeror withdraws or revokes the offer in accordance with the law
(3) The time limit for acceptance has expired and the offeree has not accepted the offer

---

meaning of the term shall be determined by reference to the phrases and sentences used in the contract, the relevant provisions of the contract, the course of dealing between the parties, and the principle of good faith. Where a contract is executed in two or more languages and it is provided that all versions are equally authentic, the words and sentences in each version shall be construed to have the same meaning. Where the words and sentences in one version are different from the other version, they shall be construed in light of the purpose of the contract. Contract Law, art. 125.

21. Contract Law, arts. 13, 25.
22. Contract Law, art. 14.
23. Contract Law, art. 14. The law recognizes that sales catalogs, advertisements, requests for proposals, and prospectuses are invitations to make offers and not offers subject to acceptance. However, an advertisement for a commodity is deemed to be an offer if the contents meet the statutory requirements for an offer. *Id.* art. 15.
24. Contract Law, art. 16. If a contract is concluded in the form of an electronic data text and the addressee designates a specific system to receive the electronic data text, the time of arrival shall be deemed to be the time that such electronic data text enters the specific system. If no particular system is designated, the time of arrival shall be deemed to be the first time of entry of the electronic data text into any system of the addressee. *Id.*
25. Contract Law, art. 17.
26. Contract Law, art. 18.
27. Contract Law, art. 19.

(4) The offeree materially alters the contents of the offer by tendering a counteroffer[28]

Under the Contract Law, an acceptance is the expression of intent by the offeree to assent to the offer.[29] The law provides an acceptance is required to be "in the form of a notice" except in situations where acceptance is provided by a method that is consistent with the customs and practice of a particular transaction.[30] The acceptance of an offer is required to be tendered to the offeror within the time limit set forth in the offer. If the offer does not provide a time limit for acceptance, the acceptance must be tendered as follows:

(1) If the offer is made verbally, the acceptance must be tendered immediately, unless otherwise agreed by the parties
(2) If the offer is in written form, the acceptance must be tendered within a reasonable amount of time[31]

An acceptance may be withdrawn, provided that notice of withdrawal of acceptance is received by the offeror prior to acceptance.[32] If a party accepts an offer after the offer expires, the acceptance constitutes a new offer to the offeror.[33] The acceptance is also required to be consistent with the contents of the offer. If the acceptance materially changes the contents of the offer, it constitutes a counteroffer. The Contract Law provides that a "material change" to an offer includes a modification of the terms concerning the subject matter, quantity, quality, price, time for performance, place and manner of performance, liability for breach, and method of dispute settlement.[34] If the acceptance contains a nonmaterial change to the contents of the offer, the acceptance is valid and a contract is formed, except in the following situations:

(1) Where the offeror timely objects to the change
(2) Where the language of the offer expressly indicates that the acceptance shall not make any changes to the content of the offer in any manner[35]

The contents of the acceptance shall form the contents of the contract, including any nonmaterial changes submitted by the offeree.[36] If the parties

28. Contract Law, art. 20.
29. Contract Law, art. 21.
30. Contract Law, art. 22.
31. Contract Law, art. 23.
32. Contract Law, art. 27.
33. Contract Law, art. 28.
34. Contract Law, art. 30.
35. Contract Law, art. 31.
36. Contract Law, art. 31.

Practice Tip: China Contract Law and Practice: Common Myths and Reality

Myth	Reality
• Contracting parties are required to use government-approved forms only.	• With the exception of certain types of contracts (e.g., insurance contracts), the parties in general have the right to negotiate contract terms.
• Government approval/registration is required for all contracts.	• Most contracts do not require approval. Exception: Import contracts involving restricted technology require approval. Technology import contracts involving unrestricted technology should be registered.
• Contracts must be in the Chinese language.	• Use of the Chinese language is not required, but for contracts that require approval or registration, the Chinese version is the controlling version.
• Contracts must be notarized.	• Notarization is limited to certain types of contracts such as real property transfer.
• Contracts must choose arbitration with the China International Economic and Trade Arbitration Commission (CIETAC) or other Chinese arbitral institutions.	• Parties to a foreign-related contract may choose arbitral institution outside of China.
• Contracts must choose Chinese law as controlling.	• Parties to a foreign-related contract may choose law of jurisdiction other than Chinese law. JV contracts and mineral/petroleum resources contracts are required to be governed by Chinese law.

enter into a written instrument, the contractual relationship is created upon signing.[37] If the parties reach an agreement by the use of letters and electronic messages, a contract is formed when the confirmation instrument is

37. Contract Law, art. 32.

signed.[38] The contract is formed at the place where the offer is accepted or, in situations involving the use of a written instrument, where the document is signed, unless otherwise agreed to by the parties.[39]

2. Validity of Contracts

If the laws or regulations specify that a contract must be approved or registered to be effective, the contract is effective upon approval and registration thereof.[40] If a contract is required by law to be in writing, the contract will not be deemed to be invalid if the parties perform the principal obligations under the contract.[41] A written contract that has been performed is not considered invalid by the failure of a party to sign the contract.[42] The parties may agree upon the validity period for the contract. A contract that includes a time limit for its entry into effect shall become effective upon the commencement of such term. A contract that includes a time limit for termination shall cease to be effective upon the expiration of such term.[43]

A contract executed by a person with limited civil capacity (i.e., a minor) is valid only upon ratification by the legal guardian of the contracting party.[44] If an agent signs a contract without authority, the contract is invalid and the agent is liable to the principal for damages.[45] The Contract Law further provides that a contract is invalid in the following circumstances:

(1) A party causes the other party to conclude the contract by fraudulent or coercive means or takes advantage of the other's difficulties to cause it to conclude a contract against its true intention

38. Contract Law, art. 33.
39. Contract Law, arts. 34–35.
40. Contract Law, arts. 36, 44. The Contract Law recognizes the principle of conditions precedent, which provides that the parties may enter into a contract subject to certain conditions. *Id.* art. 45. With-respect to the registration requirements, the SPC maintains that "[i]f the effectiveness of a contract is subject to approval and/or registration under the laws or regulations, as provided for in Article 44 of the Contract Law, which however is not obtained by the relevant party prior to conclusion of exchange of arguments at the court of trial for first instance, the contract shall be determined by the people's court as not having come into effect. Where a contract comes into effect in the absence of registration required under the laws and regulations, failure of the relevant party to obtain such registration shall not affect the validity of the contract provided that the ownership of and other property right in relation to the things as the subject matter of the contract shall not be transferred. Change, assignment, or rescission referred to in Articles 77, 87, and 96 of the Contract Law shall be handled pursuant to the first paragraph of this Article 9." SPC Contract Law Interpretation, art. 9.
41. Contract Law, art. 37. The various PRC laws require mandatory language for labor contracts, insurance contracts, real estate mortgage contracts, and other types of written obligations. For a discussion concerning labor contracts, *see* Chapter 10, Labor and Employment Law § A.1. For a discussion concerning insurance contracts, *see* Chapter 12, Insurance Law and Regulation § F. For a discussion concerning the language required for mortgage contracts, *see* Chapter 17, Land-Use, Real Estate Development, and Natural Resources § B.2.
42. Contract Law, art. 36.
43. Contract Law, art. 44.
44. Contract Law, art. 47.
45. Contract Law, art. 48. Under the law, a party to a contract with an agent lacking authority may demand that the principal ratify its agent's acts or cancel the contract. After a period of thirty days, the principal has deemed to have rejected the contract signed by its agent without authorization. The disposition of property by an agent without authorization is invalid. *Id.* art. 51.

(2) The contract is a malicious conspiracy or harms the interests of the state, a collective, or a third party
(3) The contract uses a legal form to conceal an illegal intent
(4) The contract harms the public interest
(5) The contract violates the compulsory provisions of laws and administrative laws and regulations[46]

A party may apply to the people's court or an arbitration tribunal, if applicable, to modify or cancel a contract procured under the circumstances noted above. A party to a contract may also apply to the court or tribunal to cancel or modify a contract in situations in which the con-tract is concluded as a result of a material mistake or its terms are unconscionable.[47] A contract that is ruled to be invalid is cancelled *ab initio*, or from the beginning.[48] If a contract is ruled to be partially invalid, and invalidity does not affect the validity of the remaining provisions, the remaining parts shall continue to be valid. The invalidity, cancellation, amendment, or termination of a contract shall not affect the validity of any contract provisions concerning the method of settlement of disputes that exist independently.[49]

If a contract is declared invalid or cancelled, any property that is obtained as a result of such contract shall be returned. If it is impossible or unnecessary to return such property, the property shall be valued and compensation paid based upon such valuation. The party in default shall compensate the other party for the losses incurred thereby. If both parties are in default, each party is responsible for their respective liability.[50]

3. Performance of Contracts

The Contract Law provides that each party to a contract shall perform its obligations as agreed upon in the contract.[51] If the parties agree that an obligor is required to render its performance to a third person, the obligor is liable to the obligee if it fails to perform.[52] If the parties agree that a third person is required to perform the obligations of an obligor, the obligor is liable for

46. Contract Law, art. 52. The SPC maintains that "[a] contract shall not be determined as void by the people's court only for the fact that the contract is concluded by a party thereto in excess of its business scope unless any mandate of the state as to restricted or franchised operation of business, or any provision of laws and regulations as to ban on relevant business is breached." SPC Contract Law Interpretation, art. 10.

47. Contract Law, art. 54. A party must apply to the court for cancellation of contract within one year from the date the party knows or should have known of such matter giving rise to the right of cancellation. *Id.* art. 55. The SPC maintains that the "one year" period provided for in Article 55 of the Contract Law shall be invariable, and provisions on suspension, interruption, or extension of limitation of actions shall not be applicable to such periods. SPC Contract Law Interpretation, art. 8.

48. Contract Law, art. 56.

49. Contract Law, arts. 56–57.

50. Contract Law, art. 58. If the parties collude in bad faith to the detriment of State interests, any property obtained as a result of the parties' acts may be returned to the State by the courts or arbitration tribunal.

51. Contract Law, art. 60.

52. Contract Law, art. 64.

breach of contract if the third person fails to perform the obligations.[53] The law provides that a party cannot refuse to perform its obligations under a contract as a result of a change in its name, title, or its legal representatives.[54]

A party who is required to perform first may suspend its performance if, at any time, it receives reliable information demonstrating the following circumstances involving the other party:

(1) The operational situation is seriously deteriorating
(2) Transfer of its assets or withdrawal of its capital to evade obligations
(3) Serious loss of its business reputation
(4) Other situations relating to the loss or possible loss of the obligor's ability to perform its obligations[55]

A party that desires to suspend performance based upon the above conditions is required to give the other party notice of suspension. The performance shall be resumed when the other party provides an "appropriate guarantee." After the performance is suspended, the party who suspends the performance may rescind the contract in the event that the other party fails to resume its ability for performance or fails to provide an appropriate guarantee within a reasonable period.[56] An obligor may also suspend performance if an obligee has dissolved its operation, moved its location, or engaged in any activities that make it difficult for the obligor to perform.[57]

A party may reject another party's partial performance, except in situations where the nonperforming party substantially complies with the terms of the contract and does not cause damage to the interest of the other party. The increase of costs incurred as a result of partial performance shall be the obligation of the nonperforming party.[58] Similarly, a party may refuse the obligor's early performance, except in situations in which such performance does not harm the obligee's interests. Any additional costs for early performance incurred by the obligee shall be borne by the obligor.[59]

The obligor may place the subject matter in escrow under any of the following circumstances that render it difficult for such party to perform:

(1) The obligee refuses to take delivery of the subject matter without sufficient justification
(2) The location of the obligee is unknown

53. Contract Law, art. 65.
54. Contract Law, art. 76.
55. Contract Law, art. 68.
56. Contract Law, art. 69.
57. Contract Law, art. 70.
58. Contract Law, art. 72.
59. Contract Law, art. 71.

(3) The obligee is deceased or disabled, and an heir or guardian is not determined

Where the subject matter is not fit for escrow, or the expenses of escrow are excessively high, the obligor may auction or liquidate the subject matter, and place the proceeds into an escrow account.[60] Upon delivery of the subject matter or funds to escrow, the obligor must provide notice to the obligee or its heir or guardian in a timely manner, except where the obligee cannot be located.[61] The risk of damage or loss to the items or funds in escrow shall be borne by the obligee, and all escrow fees and expenses are the responsibility of the obligee. Any interest or income derived from property or funds held in escrow shall vest in the obligee.[62] The obligee may take delivery of the subject matter in escrow at any time. However, the escrow agent, in accordance with the instructions of the obligor, may refuse to allow the obligee to take delivery of the subject matter in escrow until the obligee fully performs its obligations. The rights of the obligee to take delivery of the subject matter in escrow shall lapse if not exercised by the obligee within five years from the time the subject matter is placed in escrow. Thereafter, the subject matter in escrow shall revert to the State, after deduction of reasonable escrow expenses.[63]

Article 73 of the Contract Law recognizes the right of subrogation, namely that where an obligee sustains losses due to the obligor neglecting to exercise his or her matured obligatory rights, the obligee may make a request to the people's court that the obligee be subrogated in his or her own name to the obligor in the obligor's exercise of its claims (with the exception of situations where the obligor enjoys the said obligatory rights personally). The scope within which the right of subrogation may be exercised shall be no greater than the scope of the obligatory right enjoyed by the obligee. Necessary expenses incurred by the obligee in exercising the right of subrogation shall be borne by the obligor.[64] The SPC maintains that in order to exercise

60. Contract Law, art. 101. *See also* Contract Law, arts. 70, 91.
61. Contract Law, art. 102.
62. Contract Law, art. 103.
63. Contract Law, art. 104. The SPC maintains that the "five year" period provided for in Article 104 of the Contract Law shall be invariable, and provisions on suspension, interruption, or extension of limitation of actions shall not be applicable to such periods. SPC Contract Law Interpretation, art. 8.
64. Contract Law, art. 73. For the purpose of Article 73 of the Contract Law, the provision that "should the obligor fail to assert diligently any of its due claims and thus cause damage to the obligee" shall mean that "the obligor neither honors its due obligations owed to the obligee nor asserts any claims involving pecuniary payment it may have against any third party obligor of its own through litigation or arbitration, and as a result, the obligee is unable to realize its due claims [against the obligor]. Should any junior obligor (i.e. obligor of the obligor in question) not believe that the obligor is negligent in asserting its due claims, such junior obligor shall be subject to onus of proof." SPC Contract Law Interpretation, art. 13. The proceeding instituted by an obligee in respect of the subrogation rights under Article 73 of the Contract Law shall be governed by the people's court at the locality of domicile of the defendant. SPC Contract Law Interpretation, art. 14.

the rights of subrogation, the obligee is required to meet the following conditions: (1) claims the obligee has against the obligor are lawful; (2) the obligor fails to assert diligently any due claims of its own, causing damage to the obligee; (3) such claims of the obligor are due; and (4) such claims are not exclusively owned by the obligor.[65]

4. Amendment and Assignment of Contract

A contract may be amended by mutual consent of the parties. If approval and registration procedures for such amendments are required by law, an amendment is effective only upon approval and registration.[66] The parties to a contract may assign their rights to a contract except in situations where by law or contract an assignment is improper.[67]

5. Termination of Contract

The Contract Law provides that a contract shall terminate under any of the following circumstances:

(1) The obligations have been fully performed as agreed in the contract
(2) The contract has been rescinded
(3) The obligations have been offset
(4) The obligor has made a lodgment of the subject matter of its performance in accordance with the law
(5) The obligee has released the obligations[68]
(6) The obligations and liabilities are held by one person
(7) There are other situations in which the contract shall be terminated as set forth in the law or agreed by the parties[69]

---

65. SPC Contract Law Interpretation, art. 11. If an obligee institutes litigation against a junior obligor with the people's court a subrogation rights proceeding without naming the original obligor as a third person, the people's court may add the original obligor as a party to the action. Where two or more obligees initiate litigation for subrogation rights against the same obligor, the people's court may have all such actions consolidated. SPC Contract Law Interpretation, art. 16. If an obligee files an application with the people's court for preservation of the assets of the obligor in a subrogation rights action, the applicant is required to post adequate security. SPC Contract Law Interpretation, art. 17. In a subrogation rights action, the junior obligor may assert against the obligee any defense it may have against the obligor. If the objection raised by the obligor against the claims asserted by the obligee in a subrogation rights action is established by the people's court as a result of its examination, the proceeding instituted by the obligee shall be dismissed by the people's court. SPC Contract Law Interpretation, art. 18. An obligee is entitled to an award of litigation expenses if he or she prevails in a subrogation action. SPC Contract Law Interpretation, art. 19.

66. Contract Law, art. 77. If an amendment is ambiguous, the contract shall be deemed to have not been amended. *Id.* art. 78.

67. Contract Law, arts. 79–90. *See also* SPC Contract Law Interpretation, arts. 27–29 (addressing claims concerning third parties under assignment).

68. Where a party to a contract releases the other party of its obligations, in part or in whole, the rights and obligations under the contract shall be discharged accordingly. Contract Law, art. 105.

69. Contract Law, arts. 91, 92–106.

The parties may rescind a contract by mutual consent or in any of the following circumstances:

(1) The purpose of the contract is rendered impossible to be achieved due to an event of force majeure
(2) Prior to the expiration of the performance term, one of the parties expressly confirms, or indicates through its actions, that it will not perform its principal obligation
(3) One of the parties delays the performance of its main obligation and continues to fail to perform for a reasonable period after a performance demand
(4) One of the parties has delayed the performance of its obligations or engaged in other noncomplying actions, rendering it impossible to achieve the purpose of the contract
(5) Other circumstances of rescission as provided by law[70]

A party that desires to rescind a contract is required to provide notice to the other parties. Rescission is effective upon receipt of notice of cancellation. A party that objects to the notice may petition the people's court or an arbitration tribunal, if applicable, for an order or award affirming the validity of the contract and to demand specific performance.[71] After a contract has been rescinded, the performance shall be discontinued for contracts that have not been performed. For contracts that have been performed, a party may request to be restored to its original state or that other remedial measures be adopted in accordance with the circumstances of performance or the nature of the contract.[72] The termination of a contract shall not affect the validity of its dispute resolution and liquidation clauses and shall not affect the right of a party to demand compensation for the damages.[73] A party to a contract is entitled to a setoff of its own obligations with the other party's obligations unless such setoff is not permitted under the contract or by law.[74]

6. Remedies for Breach

If one party does not perform its contractual obligations or performs its contractual obligations in a manner not in accordance with the agreement, the

70. Contract Law, art. 95. A right to rescind the contract expires after a reasonable period of time after notice to perform has been tendered to the nonperforming party or as stipulated in the contract. *Id.* art. 96. *See also* Contract Law, art. 74; SPC Contract Law Interpretation, arts. 23–26.

71. Contract Law, art. 96. If government approval is required in order to rescind a contract, such approval is required for cancellation to be effective.

72. Contract Law, art. 97.

73. Contract Law, art. 98.

74. Contract Law, arts. 99–100.

other party has the right to demand the party in breach to perform such obligations, to take remedial measures, or to compensate him for damages incurred.[75] Where one of the parties expressly states or indicates by its action that it will not perform its contractual obligations, the nonbreaching party may hold the other party liable for anticipatory breach of contract prior to the expiration of the time limit for performance.[76]

In situations in which a party fails to perform a nonmonetary obligation, or fails to perform in accordance with the contract, the nonbreaching party may petition the people's court or an arbitration tribunal for specific performance. The remedy of specific performance is not available in situations in which performance cannot be rendered in law or in fact, the subject matter is unavailable on the market, the cost of specific performance is excessively high, or the obligee fails to demand performance within a reasonable time after breach.[77]

The Contract Law provides that amount of damages for breach of contract is equivalent to the nonbreaching party's loss resulting from the breach, including the benefit that may be derived from the performance of the contract, provided that the amount shall not exceed the damages that are foreseen or should have been foreseen by the party in breach at the time of entering into the contract.[78] Where a business engages in fraudulent activities while providing goods or services to a consumer, it shall be liable for damages in accordance with the Consumer Protection Law.[79] Moreover, the Contract Law provides that an injured party may elect to pursue either contract or tort damages as may be allowed under Chinese law.[80]

If quality is not as agreed, responsibility for the breach should be assumed in the manner agreed upon by the parties. If nothing has been agreed upon with regard to the breach, or the agreement is not clear, the party that has been harmed can, according to the nature of the object and the amount of the damage, make a reasonable choice of whether to request

75. Contract Law, arts. 107, 109.

76. Contract Law, art. 108.

77. Contract Law, art. 110.

78. Contract Law, art. 113. This rule is consistent with the Economic Contract Law (art. 33), Foreign Economic Contract Law (art. 18), and the Civil Law (art. 112).

79. Contract Law, art. 114. *See* Law of the People's Republic of China on the Protection of the Rights and Interests of Consumers (adopted October 31, 1993, by the 4th Sess. of the Standing Comm. of the 8th NPC), art. 35, *reprinted in* CHINA LAWS FOR FOREIGN BUSINESS (CCH), Business Regulation ¶ 16-480 (the "Consumer Protection Law").

80. Contract Law, art. 122. The SPC maintains that "if an obligee intends to change its claims prior to the court hearing of first instance though it made its choice under Article 122 of the Contract Law at the time the suit was lodged with the people's court, the obligee shall be permitted by the people's court to effect such change. If any objection raised by the other party in respect of the jurisdiction is upheld as a result of the review by the people's court, the proceeding shall be dismissed by the same court." SPC Contract Law Interpretation, art. 30.

repair, exchange, a remake, a return, a reduction in price, or a reduction in remuneration.[81] If the quality is not as agreed, and results in additional damage, compensation for the loss can be requested.

The parties to a contract may agree to liquidated damages or a method for calculating damages as a result of a breach.[82] The agreed-upon liquidated damages are regarded as compensation for the damage caused, but if the amount agreed upon as the cost of the breach is lower than the damage that is produced, a party can request the people's court or an arbitration organization to increase the damage award. If the agreed-upon liquidated damages are considerably higher than the damage caused, a party can petition the people's court or an arbitration organization to make an appropriate reduction.

In the event of a force majeure event, the obligations of the parties may be partially or wholly avoided. The Contract Law defines "force majeure" as "objective circumstances that cannot be foreseen, avoided or overcome."[83] A party that cannot perform a contract due to force majeure is required to notify the other party promptly, in order to reduce the loss to the other party that could result, and, in addition, shall, within a reasonable time, provide evidence of such event of force majeure.[84]

A nonbreaching party is required to take appropriate measures to prevent the loss from increasing and thereby mitigate its damages. If a nonbreaching party does not take appropriate steps to prevent further loss or damage, it is barred by law from demanding damages for the loss due to a failure to mitigate.[85] An injured party may recover all expenses incurred to mitigate its losses. If both parties are in breach, each is responsible for their respective obligations, and damages will be apportioned accordingly.[86]

7. Choice of Law/Forum

The Contract Law provides that parties to a "foreign-related" contract may choose the law applicable, except otherwise provided by law.[87] If the parties

81. Contract Law, art. 111.
82. Contract Law, arts. 114, 116.
83. Contract Law, art. 117. The original draft of the Contract Law failed to include a definition of force majeure as an unforeseeable event.
84. Contract Law, art. 118.
85. Contract Law, arts. 112, 119. This rule is consistent with the Foreign Economic Contract Law (art. 22) and the Civil Law (art. 115).
86. Contract Law, art. 120.
87. Contract Law, art. 126. The term "foreign-related" is undefined in the Contract Law. In the past, the people's courts have had a difficult time in determining which contracts are "foreign-related" in upholding awards issued by the China International Economic and Trade Arbitration Commission (CIETAC), an arbitration institution that, at one time, was allowed to assume jurisdiction only over "foreign-related" disputes. CIETAC amended its rules in April 1998 to address this problem and to ensure that its awards are upheld by the courts. The lack of a definition in the Contract Law may lead to confusion and inconsistent application. *See* Chapter 21, Mediation and Arbitration § B.1.a. China's Arbitration Law fails to provide

to a foreign-related contract fail to select the applicable law, the law of the country with the closest connection to the contract shall apply.[88] The Contract Law further provides that joint ventures, equity and contractual, and contracts for the exploration and development of natural and mineral resources performed within the territorial limits of China, shall be governed by the laws and regulations of China.

The parties to a contract may agree to resolve their dispute through arbitration. Parties to a foreign-related contract may agree to designate an arbitration institution based either in China or outside of China. If the parties fail to provide for arbitration in their contract, or if the arbitration clause is deemed to be invalid, either party may initiate litigation before the people's court with jurisdiction over the parties and the dispute. The Contract Law provides that the parties to a contract must satisfy any court judgment or arbitral award and, if a party refuses to perform its obligations, the judgment creditor or prevailing party may petition the people's court for enforcement.[89]

8. Statute of Limitations

The Contract Law provides that in the event of a dispute arising from an international sales of goods contract, the limitations period for filing a claim with the people's court or an arbitration institution is four years, commencing from the date on which the party knows or should have known that its rights have been violated.[90] A contract involving the importation of technology is also four years.[91] Other than international sales of goods contracts and technology import contracts, the Contract Law provides that the limitations periods for other types of contracts is governed by other laws.

Under the Civil Law, and in general, the limitations period for filing a lawsuit or commencing arbitration is two years calculated from the date on which a party knows or should have known that there is a violation of its

a definition of the term "foreign-related," and we must therefore look to other legislative instruments to gain an understanding of the term. In this regard, Article 304 of the *Several Opinions of the Supreme People's Court Concerning the Implementation of the Civil Procedure Law* (1992) provides that the term includes a case in which either one or both parties are of foreign nationality or a company or organization is located in a foreign country.

88. Contract Law, art. 126.

89. Contract Law, art. 128.

90. Contract Law, art. 129. The four-year rule is consistent with the FEC Law and the International Sales of Goods Convention. FEC Law, art. 39. China is a signatory to the United Nations Convention on Contracts for the International Sale of Goods [*reprinted in* 19 I.L.M. 671 (1980)].

91. Contract Law, art. 129. Under the former Technology Law, the limitations period was one year. However, the Technology Law did not apply to contracts involving foreign parties. The SPC maintains that where "a tort upon the right of a party to a dispute which arises out of a technical contract occurs prior to the effectiveness of the Contract Law, no protection shall be granted by the people's court to the extent that the lapse of time from the date such party knew or should have known such tort to the date of effectiveness of the Contract Law exceeds one year. Otherwise, such party shall have a right to take action within a period of two years." SPC Contract Law Interpretation, art. 6.

rights and interests.[92] The Civil Law provides for a one-year limitations period with respect to contractual matters involving the sale of a substandard product (i.e. breach of warranty), failure to pay rent under a lease agreement, or a loss of or damage to an item under a bailment contract.[93] The people's court may, under special circumstances, extend the limitations period.[94] The limitations period may be suspended if, within the final six months of the period of limitations, the injured party is unable to exercise its rights due to force majeure or other obstacles.[95] Calculation of the limitations period shall continue after the reason for the suspension is eliminated. The limitations period shall be suspended if legal proceedings are commenced or if an interested party demands or agrees to fulfil its obligations under the contract.[96]

B. Specialized Contracts

In addition to general contractual principals, the Contract Law governs the following types of special contracts:

(1) Purchase and Sales of Goods Contracts
(2) Electricity, Water, Gas, and Heat Power Supply and Usage Contracts
(3) Gift Contracts[97]
(4) Loan Contracts
(5) Lease Contracts
(6) Finance Lease Contracts
(7) Hire of Work Contracts
(8) Project Construction Contracts
(9) Transportation Contracts[98]
(10) Technology Contracts
(11) Bailment Contracts[99]
(12) Warehousing Contracts[100]

---

92. Civil Law, art. 135. A party that desires to perform its obligations after the limitations period is not barred from performance. Civil Law, art. 138.

93. Civil Law, art. 136. There is also a one-year limitations period for personal injury matters. The one-year limitations period on claims concerning the sale of substandard products is inconsistent with the two-year limitations period set forth in the Product Liability Law. *See* Chapter 13, Consumer Protection § A.4.

94. Civil Law, art. 137.

95. Civil Law, art. 139. *See also* Civil Law, art. 153 (definition of force majeure).

96. Civil Law, art. 140.

97. Contract Law, arts. 185–95.

98. Contract Law, arts. 288–321. The law addresses the requirements for passenger and cargo transport contracts.

99. Contract Law, arts. 365–80.

100. Contract Law, arts. 381–95.

(13) Agency Contracts
(14) Brokerage Contracts

The Contract Law covers a broad range of contractual relations that are covered under other laws and, in particular, specialized laws and regulations including, but not limited to, the following:

Electricity Usage Contracts:	Electric Power Law
Loan Contracts:	Secured Interests Law, Commercial Bank Law
Project Construction Contracts:	Construction Law, Highway Law
Transportation Contracts:	Civil Aviation Law
Finance Lease Contracts:	Secured Interests Law
Lease Contracts:	Law on the Administration of Urban Real Estate
Insurance Contracts:	Insurance Law

Since these laws have not been formally superseded by the Contract Law, a party to a specialized contract is required to understand and appreciate the standards set forth in the Contract Law and other applicable laws and regulations. Indeed, the Contract Law provides that such special laws take priority.[101]

1. Purchase and Sales of Goods Contracts

The Contract Law defines a purchase and sales contract as an agreement whereby a seller transfers title of certain goods, and the buyer agrees to pay the contract price.[102] Although not required by law, a purchase and sales contract may include terms and conditions concerning packaging, labeling, inspection procedures, controlling language, and other matters specifically relating to the sales transaction.[103] The buyer and the seller are required to follow all laws and regulations that may prohibit or restrict the transfer or sale of any property that is the subject of a purchase and sales contract.[104]

The title of the goods shall be transferred upon tender, unless otherwise set forth in the law or agreed upon by the parties. The parties to a purchase and sales contract may stipulate in the contract a provision regarding preservation of the title of the goods. Such a provision may set forth that the title of the

101. Contract Law, arts. 123–24.

102. Contract Law, art. 130. The Contract Law is consistent with China's obligations to the International Sales of Goods Convention. China is a signatory to the United Nations Convention on Contracts for the International Sale of Goods [*reprinted in* 19 I.L.M. 671 (1980)].

103. Contract Law, art. 131. If the parties do not agree upon the type of packaging materials, the seller is required to use materials that conform with industry standards or are sufficient to meet the requirements for the shipment of the specific subject matter. Contract Law, art. 156.

104. Contract Law, art. 132.

goods belongs to the seller if the buyer fails to make payment or to perform other obligations.[105]

The seller shall deliver the goods by the deadline time as prescribed in the contract. Where a period for delivery is set forth in the contract, the seller may deliver at any time within such period, provided, however, that the buyer shall be notified prior to the delivery. If the parties did not specify the deadline time for delivery of the goods in a contract, or a provision of this kind in the contract is equivocal, the seller shall deliver the goods within a reasonable period after the contract has become effective. If the goods are in the actual possession of the buyer prior to entering the contract, the time when the contract becomes effective shall be deemed to be the time of tendering the goods.[106]

The seller shall deliver the goods at the place as agreed upon in the contract. If the parties did not stipulate a place for tendering in the contract, the Contract Law provides as follows:

(1) If it has been agreed that the seller shall be responsible for delivery, the seller shall deliver the goods to the first carrier for shipment to the buyer.
(2) Where both the seller and the buyer knew of the location of the goods when the contract was executed, if it has not been agreed in the contract that the seller shall be responsible for delivery, the seller shall tender the goods at that location; if such location was unknown, the goods shall be tendered at the seller's business place where the seller was present when the contract was executed.[107]

The risks of destruction, or damage to, the goods of a purchase and sales contract shall be borne by the seller prior to tendering title of the goods and the responsibility of the buyer after tendering title.[108] In the event that the goods are not delivered by the stipulated deadline due to the buyer's breach, the risk of destruction of, or damage to, the goods during the period from the originally scheduled tendering date to the time of actual delivery shall be borne by the buyer.[109] In the event that property subject to a purchase and sales contract is in the process of shipment, the risks of destruction, or damage, shall be borne by the buyer at the time the contract becomes

105. Contract Law, arts. 133–34.
106. Contract Law, arts. 138–40.
107. Contract Law, art. 141.
108. Contract Law, art. 142.
109. Contract Law, art. 143.

effective, unless otherwise agreed by the parties.[110] If the parties failed to agree upon the location for delivery of the goods subject to a purchase and sales contract, the seller is responsible for delivery of the property to the carrier and the destruction of, or damage to, the goods shall be borne by the buyer after the seller tenders the goods to the first carrier.[111] If a buyer fails to take delivery of the property as agreed upon by the parties, the buyer is responsible for the destruction of, or damage to, the property.[112]

The seller is required to warrant that no third party claims any rights or interest in the property that is the subject of a purchase and sale agreement. A buyer may withhold payment, if applicable, to the seller if a third party lodges a claim against the subject property.[113] If the buyer was aware, at the time of entering into the contract, that a third party had a potential claim of ownership of the goods, the seller is not liable to the buyer for any subsequent claims against the goods.[114]

The Contract Law provides that a seller is required to deliver the subject property in compliance with the quality standards as agreed in the parties' contract, including any written description or specifications. If the parties did not agree upon the quality of the subject property, the seller is required to comply with the general standard concerning goods of a similar kind.[115] The buyer may claim compensatory damages for breach of contract, if the goods tendered by the seller fail to comply with the agreed-upon or customary quality standards.[116]

The Contract Law provides that a buyer is required to "timely" inspect the goods upon delivery. The buyer is required by law to make a claim to the seller that the subject goods are nonconforming with respect to quality and quantity within thirty (30) days of a determination. If the buyer fails to lodge a claim within two (2) years of receiving the subject goods, the law provides that the quantity or quality of the goods is deemed to have complied with the provisions of the contract, except if the parties' contract provides otherwise. Where the seller intentionally provides nonconforming goods, the thirty-day and two-year limitation periods do not limit a buyer's right to claim that the goods are nonconforming.[117]

110. Contract Law, art. 144.
111. Contract Law, art. 145.
112. Contract Law, art. 146.
113. Contract Law, arts. 151–52.
114. Contract Law, arts. 150–52.
115. Contract Law, arts. 153–55.
116. Contract Law, arts. 111, 155.
117. Contract Law, arts. 157–58.

The buyer shall make payment at the place and in the amount as agreed upon in the parties' contract. In the absence of such agreement on the place of payment, or in the event that the parties' agreement is ambiguous, the buyer is required to make payment at the following places:

(1) The seller's business place
(2) The place where the goods are tendered
(3) The location where the documentation relating to the goods is delivered

The buyer is required to pay the contract price at such time as agreed upon in the contract, or at the time of delivery of the goods.[118]

If the seller tenders goods in excess of the contracted quantity, the buyer may accept it or reject the excessive portion. If the buyer accepts the excessive portion, it shall pay for it at the original contract price. Where the seller tenders the goods in a deficient quantity, the law provides that the buyer is precluded from rejecting the goods except in situations in which acceptance would result in losses to the buyer. If the buyer intends to reject the goods, a "timely" notice of rejection is required to be lodged with the seller. If the buyer fails to timely notify the seller of any deficiency in the quantity, the buyer is liable to the seller for any damages that may result.[119]

The Contract Law provides that if the principal part of the goods is nonconforming, the buyer may rescind the contract to all ancillary parts of the goods. If the ancillary part of the goods is nonconforming, a buyer is precluded from seeking to rescind the contract so long as the principal part of the goods conform to the parties' contract. The buyer has the right to obtain compensation for damages resulting from any nonconforming ancillary part of the goods.[120] When the goods consist of several items and only one such item is nonconforming, the buyer may rescind the contract only with respect to the specific nonconforming item, provided, however, that if separation of such object from the other objects causes apparent damages to the value of the goods, the buyer may rescind the contract in full.[121]

118. Contract Law, arts. 159–61. The seller who accepts installment payments may request the buyer to pay an unpaid balance, or rescind the contract, when the buyer fails to make two consecutive payments and the overdue amount equals one-fifth of the total contract price. The seller who rescinds the contract may request the buyer to pay for its use of the goods. *Id.* art. 167.

119. Contract Law, arts. 162–63.

120. Contract Law, arts. 164–65. An example of this rule occurs when the tool kit that accompanies a machine is deemed to be nonconforming, but the principal part of the goods, the machine, is considered to be in compliance with the terms of the contract. A buyer thus cannot reject both the machine and the tool kit if the tool kit, as an ancillary part of the subject matter, is considered nonconforming.

121. Contract Law, arts. 164–66.

If the parties to a purchase and sales transaction rely upon samples, the subject samples are required to be maintained for safekeeping. The seller is also required to provide a description regarding the quality of the samples. The goods tendered by the seller shall have the "identical" quality to the samples. Where the buyer of a purchase and sales transaction in reliance upon samples was unaware of the hidden defects of the sample, the seller bears the obligation to tender the goods that satisfies the common criteria of the goods of the same kind, irrespective of whether the goods it actually tendered are identical to the sample provided.[122]

The parties to a purchase and sales contract may agree that the subject goods be purchased for a trial period to allow the buyer to test the subject goods. At the end of the trial period, the buyer is required to either accept or reject the goods. A buyer that fails to formally reject or accept the goods at the conclusion of the testing period is deemed to have accepted the goods.[123]

2. Electricity, Water, Gas, and Heat Power Supply and Usage Contracts

The Contract Law outlines the requirements for supply and usage contracts for electricity, water, and other utilities. A contract for the supply of utilities is required to outline the applicable fees and billing cycles. A utilities supplier is liable for any losses as a result of a utilities supplier's failure to abide by the parties' contract or as a result of a failure to abide by State safety standards.[124] If a supplier is required to terminate or suspend the supply of a utility as a result of maintenance or as a result of a limitation upon supply, it shall notify the user in advance and in accordance with the law.[125] A supplier is liable for damages for losses sustained by the user as a result of a supplier's failure to properly provide notice of termination or suspension. In situations involving natural disasters, a supplier is liable only for damages resulting from an interruption in services if repairs are not promptly

122. Contract Law, arts. 168–69.

123. Contract Law, arts. 170–71.

124. Contract Law, arts. 176–77. *See also* Electric Power Law of the PRC (adopted and promulgated on December 28, 1995, by the 17th Sess. of the Standing Comm. of the 8th NPC), *reprinted in* China Laws for Foreign Business (CCH), Business Regulation ¶ 19-604 (outlines the standards, *inter alia,* concerning the supply contracts for electricity); Provisions on Electric Power Projects Invested by Foreign Investors (issued on March 20, 1997, by the Ministry of Power Industry), *reprinted in* 127 China International Business (MOFTEC) 46 (1998) (addresses the scope of foreign investment in power projects, approval procedures, requirements for equipment purchases, pricing of electricity, requirements for contract provisions, and applicable law and dispute resolution); Interim Provisions for Submission and Approval Procedure on Electric Power Project Invested Directly by Foreigners (issued on December 9, 1997, by the Ministry of Power Industry), *reprinted in* 127 China International Business (MOFTEC) 46 (1998) (outlines detailed procedures for approval procedures including the required content of the feasibility study and project proposal).

125. Contract Law, art. 180.

made.[126] A supplier may suspend service if, after notice and demand for payment is made, the user fails or refuses to pay for the utilities.[127]

3. Loan Contracts

The Contract Law provides that a loan contract is a contract under which the borrower obtains a loan from the lender and repays the loan when the term expires. A loan contract is required to be in writing, unless otherwise agreed between the parties. A loan contract shall include provisions relating to the type, amount, intended use, rate of interest, term, and manner of repayment of the loan.[128] The Contract Law provides that a lender has a right to request that a borrower provide collateral for a loan.[129] If the lender fails to provide the loan on the agreed date or in the agreed amount, it is liable for damages to the borrower.[130]

A potential borrower is required to accurately represent its financial condition at the time of application.[131] A lender has the right to examine and supervise the use of the loan in accordance with the loan contract. If the borrower has not used the loan proceeds in a manner as agreed upon by the parties, the lender may cease further funding, demand repayment of monies loaned, and terminate the contract.[132]

The borrower is required to pay interest to the lender, unless otherwise agreed between the parties.[133] The interest rate for a loan extended by a financial institution engaging in lending operations shall be determined within the upper and lower limits of loan interest rates prescribed by the People's Bank of China. The interest rate for a loan between individuals may not be in violation of State law concerning loan interest rates. In situations in which the contract does not provide for or clearly specify the period for the payment of interest, the interest is due upon repayment of the loan. Where the term of the loan is over one year, the interest shall be paid at the end of every year within the term. Where the remaining term is less than one

126. Contract Law, art. 181.
127. Contract Law, art. 182.
128. Contract Law, arts. 196–97; *See* Commercial Bank Law of the People's Republic of China (adopted on May 10, 1995, by the 13th Sess. of the 8th NPC and as amended by the NPC on December 27, 2003), art. 37, *reprinted in* CHINA LAWS FOR FOREIGN BUSINESS (CCH), Business Regulation ¶ 8-350 (hereinafter the "Commercial Bank Law"). *See also* Chapter 11, Financial Regulation § A.2.b(1).
129. Contract Law, art. 198; Secured Interests Law of the People's Republic of China (adopted June 30, 1995, by the 14th Sess. of the Standing Comm. of the 8th NPC), *reprinted in* CHINA LAWS FOR FOREIGN BUSINESS (CCH), Business Regulation ¶ 5-605 (hereinafter the "Secured Interests Law"). *See generally* Creating & Enforcing Security in the PRC, ASIA LAW & PRACTICE (1997).
130. Contract Law, art. 201.
131. Contract Law, art. 199.
132. Contract Law, arts. 202–03.
133. Contract Law, art. 205. A loan contract between two individuals is interest-free if the parties fail to clearly specify the interest payment terms. *Id.* art. 211.

year, the interest shall be paid on repayment of the loan.[134] If the loan contract does not provide a time for the repayment of the loan, the borrower is required to tender payment of the principal and interest within a reasonable time period.[135] If the borrower fails to repay the loan when it is due, it is liable to pay to the lender the agreed-upon default payment. Where the loan contract does not provide for default payment, the borrower shall pay interest calculated for the actual period of the loan.[136]

4. Lease Contracts

The Contract Law provides that a lease contract is a contract under which a lessor delivers leased property to the lessee for the lessee's use or benefit and the lessee pays rent.[137] A lease contract shall include provisions on the description, quantity, intended use, duration of the lease, payment method and date, and maintenance and repair of the leased property.[138] The Contract Law provides that the parties may not agree to a lease term that exceeds twenty years. Any period of time extending beyond twenty years is invalid as a matter of law. Upon the expiration of the term of the lease, the parties may extend the lease contract, provided that the extended term of the lease cannot exceed a total of twenty years.[139] A lease contract is required to be in writing if the term of the lease exceeds six months. If the parties fail to

134. Contract Law, arts. 204–07. A loan contract cannot provide for the deduction of interest from the principal of a loan in advance. If interest is deducted from the principal in advance, the interest shall be calculated in accordance with the principal sum of the loan. Contract Law, art. 200.

135. Contract Law, art. 206.

136. Contract Law, arts. 207–08.

137. Contract Law, art. 212. Unless otherwise agreed by the parties, any benefits derived from the possession or use of the leased property during the term of the lease shall belong to the lessee. *Id.* art. 225. With respect to real property leasing, *see generally* Civil Law, art. 80; Law of the People's Republic of China on the Administration of Urban Real Estate (adopted on July 5, 1994, by the 8th Sess. of the Standing Comm. of the 8th NPC), arts. 31–55, *reprinted in* CHINA LAWS FOR FOREIGN BUSINESS (CCH), Business Regulation ¶ 19-593 (hereinafter the "Real Estate Law"); Provisional Regulations of the People's Republic of China Concerning the Grant and Assignment of the Right to Use State Land in Urban Areas (promulgated on May 24, 1990, by the State Council), *reprinted in* CHINA LAWS FOR FOREIGN BUSINESS (CCH), Business Regulation ¶ 14-716. With respect to contracts for the lease of civil aviation equipment, *see* Civil Aviation Law of the People's Republic of China (adopted on October 30, 1995, by the 16th Sess. of the Standing Comm. of the 8th NPC), *reprinted in* CHINA LAWS FOR FOREIGN BUSINESS (CCH), Business Regulation ¶ 15-540 (articles 26–33 outline the requirements for civil aircraft lease agreements).

138. Contract Law, art. 213. If the parties fail to provide in writing the limitations on the use of the leased property, the lessee may use the property in a manner consistent with the "nature" of the subject property. *Id.* arts. 217–18. The lessor may terminate the contract and claim compensatory damages if the leased property is damaged by the lessee while used in a manner outside the permissible scope of use. *Id.* art. 219. Also, if the parties do not agree upon maintenance of the leased property, the lessor is required to maintain the subject property. *Id.* arts. 216, 220. If the lessor refuses or fails to maintain or repair the leased property as required by contract, the lessee has the right to repair the leased property and deduct the repair costs from the rental payments. Contract Law, art. 221. A lessee has the right to terminate the lease at any time if the leased property is considered to be a danger to the life and health of the lessee, even if at the time of signing the lease contract it was known to the lessee that the leased property was substandard. *Id.* art. 233.

139. Contract Law, art. 214.

agree upon the lease term, the lease is considered a lease for an indefinite term, which may be terminated at any time by either party upon reasonable notice.[140]

The Contract Law provides that a lessee, with the consent of the lessor, may make improvements or additions to the leased property. However, the law requires that upon termination of the lease contract, the lessee may demand that the lessor reimburse a portion of the expenses incurred in connection with such improvements or additions with respect to the increase in the value of the leased property resulting from such improvements or additions as of the termination of the lease contract. If the lessee makes any improvement or addition to the leased property without the lessor's consent, the lessor may require the lessee to restore the leased property to its original condition or to pay compensation for damages.[141]

Subject to the consent of the lessor, the lessee may sublease the leased property to a third party. If a sublease is made by the lessee, the lease contract between the lessee and the lessor shall remain in effect, and the lessee shall compensate for any damages to the leased property caused by the third party. If the lessee subleases the leased property without the lessor's consent, the lessor may terminate the contract. [142]

The Contract Law provides that a lessee is required to pay the rent for the use of the leased property at the agreed date. If there is no agreement or the agreement is unclear with respect to the payment date, payment shall be made at the expiration of the term of the lease, provided that payment shall be made at the end of each one-year period if the term of the lease is one year or more, and that payment shall be made at the expiration of the term of the lease if the remaining term of the lease is less than one year.[143] If a lessee fails to pay or delays the payment of rent, the lessor may demand that the lessee tender its rental payment within a reasonable period of time. If the lessee fails to make payment within such period of time, the lessor may terminate the contract.[144] If the leased property is damaged, in whole or in part, the lessee is entitled to request a reduction or waiver of rental payments.[145]

If the lessor intends to sell leased property, the lessor shall provide notice to the lessee within a reasonable period of time prior to the sale, and the lessee shall have a right of first refusal to purchase the leased property under

140. Contract Law, arts. 215, 332.
141. Contract Law, art. 223.
142. Contract Law, art. 224.
143. Contract Law, art. 226.
144. Contract Law, art. 227.
145. Contract Law, art. 229. A lessee may also request a reduction or waiver of rent if the lessee's tenancy is interrupted by a claim of possession to the leased property by a third party. *Id.* art. 228.

the same conditions as proposed by a bona fide third-party purchaser.[146] Any change in ownership or the creation of a security interest with respect to the leased property does not affect the lease contract.[147]

The Contract Law provides that the lessee is required to return the leased property upon the expiration of the term of the lease in its original condition. The original lease contract shall remain in effect, but the term of the lease shall be of indefinite term if, upon the expiration of the term of the lease, the lessee continues to use the leased property and the lessor does not object.[148]

5. Finance Lease Contracts

The Contract Law outlines the requirements for finance lease contracts, which are required to be in writing. A finance lease contract is a contract under which the lessor, as purchaser, enters a purchase contract with a seller to purchase an object designated by the lessee for the lessee's use or benefit and the lessee pays rent.[149] The leased property under a financial lease contract is the property designated under a purchase contract. The seller shall deliver the designated object to the lessee as agreed, and the lessee shall have the rights and obligations of a purchaser with respect to the leased property. Although the lessee has possession of the leased property under the financial lease contract, the lessor is the owner of the leased property.[150] If the lessee is the subject of a bankruptcy proceeding, the leased property is excluded from the lessee's bankruptcy estate.[151] In contrast to a lease contract arrangement, the lessee under a finance lease contract is responsible for the maintenance and repair of the leased property during the term of the contract.[152]

The rent under a financial lease contract may be set by the parties. In the event of an ambiguity, the rent shall be determined on the basis of the cost of purchasing the leased property and the lessor's reasonable profit.[153] If the lessee fails to pay the rent for two consecutive payment periods, the lessor may demand payment. If the lessee still fails to pay the rent within a

146. Contract Law, art. 230.
147. Contract Law, art. 229.
148. Contract Law, arts. 235–36. If a lessee of a residence dies during the term of the lease, the persons who resided with the lessee while the lessee was alive may lease such house in accordance with the original lease contract. *Id.* art. 234.
149. Contract Law, arts. 237–38.
150. Contract Law, art. 242. The parties to a finance lease contract may agree upon the ownership rights to the leased property upon the expiration of the term of the lease. Otherwise, upon the expiration of the lease term, the lessee is required to return the leased property to the lessor or its designated agent. *Id.* art. 250.
151. Contract Law, art. 242.
152. Contract Law, art. 247.
153. Contract Law, art. 243.

reasonable period of time after receipt of a demand notice, the lessor may terminate the contract and repossess the leased property.[154] If the lessor terminates the contract and repossesses the leased property, the law provides that a lessee is entitled to demand a refund if the value of the leased property exceeds the damages, including monies due for rental payments and repair costs, if any, as a result of the lessee's breach of contract.[155]

In contrast to the obligations of a lessor in lease contract arrangements, the lessor under a lease finance contract is not liable to the lessee for the quality of the leased property unless it can be determined that the lessee relied upon the lessor in the selection of the leased property or if the lessor assisted with the selection of the leased property.[156] In addition, the lessor under a lease finance contract is also not liable for damages for property damage or personal injury to a third party caused by the use of the leased property while in the possession of the lessee.[157]

6. Contracts for Hire of Work

A contract for hire of work is a contract under which a contractor is employed to complete certain work in accordance with a principal's requirements and is paid for its finished product or services. A contract for hire of work may include contracts for processing, customized ordering, maintenance and repair, printing, photocopying, surveying and mapping, and inspection and examination.[158] The Contract Law provides that a contract for hire of work shall include provisions outlining the subject matter, quantity, quality and specifications, compensation, subcontracting, materials, completion time, and conditions for acceptance.[159] Under the Contract Law, a contractor is held to a duty of confidentiality and is prohibited from retaining or duplicating any information concerning the work for hire without the consent of the principal.[160]

A contractor is prohibited from subcontracting the "major portion" of the work to third parties without the consent and authorization of the principal. The contractor may subcontract minor tasks under the contract to a third party, unless otherwise agreed in the contract. The contractor is liable to the

154. Contract Law, art. 248.

155. Contract Law, art. 249.

156. Contract Law, art. 244. The lessor's only obligation is to guarantee that the lessee has the right of possession of the leased property during the term of the contract. *Id.* art. 245.

157. Contract Law, art. 246. The parties to a finance lease contract may provide that the lessee has the right to claim damages against the seller and manufacturer of the financed property. The lessee is usually granted the rights of a buyer in such transactions. *Id.* art. 239–40.

158. Contract Law, art. 251. A construction project contract is not considered a work for hire contract under the Contract Law. Construction project contracts are addressed in Articles 269–87.

159. Contract Law, art. 252.

160. Contract Law, art. 266.

principal for any work performed and completed by a subcontractor.[161] Either the principal or the contractor can supply the materials, components, and consumables to be used in completing the parties' contract.[162]

The principal is required, if applicable, to fully cooperate with the contractor in completing the work for hire. If the work cannot be completed due to the principal's failure to cooperate, the contractor may request that the principal perform within a reasonable period. If upon expiration of such period due performance has not been made, the contractor may rescind the contract.[163] The principal is also entitled to supervise the work of the contractor, but such supervision cannot interfere with the contractor's normal operation. Any damages or losses suffered by the contractor due to change orders or the work requirements shall be borne by the principal.[164]

The contractor is required to complete the work, and to deliver all necessary technical information and quality certifications, to the principal in accordance with the terms of the contract. The principal is required to accept or reject the work by the contractor in accordance with the contract.[165] If the completed work delivered by contractor does not conform to quality standards, the principal may demand that the contractor repair or refurbish the subject work, or demand a reduction of compensation. In addition, the principal is entitled to recover any other damages that may result from the contractor's failure to perform or partial performance.[166]

The principal is required to pay the contractor compensation within the time limit as agreed in the contract. The parties may agree upon the use of deposits, a single payment upon completion of the work, or installment payments based upon progress. If the time limit for the payment is not clearly provided by the contract, the principal shall make the payment at the same time the completed work is delivered.[167] If the principal fails to pay the contractor for compensation or expenses for materials and other disbursements

161. Contract Law, arts. 253–54. In the event the principal retains joint contractors, the Contract Law provides that joint contractors are equally liable to the principal except if provided for by contract. *Id.* art. 267.

162. Contract Law, arts. 255–56. If the principal supplies the materials, the contractor has an obligation to advise the principal that the supplied materials are insufficient to meet the terms of the contract. The contractor also has an obligation to advise the principal if the specifications or technical requirements with respect to the work for hire is unreasonable. Any damages and losses caused by the failure of the principal to timely respond to the contractor shall be borne by the principal. *Id.* art. 257. If the materials provided by the principal are in the possession of the contractor, the contractor is liable for any damages to the materials. *Id.* art. 265.

163. Contract Law, art. 259.

164. Contract Law, arts. 258, 260.

165. Contract Law, art. 261.

166. Contract Law, art. 262.

167. Contract Law, art. 263.

within the agreed time period, the contractor has a right to a lien in the completed work as a security, unless otherwise provided for in the contract.[168] The principal may rescind the contract for hire of work at any time; however, the principal is required to compensate the contractor for any damages and losses suffered as a result of the termination.[169]

7. Construction Project Contracts

A construction project contract is an agreement whereby a contractor performs certain tasks involving the construction, installation, demolition, or refurbishment of a work of improvement. In addition to traditional construction-related works, a construction project contract may also include contracts concerning architectural, design, and engineering services.[170] The law requires that a construction project contract be in writing.[171] The Contract Law provides that a contract for the construction of a work of improvement shall contain the following provisions:

(1) Scope of work
(2) Construction schedule and time for performance
(3) Quality and specifications of works
(4) Contract price and budgeting
(5) Schedule for delivery of technical information

---

168. Contract Law, art. 264. The requirements for liens are set forth in Articles 84–87 of the Secured Interests Law. *See* Secured Interests Law of the People's Republic of China (adopted June 30, 1995, by the 14th Sess. of the Standing Comm. of the 8th NPC), *reprinted in* China Laws for Foreign Business (CCH), Business Regulation ¶ 5-605 (hereinafter the "Secured Interests Law"). *See generally* Creating & Enforcing Security in the PRC, Asia Law & Practice (1997).

169. Contract Law, art. 268. This unilateral right of termination is referred to as "termination for convenience" and requires that the principal provide notice to the contractor and to pay for all work performed up to the time notice is received, including damages and a reasonable profit based upon the work performed.

170. Contract Law, art. 269, 272.

171. Contract Law, art. 270. There are a number of regulations affecting construction contracts, architectural design contracts, and real property development contracts. *See generally* Several Regulations on the Establishment of Construction Industry Enterprises with Foreign Investment (promulgated on September 18, 1995, by the Ministry of Construction and MOFTEC), *reprinted in* China Laws for Foreign Business (CCH), Business Regulation ¶ 13-596. The regulations require minimum capital requirements and other conditions for the establishment of a Foreign-Invested Construction Enterprise (FICE). *See also* Provisional Regulations on Sino-Foreign Cooperative Design of Engineering and Construction Projects (approved on March 27, 1986, by the State Council and issued on June 5, 1986, by MOFTEC and the State Planning Commission), *reprinted in* China Laws for Foreign Business (CCH), Business Regulation ¶ 19-516; Rules for the Trial Implementation of the Economic Responsibility System in Undertaking Contract Projects of Capital Construction (promulgated on March 3, 1983, by the State Council), *reprinted in* China Laws for Foreign Business (CCH), Business Regulation ¶ 12-580. *See* Notice of the State Council on Issues Concerning the Levying and Collection of Taxes on Materials and Goods Imported for Real Estate Construction (promulgated on April 23, 1995, by the State Council), *reprinted in* China Laws for Foreign Business (CCH), Customs ¶ 50-615 (provisions concerning preferential duty treatment for construction materials and equipment).

(6) Materials and equipment to be used
(7) Inspection and acceptance procedures for the work of improvement
(8) Warranty period[172]

The Contract Law provides that activity relating to the tender and evaluation of bids for construction projects must be conducted publicly and fairly. Projects for State agencies must follow procedures established by the government and the approval documents for the specific project, including feasibility studies, land-use plans, and investment plans approved by the national, provincial, and local governments.[173]

The contractor may enter into subcontract arrangements with the approval of the principal but is liable for the acts and omissions of any subcontractor.[174] The principal has the right to enter into contracts with several contractors at the same time, and may retain a project supervisor to oversee the work of the various contractors.[175]

The principal has the right to inspect the work progress so long as the inspection does not interfere with the rights of the contractor.[176] The contractor has an express statutory obligation to notify the principal of its progress to allow the principal or its agents to inspect its work, and especially with respect to the installation of framing, electrical wiring, or rough plumbing, which is eventually concealed as work progresses.[177] After the completion of the construction work, the principal must inspect the work of improvement in accordance with the construction drawings and specifications as well as the acceptance inspection regulations and quality inspections standards promulgated by the State. If the construction work passes the acceptance inspection, the principal shall pay the contract price as agreed and accept the construction project.[178]

The contractor is liable to the principal if the work of improvement fails to meet the terms of the contract or construction standards set by the State. If the quality of the construction work does not comply with the agreed

---

172. Contract Law, art. 275. Contracts concerning architectural, design, and engineering services are required to include provisions concerning payment, scope of work, and scheduling requirements. *Id.* art. 274.

173. Contract Law, arts. 172, 273.

174. Contract Law, art. 272.

175. Contract Law, art. 276.

176. Contract Law, art. 277.

177. Contract Law, art. 278.

178. Contract Law, art. 279. The principal is required to accept a contractor's work of improvement prior to conducting additional construction work at a construction project. Otherwise, the principal is liable for any alleged defects or quality problems concerning the contractor's work product that may result. This rule protects a contractor from a principal that inappropriately alters the contractor's work of improvement. *Id.*

standard due to any reason on the part of the contractor, the principal may demand that the contractor cure the defects within a reasonable time period. If the contractor fails to cure the defects within the prescribed time, the contractor shall be liable for damages for breach of the contract.[179] The contractor is also liable for any property damage or personal injuries sustained as a result of the contractor's failure to abide by the terms of the contract or to maintain workplace health and safety standards.[180]

The principal is liable to the contractor for any damages resulting from interference, delay, a failure to supply materials, access to work sites and technical information, or other reason on the part of the principal. If the principal changes the specifications or the contract terms, provides inaccurate data, or fails to provide necessary working conditions to assist the contractor in completing the work of improvement, the principal is liable for damages to the contractor. If the principal fails to pay the contract price as agreed after the completion of the construction work, the contractor may demand by notice the payment of the contract price from the principal in a reasonable period. If the principal fails to make the payment within the specified time limit, the contractor and the principal may negotiate to reduce the contract price for the construction work.[181]

8. Agency Contracts

An agency contract is an agreement whereby an agent is retained to perform services with respect to the principal's matters as agreed by the parties. The tasks performed by the agent may be general or specific.[182] The agent is required to act in a fiduciary capacity and in accordance with the principal's instructions. The agent has a duty to keep the principal informed with respect to the matters that are the subject of the agency contract. With the consent of the principal, the agent may retain a third party to accomplish the principal's tasks.[183] The principal is required to compensate the agent for his

179. Contract Law, art. 281.

180. Contract Law, art. 282.

181. Contract Law, arts. 283–86. The contractor who has not been paid for its work or materials supplied may "negotiate" with the principal to auction the project in order to receive payment from the auction proceeds. *Id.* art 286. Auctions are required to be governed by laws applicable to auction procedure. *Id.* art. 173.

182. Contract Law, arts. 396–97. Agency relationships are also generally addressed in the Civil Law. *See* Civil Law, arts. 63–70 (outlines basic standards for agency relationships). *See also* Administrative Measures of Shanghai Municipality Governing Agents (promulgated on July 11, 1994, by the Shanghai Municipal People's Government), *reprinted in* CHINA LAWS FOR FOREIGN BUSINESS (CCH), Special Zones & Cities ¶ 240-005. The Shanghai Agency Measures address the standards for agency relationships, registration requirements, mandatory content for agency contracts, requirements for commissions, liability and breach of contract issues, and dispute resolution matters.

183. Contract Law, arts. 398–402.

or her services, and to reimburse the agent for all costs incurred with respect to the subject matter of the agency relationship.[184] The law requires that any property obtained during the course of the agency relationship is owned by the principal.[185]

If an agent commits acts outside the scope of the agency relationship that result in damages to a third party, the principal is entitled to indemnification by the agent for any claim made by a third party. The agent is also liable for any damages caused by the agent's gross negligence or intentional acts.[186] On the other hand, the agent may seek compensation from the principal for any damages sustained by the agent during the course and within the scope of the agency relationship.[187]

The parties to an agency contract may terminate the relationship at any time. The agency contract terminates automatically upon the death, disability, or bankruptcy of the principal or the agent, unless the parties have agreed otherwise.[188] The Contract Law provides that, in the event of death, disability, or bankruptcy of the principal, the agent has a duty to continue to abide by the terms of the agency relationship, and to protect the interests of the principal, until such time as a successor, executor, receiver, or conservator is appointed by law or pursuant to a testamentary instrument.[189]

9. Technology Contracts

The Contract Law addresses technology contracts, including technology development contracts, technology transfer contracts, technical consulting contracts, and technical service contracts.[190] Technology contracts are required by law to facilitate "the improvement of science and technology

184. Contract Law, art. 405.
185. Contract Law, art. 404.
186. Contract Law, art. 406. Co-agents share equal liability to a principal for damages sustained by the principal. *Id.* art. 409.
187. Contract Law, art. 407. The agent may also claim damages that are sustained as a result of the principal's retention of a co-agent. *Id.* art. 408.
188. Contract Law, arts. 410–11.
189. Contract Law, arts. 412–13.
190. Contract Law, arts. 322–64. The standards for registering technology contracts are set forth in Measures for the Administration of the Authentication and Registration of Technology Contracts, Guokefazhengzi No. 63, 2000, jointly promulgated on February 16, 2000, by Ministry of Science and Technology, Ministry of Finance, State Administration of Taxation, *reprinted in* China Laws for Foreign Business (CCH), Business Regulation ¶ 5-580. These Measures apply to the work of authenticating and registering technological development contracts, technology transfer contracts, technical consultancy contracts, and technical services contracts entered into by legal persons, individuals, and other organizations in accordance with the law. Technology contracts that are not registered do not qualify for preferential tax treatment and other state-offered benefits. Art. 6.

Manufacturing Contracts in China: Protecting IP Rights[191]

An arrangement involving the manufacture of technology-related products involves a manufacturing and supplier contract, and, if applicable, should contain language that limits and/or licenses the rights to use technology. The parties have a right to choose the contractual terms under the 1999 Contract Law, and there is no required language or form terms/conditions required by law as was required prior to 1999.

- From a regulatory perspective, the tech license must be registered with the government in certain situations. The registration process is rather simple for most types of encouraged or unrestricted technology (known as "free" technology). If the technology is listed in a government-restricted list, special approval procedures must be followed. Registration is also required in order for a Chinese party to gain approval for FOREX payments for royalties due under a license contract.
- An airtight manufacturing agreement should include, among other things, (1) control of packaging or labels; (2) requirements that rejects be destroyed; (3) prohibition of diverted product and overproduction from getting in the marketplace; (4) prohibition or limitation on subcontracting; (5) language addressing post-termination details for treatment of technology; (6) language for IP and technology audits; (7) limitation of access to the technology; (8) binding on employees and anyone with access; (9) language that prohibits the Chinese party from registering IP rights in its name; (10) prohibition on improving upon, or claiming an ownership interest in improvements to, technology; and (11) prohibition of competition or circumvention.
- For IP-related technology rights (TM, Copyrights, and Patents), a foreign party in China should also register the rights to prevent others from hijacking IP rights. It is possible to secure copyright protection for manuals and manufacturing drawings. Registration is a prerequisite to asserting rights administratively or in the courts, if necessary.
- In addition to contractual protection, there are many technical or practical controls, including limiting access, that provide some protection.
- It is also important to conduct a due diligence of any proposed supplier or manufacturer. Simple due diligence may reveal that a company has a poor track record of respect for the IP rights of foreign parties.

and shall expedite the application and popularization of science and technologies."[192] Under the regulations and rules in effect prior to the adoption of the Contract Law, a *technology import contract* was required to meet

191. A sample manufacturing contract is *reprinted in* Appendix A. For a discussion of technology-related contracts and the approval/registration procedures, *see infra* § 9, Technology Contracts.

192. Contract Law, art. 323. If a contract illegally monopolizes the technology, impairs the development of technology, or infringes upon the rights of others, the contract is invalid. *Id.* art. 329.

certain conditions, such as the requirement that the technology be capable of developing new products or contribute to the advancement of scientific skills, and to obtain the approval of the government.[193] Although the Contract Law does not expressly recognize any special requirements and restrictions for imported technology, or the requirement that government approval be obtained as a prerequisite to the importation of technology, the Contract Law specifically states that regulations concerning technology import contracts would prevail over other provisions.[194]

The Contract Law requires that a technology contract be in writing, unless otherwise stipulated by the parties, and is required to "generally contain" the following provisions:

(1) Name of the project
(2) Contents, scope, and requirements of the subject matter
(3) Plan, milestones, duration, place, and method in respect of the performance
(4) Confidentiality provisions concerning the technology
(5) Liabilities and risks
(6) Ownership and sharing of technologies
(7) Standards and method of inspection and acceptance
(8) Price and payment terms
(9) Provisions relating to liquidated damages or formulas for computing damages
(10) Dispute resolution[195]

A technology contract may also include terms and conditions relating to the performance of the contract, technical specifications of the subject

193. Under prior rules, imported technology was required to be advanced and conform to at least one of the following requirements: (1) Capable of developing and producing new products; (2) Capable of improving quality and performance of products; (3) Reducing production costs and lowering consumption of energy or raw materials; (4) Uses local resources efficiently; (5) Capable of expanding product export and increasing earnings of foreign currencies; (6) Environmentally safe; (7) Facilitates and supports a safe production process; (8) Facilitates the improvement of management; or (9) Contributes to the advancement of scientific and technical skills. Regulations on Administration of Technology Import Contracts of the People's Republic of China (promulgated on May 24, 1985, by the State Council) (repealed); Detailed Rules for the Implementation of the Administrative Regulations of the People's Republic of China on Technology Import Contracts (approved December 30, 1987, by the State Council) (repealed). *See also* Provisional Regulations of Shenzhen Special Economic Zone Governing the Import of Technology (promulgated on February 8, 1984, by the Guangdong Provincial People's Government), *reprinted in* CHINA LAWS FOR FOREIGN BUSINESS (CCH), Special Zones & Cities ¶ 73-510. *See generally* Birden, *Technology Transfers to China: An Outline of Chinese Law*, 16 LOY. L.A. INT'L & COMP. L.J. 861 (1995). For a sample technology transfer contract and license agreement, *see* Appendix A.

194. Contract Law, arts. 324–25.

195. Contract Law, arts. 323–24.

technology, scheduling issues, and technology standards. Design and technical documents, as well as drawings, tables, data, and photographs, may be attached and incorporated into a technology contract. If a technology contract is deemed to be a "foreign-related" contract, the parties have a right to choose an applicable law and forum for dispute resolution of a jurisdiction other than China. However, Chinese law may govern in situations where the contract is considered a "domestic" contract, such as contracts for the establishment of a joint venture.[196]

The employer owns the right to use or transfer technology, which is developed by an employee during employment. Technology developed during employment refers to the technology that is developed during the course and scope of employment or technology developed principally by using the materials, information, technology, and facilities of the employer. The Contract Law provides that an employer is required to compensate employees that develop technology on the basis of the benefits obtained from the use or transfer of such technology.[197] The right to use or transfer technology not developed during employment belongs to the individual or entity that developed such technology, and such individuals may enter into technology contracts with respect to such technology developed outside of the scope of employment.[198]

Under the former contract standards, the term of a technology contract was limited to ten years unless approval was received by MOFCOM. The term limitation is implicitly lifted by the new rules. With respect to confidentiality provisions, the former standards limited confidentiality obligations to the duration of the contract. However, the parties are now free to negotiate a confidentiality provision that extends beyond the contract term.

a. Technology Development Contracts

A technology development contract is required to be in writing and is defined as a contract whereby the parties endeavor to develop, either jointly or in a contractor relationship, new technologies, new products, new techniques, and new materials and their systems.[199] The parties may agree upon

196. China's Arbitration Law fails to provide a definition of the term "foreign-related," and we must therefore look to other legislative instruments to gain an understanding of the term. In this regard, Article 304 of the *Several Opinions of the Supreme People's Court Concerning the Implementation of the Civil Procedure Law* (1992) provides that the term includes a case in which either one or both parties are of foreign nationality or a company or organization is located in a foreign country.

197. Contract Law, art. 325.

198. Contract Law, art. 326.

199. Contract Law, arts. 330–32.

the use and ownership of the developed technology. However, the developer is prohibited from disclosing any technical secrets to a third party prior to delivery of the developed technology to the principal.[200] If the technology that is the subject of the technology development contract has been made public by other parties, rendering the performance of the technology development contract meaningless, the parties may terminate the contract.[201] Both parties are liable for damages in the event of breach of contract.[202]

The Contract Law provides that the party that developed the technology has the right to apply for any patent rights, unless otherwise stipulated by the parties. However, the principal that retained the contractor to develop the technology has the right to use the patented technology without obligation to pay compensation to the subcontractor. The principal has a right of first refusal to obtain the patent rights of the developed technology if the subcontractor intends to transfer the patent rights to another party.[203] For an invention or creation accomplished under a cooperative development contract, the right to apply for a patent is jointly held by the parties to the joint development contract, unless otherwise stipulated by the parties.[204] If a party to a joint development contract waives its right to apply for a patent, the other party has the right to independently apply for a patent. Nevertheless, the party that has waived its right to apply for patent protection may still use the jointly developed technology without compensating the patent applicant. If a party to a joint development contract refuses to waive its rights to apply for patent protection, the other party is prohibited from applying independently.

b. Technology Transfer Contracts

A technology transfer contract includes contracts for transfer of patent rights, transfer of the right to apply for a patent, transfer of nonpatented technologies, the licensing of patent exploitation, and technology import.[205] A technology transfer contract may provide for the exercisable scope of the patent rights or use of nonpatentable technologies between the transferor and the transferee; provided, however, that no provisions of the contract shall restrict technology competition and development.[206]

A technology transfer contract in which a patent is involved shall set forth the description of the invention/creation concerned, the applicant and

200. Contract Law, art. 341.
201. Contract Law, art. 337.
202. Contract Law, arts. 333–34, 336.
203. Contract Law, art. 339.
204. Contract Law, art. 340.
205. Contract Law, art. 342.
206. Contract Law, art. 343.

owner of the patent right, the date of application, application number, patent number, and term of validity of the patent right. A patent license contract shall be valid only during the term in which the patent is valid. After the term of validity of patent rights has expired or patent rights have been declared invalid, the patent right owner shall not enter into a patent licensing contract with any person in respect of such patent.[207]

The licensor of a patent licensing contract shall grant a license to the licensee to utilize the patented technologies in accordance with the contract and is required to deliver technical information for the utilization of the patent and provide necessary technical guidance. The licensee of a patent licensing contract shall not permit any third party to utilize the patented technology, and shall pay royalties in accordance with the parties' contract.[208]

207. Contract Law, art. 344.

208. Contract Law, arts. 345–46. Chinese manufacturers and exporters have a history of ignoring their royalty obligations under technology contracts. As a manufacturer and not an inventor, China is resistant to paying others for their intellectual property (IP). China's actions are a typical response from a country that is currently the focus of worldwide manufacturing—and much like the other Asian "tigers" in the past that developed their economies as a manufacturing base. Chinese companies frequently refuse to pay royalties unless forced to do so and, even if forced to do so, the usual practice is to underreport sales or flout audit rights in a misguided effort to pay less for per-unit royalties. The Chinese government has also expressed a policy that prevents the payment of royalties that it considers to be unfair or onerous, and encourages the development of homegrown technology standards as a way to cast off the yoke of foreign royalty obligations. This includes the efforts in wireless, DVD players, and digital compression. Encouraging the development of homegrown standards for the sake of avoiding the payment of royalties to foreign IP rights holders is bad policy. What the PRC government should encourage is independent innovation instead of coming up with something that supposedly replaces existing standards. Furthermore, the PRC government should strongly encourage Chinese companies to license the right to use, develop, and improve upon existing technology, and discourage copying, reverse engineering, and pseudo inventions just for the sake of ignoring the payment of legitimate royalties for the use of technological know-how of foreigners. Developing a homegrown standard is acceptable if they are trailblazers. But it is wasteful if Chinese enterprises are developing the standard to simply avoid paying for royalties. The end result may be that Chinese companies will get hit with infringement actions and will be denied markets worldwide for their goods if they ignore the IP rights of others. Consumer demands, business opportunities, and the threat of legal action will force the good Chinese companies to accept and comply with licensing arrangements. U.S. firms must do two things: (1) educate their Chinese customers, consumers, government, and partners—manufacturers, distributors, and joint venture partners—on the benefits of using their technological innovations and standards; and (2) aggressively and decisively enforce their IP rights against Chinese companies. Such enforcement strategies should include informal, administrative, judicial, and political remedies against infringing parties. U.S. companies must exercise some patience in helping Chinese companies mature in the global business environment. Most Chinese companies are struggling to operate in the international environment while under the internal constraints of typically poorly run state-owned enterprises. They hear the conflicting messages from the Chinese government that they need to run their businesses consistent with international standards but to do so the "China way." The Chinese way of doing business is less like a multinational and more like a policy-driven government-owned enterprise. The Chinese government still preaches the dogma that Chinese companies should resist "foreign domination," which sets the wrong tone for Chinese companies in their quest to develop international markets as good corporate citizens. Despite the Chinese government's insistence on developing homegrown standards in lieu of adopting foreign technological standards, the reality is that Chinese companies need the technology and U.S. companies welcome the business opportunity. However, U.S. companies should not share their technological know-how with any Chinese party—government-sponsored or private—unless they have satisfactory contractual and technological control over their IP rights. Although the judicial system is getting better, foreigners should not rely on the Chinese courts, given that they are still very much in favor of Chinese parties. For an interview of the author on the subject of IP rights in China,

The transferor in a nonpatentable technology transfer contract is required to provide all technical information and guidance, and to "guarantee the utility and reliability of the technology."[209] The transferee of a nonpatentable technology transfer contract shall utilize the technology in accordance with the parties' contract and is required to pay royalties for the transfer and use of the technology.[210] Both parties to a transfer contract involving nonpatented technology are obligated "to assume the duty of confidentiality."[211]

The Contract Law provides that the transferor in a technology transfer contract shall warrant that it is the lawful owner of the technology provided and that the technology provided is complete, without error, effective, and able to achieve the agreed-upon objectives.[212] The law further provides that the transferee of a technology transfer contract shall, in accordance with the stipulated scope and duration, undertake the obligation to maintain confidentiality of any trade secrets relating to the subject technology provided by the transferor that have not been publicly disclosed.[213] If either party is in breach of a technology transfer agreement, such as the failure to pay royalties or by failing to transfer the subject technology, the nonbreaching party is entitled to compensation for damages.[214] A transferor of technology is liable to the transferee if the subject technology violates the rights and interests of a third party.[215] If either party improves the transferred technology, neither party can claim exclusive rights to the improvements unless provided for by contract.[216]

c. Technical Consulting Contracts and Technical Service Contracts

The Contract Law outlines the requirements for technical consulting contracts and technical service contracts.[217] A technical consulting contract is a

---

see B. Deagon, *China's Homegrown Standards Bring Headaches to U.S. Firms,* Investor's Business Daily (April 8, 2004). For a general discussion on China's perception on royalty payments, *see* Z. Kan, *Rising DVD Royalties to Hit Exports,* CHINA DAILY, Business Weekly (October 10, 2002).

209. Contract Law, art. 347. The technology import standards require that a supplier of technology guarantee quality and performance, and provide documents and specifications concerning the technology that are complete, correct, and accurate. The technology is also required to be capable of accomplishing the technical targets prescribed in the contract. The supplier must guarantee that it is the lawful owner of the technology or has the rights to transfer the technology and is liable for damages in the event that a claim for infringement is lodged against the Chinese party.

210. Contract Law, art. 348.

211. Contract Law, arts. 350–51.

212. Contract Law, art. 349.

213. Contract Law, art. 350.

214. Contract Law, arts. 351–52.

215. Contract Law, art. 353.

216. Contract Law, art. 354. Under the technology import standards, if a contract does not contain an agreement with regard to rights to use scientific or technical improvements, the party making the improvements shall enjoy rights to the improvements.

217. Contract Law, arts. 356–64.

contract that involves the engagement of a party to conduct and prepare a technical feasibility study, technical surveys, and appraisals in respect of a specific technical project. A technical service contract is defined as a contract under which one party uses its technical knowledge to solve a specific technical problem for another party. A technical consulting contract has broader application than a technical service contract, which involves the resolution of a specific technical task. Such contracts do not include contracts for construction design or installation work. Unless otherwise specified in the parties' contract, the party that developed the new technology pursuant to a technical consulting or service contract is the owner of such developments.[218]

d. Technology Import Registration Procedures

In December 2001, the State Council issued the PRC Management Regulations on Technology Import and Export (State Council Order No. 331), and MOFTEC issued the implementing rules to the regulations.[219] The new rules, including multiple catalogues and appendices, took effect January 1, 2002, and were revised to meet China's WTO obligations to eliminate mandatory technology-transfer requirements and to conduct automatic registration for (instead of administrative approval of) unrestricted imports.

The standards for technology import contracts prohibit a transferor of imported technology from requiring that the Chinese party accept requirements that are unreasonably restrictive. Technology contracts should not contain the following terms and conditions:

(1) Unreasonable restrictions on the licensee's sourcing of raw materials, components, products, or equipment
(2) Restrictions on the licensee's rights to acquire similar or competing technology
(3) Restrictions on the licensee's right to improve the technology or use of any improvements
(4) Requirements that the licensee pay for or undertake obligations for patents that have expired or been declared invalid
(5) Conditions not closely related to the technology to be imported, including requirements to purchase unnecessary additional technology, raw materials, products, equipment, or services

218. Contract Law, art. 363.

219. PRC Management Regulations on Technology Import and Export (State Council Order No. 331); Technology Import and Export Contract Registration Management Rules (MOFTEC Order No. 17); Rule on Management of Prohibited and Restricted Import Technology (MOFTEC/SETC Order No. 18); Catalogue of Prohibited and Restricted Import Technologies (MOFTEC/MOST Order No. 15); Management of Prohibited and Restricted Export Technology (MOFTEC/MOST Order No. 14).

(6) Unreasonable restrictions on licensee's export channels for products using the imported technology and
(7) Unreasonable restrictions on output, variety, or selling prices of the products produced by the licensee

Any such provisions that impose contractual restrictions that might otherwise be in violation of the law may still be permissible if they are fair, reasonable, and reciprocal.

The regulations and implementing rules classify technology imports into three categories: "unrestricted" or "free," "restricted," and "prohibited." MOFTEC released multiple regulations detailing classification and procedural requirements for each of the three categories of technology imports. Most technology is unrestricted or "free" and may be imported without the need of government approval.

The importation of technology into China is *prohibited* if (1) it will endanger the national security or the public interest; (2) the technology must be prohibited to protect human health and safety; (3) the technology would be destructive to the environment; and (4) the technology is prohibited from importation by international treaty obligations. *Restricted* technology is defined as technology that (1) will endanger national security or the public interest; (2) the import of which must be limited to protect a particular domestic industry; (3) the technology involves the importation of agricultural, animal, or fishery products that are, for health reasons, restricted; (4) the import must be restricted to maintain China's international financial status or the balance of international payments; or (5) if the restriction is required by international treaty obligations. Restrictions on technology must not conflict with China's WTO obligations.

Most technology is unrestricted or "free" and is eligible for an automatic import license. In regard to unrestricted technology, MOFTEC issued the Technology Import and Export Contract Registration Management Rules (MOFTEC Order No. 17), which detail technology contract requirements for trade of technologies that do not require an import license. Contracts for the import or export of "free" or "unrestricted" technologies are valid and binding upon execution. Although no approval is required, contracts for unrestricted technology are required to be registered with MOFCOM. Companies must register such contracts, and registration agencies must complete registration within three days of the contract's submission. Firms must register contracts online with the China International Electronic Commerce Network (http://ec.cn) and with local MOFCOM authorities. Registration with local foreign trade offices requires submission of a registration application for a free import technology contract, a copy of the contract, and proof of the legal status of both contract parties. Central-level MOFCOM registration is required for contracts involving technology for projects under the State Council and projects funded through state revenue or loans from foreign governments or organizations. Modifications to contracts must undergo the same registration process. A practical impact of a failure to register a technology contract is that payments to a foreign party for royalties or fees under the contract may be denied by the state Administration of Foreign Exchange without a proper registration number. However, a contract involving unrestricted technology is still legally binding and enforceable notwithstanding the parties' failure or refusal to register with the authorities.

With respect to restricted or prohibited technology imports, MOFTEC and the SETC jointly issued the Rule on Management of Prohibited and Restricted Import Technology (MOFTEC/SETC Order No. 18) on December 30, 2001, which bans the import of prohibited technologies and requires licensing of restricted technology. The classification of technologies appears in the Catalogue of Prohibited and Restricted Import Technologies, of which the first three batches were released on December 30, 2001. The application for approval to import restricted technologies is a two-step process. First, applicants must submit initial applications for import licenses to MOFCOM, which will respond with a decision on preliminary approval within 30 days; if successful, an applicant will receive a Proposal for Technology Import License from MOFCOM. The parties to a technology contract involving restricted technology must then submit a signed contract along with the Proposal and supporting documents to MOFCOM to receive an import license. MOFCOM is required to render a decision on the import license within 10 days.[220] Similar rules and catalogues for restricted and prohibited technologies for export were released by MOFCOM and the Ministry of Science and Technology (MOST). A technology contract involving restricted technology is not valid or enforceable until MOFCOM approval is granted and the contract is registered.

e. Tort Claims for Misuse of Technology Subject to Contract

The Unfair Competition Law of the PRC prohibits a party from obtaining technology by means of misappropriation, misrepresentation, or coercion.[221] The Unfair Competition Law applies to all legal persons, other economic organizations, and individuals who engage in commercial operations or

220. Companies that obtain import licenses must also register online at http://ec.cn.

221. Law of the People's Republic of China Against Unfair Competition (adopted September 2, 1993, at the 3rd Sess. of the Standing Comm. of the 8th NPC), *reprinted in* CHINA LAWS FOR FOREIGN BUSINESS (CCH), Business Regulation ¶ 16-640 (hereinafter the "Unfair Competition Law"). In addition to remedies under the Unfair Competition Law, the owner of technology also has rights under the various intellectual property laws and the Civil Law. *See* Chapter 14, Intellectual Property.

profit-making services.[222] Among other things, a party that reveals, uses, or allows others to use commercial secrets in violation of agreements or requests to keep the secrets confidential by the owner of the technology is liable for damages under the Unfair Competition Law.[223] Commercial secrets are technical and business information that is not known to the public; they provide economic benefits to the owner, are of practical application, and have been designated by the owner as confidential or secret.[224]

The SAIC and its local branches are empowered to investigate unfair competition claims and issue monetary penalties.[225] In addition to administrative remedies, a party has a judicial right of action for unfair competition.[226] A defendant that engages in unfair competition is required to pay compensation for damages including the profits obtained as a result of the unlawful activities. An injured party is also entitled to receive an award of "reasonable fees arising from the investigation."[227]

10. Foreign Trade Agency Contracts

Traditionally, direct sales to Chinese enterprises have been restricted, and trade involving foreign parties is required to be handled directly through a government approved trading company.[228] Under the Foreign Trade Agency Regulations, a limited number of Chinese enterprises are authorized to handle foreign trade matters including the importation of merchandise and materials into China. Post-WTO, and specifically after 2004, all organizations and entities in China shall have full trading rights and not be required to use the services of authorized trading companies. Prior to full adoption and implementation of the standards in the WTO timetables, the reliance on trading companies and trade agency contracts will continue.[229] Under the Foreign

222. Unfair Competition Law, art. 2.

223. Unfair Competition Law, art. 8. It is also unfair competition to obtain the commercial secrets of other proprietors by theft, inducement, coercion, or other illicit means or to reveal, use, or allow others to use illegally obtained commercial secrets of others. *Id.* at art. 10. *See generally* Cheng, *Legal Protection of Trade Secrets in the People's Republic of China,* 5 PAC. RIM L. & POL'Y 261 (1996). *See also* Chapter 23, Criminal Liability for FIE Activities § B.4.

224. Unfair Competition Law, art. 10.

225. Unfair Competition Law, art. 3.

226. Unfair Competition Law, art. 20.

227. Unfair Competition Law, art. 20.

228. *See* Foreign Trade Law of the People's Republic of China (adopted on May 12, 1994, by the 7th Sess. of the Standing Comm. of the 8th NPC and as amended on April 6, 2004, by the NPC's Standing Committee) (Articles 8–14 outline the requirements of foreign trade operators); Provisional Regulations Concerning the Foreign Trade Agency System (promulgated on August 29, 1991, by the Ministry of Foreign Economic Relations and Trade), *reprinted in* CHINA LAWS FOR FOREIGN BUSINESS (CCH), Business Regulation ¶ 13-566 (Article 5 outlines the written requirements for a commission agreement for a foreign trade agency). *See also* Civil Law, arts. 63–70, outlining the standards for agency relationships. The Contract Law briefly addresses trading company contracts.

229. Foreign Trade Law of the People's Republic of China (adopted on May 12, 1994, by the 7th Sess. of the Standing Comm. of the 8th NPC and amended on April 6, 2004, by the NPC's Standing

Trade Agency Regulations, an end user or purchaser is required to enter into a commission agreement with a Chinese foreign trade agent in order to purchase and import goods from outside of China.[230] The agency agreement is required to be in writing and include the following matters:

(1) Name, scope, content, price range, payment method, and currency used for the commissioned import or export commodities
(2) The scope of authority of the foreign trade agent
(3) The obligations for expenses incurred by the parties[231]
(4) Commission fees and other compensation[232]
(5) Dispute resolution
(6) Term of the agency agreement[233]

The agent has a statutory obligation to keep the principal informed of the sales process or other tasks assigned to the agent. Subject to the approval of the principal, the agent may negotiate a purchase or sales contract on the principal's behalf with a foreign party. This authority is strictly limited and, by law, the agent is prohibited from making any promises concerning the terms of the purchase or sales contract to the foreign party.[234]

The agent is required to enter into a contract on the principal's behalf with the foreign party. The agent is also required to advise the principal of the international market price for the goods imported or exported, as well as to advise the principal of international and foreign trade rules that may affect the importation or exportation.[235] If a foreign party claims compensation for damages, the agent is required to timely tender the claims documents to the principal.[236] The principal is responsible to resolve all disputes with the foreign party as per the agency agreement. If the agent is at fault, the agent is

Committee). The amended Foreign Trade Law is effective on July 1, 2004. Prior to entry into WTO, China jealously guarded trading rights issued to state-run import/export companies, which stifled competition for imports, as well as reduced domestic companies' access to export markets. In recent years, trading rights have gradually been extended to a much wider range of companies, including Chinese domestic companies, as part of China's market reforms. But the prior law prohibits individuals from undertaking foreign trade (i.e., import of export activities). Under the amendment to the Foreign Trade Law, all individuals, legal entities, and organizations may participate in foreign trade, and the examination and approval process for import and export rights has been eliminated. Companies engaged in trading are only required to register with the government. Under the law, MOFCOM is required to implement an automatic import/export licensing system for goods requiring a license.

230. Contract Law, art. 414; Foreign Trade Agency Regulations, arts. 2, 3.

231. If not agreed upon by the parties, the agent is responsible for all expenses. Contract Law, art. 415.

232. Contract Law, art. 422; Foreign Trade Agency Regulations, art. 13. An agency is entitled to a commission if the principal fails to proceed with a sale or purchase. *Id.* at art. 11.

233. Foreign Trade Agency Regulations, art. 5.

234. Foreign Trade Agency Regulations, art. 8.

235. Foreign Trade Agency Regulations, art. 18. Under the Contract Law, the agent is required to advise the principal of pricing issues and obtain the consent of the principal to sell an item below the instructed price. Contract Law, art. 418.

236. Foreign Trade Agency Regulations, art. 23.

responsible to the foreign party for damages. When the principal is at fault, the principal is required to indemnify the agent.[237]

The resulting system is an added layer of bureaucracy that is both costly and time consuming. However, the stated policy of the Chinese government is to eventually abandon the trading company monopolies and to allow foreign parties and Chinese enterprises the right to trade without intermediaries. Effective January 1, 1999, China's *private* manufacturing enterprises and research institutes are entitled to direct import and export rights. However, State-owned enterprises are still required to use State-owned trading companies for foreign trade.[238]

11. Insurance Contracts

The Contract Law does not specifically address the requirements for insurance contracts.[239] However, the rules in the Contract Law pertaining to the use of standardized clauses in contracts may increase the exposure of insurance companies that use such provisions as a matter of practice.[240] The insurance laws and regulations, and directives of the China Insurance Regulatory Commission, should be reviewed in conjunction with the rules outlined in the Contract Law.[241]

C. Secured Interests Contracts

The NPC promulgated the Secured Interests Law in 1995 in order to promote the flow of credit sources and "to ensure the satisfaction of creditors' claims."[242] The law permits creditors in financial and commercial transactions

237. Foreign Trade Agency Regulations, arts. 23–24; Contract Law, art. 421.

238. *See* Provisional Measures on Granting Self-Managing Import and Export Rights to Private Production Enterprises and Scientific Research Institutions (approved by the State Council on September 2, 1998, and promulgated by the Ministry of Foreign Trade and Economic Cooperation on October 1, 1998), *reprinted in* CHINA LAWS FOR FOREIGN BUSINESS (CCH), Business Regulation ¶ 13-532 and 136 China International Business (MOFTEC) 58 (1998) (outlines the qualifications and requirements for an application to self-manage international trading, procedures for submission and examination of applications, and rights and obligations of firms that qualify). *See also* Zhang, *Private Firms Granted Import and Export Rights,* CHINA DAILY (Oct. 16, 1998), available on Lexis, News Library, or on the Web site of the CHINA DAILY at http://www.chinadaily.com.cn.

239. For a discussion concerning the requirements and restrictions for insurance contracts, *see* Chapter 12, Insurance Law and Regulation § F.

240. Contract Law, art. 39. *See supra* footnote 16 and accompanying text.

241. Insurance Law of the People's Republic of China (adopted on June 30, 1995, by the 14th Sess. of the Standing Comm. of the 8th NPC), arts. 18, 32, *reprinted in* CHINA LAWS FOR FOREIGN BUSINESS (CCH), Business Regulation ¶ 9-620 (outlining the rules for formation and interpretation of insurance contracts and specifically property and life insurance contracts).

242. Secured Interests Law of the People's Republic of China (adopted on June 30, 1995, by the 14th Sess. of the Standing Comm. of the 8th NPC), *reprinted in* CHINA LAWS FOR FOREIGN BUSINESS (CCH), Business Regulation ¶ 5-605 (hereinafter the "Secured Interests Law"); Several Issues Concerning the Application of the PRC Secured Interests Law Interpretations (promulgated by the Supreme People's

to request and receive collateral as a means to secure a debt. The Secured Interests Law provides that secured transactions "shall be undertaken in compliance with the principles of equality, consent, fairness, honesty and mutual trust."[243]

The Secured Interests Law recognizes the use of four types of security interests, including guarantees, mortgages, pledges, and liens, and requires that a security contract be an ancillary agreement to the principal contract creating the debt.[244] If the principal contract is void, the security contract is also void as well.

While the Secured Interests Law and SPC interpretation concerning the law are positive developments, there remains uncertainty with respect to application by the courts as the law continues to evolve in this area.

1. Guarantee

a. Relationship between Guarantee and Guarantor

The Secured Interests Law defines the guarantee to mean "the act of a guarantor, pursuant to an agreement between the guarantor and the creditor, in performing the obligations of or bearing liability for a debtor when that debtor fails to perform his/her obligations."[245] The Secured Interests Law provides that "[n]o organization or individual shall coerce an enterprise or a financial institution such as a bank to provide a guarantee for any party."[246] All corporations, enterprises, and individuals who are able to perform the obligations of the debtor in a representative capacity may act as guarantors.[247] However, the following organizations and institutions are prohibited from acting as guarantors:

(1) State agencies, except where loans from foreign governments or international economic organizations are used in the form of a subloan with the approval of the State Council

(2) Nonprofit institutions and social welfare organizations, such as schools and hospitals

---

Court on December 8, 2000, and effective as of December 13, 2000), *reprinted in* China L. & Prac., Feb. 2001 (hereinafter the "SPC Secured Interests Law Interpretation"). *See* A. Godwin & Z. Lili, *Judicial Interpretation on the PRC Security Law,* China L. & Prac., Feb. 2001; D. Wang, *Developments and Prospects in China's Security Law,* China L. & Prac. (April 2003). *See also* Administration of the Provision of Security to Foreign Entities by Domestic Institutions Inside China Procedures (promulgated by the People's Bank of China, effective as of October 1, 1996), and Implementing Rules (issued by SAFE effective January 1, 1998).

243. Secured Interests Law, art. 3.

244. Secured Interests Law, arts. 2, 5.

245. Secured Interests Law, art. 6.

246. Secured Interests Law, art. 11. The financial institution or enterprise has the right to refuse such coercion.

247. Secured Interests Law, art. 7.

(3) Branch organizations, except in situations in which express written authorization from the parent corporation is provided[248]

When there are two or more guarantors for a single debt obligation, the guarantors assume liability in accordance with the proportion agreed to in the guarantee contract and, if the proportion is not specified in the contract, the guarantors assume joint and several liability for the debt.[249] As a result, a creditor may demand that one of the guarantors assume full guarantee liability. A party that assumes the guarantee liability is entitled to seek compensation from the debtor or demand other guarantors to share joint liability.

Guarantees by Chinese domestic parties issued to foreign parties, including foreign-funded financial institutions, require registration with, and approval by, the State Administration of Foreign Exchange (SAFE).[250] The Security Measures provide that the SAFE has the authority to approve, administer, and register all guarantees issued by Chinese organizations, financial and nonfinancial, to foreign creditors. Prior to issuance, all guarantees are required to obtain approval except for financing of less than one year. To obtain approval, Chinese organizations are required to maintain certain liquidity and asset/liability standards. Foreign-funded financial institutions are considered foreign parties for purposes of the Security Measures.

b. Guarantee Contract

The Secured Interests Law provides that a guarantor and the creditor enter into a written guarantee contract.[251] A guarantor and the creditor may enter a separate guarantee contract for each individual principal contract, or negotiate a single contract that covers a number of principal loans for a certain time period or set of commodity transactions, and that is limited to a maximum debt amount.[252] The law requires that a guarantee contract include certain

248. Secured Interests Law, arts. 8–10. If a branch office enters into a guarantee without authorization, the guarantee is invalid up to the portion of the contract that exceeds the authorization. *Id.* art. 29.

249. Secured Interests Law, art. 12.

250. Administrative Measures on Security Given to Foreign Parties by Domestic Institutions (promulgated on September 25, 1996, by the PBOC), *reprinted in* CHINA LAWS FOR FOREIGN BUSINESS (CCH), Business Regulation ¶ 8-698 (hereinafter the "Security Measures"). Article 6 (1) of the SPC Secured Interests Law Interpretation provides that external security is invalid if it has not been registered or approved by SAFE. *See* Foreign Debt Administration Tentative Procedures (promulgated on March 1, 2003, by the State Administration of Foreign Exchange) (provides certain new and tighter foreign debt registration standards for foreign-invested enterprises, including the requirement that an FIE's foreign debt agreements will not be effective until they have been registered with SAFE and require that the balance of existing short-term foreign debts be aggregated with existing medium-term and long-term foreign debts for the purpose of applying the borrowing limit to new foreign debt).

251. Secured Interests Law, art. 13.

252. Secured Interests Law, art. 14.

mandatory language, including the following specific information:

(1) The type and amount of the principal debt guaranteed
(2) The time limit for the debtor to discharge the debt
(3) The method of guarantee
(4) The scope of the guarantee
(5) The duration of the guarantee
(6) Other information deemed necessary by the guarantor and guarantee[253]

The Secured Interests Law provides for *ordinary* and *joint guarantee liability*.[254] An *ordinary guarantee* refers to the act of the guarantor in assuming guarantee liability when the debtor fails to perform its obligations. The guarantor under an *ordinary guarantee* may refuse to assume liability where the dispute over the principal contract has yet to be determined by judicial or arbitration proceedings, and before the debtor is found to be incapable of performing its obligations under an enforcement order against property. However, this refusal to assume liability may not be exercised in the following situations:

(1) Where the creditor is unable to locate the debtor
(2) Where collection efforts against the debtor are suspended by court order in bankruptcy proceedings[255]

The term *joint guarantee liability* refers to the stipulation in the guarantee contract that the guarantor and the debtor shall assume joint liability for the debts. When the debtor fails to perform its obligations in the time period provided by contract, the guarantor assumes guarantee liability within the scope of the guarantee.[256] The Secured Interests Law provides that *joint guarantee liability* applies when the parties have made no arrangements on the method of guarantee or when the arrangements are unclear.[257] All parties to a guarantee contract, including both an *ordinary guarantee* and a *joint guarantee liability*, have the right to seek indemnification from the other guarantors.[258]

c. Liability for Breach of Guarantee

The Secured Interests Law provides that the scope of a guarantee shall include the principal debt and interest, contractual penalties for default,

253. Secured Interests Law, art. 15. The absence of this information does not invalidate the contract. The Secured Interests Law does state that a contract that does not contain this information in its entirety "may be revised." *Id.*
254. Secured Interests Law, art. 16.
255. Secured Interests Law, art. 17.
256. Secured Interests Law, art. 18.
257. Secured Interests Law, art. 19.
258. Secured Interests Law, art. 20.

compensatory damages, and collection costs.[259] Where the guarantee contract stipulates otherwise, those stipulations shall be complied with. If the parties to a guarantee fail to specify the scope of the guarantee, the guarantor is required to assume liability for the entire debt.[260]

If during the guarantee period, the creditor transfers or assigns its rights and interests to the principal claim, the guarantor continues to be liable as a guarantor, unless provided for by contract.[261] If a creditor allows a debtor to transfer the debt to a third party, the guarantor no longer bears guarantee liability for the debt transferred without its express written approval.[262] All modifications and amendments to the principal contract require express written approval from the guarantor. Without such an approval, the guarantor no longer bears guarantee liability unless provided for by contract.[263]

The Secured Interests Law provides that if the agreement does not specify the duration of an *ordinary guarantee* or a *joint guarantee liability*, the duration of the guarantee is set by statute to be a period of six months following the date of expiration of the principal debt. In the event that the creditor fails to initiate litigation or arbitration proceedings for collection, the guarantor is exempt from guarantee liability.[264]

A guarantor of a series of commercial loans may terminate the guarantee contract at any time, but the guarantor remains liable for claims that arose before written notification is submitted to the creditor.[265] The Secured Interests Law provides that where both a guarantee and personal or real property secures a debt, the guarantor assumes liability for that proportion of the debt that is not covered by property.[266] Where the creditor relinquishes the tangible security, the guarantor is exempt from liability within the scope of rights relinquished by the creditor.

The Secured Interests Law provides that a guarantor is not liable for a debtor's obligations in the following situations:

(1) Where the creditor and debtor act in collusion to defraud the prospective guarantor into executing a guarantee

259. Secured Interests Law, arts. 21, 31.
260. Secured Interests Law, art. 21.
261. Secured Interests Law, art. 22.
262. Secured Interests Law, art. 23.
263. Secured Interests Law, art. 24.
264. Secured Interests Law, art. 25.
265. Secured Interests Law, art. 27.
266. Secured Interests Law, art. 28. If a creditor relinquishes its rights to tangible security, the Secured Interests Law provides that the guarantor is exonerated for liability up to the value of the secured property.

(2) Where the creditor induces the guarantor, by means of fraud or duress, to execute the guarantee[267]

The SPC Secured Interests Law Interpretation provides for civil liability for invalid security contracts. Specifically, a security provider and debtor may be held jointly and severally liable to a creditor for compensation for any financial loss in situations where the principal contract is valid but the security contract is invalid, provided that the creditor is not at fault.[268] If the principal contract is deemed valid, the SPC apportions the liability between the debtor and security provider, and limits the security provider's liability to one-half of the portion of the loss that the debtor is unable to discharge.

2. Mortgage

a. Mortgage and Mortgaged Property

The Secured Interests Law provides that the term "mortgage" refers to "the acts of a debtor, or a third party, who, without transferring possession, designates property . . . as security against the claims of a creditor."[269] If a debtor fails to perform its obligations under a mortgage contract, the creditor is entitled to foreclose upon the mortgaged property as security for the underlying debt. The creditor may be compensated through the transfer of the property, the value of which shall be decided through asset valuation. Alternatively, the creditor may be compensated from the proceeds of an auction or sale of the mortgaged property.[270]

The Secured Interests Law provides that the following categories of property are subject to mortgage:

(1) Buildings and other attachments to land owned by the mortgagor

---

267. Secured Interests Law, art. 30.

268. SPC Secured Interests Law Interpretation, arts. 7, 41. If the principal contract is invalid and the security provider is at fault for the invalidity, the portion of the civil liability to be borne by the security provider is limited to one-third of the portion that the debtor is unable to discharge. SPC Secured Interest Law Interpretation, art. 8.

269. Secured Interests Law, art. 33. *See also* Measures of Shanghai Municipality on Real Estate Mortgages (promulgated on August 22, 1994, by the Shanghai Municipal People's Government), *reprinted in* CHINA LAWS FOR FOREIGN BUSINESS (CCH), Special Zones & Cities ¶ 240-015. The Shanghai mortgage rules outline the types of property rights that are subject to mortgage, including land-use rights and structures, mandatory language for mortgage contracts and authentication procedures, obligations of the mortgagor to maintain the property, inspection rights of the mortgagee, legal liability of the parties to a mortgage contract, and registration procedures for mortgages. *See also* Regulations of Guangdong Province on Mortgage Loan Administration (promulgated on December 20, 1992, by the Guangdong Provincial People's Government), *reprinted in* CHINA LAWS FOR FOREIGN BUSINESS (CCH), Special Zones & Cities ¶ 70-892 (addresses the standards for mortgage rights, mandatory provisions for mortgage contracts, registration requirements for mortgages, foreclosure and sale of mortgaged property, and liability issues).

270. The Secured Interests Law defines a "mortgagor" as the debtor and the "mortgagee" as the creditor. The secured property is referred to as the "mortgaged property." Secured Interests Law, art. 33.

(2) Machinery, transport equipment, and other property owned by the mortgagor
(3) Land-use rights, buildings, and other attachments to land that the mortgagor has the right to dispose of in accordance with the law
(4) State-owned machinery, transport equipment, and other properties that the mortgagor has the right to dispose of in accordance with the law
(5) Land-use rights pertaining to unimproved land resources contracted out to the mortgagor
(6) Other properties that may be mortgaged in accordance with the law[271]

The mortgagor may mortgage any combination of the properties listed above. Where legally acquired buildings on State-owned land are mortgaged, the land-use rights pertaining to the land shall be mortgaged at the same time.[272] The parties may also enter into a maximum mortgage claim, which secures a series of creditor claims within a certain period of time and for a maximum principal sum.[273]

The law provides that a creditor's claim that is secured by the mortgage shall not exceed the value of the mortgaged property.[274] The Secured Interests Law provides that the following categories of property shall not be mortgaged:

(1) Ownership to land (since all land is owned by the state)
(2) Land-use rights pertaining to collectively owned lands such as farmlands, house sites, and lands and hills allotted for personal needs
(3) Educational, medical, and other public welfare facilities of non-profit organizations, such as schools and hospitals
(4) Property to which ownership is uncertain or disputed
(5) Property that has been seized, confiscated, or sequestered
(6) Other property that is not subject to mortgage by law[275]

271. Secured Interests Law, art. 34. The People's Bank of China adopted regulations that expand the types of instruments that may be subject to a security agreement. *See* Administrative Measures on Securities Given to Foreign Parties by Domestic Institutions (promulgated on September 25, 1996, by the People's Bank of China), *reprinted in* China Laws for Foreign Business (CCH), Business Regulation ¶ 8-698. An undertaking may also include financial securities, finance lease, securities under a countertrade program, or securities for contracted overseas engineering projects. For a discussion on the difficulties of enforcing a mortgage interest in real property in China, *see Hedging Your Bets,* EIU Business China (Feb. 1, 1999), available on Lexis, News Library.

272. Secured Interests Law, art. 36. If State-owned land is transferred and mortgaged, the buildings on the land are required to be mortgaged at the same time.

273. Secured Interests Law, art. 59.

274. Secured Interests Law, art. 35.

275. Secured Interests Law, art. 37.

b. Mortgage Contract and Registration Procedures

The Secured Interests Law provides that the mortgagor and the mortgagee shall enter into a mortgage contract in writing.[276] The mortgage contract is required to include the following information:

(1) The type and amount of the principal debt claim that is secured by the mortgaged property
(2) The time limit for performance by the debtor
(3) The description, amount, quality, condition, location, and ownership of the land-use rights of the mortgaged property
(4) The scope of the mortgage security
(5) Other matters deemed necessary by both the mortgagor and the mortgagee[277]

A mortgage contract is effective only upon registration. The Secured Interests Law provides that registration of mortgaged property is as follows:

(1) *Land-use rights without attachments:* Registration is administered by the land administration departments responsible for verification and issuing of land-use right certificates.
(2) *Urban real estate or buildings:* Departments designated by local governments administer registration.
(3) *Timber resources:* The forestry administration departments administer registration.
(4) *Aircraft, ships, and vehicles:* Departments in charge of the registration of means of transport administer registration.
(5) *Equipment and other movable property:* The local industrial and commercial administration departments administer registration.[278]

The principal contract and the mortgage contract and title or certificates pertaining to the mortgaged property demonstrating ownership must be submitted at the time of registration.[279]

---

276. Secured Interests Law, art. 38.

277. Secured Interests Law, art. 39. The absence of the required information in a mortgage contract does not invalidate the contract. The law provides that the contract "may be revised." The Secured Interests Law provides that the mortgagee and the mortgagor may not stipulate in the mortgage contract that legal ownership of the mortgaged property be transferred to the creditor in the event that the debtor fails to perform its obligations. *Id.* art. 40.

278. Secured Interests Law, arts. 41, 42. In situations involving other types of property to be mortgaged, the parties may voluntarily register the mortgaged property with the SAIC. A secured interest in a vessel is subject to the Maritime Law. *Id.* art. 95. "Movable" property under the law is anything other than land and attachments to land such as buildings and timber. *Id.* art. 92.

279. Secured Interests Law, art. 44. Registration information is available for inspection and copying at the applicable government office. *Id.* art. 45.

c. Mortgage Rights

The secured interest created by a mortgage includes the principal debt and interest, penalties for default pursuant to contract, compensatory damages, and collection costs and expenses incurred by the creditor.[280] If a debtor fails to pay the debt as required by the parties' contract, the mortgagee (i.e., the creditor) has the right to claim the income generated by the mortgaged property.[281] A debtor is required to advise any tenants that leased property is subject to mortgage.[282]

If a mortgagor-debtor intends to assign, sell, or otherwise transfer the mortgaged property, the mortgagor-debtor is required to advise the mortgagee of the transfer. A mortgagor-debtor is also required to notify the transferee that the subject property is encumbered. A failure to advise a mortgagee-creditor of an intended assignment, sale, or transfer renders the transaction invalid.[283] If the purchase price of mortgaged property is below fair market value, the mortgagee-creditor may request that the mortgagor-debtor provide additional security to support the original secured loan. A failure to provide additional security, upon request, prohibits the transfer of mortgaged property below fair market value.[284] The Secured Interests Law provides that the sales proceeds received by the mortgagor-debtor must be tendered to the creditor to pay the mortgage debt. The mortgagor-debtor is entitled to retain any sales proceeds in excess of the creditor's claim. If the purchase price is insufficient to satisfy the creditor's claim, the debtor is obligated to pay the deficiency.

If a debtor engages in any acts that may result in the destruction of, or reduction in value to, the mortgaged property, the creditor may demand that the mortgagor restore the value of the mortgaged property or provide additional security equal to the value reduced.[285] The Secured Interests Law provides that if a reduction in value of the mortgaged property is not caused by the fault of the mortgagor-debtor, the creditor may demand additional security only within the scope of the compensation received by the mortgagor for the loss, which is usually insurance proceeds.[286]

d. Satisfaction of Mortgagee-Creditor's Claims

If the debtor fails to meet its obligation on the principal loan, the Secured Interests Law provides that a mortgagee-creditor may satisfy its claim by

280. Secured Interests Law, art. 46.

281. Secured Interests Law, art. 47. Any income received from the mortgaged property is first used to meet the collection expenses.

282. Secured Interests Law, art. 48.

283. Secured Interests Law, art. 49.

284. Secured Interests Law, art. 49.

285. Secured Interests Law, art. 51.

286. Secured Interests Law, art. 51.

agreement with the mortgagor-debtor for the voluntary transfer of title of the subject property to the mortgagee. In the alternative, the creditor may initiate foreclosure proceedings before the people's court.[287] If the proceeds from auction or sale of the mortgaged property are less than the amount of the creditor's claim, the mortgagor-debtor is liable for any deficiency. The mortgagor-debtor is entitled to any excess proceeds received from the sale of the mortgaged property.

Registered mortgage contracts have priority over those that are not registered, or those registered later in time. If property is subject to multiple mortgages, the proceeds from the auction or sale of the mortgaged property shall be used to settle creditors' claims in accordance with the following requirements:

(1) Where the mortgage contracts take effect upon registration, payments will be made in the order of registration
(2) Where the mortgages in question were registered at the same time, the payments will be made in proportion to each creditor's claim
(3) Where the mortgage contracts take effect from the date of signature and the mortgaged property is registered, the payments will be made in order of registration
(4) Where the mortgaged property is not registered, the priority of payment shall be determined in order of the effective date of the respective contracts
(5) Where the respective contracts take effect on the same date, the payments will be made in proportion to the corresponding creditors' claim[288]

Improvements to land that are constructed or installed subsequent to a mortgage contract are not subject to the mortgage contract. However, if it becomes necessary to foreclose on mortgaged land, the improvements may be auctioned along with the mortgaged property, but the creditor is not entitled to demand the auction proceeds for the sale of such improvements.[289] It is therefore important for the parties to have both the land and the improvements valued separately prior to auction.

287. Secured Interests Law, art. 53. The sale of property subject to a mortgage shall be based upon fair market value. *Id.* art. 94.

288. Secured Interests Law, art. 54.

289. Secured Interests Law, art. 55. *See generally* Regulations of the Shenzhen Special Economic Zone on the Tendering and Auction of Land-Use Rights (promulgated on February 6, 1998, as Order No. 68 of the Shenzhen Municipal People's Government), *reprinted in* CHINA LAWS FOR FOREIGN BUSINESS (CCH), Special Zones & Cities ¶ 120-095 (outlines the types of residential and commercial land subject to auction, invitation and tender process, selection of tenders, auction procedures, and legal liability).

3. Pledge Contracts

a. Pledge of Movable Property

The Secured Interests Law provides that the term "pledge" refers to "the act of a debtor or a third party in transferring possession of movable property to the creditor as security for the creditor's claim."[290] If a debtor fails to perform its obligations under a loan and pledge contract, the creditor is entitled to obtain ownership of the movable property or to receive priority compensation from the proceeds of auction or sale of the property. The debtor and creditor must enter into a written pledge contract that takes effect from the date that possession of the pledged property is transferred to the creditor.[291] A pledge contract is required to include the following information:

(1) The type and amount of the creditor's claim
(2) The time limit for the debtor to perform its obligations
(3) The description, amount, quality, and condition of the pledged assets
(4) The scope of the pledge
(5) The time for the transfer of the pledge assets
(6) Other information deemed necessary by both the debtor and creditor[292]

The scope of the pledge includes the principal creditor's claim and interest, penalties for default pursuant to contract, compensatory damages, expenses incurred with respect to the storage of pledged assets, and collection costs.[293] A creditor is entitled to receive any income generated by the pledged property. Any income received is first applied to storage and collection expenses.[294]

A creditor is under an obligation to preserve and maintain the pledged property and is liable for damage to the pledged property while it is in the creditor's possession. If the creditor fails to use reasonable care with respect to the pledged property and, as a consequence, the pledged property is damaged, the debtor may request to withdraw the pledged property from the creditor's possession.[295]

If a debtor performs its obligations, the creditor is required to restore possession of the pledged property to the debtor.[296] In the event the debtor fails

290. Secured Interests Law, art. 63. "Movable" property under the law is anything other than land and attachments to land such as buildings and timber. *Id.* art. 92.
291. Secured Interests Law, art. 64.
292. Secured Interests Law, art. 65.
293. Secured Interests Law, art. 67.
294. Secured Interests Law, art. 68.
295. Secured Interests Law, art. 69.
296. Secured Interests Law, art. 71.

to perform its obligations, the pledged assets, with the consent of the debtor, may be converted to value. Alternatively, the creditor may receive payment from the proceeds acquired through auction or sale of the pledged property. In the event that the sale proceeds of the pledged property exceed the creditor's claim, the excess must to be tendered to the debtor. The debtor is liable for any deficiency between the sales proceeds and the creditor's claim.[297]

b. Pledge of Title

The Secured Interests Law provides that the parties to a loan contract may agree to pledge, as security, documents of title including the following:

(1) Bills of exchange, checks, promissory notes, securities, deposit receipts, warehouse receipts, bills of lading
(2) Legally transferable shares and share certificates
(3) Legally transferable exclusive trademark rights, patent rights, copyright and other intellectual property rights
(4) Other rights that can be pledged according to the law[298]

A pledge contract involving documents of title is effective from the date of transfer. In the event that the documents of title have redemption or delivery dates, the creditor may redeem the documents, or take delivery of the goods (i.e., goods subject to a bill of lading or warehouse receipt), prior to the expiration of the time limit for repayment of the debt. In addition, the creditor, with the debtor's consent, may use the money redeemed or the goods delivered to satisfy in advance its claims, or may deposit the money or goods with a third party.[299]

In situations involving the pledge of legally transferable share certificates, the parties are required to register the pledge with the China Securities Regulatory Commission. The pledge contract takes effect from the date of registration.[300] The proceeds acquired by the creditor from any transfer of the pledged shares may be used to satisfy the secured claim of the creditor or deposit with a third party upon agreement with the debtor. The pledge involving the shares of a limited liability company shall be subject to the relevant provisions of the Company Law relating to share transfer.[301] The pledge contract is effective on the date that the pledge of shares is recorded in the stock ledger.

297. The sale of property subject to a pledge must be based upon fair market value. Secured Interests Law, art. 94.
298. Secured Interests Law, art. 75.
299. Secured Interests Law, arts. 76–77.
300. Secured Interests Law, art. 78.
301. Company Law, art. 35.

The parties to a pledge contract involving legally transferable trademarks, patents, or copyrights are required to enter into a written pledge contract and register the pledge with the applicable government agency. The pledge contract shall take effect from the date of registration.[302] The parties to a pledge contract involving intellectual property may not further assign or transfer rights to the property without the express consent of the parties.

4. Lien Contract

The Secured Interests Law defines a "lien" as an act of the creditor in obtaining ownership of the debtor's movable property pursuant to the parties' contract.[303] Property that is subject to a lien includes property in the possession of the creditor pursuant to a contract for transport, storage, repair, or processing services.[304] If a debtor fails to perform its obligations within the agreed-upon time, the creditor is entitled to a lien over the relevant property. The creditor may convert the property to value or is entitled to receive priority compensation from the proceeds acquired at auction or sale. The scope of the lien covers the principal debt and interest, monetary penalties for default as allowed by contract, compensatory damages, expenses incurred in storage of the property subject to the lien, and collection costs.[305] A creditor has the obligation to use reasonable care with respect to property in its possession as a result of an exercise of its lien rights, and is liable for damage to the property as a result of negligence.[306]

The Secured Interests Law provides that a creditor is required to give the debtor a minimum of sixty days' notice of the creditor's enforcement rights concerning the property subject to lien. If a debtor fails to perform its obligations within the specified time limit in the notice, the creditor may, upon agreement with the debtor, convert the property to value or be compensated with the proceeds acquired from auction or sale of the property in accordance with the law.[307] The right to enforce a lien is invalid if the claim of the creditor ceases to exist or if the debtor provides alternative security which is accepted by the creditor.[308]

---

302. Secured Interests Law, art. 79. For a discussion concerning the registration requirements for the assignment of interest in intellectual property, *see* Chapter 14, Intellectual Property.

303. Secured Interests Law, art. 82. "Movable" property under the law is anything other than land and attachments to land such as buildings and timber. *Id.* art. 92.

304. Secured Interests Law, art. 84. By contract, the parties may subject other property to lien rights.

305. Secured Interests Law, art. 83. The sale of property subject to a lien shall be based upon fair market value. *Id.* art. 94.

306. Secured Interests Law, art. 86.

307. Secured Interests Law, art. 87.

308. Secured Interests Law, art. 88.

5. Deposit

The Secured Interests Law provides that parties to a contract may agree that one party is required to provide a deposit as security for a claim of the creditor. In the event that the debtor performs its obligations to the creditor, the deposit shall be set off against the purchase price or be refunded. The deposit will not be refunded if the debtor fails to perform its obligations. If the recipient of a deposit fails to perform its obligations, the recipient is required to refund double the amount of the advanced deposit.[309]

The requirement for a deposit shall be stipulated in a written contract. The parties shall set a time limit for performance or refund of the deposit. The contract takes effect from the date of the actual delivery of the deposit.[310] The amount of a deposit is based upon agreement between the parties and may not exceed 20 percent of the value of the subject matter of the principal contract.[311]

Key Laws and Regulations

Contract Law (adopted at the 2nd Session of the 9th National People's Congress on March 15, 1999)

First Interpretation of the Supreme People's Court on Certain Issues in Relation to the Application of the Contract Law of the People's Republic of China (adopted by the 1,090th Sess. of the Judicial Comm. of the Supreme People's Court on December 1, 1999, and effective on December 29, 1999)

General Principles of Civil Law of the People's Republic of China (adopted April 12, 1986, by the 4th Sess. of the 6th National People's Congress)

Secured Interests Law of the People's Republic of China (adopted June 30, 1995, by the 14th Sess. of the Standing Comm. of the 8th National People's Congress)

Several Issues Concerning the Application of the PRC Secured Interests Law Interpretations (promulgated by the Supreme People's Court on December 8, 2000, and effective as of December 13, 2000)

(Continued)

309. Secured Interests Law, art. 89.
310. Secured Interests Law, art. 90.
311. Secured Interests Law, art. 91; Contract Law, art. 115.

(Continued from previous page)

Administration of the Provision of Security to Foreign Entities by Domestic Institutions Inside China Procedures (promulgated by the People's Bank of China, effective as of October 1, 1996)

Measures for the Administration of the Authentication and Registration of Technology Contracts (jointly promulgated on 16 February 2000 by Ministry of Science and Technology, Ministry of Finance, State Administration of Taxation)

Interpretation Regarding Several Issues on the Laws Applicable to the Adjudication of Disputes Involving Technology Contracts (issued on November 10, 2003, by the Supreme People's Court)

Chapter 8

Tender Law and Government Procurement

Traditionally, government procurement in China was conducted by each administrative agency with money earmarked from the agency's budget. The lack of a regulatory code, and the absence of fiscal supervision of individuals responsible for purchasing, resulted in corruption and inefficient use of government funds. In 1996, the Chinese government started an experimental procedure requiring that all purchasing be conducted by a special administration at the municipal or provincial level. The experimental rules also call for the establishment of a purchasing process to ensure fiscal supervision and public bidding for major expenditures to ensure fair competition.

The National People's Congress has adopted a Tender Law, which is effective January 1, 2000 (hereinafter the "Tender Law").[1] The Tender Law

---

1. Tender Law of the People's Republic of China, adopted on August 30, 1999, at the 11th Meeting of the Standing Committee of the 9th National People's Congress, *reprinted in* CHINA LAWS FOR FOREIGN BUSINESS (CCH), Business Regulation ¶19-645 (hereinafter the "Tender Law"). *See also* Regulations on Scope and Scale Standards for Engineering Construction Projects for Which Tenders Must Be Invited, issued and effective on May 1, 2000, as Order No. 3 of the State Development Planning Commission of the People's Republic of China, *reprinted in* CHINA LAWS FOR FOREIGN BUSINESS (CCH), Business Regulation ¶ 19-646; Invitation and Submission of Bids for Construction Work for Construction Projects Procedures (promulgated on March 8, 2003, and effective May 1, 2003, by the State Development Planning Commission, the Ministry of Construction, the Ministry of Railways, the Ministry of Communications, the Ministry of Information Industry, the Ministry of Water Resources, and the Civil Aviation Administration of China) (hereinafter referred to as the "Construction Project Tender Rules"); Circular on Division of Responsibilities in the Administrative Supervision of Tendering and Bidding Activities by Relevant State Council Departments; The Trial Measures for Carrying out Invitation of Tender Activities by Construction Projects on Their Own; Provisional Measures on Publication of Tender Invitation Announcements; Provisional Measures on Supervising the Tendering and Bidding for State Material Construction Projects. The Tender Law originally was first drafted in June 1994. *See* The Drafting Process of the Law on Tenders and Bids, published by the Regulatory Policy Department of the State Development

is designed to standardize tendering and bidding activities, and its promulgation marked a major milestone in China's reform of its investment and financing system and the development of public procurement procedures.[2] The basic objective of the Tender Law and implementing regulations is to ensure that all contracts for major projects in which the PRC government has an interest, including infrastructure and government-funded projects, are awarded through a fair, transparent, and open system of tender that is consistent with international standards and market forces.[3] Various provincial and local governments have adopted their own regulations that supplement the standards in the Tender Law.[4] In addition, various other agencies involved with development planning, construction, railways, telecommunications, information industry, water resources, and civil aviation are responsible for managing and supervising infrastructure projects involving their related industry sectors.[5]

In 2002, the Tender Law was followed by the adoption of the Government Procurement Law, which was introduced to address concerns over corruption, lack of transparency, and inefficient procurement practices. The

---

and Planning Commission on August 31, 1999. In 1997, the State Planning Commission issued provisional regulations on standards for public tenders. *See* Invitation and Submission of Tenders for Large and Medium-Sized State Capital Construction Projects Tentative Provisions (promulgated on Aug. 18, 1997, by the State Planning Commission).

2. In October of 1998 (and effective January 1, 1999), the Standing Committee of the People's Congress of Shenzhen promulgated government purchasing regulations that cover the purchase of all goods and services with budgetary funds by State organizations in the Special Economic Zone. Under the Shenzhen regulations, public bidding is required for all contracts in excess of $12,050. *See* Zhang & Li, *Congress to Debate Purchasing Law: Regulation Urgently Required to Curb Corruption and Cut Waste in Governmental Spending,* CHINA DAILY BUSINESS WEEKLY (Nov. 15–21, 1998), available on Lexis, News Library, or on the Web site of the CHINA DAILY at http://www.chinadaily.com.cn.

3. Construction Project Tender Rules, art. 4.

4. *See* Guangdong Province, Administration of Invitation for and Submission of Tenders for Construction Projects Regulations (promulgated on Nov. 1, 1999, and effective Jan. 1, 2000); Guangdong Province, Invitation, Evaluation and Determination of Tenders for Works in Building Construction Projects and Public Infrastructure Projects Procedures (Trial Implementation) (promulgated on April 19, 2002, and effective May 1, 2002); Beijing Municipality, Administration of Invitation and Submission of Tenders for Olympic Games Construction Project Legal Persons Procedures (issued on July 28, 2002) (applicable to tenders for construction projects for the 2008 Olympics and covers each stage of tendering process, invitation, submission, evaluation of tenders); Sichuan Province, Administration of Invitation and Submission of Tenders for Construction Projects (promulgated on March 2, 2001); Beijing Municipality, Invitation and Submission of Bids Regulations (promulgated on Sept. 6, 2002).

5. Construction Project Tender Rules, art. 6. *See also* Administration of Invitation and Submission of Bids for Works on Water Transport Projects Procedures (Sept. 2000); Administration of Invitation and Submission of Bids for the Supervision of Construction on Water Transport Projects Procedures (Aug. 2002); Administration of Invitation and Submission of Bids for Highway Construction Projects Procedures (July 2002); Procedures for the Administration of Invitation and Submission of Bids for Highway Project Surveying and Design (Jan. 2002); Administration of Railway Construction Projects (promulgated on July 31, 2003, by the Ministry of Railroads) (outlines bidding standards and administration for rail construction projects). *See generally Bidding Successfully for Oil and Gas Projects in the PRC,* CHINA L. & PRAC. (Sept. 2002); S. Harter & C. Wang, *Evaluation of Competitive Tenders in China: Theory and Practice,* CHINA L. & PRAC. (Nov. 2001); T. Mahony, *Winning Bids: The New Bidding Law,* CHINA L. & PRAC. (Oct. 1999).

Government Procurement Law was also promulgated to bring China's procurement practices in line with international standards.[6]

This chapter reviews the Tender Law and Government Procurement Law, and related regulations, rules, and practices.

A. Tender Law

The Tender Law applies to all tendering and bidding activities undertaken in the People's Republic of China. Therefore, all engineering construction project tendering, and goods and service procurement tendering, either compulsory or noncompulsory tendering projects, must abide by the Tender Law.[7] Since foreign-invested projects are not specifically excluded, they are included if they otherwise would fall into one or more categories set forth in the Tender law. The law specifically provides that no party is allowed to evade the tendering requirements by dividing a project down into smaller bids or portions.[8]

The Tender Law does not define the scope of application of the law including the scope of infrastructure projects or public safety projects that involve the public interest. In support of the Tender Law, the State Development and Planning Commission adopted the Regulations on Scope and Scale Standards for Engineering Construction Projects Tendering, which specifies requirements for various compulsory tendering projects.[9] Tenders must be publicly tendered for the following project construction items undertaken

6. Law of the People's Republic of China on Government Procurement (promulgated on June 29, 2002, by the Standing Committee of the Ninth National People's Congress, effective January 1, 2003) (hereinafter the "Government Procurement Law"). *See generally China's New Government Procurement Law: A Major Step Towards Establishing a Comprehensive System,* CHINA L. & PRAC. (July 2002); Y. An, *Government Procurement and Its Legislation in China,* CHINA L. (April 2001).

7. Tender Law, art. 2.

8. Tender Law, art. 4; Construction Project Tender Rules, art. 3.

9. Regulations on Scope and Scale Standards for Engineering Construction Projects for Which Tenders Must Be Invited, issued and effective on May 1, 2000, as Order No. 3 of the State Development Planning Commission of the People's Republic of China, *reprinted in* CHINA LAWS FOR FOREIGN BUSINESS (CCH), Business Regulation ¶ 19-646 (hereinafter the "Engineering/Construction Tendering Regulations.") *See The Bidding Law Becomes Clearer,* CHINA L. & PRAC. (July 2000). *See also* Ministry of Construction, Administration of Invitation and Submission of Tenders for Construction Project Design Procedures (promulgated on Oct. 18, 2000, by the Ministry of Construction) (outline the rules governing open and private tenders, standards for information set forth in invitation documents, rules for tender evaluation committees, and standards for rejecting a tender); International Invitations for and Submission of Tenders for Mechanical and Electrical Equipment Implementing Procedures (promulgated on Oct. 8, 2000, by the Ministry of Foreign Trade & Economic Cooperation) (outlines the types of equipment subject to international tender, standards for the informational content of the tender documents, criteria for evaluating tenders from the commercial, price, and technical perspectives, and penalty provisions); State Development Planning Commission, Supervision of Invitation and Submission of Tenders for Major State Construction Projects Tentative Procedures (promulgated on Jan. 10, 2002, by the State Development Planning Commission) (rules outline that SDPC auditors will audit large state construction projects, guidelines for auditors, penalties for violations of law discovered during audits, etc.).

within the People's Republic of China, including engineering, design, construction, supervision, and management of the project, and the purchase of important equipment and materials for the project construction:

(1) Large-scale infrastructure or public utility projects relating to the public interest of society or public security
(2) Projects wholly or partly utilizing state-owned capital or state finances
(3) Projects utilizing loan or aid funds provided by international organizations or foreign governments[10]

The Engineering/Construction Tender Regulations define the scope of infrastructure projects relating to the public interest or public safety to include:

(1) Petroleum, natural gas, coal, electricity, new energy resources, and other energy resource projects
(2) Telecommunications and transportation projects such as railways, highways, pipelines, water transport, air transport, and other communication and transportation industries
(3) Postal services, telecommunication hubs, communications, information networks and other postal and telecommunication projects
(4) Flood prevention, irrigation, flood drainage, water diversion, tidal land harnessing, soil and water conservation, key irrigation systems, and other water control projects
(5) Highways, bridges, subways and light railways, sewage drainage and treatment, waste disposal, underground pipelines, public vehicle parking, and other urban infrastructure facility projects
(6) Environmental protection projects
(7) Other infrastructure projects[11]

The regulations further define the scope of public utility projects relating to the public interest or public safety to include:

(1) The supply of water, electricity, gas, heat supplies, and other urban construction projects
(2) Science and technology, education, culture, and other projects
(3) Physical education, tourism, and other projects
(4) Health, social welfare, and other projects

10. Tender Law, art. 3.
11. Engineering/Construction Tendering Regulations, art. 2.

(5) Commercial housing, including economical residential housing
(6) Other public utility projects[12]

The scope of investment projects utilizing state-owned funds includes:

(1) Projects utilizing funds from government budgets at various levels
(2) Projects utilizing various special governmental construction project funds included in government financial management
(3) Projects utilizing self-funded finance of state-owned enterprises or government institutions, which are actually controlled by the investors of the state assets[13]

The scope of projects with State financing includes:

(1) Projects utilizing funds financed by government bonds
(2) Projects utilizing funds that have been either borrowed by the State from foreign governments or for which the State has provided securities
(3) Projects utilizing State policy loans
(4) Projects utilizing investments funded by State-authorized investors
(5) Projects utilizing investments financed under special permission of the State[14]

The scope of projects utilizing funds provided by international organizations or foreign governments includes:

(1) Projects utilizing loans provided by the World Bank, the Asia Development Bank, and other international organizations
(2) Projects utilizing loan funds provided by foreign governments or other foreign government bodies
(3) Projects utilizing aid funds provided by international organizations or foreign governments[15]

For all engineering and construction projects that come within any of the above categories of projects, the project is subject to public tender if one of the following factors is satisfied:

(1) The estimated price for a single construction contract is more than RMB2 million

12. Engineering/Construction Tendering Regulations, art. 3.
13. Engineering/Construction Tendering Regulations, art. 4.
14. Engineering/Construction Tendering Regulations, art. 5.
15. Engineering/Construction Tendering Regulations, art. 6.

(2) The estimated purchase price for important equipment, materials, or other goods for a single contract is more than RMB1 million
(3) The estimated purchase price for services of surveying, design, supervision, and management or other services for a single contract is more than RMB500,000
(4) The total investment in the project is more than RMB30 million even though any one single contract price is below the standards set out above[16]

The Engineering/Construction Tendering Regulations provide that public tenders are not allowed to be restricted to bidders in a particular region, and the tender process may not discriminate against potential bidding parties.[17] Provincial and local governments may set their own tender standards so long as they comply with the national law and do not place restrictions on the tender process in excess of national legal standards.[18]

Bids for construction projects that legally require public bidding for construction work may be invited only if the following conditions are satisfied:

(1) The end user or bid inviting party has been lawfully established
(2) The preliminary design and the budgetary estimate have been approved (if subject to examination and approval)
(3) The scope, method, organization, etc. of the invitation of bids have been verified (if subject to verification)
(4) The required project funds have been approved and obtained, or funding has been effectively secured
(5) The design drawings and technical materials required for the invitation of bids are completed[19]

1. Tendering Methods

If the Tender Law applies to a particular project, the project may be tendered in one of two ways: *open tendering* (public tender) and *tender by invitation* (private tender).[20] *Open tendering* occurs when the tender organizer invites unspecified legal persons and other organizations to participate in the bidding by issuing a public notice. This invitation is required to be published in

16. Engineering/Construction Tendering Regulations, art. 7.
17. Engineering/Construction Tendering Regulations, art. 9.
18. Engineering/Construction Tendering Regulations, art. 10.
19. Construction Project Tender Rules, art. 8.
20. Tender Law, art. 10; Construction Project Tender Rules, art. 9.

the public press, information network, or other media designated by the government.[21] A public announcement of a tender is required to include the name and address of the inviting party, the nature and size of the tender project, the place and time for carrying out the project, and details as to how to obtain a copy of the tender documents.[22]

In a private tender or *tender by invitation,* the bid organizer invites several specified legal persons and other organizations to participate in the bidding by invitation. When using the invitation method, the bid invitation letters are required to be issued to no less than three legal persons or organizations that are capable of performing the project.[23] A private tender may be undertaken for a project that is not suitable for public tender that has been designated as a project of national importance.[24] For those projects listed in Articles 2 and 3 of the Engineering/Construction Tendering Regulations, private tender is not allowed in those circumstances.[25] Nevertheless, subject to government approval, construction projects involving the following circumstances shall not require public bidding:

(1) The project involves State security, State secrets, emergency rescue, or disaster relief, and is not suitable for the invitation of bids
(2) The project uses poverty relief funds to provide work instead of aid, and requires the use of peasant labor
(3) The main technology for the construction uses specific patents or proprietary technology

21. Tender Law, art. 16; Construction Project Tender Rules, art. 15. The State Development and Planning Commission also issued the *Provisional Measures on Publication of Tender Invitation Announcements* on July 1, 2000. The Measures are designed to standardize publication activities for tender invitation announcements and to ensure that potential bidders can obtain tender invitation information in an equal, convenient, prompt, and accurate manner. The Measures apply to publication activities for tender invitation announcements on projects for which the invitation of tenders is required by law. The Measures require such tender invitation announcements to be published in designated media. The designated media were announced in the *Notice of the State Development Planning Commission Designating Media for the Publication of Tender Invitation Announcements for Projects for Which Invitation of Tenders Is Required by Law,* issued on June 30, 2000. These designated media include the *China Daily,* the *China Economic Herald,* the *China Construction News* and *China Public Procurement and Bidding,* which is a Web site located at http://www.chinabidding.com.cn.

22. Tender Law, art. 16; Construction Project Tender Rules, art. 14. A bid invitation announcement or letter shall state at least the following particulars: (1) the name and address of the bid-inviting party; (2) the subject matter, scale, and source of funding of the project; (3) the location and time limit for execution of the project; (4) the time and place for obtaining the bid invitation documents or prequalification documents; (5) the fee payable for obtaining the bid invitation documents or prequalification documents; and (6) the required qualification rating of the bidders. Construction Project Tender Rules, art. 14.

23. Tender Law, art. 17; Construction Project Tender Rules, art. 13. *See also* Government Procurement Law, arts. 34, 35.

24. Tender Law, art. 11.

25. Construction Project Tender Rules, art. 3.

(4) The project is for the construction enterprise's own use, and the construction enterprise has the requisite qualifications required to complete the project
(5) The project is a small-scale project added to another project under construction or involves the addition of floors to an existing main structure, and the original winning bidder remains able to contract for the project
(6) Other circumstances specified by laws or administrative regulations[26]

In addition, private tender may be allowed in the following situations upon approval by the government:

(1) The project involves complicated technology or special requirements for which only a few prospective bidders are available for selection
(2) The project is limited by natural environment of the region
(3) The project involves State security, State secrets, emergency rescue, or disaster relief and is suitable for the invitation of bids but not for the public invitation of bids
(4) Compared to the value of the project, the cost of public invitation of bids would be prohibitive
(5) Laws or regulations stipulate that the public invitation of bids is not suitable[27]

A public tender announcement or written invitations may request that interested parties submit prequalification documents to determine their capabilities, expertise, and financial strength. However, an end user or tendering agency may not restrict or exclude potential bidders on the basis of unreasonable conditions, and must not engage in discrimination between bidders.[28] Qualification reviews shall focus on whether the prospective bidders meet the following conditions:

(1) Right to independently enter into contracts
(2) Capability and expertise (including professional and technical qualifications and capabilities), the funds, the equipment and other material facilities and material conditions, the management

26. Construction Project Tender Rules, art. 12.
27. Construction Project Tender Rules, art. 11.
28. Tender Law, art. 18; Construction Project Tender Rules, arts. 16, 17–20 (standards for prequalification).

capability, the experience, the reputation, and the corresponding personnel to perform the contract

(3) Good standing, including the absence of any order to cease business, to not have been subjected to cancellation of one's bidding qualifications, to not have one's assets subjected to receivership or frozen, and to not be in a state of bankruptcy

(4) Clear record of good corporate actions relating to the bidding process, including no record of fraudulent conduct, material breach of contract, or causing serious project quality problems, during the last three years

(5) Other conditions specified by laws or administrative regulations[29]

The tender documents are required to contain all the substantive requirements and conditions of the tender, including the technical requirements of the tender project, the criteria for investigation of the tendering party's qualifications, the pricing standards, and the criteria for tender evaluation. The tender documents should also contain the principal terms of the contract that will eventually be signed by the parties if a bid is accepted.[30] The Tender Law also prohibits the tender documents from requiring or indicating any specified producers or suppliers, and the tender documents may not include any other requirement that favors or excludes any prospective bidders.[31]

Prior to accepting bids, the end user or tendering agency has the discretion to allow prospective bidders to inspect the project site.[32] The law provides that the end user or tendering agency is prohibited from disclosing to third parties the names or number of prospective bidders who have received tender documents, or any other information relating to the invitation or submission of tenders that may affect fair competition. If the end user or tendering agency intends to impose a minimum bid limit, this limit is required to remain confidential.[33]

---

29. Construction Project Tender Rules, art. 20.

30. Tender Law, art. 19; Construction Project Tender Rules, art. 24. The bid-inviting party is required to prepare the bid invitation documents in accordance with the special characteristics and requirements of the construction bid invitation project. In general, the bid invitation documents shall contain the following: (1) the bid invitation; (2) the points to be noted by the bidders; (3) the main terms of the contract; (4) the forms of the bid documents; (5) if the bids are invited using a bill of quantities, the bill of quantities; (6) the technical terms; (7) the design drawings; (8) the standards and method for evaluating the bids; and (9) supplementary bidding materials. The bid-inviting party shall specify the substantive requirements and criteria in the bid invitation documents and indicate the same in a prominent manner. Construction Project Tender Rules, art. 24.

31. Tender Law, art. 20.

32. Tender Law, art. 21; Construction Project Tender Rules, art. 32.

33. Tender Law, art. 22.

The Tender Law requires that the end user or tendering agency provide prospective bidders with a reasonable amount of time to prepare and submit their tender proposals. For projects that are required by law to be put to public tender, the review period shall not be less than twenty days from the commencement date of the tender to the bid closing date.[34] In the event that the end user or tendering agency or tendering agent is required to amend or clarify the tender documents, all recipients of the tender documents are to receive the amendments at least fifteen days prior to the bid submission closing date. The written amendments are required to be incorporated into the principal tender documents.[35]

2. Submission of Tenders

The Tender Law requires that a bidder be fully capable of performing the work that is the subject of the tender and, if required by law, must maintain any relevant qualifications or certifications to perform the subject work.[36] A bidder must prepare its proposal in accordance with the requirements of the tender documents. Proposals must provide responses to the substantive requirements and conditions of the tender documents. When a tender project is related to construction work, proposals must include resumés of the key management and technical personnel that are anticipated to be assigned to the project, previous experience, and a list of machinery and equipment planned to be used in completing the tender project.[37]

The end user may require that bidders provide a bid security with their proposals. The security is required to take the form of cash, cashier's check, certified check, money order, or a bank guarantee letter. The bid security may not exceed 2 percent of the total bid price, or a maximum of RMB800,000. The bid security shall be valid for a period of thirty days beyond the validity of the proposals. If a bidding party fails to provide the bid security with its proposal, its bid documents may be rejected.[38] The regulations require that bid security be refunded to the unsuccessful bidders within fifteen days after the end user or bid-inviting party and the winning bidder have executed the project contract.[39]

Bidders are required to deliver proposals to the stipulated place for submission of tenders before the close of business on the final day for submission of tenders stipulated in the tender documents. Following the

34. Tender Law, art. 24; Construction Project Tender Rules, art. 31.
35. Tender Law, art. 23.
36. Tender Law, art. 26; Construction Project Tender Rules, art. 35.
37. Tender Law, art. 27; Construction Project Tender Rules, art. 36.
38. Construction Project Tender Rules, art. 37. The rules do not specify the use of bid bonds as are common in western countries. *See also* Construction Project Tender Rules, art. 45 (bid security rules for consortiums).
39. Construction Project Tender Rules, art. 63.

receipt of a proposal, the end user or tendering agency must acknowledge receipt by signature and retain the proposal without opening it. Where fewer than three proposals are received, the end user or tendering agency must invite submissions again in accordance with the Tender Law. An end user or tendering agency must refuse to accept any proposal delivered after the closing date for submission of tenders.[40]

A bidder may supplement, amend, or withdraw its proposal before the closing date for submission of tenders by written notice to the end user or tendering agency. The content of any supplement or amendment becomes part of the proposal.[41] If a bidder plans to use subcontractors to perform a portion of the work that is the subject of the tender, the bid proposal is required to describe the subcontractor arrangement.[42]

Two parties may join forces as a consortium or teaming arrangement for purposes of bidding on a tender. However, the law requires that each member of a consortium have capability to undertake the tender project individually. The members of a consortium bid team are required to sign a joint proposal agreement or teaming agreement, which must describe the delegation of work and responsibilities of each party. Such a joint proposal agreement must be forwarded to the end user or tendering agency with the proposal. Where a tender is awarded to a team or consortium, the members of the team or consortium are required to enter into the principal contract jointly with the end user, and assume joint and several liability to the end user for the project. However, an end user may not compel independent bidders to form a team or consortium for the purpose of submitting a joint proposal, and may not restrict competition between bidders by demanding that joint arrangements be formed.[43]

Practice Tip: Use of Local Partners/Consortium Members

The importance of a local partner for public procurement projects cannot be understated. In the right situation, a local partner or member of a consortium can provide much-needed political contacts, contacts with local suppliers and subcontractors, and access to utilities and other resources. At the same time, the need to conduct a thorough due diligence of a local partner's capabilities, experience, and resources cannot be understated.

40. Tender Law, art. 28.
41. Tender Law, art. 29; Construction Project Tender Rules, arts. 39–40.
42. Tender Law, art. 30.
43. Tender Law, art. 31; Construction Project Tender Rules, arts. 42–44. *See also* Government Procurement Law, art. 24.

The Tender Law prohibits any bidders from colluding in relation to the quoted price, and may not force out other bidders from fair competition or infringe the lawful rights and interests of the end user or tendering agency or other bidders.[44] Similarly, a bidder may not collude with the end user or tendering agency to the detriment of state interests or the public interest of society or the lawful rights and interests of any other person.[45] The law also prohibits any party from bribing or providing any compensation to the end user or tendering agency or any member of the tender evaluation committee for the purpose of securing a contract award.[46] A bidder is also prohibited from engaging in any fraudulent activities, such as submitting a proposal at a below-cost quoted price or tendering under the name of another person in order to win the contract award.[47]

3. Tendering Agents

An inviting party has the discretion to manage a tender on its own or to engage a tendering agency to handle the tender bid on its behalf.[48] A tendering agent is required by law to be an independent enterprise that is not connected to any governmental agency. A tendering agent and an end user are required to enter into a formal written engagement contract, and the agent may be paid based upon a fee to be negotiated by the parties.[49]

44. Construction Project Tender Rules, art. 46. The following acts are defined in the regulations as to constitute collusion by bidders on the bid price: (1) bidders agree to inflate or bring down the bid price; (2) bidders agree to each quote high, medium, and low prices for the bid invitation project; (3) bidders first conduct an internal price competition and determine a winning bidder among themselves and then participate in the bid; or (4) other acts of collusion on the bid price between bidders. Construction Project Tender Rules, art. 46.

45. Construction Project Tender Rules, art. 47. The regulations provide that the following acts shall constitute collusion between the bidders and the bid-inviting party or end user in the submission of bids: (1) the bid-inviting party opens the bid documents prior to the bid opening and informs other bidders of the details of the bids or assists a bidder in replacing its bid documents or modifying its price quote; (2) the bid-inviting party discloses the reserve price to a bidder; (3) the bid-inviting party and bidders consult on bringing down or inflating the bid price at the time of the bid submission and giving the bidders or the bid-inviting party extra compensation after the awarding of the contract; (4) the bid-inviting party internally determines the winning bidder in advance; or (5) other acts of collusion in the submission of bids. Construction Project Tender Rules, art. 47.

46. Tender Law, art. 32. *See also* Government Procurement Law, art. 25.

47. Tender Law, art. 33; Construction Project Tender Rules, art. 48.

48. Tender Law, art. 12; Construction Project Tender Rules, arts. 7, 21. A party that handles a tender in-house is required to register with the relevant supervising agency. The State Development and Planning Commission issued the *Trial Measures for Carrying out Invitation of Tender Activities by Construction Projects on Their Own* on July 1, 2000. The Measures set forth rules on how a party that needs to invite tenders can qualify to handle tender invitation on its own instead of appointing a tender invitation agency. Application is made to the State Development Planning Commission at the time the feasibility study is submitted. If all the requirements are met, approval will be given and the party inviting tenders can carry out its own invitation of tenders.

49. Construction Project Tender Rules, art. 23. The work performed by the tender agent includes, among other things, as follows: (1) drafting the bid invitation plan and preparing and selling the bid invitation documents and prequalification documents; (2) examining the qualifications of the bidders; (3) preparing the reserve price; (4) organizing site inspection by the bidders; (5) organizing the opening

A tendering agent may not act as agent without authority to do so, act as agent *ultra vires,* or act as agent in an entrusted matter that it is fully aware to be in violation of the law. A tendering agent is not allowed to be engaged as both a bid agent and consultant with respect to the same project, and the agent is not allowed to delegate the tender work to another party without the consent of the end user.[50]

4. Evaluation of Tender Proposals and Contract Awards

The Tender Law requires that the physical opening of proposals be conducted publicly on the submission closing date. The end user or tendering agency shall preside over and invite all the bidders to attend the opening of tenders. At the opening of the proposals, the end user or representative must ensure that the proposals have remained sealed prior to opening. Alternatively, a notary authorized by the end user or tendering agency may ensure and certify that the proposals have remained sealed prior to opening. After it has been ascertained that there are no irregularities, a staff member must open the documents in public and announce the names and tender prices of the bidders and other important information contained in the proposals. All proposals received by the end user or tendering agency prior to the closing time for submission of tenders must be publicly opened and announced at the opening of tenders.[51]

The Tender Law provides that a proposal evaluation committee be formed by the end user or tendering agency and be responsible for evaluation of the tender proposals. A tender evaluation committee for a project must be comprised of representatives of the end user or tendering agency, and technical, economic, and other experts. The committee must have an odd number of at least five members, of whom at least two-thirds must be technical, economic, or other experts. The evaluation committee experts must have at least eight (8) years' experience in the relevant field and hold a high-ranking professional title or have obtained an equivalent level of expertise. Any person with an interest or relationship with a bidder is prohibited from participating on a tender evaluation committee for the project, and any committee member that is an interested party is required by law to disqualify himself or herself from the process. The names of members of a tender evaluation committee are required to remain confidential until the award of tender has been confirmed.[52]

and evaluation of the bids and assisting the bid-inviting party with the determination of the winning bidder; (6) drafting the contract; and (7) other matters delegated by the bid-inviting party. Construction Project Tender Rules, art. 22.

50. Construction Project Tender Rules, art. 22.

51. Tender Law, arts. 34–36; Construction Project Tender Rules, arts. 38, 49. The opening proceedings must be recorded for reference purposes.

52. Tender Law, art. 37. Members of a tender evaluation committee are required by law to carry out their duties in an objective and impartial fashion and abide by professional ethics, and they are personally

The Tender Law provides that the end user or tendering agency must take all necessary steps to ensure that the evaluation process of tenders is conducted in strict confidence. The end user or inviting party may not, in whole or in part, use the technology or technical specifications from the bid documents from an unsuccessful proposal and, if it does so, it must obtain the consent and agree to provide financial compensation for the use of the technology.[53] The law further provides that no individual or organization is permitted to interfere with or influence the process or outcome of tender evaluation.[54]

A tender evaluation committee may require a bidder to clarify or explain any information, representation, or ambiguity set forth in a proposal. Such clarifications or explanations must not, however, exceed the scope of the original proposal or alter its substantive content of the proposal so as to give the revising bidder an unfair advantage.[55]

A tender evaluation committee is required to evaluate and compare proposals in accordance with the criteria and methodology for evaluation of tenders as set out in the tender documents. When the evaluation of tenders has been completed, a tender evaluation committee must provide a written tender evaluation report to the end user or tendering agency, and recommend a qualified candidate for the award of the tender.[56] The successful

responsible for their actions and decisions on the committee. Members of a tender evaluation committee must not make private contact with bidders, and must not accept any material or other benefit from a bidder. Members of a tender evaluation committee and staff members involved in the tender evaluation process must not divulge any information relating to the evaluation and comparison of proposals and the recommendation of a successful bidder, or any other information related to the evaluation of tenders. Tender Law, art. 44. *See also* Provisional Regulations on Bid Appraisal Committees and Bid Appraisal Measures (jointly promulgated on July 12, 2001, by the State Development Planning Commission, State Economic Trade Commission, Ministry of Construction, Ministry of Railroads, Ministry of Communication, Ministry of Information Industries, and Ministry of Water Resources) (outlines standards for bid evaluation committees and experts, bid evaluation standards, standards for technical and commercial comparison of bids, guidelines for candidate recommendations and bid determinations, and liability standards for violations of the laws and regulations).

53. Construction Project Tender Rules, art. 61.

54. Tender Law, art. 38.

55. Tender Law, art. 39; Construction Project Tender Rules, arts. 51, 52. The evaluation committee may unilaterally correct obvious errors in bid documents in limited circumstances. Construction Project Tender Rules, art. 53.

56. Construction Project Tender Rules, art. 56. After the bid evaluation committee has completed its review, the committee is required to prepare and submit a written bid evaluation report to the bid-inviting party or end user. The regulations require that the bid evaluation report be signed by all the members of the bid evaluation committee. In general, the bid-inviting party or end user is required to announce the winning proposal within fifteen days of receipt of the bid evaluation report and no later than 30 working days prior to the expiration of the term of validity of the bids. The letter of acceptance shall be issued by the bid-inviting party. Construction Project Tender Rules, art. 56. The candidates recommended for the status of winning bidder by the bid evaluation committee shall be limited to between one and three persons and they shall be listed in order. The bid-inviting party shall accept the candidates recommended for the status of winning bidder by the bid evaluation committee and may not determine the winner from persons other than the candidates recommended by the bid evaluation committee. Construction Project Tender Rules, art. 57. For projects that are legally required to be publicly bid, the bid-inviting party or

bidder must be determined on the basis of the written tender evaluation report and recommendation of the tender evaluation committee. The end user or tendering agency may also authorize the tender evaluation committee to directly select the successful bidder.[57]

The Tender Law requires that a successful proposal must satisfy one of the following conditions:

(1) The tender is able to satisfy to the greatest extent each of the composite appraisal standards stipulated in the tender documents
(2) The tender is able to satisfy the substantive requirements of the tender documents at the lowest evaluated tender price, excluding any tender price that is below cost[58]

The tender evaluation committee may reject all of the proposals if it believes that none of the tenders complies with the requirements of the tender documents.[59]

After determining the successful bidder, the end user or tendering agency must forward written notice of tender award to the successful bidder, and must simultaneously notify all unsuccessful bidders of the outcome of the tender. A written notice of tender award is binding in law on both the end user or tendering agency and the successful bidder.[60] Where the end user or

---

end user is required to select the top-ranked candidate in the evaluation report as the winning bidder. If the top-ranked candidate renounces the award on the basis that the bidder is unable to perform the contract due to force majeure or if the bid invitation documents provide for the payment of a performance security and the top-ranked candidate fails to pay the same within the specified period of time, the bid-inviting party may select the second-ranked candidate as the winning proposal. If the second-ranked candidate is unable to execute the contract for the same reasons as above, the bid-inviting party may select the third-ranked candidate as the winning bidder. Construction Project Tender Rules, art. 58.

57. Tender Law, art. 40. Before determining the successful bidder, the end user or tendering agency in not permitted to negotiate with any bidder regarding tender price, a tender proposal, or any other substantive matter. Tender Law, art. 43.

58. Tender Law, art. 41.

59. Tender Law, art. 42. The evaluation committee shall not accept bid documents if: (1) they were delivered after the deadline or were not delivered to the designated place; or (2) they were not sealed as required in the bid invitation documents. Bid documents may also be treated as invalid by the bid evaluation committee after preliminary examination if: (1) they do not bear the work unit's seal or do not bear the signature or seal of the legal representative or his authorized representative; (2) they were not completed in the specified format, there are omissions, or key segments of text are illegible and undecipherable; (3) the bidding party submitted two or more sets of different bid documents, or on one set of bid documents it quoted two or more price quotes for the same project and failed to state which quote was valid, unless such quote appears in an alternate bid plan submitted in accordance with the bid invitation documents; (4) the name of the bidding party or its organizational structure is not consistent with that at the time of pre-qualification; (5) no bid security deposit was provided as required by the bid invitation documents; or (6) the joint bid (teaming or consortium) agreement of the members of a consortium was not included with the bid by the consortium. Construction Project Tender Rules, art. 50.

60. Construction Project Tender Rules, art. 60. The bid inviting party may not demand that the winning bidder lower its price, increase the quantity of work, shorten the time limit for the work, or make other demands that run contrary to the intentions and expectations of the winning bidder and may not treat such demands as conditions for issuing the letter of acceptance and executing the contract. Construction Project Tender Rules, art. 59.

tendering agency alters the outcome of the tender or the successful bidder repudiates the tender project following the issuing of written notice of tender acceptance, the defaulting party is liable for its actions.[61] The end user or tendering agency and the successful bidder must conclude a written contract in conformity with the terms of the tender documents and the successful proposal within thirty days of the issue of a written notice of tender award. The end user or tendering agency and the successful bidder may not conclude any other agreement that is contrary to the substantive contents of the contract.[62] Where the tender document requires the successful bidder to lodge a security bond, the successful bidder must post security in the time required.[63]

Practice Tip: Bank Guarantees versus Performance Bonds

Given that the performance bond industry in China is relatively new, the traditional practice in government procurement projects is for foreign parties to put up irrevocable bank guarantees as performance security. The problem with bank guarantees is that they are demand obligations, and many foreign contractors have unfortunately realized that they can be cashed in at the whim of the Chinese tendering agency. As a result, foreign suppliers and contractors have little recourse but to arbitrate to recover bank guarantees that may have been improperly called upon. To support and encourage the use of performance bonds, the Ministry of Construction plans to adopt regulations to support the use of performance bonds which, in contrast to bank guarantees, are a form of contractual obligations that provide better protection for contractors. For more information concerning performance bonds issued by Chinese bonding companies, see the Web site of Chang An Surety Company at http://www.changan.com.cn.

The successful bidder must carry out its obligations and complete the tender project in accordance with the contract. The successful bidder may not transfer the tender project to a third party; however, the successful bidder

61. Tender Law, art. 45.

62. Construction Project Tender Rules, arts. 62, 64. The end user or inviting party is required to report the outcome of a tender and resulting contract to the relevant government agency responsible for the subject work. Construction Project Tender Rules, art. 65.

63. Tender Law, art. 46; Construction Project Tender Rules, art. 62. The regulations allow for the use of performance bonds for security purposes. The winning bidder is required to pay a performance bond or other form of performance security if the bid invitation documents require the winning bidder to do so. If the winning bidder refuses to provide such bond or security, it shall be deemed to have renounced the project that it won. If the bid inviting party requires the winning bidder to pay a performance bond or other form of performance security, the bid inviting party shall provide to the winning bidder security for the project amounts. The bid inviting party is prohibited from arbitrarily increasing the performance bond or compelling the winning bidder to advance payment of the construction funds for the project that it won. Construction Project Tender Rules, art. 62.

may subcontract portions of the contract to third parties. However, the successful bidder may in accordance with the contract or with the consent of the end user or tendering agency subcontract certain portions of the work of improvement to third-party subcontractors or suppliers. Any subcontractor retained by the bidder with the consent of the end user is required to comply with the conditions and standards relating to qualifications and expertise, and may not further subcontract the work to other parties. The successful bidder is responsible to the end user for the subcontracted work, and the subcontractor assumes joint and several liability for the subcontracted work.[64]

A violation of the law may subject a party to monetary and administrative penalties, set forth as follows:

(1) Failure to invite bidders: Fine between 0.5 percent to 1 percent of the tender contract price
(2) Disclosure of confidential information, collusion between bidding party and end user: Fine between RMB50,000 and RMB250,000, and potential criminal liability
(3) Improper restrictions/exclusions of bidders: RMB10,000 to RMB50,000
(4) Collusion by bidders: Fine of between 0.5 percent and 1 percent of the tender contract price, and potential criminal liability
(5) Fraud and misrepresentation by bidder: fine of between 0.5 percent and 1 percent of the tender contract price, invalidation of proposal, and potential criminal liability
(6) Violations by tender evaluation committee: disciplinary warning, fine of between RMB3,000 and RMB50,000, and potential criminal liability
(7) Improper subcontracting by successful bidder: fine of between 0.5 and 1 percent of the contract price, possible revocation of bidder's business license
(8) Contract inconsistent with tender documents/proposal: fine of between 0.5 and 1 percent of contract price
(9) Bidder's failure to perform the contract: possible forfeiture of performance bond/guarantee, possible debarment from other projects in China for 2–5 years, potential loss of business license[65]

64. Tender Law, art. 48; Construction Project Tender Rules, art. 67. The end user or inviting party may not force a contractor to accept any particular subcontractor. Construction Project Tender Rules, art. 66.

65. Tender Law, arts. 49–64; Construction Project Tender Rules, arts. 68–89.

B. Government Procurement Law

Government procurement in China has been plagued with transparency problems, uncertain rules and standards, favoritism for domestic suppliers, endemic corruption, and lack of effective administrative review and dispute resolution mechanisms. Under the former Procurement Regulations, which have since been repealed, foreign suppliers were required to undergo an application process in order to be considered as eligible bidders. Chinese suppliers did not face similar obstacles. Moreover, procurement agencies in China were prohibited from purchasing foreign goods, or contracting with foreign parties for engineering projects and services without permission from the Ministry of Finance.[66]

In 2002, the Government Procurement Law was promulgated to address many of these concerns and bring fairness, integrity, and transparency to the procurement process in line with international standards.[67] The law specifically incorporates the Tender Law for those procurement projects that require public and private tenders[68] and requires that all government procurement activities be disclosed to the public through approved media sources.[69] The law also specifically bars interested persons from participating

66. In 2001, total government procurement volume in the PRC reached RMB65.3 billion ($7.9 billion), which is more than double from 2000. However, the volume of government procurement is 3.7 percent of China's gross domestic product and 2 percent of government expenditure, which is far less than most developed countries. China plans to increase its government procurement for 2003 to over RMB100 billion ($12 billion) and expected to reach over RMB300 billion ($48.2 billion) in the next three years. *See generally China Pushes Government Procurement Closer to Global Standard,* Xinhua News Agency (June 29, 2002); *China to Increase Government Procurement,* Interfax-China (June 11, 2003) (citing Ministry of Finance statistics and anticipated expenditures).

67. Law of the People's Republic of China on Government Procurement (promulgated on June 29, 2002, by the Standing Committee of the Ninth National People's Congress, effective January 1, 2003) (hereinafter the "Government Procurement Law"). The law specifically calls for greater transparency, fair competition, impartial competition, and good faith. Government Procurement Law, art. 3. Various municipal governments have adopted their own set of local procurement laws. *See* Beijing Municipal Government Procurement Measures (promulgated as Order No. 26, Beijing Municipal People's Government, issued 22 April 1999), *reprinted in* China Laws for Foreign Business (CCH), Business Regulation ¶ 91-077 (outlines methods of government procurement, procurement by tender, purchase applications, budgetary arrangements, funds settlement, and supervision and inspection).

68. Government Procurement Law, art. 4.

69. Government Procurement Law, arts. 11, 63. The exception to the transparency requirement involves situations that concern "state secrets." The disclosure of "state secrets" is prohibited by law, and the relevant regulations define the terms secret information and illegal disclosure in broad terms. "State secrets" are defined as "matters that affect the security and interests of the state," and are illustrated by broad categories of information relating to national defense, "import policy decisions on state affairs," "economic and social development," "science and technology development," "criminal investigations," and "other state secrets that by decision of the state departments on protecting state secrets should be safeguarded." Law on Safeguarding State Security of the People's Republic of China (promulgated by the State Council in 1993); Detailed Rules for the Implementation of the Law on Safeguarding State Security of the People's Republic of China (promulgated by the State Council in 1994).

in any procurement decisions.[70] While the Government Procurement Law emphasizes the stated policy that domestic sources are preferred, procurement from offshore sources is acceptable when goods and services cannot be acquired under reasonable business terms within the PRC, when goods and services are procured for use outside of the PRC, or in other circumstances that justify purchasing from offshore suppliers.[71] The law does not apply to matters involving state security or secrets, or in emergency situations due to serious natural disasters or other force majeure events.[72]

The Government Procurement Law specifically defines the scope of "government procurement" to include the procurement of goods, projects, and services as specified in the centralized procurement catalog as allowed by law.[73] The law also defines "procurement" as "the act of obtaining goods, projects and services with payments in the form of contract, including purchase, leasing, commission, employment, etc."[74] "Goods" generally refer to raw materials, fuels, equipment, and products. "Projects" are limited to construction projects, and "services" mean government procurement objects other than "goods" and "projects."[75]

The Government Procurement Law specifically defines the parties involved in the government procurement process and, specifically, the procurers or procuring agencies, suppliers, and procurement agencies.[76] Procurers include government organizations, institutions, and administrative agencies that are authorized to conduct procurement activities.[77] Procurement agencies are centralized procurement organizations that are responsible for managing centralized procurement for its corresponding level of government,

70. Government Procurement Law, art. 12. The Ministry of Finance and subordinate offices are responsible for supervising procurement activities. Government Procurement Law, arts. 13, 59. The Government Procurement Law outlines various provisions concerning the supervision of procurement functions. Supervising departments are not allowed to engage in procurement activities (Article 60), and have the right to audit and examine all procurement records and activities (Articles 65, 66, 68, 69). Procurement staff are required to be trained and examined in the subjects of procurement procedures and ethics (Article 62). The law also precludes any individual or unit from pressuring procurement staff to purchase goods or services from any specific supplier (Article 64). The Government Procurement Law also provides that any individual or unit has the right to report and/or file a complaint with the courts with respect to any unlawful government procurement activities (Article 70).

71. Government Procurement Law, art. 10.

72. Government Procurement Law, art. 85.

73. Government Procurement Law, art. 2. Military procurement is guided by procedures adopted by the Central Military Commission. Government Procurement Law, art. 86. The Chinese military has taken steps to reform its procurement system. *See Military Procurement Invites Open Bids*, Xinhua News Agency (April 1, 2004).

74. Government Procurement Law, art. 2.

75. Government Procurement Law, art. 2.

76. Government Procurement Law, art. 14.

77. Government Procurement Law, art. 15.

and are required to operate on a nonprofit basis.[78] Procurers and procuring agencies are required to enter into an entrustment contract outlining the rights and obligations of the parties.[79] The Government Procurement Law provides that procurement agencies are required to operate in an efficient and cost-effective manner and shall obtain goods and services at the average market price.[80]

Suppliers refer to legal persons, organizations, or natural persons that supply goods, projects, or services to procurers.[81] In order to qualify as a supplier, an enterprise is required to meet the following conditions and qualifications:

(1) Capacity to assume civil liability
(2) Sound commercial and accounting standards and practices
(3) Sufficient supplies and capabilities to fulfill the procurement contract
(4) Compliance with tax payment obligations
(5) No history of any serious violation of the law
(6) Any other requirement stipulated by relevant laws and regulations[82]

The government may also impose special qualifications on suppliers according to the procurement activities; however, government agencies are prohibited from imposing conditions that discriminate against suppliers or impose unreasonable conditions that result in discrimination or disparate treatment between suppliers.[83] The government is also authorized under the law to review the qualifications and performance records of suppliers.[84]

The Government Procurement Law authorizes suppliers to join forces to bid and act as a single supplier, team, or consortium. In the event that two or more suppliers join together, they are required to submit a joint procurement

78. Government Procurement Law, arts. 16, 18, 19.
79. Government Procurement Law, art. 20.
80. Government Procurement Law, art. 17.
81. Government Procurement Law, art. 21.
82. Government Procurement Law, art. 22. Interim Measures for the Administration of the Registration and Qualification of Government Procurement Suppliers and the Announcement on Relevant Issues Concerning the Registration of Suppliers (issued on November 28, 2003, by the Government Procurement Center for Party and State Agencies) (hereinafter the "Qualified Government Supplier Registration Measures"). The Qualified Government Supplier Registration Measures outline the standards for becoming a registered qualified supplier and set forth registration procedures for qualified suppliers. The Measures provide that qualified procurement suppliers will receive a registration number, username, and password to download bids and to obtain information concerning centralized government procurement activities. Once registered, a qualified supplier may be a candidate for bid invitations, competitive negotiations, and procurement inquiries and, once registered, the supplier has blanket approval to participate in government procurement activities without the need to go through the approval process repeatedly. Registered suppliers are required to deposit RMB10,000 as a refundable performance guarantee.
83. Government Procurement Law, art. 22.
84. Government Procurement Law, art. 23.

contract to the government procurement agency, and are required to be jointly and severally liable for any procurement obligations of the team.[85] However, the law specifically prohibits parties from colluding to disrupt fair competition.[86]

1. Government Procurement Procedures

The Government Procurement Law approves of six methods for government procurement activities, including as follows:

(1) Public tender
(2) Private tender or tender by invitation
(3) Competitive negotiation
(4) Single-source procurement
(5) Inquiry
(6) Other methods approved by the State Council[87]

The Government Procurement Law specifically states that the principal method for the procurement of goods and services shall be by *public tender*, and procurement agencies are prohibited from apportioning procurement activities to evade the public tender requirement.[88] Under the method of *public tender*, the State Council determines the specific amount procured if the project is under the budget of the central government. If the project is part of a local budget, the authorized local authority determines the amount. Under this method, all bidders must send in their bid documentation no less than twenty days before the deadline for bidders to submit their bids.[89] A *public tender* may be invalidated if there are less than three qualified bidders that respond to a procurement bid, if an unlawful act was committed during the procurement process, if the proposals received reflect a price that exceeds the procurement budget, or if the procurement task is cancelled as a result of a "serious accident."[90]

85. Government Procurement Law, art. 24. These obligations are consistent with the consortium or team rules under the Tender Law. Tender Law, art. 31.
86. Government Procurement Law, art. 25. *See also* Tender Law, art. 32.
87. Government Procurement Law, art. 26. A government procurement project's procurement standards are open to the public, and all decisions concerning the award to a supplier are required to be publicly announced. Government Procurement Law, art. 63.
88. Government Procurement Law, art. 28. *See also* Tender Law, art. 4; Construction Project Tender Rules, art. 3.
89. Government Procurement Law, arts. 26, 27.
90. Government Procurement Law, art. 36.

Procurement by means of *private tender* may be used only under the following two circumstances:

(1) The goods and services are special and must be procured by limited suppliers; or
(2) The expenses relevant to public tender are excessive[91]

In situations involving private tender, the procuring agency must randomly select three or more suppliers among the eligible suppliers.[92]

The Government Procurement Law provides that *competitive negotiation* is an acceptable means of procurement but can be used only in the following circumstances:

(1) Where no suppliers bid for the work
(2) Where there is no qualified bidder
(3) Where the reinvitation of bids is not feasible
(4) Where the project involves complicated technologies or features that are not easily defined
(5) Where the project is time sensitive; or
(6) Where the total value of the procurement cannot be predetermined[93]

Competitive negotiation requires the establishment of a negotiation group consisting of the procurer's representatives and experts. This negotiation group drafts the negotiation documents, determines the list of suppliers to be invited to negotiate, participates in the negotiation process, and ultimately determines the successful supplier.[94]

---

91. Government Procurement Law, art. 29. *See also* Construction Project Tender Rules, arts. 11, 12.

92. Government Procurement Law, art. 34. In private tenders, the procuring agency is required to give not less than 20 days' notice of the deadline for submitting bids. Government Procurement Law, art. 35. *See also* Tender Law, art. 17; Construction Project Tender Rules, art. 13.

93. Government Procurement Law, art. 30.

94. Government Procurement Law, art. 38. The law requires that the following procedures be established when the *competitive negotiation* process is used for procurements: (1) *Establishing a negotiation group*. The negotiation group shall consist of the procurer's representatives and appropriate experts (a total of three or more in odd number), among which the number of experts shall be at least two-thirds of the total number of members. (2) *Drafting negotiation documents*. Negotiation documents shall specify negotiation procedures, negotiation items, the terms and conditions of the draft contract, and the standards to evaluate the successful supplier. (3) *Determining the list of suppliers to be invited for negotiation*. The negotiation group shall select three or more suppliers from the list of qualified suppliers to take part in negotiation, and provide them the negotiation documents. (4) *Negotiation*. All members of the negotiation group shall negotiate with suppliers one by one. In negotiation, all parties concerned shall not disclose technical data, prices, and other information of other suppliers related to negotiation. Where negotiation documents are revised substantially, the negotiation group shall notify in writing all suppliers taking part in negotiation. (5) *Determining the successful supplier*. Upon completion of the negotiation, the negotiation group shall require all suppliers taking part in negotiation to quote within a specified time limit. The procurer shall determine the successful supplier among all candidates recommended by the negotiation group in accordance with the principle of meeting stated procurement requirements, and the lowest bidding price, and to notify the results to all unsuccessful negotiation suppliers. Government Procurement Law, art. 38.

The Government Procurement Law authorizes the use of a *single source* for procurement supplies, but in only the following circumstances:

(1) The goods or services must be procured by one supplier
(2) The procurement is time sensitive as a result of an emergency situation; or
(3) The procurement from a previous supplier is necessary in order for consistency, and the total amount for continuous procurement shall not exceed 10 percent of the original contracted value[95]

The procurement of goods and services using the *single sourcing* method requires that the parties negotiate terms that ensure product quality and reasonable prices.[96]

The Government Procurement Law provides that an *inquiry* method of procurement may be used if there are uniform specifications and standards for the goods to be procured. Furthermore, there must be a sufficient supply of the good and narrow price margins for the subject goods.[97] If the *inquiry* method of procurement is used, the procurer is required to establish an inquiry group that will investigate and determine the suppliers.[98]

2. Supplier Contracts

All rights and obligations between a procurer and a supplier involving government procurement must be concluded in a written contract. Such contracts are governed by the Contract Law of the People's Republic of China.[99] The specific requirements for such contracts shall be agreed upon by the authorized departments of the State Council.[100] Upon the successful completion of the bidding process, the procurer and the successful supplier have

95. Government Procurement Law, art. 31.
96. Government Procurement Law, art. 39.
97. Government Procurement Law, art. 32.
98. Government Procurement Law, art. 40. The law requires that the following procedures be employed if the inquiry method is adopted: (1) *Organizing an inquiry group.* The inquiry group shall consist of the procurer's representatives and the appropriate experts (a total of three or more in odd number), among which the number of experts shall be at least two-thirds of the total members. The inquiry group shall stipulate the structure of the procurement project's price and the standards for evaluating the successful supplier. (2) *Determining the name list of suppliers whose quotations are inquired.* The inquiry group shall, according to the procurement demand, select three or more suppliers from the list of qualified suppliers, and send inquiry notices to them for their quotations. (3) *Inquiry.* The inquiry group shall require the suppliers to give the fixed prices at a time. (4) *Determining the successful supplier.* The procurer shall determine the successful supplier in accordance with the principle of meeting procurement requirements and the lowest bidding price, and to notify the results to unsuccessful suppliers. Government Procurement Law, art. 40.
99. Government Procurement Law, arts. 43, 44. A procurement agency may sign a supply contract on behalf of the principal, but is required to attach the power of attorney from the procurer to the supply contract.
100. Government Procurement Law, art. 45.

30 days in which they just sign a government procurement contract, which shall be legally binding.[101] Then, the supplier must, within seven working days after the signing date of the government procurement contract, submit the counterpart to the relevant department in charge of that particular procurement.[102] The supply contract may be amended to increase the quantity of the goods or services to be provided, so long as the goods and services are identical to the original contract and the increase does not exceed 10 percent of the original contract amount.[103] Both parties are bound by the terms and conditions of the supply contract, and each is liable for any breach thereto.[104]

With the approval of the government, a supplier may contract with third-party subcontractors or suppliers for the goods and services that are the subject of the procurement. The original supplier is responsible for the goods and services provided by any third-party subcontractor or supplier.[105]

3. Appeals, Inquiries, and Complaints

The Government Procurement Law includes procedures by which suppliers can formally lodge inquiries and complaints. If a supplier believes that it has sustained damages as a result of the procurement process, it may, within seven business days from the day on which it became aware or should have become aware that its interests were affected, submit a written complaint or inquiry to the procurer or procurement agency.[106] The procurer or its authorized procurement agency must thereafter respond in writing within seven business days of receiving the inquiry or complaint.[107] In the event that the complainant is not satisfied with the response, or if the response was not made in the specified time, the supplier may then, with fifteen business days, lodge a formal complaint to the relevant department in charge of government procurement.[108] Thereafter, the administrative department must issue a written decision with respect to the subject matter of the complaint within thirty business days.[109] If either party is not satisfied with the administrative

101. Government Procurement Law, art. 46.
102. Government Procurement Law, art. 47.
103. Government Procurement Law, art. 49.
104. Government Procurement Law, art. 50. A party to a supply contract may not modify, amend, or terminate the contract without consent and authorization of the other party.
105. Government Procurement Law, art. 48. *See also* Tender Law, art. 48; Construction Project Tender Rules, art. 67.
106. Government Procurement Law, arts. 52, 54.
107. Government Procurement Law, arts. 53, 54.
108. Government Procurement Law, art. 55.
109. Government Procurement Law, art. 56.

decision, the complainant may apply for reconsideration by the agency or file a complaint with the people's court under the Administrative Litigation Law.[110]

4. Legal Liability and Penalties

The Government Procurement Law authorizes the imposition of monetary and administrative sanctions for violations of the law including fines (ranging from RMB20,000–200,000 or five to ten percent of the procurement amount), administrative warnings, disqualification from future procurement activities, and civil and criminal liability.[111] The Government Procurement Law imposes sanctions directly on the responsible departments or personnel. The law lists such acts pertaining to procurers, suppliers, and administrative departments in charge of government procurement.[112]

Key Laws and Regulations

Tender Laws

Tender Law of the People's Republic of China (promulgated on August 30, 1999 at the 11th Meeting of the Standing Committee of the 9th National People's Congress)

Regulations on Scope and Scale Standards for Engineering Construction Projects for which Tenders Must be Invited (issued and effective on May 1, 2000 as Order No. 3 of the State Development Planning Commission of the People's Republic of China)

(Continued)

110. Government Procurement Law, art. 57.

111. Government Procurement Law, arts. 76–77, 82.

112. The Government Procurement Law describes the activities by procurement agencies that are subject to civil and criminal penalties including: using unauthorized means of inviting public bids; using an unqualified agency to handle government procurement; improper discrimination against suppliers; negotiating with bidders during the invitation to bid phase; failing to conclude a proper procurement contract; accepting bribes; maliciously collaborating with suppliers or procurement agencies; obstructing authorized supervision and examination; and revealing the lower limit on bids before bid opening. Government Procurement Law, arts. 71, 72. The Law also outlines the activities by suppliers that may be subject to civil and criminal penalties: using false documentation to bid; using defamation or other illegal measures to compete in bidding; maliciously collaborating with the procurer, other suppliers, or the procurement agency; bribery or offering other interests to the procurer or the procurement agency; negotiating with the procurer in the course of procurement by invitation to bid; and refusing to cooperate with authorized investigations and audits. Government Procurement Law, art. 77. Offenses involving administrative departments in charge of government procurement primarily include negligence of duties, abuse of authority, and showing improper favoritism. If an administrative department fails to properly respond to a supplier's complaint, the directly responsible official and other directly responsible personnel shall be subject to administrative sanctions. Government Procurement Law, art. 81.

(Continued from previous page)

Invitation and Submission of Bids for Construction Work for Construction Projects Procedures (promulgated on March 8, 2003, and effective May 1, 2003, by the State Development Planning Commission, the Ministry of Construction, the Ministry of Railways, the Ministry of Communications, the Ministry of Information Industry, the Ministry of Water Resources, and the Civil Aviation Administration of China)

Invitation and Submission of Tenders for Large and Medium-Sized State Capital Construction Projects Tentative Provisions (promulgated on Aug. 18, 1997, by the State Planning Commission)

Administration of Invitation for and Submission of Tenders for Construction Projects Regulations (promulgated on Nov. 1, 1999 by the Guangdong Provincial Government)

Invitation, Evaluation and Determination of Tenders for Works in Building Construction Projects and Public Infrastructure Projects Procedures (promulgated on April 19, 2002, by the Guangdong Provincial Government)

Administration of Invitation and Submission of Tenders for Olympic Games Construction Project Legal Persons Procedures (issued on July 28, 2002, by the Beijing Municipal Government)

Invitation and Submission of Bids Regulations (promulgated on Sept. 6, 2002, by the Beijing Municipal Government)

Administration of Invitation and Submission of Bids for Works on Water Transport Projects Procedures (Sept. 2000)

Administration of Invitation and Submission of Bids for the Supervision of Construction on Water Transport Projects Procedures (Aug. 2002)

Administration of Invitation and Submission of Bids for Highway Construction Projects Procedures (July 2002)

Procedures for the Administration of Invitation and Submission of Bids for Highway Project Surveying and Design (Jan. 2002)

Administration of Railway Construction Projects (promulgated on July 31, 2003 by the Ministry of Railroads)

Law of the People's Republic of China on Government Procurement (promulgated on June 29, 2002 by the Standing Committee of the Ninth National People's Congress, effective January 1, 2003)

Regulations on Scope and Scale Standards for Engineering Construction Projects for which Tenders Must be Invited (Issued and effective on May 1, 2000 as Order No. 3 of the State Development Planning Commission of the People's Republic of China)

Ministry of Construction, Administration of Invitation and Submission of Tenders for Construction Project Design Procedures (promulgated on Oct. 18, 2000, by the Ministry of Construction)

(Continued)

(*Continued from previous page*)

International Invitations for and Submission of Tenders for Mechanical and Electrical Equipment Implementing Procedures (promulgated on Oct. 8, 2000, by the Ministry of Foreign Trade & Economic Cooperation)

State Development Planning Commission, Supervision of Invitation and Submission of Tenders for Major State Construction Projects Tentative Procedures (promulgated on Jan. 10, 2002, by the State Development Planning Commission)

Provisional Regulations on Bid Appraisal Committees and Bid Appraisal Measures (jointly promulgated on July 12, 2001, by the State Development Planning Commission, State Economic Trade Commission, Ministry of Construction, Ministry of Railroads, Ministry of Communication, Ministry of Information Industries, and Ministry of Water Resources)

Government Procurement Laws

Law of the People's Republic of China on Government Procurement (promulgated on June 29, 2002 by the Standing Committee of the Ninth National People's Congress, effective January 1, 2003)

Beijing Municipal Government Procurement Measures (promulgated as Order No 26, Beijing Municipal People's Government Issued April 22, 1999)

Interim Measures for the Administration of the Registration and Qualification of Government Procurement Suppliers and the Announcement on Relevant Issues Concerning the Registration of Suppliers (issued on November 28, 2003, by the Government Procurement Center for Party and State Agencies)

Chapter 9

Taxation Law

During the 1990s, the Chinese government made an effort to simplify the implementation of its tax laws, standardize tax collection, and enforce its rules in order to quash tax evasion.[1] This chapter addresses the principal tax laws that apply to FIE operations, including the consumption, business, and value-added taxes, the enterprise income tax, and the individual income tax. This chapter further reviews the procedures for taxation of foreign investment enterprises and representative offices of foreign companies, tax accounting issues and tax return requirements, penalties for violations of the tax laws and regulations, and review procedures available to a party affected by a decision of the taxation authorities.

1. Post-WTO, the government intends to bring China's tax system into conformance with international practices. By 2006, China plans to unify its tax code by raising rates for foreign investors and lowering tax rates for domestic enterprises. The unified tax rates is anticipated to range from 24–28%.

A. Turnover Taxes

Both foreign and domestic enterprises are subject to three turnover taxes:[2] business tax,[3] value-added tax (VAT),[4] and consumption tax.[5]

2. Decision of the Standing Committee of the NPC Concerning the Application of Provisional Rules on Value-Added Tax, Consumption Tax and Business Tax for Foreign Investment Enterprises and Foreign Enterprises (Decree No. 18 of the Chairman of the PRC, promulgated December 29, 1993, by the 5th Sess. of the Standing Comm. of the 8th NPC), *reprinted in* CHINA LAWS FOR FOREIGN BUSINESS (CCH), Taxation ¶ 31-748. For a discussion of the turnover tax system, *see* Ng, *An Overview of the Turnover Tax System in China and the Tax-Planning Opportunities for Foreign Investors,* 23 INT'L TAX J. 25 (1997). *See generally* H. GENSLER & J. YANG, A GUIDE TO CHINA'S TAX & BUSINESS LAWS (1996); J. VANDERWOLK, PRACTICAL CHINA TAX PLANNING (1996).

3. Provisional Rules of the People's Republic of China on Business Tax (adopted November 26, 1993, by the 12th Sess. of the Standing Comm. of the State Council), *reprinted in* CHINA LAWS FOR FOREIGN BUSINESS (CCH), Taxation ¶ 31-739 (hereinafter the "Business Tax Rules"); Detailed Rules for the Implementation of the Provisional Rules of the People's Republic of China on Business Tax (promulgated December 25, 1993, by the Ministry of Finance), *reprinted in* CHINA LAWS FOR FOREIGN BUSINESS (CCH), Taxation ¶ 31-740 (hereinafter the "MOF Business Tax Rules"). *See also* Regulations Concerning the Handling of Business Tax Accounting (promulgated on December 27, 1993, by the MOF), *reprinted in* CHINA LAWS FOR FOREIGN BUSINESS (CCH), Taxation ¶ 35-822. *See generally* Gensler, *The People's Republic of China Business Tax of 1994,* 8 TRANSNAT'L LAW. 103 (1995).

4. Provisional Rules of the People's Republic of China on Value-Added Tax (adopted November 26, 1993, by the 12th Sess. of the Standing Committee of the State Council), *reprinted in* CHINA LAWS FOR FOREIGN BUSINESS (CCH), Taxation ¶ 31-736 (hereinafter the "VAT Rules"); Detailed Rules for the Implementation of the Provisional Rules of the People's Republic of China on Value-Added Tax (promulgated December 25, 1993, by the Ministry of Finance), *reprinted in* CHINA LAWS FOR FOREIGN BUSINESS (CCH), Taxation ¶ 31-737 (hereinafter the "MOF VAT Rules"); Regulations on Certain Detailed Issues Concerning Value-Added Tax (promulgated December 28, 1993, by the State Administration of Taxation), *reprinted in* CHINA LAWS FOR FOREIGN BUSINESS (CCH), Taxation ¶ 31-738 (hereinafter the "SAT VAT Rules"); Notice of the State Administration of Taxation on Questions Concerning the Administration of the Levying and Collection of Taxes Related to the Implementation of Value-Added Tax for Foreign Investment Enterprises and Foreign Enterprises (issued December 6, 1993, by the State Administration of Taxation), *reprinted in* CHINA LAWS FOR FOREIGN BUSINESS (CCH), Taxation ¶ 31-756. *See also* Regulations Concerning the Handling of Value-Added Tax Accounting (promulgated on December 27, 1993, by the MOF), *reprinted in* CHINA LAWS FOR FOREIGN BUSINESS (CCH), Taxation ¶ 35-818. For a discussion of the VAT system, *see* Chui & Yang, *The Value-Added Tax in China: Identifying Important Issues,* 23 INT'L TAX J. 71 (1997); Peck, Kung & Ho, *Enter the VAT,* CHINA BUSINESS REVIEW 40–43 (Mar./Apr. 1994); Xiangyuan & Huang, *China on the Horizon: Exploring Current Legal Issues: China's New VAT System,* 28 J. MARSHALL L. REV. 619 (1995).

5. Provisional Rules of the People's Republic of China on Consumption Tax (adopted November 26, 1993, by the 12th Sess. of the Standing Comm. of the State Council and promulgated on December 13, 1993, by the State Council), *reprinted in* CHINA LAWS FOR FOREIGN BUSINESS (CCH), Taxation ¶ 31-733 (hereinafter the "Consumption Tax Rules"); Detailed Rules for the Implementation of the Provisional Rules of the People's Republic of China on Consumption Tax (promulgated on December 25, 1993, by the Ministry of Finance), *reprinted in* CHINA LAWS FOR FOREIGN BUSINESS (CCH), Taxation ¶ 31-734 (hereinafter the "MOF Consumptive Tax Rules"); Regulations on Certain Detailed Issues Concerning Consumption Tax (promulgated on December 28, 1993, by the State Administration of Taxation), *reprinted in* CHINA LAWS FOR FOREIGN BUSINESS (CCH), Taxation ¶ 31-735 (hereinafter the "SAT Consumptive Tax Rules"); Notice of the SAT on Certain Issues Concerning the Levy of Consumption Tax (promulgated on May 21, 1997, by the State Administration of Taxation), *reprinted in* CHINA LAWS FOR FOREIGN BUSINESS (CCH), Taxation ¶ 31-818. *See also* Regulations Concerning the Handling of Consumption Tax Accounting (promulgated on December 27, 1993, by the MOF), *reprinted in* CHINA LAWS FOR FOREIGN BUSINESS (CCH), Taxation ¶ 35-814. *See generally* Gensler, *The 1994 Consumption Tax of the People's Republic of China,* 13 U.C.L.A. PAC. BASIN L.J. 293 (1995).

1. Business Tax

Business tax is imposed upon gross revenue of various types of services and the transfer of intangible and immovable property, which are not otherwise subject to value-added tax.

a. Scope of Taxation

China's business tax applies to nine different categories of activities, including service industries; the transfer of intangible assets such as patents, non-patented technology, commercial goodwill, trademarks, and copyrights; and the sale or transfer of land-use and real estate located within the PRC. Taxable services include transportation,[6] communications, construction,[7] finance and insurance,[8] postal services, cultural and sporting events, entertainment,[9] advertising, agency services, hotels, restaurants and catering, tourist services, storage, and rental and leasing services.[10] For example, a 3 percent tax is charged on installation services for communications-related products/services. Most business tax rates are between 3 percent and 5 percent. However, the

---

6. *See* Measures on the Levying of Tax on Revenue Derived from Vessel Transportation by Foreign Companies (promulgated on October 24, 1996, by the MOF and the SAT), *reprinted in* CHINA LAWS FOR FOREIGN BUSINESS (CCH), Taxation ¶ 32-758 (outlines liability for business and enterprise tax for foreign ship owners, charter companies, and shipping companies).

7. A taxpayer engaging in construction and repair is required to include the cost of raw materials and cost of power used in a project in determining turnover for purposes of the business tax. A taxpayer engaged in the installation of equipment must include the equipment costs if the equipment is included in the installation project. *See* MOF Business Tax Rules, art. 18.

8. *See* MOF Business Tax Rules, arts. 8 (insurance services subject to business tax), 21 (business tax applicable to reinsurance income). *See also* Notice of the Ministry of Finance, the State Administration of Taxation and the People's Bank of China on Tax Issues Concerning Foreign-Funded Financial Institutions Conducting Renminbi Business (promulgated on May 5, 1997, by the MOF, SAT, and PBOC), *reprinted in* CHINA LAWS FOR FOREIGN BUSINESS (CCH), Taxation ¶ 31-822 (application of business tax to renminbi business, requiring separate accounts and separate taxation calculations for renminbi business, and preferential treatment for renminbi business income); Notice of the Ministry of Finance and the State Administration of Taxation on the Transferred Issue of the Notice of the State Council on Issues Concerning Adjustment of Taxation Policies for the Financial and Insurance Industries (promulgated on March 14, 1997, by the MOF and the SAT), *reprinted in* CHINA LAWS FOR FOREIGN BUSINESS (CCH), Taxation ¶ 31-854 (addresses the application of business tax for income derived outside of the special economic zones for financial institutions and insurance companies, accounting requirements for income inside and outside the zones); Notice of the State Administration of Taxation on Issues Concerning the Application of Preferential Income Tax Treatment for Foreign-Funded Financial Institutions Established in Districts Other Than the Special Economic Zones (promulgated on March 13, 1995, by the SAT), *reprinted in* CHINA LAWS FOR FOREIGN BUSINESS (CCH), Taxation ¶ 32-616.

9. The business turnover of an entertainment enterprise shall be the various charges collected from the audience, including the ticket sales, table fees, fees for beverages and food, and other charges. *See* MOF Business Tax Rules, art. 23. For performances, the business turnover is calculated based upon the total ticket sales less the fees paid to performers, the performance location, production companies, and agents. MOF Business Tax Rules, art. 22.

10. *See* Notice of the State Administration of Taxation on the Handling of Taxation Issues Concerning the Contracting and Leasing of Operations by Foreign Investment Enterprises (promulgated on March 7, 1995, by the SAT), *reprinted in* CHINA LAWS FOR FOREIGN BUSINESS (CCH), Taxation ¶ 32-613; Notice of the State Administration of Taxation on Issues Concerning Taxation of Foreign Enterprise Rental Income Derived from Renting Out Houses and Buildings Within Chinese Territory (promulgated on November 20, 1996, by the SAT), *reprinted in* CHINA LAWS FOR FOREIGN BUSINESS (CCH), Taxation ¶ 32-673.

business tax rates are higher for the entertainment industry (e.g., music halls, cinemas, ballrooms, karaoke bars, bowling alleys, billiards rooms), ranging from 5 percent to 20 percent.[11]

b. Exclusions from Business Tax Turnover

The business tax is based upon the total "turnover" of the business enterprise, which includes the total consideration and other receivables of a business.[12] The items excluded from turnover and thereby allowed as deductions include the following:

(1) *Transportation:* Charges to subcontractors paid to other transportation enterprises for transportation of goods and individuals outside of China.[13]
(2) *Tourist Business:* Fees paid to tourist agencies for tours outside of China.
(3) *Construction:* Fees paid to subcontractors for work under a prime contract.[14]
(4) *Loans:* Interest incurred on money borrowed.[15]
(5) *Insurance:* Premiums paid on reinsurance by an insurance company.
(6) *Performing Arts:* Fees paid to production companies, agents, and performers.
(7) *Equipment Lease Income for Foreign Operators:* The interest income and income from the lease of tangible personal property that is derived in China by a foreign company without an established organization or premises in China is not subject to the business tax.[16]

---

11. *See* Business Tax Rules, art. 2 and accompanying table.

12. Business Tax Rules, art. 4. A taxpayer who accounts for a portion of its turnover in foreign exchange is required to convert the foreign exchange to renminbi on the day in which the income was generated for purposes of determining the correct turnover. Financial and insurance enterprises are required to convert at the rate fixed in their final accounting statements of the previous year. A taxpayer is required, in advance, to determine which conversion rate is to be adopted and shall not change this rate for a period of twelve months. *See* MOF Business Tax Rules, art. 16. *See also* Notice of the MOF and the SAT on Issues Concerning the Conversion of Foreign Exchange into Renminbi by the Finance and Insurance Industries When Calculating Business Turnover (promulgated on July 5, 1996, by the MOF and the SAT), *reprinted in* CHINA LAWS FOR FOREIGN BUSINESS (CCH), Taxation ¶ 31-798.

13. Transportation and tourist services that originate in China are subject to the business tax. *See* MOF Business Tax Rules, art. 7.

14. A foreign designer or architect may consider splitting its China-related projects into two different types of services to reduce exposure to the business tax. Any services performed outside of China should be treated separately from work performed in China. A taxpayer should document the work performed outside of China to substantiate a claim that a service contract is exempt from the business tax.

15. *See* Notice of the Ministry of Finance and the State Administration of Taxation on Relevant Issues Concerning the Levying and Collection of Business Tax on the Finance Industry (promulgated on August 11, 1995, by the MOF and SAT), *reprinted in* China Laws for Foreign Business (CCH), Taxation ¶ 31-790 (provides that financial institutions are exempt from paying business tax on inter-bank transactions).

16. Notice of the SAT on the Issue of Whether Business Tax Should Be Levied on Interest and Rental Income Derived by Foreign Enterprises Within the Territory of China (promulgated on March 14, 1997, by the SAT), *reprinted in* CHINA LAWS FOR FOREIGN BUSINESS (CCH), Taxation ¶ 31-810.

(8) *Foreign Exchange, Securities Trading:* Acquisition costs of foreign exchange may be deducted from sales proceeds.[17]

c. Exemptions from Business Tax

The tax laws provide that certain types of services are exempt from the business tax, including child care, retirement homes, medical institutions,[18] agriculture, cultural activities at religious centers,[19] and services rendered by the disabled.[20] The cultural activities of memorial centers, museums, cultural centers, libraries, and art galleries are considered entertainment activities and subject to taxation.[21]

A small business is exempt from the business tax if its monthly turnover does not exceed RMB8,000 or, if based upon a per transaction basis, a daily transaction turnover of RMB50.[22] If the business turnover of a taxpayer has reached the taxable threshold, the amount of business tax payable shall be calculated according to the full amount of the business turnover. The threshold amount, therefore, does not represent a deduction or exclusion. The business tax threshold may be modified by the taxation authorities from region to region to reflect the differences in economic development in China.

d. Payment of Business Tax

A taxpayer's liability for payment of business tax is due on the date of receipt of the business income.[23] The payment periods are set at the discretion of the taxation authorities and are either five, ten, fifteen, or thirty days after receipt of the income. If payment cannot be made on a fixed time basis, the taxation authorities have the authority to base payment on a transaction basis.[24] If the payment period is set at thirty days, the taxpayer is required to declare and pay its business tax within ten days of the expiration of the payment period. If the payment period is set for any other time period (i.e., five, ten, or fifteen days), the taxpayer has five days to declare and pay the business tax from the date of expiration of the payment period.

17. Business Tax Rules, art. 5.

18. Medical services exempt from the business tax include services rendered by hospitals and other medical institutions, including the diagnosis, treatment, and prevention of disease, birth delivery and family planning, medical equipment and pharmaceuticals, and food services relating to medical institutions. MOF Business Tax Rules, art. 26, § (2).

19. Business Tax Rules, art. 6.

20. *See also* MOF Business Tax Rules, art. 26, § (1). The labor services provided by the disabled themselves to society are exempt from the business tax.

21. MOF Business Tax Rules, art. 26, § (5).

22. Business Tax Rules, art. 8; MOF Business Tax Rules, art. 27.

23. Business Tax Rules, art. 9.

24. Business Tax Rules, art. 13.

The payment period is quarterly for the finance industry and monthly for the insurance industry.[25]

A taxpayer engaged in both an exempt and nonexempt business, or in activities with different rates of tax, is required to prepare separate accounting records.[26] If separate records are not kept, the taxation authorities may impose the highest rate applicable to all income uniformly.

2. Value-Added Tax

The value-added tax (VAT) is a component of the unified set of turnover taxes. The VAT has the broadest scope of application and is a major source of tax revenue for the PRC.

a. Scope of VAT

VAT is imposed upon both individuals and entities and has four different tax rates (from zero to 17 percent), although most goods are subject to a standard rate of 17 percent.[27] The lower rate of 13 percent applies to agricultural products; certain types of metal products; publications such as books, newspapers, and magazines; and household equipment used for water purification, hot water heaters, and air conditioning.[28] VAT is also payable on the transfer of land-use rights[29] and income derived from petroleum exploration.[30] This turnover tax is levied upon the value added to merchandise at each level of production, distribution, and sale. At each stage of the sales process, VAT is collected by the seller and advanced to the government. In general, the seller may deduct input VAT (i.e., the VAT paid at the previous level) from the tax payment to the tax authorities while certain VAT paid, such as that for the purchase of fixed assets, should be capitalized and cannot be currently deductible against output VAT.

---

25. MOF Business Tax Rules, art. 33.

26. Business Tax Rules, art. 7. *See also* MOF Business Tax Rules, art. 6.

27. VAT Rules, art. 2, § 1.

28. VAT Rules, art. 2, § 2.

29. There are special rules concerning land-use rights and the calculation of VAT on income derived from the transfer of land-use rights. *See* Provisional Rules of the People's Republic of China on Land Value-Added Tax (adopted November 26, 1993, by the 12th Sess. of the Standing Comm. of the State Council and promulgated by the State Council on December 13, 1993), *reprinted in* CHINA LAWS FOR FOREIGN BUSINESS (CCH), Taxation ¶ 31-742; Detailed Rules for the Implementation of the Provisional Rules of the People's Republic of China on Land Value-Added Tax (promulgated on January 27, 1995, by the Ministry of Finance), *reprinted in* CHINA LAWS FOR FOREIGN BUSINESS (CCH), Taxation ¶ 31-743; Notice of the Ministry of Finance and the State Administration of Taxation on Regulations on Certain Detailed Issues Concerning Land Value-Added Tax (promulgated on May 25, 1995, by the MOF and SAT), *reprinted in* CHINA LAWS FOR FOREIGN BUSINESS (CCH), Taxation ¶ 31-794.

30. Notice of the State Administration of Taxation on Questions Concerning the Payment of Value-Added Tax by Sino-Foreign Cooperative Petroleum Exploration Enterprises (promulgated April 28, 1994, by the SAT), *reprinted in* CHINA LAWS FOR FOREIGN BUSINESS (CCH), Taxation ¶ 31-726.

b. VAT Exemptions and Reductions

The tax laws provide that regions and zones are prohibited from granting special reductions or exemptions, and that all such preferential treatment can be granted only by the State Council. The tax laws provide that a number of products are exempt from VAT including the following:

(1) Agricultural products sold by the grower
(2) Contraceptive drugs and devices
(3) Antique books
(4) Imported instruments and equipment for use directly in scientific research, experiments, and teaching
(5) Materials and equipment imported for use directly by foreign governments and international organizations
(6) Equipment imported for processing, assembly, or compensation trade
(7) Products for use by disabled persons directly imported by organizations representing the interests of the disabled
(8) Sales of used articles[31]

A party that imports equipment, components, or materials that are used to process materials under a processing contract is specifically exempt from VAT.[32] FIEs involved in priority industries are exempt from VAT (and import duties) effective January 1, 1998.[33] The priority industries include textiles, mining and metallurgy, agriculture, transportation, telecommunications, aviation, energy, and petrochemicals. Foreigners investing in China's service sector, light industry, electronics, and medical equipment industries are also eligible for exemption from VAT. A general exemption also applies for high-technology imports and goods designated as new technology. However, China requires that all equipment imported by FIEs is subject to mandatory inspection, appraisal, and certification.[34] If an FIE undervalues the imported equipment, it is liable to pay the full VAT and tariffs on the merchandise and potential civil and criminal penalties if the actual value is significantly understated.

31. VAT Rules, art. 16.

32. VAT Rules, art. 16, § (6).

33. *See China Lifts Tariffs, Value-Added Tax on Capital Imports for Targeted Industries,* 15 INT'L TRADE REP. 5 (1998). Imported capital equipment by FIEs has traditionally been granted exemptions from both import tariffs and value-added tax (VAT). In 1996, China revoked the exemption in an effort to unify its treatment of foreign and domestic enterprises. In late 1997, China reversed this policy and effective January 1, 1998, imported equipment is entitled to duty-free treatment and an exemption from VAT.

34. *See Chinese Joint Venture Partners Must Watch Foreigners' Valuation of Assets, Agency Says,* 15 INT'L TRADE REP. 379 (1998). FIEs are required to have all capital imports certified by government-approved appraisers prior to clearing Customs.

Merchandise imported into China and sold wholesale for sale in duty-free stores is exempt from VAT.[35] Retail sales of imported duty-free goods by approved duty-free stores are subject to a VAT tax rate of 6 percent of the sales value of the merchandise.[36] An exporter of merchandise is not required to pay VAT on exports and may claim a VAT refund from the taxation authorities for any tax paid.[37]

35. *See* Notice on Questions Concerning the Levying of Value-Added Tax on Sales of Goods Imported Duty-Free (promulgated on March 15, 1994, by the State Administration of Taxation), *reprinted in* China Laws for Foreign Business (CCH), Taxation ¶ 31-768 (hereinafter the "Duty-Free VAT Rules").

36. Duty-Free VAT Rules, art. 2.

37. VAT Rules, art. 2, § 3. A taxpayer may apply for a refund of any VAT paid on exported items. *See* VAT Rules, art. 25. *See also* Notice of the Ministry of Finance and the State Administration of Taxation on Tax Questions Concerning Export Commodities of Foreign Investment Enterprise (promulgated on August 25, 1994, by the MOF and the SAT), *reprinted in* China Laws for Foreign Business (CCH), Taxation ¶ 32-734. On June 21, 1999, the SAT issued the *Detailed Regulations on Certain Issues Regarding Tax Refunds (Exemptions) for Exported Goods* (issued on June 21, 1999, by the SAT and effective as of date of issue), *reprinted in* China Laws for Foreign Business (CCH), Taxation ¶ 31-812 (hereinafter the Export Tax Exemption Regulations). The purpose of the Export Tax Exemption Regulations is to clarify and standardize the administration for tax exemptions for exported goods. The regulations outline specific procedures in the following categories: (1) goods exported by MOFTEC-approved private export enterprises and Sino-foreign joint venture enterprises—procedures for tax refunds are handled in accordance with current export tax refund procedures starting from the date on which the enterprise was approved; (2) projects involving mechanical and electrical products that use loans from foreign governments or international financial organizations—provides specific procedures for obtaining export refunds; (3) certain small-scale commercial enterprises and certain agricultural products for export, tax refund rates, and procedures—clarified ambiguity of previous regulations; (4) certain foreign shipping companies and production enterprises that export on a consignment basis—the regulations provide that certain tax payment certificates no longer need to be filed; (5) tax refund rate for foreign enterprises that import raw materials for processing and export shall be based upon the date recorded in the Special VAT Invoice for the materials sold; (6) manufacturing enterprises—tax refund rate is based on the date recorded in the processing trade application; and (7) export goods that are processed on consignment by foreign trade enterprises—the tax amount that should be refunded must be calculated separately according to the respective tax refund rate for raw materials and processing expenses. On August 2, 2001, the SAT issued the *Supplementary Circular Regarding the Administration of Export Refund (Exemption) Based on Classification of Enterprises* (issued on August 2, 2001, by the SAT, effective as of date of issue), *reprinted in* China Laws for Foreign Business (CCH), Taxation ¶ 31-813. In 1998, the SAT issued a circular that classified exporting enterprises into four types of operations. These categories were based upon VAT refund procedures of varying degrees of complexity. For example, Type-A enterprises are subject to simplified VAT refund procedures whereas Type-D enterprises are subject to stringent filing, verification, and approval procedures in order to receive a VAT refund. The new circular facilitates and simplifies the Type-A and Type-B procedures and requirements for enterprises located in the western region of China. Among the relaxed requirements for Type-A qualifications, the production period requirement has been reduced to a six-month period from a one-year period. The export value has been reduced from $30 million to $20 million. The export value requirement for Type-B qualifications has been reduced from $30 million in two consecutive years to $15 million for one year (which is further lowered to $10 million for manufacturing enterprises). As a result of these changes, it is easier for western-based enterprises to qualify for Type-A or Type-B qualifications and grants such enterprises better cash flow status by enabling the enterprises to receive earlier VAT refunds on exports. On October 8, 1999, the SAT issued the *Notice on Several Tax Issues Regarding the Export of Goods by Foreign-Invested Enterprises* (issued on October 8, 1999, by the SAT, and effective on November 1, 1999). This notice addresses various issues relating to the applicable VAT Export Mechanism for FIEs established before December 31, 1993. As of November 1, 1999, instead of receiving a tax exemption, an FIE established before December 31, 1993, shall receive a tax refund on goods exported either by the FIE or by its agent. *See generally* M. Mui & K. Lee, *The VAT Refund Effect: Will the New VAT Refund Changes Cut into Your Profit?*, China Bus. Rev. (January 2004). *See also* Interim Provisions Concerning Administrative Sanctions on Enterprises Fraudulently Claiming Export Tax Refunds (issued on September 27, 2000, by the Ministry of Foreign Trade and Economic Cooperation and the SAT), *reprinted in* China Laws for Foreign Business (CCH), Taxation ¶ 31-870.

Taxpayers with sales below a threshold amount are exempt from VAT.[38] The threshold amount for the sale of goods is RMB600–RMB2,000 per month, and for taxable labor services is RMB200–RMB800 per month.[39] The threshold amount on a per transaction basis is RMB50–RMB80 for one transaction per day. The VAT rate applicable to small business for taxable goods or services is 6 percent.[40] A small business is defined as a producer with annual turnover of less than RMB1 million ($870,000) or wholesalers/retailers with annual turnover of less than RMB1.8 million ($1,566,000).[41] Small businesses are prohibited from deducting any input tax already paid from the output tax they owe.

Taxpayers that intend to claim an exemption or reduction are required to maintain separate accounting records; otherwise, they are prohibited from claiming any preferences.[42] The sale and transfer of goods between related companies may constitute a taxable transfer of goods for purposes of VAT calculation.[43]

c. Payment of VAT

The tax authorities may schedule VAT assessable periods for one, three, five, fifteen, or thirty days. If the assessable period is thirty days, the VAT must be paid within ten days of the expiration of the payment period. For all other payment periods, the VAT must be paid within five days.[44] The payment of VAT on imported goods must be made by the taxpayer within seven days following notice from Customs.[45] The late fees for the untimely payment of VAT—0.2 percent per day or 73 percent per year—may be levied by the tax authorities.

A taxpayer receives a VAT number at the time of registration with the SAT and local tax authorities. An FIE is required to apply for VAT invoices from the taxation authorities for its sales transactions, and can use only

38. VAT Rules, art. 18.
39. MOF VAT Rules, art. 32.
40. VAT Rules, arts. 11–14.
41. MOF VAT Rules, art. 24.
42. VAT Rules, art. 17.
43. On August 26, 1999, the SAT issued the *Circular of the State Administration of Tax Regarding Issues in Connection with Assessment of Value-Added Tax on Movement of Goods between Subsidiaries of the Same Enterprise* (issued on August 16, 1999, by the SAT, effective as of date of issue). This circular clarifies whether the movement of goods among the subsidiaries of the same enterprise with a single set of accounts constitutes a taxable transfer of goods. According to the SAT Circular, the receiving entity of such a transfer of goods would be considered to have conducted a taxable sale activity if it has issued an invoice to the buyer or received payment for goods from the buyer.
44. VAT Rules, art. 23.
45. VAT Rules, art. 24. The taxpayer pays the VAT to Customs on imported items. VAT Rules, art. 22, § (4).

government-approved invoices.[46] A VAT invoice (also commonly referred to as a "fa piao") is required for each transaction of the taxpayer, and all unused or voided invoices must be returned to the tax authorities.[47] The amount of VAT due is determined by an analysis of the enterprise's sales and purchases (i.e., total output tax minus input tax). A taxpayer that conducts business in foreign exchange is required to convert the transaction to renminbi for purposes of VAT on the day that the sale occurred or on the first day of the current month.[48]

The rules require that a taxpayer maintain specific accounting records to substantiate its VAT transactions and tax payments. The VAT Rules empower the tax authorities to inspect and audit the records of a taxpayer.[49] The

46. Regulations on the Use of Special Value-Added Tax Invoices (promulgated December 28, 1993, by the State Administration of Taxation), *reprinted in* CHINA LAWS FOR FOREIGN BUSINESS (CCH), Taxation ¶ 31-752; Supplementary Notice on Issues Concerning the Use of Special Value-Added Tax Invoices (promulgated February 25, 1994, by the State Administration of Taxation), *reprinted in* CHINA LAWS FOR FOREIGN BUSINESS (CCH), Taxation ¶ 31-762; Notice of the State Administration of Taxation on the Issuing of the "Measures for Auditing and Inspection of Special VAT Invoices and Other Documents for Tax Calculation and Tax Deduction (Trial Implementation)" (promulgated March 24, 1995, by the State Administration of Taxation), *reprinted in* CHINA LAWS FOR FOREIGN BUSINESS (CCH), Taxation ¶ 31-780; Notice of the State Administration of Taxation on Issues Concerning the Completion and Issue of Special Value-Added Tax Invoices (promulgated on September 18, 1996, by the State Administration of Taxation), *reprinted in* CHINA LAWS FOR FOREIGN BUSINESS (CCH), Taxation ¶ 31-782; Administrative Measures of the People's Republic of China on Invoices (adopted on December 12, 1993, by the State Council and promulgated on December 23, 1993, by the Ministry of Finance), *reprinted in* CHINA LAWS FOR FOREIGN BUSINESS (CCH), Taxation ¶ 39-615 (outlining the rules governing the printing, purchase, and retention of invoices for tax purposes); Announcement of the State Administration of Taxation on Nationwide Uniform Changes to Formulate New Edition Ordinary Invoices (promulgated on September 20, 1996, by the State Administration of Taxation), *reprinted in* CHINA LAWS FOR FOREIGN BUSINESS (CCH), Taxation ¶ 39-635 (describes the uniform anti-fraud forms and requirements for use of new forms). A company or individual may retain a tax specialist to assist it with its taxation matters in China. *See* Trial Measures on Tax Agency (promulgated on October 19, 1994, by the State Administration of Taxation), *reprinted in* CHINA LAWS FOR FOREIGN BUSINESS (CCH), Taxation ¶ 39-630 (rules governing tax specialists retained by a taxpayer to handle taxation matters, including tax registration, purchase of invoices, preparation and filing of declarations or withholding statements, payment of tax or application for refunds, establishment of tax accounting system, tax consultation, and application for administrative review and tax litigation).

47. Notice on Issues Concerning the Use of Special Value-Added Tax Invoices (promulgated February 14, 1994, by the State Administration of Taxation), *reprinted in* CHINA LAWS FOR FOREIGN BUSINESS (CCH), Taxation ¶ 31-760.

48. MOF VAT Rules, art. 15.

49. *See* Measures on Annual Inspection of General Payers of Value-Added Tax (promulgated on March 17, 1998, by the State Administration of Taxation), *reprinted in* CHINA LAWS FOR FOREIGN BUSINESS (CCH), Taxation ¶ 31-764 (outlines the objectives and procedures for VAT annual inspections); Notice of the Ministry of Finance and the State Administration of Taxation on Strengthening the Administration of the Levy and Collection of Business-linked Value-added Tax (promulgated on January 9, 1998, by the Ministry of Finance and the State Administration of Taxation); Notice on Certain Questions Concerning the Levying and Collection of Value-Added Tax (promulgated on May 7, 1994, by the SAT), *reprinted in* CHINA LAWS FOR FOREIGN BUSINESS (CCH), Taxation ¶ 31-731 (addresses issues concerning the location of payment of VAT, calculation of VAT with mixed goods/services, etc.). Notice of the State Administration of Taxation on the Issuing of the "Measures for Auditing and Inspection of Special VAT Invoices and Other Documents for Tax Calculation and Tax Deduction (Trial Implementation)"(promulgated on March 24, 1995, by the State Administration of Taxation), *reprinted in* CHINA LAWS FOR FOREIGN BUSINESS (CCH), Taxation ¶ 31-780 (outlines the specific audit procedures of the tax authorities, documents to be inspected, methods of inspection, and standards for auditors).

> **Practice Tip: Pursuit of the *Fa Piao***
>
> An enterprise is required to issue a *fa piao* whenever it receives money on a sale of goods or provision of services. When an enterprise files its monthly tax report, it pays a percentage of VAT tax based upon the value of the *fa piao* issued in that month. For a party claiming a deduction for a business expense, the *fa piao* is required to claim the expense, and without the invoice a claim is unacceptable. In order to be valid, a *fa piao* is required to have two chops, or stamps, imprinted on the invoice, including one that is printed by the local tax authorities and another that is stamped by the company that issues the *fa piao*. The language in the company chop must exactly match that on the payee line of the invoice. Information concerning the payer and the service item must be included in the *fa piao* or there is a risk that the invoice may be considered invalid.

untimely payment of VAT is subject to a penalty surcharge of 0.2 percent per day, or 73 percent per year. A taxpayer is entitled to request a refund of VAT for returns of merchandise.[50]

3. Consumption Tax

The consumption tax is levied upon certain consumer goods, including liquor, cosmetics, motor vehicles, hair conditioners, jewels, pearls, jade, fireworks, motor vehicle tires, motorcycles, and tobacco products. The consumption tax rates are as follows: Grade A cigarettes (compound rates),[51] cigars (40 percent), cut tobacco (30 percent), liquor from grains or potatoes (compound rates), beer (RMB220 per ton), cosmetics (30 percent), skin and hair conditioners (17 percent), pearls/jade jewelry (10 percent), firecrackers and fireworks (15 percent), diesel fuel (RMB0.1 per liter), motor vehicle tires (10 percent), motorcycles (10 percent), and motor vehicles (3 percent–8 percent).[52] Taxable consumer goods that are exported are exempt from consumption tax.[53] Consumption tax is payable to Customs on imported items, and such payment is due seven days

50. MOF VAT Rules, art. 11.

51. *See* Notice on Adjusting the Consumption Tax Policies on Tobacco Products (issued on June 4, 2001, by the Ministry of Finance and the State Administration of Taxation) (changes tax rates for cigarettes from flat rates of 45%/30% to compound rates).

52. Consumption Tax Law, art. 2 and accompanying table. The MOF Consumption Tax Rules outline in detail the methods for calculating the consumption tax. Goods subject to the consumption tax are also subject to VAT. *See also* Notice on Adjusting the Consumption Tax Policies on Liquor Products (issued on May 11, 2001, by the MOF and SAT) (outlines use of compound rates rather than fixed percentage rates of consumption tax).

53. Consumption Tax Law, art. 11. If an exported item is returned by the overseas buyer, the exporter is required to declare with Customs the return and to pay the refunded portion of the consumption tax. MOF Consumption Tax Rules, art. 23.

from the date of notice from Customs.[54] As with the business and VAT taxes, the consumption tax may be paid, within the discretion of the tax authorities, on a per transaction basis or under a payment period plan.[55] If a consumer good is returned to the taxpayer, the taxpayer may request from the tax authorities a refund of the consumption tax paid on the returned item.[56]

B. Foreign Enterprise Tax

The tax regulations require FIEs to pay income taxes at a rate of 33 percent: the national government collects 30 percent and the local and provincial governments collect 3 percent.[57] All enterprises are subject to income tax, including FIE service organizations that collect revenue for activities in China such as overseas accounting, consulting, and law firms;[58] FIEs that provide services to related or subsidiary organizations and charge fees for such

54. Consumption Tax Law, arts. 12, 15. *See also* Notice of the General Administration of Customs on Certain Questions Concerning the Levying and Collection of Value-Added Tax and Consumption Tax on Imported Goods (promulgated on December 25, 1993, by the General Administration of Customs), *reprinted in* CHINA LAWS FOR FOREIGN BUSINESS (CCH), Taxation ¶ 31-729 (outlining rules for collection of VAT and consumption tax by Customs).

55. Consumption Tax Law, art. 14.

56. MOF Consumption Tax Rules, art. 24.

57. Income Tax Law of the People's Republic of China for Enterprises with Foreign Investment and Foreign Enterprises (the "FIE Tax Law") (promulgated on April 9, 1991, by the 4th Sess. of the 7th NPC), *reprinted in* CHINA LAWS FOR FOREIGN BUSINESS (CCH), Taxation ¶ 32-505. *See also* Detailed Rules for the Implementation of the Income Tax Law of the People's Republic of China for Foreign Investment Enterprises and Foreign Enterprises (the "FIE Tax Rules") (promulgated June 30, 1991, by the State Council), *reprinted in* CHINA LAWS FOR FOREIGN BUSINESS (CCH), Taxation ¶ 32-507. For a discussion of the income tax law of China as applied to foreigners, *see* Lam, Cho & Mak, *The Historical Development of Income Tax Law for Domestic and Foreign Enterprises in China,* 22 INT'L TAX J. 51 (1996); *China: Tax Regulations,* EIU VIEWS WIRE (Jan. 26, 1999), available on Lexis, News Library; Cheng, *Tax Incentives for Foreign Investment,* 136 CHINA INTERNATIONAL BUSINESS (MOFTEC) 5 (1998). *See also* Provisional Rules of the People's Republic of China on Enterprise Income Tax (promulgated on December 13, 1993, by the State Council), *reprinted in* China Laws for Foreign Business (CCH), Taxation ¶ 31-745 (addresses enterprise tax issues for all enterprises in China, except Foreign Investment Enterprise); Detailed Rules for the Implementation of the Provisional Rules of the People's Republic of China on Enterprise Income Tax (promulgated on February 4, 1994, by the Ministry of Finance), *reprinted in* China Laws for Foreign Business (CCH), Taxation ¶ 31-746; Regulation on Certain Policy Issues Concerning Enterprise Income Tax (promulgated on May 13, 1994, by the Ministry of Finance and the SAT), *reprinted in* China Laws for Foreign Business (CCH), Taxation ¶ 31-744 (outlines policy objectives for enterprise income tax); Notice of the Ministry of Finance and the State Administration of Taxation on Several Detailed Issues Concerning Enterprise Income Tax (promulgated on November 1, 1996, by the Ministry of Finance and the SAT), *reprinted in* China Laws for Foreign Business (CCH), Taxation ¶ 31-784. The principal office of an FIE is responsible for the taxes of its branch offices. *See* Notice of the State Administration of Taxation on Issues Concerning Applicable Income Tax Rate for the Branch Organizations of Foreign Investment Enterprises (promulgated on April 9, 1997, by the SAT), *reprinted in* CHINA LAWS FOR FOREIGN BUSINESS (CCH), Taxation ¶ 32-766. In May of 1998, the SAT developed a comprehensive set of rules concerning transfer pricing. *See* Sherwood, *Climbing Higher on the Great Wall of Transfer Pricing,* 7 TRANSFER PRICING REPORT No. 13 (Oct. 28, 1998).

58. Notice on Issues Concerning the Handling of Taxation with Respect to Foreign Investment Enterprises with Foreign Enterprises Engaged in Consulting Business (issued on May 12, 2000, by the SAT), *reprinted in* CHINA LAWS FOR FOREIGN BUSINESS (CCH), Taxation ¶ 32-638 (outlines standards and procedures for handling tax issues on income of foreign law, accounting, auditing, and consulting firms).

services;[59] income received by FIEs for stock transactions and dividends;[60] and income derived outside of China.[61]

As with domestic enterprises, an FIE is entitled to certain exemptions[62] from and credits[63] to enterprise income tax, as well as certain business deductions.[64] An FIE is required to submit an annual tax return and supporting

---

59. Notice of the State Administration of Taxation on Issues Relating to Tax Treatment for Provision of Services by Foreign-Funded Investment Companies to Subsidiary Companies (promulgated on September 28, 2002, by the SAT), *reprinted in* CHINA LAWS FOR FOREIGN BUSINESS (CCH), Taxation ¶ 32-705 (addresses tax treatment of fees collected by FIEs for services to affiliated companies).

60. Notice of the State Administration of Taxation Concerning Taxation of Income from Stock (Share Rights) Transactions and Dividends Received by Foreign Investment Enterprises, Foreign Enterprises, and Foreign Nationals (issued on July 21, 1993, by the SAT), *reprinted in* CHINA LAWS FOR FOREIGN BUSINESS (CCH), Taxation ¶ 32-706.

61. Notice of the Ministry of Finance and the State Administration of Taxation on the Promulgation of the Provisional Measures for the Calculation and Levy of Income Tax on Income Derived Outside China (Revised Version) (promulgated on November 25, 1997, by the Ministry of Finance and the State Administration of Taxation), *reprinted in* CHINA LAWS FOR FOREIGN BUSINESS (CCH), Taxation ¶ 31-719 (addresses tax treatment of overseas income of FIEs).

62. Various exemptions from income may apply to FIEs. For example, income from State treasury bonds are exempt from taxation. In this regard, on December 1, 1999, the SAT issued the *Reply on the Issue of the Tax Handling of Interest Income Obtained by Foreign-Invested Enterprises and Foreign Enterprises from the Purchase of State Treasury Bonds* (issued on December 1, 1999, by the SAT, effective as of the date of issue). This order provides that in line with the *PRC Regulations on State Treasury Bonds* (issued on March 18, 1992, by the State Council), such interest income is exempt from enterprise income tax, but tax is payable on income from state treasury bond transfers. Income items that are exempt from taxable income are listed in Article 19 of the *Income Tax Law of the PRC for Enterprises with Foreign Investment and Foreign Enterprise*.

63. FIEs may be entitled to a tax credit on the purchase of domestically produced equipment. In this regard, on January 14, 2000, the Ministry of Finance and the SAT issued the *Notice of Foreign Enterprise Income Tax Credit for FIEs Purchasing Domestically Manufactured Equipment* (issued on January 14, 2000, by the Ministry of Finance and SAT, effective July 1, 2000). This order was issued to promote sales of domestically manufactured equipment and provides that an FIE can receive credit of 40 percent of the price of domestic equipment purchased within the total investment against the increase to its foreign enterprise income tax liability over the previous year. The order sets forth items on the *List of Non-exemption Commodities Imported by Foreign Investment Projects* that are excluded from the credit program. Besides the total investment, expenditure on the purchase of domestic equipment used for technical improvement may also be credited. This tax credit may not be used to create a net loss and is subject to a maximum five-year carryforward period. FIEs currently enjoying state-level tax holidays may carry the credit forward for seven years. If the enterprise leases or transfers the equipment on which the income tax credit has been claimed in accordance with this Notice, the enterprise is required to repay the credit. Furthermore, the provisions of this Notice may be retroactively applied to purchases made after June 30, 1999. On May 18, 2000, the SAT issued the *Notice on Issuing the Management Measures for Enterprise Income Tax Credit for FIEs Purchasing Domestically Manufactured Equipment*. This Notice clarifies and provides implementing details for the *Notice on Foreign Enterprise Income Tax Credit for FIEs Purchasing Domestically Manufactured Equipment*. It defines the types of equipment that may qualify for the tax credit and specifies the amount of domestically manufactured equipment that must be purchased for qualification of the tax credit. Furthermore, the Notice provides detailed approval procedures as well as documentation requirements for foreign enterprises. In order to receive such income tax credit, enterprises are required to submit their application for credit within two months after purchasing the equipment. These applications must be submitted at each administrative level, with the final approval coming from the provincial tax bureau. The provincial tax bureau then must issue a decision within one month after receipt of the application. This Notice also sets out an additional requirement for the final settlement of the annual foreign enterprise income tax. FIEs must submit their tax returns, along with a summary statement for verification of all claimed foreign enterprise income tax credit, a copy of all invoices for the purchase of the equipment, and statements of all the credited domestically manufactured equipment items. The head office of the FIE must consolidate all such information for each of its subsidiary branches that has purchased domestically manufactured equipment.

64. *See* Administrative Measures on the Examination and Verification of the Loss Recovery of Enterprise Income Tax Before Tax (promulgated on December 16, 1997, by the SAT), *reprinted in* CHINA LAWS

documentation and materials.[65] An FIE that qualifies, and continues to qualify, as a "high technology" operation, or is located in a high-technology zone, may obtain preferential tax rates as follows:

(1) Reduced national income tax of 15 percent
(2) Tax holidays for two years following the first year of profits
(3) Tax reduction of 50 percent for the third through the fifth years of operation after the first profit-making year
(4) Refunds on profits reinvested in China of 40 percent of taxes paid[66]

FOR FOREIGN BUSINESS (CCH), Taxation ¶ 31-715 (outlines procedures for the approval of loss recovery against income tax); Administrative Measures on Enterprise Property Loss Deductions before Tax (promulgated on December 16, 1997, by the SAT), *reprinted in* CHINA LAWS FOR FOREIGN BUSINESS (CCH), Taxation ¶ 31-716 (outlines procedures for approval of enterprise property-related losses against income tax and deduction of such losses).

65. An FIE is required to register with the local tax authorities and must present its tax certificates at the time of opening a bank account and purchasing tax invoices. In addition to FIEs engaged in operations in China, the law further requires that overseas enterprises involved with construction, installation, assembly, and prospecting activities in China or providing labor services in China, to register with the SAT within 30 days of signing a contract. *See* Management Rules on Taxation Registration (promulgated on December 17, 2003, by the State Administration of Taxation). *See also* Notice of the State Administration of Taxation on the Printing and Distribution of the Administrative Measures on Income Tax Calculation and Clearance Payments for Foreign Investment Enterprises and Foreign Enterprises(promulgated on June 20, 1997, by the SAT), *reprinted in* CHINA LAWS FOR FOREIGN BUSINESS (CCH), Taxation ¶ 32-780 (outlines required forms and documents to be submitted annually by an FIE). On January 1, 2001, the SAT adopted the *Notice on Issuance of a Newly Revised Income Tax Report Form for Foreign and Foreign-Invested Enterprises*. Under this Notice, FIE income tax returns are divided into two categories. The Type A return requires a set of form attachments, and should be completed by enterprises sufficiently capable in their accounting to pay enterprise income tax on an actual basis. The type B return is for use by FIEs paying enterprise income tax on a deemed-profit or cost-plus basis. On November 15, 2000, the Beijing Local Tax Bureau issued the *Announcement from the Beijing Local Tax Bureau on Foreign Related Tax Jurisdiction*. Effective as of January 1, 2001, all FIEs (equity joint ventures, cooperative joint ventures, and wholly owned foreign enterprises) in Beijing are required to pay their local taxes to the district level local tax bureau. Previous to this Announcement, Beijing FIEs submitted their local taxes to the Foreign Affairs Branch of the Beijing Local Tax Bureau. The income tax returns for enterprises are required to be on the printed form approved by the SAT. *See* Notice of the State Administration of Taxation Regarding the Printing and Distributing of Enterprise Income Tax Returns (promulgated on May 27, 1994, by the SAT), *reprinted in* CHINA LAWS FOR FOREIGN BUSINESS (CCH), Taxation ¶ 31-786 (tax forms attached to the notice).

66. FIE Tax Rules, art. 73; Regulations on Tax Policies for State Hi-Tech Development Zones (approved March 6, 1991, by the State Council), *reprinted in* CHINA LAWS FOR FOREIGN BUSINESS (CCH), Taxation, ¶ 39-605; Notice on Certain Issues Concerning the Implementation of the Income Tax Law for Enterprises with Foreign Investment and Foreign Enterprises (issued on August 21, 2000, by the SAT), *reprinted in* CHINA LAWS FOR FOREIGN BUSINESS (CCH), Taxation ¶ 32-600 (addresses issues concerning the handling of applications for tax reductions and exemptions, tax losses, etc.); Notice on Relevant Issues Concerning Implementing Tax Exemption, Offset and Refund Policies for Foreign Investment Enterprises (issued on July 15, 1998, by the SAT), *reprinted in* CHINA LAWS FOR FOREIGN BUSINESS (CCH), Taxation ¶ 32-620 (addresses procedures for export tax refunds). *See also* Notice on Issues Relating to Enterprise Income Tax Refunds for Reinvestment by Foreign Investors (issued on July 17, 2002, by the SAT), *reprinted in* CHINA LAWS FOR FOREIGN BUSINESS (CCH), Taxation ¶ 32-621 (procedures for handling tax refunds and preferential treatment for profits reinvested by FIEs); Notice of the State Bureau of Taxation Concerning Several Questions on Tax Refunds for Funds Reinvested by Foreign Investors in Foreign Investment Enterprises (issued on June 15, 1993, by the SAT), *reprinted in* CHINA LAWS FOR FOREIGN BUSINESS (CCH), Taxation ¶ 32-702. *See also* Notice of the State Administration of Taxation on Questions Concerning the Determination of the First Profit-Making Year and Calculation of the Period of Reduction of and Exemption from Taxes for Foreign Investment Enterprises (promulgated on June 28, 1995, by the SAT), *reprinted in* CHINA LAWS FOR FOREIGN BUSINESS (CCH), Taxation ¶ 32-622; Official Response of the State Administration of Taxation on Relevant Issues Concerning Tax Refunds on Funds Re-Invested by Foreign Investment Enterprises (promulgated on April 3, 1995, by the SAT), *reprinted in* CHINA LAWS FOR FOREIGN BUSINESS (CCH),

"High technology" and "new technology" operations are defined as enterprises that engage in "research, development, production, and handling of one or more types of high and new technology and products" as outlined in the regulations.[67] Certain industries such as oil and gas exploration are subject to specific

---

Taxation ¶ 32-619 (prohibits tax preferences for the use of funds "reinvested" in enterprises); Official Response of the State Administration of Taxation on Relevant Issues Concerning Tax Refunds for Reinvestment by Foreign Investors of Foreign Investment Enterprises (promulgated on March 18, 1996, by the SAT), *reprinted in* China Laws for Foreign Business (CCH), Taxation ¶ 32-750 (requirement to obtain certificate of approval to reinvest in production exporting enterprise and technologically advanced enterprise); Notice of the State Administration of Taxation on Relevant Issues Concerning the Levying and Collection of Income Tax from Foreign Investment Enterprises Which Engage in Real Estate Development Operations (promulgated on August 3, 1995, by the SAT), *reprinted in* China Laws for Foreign Business (CCH), Taxation ¶ 32-631 (real estate development business is not considered a "production" activity and therefore not subject to preferential treatment); Notice of the State Administration of Taxation on Questions Concerning the Application of Preferential Tax Treatment for Foreign Investment Enterprises Which Engage in Special Investment Projects Such as Harbors and Wharves (promulgated on August 4, 1995, by the SAT), *reprinted in* China Laws forForeign Business (CCH), Taxation ¶ 32-634 (an FIE that engages in infrastructure projects such as harbor, wharf, airport, railroad, highway, power generation, mining, water conservation, communications, or agriculture development operation may enjoy preferential treatment); Clarification of Relevant Issues Concerning How Foreign Investment Enterprises May Enjoy the Preferential Tax Treatment of "Double-Intensive Enterprises" (promulgated on July 7, 1995, by the SAT), *reprinted in* China Laws for Foreign Business (CCH), Taxation ¶ 32-637 (addresses standards for tax preferences for technology-intensive and knowledge-intensive enterprises). *See generally* Maugue, *Tax Incentives in the People's Republic of China: Who Benefits?*, 5 Tul. J. Int'l & Comp. L. 155 (1997). For a reference to the types of technology encouraged by the government, *see* the Catalogue of Encouraged Foreign Investment in High and New Technology Products (2003) (issued on July 18, 2003, by the Ministry of Commerce and the Ministry of Science and Technology). The 2003 catalogue furthers the Chinese government's policy of encouraging foreign investment in underdeveloped industries and groups 196 product types into 11 principal categories: electronic information; software; space and aviation; optical-mechanical-electrical integration; biomedicines and medical treatment instruments; new materials; new energies and high-efficiency energies; environmental protection; earth, air, and sea; nuclear application technologies; and modern agriculture. *See also* Circular on Tax Policies for Further Encouraging Development of Software Industry and IC Industry (adopted by the Ministry of Finance and the State Administration of Taxation, effective from January 1, 2002, to December 31, 2010). Manufacturers of integrated circuits who have paid VAT will receive a rebate for all but three percent (3%) of the VAT paid. The rules require that the rebated funds be applied back into the business and specifically for the use in the manufacturing, research, and development of integrated circuit products. The rules exempt from corporate income tax for two years domestic manufacturers of integrated circuits that produce chips with a line width below 0.8 microns, and such enterprises are entitled to further exemption of fifty percent (50%) of corporate income tax for three years starting from the first profitable year. Foreign investment companies producing integrated circuits are already entitled to the 50%-over-three-years tax break, and the rule brings domestic manufacturers in parity with FIEs. Domestic and FIE chip manufacturers who invest profits in new or existing integrated circuit companies and promise to operate for at least five (5) years are eligible for a forty percent (40%) rebate on income tax paid. Manufacturers who reinvest their after-tax profits in western China and promise to operate for at least five years receive eighty percent (80%) rebate on income tax paid. *See also* Notice on Relevant Issues Concerning the Implementation of Preferential Income Tax Policies for Software Enterprises and High-technology Enterprises (issued on May 29, 2003, by the State Administration of Taxation, and effective January 1, 2003) (provides that software production enterprises established after July 1, 2000, will be considered as "newly established software production enterprises" entitled to preferential tax treatment; provides a definition of "first profit-making year"; outlines the method for determining eligibility of a software enterprise for tax reductions and exemptions; and sets forth the applicable tax rate for newly established software production enterprises and high-technology enterprises to be fifteen percent (15%)); Reply on the Enjoyment of Preferential Enterprise Income Tax Policies for Technologically Advanced Enterprises by Foreign-invested Enterprises with Investment in Installments (issued on July 9, 2003, by the State Administration of Taxation) (provides that FIEs established pursuant to an approved contract that requires the contribution of capital in installments are eligible for tax preferences and may enjoy a fifty percent (50%) reduction of enterprise income tax for an additional three years beyond the initial five-year tax holiday).

67. Regulations on Tax Policies for State Hi-Tech Development Zones (approved March 6, 1991, by the State Council), *reprinted in* China Laws for Foreign Business (CCH), Taxation, ¶ 39-605. *See also* Regulations Concerning the Conditions and Measures for the Identification of High and New Technology

registration and accounting procedures.[68] Preferential tax treatment is extended to foreign investors that make additional investments into existing operations,[69] FIEs that invest in the western regions of China,[70] or FIEs that invest in

Enterprises in the National Development Zones for High and New Technology Industries (promulgated on March 6, 1991, by the State Science and Technology Commission), *reprinted in* INVESTMENT IN CHINA (MOFTEC) 228 (1993). The regulations list the "scope of high and new technology" as follows: microelectronics, electronic information, space science and aerospace, photoelectron science, life science and genetic engineering, material science, energy science, environmental protection and ecology, geoscience and marine engineering, radiation science, and medical science. The list is subject to modification by the State Science and Technology Commission. On November 2, 1999, the Ministry of Finance and SAT issued the *Notice on Tax Issues Regarding the Implementation of the "Decision of the Central Committee of the Chinese Communist Party and the State Council Regarding Strengthening Technological Innovation, Developing High Science and Technology, and Realizing Industrialization"* (issued on October 2, 1999, by the Ministry of Finance and SAT and effective on October 1, 1999). This notice clarifies the preferential VAT, business tax, income tax, and import/export tax policies for the encouragement of investments in technology. Income generated from technology transfers, technology development, and related technical consulting and technical services are exempt from business tax. General taxpayers are allowed to utilize a 6-percent VAT rate for software development activities and to deduct the total amount of wages paid from their taxable income. FIEs and foreign enterprises, which provide funding to scientific research and educational institutions for research and development expenses, may also receive income tax deductions. The notice also provides details on other preferential treatments such as exemptions on tariffs and import-linked VAT, including taxes levied on certain software expenses and imported qualified high-tech equipment and accompanying technology and accessories. On September 19, 1999, the SAT issued the *Notice on Issues Regarding the Deduction of Taxable Income of Foreign-Invested Enterprises* (issued on September 19, 1999, by SAT and effective January 1, 2000). This notice allows further taxable income deductions for FIE R&D expenses. Upon approval from the relevant tax authorities, an FIE may deduct an additional 50 percent of its R&D expenses from the current year's taxable income. Such treatment applies only to FIEs for which R&D expenses incurred within China have increased by 10 percent over the previous taxable year. The notice also provides a detailed list of expenses that qualify for such deductions. On June 8, 2001, the SAT issued the *Supplementary Notice on Deduction of R&D Expenses from Tax Payable by Foreign Investment Enterprises.* Under the 1999 *Notice on Relevant Questions Regarding the Deduction of R&D Expenses from Tax Payable by FIEs,* FIEs may claim a 50-percent deduction from total R&D expenses on any increase in its corporate income tax payable for the relevant period. The 2001 Supplementary Notice provides further detail regarding the deductions for R&D expenses. Specifically, the Notice stipulates that enterprises must maintain detailed and separate project plans and budget accounts for R&D expenses and assign qualified personnel to manage such accounts.

68. *See* Notice of the State Administration of Taxation on Matters Concerning the Payment of Taxes by Foreign Petroleum Companies Engaged in Cooperative Mining of Petroleum Resources in China (promulgated on March 16, 1995, by the SAT), *reprinted in* CHINA LAWS FOR FOREIGN BUSINESS (CCH), Taxation ¶ 32-610.

69. Notice on Corporate Income Tax Incentives Policies for Additional Investment by Foreign-Invested Enterprises (issued on June 1, 2002, by the Ministry of Finance and State Administration of Taxation); Notice on Issues Relating to Enterprise Income Tax Refunds for Reinvestment by Foreign Investors (issued on July 17, 2002, by the SAT), *reprinted in* CHINA LAWS FOR FOREIGN BUSINESS (CCH), Taxation ¶ 32-621 (procedures for handling tax refunds and preferential treatment for profits reinvested by FIEs). The Notice applies to projects classified as "encouraged" and the investment must total at least $60 million or at least $15 million if the added investment totals more than half of the original registered capital. Separate accounting records are required to be set up for the new investment funds injected into the FIE. *But see* Circular on Questions Relating to Reinvestment Refunds to Foreign Investors (issued on July 30, 2001, by the State Administration of Taxation) (circular provides that a foreign investor may not qualify for reinvestment refunds if it effectively distributes the profits of the FIE by way of related party transaction and the profits must be directly reinvested). *See also* Supplementary Notice on Questions Related to Foreign-Invested Enterprises Enjoying Enterprise Income Tax Preferential Policies for Additional Investment (issued on March 28, 2003, by the SAT) (clarifying certain issues related to tax preferences for increased investment in foreign investment projects and provides that "encouraged projects" eligible for preferential treatment include (i) projects approved before April 1, 2002, that were in the "encouraged" or "restricted B" categories under the Catalogue for Guiding Foreign Investment in Industry issued in 1997, and (ii) projects in the "encouraged" category under the revised Foreign Investment Catalogue issued in 2002).

70. On September 17, 1999, the SAT issued the *Notice on Implementing the Preferential 3-Year Tax Rate When Levying and Collecting Income Tax on FIEs Established in Middle and Western Areas* (issued

domestically produced equipment.[71] The government bars preferential tax treatment to enterprises with less than twenty-five percent (25%) foreign ownership.[72]

In situations involving the merger, division, or equity reorganization and transfer of FIE assets, capital gains derived from the sale of assets are taxable under the foreign enterprise income tax law.[73] The uniform capital gains tax of ten percent (10%) is imposed upon the amount realized from a sale of an interest in an FIE, less the registered capital and distributable after-tax retained earnings of the FIE. In addition, preferential treatment such as reductions or exemptions is not affected by reorganizations as long as the FIE continues to meet the requirements for such treatment. If the preferential period lapses before the restructuring process, the benefits will not be

---

on September 17, 1999, by the SAT, effective on January 1, 2000). This notice clarifies the State Council's policy granting preferential treatment (i.e., three-year preferential 15-percent income tax rate) to encourage industrial FIEs to invest in the inland and western regions of China. Subject to State Council approval, FIEs categorized as "encouraged and restricted B" may be eligible for favorable treatment. The notice also provides detailed explanations of the approval procedures.

71. Measures on the Administration of the Offset or Exemption of Enterprise Income Tax for Foreign Investment Enterprises in the Purchase of Domestically Made Equipment (issued on May 18, 2000, by the SAT), *reprinted in* China Laws for Foreign Business (CCH), Taxation ¶ 32-635; Notice on Relevant Issues Concerning the Offset or Exemption of Enterprise Income Tax for Foreign Investment Enterprises in the Purchase of Domestically Made Equipment (issued on January 14, 2000, by the Ministry of Finance and SAT), *reprinted in* China Laws for Foreign Business (CCH), Taxation ¶ 32-636; Trial Measures on the Administration of Tax Rebates for the Purchase of Domestically Made Equipment by Foreign Investment Enterprises (promulgated on September 20, 1999, by the SAT), *reprinted in* China Laws for Foreign Business (CCH), Taxation ¶ 32-700 (addresses the scope and conditions for tax rebates on domestic purchases).

72. Circular Concerning Issues Relevant to Strengthening the Administration of the Examination, Approval, Registration, Foreign Exchange Issues, and Taxation of Foreign-Invested Enterprises (jointly issued on December 30, 2002, by the MOFTEC, SAT, SAIC, and SAFE). *See generally* W. Yang & S. Qin, *FIEs 25% or Less*!, China L. & Prac. (Feb. 2003); C. Han & S. Qin, *FIE Status and the 25% Rule*, China L. & Prac. (Dec. 2001).

73. *See* Provisional Regulations on the Handling of Income Tax on Reorganizations of Foreign Investment Enterprises such as Mergers, Splits, Reorganization of Equity and Asset Transfer (promulgated April 28, 1997, by the State Administration of Taxation), *reprinted in* China Laws for Foreign Business (CCH), Taxation ¶ 32-774. *See also* Dauchez & Vernay, *Tax Treatment of FIE Reorganizations*, 11 China L. & Prac. 55 (July/Aug. 1997). *See also* Notice of the State Administration of Taxation on Tax Collection Issues Relating to Foreign Investment Enterprises and Foreign Enterprises Engaged in Disposal of Financial Assets (issued on January 7, 2003, by the SAT), *reprinted in* China Laws for Foreign Business (CCH), Taxation ¶ 32-800. These Regulations address situations where FIEs obtain the equity, debt, capital, and "bundled-assets" of domestic companies and then transfer, retire, exchange, or sell these assets for profit. When an FIE acquires re-disposed assets, the amount paid upon acquistion constitutes the original price. The company may subsequently reconstitute the assets and set an original price for the entire group of assets; however, that price may not exceed the original price the company paid for the entire group of assets. Tax will be levied on income from the real capital portion of re-disposed assets if the assets in question are fixed. VAT will be levied on the sale of any commodities. Enterprise income tax will be levied on income received from re-disposed assets after the original price, expenses, and any loss has been deducted. *See also* Notice of the Ministry of Finance and the State Administration of Taxation on Issues Concerning the Handling of Relevant Income Tax on the Added Value of Enterprise Asset Valuation (promulgated on June 23, 1997, by the Ministry of Finance and the SAT), *reprinted in* China Laws for Foreign Business (CCH), Taxation ¶ 31-850. The SAT has also adopted rules addressing the tax treatment of M&A activity involving domestic enterprises and foreign investors. *See* Notice of State Administration of Taxation on Tax Collection Issues Relating to Mergers and Acquistions of Domestic Enterprises by Foreign Investors (promulgated on May 28, 2003, by the SAT), *reprinted in* China Laws for Foreign Business (CCH), Taxation ¶ 32-810.

extended. The law also allows for FIEs involved in reorganizations to carry forward previous losses over a five-year period.[74]

In April 1999, the State Administration of Taxation issued an order that addresses the tax consequences of failing to make required registered capital payments.[75] The circular is retroactive to the 1998 taxable year and is designed to provide additional guidance in regard to the criteria for evaluating whether foreign investment enterprise tax treatment is applicable to a particular enterprise. Pursuant to the circular, an enterprise is disqualified for preferential treatment if the foreign investor fails, without legal grounds, to meet capital contribution obligations in the time and manner required by the relevant laws, regulations, or investment contracts. Also, enterprises that fail to meet the 25-percent investment threshold will be taxed at the same rates as domestic enterprises are taxed.

The State Administration of Taxation issued an order concerning the application of losses to offset taxable income.[76] Pursuant to this Notice, calculated losses, which may be carried over to subsequent taxable years, must be adjusted by items of income. Such items are excluded from taxable income. With the issuance of this Notice, losses must exceed exclusions from taxable income in order to be applied in subsequent taxable years.

The government has adopted transfer pricing standards used in determining enterprise income tax, and transfer pricing investigations have become an important tool for the government to raise revenues in recent years.[77] The Transfer Pricing Rules provide guidelines for tax authorities and taxpayers on various related party transactions, including the definition of affiliation, different types of transactions, identification of targets for transfer pricing audits, implementation procedures, adjustment methods, tax consequences and penalties, review and litigation of transfer pricing decisions, and document filings, etc. Transactions between related parties should be conducted on an arm's length basis, and relevant enterprises are required to report transactions with their affiliates in the forms designated by the tax authorities together with their annual income tax returns.

74. FIE Tax Law, art. 11; FIE Tax Rules, art. 91.

75. Circular of the State Administration of Taxation on Issues Concerning the Handling of Income Tax for Foreign Investment Enterprises Where the Foreign Investment Has Not Been Paid-in (issued on April 14, 1999, by the State Administration of Taxation).

76. Notice Regarding the Compensation of Losses with an Enterprise's Tax Exempt Income (issued on March 5, 1999, by the State Administration of Taxation).

77. Tax Administration Procedures on Business Transactions Among Affiliated Enterprises (promulgated by the State Administration of Taxation on April 23, 1998) (the Transfer Pricing Rules): Tax Administration Procedures on Challenge to Certain Related Party Transactions (issued on September 26, 2003, by the State Tax Administration) (outlines procedures for valuation of used assets between related parties); Notice of the State Administration of Taxation on Issues Relating to Tax Treatment for Provision of Services by Foreign-Funded Investment Companies to Subsidiary Companies (promulgated on September 28, 2002, by the SAT), *reprinted in* CHINA LAWS FOR FOREIGN BUSINESS (CCH), Taxation ¶ 32-705 (addresses tax treatment of fees collected by FIEs for services to affiliated companies).

Taxpayers may reach advanced pricing arrangements, with tax authorities concerning transfer pricing matters.

C. Tax Issues for Specific Industry Sectors

The tax authorities have adopted scores of regulations and rules specifically for certain industry sectors with respect to VAT, business, consumption, and enterprise taxation, and investors should fully analyze their exposure on a general and industry-specific basis. A few highlights concerning industry-specific tax rules are set forth below and in the footnotes throughout this chapter.

1. Finance Leasing

In July of 2000, the SAT issued a notice that clarifies the inconsistencies between local tax bureaus when determining whether to levy business tax or VAT on finance leasing activities.[78] According to the Notice, finance leasing businesses approved by the People's Bank of China (PBOC) and China Banking Regulatory Commission (CBRC) are subject to business tax regardless of whether the title to the leased property is to be transferred to the lessee when the lease contract expires. Entities that are not approved by the PBOC or CBRC, which are conducting finance leasing activities, are subject to VAT if there is a transfer of title to the property at the end of the lease. If no such transfer occurs, business tax may be imposed. The Notice also provides a definition for finance leasing that emphasizes the lessee's influence over the lessor in the purchase of the leased equipment and the lessee's option to acquire the title to the equipment when the lease term expires.

2. Financial Institutions

In July of 2000, the SAT issued a notice that provides that the offshore banking businesses of foreign-investment financial institutions fall under the category of "services provided in China" and are therefore subject to the relevant business taxes.[79] For foreign-investment financial institutions operating in Special Economic Zones, the Notice broadens the scope of preferential tax treatment to include financial services provided to individuals and insurance activities. For financial leasing activities, financial entities may deduct interest expenses only on a loan borrowed from abroad as a cost item from the taxable income in order to calculate the business tax. The Notice also provides that interest expenses on interbank borrowings from an overseas affiliate in which a foreign-invested financial institution has deposits are

78. Notice on the Levying of Turnover Taxes on Finance Leasing (issued on July 7, 2000, by the SAT).

79. Notice on Several Policy Issues Regarding Business Tax Imposed on Foreign Investment Financial Institutions (issued on July 28, 2000, by the SAT, effective on August 1, 2000), *reprinted in* CHINA LAWS FOR FOREIGN BUSINESS (CCH), Taxation ¶ 32-627.

not deductible from the interest income if the institution re-lends the relevant amount to borrowers.

On April 25, 2001, the Ministry of Finance and the SAT issued a notice that terminates the business tax incentive given to foreign-investment institutions and branches of foreign financial institutions under previous rules adopted in 1997.[80] The 1997 rules provided foreign-investment financial institutions and branches of foreign financial institutions that are established in the Special Economic Zones (including the Shanghai Pudong and Suzhou Industrial Park) with an eight-percent business tax exemption for five years on their business income. While the new 2001 Notice is designed to level the playing field between foreign and domestic enterprises, enterprises granted the tax exemption under the 1997 rule are entitled to continue to enjoy the same exemptions.

3. Insurance Operations

In 2001, the Ministry of Finance and the SAT issued an order that provides that certain insurance companies and insurance products are exempt from business tax.[81] This exemption applied to general life insurance policies (with terms of one year or more that return the principal and the interest to the insured), pension fund insurance, and health insurance (with terms of one year or more). Furthermore, only insurance policies that are approved by the SAT and Ministry of Finance are entitled to business tax exemption. (The circular lists all categories of insurance that are eligible for exemption.) For new forms of insurance, insurance companies must first pay the taxes before applying to the appropriate tax bureau for an exemption. Upon such approval, the paid business tax can either be credited toward future tax payments or be refunded.

4. Energy and Communication Industries

On July 2, 1999, the State Council issued the *Notice of the State Council on Expanding the Scope of Application of the Regulations on Preferential Tax Treatments for Foreign Investment Enterprises Engaged in Energy and Communication Infrastructure Projects*.[82] In order to encourage more

80. Notice on Adjusting Business Tax Policies for Foreign Financial Institutions and Financial Institutions with Foreign Investment (issued on April 25, 2001, by the Ministry of Finance and the SAT, effective on May 1, 2001).

81. Circular on Several Questions Regarding the Exemption from Business Tax on Life Insurance Business (issued on August 18, 2001, by the Ministry of Finance and the State Administration of Taxation).

82. Notice of the State Council on Expanding the Scope of Application of the Regulations on Preferential Tax Treatments for Foreign Investment Enterprises Engaged in Energy and Communication Infrastructure Projects (issued on January 1, 1999, by the State Council, effective July 2, 1999).

foreign enterprises to engage in the energy and communications sectors, especially in central or western regions, this Notice expands the scope of preferential tax treatments for such projects. Under Article 73 of the *Detailed Rules of the Implementation of the Income Tax Law of the PRC for FIEs and Foreign Enterprises*, energy- or communications-related production-orientated FIEs established in central regions, western regions, or in old urban areas where Special Economic Zones or Economic and Technical Development Zones are located, may receive a 15-percent reduced income rate. The Notice eliminates these geographic restrictions on the preferential tax treatments. Under the Notice, subject to SAT approval, an FIE may receive the reduced income rate for communications and energy projects anywhere in China.

5. Real Estate

On December 21, 1999, the SAT issued the *Notice on Certain Tax Treatment on FIEs in the Real Estate Business*.[83] According to the Circular, a real estate development FIE that entrusts an overseas enterprise to sell its real estate property located in China should specify its sales income at the price at which the overseas enterprise sells the same property to overseas purchasers in order to calculate the Business Tax and Foreign Enterprise Income Tax. Any commission paid to these overseas enterprises may be deducted from the taxable income if the commission does not exceed ten percent of the total sales income.

6. Venture Capital Operations

To clarify the taxation of foreign investment venture capital enterprises (FIVCE) established inside China, the SAT issued its first ruling on the taxation of FIVCEs in June 2003 (Circular 61).[84] The FIVCE Tax Rules clarify that venture capital firms are not entitled to preferential tax treatment that is intended for production-oriented foreign investment enterprises (FIEs) under the relevant laws and regulations.[85] An FIVCE with legal person status will be taxed as a normal corporation.[86] In situations where the FIVCE

83. Notice on Certain Tax Treatment of FIEs in the Real Estate Business (issued on December 21, 1999, by the SAT, effective on January 1, 2000).

84. Notice of State Administration of Taxation on Tax Collection Issues Relating to Enterprise Income Tax Payable by Foreign-Invested Venture Capital Companies (issued on June 4, 2003, by the State Administration of Taxation), *reprinted in* CHINA LAWS FOR FOREIGN BUSINESS (CCH), Taxation ¶ 32-815 (hereinafter the "FIVCE Tax Rules").

85. FIVCE Tax Rules, art. I.

86. FIVCE Tax Rules, art. II.

is without legal person status (such as a limited liability partnership), the investors may, subject to the approval of tax authorities, elect to be taxed as a corporation at the FIVCE level or separately as individual taxpayers.[87] Although foreign investors of an FIVCE without legal person status may elect to be taxed separately, the benefits of typical partnership taxation, such as flow-through treatment, allocations of gains or losses, etc. will not be available. According to the FIVCE Tax Rules, if a foreign investor to an FIVCE without legal person status elects to be taxed individually, it will be taxed as if it has a permanent establishment in China. However, if an FIVCE is not directly involved in the management of the fund or provision of services and engages other enterprises, such as a venture capital management enterprise (VCME), to conduct venture capital business in China, foreign investors to such type of FIVCEs will not be regarded as having permanent establishments in China.

D. Individual Income Tax

A person residing in China for longer than a year is considered a resident and is liable for tax on his or her income derived inside and outside of China. Individuals who reside for less than one year are considered nonresidents and are liable for tax only on the income derived in China.[88] The expatriate employees or chief representative who works more than 183 days per calendar year in China is subject to China's individual income tax.[89] The

87. FIVCE Tax Rules, art. III.

88. *See* Notice of the State Administration of Taxation on Certain Detailed Issues Concerning the Calculation and Payment of Individual Income Tax by Individuals without Residence in the Territory of China (promulgated on April 3, 1995, by the SAT), *reprinted in* CHINA LAWS FOR FOREIGN BUSINESS (CCH), Taxation ¶ 30-580; Notice of the State Administration of Taxation on Questions Concerning the Obligation to Pay Tax on Income Derived from Wages and Salaries by Individuals without Residence within the Territory of China (promulgated on June 30, 1994, by the SAT), *reprinted in* CHINA LAWS FOR FOREIGN BUSINESS (CCH), Taxation ¶ 30-575; Notice of the State Administration of Taxation on Certain Issues Concerning the Payment of Individual Income Tax by Individuals without Residence within the Territory of China Involving Tax Agreements (promulgated on August 3, 1995, by the SAT), *reprinted in* CHINA LAWS FOR FOREIGN BUSINESS (CCH), Taxation ¶ 30-585; Notice of the Ministry of Finance and the State Administration of Taxation on Issues Concerning the Calculation of the Five-Year Residency Period for Individuals without Residence in China (promulgated on September 16, 1995, by the MOF and the SAT), *reprinted in* CHINA LAWS FOR FOREIGN BUSINESS (CCH), Taxation ¶ 30-590 (addresses the five-year rule on determining residency for purposes of Chinese income tax).

89. Individual Income Tax Law of the People's Republic of China (adopted September 10, 1980, at the 3rd Sess. of the 5th NPC, amended October 31, 1993, at the 4th Sess. of the Standing Comm. of the 8th NPC, and amended on August 30, 1999, by the 11th Sess. of the Standing Comm. of the 9th NPC), *reprinted in* CHINA LAWS FOR FOREIGN BUSINESS (CCH), Taxation ¶ 30-500 (hereinafter the "Individual Income Tax Law") (tax rate tables attached to the law); Detailed Rules for the Implementation of the Individual Income Tax Law of the PRC (promulgated January 28, 1994, by the Ministry of Finance), *reprinted in* CHINA LAWS FOR FOREIGN BUSINESS (CCH), Taxation ¶ 30-505 (hereinafter the "Individual Income Tax Rules"); Regulations on Certain Issues Concerning the Levying of Individual Income Tax (promulgated April 6, 1994, by the State Administration of Taxation), *reprinted in* CHINA LAWS FOR

183-day period is derived from a U.S./China tax treaty of January 1, 1987. The PRC law provides only a 90-day period for personnel from countries not subject to tax treaties.[90] The tax rates are in nine different brackets and range from 5 percent to 45 percent depending upon the salary and a number of exemptions that may apply. Taxable income includes wages and salaries; overseas income;[91] income derived from royalties, dividends,[92] interest, and bonuses; income derived from the leasing or assignment of property or land-use rights; and other forms of income paid for labor services.[93] In computing

---

FOREIGN BUSINESS (CCH), Taxation ¶ 30-510 (hereinafter the "Individual Income Tax Regulations"). *See generally* Gensler, *The 1994 Individual Income Tax Law of the People's Republic of China,* 26 CAL. W. INT'L L.J. 115 (1995). *See also* Provisional Measures on the Personal Lodging of Individual Income Tax (promulgated on May 26, 1995, by the SAT), *reprinted in* CHINA LAWS FOR FOREIGN BUSINESS (CCH), Taxation ¶ 30-565 (outlines obligations of individual taxpayers to file tax returns).

90. Individual Income Tax Rules, art. 7. The PRC has entered into over 80 tax treaties with various governments worldwide and, where applicable, the treaties should be consulted for purposes of determining any potential benefits in any given situation where investors have multinational operations.

91. Provisional Administrative Measures on the Levy and Collection of Individual Income Tax on Overseas Income (issued on August 11, 1998, by the SAT), *reprinted in* CHINA LAWS FOR FOREIGN BUSINESS (CCH), Taxation ¶ 30-566 (outlines requirements for payment of tax on overseas-generated income from various sources).

92. Notice of the State Administration of Taxation Concerning Taxation of Income from Stock (Share Rights) Transactions and Dividends Received by Foreign Investment Enterprises, Foreign Enterprises, and Foreign Nationals (issued on July 21, 1993, by the SAT), *reprinted in* CHINA LAWS FOR FOREIGN BUSINESS (CCH), Taxation ¶ 32-706.

93. Individual Income Tax Law, art. 2. Income derived from stock options may be subject to taxation. On March 17, 2000, the SAT issued the *Notice on the Determination of Tax Liabilities of Non-Residents on their Salary and Wage Income Received in the Form of Stock* (issued on March 17, 2000, by the SAT, effective as of date of issue). This notice addresses the income tax obligation of individuals who receive stock options as a result of performance, both within and outside of China, for the respective offices of the same firm. According to the notice, if an individual receives income on such stock options and part of the income is attributable to work performed outside of China, then that part of the income may be excluded from taxable income. Likewise, if an individual receives such income during his or her stay outside of China and part of the income is attributable to work performed in China, this portion is considered a China-source income. Income on savings deposits is also subject to taxation. *See* Implementing Measures for Levying Individual Income Tax on Interest from Savings Deposits (issued on September 30, 1999, by the State Council, effective on November 1, 1999). These Measures specify that "interest on savings deposits" is no longer exempt from income taxes as it had been under Article 4 of the *Individual Income Tax Law of the People's Republic of China.* After the implementation of these Measures, individuals who earn interest income on renminbi or foreign currency savings with savings deposit entities in the PRC are required to pay a 20-percent tax on such income. The savings deposit entity has the authority to withhold and pay due taxes and collect a service fee equaling 2 percent of the withheld tax. Certain savings accounts, such as those for education, may be exempt from such income taxes. Also, on October 25, 1999, the SAT issued the *Notice on Issues Regarding Individual Income Tax on Interest from Savings Deposits of Foreign Nationals and Residents of Hong Kong, Macao, and Taiwan.* Under this notice, foreign nationals residing in such regions may enjoy the preferential tax treatments on interest income that are stipulated in the applicable tax treaty. (Such treaties are attached to the notice as an appendix.) In order to qualify for such tax rates, a foreign national must submit an *Application Form for a Foreign Resident to Enjoy the Treatment Provided by the Avoidance of Double Taxation Treaty.* Foreign nationals of countries that have not entered into tax treaties with China, Taiwan, Hong Kong, or Macao may be subject to a 20-percent income tax rate on income generated by savings deposits. Implementing Measures for Levying Individual Income Tax on Interest from Savings Deposits (issued on September 30, 1999, by the State Council, effective on November 1, 1999). Bonuses may also be subject to individual income tax. In this regard, on May 4, 1999, the SAT issued the *Circular Regarding the Issue of Determining the Tax Obligation of Individuals without Domicile within the Boundaries of China for Their Bonuses Obtained During the Period of Working outside China* (issued on May 4, 1999, by the SAT, effective as of the date of issue). This Circular pertains to individuals who work

taxable income, a basic monthly deduction of RMB800 is allowed by citizens and RMB3200 is allowed for foreigners.[94] Chinese law also provides that, subject to certain conditions, reasonable allowances for housing, food, laundry services, business travel expenses, home leave travel expenses, educational expenses for children, language training fees, and relocation expenses are exempt from individual income tax.[95] An FIE, as a statutory withholding agent, is required to withhold the individual income tax on wages and other income paid to its employees.[96]

In May 1999, the State Administration on Taxation issued a notice that provides that the salaries of directors or partners who hold two or more titles or positions in entities established in China by foreign companies shall be considered a PRC source of taxable revenue.[97] Such persons are responsible for PRC personal income taxes. Such individuals are taxed according

---

concurrently in both the Chinese and foreign offices of the same firm. Bonuses, which are earned by such individuals during the months that the individual is working in the non-Chinese office, are not considered taxable income. However, if the individual works in China for any portion of a given month, then all accrued bonuses of that month are subject to income taxation. *Circular Regarding the Issue of Tax Levy on Bonus Obtained by Individuals without Domicile in China* (issued on October 14, 1996, by the SAT).

94. Individual Income Tax Law, art. 6; Individual Income Tax Rules, art. 28.

95. *See* Notice of the State Administration of Taxation on Issues Concerning the Implementation of an Individual Income Tax Levy or Exemption on Allowances of Foreign Individuals (promulgated on April 9, 1997, by the State Administration of Taxation), *reprinted in* China Laws for Foreign Business (CCH), Taxation ¶ 30-605 (outlines standards for various exemptions and allowances for FIEs). *See also* Notice on the Implementing Standards for the Exemption of Home Leave Expenses of Expatriate Employees from Individual Income Tax (issued on May 4, 2001, by the SAT) (allows for exemption of reasonable home leave expenses for two home leaves per year for employees and family). *See also* Notice on Relevant Income Tax Issues Concerning Overseas Insurance Premiums of Foreign Investment Enterprises and Employees of Foreign Enterprises (issued on June 26, 1998, by the SAT), *reprinted in* China Laws for Foreign Business (CCH), Taxation ¶ 32-744 (addresses tax treatment of health and insurance benefits and premiums); Notice of the State Administration of Taxation on the Handling of Tax Questions Concerning the Drawing, Expenditure and Use of Housing Accumulation Funds by Foreign Investment Enterprises and their Employees (promulgated on July 26, 1994, by the SAT), *reprinted in* China Laws for Foreign Business (CCH), Taxation ¶ 30-560 (tax treatment of housing allowances by FIEs).

96. *See* Provisional Measures on Withholding Individual Income Tax (promulgated on April 6, 1995, by the SAT), *reprinted in* China Laws for Foreign Business (CCH), Taxation ¶ 30-570 (hereinafter the "Tax Withholding Measures"). The Tax Withholding Measures also require an FIE to withhold income tax on other items of income issued to individuals including royalties, leasing income, bonuses, and dividends, as well as wages and salaries. *See also* Notice on Relevant Issues Concerning the Strengthening of the Administration of Withholding Income Tax of Foreign Enterprises (issued on May 29, 1998, by the State Administration of Taxation), *reprinted in* China Laws for Foreign Business (CCH), Taxation ¶ 32-711. The SAT issued the *Notice on the Withholding Obligations of FIEs on the Salaries and Wages of Individuals Paid by Overseas Enterprises* (issued on December 21, 1999, by the SAT, effective on January 1, 2000). The FIE Withholding Notice clarifies the obligations of FIEs to withhold the individual income tax of their employees if such employees receive their salaries and wages from both the FIE and a foreign enterprise. FIEs are obligated to withhold and pay individual income taxes for its employees, even for the portion of the salaries and wages paid by overseas associated enterprises. *See also* Notice of the State Administration of Taxation on Issues Concerning the Calculation and Levying of Individual Income Tax Borne by Employers on Behalf of Employees (promulgated on November 8, 1996, by the SAT), *reprinted in* China Laws for Foreign Business (CCH), Taxation ¶ 30-595 (addresses tax issues related to tax payments paid in part by the employer).

97. Notice on Tax Issues Concerning Directors of Foreign Companies Who Hold Concurrent Positions in China (issued on May 17, 1999, by the State Administration on Taxation).

to Articles 2 and 3 of the *Notice of the SAT on Issues Concerning the Levying and Collection of Personal Income Tax on Directors of Foreign-Invested Companies that Hold Direct Management Positions.*[98] Under this notice, tax authorities may calculate monthly wage and salary by referring to the salary levels of similar positions in enterprises in similar areas and industries.

The laws of China, consistent with international norms, levy tax on the individual income of partners rather than at the partnership level.[99] The Partnership Tax Notice specifically deals with the issue of double taxation on proprietorship and partnership enterprises. Under the Partnership Tax Notice, the enterprise level in proprietorships or partnerships is not held responsible for the tax burdens of the firm. Rather, the investors of proprietorships and partners of partnerships are responsible for the tax burden of the enterprise. The tax liability of such individuals ranges from 5 percent to 35 percent of income. Either of the two methods, the actual method or deemed method, may be used in determining the taxable income of such individuals depending on the complexity of the proprietorship or partnership accounting structure. The Notice also provides a list of pretax non-deductible items (for enterprises using the actual method) and a table of deemed profit rates for different trade and industries (for enterprises adopting the deemed method).

E. Tax Issues for Representative Offices

If a representative office stays within the confines of the law and does not engage in any profit-making activity, the RO is not liable for turnover tax (VAT and business tax) or the foreign enterprise tax.[100] If the RO performs

98. Notice of the State Administration of Taxation on Issues Concerning the Levying and Collection of Individual Income Tax on Directors of Foreign Investment Enterprises Who Directly Hold Administrative Positions (promulgated on November 21, 1996, by the SAT), *reprinted in* CHINA LAWS FOR FOREIGN BUSINESS (CCH), Taxation ¶ 30-600.

99. Notice on the Levying of Individual Income Tax on Investors in Proprietorship and Partnership Enterprises (issued on September 19, 2000, by the Ministry of Finance and the SAT, effective on January 1, 2001) (hereinafter the "Partnership Tax Notice").

100. Notice of the State Administration of Taxation on Certain Detailed Issues Concerning Tax Levies on Foreign Enterprise Resident Representative Offices (promulgated on January 2, 1997, by the SAT), *reprinted in* CHINA LAWS FOR FOREIGN BUSINESS (CCH), Taxation ¶ 32-762. *See* Zhang, *Taxation on Resident Representative Offices of Foreign Businesses,* 134 China International Business (MOFTEC) 47 (1998). *See* Notice on the Explanation of the Issue Whether Representative Offices of Foreign Companies Constitute Permanent Establishments under Tax Treaties (issued on September 13, 1999, by the SAT, effective as of the date of issue), *reprinted in* CHINA LAWS FOR FOREIGN BUSINESS (CCH), Taxation ¶ 32-760 (clarifies role of local tax authorities in making determination of permanent establishments under treaty obligations); Tax Administration Issues Relevant to Resident Representative Offices of Foreign Enterprises (issued on March 12, 2003, by the State Administration of Taxation). *See generally* I. Chan, *Re-evaluating Tax Assessment for Representative Offices,* CHINA L. & PRAC. (Sept. 2003). *See also* Notice of the State Bureau of Taxation Exempting Certain Expenses Advanced by Foreign Enterprise

preparatory and liaison services only for and on behalf of its immediate head office, the RO may be exempt from taxation. The term "immediate head office" has a very narrow definition and refers to the legal entity that directly owns the RO in China, excluding affiliate companies.[101]

To maintain the tax-exempt status, it is necessary to restrict the functions of the RO. In addition, the RO must not be directly involved in the negotiation or conclusion of the contracts of the company. An RO's local personnel must be instructed not to negotiate prices and other contractual terms. If the RO acts as an agent or a consultant and receives commissions, service fees, etc., it is liable for taxes on such income. If the RO provides after-sales services and charges for those services, such income is taxable.

It is the general practice of the tax authorities in China to impose a tax on representative offices of foreign companies on a cost-plus basis; namely, 10 percent of all costs to operate an RO is collected as a tax.[102] To further comply with WTO principles and respond to the complaints by foreign companies, on March 12, 2003, the State Administration of Taxation (SAT) issued the Circular on the Tax Administration Issues Relevant to Representative Offices of Foreign Enterprises (Guo Shui Fa (2003) No. 28). The purpose of the circular is to clarify the different tax treatments for different types of ROs and the relevant implementing procedures provided in the past SAT regulations. Under the new circular, ROs providing professional services, such as law firms or accounting firms, are required to pay taxes on the income actually

---

Resident Representative Offices on Behalf of Their Head Offices from Inclusion as Resident Representative Office Expenditure for Income Tax Calculation Purposes (promulgated on December 12, 1988, by the State Bureau of Taxation), *reprinted in* CHINA LAWS FOR FOREIGN BUSINESS (CCH), Taxation ¶ 32-665 (outlines certain exempt expenses from income tax calculation); Notice of the State Administration of Taxation on Issues Concerning Improvement of Taxation Collection Administration for Foreign Enterprise Resident Representative Offices (issued on September 13, 1996, by the SAT), *reprinted in* CHINA LAWS FOR FOREIGN BUSINESS (CCH), Taxation ¶ 32-671 (outlines the types of activities of rep offices exempt from taxation and tax collection procedures for rep offices); Notice on Certain Issues Concerning Tax Handling in Respect of Resident Representative Offices of Foreign Enterprises (issued on April 30, 1998, by the SAT), *reprinted in* CHINA LAWS FOR FOREIGN BUSINESS (CCH), Taxation ¶ 32-674 (addresses tax issues for expenditures on fixed assets, charitable donations, etc. for rep. offices).

101. The taxation authorities sometimes use a taxation method based upon office expenses for ROs that engage in profit-making activities. An RO may compute its tax based on either actual revenues and profits derived from activities in China or based on the cost of operating the RO, which is referred to as the "cost-plus" method. The tax authorities use a "deemed revenue" formula of 117.5% of the RO's expenses, and then imposes an income tax of 33% on the deemed profit, which is calculated as 10% of the "deemed revenue" of the operation. *See* Tax Administration Issues Relevant to Resident Representative Offices of Foreign Enterprise Circular (issued on March 12, 2003, by the State Administration of Taxation).

102. Circular on Taxation Methods for Representative Offices of Foreign Enterprises jointly issued by the Ministry of Finance and the State Administration of Taxation (1985), Caishuiwaizi No. 200; Circular Regarding Determination of the Taxation Methods for Representative Offices jointly issued by the Ministry of Finance and the State Administration of Taxation (1986), Caishuiwaizi No. 055; Circular Regarding the Reduction of Verified Profit Rates for Representative Offices of Foreign Enterprises Issued by the Ministry of Finance (1986), Caishuiwaizi No. 290; Circular Regarding Strengthening the Administration of Taxation on Representative Offices of Foreign Enterprises Issued by the State Administration of Taxation, Guoshuifa (1996) No. 165.

earned in accordance with the applicable tax accounting principles. For ROs engaging in agency or trading business, the cost-plus taxation method may be used and thereby disregard that the RO is actually generating any revenue.

The RO is also required to act as an income tax withholding agent if it pays its local Chinese employees wages, salaries, and various types of subsidies, allowances, or bonuses.[103] The RO is required to establish an individual income tax account book and each month lodge a monthly income adjustment tax declaration form with the local taxation authorities. By the tenth day of each month, the RO is required to file the declaration form for the previous month and to pay tax withheld based upon the progressive tax rate on income.[104] The taxation authorities provide the RO with a commission of 3 percent of the tax withheld and tendered. The RO can be penalized if it fails or refuses to comply with the withholding requirements.[105] A representative office is subject to inspection by the State Administration of Taxation and its local bureaus.[106]

F. Other Applicable Taxes

In addition to the income and turnover taxes, the PRC tax laws[107] applicable to FIEs include the resource tax,[108] urban real estate

103. *See* Tax Withholding Measures, art. 2. Notice on the Question of Levying Individual Income Adjustment Tax on Remuneration Paid to Chinese Employees by the Beijing Resident Representative Offices of Foreign Enterprises (issued February 2, 1991, by the Foreign Taxation Branch of the Beijing Municipal Taxation Bureau), *reprinted in* CHINA LAWS FOR FOREIGN BUSINESS (CCH), Taxation ¶ 30-527 (the "Beijing RO Tax Withholding Rules"). *See also* Provisional Measures of Guangdong Province on Withholding Individual Income Tax (promulgated on June 1, 1995, by the Guangdong Provincial People's Government), *reprinted in* CHINA LAWS FOR FOREIGN BUSINESS (CCH), Special Zones & Cities ¶ 270-020.

104. Beijing RO Tax Withholding Rules, arts. 1, 2.

105. Beijing RO Tax Withholding Rules, art. 4.

106. *See* Notice of the State Administration of Taxation on Issues Concerning Taxation Inspections of Foreign Enterprise Resident Representative Offices (promulgated on June 12, 1996, by the SAT), *reprinted in* CHINA LAWS FOR FOREIGN BUSINESS (CCH), Taxation ¶ 32-669 (outlining the procedures for tax audits for ROs). The tax rules for representative offices are available on the Web site of MOFCOM at http://www.mofcom.gov.cn.

107. *See* Notice of the State Administration of Taxation Concerning Applicable Categories of Taxes for Foreign Investment Enterprises, Foreign Enterprises, and Foreign Individuals (promulgated on May 9, 1994, by the SAT), *reprinted in* CHINA LAWS FOR FOREIGN BUSINESS (CCH), Taxation ¶ 32-730 (outlining the tax laws that apply to foreign parties).

108. Provisional Rules of the People's Republic of China on Resource Tax (adopted on November 26, 1993, by the 12th Sess. of the Standing Comm. of the State Council), *reprinted in* CHINA LAWS FOR FOREIGN BUSINESS (CCH), Taxation ¶ 31-774. The resource tax applies to all mining operations that extract mineral resources from the territory of the PRC. The resource tax is based upon a taxation scale and is categorized by the resource type and quality. There are exemptions to the resource tax based upon special uses of the resource materials and in situations where a taxpayer incurs losses due to casualty or other occurrence. *See also* Administrative Measures of the People's Republic of China on Withholding Resource Tax (promulgated on April 15, 1998, by the State Administration of Taxation), *reprinted in* CHINA LAWS FOR FOREIGN BUSINESS (CCH), Taxation ¶ 31-773 (outlines withholding obligations for resource tax); Regulations Concerning the Handling of Resource Tax Accounting (promulgated on February 21, 1994, by the Ministry of Finance), *reprinted in* CHINA LAWS FOR FOREIGN BUSINESS (CCH), Taxation ¶ 35-830.

tax,[109] stamp duty tax,[110] deed tax,[111] customs duties,[112] and vehicle tax and surcharge.[113]

G. Prohibition on Unauthorized Fees Assessed against FIEs

In response to complaints from foreign investors, the State Council issued a circular prohibiting the imposition of unauthorized fees, taxes, and other exactions and allowing FIEs to refuse to pay any fee assessed by a government

109. The urban real estate tax is generally imposed annually based upon the assessed value of real property. The typical tax rates are 1.8% for land and 1.2% for buildings, and certain deductions are allowed in computing the assessed value of the property. *See* Provisional Regulations Governing the Urban Real Estate Tax (promulgated on August 8, 1951, by the Administration Council), *reprinted in* China Laws for Foreign Business (CCH), Taxation ¶ 39-500 (addresses the taxes imposed upon real property, exemptions, and tax rates); Provisional Regulations of the People's Republic of China on Real Estate Tax (issued on September 15, 1986, by the State Council), *reprinted in* China Laws for Foreign Business (CCH), Taxation ¶ 39-505. *See also* Official Response of the State Administration of Taxation on Applicable Urban Real Estate Tax Policies for Buildings Newly Built by Foreign Investment Enterprises (promulgated on January 21, 1997, by the SAT), *reprinted in* China Laws for Foreign Business (CCH), Taxation ¶ 32-778 (limits the exemptions that apply to FIEs that are set forth in the Urban Real Estate Tax Law). The land VAT tax applies to the sale of land and buildings, and the tax rates range from 30–60% of the appreciation value of the real property.

110. *See* Provisional Rules of the People's Republic of China on Stamp Duty (promulgated on August 6, 1988, by the State Council), *reprinted in* China Laws for Foreign Business (CCH), Taxation ¶ 31-712. Stamp duty is a tax on the issuance of certain types of documents such as purchase and sale transactions, property leasing, loan agreements, technology contracts, and other contractual documents and documents of transfer of property title. The stamp duty is based upon the contract amount as follows: purchase and sale contracts (0.03 percent), processing contracts (0.05 percent), engineering and design contracts (0.05 percent), construction contracts (0.03 percent), property leasing contracts (0.01 percent), commodity transportation contracts (0.05 percent), storage contracts (0.01 percent), loan contracts (0.005 percent), insurance contracts (0.003 percent of insured value), and technology contracts (0.05 percent). *See also* Notice on Certain Questions Concerning the Levying and Collection of Stamp Duty from Foreign Investment Enterprises and Foreign Enterprises (promulgated on April 7, 1994, by the SAT), *reprinted in* China Laws for Foreign Business (CCH), Taxation ¶ 32-722. Detailed Rules for Implementing the Provisional Rules of the People's Republic of China on Stamp Duty (promulgated on September 29, 1988, by the Ministry of Finance), *reprinted in* China Laws for Foreign Business (CCH), Taxation ¶ 31-722. The State Council reduced the stamp duty on stock transactions from 0.4 percent to 0.5 percent in June 1998 to encourage investment. *See Stamp Duty Cut Boosts Shares,* China Daily (June 13, 1998), available on Lexis, News Library, or on the Web site of the China Daily at http://www.chinadaily.com.cn.

111. *See* Provisional Rules of the People's Republic of China on Deed Tax (promulgated on July 7, 1997, by the State Council), *reprinted in* China Laws for Foreign Business (CCH), Taxation ¶ 39-640; Detailed Rules for the Provisional Rules of the People's Republic of China on Deed Tax (promulgated on October 28, 1997, by the Ministry of Finance), *reprinted in* China Laws for Foreign Business (CCH), Taxation ¶ 39-648. The deed tax rates range from 3 percent to 5 percent and the deed tax applies to the transfer of land or building ownership rights. A taxpayer may be exempt from the deed tax in certain situations.

112. *See generally* Chapter 15, Customs and Trade Regulation § B.2.d.

113. *See* Measures for the Imposition of a Surcharge on Vehicle Purchases (promulgated on April 2, 1985, by the State Council), *reprinted in* China Laws for Foreign Business (CCH), Taxation ¶ 34-565; Provisional Regulations of the People's Republic of China on Vehicle and Vessel Usage Tax (issued on September 15, 1986, by the State Council), *reprinted in* China Laws for Foreign Business (CCH), Taxation ¶ 34-568; Provisional Regulations Governing the Vehicle and Vessel License Plate Tax (promulgated on September 13, 1951, by the Administrative Council of the Central People's Government), *reprinted in* China Laws for Foreign Business (CCH), Taxation ¶ 34-500.

agency that is unable to produce a valid License for Fee Collection issued by the Ministry of Finance.[114] The circular provides that an FIE will be issued an Enterprise Fee Payment Registration Card and will provide information concerning the fee collected, date and time of fee collection, and information concerning the agency's authorization to collect a fee. If an agency refuses to supply the information on the Card, the FIE is not required to pay the demanded fee.

H. Penalties and Administrative/Judicial Review

Since 1996, the tax authorities have increased their supervision and enforcement capabilities to ensure that both domestic and foreign enterprises are accurately and promptly paying their taxes. The State Administration of Taxation (SAT) conducts ongoing audits of FIEs and, in a special audit of 7,000 FIEs initiated in October of 1996, it discovered that one-third of the representative offices in China failed to register with the tax authorities as required by law. The SAT's 1996 audit resulted in the imposition of delinquent taxes in the sum of $204 million. In 1997, FIEs in China paid over $10 billion in corporate tax, and personal tax for FIE employees equaled $2 billion. China collected a record of $11.3 billion in tariff duties in 1997, an increase of 10.4 percent over 1996. China collected from FIEs $134.3 billion in personal and corporate tax, customs duties, VAT, and consumption taxes in 1997.[115]

114. *See generally* Harpole, *New Developments: Collecting Fees from Foreign Investment Enterprises,* 11 China Law News 16 (May 29, 1998); *Wei: Fines Not Source of Income for Units,* China Daily (May 22, 1998), available on Lexis, News Library, or on the Web site of the China Daily at http://www.chinadaily.com.cn (CCP emphasizes that fees are not to be considered income sources for law enforcement or executive departments).

115. *See generally* Administrative Law of the PRC on the Levying and Collection of Taxes (adopted on September 4, 1992, at the 27th Sess. of the Standing Comm. of the 7th NPC, amended on February 28, 1995, at the 12th Sess. of the Standing Comm. of the 8th NPC, and amended on April 28, 2001, by the Standing Committee of the National People's Congress, effective on May 1, 2001), arts. 37–56, *reprinted in* China Laws for Foreign Business (CCH), Taxation ¶ 39-621 (hereinafter the "Administrative Law on Tax Collection"). The Administrative Law on Tax Collection, as amended, governs tax compliance and collection procedures and addresses issues such as statutes of limitations for tax assessment, liabilities and penalties for noncompliance, tax return filing and audit procedures, and registration requirements. In comparison to the prior version of the law, the 2001 amendments include significant reduction with respect to penalties for late payment (from 73 percent per year to 18 percent per year), a reduction in the maximum statute of limitations from ten years to five years for tax assessments on underpayment due to the taxpayer's mistakes, and a newly introduced concept of refunding bank deposit interest on overpayment if it is discovered within three years. The law also elaborates on the rights and obligations of taxpayers, clarifies the definition of tax evasion, and provides a clearer separation between civil and criminal tax evasion. It also introduces minimum penalties in addition to the penalty ceilings provided in the previous law. In order to facilitate tax compliance, the amended law encourages electronic and postal filing of tax returns. *See generally* M. Moser & W. Zee, China Tax Guide (1993); Sommers & Phillips, *Assessing the Tax Administration Law of the People's Republic of China,* 18 Loy. L.A. Int'l & Comp. L. J. 339 (1996); Curley & Fortunato, *Tax Considerations for Investors in China: A Preliminary Look,* 20 N.C.J. Int'l L. & Com. Reg. 531 (1995).

The SAT has also reported that expatriate employees, many who worked in China full-time and more than 180 days a year, failed to register with the local tax bureaus or falsely claimed that they had no taxable income. In response, the SAT issued regulations providing that foreigners who fail to pay income taxes are prohibited from exiting China, except for taxpayers that tender a bond or monetary guarantee to cover the tax payment or in the event that they are discharged through bankruptcy proceedings.[116] In June 1998, the SAT initiated another nationwide audit to evaluate the scope and extent of tax evasion by FIEs.[117] In the same month, the NPC Standing Committee requested that the Ministry of Finance and the SAT revise the taxation laws to improve enforcement and the collection of revenue. Following its entry into WTO in 2001, and specifically as a result of China's commitment to reduce import tariffs, the tax authorities have increased their collection efforts to make up for the revenue shortfall.

A taxpayer that violates the tax laws, including a failure to register with the tax authorities, a failure to file tax returns and supporting documentation, a failure to report income, or overstating expenses, or engages in any other acts deemed to be a violation of the tax laws is subject to monetary and administrative penalties and, in serious cases, criminal penalties.[118] A taxpayer that is affected by a decision of the tax authorities has a right to seek administrative review of a decision, and has the opportunity to petition the people's court for judicial relief.[119] A request for judicial review

116. *See Record of Events (January–March 1997),* China Law 103 (1997). The Beijing Municipal Taxation Bureau pays informants a cash reward to report tax evaders. *See Cash Rewards Offered in Crackdown of Tax Dodgers,* South China Morning Post, p. 12 (October 28, 1997), available in Lexis, News Library, SCHINA File. *See also* Administrative Law on Tax Collection, art. 28 (authorization of the tax authorities to request the detention of a person that fails to pay tax obligations).

117. Tong, *State Launches National Check on Tax Evasion,* China Daily (June 2, 1998), available on Lexis, News Library, or on the Web site of the China Daily at http://www.chinadaily.com.cn.

118. Administrative Law on Tax Collection, art. 37. *See also* Supplementary Regulations of the Standing Committee of the NPC on Punishment for Tax Evasion and Refusal to Pay Tax (adopted on September 4, 1992, by the 27th Sess. of the Standing Comm. of the 7th NPC), *reprinted in* China Laws for Foreign Business (CCH), Taxation ¶ 39-610. *Revision of Taxation Law Urged to be Speeded Up,* China Daily (June 12, 1998), available on Lexis, News Library, or on the Web site of the China Daily at http://www.chinadaily.com.cn. *See also Death Penalties,* China Daily (April 23, 1998), available on Lexis, News Library, or on the Web site of the China Daily at http://www.chinadaily.com.cn.

119. Administrative Law on Tax Collection, art. 56. *See also* Official Response of the State Administration of Taxation on Issues Concerning Taxation Review Conditions (promulgated on August 4, 1997, by the State Administration of Taxation), *reprinted in* China Laws for Foreign Business (CCH), Taxation ¶ 39-644 (outlining extensions of time for appeals and conditions for appeal). *See* Trial Rules for Taxation Administrative Reviews (issued on September 23, 1999, by the SAT, effective on October 1, 1999) (hereinafter the "Tax Administrative Review Rules"). The Trial Rules are issued in anticipation of the issuance of the *Administrative Review Law of the PRC,* which was implemented on October 1, 1999, to replace the 1993 *Rules for Taxation Administrative Reviews.* The rules provide taxpayers with guidelines and procedural remedies in the event of a dispute with the tax authorities. The Tax Administrative Review Rules discuss the scope and jurisdiction of administrative reviews, application procedures, acceptance of applications, and review rulings, and contain several provisions that were not contained in the 1993 rules. For example, the respondent (e.g., the tax authority) is prohibited from collecting evidence from the applicant taxpayer during the review process.

must be filed with the people's court within fifteen days of receipt of the final decision.[120]

In October 2002, the State Council issued rules increasing the enforcement powers of the State Adminstration of Taxation.[121] Under the 2002 Tax Enforcement Rules, the SAT may disclose certain information on delinquent taxpayers in the media, and may recover overdue taxes by freezing bank accounts or selling the taxpayers' properties. The SAT is also empowered to reward informants or whistleblowers for information concerning tax evasion and other violations of the law.

The 2002 Tax Enforcement Rules set new obligations for taxpayers. Specifically, the rules require taxpayers to report all bank account numbers within a specified period from account opening and are to file tax returns regardless of whether any tax is payable. The 2002 Tax Enforcement Rules further require taxpayers to notify the SAT prior to any dissolution, bankruptcy, or intended disposition of assets if the taxpayer owes more than RMB50,000.

The 2002 Tax Enforcement Rules contain a number of new information-sharing provisions. A commercial bank may not open a bank account for those who fail to obtain a tax registration certificate. A financial institution may be fined between RMB2,000 and RMB50,000 for failure to record the tax registration certificate number on a taxpayer's account. Withholding agents are required to report to the tax authorities if a taxpayer refuses to allow withholding taxes.

The new rules clarify the parties responsible for payment of unpaid taxes. A legal representative of a corporate taxpayer may be detained and prevented from leaving China if taxes or late fees have not been paid or a guarantee/security provided. If a taxpayer fails to pay tax or pays less than the amount payable because a tax agent violates tax collection laws and regulations, a fine of between fifty percent (50%) and not more than three times the amount of overdue tax may be imposed on the tax agent. Transfer pricing enforcement will be augmented, as the tax authorities may adjust the tax payable amount on taxpayers that have structured related transactions that are not carried out on an arm's-length basis.

---

120. In the first five years since the Administrative Law on Tax Collection was adopted, the people's courts have tried 5,917 cases of tax evasion, administratively punished 6 million tax evaders, and sentenced 4,241 individuals to prison terms for violating the tax laws. *See Tax Crimes*, CHINA DAILY (June 13, 1998), available on Lexis, News Library, or on the Web site of the CHINA DAILY at http://www.chinadaily.com.cn.

121. Administration of the Levy and Collection of Taxes Law Implementing Rules (promulgated and effective on October 15, 2002, by the State Council).

A fine of RMB2,000 to RMB50,000 may be imposed on a taxpayer who illegally prints, transfers, trades, alters, or falsifies tax payment receipts. A fine of RMB10,000 or less (or up to RMB50,000 in serious circumstances) may be imposed on a taxpayer that evades, refuses, or obstructs a tax investigation.

Key Laws and Regulations

Value-Added Tax

Decision of the Standing Committee of the NPC Concerning the Application of Provisional Rules on Value-Added Tax, Consumption Tax and Business Tax for Foreign Investment Enterprises and Foreign Enterprises (Decree No. 18 of the Chairman of the PRC, promulgated December 29, 1993, by the 5th Sess. of the Standing Comm. of the 8th NPC)

Provisional Rules of the People's Republic of China on Value-Added Tax (adopted November 26, 1993, by the 12th Sess. of the Standing Committee of the State Council)

Detailed Rules for the Implementation of the Provisional Rules of the People's Republic of China on Value-Added Tax (promulgated December 25, 1993, by the Ministry of Finance)

Regulations on Certain Detailed Issues Concerning Value-Added Tax (promulgated December 28, 1993, by the State Administration of Taxation)

Notice of the State Administration of Taxation on Questions Concerning the Administration of the Levying and Collection of Taxes related to the Implementation of Value-Added Tax for Foreign Investment Enterprises and Foreign Enterprises (issued December 6, 1993, by the State Administration of Taxation)

Regulations Concerning the Handling of Value-Added Tax Accounting (promulgated on December 27, 1993, by the Ministry of Finance)

Provisional Rules of the People's Republic of China on Land Value-Added Tax (adopted November 26, 1993, by the 12th Sess. of the Standing Comm. of the State Council and promulgated by the State Council on December 13, 1993)

Detailed Rules for the Implementation of the Provisional Rules of the People's Republic of China on Land Value-Added Tax (promulgated on January 27, 1995, by the Ministry of Finance)

Notice of the Ministry of Finance and the State Administration of Taxation on Regulations on Certain Detailed Issues Concerning Land Value-Added Tax (promulgated on May 25, 1995, by the Ministry of Finance and State Administration of Taxation)

Notice of the State Administration of Taxation on Questions Concerning the Payment of Value-Added Tax by Sino-Foreign Cooperative Petroleum Exploration

(*Continued*)

(*Continued from previous page*)

Enterprises (promulgated April 28, 1994, by the State Administration of Taxation)

Notice on Questions Concerning the Levying of Value-Added Tax on Sales of Goods Imported Duty-Free (promulgated on March 15, 1994, by the State Administration of Taxation)

Notice of the Ministry of Finance and the State Administration of Taxation on Tax Questions Concerning Export Commodities of Foreign Investment Enterprise (promulgated on August 25, 1994, by the Ministry of Finance and the State Administration of Taxation)

Regulations on the Use of Special Value-Added Tax Invoices (promulgated December 28, 1993, by the State Administration of Taxation)

Notice on Issues Concerning the Use of Special Value-Added Tax Invoices (promulgated February 14, 1994, by the State Administration of Taxation)

Supplementary Notice on Issues Concerning the Use of Special Value-Added Tax Invoices (promulgated February 25, 1994, by the State Administration of Taxation)

Notice of the State Administration of Taxation on the Issuing of the "Measures for Auditing and Inspection of Special VAT Invoices and Other Documents for Tax Calculation and Tax Deduction" (promulgated March 24, 1995, by the State Administration of Taxation)

Notice of the State Administration of Taxation on Issues Concerning the Completion and Issue of Special Value-Added Tax Invoices (promulgated on September 18, 1996, by the State Administration of Taxation)

Measures on Annual Inspection of General Payers of Value-Added Tax (promulgated on March 17, 1998, by the State Administration of Taxation)

Notice of the Ministry of Finance and the State Administration of Taxation on Strengthening the Administration of the Levy and Collection of Business-Linked Value-Added Tax (promulgated on January 9, 1998, by the Ministry of Finance and the State Administration of Taxation)

Notice on Certain Questions Concerning the Levying and Collection of Value-Added Tax (promulgated on May 7, 1994, by the State Administration of Taxation)

Notice of the State Administration of Taxation on the Issuing of the "Measures for Auditing and Inspection of Special VAT Invoices and other Documents for Tax Calculation and Tax Deduction (Trial Implementation)" (promulgated on March 24, 1995, by the State Administration of Taxation)

Consumption Tax

Provisional Rules of the People's Republic of China on Consumption Tax (adopted November 26, 1993, by the 12th Sess. of the Standing Comm. of the State Council and promulgated on December 13, 1993, by the State Council)

(*Continued*)

(Continued from previous page)

Detailed Rules for the Implementation of the Provisional Rules of the People's Republic of China on Consumption Tax (promulgated on December 25, 1993, by the Ministry of Finance)

Regulations on Certain Detailed Issues Concerning Consumption Tax (promulgated on December 28, 1993, by the State Administration of Taxation)

Notice of the State Administration of Taxation on Certain Issues Concerning the Levy of Consumption Tax (promulgated on May 21, 1997, by the State Administration of Taxation)

Regulations Concerning the Handling of Consumption Tax Accounting (promulgated on December 27, 1993, by the Ministry of Finance)

Notice on Adjusting the Consumption Tax Policies on Tobacco Products (issued on June 4, 2001, by the Ministry of Finance and the State Administration of Taxation)

Notice on Adjusting the Consumption Tax Policies on Liquor Products (issued on May 11, 2001, by the Ministry of Finance and State Administration of Taxation)

Notice of the General Administration of Customs on Certain Questions Concerning the Levying and Collection of Value-Added Tax and Consumption Tax on Imported Goods (promulgated on December 25, 1993, by the General Administration of Customs)

Business Tax

Provisional Rules of the People's Republic of China on Business Tax (adopted November 26, 1993, by the 12th Sess. of the Standing Comm. of the State Council)

Detailed Rules for the Implementation of the Provisional Rules of the People's Republic of China on Business Tax (promulgated December 25, 1993, by the Ministry of Finance)

Regulations Concerning the Handling of Business Tax Accounting (promulgated on December 27, 1993, by the Ministry of Finance)

Notice of the Ministry of Finance and the State Administration of Taxation on Relevant Issues Concerning the Levying and Collection of Business Tax on the Finance Industry (promulgated on August 11, 1995, by the Ministry of Finance and State Administration of Taxation)

Notice of the State Administration of Taxation on the Issue of Whether Business Tax Should be Levied on Interest and Rental Income Derived by Foreign Enterprises Within the Territory of China (promulgated on March 14, 1997, by the State Administration of Taxation)

(Continued)

(*Continued from previous page*)

Enterprise Income Tax

Income Tax Law of the People's Republic of China for Enterprises with Foreign Investment and Foreign Enterprises (promulgated on April 9, 1991, by the 4th Sess. of the 7th NPC)

Detailed Rules for the Implementation of the Income Tax Law of the People's Republic of China for Foreign Investment Enterprises and Foreign Enterprises (promulgated June 30, 1991, by the State Council)

Provisional Rules of the People's Republic of China on Enterprise Income Tax (promulgated on December 13, 1993, by the State Council)

Detailed Rules for the Implementation of the Provisional Rules of the People's Republic of China on Enterprise Income Tax (promulgated on February 4, 1994, by the Ministry of Finance)

Regulation on Certain Policy Issues Concerning Enterprise Income Tax (promulgated on May 13, 1994, by the Ministry of Finance and the State Administration of Taxation)

Notice of the Ministry of Finance and the State Administration of Taxation on Several Detailed Issues Concerning Enterprise Income Tax (promulgated on November 1, 1996, by the Ministry of Finance and the State Administration of Taxation)

Notice of the State Administration of Taxation on Issues Concerning Applicable Income Tax Rate for the Branch Organizations of Foreign Investment Enterprises (promulgated on April 9, 1997, by the State Administration of Taxation)

Notice of State Administration of Taxation on the Printing and Distribution of Revised Working Rules and Procedures of Income Tax Calculation and Settlement for Foreign Investment Enterprises and Foreign Enterprises (issued on February 8, 2003, by the State Administration of Taxation)

Notice on Issues Concerning the Handling of Taxation With Respect to Foreign Investment Enterprises with Foreign Enterprises Engaged in Consulting Business (issued on May 12, 2000, by the State Administration of Taxation)

Notice of the State Administration of Taxation on Issues Relating to Tax Treatment for Provision of Services by Foreign-Funded Investment Companies to Subsidiary Companies (promulgated on September 28, 2002, by the State Administration of Taxation)

Notice of the State Administration of Taxation Concerning Taxation of Income from Stock (Share Rights) Transactions and Dividends Received by Foreign Investment Enterprises, Foreign Enterprises, and Foreign Nationals (issued on July 21, 1993, by the State Administration of Taxation)

Notice of the Ministry of Finance and the State Administration of Taxation on the Promulgation of the Provisional Measures for the Calculation and Levy of Income Tax on Income Derived Outside China (Revised Version) (promulgated on November 25, 1997, by the Ministry of Finance and the State Administration of Taxation)

(*Continued*)

(Continued from previous page)

Administrative Measures on the Examination and Verification of the Loss Recovery of Enterprise Income Tax Before Tax (promulgated on December 16, 1997, by the State Administration of Taxation)

Administrative Measures on Enterprise Property Loss Deductions before Tax (promulgated on December 16, 1997, by the State Administration of Taxation)

Management Rules on Taxation Registration (promulgated on December 17, 2003, by the State Administration of Taxation)

Notice of the State Administration of Taxation on the Printing and Distribution of the Administrative Measures on Income Tax Calculation and Clearance Payments for Foreign Investment Enterprises and Foreign Enterprises (promulgated on June 20, 1997, by the State Administration of Taxation)

Notice of the State Administration of Taxation Regarding the Printing and Distributing of Enterprise Income Tax Returns (promulgated on May 27, 1994, by the State Administration of Taxation)

Regulations on Tax Policies for State High-Tech Development Zones (approved March 6, 1991, by the State Council)

Notice on Certain Issues Concerning the Implementation of the Income Tax Law for Enterprises with Foreign Investment and Foreign Enterprises (issued on August 21, 2000, by the State Administration of Taxation)

Notice on Relevant Issues Concerning Implementing Tax Exemption, Offset and Refund Policies for Foreign Investment Enterprises (issued on July 15, 1998, by the State Administration of Taxation)

Notice on Issues Relating to Enterprise Income Tax Refunds for Reinvestment by Foreign Investors (issued on July 17, 2002, by the State Administration of Taxation)

Notice of the State Bureau of Taxation Concerning Several Questions on Tax Refunds for Funds Reinvested by Foreign Investors in Foreign Investment Enterprises (issued on June 15, 1993, by the State Administration of Taxation)

Notice of the State Administration of Taxation on Questions Concerning the Determination of the First Profit-Making Year and Calculation of the Period of Reduction of and Exemption from Taxes for Foreign Investment Enterprises (promulgated on June 28, 1995, by the State Administration of Taxation)

Official Response of the State Administration of Taxation on Relevant Issues Concerning Tax Refunds on Funds Reinvested by Foreign Investment Enterprises (promulgated on April 3, 1995, by the State Administration of Taxation)

Official Response of the State Administration of Taxation on Relevant Issues Concerning Tax Refunds for Reinvestment by Foreign Investors of Foreign Investment Enterprises (promulgated on March 18, 1996, by the State Administration of Taxation)

(Continued)

(*Continued from previous page*)

Notice of the State Administration of Taxation on Relevant Issues Concerning the Levying and Collection of Income Tax From Foreign Investment Enterprises which Engage in Real Estate Development Operations (promulgated on August 3, 1995, by the State Administration of Taxation)

Notice of the State Administration of Taxation on Questions Concerning the Application of Preferential Tax Treatment for Foreign Investment Enterprises Which Engage in Special Investment Projects Such as Harbors and Wharves (promulgated on August 4, 1995, by the State Administration of Taxation)

Clarification of Relevant Issues Concerning How Foreign Investment Enterprises May Enjoy the Preferential Tax Treatment of "Double-Intensive Enterprises" (promulgated on July 7, 1995, by the State Administration of Taxation)

Circular on Tax Policies for Further Encouraging Development of Software Industry and IC Industry (adopted by the Ministry of Finance and the State Administration of Taxation, effective from January 1, 2002 to December 31, 2010)

Notice on Relevant Issues Concerning the Implementation of Preferential Income Tax Policies for Software Enterprises and High-Technology Enterprises (issued on May 29, 2003, by the State Administration of Taxation, and effective January 1, 2003)

Reply on the Enjoyment of Preferential Enterprise Income Tax Policies for Technologically Advanced Enterprises by Foreign-Invested Enterprises with Investment in Installments (issued on July 9, 2003, by the State Administration of Taxation)

Regulations on Tax Policies for State High-Tech Development Zones (approved March 6, 1991, by the State Council)

Regulations Concerning the Conditions and Measures for the Identification of High and New Technology Enterprises in the National Development Zones for High and New Technology Industries (promulgated on March 6, 1991, by the State Science and Technology Commission)

Supplementary Notice on Deduction of R&D Expenses from Tax Payable by Foreign Investment Enterprises (issued on June 8, 2001, by the State Administration of Taxation)

Notice on Issues Regarding the Eligibility of Foreign Invested Enterprises for Technology-Intensive and Knowledge-Intensive Preferential Tax Policies (issued on November 7, 2003, by the State Administration of Taxation)

Notice of the State Administration of Taxation on Matters Concerning the Payment of Taxes by Foreign Petroleum Companies Engaged in Cooperative Mining of Petroleum Resources in China (promulgated on March 16, 1995, by the State Administration of Taxation)

(*Continued*)

(*Continued from previous page*)

Notice on Corporate Income Tax Incentives Policies for Additional Investment by Foreign Invested Enterprises (issued on June 1, 2002, by the Ministry of Finance and State Administration of Taxation)

Notice on Issues Relating to Enterprise Income Tax Refunds for Reinvestment by Foreign Investors (issued on July 17, 2002, by the State Administration of Taxation)

Circular on Questions Relating to Reinvestment Refunds to Foreign Investors (issued on July 30, 2001, by the State Administration of Taxation)

Supplementary Notice on Questions Related to Foreign-Invested Enterprises Enjoying Enterprise Income Tax Preferential Policies for Additional Investment (issued on March 28, 2003, by the State Administration of Taxation)

Measures on the Administration of the Offset or Exemption of Enterprise Income Tax for Foreign Investment Enterprises in the Purchase of Domestically Made Equipment (issued on May 18, 2000, by the State Administration of Taxation)

Notice on Relevant Issues Concerning the Offset or Exemption of Enterprise Income Tax for Foreign Investment Enterprises in the Purchase of Domestically Made Equipment (issued on January 14, 2000, by the Ministry of Finance and State Administration of Taxation)

Trial Measures on the Administration of Tax Rebates for the Purchase of Domestically Made Equipment by Foreign Investment Enterprises (promulgated on September 20, 1999, by the State Administration of Taxation)

Circular Concerning Issues Relevant to Strengthening the Administration of the Examination, Approval, Registration, Foreign Exchange Issues, and Taxation of Foreign-Invested Enterprises (jointly issued on December 30, 2002, by the Ministry of Finance, State Administration of Taxation, SAIC, and SAFE)

Provisional Regulations on the Handling of Income Tax on Reorganizations of Foreign Investment Enterprises such as Mergers, Splits, Reorganization of Equity and Asset Transfer (promulgated April 28, 1997, by the State Administration of Taxation)

Notice of the State Administration of Taxation on Tax Collection Issues Relating to Foreign Investment Enterprises and Foreign Enterprises Engaged in Disposal of Financial Assets (issued on January 7, 2003, by the State Administration of Taxation)

Notice of the Ministry of Finance and the State Administration of Taxation on Issues Concerning the Handling of Relevant Income Tax on the Added Value of Enterprise Asset Valuation (promulgated on June 23, 1997, by the Ministry of Finance and the State Administration of Taxation)

Notice of State Administration of Taxation on Tax Collection Issues Relating to Mergers and Acquisitions of Domestic Enterprises by Foreign Investors (promulgated on May 28, 2003, by the State Administration of Taxation)

(*Continued*)

(Continued from previous page)

Circular of the State Administration of Taxation on Issues Concerning the Handling of Income Tax for Foreign Investment Enterprises Where the Foreign Investment Has Not Been Paid-In (issued on April 14, 1999, by the State Administration of Taxation)

Notice Regarding the Compensation of Losses with an Enterprise's Tax Exempt Income (issued on March 5, 1999, by the State Administration of Taxation)

Tax Administration Procedures on Business Transactions Among Affiliated Enterprises (promulgated by the State Administration of Taxation on April 23, 1998)

Notice of the State Administration of Taxation on Issues Relating to Tax Treatment for Provision of Services by Foreign-Funded Investment Companies to Subsidiary Companies (promulgated on September 28, 2002, by the State Administration of Taxation)

Notice of State Administration of Taxation on Tax Collection Issues Relating to Enterprise Income Tax Payable by Foreign-Invested Venture Capital Companies (issued on June 4, 2003, by the State Administration of Taxation)

Notice on the Levying of Turnover Taxes on Finance Leasing (issued on July 7, 2000 by the State Administration of Taxation)

Notice on Several Policy Issues regarding Business Tax Imposed on Foreign Investment Financial Institutions (issued on July 28, 2000, by the State Administration of Taxation)

Notice on Adjusting Business Tax Policies for Foreign Financial Institutions and Financial Institutions with Foreign Investment (issue on April 25, 2001, by the Ministry of Finance and the State Administration of Taxation, effective on May 1, 2001)

Circular on Several Questions regarding the Exemption from Business Tax on Life Insurance Business (issued on August 18, 2001, by the Ministry of Finance and the State Administration of Taxation)

Notice of the State Council on Expanding the Scope of Application of the Regulations on Preferential Tax Treatments for Foreign Investment Enterprises Engaged in Energy and Communication Infrastructure Projects (issued on January 1, 1999, by the State Council, effective July 2, 1999)

Notice on Certain Tax Treatment on FIEs in the Real Estate Business (issued on December 21, 1999 by the State Administration of Taxation, effective on January 1, 2000)

Notice of State Administration of Taxation on Tax Collection Issues Relating to Enterprise Income Tax Payable by Foreign-Invested Venture Capital Companies (issued on June 4, 2003, by the State Administration of Taxation)

(Continued)

(*Continued from previous page*)

Individual Income Tax

Notice of the State Administration of Taxation on Certain Detailed Issues Concerning the Calculation and Payment of Individual Income Tax by Individuals Without Residence in the Territory of China (promulgated on April 3, 1995, by the State Administration of Taxation)

Notice of the State Administration of Taxation on Questions Concerning the Obligation to Pay Tax on Income Derived from Wages and Salaries by Individuals Without Residence Within the Territory of China (promulgated on June 30, 1994, by the State Administration of Taxation)

Notice of the State Administration of Taxation on Certain Issues Concerning the Payment of Individual Income Tax by Individuals without Residence Within the Territory of China Involving Tax Agreements (promulgated on August 3, 1995, by the State Administration of Taxation)

Notice of the Ministry of Finance and the State Administration of Taxation on Issues Concerning the Calculation of the Five-Year Residency Period for Individuals Without Residence in China (promulgated on September 16, 1995, by the Ministry of Finance and the State Administration of Taxation)

Individual Income Tax Law of the People's Republic of China (adopted September 10, 1980, at the 3rd Sess. of the 5th NPC, amended October 31, 1993, at the 4th Sess. of the Standing Comm. of the 8th NPC, and amended on August 30, 1999 by the 11th Sess. of the Standing Comm. Of the 9th NPC)

Detailed Rules for the Implementation of the Individual Income Tax Law of the PRC (promulgated January 28, 1994, by the Ministry of Finance)

Regulations on Certain Issues Concerning the Levying of Individual Income Tax (promulgated April 6, 1994, by the State Administration of Taxation)

Provisional Measures on the Personal Lodging of Individual Income Tax (promulgated on May 26, 1995, by the State Administration of Taxation)

Provisional Administrative Measures on the Levy and Collection of Individual Income Tax on Overseas Income (issued on August 11, 1998, by the State Administration of Taxation)

Notice of the State Administration of Taxation Concerning Taxation of Income from Stock (Share Rights) Transactions and Dividends Received by Foreign Investment Enterprises, Foreign Enterprises, and Foreign Nationals (issued on July 21, 1993, by the State Administration of Taxation)

Implementing Measures for Levying Individual Income Tax on Interest from Savings Deposits (issued on September 30, 1999 by the State Council, effective on November 1, 1999)

Circular Regarding the Issue of Tax Levy on Bonus Obtained by Individuals without Domicile in China (issued on October 14, 1996 by the State Administration of Taxation)

(*Continued*)

(Continued from previous page)

Notice of the State Administration of Taxation on Issues Concerning the Implementation of an Individual Income Tax Levy or Exemption on Allowances of Foreign Individuals (promulgated on April 9, 1997, by the State Administration of Taxation)

Notice on the Implementing Standards for the Exemption of Home Leave Expenses of Expatriate Employees from Individual Income Tax (issued on May 4, 2001, by the State Administration of Taxation)

Notice on Relevant Income Tax Issues Concerning Overseas Insurance Premiums of Foreign Investment Enterprises and Employees of Foreign Enterprises (issued on June 26, 1998, by the State Administration of Taxation)

Provisional Measures on Withholding Individual Income Tax (promulgated on April 6, 1995, by the State Administration of Taxation)

Notice on Relevant Issues Concerning the Strengthening of the Administration of Withholding Income Tax of Foreign Enterprises (issued on May 29, 1998, by the State Administration of Taxation)

Notice on Tax Issues Concerning Directors of Foreign Companies Who Hold Concurrent Positions in China (issued on May 17, 1999, by the State Administration on Taxation)

Notice of the State Administration of Taxation on Issues Concerning the Levying and Collection of Individual Income Tax on Directors of Foreign Investment Enterprises Who Directly Hold Administrative Positions (promulgated on November 21, 1996, by the State Administration of Taxation)

Notice on the Levying of Individual Income Tax on Investors in Proprietorship and Partnership Enterprises (issued on September 19, 2000, by the Ministry of Finance and the State Administration of Taxation, effective on January 1, 2001)

Representative Office Taxation

Notice of the State Administration of Taxation on Certain Detailed Issues Concerning Tax Levies on Foreign Enterprise Resident Representative Offices (promulgated on January 2, 1997, by the State Administration of Taxation)

Notice on the Explanation of the Issue Whether Representative Offices of Foreign Companies Constitute Permanent Establishments under Tax Treaties (issued on September 13, 1999, by the State Administration of Taxation)

Tax Administration Issues Relevant to Resident Representative Offices of Foreign Enterprises (issued on March 12, 2003, by the State Administration of Taxation)

Notice of the State Bureau of Taxation Exempting Certain Expenses Advanced by Foreign Enterprise Resident Representative Offices on Behalf of Their Head Offices From Inclusion as Resident Representative Office Expenditure for Income Tax Calculation Purposes (promulgated on December 12, 1988, by the State Bureau of Taxation)

(Continued)

(Continued from previous page)

Notice of the State Administration of Taxation on Issues Concerning Improvement of Taxation Collection Administration for Foreign Enterprise Resident Representative Offices (issued on September 13, 1996, by the State Administration of Taxation)

Notice on Certain Issues Concerning Tax Handling in Respect of Resident Representative Offices of Foreign Enterprises (issued on April 30, 1998, by the State Administration of Taxation)

Tax Administration Issues Relevant to Resident Representative Offices of Foreign Enterprise Circular (issued on March 12, 2003, by the State Administration of Taxation)

Circular on Taxation Methods for Representative Offices of Foreign Enterprises jointly issued by the Ministry of Finance and the State Administration of Taxation, (1985) Caishuiwaizi No. 200

Circular Regarding Determination of the Taxation Methods for Representative Offices jointly issued by the Ministry of Finance and the State Administration of Taxation, (1986) Caishuiwaizi No. 055

Circular Regarding the Reduction of Verified Profit Rates for Representative Offices of Foreign Enterprises issued by the Ministry of Finance, (1986) Caishuiwaizi No. 290

Circular Regarding Strengthening the Administration of Taxation on Representative Offices of Foreign Enterprises issued by the State Administration of Taxation (1996) Guoshuifa No. 65

Notice of the State Administration of Taxation on Issues Concerning Taxation Inspections of Foreign Enterprise Resident Representative Offices (promulgated on June 12, 1996, by the State Administration of Taxation)

Miscellaneous Tax Rules

Provisional Rules of the People's Republic of China on Resource Tax (adopted on November 26, 1993, by the 12th Sess. of the Standing Comm. of the State Council)

Administrative Measures of the People's Republic of China on Withholding Resource Tax (promulgated on April 15, 1998, by the State Administration of Taxation)

Regulations Concerning the Handling of Resource Tax Accounting (promulgated on February 21, 1994, by the Ministry of Finance)

Provisional Regulations Governing the Urban Real Estate Tax (promulgated on August 8, 1951, by the Administration Council)

Provisional Regulations of the People's Republic of China on Real Estate Tax (issued on September 15, 1986, by the State Council)

(Continued)

(*Continued from previous page*)

Official Response of the State Administration of Taxation on Applicable Urban Real Estate Tax Policies for Buildings Newly Built by Foreign Investment Enterprises (promulgated on January 21, 1997, by the State Administration of Taxation)

Provisional Rules of the People's Republic of China on Stamp Duty (promulgated on August 6, 1988, by the State Council)

Notice on Certain Questions Concerning the Levying and Collection of Stamp Duty from Foreign Investment Enterprises and Foreign Enterprises (promulgated on April 7, 1994, by the State Administration of Taxation)

Detailed Rules for Implementing the Provisional Rules of the People's Republic of China on Stamp Duty (promulgated on September 29, 1988, by the Ministry of Finance)

Provisional Rules of the People's Republic of China on Deed Tax (promulgated on July 7, 1997, by the State Council)

Detailed Rules for the Provisional Rules of the People's Republic of China on Deed Tax (promulgated on October 28, 1997, by the Ministry of Finance)

Measures for the Imposition of a Surcharge on Vehicle Purchases (promulgated on April 2, 1985, by the State Council)

Provisional Regulations of the People's Republic of China on Vehicle and Vessel Usage Tax (issued on September 15, 1986, by the State Council)

Provisional Regulations Governing the Vehicle and Vessel License Plate Tax (promulgated on September 13, 1951, by the Administrative Council of the Central People's Government)

Tax Collection Rules

Administrative Law of the PRC on the Levying and Collection of Taxes (adopted on September 4, 1992, at the 27th Sess. of the Standing Comm. of the 7th NPC, amended on February 28, 1995, at the 12th Sess. of the Standing Comm. of the 8th NPC, and amended on April 28, 2001 by the Standing Committee of the National People's Congress, effect on May 1, 2001)

Supplementary Regulations of the Standing Committee of the NPC on Punishment for Tax Evasion and Refusal to Pay Tax (adopted on September 4, 1992, by the 27th Sess. of the Standing Comm. of the 7th NPC)

Official Response of the State Administration of Taxation on Issues concerning Taxation Review Conditions (promulgated on August 4, 1997, by the State Administration of Taxation)

Trial Rules for Taxation Administrative Reviews (issued on September 23, 1999, by the State Administration of Taxation, effective on October 1, 1999)

Administration of the Levy and Collection of Taxes Law Implementing Rules (promulgated and effective on October 15, 2002, by the State Council)

Chapter 10

Labor and Employment Law

The rules of employment as they pertain to foreign enterprises have gone through a number of significant changes in recent years. The PRC has adopted laws specifically addressing general employment issues for local Chinese citizens employed by both domestic and foreign-invested enterprises (FIE), and foreigners employed by FIEs in China. There are also special employment regulations for representative offices with respect to employment matters. This chapter addresses the labor laws and regulations that impact FIEs and specifically with respect to issues of recruitment, labor contracts (both individual and collective bargaining agreements), equal employment opportunity, protection of minors and female workers, hours of work and wages, and labor dispute resolution. This chapter also addresses the regulations governing the permit requirements for foreigners working in China.

A. Enterprise Employment

The NPC enacted a comprehensive national labor law in 1994, which preempts all laws and regulations at the provincial, municipal, and local levels.[1]

1. Labor Law of the People's Republic of China (adopted July 5, 1994, by the 8th Sess. of the Standing Comm. of the 8th NPC), *reprinted in* China Laws for Foreign Business (CCH), Business Regulation ¶ 12-500 (hereinafter the "Labor Law"). Prior to the national Labor Law, the Shenzhen SEZ adopted a labor law of its own, which applies to all workers except for government officials. *See* Rules of the Shenzhen Special Economic Zone on Labor Contracts (adopted on August 4, 1994, by the 24th Sess. of the Standing Comm. of the 1st Shenzhen Municipal People's Congress), *reprinted in* China Laws for Foreign Business (CCH), Special Zones & Cities ¶ 73-502. The Municipality of Shanghai has also promulgated its own set of labor rules that are consistent with the national Labor Law. *See* Rules of the Shanghai Municipality on Labor and Personnel Management in Foreign Investment Enterprises (promulgated

The Labor Law applies to all enterprises, including FIEs, State-owed enterprises, and private enterprises. The Labor Law sets forth the fundamental worker rights for all employees in China, including the following:

(1) The right to equal employment opportunity
(2) The right to choice of job[2]

---

on December 20, 1994, by the Standing Comm. of the Shanghai Municipal People's Congress), *reprinted in* CHINA LAWS FOR FOREIGN BUSINESS (CCH), Special Zones & Cities ¶ 240-025 (provide for employee recruitment, dismissal, and resignation; compensation and benefits; hours of work; and dispute resolution); Shanghai Employment Contract Rules (issued by the Shanghai Labor and Social Security Bureau on May 1, 2002) (provide that FIE employment contracts are required to be in the Chinese language; that contracts set forth working conditions and compensation and that that compensation be at least equal to those set forth in an applicable collective labor contract; that an employment relationship will be deemed to exist where a person has performed the duties of an employee as required by the employer, even if there is no employment contract; that an employee may terminate employment at any time; that the employer is to provide 30 days' notice before termination; that a part-time employment relationship may be created if the employee works for not more than 50% of the legal working hours of a relevant time period; that an employer shall pay social security on behalf of the part-time employee, and the proportional share of workers' compensation obligations where applicable; that the temporary suspension of an employment contract in certain situations is permissible; that an employment contract may require an employee knowledgeable of the employer's trade secrets to provide advance notice of not more than six months to terminate the contract; that an employment contract may contain a noncompetition clause for a period not exceeding three years after employment termination and that such noncompete provision must be supported by consideration; that an employment contract may stipulate damages in case of a breach by the employee of (i) the term of the contract, or (ii) the employee's confidentiality obligation as provided in the employment contract; and that employment contracts survive company merger or division). In 2003, the Shanghai Labor and Social Security Bureau launched an inspection of foreign and domestic enterprises to determine compliance with the Shanghai Employment Contract Rules. *See Shanghai to Inspect Implementation of Employment Rules,* China Market Intelligence, THE U.S.-CHINA BUSINESS COUNCIL (July 16, 2003), available online to members at http://www.uschina.org. The city of Beijing has also adopted its own set of labor rules pursuant to the Labor Law. *See* Rules of the Beijing Municipality on the Supervision of Labor Protection (promulgated on July 27, 1995, by the Standing Comm. of the 10th Beijing Municipal People's Congress), *reprinted in* CHINA LAWS FOR FOREIGN BUSINESS (CCH), Special Zones & Cities ¶ 170-045. *See also* Rules of Dalian Municipality on Labor Protection (promulgated on October 4, 1995, by the Dalian Municipal People's Government), *reprinted in* CHINA LAWS FOR FOREIGN BUSINESS (CCH), Special Zones & Cities ¶ 180-005; Regulations of Qingdao Municipality on Labor Management in Foreign Investment Enterprises (promulgated on February 9, 1996, by the Standing Comm. of the 11th Qingdao Municipal People's Congress), *reprinted in* CHINA LAWS FOR FOREIGN BUSINESS (CCH), Special Zones & Cities ¶ 220-010; Administrative Regulations of Guangdong Province on Labor Contracts (promulgated on April 7, 1995, by the Guangdong Provincial People's Government), *reprinted in* CHINA LAWS FOR FOREIGN BUSINESS (CCH), Special Zones & Cities ¶ 270-005. *See generally* Josephs, *Labor Law in a "Socialist Market Economy": The Case of China,* 33 COLUM. J. TRANSNAT'L L. 559 (1995). For a discussion of the historical developments of the labor law in the PRC, *see* H. Josephs, Labor Law in China: Choice and Responsibility (1990). For an MOL view on the legal reform of China's labor law and social security system, *see* Wang, *Work in Progress: Labor and Social Security Reform,* 136 CHINA INTERNATIONAL BUSINESS (MOFTEC) 20 (1998). For a discussion on China's changing personnel practices and tips on retaining valuable employees, *see* J. Leininger, *The Key to Retention: Committed Employees,* China Bus. Rev. (January–February 2004). *See also* B. Athreya, *China's Changing Labor Relations,* China Bus. Rev. (January–February 2004).

2. The right to choice of job has been restricted under China's household registration (*hukou*) system, which traditionally classified Chinese citizens into rural or urban classes. The *hukou,* or identification card/booklet, are issued by municipal or township entities and limit access to social services and schools to only those citizens issued a *hukou* within the administrative entity's jurisdiction. The effect of the *hukou* system was to prevent mobility of the workforce, and especially rural workers that migrated to the larger urban areas. In recent years, China has reformed the system to relax the barriers and restrictions to improve labor mobility. *See generally* Zhang Ye, *Hope for China's Migrant Women Workers,* CHINA BUS. REV. (May–June 2002).

(3) The right to compensation for labor
(4) The right to rest periods, vacations, and holidays
(5) The right to workplace safety and healthy work conditions
(6) The right to vocational training
(7) The right to social insurance and benefits
(8) The right to resolve labor disputes[3]

The Labor Law also imposes workplace obligations on the employee, including the following:

(1) The obligation to complete work assignments
(2) The obligation to improve and develop the employee's vocational skills
(3) The obligation to adhere to workplace health and safety standards
(4) The obligation to workplace discipline and professional ethics[4]

Pursuant to the Labor Law, specific regulations have been adopted that apply to all foreign-invested enterprises.[5] According to the FIE Labor

---

3. Labor Law, art. 3. Although the Labor Law, as well as the Constitution, provides for basic and fundamental worker rights, the recognition and enforcement of such rights have been questioned by foreign governments and human rights organizations. Both the Chinese government and employers—government as well as multinationals—have been accused of violating basic worker rights. *See generally* Poole, *Chinese Disney Staff Exploited,* THE INDEPENDENT (London) 14 (Feb. 24, 1999). The U.S. Department of Labor and a number of business groups and human rights organizations encourage multinationals to adhere to worker rights codes of conduct. For information regarding worker rights codes of conduct, *see* the Web site for the Department of Labor at http://www.dol.gov or the Web site for the International Mass Retail Association at http://www.imra.org. For information concerning codes of conduct in China, *see* R. Rosoff, *Beyond Codes of Conduct: Addressing Labor Rights Problems in China,* CHINA BUS. REV. (March–April 2004). For a review of the codes of conduct program for Nike, Adidas, and Reebok, see their respective Web sites for more information. China has also been accused of exporting prison labor products. *See* Zimmerman, *U.S. Law and Convict-Produced Imports,* CHINA BUS. REV. 41 (March–April 1992). In November 2003, the U.S. DOL and the Chinese MOLSS signed an agreement on technical cooperation between the two government ministries. Pursuant to the DOL/MOLSS Agreement, China and the United States agreed to cooperate in developing labor legislation, labor law implementation, labor law education, industry relations, labor legal aid, and other issues concerning worker rights. *See Sino-U.S. Agreement on Labor Law Cooperation Signed,* Xinhua News Agency (November 24, 2003). In March of 2004, the AFL-CIO initiated a Section 301 alleging that China violated international worker rights. The AFL-CIO petition seeks U.S. government action on the basis that China's labor practices constitute "an act, policy or practice" that is "unreasonable or discriminatory and burdens or restricts United States commerce." Under Section 301, an "unreasonable" act, policy, or practice is one in which there is a *persistent pattern* of conduct that violates fundamental worker rights. For a copy of the AFL-CIO's petition, *see* http://www.afl-cio.org. The USTR rejected the petition and refused to investigate the issues.

4. Labor Law, art. 3.

5. Regulations on Labor Management in Foreign Investment Enterprises (promulgated August 11, 1994, by the Ministry of Labor and MOFTEC), *reprinted in* CHINA LAWS FOR FOREIGN BUSINESS (CCH), Business Regulation ¶ 12-626 (the "FIE Labor Regulations"). *See also* Notice of Abolishment of the Notice Concerning Strengthening Labor Management in Foreign Investment Enterprises and Private Enterprises and the Effective Safeguarding of the Legal Rights and Interests of Employees (promulgated on March 4, 1994, by the MOL, the Ministry of Public Security, and the All-China Federation of Trade Unions and abolished on February 25, 2003), *reprinted in* CHINA LAWS FOR FOREIGN BUSINESS (CCH), Business Regulation ¶ 12-503 (sets forth standards for recruitment, labor contracts, and health and safety standards, and prohibits the illegal custody of employee property or documents as a "factory pledge"). *See generally* L. Wozniak, *Companies in China Struggle to Train, Retain Managers*, WALL ST. J. (December 30, 2003) (citing a survey that found that 43% of senior managers for foreign companies voluntarily quit their jobs, making it difficult for multinationals to attract and retain talented managers).

Regulations, the board of directors of an FIE has the right to develop its personnel practices and procedures, but company policy must comply with State employment standards and objectives.

1. Labor Contracts

The Labor Law provides that all employers are required to execute labor contracts with their employees to establish the terms and conditions of the employment relationship.[6] The written labor contract must include the following matters:

(1) Employment term
(2) Duties and responsibilities of the employee
(3) Conditions of employment and labor protection
(4) Compensation and benefits
(5) Work hours, rest periods, rest days, vacation time, and holidays
(6) Disciplinary procedures and grounds for termination
(7) Dispute resolution[7]

A labor contract may also include other items pertinent to an employer's operation, including confidentiality, noncompetition, conflict of interest, nonsolicitation, intellectual property, and other similar issues.[8] A labor contract may provide for a probationary period that may not be more than six months.[9] A labor contract is invalid if it violates the law or regulations, or if the contract is executed under threat of violence, coercion, or deception. A labor contract between an individual and an FIE is required to be filed with the local labor administration one month after the execution of the agreement.[10]

In addition to and separate from an individual labor contract, the employees of an enterprise may negotiate a collective bargaining agreement with an FIE.[11] The Labor Law protects the rights of employees to join or

6. Labor Law, art. 16; FIE Labor Regulations, art. 8.
7. Labor Law, art. 19; FIE Labor Regulations, art. 8.
8. Labor Law, art. 22.
9. Labor Law, art. 21.
10. FIE Labor Regulations, art. 9.
11. Labor Law, arts. 7, 33; FIE Labor Regulations, art. 8. *See also* Trade Union Law of the People's Republic of China (adopted on April 3, 1992, at the 5th Sess. of the 7th NPC and as amended on October 27, 2001), *reprinted in* CHINA LAWS FOR FOREIGN BUSINESS (CCH), Business Regulation ¶ 12-501 (outlining the obligations of trade unions, mediation involving trade unions and employers, and internal rules for trade unions) (hereinafter the "Trade Union Law"); Regulations of Beijing Municipality on Trade Unions in Sino-Foreign Joint Equity Enterprises (adopted on November 3, 1990, at the 23rd Sess. of the Standing Comm. of the 9th Beijing Municipal People's Congress), *reprinted in* CHINA LAWS FOR FOREIGN BUSINESS (CCH), Business Regulation ¶ 12-505 (outlining the obligations and duties of trade unions in Beijing-based EJV) (hereinafter the "Beijing Trade Union Regulations"); Certain Regulations of Guangzhou Municipality on the Implementation of the Trade Union Law of the People's Republic of

organize trade unions. A collective bargaining agreement sets the minimum conditions for all employees with respect to compensation, working conditions, hours and wages, vacation and rest periods, and benefits. A collective bargaining contract is binding upon all staff and workers and must be submitted to the Ministry of Labor and Social Security (MOL) or local labor administration for approval. A collective bargaining agreement may be submitted only after it is signed by the parties and is deemed to take effect fifteen days after submission so long as no objections are raised by the labor administration.[12] Any amendments to a labor contract must be in writing.[13]

2. Recruitment

An FIE is required to give priority in recruitment to Chinese citizens over foreign nationals. When there is a need to recruit foreign personnel, including individuals from Taiwan, Hong Kong, or Macao, an FIE must receive approval (i.e., employment permit) from the MOL or local labor administration.[14] In general, an FIE should exercise caution in the selection of any employee—Chinese citizens and foreign nationals—who may still be bound by the terms of preexisting employment relationships with current employers. Under the laws and regulations, a recruiting employer is responsible for contract cancellation charges to a current employer of a recent hire.[15] In all negotiations with state-owned enterprises, a foreign party should be on guard against the pressure to hire more personnel than is necessary to accomplish the objectives of a proposed operation. As more state-owned enterprises seek to find employment for their redundant workers, a foreign party should be alert against being held responsible for an overbloated and unnecessary workforce.

China (promulgated on June 8, 1995, by the Guangzhou Municipal People's Government), *reprinted in* CHINA LAWS FOR FOREIGN BUSINESS (CCH), Special Zones & Cities ¶ 270-030 (addresses trade union rules for enterprises in the city of Guangzhou). *See generally* Li, *Legal Aspects of Labor Relations in China,* 33 COLUM. J. TRANSNAT'L L. 521 (1995); *MOLSS Issues Collective Bargaining Minimum Wage Rules*, China Market Intelligence, U.S.-CHINA BUSINESS COUNCIL (February 18, 2004). *See also* Trial Measures Governing Collective Consultation on Wages (adopted on October 10, 2000, by the Ministry of Labor and Social Security), *reprinted in* CHINA LAWS FOR FOREIGN BUSINESS (CCH), Business Regulation ¶ 12-640 (guidelines for collective bargaining).

12. Labor Law, arts. 33, 34; FIE Labor Regulations, art. 9.

13. FIE Labor Regulations, art. 10.

14. FIE Labor Regulations, art. 6. *See also* Administrative Regulations on the Employment of Foreigners in China (jointly promulgated on January 22, 1996, by the MOL, MPS, and MOFTEC), *reprinted in* CHINA LAWS FOR FOREIGN BUSINESS (CCH), Business Regulation ¶ 12-630 (hereinafter the "Employment of Foreigners Regulations").

15. Labor Law, art. 99; FIE Labor Regulations, art. 5. If an FIE recruits an employee in violation of the regulations, the MOL may impose a fine of five to ten times the average monthly wage of the employee and require that the FIE release the employee. FIE Labor Regulations, art. 28. For a discussion concerning the role of headhunters in China, *see Human Resources—The Mighty Hunters,* CHINA ECONOMIC NEWS (Aug. 23, 1998), available on Lexis, News Library.

3. Vocational Training

Article 3 of the Labor Law provides that employees have a right to vocational training. An employer is required to allocate funds for the establishment of a vocational training program to improve and enhance the work skills of its employees and increase their opportunities for advancement.[16] Employers are also required to provide training to employees in technical positions prior to the commencement of work.

Practice Tip: Training as a Way of Retaining Good Employees in China

Retaining the highly skilled Chinese workers is difficult for foreign companies, and special attention should be given to developing a strategy to recruit and retain qualified and loyal employees. The loyalty of employees created by the former cradle-to-grave system of Communism is a thing of the past, and especially for foreign companies. The highly trained managers—those who are educated overseas or have worked overseas—tend to move around from job to job to increase their compensation and to elevate their profile in the professional community. While there are many avenues for training—including in-house at foreign companies—many Chinese realize that the high-salary jobs require a solid education, English language skills, and experience in high-tech areas. Tips to increase employee loyalty and thereby retain good employees include: providing in-house training, reimbursement for continuing education classes, overseas travel for training of middle and senior managers, and salary increases and bonuses based upon the employee's efforts to enhance his or her skills.

4. Equal Employment Opportunity

The Labor Law provides that an employer may not discriminate on the basis of nationality, race, sex, or religious belief.[17] In addition, the Labor Law provides that an employer is prohibited from discriminating against female workers unless the type of work is "unsuitable for woman as stipulated by the State."[18] The written policy of the government is to encourage the employment of disabled persons, minority nationalities, and military personnel retiring from active service.[19] This encouragement policy is akin to affirmative action programs in the United States. The effectiveness of this policy in remedying underemployment in the above-referenced categories of employees is uncertain.

16. Labor Law, arts. 3, 66–69.
17. Labor Law, art. 12.
18. Labor Law, art. 13.
19. Labor Law, art. 14.

5. Social Insurance and Welfare

Chinese law provides that employees are entitled to, and employers are required to provide, social insurance and welfare benefits, even if the employee prefers to waive such benefits.[20] The Labor Law provides for a national social insurance system that includes the following social insurance and welfare benefits:

(1) Retirement and pension benefits[21]
(2) Worker compensation for job-related injuries and diseases[22]
(3) Medical care and disability benefits for injuries or diseases that are not employment related[23]
(4) Unemployment benefits[24]

---

20. Labor Law, arts. 70–72. *See generally* Harpole, *PRC Pension Fund Reforms: The Path to Uniformity,* 6 CHINA LAW NEWS 1 (December 1997) (analysis of State Council decision on pension fund matters including employee contribution, ratio of contributions, management of pension funds, and specific procedures for FIEs). The PRC is also likely to revamp its entire social insurance and welfare program for a social security system that is workable in a market-oriented system. *See* Wang, *Social Security Stressed,* CHINA DAILY (June 24, 1998), available on Lexis, News Library, or on the Web site of the CHINA DAILY at http://www.chinadaily.com.cn. The law requires that employers establish housing funds. In this regard, on April 3, 1999, the State Council issued the *Administrative Rules for Housing Mutual Funds.* These Rules require all government organizations, state-owned enterprises, urban collectively owned enterprises, foreign investment enterprises, urban privately owned enterprises, and other institutions and their employees to contribute a stipulated amount of funds to the "housing mutual fund management center." These housing mutual funds are owned by the employees and distributed to employees who are purchasing, constructing, or renovating their housing. The contribution rate is no less than five percent of the employee's monthly average salary of the preceding year. Provincial governments have the authority to promulgate rules that may increase the rate of contribution.

21. The rates charged for the PRC pension system depend upon the city or region. *See e.g.,* Rules of Guangzhou Municipality on Social Security (promulgated on July 31, 1995, by the Standing Comm. of the Guangzhou Municipal People's Congress), *reprinted in* CHINA LAWS FOR FOREIGN BUSINESS (CCH), Special Zones & Cities ¶ 270-040 (addresses the financing and administration of funds, social security insurance benefits, fund supervision, and liability issues).

22. *See e.g.,* Rules of the Shenzhen Special Economic Zone on Industrial Injury Insurance (promulgated on February 26, 1993, and as amended on January 11, 2000, by the Standing Comm. of the Shenzhen Municipal People's Congress), *reprinted in* CHINA LAWS FOR FOREIGN BUSINESS (CCH), Special Zones & Cities ¶ 73-515 (addresses requirements for worker compensation insurance, insurance fund management, worker compensation benefits, worker compensation administrative system and supervision, procedures for benefits disputes, and liability issues).

23. Under China's old planned economy system, the government developed a free medical care system under which the government and enterprises paid for State employees' medical treatment. Since the early 1990s, some regions of China have established a "shared payment system" that requires contributions from both individuals and employers. In December 1998, the MOL adopted rules that require medical insurance contributions from both individuals and enterprises. Ying, *Medical Insurance System Gets Makeover,* CHINA DAILY (Dec. 12, 1998), available on Lexis, News Library, or on the Web site of the CHINA DAILY at http://www.chinadaily.com.cn. All employees are required to pay 2 percent of their standard wages toward medical insurance. Employers are required to pool funds to pay for certain medical expenses. The government regulations are also encouraging employers to obtain supplemental insurance from private insurance carriers. The government is also in the process of revamping the country's entire pension system. *See generally* Harpole, *PRC Pension Fund Reforms: The Path to Uniformity,* 6 CHINA LAW NEWS 1 (December 1997) (analysis of State Council decision on pension fund matters including employee contribution, ratio of contributions, management of pension funds, and specific procedures for FIEs). The PRC is also likely to revamp its entire social insurance and welfare program for a social security system that is workable in a market-oriented system. *See* Wang, *Social Security Stressed,* CHINA DAILY (June 24, 1998), available on Lexis, News Library, or on the Web site of the CHINA DAILY at http://www.chinadaily.com.cn.

24. *See* Rules of the Shenzhen Special Economic Zone on Unemployment Insurance (promulgated on November 28, 1996, by the Shenzhen Municipal People's Government), *reprinted in* CHINA LAWS FOR

(5) Pregnancy and maternity benefits
(6) Death benefits for survivors[25]

The benefits provided under the PRC system are required to be consistent with the level of national economic development. The government further encourages both employers and employees to participate in supplemental private insurance programs.[26] As a practical matter, and as required by the various local labor agencies, social insurance benefits are a topic that is specifically addressed in the collective and individual labor contracts negotiated by an FIE.

More multinationals are seeking to globalize their network of benefits and personnel policies practices. Cultural and practical issues may impact a foreign company's ability to set up a uniform system of benefits and employment policies. However, there are no legal limitations or restrictions in China as to whether a company can apply its standards in a uniform and global manner.

6. Protection of Minors and Female Workers

The Labor Law prohibits the employment of persons under the age of sixteen years.[27] In the entertainment sector and in athletic events, employers may recruit minors to work but are required to obtain special approval and to ensure that the employee receives a compulsory education.[28] Underage workers (between the ages of sixteen and eighteen years) are prohibited from working in underground mining operations and pits, working with poisonous or harmful substances, or engaging in physically intense labor.[29] An employer is required, at its expense, to arrange for regular medical examinations of underage workers.[30]

The Labor Law further prohibits female employees from working in mining operations and other dangerous occupations.[31] The law further prohibits female workers from working in high altitudes, at low temperatures, or in contact with cold water, or from performing strenuous physical labor during menstruation.[32] Employers also are prohibited from having expectant

---

FOREIGN BUSINESS (CCH), Special Zones & Cities ¶ 120-075. The Shenzhen Unemployment Rules outline the standards for unemployment insurance funds, unemployment benefits, standards for unemployment insurance agencies, legal obligations, and penalties for violations. *See generally* Williams & Woo, *The "Worthy" Unemployed: Societal Stratification and Unemployment Insurance Programs in China and the United States,* 33 ÇOLUM. J. TRANSNAT'L L. 457 (1995).

25. Labor Law, art. 73.
26. Labor Law, art. 75.
27. Labor Law, art. 15.
28. Labor Law, art. 15.
29. Labor Law, arts. 58, 64.
30. Labor Law, art. 65.
31. Labor Law, art. 59. *See also* Regulations Concerning the Labor Protection of Female Staff and Workers (adopted on June 28, 1988, at the 11th Sess. of the State Council), *reprinted in* CHINA LAWS FOR FOREIGN BUSINESS (CCH), Business Regulation ¶ 12-610.
32. Labor Law, art. 60.

mothers engage in strenuous physical labor during the term of pregnancy, and expectant mothers are barred from night work or overtime during the final trimester of pregnancy.[33] The law further mandates maternity leave of a minimum of ninety days.[34] Nursing mothers are not allowed to work overtime, work night hours, or engage in strenuous physical labor for a period of up to one year after the child is born.[35]

There is no specific law or regulation dealing with sexual harassment in the workplace. Nevertheless, the courts are willing to hear cases based upon contractual theories and general tort theories as described in the Civil Code.[36]

Practice Tip: Sexual Harrassment Standards in China

More workers are lodging sexual harassment claims based upon work rules and corporate policies that are modeled after Western standards, or that have been introduced by FIEs as part of their global workplace standards. Caveat: If an FIE adopts a Western-styled policy prohibiting sexual harassment in the workplace, it should train its managers—foreign and local—with respect to the appropriate standards of conduct required under the policy. Given that China's Confucian-based style of management can be easily perceived as male chauvinism, training and monitoring is critical.

7. Workplace Health and Safety

Employers are required to establish a program of workplace health and safety and to take specific measures to guard against workplace accidents.[37] Such a program requires that employees be provided with the necessary protective equipment such as goggles, work clothes, head covering, and other

33. Labor Law, art. 61. *See also* Provisional Regulations for Health Care for Women Employees (issued on May 30, 1986, by the Ministry of Public Health), *reprinted in* CHINA LAWS FOR FOREIGN BUSINESS (CCH), Business Regulation ¶ 12-594 (detailed regulations concerning work rules for women and specifically with respect to expectant mothers, prohibitions on pregnancy for women exposed to radiation or chemicals, postnatal care, and the treatment of female employees during menopause).

34. Labor Law, art. 62.

35. Labor Law, art. 63.

36. The Chinese government is contemplating legislation preventing sexual harassment. *See China Considers Legislation Against Sexual Harassment*, CHINA DAILY (Aug. 14, 2003). The people's courts are beginning to hear cases involving sexual harassment in the workplace. *See* Plaintiff Wins in Landmark Sexual Harassment Suit, WALL ST. J., June 9, 2003, available online at http://www.wsj.com.

37. Labor Law, arts. 52–57. In 2003, the government adopted a number of regulations to protect the rights of employees that sustain work-related injuries including the Regulations on Insurance for Work-Related Injuries, Procedures for Confirming Work-Related Injuries, Measures for Casualty Compensation Paid in One Lump Sum by Illegal Employers, and the Regulations on Identification of Dependents of Employees Who Incurred Work-Related Death. *See Full Text: Progress in China's Human Rights Cause in 2003: Economic, Social and Cultural Rights*, Xinhua News Agency (March 30, 2004).

items needed to protect workers. Employers are also required to train employees concerning health and safety issues and to discipline errant employees that fail to follow company rules and labor regulations. For workers involved with dangerous occupations or hazardous substances, the employer is required to provide regular medical examinations at company expense. A worker has the right to refuse to engage in any task that is considered unsafe and has the right to seek relief from the labor authorities in situations involving uncorrected problems that jeopardize employees.[38]

The government adopted the Law on the Prevention and Control of Occupational Diseases, which was effective May 2002.[39] The law sets forth the standards for controlling and supervising occupational injuries, provides standards for the diagnosis of diseases and employee health care, and provides that employees have a right to advise regulatory authorities of any violations of the law and/or to refuse to work.[40] It is a violation of the law to produce, operate, import, or use equipment and materials that possibly could cause occupational disease hazards.[41] The law further provides that employers are required to notify prospective employees of any possible risks of occupational disease in the workplace, and are required to provide medical care to any injured worker.[42]

The State Council adopted specific regulations governing the protection of workers in operations where toxic substances are used in the workplace.[43] Under the Toxics in the Workplace Regulations, the employer is required to take effective protective measures to prevent accidental poisoning in the workplace, and to maintain worker compensation insurance according to the law.[44] In addition to licensing requirements for the use of toxic substances in

38. Labor Law, art. 56.

39. Law on the Prevention and Control of Occupational Diseases, promulgated on October 27, 2001, and effective on May 1, 2002, by the Standing Committee of the National People's Congress. *See also* Notification of the Ministry of Health on the Relevant Issues Concerning the Implementation of the Law on the Prevention and Control of Occupational Diseases, promulgated on May 8, 2002, by the Ministry of Health (outlines tasks and programs to be adopted by the MOH with respect to prevention and control of disease and injury in the workplace). The law sets forth detailed penalty provisions in the event of a violation of the law. Occupational Diseases Law, arts. 62–76. *See generally* C. Gelb & V. Hulme, *Ensuring Health and Safety of China Operations*, CHINA BUS. REV. (January–February 2002). For an interesting article concerning legal issues and the outbreak of Severe Acute Respiratory Syndrome (SARS), *see* S. Bosco, *The Impact of SARS: Guidance for Employers in the PRC*, CHINA L. & PRAC. (June 2003) (outlining employer obligations to report illness, obligations to continue to pay salaries, work stoppages, and quarantine issues).

40. Occupational Diseases Law, arts. 12, 30.

41. Occupational Diseases Law, art. 27.

42. Occupational Diseases Law, arts. 30, 39–54.

43. Regulations on Labor Protection in the Operational Fields Where Toxic Articles Are Used, adopted by the 57th Executive Meeting of the State Council on April 30, 2002, and effective on May 12, 2002 (hereinafter the "Toxics in the Workplace Regulations"). For more information concerning the regulation of the workplace, see the Web site of the Ministry of Labor and Social Security at http://www.molss.gov.cn.

44. Toxics in the Workplace Regulations, art. 5.

the workplace, the protective measures outlined in the Regulations provide that the operational areas where toxics are used must be separate from the living quarters, and that no person may reside in the operational areas that are exposed to toxic substances; that the employer install an effective ventilation system if toxics are used in an enclosed area of the workplace; that workers exposed to toxics must be provided with medical care by the employer; and equipment used with toxic substances be disposed of properly.[45] The Toxics in the Workplace Regulations also grant workers the right to receive training in regard to the handling of toxic substances, and workers are allowed to freely lodge complaints with regulatory authorities and may refuse to work in an environment without proper safeguards from toxic substances.[46] If an employer does not have the required insurance, an injured worker has the right to claim compensation against the employer.[47] The Regulations also restate the prohibition on child labor and the prohibition on exposing minor or pregnant employees to toxic substances.[48] A violation of the law may expose both an employer and management personnel to criminal and administrative penalties including, but not limited to, revocation of business license, fines of up to RMB500,000 per violation, and imprisonment of management personnel.[49]

8. Termination

An employment contract will terminate automatically upon the expiration of the term, unless the contract is renewed by mutual consent of the parties.[50] An employment contract may also be terminated "when conditions occur for termination of the labor contract as agreed by the parties concerned."[51] In order to be effective, the conditions for termination must be expressly stated in the parties' labor contract. These conditions should be clearly set forth in the labor contract. A foreign enterprise may terminate, without advanced notice to the employee, a labor contract in the following circumstances:

(1) An employee has failed to meet the conditions of employment during the company's probationary period

45. Toxics in the Workplace Regulations, arts. 11, 29, 32–36, 41.
46. Toxics in the Workplace Regulations, art. 38–40. Workers affected by toxic substances have a right to medical expenses, rehabilitation expenses, nursing services, wages and other benefits, disability subsidies, death allowances and funeral expenses, pensions, and other insurance benefits. Art. 41.
47. Toxics in the Workplace Regulations, art. 45.
48. Toxics in the Workplace Regulations, art. 7.
49. Toxics in the Workplace Regulations, arts. 56–69.
50. FIE Labor Regulations, art. 10.
51. Labor Law, art. 23; FIE Labor Regulations, art. 10.

(2) An employee has failed to adequately perform his or her obligations under an employment contract
(3) An employee has willfully violated the policies and procedures of the employer
(4) An employee has engaged in unethical conduct that results in serious losses to the employer; or
(5) An employee has been convicted of a crime[52]

After seeking the opinion of the trade union, if applicable, an employer may terminate an employment contract with thirty days' written notice in the following circumstances:

(1) The employee is "incapable of performing a job and remains incapable after receiving training or being transferred to another position"
(2) The employee has been ill or injured outside his or her place of employment and, as a result, is unable to perform the job requirements after medical treatment; or
(3) The labor contract is incapable of implementation due to circumstances that were relied upon by the parties in negotiating the contract, and the parties are unable to reach an agreement to amend the contract[53]

An employer may proceed with a reduction in workforce if it is undergoing liquidation, bankruptcy proceedings, or statutory reorganization.[54] Workers that are dismissed as a result of a reduction in workforce are entitled to compensation based upon the years of service to the company. A dismissed worker, for example, is entitled to one month's average salary for

52. FIE Labor Regulations, art. 11, § (2). Note that the Labor Law, Article 25, has similar provisions except that termination of the contract may be imposed if the employee is merely accused of a crime rather than convicted as set forth in the FIE Labor Regulations. Termination is effective only in foreign enterprises if the employee is convicted of a crime.

53. Labor Law, art. 26; FIE Labor Regulations, art. 12. Examples of situations in which the circumstances render the contract incapable of implementation include an employee's failure to qualify or maintain a license required for a position (e.g., airline pilot, truck driver, etc.).

54. Labor Law, art. 27. *See also* Measures of the Shenzhen Special Economic Zone on Enterprise Staff Reductions for Economic Reasons (promulgated on November 15, 1996, by the Shenzhen Municipal People's Government), *reprinted in* CHINA LAWS FOR FOREIGN BUSINESS (CCH), Special Zones & Cities ¶ 120-070. The Shenzhen measures address the standards for terminating employees as a result of financial considerations, the termination procedures based upon residency (permanent residents have preference), disclosure requirements to trade unions and employee representatives, procedures for rehiring employees subject to layoffs, and penalties for violations of the standards. Under the SPC Bankruptcy Case Provisions, a debtor's bankruptcy petition is required to provide information concerning its workforce and contingency plans for its workers. *See* SPC Bankruptcy Case Provisions, art. 6. The SPC Bankruptcy Case Provisions also outline the rights of workers and employees during bankruptcy proceedings. *See generally* SPC Bankruptcy Case Provisions, arts. 56–58.

every full year that the employee has been employed by the enterprise.[55] In addition, a terminated employee is entitled to a medical treatment allowance of the equivalent of three months' salary for employees with less than five years of service and six months' salary for employees with more than five years of service.[56] An FIE is prohibited from terminating a labor contract when an employee sustains a work-related injury or when an employee is pregnant or on maternity leave.[57] If an employee requests the termination of the contract as a result of a work-related injury, the FIE is required to pay an employment rehabilitation fee on behalf of the injured employee.

In June 1998 the State Council adopted new unemployment regulations to soften the impact of job cuts resulting from the ongoing government institutional reform and the move toward more efficiency in state-owned enterprises (SOEs). As SOEs struggle to meet the government's demand to dismantle the cradle-to-grave system, they have been forced to lay off a significant percentage of their workforce.[58] Although the SOE Reduction in Workforce Regulations is specifically directed to state-owned enterprises, the regulations have application to foreign-invested enterprises (FIE) in a number of situations.

In the event that either the husband or wife of an FIE employee is laid off at an SOE, an FIE is prohibited from terminating the employment relationship of its own employee. FIEs are thus required to lay off employees on a case-by-case basis, taking into account the individual employee's personal situation. The regulations ensure that the wage earners in a family unit are not rendered unemployed simultaneously and are designed to guarantee the basic living needs of employees and their families terminated as a result of a reduction in workforce.

The SOE Reduction in Workforce Regulations also require that all enterprises, including FIEs, must maintain a system of unemployment insurance contributions. Specifically, the new standards require that unemployment insurance contributions be increased nationwide from 1 percent to 3 percent. Previously, employers were required to contribute a total of only 1 percent of the enterprise's entire payroll amount, and the employees made no contribution whatsoever. Now, the regulations require that employees

---

55. FIE Labor Regulations, arts. 19, 20. FIEs are required to maintain records of their employees' length of service, wages, payment details, and expenditure on benefits and other insurance. *Id.* art. 18.

56. FIE Labor Regulations, art. 20. Service for greater than six months but less than one year is treated as service for one year for purposes of calculating the payment of allowances.

57. Labor Law, art. 29; FIE Labor Regulations, art. 13.

58. *See* Notice Regarding the Methods for Effectively Protecting the Livelihood and Re-employment of Redundant Employees of State-Owned Enterprises (promulgated by the State Council on June 29, 1998), *reprinted in* China Labor & Social Security Law—Essential Facts Explained ¶ 28-005 (hereinafter the "SOE Reduction in Workforce Regulations").

and employers contribute 1 percent and 2 percent, respectively. The effective date of this requirement, although set for June 1998, is actually determined by the local and provincial labor departments.

An employee may terminate a labor contract for any reason with thirty days' advance written notice.[59] However, an employee that fails to maintain the confidentiality of employer trade secrets, or breaches the labor contract resulting in economic losses to the employer, is legally responsible for damages to the employer.[60] Under the Criminal Law, the unlawful disclosure and use of a "business secret" is a criminal act punishable by imprisonment of up to seven years in serious cases.[61]

The Labor Law provides that the employee has the right to terminate his or her employment relationship when the employer is in violation of his or her legal and contractual duties to the worker. The employee may terminate its employment relationship, without notice, in any of the following circumstances:

(1) During the probationary period
(2) Where the employer forces an employee to work by means of threats, restrictions to freedom, or force
(3) Where the employer fails to pay any compensation to the employee; or
(4) Where the employer fails to provide work conditions consistent with the labor contract[62]

9. Wage and Hour Regulation

The State Council issued regulations in 1995 providing for a forty-hour and five-day workweek.[63] The employer may extend the hours of work after consultation with the trade union and the employee, on the condition that overtime pay is provided and the work does not exceed thirty-six hours per month.[64] In certain professions and emergency situations, the law provides that overtime work may be required of employees.[65] For example, where the

59. Labor Law, art. 31.
60. Labor Law, art. 102.
61. Criminal Law, arts. 219, 220. *See infra* Chapter 23, Criminal Liability for FIE Activities § B.4. Under the Company Law, directors, supervisors, and managers have an obligation to maintain confidentiality of company secrets, except if allowed to disclose by the board of directors. *See* Company Law, art. 62.
62. Labor Law, art. 32.
63. Regulations of the State Council Governing Working Hours for Workers (promulgated March 25, 1995, by the State Council), art. 3, *reprinted in* CHINA LAWS FOR FOREIGN BUSINESS (CCH), Business Regulation ¶ 12-622. Prior to the State Council's 1995 regulations, the Labor Law provided for a five-and-a-half-day workweek and eight-hour workday. Labor Law, art. 36.
64. Labor Law, art. 41.
65. Labor Law, art. 42.

health of workers and the safety of property are threatened due to natural disaster or accident, or where urgent repairs to production equipment, public transportation, or public facilities are in the public interest, the employer is exempt from the overtime limitations of the labor law.

FIEs are required to pay their employees the "average wage standard" of employees in the "same industry in the local area."[66] The law also requires that the average wage standard of an FIE increase progressively in line with the economic development of the enterprise. A decision concerning wages is made by the FIE's board of directors, which must take into consideration the enterprise's productivity rate, economic results, and the consumer price index and wage guidelines for the region.[67]

In addition, the FIE Wage Measures provide that FIEs are required to follow the principle of equal pay for equal work.[68] This rule applies to expatriate versus Chinese personnel as well as between male and female workers. Specifically, this rule requires that the FIE pay its Chinese senior management personnel a "nominal wage income" similar to the actual wages paid to foreign senior management personnel working in China. The "nominal wage income" is used to determine the level of benefits, social insurance, and subsidies that the FIE will be required to pay on the Chinese employee's behalf.[69] The "actual wage income" of the Chinese management employee will be set by the agency that regulates the Chinese party to the venture. The actual wage paid to the Chinese employee may be less than the nominal wage rate. The actual wage rate is based upon the enterprise's internal wage system, wage standards, profits earned by the FIE, and the average wage income of other employees in similar positions in the industry.

The employer is required to pay its employees in cash and at least once per month, and is required to withhold income taxes.[70] The employees are entitled to at least 150 percent of base wages for overtime (i.e., excess of

66. Provisional Administrative Measures on Wage Incomes of Foreign Investment Enterprises (promulgated February 14, 1997, by the Ministry of Labor) art. 4, *reprinted in* CHINA LAWS FOR FOREIGN BUSINESS (CCH), Business Regulation ¶ 12-634 (hereinafter "FIE Wage Measures"); Several Opinions on Collective Bargaining in Respect of Foreign Investment Enterprise Wages (promulgated on February 14, 1997, by the General Office of the Ministry of Labor), *reprinted in* CHINA LAWS FOR FOREIGN BUSINESS (CCH), Business Regulation ¶ 12-638 (standards for wage determinations in collective bargaining negotiations). These rules apply to all FIEs including FIEs limited by shares, *see infra* Chapter 16, Securities Regulations § C.4. *See also* Notice on the Issuing of Minimum Wage Standards for Staff and Workers of Enterprises in Guangdong Province (promulgated on May 22, 1995, by the Guangdong Provincial People's Government), *reprinted in* CHINA LAWS FOR FOREIGN BUSINESS (CCH), Special Zones & Cities ¶ 270-015 (setting minimum wage standards for the Guangdong Province).

67. FIE Wage Measures, art. 5.

68. Labor Law, art. 46; FIE Labor Regulations, art. 14.

69. FIE Wage Measures, arts. 8–10.

70. Labor Law, art. 50; FIE Labor Regulations, art. 15. For a discussion concerning the tax withholding rules, *see* Chapter 9, Taxation Law § C.

eight hours per day or forty hours per week), 200 percent of base wages for hours worked on rest days, and 300 percent of base wages for hours worked on national holidays.[71]

10. Penalties for Violations of Labor Laws

The MOL and the local labor administrative departments are responsible for supervising compliance with the Labor Law and applicable regulations.[72] Labor officials have the full right to enter the premises of an employer, inspect the work premises, and demand documentation and other tangible items, such as the safety equipment provided employees, to determine compliance.[73] The trade unions also have contractual and regulatory rights to oversee the activities of the employer.[74]

If the employer violates the Labor Law or applicable regulations, including violations of child labor standards, standards for women, and wage and hour violations, the MOL or its local labor department may issue a notice of violation, a cease and desist order, an order for compensation for the injured employee, or an order for monetary penalty against the employer.[75] For violations of workplace health and safety standards or other serious violations, the labor officials may suspend operations of the enterprise or take steps to cancel the company's business license in egregious cases.[76] For serious infractions involving false imprisonment, improper search or seizure, battery, conduct considered insulting, or physical violence, the public

71. Labor Law, art. 44.

72. In March 1998, the 9th National People's Congress (NPC) of the People's Republic of China announced an institutional reorganization of the various ministries, reducing the total number from 40 to 29. The NPC retained 27 of the original ministries and added two new ministries. The purpose of the reforms is to improve efficiency, streamline the massive government bureaucracy, separate the government from economic enterprise administration, reduce the scope of corruption, and reduce the civil service. With respect to labor matters, the Ministry of Labor and Social Security (MOL) replaces the Ministry of Labor, the Ministry of Personnel, Ministry of Civil Affairs, and the medical insurance functions of the Ministry of Health. The State Council is responsible for carrying out the reorganization plan at the national level. Although the organizational structure of the local congresses mirror the government structure, it is unclear as to whether the provincial governments will adopt the reforms initiated by the NPC in March 1998. The reorganization process has led to confusion concerning the agencies responsible for labor matters and jurisdictional conflicts over certain issues. Although the reorganization process has been anticipated to result in lax enforcement of labor law violations, the MOL has been aggressive in its efforts to develop a regulatory framework to meet the institutional and economic changes affecting the country in 1998.

73. Labor Law, arts. 85–87.

74. Labor Law, art. 88; Trade Union Law, arts. 17, 21; Beijing Trade Union Regulations, arts. 21–23.

75. Labor Law, arts. 89–96. *See also* Civil Law, art. 123. The Civil Law provides that an employer is liable for injury caused in the course of work that involves a high degree of danger, including work with poisonous, radioactive, and explosives materials; high-speed transport tools; or high-altitude conditions. An employer's responsibility is reduced if the injured party is found to be liable for his or her injuries. Civil Law, art. 131.

76. Labor Law, art. 92. The officers and directors of an FIE who are found to be personally responsible for subjecting employees to unsafe work conditions may be prosecuted criminally. Labor Law, art. 93; Criminal Law, arts. 134–139. *See infra* Chapter 23, Criminal Liability for FIE Activities § A.2.

security bureau (i.e., the Chinese police) is empowered to initiate a criminal investigation and prosecution of the responsible management personnel. In such situations, the public security bureau also has the right to detain the management personnel for up to fifteen days pending an investigation.[77]

If the employer arbitrarily arranges for employees to work extra shifts or extra hours in violation of the State Council regulations, the MOL may impose a fine of up to five times the total amount paid to those employees who worked extra hours in violation of the regulations.[78] A failure to pay the minimum wage exposes an FIE to pay compensation to the employee in the sum of 20 percent to 100 percent of the difference between the standard minimum wage and the actual wage paid to the employee.[79] If the FIE obstructs or refuses to follow the instructions of the labor administration, the FIE may be fined up to 0.1 percent of its monthly business income.[80]

11. Dispute Resolution

The parties to a labor dispute are required to resolve the dispute in stages. First, the parties, including the enterprise and the employee, are required to engage in consultation.[81] If the parties are unable to resolve the matter informally, they are required to apply to the labor dispute mediation committee of the enterprise for voluntary conciliation. Under the Labor Dispute Rules, mediation of a dispute is strongly encouraged. If such efforts fail, the parties may apply to the local labor dispute arbitration commission to initiate an arbitration proceeding. If one party disagrees with the tribunal's arbitration

77. Labor Law, art. 96.

78. FIE Labor Regulations, art. 29. The total amount paid to employees is calculated at the average hourly or daily wage actually paid for the current month for each employee.

79. FIE Labor Regulations, art. 29. *See also* Notice on the Issuing of Minimum Wage Standards for Staff and Workers of Enterprises in Guangdong Province (promulgated on May 22, 1995, by the Guangdong Provincial People's Government), *reprinted in* China Laws for Foreign Business (CCH), Special Zones & Cities ¶ 270-015; Handling of Labor Disputes Regulations (issued on July 27, 2002, by the Qingdao Municipal Government).

80. Labor Law, art. 101; FIE Labor Regulations, art. 32.

81. Labor Law, art. 77. *See also* Rules of the People's Republic of China on the Handling of Enterprise Labor Disputes (promulgated on July 6, 1993, by the State Council), art. 6, *reprinted in* China Laws for Foreign Business (CCH), Business Regulation ¶ 12-618 (hereinafter the "Labor Dispute Rules"); Official Reply Concerning the Scope of Accepting and Hearing the Labor Arbitration Cases (promulgated on December 7, 1993, by the Ministry of Labor); Official Reply Concerning Whether Labor Dispute Arbitration Commission Has the Right or Not to Change the Settlement Made by Enterprises (promulgated on June 14, 1993, by the Ministry of Labor); Circular Concerning Promulgating "Rules on Organization of Labor Dispute Arbitration Commission" (promulgated on November 5, 1993, by the Ministry of Labor); Official Reply Concerning Difficult Issues of Labor Dispute Arbitration (promulgated on February 8, 1994, by the Ministry of Labor); Circular Concerning Several Issues in the Work of Labor Dispute Arbitration (promulgated on September 1, 1995, by the Ministry of Labor); Official Reply Concerning the Issues on Procedure of Labor Dispute Arbitration (promulgated on July 25, 1996, by the Ministry of Labor); Official Reply Concerning Whether the Labor Dispute Arbitration Commission Can Reaccept the Labor Dispute Cases Which Have Been Withdrawn (promulgated on July 8, 1997, by the Ministry of Labor).

award, the disputing party may file a claim in the people's court. The Labor Dispute Rules provide that the following matters are subject to the aforementioned dispute resolution procedures:

(1) A dispute concerning the dismissal of an employee
(2) A dispute concerning the resignation or voluntary termination of employment by the employee
(3) A dispute involving compensation, insurance, welfare, training, or labor protection
(4) A dispute concerning the performance or interpretation of a labor contract[82]

a. Labor Mediation

The labor dispute mediation committee of an enterprise is required to consist of three individuals chosen by and representing the employees, employer, and the trade union.[83] If an enterprise does not have a trade union, the representatives of the employer and the employee have the discretion to either form a two-member committee or appoint an additional person. The mediation committee must complete the conciliation process within 30 days of the date the parties apply.[84] The mediation process is based upon consent and voluntary participation, and either party may cease involvement at any time. If an agreement is reached, a written settlement agreement must be prepared and signed by the mediation committee and the parties.[85]

b. Labor Arbitration

If the parties are unable to mediate a dispute, they may file an application for arbitration with the labor dispute arbitration commission established at the city or county level. A labor arbitration commission consists of representatives of the MOL or other labor authorities, trade union, and the economic affairs administrative department designated by the government.[86] In practice, the MOL or other labor authority is responsible for the administration of arbitration cases.

A party to a labor dispute is required to file a written application for arbitration within six months from the date that the party knew or should have known that there was a violation of rights that triggered the labor dispute.[87] An application for arbitration is required to specify the names and address of the parties, the legal representatives, the facts and reasoning for

82. Labor Dispute Rules, art. 2.
83. Labor Dispute Rules, arts. 7–8.
84. Labor Dispute Rules, art. 10.
85. Labor Dispute Rules, art. 11.
86. Labor Dispute Rules, art. 13.
87. Labor Dispute Rules, art. 23. An application may be filed after the six-month limitations period for extenuating circumstances beyond the control of the parties.

the claim, and the names of all potential witnesses. A party to a labor arbitration may be represented by legal counsel.[88] The applicant is also required to submit all supporting documents in favor of its claims. Within seven days of receiving the application, the commission is required to accept or reject the application for arbitration, and thereafter notifies the parties within seven days. The defendant is required to respond to the commission and to file an answer or statement in defense within fifteen days and include supporting documentation.[89] A failure by the defendant to submit an answer within the prescribed time limit does not affect the proceeding. The commission will appoint the arbitrators to the tribunal, with most cases involving three arbitrators. Individuals that are related to any of the parties or have a personal interest in the labor dispute may not act as arbitrators.[90] Either party may request that a particular arbitrator withdraw from the tribunal if bias is demonstrated. The tribunal is required to complete the entire arbitration proceeding, including a hearing, within sixty days from the date the tribunal is formed.[91]

The commission is required to give the parties at least four days' notice of the arbitration hearing. By law, the tribunal is required to attempt to resolve a dispute by mediation prior to the conclusion of the arbitration hearing.[92] If a party fails to attend an arbitration hearing after receiving written notice and fails to attend without a legitimate reason, the party is deemed to be in default and an award may be entered in his or her absence.[93] All personnel information disclosed during the course of a proceeding is confidential and may not be disclosed by the arbitrators or the commission.[94]

c. Litigation

If a party disagrees with an arbitration tribunal's award, that party is required to file a complaint with the people's court within fifteen days of receiving the award notice. If the party fails to institute legal proceedings within the required time, the award becomes final and is not subject to judicial review.[95] In the event that a party fails to implement either a mediation

---

88. Labor Dispute Rules, art. 19.
89. Labor Dispute Rules, art. 25.
90. Labor Dispute Rules, arts. 35, 36. An arbitrator may be criminally liable if he or she engages in unethical conduct such as favoritism, acceptance of payments, or disclosure of confidential information. Labor Dispute Rules, art. 38.
91. Labor Dispute Rules, art. 32. An extension of no more than thirty days may be granted in complicated cases.
92. Labor Dispute Rules, art. 27.
93. Labor Dispute Rules, art. 26.
94. Labor Dispute Rules, art. 33.
95. Labor Dispute Rules, art. 30. *See also* Several Questions Concerning the Application of Law to the Trial of Labor Dispute Cases Interpretation (issued on April 16, 2001, by the Supreme People's Court). The SPC Labor Dispute Interpretation provides that when a party to a labor dispute does not

agreement or arbitration award, the injured party may apply to the people's court for enforcement.[96] The Chinese courts have rarely addressed employment litigation other than cases to confirm or set aside labor arbitration matters. In recent years, Chinese employees have resorted to litigation to redress employment-related claims such as wrongful termination and invasions of privacy.[97]

The MOL issued an internal report in August 1998 that stated that there had been a significant increase in employment disputes over the past three years, which peaked in 1997 at 71,254 disputes.[98] This was an increase of 55 percent over 1996. These cases involved foreign and domestic employers. The MOL report found that employees that initiated arbitration were victorious 56 percent of the time while employers prevailed a mere 16 percent of the time. The balance of the cases were resolved through mediation[99] or, in 4 percent of the cases, proceeded to the people's court for a resolution. The report also found that employment-related disputes involving foreign companies increased by 131 percent between 1996 and 1997. The MOL survey also noted that 47 percent of the cases involved wage and hour issues,

accept the judgment of a labor arbitration commission, he or she may submit the case for review to the people's court. The court with jurisdiction is where the employer is located or where the employment contract was performed. SPC Labor Dispute Interpretation, art. 8. The SPC order states that in the event of a merger, the successor work unit will be a party in labor disputes arising before the merger; in the event of a division, the work unit that effectively is the employer will be the party in labor disputes arising before the merger. The order further states that when a party does not accept the judgment of the labor arbitration commission and submits a lawsuit to the people's court, the award of the arbitration commission will be invalidated. However, when some employees accept an arbitration award while others submit a lawsuit to the people's court, the arbitration award is legally effective for the workers who accepted the award.

96. Labor Dispute Rules, art. 31.

97. Chinese lawyers are increasingly taking a much bolder approach to employment litigation against foreign parties. In a case filed in the Guangzhou Yuexiu People's Court, a former employee of Procter & Gamble sued P&G China and his supervisor for defamation, invasion of privacy, and "spiritual torture," seeking compensatory damages in the sum of RMB400,000 ($48,193). Plaintiff claims that P&G took possession of his work computer and disclosed personal and private information to the public. P&G admitted that it took possession of the plaintiff's computer, which is company property, when plaintiff advised the company that he was leaving P&G to work for another company. P&G confiscated the computer to protect the company's business secrets. The outcome of the case is left for observation. *See* Zhan, *Local Employee Sues P&G in Privacy Case,* China Daily (June 11, 1998), available on Lexis, News Library, or on the Web site of the China Daily at http://www.chinadaily.com.cn. *See also* P. Pan, *Chinese Workers' Rights Stop at Courtroom Door, Washington Post,* (June 28, 2002), available online at http://www.washingtonpost.com (article illustrates the difficulties workers have in enforcing their rights before judges perceived to be corrupt). Chinese employees are increasingly using the judicial system for labor-related disputes. In 2002, the Supreme People's Court issued a report stating that in 2001 the courts in China heard 100,440 labor-related litigation matters, which was an increase of 33% over 2000. *See Labor Disputes and Wilderness Cases More Common in Courtroom,* China Daily (March 11, 2002).

98. For an analysis of the MOL report, *see* Wan & Dorn, *Labor Disputes Continue to Rise,* China Law Update 7 (Sept. 25, 1998).

99. In 1998, China had 1.57 million mediators and 17,000 arbitrators that work with 270,000 mediation committees and 3,159 arbitration committees across the nation. *See* Li, *Labor Disputes Increase, Cause Concern,* China Daily (Mar. 7, 1998), available on Lexis, News Library, or the Web site of the China Daily at http://www.chinadaily.com.cn.

26.2 percent of the cases concerned issues arising under employment contract terms, and 16.8 percent involved retirement and pension benefits.

B. Representative Office Employment

A representative office (RO)[100] is prohibited from employing Chinese nationals directly and is required to contract with an approved labor bureau or agency for purposes of its personnel needs.[101] The law requires that a written contract be executed between the labor bureau and the representative office. Traditionally, the government-owned Foreign Enterprise Services Corporation (FESCO) was the only labor bureau authorized to work with foreign parties. For years, FESCO held a monopoly on employment matters of local Chinese personnel, and its practices were frowned upon by FIEs that were required to use FESCO's services.[102] In the early 1990s, the administration for industry and commerce for major cities began to allow other labor bureaus to compete against FESCO.[103] Today, foreign companies with RO operations in major cities have a choice of labor bureaus to engage for purposes of local personnel needs. FESCO has become more and more competitive with the labor bureaus that have broken FESCO's traditional monopoly on employment matters. In response to the competition, FESCO has improved its efficiency and services.

An RO is prohibited from recruiting employees directly, and the employment of Chinese nationals independently from authorized labor bureaus may result in monetary penalties. In practice, an RO may recruit an employee independently of the labor bureau but is still required to formally retain the employee by and through the labor bureaus.[104] The labor bureaus,

100. *See supra* Chapter 4, FIE Organizational Structure and Approval Procedures, § A.1., for a discussion of the scope and limitations, and approval procedures for representative offices. *See also* Interim Regulations of the State Council of the PRC Concerning the Control of Resident Representative Offices of Foreign Enterprises (promulgated October 30, 1980, by the State Council), art. 11, *reprinted in* China Laws for Foreign Business (CCH), Business Regulation ¶ 7-500. *See also* Procedures of the State Administration for Industry and Commerce of the People's Republic of China for the Registration and Administration of Resident Representative Offices of Foreign Enterprises (promulgated March 15, 1983, by the State Council), art. 10, *reprinted in* China Laws for Foreign Business (CCH), Business Regulation ¶ 7-560.

101. Provisional Measures for the Administration of the Registration of Employees of Foreign Enterprise Representative Offices Stationed in Beijing, art. 2 (promulgated September 30, 1986, by the Beijing Municipal Administration for Industry and Commerce), *reprinted in* China Laws for Foreign Business (CCH), Business Regulation ¶ 12-586 (hereinafter referred to as "Beijing RO Employment Measures").

102. During its monopoly years, FESCO had been accused of providing employees who spied on employers. FESCO also required its employees to attend a weekly debriefing meeting.

103. Administrative Regulations of the Beijing Municipal People's Government on the Recruitment of Chinese Employees by Resident Representative Offices of Foreign Companies (promulgated on May 14, 1996, by the Beijing Municipal People's Government), *reprinted in* China Laws for Foreign Business (CCH), Special Zones & Cities ¶ 170-155.

104. Beijing RO Employment Measures, art. 5. *See infra* Sample Contract for the Employment of Chinese Citizens, Appendix A.

for a fee, assist foreign parties in recruitment, employment searches, development of policies and procedures, and supervision and training of employees. The labor bureaus also provide the retirement benefits, medical benefits, worker compensation insurance, and other benefits for the employees.

In addition, ROs are allowed to have separate nonbinding "agreements" with their local employees that usually provide for rules of conduct, personnel practices, bonuses in addition to those required by the labor bureau, and other matters. A separate agreement with the RO's "employees" may provide for, among other things, the following:

(1) Recognition of Chinese rules concerning the prohibition on profit-making activities for ROs
(2) Additional nonbonus compensation not covered in the labor bureau contract
(3) A recognition of anticorruption laws
(4) Policies concerning reimbursement of business-related expenses
(5) Confidentiality, noncompetition, conflict of interest, nonsolicitation, intellectual property, and other similar issues important to the RO

The labor bureaus encourage separate agreements but require that they obtain a copy for their records. Any agreements, correspondence, or policies directed to employees should avoid use of the language "sales" and "sales quota" to avoid tax liability. The agreement with a labor bureau may be in English (or other foreign language), but the binding version is in the Chinese language. Although FESCO and the labor bureaus prefer to use their form agreements, many of the terms are negotiable as long as a violation of the labor laws does not result. Although the Labor Law does not directly apply to ROs since a representative office must continue to employ Chinese nationals through an authorized labor bureau, the standards and requirements of the Labor Law are applicable by contract.

Employees work a five-day week, eight hours a day, and overtime is paid on an hourly basis. Salaries are calculated on a 13-month basis that includes a one-month bonus. Since employees also are provided a one-month vacation, representative offices must pay for 13 months and receive 11 months of employee time. For FESCO-referred workers, the wages are paid to the labor bureau directly and not to the employee. The FESCO worker may take home 40–45 percent of the salary. With other labor bureaus, the employee is allowed to receive a larger portion of his or her salary directly. If the employee is a highly skilled or executive level worker, the labor bureau may allow the worker to keep most of his or her salary and will only charge an administration fee for maintaining the contractual relationship. The remaining wage is withheld by FESCO to cover the employee's housing, medical care, and pensions.

C. Merger and Acquisitions: Employment Concerns

Post-WTO China has adopted a number of M&A rules and regulations that have impact on labor issues, which essentially require that merging companies prepare a plan for addressing labor-related issues prior to the completion of an acquisition. The pertinent regulations are as follows:

1. Regulations on the Merger and Division of FIEs

The regulations are formulated to regulate merger and division activities associated with FIEs. The regulations are applicable to the merger or division of EJVs, CJVs with legal person status, WFOEs, or joint-stock limited companies with foreign investment.[105] Each party to the merger agreement must guarantee that the original employees of the proposed merged FIEs will be fully employed, or the employment issues be "properly settled."[106] The FIE merger agreement must be submitted to the labor and foreign investment approval authorities, and the merger agreement must include a provision on employee settlements.[107]

2. Provisional Regulations on Utilizing Foreign Investment in Restructuring State-Owned Enterprises

The regulations are applicable to activities that use foreign investment to convert SOEs and incorporated enterprises with state-owned shares (with the exception of financial enterprises and listed companies) into incorporated FIEs, or to establish incorporated FIEs.[108] One of the mandatory requirements in utilization of foreign investment in restructuring SOEs is that "when, after restructuring, control over one enterprise is shifted to foreign investors, or all or important operative assets of one enterprise are sold to foreign investors, the restructuring party and the restructuring enterprise must make plans for the appropriate care of employees, and the plans must be approved following consideration by an employee representative

105. Regulations on the Merger and Division of Foreign Investment Enterprises (promulgated by the Ministry of Foreign Trade and Economic Cooperation (MOFTEC) and the State Administration of Industry and Commerce (SAIC) on November 22, 2001), arts 1, 2.

106. Regulations on the Merger and Division of FIEs, art. 17.

107. Regulations on the Merger and Division of FIEs, arts. 19, 22.

108. Provisional Regulations on Utilizing Foreign Investment in Restructuring State-Owned Enterprises (promulgated by the State Economic and Trade Commission (SETC), Ministry of Finance (MOF), State Administration of Industry and Commerce (SAIC), and State Administration of Foreign Exchange (SAFE) on November 8, 2002, art. 2).

congress." The restructuring enterprise must use its current assets to pay for overdue employee salaries, overdue social insurance premiums, and other employment-related expenditures. When employees choose to continue employment with the restructured enterprise, new labor contracts must be signed or changes made to the original contracts. Economic compensation payments must be paid in full to employees whose labor contracts are terminated; the enterprise at issue must pay a one-time, full social insurance fee if the employees are released to the social insurance institutions. The economic compensation payments and social insurance fees can be deducted from the restructuring enterprise's pre-restructuring net assets, or shall be paid in priority from the proceeds of transferring State-asset ownership from State-asset owners.[109]

3. Provisional Regulations on Foreign Investors Merging with or Acquiring Domestic Companies

The regulations apply to the purchase of equity rights or subscription of an additional capital increase of a nonforeign enterprise (i.e., a domestic company) by a foreign investor that results in the establishment of an FIE, purchase and operation of the assets of a domestic company by a foreign investor, or purchase of assets of a domestic company by a foreign investor who subsequently establishes an FIE with the purchased assets.[110] Foreign investors purchasing equity rights or assets of a domestic company must apply to the appropriate authorities for approval by submitting a set of mandatory documents including the employee allocation plan of the merged or acquired domestic company.[111]

D. Employment of Foreigners in China

An employer is required to apply for an employment license (the "Employment License") in order to legally hire foreign personnel. The MOL requires that foreign personnel be hired to fill only positions that have special requirements and for which there are currently no suitable domestic applicants.[112] The

109. Provisional Regulations on Utilizing Foreign Investment in Restructuring State-Owned Enterprises, art. 8 (2).

110. Provisional Regulations on Foreign Investors Merging with or Acquiring Domestic Companies, promulgated by the Ministry of Foreign Trade and Economic Cooperation (MOFTEC), State Administration of Taxation, State Administration of Industry and Commerce (SAIC), and State Administration of Foreign Exchange (SAFE) on March 7, 2003, art. 2.

111. Provisional Regulations on Foreign Investors Merging with or Acquiring Domestic Companies, arts. 12 (9), 15 (8).

112. Employment of Foreigners Regulations, art. 6.

rules are purposefully designed to make it difficult for foreign companies to employ foreign personnel and to encourage "localization," the employment of local Chinese personnel.[113] The Employment License approval process not only compounds the administrative burden and the cost of doing business in China, foreign companies have been forced to employ local Chinese citizens in positions that are traditionally filled by trained expatriate staff, or have refused to hire a Chinese citizen to fill a position that requires specialized skills or allows access to sensitive information.

In order to obtain an Employment License for a foreign worker, an employer is required to submit an application that sets forth the reasons for recruiting the specific individual, the needs of the employer, and personal information of the foreign individual including nationality, sex, level of education and profession, health condition, marital status, and information concerning prior employment experience in China.[114] The application is accompanied by various documents, including the curriculum vitae of the foreign individual, a letter of intent of the employer concerning the appointment, a report prepared by the employer setting forth the justification for the proposed recruitment of the foreign employee, the credentials of the foreigner concerning the work to be performed (i.e., engineering license or diploma, medical degree, etc.), and a health certificate of the foreigner.[115] A foreigner must be at least 18 years of age and must have the appropriate professional skills or vocational training required for the position, no criminal record, a confirmed position by an employer, and a valid passport.[116] An FIE is required to submit its application, joint venture contract, and articles of association for approval.[117] The local labor departments are responsible for issuing the Employment License.

An Employment License is not necessary to employ the Chief Representative of an RO. An RO may apply directly for an Employment Permit without justifying the need for the employment.[118] An Employment License is also

113. Melvin & Sylvester, *Shipping Out: Expatriate Employees Need More Than a Ticket and Visa Before Departing for China,* CHINA BUSINESS REVIEW 30 (May–Jun. 1997).

114. Employment of Foreigners Regulations, art. 11. The application is attached to the regulations as Appendix 2 of the Employment of Foreigners Regulations. The approved form for the Employment License is attached as Appendix 1 to the regulations.

115. Employment of Foreigners Regulations, art. 11.

116. Employment of Foreigners Regulations, art. 7. A "foreigner" is defined as any person "not of Chinese nationality." *Id.* at 2. The regulations specifically exclude the employment of individuals who are residents of Taiwan, Hong Kong, or Macao, and does not apply to employment relationships in Taiwan, Hong Kong, or Macao. *Id.* at 32, 33.

117. Employment of Foreigners Regulations, art. 13. Chinese enterprises are required to obtain preliminary approval of vocational authorities before submitting an application for an Employment License of foreigners. The vocational authorities are required to assess the labor market demands. *Id.* at arts. 11, 12. An FIE does not require approval from vocational authorities to recruit a foreign individual. Private citizens in China are prohibited from employing foreigners. *Id.* at 34.

118. Employment of Foreigners Regulations, art. 10.

not necessary for a foreign specialist hired or funded directly by the Chinese government; foreign workers with specialized skills who are employed in offshore petroleum operations;[119] and foreigners employed as performers or musicians who hold a permit issued by the Ministry of Culture.[120]

A foreigner who has obtained approval to work in China must apply overseas to a Chinese embassy, consulate, or visa office to obtain a Work Visa. The foreign employee must hold a valid work visa for entry into China.[121] After the foreigner enters China, the employer has fifteen days to submit an Employment Registration Form for Foreigners to obtain an Employment Permit for the foreign party. The registration form must be accompanied by the Employment License, the employment contract between the employer and the foreigner, and the foreigner's passport.[122] An Employment Permit is valid only within the area specified in the permit. A foreigner issued an Employment Permit is required to present the permit to the public security authority to apply for a Residence Certificate (also referred to as a Residence Card) within thirty days of entering China.[123] After entering the country, a foreign employee may commence work only after obtaining an Employment Permit and a Residence Certificate.[124] Without a permit and residence certificate, a foreigner is prohibited from legally working in China.[125]

119. Foreign workers in the offshore petroleum industry are required to hold a special work permit. Employment of Foreigners Regulations, art. 9, § (2). Foreign chambers of commerce that employ foreign workers are required to follow the procedures in the Notice Concerning the Employment of Foreign Nationals by Foreign Chambers of Commerce in China (issued on January 20, 1999, by the Ministry of Civil Affairs, Division of Administration of Civilian Organizations).

120. Employment of Foreigners Regulations, art. 9.

121. *See* Regulation on Further Simplification of Entry Procedures for Foreign Experts (promulgated on March 4, 2002; jointly issued by the Ministry of Public Security, the Ministry of Foreign Affairs, the Ministry of Education, the Ministry of Science and Technology, the Ministry of Personnel, the Ministry of Labor and Social Security, the Ministry of Foreign Trade and Economic Cooperation, the State Council Office of Overseas Chinese Affairs, and the State Bureau of Foreign Experts) (Rules allow for issuance of two- to five-year visas for foreign experts, including senior executives and technical personnel associated with multinationals. The visas issued under these rules will be "F" visas, which are meant for individuals who are in China for less than 180 days at a time and are intended for persons who reside outside of China. For those individuals residing in China, the "Z" visa or residents visa will also be issued for up to two to five years. The Regulations provide that long-term visas will be issued to senior management personnel who hold the position of assistant general manager or higher, persons who invest $1 million or more in key poverty relief projects in Western or Central China, or persons that invest over $3 million in foreign investment projects). The city of Shanghai has also relaxed its resident permit and visa requirements; *see Shanghai PSB Changes Foreign Resident Permit and Visa Procedures,* CHINA MARKET INTELLIGENCE, THE U.S.-CHINA BUSINESS COUNCIL (October 1, 2003), available to members online at http://www.uschina.org.

122. Employment of Foreigners Regulations, art. 16. The Employment Registration Form for Foreigners is attached to the regulations as Appendix 3.

123. Employment of Foreigners Regulations, art. 16.

124. Employment of Foreigners Regulations, art. 8.

125. *See* Regulations of the People's Republic of China on Consular Privileges and Immunities (adopted on October 30, 1990, at the 16th Sess. of the Standing Comm. of the 7th NPC), art. 18, *reprinted in* CHINA LAWS FOR FOREIGN BUSINESS (CCH), Business Regulation 19-526 (outlines the rights and obligations of consular employees including exemptions from taxation, work visas).

The regulations provide that a foreigner and an employer are required to enter into a written labor contract. The regulations provide that a foreign employee's wages cannot be lower than the minimum wage in the locality,[126] and the maximum term of the contract is five years and may be renewed.[127] The Employment Permit automatically expires at the end of the contract term or is terminated for reasons set forth in the parties' agreement. In the event of termination, the employer is required to surrender the employee's Employment Permit and Residence Certificate and to assist the employee with his or her departure from China.[128] If an employee intends to change professions or employers, or move to a different region of China, he or she is required to obtain approval.[129]

Any dispute between the employer and the foreigner may be resolved consistent with the parties' contract, or through the dispute resolution provisions of the Labor Law and the Labor Dispute Rules.[130] Employers are required to submit to annual inspection of Employment Permits by the MOL or its affiliates.[131] A violation of the regulations may result in deportation of the foreign employee with deportation costs borne by the employer or the foreigner. The employer and the foreigner are also subject to fines and penalties for violations of the regulations.[132]

Key Laws and Regulations

Labor Law of the People's Republic of China (adopted July 5, 1994, by the 8th Sess. of the Standing Comm. of the 8th NPC)

Regulations on Labor Management in Foreign Investment Enterprises (promulgated August 11, 1994, by the Ministry of Labor and the MOFTEC)

(*Continued*)

126. Employment of Foreigners Regulations, art. 22.

127. Employment of Foreigners Regulations, art. 18.

128. Employment of Foreigners Regulations, art. 21. If the foreigner's residence status is revoked as a result of a violation of Chinese law, the employer is required to terminate the labor contract and assist with the employee's departure from China. *Id.* at 25.

129. Employment of Foreigners Regulations, art. 24.

130. Employment of Foreigners Regulations, art. 26; Labor Law, arts. 77–88.

131. Employment of Foreigners Regulations, art. 27. The annual inspection takes place within thirty days after the end of each year of employment of the foreigner. An Employment Permit is automatically invalid if the employer does not submit to the annual inspection.

132. Employment of Foreigners Regulations, arts. 29, 30.

(Continued from previous page)

Notice of Abolishment of the Notice Concerning Strengthening Labor Management in Foreign Investment Enterprises and Private Enterprises and the Effective Safeguarding of the Legal Rights and Interests of Employees (promulgated on March 4, 1994, by the MOL, the Ministry of Public Security, and the All-China Federation of Trade Unions and abolished on February 25, 2003)

Trade Union Law of the People's Republic of China (adopted on April 3, 1992, at the 5th Sess. of the 7th NPC and as amended on October 27, 2001)

Regulations of Beijing Municipality on Trade Unions in Sino-Foreign Joint Equity Enterprises (adopted on November 3, 1990, at the 23rd Sess. of the Standing Comm. of the 9th Beijing Municipal People's Congress)

Certain Regulations of Guangzhou Municipality on the Implementation of the Trade Union Law of the People's Republic of China (promulgated on June 8, 1995, by the Guangzhou Municipal People's Government)

Trial Measures Governing Collective Consultation on Wages (adopted on October 10, 2000, by the Ministry of Labor and Social Security)

Administrative Regulations on the Employment of Foreigners in China (jointly promulgated on January 22, 1996, by the MOL, MPS, and MOFTEC)

Rules of the Shenzhen Special Economic Zone on Industrial Injury Insurance (promulgated on February 26, 1993, and as amended on January 11, 2000, by the Standing Comm. of the Shenzhen Municipal People's Congress)

Regulations concerning the Labor Protection of Female Staff and Workers (adopted on June 28, 1988, at the 11th Sess. of the State Council)

Law on the Prevention and Control of Occupational Diseases (promulgated on October 27, 2001, and effective on May 1, 2002, by the Standing Committee of the National People's Congress)

Notification of the Ministry of Health on the Relevant Issues Concerning the Implementation of the Law on the Prevention and Control of Occupational Diseases (promulgated on May 8, 2002, by the Ministry of Health)

Regulations on Labor Protection in the Operational Fields Where Toxic Articles Are Used (adopted by the 57th Executive Meeting of the State Council on April 30, 2002, and effective on May 12, 2002)

Notice Regarding the Methods for Effectively Protecting the Livelihood and Re-employment of Redundant Employees of State-Owned Enterprises (promulgated by the State Council on June 29, 1998)

Regulations of the State Council Governing Working Hours for Workers (promulgated March 25, 1995, by the State Council)

Provisional Administrative Measures on Wage Incomes of Foreign Investment Enterprises (promulgated February 14, 1997, by the Ministry of Labor)

(Continued)

(*Continued from previous page*)

Several Opinions on Collective Bargaining in Respect of Foreign Investment Enterprise Wages (promulgated on February 14, 1997, by the General Office of the Ministry of Labor)

Rules of the People's Republic of China on the Handling of Enterprise Labor Disputes (promulgated on July 6, 1993, by the State Council)

Official Reply Concerning the Scope of Accepting and Hearing the Labor Arbitration Cases (promulgated on December 7, 1993, by the Ministry of Labor)

Official Reply Concerning Whether Labor Dispute Arbitration Commission Has the Right or Not to Change the Settlement Made by Enterprises (promulgated on June 14, 1993, by the Ministry of Labor)

Circular Concerning Promulgating "Rules on Organization of Labor Dispute Arbitration Commission" (promulgated on November 5, 1993, by the Ministry of Labor)

Official Reply Concerning Difficult Issues of Labor Dispute Arbitration (promulgated on February 8, 1994, by the Ministry of Labor)

Circular Concerning Several Issues in the Work of Labor Dispute Arbitration (promulgated on September 1, 1995, by the Ministry of Labor)

Official Reply Concerning the Issues on Procedure of Labor Dispute Arbitration (promulgated on July 25, 1996, by the Ministry of Labor)

Official Reply Concerning Whether the Labor Dispute Arbitration Commission Can Reaccept the Labor Dispute Cases which have been Withdrawn (promulgated on July 8, 1997, by the Ministry of Labor)

Several Questions Concerning the Application of Law to the Trial of Labor Dispute Cases Interpretation (issued on April 16, 2001, by the Supreme People's Court)

Interim Regulations of the State Council of the PRC Concerning the Control of Resident Representative Offices of Foreign Enterprises (promulgated October 30, 1980, by the State Council)

Procedures of the State Administration for Industry and Commerce of the People's Republic of China for the Registration and Administration of Resident Representative Offices of Foreign Enterprises (promulgated March 15, 1983, by the State Council)

Provisional Measures for the Administration of the Registration of Employees of Foreign Enterprise Representative Offices Stationed in Beijing (promulgated September 30, 1986, by the Beijing Municipal Administration for Industry and Commerce)

Administrative Regulations of the Beijing Municipal People's Government on the Recruitment of Chinese Employees by Resident Representative Offices of Foreign Companies (promulgated on May 14, 1996, by the Beijing Municipal People's Government)

(*Continued*)

(*Continued from previous page*)

Provisional Regulations on Utilizing Foreign Investment in Restructuring State-owned Enterprises (promulgated on November 8, 2002, by the State Economic and Trade Commission, Ministry of Finance, State Administration of Industry and Commerce, and State Administration of Foreign Exchange)

Provisional Regulations on Foreign Investors Merging with or Acquiring Domestic Companies (promulgated on March 7, 2003, by the Ministry of Foreign Trade and Economic Cooperation (MOFTEC), State Administration of Taxation, State Administration of Industry and Commerce (SAIC), and State Administration of Foreign Exchange)

Notice Concerning the Employment of Foreign Nationals by Foreign Chambers of Commerce in China (issued on January 20, 1999, by the Ministry of Civil Affairs, Division of Administration of Civilian Organizations)

Regulation on Further Simplification of Entry Procedures for Foreign Experts (promulgated on March 4, 2002, jointly issued by the Ministry of Public Security, the Ministry of Foreign Affairs, the Ministry of Education, the Ministry of Science and Technology, the Ministry of Personnel, the Ministry of Labor and Social Security, the Ministry of Foreign Trade and Economic Cooperation, the State Council Office of Overseas Chinese Affairs, and the State Bureau of Foreign Experts)

Chapter 11

Financial Regulation

For years, foreign investors have pleaded with China for real access to foreign exchange and quality financial services in order to meet the needs of their China operations. In response, the government has made significant changes since 1995 to China's banking and financial systems, including the adoption of new banking laws, rules governing the activities of foreign-funded financial institutions, rules and regulations affecting foreign exchange, regulations concerning the establishment of trusts and trust administration, and the regulation of group finance and financial leasing companies. Post-WTO, China's domestic banking institutions are preparing for foreign competition by upgrading their information technology infrastructure and by courting potential foreign investors. This chapter addresses the regulation of China's financial system and foreign exchange control rules. This chapter also addresses the accounting and auditing standards applicable to FIEs, and the joint annual review procedures designed to allow fiscal government agencies to conduct a single review process in place of multiple reporting procedures.

A. Banking Regulation

Prior to 1978, under the centrally planned economy in China, the People's Bank of China (PBOC) was in effect the only bank operating in China.[1] The

1. In 1980, China's membership in the World Bank and the International Monetary Fund was reinstated. In December 1981, the China Investment Bank was established to make use of World Bank funds.

PBOC performed the functions of both a central bank and a commercial bank, including currency issuance, deposits, lending, settlements, and foreign exchange. In 1978, the State Council created various banks with the intent of severing the commercial bank functions from the traditional central bank functions. The four commercial banks created were designed to focus on specific industry sectors, which included the Industrial and Commercial Bank of China (ICBC),[2] the Bank of China (BOC),[3] the Agricultural Bank of China (ABC),[4] and the Construction Bank of China (CBC), formerly known as the People's Construction Bank of China.[5] In 1985, these banks were further authorized to expand their operations, and the original areas of specialty are no longer clearly defined (e.g., agricultural sector for the ABC and the project finance sector for the CBC). All four commercial banks have expanded into international business and investment banking. In 1994, the State Council created three policy banks to address policy loans such as government subsidized financing, including the Export and Import Bank of China (Eximbank),[6] National Development Bank of China (NDB), and the Agricultural Development Bank of China (ADB). The NDB is responsible for financing infrastructure projects, the Eximbank is responsible for encouraging export sales of China products, and the ADB is responsible for policy loans to the agricultural sector.

Today, there are over a dozen national and regional commercial banks that are authorized to engage in both renminbi and foreign currency business, including the following banks: Bank of Communications,[7] CITIC

2. The ICBC was established to replace the PBOC with respect to commercial banking activities in urban areas.

3. The BOC, which is the most profitable Chinese bank, has focused primarily on foreign trade and foreign currency exchange, and has over 500 overseas offices in 19 countries and regions and has a strong presence in Hong Kong. The Bank of China (BOC) was established in 1912 and is currently a legal entity under the control of the State Council. For more information regarding the BOC, *see* http://www.bank-of-china.com. The BOC adheres to the Uniform Customs and Practice for Documentary Credits (UCPDC) of the International Chamber of Commerce (ICC) for the purpose of standardizing international transactions (ICC Publication No. 500). In addition, most Chinese banks adhere to the Uniform Rules for Demand Guarantees developed by the ICC (ICC Publication No. 458).

4. The Agricultural Bank was first established in March of 1955 but was closed during the Cultural Revolution (merged with the PBOC in 1965).

5. The Construction Bank of China resumed operations in 1983 and its original principal function is to administer the funds allocated for capital construction and exploration of natural resources.

6. In 2002, the Export-Import Bank of China merged with the export credit insurance department of People's Insurance Corp. of China to form the China Export & Credit Insurance Corp., or Sinosure. The Ministry of Finance has backed the company with a RMB4 billion ($483.9 million) fund and the new entity is required to promote exports by offering export credit risk insurance. Under the WTO's national treatment principle, Sinosure provides insurance for both Chinese and foreign companies exporting from China. The address and contact information for Sinosure is No. 5 Fu Wai North Street, Beijing; Tel: 86-10-8838-2288; Fax: 86-10-6303-4714.

7. The Bank of Communications was first established in 1908 and was merged with the PBOC in 1958. In 1986, the State Council authorized the establishment of the Bank of Communications with its headquarters in Shanghai. Fifty percent (50%) of the shares of the Bank of Communications is held by the PBOC, and local enterprises hold the balance of the bank's equity interest.

Industrial Bank, China Everbright Bank, Guangdong Development Bank, Shenzhen Development Bank, Huaxia Bank, and the Shanghai Pudong Development Bank.[8] China's banking system also includes cooperative banks, rural credit cooperatives, trust and investment companies, finance companies, urban credit cooperatives, and finance leasing companies.

In addition to the various domestic institutions, foreign banks have played a significant role in China's banking market. At the present time, there are over 500 offices and branches of foreign banks in the PRC. In 1995, and as amended in 2003, the NPC adopted two important banking laws that affect foreign financial institutions with operations in China, including the PRC Bank Law and the Commercial Bank Law.

1. PRC Bank Law

The Bank Law[9] provides that the PBOC is responsible for traditional central bank functions such as developing and implementing national monetary policies; issuing and controlling the circulation of renminbi; regulating financial institutions and the banking industry; managing the foreign exchange reserves of China; managing the national treasury; and engaging in international financial activities.[10] The PBOC is authorized to use a number of tools to implement the fiscal policies of the state including the establishment of interest rates;[11] a requirement that financial institutions deposit reserve funds; conducting transactions involving bonds and foreign exchange on the open

8. For an analysis of China's banking system, *see* J. Tang and M. Doyle, *Money and Banking* § 9.2, *in* Business Law in China (1997 ICC). For a chart outlining the structure of China's Financial Institutions, *see* China Information Services' Web site "ChinaOnLine" at http://www.chinaonline.com. For a discussion concerning the Export and Import Bank of China, *see* Zhang, *Eximbank Offers Support to Exporters,* CHINA BUSINESS WEEKLY (Oct. 25–31, 1998), available on Lexis, News Library, or on the Web site of the CHINA DAILY at http://www.chinadaily.com.cn. For a discussion of China's financial sector post-WTO, *see* China's Financial Sector, U.S.-CHINA BUSINESS COUNCIL (March 2002).

9. *See* Law of the People's Republic of China on the People's Bank of China (adopted on March 18, 1995, by the 3rd Sess. of the 8th NPC), *reprinted in* CHINA LAWS FOR FOREIGN BUSINESS (CCH), Business Regulation ¶ 8-450 (hereinafter the "Bank Law"). The PBOC is under the direct supervision of the State Council. In November 1998, the Chinese government abolished the provincial branches of the PBOC and set up nine regional branches divided by geographical areas. The purpose of eliminating the central bank's provincial subsidiaries is designed to eliminate the financial risks incurred by local governments' intervention in the PBOC's work. In the past, provincial leaders have been accused of ignoring national policies and improperly forcing the local PBOC offices to support underperforming local enterprises and projects that lacked economic feasibility. *See* Xu, *Bank Reform to Tighten Control,* CHINA DAILY (Nov. 17, 1998), available on Lexis, News Library, or on the Web site of the CHINA DAILY at http://www.chinadaily.com.cn.

10. Bank Law, art. 4.

11. *See generally* Provisional Regulations on Interest Rate Control (promulgated on December 11, 1990, by the PBOC), *reprinted in* CHINA LAWS FOR FOREIGN BUSINESS (CCH), Business Regulations ¶ 8-750 (outlines the PBOC's standards for interest rate formulation and penalties for violations of interest rate control provisions); Announcement of the People's Bank of China on the Reduction of Deposit and Loan Interest Rates and the Reform of the Deposit Reserve Fund System (promulgated on March 25, 1998, by the PBOC), *reprinted in* CHINA LAWS FOR FOREIGN BUSINESS (CCH), Business Regulations ¶ 8-710.

market; and providing requirements for the issuance of commercial loans.[12] The PBOC is administered by a governor nominated by the State Council and confirmed by the NPC. The Bank Law sets forth the organizational structure for the PBOC, financial and accounting requirements, and rules governing the issuance and control of renminbi.

In 2003, the PBOC was reorganized with the creation of the China Banking Regulatory Commission (CBRC), and assumed responsibility for regulating and supervising the banking industry, which were previously the functions of several departments of the PBOC. The PRC government approved of restructuring the central bank's role in formulating and implementing monetary policy and ensuring the overall stability of China's financial system. The PBOC is also responsible for administering the PRC's credit rating system and efforts against money laundering.[13]

2. Commercial Bank Law

The second important banking law enacted in 1995 is China's first commercial bank law.[14] The stated purpose of the 1995 Commercial Bank

12. Bank Law, art. 22.

13. Pursuant to the revised Bank Law, the PBOC's Monetary Policy Committee is responsible for the formulation and adjustment of monetary policies. Bank Law, art. 12. The PBOC is also responsible for the following tasks: (1) regulate the interbank lending, bond, foreign exchange, and gold markets (Bank Law, art. 4); (2) formulate rules jointly with the CBRC for payment and settlement procedures (Bank Law, art. 27); (3) supervise financial institutions with regard to deposit payments, foreign exchange control, and money laundering activities (Bank Law, art. 32); and (4) request the intervention of the CBRC with financial institutions in matters involving monetary policies and financial stability (Bank Law, art. 33). The amendments to the Bank Law in 2003 included the establishment of various departments including the Financial Market Department, Financial Stability Bureau, Credit Reference Administration Bureau, and the Anti-Money Laundering Bureau (previously part of the PBOC's Security Bureau). *See generally* Banking Supervision and Administration Rules (promulgated on December 27, 2003, by the NPC Standing Committee) (provides the legal basis for the CBRC and the agency's formal right to implement and monitor banking policy; provides the authority to the CBRC to monitor, investigate, and examine bank records for regulatory compliance; and provides the CBRC's jurisdiction over foreign and domestic companies operating in commercial banking, urban and rural credit cooperatives, financial asset management, and other financial services operations); Rules on the People's Bank of China (promulgated on December 27, 2003, by the NPC Standing Committee) (outlines the responsibilities of the CBRC and PBOC). On April 28, 2003, the CBRC announced the creation of fifteen divisions with jurisdiction and responsibility over particular sectors. For example, the CBRC First Division will be responsible for the supervision and administration of state-owned commercial banks and asset management companies. The Second Division will be responsible for the supervision and administration of shareholding commercial banks and municipal commercial banks, and the CBRC Third Division will be responsible for the supervision and administration of policy banks, postal savings agencies, and foreign-invested banks. *See generally* S. Harner, *New Laws Boost Banking Industry Supervision and Management*, CHINA L. & PRAC. (February 2004).

14. *See* Commercial Bank Law of the People's Republic of China (adopted on May 10, 1995, by the 13th Sess. of the 8th NPC, and as amended by the NPC on December 27, 2003), *reprinted in* CHINA LAWS FOR FOREIGN BUSINESS (CCH), Business Regulation ¶ 8-350 (hereinafter the "Commercial Bank Law"). The Amendments to the Commercial Bank Law expand the scope of both foreign and domestic banks while easing government restrictions. The expanded scope of operations includes bill acceptance, financial debt purchase and sales, bank card services, and foreign exchange settlement and sales. The Amendments transfer much of the PBOC's authority to supervise and regulate China's commercial banks, credit cooperatives, policy banks, financial asset management companies, trust and investment companies,

Law is to standardize China's banking system, to promote the development of its "socialist market economy," and is an attempt to elevate China's practices to international banking standards.[15] The provisions of the Commercial Bank Law are applicable to foreign-funded commercial banks, equity joint venture commercial banks, and the branch offices of foreign commercial banks.[16] A commercial bank may engage in the following activities:

(1) Receive public deposits[17]
(2) Provide short-term, medium-term, or long-term loans[18]
(3) Conduct domestic and overseas settlements
(4) Make payments on negotiable instruments
(5) Issue financial bonds and other debt instruments
(6) Act as an agent to issue, purchase, and underwrite government bonds
(7) Purchase and sell government bonds for its own account
(8) Engage in interbank loans
(9) Purchase and sell foreign exchange on its own account or on behalf of its customers

---

financial companies, financial lease companies, and other banking institutions to the CBRC. The PBOC remains China's central bank, with authority to formulate and implement monetary policies and to monitor and safeguard financial markets, including a new power to trade bonds on the open market. In certain circumstances, the PBOC may request the CBRC to investigate a regulated financial institution. *See also* Administrative Regulations Governing Financial Institutions (promulgated on August 9, 1994, by the People's Bank of China, and as amended in 2003 by the China Banking Regulatory Commission), *reprinted in* CHINA LAWS FOR FOREIGN BUSINESS (CCH), Business Regulation ¶ 8-400 (outlines procedures for the administration of financial institutions, standards for applications, standards for control of licenses, standards for management of capital funds or working funds, qualifications for principal personnel, and penalties for violations of the law). *See* CBRC Grants New Streamlined Financial Licenses, China Market Intelligence, THE U.S.-CHINA BUSINESS COUNCIL (July 16, 2003), available online to members at http://www.uschina.org.

15. Commercial Bank Law, art. 1. As amended in 2003, the language concerning the "socialist market economy" was dropped. Article 1 now states: "This Law is formulated in order to strengthen banking regulation, to standardize regulation, to prevent and dispel banking risk, to protect the lawful rights and interests of depositors and other customers, and to encourage healthy growth of the banking industry."

16. Commercial Bank Law, art. 88. Although the Commercial Bank Law applies to foreign-funded financial institutions, they are restricted in the scope of their operations. *See infra* note 89 and accompanying text.

17. For deposits of foreign currency, *see* Regulations of the Bank of China on Foreign Currency Deposits (Category A) (promulgated on February 26, 1993, by the Bank of China), *reprinted in* CHINA LAWS FOR FOREIGN BUSINESS (CCH), Business Regulation ¶ 8-560; Regulations of the Bank of China on Foreign Currency Deposits (Category B) (promulgated on February 26, 1993, by the Bank of China), *reprinted in* CHINA LAWS FOR FOREIGN BUSINESS (CCH), Business Regulation ¶ 8-565; Administrative Regulations on Domestic Foreign Exhange Accounts (promulgated on October 7, 1997, by the PBOC), *reprinted in* CHINA LAWS FOR FOREIGN BUSINESS (CCH), Business Regulation ¶ 8-569.

18. The PRC regulates loans provided by a syndication of lending institutions. The PBOC (and now the CBRC) requires that all syndicated loans must be reported and approved. *See* Provisional Measures on Syndicated Loans (promulgated on October 7, 1997, by the PBOC), *reprinted in* CHINA LAWS FOR FOREIGN BUSINESS (CCH), Business Regulation ¶ 8-732 (outlining standards for syndicate lending, syndicated loan agreements, obligations of the lead bank, and administration of syndicated loans).

(10) Provide trade financing services such as letters of credit and guarantees[19]
(11) Act as an insurance agent
(12) Establish branch offices[20]
(13) Provide safety deposit boxes for customers
(14) Issue credit cards and other credit services[21]

A commercial bank is an autonomous entity with legal person status and must be sufficiently capitalized to engage in banking activities.[22] Commercial banks are required to act independent of governmental enterprises and free from influence of local government officials who, in the past, demanded that banks pander to local interests notwithstanding that many enterprises were financially incapable of repaying loans.[23] Commercial banks are now

19. *See* Measures on the Settlement of Domestic Letters of Credit (promulgated on June 23, 1997, by the PBOC), *reprinted in* CHINA LAWS FOR FOREIGN BUSINESS (CCH), Business Regulation ¶8-460 (outlines the standards for letters of credit, standards for issuing a letter of credit, required terms of a letter of credit, obligations of the issuing and notifying financial institutions, conditions for negotiated payments, standards for examination and approval of documents, and fees). *See also* Deutsch, *Legislation Profiles: Letter of Credit Legislation,* 4 CHINA LAW NEWS 9–10 (Oct. 1997).

20. Commercial Bank Law, arts. 19–23. A branch office of a commercial bank is required to obtain the approval of the CBRC, which involves the review of the bank's accounting records and information concerning the proposed branch office. A commercial bank is required to exercise a systemwide accounting system in order to control the activities of its branch operations. All civil liability incurred by a branch shall be borne by the head office. A commercial bank is required to publicly announce the opening of any new branch office. *But see* Administration of the Establishment of Business Network Points in the Same City by Commercial Banks Procedures (issued on February 21, 2002, by the PBOC) (The Procedures outline the pre-notification process for establishment of retail sub-branch networks and ATMs, and provide that a commercial bank applying for a sub-branch must have paid-in capital of RMB10,000,000, may only apply for one sub-branch per application, and is subject to sequencing requirements that effectively limit the number of new sub-branches to one per city per year. These Procedures apply equally to Chinese and foreign banks.)

21. Commercial Bank Law, art. 3. The use of installment loans for consumer consumption, such as with the purchase of automobiles, has yet to be fully embraced in China, but change is ongoing. *See China Credit Plans Needed to Expand Consumption,* CHINA DAILY (Aug. 17, 1998), available on Lexis, News Library, or on the Web site of the CHINA DAILY at http://www.chinadaily.com.cn. The use of credit and debit cards is increasing in China with foreign companies actively participating. Growth has been slow given China's immature consumer credit card culture. *See generally* M. Pacelle, *American Express, Chinese Bank Team Up to Provide Credit Cards,* WALL ST. J. (March 30, 2004) (in 2004, American Express teamed up with the Industrial & Commercial Bank of China to offer credit cards to Chinese consumers); J. Baglole, *Citibank Takes Risk by Issuing Cards in China,* WALL ST. J. (March 10, 2004) (in 2004 Citibank linked up with the Shanghai Pudong Development Bank to issue credit cards). With the approval of and under the supervision of the CBRC, commercial banks may be authorized to engage in various fee-based banking services such as (i) account collection and settlement; (ii) credit card services; (iii) loan commitments; (iv) fund management and custodianship; and (v) consultancy and advisory services. Commercial banks may engage in such intermediary activity upon submission of a written application to the CBRC. However, commercial banks may not issue or engage in the direct purchase or sale of securities and are limited to services related to dividend distribution. Commercial banks undertaking an intermediary business are to submit quarterly and annual reports to the CBRC. The CBRC is authorized to suspend a commercial bank for engaging in unapproved activities or for failure to submit a report as required by law. Relevant Questions in Implementing the Circular (issued on April 22, 2002, by the People's Bank of China).

22. Commercial Bank Law, art. 4.

23. Commercial Bank Law, art. 4. Article 41 of the Commercial Bank Law provides that "[n]o unit or individual is allowed to compel commercial banks to grant loans or provide guarantees. Commercial

independently liable for their liquidity and profitability, and by law are required to protect the interest of their depositors and are prohibited from exercising favoritism toward a local government in its loan writing decisions.[24]

a. Approval Procedures for Commercial Banks

The establishment of a commercial bank is subject to the approval of the China Banking Regulatory Commission (CBRC). An entity or individual is prohibited from engaging in banking activities or using the word "bank" in its company name without approval from the CBRC.[25] An applicant for a commercial bank is required to meet the following conditions in order to obtain approval to engage in banking activities:

(1) Adopt articles of association in conformity with the Company Law[26]
(2) Have registered capital of at least RMB1 billion for a commercial bank, RMB100 million for an urban cooperative bank, and RMB50 million for a rural cooperative bank
(3) The senior management must possess specialized professional expertise and experience[27]
(4) Have a sound organizational structure and management system
(5) Have adequate premises, equipment, security, and other necessary facilities[28]

---

banks shall have the authority to refuse any unit or individual which seeks to compel the issue of a loan or provision of a guarantee." Both the governmental unit demanding a loan and the bank employee are subject to discipline and personal liability in cases involving loans that are inappropriately issued to government units. Commercial Bank Law, art. 85.

24. Commercial Bank Law, art. 6.

25. Commercial Bank Law, art. 11. *See* Measures for the Administration of Finance Licenses (issued on May 26, 2003, by the China Banking Regulatory Commission, and effective July 1, 2003) (hereinafter the "CBRC Licensing Measures"). The CBRC Licensing Measures simplify the permit system introduced in 1994. As revised, the Measures provide that the CBRC will issue licenses to domestic financial institutions with the status of a legal person in China, as well as branches of foreign financial institutions, while the provincial-level CBRC offices will issue licenses to branches of domestic financial institutions and sub-branches of foreign financial institutions. The CBRC Licensing Measures provide that licenses are not subject to annual review and are required to be updated or replaced only if the financial institution changes its name, legal representative, address, or operating circumstances, or if the license is lost or destroyed. *See CBRC Grants New Streamlined Financial Licenses,* China Market Intelligence, The U.S.-China Business Council (July 16, 2003), available online to members at http://www.uschina.org.

26. A commercial bank is required to comply with the provisions of the Company Law and specifically with respect to the organizational form and institutional framework. Commercial Bank Law, art. 17.

27. A person who has been convicted of crimes of corruption, bribery, conversion of property, embezzlement, or "undermining social economic order" is prohibited from holding a senior management position in a commercial bank. A person who has held a position as a director or manager of a company declared bankrupt and liquidated due to poor management, and has personal responsibility for the losses, is prohibited from holding a senior management position with a commercial bank. A person who has personal debts in default is prohibited from working in management at a commercial bank. Commercial Bank Law, art. 27.

28. Commercial Bank Law, arts. 12–14.

An applicant for a commercial bank is required to submit to the CBRC an application, feasibility study, and a number of other documents including the following:

(1) A draft articles of association
(2) Credentials of proposed management personnel
(3) A capital verification certificate
(4) Stock ledger
(5) Certificates of creditworthiness relating to shareholders who hold more than 10 percent of the registered capital
(6) Documentation outlining the bank's management principles and plans
(7) Information on the operational premises, security measures, and other facilities relevant to the operation
(8) Other documents and information as required by the CBRC[29]

Upon approval, the commercial bank is issued a business license by the CBRC and is thereafter required to present its license to the SAIC for a business registration certificate.[30] Commercial banks are required to use their business licenses in accordance with the provisions of the law and administrative regulations. The law prohibits a party from forging, altering, assigning, leasing, and lending a business license.[31] A commercial bank is required to obtain the approval of the CBRC to change its name, registered capital, address of its principal office, or shareholders that hold more than 10 percent of the total capital or total shares of the bank. CBRC approval is also required to amend the bank's articles of association, replace the chairman of the bank, readjust the scope of the bank's business operations, or to undergo a merger or division.[32]

b. Commercial Bank Operational Standards

In general, the key operating standard for financial institutions under the Commercial Bank Law, in light of China's history of favoritism, is to closely examine the creditworthiness of borrowers and to implement collection procedures to ensure the recovery of loans per schedule.[33] By law, the banks are

29. Commercial Bank Law, art. 15.
30. Commercial Bank Law, art. 16.
31. Commercial Bank Law, art. 26.
32. Commercial Bank Law, arts. 24, 25, 28. *See also* Provisional Regulations Concerning Investment in Financial Institutions Through Purchase of Shares (promulgated on July 28, 1994, by the People's Bank of China), *reprinted in* CHINA LAWS FOR FOREIGN BUSINESS (CCH), Business Regulation ¶ 8-666 (outlining procedures for acquisition of the shares of a financial institution and provision expressly prohibiting foreign investors from investing in Chinese-funded financial institutions).
33. Commercial Bank Law, art. 7. In June 2003, the PBOC created a nationwide credit database intended to improve the risk management of Chinese bank loans. Credit information on

protected in their efforts to recover unpaid debts from borrowers. In the past, financial institutions had little leverage to force a powerful governmental enterprise to repay its loan obligations. As a result, many enterprises defaulted on their obligations, leaving the banks with large underperforming portfolios. Although commercial banks have the discretion to operate their loan facilities, they are required to adhere to the "national industrial policies" of the PRC.[34]

The Commercial Bank Law also requires financial institutions to abide by the principles of fair competition and may not engage in "unfair rivalry" when promoting their business.[35] This rule reflects the realization that competition for banking business may become heated as the system continues to evolve into a free market, and especially since foreign-funded institutions seek to become players in China's banking industry. Commercial banks are also required to meet capital adequacy requirements, which in the past were difficult for domestic banks to maintain. Specifically, banks in China are now required to maintain an eight percent (8%) capital adequacy ratio and four percent (4%) core capital ratio.[36]

(1) Rules for Loan Contracts. A commercial loan must be in writing and signed by the bank and the borrower.[37] A commercial bank is required to fully evaluate the credit of a potential borrower including the ability to repay a loan, source of funds, income, method of repayment, and assets.[38] A bank has the discretion to demand that a borrower provide a guarantee secured by a mortgage or pledge.[39] The interest rates charged by a bank

---

RMB11.2 trillion ($1.4 trillion) is compiled on four million corporate borrowers in China. *China Creates Nationwide Credit Database,* China Market Intelligence, The U.S.-China Business Council (June 25, 2003), available online to members at http://www.uschina.org. *See also* J. Baglole, *Credit Ratings in China Can Be Mere Guesswork,* Wall St. J. (Jan. 5, 2004); K. Chen & J. Areddy, *Tracking China's Consumers: Personal Loans Off, but Credit-Check System is Spotty,* Wall St. J. (March 2, 2004), available online at http://www.awsj.com.

34. Commercial Bank Law, art. 34.

35. Commercial Bank Law, art. 9.

36. For more information on capital adequacy and core capital requirements, *see* the Web site of the China Banking Regulatory Commission at http://www.cbrc.gov.cn. China adheres to the capital adequacy standards under the Basel I rules, which reflect the capital-adequacy ratio of eight percent (8%). In 2003, China rejected the use of the Basel II standard that calculates the required capital-adequacy ratio through a three-part equation on the basis that it was too complicated and open to misinterpretation. *See Banking Update: CBRC Rejects Basel II Rules, NPC to Review Banking Laws,* China Market Intelligence, U.S.-China Business Council (August 20, 2003); M. DeSombre & W. Chen, *New Capital Rules Bring China's Banking Regulation up to Global Standards,* China L. & Prac. (April 2004).

37. Commercial Bank Law, art. 37.

38. Commercial Bank Law, art. 35. The PBOC (now under the jurisdiction of the CBRC) has adopted a set of guidelines concerning the classification of loan risks. For a brief discussion of the guidelines, *see* Harpole, *New Developments: Classifying Loan Risks,* 11 China Law News 17 (May 29, 1998).

39. Commercial Bank Law, art. 36. *See also* Secured Interest Law, chap. 2; Administrative Measures on Security Given to Foreign Parties by Domestic Institutions (promulgated on September 25, 1996, by

are required to be consistent with the upper and lower limits set by the CBRC.[40]

A borrower is required to repay both the principal and interest within the time required under the loan contract. If a borrower is in default of a loan, a commercial bank has a right to attach the secured property and to sell the property to satisfy the debt due. An auction must be conducted within one year of attachment.[41]

A commercial bank is prohibited from issuing an unsecured loan to a "related party" including directors, supervisors, management personnel, credit operation personnel, and their relatives or to individuals that have an interest in the bank or have held senior management positions in the bank. However, a commercial bank may issue a secured loan to a "related party" so long as the terms and conditions of the loan are consistent with loans granted to other borrowers.[42]

(2) Protection for Depositors. Commercial banks are required to operate in compliance with the principles of voluntary deposits, freedom of withdrawal, interest on deposits, and confidentiality of depositors when handling the business of personal savings deposits.[43] Confidentiality standards provide that, except when required by law, a commercial bank may refuse to allow third persons information concerning the accounts of individuals and entities with the bank.[44] Banks are required to set and publish the deposit interest rates in accordance with the upper and lower limits set by the CBRC, and are required to maintain sufficient reserves to ensure the payment of both principal and interest on demand by depositors.[45]

---

the PBOC), *reprinted in* CHINA LAWS FOR FOREIGN BUSINESS (CCH), Business Regulation ¶ 8-698 (hereinafter the "Security Measures"). The Security Measures provide that the SAFE has the authority to approve, administer, and register all guarantees issued by Chinese organizations, financial and non-financial, to foreign creditors. Prior to issuance, all guarantees are required to obtain approval except for financing of less than one year. To obtain approval, Chinese organizations are required to maintain certain liquidity and asset/liability standards. Foreign-invested financial institutions are considered to be foreign parties for purposes of the Security Measures.

40. Commercial Bank Law, art. 38.

41. Commercial Bank Law, art. 42.

42. Commercial Bank Law, art. 40.

43. Commercial Bank Law, art. 29.

44. Commercial Bank Law, arts. 29, 30.

45. Commercial Bank Law, arts. 31–33. In September 2003, the PBOC raised the deposit reserve ratio from six percent (6%) to seven percent (7%) of the total loans that each financial institution must deposit with the PBOC. *See PBOC Raises Deposit Reserve Ratio,* CHINA MARKET INTELLIGENCE, U.S.-CHINA BUSINESS COUNCIL (August 27, 2003). In April 2004, the PBOC increased the bank reserve requirement of bank deposits to 7.5% in a move to clamp down on fast growth of money supply and credit. The order applies to China's largest banks but exempts rural and urban credit cooperatives that would continue to be bound by a 6% reserve requirement. *PBOC Hikes Reserve Requirement to 7.5%,* CHINA DAILY (April 12, 2004).

An enterprise is allowed to open one basic account for handling its deposits, payments, and transfers. An enterprise is prohibited from opening an account in the name of an individual with the enterprise's funds.[46]

Banks are required to maintain normal business hours that are publicly announced and convenient to its customers. A commercial bank is prohibited from reducing its normal business hours or closing its business.[47] A bank is allowed to charge fees for its services but is required to meet the fee standards of the CBRC.[48]

(3) Records, Accounting, and Reporting. A commercial bank is required to maintain financial accounting statements, loan application files, loan agreements, and other documents and records concerning the bank's operations.[49] A bank is also required to establish an accounting system and internal control system that is consistent with CBRC standards.[50] An institution is required to release to the public information concerning their business performance and audit reports within three months before the end of the accounting year (i.e., calendar year).[51] In addition, a commercial bank is required to submit a balance sheet, profit and loss statement, and other accounting records to the CBRC on a quarterly basis.[52]

The CBRC has the power to conduct audits and inspections of the records of a commercial bank, including an evaluation of the deposits, loans, settlement of accounts, bad debts, and other aspects of the commercial banking operation at any time and without notice.[53] A commercial bank is

46. Commercial Bank Law, art. 48.

47. Commercial Bank Law, art. 49.

48. Commercial Bank Law, art. 50. *See* Provisional Rules on the Administration of Commercial Banking Service Pricing (promulgated on June 26, 2003, by the CBRC). The bank service fee rules are effective October 1, 2003, and govern the pricing of commercial banking services. The rules categorize services into two classifications: government-regulated services and market-based services. Government-regulated services are defined as basic RMB settlement operations and other services specified by the CBRC, and such services have minimal fees. All other services may be set by the market. The rules further provide that certain banking activities are not subject to any charges such as basic services in opening an RMB bank account, closing an account, and making deposits at different branches of a bank in the same city. Banks may charge for certain activities such as withdrawals of large sums of cash and deposits in small denominations. The rules also set forth a reporting mechanism for changes to bank service charges; namely, changes must be reported to the CBRC 15 days prior to implementation and posted at each bank location at least 10 days prior to implementation.

49. Commercial Bank Law, art. 51.

50. Commercial Bank Law, arts. 54, 55, 59, 60. *See also* Guiding Principles on the Improvement of the Internal Controls of Financial Institutions (promulgated on May 16, 1997, by the PBOC), *reprinted in* CHINA LAWS FOR FOREIGN BUSINESS (CCH), Business Regulation ¶ 8-455 (hereinafter the "PBOC Internal Control Principles"). Article 12 of the PBOC Internal Control Principles outlines the standards for commercial bank accounting systems.

51. Commercial Bank Law, arts. 56, 58.

52. Commercial Bank Law, art. 61.

53. Commercial Bank Law, art. 62. *See also* Financial Institution Inspection System of the Shenzhen Special Economic Zone Branch of the People's Bank of China (promulgated on September 26, 1995, by

required to produce any requested report or document upon demand. A commercial bank is also subject to the auditing supervision of the Auditor General of the Chinese Auditing Administration, which has direct responsibility to the State Council.[54] The Commercial Bank Law outlines the standards for bank takeovers by the PBOC, the standards for takeovers, the duration of the takeover period, dissolution procedures for institutions subject to takeover, and protection of depositors and creditors.[55]

(4) Bank Employee Standards. The employees of a commercial bank are required to abide by the law and regulations applicable to banking operations. Bank employees are prohibited from engaging in the following activities:

(1) Using their professional positions to extort money, accept bribes, or receive rebates and commissions
(2) Using their professional positions to embezzle funds of the bank or its customers
(3) Practicing favoritism in granting loans to, or provisions of guarantees for, relatives and friends
(4) Holding concurrent positions in other economic organizations
(5) Disclosing State or commercial secrets obtained during the course of their employment
(6) Engaging in other activities that violate the law, administrative regulations, and standards[56]

An employee that engages in any of the activities noted above is subject to administrative penalties, criminal penalties, and civil liability.[57]

(5) Online Banking Regulations. The PBOC has adopted standards for online banking services.[58] The Online Banking Regulations apply to all banking institutions that are approved by the PBOC (and now the CBRC), including policy banks, Chinese-owned commercial banks, equity joint venture banks, wholly foreign-owned banks, and branches of foreign banks.[59]

---

the Shenzhen SEZ Branch of the PBOC), *reprinted in* CHINA LAWS FOR FOREIGN BUSINESS (CCH), Special Zones & Cities ¶ 120-055 (outlines the inspection standards for Shenzhen SEZ financial institutions and insurance companies).

54. Commercial Bank Law, art. 63. For a discussion concerning the Auditing Law of the PRC, *see supra* § F.2.

55. Commercial Bank Law, chap. 7.

56. Commercial Bank Law, arts. 52, 53.

57. Commercial Bank Law, arts. 81–85.

58. Administration of Online Banking Services Tentative Procedures (issued on June 29, 2001, by the PBOC, effective as of date of issue) (hereinafter "Online Banking Regulations").

59. Online Banking Regulations, art. 2.

Any banking institution that offers online services is required to apply to the CBRC for approval and registration.[60]

The Online Banking Regulations list the requirements for approval to offer online services. Eligible banks are required to meet or exceed the following criteria:

(1) Maintains a sound internal management system and control mechanism that can assess and regulate the risks associated with online banking
(2) Maintains the necessary hardware, software, and technical expertise to support an online banking system
(3) Maintains a sound financial position[61]

The Online Banking Regulations detail the application process, CBRC application standards and documents, and procedures for applying to provide additional online services.

The Online Banking Regulations outline the statutory precautions that must be taken by financial institutions to ensure the management of risks associated with online banking services. All online banks must take the proper security measures such as commercial encryption, physical security measures that can effectively guard against unlawful access to key equipment, and protection of customers' rights of privacy.[62]

The Online Banking Regulations provide that banks that fail to meet the requirements stipulated in the procedures may be subject to various civil penalties under the *Penalties for Illegal Financial Acts Procedures*, the *Administration of the Qualifications for Office of the Senior Management Personnel of Financial Institutions Procedures*, and other related laws and regulations. The CBRC is empowered to order a party to cease its online services in the event a financial institution engages in any of the following:

(1) Offers online services without the approval and registration of the CBRC
(2) Violates State laws or regulations and threatens social welfare through its online services
(3) Engages in unfair competition by the use of its online services

60. Online Banking Regulations, art. 4. These rules also apply to financial institutions registered in Hong Kong, Taiwan, and Macao that offer PRC clients online banking services as well as Mainland Chinese banks that offer online banking services overseas.

61. Online Banking Regulations, art. 6.

62. Online Banking Regulations, art. 14. Despite the general requirements concerning the protection of customer privacy, the legal safeguards are ineffective.

(4) Lacks the necessary resources or experienced technical persons, which leads to major capital loss through its online services
(5) Maintains inadequate systems security, which threatens customer interests and the security of the bank's organization
(6) Fails to report a major incident to the CBRC[63]

(6) Liability and Penalties. A bank is subject to civil liability to its depositors for delays or refusals to pay principal or interest on deposits, illegal withholding or freezing of deposits, and breach of confidentiality concerning depositors' accounts.[64] A commercial bank is also subject to monetary penalties, suspension of business activities, revocation of a business license, and criminal liability if it violates any provision of the bank law or related regulations.[65] If a commercial bank or employee of a bank disputes any administrative penalty issued by the CBRC, the bank or the employee may initiate litigation with the people's court pursuant to the Administrative Litigation Law.[66]

(7) Money Laundering Prevention. In 2003, the PRC government adopted a series of regulations to prevent money laundering that apply to all banks operating in China, including commercial banks, finance companies, trust and investment companies, lease financing companies, and foreign-invested financial institutions.[67] Under new rules, both foreign currency and

63. Online Banking Regulations, art. 26.

64. Commercial Bank Law, art. 73. *See also* Penalty Measures for Illegal Financial Activities (issued on February 22, 1999, by the State Council, effective as of date of issue). The Penalty Measures apply to all institutions that engage in financial services activities in the PRC, including banks, trust corporations, financial institutions, trust and investment companies, and financial leasing companies. The Penalty Measures address illegal activities committed by regulated financial institutions such as operating outside the prescribed scope of business; failure to keep proper accounting records; activities in breach of the relevant regulations with respect to securities, futures, and derivative trading; filing of false or inaccurate accounting information; and issuance of false letters of credit and other commercial documents. Financial institutions are also required to maintain the prescribed debt-equity ratio, assist the tax and customs authorities to freeze funds of enterprises engaging in illicit activities, and to report unusual foreign currency deposit and conversion activities. The Penalty Measures provide that commercial banks are prohibited from providing overdraft facilities for securities and futures settlements, and imposes a fine on such activities which range from two to five times the illegally derived profits.

65. Commercial Bank Law, chap. 8.

66. Commercial Bank Law, art. 86. For a discussion concerning the Administrative Litigation Law, *see* Chapter 22, Litigation in the People's Court § C.

67. Financial Institutions Anti–Money Laundering Provisions (promulgated by the PBOC on Jan. 3, 2003, and effective on Mar. 1, 2003) (hereinafter referred to as the "Anti–Money Laundering Provisions"); Large and Suspicious Renminbi Payment Transactions Reporting Administrative Procedures (promulgated by the PBOC on January 3, 2003, and effective on March 1, 2003) (hereinafter referred to as the "Large RMB Transaction Procedures"); Management Procedures for Financial Institutions Governing Reporting of Large and Suspicious Foreign Currency Funds Transactions (promulgated by the PBOC on January 3, 2003, and effective on March 1, 2003) (hereinafter referred to as the "Large FOREX Transaction Procedures"). The provisions apply to financial institutions under the supervision of the PBOC (and now the China Banking Regulatory Commission); namely, policy banks, commercial

renminbi transactions through financial institutions in China will receive a higher level of scrutiny in contrast to the past.[68] The new anti–money laundering provisions require the banks to "know your customer" and specifically require that financial institutions have a duty to examine for authenticity and legality the documents presented by customers requiring bank services, regardless of whether they are individuals, corporations, or other entities. These documents are to be photocopied and the copies kept in files. The second key aspect of the anti–money laundering program is reporting of large or suspicious transactions, which relates to internal book transfers as well as to cash transactions. Suspicious transactions are required to be immediately reported to the Public Security Bureau (PSB). The third important aspect of the program is record keeping. The regulations mandate that banks maintain records of customer accounts and transaction data.

Pursuant to the Anti–Money Laundering Provisions, financial institutions and their employees are obligated to participate in the prevention of money laundering, maintain the confidentiality of anti–money laundering information, and cooperate with law enforcement officials in anti–money laundering efforts. Financial institutions are required by law to assist and cooperate with judicial, customs, and taxation authorities in investigating, freezing, or withholding account funds in suspected transactions.[69] Financial institutions are also required to establish anti–money laundering internal control mechanisms, which includes establishing a specialized department to handle anti–money laundering, or designating an already established department to handle the task.[70]

The Anti–Money Laundering Provisions also require that financial institutions record client identification information.[71] According to the regulations,

---

banks, credit cooperatives, postal savings, trust and investment companies, finance lease companies, and foreign financial institutions. Excluded from the program are securities and funds management firms, which are under the supervision of the China Securities Regulatory Commission (CSRC), and insurance firms, which are under the China Insurance Regulatory Commission (CIRC). *See generally* S. Harner, *China Gets Tough on Money Laundering,* CHINA L. & PRAC. (Mar. 2003); *China Strengthens Supervision of RMB Payments,* People's Daily Online, Jan. 14, 2003; *Anti-Money Laundering War Underway in China,* People's Daily Online, July 4, 2002, available at http://www.peopledaily.com.cn; *China Issues Regulation on Money Laundering,* Xinhua News Service, Jan. 13, 2003, available online at http://www.xinhua.com.cn.

68. In September 2001, immediately following the 9/11 terrorist attack on the United States, the PBOC established an anti–money laundering working group to develop a program applicable to Chinese financial institutions. In July 2002, the PBOC set up a payment transaction monitoring office and an anti–money laundering office. The target transactions are proceeds from smuggling, drugs, corruption, and terrorism that are laundered through the mechanism of normal bank settlements. The State Administration of Foreign Exchange (SAFE) is responsible for monitoring foreign currency transactions and the PBOC Payments and Settlements Management Office monitors RMB transactions.

69. Anti–Money Laundering Provisions, art. 6.

70. Anti–Money Laundering Provisions, arts. 8, 9.

71. Anti–Money Laundering Provisions, arts. 10, 11.

customers opening a savings account or settling accounts are required to present proper identification. Bank employees are required to check the identification documents and register the names and other information in banking transactions. When a financial institution suspects that a large or suspicious transaction may be linked to criminal activities, it is required to promptly report to local public security authorities.[72] Financial institutions are required to maintain account and transaction records for a minimum of five years.[73] The Anti–Money Laundering Provisions provide for a fine of up to RMB30,000 for violations, and senior management may be disqualified from working at a financial institution in serious infractions.[74] The regulations further provide that in serious cases financial institutions failing to comply with the law may be subject to criminal prosecution.

The Large FOREX Transaction Provisions provide that a foreign exchange transaction is "large" if it involves an amount beyond a specified threshold and "suspicious" if the amount, frequency, source, direction, and application is considered unusual and "abnormal."[75] Under the Procedures, financial institutions are required to report to SAFE or its local branches all large and suspicious foreign exchange transactions on a monthly basis.[76] Where money laundering is suspected, the financial institution is required to issue a written report to SAFE.[77] Financial institutions are required to report to the local public security bureau and copy the local branch of SAFE of any transaction in which criminal activities are found within three working days of such finding.[78] Financial institutions are required to maintain records of all such transactions for at least five years from the transaction date, and such records may not be disclosed to a third party without the consent of the individual or company involved unless required by law.[79]

The Large FOREX Provisions set forth separate definitions of "large," "suspicious cash," and "suspicious noncash" foreign exchange transactions. The threshold amount of a daily single or cumulative "large foreign exchange transaction(s)" is $10,000 in the case of cash transaction, $100,000 in the case of noncash single or daily cumulative transaction(s) by an individual, and $500,000 in the case of noncash single or daily cumulative transaction(s) by an enterprise.[80] A "suspicious cash" FOREX transaction is defined as an

72. Anti–Money Laundering Provisions, art. 16.
73. Anti–Money Laundering Provisions, art. 17.
74. Anti–Money Laundering Provisions, art. 20.
75. Large FOREX Transaction Procedures, art. 2.
76. Large FOREX Transaction Procedures, arts. 11, 14, 16.
77. Large FOREX Transaction Provisions, art. 12.
78. Large FOREX Transaction Provisions, art. 15.
79. Large FOREX Transaction Provisions, arts. 6, 7.
80. Large FOREX Transaction Provisions, art. 8.

investment by a foreign-invested enterprise using foreign exchange cash in a manner outside the company's business scope.[81] The Provisions define "suspicious noncash" transactions as frequent (defined as three or more times daily, or occurring daily for a period of five or more days) movement of a large amount of foreign exchange between the foreign exchange accounts of an enterprise that is incompatible with its business nature or scope, or remittance of foreign exchange capital contributions out of the country promptly after their receipt by a foreign-invested enterprise that is incompatible with the need for its production or operation expenses.[82]

The Large RMB Provisions apply to transactions of money payments and funds settlement denominated in renminbi (including those made by negotiable instruments, bank cards, Internet payments, or cash) conducted in the course of economic activities by enterprises or individuals.[83] The Large RMB Transaction Provisions require that financial institutions integrate anti–money laundering mechanisms into their organization, and appoint personnel who will be responsible for recording, analyzing, and reporting large and suspicious transactions.[84] The Provisions define large RMB transactions to include a single transfer of RMB1 million ($121,000) or more between the accounts of legal persons, other organizations or individually owned household businesses; a single cash transaction of RMB200,000 ($24,000) or more (including deposits, withdrawals, cash transfers, money orders, and cashier's checks); and transfers of RMB200,000 ($24,000) or more between two accounts of an individual or an organization.[85]

The Large RMB Transaction Provisions also list a broad range of banking activities that may be considered suspicious transactions, including transactions in a frequency, or of an amount, that obviously do not accord with the account holder's scope of business; or a noticeable increase in transactions with bank accounts in regions where drug trafficking, smuggling, and terrorism are common.[86] The provisions require that financial institutions establish a customer database for recording pertinent data, including registered capital, scope of business, principal senders and recipients of funds, and daily average account transaction amounts.[87] Financial institutions should report large or suspicious transactions to the People's Bank of China or its branches, and when a financial institution discovers a transaction that is clearly related

81. Large FOREX Transaction Provisions, art. 9.
82. Large FOREX Transaction Provisions, art. 10.
83. Large RMB Transaction Provisions, art. 2.
84. Large RMB Transaction Provisions, art. 6.
85. Large RMB Transaction Provisions, art. 7. The RMB200,000 ($24,000) is above the usual amount of $10,000 used by most financial centers, including Hong Kong and the United States.
86. Large RMB Transaction Provisions, art. 8.
87. Large RMB Transaction Provisions, art. 10.

to illegal activity, it is required to immediately notify the public security authorities.[88]

3. FIE Financial Institutions

The State Council and the PBOC adopted rules specifically addressing the application process, capital requirements, appointment and expertise of personnel, reporting requirements, and other rules specifically applicable to foreign-funded financial institutions.[89] The FIE Financial Institution Regulations apply to a number of different types of financial institutions, including the following:

(1) *Foreign Bank:* the headquarters of a bank with foreign capital within the territory of the PRC.
(2) *Foreign Bank Branch:* a branch of a foreign bank established in the territory of the PRC.
(3) *Joint Equity Bank:* a bank established as an equity joint venture between a foreign financial institution and a Chinese enterprise within the territory of the PRC.[90]
(4) *Foreign Finance Company:* the head office of a finance company with foreign capital established in the territory of the PRC.
(5) *Joint Equity Finance Company:* a finance company established as an equity joint venture between a foreign financial institution and a Chinese enterprise.[91]

88. Large RMB Transaction Provisions, arts. 16, 18.

89. *See* Administrative Regulations of the People's Republic of China Governing Foreign-Funded Financial Institutions (promulgated on February 25, 1994, by the State Council, and as amended on December 20, 2001), *reprinted in* CHINA LAWS FOR FOREIGN BUSINESS (CCH), Business Regulation ¶ 8-692 (hereinafter the "FIE Financial Institution Regulations"); Detailed Implementing Regulations for the Administrative Rules of the People's Republic of China Governing Foreign-Funded Financial Institutions (promulgated on April 30, 1996, by the People's Bank of China, and as amended on January 29, 2002, by the PBOC), *reprinted in* CHINA LAWS FOR FOREIGN BUSINESS (CCH), Business Regulation ¶ 8-693 (hereinafter the "FIE Financial Institution Implementing Rules"). The 2002 amendments to the FIE Financial Institution Regulations implement China's WTO commitments in the financial services sector and seek to strengthen bank regulation to be more consistent with the Basel Accord. Both the FIE Financial Institution Regulations and implementing regulations are effective February 1, 2002. For a general discussion on the standards for FIE financial institutions, *see* C. Kan & S. Harder, *What Opportunities Do Foreign Banks Have in China?,* CHINA L. & PRAC. (April 2002); D. Yu, *New Legislation on Foreign-Funded Financial Institutions in China,* CHINA L. & PRAC. (February 2002).

90. Specific to joint equity banks, the CBRC issued a risk rating system to assess the risk, management systems, and profitability of joint equity banks in China. The system sets forth 100-point rating categories for such issues as capital adequacy, risk conditions, management and governance conditions, profitability, etc. The system only applies to joint equity banks in China and it is assumed that the CBRC is testing the rating system to determine whether to apply the program to all banks if successful. Provisional Risk Rating System for Joint Equity Banks (issued on February 22, 2004, by the CBRC). *See generally CBRC Issues Risk Rating System for Joint Equity Banks,* CHINA MARKET INTELLIGENCE, U.S.-CHINA BUSINESS COUNCIL (March 4, 2004).

91. FIE Financial Institution Regulations, art. 2, §§ (1)–(5). The 2002 Amendments to the Regulations provide that the Chinese party to an equity joint venture bank or equity joint venture finance company does not need to be a financial institution.

An FIE Financial Institution is required to abide by the laws of the PRC if it operates in China and may not "harm the social interests" of the PRC.[92] The law protects the legal rights and interests of FIE Financial Institutions operating in China. The CBRC is the agency with regulatory authority over institutions, and a branch office of the CBRC is responsible for the day-to-day supervision of institutions within its locale.[93]

a. Establishment and Registration

An applicant for approval of an FIE Financial Institution is required to go through a two-step approval process with the CBRC. The initial application is filed with a local branch of the CBRC, which will submit an opinion to the head office of the CBRC concerning the application.[94]

(1) Preliminary Application. In its initial submission to the CBRC, an applicant for approval of a *foreign bank* or *foreign finance company* is required to meet the following conditions:

(1) The applicant is required to be a financial institution
(2) The applicant has established and operated a representative office in China for at least two years[95]
(3) The end of the year total assets in the year prior to the submission of an application shall be in excess of $10 billion
(4) The financial institution is required to have an established financial supervision and administration system in the countries where it is located

92. FIE Financial Institution Regulations, art. 3.
93. FIE Financial Institution Regulations, art. 4.
94. PBOC FIE Rules, art. 6.
95. For more information concerning the requirements for a representative office, *see* Chapter 4, Organizational Structure § A.1. The representative offices of foreign financial institutions including commercial banks, investment banks, securities companies, insurance companies, insurance brokerage and agency firms, insurance adjusters, funds management companies, foreign exchange companies, credit card companies, and financial leasing companies, are required to follow special registration and supervision procedures. The approval and regulatory agency of these types of representative offices is the CBRC. *See* Administrative Measures on Representative Offices in China of Foreign Financial Institutions (promulgated on April 29, 1996, by the People's Bank of China and revised and repromulgated by Order No. 8 on June 27, 2002, by the People's Bank of China), *reprinted in* CHINA LAWS FOR FOREIGN BUSINESS (CCH), Business Regulation ¶ 7-540 (outlines the application procedures for financial institution rep. offices, documents required for application, termination of rep. office, supervision issues, penalties for violations, etc.). The Foreign Bank Rep Office Measures define "foreign-funded financial institutions" to include both foreign financial institutions and foreign-funded financial institutions registered and established in China. "Representative agencies of foreign-funded financial institutions" include representative offices and head representative offices that carry on non-business activities such as liaison work, consultancy activities, and market research that are established in China by foreign-funded banks. Foreign Bank Rep Offices and their staff are prohibited from signing contracts or engaging in any profit-making activities. The Foreign Bank Rep Office Measures set forth application requirements, approval procedures, the qualifications of the chief representative, reporting requirements, and other conditions and standards.

(5) The supervising body of the country or territory where the applicant is based must approve of its application
(6) Other conditions imposed by the CBRC[96]

The minimum registered capital (which is required to be the actual capital contributed) for a *foreign bank* is RMB300 million and for a *foreign finance company* is RMB200 million, both of which are required to be in freely convertible currencies. The People's Bank of China may increase the minimum level requirements of its registered or working capital and determine the applicable RMB rate in accordance with the business scope of a foreign-owned financial institution and the requirements of prudent supervision.[97]

An applicant for approval of a *foreign bank branch* is required to meet the following conditions:

(1) The applicant has established and operated a representative office in China for at least two years
(2) The end of the year total assets in the year prior to the submission of an application shall be in excess of $20 billion
(3) The financial institution is required to have an established financial supervision and administration system in the countries where it is located
(4) The supervising body of the country or territory where the applicant is based must approve of its application
(5) Other conditions imposed by the CBRC[98]

The working funds of a *foreign bank branch* from its headquarters are required to be not less than RMB100 million in freely convertible currencies.[99]

In its initial application, an applicant for approval of a *joint equity bank* or *joint equity finance company* is required to meet the following conditions:

(1) The foreign investor to the joint venture must be a financial institution
(2) The foreign party shall already have an established representative office within the territory of China

96. FIE Financial Institution Regulations, art. 6.

97. FIE Financial Institution Regulations, art. 5. The 2002 Amendments to the Regulations require that the registered capital of wholly foreign-owned banks, equity joint venture banks, wholly foreign-owned finance companies, and equity joint venture finance companies must be based on actual capital contributed. Under prior rules, the cash portion of the registered capital was required to be no less than fifty percent (50%).

98. FIE Financial Institution Regulations, art. 7. If a foreign bank applies to increase the number of branches in China, in addition to meeting the conditions of Article 7, it is also required to have an "outstanding performance record" for its existing branches in China and the most recently established branch in China has been operating for more than one year.

99. FIE Financial Institution Regulations, art. 5.

(3) The foreign party shall have end of the year total assets in the year prior to the application in excess of $10 billion
(4) The financial institution is required to have an established financial supervision and administration system in the countries where it is located
(5) The supervising body of the country or territory where the applicant is based must approve of its application
(6) Other conditions as imposed by the CBRC[100]

The minimum amount of registered capital for a *joint equity bank* is RMB300 million and for a *joint equity finance company* is RMB200 million.[101]

An applicant for a *wholly foreign-owned bank*, *wholly foreign-owned finance company*, *joint equity bank*, and a *joint equity finance company* is required to submit the following documents in support of its application:

(1) An application for the establishment of an FIE Financial Institution, which includes the intended name of the operation, its registered capital and paid-up capital, and the type of business for which the application is intended
(2) A feasibility study report[102]
(3) Draft articles of association of the *foreign bank* or *foreign finance company* to be established, or the joint venture contract and draft articles of the *joint equity bank* or *joint equity finance company* to be established
(4) The business license of the applicant(s)
(5) The annual reports of the applicant(s) for the previous three years
(6) Other information as required by the CBRC[103]

An applicant for a *foreign bank branch* is required to submit all documents listed above except for the draft contract or articles of association that do not apply in situations involving an application for a bank branch.[104] All

100. FIE Financial Institution Regulations, art. 8.

101. FIE Financial Institution Regulations, art. 5.

102. The feasibility study report is required to include at least the following: the general status of the applicant, an analysis of the market prospects of the institution to be established, plans for future business development of the institution, the organizational and administrative structure of the institution to be established, and a forecast of the amount of assets, liabilities, and profits for the first three years of the proposed operation. FIE Financial Institution Implementing Rules, art. 8.

103. FIE Financial Institution Regulations, arts. 9, 11; FIE Financial Institution Implementing Rules, art. 11. The CBRC requires that an applicant also submit information concerning the financial system and regulatory environment of the foreign institutions' home country; an organizational chart of the applicant and the corporate group that the applicant is a member, if applicable; and a recommendation on behalf of the applicant by the financial regulatory authority from the applicant's home country. FIE Financial Institution Implementing Rules, arts. 12, 16. All documents listed are required to be translated into Chinese before submission.

104. FIE Financial Institution Regulations, art. 10.

other documents to be submitted in support of an application are required to be in the Chinese language, with the exception of annual reports that may be submitted in either Chinese or English.[105] An application for an FIE Financial Institution is required to be signed by the chief executive officer of the foreign financial institution and addressed to the CBRC.[106] All business licenses and authorization letters are required to be notarized.[107]

The CBRC is required to conduct an initial examination of the application for establishing a foreign-owned financial institution before making a decision whether or not to accept the application within six (6) months after receiving all of the application documents. After the application is accepted, the CBRC will issue a formal application form to the applicant. In the event the application is denied, the CBRC is required to inform the applicant in writing, stating its reasons for rejection. An applicant that receives a rejection notice will be disallowed from applying to establish any business institution in the same city for a period of one (1) year.[108] Under special circumstances, if the CBRC is unable to complete the initial examination and reach a decision whether or not to accept the application within the six-month period of time, the CBRC, in its discretion, may extend the review period for up to three (3) months.[109]

(2) Formal Application and Registration. After initial approval is received, the applicant is required to go through a preparatory period of six months and complete certain statutory tasks and conditions: namely, the institution is required to establish an internal control system that consists of effective supervision and administration of staff including personnel involved with transactions, funds control and operations, and other sensitive business functions; to establish an audit system for deposits, loans, remittances, foreign exchange transactions, financial affairs, and investment management; and to establish security measures for facilities and funds.[110] In addition, the

105. FIE Financial Institution Regulations, art. 12; FIE Financial Institution Implementing Rules, arts. 11, 12 (annual reports in languages other than English or Chinese are required to be translated).

106. PBOC FIE Regulations, arts. 16, 17.

107. PBOC FIE Regulations, art. 9.

108. FIE Financial Institution Implementing Rules, art. 20.

109. FIE Financial Institution Regulations, art. 13. The initial application process is more particularly described in the Implementing Rules. FIE Financial Institution Implementing Rules, arts. 8–18. After the initial application is approved, an applicant must obtain an official application within fifteen (15) days of receiving notice of approval from the CBRC. FIE Financial Institution Implementing Rules, art. 19.

110. FIE Financial Institution Implementing Rules, art. 22. *See also* PBOC Internal Control Principles. The Principles apply to FIE Financial Institutions and, in detail, outline the required standards and objectives for internal controls, management and supervision of internal control systems, and the role of the PBOC (and now CBRC) in supervising the implementation of internal control systems. FIE Financial Institutions are required to satisfy prudential conditions such as an effective (i) corporate governance structure; (ii) risk management system; (iii) internal control system; (iv) information management system; (v) operating status with no record of any material violation or breach; and (vi) anti–money laundering measures.

applicant is required to complete other tasks during the preparatory stage including, but not limited to, the retention of qualified personnel required for monitoring and control of business risks; the printing of important business vouchers, receipts, and other documents for external use; establishment of safety and precautionary measures; and the engagement of an accounting firm to audit the internal control system, accounting system, and computer system of the operation.[111] At the completion of the preparatory period, or within six months of receiving the formal application form, an applicant is required to complete the official application and submit the following documents and information to the CBRC:

(1) The names and curricula vitae of the principal responsible persons involved with the proposed FIE Financial Institution
(2) The letters of authorization of the principal responsible persons, including the general managers, president of China operation, or other management personnel with equivalent powers of office, to be appointed to work at the FIE Financial Institution[112]
(3) A contribution verification certificate
(4) Information concerning the "safety and precautionary measures for the facilities" relevant to the business
(5) A letter of guarantee for tax liability and debts from the headquarters of the *foreign bank branch*[113]
(6) Other documents required by the CBRC[114]

CBRC is required to render a decision as to whether to approve a completed formal application accompanied by supporting documents for establishing a foreign-invested financial institution within two (2) months of receiving the application.[115] In the event the CBRC approves of the application, it will issue a Financial Institution Operating Certificate to the applicant. The applicant thereafter submits the Financial Institution Operation Approval Certificate to the SAIC in order to obtain a business license.[116] An approved institution is required to commence its business operations within ninety days from the date on which a business license is issued. An FIE Financial Institution is required to make a public announcement before

111. FIE Financial Institution Implementing Rules, art. 22.
112. FIE Financial Institution Implementing Rules, art. 25.
113. The guarantee letter is required to be notarized. FIE Financial Institution Implementing Rules, art. 8.
114. FIE Financial Institution Regulations, art. 14; FIE Financial Institution Implementing Rules, art. 24. The CBRC may, in its discretion, extend the preparatory period for three (3) months. FIE Financial Institution Implementing Rules, art. 23.
115. FIE Financial Institution Implementing Rules, art. 25.
116. FIE Financial Institution Regulations, arts. 15, 16.

commencing its operations.[117] An FIE Financial Institution is required to obtain the approval of the CBRC to establish additional branch offices, adjust or assign registered capital, increase or decrease working capital, and change the name of the business or business location.[118] In the event that the CBRC rejects an application, it is required to provide written notice of its decision to the applicant.[119]

b. Scope of Operations for FIE Financial Institutions

A *wholly foreign-owned bank*, *foreign bank branch*, and *joint equity bank* may engage in any of the following activities upon approval by the CBRC:

(1) Accept public deposits, with no limit on foreign currency deposits
(2) Issue short-term, mid-term, and long-term loans
(3) Handle acceptances and discounts on negotiable instruments
(4) Buy and sell government bonds, financial bonds, and other foreign currency securities other than stocks[120]
(5) Provide letter of credit services and guarantees
(6) Conduct domestic and overseas settlements and buy and sell foreign exchange on its own behalf or as an agent
(7) Conduct foreign exchange business[121]
(8) Engage in interbank loans
(9) Conduct bank card businesses
(10) Provide safety deposit box services
(11) Provide credit investigation and consulting services[122]
(12) Conduct other business operations as permitted by the CBRC[123]

117. FIE Financial Institution Regulations, arts. 27, 28.

118. FIE Financial Institution Regulations, art. 33.

119. FIE Financial Institution Implementing Rules, art. 25. An applicant that is refused a Financial Institution Operation Certificate may not apply for the establishment of another operation for one (1) year. FIE Financial Institution Implementing Rules, art. 25.

120. The Implementing Rules provide that the buying and selling of bonds and securities does not include Chinese and foreign government bonds, bonds issued by Chinese financial institutions, and bonds issued by Chinese non-financial institutions. FIE Financial Institution Implementing Rules, art. 29.

121. The Implementing Rules distinguish between foreign exchange business involving customers in Hong Kong, Macao, and Taiwan ("Greater China FOREX Business") and "comprehensive foreign exchange business with all types of customers." For Greater China FOREX Business the working capital and registered capital requirements are less than that required for "comprehensive" services. FIE Financial Institution Implementing Rules, arts. 31, 32.

122. The creditworthiness investigations and consultancy services mentioned in the Regulations are defined to include those services relating to the banking industry only. FIE Financial Institution Implementing Rules, art. 30.

123. FIE Financial Institution Regulations, art. 17, §§ (1)–(13). Pursuant to its WTO commitments, the CBRC announced in October 2003 that China has agreed to further open the market for the foreign banking industry. Specifically, eligible foreign banks will be allowed to provide renminbi services to Chinese companies, and the number of cities in which they are permitted to provide RMB currency services will increase from nine to thirteen. Procedures for the Administration of Renminbi Bank Settlement Accounts (issued on April 10, 2003, by the People's Bank of China); Notice Concerning the Further Opening of Renminbi Services to Foreign-Invested Financial Institutions (issued on October 24, 2003).

A *foreign finance company* or *joint equity finance company*, upon approval by the CBRC, may engage in the following types of activities:

(1) Accept deposits, each of which shall be no less than RMB1 million or the equivalent in a freely convertible foreign currency for a term not less than three months
(2) Issue short-term, mid-term, and long-term loans
(3) Handle acceptances and discounts on negotiable instruments
(4) Buy and sell government bonds, financial bonds, and other foreign currency securities other than stocks
(5) Provide guarantees
(6) Buy and sell foreign exchange on its own behalf or as an agent
(7) Engage in interbank loans
(8) Provide credit investigation and consulting services
(9) Provide foreign exchange trust services
(10) Conduct other business operations as permitted by the CBRC[124]

FIE Financial Institution finance companies may not engage in the bank card business, but may, unlike FIE Financial Institution banks, provide foreign exchange trust services.

FIE Financial Institutions may set up in any city within the People's Republic of China. The 2002 Amendments to the Regulations remove client restrictions on FIE Financial Institutions' foreign currency business, and remove quantitative restrictions on the foreign currency business of FIE Financial Institutions as a condition to RMB market access. Foreign-owned financial institutions conducting RMB business are required to have operated

---

See also China Accelerates Plan to Reform Banks, CHINA DAILY (Dec. 3, 2003), available online at http://www.chinadaily.com.cn. CBRC has the authority to determine an FIE Financial Institution's geographic scope and client base of its RMB business. The FIE Financial Institution Regulations provide that FIE Financial Institution RMB business applicants have operated in the PRC for three (3) years with profitability for the most recent two (2) years before they can be approved for RMB business. The CBRC continues to manage RMB interest rates for loans under $3,000,000. Since the mid-1990s, the PBOC (and now the CBRC) has increasingly allowed a limited number of foreign banks to participate in China's domestic bond market. *See China Gives Eight Foreign Banks Limited Access to Bond Market*, AAP Newsfeed (June 11, 1998), available on Nexis, News Library. Also in the 1990s, the PBOC experimented with allowing qualified foreign-funded financial institutions to engage in RMB business. For a review of practices in the past, *see generally* Guiding Principles on the Trial Conduct of Renminbi Business by Foreign-Funded Financial Institutions in Shenzhen (promulgated on August 13, 1998, by the Shenzhen Special Economic Zone Branch of the PBOC), *reprinted in* CHINA LAWS FOR FOREIGN BUSINESS (CCH), Special Zones & Cities ¶ 71-205 (outlines the rules for conducting RMB business in Shenzhen and the PBOC approval procedures); Provisional Administrative Measures of Shanghai Pudong on Foreign-Funded Financial Institutions Conducting Trial Renminbi Business Operations (promulgated on December 2, 1996, by the People's Bank of China), *reprinted in* CHINA LAWS FOR FOREIGN BUSINESS, (CCH), Special Zones & Cities ¶ 92-195 (measures address the licensing process required of foreign financial institutions doing RMB business and set forth the foreign exchange capital requirements to engage in RMB transactions).

124. FIE Financial Institution Regulations, art. 17, §§ (1)–(13).

in China for three years and engaged in business profitably for two years prior to filing an application to engage in RMB business.[125] The CBRC has the discretion to determine the geographical scope and the scope of service for the RMB business of foreign-owned financial institutions.[126] The regulations further provide that foreign-owned financial institutions are required to apply to the CBRC prior to offering new banking products or services within their approved business scope.[127] The rate of interest on a deposit or loan and the fee standards of the various types of services conducted by FIE Financial Institutions shall be determined by the institution in accordance with the CBRC.[128]

c. Reserve Funds and Liquidity Requirements

FIE financial institutions are required to maintain certain liquidity requirements and to adopt a prudential accounting system.[129] Foreign-owned financial institutions are required to maintain a deposit reserve fund with the branch of the PBOC in its locality, the ratio of which is to be determined and adjusted by the PBOC at its discretion.[130] The CBRC also requires that thirty percent (30%) of the working capital of the branches of foreign-owned banks shall be held in interest-bearing assets as specified by the CBRC and included in the deposit and other funds as specified by the CBRC.[131] A wholly foreign-owned bank, joint equity bank, wholly foreign-owned finance company, and joint equity finance company is required to maintain a capital adequacy ratio of not less than eight percent (8%).[132]

125. FIE Financial Institution Regulations, art. 20. The Implementing Rules distinguish between RMB business relating to customers in Hong Kong, Macao, and Taiwan ("Greater China RMB Business") and "comprehensive RMB business with all types of customers." For Greater China RMB Business the working capital and registered capital requirements are less than "comprehensive" services. FIE Financial Institution Implementing Rules, arts. 33–36. The Implementing Rules outline the procedures for approval to conduct or expand the scope of RMB business. FIE Financial Institution Implementing Rules, arts. 39-43. Banks approved to conduct RMB business may also conduct RMB inter-bank transactions. FIE Financial Institution Implementing Rules, art. 49.

126. FIE Financial Institution Regulations, art. 19.

127. FIE Financial Institution Regulations, art. 21. The CBRC must act on an application concerning new products and services within sixty days. The Implementing Rules outline the procedures for applications to expand a bank's business services. FIE Financial Institution Implementing Rules, arts. 44-46.

128. FIE Financial Institution Regulations, art. 22.

129. FIE Financial Institution Regulations, arts. 23–37; FIE Financial Institution Implementing Rules, art. 72.

130. FIE Financial Institution Regulations, art. 23. *See also* Regulations Governing Capital Adequacy of Commercial Banks (issued and effective on March 1, 2004, by the CBRC). In April 2004, the PBOC increased the bank reserve requirement of bank deposits to 7.5% in a move to clamp down of fast growth of money supply and credit. The order applies to China's largest banks but exempts rural and urban credit cooperatives that would continue to be bound by a 6% reserve requirement. *PBOC Hikes Reserve Requirement to 7.5%,* CHINA DAILY (April 12, 2004).

131. FIE Financial Institution Regulations, art. 24. The term "interest bearing assets" includes foreign exchange interest-bearing and RMB interest-bearing assets. FIE Financial Institution Implementing Rules, art. 65.

132. FIE Financial Institution Regulations, art. 25.

The regulations also govern transactions involving shareholders, senior management, and related or affiliated enterprises. The ratio of fixed assets to shareholders' equity of WFOE banks, JV banks, WFOE finance company, or JV finance company cannot exceed forty percent (40%).[133] The ratio of funds held by an enterprise with an affiliated enterprise may not exceed twenty-five percent (25%) unless approved by the CBRC.[134] The Implementing Rules prohibit an FIE financial institution from granting credit to a related person or enterprise on conditions that are more preferential than those that apply to any other borrower.[135]

The 2002 amendments to the FIE Financial Institution Regulations provide for methods of assessing currency risk. For a WFOE bank, an equity joint venture bank, a WFOE finance company, or an equity joint venture finance company, the ratio of RMB assets to RMB risk-weighted assets must not be less than eight percent. For a foreign bank branch, the ratio of its RMB working capital plus reserve funds to RMB risk-weighted assets must not be less than eight percent. The CBRC has the discretion to increase the RMB-related ratios in accordance with the relevant regulations.[136]

Under the 2002 Amendments, the FIE Financial Institution Regulations tighten large exposure limits, which may not exceed twenty-five percent (25%) of the FIE's capital. The regulations require that financial institutions maintain a ratio of current assets to the balance of current liabilities greater than twenty-five percent (25%).[137] Current assets are defined as cash, gold, deposits with the CBRC, deposits with other banks, interbank loans with maturities not exceeding one month, net credit balances in accounts with associated overseas banks and affiliated institutions, discounted and other purchased bills with maturities not exceeding one month, other account receivables and loans with maturities not exceeding one month, negotiable bonds with one month maturities and any other assets which can be realized

133. FIE Financial Institution Regulations, art. 27. The ratios under articles 26 and 27 for shareholders or related enterprises are calculated quarterly. FIE Financial Institution Implementing Rules, art. 74.

134. FIE Financial Institution Regulations, art. 26. An "affiliated enterprise" refers to an enterprise that controls the other enterprise directly or indirectly or has substantial influence over the enterprise. FIE Financial Institution Implementing Rules, art. 67. *See also* Z. Dingmin, *Rules Focus on Banking Supervision,* China Daily (April 7, 2004) (describing rules issued on April 6, 2004, governing transactions between commercial banks and affiliated parties).

135. FIE Financial Institution Implement Rules, art. 73. Related persons include (1) directors, supervisors, managerial personnel, credit business personnel, and their close relatives; (2) the companies, enterprises, and other economic entities in which the persons specified above invest or hold a senior management position; or (3) shareholders and the affiliated enterprises of the FIE financial institution.

136. FIE Financial Institution Regulations, art. 28; FIE Financial Institution Implementing Rules, art. 66.

137. FIE Financial Institution Regulations, art. 29. The liquidity ratio is required to be calculated on a daily basis. FIE Financial Institution Implementing Rules, art. 68.

within one month, in each case adjusted for estimated non-recoverable items.[138] FIE financial institutions are required to ensure that the ratio of foreign currency deposits received within China and total foreign currency reserves does not exceed seventy percent (70%).[139]

d. Reporting and Audits

The CBRC has the right to inspect and audit—on a regular or random basis—the business operations, management, and financial position of an FIE Financial Institution.[140] An institution is required to submit financial statements and other documents required by the CBRC including statistical data, internal audit reports, and business reports.[141] A foreign bank that has established two or more branches in China is required to select one branch as its reporting branch operation, which will be responsible for consolidated reporting of the branches to the CBRC.[142] An institution is required to report to the CBRC any major change to its financial position, amendments to its articles of association, and change in registered capital.[143]

---

138. FIE Financial Institution Implementing Rules, art. 68.

139. FIE Financial Institution Regulations, art. 30. The total amount of foreign exchange deposits accepted in China shall include interbank and non-interbank deposits. The following foreign exchange investments shall not be included in offshore foreign exchange investments: Chinese government bonds issued abroad, bonds issued by Chinese financial institutions, and bonds issued by Chinese non-financial institutions. FIE Financial Institution Implementing Rules, art. 69.

140. FIE Financial Institution Regulations, arts. 35, 36, 37. The CBRC and its delegated authorities have the right to demand that foreign-owned financial institutions follow steps to improve business management, cash management, and security precautions in accordance with the regulations governing business administration policies. *Id.* at art. 36. A foreign-owned financial institution shall accept the CBRC and its delegated authorities' supervision and investigations by tendering and not refusing, obstructing, or hiding relevant and accurate documents, information, and written reports. FIE Financial Institution Regulations, art. 37.

141. FIE Financial Institution Regulations, art. 34; FIE Financial Institution Implementing Rules, art. 64. *See* Rules on the Administration of Consolidated Financial Statements of Foreign-Invested Banks (issued on March 8, 2004, by the CBRC, and effective on April 1, 2004) (requires all foreign financial institutions to release biannual consolidated financial statements concerning their mainland operations, and include information on supervisory methods of the institution's worldwide headquarters and important information on the institution's worldwide operations). The above-referenced rules are part of the CBRC's efforts to monitor and control the banking practices in China post-WTO.

142. FIE Financial Institution Implementing Rules, art. 64.

143. FIE Financial Institution Implementing Rules, art. 33. FIE Financial Institutions are required to report to the CBRC (i) any serious financial or operational problems; (ii) major adjustments to the institution's operating strategy; (iii) important board resolutions; (iv) any change in shareholder of ten percent (10%) of the total capital or shares of an FIE Financial Institution; (v) any change to the articles of association, registered capital, or registered address of the head office of an FIE Financial Institution; (vi) reorganization of the head office of an FIE Financial Institution and changes in its chairman or president; (vii) any serious problems (financial or operational) of the head office of a foreign bank branch or a foreign joint venture party; and (viii) major changes in the laws and regulations of the place of the head office of a foreign bank branch or a foreign joint venture party. The Regulations also require that the FIE notify the local CBRC branch at least seven business days prior to a suspension of business. FIE Financial Institution Implementing Rules, art. 84. The Implementing Rules outline the procedures for applications for approval of adjustments to registered capital, name changes, changes resulting from a merger or division, change of shareholder, change of office location, or amendments to articles of association. FIE Financial Institution Implementing Rules, arts. 76–83.

e. Management Personnel

The CBRC requires that senior management personnel demonstrate certain qualifications. Under the Implementing Regulations, the CBRC manages a verification and approval system for senior management personnel of FIE financial institutions.[144] For senior management personnel such as the chairman, general manager, and bank president, the financial institution is required to obtain the approval of the CBRC before such personnel can assume a position in China. A person who holds a position of general manager or president of an FIE Financial Institution is required to have ten years' experience in the financial industry or fifteen years or more of related work experience in the economic sector (of which at least five years of such experience shall be in the financial industry), and shall have been in a position with at least five years' experience as a department manager of a branch of a financial institution.[145] A general manager or president is required to be of good character with no record of individual bankruptcy or in the capacity as a company manager, and have no criminal record.[146]

---

144. FIE Financial Institution Implementing Rules, arts. 52–56. The CBRC head office is required to approve an application for qualification of a senior manager within ninety days from receipt of the application and materials. If the application only requires CBRC branch office approval, an application must be approved or rejected in forty-five days. If an FIE is only required to record the personnel with the CBRC, the application is deemed to be approved if the CBRC fails to object in thirty days. FIE Financial Institution Implementing Rules, art. 63. *See also* Procedures for the Administration of the Qualifications for Office of the Senior Management Personnel of Financial Institutions (issued on March 24, 2000, by the People's Bank of China) (procedures outline the appointment qualifications for senior managers of FIE financial institutions).

145. FIE Financial Institution Implementing Rules, art. 53 (1). A person who assumes the position of vice chairman of the board or vice president (deputy general manager) of an FIE financial institution or the president (general manager) of a foreign bank branch shall have five years or more of experience in the financial industry or ten years or more of related work experience in the economic sector (of which three years or more such experience shall be in the financial industry), and shall have been in a position of a business department manager or equivalent or higher for two or more years. FIE Financial Institution Implementing Rules, art. 53 (2). A person who assumes the position of deputy president (deputy general manager) of a foreign bank branch or the president of a sub-branch shall have four years or more of experience in the financial industry or six years or more of related work experience in the economic sector (of which two or more years of such experience shall be in the financial industry). FIE Financial Institution Implementing Rules, art. 53 (3). All senior managers are required to hold a bachelor's degree or above or have an additional six years of related experience in the financial industry or eight years in the economic sector. FIE Financial Institution Implementing Rules, art. 53 (4).

146. FIE Financial Institution Implementing Rules, arts. 50, 51. Senior management personnel are required to be familiar with and comply with China's laws and regulations on financial regulation; have professional knowledge, work experience, and management skills that relate to the position; and have no record of improper conduct. The Implementing Regulations also provide that senior managers cannot be persons with any criminal record; persons having been "seriously penalized" due to a violation of the law; persons having taken "major responsibility" for or having been the person directly responsible for the bankruptcy, serious violation of regulations, or revocation of a permit to conduct financial business of any financial institution within five years; or persons having caused heavy losses to the financial institution or any other enterprise or company in which he or she was employed as a result of material error in the past five years. FIE Financial Institution Implementing Rules, arts. 50, 51. The Implementing Regulations outline the procedures for a verification and approval system for senior management personnel of FIE financial institutions. FIE Financial Institution Implementing Rules, arts. 52–56. The head office of the CBRC is responsible for verification and approval or revocation of qualifications with respect to

The term of office of senior management personnel is required to be at least two years and is barred from holding another operational management position concurrently with the FIE Financial Institution.[147] An FIE Financial Institution is required to obtain approval for any changes involving senior management personnel. In the event that the general manager or president of a foreign-funded financial institution or the head of any sub-branch is absent from his or her post for a continuous period of one month or more, the CBRC is required to be notified. The institution is required to appoint a replacement of any senior management personnel who is absent from his or her position for three consecutive months or more.[148]

The term "senior management personnel" is defined by the CBRC as a general manager or president of a bank or deputy general manager or vice president of a bank.[149] For other positions of importance, such as the chief accountant, compliance managers, and operations managers, the FIE financial institution is required to register such personnel with the CBRC.[150] Foreign-owned financial institutions are required to employ an accountant qualified to practice in China and approved by the CBRC.[151]

f. Liquidation

If an FIE Financial Institution intends to terminate its operations, it is required to provide notice to the CBRC thirty days prior to cessation of the operations and can commence liquidation and dissolution only after obtaining approval.[152] An institution is required to follow the liquidation procedures established by the State Council.[153]

---

the following positions: chairman of the board or president (general manager) of an FIE financial institution and the general manager of a foreign bank branch. Local branches of the CBRC may approve vice chairman of the board or vice president (deputy general manager) of an FIE institution and the deputy general manager of a foreign bank branch and the head of a sub-branch. FIE Financial Institution Implementing Rules, art. 54. The CBRC may revoke the qualifications of a senior manager if he or she is under investigation for criminal liability; refuses or interferes with government investigations; engages in unsound internal management and control practices; operates in serious violation of the law; and is involved in other circumstances that according to the CBRC justifies revocation. FIE Financial Institution Implementing Rules, art. 62.

147. FIE Financial Institution Implementing Rules, art. 56. Under prior regulations, FIE financial institutions were required to employ, within three years of commencing business operations, at least one Chinese citizen as a senior manager. This rule was dropped with the 2002 amendments.

148. FIE Financial Institution Implementing Rules, art. 61.

149. FIE Financial Institution Implementing Rules, art. 57.

150. FIE Financial Institution Implementing Rules, arts. 58, 59. Under the CBRC record system, the FIE financial institution is required to submit a power of attorney with respect to the authorization of the subject employee, resumé of the candidate, identification cards and academic credentials, and a statement from the candidate that he or she has no record of improper conduct. FIE Financial Institution Implementing Rules, art. 59.

151. FIE Financial Institution Regulations, art. 32; FIE Financial Institution Implement Rules, arts. 75, 85–86.

152. FIE Financial Institution Regulations, art. 38.

153. FIE Financial Institution Rules, arts. 40–41; FIE Financial Institution Implementing Rules, arts. 90–109 (outline procedures and materials required for voluntary dissolution and liquidation; standards

g. Supervision and Penalties

If an institution is unable to meet its obligations, the CBRC may order the institution to suspend its operations and to take corrective steps to improve the solvency of its operation.[154] An institution that engages in banking activities without approval, engages in activities outside the scope of its approval, fails to submit the required financial statements and other documents, or commits other violations of the laws is subject to fines, confiscation of profits, suspension orders, or loss of a business license.[155]

4. Foreign Investment and Equity Participation in Chinese Financial Institutions

The China Banking Regulatory Commission has adopted a set of regulations governing the investment or equity participation in Chinese-owned financial institutions by overseas investors.[156] The regulations set forth the application procedures and capital requirements for foreign investment in Chinese-owned financial institutions, and approval is on a case-by-case basis. The regulations provide that the investment or equity participation ratio in a Chinese-owned financial institution by a single overseas investor shall not

---

for liquidation committee; documentation required by FIE financial institution to start the liquidation process; deadlines for the liquidation process; standards for closing a branch office of FIE financial institution; notice procedures to creditors and governmental agencies; requirements for procurement of audit report for liquidation approval; restrictions on sales or transfers of assets; issues involving FOREX and liquidation; standards for liquidation report; standards for involuntary liquidation and dissolution; and standards for resumption of activities post-liquidation). Measures on Liquidation Procedures for Foreign Investment Enterprises (approved on June 15, 1996, by the State Council and promulgated on July 9, 1996, by MOFTEC), *reprinted in* CHINA LAWS FOR FOREIGN BUSINESS (CCH), Business Regulation ¶ 13-608 (hereinafter the "FIE Liquidation Procedures"). *See* Chapter 20, Enterprise Liquidation, Reorganization, and Bankruptcy § A.

154. FIE Financial Institution Regulations, art. 39. If an FIE financial institution is unable to timely pay its obligations, the CBRC may order that it cease operations and resolve its financial problems within a stipulated period of time. If the FIE recovers the ability to repay its debts during the rectification period, it may apply to the CBRC to resume operations or proceed to liquidation. FIE Financial Institution Regulations, art. 39.

155. FIE Financial Institution Regulations, arts. 42–49. If an FIE financial institution engages in activities in violation of the supervision and reporting requirements of the Regulations, the CBRC may issue a warning, confiscate any illegal income, and impose a monetary penalty of one to three times the amount of any gains. If an FIE financial institution refuses or interferes with the regulatory functions of the CBRC or submits false documentation or information, the CBRC may issue a warning and impose a monetary penalty ranging from RMB100,000 to RMB500,000. If an FIE financial institution fails to submit its financial statements and other documents or information in a timely manner, the CBRC may issue a warning and order it to rectify the circumstances within a specified period, and may impose a monetary penalty ranging from RMB10,000 to RMB100,000. In case of serious violations of the Regulations, the CBRC may suspend the business license of an FIE financial institution or revoke its business license, and any senior management personnel involved may be disqualified from working in China.

156. Procedures for the Administration of Investment and Equity Participation in Chinese-Invested Financial Institutions by Offshore Financial Institutions (promulgated on December 8, 2003, by the China Banking Regulatory Commission) (hereinafter the "Overseas Investment in Chinese-Owned Banks Regulations"). *See generally* T. Jones, *Foreign Strategic Investment in a PRC Domestic Bank*, CHINA L. & PRAC. (March 2003); C. Choi & C. Kan, *Giving a Boost to Foreign Equity Participation in Domestic Financial Institutions*, CHINA L. & PRAC. (March 2004).

exceed twenty percent (20%), and if the aggregate foreign investment is greater than twenty-five percent (25%), the institution will be treated as a foreign-invested financial institution and limited in its scope of business as would be an FIE financial institution.[157] The capital limits on investment in Chinese-owned financial institutions is a minimum of $10 billion for investment and equity participation in Chinese-owned commercial banks, and not less than $1 billion for investment and equity participation in Chinese-owned non-bank financial institutions.[158]

B. Foreign Exchange Regulation

A foreign investor in China has the right to repatriate funds subject to the foreign exchange rules and regulations. Historically, it has been difficult for foreign parties to remit profits and income abroad given that foreign currency is strictly controlled and China's currency, the renminbi (RMB), is not freely convertible.[159]

Since 1996, the government has restructured its foreign exchange regulatory system in order to encourage foreign companies to continue to invest in China and as a conciliatory point with its trading partners to gain admission to the World Trade Organization. The State Council promulgated regulations setting forth relatively flexible standards designed to facilitate the prompt processing of foreign exchange transactions.[160] Prior to July 1, 1996, foreign

157. Overseas Investment in Chinese-Owned Banks Regulations, art. 8.

158. Overseas Investment in Chinese-Owned Banks Regulations, art. 7.

159. FOREX Rules, art. 7.

160. Rules of the People's Republic of China on Foreign Exchange Control (promulgated January 29, 1996, by the State Council and amended on January 4, 1997, by the State Council), *reprinted in* CHINA LAWS FOR FOREIGN BUSINESS (CCH), Business Regulation ¶ 8-545 (hereinafter the "FOREX Rules"). The FOREX Rules are available on the Web site of MOFCOM at http://www.mofcom.gov.cn. *See also* Administrative Regulations on Foreign Exchange Settlements, Sales and Payments (promulgated June 20, 1996, by the People's Bank of China), *reprinted in* CHINA LAWS FOR FOREIGN BUSINESS (CCH), Business Regulation ¶ 8-780 (hereinafter "FOREX Settlement Regulations"); Notice of the State Administration of Foreign Exchange on the Printing and Distribution of the Administrative Measures on the Settlement of Foreign Exchange under Current Accounts (promulgated on July 25, 1997, by the State Administration of Foreign Exchange), *reprinted in* CHINA LAWS FOR FOREIGN BUSINESS (CCH), Business Regulation ¶ 8-670; Announcement of the People's Bank of China on the Implementation of Foreign Exchange Settlements and Sales at Banks by Foreign Investment Enterprises (promulgated June 20, 1996, by the People's Bank of China), *reprinted in* CHINA LAWS FOR FOREIGN BUSINESS (CCH), Business Regulation ¶ 8-784; Notice on the Issue of the "Provisional Measures on the Administration of Foreign Exchange Registration for Foreign Investment Enterprises" (promulgated June 28, 1996, by the State Administration of Foreign Exchange), *reprinted in* CHINA LAWS FOR FOREIGN BUSINESS (CCH), Business Regulation ¶ 8-788 (hereinafter "FOREX Registration Measures"); Administrative Regulations on Domestic Foreign Exchange Accounts (promulgated on October 7, 1997, by the People's Bank of China), *reprinted in* CHINA LAWS FOR FOREIGN BUSINESS (CCH), Business Regulation ¶ 8-569 (hereinafter the "FOREX Administrative Regulations"). *See generally China: FOREX Regulations,* EIU ViewsWire (May 28, 1998), available on Lexis, News Library. The SAFE has adopted regulations governing the administration of foreign exchange in bonded zones. *See* Administrative Measures on Foreign Exchange Control in Bonded Zones (promulgated by the SAFE on July 25, 2002), *reprinted in* CHINA LAWS FOR FOREIGN

investors with operations in China were limited to conducting foreign exchange transactions through swap centers. Today, foreign exchange transactions may be conducted through approved financial institutions, and SAFE is taking steps to continue to liberalize FOREX transactions.[161]

1. Application for an FERC

An enterprise must first file an application with the State Administration of Foreign Exchange (SAFE) to obtain a Foreign Investment Enterprise Foreign Exchange Registration Certificate (FERC) in order to open a foreign exchange bank account.[162] When applying for an FERC, an FIE is required to prepare a registration form outlining the scope of the operation and products, the capitalization and assets of the FIE, proof of its legal existence, the purpose of the proposed foreign exchange account, and other general

---

BUSINESS (CCH), Business Regulation ¶ 8-530 (outlines procedures for FOREX registration and annual inspection, administration of FOREX accounts in bonded zones, and FOREX settlement procedures). The Bonded Zone FOREX Measures specify that (i) export-processing companies and logistics firms may purchase FOREX with revenues from products sold in China; (ii) newly-registered companies may use their RMB-denominated registered capital to buy foreign currencies to pay foreign exchange obligations; (iii) companies may use RMB-denominated profits, interest income, and dividends to buy foreign exchange; (iv) upon SAFE approval, companies inside the bonded zone can open capital accounts in banks outside the zone; and (v) an FIE in the bonded zone no longer needs special SAFE registration certificates. Such companies must still buy foreign exchange at designated banks and present the necessary documentation. *See also* Notice on Relevant Issues Related to Furthering Adjustment of Import/Export Verification Management Policies (issued on July 10, 2002, by the State Administration of Foreign Exchange) (outlines reporting requirements and extends the time periods wherein traders must file for an extension of foreign exchange verification and cancellation procedures; states that exporters must report to SAFE if foreign exchange payments for exports out of China will be received more than 180 days after export; and states that importers are no longer required to report the cancellation of payments paid by letters of credit or documents against payment that are transacted 90 days after import). The government has also adopted regulations for the administration of foreign exchange in the insurance sector. *See* Provisional Regulations on Foreign Exchange Administration for Insurance Industry (promulgated on September 24, 2002, by SAFE and the China Insurance Regulatory Commission), *reprinted in* CHINA LAWS FOR FOREIGN BUSINESS (CCH), Business Regulation ¶ 9-670.

161. In April 2003, SAFE issued a notice that lists 26 administrative activities that no longer need the approval of SAFE and outlines how 21 of these listed items will be handled. Abolished tasks include approvals for FOREX activities in insurance, finance, and other industry sectors, as well as approvals that apply to FIEs. Although certain items do not require SAFE approval, registration and filing is still required. *See* the Web site of SAFE (http://www.safe.gov.cn) for a copy of the list of activities no longer requiring SAFE approval. *See also* Regulations on Border Trading of FOREX (issued on October 1, 2003, by SAFE) (rules liberalize FOREX transactions across China's borders by allowing border trading companies and individuals living at the border to conduct business in the nonconvertible currencies of neighboring countries); Notice Relating to the Publication of the "Interim Measures on the Administration of Carrying Foreign Currencies at Exit-Entry of the Border" (issued on August 28, 2003, by SAFE and the Customs General Administration). *See* Foreign Debt Administration Tentative Procedures (promulgated on March 1, 2003, by the State Administration of Foreign Exchange) (provides certain new and tighter foreign debt registration standards for foreign-invested enterprises including the requirement that an FIE's foreign debt agreements will not be effective until they have been registered with SAFE, and requires that the balance of existing short-term foreign debts be aggregated with existing medium-term and long-term foreign debts for the purpose of applying the borrowing limit to new foreign debt).

162. FOREX Registration Measures, art. 4. The SAFE (and its local offices) is the regulatory agency responsible for foreign currency exchange control.

information.[163] The FERC application should be accompanied by the enterprise's business license, the joint venture contract, articles of association of the enterprise, and an investment verification certificate.[164] The SAFE examines whether a foreign party has made its capital contributions in accordance with the terms of the joint venture contract. An application for the FERC must be filed within thirty days of obtaining a business license.[165]

2. Opening a Foreign Exchange Account

Only after obtaining an FERC may an FIE open a foreign exchange account at a bank authorized to engage in foreign exchange business.[166] An FIE, with approval, may open a foreign exchange account for current or capital accounts,[167] or may open special accounts to facilitate foreign direct investment activities.[168] In order to open a foreign exchange account, an FIE must

163. *See* Provisional Administrative Regulations on Domestic Allocation and Transfer of Foreign Exchange (promulgated on September 25, 1997, by the State Administration of Foreign Exchange), *reprinted in* CHINA LAWS FOR FOREIGN BUSINESS (CCH), Business Regulation ¶ 8-688 (hereinafter referred to as the "FOREX Allocation and Transfer Regulations") (provides detailed information and data requirements for FERC applications).

164. FOREX Registration Measures, art. 4. In the past, the SAFE reviewed feasibility studies to determine a project's ability to generate foreign exchange and issued an opinion. Such opinions had the effect of determining whether to approve a joint venture project. Under the rules, the SAFE is not authorized to issue an opinion concerning the FIE's operation.

165. FOREX Registration Measures, art. 4. A foreign party may set up a temporary account to hold foreign exchange in preparation of establishing an FIE. FOREX Administrative Regulations, art. 25.

166. FOREX Registration Measures, arts. 5, 6; FOREX Administrative Regulations, arts. 12, 28 § (3).

167. FOREX Administrative Regulations, art. 6, 20 (outlining the different types of current and capital accounts). The regulations provide that the scope of exchange control includes the regulation of foreign currency, payment instruments denominated in foreign currency, securities denominated in foreign currency, and other assets denominated in foreign currency. FOREX Rules, art. 3.

168. In 2003, SAFE issued a notice that provides foreign investors with more methods of contributing capital to its FIEs. *See* Notice from the State Administration of Foreign Exchange on Issues Relating to Improving Foreign Exchange Administration of Foreign Direct Investment (issued on March 3, 2003, by the State Administration of Foreign Exchange) (hereinafter referred to as "FDI FOREX Notice"), *reprinted in* CHINA LAWS FOR FOREIGN BUSINESS (CCH), Business Regulation ¶ 8-730. Subject to SAFE approval, foreign investors may open onshore "special FOREX accounts," in one of four categories: (1) *Investment account:* used for when a foreign investor contracts for a project; (2) *Acquisition Account:* used for when a foreign investor desires to establish an FIE, or for funds to be used for acquiring land-use rights, equipment, or other assets during the FIE's pre-establishment period; (3) *Expense Account:* used for when a foreign investor intends to establish an FIE, to be used for market research and establishment costs during the FIE's pre-establishment period; and (4) *Security Account:* used for when a foreign investor needs to provide a funding security or deposit to a domestic institution. FDI FOREX Notice, art. 1. SAFE retains discretion to determine the duration and limits on the amounts held in such special FOREX accounts. After an account is established and funds transferred therein, the investor's capital contribution that may be required to establish an FIE is deemed to have been made if placed into these special accounts. Foreign investors are allowed to open only a single special FOREX account, unless SAFE approves additional accounts. SAFE allows foreign investors to contribute funds directly to an FIE's capital account (1) from an offshore account in a designated offshore FOREX bank; or (2) by using the FOREX in an onshore nonresident individual cash remittance account. Subject to the ratio of capital contribution made to an FIE, a foreign investor also may convert specific items into an FIE's registered capital; namely, an FIE may convert into registered capital (1) a proportional amount of the FIE's development funds and reserve funds; (2) the FIE's undistributed dividends and accrued interest; (3) principal and accrued interest of the FIE's registered foreign debt held by the foreign investors; and (4) investors'

present a bank with a notice to open an account issued by the SAFE.[169] An FIE is also required to provide the bank with a certificate issued by the SAFE if it intends to open a loan account for foreign debts or foreign exchange loans.[170]

After a bank has opened a foreign exchange account for an FIE, the bank is required to specify on the FIE's FERC the account currency, account number, account type, and the date on which the account is opened.[171] Each foreign exchange account has a strictly defined scope of use.[172] The FOREX Administrative Regulations provide for the opening of foreign exchange clearance accounts employed for the purpose of revenue and expenditures on current account items and, with approval, expenditures for capital account items.[173] The rules also provide for the opening of a foreign exchange special account that can be used for the payment of foreign debts and foreign exchange loans issued by Chinese financial institutions.[174] An FIE is required to use the foreign exchange account in accordance with the FERC and, in general, is limited to the type of account, scope of the revenue and expenditures, maximum amount of currency to be held in a particular account, and the term of the account.[175] The circulation of foreign currency is prohibited and may not be quoted for settlement purposes in the PRC.

An FIE may repatriate profits, dividends, and income after taxation from its own foreign exchange account or with foreign exchange purchased at designated institutions. The banks require the submission of a resolution of the FIE's board of directors outlining the profit distribution plan before the approval of a repatriation of profits and other distributions.

SAFE has adopted rules that unify the procedures for FOREX account opening and management for FIEs and domestic enterprises.[176] Under these

early-recouped investments or assets derived from liquidation, equity transfer, or reduction of registered capital from FIEs in which they have invested. SAFE will not approve onshore transfer of FOREX funds between FIEs and their domestic investee enterprises, or the domestic investee enterprises invested by the same FIE (FIE holding companies are excluded).

169. FOREX Administrative Regulations, art. 12.

170. FOREX Administrative Regulations, arts. 6 § (11), 20 § (1), 22.

171. FOREX Registration Measures, art. 6; FOREX Administrative Regulations, art. 31.

172. FOREX Administrative Regulations, arts. 16, 17. An FIE may apply to open a foreign exchange account outside the place of its registration. FOREX Administrative Regulations, art. 36.

173. FOREX Administrative Regulations, arts. 6, 20.

174. FOREX Administrative Regulations, arts. 6 § (11), 20 § (1), 22.

175. FOREX Administrative Regulations, art. 42.

176. Notice on Issues Concerning Furthering the Adjustment of Current Foreign Exchange Account Administrative Policies (issued by the State Administration of Foreign Exchange and effective on October 15, 2002) (hereinafter the "FOREX Current Account Notice"); Foreign Exchange Accounts for Current Items by Domestic Entities Implementing Rules (issued by the State Administration of Foreign Exchange and effective on October 15, 2002) (hereinafter the "FOREX Current Account Implementing Rules").

rules, local SAFE branches have jurisdiction to supervise FOREX matters.[177] The FOREX Current Account Notice and FOREX Current Account Implementing Rules do not apply to special Customs areas, such as bonded and export-processing zones. The FOREX Current Account Notice and FOREX Current Account Implementing Rules require the consolidation of foreign exchange current settlement accounts and special-purpose foreign exchange accounts into a foreign exchange current account. These regulations relax account-opening requirements for Chinese-funded enterprises.

The FOREX Current Account Notice and FOREX Current Account Implementing Rules actively promote the expansion of SAFE's FOREX account management information system, and outline reporting requirements for financial institutions engaged in current account FOREX activities. Since SAFE can closely monitor daily transactions, banks in areas covered by the system will no longer be subject to yearly SAFE inspections. Enterprises demonstrating a need may open multiple accounts of one or more foreign currencies in one or several banks as long as the total FOREX amount does not exceed the enterprise's approved ceiling for each currency. SAFE must still approve foreign exchange payments under capital account items, as capital account controls will not be relaxed for several years.

Under the FOREX Current Account Notice and FOREX Current Account Implementing Rules all businesses are required to apply to SAFE to combine accounts, and to have the account ceiling approved by SAFE prior to December 31, 2003. The regulations specify that a domestic entity's balance of a foreign exchange current account shall not exceed twenty percent (20%) of the previous year's current account foreign exchange revenues. Local SAFE offices have the authority to modify the amount of FOREX an enterprise is allowed to maintain. If the entity has no FOREX revenues, the current foreign exchange account may not exceed $100,000. Local SAFE entities are to ensure that the total amount of FOREX kept in its jurisdiction's current FOREX accounts does not exceed twenty-five (25%) of the area's previous year FOREX income or other specified amount.

3. Control over Foreign Exchange Transactions

Financial institutions are obligated to examine foreign exchange transactions to determine whether account holders are using their respective accounts in a manner consistent with the regulations, and is bound by law

177. *See also* Announcement Regarding Transfer of Part of the Foreign Exchange Business from the State Administration of Foreign Exchange to the SAFE Beijing Branch (issued on September 21, 2001, by SAFE).

to report this information to the SAFE.[178] If the amount of foreign exchange in an account exceeds the maximum limited set by the SAFE, the excess must be sold to a foreign exchange bank or traded at foreign exchange swap centers.[179] The FERC allows an account holder to engage in foreign exchange transactions without the need to obtain approval for individual transactions.[180] The FERC is valid for a one-year period of time and must be renewed annually.

If an FIE, after completion of the FERC procedures, changes its name, address, or scope of business, or is assigned or merges with another organization, the FIE is required to apply to the SAFE for an amended FERC.[181] The approval of the SAFE is also required if the FIE intends to use profits derived from the operation for reinvestment in China or to increase its registered capital.[182] If an FIE uses its profits to increase its registered capital, approval from the SAIC or local authorities is also required.[183] A holding or investment company is required to obtain the approval of the SAFE if it intends to transfer its foreign exchange funds for investment in China.[184]

If an FIE terminates its operation or is legally liquidated and dissolved, it must, within thirty days of completing the liquidation procedures, apply to the SAFE for cancellation of the FERC.[185] Upon liquidation, an FIE is required to surrender its FERC and to close its foreign exchange account. If the funds in a foreign exchange account are exhausted, the bank may cancel the account. An FIE is also prohibited from altering its FERC and is barred from assigning, lending, leasing, or selling its FERC to other parties.[186] A violation of the registration measures may result in monetary fines issued by the SAFE.[187] The SAFE is authorized to supervise foreign exchange account transactions and may monitor the activities of financial institutions.[188]

---

178. FOREX Settlement Regulations, art. 39; FOREX Administrative Regulations, art. 40.

179. FOREX Settlement Regulations, art. 10.

180. FOREX Registration Measures, art. 7.

181. FOREX Registration Measures, art. 8; FOREX Administrative Regulations, art. 37.

182. Notice on Certain Issues Concerning the Alteration of Capital Funds by Foreign Investment Enterprises, arts. 1, 2, 4 (promulgated June 28, 1996, by the State Administration of Foreign Exchange), *reprinted in* CHINA LAWS FOR FOREIGN BUSINESS (CCH), Business Regulation ¶ 8-792 (hereinafter "FOREX Capital Funds Alteration Notice").

183. FOREX Capital Funds Alteration Notice, art. 2.

184. FOREX Capital Funds Alteration Notice, art. 3.

185. FOREX Registration Measures, art. 9; FOREX Administrative Regulations, arts. 38, 41.

186. FOREX Registration Measures, art. 11; FOREX Administrative Regulations, art. 42.

187. FOREX Registration Measures, art. 12; FOREX Administrative Regulations, arts. 42, 44.

188. The State Council authorizes an award system to allow individuals to report and expose violations of foreign exchange rules. FOREX Rules, art. 8; FOREX Administrative Regulations, art. 39. The Supreme People's Court issued a notice emphasizing that harsh penalties are to be imposed upon persons that trade in foreign exchange using false or invalid FERCs. *See* Tang, *Court Seeks Stiff Penalties for Illegal Currency Traders,* CHINA DAILY (September 1, 1998), available on Lexis, News Library, or on the Web site of the CHINA DAILY at http://www.chinadaily.com.cn. *See* Decision Concerning Punishment of Criminal Offenses Involving Fraudulent Purchase, Evasion and Illegal Trading of Foreign Exchange (issued on

The policy of the government is to eventually fully abolish the foreign exchange swap centers and require all enterprises, domestic and foreign-related, to use the interbank system currently employed.[189] Foreign-funded financial institutions, with the approval of the CBRC and SAFE, may operate as a designated foreign exchange bank, which allows them to engage in foreign exchange transactions. In addition, the government has approved a number of foreign financial institutions to conduct business in renminbi. The renminbi-approved banks are limited to commercial transactions in major cities and renminbi-denominated transactions cannot exceed 35 percent of the institution's loan portfolio.[190]

Dec. 29, 1998, by the Standing Committee of the 9th NPC), *reprinted in* 139 China International Business (MOFTEC) 50 (1999) (provides for large fines and prison terms ranging up to life imprisonment for fraudulent foreign exchange transactions). *See also* Provisional Rules of the Ministry of Foreign Trade and Economic Cooperation concerning the Imposition of Administrative Penalties on Foreign Economic and Trade Enterprises Engaged in Foreign Exchange Evasion and Illegal Arbitrage in Foreign Exchange (issued on October 9, 1998, by the MOFTEC), *reprinted in* 2 CHINA LAW UPDATE 19 (Feb. 1999) (outlines administrative penalties for violations of foreign exchange trading rules by FIEs, administrative litigation procedures for contesting penalty decisions). *See also* Provisional Regulations Regarding the Administrative Punishments on Disciplinary Measures on Activities Violating the Foreign Exchange Administrative Regulations, Including Arbitrage, Illegal Procurement, Illegal Evasion and Illegal Transactions in Foreign Exchange (issued on January 25, 1999, by the Ministry of Supervision, Ministry of Personnel, People's Bank of China, State General Administration of Customs and the State Administration of Foreign Exchange) (hereinafter the "FOREX Disciplinary Measures"). These Regulations follow the *Administrative Regulations on Foreign Exchange,* the *Provisional Regulations on State Civil Servants,* and the *Regulations Concerning the Rewards and Disciplinary Sanctions for Enterprise Employees.* The FOREX Disciplinary Measures apply to civil servants, employees of financial institutions approved to engage in foreign exchange business activities, and employees of state-owned foreign trade enterprises. The FOREX Disciplinary Measures set forth a list of illegal FOREX-related activities and detail penalties for such activities the severity of which is based upon the amount of money involved. The punishments include, in ascending order of severity, sanction of warning, recorded demerit, special recorded demerit, demotion, dismissal from office, continued employment on probation, and expulsion. In case of regulatory violations, the relevant personnel in charge and other directly responsible personnel may be held responsible, and not the enterprise. If an infraction violates both the PRC Criminal Laws and the FOREX Disciplinary Measures, criminal penalties may be imposed upon the responsible party.

189. The swap centers are exchanges that at one time were located throughout China where buyers and sellers of foreign exchange traded renminbi for other currencies. In order for a joint venture to obtain foreign exchange at a swap center, other parties had to be willing to trade foreign exchange. Since the restructuring of China's foreign exchange system at the beginning of 1994, swap centers have been open only for use by foreign investment enterprises (FIEs), such as joint ventures, so there must be sufficient foreign investment enterprises with currency to sell for trades to take place. Chinese entities other than FIEs can enter into foreign exchange transactions at designated foreign exchange banks, which differ from swap centers in that the bank itself is the counter-party for the transaction. As part of the 1994 reforms, the swap centers are now run by the foreign exchange banks, and the Chinese government has stated that it plans to abolish swap centers because all entities have been allowed access to the foreign exchange banks. During the transition period, however, the swap centers continued to operate.

190. Provisional Administrative Measures of Shanghai Pudong on Foreign-Funded Financial Institutions Conducting Trial Renminbi Business Operations (promulgated on December 2, 1996, by the People's Bank of China), *reprinted in* CHINA LAWS FOR FOREIGN BUSINESS (CCH), Special Zones & Cities ¶ 240-065. The measures address the licensing process required of foreign financial institutions interested in doing renminbi business, and sets forth the foreign exchange capital requirements to engage in RMB transactions. *See also* Notice of the Ministry of Finance, the State Administration of Taxation and the People's Bank of China on Tax Issues Concerning Foreign-Funded Financial Institutions Conducting Renminbi Business (promulgated on May 5, 1997, by the MOF, SAT, and PBOC), *reprinted in* CHINA LAWS FOR FOREIGN BUSINESS (CCH), Taxation ¶ 31-822 (requiring separate accounts and separate taxation calculations for RMB business, and a prohibition on tax preferential treatment for RMB business

4. Project Financing

The government has developed project finance regulations for infrastructure and construction projects in the PRC financed by international commercial funds.[191] Chinese law requires that project financing conditions be competitive and must be examined and approved by the State Administration of Foreign Exchange (SAFE).[192] The rules further require that the anticipated income and assets of the project are the sole source of the funds for the repayment of foreign loans. Specifically, project financing in China has the following characteristics:

(1) The creditor will not have a right of recourse to assets and income outside of the construction project

(2) The domestic enterprise is prohibited from using the assets, rights and interest, or income outside the construction project as collateral or security for a mortgage or pledge

(3) The domestic organization must not supply any form of financial security[193]

The Chinese government encourages the use of overseas financing for the construction of power generation, roads and highways, bridges, tunnels, urban water treatment facilities, waste water treatment facilities, and other

---

income). Pursuant to an order in December of 1996, nine financial institutions are authorized to conduct RMB business including the following: Citibank, the Hong Kong & Shanghai Banking Corp., Britain's Standard Chartered, the Bank of Tokyo-Mitsubishi Ltd., Industrial Bank of Japan, Sanwa Bank, and Dai-ichi Kangyo Bank of Japan, the Banque Indosuez, and a Shanghai joint venture operated by France's Banque Nationale de Paris and the State-owned Industrial and Commercial Bank of China. The Chinese government advised the public in December 1997 that it intended to authorize the trading of renminbi by more foreign financial institutions and in Beijing and Shenzhen. *See China May Allow More Foreign Banks to Trade in Local Currency,* 14 Int'l Trade Rep. 2203 (1997). The government is also allowing border trade enterprises to use any convertible currency or renminbi to settle their accounts. *See* Notice of the State Administration of Foreign Exchange on the Issuing of the Provisional Measures on Border Trade Foreign Exchange Control (promulgated on January 23, 1997, by the State Administration of Foreign Exchange), *reprinted in* CHINA LAWS FOR FOREIGN BUSINESS (CCH), Business Regulation ¶ 8-808.

191. Provisional Measures on the Administration of the Overseas Financing of Projects (promulgated on April 16, 1997, by the State Planning Commission and the State Administration of Foreign Exchange), *reprinted in* CHINA LAWS FOR FOREIGN BUSINESS (CCH), Business Regulation ¶ 8-812 (hereinafter the "Project Financing Rules"). For a discussion of the Project Financing Rules, *see* Lange & Ross, *New Project Finance Measures Further Limit Lenders' Room for Maneuver, in* CHINA L. & PRAC. 51–54 (June 1997). *See also* FOREX Rules, arts. 22 (approval for external loans), 25 (registration requirements for foreign debt). The Chinese government encourages the use of the build, operate, and transfer investment structure for infrastructure projects. *See* Chen, *BOT in China: Opportunities and Uncertainties,* 14 CHINA LAW NEWS 1 (Aug. 28, 1998). *See also* Chapter 4, FIE Organizational Structure and Approval Procedures § C.5. *See also* Procedures for Borrowing of International Commercial Loans Concerning Domestic Agencies (issued on January 1, 1998, by the People's Bank of China), *reprinted in* 128 CHINA INTERNATIONAL BUSINESS (MOFTEC) 52 (1998) (addresses the procedures for approval of international commercial loans, the authority of the State Administration of Exchange Control, restrictions on international borrowing, conditions for borrowing, and legal liability).

192. Project Financing Rules, art. 11.

193. Project Financing Rules, art. 1.

infrastructure projects. The government also encourages construction projects involving facilities that are anticipated to generate long-term and stable income.[194]

The Project Financing Rules require that the parties to project finance contracts, project construction contracts, or project operation contracts be qualified to perform the tasks under the contracts, and are required to rely upon their own economic and technical capabilities to perform the contract. Each party is required to bear their share of the risks associated with a construction project.[195] The principal investor in a construction project is not permitted to become a party to a construction contract that may result in a conflict of interest.

The Project Financing Rules prohibit a domestic financial institution from acting as a guarantor for a project. Other domestic organizations that provide security for the performance of a project finance contract are required to obtain government approval.[196]

A proposal and feasibility study must be prepared by the parties to a project and submitted to the local planning departments. After preliminary examination, the proposal and study are submitted to the State Development Planning Commission for approval.[197] Large projects are required to be examined and approved by the State Council. A construction project feasibility study, in addition to the general issues required for such reports, also include the following information:

(1) Qualifications of, and the proportion of risk to be borne by, the principal investor in the project and the parties to the contract
(2) Method of foreign currency equalization and amount of foreign exchange required for the term of operation of the project
(3) Factors for setting prices for products and services and methods for amendments or revisions to pricing
(4) Project finance program including the payment schedules, loan terms, interest rates, itemized charges under the loans, and other financing conditions
(5) Guarantee and security agreements
(6) Draft of the project finance contract and underlying construction contract[198]

194. Project Financing Rules, art. 2.
195. Project Financing Rules, art. 4.
196. Project Financing Rules, art. 5.
197. Project Financing Rules, art. 8.
198. Project Financing Rules, art. 9.

After the feasibility study is approved by the State Development Planning Commission, approval must be obtained from the SAFE.[199] The project company is required to promptly transfer into China the foreign exchange funds pursuant to the project financing contract, and such funds cannot be deposited overseas without the approval of the SAFE.[200] The funds can thereafter be used, as approved by the State Development Planning Commission, for purchase or payment of technical equipment, services, and materials.

A project company is required to establish renminbi and foreign exchange Repayment Accounts earmarked for the payment of loan principal and interest with a foreign exchange designated bank in China.[201] A project company is not permitted to set up an overseas account for domestic income generated by the project without prior approval of the SAFE. If the income from a project is insufficient to pay the loan principal and interest, the project company, with the approval of the SAFE, may purchase foreign exchange and deposit the funds in the Repayment Account.[202] Foreign exchange held in a Repayment Account earmarked for the payment of loan principal and interest must be remitted abroad in a timely manner and in accordance with State regulations and the parties' agreement.

The project company is required to register with the SAFE and to submit a report to the SAFE that outlines its income and use of funds on an annual basis. The report must be submitted before the end of each March for activities in the prior year.[203] A project company is subject to inspection and supervision by SAFE. If a project company fails to obtain the required approval, a bank is prohibited from opening a Repayment Account.

5. Domestic Enterprises and Foreign Exchange Control

Traditionally, a domestic enterprise was required to repatriate all its foreign exchange receipts relating to its capital account transactions and prohibited from depositing its foreign exchange with an overseas institution without authorization.[204] Domestic enterprises may make external payments from

199. Project Financing Rules, art. 12. An applicant is required to submit to the SAFE the documents submitted to the State Development Planning Commission and the approval certificate from the Commission.

200. Project Financing Rules, art. 13.

201. Project Financing Rules, art. 14.

202. Project Financing Rules, art. 15.

203. Project Financing Rules, art. 16.

204. FOREX Rules, arts. 9, 10. *See also* Notice on Several Issues Concerning the Adjustment of Administrative Policies for Foreign Exchange Accounts Under the International Contracting Project and Other Current Account Items (issued by the State Administration of Foreign Exchange and effective on September 1, 2003). This Notice allows domestic companies engaged in international business activities to retain 100% of their foreign currency earnings in foreign currency. Under prior rules, domestic

their own foreign exchange accounts or with foreign exchange purchased at designated banks upon presentation of commercial invoices justifying payments.[205] With the approval of SAFE, a domestic enterprise may use foreign exchange for overseas investments. A domestic enterprise is also required to obtain the approval of the SAFE to use foreign exchange for payments under guarantee contracts. Effective November 1, 2003, SAFE adopted rules that authorize FOREX purchases up to $3 million (up from a previous limit of $1 million) for qualified Chinese companies in order to facilitate overseas investment.[206]

6. Foreign Exchange Held by Individuals

An individual may hold foreign exchange personally. The State Council recognizes the principles of voluntary deposit, unrestricted withdrawal, interest on deposits, and confidentiality with respect to foreign exchange savings deposits.[207] An individual who imports or exports foreign exchange is required to declare the currency with Customs.[208] Since September 2003, Chinese citizens are allowed to purchase and travel abroad with more foreign exchange.[209] SAFE also regulates large FOREX transactions involving non-PRC and non-Mainland residents.[210]

---

companies were only allowed to retain 20% of their foreign earnings in foreign currency and required that the remaining 80% be converted into RMB. Domestic companies engaged in international transportation, overseas project contracting and labor services, and public bidding and tenders may retain their foreign earnings in their original form.

205. FOREX Rules, art. 11. The PBOC (and now the CBRC) and the SAFE have adopted a new computer system, which goes into effect November 1, 1998, and allows for financial institutions to obtain computer-generated import declaration papers to verify an enterprise's need to obtain foreign exchange to purchase imports. *See generally* Zhang, *New System to Be Used to Prevent Cheating,* CHINA DAILY (Oct. 26, 1998), available on Lexis, News Library, or on the Web site of the CHINA DAILY at http://www.chinadaily.com.cn.

206. For a Chinese version of the regulation, see the Web site of the State Administration of Foreign Exchange at http://www.safe.gov.cn. Part of the motivation behind the increased limits of FOREX available to domestic companies is the surge in foreign exchange reserves held by Chinese companies and the pressure on the PRC government to loosen financial controls and revalue the RMB. *See generally SAFE Expands Local FOREX Approval for Chinese Companies,* CHINA MARKET INTELLIGENCE, U.S.-CHINA BUSINESS COUNCIL (November 12, 2003).

207. FOREX Rules, art. 13; FOREX Administrative Regulations, arts. 6 § (13), 9, 15.

208. FOREX Rules, art. 14.

209. *See* Notice on the Provisional Management Rules on Entering and Exiting China with Foreign Currency (issued on September 1, 2003, by the State Adminstration of Foreign Exchange and the General Administration of Customs). This rule allows PRC citizens to travel abroad with $5,000 without reporting to SAFE. This is an increase over the previous $2,000 allowance. PRC citizens must report the movement of between $5,000 to $10,000 to SAFE, and prohibits the movement of a sum in excess of $10,000. *See also* Implementing Rules on the Management of Purchasing Foreign Exchange by Domestic Residents (issued and effective on August 1, 2002, by the State Administration of Foreign Exchange) (provides that all state-owned banks may apply to SAFE for approval to sell FOREX to qualified domestic residents and ends the monopoly held by the Bank of China on retail FOREX sales).

210. Effective March 1, 2004, SAFE requires that non-residents changing foreign currency, receiving foreign currency payments, purchasing foreign currency, or opening a foreign currency account to submit identification and documentation concerning the source of the funds. Transactions in excess of $5,000 require identification and transactions in excess of $50,000 require SAFE approval. A copy of the

7. Foreign Exchange Operations of Financial Institutions

A financial institution that engages in foreign exchange operations must be approved by the SAFE and issued a foreign exchange operations license.[211] A financial institution that has been approved to engage in foreign exchange operations must not exceed its approved scope of operations. An authorized institution must open specific foreign exchange accounts for its customers and adhere to the control regulations.[212] A financial institution that engages in foreign exchange operations must allocate a foreign exchange deposit reserve fund, and comply with asset-to-liability ratios concerning foreign exchange operations.[213] The foreign exchange operations of financial institutions are subject to inspection and supervision by the SAFE, and are required to submit their balance sheets, profit and loss statements, and other financial and accounting records required by the SAFE.[214] A financial institution is required to notify the SAFE if it intends to terminate its foreign exchange operations, settle its foreign exchange debts and credits, and surrender its foreign exchange operations license.[215]

8. Non-Trade FOREX Transactions for Multinationals

Under SAFE regulations, an approved financial institution may handle and approve the settlement of FIE capital account settlement transactions.[216] FIEs no longer need to seek approval from SAFE or its branches for each capital account settlement transaction. SAFE-authorized banks are responsible for inspecting and handling the transactions while reporting capital settlement status to SAFE on a regular basis. The MNE FOREX Notice streamlines procedures for handling certain non-trade foreign exchange transactions in Beijing, Shanghai, and Shenzhen. "Multinational companies" as referred to in the Notice include foreign-invested multinational companies that have established foreign investment enterprises with an investment nature inside China with approval of MOFCOM/COFTEC, and authorized Chinese group companies, which have approved foreign-related business operation rights.[217]

---

rules in Chinese is available on the Web site of SAFE at http://www.safe.gov.cn. The stated purpose of the rules is to better manage the inflows and outflows of FOREX and to control money laundering activities.

211. FOREX Rules, art. 27.

212. FOREX Rules, art. 28.

213. FOREX Rules, art. 29.

214. FOREX Rules, art. 31.

215. FOREX Rules, art. 32.

216. Notice on the Management of Non-Trade Exchange Transactions for Multinational Companies (Trial) (issued on August 18, 2003, by the State Administration of Foreign Exchange) (hereinafter the "MNE FOREX Notice").

217. MNE FOREX Notice, arts. 1, 2. Qualified companies must have a three year record of compliance with foreign exchange laws and regulations. MNE FOREX Notice, art. 11.

Qualified MNEs and domestic multinationals may remit overseas payments for non-trade transactions, including salaries and bonuses, pensions, travel and training expenses, patent fees, technology transfer fees, management fees, and other fees upon presentation of proper documentation at any designated foreign exchange bank.[218] Multinational companies can make the payments from foreign exchange accounts or convert renminbi to make the foreign exchange payments. The MNE FOREX Notice expands nationwide a similar policy enacted in Shanghai in June 2003. Both the MNE FOREX Notice and the policy in Shanghai are designed to ease the administration of foreign exchange for non-trade transactions, to improve the business operation environment, and to promote the development of the economy.[219]

9. Activities Subject to Penalties

The FOREX Rules authorize the SAFE to impose fines ranging from 30 percent to five times the amount of foreign exchange involved in an illegal transaction, including the following activities:

(1) Depositing foreign exchange earnings abroad without authorization
(2) Failing to sell foreign exchange to a designated foreign exchange bank
(3) Remitting or taking foreign exchange out of China without approval
(4) The unauthorized carrying or mailing of certificates of foreign exchange deposits or securities denominated in foreign exchange without authorization[220]

An individual or enterprise is liable for penalties of 30 percent or up to three times the foreign exchange involved for the following activities:

(1) Payments in renminbi for expenses when foreign exchange is required
(2) The use by overseas investors of renminbi funds for equipment and materials and earmarking such purchases as a "foreign investment"
(3) The fraudulent purchase of foreign exchange from designated foreign exchange banks through the use of false or invalid invoices, contracts, and other documents[221]

218. MNE FOREX Notice, arts. 4–9.
219. MNE FOREX Notice, art. 1.
220. FOREX Rules, art. 39.
221. FOREX Rules, art. 40.

If a party conducts unauthorized foreign exchange operations, SAFE may confiscate the funds and suspend the party from operating. In serious cases, the unauthorized party is subject to criminal liability.[222] If a financial institution engages in foreign exchange operations in excess of its authorized scope, the SAFE may impose a fine of between one and five times the amount of the illegal gains. If there are no illegal gains, the SAFE may still impose a fine ranging from RMB100,000 to RMB500,000. The SAFE also has the power to revoke an institution's foreign exchange operations license.[223] A foreign institution is also subject to monetary penalties if it fails to conduct foreign exchange settlement in accordance with the regulations.[224] A party that disagrees with a penalty decision by SAFE may, within fifteen days of receiving a penalty notice, apply for an internal appeal with SAFE. SAFE will respond within two months of receiving the appeal application. A party that disputes the SAFE's decision on the internal appeal may file an action with the people's court.[225]

C. Trade Finance

There are no specific laws or regulations in China governing trade finance standards. However, the Chinese banking community adheres to the international standards for documentary credits as adopted by the International Chamber of Commerce under the Uniform Customs and Practice on Documentary Credits (as amended in 1993) (also referred to as UCP 500). The UCP 500 sets forth a comprehensive guide for internationalizing and institutionalizing commercial practices for documentary credits such as letters of credit. In a supplement to the UCP 500, the ICC adopted a set of guidelines designed to reduce the number of discrepancies involving letters of credit transaction. The Supreme People's Court has adopted regulations that bar the local people's courts from addressing cases involving disputes over letters of credit.[226]

---

222. FOREX Rules, art. 41. In October 1998, the Supreme People's Court issued an order requiring lower people's courts to aggressively investigate and prosecute cases involving illegal foreign exchange transactions. *See Exchange Activities to Be Regulated,* CHINA DAILY (Oct. 14, 1998), available on Lexis, News Library, or on the Web site of the CHINA DAILY at http://www.chinadaily.com.cn; Hu, *China's Foreign Exchange Policy after the Asian Financial Storm,* 128 CHINA INTERNATIONAL BUSINESS (MOFTEC) 33 (1998) (discusses impact of regional financial crisis on government's foreign exchange policies).

223. FOREX Rules, art. 41.

224. FOREX Rules, art. 42.

225. FOREX Rules, art. 50. For a discussion of the administrative litigation process, *see* Chapter 22, Litigation in the People's Court § C.

226. Regulation on Several Issues on Jurisdiction of Overseas Civil and Commercial Lawsuits, PRC Supreme People's Court Judicial Interpretation [2002] No. 5 (promulgated by the SPC on Feb. 25, 2002, and effective on Mar. 1, 2002).

D. Group Finance, Financial Leasing, and Automotive Finance Companies

1. Enterprise Group Finance Companies

The Enterprise Group Finance Measures apply to enterprise group finance companies, including foreign investment enterprise groups.[227] The Measures provide that "finance companies" refers to nonbank financial institutions established in accordance with the Company Law and that provide financial services for the development of new products and technological upgrading of the member company subsidiaries and work units, primarily in the form of medium- and long-term financial business.[228] The Measures define the group units as subsidiaries in which the parent company holds over 51 percent of the shares, and companies in which the parent company and subsidiaries hold over 20 percent of the shares either independently or jointly, or in which they hold less than 20 percent but are the largest shareholder. Member work units of foreign investment enterprise groups also include companies within China in which the foreign investor in the foreign investment enterprise group has a direct shareholding of over 20 percent or in which the foreign investor and the enterprise group have a joint shareholding of over 20 percent.[229]

The Enterprise Group Finance Measures outline the standards and procedures for establishing a group finance company. The minimum registered capital requirement set forth in the Measures is RMB300 million or the equivalent in a freely convertible currency. Financial companies set up by foreign investment enterprise groups must have at least one Chinese citizen in their senior management. A group finance company may engage in various business activities approved in the Enterprise Group Finance Measures, including investment in negotiable securities, financial institution equity or member work unit equity, and overseas foreign currency loans.

The Enterprise Group Finance Measures outline the application procedures for establishing a group finance company and also lists the documents and information to be submitted to the CBRC for approval. The measures also state that a company must seek the approval of the CBRC if the

227. Measures on the Management of Enterprise Group Finance Companies (promulgated on June 30, 2000, as Order No. 3 [2000] of the People's Bank of China), *reprinted in* China Laws for Foreign Business (CCH), Business Regulation ¶ 8-360 (hereinafter referred to as "Enterprise Group Finance Measures"). The Measures repeal various prior PBOC rules and circulars including the Administration of Finance Companies of Enterprise Groups Tentative Procedures, Questions Relevant to Strengthening of the Administration of the Capital of the Finance Companies of Enterprise Groups Circular and PBOC, Questions Relevant to the Establishment and Management of the Finance Companies of Foreign Investment Enterprise Groups Circular.

228. Enterprise Group Finance Measures, art. 2.

229. Enterprise Group Finance Measures, art. 3.

company amends its company name, registered capital, or business scope. The Measures also outline the standards for regulatory supervision, termination of operations, and receivership issues.

2. Financial Leasing Companies

The CBRC has adopted a set of regulations regulating the financial leasing industry.[230] Under the Measures, a "financial leasing company" refers to a non-banking financial organization approved to engage in financial leasing as its principal business. A company authorized under these Measures is required to use the words "financial leasing" in the name of the company.[231] In order to be approved, a financial leasing company is required to have a corporate structure consistent with the Company Law, qualified senior management, internal controls and management systems, business premises that are appropriate for the operations, and minimum registered capital of RMB500,000,000. A financial leasing company that engages in foreign exchange business must have an additional foreign exchange minimum capital of no less than $50,000,000 (or equivalent convertible currency).[232] The CBRC requires that financial leasing companies go through a two-step establishment process before commencing operations.[233]

Upon approval, a financial leasing company may engage in the following Chinese and foreign currency business with the approval of the CBRC:

(1) Financing leasing business such as direct leasing, leasing back, subleasing, and mandate leasing[234]
(2) Business leasing operations

---

230. Measures on the Management of Financial Leasing Companies (promulgated on June 30, 2000, as Order No. 4 [2000] of the People's Bank of China), *reprinted in* CHINA LAWS FOR FOREIGN BUSINESS (CCH), Business Regulation ¶ 8-370 (hereinafter referred to as "Financial Leasing Company Measures"). *See generally* E. Tang & G. Li, *Approaching Leasing Joint Ventures*, CHINA L. & PRAC. (April 2003).

231. Financial Leasing Company Measures, art. 2. Other companies are not allowed to use the words "financial leasing" in their company names without approval of the CBRC.

232. Financial Leasing Company Measures, arts. 5, 6. The CBRC has the discretion to adjust the minimum amount of registered capital of a financial leasing company "in accordance with the requirements of the development of the financial leasing industry." *Id.* Art. 6.

233. Financial Leasing Company Measures, arts. 7–11. The CBRC is required to respond to an application to establish a financial leasing company in three (3) months. If an application is not approved, the applicant is not allowed to submit another application of the same nature within six months. Financial Leasing Company Measures, art. 9. The time limit for the preparation of the establishment of a financial leasing company is six months, which may be extended. No operational activities are allowed under the name of a financial leasing company during the preparation period. Financial Leasing Company Measures, art. 10. A financial leasing company may establish branch offices with the approval of the CBRC. Financial Leasing Company Measures, art. 13. Any changes to the company name, business scope, articles of association, business premises address, senior management personnel must be reported to the CBRC. Financial Leasing Company Measures, art. 14.

234. "Financing leasing business" is defined as a business activity whereby a lessor purchases leased articles from a seller and supplies use to a lessee, and receives rent from the lessee. The lessor retains

(3) Accepting lease funds entrusted by legal persons or organizations
(4) Accepting lease guarantee money from a leasing party
(5) Providing floating capital loans over leased property to a lessee
(6) Investing in securities and investing in financial organizations
(7) Issuing bank bonds with the approval of the People's Bank of China
(8) Borrowing money from financial organizations
(9) Borrowing foreign exchange
(10) Bank call loan business
(11) Selling off and handling the remaining value of depreciated leased goods and products
(12) Economic consultation and assurances
(13) Other business approved by the CBRC[235]

A financial leasing company is required to establish financial internal controls in accordance with state regulations. The company is also required to submit to the supervision of the CBRC, including on-site audits and inspections.[236] The Financial Leasing Company Measures requires that a company adhere to the following asset and liability ratios:

(1) The total value of capital must not be less than 10 percent of the total value of risk assets
(2) The highest amount of the surplus financing amount (lease + loan) with respect to the same lessee must not exceed 15 percent of the total amount of capital of the financial leasing company
(3) Floating asset loans provided to a lessee must not exceed 60 percent of the value of the lease contract
(4) The total value of long-term investment must not be higher than 30 percent of the total amount of capital

ownership in the leased articles and receives rent as a condition of lease. The lessee acquires the rights of possession, use, and benefit with respect to the leased articles during the term of the lease as contained in the lease contract. Financial Leasing Company Measures, art. 46. "Leasing back business" is defined as a form of lease whereby the lessee sells its articles to the lessor and signs a financing leasing contract with the lessor simultaneously, and then those articles are leased back by the lessor. In a lease-back situation, the lessee and the seller are the same person. Financial Leasing Company Measures, art. 47. "Subleasing business" means a business activity involving multiple financial leasing of the same article or property. In subleasing business, the lessee of the first lease contract is the lessor of the second lease contract at the same time, and is called the sublessor. The sublessor transfers leased articles from other lessors to a third party. The first lessor retains ownership of the leased articles. Financial Leasing Company Measures, art. 48. "Mandate leasing business" is defined as a business activity whereby a lessor accepts funds or leased articles from a principal. Financing leasing business is handled with a lessee appointed by the principal in accordance with the principal's written instructions. The ownership of the leased articles during the term of the lease remains with the principal, and the lessor may only receive processing fees and does not assume the risk of loss. Financial Leasing Company Measures, art. 49.

235. Financial Leasing Company Measures, art. 18.

236. Financial Leasing Company Measures, arts. 23, 24, 25.

(5) The proportion of lease assets (including property under mandate leases and subleases) must not be less than 60 percent of total assets
(6) The residual amount of borrowed call loan funds must not exceed 100 percent of the total amount of capital
(7) The residual amount of foreign assurances must not exceed 200 percent of the total amount of capital[237]

The CBRC retains the discretion to adjust the asset-to-liability ratios set forth above.

3. Automotive Finance Companies

The automotive finance market in China has grown considerably in recent years. In 2002, the automobile loans in China totaled RMB115 billion and as of the end of July 2003, the four major banks in China reported loans on auto sales to be RMB140 billion. In China, only 10 percent of car sales are affected by financing (through Chinese banks set up in 1998) while the percentage globally exceeds 70 percent.[238] In order to better manage the industry growth, the CBRC has adopted regulations for the establishment, administration and supervision, and termination of automobile finance companies.[239]

Automobile finance companies (AFC) are nonbank financial institutions that are regulated by the China Banking Regulatory Commission and are

237. Financial Leasing Company Measures, art. 26. A financial leasing company is required to submit asset and liability statements and profit and loss statements, together with business ratio examination and verification reports and other written reports to the CBRC for the preceding year within one month from the end of each accounting year. Management is legally responsible for the veracity of the reports submitted to the CBRC. Financial Leasing Company Measures, art. 28.

238. T. Zhengyu & C. Ling, *Auto Finance Companies Finally Get the Green Light in China,* CHINA L. & PRAC. (Nov. 2003). In December 2003, the CBRC approved auto-financing ventures for General Motors Corp., Toyota Motor Corp., and Volkswagon AG, which were the first to be approved under the new rules. The GM company is a JV between General Motors Acceptance Corporation, an automotive financial services provider, and the Shanghai Automotive Group Finance Co., a subsidiary of Shanghai Automotive Industry Corp. (Group). Although approved for business, the three FIE auto finance companies are required to submit reports on their equity capital, management structure, company development plans, and other necessary materials during a six-month preparatory stage. Upon approval of all materials during the preparatory stage, the companies may thereafter be granted operator's license. The Chinese automotive industry is likely to follow the FIEs in setting up domestic auto finance companies. *See* J. Lee, *GM, Volkswagen, Toyota Plan China Finance Arms,* WALL ST. J. (Dec. 30, 2003), available online at http://www.awsj.com; *AFC Rules Cheer Auto Financing Market,* BUSINESS WEEKLY (Oct. 14, 2003), available online at http://www.chinadaily.com.cn.

239. Administration of Auto Finance Companies Procedures (promulgated by the People's Bank of China on and effective as October 3, 2003); Administration of Auto Finance Companies Procedures Implementing Rules (promulgated on November 12, 2003, by the China Banking Regulatory Commission) (implementing regulations that outline the application procedures for establishing an auto finance company). *See generally China's WTO Compliance and Foreign Investment in the Auto Industry,* CHINA L. & PRAC. (Feb. 2003); W. Yi, *China's Post-WTO Compliance and the Pending Auto Financing Regulatory Measures,* CHINA L. & PRAC. (Nov. 2002); T. Zhengyu, *CBRC Unveils Implementing Rules for Auto Finance Companies,* CHINA L. & PRAC. (Dec. 2003). In early 2004, the PBOC and the CBRC issued draft rules for comment in regard to the management and supervision of auto finance industry. The draft

approved to provide auto finance loans to buyers and dealers in China. An AFC must have total assets of no less than RMB4 billion and annual turnover of RMB300 million.[240] The AFC investor must also be continuously profitable for a period of three years prior to the application, and the largest investor must contribute no less than 30 percent of the total capital contribution. The regulations provide that the minimum registered capital for an AFC is RMB500 million ($60,000,000) and may be subject to adjustments by the CBRC.[241] Given the high financial and registered capital requirements, the AFC rules will likely limit the business to the larger and financially strong automotive companies.

There are a number of obstacles for auto finance companies including the lack of effective judicial remedies to allow financing companies to recover or repossess vehicles from borrowers who refuse or fail to make timely payments under automobile finance contracts.

E. Trusts, Trust Property, and Trust Administration

The use of trusts and trust instruments is a relatively new concept in China. To support the development of the use of trusts and to standardize industry practices, the PRC has adopted a law governing the creation and management of trusts.[242] The Law applies to all individual, business, and public interest trust activities conducted within the territorial limits of China. The PBOC has adopted a set of rules regulating the business activities and administration of trust and investment institutions.[243]

The term "trust" is defined as a settlor entrusting property to a trustee based on confidence in that trustee, who carries out administration or disposition of such property in his/her own name in accordance with the wishes

Management Rules on Auto Loans would apply to all banks and non-bank financial institutions involved with auto financing and would outline the standards for the issuance of loans, issues concerning collateral, and guidelines for credit evaluation. *See* http://www.cbrc.gov.cn/yaowen/detail.asp?id=266.

240. AFC Regulations, art. 5.

241. AFC Regulations, art. 7.

242. Trust Law of the People's Republic of China (Adopted April 28, 2001, at the 21st Meeting of the Standing Committee of the 9th National People's Congress, Issued by Presidential Decree (No. 50) of the People's Republic of China on April 28, 2001), *reprinted in* CHINA LAWS FOR FOREIGN BUSINESS (CCH), Business Regulation ¶ 19-660 (hereinafter the "Trust Law"). The Trust Law is the first law of its kind in China. However, the Contract Law, adopted in 1999, includes articles governing the activities of entrustment contracts. *See generally The PRC's First Trust Law: Trusts Without Chinese Characteristics?*, CHINA L. & PRAC. (June 2001).

243. Measures on Administration of Trust and Investment Institutions (Promulgated January 12, 2001, by the People's Bank of China), *reprinted in* CHINA LAWS FOR FOREIGN BUSINESS (CCH), Business Regulation ¶ 8-714 (hereinafter the "Trust Institution Measures"). *See generally* D. Wang, *Plenty of Room to Grow: A Look at China's Trust Industry*, CHINA L. & PRAC. (Feb. 2003); J. Zhu, *Holding Funds in Trust in China*, CHINA L. & PRAC. (Feb. 2003).

of the settlor for the benefit of the beneficiaries or for a specific purpose.[244] When carrying out trust activities the trust parties must abide by the law and administrative regulations, and observe the principles of consent, fairness, honesty and good faith, and trust activities may not harm the interests of the State or the public interests of society.[245]

The establishment of a trust must be for a legal purpose, and to establish a trust there must be specific assets and these assets must be the lawful property of the settlor. Assets as referred to in the Trust Law include legally recognized property rights.[246] Under the Trust Law, a trust may only be created by a written trust instrument and may be in the form of a trust contract, will, codicil, or other written documentation as stipulated by provisions of the law and administrative regulations. Trusts in the form of a trust contract are established when the trust contract is signed. Other forms of written trusts are established when the trustee accepts the trust.[247] A trust instrument is required to include the following language:

(1) The purpose of the trust
(2) The name and the place of residence of the settlor and trustee
(3) The beneficiary or the range of beneficiaries
(4) The scope of the trust property, its type and condition
(5) The form and method by which the beneficiary is to receive the benefits of the trust[248]

A trust institution is required to submit for approval its standard trust instruments and contracts.[249] A trust institution is also required to provide the settlor with a risk statement outlining that losses will be paid from trust property so long as the trust corpus is managed as agreed in the trust instrument.[250]

---

244. Trust Law, art. 2.
245. Trust Law, art. 5.
246. Trust Law, arts. 6–7.
247. Trust Law, art. 8.
248. Trust Law, art. 9. In addition to the required language set forth in Article 9, a trust instrument may also include language concerning the term of the trust, the method of administering the trust property, the trustee's compensation, the method for designating a new trustee, and termination provisions. *See also* Article 7 of the Interim Measures on the Administration of Trust Money of Trust and Investment Companies (promulgated on June 26, 2002, by the PBOC), a translation is available on the Isinolaw Web site at http://www.isinolaw.com (outlining the mandatory provisions for trust instruments) (hereinafter the "Trust Funds Management Provisions").
249. Trust Institution Measures, art. 24.
250. Trust Funds Management Provisions, arts 8, 9. A trust instrument is required to contain the following language: "In managing trust property, the trustee must be devoted to his duties, and fulfill the obligation of management with honesty, good faith, prudence, and efficiency. The risk caused, when the trust money is managed strictly according to this trust contract, shall be paid by trust property, i.e. the money consigned by the trustor and the asset created after the trustee's use of such money. The risk caused, when the money is managed not in accordance with this trust deed but in the trustee's improper way, shall be compensated by the trustee." Trust Funds Management Provisions, art. 9.

If the law requires that registration procedures be carried out for trust property, the trust will have no legal effect until the registration is completed.[251] A trust is also deemed to be invalid in the following situations:

(1) The purpose of the trust violates the law or administrative regulations, or harms the common social interest
(2) The trust property cannot be determined
(3) The settlor sets up a trust using illegal assets or assets for which under the present Law a trust must not be set up
(4) The trust has been specifically set up for the purpose of litigation or to demand the repayment of a debt
(5) The beneficiary or the range of beneficiaries cannot be determined
(6) Other situations as stipulated by provisions of the law and administrative regulations[252]

The establishment of a testamentary trust is required to be consistent with the provisions relating to wills in the Inheritance Law of the People's Republic of China.[253] If an individual specified in a will refuses or is unable to act as a trustee, the beneficiary may appoint a substitute trustee. In the event that the beneficiary does not have the capacity for civil acts or has only limited capacity for civil acts, his or her legal guardian may designate a substitute trustee. If a testamentary instrument sets forth procedures for appointing a substitute trustee, said provisions will be controlling.[254]

1. Trust Property

Trust property includes all property accepted by the trust, as well as all proceeds or assets received as a result of the sale, disposition, or operation of trust property.[255] Prior to establishing a trust, the trust assets must be segregated from other assets. In the event that a settlor dies or if the trust is legally dissolved, revoked, or declared insolvent and the settlor is the only beneficiary, the trust shall terminate and the trust property shall be considered as part of the settlor's estate or as assets for liquidation. In the event that the settlor is not the only beneficiary, the trust shall continue to exist and the

251. Trust Law, art. 10. A creditor has a right to challenge the creation of a trust that harms the interests of the creditor. A creditor must seek relief in the people's court within one year from the date that it knows or should have known the grounds for seeking revocation of a trust. Trust Law, art. 12.
252. Trust Law, art. 11.
253. Inheritance Law of the People's Republic of China (promulgated on April 10, 1985, by the State Council), *reprinted in* 3 China Law Reference Service ¶ 3320.
254. Trust Law, art. 13.
255. Trust Law, art. 14. Assets that are prohibited from circulation may not be part of the trust corpus. Assets whose circulation is restricted by law and administrative regulations may only form a part of the trust corpus upon government approval.

trust assets shall not be considered as part of the settlor's estate or as assets for liquidation. However, joint trust beneficiary rights of the settlor with other beneficiaries where the settlor dies or is legally dissolved, revoked, or declared insolvent shall be considered as the settlor's estate or as assets for liquidation.[256]

The assets of the trustee and the trust assets are required to be segregated and may not be commingled. In the event that the trustee dies or is legally dissolved, revoked, or declared insolvent, the trust property will not become a part of the trustee's estate or assets for liquidation.[257]

Trust assets are not subject to enforcement measures, except in the following situations:

(1) Prior to the establishment of a trust a creditor already has the rights of a priority creditor in relation to the trust property and has exercised these rights in accordance with the law
(2) In administering trust affairs trustees have run up debts and creditors have demanded the discharging of these debts
(3) Tax that shall be borne by the trust estate itself needs to be paid
(4) Other situations stipulated by the law

In the event that enforcement measures are taken against trust property, the settlor, the trustees, or the beneficiaries have a statutory right of action to seek relief before the people's court.[258]

2. Parties to a Trust

A settlor may be an individual or legal entity that has the legal civil capacity. A settlor has the right to be fully advised of trust activities by the trustee, and has express rights of action against a trust that fails to perform its obligations or breaches its fiduciary duties. A settlor must take action, including the filing of a complaint with the people's court, within one year from the date that it knew or should have known of the offending actions by the trustee.[259]

A trustee may be an individual or legal entity that has full civil capacity, and is required to comply with the terms and conditions of the trust instrument or contract to the benefit of the trust beneficiaries.[260] The Trust Law provides that in administering the trust property, the trustee is required to fulfill its duties and

256. Trust Law, art. 15.
257. Trust Law, art. 16.
258. Trust Law, art. 17.
259. Trust Law, arts. 19–23; Trust Institution Measures, arts. 32–38.
260. Trust Law, art. 24. A trust instrument may provide that a trust be managed by joint trustees. Joint trustees assume joint and several liability to the trust. Any communications to one trustee is valid for all joint trustees. Trust Law, art. 31, 32.

carry out its obligation to administer the trust property honestly, in good faith, and with prudence and efficiency.[261] A trustee has a statutory duty prohibiting the use of trust property for the trustee's own personal gain or interests, and in the event of any self-dealing the benefits thereof become trust property and any losses are the responsibility of the trustee.[262] A trustee is required to separate the trust assets from the assets of a third party or assets of the trustee.[263] A trustee is entitled to compensation for its services pursuant to the terms and conditions of the trust instrument or other agreement of the parties.[264]

A trustee may resign at any time after a trust is formed, but will continue with his or her duties until a substitute trustee is appointed.[265] A trustee's position may be terminated in the following situations:

(1) Death
(2) Legal proclamation of lack of capacity for civil acts or restricted capacity for civil acts
(3) Revocation in accordance with law or declaration of insolvency
(4) Legal dissolution or forfeiture of official capacity
(5) Resignation or dismissal
(6) Other situations as stipulated by law and administrative regulations[266]

When a trustee's duties are terminated, the successor trustee or the estate administrator, guardian, or liquidator shall administer the trust property and manage trust affairs.

The Trust Law provides that the beneficiary of a trust is the person or entity that is to receive the benefits of the trust. A settlor may be a beneficiary of a trust and may be the sole beneficiary of the trust. A trustee may be a beneficiary but is not allowed to be the sole beneficiary of the same trust.[267]

---

261. Trust Law, arts. 24, 25. A trustee is required to manage trust affairs personally unless the trust instrument provides otherwise. If the trustee delegates the duty to manage the trust assets to another party, the trustee remains liable for trust affairs. Trust Law, art. 30. A trustee is required to prepare reports on trust affairs for the settlor and beneficiaries. Trust Law, 33.

262. Trust Law, arts. 26, 27. Trustees may engage in transactions between trust property and their own property if allowed in the trust instrument, and if the subject transaction is carried out in an arms-length manner and for a fair market price. Trust Law, art. 28.

263. Trust Law, art. 29; Trust Institution Measures, art. 36.

264. Trust Law, art. 35; Trust Institution Measures, art. 38. A trustee cannot claim compensation if it violates the terms of the trust instrument and causes losses to the trust or improperly disposes of trust property. Trust Law, art. 36; Trust Institution Measures, art. 39. Expenses of the trust are paid from trust property except in situations where the trustee violates the law or the trust instrument, and in that situation the trustee is liable for said expenses. Trust Law, art. 37; Trust Institution Measures, art. 40.

265. Trust Law, art. 38. A trustee for a charitable trust may not resign without approval. Trust Law, art. 66.

266. Trust Law, art. 39. A trustee terminated under Article 39, items (3) through (6), is required to prepare a report on the trust affairs. Trust Law, art. 41. If the position of one joint trustee is terminated, the other joint trustee carries out the duties of the trust management. Trust Law, art. 42.

267. Trust Law, art. 43.

Beneficiaries have the right to receive benefits from the trust from the date the trust is created.[268] Joint beneficiaries may receive benefits from a trust in accordance with the terms and conditions of the trust instrument, or in equal proportions if the trust instrument is silent.[269] Beneficiaries may give up their right to receive trust benefits. If all of the beneficiaries of a trust give up their right to receive trust benefits, the trust will be terminated automatically. In situations where some but not all the beneficiaries give up their rights to a trust, the trust benefits and property will be apportioned consistent with the trust instrument.[270] A beneficiary to a trust may use trust proceeds to pay off debts or transfer rights under a trust, except where the trust instrument contains restrictive covenants.[271] Any dispute between beneficiaries may be heard before the people's court.[272]

3. Changes to and Termination of a Trust

If a settlor is the sole beneficiary under a trust, the settlor or his successor may terminate the trust, unless otherwise provided in the trust instrument.[273] After the establishment of a trust, the settlor may change the beneficiary or dispose of the beneficiary's right to benefit from the trust in the following situations:

(1) A beneficiary commits a major tortious act against the settlor
(2) A beneficiary commits a major tortious act against other joint beneficiaries
(3) Agreement has been given by a beneficiary
(4) Other situations stipulated by the trust document occur[274]

In the circumstances stipulated in items (1), (3), and (4) above, the settlor has the right to dissolve the trust.

A trust shall not terminate due to the death, loss of the capacity for civil acts, legal dissolution, revocation in accordance with the law, or bankruptcy of the settlor or trustee, except in situations provided by law or the trust instrument.[275] A trust shall terminate in the following circumstances:

(1) A termination event stipulated in the trust instrument occurs
(2) The continued existence of the trust violates the objectives of the trust

268. Trust Law, art. 44.
269. Trust Law, art. 45.
270. Trust Law, art. 46.
271. Trust Law, arts. 47, 48.
272. Trust Law, art. 49.
273. Trust Law, art. 50.
274. Trust Law, art. 51.
275. Trust Law, art. 52.

(3) The intent of the trust has already been realized or cannot be realized
(4) Parties to the trust consult and reach agreement for termination of the trust
(5) The trust is revoked or nullified
(6) The trust is dissolved or terminated[276]

When a trust terminates, the trust property shall vest in the persons stipulated by the trust instrument. In the event the trust instrument is silent on the disposition of trust property upon termination, ownership of the trust property is to be determined according to the following order: (1) beneficiaries or their heirs; (2) settlors or their heirs.[277]

4. Charitable Trusts

The Trust Law outlines the standards for the establishment and management of charitable trusts.[278] Trusts that are established for one of the following public interest purposes are considered "charitable trusts":

(1) Poverty relief
(2) Relief of disaster victims
(3) Support for the disabled
(4) The development of education, science and technology, culture, the arts, and sport
(5) The development of medical and health services
(6) The development of environmental protection and the preservation of the ecological environment
(7) The development of other public interests[279]

The Trust Law provides that the establishment of charitable trusts and the determination of trustees for such shall be approved by the relevant charitable public welfare administrative body. Trusts that have not received approval from the public welfare administrative body are not allowed to engage in activities in the name of a charitable trust.[280] Public welfare administrative organizations are required to supervise and audit the activities of

276. Trust Law, art. 53.

277. Trust Law, art. 54. Provisions dealing with trust termination and liquidation are set forth in articles 55–58 of the Trust Law.

278. Trust Law, arts. 59–72. The establishment of charitable trusts is encouraged by the PRC government. Trust Law, art. 61. The law requires that public welfare organizations support the establishment of charitable trusts. Trust Law, art. 62.

279. Trust Law, art. 60.

280. Trust Law, art. 62. If a public welfare administrative organization violates the law, the trustees, the settlor, or the beneficiaries of the charitable trust have standing to bring a claim before the people's court. Trust Law, art. 73.

charitable trusts. Trustees must report the affairs of the trust and trust property on an annual basis to the relevant public welfare administrative organization.[281] If a trustee of a charitable trust violates his/her fiduciary obligations or fails to perform his/her obligations to the trust, the public welfare administrative organization may replace the trustee.[282] The law provides that trust property and income of charitable trusts must not be used for non-public welfare purposes.[283] Termination or liquidation of a charitable trust must be made with the approval and oversight of the public welfare administrative organization charged with supervision of the trust.[284]

5. Trust and Investment Institutions

The PBOC has adopted a set of rules regulating the business activities and administration of trust and investment companies.[285] The Trust Institution Measures provide that "trust and investment companies" are financial institutions established in accordance with the *Company Law of the People's Republic of China* and the Trust Institution Measures, and which engage mainly in the operation of trust business.[286] The term "trust" used in the Trust Institution Measures refers to the activities in which a commissioning party has entrusted property to the trustee, and the trustee will, in accordance with the will of the commissioning party, manage and dispose of the property for the benefit of the beneficiary of the trust or for a specific

281. Trust Law, art. 67. Trustees shall prepare a report on their handling of trust affairs and the state of trust assets at least once a year. After ratification of the report by the trust supervisor the report shall be submitted to the public welfare administrative body to be verified and approved and shall be announced by the trustee.

282. Trust Law, art. 68. Trustees are not allowed to resign without the approval of the public welfare administrative organization supervising the charitable trust. Trust Law, art. 66.

283. Trust Law, art. 63.

284. Trust Law, arts. 70–72. If a charitable trust is terminated and if there are no owners of rights of the trust property, after approval from the public welfare administration body the trustees shall use the trust property for purposes that are similar to the original charitable trust intent or transfer the property to public welfare organizations or charitable trusts that have aims similar to those of the original trust intent. Trust Law, art. 72.

285. Measures on Administration of Trust and Investment Institutions (Promulgated January 12, 2001, by the People's Bank of China), *reprinted in* CHINA LAWS FOR FOREIGN BUSINESS (CCH), Business Regulation ¶ 8-714 (hereinafter the "Trust Institution Measures"). The CBRC is the regulatory authority responsible for supervision of trust institutions. Trust Institutions Measures, art. 10. *See also* Trust Law of the People's Republic of China (adopted April 28, 2001, at the 21st Meeting of the Standing Committee of the 9th National People's Congress, issued by Presidential Decree (No. 50) of the People's Republic of China on April 28, 2001), *reprinted in* CHINA LAWS FOR FOREIGN BUSINESS (CCH), Business Regulation ¶ 19-660 (hereinafter the "Trust Law"). *See also* Interim Measures on the Administration of Trust Money of Trust and Investment Companies (promulgated on June 26, 2002, by the PBOC), available on the Web site of Isinolaw at http://www.isinolaw.com (outlines the standards for management of trust funds). *See generally Trust Investment Companies—A Vehicle for a Corporate Restructuring in China,* CHINA L. & PRAC. (Mar. 2001); D. Wang, *Plenty of Room to Grow: A Look at China's Business Trust Industry,* CHINA L. & PRAC. (Feb. 2003).

286. Trust Institution Measures, art. 2.

purpose as set forth in a trust instrument.[287] The Trust Institution Measures provide that a "commissioning party" refers to a natural person, a legal person, or any other type of organization established in accordance with the law, that has full capacity for civil action. A "beneficiary" refers to a natural person, a legal person, or any other type of organization established in accordance with the law, that is entitled to the benefits of a trust. A commissioning party and a beneficiary may or may not be the same person.[288]

The Trust Institution Measures define the term "trust business" as the business activities of a trust and investment company that, for compensation, acts as a trustee and handles trust affairs. The term "trust property" used in the Trust Institution Measures refers to the property acquired by a trust and investment company in the course of acceptance of trust. Property acquired by a trust and investment company from the management or disposition of trust property or from other activities is also considered the property of the trust. Property prohibited from circulation by laws and regulations shall not be used as trust property. Property restricted from circulation by laws and regulations may be used as trust property upon approval by the relevant competent department in accordance with the law.[289]

The Trust Institution Measures prohibit a trust and investment company from owning, benefiting from, or encumbering trust property. In the event of liquidation, trust property is not considered an asset of the trust and investment company, and the trust will not terminate as a result of the dissolution, bankruptcy, or liquidation of the trust institution.[290] A trust institution is required to comply with the principles of honesty, trustworthiness, prudence, and efficiency, and its activities may not violate public interests. A trust and investment company shall not engage in deposit business or issue bonds or undertake overseas borrowing.[291]

A trust and investment company shall be established as a limited liability company or company limited by shares. A trust institution shall apply for approval of the CBRC in order to obtain a "Trust Institution Legal Person License."[292] The CBRC has the discretion to approve or reject applications

287. Trust Institution Measures, art. 3.
288. Trust Institution Measures, art. 3.
289. Trust Institution Measures, art. 4.
290. Trust Institution Measures, arts. 5–6.
291. Trust Institution Measures, arts. 7–9.
292. Trust Institution Measures, arts. 10–11, 19. A trust and investment company shall apply for approval from the CBRC in any of the following situations: (1) change of name; (2) change of registered capital; (3) change of the location of the company; (4) change of organizational structure; (5) adjustment of business scope; (6) change of senior management personnel; (7) change of key shareholders or adjustment of the structure of share ownership; (8) revision of articles of association; (9) merger or division; or (10) other changes as prescribed by the CBRC. Trust Law, arts. 15–20.

in light of the needs of economic development and situations of the industry. The Trust Institution Measures provide that a trust and investment company meet the following conditions:

(1) Have articles of association that conform to the *Company Law of the People's Republic of China* and provisions of the People's Bank of China
(2) Have shareholders with qualifications for holding shares as prescribed by the People's Republic of China
(3) Have registered capital that meets the minimum requirement set by the Trust Institution Measures
(4) Have senior management personnel who possess qualifications required for their positions by the People's Republic of China, and have appropriate professional personnel for the trust business
(5) Have a sound organizational structure, rules for trust business operations, and a system for risk control
(6) Have business premises, safety measures, and other facilities related to the business, which meet the requirements
(7) Have met other conditions stipulated by the People's Bank of China and CBRC[293]

The Trust Institution Measures provide that the registered capital of a trust and investment company shall not be less than RMB300 million.[294] For trust institutions that engage in foreign exchange business, the registered capital shall include an amount of foreign exchange equivalent to the value of not less than $15 million.[295] The PBOC retains the right to increase the minimum registered capital "in light of the needs for the development of trust and investment companies."[296]

With the approval of the CBRC, a trust and investment company may engage in all or part of the following business:

(1) Operating trust funds upon entrustment; that is, the commissioning party commissions funds, which he/she is unable to manage or is restricted from managing by relevant regulations of the State, to

293. Trust Institution Measures, art. 13.

294. Trust Institution Measures, art. 14. A trust and investment company shall comply with the following provisions when accepting trust funds for which it is authorized to decide the forms of management: (1) the total balance of the trust funds shall not exceed ten times of its registered capital; (2) the term of the trust shall not be less than one year; and (3) a single trust fund shall not be less than RMB50,000. Trust Law, art. 46.

295. With FOREX management issues, a trust and investment company is required to follow SAFE laws and regulations. Trust Institution Measures, art. 48.

296. Trust Institution Measures, art. 14.

a trust and investment company for management, operation, and disposal of in accordance with conditions and purposes as agreed upon

(2) Managing personal property, real property, and other property upon entrustment; that is, the commissioning party entrusts his/her own property or property rights, such as personal property, real estate, copyrights, or intellectual property, to a trust and investment company for management, operation, and disposal of in accordance with conditions and purposes as agreed upon
(3) Operating, upon entrustment, investment fund business that is permitted under relevant regulations of the State, and acting as the promoter of the fund management company to engage in investment fund management
(4) Providing intermediary services such as enterprise asset restructure, purchase or merger, project financing, company financial management, or financial consultancy
(5) Consigning, upon entrustment, treasury bonds and enterprise bonds approved by relevant departments of the State Council
(6) Managing, operating, and disposing of property as agents
(7) Acting as custodians
(8) Certifying and investigating creditworthiness and providing economic consultancy
(9) Providing guarantees with self-owned property for others
(10) Other business approved by the People's Bank of China or CBRC[297]

A trust institution is required to adopt and submit for approval its standard trust instruments and contracts.[298] A written document for the acceptance of a trust by a trust and investment company shall state clearly the following matters unless laws and regulations provide otherwise:

(1) Names and addresses of the commissioning party, trustee, and beneficiary

297. Trust Institution Measures, art. 21. The business scope of a trust institution is required to be defined in the articles of association of the entity, and as approved by the CBRC. Trust Institution Measures, art. 27. The business scope of a trust institution also may include FOREX business. With CBRC approval, a trust and investment company may be established to engage in the following public welfare activities: (1) poverty relief; (2) assistance for the disabled; (3) development of education, science, technology, sports, culture, and arts; (4) development of medical care and health system, and environmental protection; or (5) development of other public interest or charitable activities that are beneficial to the society. Trust Institution Measures, art. 22. For the standards for charitable trusts, *see* articles 59–73 of the Trust Law. A trust and investment company may engage in leasing, sale, loan, investment and interbank loans. Trust Institution Measures, arts. 23–26.

298. Trust Institution Measures, arts. 24, 28.

(2) Purpose of the trust
(3) Scope, type, and conditions of the trust property
(4) Rights and obligations of the parties to the trust
(5) Requirements for risk disclosure and risk bearing in the management of trust property
(6) Forms of management of trust property and means for distribution of trust interests
(7) Compensation for the trust and investment company
(8) Tax and fee payment for the trust property and calculation of relevant management fees
(9) Term of the trust and termination of the trust
(10) Ownership of the trust property upon termination of the trust
(11) Liabilities of the parties to the trust for breach of contract and the methods of dispute arbitration
(12) Other matters that the commissioning party and the trustee consider necessary to be specified[299]

A trust and investment company has a statutory obligation to maximize the beneficiaries' interests and manage the trust property prudently and effectively.[300] A trust and investment company is required to abide by the statutory duties in the Trust Law, and is required to maintain confidentiality with respect to trust business and trust property.[301] A trust and investment company is required to set aside five percent of its after-tax profit as a compensation reserve fund on an annual basis, to a limit of twenty percent of the company's registered capital. The compensation reserve fund of a trust and investment company may only be deposited in a State-owned commercial bank or be used for purchasing treasury bonds.[302]

A trust and investment company is required to establish internal controls, adopt internal accounting and audit procedures in accordance with the law.[303] The CBRC has the authority to audit and inspect the records of a trust and investment company, and has the right to question senior management concerning trust activities.[304] A trust and investment company and its personnel are liable for statutory penalties in the event of a violation of the law.[305]

299. Trust Institution Measures, art. 29.
300. Trust Institution Measures, art. 30. *See also* Trust Law, arts. 24, 25.
301. Trust Institution Measures, arts. 32–37.
302. Trust Institution Measures, art. 51.
303. Trust Institution Measures, arts. 52–55.
304. Trust Institution Measures, arts. 56–61.
305. Trust Institution Measures, arts. 72–76.

F. Accounting, Auditing, and Joint Annual Review Procedures

The NPC and various government agencies responsible for fiscal matters, including the Ministry of Finance and the National Audit Office (NAO), have promulgated accounting standards[306] and auditing procedures for FIEs.[307]

1. Accounting System for Enterprises

Under previous rules, the Ministry of Finance developed an *Accounting System for Foreign-Invested Enterprises,* which was specifically applicable to foreign-invested enterprises, including joint ventures and wholly foreign-owned enterprises, established within the People's Republic of China.[308] In

306. Accounting Law of the People's Republic of China (adopted on January 21, 1985, by the 9th Sess. of the Standing Comm. of the 6th NPC and amended on December 29, 1993, by the 5th Sess. of the Standing Comm. of the 8th NPC, and amended and revised on October 31, 1999, at the 12th Meeting of the Standing Comm. of the 9th NPC), *reprinted in* CHINA LAWS FOR FOREIGN BUSINESS (CCH), Taxation ¶ 35-510; Regulations on Issues Concerning Implementation of "Accounting System for Business Enterprises" by Foreign Investment Enterprises (promulgated on November 29, 2001, by the Ministry of Finance), *reprinted in* CHINA LAWS FOR FOREIGN BUSINESS (CCH) Taxation ¶ 35-502 (these regulations repealed the "Accounting System of the People's Republic of China for Foreign Investment Enterprises" promulgated on June 24, 1992, by the Ministry of Finance), *reprinted in* CHINA LAWS FOR FOREIGN BUSINESS (CCH), Taxation ¶ 35-501 (hereinafter the "Regulations Concerning the Accounting System for Foreign-Invested Enterprises"). *See also* Classification of Accounts and Accounting Statements for Foreign Investment Industrial Enterprises (issued on May 25, 1992, by the MOF), *reprinted in* CHINA LAWS FOR FOREIGN BUSINESS (CCH), Taxation ¶ 35-540 (outlines standards for accounting classification system); Regulations of the People's Republic of China on Financial Administration of Foreign Investment Enterprises (issued on June 24, 1992, by the MOF), *reprinted in* CHINA LAWS FOR FOREIGN BUSINESS (CCH), Taxation ¶ 35-550 (outlines the financial management standards for FIEs). The MOF has developed accounting standards for shareholder enterprises. *See* Accounting System for Experimental Shareholding Enterprises (promulgated on May 23, 1992, by the MOF and the State Commission for Restructuring the Economic System), *reprinted in* CHINA LAWS FOR FOREIGN BUSINESS (CCH), Taxation ¶ 35-505. *See generally* Y.W. TANG, B. COOPER & L. CHOW, ACCOUNTING STANDARDS AND FINANCE IN CHINA (1996).

307. Auditing Law of the People's Republic of China (promulgated on August 31, 1994, by the 9th Sess. of the Standing Comm. of the 8th NPC), *reprinted in* CHINA LAWS FOR FOREIGN BUSINESS (CCH), Taxation ¶ 35-805 (hereinafter the "Auditing Law"); Detailed Rules for the Implementation of the Auditing Law of the People's Republic of China (promulgated on October 21, 1997, by the State Council), *reprinted in* CHINA LAWS FOR FOREIGN BUSINESS (CCH), Taxation ¶35-850. *See also* Auditing Procedures for Chinese-Foreign Equity and Contractual Joint Ventures (promulgated January 12, 1993, by the State Auditing Bureau), *reprinted in* CHINA LAWS FOR FOREIGN BUSINESS (CCH), Taxation ¶ 35-810 (hereinafter the "FIE Auditing Procedures"). *See generally* H. GENSLER, AUDITING STANDARDS OF THE PEOPLE'S REPUBLIC OF CHINA (1996); Chong, *Chinese Auditing Systems,* 76 MANAGEMENT ACCOUNTING 66 (July/Aug. 1998), available on Nexis, News Library.

308. Accounting System of the People's Republic of China for Foreign Investment Enterprises (promulgated on June 24, 1992, by the Ministry of Finance, and repealed in 2001). The special accounting system for FIEs was repealed in November 2001. *See* Regulations on Issues Concerning Implementation of "Accounting System for Business Enterprises" by Foreign Investment Enterprises (promulgated on November 29, 2001, by the Ministry of Finance), *reprinted in* CHINA LAWS FOR FOREIGN BUSINESS (CCH), Taxation ¶ 35-502 (requiring that all FIEs follow the Accounting System for Business Enterprises adopted in December 2000 and outlining specific rules for implementing the Accounting System to FIEs and retroactive application); Answers to Questions Relevant to the Implementation of the Enterprise Accounting System by Foreign Investment Enterprises (issued on May 26, 2002, by the Ministry of Finance) (clarifies several issues with respect to the adoption of the Accounting System for Enterprises by FIEs). *See* Accounting System for Business Enterprises (promulgated on December 29, 2000, by the Ministry of Finance and effective January 1, 2001). The MOF and the Chinese Institute of Certified Public

2000, the MOF adopted a new Accounting System for Enterprises and in 2001 required that FIEs comply with the unified standards. The Ministry of Finance is the regulatory agency responsible for administering a uniform national accounting system for all enterprises including foreign-invested enterprises. The *Accounting System for Enterprises* is required to follow a number of general principles, including the following:

(1) The system should be divided into accounting periods (i.e., monthly, quarterly, and annually)
(2) The fiscal year of the system must be based on the calendar year
(3) The accounting system should be based on actual transactions that have been accurately and completely recorded
(4) The accounting system should adopt the accrual method of accounting
(5) Income and expenses of an enterprise must balance
(6) Assets of an enterprise shall be stated at their original cost
(7) The accounting system must clearly distinguish between capital expenditure and revenue expenditure
(8) Accounting methods adopted by an enterprise shall be consistent from one period to another and shall not be arbitrarily changed[309]

The accounting system of an enterprise shall adopt a debit and credit double-entry bookkeeping procedure.[310] An enterprise may adopt renminbi or a foreign currency as its bookkeeping base currency.[311] However, once a currency is chosen, an enterprise may not change the type of currency without approval from the MOF or its subordinate departments. An enterprise that engages in business operations using various currencies may establish separate records for the various currencies. If the enterprise chooses a foreign currency, it must use a currency that has an exchange rate quoted by the State Administration of Foreign Exchange.[312] The accounting system of an enterprise shall be maintained in Chinese or, at the same time, in both

Accountants have adopted a number of explanatory circulars and notices on various accounting standards questions. The China Securities Regulatory Commission has also issued a number of circulars and notices concerning accounting practices for publicly traded companies. *See* Notice on Questions and Answers for Criteria on the Information Disclosure of Publicly Traded Companies, CSRC Notice No. 6 (issued on December 21, 2001, by the China Securities Regulatory Commission). The MOF has adopted accounting standards specifically for financial institutions. *See* Financial Enterprise Accounting System (promulgated on November 27, 2001, by the MOF and effective on January 1, 2002).

309. Accounting System for Enterprises, arts. 7, 11.

310. Accounting System for Enterprises, art. 9.

311. Accounting System for Enterprises, art. 8.

312. Accounting System for Enterprises, art. 8. An enterprise that uses a foreign currency as its base currency is required to convert its accounting reports, which are submitted to the tax authorities and financial departments, to renminbi.

Chinese and another language.[313] An enterprise's accounting system is required to consist of three principal types of accounting books, which include journals, general classification ledgers and subsidiary ledgers, and supplementary books if applicable. An enterprise is required to maintain its books using a system of prompt registration, complete documentary substantiation to support each entry, and the use of accurate figures and clear description on the basis of original documents and vouchers.[314] For joint venture operations where the JV partners pay separate tax, the parties are required to maintain joint ledgers that reflect the joint assets and liabilities of each joint venture partner.[315] An enterprise that keeps its accounts on computer is required to ensure that the software system employed satisfies the accounting system requirements in the regulations.

The accounting system of an enterprise is required to include records of the following:

(1) Current assets[316]
(2) Long-term investments[317]
(3) Fixed assets[318]
(4) Construction in progress[319]
(5) Intangible assets[320]
(6) Short and long-term liabilities[321]

313. Accounting System for Enterprises, art. 10. The Regulations provide that an enterprise in an autonomous zone may use the language of local nationalities in preparing financial records.

314. Accounting System for Enterprises, art. 11.

315. Accounting System for Enterprises, arts. 80, 110, 147.

316. Accounting System for Enterprises, arts. 14–20. The accounting system of an enterprise includes journals that itemize cash and bank transactions in chronological order. Current assets include cash, bank deposits, marketable securities, accounts receivable, advance payments and deposits, and inventory. *Id.* art. 14. The different types of current assets must be accounted separately. The inventory of the enterprise must be recorded at actual cost. *Id.* art. 20.

317. Accounting System for Enterprises, arts. 21–24. Long-term investments include the investment of cash, materials, and intangible assets in other enterprises or the purchase of stocks and bonds with a return on investment that is not expected to be realized within one year. *Id.* art. 21. The Regulations outline the accounting standards for long-term investments.

318. Accounting System for Enterprises, arts. 25–42. The Regulations outline the standards for recording fixed assets, depreciation of fixed assets, and the inventory of fixed assets. Fixed assets are required to be separately accounted for and recorded at their original cost. An enterprise is required to adopt the straight-line method for calculating the depreciation of fixed assets or the workload method if appropriate. The Accounting System for Enterprises addresses the methods for devaluation and depreciation of assets. *Id.* at 51–66.

319. Accounting System for Enterprises, arts. 28–33. The Regulations outline the accounting standards for construction in progress of an enterprise and specifically the record keeping for construction materials, purchased equipment to be installed, advance payments and deposits for construction purposes, administrative expenses for construction purposes, and final settlement of completed construction.

320. Accounting System for Enterprises, arts. 43–50. The Regulations outline the standards for recording intangible assets, which include industrial property rights, proprietary technology, licensed rights, land-use rights, and other intangible assets. Intangible assets contributed by a foreign party as part of a joint venture must be accounted for according to the amount in the JV contract.

321. Accounting System for Enterprises, arts. 68–70 (current liabilities), 71–77. The Regulations outline the accounting standards for current liabilities, long-term liabilities, other liabilities, and interest payments on loans.

(7) Investors' equity[322]
(8) Costs and expenses[323]
(9) Income, profit, and profit distribution[324]
(10) Foreign currency transactions[325]
(11) Income taxes[326]
(12) Liquidation transactions[327]

a. Accounting Reports

The accounting reports of an enterprise are required to generally be classified into four broad categories: assets, liabilities, investors' equity, and profit and loss. The accounting reports of an enterprise include the accounting statements, which include the balance sheet, profit and loss statement, and statement of change in financial condition, and a description of the enterprise's financial condition.[328] The Regulations require that an enterprise's quarterly and annual accounting statements must be submitted to the MOF or its subordinate office and the taxation authorities. The quarterly accounting statement must be submitted within 15 days after the end of each quarter. The annual accounting statement must be submitted together with the audit report of a certified public accountant within four months after the end of the calendar year.[329]

322. Accounting System for Enterprises, arts. 79–84. Investors' equity in an FIE includes the paid-up capital, accumulated capital, reserve funds, expansion funds, and undistributed profits. Each of the different types of investors' equity are required to be accounted for separately. The paid-up capital includes the capital actually contributed pursuant to a JV contract and may consist of cash, materials, or intangible assets. Cash investment is recorded based on the amount actually deposited by a party into the bank account of the enterprise. Investments in materials or intangible assets are recorded based on the amount shown in the parties' contract.

323. Accounting System for Enterprises, arts. 99–105. The Regulations outline the accounting standards for the treatment of costs and expenses of an enterprise, including the cost of goods and materials, wages and salaries, operational expenses, administrative expenses, and other expenses.

324. Accounting System for Enterprises, arts. 85–98 (income), 106, 108 (profits), 109–112 (profit distribution). The Regulations address the accounting standards for recording income, profit, profit distribution, reserve funds, welfare funds, and enterprise expansion funds.

325. Accounting System for Enterprises, arts. 15, 77, 80, 117, 119, 120.

326. Accounting System for Enterprises, art. 107.

327. Accounting System for Enterprises, arts. 57, 58. The Regulations outline the accounting standards for liquidation transactions, the valuation of assets during liquidation, and the liquidation expenses. The Regulations provide that accounting statements concerning liquidation are required to be prepared and approved prior to cancellation of an enterprise's business license.

328. Accounting System for Enterprises, arts. 152–157. The content of the financial condition description is required to include the following information: (a) total amount of investment, investment components and investment progress; (b) condition of changes in capital; (c) condition of production and operation; (d) condition of gains and losses and profit distribution; (e) condition of changes in capital and capital turnover; (f) condition of foreign exchange balance; (g) condition of payment of major taxes; (h) condition of overage, shortage, deterioration, spoilage, damage, and asset write-offs; (i) changes in accounting methods; and (j) other issues requiring explanation.

329. Accounting System for Enterprises, art. 157.

b. Financial Reports and Public Disclosure

The Regulations provide that the accounting files of an enterprise, which include the accounting books, accounting reports, capital verification reports, audit reports, the financial accounting system, as well as other important documents related to the operation and management and investors' equity, such as contracts, articles of association, resolutions of the board of directors, and long-term economic contracts, are required to be maintained in China for a minimum of 15 years. The annual accounting statements, including the liquidation accounting statements, are required to be maintained permanently. If an enterprise is subject to liquidation proceedings, the accounting files must be transferred to the regulatory authorities prior to termination of the operation.

The PRC government has adopted regulations governing the preparation of financial and accounting reports for enterprises to ensure the veracity and completeness of such reports.[330] The Regulation on Financial and Accounting Reports of Enterprises outlines various monetary penalties, administrative sanctions, and possible criminal penalties for violations of the law in regard to the preparation of financial and accounting reports.[331]

All enterprises, including FIEs, are subject to the Regulation on Financial and Accounting Reports of Enterprises with regard to the preparation and release of financial and accounting reports. As defined in the Regulations, "financial and accounting reports" refers to documents of an

330. Regulations on Financial and Accounting Reports of Enterprises (promulgated on June 21, 2000, by the State Council and effective from January 1, 2001), *reprinted in* China Laws for Foreign Business (CCH), Taxation ¶ 35-525 (hereinafter the "Regulations on Financial and Accounting Reports of Enterprises"). If an enterprise is required to prepare multiple financial and accounting reports to different parties, it is required to be consistent with its information and methods in preparing the subject reports. Regulation on Financial and Accounting Reports of Enterprises, art. 36.

331. Regulation on Financial and Accounting Reports of Enterprises, arts. 39–43. A monetary fine of RMB5,000 to RMB100,000 may be imposed on an enterprise, and a fine of RMB3,000 to RMB50,000 may be imposed on a responsible individual for intentionally falsifying reports. In severe situations, criminal liability may be imposed for falsifying reports. Regulation on Financial and Accounting Reports of Enterprises, art. 40. A fine of RMB3,000 to RMB50,000 may be imposed on an enterprise, and a fine of RMB2,000 to RMB20,000 may be imposed on a responsible individual for engaging in the following activities: (1) arbitrarily changing the standards for confirmation and calculation of essential accounting factors; (2) arbitrarily changing the foundation, basis, principles, and method behind the formulation of financial and accounting reports; (3) performing account settlement before or after the account settlement day; (4) not verifying assets and liabilities completely in accordance with the provisions of the Regulations before drawing up an annual financial and accounting report; and (5) refusing to allow supervision and examination, in accordance with law, of a financial and accounting report by the finance department or other relevant department, or providing details of relevant circumstances that misstate the facts. Accounting personnel who engage in unlawful activity may also lose their qualifications and certification to engage in accounting work. Regulation on Financial and Accounting Reports of Enterprises, art. 39. An individual or entity that encourages, instructs, or compels accounting personnel to falsify accounting reports or conceal information may be subject to criminal liability or a monetary fine of RMB5,000 to RMB50,000. Regulation on Financial and Accounting Reports of Enterprises, art. 41.

enterprise released publicly that reflect the financial position of the enterprise over a specified period and the business results and cash flow over a particular accounting period.[332] The Regulations provide that the legal representative of an enterprise is responsible for the truthfulness and completeness of financial and accounting reports of the enterprise,[333] and that it is unlawful for any individual or entity to encourage, instruct, compel, or order an enterprise to draft and release externally false financial and accounting reports or reports that conceal material facts.[334] The Regulations provide that a registered accountant or accounting firm is required to complete the auditing of the financial and accounting reports of an enterprise in accordance with applicable laws and administrative rules and regulations.[335]

The Regulation on Financial and Accounting Reports of Enterprises provides that financial and accounting reports are required to be divided into yearly, half-yearly, quarterly, and monthly financial and accounting reports. Yearly and half-yearly financial and accounting reports are required to include: (1) accounting statements; (2) annotations to accounting statements; and (3) an explanation of the financial position of the enterprise.[336] Accounting statements are required to include assets and liability statements,[337] profit

332. Regulation on Financial and Accounting Reports of Enterprises, art. 2.

333. Regulation on Financial and Accounting Reports of Enterprises, art. 3.

334. Regulation on Financial and Accounting Reports of Enterprises, art. 4.

335. Regulation on Financial and Accounting Reports of Enterprises, art. 5.

336. Yearly and half-yearly accounting reports are required to reflect comparative data of at least two years or two interrelated periods. Regulation on Financial and Accounting Reports of Enterprises, art. 13.

337. The Regulation on Financial and Accounting Reports of Enterprises provide that an asset and liability statement is a document that outlines the financial position of an enterprise over a specified period of time. An assets and liability statement is required to list each item separately according to the classification of assets, liabilities, or ownership rights (or "shareholder rights"). The Regulations further define the terms that follow. "Assets" are the resources obtained from past transactions and events, which are in the possession or control of the enterprise. These resources are expected to bring economic benefits to the enterprise. Assets set forth in an assets and liability statement are required to be classified and listed separately according to their liquidity, including floating assets, long-term investment, fixed assets, intangible assets and other assets. Where the assets of banks, insurance companies, and non-bank financial institutions have particular characteristics, each item is required to be classified and listed separately according to its characteristics. "Liabilities" refers to current obligations formed from past transactions and events, and the economic benefits that are expected to flow out from the enterprise in order to fulfill those obligations. Liabilities on an assets and liability statement are required to be classified and listed separately according to their liquidity, and include floating liabilities, long-term liabilities, etc. Where the liabilities of banks, insurance companies, and non-bank financial institutions have particular characteristics, each item is required to be classified and listed separately according to its characteristics. "Ownership rights" are economic benefits that a shareholder or owner enjoys in the assets of an enterprise. The value of the benefit is the surplus after the liabilities of the enterprise are subtracted from its assets. Ownership rights on an assets and liability statement must be listed separately according to capital actually received (including capital stock), capital public reserve funds, net profit public reserve funds, and undistributed profits. Regulation on Financial and Accounting Reports of Enterprises, art. 9.

and loss statements,[338] cash flow statements[339] and related attachments.[340] Quarterly and monthly financial and accounting reports are usually referred to as accounting statements and are required to include asset and liability statements and profit and loss statements.[341]

The Regulation on Financial and Accounting Reports of Enterprises provides that "annotations to accounting statements" means explanations of the foundation, basis, principles, and method behind the statement's formulation together with the key items of the report in order to assist the user of an accounting statement to understand the content. Annotations to accounting statements are required to include at least the following:

(1) An explanation of a conclusion that does not accord with basic accounting
(2) Important accounting policies and accounting estimates together with the circumstances and reasons for any alteration, and the effect of such alteration on the financial position and business activities
(3) An explanation of possible matters and matters that occur after the making of the assets and liability statement
(4) An explanation of the relationship with related parties together with any transactions with those parties
(5) The transfer of major assets and the circumstances of sale
(6) Any merger or division of the enterprise
(7) Major investment and financing activities
(8) Detailed information of important matters in the accounting statement
(9) Other matters that require explanation in order to assist in understanding and analyzing the accounting report[342]

338. Each item in a profit statement is required to be classified and listed separately according to each kind of income and expense together with the various items that constitute the profit of the enterprise. The regulations define the terms income, expenses, and profit. Regulation on Financial and Accounting Reports of Enterprises, art. 10.

339. Regulation on Financial and Accounting Reports of Enterprises, arts. 6, 7. A cash flow statement is a statement that reflects the incoming and outgoing cash and articles equivalent to cash of an enterprise over a particular accounting period of time. A cash flow statement is required to classify and list separately cash flow according to business activities, investment activities, and fund-raising activities. The regulations set forth the definitions of the terms "business activities," "investment activities," and "fund-raising activities." Regulation on Financial and Accounting Reports of Enterprises, art. 11.

340. Corresponding attachments are supplementary statements that reflect the financial position, business activities, and cash flow of an enterprise, and mainly include a distribution of profits statement together with other attachments as may be required by accounting practices. A profits distribution statement is a statement that reflects the distribution of net profits realized over a particular accounting period together with undistributed profits or losses carried forward from the previous year of an enterprise. Regulation on Financial and Accounting Reports of Enterprises, art. 12.

341. Regulation on Financial and Accounting Reports of Enterprises, art. 8.

342. Regulation on Financial and Accounting Reports of Enterprises, art. 14.

The explanation of an enterprise's financial status in the yearly and half-yearly financial and accounting reports is required to provide information on the following matters:

(1) The basic situation of the enterprise's production and operation
(2) The situation of profit realization and distribution
(3) The circumstances of increase, decrease, and flow of funds
(4) Other matters that have a major effect on an enterprise's financial status, business activities, and cash flow[343]

An enterprise is required to verify its assets and liabilities in the preparation of its annual report, including a determination of actual value of assets and inventory, verification of accounts receivables, verification of liabilities and accounts payable, etc.[344] An enterprise is required to prepare accounting statements that are complete in content, accurate in figures, and correct in calculation, and must not leave out or arbitrarily accept and reject items.[345] Related figures, data, and explanatory annotations in accounting statements for a current period of time are required to be consistent with figures used in previously issued accounting statements.[346] For enterprises undergoing liquidation, financial and accounting reports must be prepared for the time period up to the termination of operations, along with a separate report reflecting the activities during the liquidation period.[347]

The accounting information reflected in a financial and accounting report that is released publicly is required to be accurate and complete, and enterprises are required to publicly release such reports in a timely manner as required by law.[348] If an entity or individual receives an enterprise's financial and accounting report before the report has been formally released to the public, the recipient is required to maintain confidentiality of the reports' contents.[349] The Regulation on Financial and Accounting Reports of Enterprises provides that financial and accounting reports released publicly by an enterprise are required to have numbered pages and a front cover, to be bound, and to include the company seal. The Regulations provide that

343. Regulation on Financial and Accounting Reports of Enterprises, art. 15.
344. Regulation on Financial and Accounting Reports of Enterprises, arts. 20, 21.
345. Regulation on Financial and Accounting Reports of Enterprises, art. 23.
346. Regulation on Financial and Accounting Reports of Enterprises, arts. 24, 25.
347. Regulation on Financial and Accounting Reports of Enterprises, art. 27.
348. Regulation on Financial and Accounting Reports of Enterprises, arts. 29, 30. An enterprise may not be forced to provide financial reports and accounting data in whole or in part other than in accordance with the law. An enterprise may refuse to comply with any request for information that is inconsistent with the requirements of the law. Regulation on Financial and Accounting Reports of Enterprises, art. 34. SOEs are required to release financial reports at least once a year to a meeting of the employee representatives. Regulation on Financial and Accounting Reports of Enterprises, art. 35.
349. Regulation on Financial and Accounting Reports of Enterprises, art. 38.

certain information must appear on the cover page of financial reports, including the name of the enterprise, the unified enterprise code number, the organizational form and address of the enterprise, the time period covered by the statements, and the date of the report. The report must be signed and sealed by the legal representative of the enterprise, a person responsible for the enterprise's accounting practices.[350] If a financial and accounting report is audited by a registered accountant, the enterprise is required to attach the audit report to the subject report for release to the public.[351]

2. Auditing Procedures

The Auditing Law outlines the procedures for fiscal and operational audits of organizations and entities in China, and addresses the administrative guidelines and standards for auditors under the jurisdiction of the National Audit Office (NAO) and its subordinate organizations. Given that FIEs are subject to audits as domestic enterprises and as taxpayers, the requirements of the Auditing Law have application to foreign investors in China.

In general, the Audit Law provides that the NAO and its subordinate offices exercise independent audit supervision rights in accordance with the law and no other administrative organization, institution, or individual shall be permitted to interfere with the NAO's obligations.[352] In handling audit matters, auditing offices and auditors are required to be "objective and impersonal, practical and realistic, and honest when performing their official duties."[353] The Audit Law provides that an auditor must have the requisite training, experience, and qualifications suitable to conduct auditing work.[354] In addition, the law provides that an auditor must withdraw from handling an audit matter in situations involving real or potential conflicts of interest.[355] The law further requires auditors to maintain confidentiality concerning State or commercial secrets that may be disclosed during the course of an audit.[356]

The auditing office has broad discretion to audit the assets, liabilities, losses, and profits of State-owned enterprises, State-funded construction and

350. Regulation on Financial and Accounting Reports of Enterprises, art. 31.
351. Regulation on Financial and Accounting Reports of Enterprises, art. 37.
352. Auditing Law, art. 5.
353. Auditing Law, art. 6. The law also provides for criminal prosecution and administrative penalties if an auditor abuses the powers of office. *Id.* art. 49.
354. Auditing Law, art. 12.
355. Auditing Law, art. 13.
356. Auditing Law, arts. 14, 36. Auditors receive special protection under the law. No organization or individual may obstruct an auditor in the exercise of that auditor's powers of office, or retaliate against that auditor. Senior management personnel of an audit office may not be dismissed from their posts without justification. *Id.* art. 15. If an individual, enterprise, or organization retaliates or attempts to retaliate against an auditor, the law provides for administrative and criminal penalties. *Id.* art. 48.

infrastructure projects, projects funded by foreign capital loans and recipients of international assistance, FIEs, financial institutions, social welfare funds, and State social institutions.[357] An auditing office is also authorized to conduct ongoing audits and enterprise supervision with respect to State-owned enterprises that are considered important to the national economy, receive excessive financial subsidies, or have incurred relatively large amounts of losses.[358] The NAO is also authorized to conduct special audits of local government authorities on matters relating to State fiscal revenues and expenditures, and an audit investigation report must be reported to the people's government at the equivalent level and to the superior level auditing office.[359]

Prior to initiating an audit, the auditing office is required to provide three days' written notice of commencement of audit to the targeted enterprise or organization.[360] The auditors are required to produce their employment credentials and a copy of the audit notice when visiting an audited enterprise's facilities. [361] An enterprise or organization subject to an audit must cooperate with the work of the auditing office and provide the necessary facilities to assist the auditors in completing their work.[362] The NAO and its subordinate offices have the authority to demand that an enterprise or government agency produce its financial records for inspection and review.[363] The auditors further have the authority to interview and question the employees and management personnel of audited enterprises and organizations.[364] During the course of an audit, an enterprise or organization may not transfer, conceal, alter, or destroy its accounting records and other materials relating to its expenditures and income.[365]

At the conclusion of an audit, the individual auditors are required to issue a preliminary audit report to the auditing office. The Auditing Law provides that the audited enterprise or organization is entitled to submit additional information and documentation prior to the submission of a final

357. Auditing Law, arts. 16–25.
358. Auditing Law, art. 21.
359. Auditing Law, art. 27.
360. Auditing Law, art. 37.
361. Auditing Law, art. 38.
362. Auditing Law, arts. 38, 41. A failure to cooperate with an audit opens an enterprise and organization to penalties.
363. Auditing Law, arts. 31, 32.
364. Auditing Law, art. 33.
365. Auditing Law, arts. 34, 38. The auditors have the power to instruct the financial departments of the local governments to suspend access to government funds if the audited enterprise or organization removes, alters, or destroys its financial records during the course of an audit. A violation of the rule against destruction or transfer of records exposes an enterprise or organization to administrative and criminal penalties. *Id.* arts. 42–47.

audit report to the auditing office. The audited enterprise or organization has ten days from the date of receiving the preliminary audit report to file a written submission with the auditors or the auditing office directly.[366] After the submission of a final audit report, the NAO and its subordinate offices are required to issue a formal opinion within thirty days concerning the enterprise or organization audited. In matters involving financial irregularities and violations of law, the auditing office may refer its findings to the judicial authorities for prosecution or relevant government finance department for administrative penalty proceedings.[367]

Effective January 1, 2004, the law requires that auditors retained by companies in China have a limited tenure. Specifically, companies are required to change auditing staff every five years and must wait two years before hiring a previously retained auditor. Auditors for newly listed firms are limited to a two-year engagement. This rule applies to auditors of listed companies, underwriters, securities and futures market firms, stock and futures exchanges, securities investment funds, and settlement institutions.[368]

3. Joint Annual Review Procedures

The various revenue branches of the government and agencies responsible for supervision of foreign-invested enterprises issued a notice on December 26, 1996, setting forth a joint annual review procedure for FIEs.[369] Under the Joint Annual Review Procedures, the government has established national review procedures for FIEs, which are required to take place annually from January 1 to April 30 of each year. The procedures are similar to review programs established by local branches of the SAIC and other government agencies and apply to all FIEs and enterprises from Hong Kong, Taiwan, and Macao. The stated objective of the annual review is to "further improve the investment environment and to lessen the burden on enterprises."[370] In reality, the audit procedures are designed to provide the various government agencies

366. Auditing Law, art. 39.

367. Auditing Law, art. 40.

368. *See PRC Bolsters Corporate Governance with Auditor Rotation*, CHINA MARKET INTELLIGENCE, THE U.S.-CHINA BUSINESS COUNCIL (November 5, 2003), available online to members at http://www.uschina.org.

369. Notice of the Ministry of Foreign Trade and Economic Cooperation, the State Administration for Industry and Commerce, the State Economic and Trade Commission, the Ministry of Finance, the State Administration of Taxation, and the General Administration of Customs on Joint Annual Review of Foreign Investment Enterprises (promulgated December 26, 1996), *reprinted in* CHINA LAWS FOR FOREIGN BUSINESS (CCH), Business Regulation ¶ 13-365 (hereinafter the "Joint Annual Review Procedures"). *See also Law Bulletin: Reports on Legal Developments from the Chinese Press*, 11 CHINA L. & PRAC. 19 (March 1997).

370. Joint Annual Review Provisions, preamble.

more control over FIEs which, in the past, have either ignored reporting requirements or provided incomplete responses in order to circumvent certain regulations, especially in the area of foreign exchange, taxation, and the scope of business of the FIE.

a. Review Questionnaire

The questionnaire/report book is uniformly printed and distributed by the SAIC. An FIE is required to obtain a copy of the questionnaire/report book from the SAIC after the first of each year, and must complete it in accordance with the instructions. The questionnaire/report book requests information concerning the scope of business operation; the industry sector of the FIE; the type of enterprise of the FIE (e.g., EJV, CJV, WFOE, holding company, etc.); the total number of local and foreign employees; the officers and board leadership; various registration numbers such as customs registration number, foreign exchange registration certificate number, and taxation registration number; the registered capital per agreement and the actual contributions to registered capital by parties to the FIE; profits reinvested by the foreign party; the FIE's gross sales including export sales; foreign exchange earnings; amount of taxes and customs duties paid; a description of the FIE's operations; justifications for losses or abnormal production; name of the contractor for enterprises under contract management; information concerning foreign exchange accounts, revenue, trading, borrowing, and expenditures; and information concerning branch offices, if any.[371]

b. Documents Required

A foreign-invested enterprise is required to submit copies of its annual report, business license, financial statements, capital verification report, and registration certificates with the tax authorities. The various joint annual review agencies will have the right to examine the questionnaire/report book and accompanying documentation. If an FIE fails to prepare the questionnaire/report book in the proper format or fails to include the required information, it will be given an opportunity by the SAIC to provide the corrected information. A subsequent failure to correct the deficiency may result in a monetary penalty to the FIE and the consultants hired to prepare the reports such as accounting firms. The SAIC also has the authority to cancel the

371. Joint Annual Review Procedures, attached questionnaire/report book.

approval certificate and business license of an FIE that fails to properly prepare the questionnaire/report book.[372] On-site inspections will focus on those FIEs that fail to comply with the Joint Annual Review Procedures. The deadline for submitting the review questionnaire and supporting documents is March 15 of each year.

Key Laws and Regulations

Banking Regulations

Law of the People's Republic of China on the People's Bank of China (adopted on March 18, 1995, by the 3rd Sess. of the 8th NPC)

Banking Supervision and Administration Rules (promulgated on December 27, 2003, by the NPC Standing Committee)

Rules on the People's Bank of China (promulgated on December 27, 2003, by the NPC Standing Committee)

Commercial Bank Law of the People's Republic of China (adopted on May 10, 1995, by the 13th Sess. of the 8th NPC, and as amended by the NPC on December 27, 2003)

Administrative Regulations Governing Financial Institutions (promulgated on August 9, 1994, by the People's Bank of China, and as amended in 2003 by the China Banking Regulatory Commission)

Regulations of the Bank of China on Foreign Currency Deposits (Category A) (promulgated on February 26, 1993, by the Bank of China)

Regulations of the Bank of China on Foreign Currency Deposits (Category B) (promulgated on February 26, 1993, by the Bank of China)

Administrative Regulations on Domestic Foreign Exchange Accounts (promulgated on October 7, 1997, by the PBOC)

Provisional Measures on Syndicated Loans (promulgated on October 7, 1997, by the PBOC)

Measures on the Settlement of Domestic Letters of Credit (promulgated on June 23, 1997, by the PBOC)

Administration of the Establishment of Business Network Points in the Same City by Commercial Banks Procedures (issued on February 21, 2002, by the PBOC)

(Continued)

372. A condition of a business license and registration is to cooperate with the annual review procedures. *See* Administrative Regulations of the People's Republic of China Governing the Registration of Legal Corporations (promulgated June 3, 1988, by the State Council) art. 24, *reprinted in* CHINA LAWS FOR FOREIGN BUSINESS (CCH), Business Regulation ¶ 13-542.

(Continued from previous page)

Measures for the Administration of Finance Licenses (issued on May 26, 2003, by the China Banking Regulatory Commission, and effective July 1, 2003)

Provisional Regulations Concerning Investment in Financial Institutions Through Purchase of Shares (promulgated on July 28, 1994, by the People's Bank of China)

Administrative Measures on Security Given to Foreign Parties by Domestic Institutions (promulgated on September 25, 1996, by the PBOC)

Provisional Rules on the Administration of Commercial Banking Service Pricing (promulgated on June 26, 2003, by the CBRC)

Guiding Principles on the Improvement of the Internal Controls of Financial Institutions (promulgated on May 16, 1997, by the PBOC)

Administration of Online Banking Services Tentative Procedures (issued on June 29, 2001, by the PBOC, effective as of date of issue)

Penalty Measures for Illegal Financial Activities (issued on February 22, 1999, by the State Council, effective as of date of issue)

Financial Institutions Anti-Money Laundering Provisions (promulgated by the PBOC on January 3, 2003, and effective on March 1, 2003)

Large and Suspicious Renminbi Payment Transactions Reporting Administrative Procedures (promulgated by the PBOC on January 3, 2003, and effective on March 1, 2003)

Management Procedures for Financial Institutions Governing Reporting of Large and Suspicious Foreign Currency Funds Transactions (promulgated by the PBOC on January 3, 2003, and effective on March 1, 2003)

Administrative Regulations of the People's Republic of China governing Foreign-Funded Financial Institutions (promulgated on February 25, 1994, by the State Council, and as amended on December 20, 2001)

Detailed Implementing Regulations for the Administrative Rules of the People's Republic of China Governing Foreign-Funded Financial Institutions (promulgated on April 30, 1996, by the People's Bank of China, and as amended on January 29, 2002, by the PBOC)

Administrative Measures on Representative Offices in China of Foreign Financial Institutions (promulgated on April 29, 1996, by the People's Bank of China and revised and re-promulgated by Order No. 8 on June 27, 2002, by the People's Bank of China)

Procedures for the Administration of Renminbi Bank Settlement Accounts (issued on April 10, 2003, by the People's Bank of China)

Notice Concerning the Further Opening of Renminbi Services to Foreign-Invested Financial Institutions (issued on October 24, 2003)

(Continued)

(Continued from previous page)

Notice Concerning the Further Opening of Renminbi Services to Foreign-Invested Financial Institutions (issued on October 24, 2003)

Regulations Governing Capital Adequacy of Commercial Banks (issued and effective on March 1, 2004, by the CBRC)

Rules on the Administration of Consolidated Financial Statements of Foreign-Invested Banks (issued on March 8, 2004, by the CBRC, and effective on April 1, 2004)

Procedures for the Administration of the Qualifications for Office of the Senior Management Personnel of Financial Institutions (issued on March 24, 2000, by the People's Bank of China)

Procedures for the Administration of Investment and Equity Participation in Chinese-Invested Financial Institutions by Offshore Financial Institutions (promulgated on December 8, 2003, by the China Banking Regulatory Commission)

Rules of the People's Republic of China on Foreign Exchange Control (promulgated January 29, 1996, by the State Council and amended on January 4, 1997, by the State Council)

Administrative Regulations on Foreign Exchange Settlements, Sales and Payments (promulgated June 20, 1996, by the People's Bank of China)

Notice of the State Administration of Foreign Exchange on the Printing and Distribution of the Administrative Measures on the Settlement of Foreign Exchange under Current Accounts (promulgated on July 25, 1997, by the State Administration of Foreign Exchange)

Announcement of the People's Bank of China on the Implementation of Foreign Exchange Settlements and Sales at Banks by Foreign Investment Enterprises (promulgated June 20, 1996, by the People's Bank of China)

Notice on the Issue of the "Provisional Measures on the Administration of Foreign Exchange Registration for Foreign Investment Enterprises" (promulgated June 28, 1996, by the State Administration of Foreign Exchange)

Administrative Regulations on Domestic Foreign Exchange Accounts (promulgated on October 7, 1997, by the People's Bank of China)

Administrative Measures on Foreign Exchange Control in Bonded Zones (promulgated by the SAFE on July 25, 2002)

Notice on Relevant Issues Related to Furthering Adjustment of Import/Export Verification Management Policies (issued on July 10, 2002, by the State Administration of Foreign Exchange)

Provisional Regulations on Foreign Exchange Administration for Insurance Industry (promulgated on September 24, 2002, by SAFE and the China Insurance Regulatory Commission)

(Continued)

(Continued from previous page)

Regulations on Border Trading of FOREX (issued on October 1, 2003, by SAFE)

Notice Relating to the Publication of the "Interim Measures on the Administration of Carrying Foreign Currencies at Exit-Entry of the Border" (issued on August 28, 2003, by SAFE and the Customs General Administration)

Foreign Debt Administration Tentative Procedures (promulgated on March 1, 2003, by the State Administration of Foreign Exchange)

Provisional Administrative Regulations on Domestic Allocation and Transfer of Foreign Exchange (promulgated on September 25, 1997, by the State Administration of Foreign Exchange)

Notice from the State Administration of Foreign Exchange on Issues Relating to Improving Foreign Exchange Administration of Foreign Direct Investment (issued on March 3, 2003, by the State Administration of Foreign Exchange)

Notice on Issues Concerning Furthering the Adjustment of Current Foreign Exchange Account Administrative Policies (issued by the State Administration of Foreign Exchange and effective on October 15, 2002)

Foreign Exchange Accounts for Current Items by Domestic Entities Implementing Rules (issued by the State Administration of Foreign Exchange and effective on October 15, 2002); Announcement Regarding Transfer of Part of the Foreign Exchange Business from the State Administration of Foreign Exchange to the SAFE Beijing Branch (issued on September 21, 2001, by SAFE)

Notice on Certain Issues Concerning the Alteration of Capital Funds by Foreign Investment Enterprises, arts. 1, 2, 4 (promulgated June 28, 1996, by the State Administration of Foreign Exchange)

Provisional Measures on the Administration of the Overseas Financing of Projects (promulgated on April 16, 1997, by the State Planning Commission and the State Administration of Foreign Exchange)

Notice on Several Issues Concerning the Adjustment of Administrative Policies for Foreign Exchange Accounts Under the International Contracting Project and Other Current Account Items (issued by the State Administration of Foreign Exchange and effective on September 1, 2003)

Notice on the Provisional Management Rules on Entering and Exiting China with Foreign Currency (issued on September 1, 2003, by the State Administration of Foreign Exchange and the General Administration of Customs)

Notice on the Management of Non-Trade Exchange Transactions for Multinational Companies (Trial) (issued on August 18, 2003, by the State Administration of Foreign Exchange)

Regulation on Several Issues on Jurisdiction of Overseas Civil and Commercial Lawsuits, PRC Supreme People's Court Judicial Interpretation [2002] No. 5 (promulgated by the SPC on Feb. 25, 2002, and effective on March 1, 2002)

(Continued)

(Continued from previous page)

Measures on the Management of Enterprise Group Finance Companies (promulgated on June 30, 2000, as Order No. 3 [2000] of the People's Bank of China)

Measures on the Management of Financial Leasing Companies (promulgated on June 30, 2000, as Order No. 4 [2000] of the People's Bank of China)

Administration of Auto Finance Companies Procedures (promulgated by the People's Bank of China on and effective as October 3, 2003)

Administration of Auto Finance Companies Procedures Implementing Rules (promulgated on November 12, 2003, by the China Banking Regulatory Commission)

Accounting and Auditing

Accounting Law of the People's Republic of China (adopted on January 21, 1985, by the 9th Sess. of the Standing Comm. of the 6th NPC and amended on December 29, 1993, by the 5th Sess. of the Standing Comm. of the 8th NPC, and amended and revised on October 31, 1999, at the 12th Meeting of the Standing Comm. of the 9th NPC)

Regulations on Issues Concerning Implementation of "Accounting System for Business Enterprises" by Foreign Investment Enterprises (promulgated on November 29, 2001, by the Ministry of Finance)

Auditing Law of the People's Republic of China (promulgated on August 31, 1994, by the 9th Sess. of the Standing Comm. of the 8th NPC)

Detailed Rules for the Implementation of the Auditing Law of the People's Republic of China (promulgated on October 21, 1997, by the State Council)

Auditing Procedures for Chinese-Foreign Equity and Contractual Joint Ventures (promulgated January 12, 1993, by the State Auditing Bureau)

Regulations on Issues concerning Implementation of "Accounting System for Business Enterprises" by Foreign Investment Enterprises (promulgated on November 29, 2001, by the Ministry of Finance)

Answers to Questions Relevant to the Implementation of the Enterprise Accounting System by Foreign Investment Enterprises (issued on May 26, 2002, by the Ministry of Finance)

Accounting System for Business Enterprises (promulgated on December 29, 2000, by the Ministry of Finance and effective January 1, 2001)

Financial Enterprise Accounting System (promulgated on November 27, 2001, by the MOF and effective on January 1, 2002)

Regulations on Financial and Accounting Reports of Enterprises (promulgated on June 21, 2000, by the State Council and effective from January 1, 2001)

(Continued)

(*Continued from previous page*)

Trust Law and Administration

Trust Law of the People's Republic of China (adopted 28 April 2001 at the 21st Meeting of the Standing Committee of the 9th National People's Congress, Issued by Presidential Decree [No. 50] of the People's Republic of China on April 28, 2001)

Measures on Administration of Trust and Investment Institutions (promulgated January 12, 2001, by the People's Bank of China)

Interim Measures on the Administration of Trust Money of Trust and Investment Companies (promulgated on June 26, 2002, by the PBOC)

Measures on Administration of Trust and Investment Institutions (promulgated on January 12, 2001, by the People's Bank of China)

Chapter 12

Insurance Law and Regulation

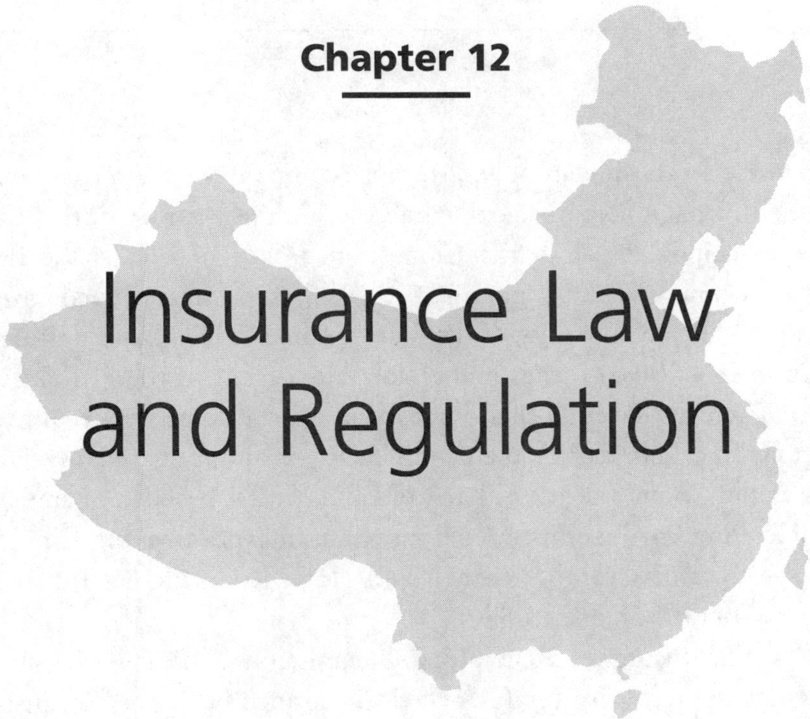

Prior to the economic reforms in the early 1980s, China's insurance laws and regulations were incomplete. To support the economic reform process, the State Council in 1983 issued regulations concerning property insurance that outline the standards for property insurance contracts, the liability and procedures for insurance companies, and the obligations of the insured party.[1] In 1985, the State Council issued regulations with respect to the standards for establishing and operating an insurance business.[2] After several years of consideration, in 1995, the NPC adopted the Insurance Law which is the PRC's first comprehensive law governing insurance contracts, insurance business operating rules, supervision of the insurance industry, standards for agents and brokers, and liability matters.[3] The Insurance Law

1. *See* Regulations of the People's Republic of China on Contracts of Property Insurance (promulgated on September 1, 1983, by the State Council), *reprinted in* CHINA LAWS FOR FOREIGN BUSINESS (CCH), Business Regulation ¶ 9-580 (repealed).

2. Provisional Regulations Governing the Management of Insurance Enterprises (promulgated on March 3, 1985, by the State Council), *reprinted in* CHINA LAWS FOR FOREIGN BUSINESS (CCH), Business Regulation ¶ 9-600 (repealed).

3. Insurance Law of the People's Republic of China (adopted on June 30, 1995, by the 14th Sess. of the Standing Comm. of the 8th NPC and revised on October 28, 2002, by 30th Sess. of the Standing Comm. of the 9th NPC), *reprinted in* CHINA LAWS FOR FOREIGN BUSINESS (CCH), Business Regulation ¶ 9-620 (hereinafter the "Insurance Law"). *See also* Simms, *China's Insurance Law,* CHINA BUSINESS REVIEW 30 (Sept./Oct. 1996); Qinhuo, *The Legal Protection of the Insured's Rights and Interests under the Insurance Law of China,* 4 CANBERRA L. REV. 189 (1997/98); Chaput, *An Introduction to Insurance Law and Coverage in the People's Republic of China,* 30 TORT & INS. L. J. 871 (1995); *Profile: China's Insurance Industry,* ASIA PULSE (Jan. 20, 1999), available on Lexis, News Library; Y. Lee, *Insurance in China: Pre- and Post-WTO,* CHINA BUSINESS REVIEW (May/June 2002), available on the Web site of the U.S./China Business Council at http://www.uschina.org; G. Xu, Amending the Insurance Law: Long-Term Policy or Expedient Measures, CHINA L. & PRAC. 21 (Dec. 2002/Jan. 2003).

applies to the establishment of an insurance company with foreign equity and branches of foreign insurance companies within the territory of the PRC.[4]

The principal player in the Chinese insurance market is the People's Insurance Company of China (PICC), which is a State-owned insurance company under the authority of the State Council. PICC has a national network of over 4,000 branches and claims 90 percent of the PRC insurance market.[5] There are several other domestic insurance companies that focus on the regional markets such as the China Pacific Insurance Company, which is owned by the Communications Bank of China and is based in Shanghai, and the China Ping An Insurance Company, an enterprise of the China Merchants Group and several Shenzhen and Hong Kong financial institutions and is based in the Shenzhen SEZ.

The China Insurance Regulatory Commission (CIRC) is the approval and regulatory authority for FIE-related insurance business.[6] An insurance company can engage in insurance business only if it is established in China in accordance with the law.[7] Applicants are required to go through stringent

4. Insurance Law, art. 154.

5. The reality is that PICC holds about 70% of China's property and casualty insurance market. In November 2003, PICC listed on the Hong Kong stock exchange and net $693 million in the IPO.

6. Insurance Law, art. 9. *See* Provisional Regulations on Insurance Administration (promulgated on August 16, 1996, by the People's Bank of China), art. 2, *reprinted in* China Laws for Foreign Business (CCH), Business Regulation ¶ 9-630. CIRC has prepared a draft set of revised Regulations on the Administration of Insurance Companies, which were released to the public for comment in August 2003. An unofficial translation of the draft regulations is available on the Web site of the U.S./China Business Council at http://www.uschina.org. The CIRC replaced the Insurance Department of the People's Bank of China in November 1998 as the regulatory agency responsible for the insurance industry. CIRC operates a Web site at http://www.circ.gov.cn. *See* Xu, *Insurance Sector to Be Regulated by New Body,* China Daily (Nov. 19, 1998), available on Lexis, News Library, or on the Web site of the China Daily at http://www.chinadaily.com.cn. The State Council has also restructured the PICC. Zhang, *New Body Regulates China's Insurance Sector,* 138 China International Business (MOFTEC) 17 (1999) (discusses the China Insurance Regulatory Commission, its departments, leadership, and policies); Wang, *China's Insurance Market Restructuring,* China Daily (March 22, 1999), available on Lexis, News Library, or on the Web site of the China Daily at http://www.chinadaily.com.cn. The CIRC established a hotline in February 1999 to allow the public to register complaints concerning insurance regulatory staff and the insurance industry. *CIRC Opened to Guarantee Legal Rights,* China Daily (Feb. 2, 1999), available on Lexis, News Library, or on the Web site of China Daily at http://www.chinadaily.com.cn. CIRC has established administrative reconsideration standards designed to allow affected companies or individuals the right to appeal any adverse decision of CIRC. *See* Measures on Administrative Reconsideration of the China Insurance Regulatory Commission (issued on July 5, 2001, by the CIRC). (The CIRC Administrative Reconsideration Measures outlines procedures for submission of applications for reconsideration, which must be made within 60 days of receipt of the decision. CIRC must respond in five days to an application and a failure to do so will be deemed an acceptance of the application.)

7. Insurance Law, art. 9. In December 2003, CIRC issued a notice allowing domestic insurance companies to expand their geographical scope by conducting business through intermediaries or their own marketing entities in provinces where they only currently maintain branches. Notice Regarding Fulfillment of Relevant WTO Accession Commitments (issued on December 11, 2003, by the China Insurance Regulatory Commission) (provides that foreign-invested property insurance companies may conduct all non-life insurance business, with the exception of statutory insurance, and further opens to foreign investment in the insurance sector five additional cities: Fuzhou, Xiamen, Ningbo, Shenyang and Wuhan). *See generally PRC Insurance Update,* China Market Intelligence, The U.S.-China Business Council (October 1, 2003); *CIRC Opens Five More Cities to Foreign Insurers,* China Market Intelligence, The U.S.-China Business Council (January 7, 2004).

approval procedures with approval taking several years to obtain. The law requires that insurers maintain certain capital requirements, deposit guarantee funds with the CIRC, and allocate reserve funds to cover claims. The law also regulates premium rates and sets forth reporting requirements.

China's WTO obligations provide that China will allow foreign insurers selling non-life insurance to establish joint ventures with 51% ownership upon accession, and, after two years (December 2003), will be allowed to establish wholly foreign-owned branches with "no form of establishment restrictions." Foreign life insurers will be permitted to establish joint ventures with 50% ownership upon accession.

Brokerage firms for insurance of large-scale commercial risks (including reinsurance and international marine, aviation, and transport insurance and reinsurance) will be allowed to establish joint ventures with foreign equity to a maximum of 50% upon accession, 51% after three years, and, after five years, wholly-owned subsidiaries will be authorized. China has further committed to seven new insurance licenses—five for life insurance companies and two for non-life insurance companies—and an additional two foreign insurance companies will be allowed to establish in a second city.[8]

This chapter addresses the insurance laws and regulations of China including the laws governing the establishment of domestic insurance companies, foreign-invested insurance companies, regulatory standards, standards for reinsurance, claims procedures, and standards for insurance asset management companies.

A. Conditions for Operation

An insurance company is required to be organized as either a company limited by shares or a wholly State-owned company, and must be approved by the CIRC.[9] A party who engages in insurance business activities must abide by the insurance laws and regulations, and observe the principles of free will, honesty, trustworthiness, and fair competition.[10] In addition, an insurance

8. For information concerning China's WTO commitments in the insurance industry, see the Web site of the China Insurance Regulatory Commission at http://www.circ.gov.cn. On December 18, 2002, CIRC issued a press release that outlines the progress made to date concerning market access in the insurance industry.

9. Insurance Law, arts. 70, 71. The Insurance Law provides that the organizational structure of an insurance company is required to conform to the provisions of the Company Law. *Id.* at 83. For a discussion of the standards under the Company Law, *see* Chapter 4, FIE Organizational Structure and Approval Procedures § D.1.; Chapter 16, Securities Regulations § B.

10. Insurance Law, arts. 4, 8; Insurance Regulations, art. 4 § (3). For example, the promotional materials for an insurance company are required to state the company's name and must not include a company's forecast for profits or dividends. *Id.* at 57.

company seeking to establish an operation in China must comply with the following principles, conditions, and requirements:

(1) Conform to the development requirements of the national economy
(2) Maintain separate business operations in the areas of property insurance and personal insurance
(3) The company's articles of association must conform to the provisions of the Company Law
(4) The company's registered capital complies with the minimum requirements of RMB200 million[11]
(5) The company's senior management are required to have professional experience in the insurance industry[12]
(6) The company is required to have an organizational and management system sufficient to meet the needs of the insurance business[13]
(7) The company is required to have business premises and facilities that meet the requirements for engaging in an insurance business[14]

1. Solvency Requirements

An insurance company operating in the PRC must meet minimum solvency requirements and standards set forth in the Insurance Regulations.[15] The minimum solvency of an insurance company must be commensurate with the operation's business scale and is defined as its "actual assets" minus its "actual debts."[16] The minimum solvency standards for property insurance companies are no less than RMB100 million for premium proceeds of less than or equal to RMB200 million; no less than RMB100 million, or one-third

11. Insurance Law, art. 73. The minimum registered capital must be in the form of monetary capital, and CIRC retains the discretion to increase the registered capital. Insurance Law, art. 73. *See also* Insurance Regulations, art. 5 § (1).

12. Insurance Law, art. 72; Insurance Regulations, art. 5 § (2). At least 60 percent of the employees of an insurance company must have experience in insurance work and be graduates of professional insurance departments at universities or colleges. An insurance company engaging in life insurance business must employ at least one actuary recognized by the CIRC. Insurance Regulations, art. 5 § (3). The CIRC requires that insurance company employees submit to a qualification examination before commencing work. *Id.* at 15. *See also* Implementing Principles of Employment Qualifications of Senior Managers in Insurance Organizations (promulgated by the China Insurance Regulatory Commission in 1999).

13. *See* PBOC Internal Control Principles, art. 13 (outlines standards for internal control systems for insurance companies).

14. Insurance Law, art. 72; Insurance Regulations, arts, 4, 5 § (4).

15. Insurance Law, art. 98; Insurance Regulations, arts. 48–52. *See also* Provisions on Administration of Solvency Line and Guiding Principles of Supervision for Insurance Companies (promulgated on March 24, 2003, by the China Insurance Regulatory Commission); a translation is available on the Isinolaw Web site at http://www.isinolaw.com (contains specific formulas on solvency standards).

16. Insurance Regulations, arts. 48–49. In determining solvency, the "actual assets" do not include certain advanced payments, deferred assets, intangible assets, low-cost and easily depleted articles, bad debts, the cost of marketable securities in excess of current market value, one-tenth of the insurance company's immovable property and fixed assets, and other nonliquid assets. *Id.* at 49. The "actual debt" of an insurance company is the amount remaining after deducting the paid-up capital fund, accumulation fund, public welfare fund, and undistributed profits from its total assets. *Id.*

of the retained premiums, whichever is greater, when annual premiums are more than RMB200 million but less than RMB300 million; and no less than RMB1 billion, or one-quarter of the retained premiums, whichever is greater, when annual premiums are more than RMB3 billion.[17]

The minimum solvency standards for personal insurance operations are no less than RMB100 million when the actual debt of the company is less than or equal to RMB300 million; no less than RMB100 million or one-quarter of the actual debt, whichever is greater, when the actual debt is more than RMB300 million but less than RMB1 billion; no less than RMB250 million or one-sixth of the actual debt, whichever is greater, when the actual debt is more than RMB1 billion but less than RMB3 billion; and no less than RMB500 million or one-eighth of the actual debt, whichever is greater, when the actual debt is more than RMB3 billion.[18]

If a company's minimum solvency is less than 5 percent of the standards, the insurance company is required to undertake reinsurance or other transfer approved by the CIRC in order to revise its asset to liability structure within thirty days, or until the minimum solvency standard is met.[19] If the amount required to maintain minimum solvency is more than 5 percent and less than 20 percent of the standard, the insurance company is required to cease its underwriting business and, within ten days, submit a report to the CIRC that outlines a remedial plan. A remedial plan is required to set forth the measures to improve the company's financial performance, including reinsurance, asset transfer, increase in capital from shareholders, and other measures approved by the CIRC.[20] If the amount required to maintain minimum solvency is more than 20 percent and less than 40 percent of the solvency standards, the CIRC has the power to order the insurance company to improve its financial situation or terminate its operation.[21] If the amount required to maintain minimum solvency is greater than 40 percent, an insurance company is required to apply to the CIRC for bankruptcy relief.[22]

2. Approval Procedures

The Insurance Regulations require that the approval procedures for insurance business enterprises be in a two-step process including the preparatory establishment stage and the business commencement stage.[23] The two-step process is required to establish a registered (principal PRC) office or any branch,

17. Insurance Regulations, art. 50.
18. Insurance Regulations, art. 51.
19. Insurance Regulations, art. 52 § (1).
20. Insurance Regulations, art. 52 § (2).
21. Insurance Regulations, art. 52 § (3).
22. Insurance Regulations, art. 52 § (4). For a discussion concerning bankruptcy procedures, *see* Chapter 20, Enterprise Liquidation, Reorganization, and Bankruptcy § B.
23. Insurance Regulations, art. 9.

sub-branch, or liaison offices. An insurance company may not engage in any insurance business during the preparatory establishment period.[24]

a. Preparatory Establishment Stage

A company that desires to do business in China is required to file an application for preparatory establishment of a PRC insurance enterprise. The applicant is required to submit a preparatory establishment application, feasibility study, schedule of operations, resumés of management personnel, and background information concerning the foreign investor(s). The background information concerning the foreign party must include financial information for the previous three years, information concerning its approval by its host-country insurance regulatory authorities, and any other information requested by the CIRC.[25] The period for approval of the application for preparatory establishment of an insurance company by the CIRC is three months. If an applicant does not receive approval during this three-month period of time, it is barred from submitting the same application again for six months.[26] After approval is received by the CIRC, an insurance company is required to complete its preparatory establishment work within six months. If a company is unable to complete its preparatory establishment work within the six-month period, the approval documents are automatically invalid if an extension is not received by the CIRC.[27]

b. Business Commencement Stage

After the completion of the preparatory establishment stage, an insurance company may file an application with the CIRC for approval to commence its business operations. An application for approval must be submitted with capital verification certificates including the original proof of deposit of working capital funds, resumés of key management personnel for the China operation, documentary evidence demonstrating the right to use the intended business premises, articles of association,[28] reinsurance program, and other information requested by the CIRC.[29] The CIRC is required to evaluate and render a decision on an application to commence business operations within six months of filing by the insurance company.[30] If the application is approved,

24. Insurance Regulations, art. 12.

25. Insurance Law, art. 74; Insurance Regulations, art. 10.

26. Insurance Regulations, art. 11.

27. Insurance Regulations, art. 12. If an extension of time is received, the insurance company must complete its preparatory work within one year.

28. Insurance Regulations, art. 13 § (5). The articles of association are required to be in compliance with the Insurance Law and the Company Law. The articles must include details about the insurance company's operating policy, business scope, organizational structure, business management, registered capital, business premises, and liquidation procedures.

29. Insurance Law, art. 75; Insurance Regulations, art. 13.

30. Insurance Law, art. 76.

the CIRC will issue an insurance business permit to the insurance company.[31] The insurance company is then required to obtain a business license from the SAIC.[32] An insurance company may engage in business activities only after it has been issued a business license.[33]

An insurance company is required to obtain the approval of the CIRC if it intends to increase or reduce the amount of its registered capital, adjust its share ownership, alter its organizational structure, adjust business scope, change its name, amend its articles of association, or change its business premises.[34] If an insurance company intends to replace the chairman of the board of directors of the China operation or its general manager, approval must be received from the CIRC.[35] An insurance company is also required to obtain the approval of the CIRC to terminate its business operations.[36] If an insurance company terminates its operation, the insurance business permit is automatically revoked.[37]

c. Branch Office Approval Standards

An insurance company applying to establish a branch office or representative office must obtain the approval of the CIRC.[38] An insurance company may operate only in approved regions and cities and employ agents that are

31. Insurance Law, art. 77. An insurance business permit is a legal certificate authorizing an insurance company to undertake insurance business. Insurance business permits are divided into two categories: an insurance organization license and a permit for operating an insurance business. The CIRC has the exclusive right to design, print, issue, confiscate, and revoke insurance business permits. A permit includes the original and a duplicate and sets forth the name of the organization, the nature and organizational structure of the insurance company, amount of registered capital or working capital, names of the legal representative and principal senior management, business scope, date of issue, and term of validity. An insurance company is required to display the original of its insurance business permit in a prominent position at its business premises. The duplicate is required to be placed for safekeeping in a separate location but available for inspection. It is prohibited to forge, alter, lease, lend, assign, or sell a permit. A permit must be renewed every three years. If the permit is lost, the insurance company is required to issue a public notice in a newspaper designated by the CIRC within fifteen days of discovering the loss. Insurance Regulations, arts. 34–39.

32. Insurance Law, art. 77. An insurance business permit expires in six months if the company fails to complete registration procedures with the SAIC. *Id.* at 78.

33. Insurance Regulations, art. 14.

34. Insurance Law, arts. 82, 85; Insurance Regulations, art. 18. Engaging in activities without approval of CIRC with respect to any item requiring approval by law subjects the insurance company to fines ranging from RMB10,000 to RMB100,000. Insurance Law, art. 144.

35. Insurance Law, art. 82.

36. Insurance Law, arts. 86, 87–90; Insurance Regulations, art. 19. The Insurance Law sets forth a number of special provisions for insolvent companies and bankruptcy procedures. Distributions from the bankruptcy estate of an insurance company are in the following priority order: bankruptcy expenses, wages and employment benefits to employees, compensation to claimants, taxes, and company debts. Insurance Law, art. 88. Matters concerning company establishment, alteration, dissolution, and liquidation are subject to the provisions of the Company Law, FIE Liquidation Procedures, and Bankruptcy Law. Insurance Law, art. 91. *See generally* Chapter 4, FIE Organizational Structure and Approval Procedures § D.1.; Chapter 20, Enterprise Liquidation, Reorganization, and Bankruptcy § B.

37. Insurance Law, art. 90.

38. Insurance Law, arts. 80–81. An insurance company may apply to establish a branch, a sub-branch, or a liaison office. The difference between the three types of "branch" offices is determined by the activities, staffing needs, and level of anticipated business of the individual office.

approved by the CIRC.[39] A branch, sub-branch, or liaison office of an insurance company does not have separate corporate status, and all civil liability created by a branch is borne by the insurance company. Approval for a branch is predicated on demonstrating that the insurance company has been operating for at least one year with a good financial performance record and no record of any serious violations of the laws and regulations.[40] The Insurance Regulations provide that an insurance company may apply to establish a branch based upon increases in the amount of its premium proceeds.[41] An insurance company may establish the following types of branch offices based upon the following premium increases:

(1) RMB100 million: Establish a company branch within its own operational region.
(2) RMB50 million: Establish a sub-branch within its own area of jurisdiction.
(3) RMB20 million: Establish a liaison office within its own area of jurisdiction.

An insurance company may establish only one company branch within any one city in China. An insurance company's sub-branch may apply to change its name from a sub-branch to a branch office if its premium proceeds reach RMB40 million, and a liaison office may apply to change its name to a sub-branch office if its premium proceeds reach RMB10 million.[42] The Insurance Regulations require that the branch office's name identify the location and whether the organization is a branch, sub-branch, or liaison office.[43] An insurance company that has not established branch offices may engage in business activities only from its registered premises.[44]

B. Scope of Operations

An insurance company is prohibited from engaging in both personal insurance and property insurance at the same time. The scope of business of a property insurance company is limited to property loss insurance, liability insurance, credit insurance, agricultural insurance, and other forms of property insurance matters.[45] Property insurance carriers may also engage in reinsurance of property-related insurance business. The scope of business for

39. Insurance Regulations, arts. 54, 58. An insurance company is also prohibited from accepting business from unlicensed agents. *Id.* at 54.
40. Insurance Regulations, art. 5 § (6).
41. Insurance Regulations, art. 6.
42. Insurance Regulations, art. 7.
43. Insurance Regulations, art. 16.
44. Insurance Regulations, art. 17.
45. Insurance Regulations, arts. 20, 21.

a personal insurance company includes life insurance, accidental injury insurance, and health insurance.[46] A personal insurance company may also engage in reinsurance of personal-related insurance business. A company involved in the reinsurance business may handle both domestic and international reinsurance matters.

The CIRC approves of the different types of product categories for sale by insurance companies. The Insurance Regulations list the different categories of products including the following:

Property Insurance Categories

Basic risk property insurance
Comprehensive risk property insurance
All risk construction project insurance
All risk installation project insurance
Machinery damage insurance
Shipbuilding insurance
Foreign-related property insurance
All risk foreign-related property insurance

Transport Insurance Categories

Motorized vehicle insurance
Tractor insurance
Vessel insurance
Fishing vessel insurance
Aircraft insurance
Automobile insurance
Coastal and inland river boat insurance

Freight Transport Insurance Categories

Domestic freight transport insurance
Ocean freight transport insurance
Land freight transport insurance
Container insurance
Parcel post insurance

Liability Insurance Categories

Third-party liability insurance
Public liability insurance
Employer liability insurance

46. Insurance Regulations, art. 22.

Product liability insurance
Credit card insurance

Guarantee Insurance Categories

Investment insurance
Guarantee and compensation insurance
Employer loyalty guarantee insurance

Life Insurance Categories

Basic life insurance
Welfare, life, safety, and health insurance
Collective (group) personal insurance
Collective (group) life insurance
Children's education and marriage insurance

Injury Insurance Categories

Personal accident injury insurance
Collective (group) accident injury insurance

Health Insurance Categories

Sickness and medical insurance

An insurance company may apply to the CIRC for a new category of insurance product. The Insurance Regulations provide that a company that develops a new product is entitled to be awarded a six-month "protection period" that prohibits competitors from marketing or offering the same or similar type of product.[47]

An insurance company operating in China may apply to the State Administration of Foreign Exchange (SAFE) for approval to engage in foreign-currency–based insurance transactions.[48] If approved to engage in FOREX business, SAFE will issue an insurance company a special license to engage in foreign currency transactions. Approval will be granted only if the applicant has satisfied its registered capital requirements, established proper internal controls for FOREX-based business, and employed personnel that meet the qualifications of SAFE.

47. Insurance Regulations, art. 45. An insurance company may also obtain trademark and copyright protection. *See* Chapter 14, Intellectual Property §§ A, B.

48. *See* Provisional Regulations on Foreign Exchange Administration for Insurance Industry (promulgated on September 24, 2002, by SAFE and the China Insurance Regulatory Commission), *reprinted in* China Laws for Foreign Business (CCH), Business Regulation ¶ 9-670. *See also* Notice Concerning Intra-Company Lending of Foreign Exchange by Insurance Companies within China (issued on September 1, 2003, by the State Administration of Foreign Exchange) (permits intra-company foreign exchange lending in insurance industry, and with loan terms limited to four months and aggregate principal amounts not to exceed 50% of the toal FOREX capital of the borrower or lender).

C. Administration of Insurance Funds

An insurance company is required to maintain certain funds, including a guarantee fund, a reserve fund, an accumulation fund, a public welfare fund, and other funds that may be required by the CIRC.[49] The Insurance Regulations place restrictions on the allocation and use of the various funds, including the types of investments that may be purchased or designated by insurance funds.[50] A failure to allocate the required funds, or to use the funds for an improper purpose, subjects an insurance company to penalties and potential revocation of its insurance business permit.[51]

1. Guarantee Funds

Upon receipt of an insurance business permit, a company is required to deposit 20 percent of its registered capital in a bank designated by the CIRC as guarantee funds. An insurance company is also required to allocate 1 percent of its annual insurance premiums to its guarantee fund. Allocations to the guarantee fund may cease when the fund reaches 10 percent of the total assets of the insurance company.[52] The insurance company may not use the guarantee funds for any purpose other than payment of debts upon liquidation.[53]

2. Reserve Funds

An insurance company is required to set aside a portion of its premiums to cover unmatured liability claims made by insureds. With respect to property-related insurance, the reserve fund allocations must not be less

49. Insurance Regulations, art. 24.

50. Insurance Law, art. 105; Insurance Regulations, art. 33. CIRC permits the establishment of insurance asset management companies (IAMC). For a discussion concerning the standards for an IAMC, *see infra* § K Insurance Asset Management Companies. The types of permissible investments include bank savings, trading in government bonds, trading in financial bonds, and other investments approved by the State Council. An insurance company may not use its reserve funds to establish a securities trading operation or to invest in enterprises. Insurance Law, art. 105. The CIRC has the discretion to supervise and regulate the types of investments for company funds and the specific percentages of company premiums and profits allocated to the funds. *See also* Administration of Insurance Company Investment in Corporate Bonds (promulgated by the China Insurance Regulatory Commission in 2003) (provisions expand the investment channels open to insurers by permitting insurance companies to invest up to 20% of the value of their total assets in corporate bonds rated AA and higher, and limits the amount of a bond issue that an insurance company may acquire to 15% of the total bond issue or an amount equal to 2% of the value of its total assets); Notice Concerning Intra-Company Lending of Foreign Exchange by Insurance Companies within China (issued on September 1, 2003, by the State Administration of Foreign Exchange) (rules permit foreign and domestic insurers to make intra-company FOREX loans with terms limited to four months and aggregate principal amounts not to exceed 50% of the total FOREX capital of the borrower or lender).

51. Insurance Law, art. 110.

52. Insurance Law, arts. 79, 97; Insurance Regulations, art. 32.

53. Insurance Law, art. 79; Insurance Regulations, art. 26.

than 50 percent of the insurance premiums generated annually.[54] The allocations for life insurance reserve funds are based upon the total net value of all its valid life insurance policies. An insurance company is required to set aside additional reserve funds for pending compensation claims.[55]

3. Accumulation Fund

An insurance company is required to establish an accumulation fund to cover its losses, expand its business operations, or to increase its capital fund. An insurance company is required to allocate the first 10 percent of its after-tax profit to the accumulation fund. A company may cease to contribute to the accumulation fund when the fund amounts to 50 percent or more of the company's registered capital.[56] In contrast to guarantee funds, an insurance company may draw from its accumulation fund at its discretion, subject to a favorable resolution adopted at a meeting of the shareholders. If, with the approval of the shareholders a company transfers its accumulation fund into its capital fund, the amount of shares held by shareholders will increase proportionately. The company cannot reduce its accumulation fund to less than 25 percent of the company's registered capital.[57]

4. Public Welfare Fund

A company is required to establish a public welfare fund on behalf of, and for the benefit of, its employees. An insurance company is required to allocate between 5 percent and 10 percent of its after-tax profit to the public welfare fund.[58]

D. Reinsurance Requirements

An insurance company is required to reinsure 20 percent of its business to reduce its risks.[59] In the past, reinsurance was not an established practice but has gained acceptance in recent years with the domestic reinsurance market having established ties to the international reinsurance market. The CIRC has the right to restrict or prohibit an insurance company from conducting reinsurance business with firms outside of China.[60] In this regard, the CIRC

54. Insurance Law, art. 94; Insurance Regulations, art. 27.
55. Insurance Law, art. 95; Insurance Regulations, art. 28.
56. Insurance Law, art. 96; Insurance Regulations, arts. 29, 30.
57. Insurance Regulations, art. 30.
58. Insurance Regulations, art. 29.
59. Insurance Law, arts. 29, 30, 102; Insurance Regulations, art. 62.
60. Insurance Law, art. 104. Prior to China's entry in the WTO, the government restricted the foreign reinsurers from doing business in the domestic market. Linn, *Cautious China Makes Reinsurers Wait,*

requires that domestic insurance companies be given priority for reinsurance business. An insurance company must first attempt to obtain reinsurance through companies based in China and may procure reinsurance from an overseas firm only if a domestic company declines to provide reinsurance or if an overseas insurance company offers terms that are "significantly better" than the domestic company.[61]

The original insurance company, the reinsurance assignor, is required to provide the reinsurance assignee with all information concerning the original insurance policy. Both the reinsurance assignor and assignee are required to maintain the confidentiality of the information concerning the policyholder.[62] The reinsurance assignee is prohibited from demanding that the policyholder pay premiums, and the insured and the beneficiary are not allowed to lodge a claim for compensation with the reinsurance assignee.[63] The original insurer may not refuse to perform its obligations under the original insurance contract, including the payment of claims, on the grounds that the reinsurance assignee has not performed its reinsurance obligations.

CIRC has adopted regulations concerning the establishment of reinsurance companies.[64] The regulations provide that foreign insurance companies may establish businesses in China as joint ventures or WFOEs so long as they comply with the WTO commitments.[65] The minimum registered capital requirement for life reinsurance companies and nonlife reinsurance companies is no less than RMB200 million, and the minimum registered capital requirement for comprehensive reinsurance companies is no less than RMB300 million.[66]

E. Internal Control, Reports, Record Keeping, and Inspection

The CIRC requires that insurance companies maintain a system of internal controls including procedures for financial controls, claims investigations

J. OF COMMERCE 6A (Feb. 8, 1999), available on Lexis, News Library. *See generally* Golden, *Market Report: China & Hong Kong, Preparing for the Great Leap Forward,* REINSURANCE MAGAZINE, p. 12 (Feb. 3, 1999); Leonard, *China Rings in the Changes,* REINSURANCE MAGAZINE, p. 15 (Feb. 3, 1999) (discusses the institutional changes in China's insurance regulatory environment and the impact on reinsurers), both available on Lexis, News Library.

61. Insurance Regulations, art. 64.

62. Insurance Law, arts. 29, 32.

63. Insurance Law, art. 30.

64. Regulations on Establishment of Reinsurance Companies (Order No. 4 [2002], promulgated on September 17, 2002, by the China Insurance Regulatory Commission), *reprinted in* CHINA LAWS FOR FOREIGN BUSINESS (CCH), Business Regulation ¶ 9-660. *See also* Y. Li, *Reinsurance: New Area Open for Foreign Investment,* CHINA L. & PRAC. 63 (Nov. 2002).

65. CIRC Reinsurance Regulations, art. 7.

66. CIRC Reinsurance Regulations, art. 5.

and payments, actuarial activities, insurance contract management, and reinsurance.[67] An insurance company is also required to maintain its accounting and other records for at least ten years after the termination of any particular insurance contract.[68] A failure to maintain and produce accounting records and reports may result in monetary penalties.[69] An insurance company that prepares and submits false accounts and reports is subject to heavy penalties and potential criminal prosecution.[70]

An insurance company is required to undergo an annual inspection of its books and records by the CIRC.[71] In general, the reporting requirements provide that an insurance company submit information concerning its annual compensation rates, premium rates, and losses or profits with respect to its insurance products. The CIRC conducts its annual inspections during the first quarter of the calendar year. Upon receipt of notice of inspection, an insurance company is required to present an inspection report and accounting records to the CIRC within fifteen days. In addition to the annual inspection, the CIRC has the authority to inspect the records of an insurance company at any time and without notice. A refusal to submit to the supervision of the CIRC exposes an insurance company to monetary penalties, loss of insurance business permit, and criminal penalties.[72]

F. Insurance Contracts

Under the Insurance Law, a property insurance contract is defined as an agreement in which the insurer receives premiums and agrees to pay compensation for property losses caused by an occurrence involving an insurable event agreed upon in the contract.[73] The parties to an insurance contract are required to observe the principles of fairness, mutual benefit, and mutual consent, and shall "not harm the public interest."[74] When an insurance contract is concluded, the policyholder is required to pay the insurance premium and thereafter the insurer assumes liability under the contract.[75] A policyholder has the right to terminate an insurance contract at any time but an

67. Guiding Principles on the Improvement of the Internal Controls of Financial Institutions (promulgated on May 16, 1997, by the PBOC), art. 13, *reprinted in* CHINA LAWS FOR FOREIGN BUSINESS (CCH), Business Regulation ¶ 8-455 (hereinafter the "PBOC Internal Control Principles").
68. Insurance Law, art. 124; Insurance Regulations, art. 47.
69. Insurance Law, art. 146.
70. Insurance Law, art. 147.
71. Insurance Law, arts. 109, 119; Insurance Regulations, arts. 65–68.
72. Insurance Law, art. 147 § (2).
73. Insurance Law, art. 2.
74. Insurance Law, art. 11. The Law also prohibits a government unit or official from coercing a person to enter into an insurance contract except if required by law.
75. Insurance Law, art. 14.

insurance company is prohibited from terminating the contract, except if otherwise provided for by law or under the parties' contract.[76]

1. Mandatory Contract Language

Insurance contracts are required to be in writing and, if issued in China, are required to be printed in Chinese. A foreign language version may be attached if necessary but the Chinese language version is controlling.[77] The CIRC has developed form clauses that are required to be used in insurance contracts. An insurance company may submit sample contract language for approval to the CIRC.[78]

The Insurance Law requires that insurance contracts contain certain mandatory language, including the following:

(1) Name and address of the insurer
(2) Names and addresses of the insurance policyholder and the insured party and the name and address of the beneficiary, if any
(3) Insured subject matter
(4) Insurance liability and liability exemptions
(5) Insurance period and the time of commencement of insurance liability
(6) Insured value
(7) The total sum insured
(8) Insurance premium and method of payment
(9) Methods of paying compensation or claims
(10) Liability for breach of contract and dispute resolution
(11) The date the contract is executed[79]

The parties to an insurance contract may stipulate to other terms and conditions in an insurance contract in addition to the mandatory terms. The parties to an insurance contract may amend an original contract during the policy period, but any amendments are required to be in writing.[80]

2. Exclusions

An exclusion or exemption is required to be in written form and is not binding on a policyholder unless the insurance company clearly provides notice

76. Insurance Law, arts. 15, 16.
77. Insurance Regulations, art. 40.
78. Insurance Regulations, art. 42. Proposed language is deemed to be approved if the CIRC does not raise objections within thirty days.
79. Insurance Law, art. 19.
80. Insurance Law, art. 21.

of the exclusion or exemption to the policyholder's attention at the time of entering into a contract.[81]

3. Property Insurance Contracts

The insured party is required to notify the insurer if the insured subject matter is transferred to another party. The insured value of the insured subject matter may be agreed upon by the policyholder and the insurer and specified in the contract. If not specified, the insured value of the property is determined on the basis of actual value at the time of the occurrence of the insured event.[82] The policy limits may not exceed the insured value of the property, and any claim in excess of the policy limits is invalid.

The insured party is required to observe all State laws and regulations concerning labor protection, production operation, safety, and other relevant standards affecting the insured subject matter. The insurance company has a right to inspect the insured subject matter to verify that the policyholder is abiding by safety standards and may increase the insurance premiums or terminate the contract if the policyholder fails to ensure the safety of the insured subject matter.[83] If there is an increase in the degree of risk to the insured subject matter within the policy period, the policyholder is required to advise the insurer. An insurer is not liable for a claim if it results from an increased degree of risk that the policyholder failed to bring to the attention of the insurance company.[84]

G. Insurance Premium Rates

The CIRC is responsible for setting insurance premium rates.[85] The rates set by the CIRC take into account both international rates, market conditions,

81. Insurance Law, art. 18. The Contract Law places the burden on a party providing "standardized clauses" to "remind the other party to pay attention to any clauses which release or limit its liabilities" and "shall explain the clauses if requested by the other party." Contract Law, art. 39. The definition of "standardized clauses" are "clauses which have been drafted in advance by a party for repeated use." The Contract Law also provides that attempts to release a party from its obligations or designed to deny the other party certain critical rights, is invalid. If a dispute arises concerning the understanding of a standardized clause, the Contract Law provides that the clause will be interpreted against the party that provided the contractual language. In the event of a discrepancy between a standardized clause and a nonstandardized clause, the nonstandardized clause shall prevail. *Id.* arts. 41–42, 53. This rule is recognized in the Insurance Law concerning the interpretation of standard insurance contracts. *See* Insurance Law, art. 30. The Contract Law provides that a provision that seeks to exempt a party from liability as a result of intentional misconduct or gross negligence, which results in loss of property or bodily injury to the other party, is invalid. Contract Law, art. 53.

82. Insurance Law, art. 40.

83. Insurance Law, art. 36.

84. Insurance Law, art. 37.

85. Insurance Law, art. 107; Insurance Regulations, art. 41.

and the rates applied by the People's Insurance Company of China (PICC). Insurance companies are allowed to charge premiums based upon regional standards set by the CIRC that outline a range of rates for the different types of product categories. The actual premium charged may not be greater or less than 30 percent of the regional standards.[86]

An insurance company is prohibited from providing a policyholder, an insured party, or a beneficiary with a premium rebate or other benefits that are not specifically provided for in the insurance contract.[87] An insurer is required to reimburse any unused premiums if the policyholder requests the termination of the contract before the end of the contract term.[88] An insurer is required, except where otherwise agreed to in the insurance contract, to reduce the premium on a property insurance contract if the value of the insured subject matter, or the degree of risk to the insured subject matter, is significantly reduced.[89]

H. Insurance Agents and Brokers

Chapter 6 of the Insurance Law sets forth the standards for insurance agents and brokers.[90] An insurance agent is a party that handles business for an insurance company and is paid a commission by the insurer. A life insurance agent is prohibited from accepting commissions from more than two insurers concurrently.[91] An insurance broker, on the other hand, works in the interests of a policyholder, and provides intermediary services between the insured party and the insurer.[92] The broker is also entitled to a commission for its work.

An insurer is responsible for the acts of its insurance agents that handle insurance business on its behalf and is required to establish a register of its insurance agents.[93] An insurance broker, on the other hand, is liable for compensation of any losses incurred by an insured party due to its errors

86. Insurance Regulations, art. 46.
87. Insurance Regulations, art. 55.
88. Insurance Law, art. 39.
89. Insurance Law, art. 38.
90. Insurance Law, arts. 125–37. *See also* Administrative Regulations on Insurance Brokerage Companies (promulgated on January 1, 2002, by the China Insurance Regulatory Commission); an unofficial translation is available on the Web site of the U.S./China Business Council at http://www.uschina.org (outlining standards for establishment of insurance brokerage business, professional qualifications, administrative issues, regulatory supervision and penalties, etc.) (hereinafter referred to as "CIRC Insurance Brokerage Regulations"); Public Announcement of China Insurance Regulatory Commission on the Procedures for Examination and Approval of Insurance Agency Companies and Insurance Assessment Companies (issued on Sept. 13, 2001, by the CIRC).
91. Insurance Law, art. 129.
92. Insurance Law, art. 126.
93. Insurance Law, art. 128.

and omissions.[94] Both an agent and a broker are prohibited from concealing material information related to insurance contracts from the policyholder, improperly influencing or forcing a party to enter into an insurance contract, or promising a rebate of an insurance premium and other benefits not provided for in the insurance contract.[95]

Both agents and brokers are required to obtain operation permits to act as agents or brokers from the CIRC and are required to submit to the inspection and supervision of the CIRC, including a requirement to file business, financial, and accounting reports on an annual basis.[96] Brokers and agents are also required to obtain a business license from the SAIC and to purchase professional liability coverage or deposit guarantee funds.[97] CIRC requires the use of the language "insurance brokerage" in the legal title of the company.[98] Any party that conducts business as a broker or agent without authorization is subject to monetary penalties, including a confiscation of illegal proceeds.[99]

The minimum registered capital requirement for brokerage firms is RMB10 million, and at least one-half of the company personnel are required to be qualified and certified for insurance brokerage business.[100] CIRC is required to approve or reject an application within thirty days and shall provide a written explanation if the application is rejected.[101] The approval of CIRC is required for any dissolution, merger, bankruptcy, or amendments to the scope of business, shareholders, or management of a brokerage company.[102] A license to operate an insurance brokerage business is valid for three years and must be renewed within sixty days prior to expiration.[103]

I. Claims Procedures

A policyholder, the insured party, and the beneficiary under a policy are required to promptly notify an insurer of the occurrence of any events under the insurance policy triggering coverage.[104] A claim under an insurance contract, other than life insurance, must be exercised within two years from

94. Insurance Law, art. 130; CIRC Insurance Brokerage Regulations, art. 7.

95. Insurance Law, arts. 106, 131. An insurance broker and agent is subject to administrative and criminal penalties for violating his or her duties.

96. Insurance Law, arts. 119, 133.

97. Insurance Law, art. 132.

98. CIRC Insurance Brokerage Regulations, art. 11.

99. Insurance Law, art. 149. A CIRC official that improperly approves of a broker/agent license is subject to criminal prosecution.

100. CIRC Insurance Brokerage Regulations, arts. 10, 13–14. The professional qualifications for brokerage company staff is outlined in articles 28–39 of the CIRC regulations.

101. CIRC Insurance Brokerage Regulations, art. 18.

102. CIRC Insurance Brokerage Regulations, art. 26.

103. CIRC Insurance Brokerage Regulations, art. 25.

104. Insurance Law, art. 22.

the date of the insurable event or occurrence.[105] A claim under a life insurance contract must be made within five years from the date of the death of the insured party.[106] The insurer is required to pay all necessary and reasonable expenses incurred by both the insurer and the insured party in the investigation and determination of the nature and cause of and the degree of the loss caused by the insured event.[107] The insurer is also required to defend an insured party, and pay all litigation or arbitration expenses incurred in the defense of any claim lodged against an insured party.[108]

The policyholder, the insured party, and the beneficiary have a duty, to the best of their ability, to provide to the insurer all "relevant evidence and information for the determination of the nature and cause of and degree of loss relating from the insured event."[109] If the insured party or the beneficiary lodges a false claim, including a claim based upon the falsification of documents, the staging of an occurrence, or the exaggeration of losses, the insurer has the right to terminate the insurance contract and refuse to refund any premium paid.[110] Any compensation paid on a false claim is required to be refunded or reimbursed to the insurer.

In the event of an occurrence of an insured event, the policyholder is required to take all necessary measures to prevent or reduce additional loss or damage. The insurer is required to reimburse a policyholder for any mitigation expenses incurred to prevent or reduce losses sustained by the insured subject matter. The amount borne by the insurer shall be in addition to any claims paid with respect to the loss but shall not exceed the policy limits.[111]

An insurance company must promptly adjust a claim for compensation from the insured party or beneficiary. If a claim is legitimate, the insurance company must settle the claim within ten days of reaching an agreement on the matter with the insured party or beneficiary.[112] If the insurance company fails to adhere to the terms of the insurance contract, it is liable for the economic loss of the insured party or beneficiary if a payment on a claim is delayed.[113] An insurance company is required to make an advanced payment within sixty days of a claim that has not been fully determined. The balance is due when the insurance company completes its investigation.[114] The insurance

105. Insurance Law, art. 27.
106. Insurance Law, art. 27.
107. Insurance Law, art. 49.
108. Insurance Law, art. 51.
109. Insurance Law, art. 23.
110. Insurance Law, art. 28.
111. Insurance Law, art. 42.
112. Insurance Law, art. 24.
113. Insurance Law, art. 24; Insurance Regulations, art. 59.
114. Insurance Law, art. 26; Insurance Regulations, art. 60.

company is liable for damages for economic loss if it refuses to pay for a claim, or any portion of a claim, that is not in dispute. The insurer is required to issue a notice of refusal to honor a claim for matters not covered under the policy.[115]

An insurance company has a right to investigate and inspect the insured subject matter and to obtain information concerning the policyholder, prior to entering into an insurance contract.[116] An insurance company has the right to terminate a contract, as well as the right to refuse payment of a claim, if the policyholder conceals or fails to disclose material facts concerning the insured subject matter.[117] If a failure to disclose is willful, the insurer has the right to refuse reimbursement of any premiums paid by the policyholder.

An insurance company has a right of subrogation against a third party that may be responsible for damage to the insured subject matter.[118] The insured party has a duty to assist an insurance company in its subrogation efforts.[119] An insurer may not seek subrogation from the insured party's family members, except for losses that are deliberately caused by family members of the insured party.[120] The insurer's right of subrogation does not affect the insured party's right to claim compensation against a third party for injury or damages. The insurer, however, has a right of reimbursement for any monies that the insured party may receive from a third party for the loss or damage.[121]

The people's court and arbitration tribunals have a statutory duty to "make an interpretation favorable to the insured party or the beneficiary" in all disputes concerning the terms of an insurance contract.[122] This principle is consistent with the rule of *contra proferentem* recognized by various jurisdictions in the United States.[123]

J. Regulation of Foreign-Invested Insurance Companies

The State Council has adopted regulations concerning the administration of foreign-invested insurance companies in China.[124] The FIE Insurance

115. Insurance Law, art. 25.
116. Insurance Law, art. 17.
117. Insurance Law, art. 17.
118. Insurance Law, art. 45.
119. Insurance Law, art. 48.
120. Insurance Law, art. 47.
121. Insurance Law, art. 45.
122. Insurance Law, art. 31.
123. *See* 2 G. Couch, R. Anderson, and M. Rhodes, *Couch on Insurance 2d*, § 15.83, at 399 n. 4 (rev. ed. 1984) (citing cases from the District of Columbia and 47 states, with no cases cited for a contrary position); *Kunin v. Benefit Trust Life Ins. Co.*, 910 F.2d 534 (9th Cir. 1990); *Lang v. Long Term Disability Plan*, 125 F.3d 794, 799 (9th Cir. 1997).
124. Regulations of the People's Republic of China on the Administration of Foreign Investment Insurance Companies (Order No. 336 of the State Council of the People's Republic of China, adopted

Regulations were effective February 1, 2002. The FIE Insurance Regulations define "foreign investment insurance companies" to refer to the following insurance companies, which have been given approval to establish themselves and operate in China's territory in accordance with the relevant laws and administrative regulations of the People's Republic of China:

(1) Insurance companies jointly operated by foreign insurance companies and Chinese companies or enterprises within Chinese territory (hereinafter referred to as "joint-venture insurance companies")
(2) Foreign-capital insurance companies invested and operated by foreign insurance companies within Chinese territory (hereinafter referred to as "wholly foreign-owned insurance companies")
(3) Subsidiaries of foreign insurance companies operating within Chinese territory (hereinafter referred to as "subsidiaries of foreign insurance companies")[125]

The FIE Insurance Regulations provide that FIE insurance companies receive the full protection of Chinese law, and are required to follow the law and "must not infringe upon the social and public interests of China."[126] The China Insurance Regulatory Commission is responsible for the supervision and administration of FIE insurance companies, and all applications for establishing an FIE insurance company must be approved by CIRC or one of its branch offices.[127]

December 5, 2001 by the 49th Executive Meeting of the State Council, promulgated December 12, 2001, effective from February 1, 2002), *reprinted in* CHINA LAWS FOR FOREIGN BUSINESS (CCH), Business Regulation ¶ 9-650 (hereinafter referred to as "FIE Insurance Regulations"). Where the FIE Insurance Regulations do not make stipulations in respect of the administration of foreign investment insurance companies, the *Insurance Law of the People's Republic of China,* other relevant laws, regulations, and other State regulations shall apply. FIE Insurance Regulations, art. 38. These Regulations are also applicable to insurance companies from Hong Kong Special Administrative Region, Macao Special Administrative Region, and Taiwan region that are established and operating in mainland China. FIE Insurance Regulations, art. 39. In 2004, CIRC adopted regulations concerning the administration of representative offices for foreign insurance institutions, which replace the 1999 regulations on the same topic. *See* Management Rules for Foreign Insurance Organizations (issued on January 15, 2004, by the China Insurance Regulatory Commission, and effective on March 1, 2004) (outlines the procedures for registering and establishing foreign insurance company representative offices). *See also* Implementation Regulations for the Regulations of the People's Republic of China on Administration of Foreign Investment Insurance Companies (promulgated on May 13, 2004, by the China Insurance Regulatory Commission), *reprinted in* China Laws for Foreign Business, Business Regulation ¶ 9-651 (provides details on administrative procedures and standards for FIE insurance companies and applications procedures).

125. FIE Insurance Regulations, art. 2.
126. FIE Insurance Regulations, art. 3.
127. FIE Insurance Regulations, arts. 4, 5.

1. Registration and Establishment

The registered capital of a JV and WFOE FIE insurance company is required to be a minimum of RMB200 million or the equivalent in convertible currency. The minimum registered capital must be the actual cash contribution and not other forms of registered capital items such as technology. The capital invested by a foreign investor shall be in convertible currency. The regulations provide that CIRC reserves the right to increase the minimum registered capital or minimum operational capital on the basis of the scope and scale of business of the FIE.[128]

A foreign insurance company applying for the establishment of an FIE insurance company in China is required to meet the following conditions:

(1) Having conducted insurance business for more than thirty years
(2) Having already established representative offices within the Chinese territory for more than two years
(3) One year before applying for the establishment, having had a total capital of no less than $5 billion by the end of the year
(4) The country or region to which the foreign insurance company is based shall have a complete system regarding the supervision and administration of insurance business, and the foreign insurance company shall already be under the effective supervision and administration of the responsible authorities of the country or region
(5) Having met the criteria of possessing the capacity to indemnify as specified by the country or region to which the company is based
(6) Having obtained the approval for the application from the country or region
(7) Other precautionary conditions as stipulated by the CIRC[129]

In support of its application for approval of an FIE insurance company, an applicant is required to submit the following data to CIRC for examination:

(1) A *preliminary application form* signed by the legal representative of the applicant; where there is an application for the establishment of a joint-venture insurance company, the application form shall be jointly signed by the legal representatives of the parties in the joint venture
(2) The business license (copies), and certificate proving that the applicant meets the criteria of having the capacity to indemnify, and an

128. FIE Insurance Regulations, art. 7. The potential to increase the minimum registered capital requirements leaves open the possibility of abuse and capricious actions by regulatory authorities.
129. FIE Insurance Regulations, art. 8.

opinion regarding the application issued by the responsible departments of the country or region to which a foreign applicant is based

(3) Articles of association of the foreign insurance company and the annual reports of the preceding three years
(4) Where there is an application for the establishment of a joint venture insurance company, relevant data concerning the Chinese applicant
(5) A feasibility study report and preparation plan regarding the proposed company
(6) A list of the persons in charge of the preparations for the proposed company, their resumes, and certificates of their qualifications
(7) Other materials that the CIRC requires to be submitted[130]

Upon receipt of the application materials, the CIRC shall conduct an initial examination of the application for the establishment of a proposed foreign investment insurance company. The CIRC shall decide whether or not to accept the application within six months from the date of receipt. Where the CIRC decides to accept an application, it shall issue a *formal application form* to the applicant. If an application is rejected, CIRC is required to issue a written notice to the applicant and explain the reasons for the rejection.[131]

After receiving preliminary approval, an applicant for an FIE insurance company is required to complete the establishment procedures within one year from the date of receiving the *formal application form*. In the event that an applicant is unable to complete the preparations for establishing the company within the time limit, upon application for an extension and based upon justified reasons, CIRC has the discretion to approve a one-time extension of up to three months. Where preparations are still not completed at the conclusion of the extension period, the CIRC decision of preliminary acceptance shall automatically terminate. After the completion of preparations, an applicant shall submit to the CIRC the completed application form together with the following documents:

(1) A preparation report
(2) The articles of association of the proposed company
(3) A list of investors and the amount of their investment
(4) Capital rating certificates issued by legal capital rating bodies
(5) A letter of authorization issued to the persons in charge of the proposed company

130. FIE Insurance Regulations, art. 9.

131. FIE Insurance Regulations, art. 10. The six-month time period for approval has been criticized by observers as a violation of China's WTO commitments given that it delays application approval.

(6) A list of the senior managers of the proposed company, their resumés, and certificates of their qualifications
(7) The business plans and coinsurance plans of the proposed company in the coming three years
(8) Statements on insurance clauses, insurance premiums, and the calculation of reserve funds for commitment of various insurance policies to be offered within Chinese territory
(9) The business venue of the proposed company and other data concerning facilities related to the insurance business
(10) Where a subsidiary of a foreign insurance company is to be established, a letter of guarantee issued by the head office to ensure that the head office is responsible for the tax and debts of the said subsidiary
(11) Where a joint-venture insurance company is to be established, the contracts concluded for joint operation
(12) Other documents required by the CIRC[132]

CIRC is required to approve or reject the formal application within sixty days of receipt of the application materials. If approved, CIRC will issue an operating permit for the FIE insurance company. If rejected, CIRC is required to notify the applicant in writing and explain the reasons for the rejection. When a foreign investment insurance company is approved, the applicant is required to complete the registration formalities with the administrative authorities responsible for industry and commerce and obtain a business license.[133]

After the establishment of an FIE insurance company, the company is required to deposit 20 percent of its registered capital or of the total operating capital as security in a bank specified by the CIRC. The security may not be withdrawn unless the FIE insurance company needs to pay debts with this security in the course of liquidation or as may be approved by CIRC.[134]

2. Scope of Business, Supervision, and Administration

Upon approval by CIRC, an FIE insurance company may engage in the business of insurance as defined by its approved business scope.[135] Unless otherwise approved by the SAFE, an FIE insurance company engaging in

132. FIE Insurance Regulations, art. 11.
133. FIE Insurance Regulations, art. 12.
134. FIE Insurance Regulations, art. 13.
135. FIE Insurance Regulations, arts. 14–18.

insurance business within Chinese territory is required to conduct business in Chinese currency.[136]

An FIE insurance company is subject to the supervision of CIRC, and CIRC has the right to conduct an examination of company records and activities, and to impose penalties for violations.[137] An FIE insurance company is also required to file an annual report with CIRC, and a special report is required to notify CIRC within ten days any of the following actions or circumstances:

(1) A change of name of the chief responsible person or the place of the registration
(2) A change of capital funds
(3) A change of the shareholders holding 10 percent of the entire capital sum or 10 percent of the total shares
(4) An adjustment of the business scope
(5) Any punishment imposed by the responsible authorities in the country or region to which the head office is based
(6) Any significant losses incurred
(7) A division, merger, dissolution, or the head office being closed down or declared bankrupt in accordance with the law[138]
(8) Other circumstances stipulated by the CIRC[139]

3. Termination and Liquidation

In the event that an FIE insurance company is to be dissolved as a result of a division, merger, or the provisions of articles of association, the company is required to obtain the approval for dissolution from CIRC. Companies in the life insurance business may be dissolved only through division or merger.[140]

A liquidation committee is required to be established by the FIE insurance company to handle liquidation matters. If CIRC revokes the license of an insurance company, CIRC will establish a liquidation committee to handle the company's liquidation affairs.[141] During the liquidation process, the

136. FIE Insurance Regulations, art. 24. If approved to conduct business in foreign currency, the company is required to abide by the State regulations concerning foreign exchange control.

137. FIE Insurance Regulations, arts. 19–20.

138. Where the head office of a foreign insurance subsidiary is dissolved, closed down, or declared bankrupt in accordance with the law, CIRC shall prohibit the said subsidiary from carrying out new business. FIE Insurance Regulations, art. 23.

139. FIE Insurance Regulations, arts. 21–22. Within three months after the end of each fiscal year, a subsidiary of a foreign insurance company is required to submit to CIRC the annual financial report of said company and its head office of the prior year, and shall publish the annual financial report. FIE Insurance Regulations, art. 22. Where, according to these Regulations, there are documentation, data, and written reports to be submitted to the CIRC, a Chinese-language version shall be submitted including all company annual reports. FIE Insurance Regulations, art. 25.

140. FIE Insurance Regulations, art. 26.

141. FIE Insurance Regulations, arts. 26–27.

liquidation committee is required to publish a public notice of intent to dissolve the company. The public notice must be published at least three times within sixty days of the date of establishing the liquidation committee, and the content of the notice must be approved by CIRC.[142]

In the event an FIE insurance company is unable to pay its debts, the people's court may declare the company bankrupt with the consent of CIRC. A bankrupt FIE insurance company is prohibited from transferring assets offshore prior to paying debts incurred on the Mainland.[143]

4. Legal Liabilities

The FIE Insurance Regulations provide that CIRC may impose a variety of monetary and nonmonetary sanctions for various offenses. In serious cases, CIRC is authorized to pursue criminal penalties against the operators. In cases involving the unauthorized establishment or operation of an FIE insurance company, CIRC may order the closure of the business and seize any illegal income received. CIRC may impose a fine of between two and five times of the illegal earnings. Where there are no illegal earnings or the illegal earnings are less than RMB200,000, a fine of between RMB200,000 and RMB1 million may be imposed.[144]

If an FIE insurance company is operating outside its approved business scope, territorial business scope, or the scope of service recipients to carry out insurance business activities, CIRC may order corrective action to be taken, order the refund of the collected insurance premium, confiscate the illegal earnings, and impose a fine between two and five times the illegal earnings. Where there are no illegal earnings or the illegal earnings are less than RMB100,000, a fine between RMB100,000 and RMB500,000 may be imposed. Where no corrective action is taken within the time limit or serious consequences are incurred, the CIRC shall order the company to close business or revoke the permit for operation of insurance business.[145]

142. FIE Insurance Regulations, art. 28.

143. FIE Insurance Regulations, arts. 29–30. Where a foreign investment insurance company violates the provisions of these Regulations and transfers its assets out of China, the CIRC may order the company to return the assets and impose a fine of up to 20 percent of the sum of the total transferred assets. FIE Insurance Regulations, art. 36.

144. FIE Insurance Regulations, art. 31. CIRC may bar a company's senior managers from working in China in the event of any violations of the law. FIE Insurance Regulations, art. 37. CIRC has issued warnings to Hong Kong and Macao insurance companies and agents that seek to sell policies on the Mainland without an approved branch office, and especially within the bordering Guangdong Province. *HK, Macao Insurers Warned,* CHINA DAILY (March 20, 2004) (article mentions that CIRC estimates that illegal sales proceeds from cross-border policy sales exceeds $1.3 million, and that CIRC intends to pursue civil and criminal penalties against violators).

145. FIE Insurance Regulations, art. 32.

CIRC may order corrective action, suspend an operator's permit, or impose a fine between RMB50,000 and RMB300,000, if a company engages in the following activities:

(1) The company fails to deposit a security or uses the security in violation of regulations
(2) The company conducts transactions with its associated enterprises in violation of regulations
(3) The company fails to make up for a shortfall of the registered capital or operational fund[146]

CIRC may order corrective action or impose a fine between RMB10,000 and RMB100,000, if a company engages in the following activities:

(1) The company fails to observe the regulations to submit or send relevant documentation, data, or written reports
(2) The company fails to make public announcements in accordance with the regulations[147]

CIRC may order corrective action or impose a fine between RMB100,000 and RMB500,000, if a company engages in the following activities:

(1) The documentation, data, or written reports provided by the company are false
(2) The company refuses or obstructs supervision or examination which is conducted in accordance with the law[148]

K. Insurance Asset Management Companies

To address the increased growth in insurance premiums and to give insurers more tools to increase their investment yields, CIRC adopted regulations in 2004 that allow for the establishment of insurance asset management companies (IAMC) by qualified domestic and foreign insurance companies.[149]

146. FIE Insurance Regulations, art. 33.

147. FIE Insurance Regulations, art. 34.

148. FIE Insurance Regulations, art. 35.

149. Insurance Asset Management Company Interim Regulations (issued on April 30, 2004, by the China Insurance Regulatory Commission). The regulations and press release are available in Chinese on the Web site of CIRC at http://www.circ.gov.cn. Insurance companies in China have increasingly pressured CIRC to allow for greater flexibility with respect to the investment options for insurance premium income. Insurance premium income in 2004 increased to RMB1 trillion ($120 billion) annually, an increase of one-third per year over the past years. The current practice in China is to have a separate asset management department within an insurance company, and the IAMC concept is to allow insurers added flexibility in managing their premium income assets. The use of IAMCs is more in line with international practices where most large insurance companies have IAMCs to manage their portfolios. CIRC has indicated that insurance companies will eventually be allowed to invest directly in stock and issue subordinate bonds to boost their capital base. *See More Investment Options for Insurers,* CHINA DAILY

In 2003–2004, CIRC approved IAMCs for four domestic companies, namely, the People's Insurance Company of China, China Life, Huatai Insurance, and Taikang Life Insurance.

Under the IAMC Regulations, a qualified applicant is required to meet the following conditions:

(1) The shareholder(s) of the IAMC shall include at least one entity that is qualified as an insurance company or insurance holding company
(2) The applicant(s) must have eight years of operational experience in the insurance industry in China and a "clean" record for at least three years
(3) The applicant(s) must have net assets of at least RMB1 billion ($120 million)
(4) The applicant(s) total assets must be at least RMB5 billion ($600 million)
(5) The IAMCs must have minimum registered capital of RMB30 million ($3.6 million)

Under the regulations, a foreign-invested insurance company may establish a WFOE IAMC; however, the rules forbid foreign investment of more than 25% in a domestic IAMC and therefore effectively prevent foreign insurance companies from assuming control of existing domestic IAMCs through equity purchase arrangements. Insurance companies may team up to establish asset management companies, and foreign and joint venture insurance companies are also allowed to set up asset management companies if conditions are met.

The IAMC Regulations do not allow insurance companies to use their IAMCs to broaden the scope of their investments. As with insurance company investments in general, IAMCs are also limited to investing in bank deposits, bonds, and mutual funds, although CIRC has indicated that further flexibility will be granted in the future. The Regulations provide that an IAMC can only manage and dispose of insurance-related assets and that no assets from other industries or investments may be part of the IAMC portfolio and specifically from the company's non-insurance shareholders. Nevertheless, CIRC maintains that the IAMC Regulations provide the tools to allow insurance companies to position themselves to tap into China's capital markets once the regulatory authorities permit such investments.[150]

(February 11, 2004). CIRC has also adopted risk management guidelines for IAMCs. *See* X. Zhang, *CIRC Releases Rules on Risk Prevention,* China Daily (May 10, 2004).

150. Z. Rengfeng, *Regulation on Insurance Asset Unveiled,* China Daily (April 26, 2004).

The IAMC Regulations provide that CIRC has three months to review an application to establish an IAMC and, after receipt of preliminary approval, the applicant has six months to complete the preparatory process. The Regulations outline the application procedures and documentation required.

The IAMC Regulations are a step in the right direction, but further flexibility of investment options for insurance companies is necessary to allow them to better manage their money and to increase their potential yield.

Key Laws and Regulations

Insurance Law of the People's Republic of China (adopted on June 30, 1995, by the 14th Sess. of the Standing Comm. of the 8th NPC and revised on October 28, 2002, by 30th Sess. of the Standing Comm. of the 9th NPC)

Provisional Regulations on Insurance Administration (promulgated on August 16, 1996, by the People's Bank of China)

Notice Regarding Fulfillment of Relevant WTO Accession Commitments (issued on December 11, 2003, by the China Insurance Regulatory Commission)

Provisions on Administration of Solvency Line and Guiding Principles of Supervision for Insurance Companies (promulgated on March 24, 2003, by the China Insurance Regulatory Commission)

Provisional Regulations on Foreign Exchange Administration for Insurance Industry (promulgated on September 24, 2002, by SAFE and the China Insurance Regulatory Commission)

Regulations on Establishment of Reinsurance Companies (Order No. 4 [2002], promulgated on September 17, 2002, by the China Insurance Regulatory Commission)

Guiding Principles on the Improvement of the Internal Controls of Financial Institutions (promulgated on May 16, 1997, by the PBOC)

Administrative Regulations on Insurance Brokerage Companies (promulgated on January 1, 2002, by the China Insurance Regulatory Commission)

Regulations of the People's Republic of China on the Administration of Foreign Investment Insurance Companies (Order No. 336 of the State Council of the People's Republic of China, adopted December 5, 2001, by the 49th Executive Meeting of the State Council, promulgated December 12, 2001, effective from February 1, 2002)

Management Rules for Foreign Insurance Organizations (issued on January 15, 2004, by the China Insurance Regulatory Commission, and effective on March 1, 2004)

Insurance Asset Management Company Interim Regulations (issued on April 30, 2004, by the China Insurance Regulatory Commission)

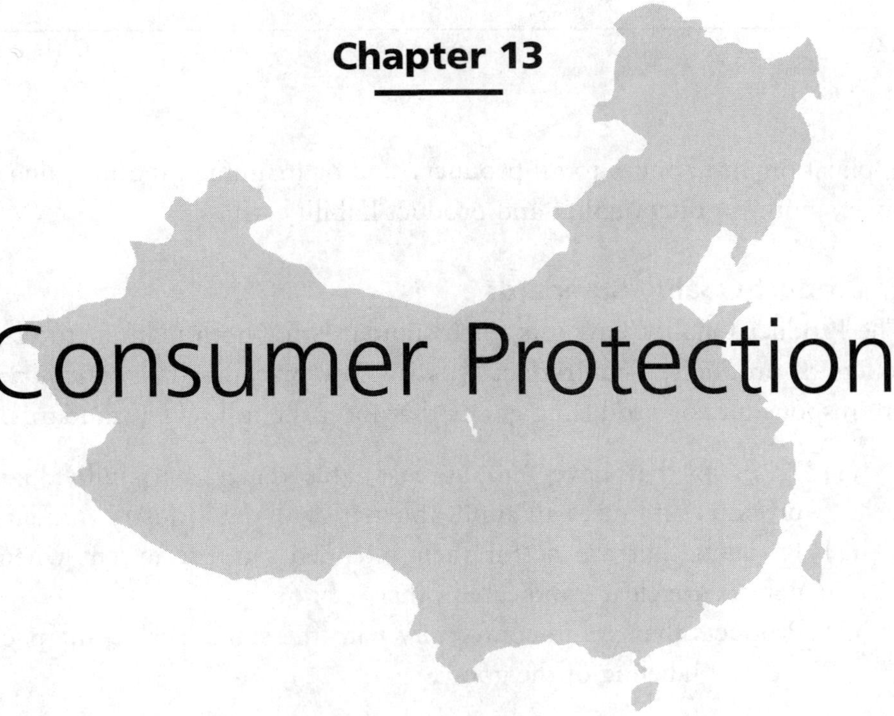

Chapter 13

Consumer Protection

With the increase in disposable income and available product selection in China, consumers have become more sophisticated in their purchasing habits and demand value for their purchases. The demand for better quality and service has also led to the introduction of new laws and regulations protecting the rights of Chinese consumers and controlling the quality of products manufactured or sold in China. This chapter addresses the product quality, standardization, consumer protection, pricing, advertising, and unfair competition laws of China.

A. Product Quality

Manufacturers have a duty to produce, and sellers have a duty to sell, quality products that are free of defects.[1] The Product Quality Law has broad

1. Product Quality Law of the People's Republic of China (adopted February 22, 1993, by the 30th Sess. of the Standing Comm. of the 7th NPC, and amended on July 8, 2000), *reprinted in* CHINA LAWS FOR FOREIGN BUSINESS (CCH), Business Regulation ¶ 16-635 (the "Product Quality Law"); Law of the People's Republic of China on the Protection of the Rights and Interests of Consumers (adopted October 31, 1993, by the 4th Sess. of the Standing Comm of the 8th NPC), *reprinted in* CHINA LAWS FOR FOREIGN BUSINESS (CCH), Business Regulation ¶ 16-480 (the "Consumer Protection Law"). The Shenzhen SEZ has developed its own rules governing product quality and provides for stringent inspection rules and authority of the government to suspend production or sale of products found in violation of product quality standards. *See* Administrative Rules of the Shenzhen Special Economic Zone on Product Quality (adopted on March 30, 1995, by the 29th Sess. of the Standing Comm. of the 1st Shenzhen Municipal People's Congress), *reprinted in* CHINA LAWS FOR FOREIGN BUSINESS (CCH), Special Zones & Cities ¶ 120-015.

application and applies to all products sold or manufactured in China, and covers both product quality and product liability issues.[2]

1. Product Quality Standards

The Product Quality Law sets forth standards for both manufacturers and sellers of products. The Product Quality Law provides that *manufacturers* are responsible for producing goods that meet the following standards:

(1) Products that have "no unreasonable danger" to individuals or property and meet all applicable national and industry standards
(2) Products that are fit for their intended purpose except when the defects are clearly indicated otherwise; or
(3) Products that are in conformity with the standards on the packaging and labeling of the goods[3]

The Product Quality Law further provides that *manufacturers* are prohibited from engaging in the following activities:

(1) Falsely designating the place of origin of the goods on the product packaging
(2) Falsely stating the origin of the goods as originating from a facility of another party
(3) Falsely using the quality certification marks or famous brand marks of another party
(4) Selling substandard products that are claimed to meet particular standards
(5) Selling products that have been declared by the State to be obsolete; or
(6) Selling counterfeit products as genuine merchandise[4]

Product packaging is required to include, in the Chinese language, a description of the product quality inspection certificate, the name and address of the manufacturing facility, the product expiration date, necessary warnings concerning the product, and the product's specifications, contents, and principal ingredients.[5] For products that are highly toxic, hazardous, or

---

2. Product Quality Law, art. 2. The Product Quality Law does not apply to construction projects. *See* General Principles of Civil Law of the People's Republic of China (adopted April 12, 1986, by the 4th Sess. of the 6th NPC), art. 122, *reprinted in* CHINA LAWS FOR FOREIGN BUSINESS (CCH), Business Regulation ¶ 19-150 (hereinafter the "Civil Law").

3. Product Quality Law, art. 26.

4. Product Quality Law, arts. 30–32. The sale of counterfeit goods and the misuse of a certification mark or famous brand mark also violate the intellectual property laws of China. *See* Chapter 14, Intellectual Property § A.7.

5. Product Quality Law, art. 27.

fragile, the packaging is required to include appropriate warnings indicating proper handling during transportation and storage.[6]

In addition to manufacturers, the Product Quality Law sets forth a number of obligations for *sellers* of products. *Sellers* are required to

(1) Adopt measures to maintain the quality of products that they sell
(2) Implement an examination and acceptance system for the purchase of inventory to ensure that purchased goods include the required product quality certificates
(3) Examine the packaging of merchandise sold to ensure that the information concerning product specifications, warnings, and facility location are included on the printed packaging

Sellers are also prohibited from

(1) Selling expired or damaged goods
(2) Falsely designating the place of origin of the goods on the product packaging
(3) Falsely stating the origin of the goods as originating from a facility of another party; or
(4) Falsely using the quality certification marks, famous brand marks, and marks of excellence of another party[7]

A violation of the standards set forth in the Product Quality Law, as noted below, is grounds for administrative penalties and civil liability.

2. Product Certification and Industry Standards

The Product Quality Law requires that manufacturers produce products under conditions that entitle them to display a certificate of product quality. The State Bureau of Technical Supervision (SBTS) and its local branches are responsible for issuing quality certificates. The certification process is consistent with internationally recognized quality control standards.[8] An enterprise

6. Product Quality Law, art. 28.
7. Product Quality Law, arts. 33–39.
8. In order to comply with its WTO obligations on national treatment, China unified its two different certification systems for foreign and domestic products on May 1, 2002. The "CCIB" mark for imported goods and the "CEEE" mark (or "Great Wall" mark) have been replaced by the "CCC" mark (which stands for "China Compulsory Certification"). The China Quality Certification Center (CQCC) and eight other authorized organizations by the China National Certification and Accreditation Administration (CNCAA) are responsible for CCC applications. CNCAA has also approved 68 laboratories throughout China to test and inspect products that are subject to CCC inspection. Information concerning the certification organizations may be obtained at http://www.aqsiq.gov.cn. Goods that do not include the CCC mark may not be distributed in China, unless the goods bear one of the old marks and were imported before August 1, 2003. CCC marks may be issued at one of the designated testing laboratories or nine designated certification centers throughout China. The certification process must be accomplished in 90 days from the date of the initial inspection of the overseas manufacturing facility.

that applies for and receives a certificate of product quality from an approved certification institution may then use a product quality mark on its products or packaging.[9]

The Chinese government has developed uniform quality control standards that are categorized as *compulsory* or *recommended standards.*[10] The agency responsible for developing and regulating national standards is the SBTS. Compulsory standards are usually established to address products that have a potential impact on the health and safety of individuals and the safety of property, or which are mandatory by law.[11] Products that fail to meet compulsory standards are prohibited from being manufactured, sold, or imported.[12] A party that manufactures, sells, or imports products that fail to meet compulsory standards is liable for penalties, confiscation of goods, and, in serious cases, criminal prosecution.[13] A party that misuses quality certificates is liable for penalties and criminal prosecution.[14] In addition to administrative penalties, an injured party has the right to file an action against an enterprise that violates that standardization laws and regulations.[15] Standards that are not compulsory are considered recommended standards, and the State encourages producers to voluntarily comply with such standards.[16] In general, national standards take priority over industry, local, and enterprise standards.[17] An enterprise that develops its own

The rules allow for exemption from the CCC requirements in a number of circumstances including imported items such as products imported for a research purpose, products imported as parts for assembly and re-export, products imported where the end products are exclusively for export, products imported to develop new product lines, products imported for equipment maintenance, and obsolete products. The validity period for most exemption certificates is 30 days and exemption certificates are, in general, for a single use. CCC certificates may be valid for up to one year.

9. Product Quality Law, art. 14.

10. Law of the People's Republic of China on Standardization (adopted December 29, 1988, at the 5th Sess. of the Standing Comm. of the 7th NPC), *reprinted in* China Laws for Foreign Business (CCH), Business Regulation (CCH) ¶ 16-590 (hereinafter the "Standardization Law"). *See also* Detailed Rules for the Implementation of the Law of the People's Republic of China on Standardization (promulgated on April 1, 1990, by the State Council), *reprinted in* China Laws for Foreign Business (CCH), Business Regulation ¶ 16-602 (hereinafter the "Standardization Rules"). The stated government policy of standards is to guarantee the safety and health of individuals, to protect the rights and interests of consumers, and to protect the environment. Standardization Law, art. 8. The government also mandates the use of standards in order to encourage the best use of natural resources and to encourage uniformity. Standardization Law, art. 9.

11. Product Quality Law, arts. 13–14; Standardization Rules, art. 18 (outlines the different types of products subject to compulsory standards).

12. Standardization Law, art. 14; Standardization Rules, art. 23; Product Quality Law, art. 8.

13. Standardization Law, art. 20; Standardization Rules, arts. 32–36. A party that is subject to penalties has the right to lodge an administrative appeal or request judicial review by the people's court. An administrative appeal or request for judicial review must be filed within fifteen days of receiving a decision. Standardization Law, art. 23; Standardization Rules, art. 37.

14. Standardization Law, art. 22.

15. Standardization Rules, art. 38.

16. Standardization Law, art. 7; Standardization Rules, art. 18.

17. Standardization Law, art. 6. The State encourages the implementation of international standards. Standardization Law, art. 4; Product Quality Law, arts. 6, 14. The policy of the government is to develop

internal standards is required to report the application of its standards to the SBTS.[18]

In September 2003, the State Council issued regulations to develop a uniform set of catalogues, technical standards, marks, and fees used in the certification and authentication of important domestic and imported products, services, and management systems to ensure overall public and consumer safety.[19] The 2003 Certification Regulations implement a licensing system for certification institutions, a qualifications recognition system for testing laboratories and institutions, and a two-track system of product certification (i.e., voluntary certification and compulsory certification for products). Foreign-invested certification enterprises may be established in China; however, by law a foreign certification institution may only establish a representative office and is prohibited from engaging in certification activities in China.

3. Product Liability

The law of China provides that a *manufacturer* and a *seller* are both liable when a product with an inherent defect causes personal injury or damage to property. Under the Product Liability Law, the injured party need prove only that he or she has sustained personal injury or property damage caused by the defective product manufactured or sold by the defendant. The injured party is not required to prove whether the defendant was at fault in any manner. The issue of causation is the principal factor in determining liability under Chinese law. Under the Product Liability Law, both the *seller* and the *manufacturer* have specific statutory obligations.

---

standards that encourage foreign economic and technological cooperation and trade. Standardization Law, art. 11. Parties to an export contract are required to agree to the technical standards for an export product. Standardization Rules, art. 25. When export products are sold on the domestic market, products that are subject to compulsory standards must comply with such standards. Standardization Rules, art. 25. All foreign-produced goods are subject to inspection by both China Customs and the import-export commodity inspection agency. The Chinese language requirement for labeling also applies to imports as well as domestically produced goods. *See also* Food Hygiene Law of the People's Republic of China (adopted October 30, 1995, by the 16th Sess. of the Standing Comm. of the 8th NPC), *reprinted in* CHINA LAWS FOR FOREIGN BUSINESS (CCH), Business Regulation ¶ 16-535 (sets forth specific hygiene requirements for food production including packaging, disinfection, storage, transportation, waste disposal, and personal hygiene of food industry personnel); Law of the People's Republic of China on the Administration of Drugs (adopted September 20, 1984, at the 7th Sess. of the Standing Comm. of the 6th NPC), *reprinted in* CHINA LAWS FOR FOREIGN BUSINESS (CCH), Business Regulation ¶ 16-545; General Standards for the Labeling of Food (promulgated February 4, 1994, by the State Bureau of Technical Supervision), *reprinted in* CHINA LAWS FOR FOREIGN BUSINESS (CCH), Business Regulation ¶ 16-586 (requires food producers to comply with national labeling standards for prepackaged foods sold in China and sets forth mandatory and optional items to be include in labels for food products).

18. Standardization Law, art. 6; Standardization Rules, art. 17.

19. Regulations of the People's Republic of China on Certification and Authentication (promulgated on September 3, 2003, by the State Council and effective on November 1, 2003).

A *seller* of a product is responsible for the repair, replacement, or refund of the purchase funds and return of the product in the following instances:

(1) Where the product does not function or have the properties for use that it should possess, and no prior warning or advisement is provided
(2) Where the product does not conform to nationally recognized standards or the specifications on the product packaging
(3) Where the product does not conform with the product description in advertisements or to physical samples[20]

If a user or consumer who purchased the product incurs losses as a result of the product, the *seller* is liable for damages and must provide compensation.[21] After a *seller* has taken responsibility for repair or replacement, or has paid compensation to the injured party, the *seller* has a right to indemnification from both the *manufacturer* and the supplier of the goods.[22] If a product is rendered defective as a result of the negligence of the *seller*, the *seller* is liable for damages.[23]

Under the Product Quality Law, a *manufacturer* is liable for personal injury or property damage caused by a defective product.[24] A *manufacturer* is not liable for personal injury or property damage if the subject product has not been placed in the stream of commerce, the alleged defect causing the damage did not exist when the product was sold, or the level of science and technology at the time the product was sold was insufficient to detect the existence of the alleged defect.[25]

A third party that sustains injuries as a result of a defective product may seek compensation against both the *seller* and the *manufacturer* of the

20. Product Quality Law, art. 40.

21. Product Quality Law, art. 40. If a seller fails to repair or replace the product, or fails to provide compensation for losses, the government may order the seller to resolve the consumer's concerns. A business operator may not unreasonably delay repair, replacement, or refunds to consumers. Consumer Protection Law, art. 23. *See also* Regulations on the Responsibility for Repair, Replacement and Return of Certain Commodities (promulgated on August 25, 1995, by the State Bureau of Technical Supervision).

22. Product Quality Law, art. 40. The seller has a right to pursue the suppliers, distributors, or other third parties that supplied the products causing damages.

23. Product Quality Law, art. 42. If the seller is unable to identify the manufacturer or supplier of a defective product, the seller is legally liable for damages.

24. Product Quality Law, art. 41. Damages that may be recovered include medical expenses, loss of income, and an allowance for a person that is rendered disabled. *Id.* at 44. If death results from a defective product, damages include funeral expenses, a pension to the family of the deceased, and living expenses for the dependents of the deceased. *Id.* If a defect in a product causes damage to property, the seller or the manufacturer is required to either restore the property or to pay the fair market value of the subject property. *Id.* The Consumer Protection Law provides that consumers have a right to obtain compensation as a result of personal injury or property damage resulting from the use of a product. Consumer Protection Law, art. 11.

25. Product Quality Law, art. 41. The law does not further explain what is meant by the "level of science and technology." This exemption from liability is open to interpretation by the testimony of expert witnesses.

product.[26] *Manufacturers* and *sellers* are held jointly and severally liable for damages caused by defective goods, and indemnification is allowed in cases in which a party can prove that the defect was not caused by his or her own misconduct.

The Product Quality Law defines a "defect" as an unreasonable danger inherent in the product wherein such danger threatens personal safety or another's property, and no clear warning is provided to the consumer.[27] When the product is governed by national or industry health and safety standards, noncompliance with the standards deems the product defective as a matter of law.[28]

4. Counterfeit Products

Under the 2001 amendments to the Product Quality Law, the SBTS is responsible for taking action against parties that produce or sell counterfeit products. The SBTS is responsible for the investigation and application of penalty and liability guidelines. Under the revised law, the SBTS has the authority to impose the following penalties:

(1) Order to cease production and sale of products in question
(2) Confiscation of the products
(3) Imposition of a monetary penalty of more than 50 percent and less than three times the value of the products
(4) Confiscation of any illegal income, if any
(5) Cancellation of business license
(6) Possible criminal liability[29]

A party that aids and abets in the violation of the Product Quality Law may be subject to penalties. The Product Quality Law defines such secondary parties as any individual or entity who "knows or ought to know that production or sale of products have been banned by this Law, yet still provides transport, custody, warehousing or other favorable conditions, or one that provides techniques for the production of fake products that imitate genuine ones,"[30] and "an operator in the services industry that uses products banned under this Law."[31]

26. Product Quality Law, art. 43.
27. Product Quality Law, art. 46.
28. Product Quality Law, art. 46.
29. Product Quality Law, art. 61.
30. Product Quality Law, art. 61.
31. Product Quality Law, art. 62.

5. Administrative and Judicial Remedies

The Product Quality Law provides that manufacturers, sellers, and secondary parties in violation of the law may be subject to administrative penalties, including orders to cease and desist manufacturing and sales, monetary penalties, and closure orders and confiscation of an enterprise's business license. Violators are also subject to criminal prosecution for willful violations of the law or in situations in which persons sustained injuries as a result of the product quality problems.[32] The SBTS and the SAIC have the power to investigate and impose penalties pursuant to the Product Quality Law.[33] In the event the government imposes an administrative penalty, an interested party has fifteen days to either administratively appeal a penalty decision or file a suit in the people's court for judicial review.[34]

The Product Quality Law provides that disputes involving defective products may be resolved by mediation between the parties. If the parties are unwilling to settle a dispute informally, the injured party may file a complaint with the people's court, or arbitration if agreed to by contract.[35] In recent years, more consumer litigation claims have been filed with the people's courts and usually with respect to expensive consumer items. A claim under the Product Quality Law is barred if it is filed more than two years

32. Product Quality Law, arts. 49–72. The SBTS has increased its supervision and level of penalties to reduce the production of low-quality and counterfeit goods. *See* Su, *Product Quality Is Now a Priority,* CHINA DAILY (Oct. 27, 1998), available on Lexis, News Library, or on the Web site of the CHINA DAILY at http://www.chinadaily.com.cn. The government has issued regulations that govern product recalls. *See* Defective Auto-Product Recall Management Rule (issued by the National Development and Reform Commission, Ministry of Commerce, General Administration of Customs, and State Administration of Quality Supervision, Inspection, and Quarantine, effective on October 1, 2004) (provides that recalls are mandatory if testing and inspection prove that the vehicle does not comply with technical safety regulations, if design or manufacturing defects have caused damage to persons or property, and if tests prove that defects may cause such damage under certain given circumstances).

33. Consumers have the right to appeal to the government for relief as a result of defective products. Product Quality Law, art. 10.

34. Product Quality Law, art. 46. *See* Law of Administrative Litigation of the People's Republic of China (adopted on April 4, 1989, by the 2nd Sess. of the 7th NPC), art 14, § (i), *reprinted in* CHINA LAWS FOR FOREIGN BUSINESS (CCH), Business Regulation ¶ 19-558 (hereinafter the "Administrative Litigation Law"). For a brief discussion concerning administrative litigation, *see* Chapter 22, Litigation in the People's Court § C.

35. Product Quality Law, art. 47. The Product Quality Law provides that an arbitration panel or the people's court has the right to delegate to the SBTS the obligation to inspect a product and render an opinion concerning the product's alleged defectiveness. *Id.* at 48. The China Consumer Association (CCA) is a government-sponsored consumer advocacy organization that investigates product quality complaints, issues product recalls and warnings to the public, and supports consumers in filing administrative complaints with the SAIC and litigation in a people's court for damages against enterprises. Product Quality Law, art. 13. The Beijing AIC opened a consumer complaint telephone hotline on March 12, 1998, to field calls from consumers concerning disputes with products. In 1997, the SAIC and its local branches investigated over 47,000 consumer rights cases and obtained RMB296 million ($35.66 million) in compensation for consumers against producers. *See* Ma, *Special Consumer Phone Line Opened,* CHINA DAILY (March 13, 1998), available on Lexis, News Library, or on the Web site of the CHINA DAILY at http://www.chinadaily.com.cn; *Consumer Rights: Buyers Bite Back,* China Economic Review (Jan. 23, 1999), available on Lexis, News Library.

from the time that the injured party was aware that his or her rights had been violated.[36] A claim for compensation for damages caused by a defective product expires ten years from the date the product was delivered to the first user or consumer.[37]

B. Consumer Protection

Under the Consumer Protection Law, enterprises are required to engage in consumer transactions in a fair and honest manner.[38] The law provides that the rights and interests of consumers shall be protected by the State.[39] The law further mandates that the national media "safeguard" consumers' legal rights and "shall use public opinion to control acts harmful to consumers' legal rights and interests."[40]

1. Standards under the Consumer Protection Law

The key principle under the Consumer Protection Law is the requirement that business enterprises guarantee that their goods and services conform to applicable health and safety standards.[41] Potentially hazardous goods must

36. Product Quality Law, art. 45. The two-year limitations period in the Product Quality Law is inconsistent with the one-year period of time set forth in the Civil Law. *See* Civil Law, art. 136.

37. Product Quality Law, art. 45. The ten-year period of time is tolled if there is evidence that the ten-year "period of safe use" has not yet expired.

38. Consumer Protection Law, art. 4. *See generally* D. KING & G. TONG, CONSUMER PROTECTION IN CHINA: TRANSLATIONS, DEVELOPMENTS, AND RECOMMENDATIONS (1991). The Pricing Law sets forth a number of consumer protection standards with respect to fair pricing practices. *See infra* Pricing Prohibitions and Consumer Protection § E.3. The Shanghai municipal government has adopted its own stringent set of consumer protection regulations. *See* Regulations on Protecting the Interests of Consumers (issued on Oct. 28, 2002, and effective on January 1, 2003, by the Shanghai Municipal People's Congress) (outlining consumer protection rules, consumer privacy standards, marketing and advertising standards, standards for direct sales, standards for gifts/bonuses, standards for returns and refunds, and punitive damages of 100 percent of the sales price in addition to refund/return.). *See generally* R. Cai, *Shanghai's New Consumer Protection Rules: Changing the Rules of Business,* CHINA L. & PRAC. (Nov. 2002). *See also* Provisions to Protect the Rights and Interests of Consumers (promulgated on March 12, 2004, by the State Administration of Industry and Commerce). The Consumer Protection Provisions list the basic responsibilities of companies that offer products and services, including liability for defective products, customer contract terms and conditions, provision of warranty obligations, provisions concerning invoices, veracity of product marketing, sales by mail or other delivery services, and liability for damages caused by defective products. The Provisions provide that defective products must be removed from circulation when serious defects are reported and that companies will be liable for injuries and other harm caused by defective products. Contracts with consumers are required to have reasonable conditions, and companies must complete their contractual obligations in a timely manner, including responsibilities involving delivery. The SAIC Provisions also require that advertisements must accurately describe or depict their respective products. The Consumer Protection Provisions fail to provide information on the methods to report violations and punish violators.

39. Consumer Protection Law, arts. 1–5.

40. Consumer Protection Law, art. 6. The law provides, too, that the "whole society shall bear responsibility for the protection of consumer's legal rights and interests."

41. Consumer Protection Law, arts. 7, 18. The Consumer Protection Law provides that a consumer has a right to expect that his or her safety is guaranteed.

provide clear and unambiguous warnings to users, as well as specific instructions for proper use and handling.[42] The law also provides that business operators have an affirmative duty to advise the government and consumers that a product is defective which may cause harm to the safety of individuals or property. The law further mandates that consumers are entitled to the following protection:

(1) Right to free choice in purchasing commodities and services[43]
(2) Right to fair dealing in consumer transactions[44]
(3) Right to obtain compensation for personal injuries or property damage as a result of the purchase or use of a product or service[45]
(4) Right to establish consumer interest groups and associations to assist with their legal rights[46]
(5) Right to report or complain of acts infringing upon the rights and interests of consumers[47]

A business operator has a statutory obligation to provide true and unambiguous answers to questions raised by consumers concerning the quality and use of products or services. The Consumer Protection Law provides that consumers have a right to all information pertaining to products including the country of origin, the manufacturer, date of production, product expiration dates, applicable product grade or level of quality, certificate of inspection and quality, operation manual, and after-sale service.[48] The Consumer Protection Law also provides that consumers have an obligation to "master" the ability to operate a product in order to ensure safe operation.[49]

42. Consumer Protection Law, art. 18.

43. Consumer Protection Law, art. 9. A consumer has the right to freely choose the business operator providing commodities and services, the types of commodities and services offered, and whether to even purchase such commodities and services. A consumer also has the right to compare, appraise, and select when choosing a commodity or service.

44. Consumer Protection Law, art. 10. A consumer has the right to fair terms of trade and conditions such as quality guarantee, reasonable price, and accurate measurements when purchasing goods or services. Consumers also have the statutory right to reject coercive transactions by business operators.

45. Consumer Protection Law, art. 11.

46. Consumer Protection Law, art. 12. A consumer protection association may provide information and advice services to consumers, participate in the supervision and inspection of products and services by the government, report to or make suggestions to the government concerning consumer rights and interests, accept complaints by consumers and conduct investigations, attempt to mediate consumer disputes, assist injured consumers in instituting litigation against business operators, and to issue press releases to the media concerning consumer affairs issues. *Id.* at art. 32. Consumer organizations are required to operate on a nonprofit basis. *Id.* at art. 33.

47. Consumer Protection Law, art. 15.

48. Consumer Protection Law, arts. 8, 13. A business operator is obligated to use its true name when conducting consumer transactions. *Id.* at art. 20.

49. Consumer Protection Law, art. 13.

Under the Consumer Protection Law, false or misleading advertising is strictly prohibited, and prices are required to be clearly marked on the products by retailers.[50] A business operator is also prohibited from setting unreasonable or unfair terms in consumer transactions.[51] The Consumer Protection Law also bars a manufacturer or seller from attempting to obtain a release from civil liability by the use of standardized contracts.[52] A business operator is further prohibited from conducting searches of a consumer or his or her personal articles while at an operator's business premises.[53]

2. Administrative and Judicial Remedies

A business operator that violates the Consumer Protection Law may be liable for administrative penalties including monetary fines, confiscation of merchandise and sales proceeds, and revocation of a business license.[54] The SAIC is the agency responsible for protecting the rights of consumers and imposing administrative penalties.[55] A business operator has the right to file an administrative appeal to a penalty decision or to seek judicial review of a penalty decision with the people's court. An administrative appeal or request for judicial review must be made within fifteen days of receipt of the decision.[56]

Under the Consumer Protection Law, as with the Product Liability Law, an injured party has a right to compensation for injuries or property damage caused by a defective product.[57] A dispute under the Consumer Protection Law may be resolved through conciliation, administrative complaint procedures, arbitration, or litigation.[58]

---

50. Consumer Protection Law, arts. 19, 22. These obligations are also covered under the Advertising Law and the Pricing Law. *See infra* § C.1., General Standards for Advertisers; § E.3., Pricing Prohibitions and Consumer Protection.

51. Consumer Protection Law, art. 24.

52. Consumer Protection Law, art. 24. The Contract Law places the burden on a party providing "standardized clauses" to "remind the other party to pay attention to any clauses which release or limit its liabilities" and "shall explain the clauses if requested by the other party." Contract Law, art. 39. The definition of "standardized clauses" are "clauses which have been drafted in advance by a party for repeated use." The Contract Law also provides that attempts to release a party from its obligations, or designed to deny the other party certain critical rights, are invalid. If a dispute arises concerning the understanding of a standardized clause, the Contract Law provides that the clause will be interpreted against the party that provided the contractual language. In the event of a discrepancy between a standardized clause and a nonstandardized clause, the nonstandardized clause shall prevail. *Id.* arts. 41–42, 53. This rule is recognized in the Insurance Law concerning the interpretation of standard insurance contracts. *See* Insurance Law, art. 30. The Contract Law provides that a provision that seeks to exempt a party from liability as a result of intentional misconduct or gross negligence, which results in loss of property or bodily injury to the other party, is invalid. Contract Law, art. 53.

53. Consumer Protection Law, art. 25.

54. Consumer Protection Law, art. 50.

55. Consumer Protection Law, art. 28.

56. Consumer Protection Law, art. 51.

57. Consumer Protection Law, art. 35.

58. Consumer Protection Law, art. 34.

C. Standards for Advertisers

In 1994, the Chinese government adopted the Advertising Law of the PRC.[59] The purpose of the Advertising Law is to standardize the industry and to "promote the positive role of advertising in the socialist market economy."[60]

1. General Standards for Advertisers

The Advertising Law provides that the contents of an advertisement are required to be truthful and "shall conform with socialist spiritual values."[61] The standards apply to advertisers, agents, and publishers of advertisements. The SAIC and its local branches are responsible for supervising advertising activities. The Advertising Law sets forth a number of "guiding principles" for the content of advertisements. In particular, an advertisement shall not be detrimental to the mental and physical health of the consumers; shall promote the improvement in quality of goods and services; shall protect the rights and interests of consumers; shall conform to social, public, and professional ethics; and shall safeguard the dignity and interests of the State.[62]

The Advertising Law also prohibits the use of the following in any advertisement:

(1) The national flag, national emblem, or national anthem of the PRC
(2) The names of government organizations
(3) The language "State level," "highest level," or "the best"
(4) Contents that may be injurious to social stability, present a danger to individuals or property, or harm the public interest
(5) Contents that may jeopardize social and public order or violate good social conventions
(6) Contents that are obscene, superstitious, or of a terrorist nature, violent, or "evil"
(7) Contents that discriminate on the basis of nationality, race, religion, or sex
(8) Contents that are harmful to the protection of the environment and natural resources

59. Advertising Law of the People's Republic of China (adopted October 27, 1994, by the 10th Sess. of the Standing Comm. of the 8th NPC), *reprinted in* CHINA LAWS FOR FOREIGN BUSINESS (CCH), Business Regulation ¶ 16-495 (hereinafter "the Advertising Law").

60. Advertising Law, art. 1.

61. Advertising Law, art. 3. The language "socialist spiritual values" is not defined in the Advertising Law.

62. Advertising Law, art. 7. Many of the guiding principles are purposefully vague and ambiguous to allow the SAIC the flexibility to assert control over objectionable advertising materials.

(9) Contents that are deemed to be injurious to the physical and mental health of minors or the disabled[63]

Advertisers are also strictly prohibited from using comparative advertising which "denigrates" the goods and services of competitors.[64] An advertisement must be clearly recognizable by the consumer as an advertisement, and shall not be disguised as a News report.[65] If an advertisement appears to represent a News report or article, the advertiser is required to clearly indicate that the publication is an advertisement to distinguish it from other nonadvertisement materials.

An advertiser may attach or include a gift article to the advertised product but is required to clearly define the type and quality of the subject gift.[66] If any data, statistics, or survey results are cited in an advertisement, the sources must be clearly indicated and accurately described.[67] With respect to patented products, the advertisement is required to specify the patent number. It is unlawful to claim that a patent application is pending approval, or to claim that patent rights exist when a patent has been cancelled, terminated, or otherwise deemed invalid.[68]

---

63. Advertising Law, arts. 7, 8. *See also* Administration of the Broadcasting of Advertisements on Radio and Television Tentative Procedures (promulgated on Sept. 15, 2003, by the State Administration of Radio, Film, and Television) (hereinafter the "SARFT Advertisement Procedures"). The SARFT Advertisement Procedures set forth general principles for the content of advertisements on both radio and television. Consistent with the Advertising Law, the SARFT Advertisement Procedures prohibit the use of the national flag, emblem, or anthem, or the image or voice of State leaders, and require that the advertisements respect State policies on race and religion, be beneficial to health of children, and respect disabled persons and women. SARFT Advertisement Procedures, arts. 6, 7, 9, 10. Advertisements must not promote gambling or violence, or induce people to engage in criminal activities. SARFT Advertisement Procedures, art. 11. Advertisements must respect science and must not contain any contents that promote superstition, cults, or false scientific information. SARFT Advertisement Procedures, art. 12. The SARFT Advertisement Procedures set strict limits on the timing and length of advertisements (i.e., advertisements may comprise only 20 percent of the total programming time each day and 15 percent of the programming time per hour from the hours of 11:00–13:00 on radio, and 19:00 and 21:00 on television). SARFT Advertisement Procedures, art. 17. The SARFT Advertisement Procedures also state that commercials concerning hemorrhoids, athlete's foot, and sanitary napkins may not be shown during mealtimes, and advertisements for alcoholic beverages are limited to twelve per day and only two during the prime time hours of 19:00 to 21:00. SARFT Advertisement Procedures, arts. 19, 20.

64. Advertising Law, art. 12. The ban on comparative advertising has precluded the Energizer Bunny from competitively racing its Chinese counterparts and stripped Budweiser of its claim as the "King of Beers." For a discussion concerning Chinese advertising practices and the prohibition on comparative advertising, *see* Drobis, *Chinese Consumers: The Riches Beyond the Wall,* 41 PUB. REL. Q. 23 (March 22, 1996), available on Lexis, News Library; *China: Advertising Industry Reform,* MARKET REP. 1 (January 14, 1994).

65. Advertising Law, art. 13. *See also* Further Strengthening the Administration of Advertising Promotion through Mass Media Circular (issued on February 5, 2001, by the State Administration of Radio, Film and Television and the State Press and Publication Administration) (circular prohibits the use of news format, interviews, professional advice, and articles to publish or broadcast an advertisement in disguised form).

66. Advertising Law, art. 9.

67. Advertising Law, art. 10.

68. Advertising Law, art. 11.

2. Rules Governing Specific Industries

Although the Advertising Law applies to all industry sectors, the law contains special provisions concerning specific products.

a. Pharmaceuticals and Medical Devices

The Advertising Law contains specific rules governing pharmaceuticals and medical devices. In such instances, an advertisement is prohibited from containing the following:

(1) Any unscientific claims or assurances
(2) Any treatment success or curative rates
(3) Comparison with other medicines or medical apparatus in terms of the effectiveness of the subject drug or device
(4) Titles or images of medical research institutes, academic institutions, medical organizations or experts, doctors, or patients[69]

The content for an advertisement for medication is required to be approved by the State Food & Drug Administration (SFDA) or the public health departments at the provincial level.[70] The Advertising Law prohibits the use of advertisements with respect to the sale of special-purpose medications such as anesthetics, psychotropic drugs, toxic drugs, or radioactive drugs.[71] An advertisement for prescription medication is required to indicate that it should be taken only on the advice of a medical practitioner.

b. Chemical Fertilizers

An advertisement concerning chemical fertilizers is prohibited from making claims of safety and specifically with respect to the absence of toxicity of the chemicals. Fertilizer advertising is also barred from making unscientific and unsupported claims or guarantees of effectiveness. Such advertisements are allowed only if supported by research data and documentation. The Advertising Law also prohibits the use of written, oral, or pictorial depictions of the improper use of the chemicals.[72]

---

69. Advertising Law, art. 14. *See infra* § G.6., Drug Advertising.

70. Advertising Law, art. 15. The trademarks and advertisements of medication, medical devices, and pesticides must be approved prior to publication. *Id.* at art. 34. The SFDA is responsible for supervising drug manufacturers. *See* Law of the People's Republic of China on the Administration of Drugs (adopted September 20, 1984, at the 7th Meeting of the Standing Committee of the 6th National People's Congress; amended February 28, 2001, at the 20th Meeting of the Standing Committee of the 9th National People's Congress; re-promulgated February 28, 2001, by Presidential Order No. 45 of the People's Republic of China) *reprinted in* CHINA LAWS FOR FOREIGN BUSINESS (CCH), Business Regulation ¶ 16-545 (hereinafter the "Drug Administration Law").

71. Advertising Law, art. 16.

72. Advertising Law, art. 17.

c. Tobacco Products

The Advertising Law bars tobacco advertisements from broadcast, film, television, newspaper, and periodical publication. Advertisers of tobacco products are limited to outdoor media such as billboards. However, the law prohibits the posting of tobacco advertisements in any waiting room, cinema or theater, meeting hall, sports facility, gymnasium, or other public place.[73] An advertisement of tobacco products must indicate that "Smoking Is Hazardous to Your Health."[74]

d. Food, Alcohol, and Cosmetics

The contents of advertisements for food, alcohol, and cosmetics may not contain medical language or terminology that can easily confuse the goods with those with medicinal properties.[75] The Advertising Law also prohibits food labels from containing misleading statements that describe or introduce the food product in a fraudulent manner or in a manner that confuses the product with another well-known product.[76]

e. Real Estate Sales and Promotions

In response to practices in the real estate industry, the Supreme People's Court has issued an interpretation that provides guidelines with respect to the advertisements and promotional materials for real property commercial developers.[77] The SPC interpretation provides that advertisements and promotional materials for sales of commercial premises are *invitations* for offers and not binding offers. However, if the representations and promises made

---

73. Advertising Law, art. 18. *See China: Tobacco Ads Must Obey the Law,* CHINA DAILY (Aug. 13, 1998), available on Lexis, News Library, or on the Web site of the CHINA DAILY at http://www.chinadaily.com.cn.

74. Advertising Law, art. 18.

75. Advertising Law, art. 19.

76. General Standards for the Labeling of Food, arts. 4.1, 4.2. The State Environmental Protection Administration has developed standards for the organic food industry in China. *See* Administration of the Certification of Organic Food Procedures (issued on June 19, 2001, by the State Environmental Protection Administration, effective as of date of issue) (hereinafter the "Organic Food Standards"). *China Law and Practice* September 2001, Vol. 15, No. 7, p. 7. The Procedures define "organic foods" as food that complies with State food hygiene standards and organic specifications and is produced without using agricultural chemicals, chemical fertilizers, growth hormones, chemical additives, artificial colorings, chemical preservatives, and genetic engineering technology. The Organic Food Standards apply to the production, certification, distribution, and sale of organic foods in the PRC. All organic food producers and sellers must submit applications to the organic food certification committee of SEPA for approval and registration. Certification is valid for two years and enables the certified entity to label their food products as "organic" in the manner stipulated by the certification body.

77. Several Issues Concerning the Application of the Law to Trial of Disputes Over Commercial Premises Sales and Purchase Contracts Interpretation (issued on April 28, 2003, by the Supreme People's Court) (hereinafter the "SPC Real Property Dispute Interpretation"). *See generally* J. Jiang & Z. Li, *Clearing Up the Law: China's New Judicial Interpretation on the Sale of Commercial Premises,* CHINA L. & PRAC. (June 2003).

by the seller with respect to the structure and relevant facilities within a development zone boundaries, which are specific and have significant impact on the formation of the purchase contract and the purchase price of the premises, then such representations and promises are regarded as binding offers.[78] As a result, sellers of real estate must be more prudent with respect to representations and promises set forth in advertisements and promotional materials.

3. Advertising Activities

The Advertising Law sets forth the requirements for advertisers, agents, and publishers engaged in the business of publishing advertisements, including the requirement that a business license be obtained and the need for sufficient staff and equipment to accomplish advertising activities.[79] Specifically, the Advertising Law provides that advertisers, agents, and publishers are required to execute written contracts outlining the rights and obligations of the parties.[80] Advertisers are required to maintain evidence that the contents of advertisements are accurate and truthful, and publishers are required to verify the factual information in advertisements.[81] If an advertisement uses the name or image of sponsors or product supporters, the advertisers are required to obtain written consent.[82] The fees charged by advertising agents and publishers are required to be reasonable, and fee schedules must be published.[83]

Advertisements posted outdoors are restricted in a number of instances. In particular, advertisements may not be affixed to traffic markers or road safety facilities such as traffic kiosks. Nor can outdoor advertisements be posted at scenic locations, historical sites, or in areas in which the advertisement would be detrimental to the environment.[84] Local authorities are allowed control over outdoor advertisements in order to ensure that the local conditions are taken into consideration. The State Administration of Industry and Commerce has adopted procedures that govern printed advertisements such as flyers, posters, brochures, and leaflets.[85] The Printed Advertisement Procedures specify the situations where registration of

78. SPC Real Property Dispute Interpretation, art. 3.
79. Advertising Law, arts. 20–33.
80. Advertising Law, art. 20.
81. Advertising Law, arts. 24, 27.
82. Advertising Law, art. 25.
83. Advertising Law, art. 29.
84. Advertising Law, art. 32. *See also* Administration of Installation of Signboard Advertisements Provisions (promulgated on February 2, 2000, by the Guangzhou Municipal Administration of Industry and Commerce).
85. Administration of Printed Advertisement Procedures (promulgated on January 13, 2000, by the State Administration of Industry and Commerce) (hereinafter the "Printed Advertisement Procedures"). Specifically excluded from the Printed Advertisement Procedures are advertisements to be found in the mass media such as newspapers, periodicals, and books, which are addressed by other statutes.

printed advertisements is required and specify the guidelines for what types of information may be included on the printed materials. The product categories requiring registration of advertisements, with an emphasis on consumer protection, include pharmaceuticals, medical treatments and equipment, pesticides, veterinary medicine, real estate, health products, and cosmetics. Printed advertisements that do not fall in any of these categories are exempt from the registration procedures unless registration is required by another law or regulation. If registration is required, the Printed Advertisement Procedures provide that registration may take place at the provincial level of the State Administration of Industry and Commerce. In contrast to former rules that required automatic registration of all printed advertisements, the Printed Advertisement Procedures reduce the bureaucratic steps faced by advertisers, and place the burden of checking the veracity of advertising materials on operators.

4. Administrative and Judicial Remedies

In general, a violation of the Advertising Law may result in penalties ranging from double to five times the amount of the advertising expenses for the violating advertisement.[86] For violations considered minor, such as a failure to clearly distinguish an advertisement from a news report, the penalty ranges from RMB1,000 to RMB10,000.[87] In more serious cases involving the falsification of documents, heavy penalties and criminal liability may be imposed.[88] The Advertising Law sets forth an appeal process, including court relief, for decisions concerning fines imposed as a result of violations. In addition to administrative sanctions, advertisers, advertising agents, and publishers have civil liability for engaging in activities in violation of the Advertising Law.[89]

D. Unfair Competition

In 1993, China adopted the Unfair Competition Law, which is designed to promote and protect fair competition in the marketplace for the benefit of consumers, business enterprises, and the general public.[90] The Unfair

86. Advertising Law, chap. V.
87. Advertising Law, art. 40.
88. Advertising Law, art. 44.
89. Advertising Law, art. 47.
90. Law of the People's Republic of China Against Unfair Competition (adopted September 2, 1993, at the 3rd Sess. of the Standing Comm. of the 8th NPC), *reprinted in* CHINA LAWS FOR FOREIGN BUSINESS (CCH), Business Regulation ¶ 16-640 (hereinafter the "Unfair Competition Law"). The Civil Law also prohibits, in general terms, unfair competition and unfair business practices. Civil Law, arts. 117–22.

Competition Law is also designed to protect the intellectual property rights and business secrets of business enterprises, and to prohibit business enterprises from engaging in corrupt practices.

1. Standards for Unfair Competition

The Unfair Competition Law, in general, provides that business enterprises are required to adhere to the principles of fairness and honesty.[91] The standards apply to all enterprises and individuals, including domestic and foreign-invested enterprises, that engage in commercial and business operations.[92] The specific activities of a business operator that are considered to be unfair competition include the following:

(1) To use the registered trademark of another party in a counterfeit manner[93]

(2) To use the same or similar names, packages, or decorations of well-known brand-named products so as to mislead consumers without permission[94]

(3) To use the names of other enterprises or individuals so as to mislead consumers without permission

(4) To use the identification marks, marks indicating quality products, and other quality marks on commodities in a counterfeit manner or to falsify the place of origin to mislead consumers with regard to quality of a product or service[95]

(5) To falsely advertise with respect to quality, composition, property, purposes, producers, validity period, and places of origin of commodities by business operators or advertising agents who knowingly provide false advertising or provide advertising that the agents should know is false[96]

(6) To obtain the commercial secrets of other proprietors by theft, inducement, coercion, or other illicit means[97]

(7) To reveal, use, or allow others to use illegally obtained commercial secrets of others[98]

---

91. Unfair Competition Law, art. 2.
92. Unfair Competition Law, art. 2.
93. *See also* Chapter 14, Intellectual Property § A.8.
94. *See also* Chapter 14, Intellectual Property § A.7.
95. Unfair Competition Law, art. 5.
96. Unfair Competition Law, art. 9.
97. Unfair Competition Law, art. 10. Commercial secrets are technical and business information that is not known to the public, provides economic benefits to the owner, is of practical application, and has been subject to steps by the owner to maintain its secrecy. A misuse of business and commercial secrets is grounds for criminal prosecution. *See* Chapter 23, Criminal Liability for FIE Activities § B.4.
98. Unfair Competition Law, art. 10.

(8) To reveal, use, or allow others to use commercial secrets of others in violation of agreements or requests to keep the secrets confidential by the owners

(9) To sell commodities at prices below cost with the intent to undermine and harm the interests of competitors[99]

(10) To tie in other goods or impose unreasonable conditions on buyers against their intentions[100]

(11) To disseminate misrepresentations intended to harm the commercial credit and reputation of a competitor's commodities[101]

(12) To engage in collusive activities intended to raise or lower the offers in a competitive bid[102]

(13) To offer or accept bribery or undisclosed rebates[103]

The Unfair Competition Law also prohibits public utilities or other certified monopolies from forcing consumers to purchase from their designated business operators thereby squeezing out other business operators from fair competition.[104] Government agencies are prohibited from forcing private business and individuals from purchasing commodities or services from designated business operators, or restricting the free flow of interprovince commerce.[105]

2. Administrative and Judicial Remedies

The SAIC and its branches have the authority to investigate unfair competition practices.[106] The SAIC may order violators to pay compensation for damages suffered by other business operators or restitution for profits

99. Unfair Competition Law, art. 11. Below-cost sales are allowed when a party is selling fresh and live commodities, commodities whose validity period will soon expire, overstocked commodities, commodities at seasonally reduced prices, or commodities at reduced prices due to debt clearing, shifting product lines, or business closure. Below-cost sales by foreign parties are prohibited under the Anti-Dumping Law. *See* Chapter 15, Customs and Trade Regulation § E.

100. Unfair Competition Law, art. 12.

101. Unfair Competition Law, art. 14.

102. Unfair Competition Law, art. 15.

103. Unfair Competition Law, art. 8.

104. Unfair Competition Law, art. 5.

105. Unfair Competition Law, art. 7. The State Council has adopted regulations that attempt to prohibit local protectionism. In this regard, the State Council issued the *Regulations on Prohibition of Local Blockades in Market Economic Activities* in 2001. Regulations on Prohibition of Local Blockades on Market Economic Activities (issued on April 21, 2001, by the State Council, effective as of date of issue). The purpose of these Regulations is to create a unified national market system established on the premises of fair competition and regulatory order. Based thereon, the Regulations prohibit local blockades, boycotts, or favoritism in market economic activities, thereby mitigating local protectionism and promoting fair market competition on a nationwide level. The Regulations provide that individuals and companies may not obstruct out-of province merchandise or construction services companies from entering the provincial market. Local governments are also prohibited from engaging in protectionist behavior and are forbidden from promulgating any rules that may alter the impact of these Regulations. A failure to comply with the rules is grounds for penalties.

106. Unfair Competition Law, art. 16.

gained where the damages cannot be ascertained, and the cost of the investigation. The SAIC may also order violators to cease and desist unfair trade practices, impose fines of up to three times the profits or up to RMB200,000, suspend or revoke business licenses, or initiate criminal prosecution.[107] Individuals and enterprises harmed by unfair trade practices have private rights of action under the Unfair Competition Law and may initiate a complaint in the people's court against a party in violation of the law.[108] Where unfair competition practices constitute violation of other laws, such as the Patent Law, Trademark Law, or Copyright Law, remedies may be sought under those laws.

E. Pricing Standards

1. Market-Oriented Standards under the Pricing Law

The NPC promulgated the Pricing Law of the People's Republic of China, effective May 1, 1998, which gave most business operators, including private and State-owned enterprises, the discretion to set their own prices for general commodities and services.[109] The Pricing Law is viewed by observers

107. Unfair Competition Law, arts. 20, 21, 22.

108. Unfair Competition Law, art. 20. The Chinese courts are increasingly using the Unfair Competition Law to protect consumers and business enterprises subject to unfair trade practices and intellectual property cases. In June 1998, Beijing-based China Area Development Promoting Committee, a government agency with supervisory authority over the Tongyi Advertising Co., was ordered by the Beijing Intermediate People's Court to pay RMB100,000 ($12,048) and issue a public apology to a local clothing factory in an unfair competition case. In April 1994, Tongyi Advertising, an agent of Crocodile International Co Ltd. in Beijing, bought 26 men's trousers from the No. 1 Clothing Factory at the price of RMB188.03 ($22.65) each and changed their original "Maple" brand to "Carteld." The trousers were then sold at the Crocodile counter in the Parkson Shopping Center for RMB560 ($67) each. The No. 1 Clothing Factory registered the "Maple" brand for its clothes in the State Bureau of Trademarks in October 1979. At the request of the factory, in May 1994, the court ordered the unsold trousers to be confiscated. In August, the Crocodile International Co told the Tongyi Advertising Co. to stop selling Crocodile products. The Parkson Shopping Center also detained over RMB170,000 ($20,481) in sales revenues from all the relabeled goods. During the course of the investigation, the business license of Tongyi Advertising was revoked by the Beijing Bureau of Industry and Commerce. Since it no longer had the capability to bear civil responsibility, its supervisor, the China Area Development Promoting Committee, became the defendant of the case in June 1994. The court ruled that the Tongyi Advertising was not the end user of the trousers and had no right to change the product labels. By reaping excessive profit through the high-quality products of the plaintiff, the defendant's action had damaged the business prestige of the plaintiff and thus amounted to unfair competition. The case raises questions concerning the liability of government agencies responsible for supervising the activities of its sponsored enterprises. *See* Shao, *Court Punishes Committee for Unfair Play,* CHINA DAILY (June 15, 1998), available on Lexis, News Library, or on the Web site of the CHINA DAILY at http://www.chinadaily.com.cn. For an interesting discussion concerning an unfair competition case between a Chinese Newspaper and a Chinese television station concerning television shopping programs, *see TV Shopping Invites Criticism,* CHINA DAILY (Jan. 28, 1999), available on Lexis, News Library, or on the Web site of the CHINA DAILY at http://www.chinadaily.com.cn.

109. Pricing Law of the People's Republic of China (promulgated on December 29, 1997, by the Standing Committee of the NCP), art. 11, *reprinted in* CHINA LAWS FOR FOREIGN BUSINESS (CCH), Business Regulation ¶ 16-660 (hereinafter the "Pricing Law"). The Pricing Law replaced prior regulations

as a milestone in China's economic reform plan and necessary to create an environment of fair competition.[110] The Pricing Law was also enacted in response to a series of price wars in China's consumer products markets.[111] The law does not apply to interest rates, securities prices, futures prices, insurance premium rates, or foreign exchange rates.[112]

2. Exception for Government-Guided Prices

Although most products are not subject to price controls, the Pricing Law provides that the government may set "governmental guided prices" for a limited number of commodities and services, including grain, cotton, crude oil, and natural gas; rare resources such as gold and silver; public utilities such as electricity and centralized heating; transportation and telecommunications; and social services such as schools, hospitals, and parks.[113] The Pricing Law further provides that when formulating government-guided

---

adopted in 1987. Prior to 1979, the central government set prices for most commodities and means of production. At present, approximately 95% of commodity prices are set by producers. *See New China Price Law,* EAST ASIAN BUS. INTELLIGENCE (May 10, 1998), available on Lexis, News Library. In accordance with the Pricing Law, the State Development Planning Commission and the State Economic and Trade Commission jointly issued a set of regulations in December 1998 prohibiting the sale of merchandise below market cost in an effort to preclude price wars. The regulations further provide that companies that attempt to exclude competitors from the market with malicious intent are subject to penalties. *See New Rule Aiming to Ban Price Wars,* CHINA DAILY (Dec. 10, 1998), available on Lexis, News Library, or on the Web site of the CHINA DAILY at http://www.chinadaily.com.cn; Roberts, *So Much for Competition,* BUSINESS WEEK 28 (Int'l Ed., Nov. 30, 1998), available on Lexis, News Library.

110. *See generally China New Pricing Law Follows the Market Rules,* CHINA DAILY (Apr. 30, 1998), available on Lexis, News Library, or on the Web site of the CHINA DAILY at http://www.chinadaily.com.cn. *See also* Suppression of Acts of Price Monopoly Tentative Procedures (promulgated on June 18, 2003, and effective on November 1, 2003, by the State Development and Reform Commission) (outlines standards for dominant market position and abusive/predatory pricing practices, and the role of industry associations in China). The SDRC Regulation on Price Discrimination is designed to combat price monopoly activities by business operators in China. Pursuant to the regulation, "price monopoly" is defined as any activity where a business operator manipulates the market price to disturb the normal business order, to harm the legal interests of other business operators or consumers, or to damage the public interests of the society through conspiracy or by abusing their dominant market position ("DMP"). A DMP will be determined on the basis of market share, whether substitutes of the subject product are available, and the difficulties of market entry by new competitors. The authorities responsible for pricing issues are empowered to determine whether or not activities constitute a price monopoly. Under the new regulation, business operators may not engage in price monopoly activities, such as price fixing or restricting production quantities, through agreements, resolutions, or coordination. Moreover, business operators may not (a) restrict the resale prices of its distributors by taking advantage of their DMP; (b) make predatory profits; (c) dump goods with the purpose of harming competitors, or sell goods below cost in the form of kickback, subsidy, or donation; or (d) conduct price discrimination. The regulation is effective from November 1, 2003. *See generally* P. Neumann & J. Guo, *The Slow Boat to Antitrust Law in China: An Examination of New Regulations on Monopoly Pricing,* CHINA L. & PRAC. (Sept. 2003); *NDRC Issues Rule Against Monopolistic Pricing,* CHINA MARKET INTELLIGENCE, THE U.S.-CHINA BUSINESS COUNCIL (July 9, 2003), available online to members at http://www.uschina.org.

111. *See China Price Law Will Set Benchmark,* CHINA DAILY (Apr. 24, 1998), available on Lexis, News Library, or on the Web site of the CHINA DAILY at http://www.chinadaily.com.cn.

112. Pricing Law, art. 47.

113. Pricing Law, art. 18. *See also* Catalogue on the Pricing of Items (issued on July 4, 2001, by the State Development Planning Commission) (categorizes the products subject to government guided and fixed prices).

prices for monopolies or public utilities, business operators, retailers, wholesalers, consumers, and other interested parties may lodge opinions with respect to the proposed price levels to ensure that pricing meets current needs and is feasible.[114]

The Pricing Law further provides that government-guided prices should be subject to public hearings in order to curb arbitrary charges and price setting.[115] Pursuant to the Pricing Law, government agencies responsible for setting prices are required to evaluate the average costs of similar commodities and services, market supply and demand, requirements for the national economy, and society's economic capacity to support the government-guided prices.[116]

3. Pricing Prohibitions and Consumer Protection

The Pricing Law prohibits business operations from engaging in price collusion, below-market pricing that amounts to market dumping, deceptive pricing practices, and price discrimination.[117] With respect to deceptive pricing practices, business operators are prohibited from making claims of price reductions when the actual price of a product is being increased. Business operators are also precluded from using ambiguous language that claims lower prices to intentionally lure consumers, or using double pricing schemes (e.g., bait-and-switch), where low prices are advertised to entice consumers to purchase products but the ultimate price is much higher than advertised or the product actually purchased is of a different quality.[118] A violation of the law may result in administrative penalties, including monetary fines, confiscation of profits, cease-and-desist orders, and revocation of a business license.[119] Although the Pricing Law does not provide for judicial relief for an aggrieved party, a business operator that violates the law is required to compensate a consumer or other business operator for any damages caused by a violation.[120]

---

114. Pricing Law, arts. 22, 23, 24, 25.

115. *See* Trial Measures Regarding the Hearing on Decision-Making for Government Pricing (issued on July 2, 2001, by the State Development and Planning Commission) (outlines the standards and guidelines for public hearings on price issues).

116. Pricing Law, art. 21.

117. Pricing Law, arts. 13, 14. Within thirty days after the effective date of the Pricing Law, the Shanghai price control authorities levied an RMB3000 ($361) fine against a Shanghai supermarket for illegally selling detergent at less than its cost. Although the practice was deemed to benefit consumers, the pricing authorities maintained that the result was market disorder and harm to the public interest. *See Shanghai Supermarket Fined for Dumping Sale*, China Bus. Info. Network (June 1, 1998), available on Lexis, News Library; *Authorities Fine Shanghai Supermarket in Dumping Case*, Xinhua News Agency (May 29, 1998), available on Lexis, News Library. Collusive activities are also prohibited under the Unfair Competition Law, art. 15.

118. Pricing Law, arts. 13, 14.

119. Pricing Law, arts. 39–46.

120. Pricing Law, art. 41.

F. Food Processing

1. Health and Safety Standards

a. Food Hygiene Law

The Food Hygiene Law outlines the standards for the safety of food and its production.[121] The legislative purpose of the Food Hygiene Law is to ensure that food hygiene standards are enforced, and to prevent food contamination. The Food Hygiene Law is applicable to all *food production and operations* within the territory of the People's Republic of China,[122] as well as imported food products.[123] The Food Hygiene Law applies to all food, food

121. Food Hygiene Law of the People's Republic of China (adopted October 1995, by the 16th Sess. of the Standing Comm. of the 8th NPC), *reprinted in* CHINA LAWS FOR FOREIGN BUSINESS (CCH), Business Regulation ¶ 16-535. The export of food products produced in China is regulated by the Procedures of the People's Republic of China on the Hygiene Management of Foods for Export (for Trial Implementation), promulgated on July 16, 1984 by the State Administration of Import and Export Commodity Inspection and the Ministry of Public Health, *reprinted in* CHINA LAWS FOR FOREIGN BUSINESSS (CCH), Business Regulation ¶ 16-555 (covers supervision and management, inspection and release, registration procedures, and legal liability and penalties). The Ministry of Health also adopted food hygiene rules for the restaurants and establishments that serve beverages. *See* Administrative Rules for Food Hygiene of the Restaurant and Beverage Industry, issued by MOH on January 16, 2000, and effective on June 1, 2000 (Chinese version available on the Web site of the Ministry of Health at http://www.moh.gov.cn). The State Environmental Protection Administration has developed standards for the organic food industry in China. *See* Administration of the Certification of Organic Food Procedures (issued on June 19, 2001, by the State Environmental Protection Administration, effective as of date of issue) (hereinafter the "Organic Food Standards"). *China Law and Practice* September 2001, Vol. 15 No. 7, p.7. The Procedures define "organic foods" as food that complies with State food hygiene standards and organic specifications and is produced without using agricultural chemicals, chemical fertilizers, growth hormones, chemical additives, artificial colorings, chemical preservatives, and genetic engineering technology. The Organic Food Standards apply to the production, certification, distribution, and sale of organic foods in the PRC. All organic food producers and sellers must submit applications to the organic food certification committee of SEPA for approval and registration. Certification is valid for two years and enables the certified entity to label its food products as "organic" in the manner stipulated by the certification body.

122. Food Hygiene Law, arts. 1, 4. "Food production and operation" refers to all activities involved in food production (except cultivation of crops and raising of livestock), collection, purchasing, processing, storage, transport, display, supply, and sales. *Id.* art. 54.

123. Food Hygiene Law, art. 30. Foods, food additives, food containers and packaging materials, and food-related utensils and equipment that have been imported must comply with national hygiene standards and the stipulations of hygiene control. Food imports are also subject to various inspection and quarantine procedures. *See* Administrative Measures on the Inspection and Quarantine of Imported/Exported Meat Products (issued on October 1, 2002, by the Administration of Quality Supervision, Inspection, and Quarantine [AQSIQ]) (provides that all meat product exporters must register with AQSIQ before exporting; meat importers must have animal and plant quarantine licenses before signing the import contract; and imported meat products are to arrive at AQSIQ-designated ports for inspection and quarantine before entering the Chinese market); Administrative Measures on the Examination and Approval of the Quarantine of Imported Animals and Plants (issued on September 1, 2002, by the AQSIQ) (provides that importers of animals or plants must have an AQSIQ quarantine license in order to clear customs, and that importers must have legal person status and import and export rights); Measures on Inspection Exemptions for Imported/Exported Commodities (issued on October 1, 2002, by the AQSIQ) (provides that commodities with good quality records may be exempted from inspection for three years; that commodities' consignee, consignor, or manufacturer may apply for such exemption if the commodity satisfies requirements for quality, reputation, and standards; and that certain items, such as food, animal/plant products, hazardous products and their packages, commodities of a highly unstable nature, and bulk goods are not eligible for an exemption).

additives, food containers, packaging materials, and related utensils and equipment. It also applies to surrounding premises and facilities used in *food production and operations*.[124] China has developed rules to govern the safety of genetically modified agricultural products.[125]

Under the Food Hygiene Law all foods manufactured or imported into China are forbidden to contain toxic or other harmful substances.[126] Foods at all times, including during and after production, are subject to basic sensory tests for appropriate color, smell, and taste. This is to ensure that spoiled or contaminated foods do not enter the market.[127]

Hygiene standards and inspection rules for all food, food-related products, and manufacturing facilities are set by the Ministry of Health (MOH) and SFDA. In the event that the MOH or SFDA have not formulated specific hygiene standards, the local government authority is authorized to formulate its own hygiene standard. However, the local authority is required to report these new standards to the appropriate department of the Ministry of Health SFDA for approval.[128] Food commodities geared toward infants and young children should also comply with nutritional and hygiene standards stipulated by the Ministry of Health (MOH).[129]

The Food Hygiene Law requires that *food production and operations* processes comply with the following hygiene standards:

(1) The production and storage facilities, containers, and packaging must be clean, internally and externally

124. Food Hygiene Law, art. 4.

125. *See* Regulation on the Management of Agricultural Genetically Modified Organisms, promulgated on July 11, 2001, by the Ministry of Agriculture. The PRC Ministry of Agriculture (MOA) released long-awaited clarifications to the Regulation on the Management of Agricultural Genetically Modified Organism (Ag GMO) Safety (Order No. 304) issued on July 11, 2001. The clarifications, released on January 5 and effective on March 20, 2002, are in the form of three rules that cover management of safety evaluation, import procedures, and labeling requirements for agricultural products. The Chinese text of the rules is available on the Web site of the MOA at http://www.agri.gov.cn. *See generally Genetic Modification in Agriculture: The Impact of China's Regulations on Foreign Trade and Investment,* CHINA L. & PRAC. (Nov. 2001) (author describes the regulatory system for GM agriculture in China, IP rights for breeders, and bio-safety regulations and standards); D. Yearman, *Seeds of Change: New Opportunities for Commercializing PVRs in China,* CHINA L. & PRAC. (October 2002) (author discusses plant variety regulations and standards, standards for compulsory licenses, term of protection for plant varieties, penalties for infringement, and application and approval process). In July 2003, it was reported that the Chinese Ministry of Agriculture had pushed back the launch date of its safety evaluation approval mechanism for genetically modified organism imports to April 20, 2004. *See generally MOA Extends Temporary GMO Administrative Regime,* CHINA MARKET INTELLIGENCE, THE U.S.-CHINA BUSINESS COUNCIL (June 4, 2003), available online to members at http://www.uschina.org.

126. On October 24, 2003, the MOH notified the WTO of 17 new food safety standards that set limits on the amount certain substances in food and agricultural products. *See* http://www.tbt-sps.gov.cn for copies of the food standards.

127. Food Hygiene Law, arts. 6, 7.

128. Food Hygiene Law, arts. 14, 15.

129. The Ministry of Health, Department of Law and Supervision specifically regulates food law issues and sets the standards for nutrition.

(2) The facilities used for storage or transport must be free of any toxic substances or vermin such as insects or rodents
(3) The manufacturer is required to provide sanitary storage, packing, and processing facilities for raw food materials
(4) The manufacturer is required to provide appropriate disinfection facilities, washrooms, lighting, and ventilation to protect the food from decay or undesirable substances
(5) The production machinery should be placed appropriately to prevent cross contamination of processed and unprocessed foods
(6) All equipment used in food production should be washed and disinfected before subsequent use, and is required to be maintained in sanitary conditions
(7) Routine maintenance to prevent contamination of food is required for all manufacturing equipment, facilities, and food containers
(8) The packaging of ready-to-eat foods should be nontoxic and clean
(9) The employees are required to wash their hands and wear clean clothing and head wear during production and sales of food
(10) The water used in food production must comply with national hygiene standards
(11) The detergents and disinfectants used in the food production process are required to be safe for humans[130]

Meat and meat products that have not undergone veterinary health inspection or fail to pass inspection, as well as live animals whose reasons of death are unknown or a result of disease, are not allowed entry into the country.[131] Damaged food goods and food transported in undesirable conditions resulting in contamination may also be excluded from entry.[132]

In the event that a manufacturer wishes to change the production or packaging of an existing approved food product, the Food Hygiene Law states that a manufacturer should submit the details necessary for hygiene and nutritional evaluation of a product before commencing changes. This requires the provision of samples of the product with the proposed changes and then submission of an application for approval.[133] Importers should note that inspection reports and details regarding agricultural chemicals, additives, and fumigants used in the exporting country

130. Food Hygiene Law, art. 8.
131. Food Hygiene Law, art. 9.
132. Food Hygiene Law, art. 9.
133. Food Hygiene Law, art. 20. An application should be submitted to the appropriate government agency. This may be different for different food products.

or region are required to be included in the declaration of goods for hygiene inspection.[134]

b. Food Additives and Food Packaging

Food additives are often excluded from ingredient lists of food products manufactured or imported into China. The State intends on remedying this and defines a food additive as a food substance that is a chemical compound or natural substance added to food in order to improve its quality, color, smell, or flavor, or a preservative or processing requirement.[135] The Food Hygiene Law also applies to food additives. Additives are required not to contain toxins or be detrimental to the health of the consumer. All equipment associated with the production of food and its packaging should comply with hygiene requirements. These items should be easy to clean and disinfect.[136]

c. Enforcement of the Food Hygiene Law

In the event of a violation of the Food Hygiene Law, the health authorities have the power to order product recall, halt production or operations, confiscate income and profits, and impose a monetary fine between one and five times the amount of the illegal income. A party in violation of the law is liable for a fine ranging from RMB1,000 to RMB50,0000 for a product that has entered the market and resulted in illness or food poisoning.[137] If the food has not entered the marketplace, the health authorities may impose monetary penalties for violations of the law ranging from RMB1,000 to RMB5,000. In the event of a serious case of food poisoning or serious disease endangering human health or if toxic harmful nonfood raw materials are added to the produced food, criminal liability may be pursued by the health authorities.[138] A company in violation of health laws also risks the loss of its health permits and business license.[139] A manufacturer is also legally liable if it engages in food production or operations without first obtaining a sanitation permit, or uses a forged or altered permit.[140]

134. Food Hygiene Law, art. 30.
135. Food Hygiene Law, art. 54.
136. Food Hygiene Law, arts. 12, 13.
137. Food Hygiene Law, arts. 51–53. Criminal liability may be imposed for corruption and other abuses of power by heath officials. A party that interferes with the work of the health authorities is also liable for civil penalties and potential criminal liability.
138. Food Hygiene Law, art. 39.
139. Food Hygiene Law, art. 30.
140. Food Hygiene Law, arts. 40–42.

2. Labeling

a. General Labeling Requirements

The Chinese government has promulgated the General Standard for the Labeling of Foods, which applies only to packaged food and beverages sold directly to consumers and does not apply to shipping units or individual packages not designed for individual sale.[141] The five fundamental elements required on all food labels are:

(1) Name of the food
(2) Ingredient list
(3) Name and address of manufacturer or distributor
(4) Net contents
(5) Country of origin
(6) Date of production
(7) Quality guarantee period and/or storage period

According to the General Standard for the Labeling of Foods, each packaged food and beverage product sold must also contain, at minimum, the following properties:

(1) A label attached to the packaging container that clearly indicates the product and ingredients in an easy-to-understand, accurate, and scientific manner
(2) Food name indicated on the label at an eye-catching level
(3) Languages used must include standard Chinese
(4) Other languages can use only letters and characters that are the corresponding size of the Chinese characters
(5) Other languages used, if any, must be consistent with the Chinese characters
(6) Standard measurements must be in the metric system
(7) Storage period or shelf life must be clearly marked on the package in a sequence of year, month, and date, referring to the date up until which quality of the food product can be assured for sale
(8) Ingredient table arranged in order retrogressively according to the amount used; all ingredients, including food additives, must be listed

141. General Standards for the Labeling of Foods (promulgated February 4, 1994, by the State Bureau for Technical Supervision for implementation from February 1995), *reprinted in* China Laws for Foreign Business (CCH), Business Regulation ¶ 16-586. As of September of 1996 all imported food products must meet China's labeling standards or otherwise product entry may be blocked into China.

(9) Product standard code and/or serial numbers of State or industry standards should be present as well as batch number and address of manufacturer
(10) Nutritional value[142]

The Chinese government allows importers of prepackaged foods to use sticker labels to display the required information. In practice, the Chinese government has been flexible with the labeling laws as they apply to food product imports.

Importers of food products are required to apply for entry of their products through the State Bureau of Technical Supervision (SBTS). The approval procedure takes approximately one year for labeling requirements. In the interim, a manufacturer may obtain a temporary labeling approval through the State Health Quarantine Bureau.[143]

The Product Quality Law also outlines the basics of China's labeling laws. It further provides that *manufacturers* are prohibited from engaging in the following activities:

(1) Falsely designating the place of origin of the goods on the product packaging
(2) Falsely stating the origin of the goods as originating from a facility of another party
(3) Falsely using the quality certification marks or famous brand marks of another party
(4) Selling substandard products that are claimed to meet particular standards
(5) Selling products that have been declared by the State to be obsolete
(6) Selling counterfeit products as genuine merchandise[144]

The Product Quality Law provides that product packaging is required to include, in the Chinese language, a description of the product quality inspection certificate, the name and address of the manufacturing facility, the product expiration date, necessary warnings concerning the product, and the product's specifications, contents, and principal ingredients.[145] For products that are highly toxic, hazardous, or fragile, the packaging is required to

142. Labeling of nutrients must comply with chapter IV of GB 7718-General Standard for Food Labeling.

143. Due to frequent changes in requirements and bureaucratic procedures, readers are advised to consult with local authorities on current practices to obtain labeling approval.

144. Product Quality Law, arts. 17–20. The sale of counterfeit goods and the misuse of a certification mark or famous brand mark also violate the intellectual property laws of China.

145. Product Quality Law, art. 15.

include appropriate warnings indicating proper handling during transportation and storage.[146]

b. Enforcement of Labeling Standards

Violations of the labeling laws are set forth in the Regulations for the Investigation and Punishment for Food Labeling.[147] In most instances in which labeling violations occur, the authorities will order the violation to be corrected within a specific period of time. If the matter is not resolved before the imposed deadline, the government authorities would order the suspension of production and sales of the product. Fines ranging between RMB500 and RMB5,000 may be imposed, or fines ranging from 10 percent to 3 times the value of the product in addition to the suspension of the sale of the product are possible. The amount fined depends on the severity of the labeling violation. For example, RMB500 to RMB1,000 or 10 percent of the value of the said imported product will be fined when:

(1) The labeling on the foodstuff fails to note one or more of the required items of the quality grading, the product standard number, or specification of a product that has undergone ionization
(2) The items required to be noted on the label are complete but fail to comply with one of the Basic Principles of the General Labeling Standards

A more substantial penalty of RMB1,000–3,000 or 15 percent of the value of the batch of foodstuffs may be imposed if the product name or net content of the foodstuff is not noted on the labeling. Penalties will range for specific violations.[148]

c. Inspection

Imported and domestic food commodities are subject to inspection for quality, safety, labeling, and customs purposes. If an import commodity passes the safety and quality licensing system of the State, a quality certification mark known as the CCIB safety mark may be affixed to the product. The Administration for Commodity Inspections Department (ACI) provides

146. Product Quality Law, art. 16.

147. Regulations for the Investigation and Punishment for Food Labeling Violations (Issued June 20, 1995, by the State Bureau for Technical Supervision), *reprinted in* CHINA LAWS FOR FOREIGN BUSINESS (CCH), Business Regulation (CCH) ¶ 16-587 (hereinafter "Regulations on Food Labeling Violations") (Chinese version is available on the Web site of the Ministry of Health at http://www.moh.gov.cn).

148. *See* Regulations on Food Labeling Violations, arts. 3–9.

qualified applicants with a CCIB holographic certification mark for imported products that are not manufactured in China.[149]

Inspections of food products manufactured in China by foreign companies are subject to the same rules as local companies. Inspections for hygiene and quality standards are carried out at both the State and local levels, and may be conducted without notice or search warrant.[150] Imported goods will be subjected to an additional customs inspection to determine if the quality of the product is consistent with CCIB standards to ensure that sanitation standards are met.[151]

d. Supervision and Administration

In 1997, the Ministry of Health promulgated additional rules that impose administrative and criminal liability for violations under the Food Hygiene Law.[152] In addition to a suspension or revocation of a violating party's health permit, the MOH is empowered to issue penalties as follows:

(1) If there are illegal profits, the health authority shall confiscate the profits and impose a fine ranging from one to three times the amount of the illegal profits; or
(2) If there are no illegal profits, the health authority may impose a monetary fine ranging from RMB500 to RMB10,000[153]

MOH has also issued the procedural rules for the MOH's (and SFDA's) regulatory activities.[154] The Food Hygiene Procedural Rules set forth provisions regarding the scope of jurisdiction of the health authorities[155] and application standards for health permits.[156] For instance, the health authority is required to review and respond in writing within 30 days after receiving an application for a newly established, enlarged, or modified product of a food producer or processor. [157]

149. Methods on Supervision and Administration of the Quality of Imported Commodities in the Circulation Sector, *printed in* International Business, Vol. 130 Issue 4, p. 51 (1998).

150. Food Hygiene Law, art. 32.

151. Food Hygiene Law, arts. 34–36. The law requires that food hygiene inspectors be qualified and must execute their duties confidentially due to technical information provided by food producers and operators.

152. Food Hygiene Penalty Rules, art. 1.

153. Food Hygiene Penalty Rules, art. 12.

154. Rules for Procedure for Supervising the Food Hygiene Law, issued on March 15, 1997, by the Ministry of Health and effective on June 1, 1997 (hereinafter the "Food Hygiene Procedural Rules") (Chinese version available on the Web site of the Ministry of Health at http://www.moh.gov.cn).

155. Food Hygiene Procedural Rules, arts. 5–11.

156. Food Hygiene Procedural Rules, arts. 12–16.

157. Food Hygiene Procedural Rules, arts. 18, 19.

G. Pharmaceuticals

The NPC has adopted a national Drug Administration Law that sets forth the general standards for pharmaceutical manufacturers and standards for marketing and sale of pharmaceutical products, regulatory issues, and liability standards.[158] The Drug Administration Law was first adopted in 1984 but subsequently amended in 2001, and applies to all enterprises engaged in the research, manufacture, trade, use, supervision, and management of drugs within the territory of the People's Republic of China.[159] The State Food and Drug Administration (SFDA), formerly known as the State Pharmaceutical Administration, is responsible for supervising drug manufacturers.[160]

The policy of the government, as set forth in the Drug Administration Law, is to support the development of both modern and traditional medicine. In addition, the government's stated policy is to support the development of new drugs and to protect the rights of parties that develop or invent new medicines or applications.[161]

---

158. Law of the People's Republic of China on the Administration of Drugs, Adopted September 20, 1984, at the 7th Meeting of the Standing Committee of the 6th National People's Congress and Amended February 28, 2001, at the 20th Meeting of the Standing Committee of the 9th National People's Congress, Repromulgated February 28, 2001, by Presidential Order No. 45 of the People's Republic of China, *reprinted in* CHINA LAWS FOR FOREIGN BUSINESS (CCH), Business Regulation ¶ 16-545 (hereinafter the "Drug Administration Law"). *See generally WTO and China's Drug Makers,* Market Letter, January 7, 2002, available on Lexis, News File; *China's Pharmaceutical Industry,* Xinhua Economic News Service, June 5, 2002, available on Lexis, News Library; Li, *New Developments in China's Pharmaceutical Regulatory Regime,* J. COMM. BIOTECHNOLOGY 241 (Winter 2002); Beach, *China Opens Drug Market by Revising Pharmaceutical Law,* Lancet, pg. 942, March 24, 2001 (the author states that "Chinese health leaders aim to promote a uniform code of conduct for manufacturers and importers and strengthen law enforcement to overcome the strong influence of local protectionism rackets that are currently stifling the pharmaceutical market"); *A Legislative Prescription for the Ills of the Drug Industry,* CHINA L. & PRAC. (April 2001) (analyzes the 2001 amendments to the Drug Administration Law). The Drug Administration Law defines a "drug" as a "substance used for the prevention, treatment and diagnosis of human diseases, and with the object of regulating human physiological functions, with stipulated indications, main functions of treatment, usage and dosage. It includes Chinese medicinal materials and Chinese medicinal liquids and tablets, prepared Chinese medicines, chemical raw material drugs and their components, antibiotics, biochemical drugs, radioactive drugs, blood serums and vaccines, blood products, diagnostic drugs and so on." Drug Administration Law, art. 102. The State Drug Administration has adopted a number of rules and regulations concerning traditional Chinese medicine production and sale. *See* Tentative Norms for the Quality Management of the Production of Chinese Medicinal Materials, promulgated on April 17, 2002, by the State Drug Administration (standards for medicinal material cultivation and production, environmental protection– and endangered species–related issues, processing standards, quality control, standards for equipment and personnel, and recordkeeping). *See generally China: Traditional Medicine Gets Tonic,* CHINA DAILY, May 21, 2001, available on Lexis, News Library; *China Revamps Traditional Medicine,* Xinhua Economic News Service, May 22, 2001, available on Lexis, News Library.

159. Drug Administration Law, art. 2.

160. The SDA was created in 1998 and took over the functions of the State Pharmaceutical Administration, the Drug Administration Bureau of the Ministry of Health, and the State Administration of Traditional Chinese Medicine. The entity is now known as the State Food and Drug Administration, or SFDA.

161. Drug Administration Law, arts. 3, 4.

1. Standards for Drug Manufacturers

Manufacturers of pharmaceuticals are required to apply for a Drug Production License from the SFDA or local branch, and no production may take place until a license is received.[162] A producer is limited to production that meets the scope of the license and must meet the following conditions:

(1) Have on staff pharmacists, engineering technicians, and other relevant technical workers whose qualifications have been recognized in accordance with the law
(2) Have factory facilities appropriate for drug production
(3) Have sufficient management personnel capable of carrying out quality assessment of the drugs produced
(4) Have rules and regulations to guarantee drug quality[163]

Pharmaceutical manufacturers are required to manage their production in accordance with the *Standards for Quality Control of Drug Production* stipulated by the SFDA. The SFDA conducts inspections of manufacturer facilities to determine compliance with the Standards and issues assessment reports certifying whether a factory is in compliance.[164] All pharmaceutical manufacturers are required to maintain production records, which are accessible to the SFDA inspectors upon request. Where a pharmaceutical manufacturer makes changes to its production techniques that affect the quality of the drugs, the enterprise is required to submit a report for examination and approval to the SFDA or local branch. Raw materials and supplementary materials required for drug production must meet the standards required for pharmaceutical use. Pharmaceutical manufacturers are required

162. Production or trading of drugs without a Drug Production License, Drug-trading License, or Dispensing License is prohibited. Drugs produced or sold in violation of the law and any illegal earnings must be confiscated. A fine of two to five times the value of the illegally produced or sold drugs (including sold or unsold drugs) may be imposed. In serious situations, the government may pursue criminal penalties. Drug Administration Law, art. 73.

163. Drug Administration Law, art. 7, 8. Drug manufacturers are required to comply with good manufacturing practices (GMP). A party that secures a production, sales, or dispensing license by means of misrepresentation or falsification of documents may be fined, imprisoned, and/or debarred from the industry. Drug Administration Law, art. 82, 83. For a list of GMP-certified manufacturers, *see* http://www.sda.gov.cn. *See also* Notice on Issues Regarding Strengthening the Administration of Applications to Produce Generic Pharmaceutical Products (effective June 1, 2002, by the SFDA) (producers of generic drugs are limited to apply for the right to produce no more than five drugs at a time or until the SFDA reviews all pending applications).

164. Drug Administration Law, art. 9. Where pharmaceutical manufacturers or sellers fail to implement the *Standards for Quality Control of Drug Production, Standards for Quality Control of Drug-trading,* quality control standards for nonclinical drug research, or quality control standards for clinical drug testing, warnings and orders may be issued for corrective measures to be taken within a time limit. If, after notice, no corrective measures have been taken, the SFDA may issue an order to stop production of an enterprise or to issue a monetary penalty of between RMB5,000 and RMB20,000. Where the situation is serious, the Drug Production License, Drug-trading License, and qualifications as a clinical drug-testing body may be revoked. Drug Administration Law, art. 79.

to implement a quality control program that meets State compliance standards. Drugs that are not produced in accordance with State standards may not be distributed or sold.[165]

The Drug Administration Law prohibits the production and sale of pharmaceuticals that make unfounded or spurious claims. A drug is spurious if any one of the following circumstances exists:

(1) The ingredients contained in the drug are inconsistent with State-approved drug standards
(2) The drug product is replaced by a nondrug substance, or a drug is replaced by another drug

Pharmaceuticals shall be treated as spurious drugs if one of the following circumstances exists:

(1) The SFDA has prohibited its use
(2) The drug is produced or imported without approval, or where the drug is sold without undergoing the testing required by law
(3) The drug product has deteriorated
(4) The drug product is contaminated
(5) The drug product is produced using unapproved raw medicinal materials or component parts
(6) The indicated suitability or the main functions of treatment exceed regulated scopes[166]

The Drug Administration Law also prohibits the production and sale of inferior drug products, which include the following:

(1) Drug products with packaging that does not indicate the expiration date or where the expiration date is altered
(2) Drug products with packaging on which the batch number is not indicated or has been altered

---

165. Drug Administration Law, arts. 10–12. The revised Drug Administration Law does away with local product registration and local product quality standards. The law requires that employees of producers, distributors, and sellers are required to go through annual medical examinations, and persons suffering from contagious diseases or any other disease that may cause contamination must not engage in work involving direct contact with pharmaceuticals. Art. 51.

166. Drug Administration Law, art. 48. Where spurious drugs are produced or sold, the illegally produced or sold drugs and the illegal earnings may be confiscated. A fine of two to five times the value of the illegally produced or sold spurious drugs may be imposed. Where a drug approval certificate has been issued, the certificate may be cancelled, and the parties involved may be ordered to stop production or stop operations for rectification. Where the situation is serious, the Drug Production License, Drug-trading License, or Dispensing License may be revoked. Drug Administration Law, art. 74. The law also provides that in serious cases involving the production and sale of spurious drugs, the liable party may be barred from the industry for ten years. Drug Administration Law, art. 76. The law also empowers the SFDA to pursue the responsible personnel at any company that produces spurious drugs. Drug Administration Law, art. 97.

(3) Drug products that have passed the expiration date
(4) Drug products for which the packing materials or containers directly in contact with the drugs have not been approved
(5) Drug products to which unauthorized coloring agents, preservatives, spices, sweeteners, or supplementary materials are added
(6) Drug products with ingredients that do not comply with state drug standards
(7) Products with other issues that do not comply with drug standards regulations[167]

2. Standards for Drug Wholesalers and Retailers

A company that engages in the wholesale or retail trade of pharmaceuticals is required to apply to the SFDA or its local branch for a Drug Trading License. No enterprise or individual may distribute or sell pharmaceuticals unless they hold a valid Drug Trading License. In order to secure approval for a license, an enterprise interested in engaging in the wholesale or retail trade of pharmaceuticals is required to meet the following conditions:

(1) Have pharmacists on staff that are certified in accordance with the law
(2) Have business premises, equipment, storage facilities, and a hygienic environment appropriate for wholesale and retail trading[168]

167. Drug Administration Law, art. 49. Where inferior drugs are produced or sold, the illegally produced or sold drugs and the illegal earnings may be confiscated. A fine of two to three times the value of the illegally produced or sold inferior drugs may be imposed. Where a drug approval certificate is issued, the certificate may be cancelled, and the parties involved may be ordered to stop production or stop operations for rectification. Where the situation is serious, the Drug Production License, Drug-trading License, or Dispensing License may be revoked. Where a crime is constituted, criminal liability may be pursued. Drug Administration Law, art. 75. The law also provides that in serious cases involving the production and sale of inferior drugs, the liable party may be barred from the industry for ten years. Drug Administration Law, art. 76. A violation of the law exposes a producer to civil liability for compensation to any injured consumer. Drug Administration Law, art. 93. *See also* Notification on Further Strengthening Supervision over the Drug Quality and on Preventing Serious Drug-Related Accidents along with the Major Inspection of Work Safety, promulgated on June 12, 2002, by the State Drug Administration (instructions to SFDA branches to crack down on counterfeit and inferior drugs and to enhance supervision of drug advertisements).

168. The law requires that employees of producers, distributors, and sellers are required to go through annual medical examinations and persons suffering from contagious diseases or any other disease that may cause contamination must not engage in work involving direct contact with pharmaceuticals. Drug Administration Law, art. 51. *See also* Notification on the Relevant Issues Concerning Accreditation of Qualifications of Practicing Pharmacists in Enterprises Dealing in Drugs, promulgated April 18, 2002, by the State Drug Administration (outlining the examination guidelines for qualifying pharmacists). A wholesaler of drugs is required to obtain approval at the provincial level of the SFDA, whereas retailers are required to be approved by the local level of the SFDA. On February 4, 2004, the SFDA issued regulations setting forth the requirements and procedures for the issuance of business licenses to drug retailers and wholesalers. *See* Rules on the Administration of Drug Operating Licensing (issued on February 4, 2004, by the SFDA) (outlining requirements for wholesale and retail companies involved with drugs, biological products, herbal medicine, pharmaceutical raw materials, and biochemical products).

(3) Have quality control policies appropriate for wholesale and retail trading

(4) Have rules and regulations to guarantee the quality of the drugs it distributes or sells[169]

Pharmaceutical sellers shall handle drugs in accordance with the *Standards for the Quality Control of Drug-Trading* adopted by the SFDA. Pharmaceutical sellers are required to establish procedures to verify the quality certificates of products they purchase, and maintain complete inventory and sales records. Sales records should indicate the general names of the drugs, the forms of the drugs, specifications, batch numbers, periods of validity, manufacturers, units of purchase or sale, quantities of purchase or sale, prices of purchase or sale, dates of purchase or sale, and other contents required by the SFDA.[170] Drug products sold by sellers must clearly indicate the method of use and dosage. In dispensing prescriptions, the seller is required to check and verify the prescription to ensure validity, and drugs dispensed pursuant to a prescription should not be altered in any way by the seller. If a prescription contains ingredients that are incompatible or amounts of ingredients in excess of the proper dosage, the prescription must be rejected, or after the prescribing physician has made the appropriate corrections. A pharmaceutical seller should also establish an inventory system governing drug storage and shall take necessary measures for cold storage, anti-freeze, anti-damp, insect-free, rodent-free, and other storage facilities to guarantee drug quality.[171]

3. Importation of Pharmaceuticals

The importation of drugs is regulated by the SFDA, and import approval is granted only if the drugs comply with quality standards and are safe for use. After examination, the SFDA will issue a Registration Certificate for Imported Drugs.[172] The Drug Administration Law prohibits importing drugs that give no effective results for treatment, that result in serious side-effects to users, or that are harmful to human health for any reason. The law also prohibits the importation of counterfeit, contaminated, diluted, and decomposed drug materials.

169. Drug Administration Law, arts. 14, 15.

170. Drug Administration Law, arts. 16–18. A violation of these provisions is grounds for revocation of license. Art. 85.

171. Drug Administration Law, arts. 19–20.

172. Drug Administration Law, arts. 38, 39, 45. *See* Regulation on Managing Imported Drugs (issued on August 18, 2003, and effective on January 1, 2004, by the State Food & Drug Administration). *See generally SFDA Releases Regulation on Management of Imported Drugs,* China Market Intelligence, The U.S.-China Business Council (September 24, 2003). Although importers must go through a cumbersome approval

Drugs may only be imported through designated ports of entry, and the importer of record is required to register the importation with SFDA officials at the port of entry. The importer is required to produce a Customs Clearance Sheet for Imported Drugs issued by the SFDA in order to complete processing with Customs. Without the Customs Clearance Sheet for Imported Drugs, the customs office is barred from allowing entry of the goods. The SFDA may require that imported drugs go through random tests for purposes of quality control. Testing may also be required for biological products and drugs to be sold in China for the first time.[173]

4. Packaging of Pharmaceuticals

The containers and packaging materials that have direct contact with drugs are required to be approved by the SFDA and must comply with the requirements for pharmaceutical use and the standards for human health and safety. Manufacturers are prohibited from using unapproved packaging materials or containers, and the SFDA may order the suspension of any use of unapproved containers or packaging materials. Drug packages are required to include a label or instruction booklet that provides the name of the drug, its ingredients, specifications, the manufacturing enterprise, approval number, product batch number, date of production, expiry date, suitability for symptoms or main function, methods of use, dosage, contraindications, side effects, and important points to note. The labels of narcotic drugs, psychotropic drugs, poisonous drugs, radioactive drugs, drugs for external use only, and nonprescription drugs must include the appropriate warning information.[174]

---

procedure before imported drugs can be introduced to the market, once approved foreign companies will enjoy unrestricted access to the Chinese market. The import of a small amount of drugs for urgent clinical needs of a medical organization or for individual personal use pursuant to prescription may be allowed without a Registration Certificate. With respect to the export of pharmaceuticals, the export of drugs may be restricted if the local supply is insufficient to supply the domestic market. Arts. 43, 44, 45. Where the import of drugs that have been granted a registration certificate for drug import has not been registered for the record, in accordance with the provisions of this Law, with the drug control and administrative departments at the place where the port permitted to import the drugs is located, warnings shall be issued. The parties involved shall be ordered to take corrective action. If no corrective action is taken within the time required, the registration certificate for the drug import may be revoked. Drug Administration Law, art. 81.

173. Drug Administration Law, arts. 40, 41. If the imported drugs fail the quality tests, they may not be imported or sold in China. *See also* Administrative Measures on Customs Clearance, Recordkeeping, and Inspection of Imported Drugs, promulgated on May 27, 2002, by the State Drug Administration (outlines procedures for customs clearance, port drug inspectors, inspection procedures, supervision, and penalties for importations in violation of the law). The SFDA also regulates the export of pharmaceuticals. *See* Provisional Regulation for Drug Export Processing (issued on June 29, 2003, by the SFDA).

174. Drug Administration Law, arts. 52, 53, 54. A violation of these provisions is grounds for revocation of the production license. Art. 86. *See also* Administrative Rules on Packing Materials, Labels, and Specifications for Drugs, promulgated by the State Drug Administration (outlines standards for packaging and labels of pharmaceuticals); Notice on Issuing the Detailed Rules on Criteria for Packing Materials and Labels for Drugs (Trial Implementation), promulgated on November 11, 2001; Announcement Regarding the Expiration of Pharmaceutical Products' Packaging Labels and Explanatory Notes

5. Pricing of Pharmaceuticals

The price of pharmaceuticals is either determined by the market or subject to government-fixed or recommended prices.[175] The Drug Administration Law provides that if the government sets or issues a recommended price, the drug price should take into consideration the basis of social average cost, market supply and demand, and social endurance, so as to make the price comply with quality, eliminate abnormally high prices, and protect the proper rights and interests of consumers. Pharmaceutical manufacturers and sellers are required to implement the drug prices fixed or recommended by the government. Manufacturers are required to submit their production costs to pricing authorities for pharmaceuticals subject to price controls.[176] The Drug Administration Law provides that manufacturers and sellers are

---

(promulgated by the State Drug Administration as Order No. 156 and effective on May 24, 2002) (announcement requires that drug manufacturers replace and update labels within six months of receiving product approval numbers).

175. For pricing purposes, the Chinese government classifies all medicines into two general categories, namely, medicine listed in the Pharmaceutical Catalogue for National Basic Medical Insurance and nonlisted medicine. Listed medicines are classified into Class A and Class B medicines and are defined as follows: *Class A Pharmaceuticals* refers to those raw materials and preparations that are first invented as well as those that have research release in foreign countries but have not been approved for public sale by any countries. *Class B Pharmaceuticals* refers to those drugs that have been allowed for sale but are not included in the international pharmaceutical catalogue and are not imported into China. The Chinese government will make fixed prices for all listed medicines. For Class A medicines and some monopolized and patent pharmaceuticals, the State Development and Reform Commission (SDRC) will approve and establish the highest price allowed for sales to the public, and no pharmacy or medical facility is permitted to sell above the approved maximum price. Drug manufacturers, however, have the freedom to set their own wholesale prices. In determining fixed maximum prices or pricing guidelines, the SDRC will consider a number of factors, including manufacturing costs, prices of similar drugs domestically and internationally, and reasonable profits. The SDRC will also review the Sales Cost Ratio (SCR) and the Sales Profit Ratio (SPR) when setting drug prices. The SCR refers to the percentage of sales cost in sales revenue and the SPR refers to the percentage of sales profit in sales revenue. For Class A pharmaceuticals, the highest SCR is 30% and the highest SPR is 45%. For Class B pharmaceuticals, the highest SCR is 20% and there is no limit for the SPR. For Class B pharmaceuticals, the SDRC will establish pricing guidelines, in contrast to a set maximum sales price for provincial-level pricing authorities to follow. For nonlisted pharmaceuticals, prices by manufacturers, retailers, or medical institutions are based on market conditions. For preparations made in-house by medical facilities, the sales price is generally calculated by manufacturing cost plus 5% profit. *See* Measures on Government Pricing of Pharmaceuticals (issued in 2000 by the National Development Reform Commission); Implementing Rules on the Law of Pharmaceutical Administration (issued in August 2002 by the SDFA).

176. Drug Administration Law, arts. 55, 57. Violations of the provisions on the management of drug prices may result in penalties imposed in accordance with the *Price Law of the People's Republic of China*. Art. 89. *See* Pricing Law of the People's Republic of China (promulgated on December 29, 1997, by the Standing Committee of the NCP), art. 11, *reprinted in* CHINA LAWS FOR FOREIGN BUSINESS (CCH), Business Regulation ¶ 16-660 (hereinafter the "Pricing Law"). *See also* Supplementary Notification of the State Development Planning Commission's General Office on the Relevant Issues Concerning Declaration Materials for Enterprises' Independent Drug Price Fixing, promulgated on June 10, 2002, by the State Development Planning Commission's General Office (outlining procedures for submitting materials in support of independent price setting by drug manufacturers). The State Development Planning Commission issued a notice requiring that all drug prices be published in approved State Media before implementation. *See generally China: New Rules Mandate Drug Prices Get Published First,* CHINA ONLINE, April 26, 2001, available on Lexis, News Library; Qi, *Paying the Price for Medicine,* CHINA BUSINESS REVIEW, pgs. 8–11, Sept./Oct. 2000 (addresses the pricing policies for drugs in the PRC and the pricing formulas and procedures for the China market).

required to set market-regulated prices based upon and in accordance with the principles of "being fair, reasonable, honest and trustworthy, and of matching the price with the quality so as to provide drug-users with reasonably priced drugs" and that it is "prohibited to make unjustified large profits and engage in any deceiving behavior that shall jeopardize the rights and interests of drug users."[177] The law further provides that manufacturers and sellers are prohibited from giving or accepting commissions or other benefits when purchasing or selling drugs, and may not offer money, goods, or other benefits, in any form, to the responsible purchasing authorities of a hospital, clinic, or other medical institution.[178]

6. Drug Advertising

The law requires that advertisements for pharmaceutical sales be approved by the SFDA. Without approval, the advertisement is not allowed to be shown publicly.[179] The content of an advertisement is required to be accurate; may not contain expressions or guarantees of effectiveness that are unscientifically based; and must not use as evidence the names or images of state authorities, pharmaceutical research units, academic bodies, specialists, scholars, doctors, or patients.[180] In addition to the Drug Administration

177. Drug Administration Law, art. 56.

178. Drug Administration Law, art. 58. A violation of the prohibition on receiving commissions or compensation for drug sales is grounds for penalties under Articles 90 and 91 of the law, which include penalties, confiscation of income, loss of license, and potential criminal liability.

179. Drug Administration Law, arts. 60–63. The advertiser is required to obtain an approval number for each ad from the SFDA in advance of public distribution and showing of an advertisement concerning drugs. Information concerning a drug may be distributed in authorized medical journals without an advertisement number. In the event of violations, penalties may be imposed in accordance with the provisions in the Law of Advertising of the People's Republic of China; and the SFDA, which issued approval numbers for advertisements, shall cancel the approval numbers of the advertisements. A reapplication for an approval number for advertising of the drugs in question may not be accepted for one year. Drug Administration Law, art. 92. *See also* Notification on Further Strengthening Supervision over the Drug Quality and on Preventing Serious Drug-Related Accidents along with the Major Inspection of Work Safety, promulgated on June 12, 2002, by the State Drug Administration (instructions to SFDA branches to crack down on counterfeit and inferior drugs and to enhance supervision of drug advertisements). *See also* Articles 14–16 of the Advertising Law of the People's Republic of China (adopted October 27, 1994, by the 10th Sess. of the Standing Comm. of the 8th NPC), *reprinted in* CHINA LAWS FOR FOREIGN BUSINESS (CCH), Business Regulation ¶ 16-495. *See also* Notification on Further Strengthening Supervision over the Drug Quality and on Preventing Serious Drug-Related Accidents along with the Major Inspection of Work Safety, promulgated on June 12, 2002, by the State Drug Administration (instructions to SFDA branches to crack down on counterfeit and inferior drugs and to enhance supervision of drug advertisements). *See generally Supervision of TV Commercials to Be Stressed,* Xinhua General News Service, October 16, 2001, available on Lexis, News Library (described a survey that found that over 1,600 drug commercials, or 34.8 percent of total drug commercials inspected, were found to violate China's advertisement laws and regulations).

180. Drug Administration Law, art. 61. The drug names listed in the state drug standards are the common names of the drugs. Where common names of drugs have been used, the names must not be used as trademarks for the drugs. Drug Administration Law, art. 50. *See also* Notification on Strengthening the Supervision and Administration of Web sites Owned by Enterprises and Institutions of Drugs and Medical Instruments, promulgated on May 29, 2002, by the State Drug Administration (outlines requirements for Web sites that display information concerning drugs and medical instruments on the

Law, advertisements must comply with the Law of Advertising of the People's Republic of China.

7. Supervision and Examination

Clinical tests of new drugs may be initiated only after approval is received from the SFDA.[181] The production of new drugs or drugs already having national standards must be approved by the SFDA and a drug approval number must be issued. Drugs shall be produced only after approval numbers are obtained and must satisfy state drug standards.[182] Pharmaceutical manufacturers, sellers, and medical organizations are required to purchase drugs from enterprises with qualifications for drug production and trade.[183] The SFDA is authorized to carry out investigations into the drugs that have already been approved for production or importation. Where drugs are found not to be effective, or to have serious side effects, or to be harmful to human health for any reason, the approval number or Registration Certificate for Imported Drugs may be cancelled. Any drugs whose approval number or Registration Certificate of Imported Drugs has been cancelled must not be produced, imported, sold, or used in China. Where the drugs have already been produced or imported, they must be destroyed or disposed of by the SFDA or local drug control and administrative department.[184]

The SFDA has the authority to supervise the pharmaceutical industry, including all producers, drug sellers, and medical institutions.[185] The SFDA

Internet); Notification on the Explanation Concerning the Administration of Internet Drug Information Services, issued on June 1, 2002, by the State Drug Administration. *See China's Drug Administration Tightens Regulations on Online Drug Sales,* CHINA BUSINESS, October 12, 2001, available on Lexis, News Library (noting that as of October 2001, the SFDA had approved only sixteen enterprises to provide online pharmaceutical information); *China: New Regulations Target Drug Information Web sites,* CHINA ONLINE, January 25, 2001.

181. Drug Administration Law, art. 29. In order to secure approval to conduct clinical tests, an applicant is required to issue a report concerning the drug development process and the results of pharmacological and toxicological tests. *See also* Administration of the Quality of Non-Clinical Trials for Pharmaceuticals Guidelines (promulgated by the State Food & Drug Administration on Aug. 6, 2003).

182. Drug Administration Law, art. 31, 32. *The Pharmacopoeia of the People's Republic of China* and drug standards promulgated by the drug control and administrative department of the State Council are the state drug standards.

183. Drug Administration Law, art. 34. Where pharmaceutical manufacturers, pharmaceutical sellers, or medical organizations, in violation of the provisions in Article 34 of this Law, purchase drugs from enterprises that do not have a Drug Production License or Drug-trading License, they shall be ordered to make corrections. Illegally purchased drugs shall be confiscated. A fine of between two times and five times the value of the illegally purchased drugs shall be imposed. Where there are illegal earnings, they shall be confiscated. Where the situation is serious, Drug Production Licenses, Drug-trading Licenses, or the operation licenses of medical organizations shall be revoked. Drug Administration Law, art. 80.

184. Drug Administration Law, art. 42.

185. Drug Administration Law, arts. 64, 68. The SFDA is authorized to conduct follow-up tests and inspections of any producer or seller of drugs. The SFDA and its staff are not allowed to engage in drug production or sales. Drug Administration Law, art. 70.

is authorized to take random tests of pharmaceuticals to determine quality, and has the power to confiscate drugs that jeopardize human health. In urgent situations, the SFDA is required to render a decision to impose administrative sanctions within seven (7) days and to issue a public notice of any action taken.[186] An interested party who disagrees with a decision of the SFDA may, within seven days of receipt of a decision or test results, apply for review.[187] The SFDA is required to establish a reporting system that allows drug producers and sellers to report any serious side effects that may result from the use of a drug that it produces or sells.[188] The law provides for civil and criminal liability in the event that regulatory officials engage in corruption, favoritism, or dereliction of duty.[189]

H. Medical Devices and Instruments

Effective May 1, 2002, the State Drug Administration (renamed as the State Food and Drug Administration) adopted standards for the approval of medical devices and instruments.[190] The Medical Instruments Measures apply to all enterprises and individuals that develop, manufacture, operate, use, or supervise medical instruments in China and provides that standards for medical instruments are divided into national standards, trade standards, and standards for product registration. Instruments that fail to meet the required standards may not be manufactured, sold, or operated.[191] The national and trade standards refer to the standards that have uniform technical requirements nationwide. The standards for production registration refer to the product standards that are formulated by a manufacturer, meet

186. Drug Administration Law, arts. 65, 66.
187. Drug Administration Law, art. 67.
188. Drug Administration Law, art. 70. In emergency situations, the SFDA may act to confiscate any drugs causing serious side effects and order a cessation of production or sales.
189. Drug Administration Law, art. 99.
190. Measures on the Administration of the Standards for Medical Instruments (Trial Implementation), promulgated on January 4, 2002, by the State Drug Administration (hereinafter the "Medical Instruments Measures"); Regulation on Supervision and Administration of Medical Devices (promulgated by the State Council on December 28, 1999); Management Provisions on Registration of Medical Devices (promulgated on April 10, 2000, by the State Drug Administration); Regulation for Medical Device Classification (promulgated on April 10, 2000, by the State Drug Administration). *See generally Medical Equipment Industry,* China Business, May 25, 2001, available on Lexis, News Library. The SFDA issued regulations effective May 1, 2002, which require medical device manufacturers to obtain approval for product manuals. Administrative Regulations for Medical Equipment (promulgated as SFDA Order No. 30 by the SFDA and effective May 1, 2002).
191. Medical Instruments Measures, arts. 20, 21.

certain safety and effectiveness requirements, and meet national or trade standards upon application for registration of the instruments.[192] The law further provides that all medical instruments manufactured and sold, including imported instruments, are required to be registered with the SFDA.[193]

Key Laws and Regulations

Consumer Protection Laws and Standards

Product Quality Law of the People's Republic of China (adopted February 22, 1993, by the 30th Sess. of the Standing Comm. of the 7th NPC, and amended on July 8, 2000)

Law of the People's Republic of China on the Protection of the Rights and Interests of Consumers (adopted October 31, 1993, by the 4th Sess. of the Standing Comm. of the 8th NPC)

Law of the People's Republic of China on Standardization (adopted December 29, 1988, at the 5th Sess. of the Standing Comm. of the 7th NPC)

Detailed Rules for the Implementation of the Law of the People's Republic of China on Standardization (promulgated on April 1, 1990, by the State Council)

Regulations of the People's Republic of China on Certification and Authentication (promulgated on September 3, 2003, by the State Council and effective on November 1, 2003)

Regulations on the Responsibility for Repair, Replacement and Return of Certain Commodities (promulgated on August 25, 1995, by the State Bureau of Technical Supervision)

Regulations on Protecting the Interests of Consumers (issued on Oct. 28, 2002, and effective on January 1, 2003, by the Shanghai Municipal People's Congress)

(Continued)

192. Medical Instruments Measures, arts. 2, 3. The SFDA is responsible for setting and enforcing the standards. Medical Instruments Measures, arts. 5–9. The procedures for setting national and trade standards are set forth in Articles 10–12 of the Medical Instruments Measures. The procedures for the establishment, examination, and verification of standards for product registration are set forth in Articles 12–19.

193. Administrative Measures on the Registration of Medical Instruments, promulgated by the State Drug Administration; Notice on Several Supplemental Explanations on Registration of Imported Medical Instruments, promulgated on November 8, 2001, by the State Drug Administration (outlining the specific documentation required for imported medical instruments). *See generally* Medical Device Regulatory Requirements for China, Office of Microelectronics, Medical Equipment and Instrumentation, U.S. Dept. of Commerce (March 16, 2001); U.S. Medical Device Industry Consultations in China, Office of Microelectronics, Medical Equipment and Instrumentation, U.S. Dept. of Commerce (April 2001).

(Continued from previous page)

Advertising Law of the People's Republic of China (adopted October 27, 1994, by the 10th Sess. of the Standing Comm. of the 8th NPC)

Administration of the Broadcasting of Advertisements on Radio and Television Tentative Procedures (promulgated on Sept. 15, 2003, by the State Administration of Radio, Film, and Television)

Further Strengthening the Administration of Advertising Promotion Through Mass Media Circular (issued on February 5, 2001, by the State Administration of Radio, Film and Television and the State Press and Publication Administration)

Several Issues Concerning the Application of the Law to Trial of Disputes Over Commercial Premises Sales and Purchase Contracts Interpretation (issued on April 28, 2003, by the Supreme People's Court)

Administration of Printed Advertisement Procedures (promulgated on January 13, 2000, by the State Administration of Industry and Commerce)

Law of the People's Republic of China Against Unfair Competition (adopted September 2, 1993, at the 3rd Sess. of the Standing Comm. of the 8th NPC)

Pricing Law

Pricing Law of the People's Republic of China (promulgated on December 29, 1997, by the Standing Committee of the NCP)

Catalogue on the Pricing of Items (issued on July 4, 2001, by the State Development Planning Commission)

Trial Measures Regarding the Hearing on Decision-Making for Government Pricing (issued on July 2, 2001, by the State Development and Planning Commission)

Food Quality Standards

Food Hygiene Law of the People's Republic of China (adopted October 1995, by the 16th Sess. of the Standing Comm. of the 8th NPC)

Administrative Rules for Food Hygiene of the Restaurant and Beverage Industry (issued by MOH on January 16, 2000, and became effective on June 1, 2000)

Administrative Measures on the Inspection and Quarantine of Imported/Exported Meat Products (issued on October 1, 2002, by the Administration of Quality Supervision, Inspection, and Quarantine [AQSIQ])

Administrative Measures on the Examination and Approval of the Quarantine of Imported Animals and Plants (issued on September 1, 2002, by the AQSIQ)

Measures on Inspection Exemptions for Imported/Exported Commodities (issued on October 1, 2002, by the AQSIQ)

(Continued)

(*Continued from previous page*)

General Standards for the Labeling of Foods (promulgated February 4, 1994, by the State Bureau for Technical Supervision for Implementation from February 1995)

Regulations for the Investigation and Punishment for Food Labeling Violations (issued June 20, 1995 by the State Bureau for Technical Supervision)

Drugs and Medical Devices

Law of the People's Republic of China on the Administration of Drugs (adopted September 20, 1984 at the 7th Meeting of the Standing Committee of the 6th National People's Congress and Amended February 28, 2001, at the 20th Meeting of the Standing Committee of the 9th National People's Congress, Re-promulgated February 28, 2001, by Presidential Order No. 45 of the People's Republic of China)

Notice on Issues Regarding Strengthening the Administration of Applications to Produce Generic Pharmaceutical Products (effective June 1, 2002, by the SDA)

Notification on Further Strengthening Supervision Over the Drug Quality and on Preventing Serious Drug-Related Accidents Along with the Major Inspection of Work Safety (promulgated on June 12, 2002, by the State Drug Administration)

Notification on the Relevant Issues Concerning Accreditation of Qualifications of Practicing Pharmacists in Enterprises Dealing in Drugs (promulgated April 18, 2002, by the State Drug Administration)

Rules on the Administration of Drug Operating Licensing (issued on February 4, 2004, by the SFDA)

Regulation on Managing Imported Drugs (issued on August 18, 2003, and effective on January 1, 2004, by the State Food & Drug Administration)

Administrative Measures on Customs Clearance, Recordkeeping, and Inspection of Imported Drugs (promulgated on May 27, 2002, by the State Drug Administration)

Administrative Rules on Packing Materials, Labels, and Specifications for Drugs (promulgated by the State Drug Administration in November 2001)

Notice on Issuing the Detailed Rules on Criteria for Packing Materials and Labels for Drugs (Trial Implementation) (promulgated on November 11, 2001, by the State Drug Administration)

Announcement Regarding the Expiration of Pharmaceutical Products' Packaging Labels and Explanatory Notes (promulgated by the State Drug Administration as Order No. 156 and effective on May 24, 2002)

Notification on Further Strengthening Supervision Over the Drug Quality and on Preventing Serious Drug-Related Accidents Along with the Major Inspection of Work Safety (promulgated on June 12, 2002, by the State Drug Administration)

(*Continued*)

(Continued from previous page)

Notification on Further Strengthening Supervision Over the Drug Quality and on Preventing Serious Drug-Related Accidents Along with the Major Inspection of Work Safety (promulgated on June 12, 2002, by the State Drug Administration)

Notification on Strengthening the Supervision and Administration of Web sites Owned by Enterprises and Institutions of Drugs and Medical Instruments (promulgated on May 29, 2002, by the State Drug Administration)

Notification on the Explanation Concerning the Administration of Internet Drug Information Services (issued on June 1, 2002, by the State Drug Administration)

Administration of the Quality of Non-Clinical Trials for Pharmaceuticals Guidelines (promulgated by the State Food & Drug Administration on Aug. 6, 2003)

Measures on the Administration of the Standards for Medical Instruments (Trial Implementation) (promulgated on January 4, 2002, by the State Drug Administration)

Regulation on Supervision and Administration of Medical Devices (promulgated by the State Council on December 28, 1999)

Management Provisions on Registration of Medical Devices (promulgated on April 10, 2000, by the State Drug Administration)

Regulation for Medical Device Classification (promulgated on April 10, 2000, by the State Drug Administration)

Administrative Regulations for Medical Equipment (promulgated as SDA Order No. 30 by the State Drug Administration and effective May 1, 2002)

Notice on Several Supplemental Explanations on Registration of Imported Medical Instruments (promulgated on November 8, 2001, by the State Drug Administration)

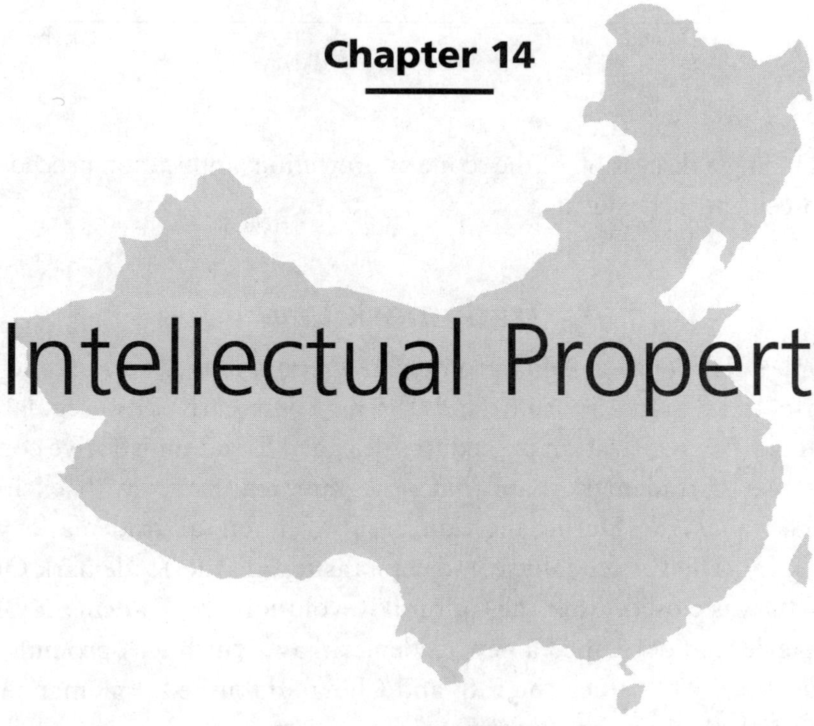

Chapter 14

Intellectual Property

The protection of intellectual and industrial property under Chinese law has received considerable attention as the country has opened its markets to the West. Since 1979, China has promulgated laws in the three major areas of intellectual property: trademarks, copyrights, and patents. Although the NPC and the State Council have aggressively adopted laws and regulations designed to protect the interests of both domestic and foreign parties, the effective enforcement of China's intellectual property laws is still in an embryonic stage.[1] This chapter addresses the copyright, patent, and trademark laws of the

1. Since the early 1990s, the relationship between the United States and China with respect to intellectual property issues can be characterized as tense. On April 26, 1991, the United States Trade Representative identified China as a "priority foreign country" and on May 26, 1991, initiated a Super 301 investigation into the intellectual property laws and enforcement of the PRC. A "priority foreign country" is one "whose inadequate protection of intellectual property is most egregious, with the greatest adverse impact on U.S. products, and who have not made significant progress in intellectual property negotiations." 19 U.S.C. §§ 3103–3106. The USTR found that the absence of effective copyright protection for computer software and piracy cost American industry an estimated $70–150 million annually. *See* Office of the United States Trade Representative, 1989 National Trade Estimate Report on Foreign Trade Barriers 42–43 (1989). In January of 1992, China and the U.S. reached an agreement in which China recognized the concerns of the U.S. and agreed to take steps to protect the IP interests of foreign investors. The U.S. also agreed to cease the Super 301 investigation. On January 17, 1992, China and the U.S. signed a Memorandum of Understanding on the Protection of Intellectual Property. The text of the MOU is reprinted in 4 J. INT'L L. & PRAC. 403 (1995) (hereinafter the "1992 U.S./China IP MOU"). In 1995, the U.S. again accused China of failing to protect the IP interests of U.S. companies and threatened to impose trade sanctions against China. The U.S. and China reached another agreement after China agreed to close factories suspected of producing pirate compact and laser disks. *See* Letter from Michael Kantor, U.S. Trade Representative, to Wu Yi, Minister of Foreign Trade and Economic Cooperation of the PRC, and Annex I (February 26, 1995), *reprinted in* 34 I.L.M. 881 (1995). *See generally* Butterton, *Pirates, Dragons and U.S. Intellectual Property Rights in China: Problems and Prospects of Chinese Environment,* 38 ARIZ. L. REV. 1081 (1996); Endeshaw, *A Critical Assessment of the U.S.-China Conflict on Intellectual Property,* 6 ALB. L. J. SCI. & TECH. 295 (1996); Dessler, *China's Intellectual Property Protection: Prospects for Achieving International Standards,* 19 FORDHAM INT'L

PRC, including a discussion of the scope of protection, application procedures, and enforcement mechanisms.

A. Trademark Law

The People's Republic of China promulgated regulations governing the registration of trademarks in 1950 and 1963.[2] These early PRC regulations were compulsory registration procedures designed for administrative control over the use of trademarks, and did not grant registrants with exclusive rights to a trademark. During the Cultural Revolution, all trademarks were effectively cancelled as feudalistic and capitalistic, and the Trademark Office of the SAIC was closed. After the Cultural Revolution, the Trademark Office was reopened and developed a new trademark law, which was promulgated on August 23, 1982. When the U.S. and China established diplomatic relations in 1979, they signed a trade agreement that provides that each party will provide national treatment for the protection of intellectual property.[3] In 1993 and again in 2001, China revised the Trademark Law and adopted new implementing rules to coincide with the revisions to the Trademark Law.[4] As of the end of 2001, more than 1.45 million trademarks have been

L. J. 181 (1995); Prohaska, *The 1995 Agreement Regarding Intellectual Property Rights between China and the United States: Promises for International Law or Continuing Problems with Chinese Piracy?*, 4 TULSA J. COMP. & INT'L L. 169 (1996); Berkman, *Intellectual Property Rights in the P.R.C.: Impediments to Protection and the Need for the Rule of Law*, 15 USCLA PAC. BASIN L.J. 1 (1996). For an outline of the complete history of the Section 301 investigations of China's IP laws and enforcement, *see* the Web site of the United States Trade Representative at http://www.ustr.gov/reports/301report/act301.htm#301–86 and http://www.ustr.gov/reports/301report/act301.htm#301–92.

2. Trademark Law of the People's Republic of China (adopted August 23, 1982, at the 24th Sess. of the Standing Comm. of the 5th NPC, revised in 1993 by the 30th Sess. of the Standing Comm. of the 7th NPC and revised in 2001 by the 24th Sess. of the Standing Comm. of the 9th NPC), art. 43, *reprinted in* CHINA LAWS FOR FOREIGN BUSINESS (CCH), Business Regulation ¶ 11-500 (hereinafter the "Trademark Law"). The purpose of the 2001 amendments was to bring China's IP regime closer in line with basic TRIPS requirements and primarily relate to enforcement issues, judicial review, and cancellation of marks. The Trademark Law is also available at the Web site of the State Intellectual Property Office at http://www.sipo.gov.cn and the Trademark Office at http://www.tmo.gov.cn. *See generally* J. Chang & C. Conroy, *Trademark Law in the People's Republic of China, in* FOREIGN TRADE, INVESTMENT AND THE LAW OF THE PEOPLE'S REPUBLIC OF CHINA 267 (M. Moser, ed. 1984); W. ALFORD, TO STEAL A BOOK IS AN ELEGANT OFFENSE: INTELLECTUAL PROPERTY LAW IN CHINESE CIVILIZATION (1995); Birden, *Trademark Protection in China: Trends and Directions*, 18 LOY. L.A. INT'L & COMP. L.J. 89 (1996).

3. Agreement on Trade Relations between the United States of America and the People's Republic of China, July 7, 1979, art. VI, ¶ 3 & 5, 31 U.S.T. 4652, T.I.A.S. No. 9630.

4. Detailed Rules for the Implementation of the Trademark Law of the People's Republic of China (amended January 3, 1988, July 15, 1993, and April 23, 1995, by the State Council, and revised on August 3, 2002 by the State Council), *reprinted in* CHINA LAWS FOR FOREIGN BUSINESS (CCH), Business Regulation ¶ 11-505 (hereinafter the "Trademark Regulations"). *See China Promulgates New Regulations on Trademark Law*, PEOPLE'S DAILY (Aug. 12, 2002), available online at http://www.peopledaily.com.cn. The Trademark Regulations are available on the Web site of the Trademark Office at http://www.tmo.gov.cn. In addition, China adopted the "International Classification of Commodities and Services with Registered Trademark" system in 1988 to conform with international practices. *See also* Notice of the State Administration for Industry and Commerce on Implementing an International

registered with the Trademark Office, applicants coming from 92 different countries.[5]

1. General Principles of China's Trademark Law

The Trademark Law provides that both trademarks and service marks[6] may be registered and that a registrant "shall enjoy an exclusive right to use the trademark."[7] A registered owner has the right to transfer the trademark or service mark, including a transfer by assignment, licensing, succession, or merger. The use of a trademark referred to in the Trademark Law includes the use of the trademark on goods, packages, or containers of the goods; in trading documents; and in advertising, exhibition, or any other business activities.[8] The owner of a registered trademark is allowed to use the circle-R (®) symbol in the upper-right-hand quarter of the mark.[9] Under prior versions of the law and

---

Classification of Commodities with Registered Trademarks (promulgated September 15, 1988, by the SAIC), *reprinted in* China Laws for Foreign Business (CCH), Business Regulation ¶ 11-529 (listing the international classifications). China is a contracting party to two international treaties pertaining to trademarks: the Madrid Agreement for International Registration of Trademarks on October 4, 1989 (the "Madrid Treaty") and the Paris Convention for the Protection of Industrial Property on March 19, 1989 (the "Paris Convention"). The Paris Convention is available on the Web site of the State Intellectual Property Office at http://www.sipo.gov.cn. The Madrid Treaty provides that "nationals of any of the contracting countries may, in all the other countries party to this Agreement, secure protection for their marks applicable to goods or services, registered in the country of origin, by filing the said marks at the International Bureau of Intellectual Property." Madrid Agreement Concerning the International Registration of Marks, Apr. 14, 1891, art. 1(2), *reprinted in* 9 World Intellectual Property Org., Industrial Property Laws and Treaties, WIPO Pub. No. 609 (E) (Oct. 1986). The Paris Convention, as last revised at the Stockholm Revision Conference, July 14, 1967, may be found at 21 U.S.T. 1538, 828 U.N.T.S. 305.

5. *China Steps Up Trademark Protection,* Xinhua News Agency (February 21, 1998), available on Lexis, News Library; *International Trademark Registrations Continue to Grow in 2001,* People's Daily (February 13, 2002), available online at http://www.peopledaily.com.cn (article mentions that international trademark applications in 2001 increased by 4.4 percent over 2000); *China Sets World Record for Trademark Registration,* People's Daily (January 26, 2002) (article cites Ma Lianyuan, the deputy director of SIPO, who claims that 270,000 trademarks were registered in 2001 in China).

6. Trademark Regulations, art. 2. Article 2 provides that "[t]he provisions made in the Regulation concerning goods trademarks shall apply to service trademarks." Prior to 1993, the law did not expressly provide for the registration of service marks. Where a service mark has been in continuous use up to the effective date of the amendments (July 1, 1993) and it is identical or similar to a registered service mark of another party of the same or similar service operations, it may continue to be used as allowed under the regulations. Trademark Regulations, art. 54.

7. Trademark Law, art. 3. Article 96 of the Civil Law of the PRC recognizes the exclusive rights to the use of trademarks. The exclusive right to use a registered trademark is limited to the mark that has been approved for registration and to the designated category of goods for which the mark has been approved. Trademark Law, art. 51.

8. Trademark Regulations, art. 3. Certain types of goods are required, by law, to obtain a registered trademark for sale. Trademark Law, art. 6; Trademark Regulations, art. 4.

9. Trademark Regulations, art. 37. The Paris Convention (art. 5d) states that no indication or mention of the registration of the trademark shall be required to be placed on goods as a condition of recognition of the right to protection. According to the 1993 Trademark Law, all registered trademarks were required to be accompanied by either the Chinese characters indicating a registered trademark or the circle-R registration symbol (®). Under the Trademark Law, as amended in 2001, the law provides that a trademark registrant shall "have the right," instead of the obligation, to indicate the wording "registered trademark" or "registration symbol" on its goods or services. Trademark Law, art. 9. Nevertheless, it is recommended that a trademark owner use the circle-R symbol to ensure that potential infringers are on

regulations, certain commodities were required to obtain a registered trademark before being marketed for sale, specifically pharmaceuticals and tobacco products.[10]

The agency responsible for registration and enforcement is the Trademark Office, which is under the control of the SAIC. The SAIC has also established the Trademark Review and Adjudication Board, which is responsible for reviewing and evaluating the decisions of the Trademark Office.[11] The Trademark Law grants the SAIC the authority to use the trademark registration process to supervise the quality of goods and to bar registrants from using trademarks or service marks from engaging in any practice that deceives consumers.[12]

The Trademark Regulations provide that collective marks are entitled to trademark protection. A collective mark is a trademark or service mark used by the members of an industrial or commercial group, association, or other collective organization for the purpose of demonstrating that the members are affiliated with the group. The use of a collective mark is based upon membership in an organization (which usually requires certain standards for use of its collective marks).[13] Similarly, the Trademark Office will also allow the registration of certification trademarks and service marks. The purpose of certification marks is to verify and substantiate the geographical origin, materials or components, manufacturing process, quality, accuracy, or other characteristics of the subject goods or services.[14] To ensure the protection of

---

notice that the trademark is registered and especially to counter any argument that the infringing party is not responsible for damages on the basis that it was unaware of the registrant's exclusive use of a trademark. Trademark Law, art. 56 (subparagraph 3). The SAIC may impose a fine on a party that improperly uses or claims that a trademark is registered. Trademark Law, arts. 47, 48.

10. The prior rule under Article 7 of the superseded Trademark Implementing Rules specifies that any pharmaceuticals intended for human use, as well as any tobacco products, must bear registered trademarks. This rule appears to have been dropped in the 2002 implementing regulations.

11. Trademark Law, arts. 2, 41–43.

12. Trademark Law, art. 7. In July 1998, the SAIC revoked 67 trademarks deceptively registered by a Shenzhen company. *See China Trademark Protection Urged,* CHINA DAILY (July 16, 1998), available on Lexis, News Library, or on the Web site of the CHINA DAILY at http://www.chinadaily.com.cn.

13. Trademark Law, art. 3.

14. Trademark Law, art. 3, 16. The trademark of Underwriter's Laboratories (i.e., "UL") is an example of a certification mark. The 2001 amendments to the Trademark Law formally recognize the rights to a trademark based upon geographical location or symbols. Trademark Law, arts. 3, 16; Trademark Regulations, art. 6. Article 6 of the Trademark Regulations provide in pertinent part: "Where a geographical indication is used as the certificate mark for the registration, natural persons, legal persons or other organizations, whose goods are provided with the relevant circumstances regarding the geographical indication, may request to use the trademark and the organization that controls the certificate mark shall permit. Where a geographical indication is used as the collective mark for the registration, natural persons, legal persons and other organizations, whose goods are provided with the relevant circumstances regarding the geographical indication, may request to join into the groups, societies and other organizations, who use the geographical indication as collective marks for registration, and the groups, societies and other organizations shall accept them as members according their statutes; where they do not request to join into the groups, societies and other organizations, who use the geographical indication as collective marks for registration, they may also use the geographical indication properly and the

the public, the Trademark Office will permit only qualified organizations to register certification marks.

Any word, design, or combination thereof that is distinctive so that it is distinguishable may be registered as a trademark in China.[15] In contrast to the prior standards, the 2001 Trademark Law's scope of marks qualified to be used as trademarks has been enlarged. The law now allows for protection for words, devices, letters, numbers, three-dimensional marks, colors, or any combinations thereof used as trademarks.[16] Chinese law, however, does not expressly recognize the shape of an object as subject matter entitled to trademark protection. Distinctiveness requires that the word, design, or their combination be easily recognizable as a trademark and different from the product itself. Article 9 of the Trademark Law, as amended in 2001, requires that "a trademark that is applied for registration shall be so distinctive as to be distinguishable, and shall not conflict with any legal rights obtained in prior by other persons." Article 11 prohibits the registration, as trademarks, of any marks or signs that:

(1) Relate only to generic names, designs, or types of the goods in respect of which the trademark is used
(2) Have direct reference only to the quality, main raw materials, function, use, weight, quantity, or other features of the goods in respect of which the trademark is used
(3) Lack distinctive features

Article 11 of the Trademark Law also addresses the registration of nondistinctive trademarks, which has been consistent with the TRIP's relevant provisions and provides that, where originally nondistinctive, trademarks may be registered if they acquire distinctiveness as a result of use in the marketplace.

---

groups, societies and other organizations shall not have the right to prohibit." *See also* Measures for Registration and Administration of Collective Marks and Certificate Marks (issued by the SAIC on December 30, 1994) (provide that certificate marks include those signs and marks used to indicate the origin of goods or services). In addition, the Ministry of Foreign Trade and Economic Cooperation ("MOFTEC") and the State Administration for Quality and Technical Supervision and Inspection provide protection for geographical language in trademarks. *See* Regulations governing the Protection of Products of Origin (issued by the State Administration for Quality and Technical Supervision in August 1999) (provides protection for Chinese products of origin); Rules of People's Republic of China on the Origin of Exported Goods, issued by MOFTEC in 1992) (govern the administration of certificate of origin for exported goods). The SAIC has also issued specific orders concerning select cases. The most significant case involved the protection of the French language "Champagne." Based upon the SAIC order of October 26, 1989, the SAIC prohibited continued use by Chinese entities or individuals of the word "Champagne" or its Chinese equivalent on any wine products marketed in China. In practice, cases arising from the protection of geographical indications are generally settled on the basis of the requirements of the Paris Convention.

15. Trademark Law, art. 7.

16. Trademark Law, art. 8.

A trademark that is identical or similar to a registered trademark of another party with respect to the same or similar type of goods may not be registered.[17] The Trademark Law, as amended in 2001, provides that the application for registration of a trademark shall not impair the existing right that others have first obtained, nor shall an applicant unlawfully file for registration of a trademark that has been used by another and had certain influence.[18] If two or more applicants apply for registration of identical or similar trademarks for the same or similar goods, registration will be granted to the party that is first to file. If two or more applicants apply to register identical or similar trademarks for the same or similar goods on the same day, each applicant is required to supply the Trademark Office with evidence of the date of first use of the trademark.[19] The trademark regulations require competing applicants that are unable to demonstrate first use to consult one another to mediate the dispute. If an agreement is reached through consultation, the competing applicants are required to submit a written contract to the Trademark Office within thirty days.[20]

The Trademark Law prohibits a party from using the following types of words or designs in a trademark or service mark:

(1) That are identical or similar to the State name, national flag, national emblem, or military flag of the People's Republic of China, a foreign country, or international organization[21]

17. Trademark Law, arts. 13, 28.

18. Trademark Law, art. 31.

19. Trademark Law, art. 29. The competing applicants are required to submit evidence of first use within thirty days of request. Trademark Regulations, art. 19.

20. Trademark Regulations, arts. 19, 20. If no agreement is reached, the parties are required to draw lots under the supervision of the Trademark Office to determine which party is selected as the trademark holder.

21. Various regulations have been adopted to protect the IP rights for the 2008 Olympics to be held in Beijing. *See* Measures on the Registration and Administration of Olympic Symbols (promulgated on May 15, 2002, by the State Administration for Industry and Commerce), available online at http://www.isinolaw.com (outline the registration procedures for Olympic symbols or the licenses for use of Olympic symbols); Protection of Olympic Intellectual Property Rights Provisions (promulgated by the Beijing Municipal Government on October 11, 2001). The regulations seek to protect the International Olympic Committee (IOC), the Chinese Olympic Committee (COC), the Beijing Organizing Committee for the Olympic Games (BOCOG) and authorized licenses, and to cover trademark, patent, and copyright protection for property such as the Olympic symbol, flag, anthem, motto, and items containing the words "OLYMPIC," "OLYMPICS," "OLYMPIAD," and "OLYMPIC GAMES." The regulations also cover the logos, mascots, names, symbols, anthem, and slogans specific to the Beijing games, and have a catch-all clause covering other aspects of Olympic intellectual property rights. The Olympic intellectual property regulations do not require trademark registration as a prerequisite to enforcement of rights. Trademark protection extends to all classes of goods and services and all uses of Olympic-related intellectual property. Owners or licenses of Olympic intellectual property may file a complaint with enforcement agencies or file suit in the people's courts to enforce their rights and to stop infringement activities. Enforcement activity related to Olympic intellectual property is within the jurisdiction of the Beijing Municipal Government (the local SAIC), the SIPO, the Copyright Bureau, the Bureau of Culture, the Public Security Bureau, and the GAC. Such entities are empowered to take a number of measures

(2) That relate to generic names or designs of the goods the subject of the trademark
(3) That relate to names of administrative regions at county level or above, or common place names of foreign countries except geographical names that have acquired a secondary meaning[22]
(4) That are a direct reference to the quality, main raw materials, function, use, weight, quantity, or other features of the goods the subject of the trademark
(5) That tend to discriminate against any nationality
(6) That tend to exaggerate and deceive in advertising the goods
(7) That are detrimental to the socialist morals and customs or have "other unhealthy influences"[23]

The registration of trademarks by foreign applicants is controlled by agreements between China and the country of the applicant, international treaties or conventions, or on the basis of reciprocity.[24] A foreign applicant must use an authorized trademark agent in order to register a trademark in China.[25] An applicant who commissions a trademark agency to apply to register a trademark must provide the agent with a written letter of authorization setting forth the contents and scope of the delegated authority.[26] For a foreign party, the letter of authorization must set forth the nationality of the applicant.

2. Application Procedures

An applicant for trademark registration may be any individual or legally established enterprise, institution, social entity, small industrial or commercial business, or individual partnership business.[27] An applicant can also be a foreigner or foreign enterprise that is a national of a country with which China has treaty obligations or that provides reciprocity of treatment of trademarks for Chinese citizens.[28] Prior to 2001, the Trademark Law allowed only foreign natural persons to register trademarks in China, while

against infringers, such as confiscation and destruction of goods. The regulations authorize fines of up to RMB30,000 against infringers, in addition to any other civil liability.

22. Trademark Law, art. 16; Trademark Regulations, art. 6.

23. Trademark Law, art. 10. The term "unhealthy influence" is not defined in the law or regulations. The SAIC is taking steps to eliminate the use of trademarks and advertisements that "advocate a decadent lifestyle" or that "reflect superstitious beliefs." *See* Su, *Improper Trademarks to Be Eliminated*, China Daily (Oct. 24, 1998), available on Lexis, News Library, or on the Web site of the China Daily at http://www.chinadaily.com.cn.

24. Trademark Law, art. 17.

25. Trademark Law, art. 18; Trademark Regulations, art. 7.

26. Trademark Regulations, art. 7.

27. Trademark Law, art. 4.

28. Trademark Law, art. 17; Trademark Regulations, art. 7.

domestic natural persons were not qualified to register trademarks in their own name. Following the principle of "national treatment" for IPR protection, provided by both TRIPS and the Paris Convention, the 2001 amendments expressly provide that natural persons may apply for registration of trademarks provided they intend to acquire the exclusive rights to use the trademark for the goods produced, manufactured, processed, selected, or marketed by them.[29] The Trademark Law, as amended in 2001, allows two or more parties to jointly apply for registration of trademarks and to jointly own and exercise the exclusive rights to the registered trademarks.[30]

a. Trademark Application Formalities

The trademark application must be in Chinese, and supporting documents in a foreign language are required to have a Chinese translation attached.[31] The applicant is required to tender the prescribed fees at the time of filing the application.[32] The regulations require that the applicant submit five copies of the trademark specimen with the application for registration.[33] The specimen of a trademark is required to be clear, on smooth and durable paper, and must not exceed a length of ten centimeters and a width of five centimeters.[34]

The law requires that an applicant specify on its application the types of goods that will be covered by the registered trademark if it intends to use its trademark for different classes of goods.[35] If the name of the commodity is not included in the commodity classification tables, the applicant is required to include a description of the goods with its application.[36] The law also requires that separate applications be submitted if different goods of the same class will be covered under the same trademark.[37] A new application

29. Trademark Law, art. 4.
30. Trademark Law, art. 5.
31. Trademark Regulations, art. 8. Application procedures and application forms are available on the Web site of the Trademark Office at http://www.tmo.gov.cn. Personnel of the Trademark Office and Trademark Review and Adjudication Board are required to withdraw from participating in any applications or cases involving situations in which he or she is a party to an application/case, has a close relative or "other relations" that are a party or the party's representative, or have an interest in the matter. Trademark Regulations, art. 9. The Trademark Law requires that matters set forth in a trademark application and materials submitted in support of the application are required to be "true, accurate, and complete." Trademark Law, art. 26.
32. Trademark Law, art. 63; Trademark Regulations, art. 58.
33. Trademark Regulations, art. 13. If the trademark specimen is a color design, the applicant is required to submit five color design specimens and one black-and-white specimen to be used for publication.
34. Trademark Regulations, art. 13. If the trademark is a three-dimensional mark, the application is required to specify and describe the three-dimensional design of the mark. If a trademark involves a foreign language, the applicant is required to define the meaning of the foreign words in the application. With respect to collective or certification trademarks, the regulations require that the applicant include supporting documents demonstrating the right to use the mark. Trademark Regulations, art. 13.
35. Trademark Law, arts. 19–21; Trademark Regulations, art. 13.
36. Trademark Regulations, art. 15.
37. Trademark Law, arts. 20, 21; Trademark Regulations, art. 13.

must be filed if a party alters or amends the words or designs of its registered trademark, or if the trademark holder changes its name or address.[38]

The date of application for the registration of a trademark is the date on which the Trademark Office receives the application.[39] The filing date is important to give the applicant rights of priority over other potential users of the mark. The Trademark Office will issue a registration number and a Notice of Acceptance of Application demonstrating that the application has been recorded if it is deemed to be complete.

The "file first, register first" principle recognized under Chinese law provides that trademark registration should be granted to the applicant that files for registration first, rather than those that are first used but are not filed for registration or are filed later. The Trademark Law provides that, where two or more applicants apply for the registration of identical or similar trademarks for the same or similar goods, the first filed trademark shall be obtained for preliminary examination and publication. If applications are filed on the same day, the trademark that was used the earliest shall be accepted, and applications of the others shall be refused.[40] The first-to-file rule is qualified by several exceptions including: (i) if the registration of the previously registered trademark is made with malice, such party may request the Trademark Review and Adjudication Board to cancel the registration of the previously filed trademark;[41] (ii) if trademarks previously filed are a copy, imitation, or translation of others' well-known trademarks not yet registered in China for the same or similar classes of goods, the registration of such trademark should not be approved.[42]

If the application appears to be incomplete, the application may be returned to the applicant by the Trademark Office.[43] The Trademark Office is also empowered to request that an applicant provide additional information supplementing its application. An applicant is required to provide supplemental information to the Trademark Office within thirty days of receipt of notice. If the requested information is timely submitted, the Trademark Office will record the application and a Notice of Acceptance of Application will be issued.[44]

38. Trademark Law, arts. 22, 23; Trademark Regulations, arts. 17, 24. The Trademark Office has developed applications to modify the name of the registrant and address. There is no need to go through the trademark registration process or to obtain a new registration number for name or address changes. Trademark Regulations, art. 24.

39. Trademark Regulations, art. 18.

40. Trademark Law, art. 29.

41. Trademark Law, art. 41.

42. Trademark Law, art. 13.

43. Trademark Law, art. 36.

44. Trademark Regulations, art. 18.

If an application is acceptable, the Trademark Office issues preliminary approval to the applicant. If preliminary approval is granted, the trademark is published in the Trademark Gazette.[45] The Trademark Office will issue a rejection notice if the application fails to meet the standards of the laws and regulations such as the prohibition on trademarks using national symbols.[46]

An applicant that receives a rejection notice may file an Application for Review of a Rejected Trademark with the Trademark Review and Adjudication Board within fifteen days of receiving the notice. The applicant is required to file an Application for Review with the Board, providing ten copies of the original application documents and the rejection notice.[47] The Board is required to provide the applicant with written notification of its final decision and, if favorable to the applicant, the matter will be transferred to the Trademark Office for recordation of the application and processing for preliminary approval. An interested party may challenge the rejection decision of the Trademark Review and Adjudication Board by filing an action in the people's court within thirty days from the date of receipt of notification.[48]

b. Objections to Preliminary Approval of Trademark

Any party has the right to oppose the preliminary approval of a trademark. A party that intends to object to a trademark is required to file a written objection within three months from the date of publication.[49] The objecting party is required to file two copies of its Statement of Objection to the Trademark Office, which is required to set forth the reasons for its opposition to the applicant's claims. The Trademark Office is required to provide the applicant with a copy of the Statement of Objection and an opportunity to respond. Within thirty days of receiving a Statement of Objection, the trademark applicant must file a statement in defense of its trademark registration. The Trademark Office is required to make a determination concerning the arguments raised and evidence introduced by the objecting party and the applicant. The Trademark Office will provide the parties with notice

45. Trademark Law, art. 27; Trademark Regulations, art. 18.
46. Trademark Law, art. 28; Trademark Regulations, art. 21.
47. Trademark Law, art. 32.
48. Trademark Law, art. 32.
49. Trademark Law, arts. 30, 33; Trademark Regulations, arts. 5, 22. An objection to a trademark application may be made on the grounds that the trademark constitutes an internationally well-known trademark. The Trademark Office and Trademark Review and Adjudication Board will review the following factors in determining whether a trademark is well-known: (1) the degree to which the public knows of the trademark; (2) the duration of the trademark's usage; (3) the duration, amount, and geographic scope of any publicity for the trademark; (4) the record of protection that the trademark has received as a well-known trademark; and (5) other factors that are part of the trademark being well-known. Trademark Law, art. 14.

of its final determination.[50] A party in disagreement with a ruling of the Trademark Office is entitled to request review of the decision to the Trademark Review and Adjudication Board by filing an Application for a Review of a Trademark Objection.[51] The petitioner is required to submit two copies of the original application, objection, and response thereto, and the determination of the Trademark Office to the Board within fifteen days of receiving the decision.[52]

c. Registration of a Trademark

If no objection to registration is made within the prescribed time, or if an objection is filed but found to be without merit, the Trademark Office will approve the trademark or service mark for registration. A registered trademark or service mark is provided a number and recorded on the Trademark Register.[53] The registrant is provided with a Certificate of Trademark Registration.

3. Application for Renewal of Registered Trademark

A trademark is valid for a period of ten years gauged from the date of registration, and may be renewable for an additional ten-year period.[54] A registrant that intends to renew its registration is required to file with the Trademark Office an Application to Renew a Registered Trademark within six months of expiration of the validity period.[55] If the renewal application is accepted, the original Trademark Registration Certificate is cancelled and a new Trademark Registration Certificate is issued by the Trademark Office. If a registered trademark is not renewed, the Trademark Office will not approve any application for registration of any trademark that is identical or similar to the formerly registered mark for a period of one year.[56] A trademark that is not renewed is removed from the Trademark Register.

4. Application for Assignment of Registered Trademark

A registered trademark owner may assign its trademark rights to a third party. An assignment is effective upon the filing of an Application to Assign

50. Trademark Law, art. 33; Trademark Regulations, art. 22.
51. Trademark Law, art. 33; Trademark Regulations, art. 22.
52. Trademark Law, arts. 33, 34; Trademark Regulations, arts. 22, 23.
53. Trademark Law, arts. 30, 34; Trademark Regulations, art. 23.
54. Trademark Law, arts. 37, 38. If a registered trademark has been cancelled or has not been renewed after expiration, the Trademark Office is barred from approving an application from another party for the same trademark for one year. This rule is to give trademark owners time to renew their applications. Trademark Law, art. 46.
55. Trademark Law, art. 38; Trademark Regulations, art. 27. A party may receive a six-month extension to file upon request. If a renewal application is not filed within the six-month extension period, the registered trademark is cancelled.
56. Trademark Law, art. 46.

a Registered Trademark with the Trademark Office.[57] The registrant is required to assign all identical or similar trademarks for the same or similar commodities. An assignment can be made only to an entity that has legal standing to apply for registration as the original applicant. If an assignment concerns pharmaceuticals or tobacco products, the assignee is required to submit certification that it is approved by the relevant authorities to produce such products. If the Trademark Office finds that an assignment is likely to result in misinterpretation, confusion, or "other detriment," an application for an assignment may be rejected.

5. Licensing of Registered Trademarks

Under the Trademark Law, a registrant may authorize other parties to use its registered trademark.[58] Under a licensing agreement, a licensee has the rights to use the trademark or service mark, usually under certain conditions. The registered owner still maintains ownership of the mark and, by law, is required to supervise and guarantee the quality of the goods the subject of the license. The product's place of manufacture is required to be clearly labeled on the products using the registered trademark pursuant to a license agreement. The trademark license contract is required to be submitted to the Trademark Office and the local administration for industry and commerce within three months of entering into the license agreement.[59]

6. Objections to Registered Trademark

A party that disputes the registration of a trademark may file an Application for Adjudication of the trademark dispute with the Trademark Review and Adjudication Board. An objection to registration must be filed within five years of the date of public announcement of the trademark registration.[60] The owner of a well-known trademark is not bound by the five-year limitation period if a party registers the trademark in bad faith.[61] Any party that desires to challenge a decision of the Trademark Review and Adjudication Board may file an action for judicial review in thirty days with the people's court.[62]

57. Trademark Regulations, arts. 25–26, 39.
58. Trademark Law, art. 40; Trademark Regulations, art. 43.
59. Trademark Regulations, art. 43. A failure to notify the Trademark Office of the license agreement exposes the registrant to monetary penalties and possible cancellation of the trademark registration. A failure to supervise a licensee may also subject the registrant to monetary penalties.
60. Trademark Law, arts. 41–44; Trademark Regulations, arts. 29–31.
61. Trademark Law, art. 41.
62. Trademark Law, art. 43. Both the applicant for cancellation and the registrant of the trademark have the right to submit evidence to the Trademark Review and Adjudication Board, as well as the right to request a public hearing of the cancellation request.

7. Administration of Trademarks in Foreign Trade

MOFTEC (now MOFCOM) has promulgated special regulations governing the protection of trademarks used in foreign trade.[63] The regulations are designed to protect the owners of trademarks in import and export transactions. A foreign trade operator is required to obtain the approval of an owner of a trademark and enter into a license agreement prior to engaging in foreign trade transactions involving a registered trademark.[64] A foreign trade operator is also prohibited from purchasing goods that depict trademarks without authorization of the trademark owner. The operator has an affirmative duty to scrutinize the license agreement between the supplier and the trademark owner prior to purchase.[65] A foreign trade operator is also barred from registering a trademark overseas that is registered in China by another party.[66] A foreign trade operator is liable for monetary penalties and a potential loss of export quotas or rights to engage in foreign trade if it misuses another party's trademarks.

An equity or cooperative joint venture enterprise that proposes to use the registered trademarks of the partners must specify that it is the intent of the parties to grant the JV company the right to use the subject marks.[67] If the parties to a JV jointly intend to register a mark in China, the parties are required to sign a notarized agreement that provides which party will be the owner of the trademark upon termination of the joint venture.

8. Certification and Protection of Well-Known Trademarks

The Trademark Office has established a set of procedures for foreign and domestic entities to obtain certification that their trademarks are "well-known" in China and entitled to protection.[68] The certification is good for a period of three years and can be renewed after the expiration of the three-year period. In order to establish the "well-known" status of a trademark, the regulations require that evidence be submitted to the Trademark Office that details the volume of sales within and outside of China, industry sector, date of first use, proof

63. Regulations of the Ministry of Foreign Trade and Economic Cooperation and the State Administration of Industry and Commerce Concerning the Administration of Trademarks for Foreign Trade (promulgated on August 25, 1995, by MOFTEC and the SAIC), *reprinted in* China Laws for Foreign Business (CCH), Business Regulation ¶ 11-535 (hereinafter the "Regulations for the Administration of Trademarks in Foreign Trade").

64. Regulations for the Administration of Trademarks in Foreign Trade, art. 9.

65. Regulations for the Administration of Trademarks in Foreign Trade, art. 12.

66. Regulations for the Administration of Trademarks in Foreign Trade, art. 13, § (2).

67. Regulations for the Administration of Trademarks in Foreign Trade, art. 11.

68. The Unfair Competition Law permits rights of action through administrative agencies or the people's court in order to protect the holders of "well-known" trademarks. *See* Unfair Competition Law, arts. 5 § (2), 21. It is a violation of the Product Quality Law to misuse a well-known trademark. *See* Product Quality Law, arts. 4, 19, 26. For a discussion of the Product Quality Law, *see* Chapter 13, Consumer Protection § A. *See generally* R. Ran, *Recognition of Well-Known Trademarks by Administrative Authorities*, China L. & Prac. (July 2003).

of continuous use, proof of registration within and outside of China, proof of advertisement and promotion, and statistical information demonstrating the applicant's economic ranking as against its competitors over the previous three years. If "well-known" status is granted, confirmation will be published by the Trademark Office, and the holder has the exclusive rights to bar other parties from obtaining registration or using an identical or similar trademark.[69]

9. Enforcement of Trademark Rights

Under the Trademark Law, infringement of the exclusive rights to use a trademark or service mark includes the following activities:

(1) Use of a trademark that is identical or similar to the registered trademark with respect to the same or similar goods without authorization of the registrant
(2) Sale of goods knowing that a counterfeit trademark is being used as a registered trademark
(3) Forgery or falsification of representations of the registered trademark, or the sale of forged representations made without authorization of the trademark owner

69. The Paris Convention requires member countries to protect well-known trademarks registered in other signatory countries. The Trademark Law, as amended in 2001, provides some level of protection. Prior to 2001, the legal provisions regarding the protection of well-known marks are set forth in the *Provisional Regulations on Recognition and Administration of Well-Known Trademarks,* promulgated by the SAIC on August 14, 1996, which offered official recognition and protection of well-known trademarks. Well-known trademarks are defined as those which "enjoy a relatively high reputation in the market and are known to the relevant public." The regulations stipulate the criteria for the recognition of well-know trademarks as well as enhanced protection for these marks. A special provision in these regulations is that use of a well-known trademark as a trade name (which would imply a relationship between the enterprise and the trademark owner) is prohibited, and applications to oppose or cancel such use must be filed within two years of the date that the trademark owner is alerted to the registration or use of the trademark in this manner. Article 4 of these regulations provides that, if a trademark registrant desires his rights on a well-known trademark to be protected, he shall apply for the recognition of well-known trademark with the Trademark Office. However, the implementation of said regulations has been disappointing for most foreign entities. From the issuance of the regulations until now, the Trademark Office has officially determined and announced a total of 196 domestic "well-known" trademarks covering various classes of goods, but up to now, no recognition of any foreign well-known trademark has been granted in accordance with these regulations, and the protection of foreign well-known trademarks is generally ensured by the SAIC on a case-by-case basis. To comply with the Paris Convention and TRIPS Agreement, the 2001 amendments to the Trademark Law have incorporated several articles in relation to the protection of well-known trademarks. These articles can be summarized as the following two points: (i) The protection of unregistered well-known trademarks. In accordance with Articles 13 and 14 of the Trademark Law, if a trademark applying for registration on identical or similar goods is a copy, imitation, or translation of another person's well-known trademark that has not been registered in China, and the public may be confused by this trademark, then it shall not be registered nor allowed to be used. As the current version of the Trademark Implementing Rules, which entered into force in 1999 before the adoption of the 2001 Trademark Law, does not reflect the new amendments of the 2001 Trademark Rules, no detailed provision is available now for the interpretation of standards as to the "copy, imitation or translation" of a well-known trademark causing confusion to the public. In practice, the SAIC makes decisions at its discretion and on a case-by-case basis. One of the most important measures for the protection of well-known trademarks that have not been registered in China is the prevention of malicious registration of such well-known trademarks by others.

(4) Causing prejudice to the exclusive rights to use the registered trademark of another person[70]

The regulations further provide that the following activities constitute infringement of the exclusive rights of a trademark owner:

(1) Using, as a product or label, written script or a design that is identical or similar to the registered trademark of another person who uses it on the same or similar goods, with the similarity being sufficient to cause confusion; or
(2) Intentionally providing storage, transport, postage, or harboring offenders in order to facilitate the infringement of the exclusive rights of another person to use a registered trademark[71]

The owner of a trademark may seek administrative relief from the administration of industry and commerce.[72] If the SAIC has reason to believe that a person is infringing upon the trademark rights of a registered owner, it has the power to obtain evidence by the following means:

(1) Investigating and questioning the persons involved
(2) Inspecting the goods and, if necessary, confiscating the goods; or
(3) Obtaining copies of contracts, accounting books, or other business documents that relate to the alleged infringement[73]

70. Trademark Law, art. 52. *See generally* A. Adcock, *Updating IP: Shanghai Addresses Its Own Intellectual Property Concerns*, China L. & Prac. (July 2003).

71. Trademark Regulations, art. 50.

72. Trademark Law, arts. 53–55; Trademark Regulations, arts. 45, 51. Any party, including a consumer, has the right to file a complaint with the SAIC concerning the alleged violation of trademark rights. Trademark Regulations, art. 51. The penalties issued by the SAIC have been characterized as inadequate in a number of high-profile cases. In 1992, the SAIC imposed a penalty of $260 for trademark infringement against the Shenzhen Reflective Materials Institute at Shenzhen University for producing pirated hologram labels designed by Microsoft to identify its software products. Microsoft claims the potential lost sales resulting from the pirated holograms was estimated at $30 million. *See* H. King, *Microsoft Nails Some Pirates,* N.Y. Times, May 10, 1992, § 3, at 7. A Chinese enterprise that was found to have infringed upon Walt Disney's trademarks for Mickey Mouse was fined by SAIC only $91. *See* L. Chua, *China Steps Up Enforcement of Piracy Laws,* L.A. Times, Apr. 4, 1994, at D3. *See also* R. Youngblood, *China Fights Trademark Abuse,* UPI, Apr. 12, 1994, Lexis, News Library, UPI File (fine of $1,712 for infringement of rights of Chinese-French joint venture). The SAIC claims that it investigated approximately 35,000 trademark infringement claims in 1995, and 30,000 trademark infringement cases in 1996. The SAIC stated that it levied fines totaling over $9.5 million and $9.7 million in 1995 and 1996, respectively. In addition, the SAIC reported that only $650,000 in economic compensation was awarded to affected parties. *China Trademark Violations Show a 15% Decrease,* China Daily (May 23, 1997), available on Lexis, News Library, or on the Web site of the China Daily at http://www.chinadaily.com.cn. *See also* Fung, *Can Mickey Mouse Prevail in the Court of the Monkey King? Enforcing Foreign Intellectual Property Rights in the People's Republic of China,* 18 Loy. L.A. Int'l & Comp. L.J. 431 (1996).

73. Trademark Regulations, art. 55.

The SAIC has the authority to take the following actions in response to violations to trademark rights:

(1) Issue an order demanding the infringing party to cease and desist its activities
(2) Confiscate and destroy products, advertising materials, and other tangible items that depict the infringing trademark
(3) Issue an order demanding the infringing party to remove the registered trademarks from goods that are involved in the infringement
(4) Confiscate molds, dies, printing plates, and other tools that are specifically used to produce the protected trademark symbols
(5) Impose a monetary fine of up to 50 percent of the total sales involving the infringing goods or up to five times the profit generated from the infringement
(6) Impose a monetary fine of up to RMB10,000 on those individuals directly responsible for the infringement activities
(7) Upon the request of the rightful trademark owner, order the offender to compensate the trademark owner[74]

The most significant amendments to the Trademark Law in 2001 pertain to enforcement. Under the amended law, trademark holders have access to a wider range of remedies available to check infringement and claim damages. Trademark owners may now apply directly to the people's courts for injunctive relief.[75]

Under the prior law, vendors of infringing goods were exempt from civil and administrative liability unless the trademark owner could prove that the vendor knew, or should have known, that the goods were infringing upon the rights of another. The amended Trademark Law eliminates the knowledge requirement for registered trademarks, and any party that infringes

74. Trademark Law, art. 56; Trademark Regulations, arts. 44, 52. Article 118 of the Civil Law of the PRC provides that the owner of a trademark has the right to demand cessation of the infringement, elimination of its effects, and compensation for losses.

75. Trademark Law, art. 57. *See* Interpretation of Several Questions on the Application of Law in Trial of Trademark Civil Dispute Cases (promulgated by the Supreme People's Court on October 12, 2002) (hereinafter the "SPC Trademark Law Interpretation") (providing court management rules for trademark disputes including provisions concerning the calculation of damages, scope of infringing activities, application of the law to services, and provision concerning trademark licensing), *summarized in* China L. & Prac., November 2002, pg. 8. The amendments to the Trademark Law with respect to enforcement issues follows the provisions set forth in the January 2001 circular issued by the Supreme People's Court. *See* Interpretation on Protective Measures for Registered Trademark Rights (issued on January 2, 2001, by the Supreme People's Court, effective on January 21, 2001), *available online at* http://www.isinolaw.com (which granted the courts the power to issue protective orders and injunctive relief in cases involving infringement). For an analysis of a trademark case involving a well-known mark, *see* S. Yusheng, *Trademark Infringement and Unfair Competition Case Study: Toyota Motors vs. Zhejiang Geely*, China L. & Prac. (Dec. 2003).

upon the trademark rights of another is liable for infringement unless he or she can demonstrate that the goods came from a legal source.

Furthermore, the SAIC and the people's courts are now authorized to confiscate and destroy the infringing goods, as well as the tools, machinery, or equipment used for manufacturing the infringing goods. The SAIC and the courts are also empowered to impose monetary fines and to order the infringing party to immediately cease and desist the infringing activities.[76] If the SAIC determines that the infringing acts constitute criminal offenses, the SAIC is required to transfer the case to the Public Security Bureau (PSB) for criminal investigation and prosecution.

The standards for establishing damages under both the prior and current Trademark Law are based upon the calculation of "benefits obtained by the infringer during the period of infringement, or the losses incurred by the infringed-upon party during the period of infringement, including the reasonable expenses incurred by the infringed-upon party for the purpose of stopping the infringement."[77] Under the amended Trademark Law, in cases for which damages are difficult to ascertain, the people's court may award statutory damages up to RMB500,000 ($60,000).[78] The applicant is also entitled to an award of legal and investigative costs to pursue the infringing party.

10. Cancellation of a Registered Trademark and Supervision by Trademark Office

A registered trademark or service mark may be cancelled for a violation of the Trademark Law and implementing regulations.[79] A mark that has been cancelled loses its exclusive rights. Prior to the 2001 amendments, applications for cancellation against registered trademarks had to be filed within one year after the date the trademark was registered. The term has been extended to five years. Furthermore, if the registration is malicious, the owner of the well-known trademark and applicant for cancellation is not limited to the five-year limitations period.[80]

If a registrant disagrees with the decision of the Trademark Office concerning revocation or cancellation, it may, within thirty days of receiving notice of the decision, file an Application for Review of the Revocation of a Trademark with the Trademark Review and Adjudication Board.[81]

76. Trademark Law, art. 53.
77. Trademark Law, art. 56.
78. Trademark Law, art. 56.
79. Trademark Law, art. 41.
80. Trademark Law, art. 41.
81. Trademark Law, art. 43.

One ground for revocation is a failure to use a registered mark for a period of three consecutive years.[82] Although the Trademark Office has the regulatory authority to supervise whether registrants are actually using their marks, as a practical matter the Trademark Office will initiate revocation proceedings only if an interested person petitions the Trademark Office to revoke a registered trademark and submits evidence that a mark has, in effect, been abandoned by the registrant. The trademark registrant is provided three months' notice to provide evidence of use of the trademark or an adequate explanation for not using the mark. If proof is not submitted in a timely manner, the Trademark Office is empowered to revoke the registration.

The Trademark Office can also revoke the registration of a trademark when the words or designs of the registered mark are modified without advising the Trademark Office, or when the trademark is assigned to another party without approval.[83] Revocation is also appropriate when a registered trademark is used to sell poorly manufactured goods.[84]

11. Judicial Remedies

A party may appeal a decision of the Trademark Review and Adjudication Board by filing an action with the people's courts within thirty days of receiving notice of the Board's decision.[85] Where the party concerned does not apply for judicial review, the decision of the Board is conclusive.[86]

If a party disagrees with the SAIC's decision concerning infringement investigations, it may file a complaint with the people's court within fifteen days of receipt of the decision. If any party disputes the enforcement decision of the SAIC, it may file a civil action in the people's court within fifteen days of notice of the decision.[87] The decision becomes conclusive after the passage of the notice period.

In addition to administrative relief, the holder of intellectual property rights may seek judicial relief before the intermediate-level people's court. Under the 2001 amendments to the Trademark Law, all cases pertaining to registration, trademark applications, oppositions, and cancellations are subject to judicial review, in addition to administrative review.[88]

82. Trademark Law, art. 44.
83. Trademark Law, art. 44.
84. Trademark Law, arts. 7, 45; Trademark Regulations, art. 40.
85. Trademark Law, arts. 32, 33, 43, 49.
86. Trademark Law, art. 34.
87. Trademark Law, art. 50.
88. Trademark Law, arts. 32, 33, 43, 49.

The major cities in China have developed specialized intellectual property courts to address complicated IP-related issues. In 1993, the Beijing Intellectual Property Trial Division was established within the Beijing Intermediate People's Court and specifically authorized to hear cases concerning trademark, copyright, and patent infringement. The IP Division has exclusive jurisdiction for matters arising in the Beijing District for IP cases. By early 1994, analogous IP trial courts were established in Fujian, Haikou, Shanghai, Shenzhen, and Xiamen.[89]

12. Criminal Penalties for Trademark Infringement

The Criminal Law provides that it is a crime to intentionally use a trademark of a registered trademark. The law further provides that it is unlawful to manufacture any representation of a registered trademark without permission of the registered owner. A person who violates the law is subject to imprisonment of up to three years; and in serious cases, including repeated incidents of infringement or where the sales volume of infringing goods is relatively large, the term of imprisonment may be from three to seven years.[90]

B. Copyright Law

The People's Republic of China promulgated its first copyright law and implementing regulations in 1990.[91] In 1992, the State Council issued the Regulations on Implementation of International Copyright Treaties, which

89. *See* Ma Chenguang, *China: More Courts to Protect Trademarks and Patents,* CHINA DAILY (March 29, 1994), available on Lexis, News Library, or on the Web site of the CHINA DAILY at http://www.chinadaily.com.cn; *China Courts Hear More Intellectual Property Cases,* CHINA DAILY (January 9, 1997), available on Lexis, News Library, or on the Web site of the CHINA DAILY at http://www.chinadaily.com.cn; *China Courts Handle More IPR Lawsuits,* CHINA DAILY (July 17, 1997), available on Lexis, News Library, or on the Web site of the CHINA DAILY at http://www.chinadaily.com.cn. For example, the Shenzhen Intermediate People's Court ordered Maxell (Japan) to stop infringing upon the trademark of the Huayuan Co. and to pay compensation in the sum of $375,000 and court costs in the sum of $14,460 in April of 1997. *Trademark Saved,* CHINA DAILY (April 21, 1997), available on Lexis, News Library, or on the Web site of the CHINA DAILY at http://www.chinadaily.com.cn.

90. Criminal Law of the People's Republic of China (promulgated March 14, 1997, by the NPC), arts. 213–15, *reprinted in* 11 CHINA L. & PRAC. 44 (June 1997) (hereinafter the "1997 Criminal Law"). *See also* Decision of the Standing Committee of the National People's Congress Concerning Punishment of the Crime of Copyright Infringement (adopted on July 5, 1994, by the 8th Sess. of the Standing Comm. of the 8th NPC), *reprinted in* CHINA LAWS FOR FOREIGN BUSINESS (CCH), Business Regulation ¶ 11-701. *See* Chapter 23, Criminal Liability for FIE Activities § B.1.

91. Copyright Law of the People's Republic of China (adopted on September 7, 1990, at the 15th Sess. of the Standing Comm. of the 7th NPC, amended on October 27, 2001, at the 24th Sess. of the Standing Comm. of the 9th NPC), *reprinted in* CHINA LAWS FOR FOREIGN BUSINESS (CCH), Business Regulation ¶ 11-700 (the "Copyright Law"). The Copyright Law is also available on the Web site of the State

grant foreigners the same level of copyright protection as Chinese citizens.[92] The National Copyright Administrative Office (NCA) of the People's Republic of China is the regulatory agency responsible for developing regulations, investigations, registration, and enforcement.[93] The NCA is also responsible for supervising the provincial and local-level copyright offices.[94]

1. General Principles of China's Copyright Law

The works of all Chinese citizens, regardless of whether they are published, are entitled to copyright protection. The published works of foreigners that are first published in China are also protected under the Copyright Law. The works of foreign persons published outside of China are entitled to copyright protection pursuant to bilateral agreements and international treaties to which both countries are parties.[95] The Copyright Law defines "works"

Intellectual Property Office at http://www.sipo.gov.cn. See also Regulations for the Implementation of Copyright Law of the People's Republic of China (promulgated on August 2, 2002, and effective September 15, 2002, by the State Council), *reprinted in* CHINA LAWS FOR FOREIGN BUSINESS (CCH), Business Regulation ¶11-702 and also available online at http://www.isinolaw.com (hereinafter the "Copyright Implementing Regulations"). *See NPC Members Debate Revision of Copyright Law,* Xinhua News Agency (Dec. 26, 1998), available on Lexis, News Library. For a discussion of contemporary copyright issues, *see generally* Hu, *"Mickey Mouse" in China: Legal and Cultural Implications in Protecting U.S. Copyrights,* 14 B.U. INT'L L.J. 81 (1996); Feaver, *China's Copyright Law and the TRIPS Agreement,* 5 J. TRANSNAT'L L. & POL'Y 431 (1996); Kolton, *Copyright Law and the People's Courts in the People's Republic of China: A Review and Critique of China's Intellectual Property Courts,* 17 U. PA. J. INT'L ECON. L. 415 (1996). For a history of copyright laws and protection in China, *see* Shoukang, *China* in INTERNATIONAL COPYRIGHT LAW AND PRACTICE (P. Geller ed. 1997). In September 1993, the NPC adopted China's first Unfair Competition Law, which encompasses the protection of copyrights. Law of the People's Republic of China Against Unfair Competition (adopted September 2, 1993, at the 3rd Sess. of the Standing Comm. of the 8th NPC), *reprinted in* CHINA LAWS FOR FOREIGN BUSINESS (CCH), Business Regulation ¶ 16-640 (hereinafter the "Unfair Competition Law"). For a discussion of the Unfair Competition Law, *see* Chapter 13, Consumer Protection § D.; Chapter 7, Contract Law § B.9.d.

92. Regulations on Implementation of International Copyright Treaties (issued on September 25, 1992, by the State Council and amended on August 2, 2002, by the State Council), *reprinted in* CHINA LAWS FOR FOREIGN BUSINESS (CCH), Business Regulation ¶ 11-703 (hereinafter the "International Copyright Treaties Implementing Regulations"). In 1992–93, China became a contracting party to the Bern Convention for the Protection of Literary and Artistic Works, the Universal Copyright Convention, and the Convention for the Protection of Producers of Phonogram against Unauthorized Duplications (Geneva Convention). *See also* Copyright Implementing Regulations, arts. 33, 34 (provides that performance by foreigners or stateless persons taking place in China shall be protected under the Copyright Law).

93. Copyright Law, art. 7. Copyright Implementing Regulations, arts. 37. The NCA is authorized to promulgate all administrative rules relating to implementation of the Copyright Law; investigate and adjudicate copyright violations; resolve issues for foreign-related copyright matters; approve and supervise copyright management matters; manage copyrights owned by the State. In contrast, the U.S. Copyright Office of the Library of Congress is primarily responsible for managing the copyright registration system.

94. Copyright Law, art. 7.

95. Copyright Law, art. 2. The 2001 amendments to the Copyright Law provide that "[w]orks of foreigners or stateless persons shall receive protection in accordance with this Law where the relevant country has not signed an agreement or joined an international treaty with China but where the works have first been published in a member state of the international treaty to which China is a participant, or have been published simultaneously in member and non-member states of the said treaty." Copyright Law, art. 2. The Copyright Implementing Regulations provide that a copyright of the works of foreigners and stateless persons is protected from the day the work is published for the first time. Copyright

to include the following types of publications in such fields as literature, art, natural science, social science, and engineering technology:

(1) Written literary works
(2) Orally delivered works
(3) Musical, dramatic, folk art, and dance works
(4) Artistic and photographic works
(5) Film, television, and video works[96]
(6) Engineering designs, product design blueprints, and related explanations[97]
(7) Maps, schematic diagrams, and other graphic works
(8) Computer software[98]
(9) Other works granted protection by law or administrative regulations[99]

The Copyright Implementing regulations further define the term "works" in the Copyright Law to mean the following:

(1) Written works are works expressed in writing, such as novels, poems, essays, and thesis

---

Implementing Regulations, art. 7. Works of foreigners and stateless persons first published outside of China shall be deemed to be published in China at the same time if published in China within 30 days. Copyright Implementing Regulations, art. 8.

96. The work of film directors, screenwriters, lyricists, composers, photographers, and other persons involved in film, television, and video works are acknowledged by law and entitled to copyright protection. Copyright Law, art. 15.

97. Scientific and technological works also receive protection under the Patent Law.

98. In addition to the Copyright Law, the State Council has adopted a number of other rules specifically addressing computer software. *See* Regulations on Computer Software Protection (Order No. 339 of the State Council, promulgated on December 20, 2001, and effective from January 1, 2002), *reprinted in* CHINA LAWS FOR FOREIGN BUSINESS (CCH), Business Regulation ¶ 11-704 (hereinafter the "Computer Software Protection Regulations"). Measures for Computer Software Copyright Registration (issued on April 6, 1992, by the Ministry of Electronics Industries of the People's Republic of China, and amended on May 26, 2000), *reprinted in* CHINA LAWS FOR FOREIGN BUSINESS (CCH), Business Regulation ¶ 11-706 (hereinafter the "Computer Software Copyright Registration Measures"). *See also* Lam, *Copyright Protection of Foreign Computer Software in the People's Republic of China: Significant Progress in Two Years,* 17 LOY. L.A. INT'L L. J. 861 (1995); Duvanel, *The Evolution and Enforcement of Computer Software Copyright in the People's Republic of China,* 16 N.Y. L. SCH. J. INT'L & COMP. L. 337 (1996); Simpson, *Copyright Law and Software Regulations in the People's Republic of China: Have the Chinese Pirates Affected World Trade?,* 20 N.C. J. INT'L LAW & COM. REG. 575 (1995); T. Zhengyu, X. Hu & C. Ling, *China's Rocky Road to Computer Software Protection,* CHINA L. & PRAC. (Nov. 2002).

99. Copyright Law, art. 3; Copyright Implementing Regulations, art. 4. The 2001 amendments to the Copyright Law added choreographic and acrobatics works, architectural works, and model works to the list of protected works. The Copyright Law also sets forth the political qualification of a work and specifically encourages "the creation and publication of works which contribute to the development of the socialist material and spiritual culture and to promote the development and prosperity of socialism's cultural and scientific institutions." Copyright Law, art. 1. The Copyright Implementing Regulations further define the term "works" to refer to "original intellectual creations in the literary, artistic and scientific domain, in so far as they are capable of being reproduced in a certain tangible form." Copyright Implementing Regulations, art. 2. The Copyright Implementing Regulations define the term "creation" to mean "intellectual activities from which literary, artistic and scientific works are directly resulted." Copyright Implementing Regulations, art. 3.

(2) Oral works are works, such as unprepared speeches, lectures, and court debates, that are expressed in spoken-word form
(3) Musical works are works, with or without accompanying words, that can be sung or performed, such as songs and symphony
(4) Dramatic works are works, such as dramas, operas, and local art forms, that are created for stage performance
(5) Qu Yi works are works created mainly for being performed in a way involving recitation, singing, or both, such as cross talk, clapper talk, ballad singing, and storytelling
(6) Choreographic works are works that express thought and emotion in successive body movements, gestures, and facial movements
(7) Acrobatics works are works that are expressed by body movement and skill, such as acrobatics, magic, and circus
(8) Works of fine art are two- or three-dimensional works created in lines, colors, or other media that, when viewed, impart aesthetic effect, such as paintings, works of calligraphy, and sculptures
(9) Building works are works with aesthetic meaning that are expressed in the form of the building or the structures
(10) Photographic works are the kind of artistic works created by recording images on light-sensitive materials or other media with the aid of devices
(11) Cinematographic works and works that are created with similar method to that of producing a film are works that, being recorded on some medium, consist of a series of frames of images, with or without accompanying sound, and can be projected with the aid of devices suitable in relation to a specific works or spread in other ways
(12) Graphic works are drawings of engineering designs and product designs that are made for the purpose of actual construction and manufacturing, and works that show geographical phenomena and demonstrate the fundamentals or the structure of a thing or an object, such as maps, diagrams
(13) Model works are the three-dimensional works made in certain proportion according to the form and structure of the object for the purpose of showing, testing, observing, etc.[100]

100. Copyright Implementing Regulations, art. 4. Article 5 of the Copyright Implementing Regulations specify a number of additional definitions as used in the Copyright Law: (1) "News of current events" refers to the mere report of facts or happenings conveyed by newspapers, periodicals, broadcasting stations, and television stations, etc.; (2) "Sound recordings" refers to the recordation of any sound of performing and other sounds; (3) "Video recordings" refers to the recordation of a series of

Copyright protection is not available to government-issued laws, regulations, decisions, or orders and any translation thereof. The Copyright Law also specifically excludes current affairs news reports, laws and regulations, or calendars, general tables, or formulas from copyright protection.[101] The law is unclear as to whether customer lists, supplier lists, and similar types of business secrets are subject to copyright protection.[102]

The scope of protection granted to a copyright holder includes the following personal rights and property rights:

(1) Right of publication, namely, the right to determine whether a work is made public
(2) Right of acknowledgment, namely, the right to state the identity of the author on the work
(3) Right of revision, namely, the right to revise or authorize another party to revise work
(4) Right to preserve the integrity of a work, namely, the right to ensure a work is not subject to misrepresentation or distortion
(5) Right of reproduction, namely, the right to produce a copy or more than one copy of a work by such means as printing, copying, dubbing, sound recording, videotaping, duplication, or photographic reproduction
(6) Right of distribution, namely, the right to supply the original or copies of a work to the public by means of sale or donation
(7) Right of lease or license, namely, the right to permit another party to pay for the temporary use of a film work, other works created in the style of film production, and computer software, except where the computer software is not the main subject matter of a lease or license

---

related images, with or without accompanying sounds, other than cinematographic works and works that are created with similar method to that of producing a film; (4) "Producer of sound recordings" refers to the initial producer of sound recordings; (5) "Producer of video recordings" refers to the initial producer of the video recordings; (6) "Performer" refers to the actor or actress, the group for performance, or other persons who perform literary and artistic works.

101. Copyright Law, arts. 5, 22 § (4). The Computer Software Protection Regulations specifically provide that the rules shall not be interpreted to provide copyright protection for thoughts, concepts, discoveries, principles, algorithms, processing procedures, and operational methods employed in the development of software. The software program and related files, including the coded command sequences or symbolic statement sequences embodied in software, are granted protection. *See* Computer Software Protection Regulations, art. 6.

102. *See generally Business Secrets and Laws,* China Economic Review, April 23, 1998, available on Lexis, News Library; Cheng, *Legal Protection of Trade Secrets in the People's Republic of China,* 5 PAC. RIM L. & POL'Y 261 (1996). In December of 1998, in a case of first impression, the Beijing No. 2 Intermediate People's Court ruled that a market research company violated the rights of a client by disclosing the business secrets of the client to the media. *Survey Firm Loses First Secrets Case,* CHINA DAILY (Dec. 23, 1998), available on Lexis, News Library, or on the Web site of the CHINA DAILY at http://www.chinadaily.com.cn.

(8) Right of exhibition, namely, the right to publicly exhibit the original or copies of artwork or photographic work
(9) Right of performance, namely, the right to publicly perform a work and to use various media to publicly broadcast the performance of a work
(10) Right of screening, namely, the right to publicly reproduce an art, photographic, or film work or other works created in the style of film production, etc., through a projector, slide projector, or other technological equipment
(11) Right of broadcasting, namely, the right to publicly broadcast a work over the radio, to broadcast or transmit broadcasted works to the public over a wired broadcasting station, or to broadcast works to the public by an audio amplifier or other means of transmitting symbols, sound, or images
(12) Right of broadcasting over the information network, namely, the right to provide works to the public through wired or radio broadcasting, and to enable the public to select their own time and place to access a work
(13) Right of filming, namely, the right to produce a work on a media carrier through film production or through a method similar to film production
(14) Right of adapting, namely, the right to adapt a work so as to create a new work involving creativity
(15) Right of translation, namely, the right to convert the written text of a work from one language to another
(16) Right of compilation, namely, the right to select or arrange works or extracts of works to be compiled into a new work
(17) Any other rights that shall be enjoyed by the copyright holder[103]

A copyright holder may wholly or partially transfer any of the rights set forth in items (5) through (17) above. A transfer of ownership of an original work, such as artwork, is not deemed to be a transfer of the work's copyright, but the right to exhibit an original work of art shall passed on to the

103. Copyright Law, art. 10; Copyright Implementing Regulations, arts. 4, 5. Under China's copyright laws, copyrights are entitled to enjoy both moral rights (personal rights) and property rights. Moral rights (the rights of publication, authorship, alteration, and integration of works) are protected under Article 10 of the Copyright Law. The same article also provides for the protection of property rights. Prior to 2001, Article 10 was vague and limited both in content and in form (only the rights of exploitation and remuneration are mentioned). The 2001 amendments to the Copyright Law have brought a major change to this article by clarifying different types of property rights conferred to a copyright holder, which include the following: reproduction rights, distribution rights, rental rights, exhibition rights, performance rights, projection rights, broadcasting rights, information network distribution rights, production rights, adaptation rights, translation rights, and compilation rights.

transferee.[104] An author's exercise of his or her copyright cannot violate the PRC Constitution or any law, and cannot harm the public interest.[105]

The owner of a Copyright may be the original author of the work, or any other individual citizen, or corporate or noncorporate entities granted the rights to a copyright pursuant to the Copyright Law or applicable foreign laws.[106] Any work by a foreign author that is first published within the territory of China is accorded all the rights and privileges available to domestic authors under the Copyright Law.[107] Prior to 2001, a foreign author's work first published outside the territory of China was protected only if the author was a national of a country that was a party to a copyright treaty with China.[108] This rule has changed, and foreign authors may receive protection if the work is published in a country that is a member of a copyright treaty with China. In contrast, U.S. copyright law protects all unpublished works of all nationals regardless of whether they are domiciled in the U.S. Only Chinese citizens are afforded the full protection of Chinese copyright laws and unpublished works of foreign authors are not protected under the Copyright Law.

A work created by two or more authors entitles them to common rights as joint authors. A party who does not contribute to the creation of a work is not regarded as a joint author. A joint work may be divided for usage, and each of the authors may be awarded independent copyright for that portion of the work that they created.[109] Copyright protection may be granted to a person who creates a separate work by editing, rearranging, translating, annotating, or collating the original work. However, such tasks are prohibited if they infringe upon the rights of the original copyright owner.[110]

Under the Copyright Law, an employee maintains the right to "occupational" or "professional" work created on behalf of his or her employer, even though the work is created on the employer's time and with the

---

104. Copyright Law, art. 18.

105. Copyright Law, art. 4.

106. Copyright Law, art. 9.

107. Copyright Law, art. 2. Under the Copyright Implementing Regulations, copyright protection is granted to books published within thirty days from the initial foreign publication. Copyright Implementing Regulations, art. 8.

108. Under the Bern Convention, foreign works are protected whether published or not. *See* International Copyright Treaties Implementing Regulations, art. 5. The Bern Convention also provides that foreign works or applied art are protected for twenty-five years from the date on which they are created (*Id.* at art. 6); foreign computer programs are protected as literary works for a term of fifty years commencing from the end of the year of initial release of the program (*Id.* at art. 7); and foreign copyright holders have the exclusive rights to import their works into China (*Id.* at art. 15).

109. Copyright Law, art. 13; Copyright Implementing Regulations, art. 9. If joint authors are unable to agree to usage, neither party can prevent the other from exercising rights. *See also* Computer Software Protection Regulations, art. 10 (rule governing joint developers of software). The death of one co-author does not affect the rights of another co-author. Copyright Implementing Regulations, art. 14.

110. Copyright Law, arts. 12, 14; Copyright Implementing Regulations, art. 10.

employer's equipment and facilities.[111] The employer-entity has the exclusive right to use occupational or professional work within the scope of its business for a period of two years. Nevertheless, the employee still retains the right to be credited as the author of the work. The personal rights thus remain with the employee, and the employer maintains the right of exploitation for a period of two years. If an author is commissioned to create a work, the parties are required to enter into a contract that specifically addresses copyright title to the commissioned work.[112]

The term of copyright protection with respect to the author's right of accreditation, right to amend the work, and right to protect the integrity of the work is indefinite.[113] The period of copyright protection for rights of publication, use, and to receive compensation with respect to the work of authorship is the lifetime of the author plus an additional fifty years.[114] The protection period for corporate or noncorporate entities, including the rights of publication, use, and compensation, is fifty years measured from the date of publication.[115] The protection period for computer programs is fifty years from the initial public release of the program. An author's interest in a copyright may be transferred by succession.[116] The Copyright Law provides that a work of authorship that is not published within fifty years of completion is not entitled to statutory protection.

2. Standards for Copyright Infringement

The Copyright Law provides that the following activities constitute infringement:

(1) Publishing a work without the consent of the copyright holder
(2) Publishing, as one's own independent work, a work jointly created with others without the consent of the other parties

111. Copyright Law, art. 16; Copyright Implementing Regulations, arts. 11, 12. *See also* Computer Software Protection Regulations, arts. 12–13 (rule governing ownership of software developed in the workplace). The employer is entitled to copyright on software developed as a "work task" by an employee. Computer Software Protection Rules, arts. 12–13. Under U.S. copyright laws a "work for hire" is defined as work prepared by an employee within the scope of his or her employment, or a work specially ordered or commissioned for use by the employer. *See* 17 U.S.C. §§ 101, 201 (b).

112. Copyright Law, art. 17. The copyright is owned by the commissioning party if not specifically addressed in the commission agreement. *See also* Computer Software Protection Regulations, art. 11 (rule governing software developed by commission).

113. Copyright Law, art. 20.

114. Copyright Law, arts. 20, 21. *See also* Computer Software Protection Regulations, art. 14. Prior to January 1, 2002, the term of copyright for software was twenty-five years and renewable for an additional twenty-five-year period for a total of fifty years. Under the revised rules, software is granted protection for fifty years.

115. Copyright Law, art. 21.

116. Copyright Law, art. 19. *See also* Computer Software Protection Regulations, art. 15 (rights of inheritance for software).

(3) Placing one's name on the work of another without taking part in the creation of the work for the purpose of personal gain
(4) Misrepresenting another's work
(5) Plagiarizing the work of another person
(6) Using a work in a performance, broadcast, exhibition, publication, film, television, or video performance or in an adapted, translated, annotated, or edited form without the consent of the copyright holder
(7) Using another's work and not paying compensation
(8) Renting an audio-visual recording or DVD of a film without the consent of the copyright holder
(9) Broadcasting a performance live without the consent of the performer
(10) Using the format design of a published book or periodical without the consent of the publisher
(11) Any other act that violates the rights of a copyright holder[117]

3. Restrictions on Rights: "Fair Use" under Chinese Copyright Law

Under the Copyright Law, a party may quote from a work of authorship for purposes of introducing or providing a commentary, provided that the quoted passage is not the essence of the work of authorship.[118] It is also not considered infringement for a work to be quoted in newspapers, periodicals, broadcasts, television programs, or news documentaries when reporting current affairs news.[119] The reproduction in minimal quantities of a published work of authorship for educational or research purposes, provided that the reproduction is not intended for commercial objectives, is not considered an infringing activity.[120] Neither the law nor the regulations define

117. Copyright Law, art. 46. *See also* Computer Software Protection Regulations, arts. 23–31 (outlining acts of infringement specifically relating to computer software). Copyright infringement is much more prevalent than trademark protection as a result of a number of factors. In addition to lax enforcement, the recognition of copyright is inconsistent cultural issues such as the contempt for protecting the individual over the interests of the community. Most Chinese are also unwilling to shut down a factory that produces pirated videotapes or software disks when the results are a loss of jobs and economic benefits. *See generally* W. Alford, To Steal a Book is an Elegant Offense: Intellectual Property Law in Chinese Civilization (1995) (reviews historical aspects of conflicting notions of IP protection). *See also* Measures for Implementing Copyright Enforcement (issued on July 24, 2003, by the National Copyright Administration of China) (Measures outline national policies regarding counterfeiting and copyright protection, and specifically grant the Copyright Office the authority to seize infringing goods and evidence immediately). For a Chinese version of the Measures, *see* the Web site of the Copyright Office at http://www.ncac.gov.cn.

118. Copyright Law, art. 22 §(2).

119. Copyright Law, art. 22 § (3); Copyright Implementing Regulations, art. 5. The Copyright Implementing Regulations defines "current affairs News" as "factual information reported through such communications media as Newspapers, periodicals, radio, and television stations." Copyright Implementing Regulations, art. 5 § (1).

120. Copyright Law, art. 22 §§ (1), (6).

the permissible number of copies that may be reproduced from published works of authorship. This rule is similar to the fair use defense under U.S. copyright laws.

The Copyright Law further provides that the following does not constitute infringement and no compensation is paid to the author:

(1) The use by government officials of published works in the execution of their official duties
(2) Performances of published works that are made without compensation
(3) Reproductions of works by libraries, archives, and museums to allow the preservation of the original work
(4) Translations of published works originally published in Chinese to the languages of minority nationalities for domestic publication and use[121]
(5) Translation into Braille of a previously published work
(6) Copying, painting, photographing, or videotaping art works installed or displayed in public places[122]

4. License and Assignment of Copyright

The Copyright Law provides that the use of a copyright may be licensed or assigned to another party if written permission is granted; otherwise, no party may use a copyright work. A copyright license contract is required to include the following terms and conditions:

(1) Form of authorized use of the work
(2) Whether the authorized use is exclusive or nonexclusive[123]
(3) Scope and duration of authorized use
(4) Payment standards and methods
(5) Liability for breach of contract
(6) Other items affecting the use of the copyright[124]

Prior to 2001, a copyright license contract could not exceed a period of ten years although it was renewable by the parties. Currently, the ten-year

121. Under the regulations implementing the Bern Convention, a party that desires to translate a foreign work originally created in Chinese into languages for the Chinese minorities is required to obtain the permission of the copyright holder. International Copyright Treaties Implementing Regulations, art. 10.

122. Copyright Law, art. 22.

123. A failure to specify whether the use is exclusive or nonexclusive may give a party the right to exclusive use, with the exception of a transfer or sublicense of rights. Copyright Implementing Regulations, art. 24. *But see* Copyright Law, art. 26 (Any rights of authorization or transfer that have not been stipulated by the copyright holder in a license agreement may not be exercised by the other party without consent). The parties to an exclusive license arrangement may file the agreement with the NCA. Copyright Implementing Regulations, art. 25.

124. Copyright Law, arts. 24–28; Copyright Implementing Regulations, arts. 23–25. *See also* Computer Software Protection Regulations, arts. 18–22 (rules governing license of software rights).

maximum license term has been deleted from the law, and there are no restrictions on the duration of a copyright license agreement.[125] A party that fails to perform its obligations under a copyright license agreement is liable for infringement.[126]

5. Rules for Specific Types of Works

a. Software

Although computer software is specifically mentioned in the Copyright Law as protectable subject matter, the law also provides that separate measures are to be developed to protect such works.[127] In 1991, the State Council issued regulations specifically addressing the protection of computer software programs and later revised the regulations effective January 1, 2002.[128] Under the Computer Software Copyright Regulations, the term "computer software" refers to computer programs and related documentation.[129] The regulations outline the key terminology as follows:

(1) *Computer programs:* coded instructional sequences, or those symbolized instructional sequences or numeric language sequences that can be automatically converted into coded instructional sequences, that are for the purpose of obtaining a certain result, and that are

125. Copyright Law, arts. 24–28.
126. Copyright Law, art. 53.
127. Copyright Law, arts. 3 § (8), 10 § (7), 46 § (8), 52, 58.
128. Regulations on Computer Software Protection (promulgated on December 20, 2001, and effective January 1, 2002, by Decree No. 339 of the State Council of the People's Republic of China), *reprinted in* CHINA LAWS FOR FOREIGN BUSINESS (CCH), Business Regulation ¶ 11-704, available online at http://www.isinolaw.com (hereinafter the "Computer Software Protection Regulations"). *See also* Measures for the Registration of Computer Software Copyright (promulgated on February 20, 2002 by the State Copyright Administration), *reprinted in* CHINA LAWS FOR FOREIGN BUSINESS (CCH), Business Regulations ¶ 11-706, and *available online at* http://www.isinolaw.com. These Measures outline provisions for the registration of software copyrights and the copyright license contracts and apply to foreign parties. Registration is not required but encouraged under the Measures. The China Copyright Protection Center is the organization that handles the registration process for software copyrights. The purpose of the Measure for Computer Software Registration, as amended in 2002, is to simplify registration procedures and promote the efficiency of the registration examination. Applicants must file an original copy of an application form for software copyright registration, the copyright guarantee certificate, authentication material on said software, and other required certificates and documentation with the Software Registration Center. The Copyright Registration Center must examine the application within sixty days after the date is accepted for hearing (shortened from 120 days). The software registration holder must provide a written response within sixty days after receiving the photocopy of a petition (also shortened from 120 days). Furthermore, an applicant may apply to the software registration agencies established by the Software Registration Center in provinces and municipalities for software registration. The Chinese government also controls the manufacture and sale of computer software programs. Provisional Measures on the Administration of Software Products (issued on March 4, 1998, as Document No. 166 by the Ministry of Electronics Industry), *reprinted in* 14 CHINA LAW NEWS 10 (Aug. 28, 1998) (outlines standards for registration of software producers, technical and quality requests for software, and standards for importation of software products).
129. Computer Software Copyright Regulations, art. 2.

operated on information processing equipment such as computers. The source program and the object program of a piece of software shall be seen as one work.

(2) *Documentation:* written materials and diagrams that are used to describe the contents, organization, design, functions and specifications, development circumstances, testing results, and method of use of the program (e.g., program design explanations, flow charts, user manuals).

(3) *Software developers:* those legal persons or other organizations that actually organize the development, directly undertake the development, and take responsibility for the finished software as well; or natural persons who rely on their own conditions to independently complete software and who take responsibility for the software.

(4) *Software copyright owners:* those natural persons, legal persons, or other organizations that, in accordance with these Regulations, enjoy the copyright of computer software.[130]

The Computer Software Copyright Regulations provide that any software protected by the law must be developed by the software developer independently, and be fixed on a certain tangible object. Chinese citizens, legal persons, or other organizations are entitled to the benefits of the copyright in their software developed by them, whether published or unpublished, in accordance with the Regulations. Foreign software developers are entitled to the benefits of copyright protection in their software first published within the territory of the People's Republic of China in accordance with the Regulations or by treaty obligations.[131]

The Computer Software Copyright Regulations specifically exclude "ideas, concepts, processing procedure, operating methods, [and] mathematical concepts" from copyright protection as may be used in the development of software.[132] Consistent with the Copyright Law, as amended, the Computer Software Copyright Regulations provide that software copyright owners have the following rights:

(1) The right of publication, that is, the right to decide whether to publish a piece of software

(2) The right of authorship, that is, the right to indicate the developer's identity and to place his name on the software

130. Computer Software Copyright Regulations, art. 3.
131. Computer Software Copyright Regulations, arts. 4, 5.
132. Computer Software Copyright Regulations, art. 6.

(3) The right of revision, that is, the right to supplement, abridge, or change the instructions or the sequence of statement
(4) The right of reproduction, that is, the right to make a copy or copies of the software
(5) The right of issuance, that is, the right to provide original or copies of the software to the public by means of selling or donation
(6) The right of leasehold, that is, the right to license, with consideration, others to temporarily use the software, except in circumstances in which the software is not the major subject matter
(7) The right of information network propagation, that is, the right to provide the software to the public by wireless or cable means, so that the public may obtain the software at their respectively selected places and time
(8) The right of translation, that is, the right to translate the software from a natural language to another natural language
(9) Other rights that should be enjoyed by copyright owners[133]

The Regulations also provide that software copyright owners may license or transfer, in whole or in part, their software copyright.[134]

Joint developers of software are required to stipulate in writing the ownership of copyright between the parties. In the absence of a written joint development agreement, the co-developers have equal rights to the subject software jointly developed. If the jointly developed software cannot be used in separate parts, the copyright is jointly owned by the co-developers, and the co-developers may exercise the copyright by consensus. If consensus cannot be reached, neither party shall prevent any other from exercising its rights to the software, with the exception of the right of transfer.[135]

The copyright of software that is commissioned to be developed by another person must be governed by a written agreement signed by and between the person who commissioned the work and the person who undertook the commission. If there is no written agreement or if it is not explicitly stipulated in the agreement, the copyright shall be enjoyed by the person undertaking the commission.[136] If software developed by an individual within the scope of his or her employment for the purposes of the work, research, and objectives of the employer, the copyright is owned by employer.[137]

133. Computer Software Copyright Regulations, art. 8.
134. Computer Software Copyright Regulations, art. 8.
135. Computer Software Copyright Regulations, art. 10.
136. Computer Software Copyright Regulations, art. 11.
137. Computer Software Copyright Regulations, art. 13. Software developed for a government department is owned by the organization that assigned the task. Computer Software Copyright Regulations, art. 12.

The software's copyright is effective when the software's development is completed. The term for protection of a software copyright shall be the lifetime of the developer plus fifty years after his or her death, or fifty years after the completion of the software's development with respect to entities or organizations.[138]

Under the Computer Software Copyright Regulations, a party that owns a legal reproduction of software is expressly allowed to install the software in a computer and other devices with the information processing capacity, to make backup copies in order to prevent damage to the original reproduction, and to make necessary revisions in order to use the software or to improve the software's performance or functions. A party that lawfully owns a software reproduction is prohibited from providing backup copies to other persons by any means. A party is also prohibited from providing any revised software to any third party without the express agreement of the software copyright owner.[139]

A license to use a software copyright must be demonstrated by a written license contract. A licensee of a software copyright is prohibited from exercising any rights beyond the scope of a license contract.[140] A written contract is especially required when the rights to a software copyright are exclusive. If a written license contract is not concluded or the exclusive license is not specified in the contract, the licensed rights shall be deemed nonexclusive rights.[141] The Computer Software Copyright Regulations also require that the transfer of a software copyright be demonstrated in writing.[142] The government encourages, but does not require, that copyright software license or transfer contracts be registered.[143]

The Computer Software Copyright Regulations require that Chinese citizens, legal persons, or other organizations are required to abide by China's

---

138. Computer Software Copyright Regulations, art. 14. Where the software copyright belongs to a natural person, and the natural person is deceased, during the term for protection of the software copyright, the inheritors of the software copyright may, according to the relevant provisions of the Succession Law of the Peoples' Republic of China, inherit rights other than the authorship. Computer Software Copyright Regulations, art. 14.

139. Computer Software Copyright Regulations, art. 16. If a holder of a software reproduction is unaware that, or has no reasonable basis to believe that, the software he or she is using infringes upon the rights of a copyright holder, he or she shall not bear the liability of compensation. However, the infringing party is required to cease the use of, and destroy, such infringing reproduction upon notice of the infringement. Liability will be triggered if, after notice, the party continues to use the infringing reproduction or pays reasonable fees to the software copyright owner. Computer Software Copyright Regulations, art. 30.

140. Computer Software Copyright Regulations, art. 18.

141. Computer Software Copyright Regulations, art. 19.

142. Computer Software Copyright Regulations, art. 20.

143. Computer Software Copyright Regulations, art. 21.

export control rules when licensing foreigners to use, or transferring to foreigners, software copyrights.[144]

A party that engages in the following activities is in violation of the Computer Software Copyright Regulations and is liable to the copyright owner:

(1) Publishing or registering a software work without the consent of the software copyright owner
(2) Publishing or registering a software work of others in his or her own name
(3) Publishing or registering a piece of software jointly developed with others as a work developed by him- or herself alone without the consent of co-developers
(4) Signing his or her name to a piece of software developed by another person or altering the signature on the software developed by another
(5) Revising or translating a software work without the license of the software copyright owner; or
(6) Other acts infringing upon the software copyright[145]

The Computer Software Copyright Regulations also provide that a party may be civilly or criminally liable for the following activities:

(1) Copying, in whole or in part, software of the software copyright owners
(2) Issuing, leasing, or disseminating through the information network software of copyright owners to the public
(3) Intentionally avoiding or damaging the technical measures adopted by the copyright owners to protect their software copyrights
(4) Intentionally deleting or changing the electronic information of the control over the software rights
(5) Transferring, or licensing others to exercise, copyright owners' software copyrights[146]

A publisher or producer of software is liable for making any unsubstantiated claims of infringement against any party.[147]

144. Computer Software Copyright Regulations, art. 22.
145. Computer Software Copyright Regulations, art. 23.
146. Computer Software Copyright Regulations, art. 24. In addition to the remedies available under the Copyright Law, a party that copies or releases copyright materials via the Internet (items (1) and (2) above) is liable to a monetary fine of RMB100 per item copies or five times the total value, whichever is less. A party that engages in the activities specified in Item (3), Item (4), or Item (5) above may be liable for a monetary fine of up to RMB50,000. A copyright owner has a right to file an action with the people's court for provisional remedies such as to enjoin acts of infringement or for property/evidence preservation. Computer Software Copyright Regulations, arts. 26, 27.
147. Computer Software Copyright Regulations, art. 28.

b. Book Publishers

Under the Copyright Law, a book publisher is required to enter into a publishing contract with the copyright holder and to pay compensation for the right to publish.[148] A book publisher has the exclusive right of publication of the work for the duration of the publishing contract, which may not exceed a period of ten years but may be extended. A book publisher is liable for compensation to the copyright holder if it does not publish the work within the time set forth in the contract.[149] A book publisher may not condense or alter a work without obtaining the consent of the copyright holder. However, a book publisher may edit the work pursuant to the quality standards set forth in the publishing contract.[150] Under the 2001 amendments to the Copyright Law, a publisher has the right to permit or prohibit another party from using the format/layout design of its published books or periodicals, and the term of such protection is ten years.[151]

A copyright holder that submits a manuscript to a newspaper or magazine is entitled to send the work to another newspaper or magazine if it receives no notice of acceptance or rejection from the original newspaper or magazine editors.[152] A newspaper or magazine publisher may edit a work without permission; however, the consent of the copyright holder is required if it intends to alter the content of the work.[153]

c. Performances

A performer, including an individual or company, is required to obtain the consent of the author of an unpublished work prior to performance. A performer may perform a published work without the consent of the copyright

148. Copyright Law, art. 29; Copyright Implementing Regulations, art. 28. Publishers are also bound by other rules affecting the printing and publishing industry. *See* Administrative Rules on the Printing Industry (promulgated originally on March 8, 1997, by the State Council and amended on August 2, 2001), *reprinted in* CHINA LAWS FOR FOREIGN BUSINESS (CCH), Business Regulation ¶ 19-616 (standards for printing industry and penalties for unauthorized printing of foreign works without approval); Administrative Rules on Publishing (promulgated on January 2, 1997, by the State Council), *reprinted in* CHINA LAWS FOR FOREIGN BUSINESS (CCH), Business Regulation ¶ 19-612 (standards for unlawful distribution of foreign works without the consent of the copyright holder). The Administrative Rules on the Printing Industry specifically prohibit the misuse of another party's copyright. *See* Administrative Rules on the Printing Industry, arts. 21, 33, 38, 39. *See also* Administrative Regulations on the Printing of Publications (promulgated August 18, 1997 by the Press and Publications Administration of the People's Republic of China), *reprinted in* CHINA LAWS FOR FOREIGN BUSINESS (CCH), Business Regulation ¶ 19-624 (requires domestic publishers to obtain proof of copyright from foreign parties prior to publication of a commissioned work).

149. Copyright Law, arts. 30, 31.

150. Copyright Law, art. 31.

151. Copyright Law, art. 35.

152. Copyright Law, art. 32. A magazine has thirty days to respond to an author and a newspaper has fifteen days to respond to an author. The right to send a manuscript to another newspaper or magazine publisher is restricted by any agreement between the parties.

153. Copyright Law, art. 33.

holder but is required to pay remuneration for the performance.[154] The performer has the right to credit for the performance, to protect the style of performance from interference, and to authorize other persons to broadcast or to make audio-visual recordings of the performance.[155]

d. Audio-Visual Recordings

A person may make an audio recording of an unpublished work only with the permission of the author. A person may make an audio recording of a published work without permission but is required to pay compensation to the copyright holder.[156] A party that is interested in making an audio-visual recording of performers is required to enter into a written contract with the performers and to pay compensation.[157] A party that has the lawful rights to produce an audio-visual recording may authorize other persons to copy and distribute the recordings for compensation.[158]

e. Broadcasts

A radio or television station using another person's unpublished work to produce a program is required to obtain the consent of the copyright holder and to pay compensation. Consent is not required if the work is published, but the station is required to pay compensation.[159] A radio or television station that broadcasts a previously released audio recording during a not-for-profit broadcast is not required to obtain the consent of the copyright holder, or required to pay compensation.[160]

6. Administrative Remedies for Copyright Infringement

Any party may apply to the NCA or lower-level copyright administrative authorities to initiate an investigation of an alleged infringement. The NCA requires that an application be filed to initiate an investigation including information on the alleged acts of infringement, samples of the works and

---

154. Copyright Law, arts. 36–38.
155. Copyright Law, art. 37.
156. Copyright Law, art. 39. *See* Regulations on Copyrights in the Production of Digital Reproductions (issued on December 9, 1999, and published in April 2000 by the National Copyright Administration, effective on March 1, 2000). These regulations address several issues concerning the copyright protection and licensing of reproductions of copyrighted works as digital devices. Such devices include CD, LD, VCD, DVD, FD, CD-ROM, CD-I, Photo-CD, DVD-ROM, and IC Card. The Regulations clarify that under the law the making of digital reproductions by copying works constitutes "the act of reproducing works." As a result, authorization must first be obtained from the copyright owner or from the collective copyright management organization before such reproduction commences.
157. Copyright Law, art. 40.
158. Copyright Law, art. 41.
159. Copyright Law, art. 42; Copyright Implementing Regulations, art. 35.
160. Copyright Law, art. 43.

infringing activities or goods, and the relief sought (i.e., confiscation, compensation, etc.).[161] The NCA is required to accept or reject an application initiating an investigation within fifteen days and to notify the applicant.[162] Upon the completion of an investigation, the investigating officials are required to prepare and submit to the NCA an "Opinion on Administrative Penalties for a Copyright Infringement," which addresses the circumstances the subject of the investigation and the proposed penalties, if any. The administrative penalties for copyright infringement may include one or more of the following:

(1) Issuance of a warning
(2) Order directing the infringing party to cease production or sales of infringing merchandise
(3) Confiscation of income obtained from the sales of infringing merchandise
(4) Confiscation of infringing merchandise and production equipment
(5) Imposition of monetary penalties ranging from RMB100 to RMB100,000 or two to five times the total sales price of the infringing article[163]

The copyright owner may also demand that the infringing party provide compensation for losses suffered as a result of the infringement.[164]

Before issuing a decision, the NCA is required to notify the parties to give them an opportunity to be heard to contest the proposed decision.[165] In the event the NCA issues a penalty, the affected party has three days to respond to a notice of penalty. A penalty must be paid within fifteen days after imposition. The NCA may impose a late payment fine of 3 percent for each day the penalty is in arrears.[166] Although strongly criticized by

161. Copyright Law, arts. 46–55; Copyright Administrative Penalties Measures, art. 14.

162. Copyright Administrative Penalties Measures, art. 15.

163. Copyright Law, art. 47; Copyright Implementing Regulations, art. 36 (authorizes the NCA to impose a fine under three times the illegal sales of an infringing party or impose a fine less than RMB100,000 if it is difficult to calculate the illegal income), art. 37 (authorizes the NCA to take steps to "redress infringements against copyright").

164. Copyright Law, art. 47; Copyright Implementing Regulations, arts. 36, 37. *See also* Implementing Measures for Copyright Administrative Penalties (promulgated on January 28, 1997, by the State Copyright Bureau), *reprinted in* CHINA LAWS FOR FOREIGN BUSINESS (CCH), Business Regulation ¶ 11-715 (hereinafter the "Copyright Administrative Penalties Measures"). The Civil Law of the PRC sets forth the basic right to pursue damages for violations of intellectual property rights. *See* Civil Law, art. 118. The Civil Law also creates a right of action for improper use of a person's name, likeness, reputation, or honor. *See* Civil Law, art. 120. The parties to a copyright dispute may mediate their claims or, if required by contract, proceed with arbitration. Copyright Law, art. 48–49. *See also* Computer Software Protection Rules, arts. 34–35.

165. Copyright Administrative Penalties Measures, art. 20.

166. Copyright Administrative Penalties Measures, art. 28.

its trading partners, the PRC has increasingly made progress against copyright infringement.[167]

7. Judicial Remedies

A party that disagrees with an administrative decision or penalty concerning a copyright may file an action with the people's court within three months of receiving notice of the decision. If an affected party fails to seek judicial relief within the required time period, the NCA may petition the people's court for enforcement of a penalty order.[168]

An injured party may also proceed with an infringement action directly in the intermediate people's court and specifically before the specialized courts addressing IP-related issues.[169] In copyright infringement cases, the infringing party is liable for the actual losses of the copyright owner. In situations where actual losses are unascertainable, the court may order a damage award based upon the illegal income resulting from the infringement. The Copyright Law also provides that the injured party is entitled to reasonable expenses incurred in order to stop the infringing acts. In situations where the actual losses or the illegal income is difficult to determine, the court has the power to impose statutory damages up to RMB500,000 ($61,000).[170] A copyright holder is also entitled to request provisional remedies from the people's court to either enjoin the infringing acts or to preserve evidence of infringement that may otherwise be destroyed.[171] A people's court is also

167. *See generally* Hong, *Crackdown Aims to Protect Copyright in Anhui Province,* CHINA DAILY (Apr. 18, 1998), available on Lexis, News Library, or on the Web site of the CHINA DAILY at http://www.chinadaily.com.cn (Anhui officials seized 48,000 counterfeit books and 27,000 copies of pirated VCDs including copies of the Academy Award winning movie *Titanic* in the first quarter of 1998, and imposed prison sentences and fines against the violators. Anhui officials paid informants to provide information concerning the pirate operations.). Huang, *Illegal Discs Crushed as Piracy Campaign Rolls On,* CHINA DAILY (June 17, 1998), available on Lexis, News Library, or on the Web site of the CHINA DAILY at http://www.chinadaily.com.cn; Zhan, *Pirated VCSs Destroyed in Guangdong,* CHINA DAILY (June 24, 1998), available on Lexis, News Library, or on the Web site of the CHINA DAILY at http://www.chinadaily.com.cn.

168. Copyright Law, art. 55. *See also* Computer Software Protection Rules, art. 36 (right to judicial relief for software-related administrative decisions).

169. Copyright Law, art. 54. Interpretation of Several Questions on the Application of Law in Trial of Copyright Civil Dispute Cases (promulgated on October 12, 2002, by the Supreme People's Court), summarized in CHINA L. & PRAC., Nov. 2002, pg. 9. *See also* Computer Software Copyright Regulations, art. 31 (in the absence of an arbitration clause, the parties may file an action in the people's court involving computer software copyright disputes). In February 1999, Microsoft won its first software piracy case in China as a result the unauthorized use of its products by two Chinese companies. Microsoft received a judgment in the sum of $100,000, and the two infringing companies were required to issue a public apology. *See Microsoft Wins Software Piracy Lawsuit in Beijing Court,* Agence France Presse (Feb. 13, 1999), available on Lexis, News Library; *The Politics of Piracy,* The ECONOMIST 64 (Feb. 20, 1999), available on Lexis, News Library.

170. Copyright Law, art. 48.

171. Copyright Law, arts. 49–50. Provisional remedies are available under Articles 93–96 and 99 of the Civil Procedure Code. Upon application by the copyright holder, the people's courts are required to render a decision on an application for the preservation of evidence within 48 hours of filing. Copyright

authorized to order the confiscation of illegal income, infringing goods, and any property or equipment that is used to engage in illegal activity.[172] The burden of proof to demonstrate that a reproduction or infringing article is from a legal source is on the party that produces or distributes the infringing work or goods.[173]

8. SPC Copyright Infringement Case Rules: Internet Copyright Infringement

The Supreme People's Court has issued several orders concerning the management of copyright infringement cases. Of particular importance is the circular concerning cases involving copyright infringement that occurs with the use of a computer network or over the Internet.[174] In the SPC Internet Copyright Interpretation, the SPC holds that the jurisdiction of the people's court is based upon where the infringing act took place or the residential location of the defendant. The SPC defines the "location of the infringing act" to include the location(s) of the network server, or of the computer terminal and other facilities involved in the alleged act of infringement.[175] If it is difficult to determine the location of the infringing act or residential location of the defendant, the location of the computer terminal or other relevant facilities involved in the infringement will be regarded as the location of the act of infringement.

The SPC Internet Copyright Interpretation also provides that all digitalized form of works and all "intellectual works" in the Internet environment, even if not listed in Article 3 of the Copyright Law, shall be given copyright protection by the court if they display a literary, artistic, or scientific field.[176] The SPC further maintains that digitalized works are to receive all the protection set forth in Article 10 of the Copyright Law, including the right to restrict or authorize others from using or distributing a work via the Internet and to receive compensation for the work.[177] The reprinting or publishing of works on the Internet is copyright infringement if publication is conducted without the permission of the author.[178]

Law, art. 50. The people's court may order that the applicant post security before issuing an evidence preservation order.

172. Copyright Law, art. 51.

173. Copyright Law, art. 52.

174. Interpretation of the Supreme People's Court on Certain Issues Concerning the Application of Laws in the Hearing of Cases Involving Computer Network Copyright Disputes (adopted November 22, 2000 at the 1144th Session of the Judicial Committee of the Supreme People's Court, Fa Shi (2000) No. 48, promulgated December 19, 2000, and effective from December 21, 2000), *reprinted in* CHINA LAWS FOR FOREIGN BUSINESS (CCH), Business Regulation ¶ 11-720 (hereinafter the "SPC Internet Copyright Interpretation").

175. SPC Internet Copyright Interpretation, art. 1.

176. SPC Internet Copyright Interpretation, art. 2.

177. SPC Internet Copyright Interpretation, art. 2.

178. SPC Internet Copyright Interpretation, art. 3.

An Internet service provider (ISP) may be jointly liable for the copyright infringement of another party if the ISP instigates or assists an infringing party in violating the rights of a copyright owner.[179] An ISP may also be jointly liable together with an infringing party if it knows, or should have known, that an act of infringement occurs on its content service but fails to take remedial action to remove the infringing content.[180] The SPC further provides that an ISP is required to provide a copyright owner, upon request, with the registration information of an infringing party, and a failure to cooperate triggers the liability of the ISP.[181] A copyright owner may seek both damages and provisional remedies to stop infringing acts from the people's court.[182] A copyright owner that wrongfully accuses another party of infringement may be liable for damages.[183]

9. Criminal Penalties for Copyright Infringement

Under the 1997 Criminal Law, intentional copyright infringement for profit is a crime.[184] The law provides that the intentional reproduction and distribution of copyrighted materials is punishable by imprisonment of not more than three years and up to seven years if the illegal income is exceptionally large.

C. Patent Law

China's first law in the area of patent rights was issued by the Qing government in 1911 and revised in 1923.[185] Under this law, new and unique inventions were

179. SPC Internet Copyright Interpretation, art. 4. Joint liability may be pursued based upon Article 130 of the Civil Law.

180. SPC Internet Copyright Interpretation, art. 5. The law provides that the ISP be given a warning by the copyright holder.

181. SPC Internet Copyright Interpretation, art. 6. The ISP is not required to cooperate with a copyright holder if he or she fails to provide information substantiating his or her copyright claim and information concerning the alleged acts of infringement. SPC Internet Copyright Interpretation, art. 7. An infringing party is barred from making a claim of breach of contract or violation of privacy against an ISP that cooperates with a copyright owner. SPC Internet Copyright Interpretation, art. 8.

182. SPC Internet Copyright Interpretation. art. 7. Damages are based upon actual losses and lost profits, and also may be calculated by the income generated by the infringing party. If damages or profits are difficult to ascertain, the people's court has the authority to award statutory damages in an amount ranging from RMB500 to RMB300,000 (with a maximum of RMB500,000). SPC Internet Copyright Interpretation, art. 10.

183. SPC Internet Copyright Interpretation, art. 8.

184. Copyright Law, art. 47; Computer Software Copyright Regulations, art. 24. Criminal Law of the People's Republic of China (promulgated March 14, 1997, by the NPC), arts. 217, 218, *reprinted in* 11 CHINA L. & PRAC. 44 (June 1997) (hereinafter the "1997 Criminal Law"). *See also* Decision of the Standing Committee of the National People's Congress Concerning Punishment of the Crime of Copyright Infringement (adopted on July 5, 1994, by the 8th Sess. of the Standing Comm. of the 8th NPC), *reprinted in* CHINA LAWS FOR FOREIGN BUSINESS (CCH), Business Regulation ¶ 11-701. *See* Chapter 23, Criminal Liability for FIE Activities § B.3.

185. Z. Chengsi, Chinese Intellectual Property and Technology Transfer Law 51 (1987).

protectable for a period of five years but were issued to Chinese nationals only or by treaty to foreigners. In 1950, the PRC issued the *Provisional Regulations Concerning the Protection of the Invention and Patent Rights,* which provided that inventions in China were State property. These regulations were modeled after the Soviet Union's patent law.

In 1980, the China Patent Bureau was formally established and assigned the obligation of developing China's patent law and regulations. In 1984, the NPC promulgated the Patent Law, and the China Patent Bureau adopted the implementing regulations in 1985.[186] The State Intellectual Property Office (SIPO), formerly known as the China Patent Bureau, is the agency responsible for registration and enforcement matters and SIPO is under the direct authority of the State Council.[187] SIPO has increased its level

186. Patent Law of the People's Republic of China (adopted March 12, 1984, at the 4th Sess. of the Standing Comm. of the 6th NPC, amended September 4, 1992, and amended on August 25, 2000, at the 17th Sess. of the Standing Comm. of the 9th NPC), *reprinted in* CHINA LAWS FOR FOREIGN BUSINESS (CCH), Business Regulation ¶ 11-600 (hereinafter the "Patent Law"); Implementing Regulations of the Patent Law of the People's Republic of China (issued on December 21, 1992, by the Patent Office, and revised and re-promulgated on December 28, 2002, by the State Council), *reprinted in* CHINA LAWS FOR FOREIGN BUSINESS (CCH), Business Regulation ¶ 11-603 (hereinafter the "Patent Law Implementing Rules"). The Patent Law and Patent Rules are available on the Web site of the State Intellectual Property Office at http://www.sipo.gov.cn. *See generally* PRACTICAL HANDBOOK OF LAWS OF THE PEOPLE'S REPUBLIC OF CHINA GOVERNING INTELLECTUAL PROPERTY (eds. J. Min, L. Qin, C. Tian) (PRC Publishing House of Law, 1994); Hill & Evans, *Chinese Patent Law: Recent Changes Align China More Closely with Modern International Practice,* 27 GW. J. INT'L L. & ECON. 359 (1993–94); Wang, *The Chinese Traditions Inimical to the Patent Law,* 14 J. INT'L L. BUS. 15 (1993); Ou, *The Practice of Patent Law in China: Some Firsthand Observations,* 15 WIS. INT'L L.J. 313 (1997). In 1992, the NPC amended the Patent Law to expand protection. The Patent Regulations were amended to reflect the amendments to the Patent Law on December 12, 1992, by the State Council. The 1992 amended Patent Law and Patent Regulations were both effective on January 1, 1993. In 1992, China became acceded to the Patent Cooperation Treaty. Patent Cooperation Treaty, June 19, 1970, 28 U.S.T. 7645, 1160 U.N.T.S. 231. The Patent Cooperation Treaty is available on the Web site of the State Intellectual Property Office at http://www.sipo.gov.cn and the Web site of the U.S. Patent and Trademark Office at http://www.uspto.gov. Between 1992 and 1995, the applications for patents in China increased at an annual rate of 17 percent. During the first ten months of 1996, foreign applications of patents increased by 57 percent over 1995. The countries with the largest number of applications includes Japan, the U.S., and Germany. *See Record of Events (October–December 1996),* China Law 102, 106–07 (1997). In general, the 2000 amendments to the Patent Law and Patent Law Implementing Rules are designed to simplify the application process and strengthen the protection of patent rights.

187. Patent Law, art. 3. The State Intellectual Property Office is revising the Patent Law to provide for protection and cooperation between Hong Kong and Mainland patents. *China New IPR Commissioner Interviewed,* China Business Information Network (CBNET), April 14, 1998, available on Lexis, News Library; Cui, *New Office Established Patent Law to Be Revised,* CHINA DAILY (April 14, 1998), available on Lexis, News Library, or on the Web site of the CHINA DAILY at http://www.chinadaily.com.cn. SIPO is required to address patent applications in an "objective, fair, accurate, and timely manner, and in accordance with the law," and all SIPO personnel are required to maintain confidentiality with respect to the contents of patent applications received by the agency. Patent Law, art. 21. SIPO is not allowed to engage in any business activities that promote patented products. Patent Law, art. 66. SIPO officials are prohibited from engaging in favoritism, and any abuse of power is subject to administrative sanctions. Patent Law, art. 67. SIPO officials are also required to withdraw from participating in any application or petition where he or she is an interested party. Patent Law Implementing Rules, art. 38. In February 2004, SIPO launched a Web site dedicated to intellectual property issues that provides information on patent filings and a database of patented products and services. *See* http://www.cipmun.net.

of cooperation with foreign governments and intellectual property rights–related organizations.[188]

The Patent Law and implementing regulations provide that an invention, utility model, or design that is a "technical solution" relating to a product, process, or improvement is subject to patent protection.[189] The Patent Law requires that the utility model, design, or invention possess novelty, inventiveness, and practical application.[190] Patent protection under Chinese law is available to both the manufacturing process and chemical process, including that related to the production of pharmaceuticals, chemicals, food, beverages, and flavorings.[191] Supplemental protection for proprietary rights to integrated circuit design is provided by law.[192]

188. SIPO signed a cooperation agreement with the World Intellectual Property Office (WIPO) on May 21, 2002. The agreement provides that SIPO and WIPO are to cooperate on certain issues, including reform of the Patent Cooperation Treaty, development and protection of IPR by small and medium enterprises, and application of information technology to IPR protection.

189. Patent Law, arts. 1, 2. The term "invention" is defined as "any new technical solution relating to a product, a process or improvement thereof." The term "utility model" is defined as "any new technical solution relating to the shape, the structure, or their combination, of a product which is fit for practical use." The term "design" is defined as "any new design of the shape, pattern, color, or their combination, of a product, which creates an aesthetic feeling and is fit for industrial application." Patent Law Implementing Rules, art. 2.

190. Patent Law, art. 22. The Patent Law provides that the term "novelty" means that, prior to the date of the patent application, no identical invention or practical and new model had been publicly disclosed in Chinese or foreign publications or has been publicly used or made known to the public by any other means in China; nor has any other person filed an application previously with SIPO that describes the identical invention; nor has the invention been recorded in any patent application document published after the said date of application. The term "creativity" is described in the law to mean that, as compared with the technology existing before the date of application, the invention has significant substantive features and represents notable progress. The term "practicability" is defined to mean that the invention or practical and new model is able to be manufactured or used and can produce positive results. Patent Law, art. 22.

191. Under the 1985 Patent Law, the manufacturing process was subject to patent protection, but pharmaceuticals or chemicals that utilize a chemical process were not considered patentable subject matter. Under the amended law, chemicals and pharmaceuticals are subject to patent protection. In addition, food, beverages, and flavorings are subject to patent protection but, under the former law, were exempt from protection. Patent Law, art. 25. For a discussion of the types of protection available to pharmaceuticals and chemicals under the former law, *see* Liu & Wei, *Technology Transfer to China: The Patent System,* 5 SANTA CLARA COMPUTER & HIGH TECH. L.J. 363, 382 (1989). China has also agreed to offer retroactive protection to some preexisting U.S. patents on pharmaceuticals and agricultural products. To be eligible, the product must have been patented in the U.S. after January 1, 1986, and before the amendments to the Chinese patent law (January 1, 1993). The product must not have been previously marketed in China. If retroactive protection is applied for and granted, the patentee has the exclusive right to manufacture and sell the product in China for seven and one-half years. *See* 1992 U.S./China IP MOU, art. 2. *See also* Regulations on Administrative Protection of Pharmaceuticals (approved by the State Council on December 12, 1992, and promulgated by Decree No. 12 of the State Pharmaceutical Administration on December 19, 1992). *But see Eli Lilly's Prozac Appeal Fails,* NAT. L. J., June 29, 1998, available on Lexis, News Library; *China Depressed,* EIU BUSINESS CHINA, July 6, 1998, available on Lexis, News Library; Bassolino & Dame, *Battling Weak IP Protection in Pharmaceuticals,* CHINA BUS. REV. 22 (Jan./Feb. 1999).

192. Regulations for the Protection of the Layout Design of Integrated Circuits (adopted on March 28, 2001, at the 36th Sess. of the Executive Meeting of the State Council and promulgated on April 2, 2001), *reprinted in* CHINA LAWS FOR FOREIGN BUSINESS (CCH), Business Regulation ¶ 11-730 (hereinafter the "Integrated Circuit Regulations"); Detailed Implementation Rules for the Regulations for the Protection of the Layout Design of Integrated Circuits (Order No. 11 of the State Office for Intellectual Property, promulgated on September 18, 2001), *reprinted in* CHINA LAWS FOR FOREIGN BUSINESS (CCH), Business Regulation ¶ 11-731. Both the Integrated Circuit Regulations and implementing rules are effective October 1, 2001. The Integrated Circuit Regulations provide that a layout design is protected only

The Patent Law provides that patent applications involving inventions concerning State security issues or "other vital interests" are to remain confidential pursuant to state secrecy statutes.[193] An invention that is contrary to the laws of China or to "social morality" or that is "detrimental to the public interest," is prohibited from receiving a patent from SIPO.[194]

An applicant for a patent may be an individual, a State-owned enterprise, a private enterprise, foreign party, or institution. A foreign applicant must retain an authorized patent agent to represent its interests in the application process.[195] A Chinese enterprise or individual is required to obtain approval from SIPO prior to applying for a patent in a foreign country.[196] Two or more individuals or entities may cooperate to develop an invention and may jointly apply for a patent. Unless otherwise agreed in writing, all joint inventors have a right to patent rights to an invention.[197]

After a patent application is published, the applicant has the right to require an individual or entity to pay a royalty for using the patented technology.[198]

---

if it is unique and original, and not "conventional." *Id.* art. 4. SIPO is responsible for the registration and enforcement of IP protection for integrated circuit designs, and proprietary rights to such designs are not effective until a designer registers with SIPO. *Id.* art. 8. Protection is granted for ten years with a maximum of fifteen years' protection from the time of development. *Id.* art. 12.

193. Patent Law, art. 4.

194. Patent Law, art. 5. *See also* Patent Law Implementing Rules, art. 9.

195. Patent Law, arts. 18, 19; Patent Law Implementing Rules, arts. 99–105. Patent agents are subject to licensing rules. *See* Patent Agent Administrative Rules (issued by the State Intellectual Property Office on June 6, 2003) (outlines the requirements and qualifications for patent agents). An application for a patent by any applicant without a residence or business office in China, when the right of foreign priority is claimed by any applicant having no habitual residence or business office in China, SIPO may, if necessary, require the applicant to submit the following documents: (1) a certificate concerning the nationality of the applicant; (2) a certificate concerning the locality of the business office or the headquarters, if the applicant is an enterprise or any other organization; and (3) a testimonial showing that the country to which the foreigner, foreign enterprise, or other foreign organization belongs recognizes that Chinese citizens and entities are, under the same conditions applied to its nationals, entitled to patent right, right of priority, and other related rights in that country. Patent Law Implementing Rules, art. 34.

196. Patent Law, art. 20. A violation of Article 20 that results in the disclosure of State Secrets will subject a person to administrative and possibly criminal liability. Patent Law, art. 64. The disclosure of "state secrets" is prohibited by law, and the relevant regulations define the terms secret information and illegal disclosure in broad terms. "State Secrets" are defined as "matters that affect the security and interests of the state" and are illustrated by broad categories of information relating to national defense, "import policy decisions on state affairs," "economic and social development," "science and technology development," "criminal investigations," and "other state secrets that by decision of the state departments on protecting state secrets should be safeguarded." Law on Safeguarding State Security of the People's Republic of China (promulgated by the State Council in 1993); Detailed Rules for the Implementation of the Law on Safeguarding State Security of the People's Republic of China (promulgated by the State Council in 1994). *See also* Patent Law Implementing Rules, Article 8, which provides that "[w]here an invention for which a patent is applied for relates to state secrets concerning national defense and is required to be kept secret, the application for patent shall be filed with the national defense patent organization."

197. Patent Law, art. 8. The "inventor" or "creator" as referred to in the Patent Law shall mean any person who has made creative contributions to the substantive features of the invention-creation. Any person who, during the course of accomplishing the invention-creation, is responsible only for organizational or administrative tasks, or who offers facilities for making use of material means, or who takes part in other auxiliary functions, shall not be considered as inventor or creator. Patent Law, art. 12.

198. Patent Law, art. 13. The Patent Law prohibits a party from passing off an unpatented product as a patented product. SIPO is authorized to impose a fine of up to RMB50,000 for falsely claiming that

A patent holder has the right to include the patent number on its products and product packaging as a notice that the products, or technology contained therein, are patented.[199]

The law provides that an invention that is developed by an employee of an enterprise using tools, technology, and equipment of the enterprise is the work product of the enterprise and not the employee. In such situations, the enterprise has the right to apply to SIPO as the patentee and not the employee. For any invention produced by an employee outside the scope of his employment, the employee-inventor has the right to file an application for a patent. Any contracts between employees and an employer will govern the relationship regarding the right to inventions in the workplace.[200] No individual or entity can prohibit an inventor from filing an application for patent rights with respect to non–work related inventions.[201]

The law provides that an enterprise that has been granted a patent is required to reward the inventor of any work-related invention and, upon commercialization, to provide the inventor with reasonable compensation based upon the economic benefits received as a result of the patent.[202] The inventor of a patented invention has a statutory right to be given credit as the inventor in the patent documentation.[203]

1. Application and Approval of Patents

If two or more applicants file applications for patent protection for the identical invention, the patent rights, by law, are granted to the applicant whose

---

a product is patented. Patent Law, art. 59; Patent Law Implementing Rules, art. 85 (outlines violations of patent misuse for nonpatented technology and products).

199. Patent Law, art. 15.

200. Patent Law, art. 6. The "service invention-creation made by a person in execution of the tasks of the entity to which he belongs" as referred to in Article 6 of the Patent Law shall mean any invention-creation made: (1) in the course of performing his or her duties within the scope of employment; (2) in execution of any task, other than his or her own duty, which was entrusted to him by the entity to which he or she is employed; (3) within one year from his or her resignation, retirement, or change of work, where the invention-creation relates to his or her own duty or the other task entrusted by the entity to which he or she was formerly employed. "The entity" as referred to in Article 6 of the Patent Law shall include the temporary working unit, as in the case of a contract or temporary worker. The "material means of the entity" as referred to in Article 6 of the Patent Law refers to entity's funds, equipment, spare parts, raw materials, or technical data that are not disclosed to, or remain confidential from, the public. Patent Law Implementing Rules, art. 11.

201. Patent Law, art. 7. The Patent Law provides for liability of individuals or employers that interfere with the rights of an inventor or designer to apply for a patent for a non-work-related invention or other rights or interests of an inventor or designer. Patent Law, art. 65.

202. Patent Law, art. 16; Patent Law Implementing Rules, art. 74 (outlines that the reward amounts for patents for inventions and patents for designs shall not be lees than RMB2000 ($240) or RMB500 ($61), respectively). *See also* Patent Law Implementing Rules, arts. 75–77 (other provisions outline rewards for inventors in Chinese enterprises).

203. Patent Law, art. 17.

application was filed first.[204] The "first to file" system of China is in sharp contrast to the United States' patent system, which issues patents on a "first to invent" basis.

A party seeking a patent is required to file an application, a description of the invention, and an abstract of the invention.[205] The description of the technology is required to provide a clear and comprehensive explanation of the invention so that it can be reconstructed by a technician in the same field of technology.[206] If applicable, the applicant is required to include technical drawings for the invention. The abstract of the invention is required to briefly

204. Patent Law, art. 9. The date an application is received by SIPO is the filing date of the application. If mailed, the date of application is the date that it is postmarked. Patent Law, art. 28; Patent Law Implementing Rules, art. 10. All proceedings before SIPO must be in written form and in the Chinese language. Patent Law Implementing Rules, arts. 3, 4. For any identical invention-creation, only one patent right shall be granted. Two or more applicants who file, on the same day, application for patent for the identical invention-creation, as provided for in Article 9 of the Patent Law, shall, after receipt of a notification from SIPO, hold consultation among themselves to decide the person or persons who shall be entitled to file the application for patent rights. Patent Law Implementing Rules, art. 13. The law requires that applicants for patent, renewal, transfer, etc. are required to advance the required fees to SIPO. Patent Law Implementing Rules, arts. 90–98. Effective March 12, 2004, SIPO implemented an electronic patent filing system. *See* Provisions on Electronic Patent Application Filing (issued on February 12, 2004, by SIPO), available online at http://www.cponline.gov.cn. Foreign patent applicants may submit documents required under the patent cooperation treaty.

205. Patent Law, art. 26. The application and supporting documents filed with SIPO are required to be filed in duplicate. Patent Law Implementing Rules, art. 16. A party that uses a patent agent is required to submit a power of attorney with the application. Patent Law Implementing Rules, art. 16. The application for a patent is required to also include the following information: (1) the nationality of the applicant; (2) the name of the country in which the applicant has the principal business office where the applicant is an enterprise or other organization; (3) the relevant matters that should be indicated if the applicant has entrusted a patent agency; the name, address, postal code, and contact telephone number of the contact person if the applicant has not entrusted a patent agency; (4) the relevant matters that should be indicated if the priority of an earlier application is claimed; (5) the signature seal of the applicant or the patent agency; (6) a list of the documents constituting the application; (7) a list of the documents appending the application; and (8) any other related matter that needs to be provided. Patent Law Implementing Rules, art. 17.

206. Article 18 of the Patent Law Implementing Rules provides detailed information to be included in the description. Article 18 provides: "The description of an application for a patent for invention or utility model shall indicate the name of the invention or utility model. This name shall be consistent with the name in the application. The description shall include the following contents: (1) Technical field: specifying the technical field to which the invention or utility model relates; (2) Background technology: indicating the background technology that, as far as known to the applicant, can be regarded as useful for the understanding, searching, and examination of the invention or utility model, and citing the documents reflecting such technology, if possible; (3) Invention content: indicating the technical problem to be solved by the invention or utility model and the technical scheme adopted to solve the technical problem, and writing down the beneficial effect of the invention or utility model comparing the current technology; (4) Explanation for the drawings: briefly describing the drawings, if any; and (5) Specific implementation means: describing in detail the best mode contemplated by the applicant for carrying out the invention or utility model; this shall be done in terms of examples, where appropriate, and with reference to the drawings, if any. The manner and order as referred to in the preceding Paragraph shall be observed by the applicant of a patent for invention or a patent for utility model, and titles shall be indicated before each part of the description unless, because of the nature of the invention or utility model, a different manner or order would afford a better understanding and a more economical presentation. The description of the invention or utility model shall be with standard use of terms and distinct expressions, shall not contain such references as: 'as described in part ___ of the claim,' nor shall it contain commercial advertising." The Patent Law Implementing Rules also provide information concerning the claims for protection sought. *See* Patent Law Implementing Rules, arts. 20–23.

state the main technical points of the invention.[207] In addition to providing information concerning the applicant and the inventor, the application is required to state the scope of patent protection requested. Applications for patents involving exterior designs are required to include drawings or photographs of the exterior design the subject of the application and the product that incorporates the exterior design.[208] Patent applications involving inventions concerning biological materials are required to deposit samples of the inventions with a depository institution designated by SIPO.[209]

In accordance with applicable bilateral and multilateral patent treaties, an applicant has a right of priority in China if the application to SIPO is filed within twelve months from the date the applicant first filed an application for an identical invention or new model in a foreign country. An applicant for a patent regarding an exterior design has a right of priority if the application with SIPO is filed within six months of filing in a foreign country.[210] Within three months of making a request for priority, an applicant is required to provide SIPO with a copy of the previous patent application and declaration.[211] An application for a patent for invention or a practical and new model is required to be limited to one invention or one practical and new model. However, two or more inventions or practical and new models belonging to a single general inventive concept may be filed as one application. An application for a patent for an exterior design shall be limited to

207. The abstract is required to outline the content of the application for a patent for an invention or utility model, including the title of the invention or utility model, the technical field to which the invention or utility model pertains, the technical problems to be solved, the essential technical scheme to solve these problems, and the main purposes of the invention or utility model. The abstract may contain the chemical formula that best characterizes the invention. In an application for a patent that contains drawings, the applicant shall indicate and provide a drawing that best characterizes the invention or utility model. The scale and the distinctness of the drawings shall be such that a reproduction with a linear reduction in size to 4cm × 6cm would still enable all details to be clearly distinguished. The whole text of the abstract shall contain not more than 300 Chinese characters. Patent Law Implementing Rules, art. 24.

208. Patent Law, art. 27. An application for a patent of an exterior design must not be identical with or similar to any exterior design that, before the date of application, has been openly published in Chinese or foreign publications or has been publicly used in China, nor must it conflict with any other person's previously acquired lawful rights. Patent Law, art. 23. The size of drawings or photographs of a design submitted in accordance with the provisions of Article 27 of the Patent Law shall not be smaller than 3cm × 8cm, nor larger than 15cm × 22cm. Where an application for a patent for design seeking concurrent protection of colors is filed, a drawing or photograph in color in duplicate shall be submitted. The applicant shall submit, in respect of the subject matter of the product incorporating the design that is in need of protection, the relevant views and stereoscopic drawings or photographs, so as to clearly show the subject matter for which protection is sought. Patent Law Implementing Rules, art. 27. Upon request from SIPO, an applicant for design patent may be required to submit a sample or model of the product incorporating the design. The volume of the sample or model submitted shall not exceed 30cm × 30cm × 30cm, and its weight shall not surpass 15 kilograms. An applicant is not allowed to submit samples or models that are perishable, fragile, or a safety hazard. Patent Law Implementing Rules, art. 29.

209. Patent Law Implementing Rules, arts. 25–26.

210. Patent Law, art. 29; Patent Law Implementing Rules, art. 107–9.

211. Patent Law, art. 30; Patent Law Implementing Rules, arts. 32–33.

one exterior design incorporated in one specific product. Two or more exterior designs that are incorporated in products belonging to the same class and are sold or used in sets may be filed as one application.[212]

An application for patent may be withdrawn at any time before the patent is granted.[213] An application may be amended at any time up to the grant of patent; however, the amendment to an application for a patent for an invention or a practical and new model may not go beyond the scope contained in the initial description and claims. An amendment to an application for a patent for an exterior design may not go beyond the scope of the design as depicted in the original drawings or photographs submitted with the application.[214]

Upon receipt of an application, SIPO is required to review a patent application and supporting materials. If a preliminary examination of the application indicates that the application is in conformity with the requirements of the law, SIPO is required to publish the application within eighteen months of the date of the application.[215] After filing an application for patent, an applicant is required to request that SIPO conduct a substantive review and examination of the application. A request for a substantive review must take place within three years or early at the initiative of SIPO. If a request is not made by the applicant within the time required, the application may be deemed to have been withdrawn.[216]

If, after a substantive review, SIPO finds that the application is not in conformity with the law, the application may be rejected and/or deemed to have been withdrawn.[217] If SIPO finds that the application conforms with the law, the patent will be granted and a certificate of registration issued. The patent is effective on the date of public notice of the patent grant.[218]

2. Novelty Requirement and Exceptions

The Patent Law requires that an invention be novel and denies protection for any invention that is disclosed in a publication anywhere in the world or an invention that has been used or made known to the public before the filing

212. Patent Law, art. 33.

213. Patent Law, art. 32; Patent Law Implementing Rules, art. 37.

214. Patent Law, art. 33; Patent Law Implementing Rules, arts. 51–52.

215. Patent Law, art. 34.

216. Patent Law, art. 35; Patent Law Implementing Rules, art. 50. An applicant is required to submit search results concerning prior art. A failure to submit documentation as required by SIPO may be grounds for rejection. Patent Law, art. 36.

217. Patent Law, arts. 37, 38; Patent Law Implementing Rules, arts. 40–49, 53 (outlining reasons for rejecting an application for patent).

218. Patent Law, arts. 39, 40; Patent Law Implementing Rules, art. 54. See also Patent Law Implementing Rules, arts. 88–89, requiring SIPO to maintain a registry system for all patent grants and patent transfers, as well as the requirement of publishing the *Patent Gazette*.

date of the application.[219] The only exception to the prohibition on the prior publication is the allowance of a six-month grace period in the following specific circumstances:

(1) Where the invention was first exhibited at an international exhibition sponsored or recognized by the Chinese government
(2) Where the invention was first made public at a prescribed academic or technological meeting; or
(3) Where the invention was disclosed by any person without the consent of the applicant[220]

Chinese law does not recognize a general one-year grace period comparable to the U.S. patent system.[221] As a result, inventors are required to apply for a patent in China before publishing any report describing the inventions except in the limited situations noted above.

The Patent Law provides that no patent shall be granted to (1) scientific discoveries; (2) rules and methods for intellectual activities; (3) methods for the diagnosis or treatment of diseases; (4) animal and plant varieties; and (5) substances obtained by means of nuclear transformation. However, the Patent law provides that the processes used in producing new animal and plant varieties may receive patent protection.[222]

3. License/Assignment of Patent Rights

The law prohibits any party from exploiting patented technology without obtaining a license from the patent holder.[223] The Patent Law provides that the right to apply for a patent, and the patent rights themselves, may be assigned by the inventor.[224] The Patent Law, however, requires that all assignments be substantiated by a written contract, which must be registered

219. Patent Law, art. 22. The existing technology as referred to in Paragraph III Article 22 of the Patent Law shall mean any technology that has been publicly disclosed in publications in the country or abroad, or has been publicly used or made known to the public by any other means in the country, before the date of application (or the priority date where priority is claimed), that is, current technology. Patent Law Implementing Rules, art. 30.

220. Patent Law, art. 24; Patent Law Implementing Rules, art. 31.

221. 35 U.S.C. § 102 (b). Under the U.S. system, an applicant may obtain a patent on an invention so long as the invention was not published, in public use, or on sale more than one year before the application filing date in the U.S.

222. Patent Law, art. 25.

223. Patent Law, arts. 11, 12. Article 11 provides: "After the granting of a patent for an invention or a practical and new model, unless stipulated otherwise by this Law, no unit or individual may, without the authorization of the patentee, exploit the patent, or manufacture, use, promise to sell, sell, or import the patented product, or use the patented process, or use, promise to sell, sell or import products directly obtained through the patented process for production or business purposes. After the granting of a patent for an exterior design, no unit or individual may, without the authorization of the patentee, exploit the patent, or manufacture, sell or import products incorporating the patented exterior design for production or business purposes."

224. Patent Law, art. 10.

with the State Intellectual Property Office in order to be effective. The assignment of patents between Chinese and foreign parties requires approval by the State Intellectual Property Office.[225]

4. Compulsory Licensing

The Chinese patent system allows for compulsory licenses for invention or utility model patents when a qualified party is unable to obtain the patentee's authorization under "reasonable terms" and within a "reasonable period of time."[226] An applicant for a compulsory license is required to "furnish proof that it or he has not been able to conclude with the patentee a license contract for exploitation on reasonable terms."[227] The Patent Law Implementing Rules provide that a party requesting a compulsory license may only apply for such a license three years after the patent is granted.[228]

The State Intellectual Property Office may also grant a compulsory license if there is a state of emergency or in the national interest, or for non-commercial public purposes.[229] When a compulsory license is granted, the patentee and the licensee may agree on the terms of the exploitation of the patent including the scope of use and compensation. If the parties cannot reach an agreement, the State Intellectual Property Office will determine the terms. However, the Patent Law provides that a compulsory license is limited in scope, is nonexclusive, and may not be assigned.[230] A compulsory license is also limited to the domestic market, and the patentee is entitled to be provided with adequate compensation.[231] The patentee may seek to terminate a compulsory license when the circumstances indicate that compulsion is no longer justified.[232]

5. Duration of Patent Rights

The patent protection period for an invention is twenty years from the date of application. The protection period for utility model and design patents is ten years from the date of application.[233] Under the prior patent laws, an invention patent was only entitled to a fifteen-year protection period and

225. Patent Law, art. 10; Patent Law Implementing Rules, art. 14.
226. Patent Law, arts. 48–55.
227. Patent Law, art. 51.
228. Patent Law Implementing Rules, art. 72.
229. Patent Law, arts. 49, 52. *See also* Compulsory Licensing Implementing Rules (issued by SIPO on June 13, 2003) (provisions provide details on applying for and terminating compulsory licenses, and arbitration procedures for disputes related to compulsory licensing).
230. Patent Law, art. 53.
231. Patent Law, art. 54. Issues concerning the royalty fees for compulsory licenses may be adjudicated before SIPO; Patent Law Implementing Rules, art. 72–73.
232. Patent Law, art. 57; Patent Law Implementing Rules, art. 72–73.
233. Patent Law, art. 42.

utility and design patents were entitled to a five-year protection period. A patent owner is required to pay an annual fee to SIPO to maintain its patent rights; otherwise, the patent rights will be terminated.[234]

6. Cancellation/Invalidation Proceedings

An individual or enterprise that disputes the patent rights granted by SIPO has a right to file a petition for cancellation to the SIPO Re-examination Board to have the patent invalidated.[235] A party that is not satisfied with a decision to invalidate or uphold a patent has a right to seek judicial review within three months of notification of the Board's decision.[236] A patent that has been declared invalid pursuant to cancellation proceedings shall be deemed to be invalid from the original application date; however, a decision to invalidate a patent will have no retroactive effect as it relates to any judgment or order issued or enforced by a people's court.[237] The law also provides that an invalidation decision will have no effect on existing license contracts or assignments currently in force; however, a patent licensor or assignor is liable for compensation for damages that include the fees and royalties previously paid.

7. Enforcement of Patent Rights

The scope of patent protection for an invention or model is determined by the terms set forth in the patent claims. The description and supporting documents filed with an application may be used to interpret the patent claims. The scope of protection for exterior design patents is determined by a review of the drawings or photographs submitted with the application.[238]

The unauthorized use of a patent is considered patent infringement.[239] In the event of a patent dispute, the law, reflecting the Chinese emphasis on

234. Patent Law, arts. 43, 44. Patent rights may also be terminated if the patent holder files a written application that indicates that the patent holder abandons its rights. If patent rights are terminated, SIPO is required to publish a notice of termination. Patent Law, art. 44.

235. Patent Law, art. 45.

236. Patent Law, art. 46.

237. Patent Law, art. 47.

238. Patent Law, art. 56. *See* Opinion Concerning the Strengthening Patent Administration of Foreign Trade (issued on December 20, 2002, by the Ministry of Foreign Trade & Economic Cooperation) (outlining procedures for enforcement of patent rights for imported technology); Provisions for the Handling of Cases of Infringement of Rights to New Varieties of Agricultural Products (issued on December 30, 2002, by the Ministry of Agriculture) (outlining administrative and judicial remedies for infringement of patented agricultural products).

239. Patent Law Implementing Rules, art. 84. Article 84 provides that the following actions constitute infringement of patent rights: (1) labeling other's patent number on their manufactured or sold products or packing of these products without authorization; (2) using other's patent number in advertisements or other advertising materials without authorization, and misguiding others to consider that the technology concerned is other's patent technology; (3) using other's patent number in the contract without authorization, and misguiding others to consider that the technology concerned is other's patent technology; and (4) forging or altering patent certificates, patent documents, or application documents for the patent rights of others.

mediation, requires that the interested parties attempt to resolve their differences by consultation. If consultation is unsuccessful, any interested party may institute an action in the people's court or may request that SIPO intervene with the dispute. In the event that SIPO finds that a party is engaging in acts of infringement, it may order the infringing party to cease and desist its activities.[240] Any party dissatisfied with the order of SIPO to cease infringement may seek judicial review of the decision within fifteen days from the receipt of notice.[241] If an infringing party does not initiate legal action within the statutory time limit and refuses to cease the infringing activities, SIPO has the discretion of filing an action with the people's court for an order for provisional relief and compulsory enforcement.[242] SIPO may suggest that the parties engage in formal mediation of the dispute and, if unsuccessful, the affected party may file an action in the people's court.

In cases involving patent infringement, SIPO has the authority to order that a party case its acts of infringement, and may confiscate illegal income and production equipment used in the infringement. SIPO is empowered to impose a monetary fine of up to three times the illegal income derived from the infringing activities. In the event that there is no illegal income or it is unascertainable, SIPO has the authority to impose a statutory fine of up to RMB50,000. If the infringement constitutes a crime, SIPO is required to refer the matter for criminal prosecution.[243]

The Patent Law provides that compensatory damages are to be paid to a patent holder based upon the actual losses sustained. Damages may also be calculated by the income received by the infringing party or, if losses are difficult to ascertain, damages may be "equitably determined with a multiple figure of the patent license use fee."[244] In addition to damages, a patent holder may file an action with the people's court for provisional remedies, including injunctive relief, in situations where an act of infringement causes

240. Patent Law, art. 57; Patent Law Implementing Rules, art. 79–82. *See also* Several Regulations of the Supreme People's Court on the Specific Applicable Laws for Stopping Patent Right Infringement Before Legal Action (issued on June 7, 2001, by the Supreme People's Court) (hereinafter the "SPC Patent Infringement Regulations"). Under the SPC Patent Infringement Regulations, an applicant may file a petition with the court requesting an order stopping a party from engaging in acts of infringement. The applicant is required to post a bond or collateral, the scope of which is within the discretion of the court. The courts are required to issue a ruling on an application within 48 hours of acceptance. A party found to have engaged in infringement may apply to the court challenging the original decision, and the court must decide within ten days whether the injunctive order is to remain in effect.

241. Patent Law, art. 57.

242. Patent Law, art. 57.

243. Patent Law, art. 58.

244. Patent Law, art. 60.

irreparable injury to the patent holder.[245] The limitations period for patent infringement litigation is two years from the date on which the patent holder or any interested party knows, or should have known, about the acts of patent infringement.[246]

The Patent Law provides that the following activities do not constitute patent infringement:

(1) Where, after the sale of a patented product that was made or imported by the patent holder, or made or imported with the authorization of the patent holder, or of a product derived directly from a patented process, any other person uses, promises to sell, or sells that product
(2) Where, before the date of the application for a patent, any identical product has been manufactured, any identical process has been used, or any necessary preparation for the manufacture or the use has been made, and the product or process will continue to be manufactured or used within the original scope only
(3) Where any foreign means of transport that temporarily passes through the territory, territorial waters, or territorial airspace of China uses the patent concerned, in accordance with any agreement concluded between the country to which the foreign means of transport belongs and China, or in accordance with any international treaty to which both countries are party, or on the basis of the principle of mutual benefit, for its own needs in its devices and equipment
(4) Where the patent concerned is used solely for the purposes of scientific research and experimentation[247]

The Patent Law further provides that any patented product or product derived directly from a patented process made and sold without knowledge of the patent holder's authorization, or can be proved to have come from a legal source, shall not be subject to liability and claims for damages.[248]

8. Administrative/Judicial Remedies

A party dissatisfied with a decision of SIPO in regard to a patent application or a decision concerning compensation under a compulsory license, may file

245. Patent Law, art. 61. Court actions for provisional remedies are addressed under Articles 93–96 and 99 of the Civil Procedure Code of the PRC. SIPO is required to suspend its procedures after a party files an action for provisional remedies with the people's court. Patent Law Implementing Rules, art. 87.
246. Patent Law, art. 62. A patent holder is limited to demanding a license fee for two years.
247. Patent Law, art. 63.
248. Patent Law, art. 63.

a request for review by the SIPO Re-examination Board.[249] A party that seeks to invalidate a patent has the right to file a petition for cancellation directly with the SIPO Re-examination Board.[250] A party that disputes the decisions or orders of the SIPO Re-examination Board may file an action for review to the people's court.[251] Upon request of an applicant, the patent approval process may be suspended pending the resolution of a dispute.[252]

On June 7, 2001, the Supreme People's Court issued orders that provide for better court management of intellectual property cases, including patent infringement matters.[253] The SPC Patent Infringement Provisional Remedies Regulations set forth more detailed procedures for the lower courts with regard to the handling of requests for provisional remedies, such as injunctive relief, and requests for preservation of evidence and property. Under the Regulations, an applicant is required to post security or collateral as a condition for issuance of provisional remedies, and it is within the court's discretion to set the amount of such security. Upon acceptance of a petition for injunctive relief, the court is required to render a decision on the application within 48 hours. The SPC regulations further provide that the court's ruling shall be immediately executed and enforced. The infringing party or other party affected by a court order may apply for a review of the court's decision with ten days of the ruling; however, the ruling remains effective during the ten-day period for filing a request for review. The applicant for provisional remedies is required to file an action for patent infringement setting for the applicants full claims within fifteen days of the ruling on injunctive relief, or the injunction order will be dismissed by the court. Similarly, on September 29, 2001, the Higher People's Court of Beijing (which is the highest-level court within the Municipality of Beijing and is equal in status to the

249. A party adversely affected by a decision of SIPO is required to file a petition for review within three months from the date of notice of the decision. Patent Law, art. 41 (review procedures for patent applications); arts. 54–55 (review procedures for decisions on compulsory license orders); Patent Law Implementing Rules, arts. 59–61.

250. Patent Law, art. 45; Patent Law Implementing Rules, art. 64–71 (outlines procedures for review of invalidation petitions).

251. Patent Law, art. 41 (judicial review of application-related issues); art. 46 (judicial review of decisions to cancel or uphold a patent pursuant to invalidation proceedings). Under the Administrative Litigation Law, an interested party has the right to file an action challenging the decision of the State Intellectual Property Office directly to the Intermediate People's Court. *See* Law of Administrative Litigation of the People's Republic of China (adopted on April 4, 1989, by the 2nd Sess. of the 7th NPC), art 14, § (i), *reprinted in* CHINA LAWS FOR FOREIGN BUSINESS (CCH), Business Regulation ¶ 19-558 (hereinafter the "Administrative Litigation Law"). For a brief discussion concerning administrative litigation, *see* Chapter 22, Litigation in the Peoples' Court § C.

252. Patent Law, art. 43.

253. Several Regulations of the Supreme People's Court on the Specific Applicable Laws for Stopping Patent Right Infringement before Legal Action (issued on June 7, 2001, by the Supreme People's Court, effective on July 1, 2001) (hereinafter the "SPC Patent Infringement Provisional Remedies Regulations").

highest court at the provincial level) issued the *Opinions on Several Issues Regarding Judgment of Patent Torts*.[254] This Patent Tort Opinion sets forth the case management standards for patent infringement acts in the people's court within the Beijing Municipality.

9. Criminal Penalties for Patent Infringement

In addition to administrative penalties and civil liability, the Criminal Law provides that it is unlawful to intentionally misrepresent ownership of a patent belonging to another party. In such cases, the infringing party is liable for imprisonment of not more than three years and potential monetary penalties.[255]

D. Customs Protection of Intellectual Property Rights

The Chinese government has adopted specific regulations that require China Customs to enforce intellectual property laws in relation to the import and export of goods.[256] Customs is required to confiscate any infringing goods, or to pursue payment from the consignee equivalent to the CIF price of the imports if the goods are unrecoverable after being released from Customs' custody.[257] Customs has the discretion to destroy the infringing goods or to preserve the goods for public welfare purposes, unless an action has been filed with an administrative agency or the court. Customs may also refer the matter to judicial authorities for criminal prosecution.[258]

---

254. Opinions on Several Issues Regarding Judgment of Patent Torts (issued on September 29, 2001, by the Higher People's Court of Beijing, effective on October 10, 2001).

255. Criminal Law, art. 216.

256. For more information concerning customs protection of intellectual property rights, *see* Chapter 15, Customs and Trade Regulation § D. Rules of the People's Republic of China on Customs Protection of Intellectual Property Rights (promulgated July 5, 1995), reprinted in China Laws for Foreign Business (CCH), Customs ¶ 50-610 (the "Customs IP Protection Rules"); Implementing Measures of the Customs of the People's Republic of China for the Protection of Intellectual Property Rights (promulgated September 28, 1995, by the General Administration of Customs), reprinted in China Laws for Foreign Business (CCH), Customs ¶ 50-612 (the "Customs IP Protection Measures"). See also Regulations on Certain Issues Concerning the Implementation of Customs Protection on Patent Rights (promulgated on March 11, 1997, by the General Administration of Customs and the China Patent Bureau), reprinted in China Laws for Foreign Business (CCH), Customs ¶ 59-026. In the three years that the regulations have been in effect, Customs in Shenzhen has uncovered more than 200 copyright, trademark, and patent violations and destroyed over 3.2 million pirated CDs. See IP Protection, China Daily (June 12, 1998), available on Lexis, News Library, or on the Web site of the China Daily at http://www.chinadaily.com.cn; Dan, Elimination of Fake UL Labels Urged, China Daily (Sept. 9, 1998), available on Lexis, News Library, or on the Web site of the China Daily at http://www.chinadaily.com.cn.

257. Customs IP Protection Rules, art. 23; Customs IP Protection Measures, art. 28.

258. Customs IP Protection Rules, art. 31.

Key Laws and Regulations

Trademark

Trademark Law of the People's Republic of China (adopted August 23, 1982, at the 24th Sess. of the Standing Comm. of the 5th NPC, revised in 1993 by the 30th Sess. of the Standing Comm. of the 7th NPC and revised in 2001 by the 24th Sess. of the Standing Comm. of the 9th NPC)

Detailed Rules for the Implementation of the Trademark Law of the People's Republic of China (amended January 3, 1988, July 15, 1993, and April 23, 1995, by the State Council, and revised on August 3, 2002, by the State Council)

Regulations of the Ministry of Foreign Trade and Economic Cooperation and the State Administration of Industry and Commerce Concerning the Administration of Trademarks for Foreign Trade (promulgated on August 25, 1995, by the MOFTEC and SAIC)

Interpretation of Several Questions on the Application of Law in Trial of Trademark Civil Dispute Cases (promulgated by the Supreme People's Court on October 12, 2002)

Copyright

Copyright Law of the People's Republic of China (adopted on September 7, 1990, at the 15th Sess. of the Standing Comm. of the 7th NPC, amended on October 27, 2001, at the 24th Sess. of the Standing Comm. of the 9th NPC)

Regulations for the Implementation of Copyright Law of the People's Republic of China (promulgated on August 2, 2002, and effective September 15, 2002, by the State Council)

Regulations on Implementation of International Copyright Treaties (issued on September 25, 1992, by the State Council and amended on August 2, 2002, by the State Council)

Regulations on Computer Software Protection (Order No. 339 of the State Council, promulgated on December 20, 2001, and effective from January 1, 2002)

Measures for Implementing Copyright Enforcement (issued on July 24, 2003, by the National Copyright Administration of China)

Measures for the Registration of Computer Software Copyright (promulgated on February 20, 2002, by the State Copyright Administration)

Provisional Measures on the Administration of Software Products (issued on March 4, 1998, as Document No. 166 by the Ministry of Electronics Industry)

Regulations on Copyrights in the Production of Digital Reproductions (issued on December 9, 1999, and published in April 2000, by the National Copyright Administration, effective on March 1, 2000)

Implementing Measures for Copyright Administrative Penalties (promulgated on January 28, 1997, by the State Copyright Bureau)

(*Continued*)

(*Continued from previous page*)

Interpretation of Several Questions on the Application of Law in Trial of Copyright Civil Dispute Cases (promulgated on October 12, 2002, by the Supreme People's Court)

Interpretation of the Supreme People's Court on Certain Issues Concerning the Application of Laws in the Hearing of Cases Involving Computer Network Copyright Disputes (adopted November 22, 2000 at the 1144th Session of the Judicial Committee of the Supreme People's Court, Fa Shi [2000] No. 48, promulgated December 19, 2000)

Decision of the Standing Committee of the National People's Congress Concerning Punishment of the Crime of Copyright Infringement (adopted on July 5, 1994, by the 8th Sess. of the Standing Comm. of the 8th NPC)

Patents

Patent Law of the People's Republic of China (adopted March 12, 1984, at the 4th Sess. of the Standing Comm. of the 6th NPC, amended September 4, 1992, and amended on August 25, 2000, at the 17th Sess. of the Standing Comm. of the 9th NPC)

Implementing Regulations of the Patent Law of the People's Republic of China (issued on December 21, 1992, by the Patent Office, and revised and re-promulgated on December 28, 2002, by the State Council)

Patent Agent Administrative Rules (issued by the State Intellectual Property Office on June 6, 2003)

Provisions on Electronic Patent Application Filing (issued on February 12, 2004, by SIPO)

Compulsory Licensing Implementing Rules (issued by SIPO on June 13, 2003)

Opinion Concerning the Strengthening Patent Administration of Foreign Trade (issued on December 20, 2002, by the Ministry of Foreign Trade & Economic Cooperation)

Several Regulations of the Supreme People's Court on the Specific Applicable Laws for Stopping Patent Right Infringement Before Legal Action (issued on June 7, 2001, by the Supreme People's Court)

Chapter 15

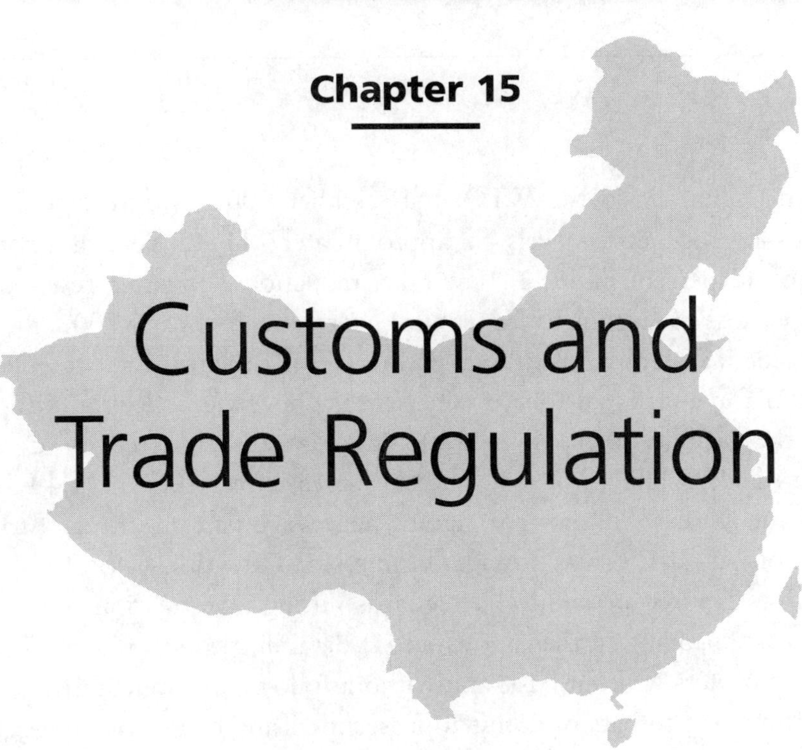

Customs and Trade Regulation

China has taken steps to reform and modernize its customs laws and regulatory system in its bid to enter the World Trade Organization (WTO), and as a result of pressure from its trading partners. China has been under particular pressure from the United States to publish its customs laws and regulations to encourage market access, and to mobilize China Customs to enforce its intellectual property laws in order to protect the interests of foreign investors.[1] While implementation of these reforms has been inconsistent, particularly as it pertains to tariff exemption and preference programs, the overall improvements to the Customs regulatory system are evident. In 1996 alone, China cut tariffs on more than 4,000 items from 35.9 percent to 23 percent, and eliminated quota, licensing, and other import-control regulations on an additional 170 items.[2]

---

1. Note that the 1992 PRC-U.S. Memorandum of Understanding Concerning Market Access specifically requires that the PRC government publish on a regular basis all laws, regulations, decrees, administrative guidance, and policies pertaining to the classification or valuation of products for customs purposes, or to rates of duty, taxes, or other charges, or to the requirements, restrictions, or prohibitions on imports or exports. *See* People's Republic of China—United States: Memorandum of Understanding Concerning Market Access, 31 I.L.M. 1274, art. I, ¶ 1 (1992). The Market Access MOU further provides that the PRC will not enforce any customs laws, regulations, decrees, rulings, or policies that are not published and readily available. *Id.* at art. I, § 2.

2. In 1996, China lowered its average import tariff from 42.1 percent to 23 percent, and on October 1, 1997, further reduced the average import tariff to 17 percent. *1998 National Trade Estimate, Foreign Trade Barriers: People's Republic of China,* United States Trade Representative, March 31, 1998, available at the USTR's Web site at http://www.ustr.gov/reports/nte/1998/china.pdf. The USTR noted that many of the tariff reductions claimed by China are with respect to imports on low-volume goods. Other goods, such as automobiles, are subject to tariffs as high as 100 percent. High tariff rates coupled with import restrictions and foreign exchange controls render importing to China a dismal experience for some types of products.

When China joined the WTO in December 2001, it agreed to further reduce its average tariff levels to approximately 11–12 percent (from an average of 42 percent in 1992). The tariff reductions, however, resulted in a tremendous loss of revenue to the Chinese government. In early 2002, the PRC Government initiated a policy (per Premier Zhu Rongji's own statement in July 2002) for China Customs to increase its revenue collection efforts to counter the tariff reductions. In 2002, the revenue collected by Customs jumped to $44.95 billion, or a 43 percent increase over 2001 ($31.4 billion). The revenue increase follows an ongoing aggressive pattern of investigations against both domestic and foreign businesses. Oftentimes, local Customs investigators ignored procedural safeguards during investigations by, among other things, engaging in the following: (1) detaining goods, employees, and assets of importers without basis and without following administrative procedures; (2) making threats of criminal prosecution and claims of "smuggling" without basis, and with the intent to frighten local Chinese employees, who usually will cooperate with authorities in a manner that places a foreign company in an adversarial position with its staff; (3) refusing to conclude investigations until importers compromise spurious claims; or (4) other tactics designed to increase the level of revenue collection. In response, it is important for companies importing into China to establish a Customs compliance system, monitor its Customs practices, and to be prepared to take a stand against China Customs if action is taken against a company that is contrary to the law.

This chapter addresses China's customs regulatory system, import and export procedures, enforcement of China customs laws, customs protection of intellectual property, and trade remedies regulations such as anti-dumping, anti-subsidy, and import safeguard measures.

A. Customs Regulatory System

The General Administration of Customs is responsible for customs operations and is charged with ensuring that the Customs laws and regulations are administered throughout the country.[3] Customs personnel are under a statutory duty to enforce the law in an impartial and diligent manner and are empowered to seek the assistance of the public security officials or other

3. Customs Law of the People's Republic of China (adopted January 22, 1987, at the 19th Sess. of the Standing Comm. of the 6th NPC, and as amended and approved July 8, 2000, at the 16th Sess. of the Standing Comm. of the 9th NPC), art. 3, *reprinted in* CHINA LAWS FOR FOREIGN BUSINESS (CCH), Customs ¶ 50-300 (hereinafter the "Customs Law"). *See* Zhao, *Custom Duty: The Role of China's Customs Service,* 136 CHINA INTERNATIONAL BUSINESS (MOFTEC) 16 (1998); R. Chan, *Customs Law Gets a Facelift,* CHINA BUS. REV. (March–April 2001).

government authorities in the performance their duties.[4] Local Customs offices are established at ports of entry throughout China and operate independently, subject to the supervision of the General Administration of Customs.[5] This responsibility extends to the following matters:

(1) To monitor and control merchandise that passes through the customs territory of China (i.e., imports and exports)
(2) To assess and collect any applicable duties, taxes, and fees on imported merchandise
(3) To investigate and prevent smuggling into the country
(4) To compile trade statistics
(5) In general, to enforce and carry out the provisions of the customs laws and regulations[6]

B. Import/Export Procedures

1. Inward- and Outward-Bound Means of Transport

A transportation operator, including the operator of a vessel, motor vehicle, or aircraft, arriving or departing from any port of entry in China is required to make a declaration to the local Customs office, present necessary documentation, and accept the supervision of Customs.[7] Departure from any port of entry requires prior permission from Customs, as does movement between ports of entry. A transportation operator is required to provide advance notice to China Customs regarding the planned arrival and departure schedule for each means of transport.[8] The loading and unloading of inward- and outward-bound goods and articles, and the boarding and disembarking of passengers, are subject to Customs supervision and control.[9] The transportation operator

4. Customs Law, art. 7; Detailed Rules for the Implementation of the Administrative Penalties of the Customs Law of the People's Republic of China (approved June 30, 1987, by the State Council and promulgated on July 1, 1987, by the General Administration of Customs, amended and approved February 17, 1993, by the State Council and repromulgated April 1, 1993, by the General Administration of Customs), *reprinted in* China Laws for Foreign Business (CCH), Customs ¶ 50-315 (hereinafter the "Administrative Penalties Rules").

5. Customs Law, art. 3.

6. Customs Law, art. 6. Customs is vested with the following powers: (1) to inspect and examine inward and outward means of transport, goods, and articles; (2) to detain individuals entering or leaving the territory in violation of the Customs Law and other related laws and regulations; (3) to examine the papers of persons entering or leaving the territory; and (4) to examine documentation supporting customs transactions including contracts, invoices, accounts, bills, records, documents, business letters and cables, audio and video recordings, and other data related to the inward and outward means of transport, goods, and articles.

7. Customs Law, art. 8.

8. Customs Law, art. 10.

9. Customs Law, art. 17.

is required to remain present during inspection by Customs, and is required to assist as may be required by Customs.[10] No change in control of the vehicle, vessel, or aircraft is permitted until the completion of Customs formalities.[11] Whenever a transportation operator is forced to discharge cargo as a result of force majeure at a location without Customs present, the transportation operator is required to immediately notify China Customs.[12]

2. Inward- and Outward-Bound Goods

In general, all import and export goods may be processed through Customs either by the consignee of import goods and consignor of export goods or by registered clearing agents or customhouse brokers.[13] Import goods are subject to Customs supervision from the time of arrival in the Customs Territory of China until the completion of Customs clearance procedures.[14] Export goods are subject to Customs supervision from the time of declaration for export to departure from Chinese territory. Merchandise that is transported under bond is subject to Customs' supervision and control until it is released or exported.

a. Declaration and Examination

The consignee of import goods and the consignor of export goods are required to make accurate declarations at the time of import or export.[15] The consignee or consignor is required to obtain and submit all relevant licenses, and goods without the required license may not be released. Import goods must be declared to Customs within fourteen days of the arrival of the means of transport, while declaration of export goods must generally be made at least twenty-four hours prior to loading. A fee may be assessed where the consignee of imported goods fails to make declaration within the required time period. The consignee or consignor is required to be present during any required examinations, and all imported and exported merchandise is subject to inspection.[16] The General Administration of Customs may authorize an

---

10. Customs Law, art. 18.
11. Customs Law, art. 14.
12. Customs Law, art. 22.
13. Customs Law, art. 9.
14. Customs Law, art. 23.
15. Customs Law, art. 9. The Customs clearance process is conducted electronically. *See* Provisions of the General Administration of Customs for the Administration of Declarations for Imported and Exported Goods (issued on September 18, 2003, by the General Administration of Customs) (outlines procedures for obtaining customs clearance for imported and exported goods; provides that trading enterprises are to register with GAC upon establishment and conduct Customs clearance procedures in their own name or through a professional agent; and provides that Customs declarations must be made through an electronic data declaration form that carries the same legal validity as the hard-copy paper declaration form used in the past).
16. Customs Law, art. 24.

exemption from examination upon receipt of application from the consignee or consignor.[17]

b. Valuation of Goods, Assessment, and Payment of Duties

The clearance and release of import and export goods will not be granted before applicable duties and fees are paid in full, unless special authorization for release is granted by Customs.[18] Customs duties are levied in accordance with the established import or export tariff rates and as may have been reduced pursuant to WTO tariff reduction commitments.[19] Tariffs are generally assessed on an ad valorem basis. The consignee of import goods and the consignor of export goods are legally responsible for payment of Customs duties and fees.[20]

Generally, payment of import or export duties must be made within fifteen days from the issuance of a duty memo by Customs.[21] Failure to meet this time limit will result in the assessment of a penalty by Customs. Where the delay exceeds three months, Customs may issue a demand for payment or may proceed with forfeiture and auction of the goods.

Post-WTO China has committed to abide by the Agreement on Implementation of Article VII of the GATT (i.e., Customs Valuation Agreement, which sets forth rules to unify the procedures for customs valuation by laying out in hierarchical order the five methods to determine Customs value of imported goods).[22] Similar to the rules used for transfer pricing, the first method is the transaction value, followed by valuation based upon transactions involving similar goods and other methodologies. To meet its commitments to abide by WTO Customs Valuation Agreement, China adopted the Measures of Customs of the People's Republic of China for the Examination and Approval of the Dutiable Value of Import and Export Goods.[23]

---

17. Customs maintains a "red list" of manufacturing enterprises that are large importers determined to operate in compliance with the law. Companies on the "red list" are generally provided more favorable treatment during the importation clearance process. For a review of the list, see the Web site of Customs at http://www.customs.gov.cn.

18. Customs Law, art. 23. A party may post a deposit covering any duties or fees to be paid at the time of importation.

19. Customs Law, art. 55.

20. Customs Law, art. 54.

21. Customs Law, art. 60.

22. *See* Agreement on Implementation of Article VII of the General Agreement on Tariffs & Trade of 1994, available online at http://www.wto.org (hereinafter referred to as "WTO Customs Valuation Agreement").

23. Measures of Customs of the People's Republic of China for the Examination and Approval of the Dutiable Value of Import and Export Goods, promulgated on December 31, 2001, and effective on January 1, 2002, by the General Customs Administration (hereinafter the "Customs Valuation Measures"). The General Administration of Customs is responsible for interpreting these Measures. *Id.* art. 46. These Measures shall not be applicable to the verification and determination of (i) the dutiable value of the baggage and articles accompanying incoming passengers, personal postal articles, and other personal

Practice Tip: Customs' Use of Price Lists

Customs still uses Price Lists or Referenced Prices for determining dutiable value without regard to true transaction value. In negotiations for China's accession to the WTO, WTO members expressed concern regarding the methods used by China to determine the customs value of goods, in particular regarding the practice of using minimum or reference prices for certain goods, which would be inconsistent with the Customs Valuation Agreement. Other WTO-consistent means were available to members doubting the veracity of declared transaction values. In response, China stated that it had ceased to use and would not reintroduce minimum or reference prices as a means to determine customs value. Importers should be alert to determine if Customs attempts to use Reference Prices to determine dutiable value for imports and to protest the use of such lists if appropriate.

The Customs Valuation Measures provide that dutiable value of import goods shall be examined and determined by Customs on the basis of the transaction price of the goods.[24] The transaction price is required to include the freight, relevant expenses, and insurance incurred before the unloading of the goods at the port of discharge inside the PRC.[25] The transaction price of the import goods is defined as the price actually paid or payable by the buyer for purchasing the goods, subject to any adjustments for fees, costs, or royalties.[26]

articles for self-use that are permitted for import, and (ii) the dutiable value of the import and export goods and articles suspected of having been smuggled. *Id.* art. 45. Customs Valuation Measures supersede the "Measures of Customs of People's Republic of China for the Examination and Approval of Dutiable Value of Import and Export Goods" implemented as from September 1, 1992, and the "Measures of Customs of People's Republic of China for the Examination and Approval of Dutiable Value of the Goods Imported for Processing Trade" implemented as from October 1, 1999. *See also* Regulations of the People's Republic of China on Import and Export Duty (promulgated on November 23, 2003, by the State Council and effective January 1, 2004). The Import/Export Duty Regulations expand tariff categories to include most-favored-nation tariffs, treaty tariffs, preferential tariffs, and quota tariffs. The Regulations set out the method for calculating duties and extend the deadline for the payment of tariffs to fifteen days from issuance of a payment notice by the GAC and reduce late payment fees to 0.05% of the balance of the unpaid duty. The Import/Export Duty Regulations further authorize Customs to impose retaliatory tariffs against goods imported from countries or regions in violation of bilateral or multilateral trade agreements. Under the Regulations, an enterprise that is the subject of a merger or acquisition is required to notify Customs of the intended corporate change of ownership.

24. Customs Valuation Measures, art. 3. *See also* WTO Customs Valuation Agreement, arts. 1, 8. Article 1 is to be read together with Article 8, which provides, *inter alia,* for adjustments to the price actually paid or payable in cases where certain specific elements that are considered to form a part of the value for customs purposes are incurred by the buyer but are not included in the price actually paid or payable for the imported goods. Article 8 also provides for the inclusion in the transaction value of certain considerations that may pass from the buyer to the seller in the form of specified goods or services rather than in the form of money.

25. Customs Valuation Measures, arts. 3, 24–30 (guidelines for calculation of freight, expenses, insurance); WTO Customs Valuation Agreement, art. 8.

26. "Price actually paid or payable" shall mean the total amount paid by the buyer, directly or indirectly, for the purchase of the goods, i.e., the aggregate sum of money already paid or to be paid by the

The Customs Valuation Measures provide that the transaction price of the import goods is required to satisfy the following requirements:

(1) The buyer shall not be subject to any restriction in disposing of or using the import goods, with the exception of the restrictions imposed by domestic laws and/or administrative regulations, restrictions to the territories for the resale of the goods, and the restrictions having no material influence on the price of the goods
(2) The price of the goods shall not be affected by any conditions or factors that may cause the transaction price of the goods unable to be determined
(3) The seller shall not directly or indirectly obtain any proceeds generated from the resale, disposal, or use of the import goods by the buyer, unless an adjustment can be made according to Article 4 of these Measures
(4) There is no special relationship between the buyer and the seller. If there is any such special relationship, the provisions set forth in Article 6 of these Measures must be followed[27]

When determining the dutiable value of import goods, the following *expenses* or costs shall be added thereto:

(1) The following fees borne by the buyer:
  a. commissions and brokerage charges except the purchasing commissions[28]

---

buyer to the seller, or to a third party for performing the obligation as a seller, as a consideration for the seller's sale of the import goods. Customs Valuation Measures, art. 41. The payment need not necessarily take the form of a transfer of money. Payment may be made by way of letters of credit or negotiable instruments. Payment may be made directly or indirectly. An example of an indirect payment would be the settlement by the buyer, whether in whole or in part, of a debt owed by the seller. The price actually paid or payable refers to the price for the imported goods. Thus the flow of dividends or other payments from the buyer to the seller that do not relate to the imported goods are not part of the customs value. WTO Customs Valuation Agreement, note to art. 1.

27. Customs Valuation Measures, art. 3. The buyer and the seller shall be deemed to have special relationship under any of the following circumstances: (i) The buyer and the seller are members of the same family; (ii) The buyer and the seller are respectively the senior officer or director in business of one another; (iii) Either of the buyer and the seller is under direct or indirect control of the other; (iv) Both of the buyer and the seller are under direct or indirect common control of a third party; (v) Both of the buyer and the seller are directly or indirectly controlling a third party; (vi) Either of the buyer and the seller directly or indirectly owns, controls, or holds 5 percent or more of the publicly listed voting stocks or shares of the other; (vii) Either of the buyer and the seller is the employee, senior officer, or director of the other; (viii) Both the buyer and the seller are members of the same partnership. In the event that the buyer and the seller have certain contacts with each other in terms of business operations, or either of them is the exclusive agent, distributor, or assignee of the other, where any of the above mentioned circumstances exists, they shall be deemed to have a special relationship. Customs Valuation Measures, art. 42.

28. "Purchasing commissions" are defined in the Measures to mean the expenses for labor services paid by the buyer to its buying agent, for the purpose of purchasing the import goods. "Brokerage charges" shall mean the expenses for labor services paid by the buyer to the broker representing the benefits of both the buyer and the seller, for the purpose of purchasing the import goods. Customs

b. expenses for the containers deemed as an integral part of the goods
c. expenses for packing materials and packing services

(2) The value for the following items or services directly or indirectly provided free of charge, or sold at a price lower than the cost price, by the buyer to the seller or the relevant party:
a. materials, components, parts, and similar items contained in the import goods
b. tools, molds, and similar items used in the course of production of the import goods
c. materials consumed in the course of production of the import goods
d. engineering design, technical R&D, process, and drawings required for the production of such goods conducted outside the PRC

(3) The franchise royalties that are payable by the buyer, either directly or indirectly, that are related to the goods and constitute a condition for the seller for the sale of the goods within the People's Republic of China[29]

(4) The proceeds obtained by the seller directly and indirectly from the income generated by the buyer's resale, disposal, or use of the imported goods

For the expenses or value specified above, the consignee shall provide Customs with objective and quantified data and information.[30]

Valuation Measures, art. 41. *See also* WTO Customs Valuation Agreement, note to art. 8, ¶ 1 (a) (i). The term "buying commissions" means fees paid by an importer to the importer's agent for the service of representing the importer abroad in the purchase of the goods being valued.

29. "Franchise royalties" shall mean the fees paid by the buyer for obtaining the license to use the works, patents, trademarks, proprietary technology, and other rights related to the imports and protected under copyrights. However, in assessing the dutiable value, the fees for the right of reproduction of the import goods inside the PRC shall not be added into the price of the goods actually paid or payable. Customs Valuation Measures, art. 41. *See also* WTO Customs Valuation Agreement, 8 (1) (c). The royalties and license fees referred to in paragraph 1(c) of Article 8 of the WTO Customs Valuation Agreement may include, among other things, payments in respect to patents, trademarks, and copyrights. However, the charges for the right to reproduce the imported goods in the country of importation shall not be added to the price actually paid or payable for the imported goods in determining the customs value. Payments made by the buyer for the right to distribute or resell the imported goods shall not be added to the price actually paid or payable for the imported goods if such payments are not a condition of the sale for export to the country of importation of the imported goods. WTO Customs Valuation Agreement, note to art. 8 (1) (c). *See also* Regulation on Valuation of Royalties Related to Imported Goods (promulgated on May 30, 2003, by the General Administration of Customs). (Provides that a royalty/license fee includes payments for patents, trademarks, copyrights, and rights of resale/distribution. These fees, when related to the imported goods and a condition of sale, must be added to the dutiable value of the goods and be subject to duties and VAT.)

30. Customs Valuation Measures, art. 4. In the absence of such objective and quantified data and information, the dutiable value shall be assessed by Customs in accordance with Articles 7 to 11 of the Customs Valuation Measures.

The Customs Valuation Measures provide that the following expenses shall not be added for purposes of determining dutiable value:

(1) The expenses for the after-import capital construction, installation, assemblage, maintenance, and technical services of the plants, machines, equipment, and other items
(2) The freight incurred after the arrival of the goods at the port of discharge inside the PRC
(3) The import duty and other internal taxes[31]

The Customs Valuation Measures provide that, in the event that there is a special relationship between the buyer and the seller, Customs is required to accept the transaction price in the following situations:

(1) The transaction price at which the seller sells an equivalent or similar item to a domestic buyer having no special relationship
(2) The dutiable value of an equivalent or similar item as determined pursuant to the price deduction or price calculation methods[32]

When making comparison by using the price methods listed above, Customs is required to take into consideration the variation in the quantities, and must take into consideration the expenditure differences that may result if there is any special relationship between the buyer and seller.

The Customs Valuation Measures provide that in the event that the dutiable value of the import goods is unable to be determined pursuant to the transaction value, Customs shall apply the following methods in a sequence set forth below to determine the dutiable value of the imported goods:

(1) Method of transaction price for an equivalent item
(2) Method of transaction price for a similar item
(3) Price deduction method
(4) Price calculation method
(5) Reasonable methods[33]

---

31. Customs Valuation Measures, art. 4. *See also* WTO Customs Valuation Agreement, art. 8 (2).

32. Customs Valuation Measures, arts. 6, 9, 10. The Customs Valuation Measures provide that the term "equivalent item" shall mean an item that is produced in the same country or region as the import goods, and that is identical to the import goods in physical property, quality, goodwill, and all other aspects, provided that the existence of superficial and minor diversities shall be acceptable. "Similar item" shall mean an item that is produced in the same country or region as the import goods, and that, even if not being completely identical to the import goods in all aspects, has the characteristics and constructional materials similar to the import goods, has the same function as the import goods, and is interchangeable with the import goods in the trade. Customs Valuation Measures, art. 41.

33. Customs Valuation Measures, art. 7.

When applying the valuation method of transaction price for an *equivalent or similar item*, Customs shall assess the dutiable value on the basis of the transaction price of an item equivalent or similar to the assessed goods, and imported at the same time or approximately the same time as the assessed goods. In addition, Customs is required to use the transaction price of an equivalent or similar item at the same commercial level and same quantity, provided that an adjustment shall be made, on the basis of the objective and quantified data and information, with respect to the differences in costs and other expenses arising from the variation in transportation distances and shipment methods between the import goods and the equivalent or similar item.[34] In the absence of the transaction price for an equivalent or similar item, Customs may use the transaction price for an equivalent or similar item at a different commercial level or in different import quantity, provided that an adjustment be made with respect to the differences in prices, costs, and other expenses arising from the variation in commercial levels, import quantity, transportation distances, and shipment methods between the import goods and the equivalent or similar item.[35]

The Customs Valuation Measures provide that when using the *price deduction method* for determining dutiable value, Customs shall assess the dutiable value on the basis of the price for the sale inside China of an import item equivalent or similar to the assessed goods. The item sold at such price shall satisfy the following conditions:

(1) The item is sold at the same time or approximately the same time as the assessed goods
(2) The item is sold in such conditions as at the time of import
(3) The item is sold at the first link inside the PRC
(4) The aggregate sales volume of the item is the largest
(5) The buyer of the item has no special relationship with the seller

34. Customs Valuation Measures, art. 8. See also WTO Customs Valuation Agreement, arts. 2–5.

35. *See* WTO Customs Valuation Agreement, note to art. 2. A condition for adjustment because of different commercial levels or different quantities is that such adjustment, whether it leads to an increase or a decrease in the value, be made only on the basis of demonstrated evidence that clearly establishes the reasonableness and accuracy of the adjustments, e.g., valid price lists containing prices referring to different levels or different quantities. As an example of this, if the imported goods being valued consist of a shipment of ten units and the only identical imported goods for which a transaction value exists involved a sale of 500 units, and it is recognized that the seller grants quantity discounts, the required adjustment may be accomplished by resorting to the seller's price list and using that price applicable to a sale of ten units. This does not require that a sale had to have been made in quantities of ten as long as the price list has been established as being bona fide through sales at other quantities. In the absence of such an objective measure, however, the determination of a customs value under the provisions of Article 2 is not appropriate.

When assessing the dutiable value of the import goods based upon the *price deduction method*, Customs shall deduct the following items:

(1) The profit and general expenses for an item of the same grade or kind as the import goods upon its sale inside the PRC as well as the commissions customarily paid in respect of such item
(2) The freight, insurance, handling charges, and other relevant expenses incurred after the arrival of the import goods at the port of discharge inside the PRC
(3) The import duty, import-linked taxes, and other internal taxes relating to the import or sale of the aforementioned goods[36]

When assessing the dutiable value of the import goods pursuant to clauses 1 and 2 of Article 9, if the equivalent or similar item is not sold in the PRC at the same time or approximately the same time as the assessed goods, Customs may extend the period for the domestic sale to ninety days from the date upon which Customs accepts the declaration of the assessed goods, provided that all other conditions specified in clause 1 of this Article are satisfied.[37]

If the equivalent or similar item is not sold in the PRC in such conditions as at the time of import, then, at the request of the consignee of the import goods, the sales price for the item after being further processed may be used for assessing the dutiable value, provided that all other conditions specified in clause 1 of this Article are satisfied, and provided further that the value added by processing shall be deducted simultaneously.[38]

36. Customs Valuation Measures, art. 9. The "profit and general expenses" referred to in Article 9 of the Measures shall be determined on the basis of the materials provided by the consignee of the import goods. In the event that the profit and general expenses of the consignee are inconsistent with the profit and general expenses of the items belonging to the same grade or same kind which are sold inside the PRC, then the latter shall be taken as the basis for determination. "General expenses" shall include the direct and indirect expenses in connection with the sale of the goods. Customs Valuation Measures, art. 43. When deciding the deductible items under Article 9, Customs is required to apply generally accepted accounting principles in China. Customs Valuation Measures, art. 41. *See also* WTO Customs Valuation Agreement, art. 5. The WTO Customs Valuation Agreement provides that if the imported goods or identical or similar imported goods are sold in the country of importation in the condition as imported, the customs value of the imported goods under the provisions of Article 5 shall be based on the unit price at which the imported goods or identical or similar imported goods are so sold in the greatest aggregate quantity, at or about the time of the importation of the goods being valued, to persons who are not related to the persons from whom they buy such goods, subject to certain deductions. The term "unit price at which . . . goods are sold in the greatest aggregate quantity" means the price at which the greatest number of units is sold in sales to persons who are not related to the persons from whom they buy such goods at the first commercial level after importation at which such sales take place. WTO Customs Valuation Agreement, note to art. 5.

37. Customs Valuation Measures, art. 9. The Measures provide that the term "approximately the same time" shall mean within forty-five days prior to and after, respectively, the date upon which Customs accepts the import declaration for the assessed goods. Customs Valuation Measures, art. 41.

38. Customs Valuation Measures, art. 9.

The Customs Valuation Measures provide that when using the *price calculation method*, Customs shall assess the dutiable value of the import goods on the basis of the aggregation of the following:

(1) The value of raw materials used in the production of the import goods, and the expenses for the assemblage and other processing
(2) The profit and general expenses consistent with those of the items exported to and sold in the PRC that are of the same grade or kind as the import goods
(3) The freight, relevant expenses, and insurance incurred prior to the unloading of the import goods at the port of discharge inside the PRC

When assessing the dutiable value based upon the *price calculation method*, Customs may verify, outside the PRC, the relevant materials provided by the enterprise, after obtaining the consent of the foreign manufacturer and informing in advance the government of the relevant country or region.[39]

The Customs Valuation Measures provide that when Customs applies *reasonable methods* for determining dutiable value, the agency shall assess the dutiable value of the goods on the basis of information and materials obtained in China, provided that the following prices shall not be used:

(1) The domestic selling price applicable in China for goods produced in China
(2) The higher price available for choice
(3) The sales price of the goods prevailing in the market of the exporting region
(4) The price calculated based on the value or expenses other than those set forth under Article 10 of the Customs Valuation Measures

39. Customs Valuation Measures, art. 10. *See also* WTO Customs Valuation Agreement, art. 6. Under Article 6 of the WTO Customs Valuation Agreement, Article 6(1), the customs value of imported goods may be based upon computed value. Computed value shall consist of the sum of: (a) The cost or value of materials and fabrication or other processing employed in producing the imported goods; (b) An amount for profit and general expenses equal to that usually reflected in sales of goods of the same class or kind as the goods being valued that are made by producers in the country of exportation for export to the country of importation; (c) The cost or value of all other expenses necessary to reflect the valuation option chosen by the member State under paragraph 2 of Article 8 of the treaty. The WTO Customs Valuation Agreement further provides that no member state may require or compel any person not resident in its own territory to produce for examination, or to allow access to, any account or other record for the purposes of determining a computed value. However, information supplied by the producer of the goods for the purposes of determining the customs value under the provisions of this Article may be verified in another country by the authorities of the country of importation with the agreement of the producer and provided they give sufficient advance notice to the government of the country in question and the latter does not object to the investigation.

(5) The sales price for the goods exported to a third country or region
(6) The minimum fixed price or an arbitrary and/or fictitious price[40]

The Customs Valuation Measures provide specific rules for determining dutiable value with respect to materials and components imported for processing trade, bonded zones or export processing zones, items reimported after undergoing repairs overseas, temporary imports, leased goods, trade samples and exhibits, goods subject to partial or full tariff exemption, barter trade, consignment sales, and gifts.[41]

The consignor and consignee of the import goods are required to truthfully declare to Customs the transaction price of the import and export goods, and provide Customs with the invoices, contracts, packing lists, and other documentation, written materials, and electronic data necessary to demonstrate the validity of the declared value. Upon request from Customs, the consignor and consignee of the import goods are required to provide supplemental information to substantiate the relationship and transaction activities between the buyer and the seller, as well as other materials in relation to the declared value.[42] Customs has the authority to take the

40. Customs Valuation Measures, art. 11. *See also* WTO Customs Valuation Agreement, art. 7. If the importer so requests, the importer shall be informed in writing of the customs value determined under the provisions of this Article 7 of the WTO Customs Valuation Agreement (reasonable method) and the method used to determine such value.

41. Customs Valuation Measures, arts. 12–20. The dutiable value for goods in bonded zones is based upon the prices for the sale of the goods outside the bonded area or the price for the delivery from the bonded warehouses for sales in the domestic market, as approved by Customs. *Id.* at 13. The dutiable value for imports re-exported after repair is based upon the repair costs outside of China. *Id.* at 14. *See also* Supervising Measures on Goods Imported and Exported Under ATA Certificates (promulgated on December 24, 2001, by the General Administration of Customs). (These regulations apply to goods temporarily imported/exported for exhibit or use in exhibits, conferences, trade fairs, and other similar activities. No tariff is imposed on temporary imported goods. China's ATA system is consistent with the ATA Carnet practices employed worldwide. Application for ATA certificates is through the China Council for the Promotion of International Trade.) *See also* Regulations on Taxation Issues Related to Import Taxes Levied by Customs on Imported Goods (issued on March 16, 2004, by the Ministry of Finance, General Administration of Customs, and State Administration of Taxation) (exempting most goods imported for use in exhibitions from VAT and consumption tax as long as the importer posts security).

42. Customs Valuation Measures, art. 31. Recognizing that the customs administration may have to address cases for which it has reason to doubt the truth or accuracy of the particulars or of documents produced by traders in support of a declared value, the WTO Committee on Customs Valuation has emphasized that, in so doing, the customs administration should not prejudice the legitimate commercial interests of traders. Having regard to Article 17 of the Agreement, paragraph 6 of Annex III to the Agreement, and the relevant decisions of the Technical Committee on Customs Valuation, the Committee on Customs Valuation has determined that: When a declaration has been presented and where the customs administration has reason to doubt the truth or accuracy of the particulars or of documents produced in support of this declaration, the customs administration may request the importer to provide further explanation, including documents or other evidence, that the declared value represents the total amount actually paid or payable for the imported goods, adjusted in accordance with the provisions of Article 8 of the Customs Valuation Agreement. If, after receiving further information, or in the absence of a response, the customs administration still has reasonable doubts about the truth or accuracy of the declared value, it may, bearing in mind the provisions of Article 11 of the Customs Valuation Agreement, be deemed that the customs value of the imported goods cannot be determined under the provisions of Article 1 thereof. Before taking a final decision, the customs administration must communicate to the

following actions in investigating the validity of any declared value: (i) to review and reproduce the contracts, invoices, account books, vouchers for settlement and payment of foreign exchange, bill of documents, business correspondence, and other written materials and electronic data reflecting the relationship and transaction activities between the buyer and the seller; (ii) to investigate into the issues relating to the price of the import and export goods with the consignor and consignee as well as other companies and enterprises having fund dealings or other business dealings with the consignor and consignee of the goods; (iii) to examine the import and export goods or draw samples from the goods to inspect or test the same; (iv) to enter the production and operation sites and/or goods storage sites of the consignor and consignee for inspecting the goods, production, and operation conditions in relation to the import and export activities; (v) to consult and inquire of the relevant financial institutions or tax authorities about the information of receipt and payment in foreign exchange or payment of domestic taxes in relation to the import and export goods. The law prohibits a party from preventing or refusing to cooperate with Customs in its investigation concerning valuation issues.[43]

If Customs questions the accuracy of the declared value, Customs is required to inform the consignor and consignee in writing of the reasons for its concerns and may request further clarification in response. If, within fifteen days of the service of such written notice by Customs, the consignor and consignee fail to provide supplemental information, or, after verifying the provided materials, Customs still has reason to question the accuracy of the declared value, Customs is authorized to reject the declared value and may assess the dutiable value in accordance with Articles 7 to 11 of the Customs Valuation Measures.[44]

If Customs has reason to believe that a special relationship between the buyer and the seller impacts the transaction value of imported goods, Customs is required to provide notice to the parties and may request additional information that indicates that any special relationship does not affect the transaction value as declared. If, within fifteen days of the service of such written notice by Customs, the consignee fails to make further presentation,

importer, in writing if requested, its grounds for doubting the truth or accuracy of the particulars or documents produced, and the importer must be afforded a reasonable opportunity to respond. When a final decision is made, the customs administration must communicate to the importer in writing its decision and the grounds therefore.

43. Customs Valuation Measures, art. 32. Customs is required to maintain the confidentiality of the materials, which are business secrets provided by the buyer, seller, or the relevant trading parties. Customs Valuation Measures, art. 38.

44. Customs Valuation Measures, art. 33.

or, after verifying the provided materials or evidence, Customs still has reason to believe that the relationship between the buyer and the seller affects the transaction price, Customs is authorized to reject the declared value and assess the dutiable value in accordance with Articles 7 to 11 of the Customs Valuation Measures.[45]

Under the law, the parties to an import transaction may submit a written application to Customs for the issuance of an advanced ruling with respect to the method for determination of the dutiable value of their goods.[46] In the event that Customs is required to postpone a determination with respect to valuation, the goods may still clear customs subject to the posting of security to cover the duty. However, Customs is required to complete the valuation assessment process within ninety days after posting of the security.[47]

If the consignor and consignee of the import goods disagree with the assessment decision of Customs, they have the right to file an application for reconsideration according to Customs Law of the People's Republic of China and the Regulations of the People's Republic of China on Import and Export Duty.[48] If the application is rejected, the affected party may file an action in the people's court for review.

c. Tariff Classification

In 1993, China became a contracting party to the International Convention on the Harmonized Commodity Description and Coding System and thereby adopted the Harmonized Tariff Schedule (HTS) for purposes of its tariff organization, nomenclature, interpretive rules, and numbering system. If an importer is uncertain with respect to the classification of its goods, it may consult with China Customs on classification issues prior to importation.[49]

---

45. Customs Valuation Measures, art. 34.

46. Customs Valuation Measures, art. 35. *See also* Provisional Administrative Regulations on Customs Administrative Rulings (promulgated on December 24, 2001, by the General Administration of Customs). (Regulations outline the standards for applying for ruling on issues such as classification of goods, determination of country of origin, import/export restrictions and license issues, and other matters involving customs. Customs must make a ruling within 60 days of receipt of an application and the ruling must be published and be effective for all Customs offices in China.)

47. Customs Valuation Measures, art. 37.

48. Customs Valuation Measures, art. 39.

49. Provisional Administrative Regulations on Customs Administrative Rulings (promulgated on December 24, 2001, by the General Administration of Customs) (Regulations outline the standards for applying for ruling on issues such as classification of goods). Customs must make a ruling within 60 days of receipt of an application. *See generally* Announcement 58, The Declaration of Import and Export Goods (issued October 2003 by the General Administration of Customs) (provides that in the case of incomplete multifunctional machinery and electrical products, the tariff classification will be based on the products' intended function or end use, so long as the declared goods demonstrate the basic features of the complete goods when declared).

d. Tariff Levels, Reductions, and Exemptions

(1) Tariff Levels. China provides its trading partners with preferential tariff rates ranging from 3 percent to 150 percent and depending upon the subject merchandise or commodity. Prior to 1996, China duty rates ranged as high as 220 percent. For countries without bilateral trade relations with China, the tariff rates range from 8 percent to 180 percent (previously 8 percent to 270 percent). In 1992, the average tariff rate was 43.2 percent, which has been reduced down to an average tariff rate in 2004 of 11 percent. This amounts to an overall reduction of the average tariff rate by more than 60 percent in 10 years. Notwithstanding the tariff reductions post-WTO, imported goods are still, in general, subject to import VAT and consumption tax where applicable. Import VAT—in a similar fashion as import duties—is based on the dutiable value of the imported goods. Consumption tax is due on imports involving certain luxury goods and fuels and may be based on dutiable value or the imported volume/quantity.

(2) Reductions and Exemptions. For much of the past two decades, China has utilized a complex assortment of tariff reductions and exemptions in order to achieve various local and national goals. These reductions and exemptions have often worked at cross purposes, creating confusion and uncertainty among both foreign and domestic parties.

In an attempt to address this problem, in 1995 the State Council issued the Notice of the State Council on the Reform and Adjustment of Import Tariff Policy (hereinafter the "1995 Notice on Reform of Tariff Policy").[50]

---

50. Notice of the State Council on the Reform and Adjustment of Import Tariff Policy (promulgated on December 26, 1995, by the State Council of the PRC), *reprinted in* China Laws for Foreign Business (CCH), Customs ¶ 50-635 (hereinafter referred to as the "1995 Notice on Reform of Tariff Policy"). The introduction to this notice sets forth the fundamental issues as follows:

> Since the Third Plenary Session of the Eleventh Central Committee of the Communist Party of China, in order to promote the policy of opening up to the outside world and the development of the national economy, China has formulated a series of preferential import policies that have played an important role in expanding foreign trade, attracting foreign funds, and introducing advanced technology. With the constant deepening of the reform and opening-up process and the gradual establishment of the socialist market economic system, the contradictions between those policies and generally accepted international rules and the principle of fair competition in the market economy are becoming increasingly prominent. In recent years the State Council has amended and revised some of the regulations on the reduction and exemption of import duty and has reduced the overall tariff level from 42 percent to 35.9 percent. However, from an overall perspective, the problem of "high tariff rates, numerous tariff reductions and exemptions and small tariff bases" remains significant. A multitude of tariff reductions and exemptions is causing unfair competition between regions and between enterprises, and is, therefore, unfavorable to State-owned enterprises transforming their operating mechanisms and is also unfavorable for coordinated inter-regional economic development. The reform and adjustment of import tariff policies must, therefore, be accelerated and the general import tariff level further reduced. Excessive and unequal regulations on the reduction of and exemption from tariffs will be rescinded. In their place a uniform, standardized, fair, and rational import policy will be established in accordance with the requirements

The major components of the 1995 Notice on Reform of Tariff Policy included the implementation of a gradual reduction of China's general tariff level from the then-current level to the average level of developing countries.

The 1995 Reform of Tariff Policy also provides that duty and import-related taxes on imported equipment and raw materials are levied at statutory duty rates with no exceptions. Effective April 1, 1996, previous reduction and exemption plans were affected as follows:

(1) Equipment and raw materials imported by newly approved FIEs (including Sino-Foreign joint and cooperative enterprises and foreign-owned enterprises) are subject to Customs duty and import-related tax at the statutory tariff and tax rates without exception[51]
(2) Equipment imported for newly approved technical transformation projects would be subject to Customs duty and import-related tax at the statutory tariff and tax rates without exception[52]
(3) Equipment imported for major construction projects as approved by the State Council would be subject to the Customs duty and import-related tax at the statutory duty rates without exception[53]
(4) Goods and materials imported into special regions (including special economic zones, economic and technological development zones, high and new technology industrial development zones, open border cities, border economic cooperation zones, open cities on rivers, state tourist zones, Shanghai Pudong new area, and other development zones) would be subject to Customs duty and import-related tax at the statutory duty rates without exception[54]
(5) All reductions or exemptions for Customs duty and import-related tax on barter trade with neighboring countries or under economic cooperation projects would be abolished
(6) All reductions or exemptions for Customs duty and import-related tax on processing equipment imported under processing trade and counter trade programs would be abolished

of the socialist market economic system and generally accepted international rules. By these means China can take a moreopen position in participating in international competition and international economic cooperation and so promote the development of the national economy.

51. Preferential treatment for FIEs established prior to April 1, 1996, was to continue for stipulated periods as approved by the MOFTEC.

52. Preferential treatment would continue for technological transformation projects incorporated into State or provincial operating plans prior to April 1, 1996.

53. Preferential treatment would continue for major construction projects approved by the State Council prior to April 1, 1996.

54. Goods and materials imported into special economic zones and the Shanghai Pudong New Area by enterprises other than FIEs would be eligible for a duty and tax refund plan.

The 1995 Reform of Tariff Policy retained the following import tariff reductions and exemptions:

(1) Articles imported for scientific and educational use, articles imported for disabled persons, articles imported by foreign diplomatic and consular missions, and articles donated by foreign governments
(2) Regulations linking differential tariff rates to domestically produced motor cars and video camera recorders (retained for the ninth five-year period)
(3) Regulations for exploration and development of offshore oil or natural gas (retained for the ninth five-year period)
(4) Regulations on VAT for importations of civil aircraft (retained for the ninth-five year period)
(5) Regulations on the importation of personal articles by Chinese residents abroad (retained temporarily)
(6) Duty-free shops at exit ports
(7) Articles 27, 28, 29, and 30 of the Duty Regulations would continue to be implemented[55]

The 1995 Notice on Reform of Tariff Policy eliminated the preferences and exemptions previously available to the processing trade, special economic zones, and FIEs. However, implementation of the Notice proved to be counterproductive to its stated purpose.[56] This was particularly so with respect to FIEs, where the elimination of tariff reductions and preferences led to a significant drop in foreign investment in China. In response, the State Council modified its position and reinstated, as of January 1, 1998, the duty and VAT preferences for capital equipment imports for select FIE and domestic projects.

In September 2002, the MOF and five other government bureaus issued a notice that revises the preferential policies for imported equipment.[57] The notice addresses preferential policies for imported equipment in the Catalogue's "permitted" category that qualify for a tax exemption for export

55. These provisions included duty preferences for *de minimis* imports, advertising and trade samples, ship's stores, damaged or lost goods, and temporary importations under bond. The retained Article 29 provided for reduction or exemptions from duties in accordance with provisions of international treaties to which the People's Republic of China is a party.

56. See *China's New Foreign Investment Regs: Duty-free Import of Some Capital Equipment Reinstated,* prepared by U.S. Embassy Beijing's Economic Section, January 12, 1998. At the same time, a revised list has been published that outlines sectors in which foreign investment is encouraged or restricted. *See* Wu, *Preferential Tariff for Imported Equipment,* 127 CHINA INTERNATIONAL BUSINESS (MOFTEC) 6 (1998).

57. Notice on Partial Adjustment to Incentive Policies on Import Taxes (issued on September 5, 2002, by the Ministry of Finance and effective October 1, 2002).

production, and are now required to pay applicable tariffs and VAT on imported equipment. However, the rules provide that qualified companies may receive rebates of paid tariffs and VAT of 20 percent per year for five years after importation of the equipment. Imported raw materials for production and imported vehicles for large-scale activities, which enjoyed tariff exemptions on a project-by-project basis in the past, are no longer eligible for tax exemptions. The rule does not apply to companies that imported equipment prior to October 1, 2002. China's long-term objective will be to eliminate the preferential treatment for foreign investors and to institute a uniform national duty and tax plan.

e. Rules of Origin

For purposes of determining rates of duty, China Customs has adopted regulations that outline the rules of origin. The regulations define the country of origin as the country where the goods are "wholly obtained or produced."[58] Goods that are produced in more than one country are deemed to originate in the country where they underwent the "last, substantial, economically justified processing."[59] The term "substantial economically justified processing" means that the goods resulting from the manufacturing process went through a tariff shift or a value-added of 30 percent or more was added to the final product.[60] The regulations allow that a reasonable quantity of accessories, spare parts, and tools may be deemed to originate from the same country from which a machine, appliance, apparatus, or vehicle has originated, provided that the tools and the machine are imported together.[61] If the tools and accessories are imported separately or are in a quantity in excess of the principal merchandise, Customs will determine the origin independently. The importer, upon request from China Customs, may be required to provide a certificate of the origin issued by a foreign

58. Provisional Regulations of the Customs of the People's Republic of China on the Origin of Imported Goods (promulgated on December 6, 1986, as amended and approved October 26, 1993, by General Administration of Customs) (hereinafter referred to as the "Country of Origin Regulations").

59. Country of Origin Regulations, art. 3.

60. Country of Origin Regulations, arts. 2, 3. Goods that undergo production in more than one country are "deemed to originate in the country where they underwent their last, substantial, economically justified processing or working." *Id.* art. 3. The Regulations define "substantial processing or working" as a tariff shift or value-added process of more than 30 percent. Generally, this rule provides that a product composed of foreign materials will be considered originating from the country where it is processed to an extent sufficient to result in a change in tariff classification under the Harmonized Tariff System. This rule is supplemented by a regional-value rule whereby an article will be considered originating from a particular country if a sufficient amount of the final value (i.e., at least 30 percent) of the product can be attributed to the originating country.

61. Country of Origin Regulations, art. 5.

competent authority.[62] A false declaration of the country of origin is subject to administrative penalties and criminal sanctions.[63]

f. Excluded and Restricted Merchandise

China excludes from entry certain merchandise including firearms, imitation weapons, ammunition, or explosives; counterfeit securities and negotiable instruments; printed matters, films, photographs, audio tapes, computer disks, and other media that are considered detrimental to China's politics, economy, culture, or morality; narcotics and other controlled substances; and animals, plants, and by-products infected with diseases.[64] While not prohibited from entry, certain types of products are subject to inspection, import licensing, and approval, such as pharmaceutical products and medical devices, used mechanical and electrical equipment,[65] food products,[66] and audio visual products.[67] Customs also restricts the importation of radio

62. Country of Origin Regulations, art. 7.

63. Country of Origin Regulations, art. 8.

64. Order of the General Customs Administration of the PRC (issued February 26, 1993), *reprinted in* CHINA LAWS FOR FOREIGN BUSINESS (CCH), Customs ¶ 50-306 (hereinafter the "Customs Order"). Items subject to import licenses are required to go through an application process. The Chinese government has developed an online application process for import and export licenses. *See* the Web site of MOFCOM for more information at http://www.mofcom.gov.cn. For example, the State Food and Drug Administration prohibits the importation of used medical devices. *See* Zhu, *Imports of Used Medical Gear Banned,* CHINA DAILY (June 16, 1998), available on Lexis, News Library, or on the Web site of the CHINA DAILY at http://www.chinadaily.com.cn.

65. Measures for the Administration of the Inspection and Supervision of Imported Used Mechanical and Electrical Products (issued on August 1, 2003, by the State Administration for Quality Supervision, Inspection and Quarantine [SAQSIQ]). Under the SAQSIQ Measures, all importers, including foreign-invested enterprises, must apply to SAQSIQ and file for the record at least 90 days prior to the importation of used mechanical and electrical goods. Within five business days after receipt of an application to import used goods, SAQSIQ is required to decide whether the products should undergo a pre-shipping inspection. Pre-shipping inspections will be mandatory for products related to health, safety, hygiene, and environmental protection, products that require approval by the department-in-charge of MOFCOM, and products that were produced at least eight years prior to the application.

66. Food imports are also subject to various inspection and quarantine procedures. See Administrative Measures on the Inspection and Quarantine of Imported/Exported Meat Products (issued on October 1, 2002, by the Administration of Quality Supervision, Inspection, and Quarantine [AQSIQ]) (provides that all meat product exporters must register with AQSIQ before exporting; meat importers must have animal and plant quarantine licenses before signing the import contract; and imported meat products are to arrive at AQSIQ-designated ports for inspection and quarantine before entering the Chinese market); Administrative Measures on the Examination and Approval of the Quarantine of Imported Animals and Plants (issued on September 1, 2002, by the AQSIQ) (provides that importers of animals or plants must have an AQSIQ quarantine license in order to clear customs, and that importers must have legal person status and import and export rights); Measures on Inspection Exemptions for Imported/Exported Commodities (issued on October 1, 2002, by the AQSIQ) (provides that commodities with good quality records may be exempted from inspection for three years; that commodities' consignee, consignor, or manufacturer may apply for such exemption if the commodity satisfies requirements for quality, reputation, and standards; and that certain items, such as food, animal/botanic products, hazardous products and their packages, commodities of a highly unstable nature, and bulk goods are not eligible for an exemption).

67. *See* Administration of Import of Audio and Video Products Procedures (issued on June 1, 2002, by the Ministry of Culture (MOCT) and General Administration of Customs) (hereinafter the "Audio-Visual Products Import Procedures"). The Audio-Visual Products Import Procedures cover the importation of

transmitter-receivers and voice encoding units; tobacco and alcohol products; endangered species; and Chinese currency. Customs also prohibits the exportation of certain items, including materials containing State secrets, cultural relics and antiques, and endangered species.[68]

g. FIE Import Control Standards

MOFTEC (now MOFCOM) has adopted import control rules that address the guidelines for import license applications and quota compliance requirements for foreign-invested enterprises.[69] Customs has adopted separate regulations on issues concerning tourists, overseas Chinese, and diplomats.[70] The import of commodities by foreign investment enterprises, including joint ventures and wholly foreign-owned enterprises, is subject to the FIE Import Control Rules.[71]

---

finished audio-visual goods including audiotapes, videotapes, phonograph records, compact discs, and video compact discs with recorded content (Audio-Visual Products). Importation of certain types of content, such as content that opposes the basic principles of the Chinese Constitution and is viewed as harmful to the sovereignty of the State or its territorial integrity, is prohibited. The Audio-Visual Products Import Procedures create an import licensing system to be carried out by MOCT or branch entities, and prohibits any person from publishing, duplicating, distributing by means of wholesale or retail, renting, screening for commercial purposes, or disseminating through an information network any Audio-Visual Products that are not approved. Approval is also required for products to be given away at corporate events or exhibitions. In order to obtain an import license, the importer is required to submit the product to the MOCT for content examination. The application is to include the text of the content in Chinese and the relevant foreign language and the import agreement. If the product is imported for publishing purposes, the copyright trade agreement (in both Chinese and the relevant foreign language), the original copyright certificate, the copyright authorization certificate, and the registration and certification documents must also be included. MOCT has 30 days from the date of receipt of the application materials to evaluate and approve or reject the application. Approval is provided on a single import shipment basis only.

68. Customs Order, List of Restricted Outbound Articles of the PRC, art. I. Customs also restricts the exportation of precious metals, products produced by China's prison system, and valuable traditional Chinese medicines. In December 2003, the Ministry of Commerce and General Administration of Customs introduced an export registration and licensing system for sensitive items and technologies such as nuclear, biological, chemical, missile and arms materials, etc. Under the 2003 rules, MOFCOM will lead in terms of the acceptance, examination, and issuance of export licenses for sensitive items and technologies. The rules are designed to implement international standards with respect to nonproliferation measures. *See New Export Rules to Regulate Sensitive Items, Technologies,* CHINA DAILY (December 27, 2003), available online at http://www.chinadaily.com.cn. For a discussion concerning the regulation of cultural resources, *see* Chapter 17, Land-Use, Real Estate Development, and Natural Resources § D. For a discussion of the U.S. customs standards prohibiting the importation of prison-made products, *see* Zimmerman, *U.S. Law and Convict-Produced Imports,* CHINA BUSINESS REVIEW 41 (Mar./Apr. 1992).

69. Detailed Implementing Rules on Import Control for Foreign Investment Enterprises (promulgated June 9, 1995, by the MOFTEC), *reprinted in* CHINA LAWS FOR FOREIGN BUSINESS (CCH), Customs ¶ 50-637 (hereinafter the "FIE Import Control Rules").

70. Customs Law, art. 34; *See also* Regulations of the People's Republic of China on Consular Privileges and Immunities (adopted on October 30, 1990, at the 16th Sess. of the Standing Comm. of the 7th NPC), art. 19, *reprinted in* CHINA LAWS FOR FOREIGN BUSINESS (CCH), Business Regulation 19-526. Article 19 of the Consular Regulations provide that imported articles for official use by a consulate and items for personal use by consular officials are exempt from duties. The personal baggage of consular officials is exempt from inspection unless Chinese authorities have serious grounds for believing that it contains articles that are not covered under the regulations, and inspections must take place in the presence of a consular official. A consular official may import a firearm for personal use with permission of the government. *Id.* at art. 20.

71. FIE Import Control Rules, art. 1. The import of crude oil, processed oil products, and steel products by a foreign investment enterprise is not subject to the FIE Import Control Rules. *Id.* at art. 14.

The term "import commodities" refers to all commodities other than machinery and electrical products, and includes quota commodities, specific registered commodities, and other commodities.[72] For imports of commodities that are subject to national import allocation plans, *quota certificates* are required.[73] In order to obtain an import license, an FIE is required to submit its *quota certificate*. Quota commodities are products required by FIEs for the purpose of producing goods for sale within China. The PRC government restricts and controls such imports in order to protect domestic industry and to ensure that the government's overall policy on imports is met.

A foreign investment enterprise that applies for an import *quota certificate* must submit its contract, articles of association, and business license to MOFCOM or its local department in charge of foreign trade and economic cooperation. The department will approve and issue a *quota certificate* based on the enterprise's actual production capacity and its import requirements.[74] In the event of a refusal to issue a quota certificate, the department concerned must give an official reply within ten working days.

A *quota certificate* is not required for commodities that are imported by a foreign investment enterprise as part of its joint venture contribution or investment.[75] A foreign investment enterprise that intends to import commodities as part of its investment in China only needs to apply for an import license. Customs will inspect and release such import equipment and materials based on the presentation of the import license. Commodities (including quota commodities, specific registered commodities, and other commodities) imported by a foreign investment enterprise for the purpose of producing export products are treated as bonded goods by Customs.[76]

Imported capital equipment by FIEs has traditionally been granted exemptions from both import tariffs and value-added tax (VAT). In 1995, China eliminated some preferential treatment for FIEs in an effort to unify

72. FIE Import Control Rules, art. 3.

73. The MOFCOM develops a national import quota plan annually. As China continues to develop its market economy, the importance of the national quota commodities import plan is anticipated to diminish. FIE Import Control Rules, art. 7.

74. FIE Import Control Rules, art. 10. MOFCOM authorizes the local departments in charge of foreign trade and economic cooperation to review and approve applications for the import of quota commodities for the purpose of producing goods for domestic sale; to sign and issue quota certificates; to handle import registration procedures for specific registered commodities that have been imported for the purpose of producing goods for domestic sale; and to sign and issue import registration certificates. The authority to sign and issue import quota certificates and import registration certificates will not be delegated to lower levels. MOFCOM is responsible for approving applications for the import of quota commodities and specific registered commodities for enterprises that are under the direct supervision of the State Council. FIE Import Control Rules, art. 9.

75. FIE Import Control Rules, art. 4.

76. FIE Import Control Rules, art. 6.

its treatment of foreign and domestic enterprises.[77] In late 1997, China reversed this policy to encourage foreign investment, and effective January 1, 1998, imported equipment is entitled to duty-free treatment and an exemption from VAT. However, China requires that all equipment imported by FIEs is subject to mandatory inspection, appraisal, and certification.[78] If an FIE undervalues the imported equipment, it is liable to pay the full tax and tariffs on the merchandise and potential civil and criminal penalties if the actual value is significantly understated.

3. Customs Rules on Processing Trade, Bonded Warehouses, and Factories

Since China initiated the Open Door policy, the PRC government has encouraged export production to stimulate economic growth and foreign exchange earnings. The exemption from tariffs and taxation for export production enterprises has been the cornerstone of this policy.

a. Processing Trade

The Import Processing Measures define a "processing enterprise" as "an export production enterprise with legal person status which engages in the processing and re-export of imported materials and parts."[79] Import and export materials involved in import processing are defined as "raw and other materials, supplementary materials, components, spare parts, accessories and packaging materials which are purchased using foreign exchange and imported by operating units exclusively for processing products for

77. *See supra* 1995 Notice on Reform of Tariff Policy.

78. *See Chinese Joint Venture Partners Must Watch Foreigners' Valuation of Assets, Agency Says,* 15 INT'L TRADE REP. 379 (1998). FIEs are required to have all capital imports certified by government-approved appraisers prior to clearing Customs. China's Import Tariff Policy of 1995 abolished the preferential treatment previously enjoyed by foreign investors on processing equipment imported under processing trade and counter trade.

79. Administrative Measures of the Customs of the People's Republic of China Governing Import and Export Commodities Involved in Import Processing (promulgated May 6, 1988, by the General Administration of Customs of the People's Republic of China), art. 2, *reprinted in* CHINA LAWS FOR FOREIGN BUSINESS (CCH), Customs ¶ 50-675 (hereinafter the "Import Processing Measures"). *See also* Notice on Several Issues Concerning the Import of Equipment for the Processing Trade (promulgated on July 1, 1998, by MOFTEC and China Customs), *reprinted in* CHINA LAWS FOR FOREIGN BUSINESS (CCH), Taxation & Customs ¶ 31-807 (outlines exemption standards for imported equipment for processing trade). *See also* Provisional Measures for the Administration of Tax Collection in Export Processing Zones (issued on October 26, 2000, by the SAT), *reprinted in* China Laws for Foreign Business (CCH), Taxation ¶ 31-730; Decision to Amend the Interim Measures of the People's Republic of China on the Supervision of Export Processing Zones (issued on September 2, 2003, by the State Council) (allows China Customs to provide clearance for the importation into China of processed products, defective products, scrap, and waste from Export Processing Zones). Commencing in April 1, 2004, China Customs intends to repeal 258 processing trade rules that were issued between 1980 and 2003. *See Customs to Repeal 258 Obsolete Processing Trade Rules,* CHINA MARKET INTELLIGENCE, THE U.S.-CHINA BUSINESS COUNCIL (March 31, 2004).

export, as well as the finished and semi-finished products for export and resale which result from the processing operations."[80]

Under the Import Processing Measures, materials and components imported for processing trade operations are generally exempt from import duty and VAT. Likewise, the finished products of processing trade operations are exempt from export duty.[81] Under these same measures, all materials and components for processing trade are considered "bonded goods."[82]

The Import Processing Measures authorize duty-free treatment on a contract-by-contract basis. Customs requires that an export production enterprise maintain separate books of account for recording details such as the import, storage, custody, withdrawal, and use of materials and parts or their transfer for processing to another factory location, as well as storage, export, and sale of finished products.[83] When importing materials and parts or exporting finished products, the export production enterprise is required to make an accurate declaration to Customs.[84] The Import Processing Measures empower Customs to conduct random on-site inspections in order to ensure compliance.[85] The facility operators are required to submit their books of accounts to Customs for verification after the fulfillment of each contract.

The Import Processing Measures require that imported materials and parts be processed into finished products and exported within one year from the date of entry. An extension of time to continue to store the parts or finished product may be granted in extenuating circumstances. Within thirty days of fulfilling a production contract, an export production enterprise is required to report to Customs in order to justify and substantiate the duty-free treatment of the imported component parts and materials.[86]

b. Bonded Warehouses, Factories, and Zones

Customs has adopted regulations that address the requirements for establishing a bonded factory or warehouse.[87] Historically, China encouraged the

80. Import Processing Measures, art. 2.

81. Import Processing Measures, art. 3.

82. Import Processing Measures, art. 4. Under the 1995 Notice on Reform of Tariff Policy, the reduction of, or exemption from, Customs duty and imported related tax on processing equipment imported under processing trade was abolished. 1995 Notice on Reform of Tariff Policy, art. 2. The Notice is silent on any specific mention of materials and components for processing trade and in practice, materials and components used in the production of export commodities continue to be treated as duty free and tax free.

83. Import Processing Measures, art. 6.

84. Import Processing Measures, art. 7. Processing trade enterprises may subcontract work to other processing or nonprocessing trade enterprises for finishing. *See* Regulation on the Supervision of Goods Under Processing Trade (issued on February 26, 2004, by the General Administration of Customs).

85. Import Processing Measures, art. 6.

86. Import Processing Measures, art. 9.

87. Administrative Measures of the Customs of the People's Republic of China Governing Bonded Factories Engaged in Processing Trade (promulgated April 6, 1988, by the General Administration of

establishment of bonded warehouses, factories, and zones in cities such as Shanghai, Shenzhen, and Guangzhou in order to promote export production. Generally, any enterprise in any city is authorized to apply to establish a bonded warehouse or factory, but only if the operation meets the requirements of the regulations.

A bonded warehouse is a facility established to store merchandise for export that has undergone processing in China.[88] A bonded factory is a facility that engages in processing trade operations specially approved by Customs to engage in the processing of bonded goods for re-export.[89] Under the bonded factory program, certain imported items used in the manufacture of goods, and finished goods processed in the bonded zones, are exempted from import and export licensing requirements, and are further exempted from Customs duties and VAT.[90] Goods may be stored at a bonded warehouse or factory

---

Customs), *reprinted in* CHINA LAWS FOR FOREIGN BUSINESS (CCH), Customs ¶ 59-010 (hereinafter the "Bonded Factories Measures"); Administrative Measures of the Customs of the People's Republic of China Governing Bonded Warehouses and the Goods Stored Therein (promulgated April 14, 1988, by the General Administration of Customs), *reprinted in* CHINA LAWS FOR FOREIGN BUSINESS (CCH), Customs ¶ 59-014 (the "Bonded Warehouse Measures"). *See also* Administrative Measures of the Customs of the People's Republic of China Governing Goods, Means of Transport and Personal Articles Entering and Leaving the Shanghai Waigaoqiao Bonded Zone (promulgated September 1990 by the General Administration of Customs), *reprinted in* CHINA LAWS FOR FOREIGN BUSINESS (CCH), Special Zones & Cities ¶ 91-012 (addresses control and inspection standards for goods entering Shanghai's boned zone); Administrative Measures for the Shanghai Waigaoqiao Bonded Zone (promulgated on September 10, 1990, by the Shanghai Municipal People's Government), *reprinted in* CHINA LAWS FOR FOREIGN BUSINESS (CCH), Special Zones & Cities ¶ 91-013 (same). *See also* Administrative Measures on Foreign Exchange Control in Bonded Zones (promulgated by the SAFE on July 25, 2002), *reprinted in* CHINA LAWS FOR FOREIGN BUSINESS (CCH), Business Regulation ¶ 8-530 (outlines procedures for FOREX registration and annual inspection, administration of FOREX accounts in bonded zones, and FOREX settlement procedures). *See also* Administration of Bonded Warehouses and the Goods Stored Therein Provisions (issued on December 5, 2003, by the General Administration of Customs). With GAC approval, certain types of goods such as imported goods for processing trade, transit goods, and goods of foreign investors for temporary storage may be stored in qualified bonded warehouses. Among other requirements, an enterprise must have registered capital of at least RMB3 million to establish a bonded warehouse. Bonded warehouses cannot be leased to other parties to manage and are subject to customs inspection and annual review. Goods stored in warehouses may undergo simple processing such as packaging, dissembling, and assembling; however, substantial processing or manufacturing is not allowed in bonded warehouses. Such goods cannot be sold, assigned, mortgaged, or disposed of in other ways without the express consent of China Customs. Goods stored in bonded warehouses can only be stored for one year or less, and are required to be exported or transferred to bonded zones, export processing zones, or other bonded warehouses; or to be sold to the domestic market.

88. Bonded Warehouse Measures, art. 2.

89. Bonded Factories Measures, art. 2. The Bonded Factories Measures allow for overall approval of a particular facility. In contrast, the Import Processing Measures allow for duty-free treatment on a contract-by-contract basis.

90. While the effect of the 1995 Notice on Reform of Tariff Policy on the overall status of the processing trade is unclear, subsequent measures promulgated by the General Administration of Customs indicate that the duty exemptions for processing trade goods in bonded zones have been retained. Specifically, the 1997 Measures on Customs Supervision and Administration in Bonded Zones states that "raw materials, spare parts, components and packaging needed for processing export products of a bonded zone enterprise will be duty free." Measures on Customs Supervision and Administration in Bonded Zones (promulgated August 1, 1997, by the General Administration of Customs) art. 12, § (4), *reprinted in* CHINA LAWS FOR FOREIGN BUSINESS (CCH), Customs ¶ 59-030 (hereinafter the "Bonded Zone Measures").

for a maximum period of one year, which may be extended in special circumstances and with the approval of Customs. Both types of operations are subject to the supervision of Customs.[91]

4. Passengers and Personal Use Articles

In 1996, Customs adopted a set of regulations concerning the clearance of entering and departing passengers at ports of entry.[92] The Passenger Clearance Regulations simplify the entry process for passengers through the use of a unified written declaration form. All passengers entering or leaving China must declare their baggage and articles to Customs. However, passengers may forgo the declaration process if they are not importing dutiable goods or restricted merchandise.

The items imported into China by international travelers are limited to reasonable quantities for personal use. The traveler upon departure from China must export such items. Any articles imported in excess of the personal use limits are not permitted for importation unless duties are paid, and articles imported on behalf of another person are prohibited.

C. Enforcement of Customs Laws

Customs has a number of administrative tools at its disposal to enforce the Customs laws and regulations, including monetary penalties, detention, exclusion, confiscation, and forfeiture.[93] Customs may also refer a matter for criminal prosecution for smuggling offenses or other serious violations of the Customs law and regulations.

Customs has the authority to pursue administrative sanctions for the following violations of Customs laws and regulations:

(1) Undervaluation of dutiable value of imports
(2) Failure or refusal to properly mark imported merchandise with the country of origin
(3) Misclassification of merchandise
(4) Inadequate records and documentation to substantiate a Customs transaction (*e.g.*, absence of an import license)

---

91. Bonded Factories Measures, art. 10.

92. Regulations of the Customs of the People's Republic of China on the Clearance of Entering and Departing Passengers (promulgated on December 25, 1995, by the General Administration of Customs of the PRC), *reprinted in* CHINA LAWS FOR FOREIGN BUSINESS (CCH), Customs ¶ 50-639 (hereinafter the "Clearance of Passengers Regulations"). The Clearance of Passenger Regulations are available on the Web site of MOFCOM at http://www.mofcom.gov.cn.

93. Customs also issues a blacklist of companies that engage in smuggling and, once the company is listed, Customs will closely scrutinize the operations of companies on the list. For a review of the list, see the Web site of China Customs at http://www.customs.gov.cn.

(5) Importation or exportation of prohibited or restricted merchandise that is declared to Customs
(6) Other violations of a less serious nature

The Administrative Penalties Rules apply to acts of smuggling that do not constitute a criminal offense, or that constitute a criminal offense but are exempt from prosecution or from penalties in accordance with the law.[94] Article 3 of the Administrative Penalties Rules defines the following acts as "smuggling":

(1) Transporting prohibited goods, restricted imports or exports, or goods or articles subject to Customs duty payments in accordance with the law, into or out of Chinese territory through a place where there is no Customs establishment and without approval from Customs
(2) Concealing, disguising, failing to declare, falsely declaring, or using other means to evade Customs supervision and control when passing through a Customs establishment, in order to transport, carry, or mail into or out of Chinese territory, prohibited or restricted goods
(3) Falsely declaring or failing to declare prices of imports or exports in order to evade Customs duty
(4) Conducting, without Customs permission and without payment of the duty payable, the unauthorized sale of goods entered within a bonded zone and subject to Customs supervision
(5) Conducting, without Customs permission and without payment of duty, the unauthorized sale of duty-exempt goods imported for use by specific enterprises or for specific purposes[95]

Article 4 of the Administrative Penalties Rules provides that the following acts shall be subject to the same penalties as an act of smuggling:

(1) Illegally purchasing smuggled goods or articles directly from a smuggler
(2) Transporting, purchasing, or selling within China's inland sea or its territorial waters, articles prohibited by the State from being brought into or out of Chinese territory, or transporting, purchasing, or selling State-restricted imports or exports without the necessary legal documents[96]

94. Detailed Rules for the Implementation of the Administrative Penalties of the Customs Law of the People's Republic of China (approved June 30, 1987, by the State Council and promulgated on July 1, 1987, by the General Administration of Customs, amended and approved February 17, 1993, by the State Council and repromulgated April 1, 1993, by the General Administration of Customs), *reprinted in* CHINA LAWS FOR FOREIGN BUSINESS (CCH), Customs ¶ 50-315 (hereinafter the "Administrative Penalties Rules").
95. Administrative Penalties Rules, art. 3.
96. Administrative Penalties Rules, art. 4.

The Administrative Penalties Rules provide that violations of Articles 3 and 4 above shall be subject to the following penalties:

(1) If State-prohibited articles are smuggled into or out of Chinese territory, in addition to confiscation of such articles and any resulting illegal gains, a fine of up to RMB50,000 may be imposed
(2) If State-restricted imports or exports or goods and articles subject to Customs duty in accordance with the law are smuggled into or out of Chinese territory, in addition to confiscation of such goods and articles and any resulting illegal gains, a fine of up to an equivalent value of the smuggled goods and articles or up to three times the Customs duty payable may be imposed
(3) If prices of imports or exports are falsely declared or not declared in order to evade Customs duty, in addition to confiscation of any resulting illegal gains, a fine of up to three times the evaded Customs duty payable may be imposed
(4) Items specifically used to cover smuggled goods or articles shall be confiscated and equipment specifically designed to conceal smuggled goods or articles shall be confiscated or ordered to be destroyed

If smuggled goods or articles are not able to be confiscated, a sum equal to the value of the said item may be recovered by Customs.[97]

If an act of smuggling is committed by two or more persons, Customs is authorized to issue penalties individually in accordance with the seriousness of each case and in accordance with each person's level of culpability. If an individual has knowledge of an act of smuggling and fails to report the matter, thereby facilitating the smuggler's operations, in addition to the confiscation of any resulting illegal gains, a fine of up to two times the amount of the illegal gains may be imposed. If there are no illegal gains, a fine of up to RMB5,000 may be imposed against an individual with knowledge of smuggling who fails to report the activities.[98] A person who prepares equipment or brings about conditions to facilitate smuggling shall also be subject to penalties.[99]

Any of the following acts shall be subject to a lesser penalty or shall be exempt from a penalty:

(1) Minor smuggling (which is undefined in the law)
(2) Where the party concerned voluntarily discloses the smuggling activities to Customs

97. Administrative Penalties Regulations, art. 5.
98. Administrative Penalties Regulations, art. 6.
99. Administrative Penalties Regulations, art. 7.

(3) Where the act of smuggling is not discovered until at least three years later[100]

For violations of the law that do not fall within the definition of smuggling, Customs has the authority to impose a monetary penalty ranging from RMB5000 up to the value of the imported goods.[101] The Administrative Penalties Rules provide that any of the following activities may be subject to a monetary penalty of an amount up to the value of the goods or articles or of up to two times the Customs duty payable:

(1) Evading Customs supervision and control and subsequently transporting, carrying, or mailing into or out of Chinese territory goods or articles that are not prohibited by the State from being brought into or out of Chinese territory, are not State-restricted imports and exports, and are not subject to Customs duty payments in accordance with the law
(2) Opening, extracting, delivering, forwarding, changing, repacking, mortgaging, or transferring without Customs approval, goods under Customs supervision and control or articles entering or leaving Chinese territory that have yet to be released by Customs
(3) Failing to provide authentic records or appropriate reasons to explain a shortage in the amount of bonded goods during transportation, storage, processing, assembly, or consignment operations
(4) Using, without prior approval from Customs, specially authorized duty-reduced or duty-exempt goods and articles for purposes other than those approved
(5) Failing to declare the name, quantity, specifications, price, country of origin, method of the trade, consumer country, trader country, or other declarable items when entering or leaving Chinese territory
(6) Failing to re-import or re-export, within the stipulated period, goods that are granted entry or exit approval on a temporary basis only, and keeping the goods within Chinese territory or abroad without authorization
(7) Failing to transport out of Chinese territory, within the stipulated period, goods in transit, trans-shipment, or through-shipment, and keeping the goods within Chinese territory without authorization

100. Administrative Penalties Regulations, art. 8. The duration period stipulated in item (3) above shall be calculated from the day the act of smuggling is committed. If there are successive acts, the duration shall be calculated from the day the last act of smuggling is committed.

101. Administrative Penalties Regulations, arts. 9–18. *See generally* B. Ostrov, *The Fight Against Smuggling*, CHINA BUS. REV. (July 2000).

(8) Unauthorized assigning, without Customs approval or payment of the Customs duty payable, of materials or articles attached to means of transport brought into or out of Chinese territory[102]

Customs has the authority to impose monetary penalties of up to RMB50,000 for the following violations:

(1) The entry into or exit from Chinese territory of a means of transport through a place where there is no Customs establishment without approval from the State Council or a State Council–authorized authority
(2) The exit from a Customs surveillance zone of an inbound or outbound means of transport without prior approval from Customs
(3) The traveling of an inbound or outbound means of transport from one Customs point to another, prior to completion of Customs procedures and without Customs approval, where the means of transport changes course midway, leaves Chinese territory, and travels to a place without a Customs establishment[103]

The Administrative Penalties Rules authorize Customs to impose a monetary penalty of up to RMB30,000 for the following violations:

(1) The entry into or exit from Chinese territory of a means of transport through a place where there is a Customs establishment, but where relevant documents for Customs inspection are not provided in accordance with regulations, or the documents provided are not authentic
(2) The failure to submit inbound or outbound means of transport, goods, or articles for examination and inspection in accordance with regulations
(3) Loading or unloading of goods or articles of an inbound or outbound means of transport, or allowing inward or outward passengers to board or disembark without Customs permission
(4) Concurrent use of an inbound or outbound means of transport in domestic freight or passenger transportation, or its use for purposes other than transportation of inbound or outbound goods without Customs permission
(5) The unauthorized change of the scope of business of an inbound or outbound means of transport to domestic transportation without completing Customs procedures in accordance with regulations

102. Administrative Penalties Regulations, art. 11.
103. Administrative Penalties Regulations, art. 12.

(6) Failing to complete, in accordance with regulations, procedures for the receiving, delivery, or sales verification of bonded goods when such services as storage, processing, assembly, and consignment sale of these goods are undertaken, or failing to complete procedures for the termination, extension, or transfer of a relevant contract
(7) Placing goods requiring Customs supervision and control outside the Customs Surveillance Zone without Customs permission or refusing to accept Customs supervision
(8) Opening or destroying, without permission, a Customs seal attached to a means of transport, a warehouse, or goods[104]

Customs is also empowered to issue penalties of up to RMB20,000 for the following activities:

(1) Failure to travel along a route specified by the authority in charge of traffic or by Customs, by an inbound means of transport that has entered Chinese territory but has not made a Customs declaration, or which has completed Customs procedures but has not left Chinese territory
(2) Failure by an inbound or outbound vessel or vehicle carrying goods requiring Customs supervision and control to travel along the route specified by Customs
(3) Failure, without due reason, to report to the nearest Customs establishment by an inbound or outbound vessel or aircraft that is forced, due to force majeure, to stop or land at a place where there is no Customs establishment and is forced to cast overboard or unload goods or articles[105]

The Administrative Penalties Rules provide that, in addition to ordering retroactive payment of Customs duty or the return of the goods concerned, a fine of up to the equivalent value of the goods may be imposed for any of the following acts:

(1) Failing to declare to Customs articles carried or mailed into or out of Chinese territory in quantities that exceed the limit specified by Customs, but that are in comparatively small numbers and are still intended for personal use
(2) Falsely declaring or refusing to accept Customs inspection of articles carried or mailed into or out of Chinese territory

104. Administrative Penalties Rules, art. 13.
105. Administrative Penalties Rules, art. 14.

(3) Failure to take out of or into Chinese territory, in accordance with regulations, goods approved and registered with Customs for temporary exemption from Customs duty when taken into or out of Chinese territory
(4) Leaving the accompanying luggage of a transit passenger within Chinese territory without Customs permission[106]

A penalty of up to RMB1,000 may be imposed for the following violations:

(1) Failing, without special reason, to advise Customs of the arrival time, place of stopover, or changes to time or place details of a vessel, train, or aircraft that is to enter or leave Chinese territory
(2) Opening or destroying, without authorization, a seal attached to an article by Customs
(3) Violating Customs laws and regulations to such an extent that the Customs authority is unable to carry out or has to suspend its supervision and control over an inbound or outbound means of transport, goods, or articles[107]

If a minor violation of Customs supervisory or control provisions is committed or the party concerned voluntarily discloses the offense, Customs has the authority to impose a lower penalty than provided for in the Rules. If a violation of Customs supervisory or control provisions is not discovered until at least three years after the violation occurred, the party concerned is exempt from a penalty.[108]

Customs also has the discretion to detain goods or means of transport with respect to any suspected violation of the law. Customs may release the items and demand a security deposit or collateral in the same amount of value as the impounded items in certain situations.[109] The law requires that Customs issue a receipt when impounding goods, articles, or means of transport in suspected smuggling cases.[110] If it is not possible to impound goods, articles, or means of transport, Customs may demand from the interested party a security deposit or collateral that is equivalent to the value of the item subject to detention.[111] Goods, articles, and means of transport impounded in accordance with the law shall not be disposed of before a decision of the people's court or a Customs penalty decision is effective. However, Customs,

106. Administrative Penalties Rules, art. 15.
107. Administrative Penalties Rules, art. 16.
108. Administrative Penalties Rules, art. 18.
109. Administrative Penalties Rules, arts. 20, 21.
110. Administrative Penalties Rules, art. 20.
111. Administrative Penalties Rules, art. 21.

with notice to the interested party, has the authority to sell fresh, live, or perishable goods that may lose their value if impounded, and any sales proceeds of such goods shall be retained in trust by Customs.[112]

The law also grants Customs the power to issue written notification to a bank or post office to temporarily stop withdrawal or payment of a deposit or money order if the money has been proved through Customs investigation to be illegal income derived from acts of smuggling. The party who deposited the money or sent the money order shall, at the same time, be notified by Customs. The period of suspension of payment shall not exceed three months. After the Customs penalty decision takes effect, Customs may order the funds forfeited in accordance with the law.[113]

A foreigner that fails to pay duties or a penalty imposed by Customs is required to post a surety bond or other form of collateral equivalent to the amount due.[114] Customs may confiscate a foreigner's bank account if it has reasons to believe that the funds are the result of a violation of Customs laws and regulations.[115]

Under the Administrative Penalty Rules, Customs is required to issue a written penalty notice to the interested party with respect to any act of smuggling or other violation of the Customs laws and regulations. If an interested party disagrees with a penalty decision of Customs, such party may file an application for review with a higher level of Customs within thirty days of receipt of the penalty notice, and a decision on a review application must be made within ninety days. An interested party may appeal an administrative review decision by filing a complaint with the people's court within thirty days of receiving the decision. In addition to an appeal of an administrative review, an interested party may also file an action directly with the people's court for review of an original penalty notice. A party that elects the remedy of judicial review is not allowed to file an application for administrative review with Customs.[116]

A penalty notice will take effect if an interested party fails to file an application for administrative or judicial review in the time required.[117] If the party concerned fails to pay the fine imposed under the Customs decision and

112. Administrative Penalties Rules, art. 22.
113. Administrative Penalties Rules, art. 23.
114. Administrative Penalties Rules, art. 29. Customs also is empowered to detain a party suspected of violating the laws and regulations. With respect to foreigners, the usual practice is to confiscate the suspect's passport, which effectively bars the individual from leaving the country. If smuggling or other offenses are suspected, Customs and the Public Security Bureau have the authority to arrest a suspect, including a foreign individual.
115. Administrative Penalties Rules, art. 23.
116. Administrative Penalties Rules, art. 26.
117. Administrative Penalties Rules, art. 28.

fails to lodge a review application or an appeal application within the time limit, Customs has the power to confiscate the security deposit or auction goods, articles, or means of transport that have been impounded or pledged, or may request the people's court to enforce the penalty decision.[118]

Customs has the authority to pursue criminal prosecution for the following violations:

(1) Significantly understating dutiable value
(2) Intentionally failing to declare the importation or exportation of prohibited or restricted merchandise (i.e., smuggling)
(3) Falsifying records and documents used to substantiate a Customs transaction

Criminal penalties under the Customs laws and the Criminal Law include capital punishment, imprisonment, detention, confiscation, and fines.[119]

Customs has the authority to revalue goods and to pursue additional duties from an importer within one year from the date of importation. If the underpayment is a result of a violation of customs laws and regulations, the limitations period for collection is three years from the date of importation.[120] The statute of limitations for a minor violation of Customs laws and regulations is three years from the date of importation.[121] For actions that are considered criminal violations, there is no statute of limitations.

1. Customs Audits and Inspections

In 1997, the State Council promulgated regulations that clarify Customs' authority to inspect the accounting records of an importer.[122] Under the Customs Inspection Rules, Customs may demand to review the customs

118. Administrative Penalties Rules, art. 30.

119. *See* Guo, *Smuggling Cases Cracked,* CHINA DAILY (June 24, 1998), available on Lexis, News Library, or on the Web site of the CHINA DAILY at http://www.chinadaily.com.cn; Zhao, *Crackdown Slows Smuggling Actions,* CHINA DAILY (Oct. 27, 1998), available on Lexis, News Library, or on the Web site of the CHINA DAILY at http://www.chinadaily.com.cn. China Customs claims that they had cracked 2,322 smuggling cases in the first five months of 1998 and seized commodities valued at RMB2.78 billion ($334 million). Customs claims to have confiscated 5.27 million pirated VCDs, 188,000 pieces of pornography; 96,000 items of counter-revolutionary propaganda and propaganda promoting superstitious beliefs; counterfeit currency with a face value of RMB480,000 ($57,800); 986 cultural relics; 124 sets of weapons and ammunition; and 107 shipments of endangered species products. Other smuggled commodities include automobiles, motorcycles, oil products, edible oil, and household electrical appliances. A court in Guangdong Province imposed the death penalty on a Hong Kong resident who was accused of evading RMB2.4 billion in tariffs and paying $1.3 million in bribes to officials of the Shenzhen Customs and Huizhou Customs. *China Co. Manager Sentenced to Death for Smuggling Vegoils*, WALL ST. J. (Jan. 18, 2004).

120. Customs Law, art. 62.

121. Administrative Penalties Rules, art. 18.

122. Customs Inspection Rules of the People's Republic of China (promulgated on January 3, 1997, by the State Council), *reprinted in* CHINA LAWS FOR FOREIGN BUSINESS (CCH), Customs ¶ 52-566 (hereinafter the "Customs Inspection Rules").

declaration documents, accounting books, financial statements, accounting vouchers, computer records, and other relevant data that have a direct relationship to the import/export activities of the company in question.[123] Under the Customs Inspection Rules, Customs has the authority to demand documentation supporting a customs transaction within three years of the date of importation.[124] Customs can demand records from any firm engaging in foreign trade, foreign processing trade, bonded warehouses, enterprises that claim preferential duty treatment, and customs brokerage firms.[125] Customs is only required to give an enterprise three days' written notice before conducting an inspection and may exercise the following authority:

(1) Review and reproduce the books, documents, and other relevant data of the party subject to the inspection
(2) Enter and inspect the production facilities of the party subject to inspection with respect to the merchandise relating to the import/export transactions
(3) Interview and question the legal representative of the company the subject of the inspection with respect to the import/export transactions of the company
(4) Investigate the banking records of the company the subject of the inspection with the approval of the head of Customs[126]

Customs inspectors are required to obtain the opinions of the company the subject of the inspection before it submits its audit results to Customs. Customs will then render a decision based upon the audit results within thirty days.[127] A party that fails to cooperate with an inspection, conceals documents or information, or falsifies records is subject to administrative fines or criminal liability.[128]

2. Administrative and Judicial Remedies

A party affected by a decision of Customs has the right to appeal internally.[129] If an importer disputes the classification or valuation imposed by Customs, the importer is required to pay the disputed amount of duty and then apply to Customs for reconsideration.[130] Within fifteen days of receipt of the

123. Customs Inspection Rules, arts. 5–8.
124. Customs Inspection Rules, art. 2.
125. Customs Inspection Rules, art. 3.
126. Customs Inspection Rules, arts. 9–22.
127. Customs Inspection Rules, arts. 23–28.
128. Customs Inspection Rules, arts. 29–31.
129. Customs Law, art. 77.
130. Customs Duty Regulations, art. 36.

Practice Tip: China Customs Compliance Strategies

Given the uncertainty of the law and practice in China, it is important for companies importing into China to establish a customs compliance system and to monitor its Customs practices. Importers are recommended to adopt a China-tailored customs compliance program that is based upon the reasonable care standard that is engrained in US customs compliance programs; namely, that company policy requires that customs transactions be handled with reasonable care, comply with both the law and practice, and are fully substantiated by supporting documentation. Documentation should be maintained to reflect the basis for decisions concerning valuation and classification, and legal opinions obtained with respect to these issues.

An overall compliance strategy should also include internal and/or neutral third-party audit of customs practices to determine if practices are inconsistent with current requirements. There is no substitute for independent review of a company's customs practices, and especially by experienced China hands that know and understand the on-the-ground practices of China Customs, the red-flag issues that may create potential Customs scrutiny, and the commitments created by China's WTO membership and the relationship that such commitments have on practices in the field.

A critical area that should not be ignored is to require that employees and managers in China be fully trained in China's customs laws, regulations, and practices, and company policy concerning customs compliance. Since the "Chinese way" of addressing customs issues may be inconsistent with China's written laws and WTO obligations, employees should be trained to exercise caution in dealing with customs transactions. As an example, corruption by underpaid customs officials is still rampant and while to engage in corrupt practices may be the "Chinese way" of addressing a customs issue, such practices violate China's own written laws (as well as US law). In addition, communications with Customs should be delegated to trained and loyal employees. Problem investigations oftentimes are triggered by disgruntled employees over practices that they themselves created. Hence, don't rely upon local employees to manage customs compliance practices in a country whose legal system is going through significant transition.

Given that the practices of customs officials at the local level may be at odds with China's WTO obligations and/or national laws, importers should closely monitor the practices of customs officials at the local level and raise any non-compliance issues with Customs at the national level (which has a spotty history of actually doing something about a non-compliance issue). Similarly, it is important that importers raise any non-compliance issues with the US Embassy personnel that actively monitor China's WTO compliance record (and specifically the Trade Facilitation Office).

A compliance strategy should also include full cooperation with Customs. If in doubt, careful discussions with local and national authorities will help improve

(Continued)

(*Continued from previous page*)

an importer's relationship with Customs and better gauge how Customs will react to certain issues.

Overall, time is of the essence for importers to carefully assess and act to improve corporate customs practices in light of the heavy pressure on China Customs to collect revenue to make up for the significant shortfall in state revenues post-WTO.

application, Customs is required to render a decision. After exhausting its administrative appeals, a party may seek judicial review in the intermediate people's court.[131] If an importer discovers that duties have been overpaid to Customs, a refund must be requested within one year from the date the duty payment was made.[132]

D. Customs Protection of Intellectual Property Rights

Since 1995, the holder of intellectual property rights (i.e., trademark, copyright, or patent) is entitled to obtain the cooperation of China Customs in the enforcement of his or her rights with respect to imported and exported merchandise.[133] Until 2004, such protection was available only to IP holders that were registered in China. Today, registration is optional and an IP holder may file a registration application with China Customs that includes specific information concerning the intellectual property rights, and the types of goods

131. Customs Law, art. 46; Customs Duty Regulations, arts. 37, 38. Under the Administrative Litigation Law, an interested party has the right to file an action challenging the decision of Customs directly to the intermediate people's court. *See* Law of Administrative Litigation of the People's Republic of China (adopted on April 4, 1989, by the 2nd Sess. of the 7th NPC), art. 14, § (i), *reprinted in* CHINA LAWS FOR FOREIGN BUSINESS (CCH), Business Regulation ¶ 19-558 (hereinafter the "Administrative Litigation Law"). For a brief discussion on administrative litigation, *see* Chapter 22, Litigation in the People's Court § C. Note that the 1992 PRC-US Memorandum of Understanding Concerning Market Access specifically required that the PRC government provide importers with the right to appeal customs decisions on a prompt and impartial basis. *See* People's Republic of China—United States: Memorandum of Understanding Concerning Market Access, 31 I.L.M. 1274, art. I, ¶ 6 (1992).

132. Customs Law, arts. 44, 45.

133. Rules of the People's Republic of China on Customs Protection of Intellectual Property Rights (promulgated July 5, 1995, and amended on December 2, 2003); Implementing Measures of the Customs of the People's Republic of China for the Protection of Intellectual Property Rights (promulgated May 25, 2004, by the General Administration of Customs), *reprinted in* CHINA LAWS FOR FOREIGN BUSINESS (CCH), Customs ¶ 50-612 (hereinafter the "Customs IP Protection Measures").

and services subject to protection.[134] An applicant is required to submit copies of its certificates issued by the copyright, trademark, and patent authorities, including agencies of the IP holder's home country, in support of registration. All documents submitted in a foreign language must be translated into Chinese.[135]

A foreign IP holder without a presence in China is required to retain an agent in China to file for registration. The agent is required to submit a power of attorney on behalf of the IP holder at the time of registration.[136] Upon approval by Customs, a registration is valid for a period of ten years and is renewable.[137] The registration is valid only to the extent of the original intellectual property rights. An IP holder is required to advise Customs of any changes to its rights to, or interests in, the intellectual property.[138] Customs must act on an application within 30 days of receipt thereof.

Customs has the authority to detain merchandise pending an investigation if it discovers, or if it is brought to its attention, that imports or exports are suspected of infringing upon the intellectual property rights of an IP holder. Customs will issue a detention notice to the IP holder and the importer or exporter, and will require that the IP holder initiate an administrative or judicial action for relief.[139] If an IP holder receives information concerning a violation of its rights, it may apply to Customs at the port of entry or exit for protection. Customs will require that the IP holder post security in order to protect the interests of the consignor or consignee if the allegations prove to be false.[140]

An interested party may request that Customs release detained merchandise upon the payment of surety equal to the value of the imported or exported goods.[141] Customs is required to reject an application for release of detained merchandise if the merchandise is clearly in violation of the rights of an IP holder or if the people's court has issued an order requiring the detention or confiscation of the subject merchandise.[142]

After an investigation, including the receipt and review of information from interested parties, Customs will either release the merchandise or

134. Customs IP Protection Rules, art. 7.
135. Customs IP Protection Measures, arts. 5, 7.
136. Customs IP Protection Measures, art. 2.
137. Customs IP Protection Rules, art. 10.
138. Customs IP Protection Rules, art. 11.
139. Customs IP Protection Measures, art. 27.
140. Customs IP Protection Rules, art. 14.
141. Customs IP Protection Rules, art. 24(3); Customs IP Protection Measures, art. 24.
142. Customs IP Protection Rules, art. 27. Customs IP Protection Measures, art. 24.

proceed with forfeiture and destruction. Customs has the discretion to destroy the goods or preserve the goods for public welfare purposes. In situations involving large infringement cases, Customs has the discretion to refer the matter for criminal prosecution.[143]

A party affected by a decision of Customs is required to file an administrative appeal within thirty days after receipt of a penalty notice. Customs is then required to act on an appeal decision within ninety days of receiving an application for appeal. A party may seek judicial review before the intermediate people's court within thirty days after receiving a final decision from Customs. An interested party has the right to waive the administrative appeal process and file an action directly with the intermediate people's court within thirty days of receipt of a decision.[144]

E. Trade Remedies: Anti-Dumping, Anti-Subsidy, and Safeguard Regulations

As China opens its markets post-WTO, some domestic industries may be unable to compete with imported products as tariff and nontariff barriers of pre-WTO are relaxed. In order to protect domestic injury from unfair trade practices, China, as well as other WTO member countries, takes advantage of trade remedies procedures that are permissible under the international trade regime. The trade remedies authorized under the WTO to counter injury from imports include anti-dumping measures; safeguard measures; and countervailing duties for subsidized imports. China has promulgated regulations providing standards and procedures for all three types of trade remedies. Since 1997, China has initiated over twenty anti-dumping investigations and one safeguard investigation. China has not initiated an anti-subsidy (or countervailing duty) investigation.

1. Anti-Dumping

The State Council promulgated anti-dumping and anti-subsidy regulations in 1997, which were later revised and repromulgated in 2001.[145] The rules

143. Customs IP Protection Rules, art. 30.

144. Administrative Penalties Rules, art. 28.

145. Regulations of the People's Republic of China on Anti-Dumping and Anti-Subsidies (promulgated on March 25, 1997, revised and repromulgated on November 26, 2001, and effective from January 1, 2002, by Order No. 328 of the State Council), *reprinted in* CHINA LAWS FOR FOREIGN BUSINESS (CCH), Customs ¶ 50-735 (hereinafter the "Anti-Dumping Regulations"). *See also* Anti-Dumping Price Security Tentative Rules (promulgated by MOFTEC on March 13, 2002); Anti-Dumping Review of New Exporters Tentative Rules (promulgated by MOFTEC on March 13, 2002); Anti-Dumping Tax Refund Tentative Rules (promulgated by

require MOFCOM to take steps against imports that result in "substantial damage or the threat of substantial damage" to the domestic industry.[146] The rules define "dumping" as a situation in which the "export price of an imported product is lower than its normal price."[147] The "normal" price is

MOFTEC on March 13, 2002); Information Disclosure for Anti-Dumping Investigation Tentative Rules (promulgated by MOFTEC on March 13, 2002); Public Consultation of Information of Anti-Dumping Investigation Tentative Rules (promulgated by MOFTEC on March 13, 2002); Sampling for Anti-Dumping Investigation Tentative Rules (promulgated by MOFTEC on March 13, 2002). The Anti-Dumping Regulations have been adopted pursuant to Articles 30–32 of the Foreign Trade Law. *See* Foreign Trade Law of the People's Republic of China (adopted on May 12, 1994, by the 7th Sess. of the Standing Comm. of the 8th NPC and as amended on April 6, 2004, by the NPC Standing Committee), *reprinted in* CHINA LAWS FOR FOREIGN BUSINESS (CCH), Business Regulation ¶ 19-586. The Foreign Trade Law authorized governmental authorities to impose "counter-measures" against foreign products imported at less than their "normal value" if those imports "substantially injured" a domestic industry. The Anti-Dumping Regulations were developed in response to the dumping charges imposed against numerous Chinese products worldwide where Chinese goods have been subject to over 500 anti-dumping cases. China claims that dumping cases in the U.S. and Europe are protectionist measures that ignore China's competitive advantage of low production costs. MOFTEC (now MOFCOM) also claims that dumping of foreign goods in China caused billions of dollars in damages to Chinese enterprises and results in the unemployment of hundreds of thousands of people. *See* Zhou, *Unfair Play: China Victimized by Anti-Dumping Moves,* 138 CHINA INTERNATIONAL BUSINESS (MOFTEC) 27 (1999); *Record of Events (January–March 1997)*, CHINA LAW 107 (1997). Shang, *China's Anti-Dumping Legislation and Investigation Procedures,* 132 CHINA INTERNATIONAL BUSINESS (MOFTEC) 48 (1998) (discusses the government authorities responsible for investigating anti-dumping complaints and procedures for investigations). On December 10, 1997, MOFTEC initiated the first anti-dumping investigation under the new regulations by targeting Newsprint (HTS 4801.000) imported from the United States, Canada, and South Korea. The investigation is the result of a petition filed by nine Chinese Newsprint manufacturers. Zhang & Li, *First Sword Against Dumping,* 135 CHINA INTERNATIONAL BUSINESS (MOFTEC) 8 (1998) (discusses newsprint dumping case). In March 1999, the Wuhan Iron & Steel (Group) Co. in Hubei Province initiated the second anti-dumping case against producers of cold rolled silicon steel from Russia. *See* Gao, *Second Anti-Dumping Case Launched,* CHINA DAILY BUSINESS WEEKLY (March 21, 1999), available on Lexis, News Library, or the Web site of the CHINA DAILY BUSINESS WEEKLY at http://www.chinadaily.com.cn. M. Dudek, A. Wang & C. Zhang, *Anti-Dumping and Safeguards with Chinese Characteristics,* CHINA L. & PRAC. July 2003 (authors state that Chinese products have been the subject of more than 300 anti-dumping investigations worldwide); P. Norton & K. Almstedt, China's *New Anti-Dumping Rules: Battleground for A New Protectionism,* CHINA L. & PRAC. (Feb. 2002). Post-WTO, China's anti-dumping rules and practices must now conform to China's obligations under the WTO Anti-Dumping Agreement, more specifically known as the Agreement on Implementation of Article VI of the General Agreement on Tariffs and Trade, set forth in the Results of the Uruguay Round of Multilateral Trade Negotiations: The Legal Texts, GATT Secretariat, 1994, pp. 168–69 (hereinafter referred to as the "WTO Anti-Dumping Agreement"). If a signatory country believes that China has failed to meet its obligations under the WTO, it may take China to compulsory WTO dispute resolution procedures in Geneva. *See generally* China's official anti-dumping Web site: http://www.cacs.gov.cn; *MOFCOM Revises Investigation Rules on Anti-dumping, Antisubsidy, and Safeguard Cases,* CHINA MARKET INTELLIGENCE, THE U.S.-CHINA BUSINESS COUNCIL (November 19, 2003). The anti-dumping, anti-subsidy, and safeguard regulations were amended in June 2004 to reflect the expanded role of the Ministry of Commerce in these cases. *State Council Issues Revised Antidumping, Antisubsidy, and Safeguard Rules,* CHINA MARKET INTELLIGENCE, THE U.S.-CHINA BUSINESS COUNCIL (April 21, 2004).

146. Anti-Dumping Regulations, art. 2.

147. Anti-Dumping Regulations, art. 3. The WTO Anti-Dumping Agreement mandates three criteria for a determination of dumping and the imposition of anti-dumping duties: (1) that the imported products were "dumped" on the domestic market; namely, that they were imported at a price lower than the price in the home market, with appropriate adjustments for shipping costs and other expenses; (2) that the domestic industry sustained injury; and (3) that the injury was caused by the "dumped" imports. The three criteria are generally referred to as dumping, injury, and causation.

the price of the same or similar goods as the imported product sold on the market in the exporting country.[148]

Damages include the actual or threatened harm to the domestic industry or "an actual obstruction to the establishment of the related domestic industries."[149] In determining whether dumping has caused damage to a domestic industry, the rules require the examination of the quantity of the product imported into China, the price of the dumped product, the impact of the dumped product on the domestic industry, and the production capacity of the dumped product in the country of origin.[150]

A domestic producer of goods or commodities that are the same or similar products as imported goods, or an organization representing domestic industry, may file an application with MOFCOM for an anti-dumping investigation.[151] An application must include the following information and documentation:

(1) The name and HTS category of the imported product
(2) The quantity and price of the alleged dumped product and its impact on the domestic industry

---

148. Anti-Dumping Regulations, art. 4. If there is no comparable price for a similar product from the country of export, the comparable price for export of the same or similar product from a third country may be used as the "normal" price. The rules also provide that the "normal" price may be determined by taking the cost of producing a similar product and adding reasonable expenses and profit. One stipulation in the China/WTO Agreement requires WTO Members to apply their dumping and countervailing duty laws in such a way that the Chinese exporter is permitted to use China costs and prices for comparison, if the producer "can clearly show that market economy conditions prevail in the industry producing the like products." In the event that the Chinese producer or importer is unable to substantiate its position, then the importing WTO Member country may use surrogate-based pricing data to determine injury and countervailing duties.

149. Anti-Dumping Regulations, art. 7.

150. Anti-Dumping Regulations, art. 8. In contrast to the prior rules adopted in 1997, the new regulations are more consistent with the standards and objectives of the WTO agreements (Agreement on Implementation of Article VI of the General Agreement on Tariffs and Trade and the Agreement onSafeguards). Specifically, under the new Anti-Dumping Regulations three elements must be determined before anti-dumping measures may be imposed: (1) the existence of dumping (in the case of an anti-dumping action) or a significant increase in the import volume of the products (in the case of a safeguard action); (2) material injury to the relevant domestic industry; and (3) causation between the dumping/import increase and the injury.

151. Anti-Dumping Regulations, art. 13. On June 25, 2002, MOFTEC established the Office of Public Information on Investigation and Reporting of Antidumping, under the Bureau of Fair Trade for Import and Export. *See* Provisional Measures on Public Information on Investigation and Reporting of Anti-Dumping (issued on June 25, 2002, by the Ministry of Foreign Trade & Economic Cooperation). Prior to the release of the Measures, on June 20, 2002, MOFTEC issued its report detailing MOFTEC's and SETC's findings related to the dumping of methylene chloride by six foreign companies on China's market, which was the first such report publicly issued by the PRC government. The Measures are intended to increase the transparency of the anti-dumping case investigation and decision processs. In March 2003, MOFTEC and the SETC were reorganized into the Ministry of Commerce (MOFCOM), and MOFCOM thereby became the sole authority in charge of anti-dumping investigations. The MOFCOM Bureau of Fair Trade for Import and Export is responsible for accepting or rejecting anti-dumping petitions, investigating dumping margins or import increases, and determining preliminary and final anti-dumping measures. The MOFCOM Bureau of Industrial Injury Investigation is authorized to investigate injuries or threats to domestic industries. Given that most industries adversely affected by international trade are state-owned-enterprises, it appears to be a conflict of interest for government agencies such as MOFCOM to also play the role of reviewing and deciding on trade remedies cases involving SOEs.

(3) The connection between the act of dumping the product and the damage sustained
(4) All necessary supporting documentation[152]

Within sixty days of receiving an application, MOFCOM will decide whether to proceed with a formal investigation and thereafter notify the parties, known exporters of the subject products, and the interested foreign governments involved.[153] MOFCOM will not initiate a proceeding if less than 25 percent of the domestic producers support the application, and is required to initiate an investigation if greater than 50 percent of the domestic producers support the application.[154] Under "special circumstances" MOFCOM may initiate an investigation even if a formal application has not been filed by the domestic industry.[155]

MOFCOM is required to make a public announcement concerning the investigation and to notify interested parties.[156] MOFCOM may request that interested parties, including foreign producers, complete questionnaires with respect to the imported product and pricing/cost issues, and submit product samples.[157] The interested parties are also entitled to the opportunity to state

152. Anti-Dumping Regulations, arts. 14–15. An application must include the following items: (1) the name, address, and relevant information of the applicant; (2) a complete description of the imported products for which the application for investigation is made, including the names of the product, of the exporting country/region or the country/region of origin, of the exporter or the producer, the price of the product in the market of the exporting country/region or the country/region of origin, the export price, etc; (3) description of the quantity and value of the same product in the domestic market; and (4) the impact on the domestic industry caused by the quantity and price of the imported product for which the investigation is applied. Anti-Dumping Regulations, art. 14.

153. Anti-Dumping Regulations, arts. 16, 19. The regulations provide that all public notices and announcements "shall contain important information, facts, reasons, references, evidences, results and conclusions." Anti-Dumping Regulations, art. 54. In the past, anti-dumping decisions failed to provide sufficient detail concerning the basis for the government's decision. The WTO Anti-Dumping Agreement requires that the determinations of investigating agencies be transparent and complete. Decisions are required to identify all of the evidence on which they are based, the methodology used in any calculations, and the reasons for accepting or rejecting the basic contentions of the parties to the proceeding.

154. Anti-Dumping Regulations, art. 17.

155. Anti-Dumping Regulations, art. 18. This provision has never been invoked.

156. Anti-Dumping Regulations, arts. 20.

157. Anti-Dumping Regulations, arts. 20, 23. Article 20 simply states that interested parties be provided "opportunities to state their opinions and arguments." Article 23 states that the "investigating authorities shall allow the petitioner and interested parties access to the files of the case with the exception of information treated as confidential." There are no provisions that allow for the timely exchange of evidence and materials to allow interested parties to comment on the submissions of the other parties. The WTO Anti-Dumping Agreement prescribes that the anti-dumping investigative procedures must be transparent, and that each party to the investigation be given an opportunity to review the evidence and legal arguments submitted. Under WTO, an investigating agency in an anti-dumping proceeding can rely only on evidence that has been submitted to all of the parties for comment. The Anti-Dumping Regulations do not provide details on investigation procedures, and one must look to the WTO for guidance on proper procedural standards. The WTO Anti-Dumping Agreement requires that "[t]hroughout the anti-dumping investigation all interested parties have a full opportunity for the defense of their interests." This must include, on request, "opportunities for all interested parties to meet those parties with adverse interests, so that opposing views may be presented and rebuttal arguments offered." WTO Anti-Dumping

their opinions to MOFCOM during the investigation. However, if an interested party provides false information or interferes with the investigation, MOFCOM has the authority to disregard the opinions and information of the interested party and render a decision.[158] Prior to making a final ruling, MOFCOM is required to give all interested parties notice of the proposed final ruling and opportunity for comment.[159]

The time limit for an anti-dumping investigation is twelve months from the date on which the decision to investigate is announced. In special circumstances, the time limit for an investigation may be extended for an additional six months for a total investigation period of eighteen months.[160]

Agreement, art. 6.2. The WTO also requires that investigating authorities provide opportunities for the parties "to see all information that is relevant . . . and that is used by the authorities in an anti-dumping investigation, and to prepare presentations on the basis of this information." WTO Anti-Dumping Agreement, art. 6.4. Article 6.1.2 of the WTO Anti-Dumping Agreement requires that the authorities make "available promptly" evidence submitted by each "interested party . . . to other interested parties participating in the investigation." These provisions are usually understood to require that all legal and evidentiary submissions be served on all parties, and that each party have the opportunity to examine and comment on submissions of the other parties.

158. Anti-Dumping Regulations, art. 21. Although an interested party may request access to the investigation file, confidential matters will not be released to the public. *Id.* arts. 22–23. Under China's Anti-Dumping Regulations, there is no express requirement that the parties be allowed to review the evidence submitted in a proceeding. Chinese parties in past investigations have claimed that their evidence is confidential state secrets to deny a foreign party the right to access to the information. In response to criticism from foreign parties in such cases, MOFCOM has submitted summaries of the confidential information, and such summaries in themselves indicated that the claimed confidential information was basic economic and market-specific information, rather than business or state secrets. In order to be in compliance with WTO obligations, MOFCOM will need to make all evidence and legal arguments available to interested parties, or risk facing a complaint before WTO. The WTO requires that detailed public summaries be provided for any "confidential information" submitted by a party. WTO Anti-Dumping Agreement, art. 6.5. To ensure transparency, an accepted practice of the WTO is to encourage the release of confidential information to other parties under strict protective orders. WTO Anti-Dumping Agreement, art. 6.5, n. 17.

159. Anti-Dumping Regulations, art. 24. This provision follows the practice in Article 6.9 of the WTO Anti-Dumping Agreement. However, the Anti-Dumping Regulations do not provide the specificity that is set forth in the WTO Anti-Dumping Agreement with respect to transparency in issuing formal decisions. The WTO Anti-Dumping Agreement requires that any final determinations "set forth . . . in sufficient detail the findings and conclusions reached on all issues of fact and law." WTO Anti-Dumping Agreement, art. 12.3. The Agreement also requires that the methodology in determining a dumping margin calculation be specifically described. WTO Anti-Dumping Agreement, art. Article 12.2.1 (iii). The WTO agreement provides in detail the factors that must be considered in the injury and causation determinations, and requires, in particular, that all other possible causes of injury be considered and not be attributed to the imported products under investigation. WTO Anti-Dumping Agreement, arts. 3, 3.5. The WTO also requires that the factors enumerated in Article 3 be reported in detail in the final determinations. WTO Anti-Dumping Agreement, art. 12.2.1 (iv). Article 6.8 authorizes investigating authorities to rely on "facts available" from sources other than the parties but only under narrow circumstances and subject to the requirement that the data be verified independently. In contrast, MOFCOM is merely empowered to render preliminary and final determinations "based on their investigations." Anti-Dumping Regulations, arts. 24, 25. There is no requirement that the findings in PRC proceedings provide any of the detail required by the WTO. The Chinese authorities are also authorized to rely on "facts available" under very general criteria and with no protection that the data be verified as to its accuracy or completeness as is required by the WTO Anti-Dumping Agreement. Anti-Dumping Regulations, art. 21.

160. Anti-Dumping Regulations, art. 26.

An anti-dumping investigation may be terminated in the event of the following circumstances:

(1) Withdrawal of the application by the applicant
(2) There is insufficient evidence to prove the existence of dumping or injury to the domestic industry, or the connection between the dumping and injury
(3) The dumping margin is lower than 2 percent
(4) The actual or potential imported volume or injury caused by the imported products is negligible
(5) MOFCOM decides that it is inappropriate to continue the anti-dumping investigation[161]

If a preliminary finding reveals damage to the domestic industry as a result of dumping, MOFCOM may impose against an importer provisional anti-dumping measures including interim anti-dumping duties or the imposition of cash deposit or other guarantee.[162] China Customs is required to implement all interim anti-dumping duties. The amount of the interim duty or cash deposit is based upon the dumping margin determined by the preliminary investigation. The time limit for imposing interim anti-dumping duties is four months from the date of public announcement of a decision and, under special circumstances, may be extended for up to nine months.[163] At the conclusion of its investigation, MOFCOM may issue permanent anti-dumping duties for a period of five years.[164] MOFCOM may only set the anti-dumping duty in an amount that does not exceed the dumping margin. The importer of a dumped product is the party that is required to pay anti-dumping duty.[165]

MOFCOM will, within twelve months of commencing the review, render a decision to amend, cancel, or retain the permanent anti-dumping duties. The Anti-Dumping Rules provide that the MOFCOM has the authority to impose sanctions retroactively for a period of ninety days if the import operator has previously caused damage to a domestic industry or

161. Anti-Dumping Regulations, art. 27.

162. Anti-Dumping Regulations, art. 28. The imposition of provisional anti-dumping measures must be publicly announced by MOFCOM.

163. Anti-Dumping Regulations, art. 30.

164. Anti-Dumping Regulations, arts. 48, 49. The five years may be extended if there is evidence that dumping will reoccur.

165. Anti-Dumping Regulations, arts. 40, 42. The anti-dumping duties shall be determined by the dumping margins set for the different exporters. MOFCOM may set a duty based upon a reasonable manner for exporters that are not included in an investigation and in circumstances where MOFCOM believes that anti-dumping duties should be imposed. Anti-Dumping Regulations, art. 41.

in situations where most of the dumped products have been imported within a short period of time and have already caused damage to the domestic industry.[166]

MOFCOM may terminate an investigation if the importer of the dumped product or the government of the country of export proposes to take effective measures to eliminate the damage caused by dumping, including accepting price commitments.[167] If the importer of a dumped product has evidence to substantiate that the amount of anti-dumping duty paid is in excess of the dumping margin, it may file an application for a refund with MOFCOM.[168]

An interested party that disputes any anti-dumping decision may apply for administrative review or petition the people's court for review.[169]

The Anti-Dumping Regulations provide that the PRC government may take reciprocal action against any country or region that adopts discriminatory anti-dumping or anti-subsidy measures on goods exported from the People's Republic of China.[170]

2. Anti-Subsidy Regulations

The Anti-Subsidy Regulations, which were adopted in 2001, set forth the standards and procedures for addressing trade distortions created by subsidization of an industry by direct or indirect financial assistance of government or quasi-government institutions.[171] MOFCOM has authority to impose anti-subsidy measures (countervailing duties) to offset improper subsidies that benefit

166. Anti-Dumping Regulations, arts. 43, 44.

167. Anti-Dumping Regulations, arts. 31–36.

168. Anti-Dumping Regulations, art. 46.

169. Anti-Dumping Regulations, art. 53. *See also* Several Questions Concerning the Application of Law on Trial Anti-Dumping Administrative Case Provisions (promulgated by the Supreme People's Republic of China on Nov. 21, 2002, and effective January 1, 2003) (outlines the standards and procedures for administrative cases involving anti-dumping investigations including final decisions on dumping, the dumping margin, injury, and the degree of injury).

170. Anti-Dumping Regulations, art. 56. The imposition of retaliatory measures may be in violation of WTO unless previously authorized as retaliatory sanctions in response to a WTO panel's finding.

171. Anti-Subsidy Regulations of the People's Republic of China (promulgated November 26, 2001, and effective on January 1, 2002, by Order No. 329 of the State Council), *reprinted in* CHINA LAWS FOR FOREIGN BUSINESS, Customs ¶ 50-736 (hereinafter the "Anti-Subsidy Regulations"). The WTO Agreement on Subsidies and Countervailing Measures (hereinafter the "WTO SCM Agreement") authorizes a WTO member country to take a dispute over improperly subsidized imports directly to a WTO dispute resolution panel. Under the WTO SCM Agreement, China is authorized to apply "countervailing measures" to counter the effects of improper subsidies to eliminate the impact of the subsidy and to allow domestic industry to compete on an equal footing. The WTO SCM Agreement defines a "subsidy" as including four elements: (1) a "financial contribution" (2) by a government (3) conferring a "benefit" that (4) is "specific."

imports and harm, or threaten to harm, China's domestic industry.[172] The Anti-Subsidy Regulations are procedurally similar to the Anti-Dumping Regulations, and MOFCOM is the agency responsible for investigating petitions for relief.[173] Anti-subsidy investigations are more complicated than anti-dumping investigations because of the particular difficulties of identifying and substantiating improper subsidies and quantifying the impact thereof.

The procedures for investigating the injury and causation issues in anti-subsidy cases parallel those for Chinese anti-dumping investigations. As with the other trade remedy investigations, MOFCOM is primarily responsible for the injury and causation determinations. The Ministry of Agriculture, however, is given joint responsibility in cases involving agricultural products.[174]

172. Anti-Subsidy Regulations, arts. 2, 5. K. Almstedt & P. Norton, *China's Anti-Subsidy Regulations: The Latest Weapon in China's Trade Law Enforcement,* CHINA L. & PRAC. (Dec. 2002). The regulations provide that the government subsidies at issue include the following: (1) subsidies for enterprises or industries provided by the government of the exporting country for export achievements; (2) foreign exchange portion retaining or similar means related to export rewarding; (3) conditions provided for exports' domestic transportation or freight more favorable than those for domestic cargoes, as provided for or approved by the government of the exporting country or region; (4) Conditions for provision of products or services by the government of the exporting country or region directly or indirectly for manufacturing exports more favorable than those for manufacturing domestic products, unless under special circumstances; (5) deduction and exemption in total or in part, or payment postponement of direct taxes or social welfare fees specially related to exports that have been paid or shall be paid by enterprises; (6) deduction directly related to exports or export achievements more favorable than the deduction for domestic products in calculating the base for the direct taxes; (7) deduction, exemption, or refund of indirect taxes related to manufacture and circulation of exports exceeding the indirect taxes imposed on domestic similar or identical products; (8) deduction, exemption, refund, or payment postponement for earlier accumulated indirect taxes imposed on cargoes or services for manufacturing exports more favorable than those for manufacturing domestic similar or identical products, unless under certain special circumstances; (9) deduction or exemption of import investment related to the manufacture of exports, or refund of import expenses exceeding charges collected upon import of such investment, unless under certain special circumstances; (10) export credit guarantee or insurance provided by the government of the exporting country or region with the rate based on which the long-term business costs and deficits are difficult to be offset, or the insurance or guarantee provided against the cost increase or foreign risk for exports; (11) interest of export credit provided by the government of the exporting country or region lower than the actual interest accrued, or payment of expenses in total or in part for exporters or other financial institutions to obtain loans so that they obtain advantages in the export credit, unless under certain special circumstances; and (12) other expenses from the public accounts constituting export subsidies.

173. Anti-Subsidy Regulations, arts. 13–28. Domestic industries and their representatives may file applications to initiate anti-subsidy investigations. An application is required to include the following items: (1) the name, address, and detailed information concerning the applicant; (2) a full description of the imported product that is the subject of review, including the product name, the country or region of origin, and the exporter or producer, if known; (3) an explanation of the quantity and value of similar or identical domestic products; (4) the adverse impact of the quantity and prices of the imported product or investigation on domestic industry; and (5) other matters that should be explained in the opinion of the applicants. The following evidence should be included with an application: (1) evidence proving the existence of a subsidy granted to the imported product that is the subject of the application; (2) proof of damages to the domestic industries; and (3) the causal relationship between the alleged subsidy and damages. Anti-Subsidy Regulations, arts. 14, 15. MOFCOM has 60 days to review an application. Anti-Subsidy Regulations, art. 16.

174. Anti-Subsidy Regulations, art. 7.

The Anti-Subsidy Regulations are consistent with the WTO SCM Agreement in a number of respects. For example, "injury" may take one of three forms: "material injury" to a domestic industry; the "threat of material injury" to a domestic industry; or "material retardation of the establishment of" a domestic industry.[175] The injury to domestic industry must be analyzed on a "like product" basis; namely, imported goods must be compared with the specific domestic products with which they compete and the subject goods must be defined narrowly.[176] Determinations of injury and causation must be based upon evidence, and an injury caused by factors other than subsidies must not be attributed to the imports that are allegedly subsidized.[177]

The Anti-Subsidy Regulations fail to provide details concerning several issues, such as the standards for determining a "threat" of injury to domestic industry and standards for causation. In contrast, the WTO SMC Agreement provides that any determination of a threat "be based on facts and not merely on allegation, conjecture or remote possibility" and more specific detail on the definition of causation.[178] Since China is a party to the WTO SCM Agreement, reliance upon treaty obligations may provide the regulatory detail needed to clarify the applicable standards in these cases.

An interested party that disputes a decision under the Anti-Subsidy Regulations may seek administrative review, as well as review before the people's court.[179]

3. Trade Safeguard Measures

The government has adopted standards and procedures for safeguard measures to counter distortions in trade caused by foreign producers and importers.[180] The Trade Safeguard Regulations provide that domestic industry

175. Anti-Subsidy Regulations, art. 7; WTO SCM Agreement, art. 15, n. 45.

176. Anti-Subsidy Regulations, arts. 10, 12; WTO SCM Agreement, arts. 15.1, 15.6.

177. Anti-Subsidy Regulations, art. 9; WTO SCM Agreement, arts. 15.1, 15.5.

178. WTO SCM Agreement, arts. 15.4, 15.5, 15.7. Comparable detailed provisions are not set forth in the Anti-Subsidy Regulations.

179. The Supreme People's Court has issued an order that provides that the Intermediate Court in Beijing would have jurisdiction over appeals of anti-subsidy cases beginning October 1, 2002. The court issued more specific rules for handling such cases on November 21, 2002. The WTO SCM Agreement mandates that, besides providing interested parties with the right to seek an administrative review, the WTO member must through national legislation "maintain judicial, arbitral or administrative tribunals or procedures for the purpose of . . . the prompt review of administrative actions relating to final determinations and reviews of determinations (and) . . . such reviews shall be independent of the authorities responsible for the determination or review in question." WTO SCM Agreement, art. 23.

180. Regulations of the People's Republic of China on Safeguard Measures (promulgated on November 21, 2001, and effective January 1, 2002, by Order No. 330 of the State Council), *reprinted in* China Laws for Foreign Business, Customs ¶ 50-737 (hereinafter the "Trade Safeguard Regulations"). The Trade Safeguard Regulations authorize MOFCOM to impose reciprocal safeguard measures against foreign governments that engage in discriminatory trade practices. Trade Safeguard Regulations, art. 32.

may petition to MOFCOM for relief when the quantity of an imported product significantly increases and consequently results in substantial injury, or a threat of substantial injury, to the domestic industry that produces a similar product or a directly competitive product.[181] MOFCOM can also initiate its own investigation even if an application for safeguard measures by domestic industry has not been formally filed.[182] The increase in imports at issue is defined under the regulations as the relative increase of the imported product in comparison to domestic production.[183]

The Trade Safeguard Regulations provide that the following factors shall be reviewed when the injury to domestic industry is determined to have been caused by the increase of the quantity of imported products: (1) the absolute and relative rates and volumes of the increase; (2) the percentage increase of imported products in the domestic market; (3) the impact of the imported products on the domestic industry, including the impact on the output, sales volume, market share, productivity, equipment availability, profit and loss, employment, and other aspects of the domestic industry; and (4) other factors that may have caused the injury to the domestic industry. MOFCOM will ignore other factors that may have caused damages to the domestic injury so long as there is evidence that the increase in imports caused some damage.[184]

There is no time limit as to when MOFCOM is to complete its investigation and announce a decision on a petition, except to do so in a "timely manner."[185] MOFCOM is required to provide importers, exporters, or other interested parties with an opportunity to be heard. MOFCOM has the authority to carry out an investigation using questionnaires, public hearings, and other appropriate methods of gathering evidence.[186] All communications and materials submitted by any party concerning an investigation are to remain confidential, and disclosure is prohibited without the consent of the submitting party.[187]

181. Trade Safeguard Regulations, art. 2. The domestic industry refers to all the domestic producers of the similar products or directly competitive products in the People's Republic of China or the producers whose total output accounts for a major part of the total domestic output of the similar products or directly competitive products. Trade Safeguard Regulations, art. 10.
182. Trade Safeguard Regulations, art. 4.
183. Trade Safeguard Regulations, art. 7.
184. Trade Safeguard Regulations, art. 8.
185. Trade Safeguard Regulations, art. 9.
186. Trade Safeguard Regulations, art. 12.
187. Trade Safeguard Regulations, art. 13.

MOFCOM is empowered to make a preliminary determination that the increase in imports has caused irreparable injury to the domestic industry, and thereafter order provisional import safeguard measures including tariff increases or quantity restrictions.[188] The duration of provisional safeguard measures may not extend for more than two hundred days from the date of implementation. If, after an investigation, MOFCOM determines that the quantity of imported products has increased and caused damages to the domestic industry, safeguard measures may be made in the form of a permanent decision.[189] Before imposing trade safeguard measures, MOFCOM is authorized to negotiate with the foreign governments that are involved with the subject imports.[190] Trade safeguard measures are required to be imposed upon all products at issue regardless of their country of origin and shall not be implemented for more than four years.[191] If the final decision issued by MOFCOM determines that safeguard measures are not necessary, the provisional tariffs that may have been paid by an importer are required to be refunded.[192]

188. Trade Safeguard Regulations, arts. 17, 18. Any tariff increase will be determined by the Tariff Commission of the State Council. Quantitative restrictions will be determined by MOFCOM. Trade Safeguard Regulations, art. 21.

189. Trade Safeguard Regulations, art. 20.

190. Trade Safeguard Regulations, art. 25.

191. Trade Safeguard Regulations, arts. 23, 27. The time limit of four years may be extended in appropriate circumstances. If trade safeguard measures extend for more than one year, the implementation order must allow for an easing of restrictions over time. Trade Safeguard Regulations, art. 28. If the safeguard measures are in place for more than three years, MOFCOM is required to conduct a mid-term review. Trade Safeguard Regulations, art. 29.

192. Trade Safeguard Regulations, art. 26.

Chinese Anti-Dumping Cases (as of December 2003)

Notice # (The most updated notice issued by MOFCOM)	Date of Issuance	Product	Initiating Date of the Investigation
28/2003	July 1, 2003	newsprinting paper 新闻纸	Dec. 10, 1997
8/2000	Sep. 11, 2000	cold-rolled silicon steel sheet 冷轧硅钢片	Mar. 12, 1999
7/2000	Aug. 25, 2000	polyester film 聚酯薄膜	Apr. 16, 1999
15/2000	Dec. 18, 2000	flat cold-rolled stainless sheet 不锈钢冷轧薄板	June 17, 1999
5/2001	June 9, 2001	propenoid acid ester 丙烯酸酯	Dec. 10, 1999
20/2002	June 20, 2002	Carrene 二氯甲烷	Dec. 20, 2000
13/2001	Nov. 6, 2001	Polysterine 聚苯乙烯	Feb. 9, 2001
23/2002	Sep. 29, 2002	fodder level L-lysine hydrochloride 饲料级 L-赖氨酸盐酸盐	June 19, 2001
3/2003	Feb. 3, 2003	polyester section 聚酯切片	Aug. 3, 2001
4/2003	Feb. 3, 2003	polyester short fiber 涤纶短纤维	Aug. 3, 2001
3/2003	Apr. 10, 2003	propenoid acid ester 丙烯酸酯	Oct. 10, 2001
22/2003	June 6, 2003	caprolactam 己内酰胺	Dec. 7, 2001
35/2003	Aug. 6, 2003	coated art paper 铜版纸	Feb. 6, 2002
41/2003	Aug. 28, 2003	catechol 邻苯二酚	Mar. 1, 2002
40/2003	Aug. 31, 2003	phthalic anhydride 邻苯二甲酸酐	Mar. 6, 2002
49/2003	Sep. 9, 2003	styrene butadiene rubber 丁苯橡胶	Mar. 19, 2002
50/2003	Sep. 23, 2003	cold-rolled steel products 冷轧板卷	Mar. 23, 2002
53/2003	Sep. 29, 2003	polyvinyl chloride 聚氯乙烯	Mar. 29, 2002
61/2003	Nov. 22, 2003	toluene diisocyanate 甲苯二异氰酸酯 (TDI)	May 22, 2002
15/2003	May 30, 2003	chloroform 三氯甲烷	May 30, 2002
33/2003	July 29, 2003	Phenol 苯酚	Aug. 1, 2002
66/2003	Nov. 18, 2003	Pure MDI, Polymeric MDI 纯 MDI 和聚合 MDI	Sep. 20, 2002
12/2003	May 14, 2003	Monoethanolamine & diathanolamine 乙醇胺	May 14, 2003
24/2004	July 1, 2003	Dispersion Unshifted Single-Mode Optical Fiber 非色散位移单模光纤	July 1, 2003
56/2003	Oct. 31, 2003	Nylon 6, 66 Filament Yarn 锦纶 6, 66 长丝	Oct. 31, 2003
59/2003	Nov. 10, 2003	chloroprene rubber 氯丁橡胶	Nov. 10, 2003

Countries and Regions at Issue	Status
U.S., Canada, Korea	reviewed after anti-dumping duty imposed
Russia	anti-dumping duty imposed
Korea	anti-dumping duty imposed
Japan, Korea	anti-dumping duty imposed
Japan, Germany, U.S.	anti-dumping duty imposed on products from Japan and U.S., investigation on Germany terminated
U.K., U.S., Holland, France, Germany, Korea	anti-dumping duty imposed on products from U.K., U.S., Holland, Germany, Korea, investigation on France terminated
Japan, Korea, Thailand	investigation terminated with no penalty imposed
U.S., Korea, Indonesia	investigation terminated with no penalty imposed
Korea	anti-dumping duty imposed
Korea	anti-dumping duty imposed
Korea, Malaysia, Singapore, Indonesia	anti-dumping duty imposed
Japan, Belgium, Korea, Russia, Holland	anti-dumping duty imposed
Japan, Korea, Finland, U.S.	anti-dumping duty imposed on products from Japan and Korea, no anti-dumping measure against U.S. and Finland
EU	anti-dumping duty imposed
India, Korea, Japan	anti-dumping duty imposed
Russia, Korea, Japan	anti-dumping duty imposed
Russia, Korea, Ukraine, Kazakhstan, Taiwan	no anti-dumping duty imposed by final award that decided it was dumping
Russia, Japan, Korea, U.S., Taiwan	anti-dumping duty imposed, price guarantee agreement with a Russian company
Japan, U.S., Korea	anti-dumping duty imposed
EU, U.S., India, Korea	pending
Japan, Korea, U.S., Taiwan	investigation extended
Japan, Korea	investigation terminated upon request of applicants
Japan, U.S., Germany, Iran, Malaysia, Taiwan, Mexico	pending
U.S., Japan, Korea	pending
Taiwan	pending
Japan, U.S., EU	pending

Key Laws and Regulations

Customs Regulations

Customs Law of the People's Republic of China (adopted January 22, 1987, at the 19th Sess. of the Standing Comm. of the 6th NPC, and as amended and approved July 8, 2000, at the 16th Sess. of the Standing Comm. of the 9th NPC)

Detailed Rules for the Implementation of the Administrative Penalties of the Customs Law of the People's Republic of China (approved June 30, 1987, by the State Council and promulgated on July 1, 1987, by the General Administration of Customs, amended and approved February 17, 1993, by the State Council and repromulgated April 1, 1993, by the General Administration of Customs)

Provisions of the General Administration of Customs for the Administration of Declarations for Imported and Exported Goods (issued on September 18, 2003, by the General Administration of Customs)

Regulations of the People's Republic of China on Import and Export Duty (promulgated on November 23, 2003, by the State Council and effective January 1, 2004)

Regulation on Valuation of Royalties Related to Imported Goods, (promulgated on May 30, 2003, by the General Administration of Customs)

Supervising Measures on Goods Imported and Exported Under ATA Certificates (promulgated on December 24, 2001, by the General Administration of Customs)

Regulations on Taxation Issues Related to Import Taxes Levied by Customs on Imported Goods (issued on March 16, 2004, by the Ministry of Finance, General Administration of Customs, and State Administration of Taxation)

Provisional Administrative Regulations on Customs Administrative Rulings (promulgated on December 24, 2001, by the General Administration of Customs)

Measures Concerning the Declaration of Import and Export Goods (issued October 2003 by the General Administration of Customs)

Notice on Partial Adjustment to Incentive Policies on Import Taxes (issued on September 5, 2002, by the Ministry of Finance and effective October 1, 2002)

Measures for the Administration of the Inspection and Supervision of Imported Used Mechanical and Electrical Products (issued on August 1, 2003, by the State Administration for Quality Supervision, Inspection and Quarantine [SAQSIQ])

Administrative Measures on the Inspection and Quarantine of Imported/Exported Meat Products (issued on October 1, 2002, by the Administration of Quality Supervision, Inspection, and Quarantine [AQSIQ])

(*Continued*)

(*Continued from previous page*)

Administration of Import of Audio and Video Products Procedures (issued on June 1, 2002, by the Ministry of Culture [MOCT] and General Administration of Customs)

Detailed Rules for the Implementation of the Administrative Penalties of the Customs Law of the People's Republic of China (approved June 30, 1987, by the State Council and promulgated on July 1, 1987 by the General Administration of Customs, amended and approved February 17, 1993 by the State Council and re-promulgated April 1, 1993 by the General Administration of Customs)

Customs Inspection Rules of the People's Republic of China (promulgated on January 3, 1997, by the State Council)

Rules of the People's Republic of China on Customs Protection of Intellectual Property Rights (promulgated July 5, 1995, and amended on December 2, 2003)

Processing Trade

Administrative Measures of the Customs of the People's Republic of China Governing Import and Export Commodities Involved in Import Processing (promulgated May 6, 1988, by the General Administration of Customs of the People's Republic of China)

Notice on Several Issues Concerning the Import of Equipment for the Processing Trade (promulgated on July 1, 1998, by the MOFTEC and China Customs)

Provisional Measures for the Administration of Tax Collection in Export Processing Zones (issued on October 26, 2000, by the SAT)

Decision to Amend the Interim Measures of the People's Republic of China on the Supervision of Export Processing Zones (issued on September 2, 2003, by the State Council)

Regulation on the Supervision of Goods Under Processing Trade (issued on February 26, 2004, by the General Administration of Customs)

Bonded Zones and Factories

Administrative Measures of the Customs of the People's Republic of China Governing Bonded Factories Engaged in Processing Trade (promulgated April 6, 1988, by the General Administration of Customs)

Administrative Measures of the Customs of the People's Republic of China Governing Bonded Warehouses and the Goods Stored Therein (promulgated April 14, 1988, by the General Administration of Customs)

Administrative Measures of the Customs of the People's Republic of China governing Goods, Means of Transport and Personal Articles Entering and Leaving the Shanghai Waigaoqiao Bonded Zone (promulgated September 1990, by the General Administration of Customs)

(*Continued*)

(*Continued from previous page*)

Administrative Measures for the Shanghai Waigaoqiao Bonded Zone (promulgated on September 10, 1990, by the Shanghai Municipal People's Government)

Administrative Measures on Foreign Exchange Control in Bonded Zones (promulgated by the SAFE on July 25, 2002)

Administration of Bonded Warehouses and the Goods Stored Therein Provisions (issued on December 5, 2003, by the General Administration of Customs)

Trade Remedies Laws and Regulations

Regulations of the People's Republic of China on Anti-Dumping (promulgated on March 25, 1997, revised and re-promulgated on November 26, 2001, and effective from January 1, 2002, by Order No. 328 of the State Council)

Anti-Dumping Price Security Tentative Rules (promulgated by MOFTEC on March 13, 2002); Anti-Dumping Review of New Exporters Tentative Rules (promulgated by MOFTEC on March 13, 2002)

Anti-Dumping Tax Refund Tentative Rules (promulgated by MOFTEC on March 13, 2002)

Information Disclosure for Anti-Dumping Investigation Tentative Rules (promulgated by MOFTEC on March 13, 2002)

Public Consultation of Information of Anti-Dumping Investigation Tentative Rules (promulgated by MOFTEC on March 13, 2002)

Sampling for Anti-Dumping Investigation Tentative Rules (promulgated by MOFTEC on March 13, 2002)

Foreign Trade Law of the People's Republic of China (adopted on May 12, 1994, by the 7th Sess. of the Standing Comm. of the 8th NPC and as amended on April 6, 2004, by the NPC Standing Committee)

Provisional Measures on Public Information on Investigation and Reporting of Antidumping (issued on June 25, 2002, by the Ministry of Foreign Trade & Economic Cooperation)

Several Questions Concerning the Application of Law on Trial Anti-Dumping Administrative Case Provisions (promulgated by the Supreme People's Republic of China on Nov. 21, 2002, and effective January 1, 2003)

Anti-Subsidy Regulations of the People's Republic of China (promulgated November 26, 2001, and effective on January 1, 2002, by Order No. 329 of the State Council)

Regulations of the People's Republic of China on Safeguard Measures (promulgated on November 21, 2001 and effective January 1, 2002, by Order No. 330 of the State Council)

Chapter 16

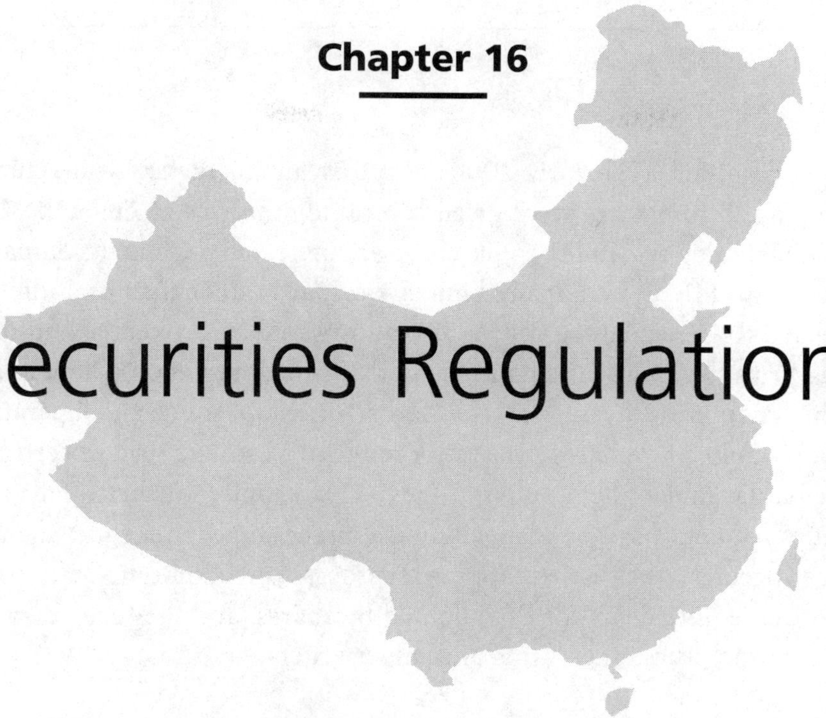

Securities Regulations

In 1981, China began allowing private enterprises to operate independently from the state. To encourage the growth of private enterprise, the Chinese Constitution was amended in 1982 to recognize the "rights" of individual businesses and private enterprises and, again, in 1988 and 2003 to grant legal protections to the "individual economy" and private property rights.[1] In the mid-1980s, China began to experiment with conversion of SOEs into shareholding enterprises as a means to raise capital and to shift the risk of operations from the state to private investors.[2] Since the early 1990s China has opened its securities markets and has developed a regulatory system to control the sale of securities on a national level. In the late 1990s, the lack of regulatory supervision led to market manipulation, embezzlement, falsified records, and other misdeeds that resulted in significant losses for investors.[3] In response, the early 2000s saw an increase in regulatory oversight, a crackdown against market manipulators, and more emphasis on corporate governance

1. Const., art. 11. The Constitution further provides that the private enterprise system is to be a "complement to the socialist public economy," and the socialist public economy, which includes state-owned enterprises and collectives, remains the "leading force in the national economy." Const., arts. 6, 7, & 11.

2. The process of selling the shares of SOEs has been defined as "corporatization," a limited form of privatization. Corporatization involves the restructuring of SOEs to allow for minority ownership without relinquishing state control of the enterprise. The state thus conveys the operational risks to SOEs while maintaining the benefits of majority ownership. *See* Bersani, *Privatization and the Creation of Stock Companies in China,* 1993 COLUMBIA BUS. L. REV. 301, 303 (1994); Zhang, *Securities Markets and Securities Regulation in China,* 22 N.C.J. INT'L LAW & COM. Reg. 557 (1997); Vandevelde, *Realizing the Re-Emergence of the Chinese Stock Market: Fact or Fiction?,* 30 V AND. J. TRANSNAT'L L. 579 (1997); Gu & Art, *Securitization of State Ownership: Chinese Securities Law,* 18 MICH. J. INT'L L. 115 (1996).

3. In 2001, a subsidiary of Sanjiu (999) Group embezzled 96 percent of the funds it raised through public offerings. *See generally* CHINA'S FINANCIAL SECTOR, THE U.S.-CHINA BUSINESS COUNCIL (March 2002).

and accountability. The early 2000s also saw an emergence of institutional investors, and foreigners were given several alternatives to enter the China market, including the ability to purchase an interest in a Chinese company or to operate an FIE as a company limited by shares rather than as a joint venture. The PRC's regulatory system also allows foreign brokerage and underwriting firms the ability to participate in the China market on a limited basis.

This chapter addresses the standards for establishing and operating a company limited by shares, the entity authorized to issue share certificates to the public under the Company Law. This chapter further analyzes the securities regulations of China including a discussion of the requirements for public offerings, the listing approval process for domestic and foreign shares, the requirements for FIEs limited by shares, and the regulatory standards for stock brokerage firms and underwriters.

A. Securities Regulatory System

In 1991, regulations were issued specifically for the Shanghai and Shenzhen stock exchanges that expressly provided for the participation of foreign investors as issuers and investors, and on a limited basis as brokers.[4] The government approved the issuance of a special class of shares—also known as "B-shares"—that are denominated in renminbi but tied to foreign currency. Since then, several Chinese companies, including foreign-invested companies, have listed on the Shenzhen Stock Exchange[5] and Shanghai Stock Exchange, as well as foreign exchanges, including Hong Kong and United States stock exchanges.[6]

4. Measures of Shanghai Municipality Governing Renminbi Special Category Shares (promulgated on November 22, 1991, by the Shanghai Branch of the People's Bank of China and the Shanghai Municipal People's Government), *reprinted in* China Laws for Foreign Business (CCH), Special Zones & Cities ¶ 91-056; Provisional Measures of Shenzhen Municipality for the Administration of renminbi Special Category Shares (jointly issued on December 5, 1991, by the People's Bank of China and the Shenzhen Municipal People's Government), *reprinted in* China Laws for Foreign Business (CCH), Special Zones & Cities ¶ 73-559; Provisional Measures of Shenzhen Municipality on Share Issuing and Trading (promulgated on May 15, 1991, by the Shenzhen Municipal People's Government), *reprinted in* China Laws for Foreign Business (CCH), Special Zones & Cities ¶ 73-553. The government is contemplating a merger of the Shanghai and Shenzhen Class B stock exchanges. Each exchange lists approximately fifty "B-share" companies, which are designed to encourage hard currency investment in Chinese companies. Shanghai's shares are traded in U.S. dollars and Shenzhen's shares are traded in Hong Kong dollars. The merger would require that B-share companies currently listed in Shenzhen be relisted as U.S. dollar–denominated shares on the Shanghai exchange. *See* Leggett, *China Weighs Plan to Merge Class B Markets,* Asian Wall Street Journal § 2, p. 11, col. 3 (Mar. 4, 1999).

5. In 2004, the Shenzhen Stock Exchange opened a sub-board for the listing of small- and medium-sized enterprises (SME Board). The SME Board includes listings of companies with less than 50 million tradable shares. The SME Board is transitional in nature pending the opening of an independent second board. The SME Board has been informally characterized as China's alternative to NASDAQ. *See generally* S. Min, *Shenzhen Exchange Ready for SME Board,* China Daily (April 6, 2004).

6. Securities Law, arts. 95–116 (outlining general standards for stock exchanges in China); Provisional Regulations on the Administration of the Issuing and Trading of Stocks (promulgated on April 22,

The Regulations Regarding the Issuing and Trading of Stock have been issued to develop the "socialist market economy" and to unify the national stock market. The Regulations Regarding the Issuing and Trading of Stock govern the issuance of all shares and trading activities within the PRC, including securities that have the function and characteristics of shares. Although the Regulations Regarding the Issuing and Trading of Stock apply to all types of trading activities, the requirements for "B-shares" are further addressed under a separate set of regulations adopted by the State Council in 1995 and a set of detailed rules adopted by the State Council Securities Commission (SCSC) in 1996.[7]

Prior to 1993, the People's Bank of China (PBOC) was the principal regulatory organization responsible for the supervision of the securities market in

---

1993, by the State Council), *reprinted in* CHINA LAWS FOR FOREIGN BUSINESS (CCH), Business Regulation ¶ 13-574 (hereinafter the "Regulations Regarding the Issuing and Trading of Stock"). In early 1998, there were over a dozen over-the-counter (OTC) stock exchanges throughout China. Provincial and municipal governments set up exchanges without the approval from the central government to allow trading for smaller companies in order to raise capital and to allow individuals to invest their money locally. In early 1998, the State Council issued regulations to close the unofficial OTC exchanges. See Chen, *Beijing Orders Cleanup of Financial Markets,* WALL ST. J. p. A12, col. 4 (Jan. 26, 1998). The central government also plans to take control over the commodities futures exchanges that are under the control of local governments. *See China to Overhaul Futures Trading,* WALL ST. J. p. A15, col. 1 (Mar. 11, 1998). *See also* Provisional Measures on the Administration of the Registration of Companies Dealing in Futures (promulgated on April 28, 1993, by the SAIC), *reprinted in* CHINA LAWS FOR FOREIGN BUSINESS (CCH), Business Regulation ¶ 13-578 (outlining conditions and requirements for commodities futures trading companies); Provisional Regulations on the Administration of Futures Trading (Order No. 267, promulgated on June 2, 1999, by the State Council), *reprinted in* CHINA LAWS FOR FOREIGN BUSINESS (CCH), Business Regulation ¶ 8-425 (outlining standards for futures exchanges, futures brokerage firms, trading rules, CSRC supervision, and penalties for violations of the law); Circular Concerning Issues Relevant to Capital Contributions to Futures Brokerages (issued on January 14, 2003, by the China Securities Regulatory Commission) (outlining the capital and prudential requirements for futures brokerage operations); Circular Concerning the Criteria, Procedure and Submission of Materials for Approving the Qualifications of Shareholders of Futures Brokerages (issued on July 2, 2002, by the China Securities Regulatory Commission). *See generally* Hou, *Derivatives and Dialectics: The Evolution of the Chinese Futures Market,* 72 N.Y.U.L. REV. 175 (1997); T. Jones, *The Uncertain State of Futures Trading in China,* CHINA L. & PRAC. (March 2003); *New Rules to Govern Futures Market Firms,* PEOPLE'S DAILY (March 24, 2004). *See* Several Issues Concerning the Trial of Futures Dispute Cases Provisions (issued on May 16, 2003, by the Supreme People's Court). The SPC Futures Litigation Provisions provide guidance to the lower courts with respect to the management of litigation matters involving claims against futures brokerage firms. Specifically, the provisions authorize a claimant to initiate a lawsuit based on both tort and contract theories of liability, and provide that a futures brokerage firm is liable for any act or omission by their brokers, subsidiaries, or any other parties that act on behalf of a brokerage firm. Further, the SPC Futures Litigation Provisions impose an obligation on futures brokerage firms to inform their clients of the risks of futures trading prior to signing a brokerage contract; otherwise, a firm will be held liable for any losses suffered by the client. *See generally* C. Jin, *The New SPC Regulations on the Hearing of Futures Disputes: Striking a Better Balance,* CHINA L. & PRAC. (September 2003); *CSRC Allows Foreign Investment in Futures Brokerages,* CHINA MARKET INTELLIGENCE, THE U.S.-CHINA BUSINESS COUNCIL (January 29, 2003).

7. Regulations of the State Council on Foreign Capital Shares Listed in China by Companies Limited by Shares (promulgated on December 25, 1995, by the State Council), *reprinted in* CHINA LAWS FOR FOREIGN BUSINESS (CCH), Business Regulation ¶ 13-600 (hereinafter "B-Share Regulations"); Detailed Rules for the Implementation of the Regulations of the State Council on Foreign Capital Shares Listed in China by Companies Limited by Shares (promulgated on May 3, 1996, by the State Council Securities Commission), *reprinted in* CHINA LAWS FOR FOREIGN BUSINESS (CCH), Business Regulation ¶ 13-604 (hereinafter "SCSC B-Share Rules").

China. In 1992, the SCSC and its administrative entity, the China Securities Regulatory Commission (CSRC), replaced the PBOC as the regulatory agencies responsible for the securities market. The SCSC consists of ministers from different government agencies including MOFTEC (now MOFCOM), the PBOC,[8] the State Development Planning Commission, Ministry of Finance, and the State Commission for the Restructuring of the Economic System (SCRES).[9] The SCSC is responsible for drafting laws and regulations concerning the securities market, developing policy for the regulations of securities, and monitoring the activities of departments and agencies related to the securities industry. In practice, the SCSC delegates its rule-making functions to the CSRC. The CSRC is the government regulatory agency that supervises the issuing and trading of stocks in China.[10] The CSRC has a number of departments responsible for specific activities including, but not limited to, the following:

(1) Department of Public Offering, which is responsible for the administration and supervision of public offerings
(2) Department of Trading and Market Supervision, which supervises the activities of the Shanghai and Shenzhen stock exchanges
(3) Department of Securities Institutions, which supervises the activities of underwriters[11]
(4) Department of Continuous Compliance, which is responsible for supervising listed companies

---

8. The PBOC is China's central bank and, prior to the creation of the CSRC, was responsible for the licensing of securities institutions such as stock brokerage firms, underwriters, and investment and mutual funds firms. For a discussion concerning the PBOC, *see* Chapter 11, Financial Regulation § A.

9. SCRES is responsible for supervising China's privatization process. SCRES must approve of the reorganization, merger, buy-out, liquidation, and sale of state-owned enterprises. As part of the institutional restructuring initiated in March 1998, the SCRES is targeted for downsizing and is to be reorganized as a research institution under the control of the State Council. For more information on the reorganization process, *see* Chapter 3, Legislating, the Judiciary, and Lawyers in China § A.3.

10. Regulations Regarding the Issuing and Trading of Stock, art. 5. The CSRC has made efforts to streamline the administrative and regulatory burdens imposed on the securities industry. In December 2002, the CSRC issued a notice abolishing 32 administrative approval items, including the preliminary examination for proposed representative offices of foreign securities firms, approval of law firms engaged in securities business, and approval for the establishment of securities investment consulting firms. State Council Decision on Abolishing First Batch of Administrative Approval Items (issued on November 1, 2002, by the State Council). *See* the Web site of the CSRC for a list of the abolished administrative approval items at http://www.csrc.gov.cn.

11. Although the PBOC (and now the CSRC) is responsible for approving the establishment of securities firms, the Department of Securities Institutions is responsible for licensing and oversight matters. This department is also involved in the supervision of law firms, accounting firms, and asset evaluation firms in conjunction with other ministries such as the Ministry of Finance and the Ministry of Justice. The MOF is the principal government agency responsible for the administration of registered accountants and accounting firms. *See* Regulations Governing the Confirmation of Qualifications of Accounting Firms and Certified Public Accountants Engaging in Securities Business Operations (promulgated on February 23, 1993, by the MOF), *reprinted in* China Laws for Foreign Business (CCH), Taxation ¶ 35-515. The MOJ is the ministry responsible for the regulation of lawyers and law firms and, together with the CSRC, it registers those lawyers that are qualified to engage in securities matters.

(5) Department of Regulations and Enforcement, which is responsible for drafting of securities laws and regulations
(6) Department of International Operations, which is responsible for the administration and supervision of overseas share listings

B. Company Law

Effective January 1, 1994, China created a national framework for the establishment of independent market-oriented entities with the promulgation of the Company Law.[12] Of relevance to the securities industry, the Company Law provides for the establishment of a company limited by shares, also referred to as a joint stock company. A company limited by shares is a corporate entity with limited liability status and can have an unlimited number of shareholders.[13] The shareholders are liable for corporate debts up to the amount of their investment. Under the Company Law, all shares must be of equal value and the minimum registered capital is RMB10,000,000 (approximately $1,168,000).[14] The stock of companies limited by shares is issued in the form of share certificates carrying equal rights and benefits for each class of stock, and at or above the par value.[15]

1. Establishment of a Company Limited by Shares

A company limited by shares may adopt the promoter method or share offering method of establishment.[16] The promoter method of establishing a company limited by shares is the purchase by promoters of all of the outstanding shares

12. Company Law of the PRC (adopted December 29, 1993, by the 5th Sess. of the Standing Comm. of the 8th NPC, revised and repromulgated on December 25, 1999, by the 13th Sess. of the Standing Comm. of the 9th NPC), *reprinted in* CHINA LAWS FOR FOREIGN BUSINESS (CCH), Business Regulation ¶ 13-518 (hereinafter referred to as the "Company Law"). For an analysis of the Company Law, *see* Torbert, *Broadening the Scope of Investment: China's New Company Law Codifies Investor Protection,* CHINA BUSINESS REVIEW 48 (May–June 1994); Han, *China's Company Law: Practicing Capitalism in a Transitional Economy,* 5 PAC. RIM L. & POL'Y 457 (1996). *See also* Provisions Regarding Several Issues on the Adjudication of Cases Involving Company Disputes (issued on November 4, 2003, by the Supreme People's Court). The SPC Company Law Disputes Interpretation introduces and defines several new concepts to Chinese law, including "nominal shareholder" (similar to a trustee shareholder), stock buy-backs, bonus stocks, and the use of securities as part of a capital contribution. The SPC interpretation also addresses the standards for the protection of minority shareholders, the fiduciary duties of directors and senior management personnel, and the circumstances under which a court may pierce the corporate veil.

13. In contrast, a limited liability company under the Company Law must have at least two but no more than fifty shareholders and is jointly established by its shareholders.

14. Company Law, art. 78.

15. Company Law, arts. 129–132.

16. Company Law, art. 74. *See also* Provisional Measures of Shanghai Municipality on the Examination and Approval of Companies Limited by Shares (promulgated on June 26, 1997, by the Shanghai Municipal People's Government), *reprinted in* CHINA LAWS FOR FOREIGN BUSINESS (CCH), Special Zones & Cities ¶ 240-095 (special requirements for approval process for companies limited by shares in Shanghai).

issued by the company (i.e., the promoters subscribe for the entire registered share capital). The share offer method, also referred to as the share float method or a public offering, refers to situations in which the promoters purchase a portion of the shares with the balance made available to the public in a public offering.[17] The consideration for stock may include cash, capitalized goods, industrial property rights, technology and nonpatented rights, land-use rights, and other forms of consideration of value.[18] All noncash forms of consideration must be evaluated and verified by a certified PRC accountant. The value of consideration from industrial property rights and technology with nonpatented rights cannot exceed 20 percent of the registered capital of a company limited by shares.

If a company limited by shares is established through the promoter method, the board of directors and the supervisory committee members are elected immediately after the promoters tender the total capital for their shares.[19] If a company is established by public offering, the promoters are required to purchase a minimum of 35 percent of the company's total shares.[20] If shares are made available in a public offering, the promoters are required to file a share offering application with the CSRC and include a number of documents concerning the company, including a prospectus, the articles of association, and information concerning the promoters.[21] A prospectus is required to provide the following information:

(1) The amount of shares subscribed to by the promoters
(2) Face value of each share and share issue price
(3) Total amount of bearer shares issued
(4) Rights and obligations of subscribers
(5) Time limits for share subscription and notification that subscribers may revoke their subscription if the offering is undersubscribed[22]

Shares that are sold in a public offering may only be underwritten by authorized securities brokerage firms. The Company Law further requires that a consignment sales agreement be executed between the brokerage firm, the promoters, and the company.[23] The name of the brokerage firm must be disclosed at the time of application.

The promoters of shares offered in a public offering are also required to contract with a financial institution for purposes of collecting share funds

17. Company Law, art. 74.
18. Company Law, art. 80.
19. Company Law, art. 82.
20. Company Law, art. 83.
21. Company Law, art. 84.
22. Company Law, arts. 87–88.
23. Company Law, art. 89.

from subscribers. The financial institution responsible for collecting share funds is required to hold the funds in trust and to provide subscribers with receipt of payment.[24] After an offering is completely sold, the capital funds are verified and a capital verification certificate is issued.

Within thirty days of receipt of issuance of the verification certificate, the promoters are required to schedule an organizational meeting that is open to the subscribers. If the issued shares have not been fully subscribed, or if the promoters fail to timely schedule an organizational meeting, the subscribers have the discretion to request a refund from the promoters and all interest on the monies held by the financial institution.[25] The promoters are required to notify the various subscribers of the date of the organizational meeting fifteen days in advance of the meeting. The Company Law requires that a subscriber with more than one-half of the total share amount be required to attend the organizational meeting. The organizational meeting shall address the following issues and concerns:

(1) Evaluate the report of the promoters with respect to the status of the establishment of the company
(2) Adopt the company's articles of association
(3) Elect members of the board of directors and the supervisory committee
(4) Examine and verify the expenses incurred with respect to the establishment of the company
(5) Examine and verify the share valuation methods of the promoters

The promoters and subscribers can also adopt a resolution not to establish the company due to major changes in business conditions, force majeure, or other factors that directly affect the viability of the enterprise.[26]

Within thirty days of the organizational meeting, the board of directors of the company is required to apply for registration with the SAIC. The registration application must include the minutes of the organizational meeting, articles of association, financial audit report concerning the company's organizational expenses, capital verification certificate, and information concerning the board members and legal representative.[27] The SAIC has thirty days to approve or reject the registration application. Upon receipt of a business license, the company is required to make a public announcement concerning its establishment. A company limited by shares is required to promptly deliver share certificates to the shareholders after registration is

24. Company Law, art. 90.
25. Company Law, art. 91.
26. Company Law, art. 92.
27. Company Law, art. 94.

approved.[28] The promoters of the company assume responsibility for all debts, losses, and expenses incurred during the course of the organizational period. In the event that the company is unable to secure registration and approval, the promoters are liable for repayment of share subscription funds and bank deposit interest amounts to the subscribers.[29]

A subsequent public offering may be made only after one year from the date of the most recent issue, and all prior offerings must be fully subscribed.[30] Additional offerings can be made only if the company has been continuously profitable and paying dividends for a period of three consecutive years, and that the profit rate is equal to or in excess of the interest rate on a bank deposit for the same time period.[31] A company may issue new shares only with the approval of the shareholders.[32]

The transfer or trading of shares is permitted under the Company Law subject to certain restrictions. The stock held by the promoters may not be transferred for a period of three years from the date of establishment of the company.[33] An application for the listing of shares requires approval by the CSRC and is based upon the following conditions:

(1) That the shares to be listed have already been issued to the public with the approval of the CSRC
(2) That the total amount of the company's share capital shall not be less than RMB50,000,000
(3) That the company has been profitable for three years
(4) That the number of shareholders who each hold shares with a face value of more than RMB1,000 shall not be less than 1,000 individuals or entities, and that the shares issued to the public shall be more than 25 percent of the total amount of the company's shares[34]
(5) That the company has not committed any significant illegal acts for three years
(6) That the company has not made any false statements in its financial statements for a period of three years[35]

28. Company Law, art. 136.
29. Company Law, art. 97.
30. Company Law, art. 137, § 1. A subsequent offering may be made in less than twelve months involving public offerings or domestic shares listed overseas (i.e., H-Shares, N-Shares) and foreign capital shares (i.e., B-Shares). *See* Overseas Shares Regulations, art. 10; B-Shares Regulations, art. 13.
31. Company Law, art. 137.
32. Company Law, art. 138.
33. Company Law, art. 147.
34. When a company with share capital exceeds RMB400 million, the shares issued to the public shall be more than 15 percent of the total shares of the company. Company Law, art. 152, § 4.
35. Company Law, art. 152.

A publicly listed company is required to periodically to disclose to the public its financial and operational condition, and financial and accounting statements are to be published twice a fiscal year.[36]

The CSRC may suspend or terminate the trading activities of a listed company in a number of circumstances, including the following:

(1) The total share capital, distribution of share rights, or other circumstances changed such that the company no longer meets the listing requirements
(2) The company fails to make public its financial position pursuant to the law
(3) The company is found to have made false entries in its financial accounting statements
(4) The company has committed acts in violation of the law
(5) The company has incurred losses over the last three consecutive years
(6) The company has decided to dissolve, has been ordered to terminate its operations, or has filed for bankruptcy protection[37]

2. Recordkeeping/Articles of Association

A company limited by shares is required to maintain its records, including the articles of association, shareholders' list, minutes of the directors and shareholders meetings, and the financial and accounting records of the company.[38] The Company Law mandates that certain provisions be included in the articles of association, including the following matters:

(1) Name and address of the company
(2) Scope of business operations of the company
(3) Method of establishment of the company
(4) Total amount of the company's shares, value of each share, and registered capital
(5) Names or titles of the promoters and the amount of shares subscribed to by the promoters
(6) Rights and obligations of the shareholders
(7) Appointment procedures, duties, authority, and rules of procedure for the board of directors

36. Company Law, art. 156. The company is required to issue annual and midterm reports.
37. Company Law, arts. 157, 158.
38. Company Law, art. 101.

(8) The company's legal representative
(9) Appointment procedures, duties, authority, and rules of procedure for the company's supervisory committee
(10) The company's method of profit distribution
(11) The company's liquidation and dissolution procedures
(12) The company's notice procedures and methods of public announcements
(13) Items and issues requiring the approval of the shareholders at the shareholders' meeting[39]

3. Shareholders' Meetings

Under the Company Law, there are three categories of corporate governance: the shareholders take action through a shareholders' meeting, the board of directors, and the supervisory board or committee. The Company Law provides that a company limited by shares is required to hold an annual meeting of the shareholders.[40] The shareholders are the ultimate authority of a company limited by shares. A shareholders' meeting is empowered to exercise the following:

(1) Determine the company's business policies and investment plans
(2) Elect, remove, and replace directors of the company and determine the level of director compensation
(3) Elect, remove, and replace members of the supervisory committee and determine the level of compensation for supervisors
(4) Review and approve reports by the board of directors and supervisory committee
(5) Review and approve the company's budget and accounting plans
(6) Review and approve the company's plans for profit distribution and loss recovery
(7) Approve capital expenditures
(8) Approve the issuance of corporate bonds
(9) Evaluate and approve any change in the corporate status, including merger, division, dissolution, and liquidation
(10) Approve amendments to the articles of association[41]

39. Company Law, art. 79.
40. Company Law, art. 104.
41. Company Law, art. 103.

In addition to the annual meeting, the shareholders are required to convene within sixty days in the following circumstances:

(1) The number of directors is less than two-thirds of the director positions stipulated in the Company Law (i.e., five) or in the company's articles of association
(2) The company's losses are equal to or exceed one-third of the total amount of share capital
(3) A shareholder or group of shareholders holding 10 percent or more of the total outstanding shares requests a meeting
(4) The board of directors or the supervisory committee believes that a shareholders' meeting is necessary[42]

The board of directors is required to give notice of the shareholders' meeting at least thirty days prior to the meeting. The notice shall include a written agenda of the items to be addressed at the meeting, and resolutions on issues that are not listed in the agenda may not be addressed.[43] Each shareholder present at the meeting is entitled to one vote per share. Most issues are resolved by a majority vote, but amendments to the articles of association or decisions concerning a merger, division, or dissolution require the approval of a two-thirds' majority of the shareholders present at the meeting to be effective.[44] The Company Law also permits the use of a proxy vote so long as the proxy is in writing.[45]

The chairman of the board of directors is required to preside over a shareholders' meeting and, in the event the chairman is unable to preside over the meeting, the chairman may appoint the vice-chairman of the board or another director to preside over the meeting. The minutes of the shareholders' meeting shall be signed by the directors present at the meeting. The minutes, proxy letters, and resolutions are required to be maintained by the company.[46] A shareholder has the right to seek judicial relief in the people's court if any action taken at a shareholders' meeting is in violation of the laws and regulations or infringes upon the rights and interests of the shareholders.[47]

4. Board of Directors

The board of directors of a company limited by shares is elected by, and responsible to, the shareholders and is, in general, responsible for managing

42. Company Law, art. 104.
43. Company Law, art. 105.
44. Company Law, arts. 106, 107.
45. Company Law, art. 108; *see also* Regulations Regarding the Issuing and Trading of Stock, art. 65.
46. Company Law, art. 109.
47. Company Law, art. 111. For a discussion of the procedural issues for civil actions in the people's court, *see* Chapter 22, Litigation in the People's Court § A.1.

the affairs of the company. A company limited by shares is governed by a board of directors consisting of no less than five and no more that nineteen directors. A director's term may be for any length of time up to a maximum of three years, and may be re-elected to consecutive terms. Although the directors serve at the will of the shareholders, a director may be removed prior to a shareholders' meeting only for "proper" reasons.[48] The board of directors exercises the following powers:

(1) Responsibility for convening the shareholders' meetings and preparing reports for the meetings
(2) Implementation of resolutions adopted by the shareholders
(3) Development of the company's business and investment plan
(4) Development of the company's financial budget and accounting plan
(5) Development of the company's profit distribution and loss recovery plan
(6) Development of the company's plans for capital expansion and corporate bond issues[49]
(7) Development of plans for company merger, division, or dissolution
(8) Appointment and approval of the company's management and determination of management compensation
(9) Development of the company's general management system and internal administrative structure[50]

A board of directors is required to have one chairman and may have one or two vice-chairmen. The board of directors with the approval of a majority of the directors shall elect a chairman and vice-chairman. The chairman of the board of directors shall be the company's legal representative and shall preside over all meetings of the shareholders and directors, and is required to implement the resolutions of the board of directors. The chairman is also responsible for signing the company's share certificates and corporate bonds.[51]

48. Company Law, art. 115.

49. The standards for issuing corporate bonds are addressed in Chapter 6, Articles 159–173 of the Company Law. Although authorized by the Company Law, the corporate bond market is underdeveloped. Part of the problem is that the government exercises tight control over foreign debt, which includes foreign issue corporate bonds since they are denominated in foreign currency. The domestic bond market is much more active and is regulated by the CSRC. In order to obtain approval, an application is filed with the CSRC, which discloses basic information about the company and the financial aspects of the issue. The application is accompanied by the company's business registration, articles of association, asset valuation report, and investment verification report. A company may also issue bonds convertible into shares. *See* Procedures for the Control of Issuing of Bonds in Foreign Currencies by Domestic Institutions (issued on January 1, 1998, by the State Administration of Foreign Exchange), *reprinted in* 128 CHINA INTERNATIONAL BUSINESS (MOFTEC) 51 (1998) (requires the approval of SAFE for all convertible bond issues).

50. Company Law, art. 112.

51. Company Law, art. 114.

The board of directors is required to meet at least twice a year. The Company Law provides that the directors are required to receive at least ten days' notice of a board meeting unless the notice is waived by the individual directors.[52] A meeting of the directors may not be held unless a quorum (i.e., majority of the directors) is present. In order to be valid, resolutions require approval of the majority of the board members present at the meeting.[53] A board member may provide written authorization to another director to act as his or her proxy. The proxy letter is required to state the scope of the proxy's authority.

The Company Law provides that directors are legally responsible for the decisions adopted by the board. If a decision of the board of directors is found to be in violation of the law, statutory regulations, or the company's articles of association, those directors that participated in the decision are legally responsible for compensating the company for any losses sustained as a result of the improper decision.[54] The Criminal Law also provides for criminal liability for director misconduct.[55] Directors are prohibited from using their positions to usurp corporate opportunities or for personal gain.[56]

A company limited by shares is required to have a general manager who serves at the will of the board of directors. The general manager is responsible for the day-to-day management functions of the company, including the appointment of personnel, developing company policies and procedures, and financial management.[57]

5. Supervisory Committee

In addition to a board of directors, the Company Law requires that a company limited by shares establish a supervisory committee that is responsible for oversight activities and consists of at least three members. The supervisory committee is required to consist of individuals representing the interests of shareholders and employees. The exact proportion of the representatives may be set forth in the company's articles of association. A director, manager, or chief financial officer of a company may not hold a position on the supervisory committee. The term of office of a supervisor is three years and shall be elected by both the shareholders and the employees. In practice, the shareholder representatives usually are in the majority over the employee representatives.

52. Company Law, art. 116.
53. Company Law, art. 117.
54. Company Law, art. 118.
55. *See* Chapter 23, Criminal Liability for FIE Activities § A.
56. Company Law, art. 123.
57. Company Law, art. 119.

The rules of procedure and voting procedures for supervisory committees are usually set forth in the company's articles of association. The supervisory committee has the statutory authority to do the following:

(1) The right to investigate the company's financial affairs
(2) The right to supervise the activities of the directors and managers during the performance of their duties to ensure compliance with the law, statutory regulations, or the company's articles of association
(3) The right to request directors and managers to address and resolve problems that impact the interests of the company
(4) The right to propose the scheduling of an interim meeting of the shareholders
(5) The exercise of other powers of office as stipulated in the company's articles of association[58]

C. Securities Regulations

There are two categories of shares issued by companies limited by shares. The first category is ordinary shares, denominated and traded in RMB, that may be held only by Chinese individuals, legal entities, or the State. These shares are referred to as "A-Shares." The second category is special shares, which are denominated in RMB but quoted and traded in foreign exchange and may be held only by foreigners. Special shares include "B-Shares," which are traded on the Shanghai and Shenzhen stock exchanges; "H-Shares," which are traded on the Hong Kong Stock Exchange; and "N-Shares," which are traded on the New York Stock Exchange. To supplement the Company Law, the State Council, the SCSC, and the CSRC have developed a number of regulations, measures, and rules that further address the issuance and listing of stock by a company limited by shares. In 1999, the NPC promulgated the Securities Law to replace and supplement the various regulations, circulars, and policy statements issued by the State Council, the PBOC, and the CSRC.[59] Under the Securities Law, the government specifically states that it

58. Company Law, art. 126.

59. The Securities Law, which is effective July 1, 1999, and is divided into 214 articles under 12 chapters, addresses such issues as the issuance of securities, trading standards, acquisition of listed companies, rules for stock exchanges, registration requirements for list companies, standards for regulatory agencies, and liability issues. The objective of the new Securities Law is to regulate the markets at a national level, to require that all securities issued to the public comply with disclosure standards, to require that all trading be conducted on exchanges approved by the State Council, to standardize clearing and settlement methods, to require that officers of listed companies be held to certain standards, to require that stockbrokers and other intermediaries be licensed and maintain certain capital requirements, to require all decisions of regulators to be fully documented and subject to court review, and to prohibit insider trading and market manipulation. Although most of the standards set forth in the Securities Law are

encourages companies that operate in compliance with the law and "industry policies" to list their shares for public trading.[60]

1. Domestic Share Regulations: A-Shares

Under the Regulations Regarding the Issuing and Trading of Stock, the issuer must be a limited liability company that has been authorized to issue stock.[61] In applying to issue stock and to establish a new entity as a limited liability company, the following requirements must be met:

(1) Production and management plans must conform to the industrial policies of the State
(2) Only one type of common stock can be issued with equal rights for equal shares
(3) The promoter's stock shall constitute not less than 35 percent of the total stock capital planned to be issued by the company

---

expressed in a number of existing laws and regulations, this law incorporates such standards in a nationally recognized basic law. The law reconfirms the current ban on foreigners trading in A-Shares, and the use of bank funds to speculate in shares, and prohibits brokers from allowing clients to trade on margin and engage in short sales. The law also has a provision that allows share issuers and underwriters to determine the issue price of stock, which is an abandonment of the administrative rules of the CSRC, which provide guidelines on how initial public offerings are to be priced. The Securities Law includes new provisions requiring stock exchanges, brokerage firms, and other financial firms to establish compensation funds to protect clients against wrongdoing of exchange members. The law further prohibits state companies—which control the majority of China's publicly traded firms—from interfering with the management of their publicly traded subsidiaries. However, it is uncertain at this time if the law covers B-Shares, which are purchased by foreigners. *See* Yu, *Draft of Securities Law Revised,* 138 China International Business (MOFTEC) 40 (1999); Sun, *Securities Law Given Overwhelming Approval,* China Daily (Dec. 30, 1998), available on Lexis, News Library or on the Web site of China Daily at http://www.chinadaily.com.cn; *China Finance: New Rules for Securities,* EIU Views Wire (Mar. 2, 1999), available on Lexis, News Library; Kentouris, *China's New Securities Law Unclear on B-Shares,* Securities Industry News 16 (Feb. 8, 1999), available on Lexis, News Library; Peng, *CSRC Seen Lifting Curbs on IPOs, Giving Issuers More Say on Price,* South China Morning Post, Business Post, p. 4 (Jan. 20, 1999), available on Lexis, News Library, or the Web site of the South China Morning Post at http://www.scmp.com.

60. Securities Law, art. 44.

61. Regulations Regarding the Issuing and Trading of Stock, art. 7. The CSRC has issued guidelines that authorize overseas-funded companies to list on the PRC stock exchanges in November 2001. *See* Foreign Investment Issues Relating to Listed Companies Several Opinions (issued on November 8, 2001, by the Ministry of Foreign Trade & Economic Cooperation and the China Securities Regulatory Commission). Subject to the conditions in the regulations, such as MOFCOM approval, an FIE may convert into a foreign-funded company limited by shares and may raise capital through a public equity offering. The listing FIE must satisfy the requirements in the Company Law, the Securities Law, and relevant CSRC listing regulations. An applicant for listing is required to have (i) passed the foreign investment enterprise joint annual examinations for three consecutive years prior to the listing application; (ii) have a business scope consistent with applicable laws and regulations; and (iii) have a Chinese partner that has a controlling interest. The regulations apply to initial and subsequent public offerings. If the foreign parties' interest falls below 25 percent (in the conversion or offering process), the FIE must return its FIE Approval Certificate to MOFCOM. In response to the 2001 regulations, several foreign companies were authorized to list A-shares, and in December 2003, the first foreign-controlled company was allowed to list A-shares in China. Zhejiang King Refrigeration Industry Co., which is based in Shangyu, Zhejiang Province, is controlled by Taiwan's largest manufacturer of industrial air conditioners and was allowed to list under the new rules. *See First Overseas Company Lists on Shanghai Exchange,* China Market Intelligence, The U.S.-China Business Council, Jan. 21, 2004; *First Overseas Company Floats A-Shares,* China Daily (December 31, 2003).

(4) Of the total stock capital to be issued by the company, the promoter's share shall not be less than RMB30 million, except where otherwise provided for by the State
(5) The portion of stock to be issued to the public shall not be less than 25 percent of the total stock capital to be issued, and the portion to be issued to the management personnel and staff of the company shall not exceed 10 percent of the amount to be issued to the public[62]
(6) The promoter has committed no major violations of the law within the previous three years
(7) Other requirements provided by the CSRC[63]

In addition to the requirements set forth above, an existing enterprise that desires to issue stock and establish a limited liability company must meet the following requirements:

(1) The net assets of the existing enterprise may account for no less than 30 percent of the total assets, and the intangible assets may account for no more than 20 percent of the net assets at the end of the year prior to issuing stock except where otherwise provided by the CSRC
(2) The existing enterprise has been profitable for three years prior to issuing the stock[64]

An enterprise company that intends to increase its equity, in addition to meeting the requirements noted above, is also required to demonstrate the following:

(1) The proceeds from the previous stock issue are used profitably in full compliance with the terms and conditions of the enterprise's prospectus
(2) The interval since the previous stock issue is no less than twelve months

62. If the total amount of stock to be issued is in excess of RMB400 million, the CSRC may reduce the proportion to be issued to the public but no less than 10 percent of the total stock of the company. Regulations Regarding the Issuing and Trading of Stock, art. 8, § (5).

63. Regulations Regarding the Issuing and Trading of Stock, art. 8.

64. Regulations Regarding the Issuing and Trading of Stock, art. 9. In September 2003, the CSRC tightened the rules under which a company limited by shares may conduct an initial public offering. As of January 1, 2004, a company must be established for at least three years and must not have undergone significant restructuring (in either its business or management team) for at least three years before it can apply for an initial public offering. The CSRC also mandates that an IPO's total value is limited to twice the unaudited net asset value of the company in the year prior to the public offering. The CSRC further provides that controlling shareholders may purchase no more than 30 percent of the total value of the new offering. *See* Notice on the Further Standardization of Work Related to Initial Public Offerings (issued on September 19, 2003, by the China Securities Regulatory Commission and effective October 1, 2003). *See generally CSRC Tightens IPO Requirements,* CHINA MARKET INTELLIGENCE, THE U.S.-CHINA BUSINESS COUNCIL (September 24, 2003).

(3) The company has committed no major violations of the law since its previous stock issue
(4) Other requirements provided for by the CSRC[65]

a. Application Procedures for Public Offering

A party that intends to issue stock to the public is first required to submit an application for preliminary approval to the State Administration of Industry and Commerce or subordinate office. The application must be accompanied by the prospectus and other supporting documents prepared by an accounting firm, asset appraisal organization, law firm, and other professional institutions.[66] An application for approval to issue shares is required to include the following information and documentation:

(1) Agreement between the promoters concerning the share issue
(2) Approval documents demonstrating the establishment of a limited liability company
(3) Business license or registration certificate for the company issued by the SAIC
(4) Articles of association
(5) Prospectus
(6) Feasibility study for the company
(7) Verified financial reports for the last three years
(8) Legal opinions of MOJ-approved securities lawyers[67]
(9) Asset appraisal report
(10) Consignment sales agreement with underwriter for the stock issue[68]

---

65. Securities Law, arts. 19, 20; Regulations Regarding the Issuing and Trading of Stock, art. 10.

66. Regulations Regarding the Issuing and Trading of Stock, art. 12, § (1).

67. A legal opinion is one of the documents required when an issuer applies to the CSRC for approval of a public offering. The required contents and format of a legal opinion prepared by a PRC attorney are outlined in a circular issued by the CSRC. *See* Code No. 12 on the Rules for the Compilation of Reports of Information Disclosure by Public Shares Issuing Companies—Legal Opinions and Lawyer's Reports on the Public Issuing of Shares (promulgated on March 1, 2001, by the CSRC), *reprinted in* China Laws for Foreign Business (CCH), Business Regulation ¶ 13-528. A legal opinion must state conclusive opinions concerning a number of topics affecting the issuer including, but not limited to, the major claims and debts, assets, environmental protection standards, tax liability, and the purpose of the funds to be raised in the public offering. An attorney may request an issuer to provide a written guarantee for certain factual information; however, the attorney is still bound by an obligation to exercise due diligence in its investigation and evaluation, and is not permitted to formulate a legal opinion containing false or misleading information. Under Article 35 of the Regulations Regarding the Issuing and Trading of Stock, an attorney is required to verify the truthfulness, accuracy, and completeness of the opinions he or she prepares. For other statutory obligations of PRC legal counsel, *see* Law of the People's Republic of China on Lawyers (adopted May 15, 1996, by the 19th Sess. of the Standing Committee of the 8th NPC), *reprinted in* China Laws for Foreign Business (CCH), Business Regulation ¶ 16-650.

68. Regulations Regarding the Issuing and Trading of Stock, arts. 13, 14. *See* Notice on Further Standardizing the Activities Related to Initial Public Offerings (issued on September 19, 2003, by the CSRC). Under the IPO Notice, a joint stock company must have been established for at least three years

If preliminary approval is granted by the SAIC or subordinate office, the application is forwarded to the CSRC for further review and evaluation. If the application is approved by the CSRC, the company is authorized to issue stock to the public.[69] However, the issuer is required to publish an approved prospectus within five business days before the stock sale commences. Prior to approval for the public offering, the prospectus and its contents cannot be released to the public.[70] The regulations provide that a prospectus is valid for a period of six months and is required to contain the following information:

(1) The name and address of the company
(2) Curriculum vitae of the promoter and the issuer
(3) Purpose of raising the funds
(4) The total amount of the current capital stock, the category and amount of stock to be issued, face value and selling price of each share, the net capital value of each stock before the issue and the net capital value of each stock after the issue, and expenses and commissions for the issuing of stock
(5) The percentage of stock subscribed to by the promoter in the first issue, the structure of stock rights and certificates for capital verification
(6) Name of the underwriter of the public offering
(7) Time, location of the public offering, and the method of subscription and payment
(8) Purpose for the funds to be raised
(9) Anticipated losses and profits of the company, and risks of investment
(10) The short-term development plans of the company
(11) Important contracts of the company
(12) Significant litigation and claims against the company
(13) Biographies of the directors and supervisors of the company

to apply for an IPO, versus the prior one year rule. The applicant must have no significant changes in its business activities and corporate management personnel in the last three years. The IPO Notice gives the CSRC more time to track the performance of a joint stock company interested in an IPO and may discourage companies from misrepresenting financial performance. The IPO Notice focuses on protecting the interests of small and medium size shareholders by requiring that the transactions between the stock issuer and its large shareholders not exceed 30 percent of the stock issuer's total transaction volume, which will prevent large shareholders from manipulating the company by share transactions. This requirement may help ensure the independence of the listed company from any affiliated companies. The IPO Notice further requires IPO applicants to describe the use of the funds raised through the offering, and the funds raised must not exceed twice the unaudited net asset value of the company in the previous year.

69. Regulations Regarding the Issuing and Trading of Stock, art. 12. *See also* Guidelines of the CSRC Issue Examination Board on the Examination and Approval of Initial Public Offerings (issued on May 11, 2001, by the CSRC) (outline the standards for which the CSRC Issue Examination Board may approve or reject an application to issue securities); Guidelines on the CSRC Issue Examination Board on Examination and Approval of New Issues by Listed Companies (issued on May 11, 2001, by the CSRC).

70. Regulations Regarding the Issuing and Trading of Stock, art. 19.

(14) Description of the production and operations of the company for the past three years
(15) The financial reports audited by an accounting firm over the past three years
(16) The use and application of funds raised in previous public offerings
(17) Other information required by the CSRC[71]

The promoters or directors of the company's board of directors and the representatives of the underwriters are required to confirm by signature that the prospectus contains no false or misleading statements or omissions of fact, and that the signatories promise to be jointly responsibile for the issue.[72] The prospectus is also required to print the following disclaimer on its cover:

> The promoter shall guarantee that the prospectus is true, accurate and complete. Any decision made by the government and State securities management departments concerning the current issue does not necessarily show substantial judgment or guarantee the value of the stock to be issued or the gains of investors.[73]

After the expiration of the six-month validity period, the prospectus is invalid and the stock sales activities must cease.[74]

b. Consignment Sales/Underwriters

All shares issued to the public are required to be distributed to the public by underwriters in conformance with a consignment or underwriting agreement.[75] A consignment agreement is required by the Securities Law to contain certain mandatory language.[76] An underwriter is required to verify the truthfulness, accuracy, and completeness of the prospectus and other

71. Regulations Regarding the Issuing and Trading of Stock, art. 15.
72. Regulations Regarding the Issuing and Trading of Stock, art. 17.
73. Regulations Regarding the Issuing and Trading of Stock, art. 16.
74. Regulations Regarding the Issuing and Trading of Stock, art. 19.
75. Regulations Regarding the Issuing and Trading of Stock, art. 20. A securities company should, in accordance with laws and administrative regulations, sell on consignment those securities publicly issued by the issuer. The sale of securities on consignment may be on a commission basis or exclusive sale basis. A sale on a commission basis is where the securities company sells the securities on behalf of the issuer, and at the conclusion of the consignment sale period those securities that have not been sold are returned to the issuer. The exclusive sale method of consignment is where the securities company purchases all the issuer's securities in accordance with an agreement, or purchases all those securities remaining at the conclusion of the consignment sale period. Securities Law, art. 21. The issuer of publicly issued securities has the right to freely choose the securities company that will conduct the consignment sale. Securities companies are prohibited from engaging in tactics that involve unfair competition for the purpose of soliciting business relating to the consignment sale of securities. Securities Law, art. 22.
76. The Securities Law requires that a consignment agreement include the following items: (1) the parties' names, addresses, and the names of their respective legal representatives; (2) the type, quantity, total value, and issue price of the securities that are the subject of the commission sale or exclusive sale; (3) the period of the commission sale or exclusive sale as well as the starting and finishing dates; (4) the

publicity materials for the public offering. If an underwriter discovers a false or misleading statement in a prospectus, it is prohibited from proceeding with a public offering.[77] If the total face value of the stock to be issued to the public exceeds RMB30 million or the total amount to be sold is expected to exceed RMB50 million, the public offering must be sold by a consignment sales group made up of at least two underwriters.[78] The public offering shall not be less than ten days nor greater than ninety days.[79] The underwriters are required to submit written status reports of the public offering to the CSRC within fifteen days after the expiration of the sales period.[80]

c. Stock Listing

The listing and trading of stock may be conducted only at an exchange approved by the CSRC.[81] In order to be approved for listing, a company must meet the following requirements:

(1) The stock of the company has been issued to the public
(2) The total capital stock after the public offering is not less than RMB50 million
(3) There are at least 1,000 individual stockholders who each hold more than RMB1,000 of stock at par value to make the total par value of the shares not less than RMB10 million
(4) The company has made a profit for the last three years consecutively; and
(5) Other requirements as provided for by the CSRC[82]

---

method of, and date for, payment in relation to the commission sale or exclusive sale; (5) expenses relating to the commission sale or exclusive sale and the method of account settlement; (6) liabilities for breach of the agreement; and (7) other matters stipulated by the CSRC. Securities Law, art. 23.

77. Securities Law, art. 24; Regulations Regarding the Issuing and Trading of Stock, art. 21. If false information is discovered and sales have already commenced, the underwriter is required to cease all sales activities and to take corrective action.

78. In contrast to the regulations, the Securities Law provides that where the total face value of securities to be issued publicly exceeds RMB50 million, the consignment sale must be conducted by a consignment sales group. The consignment sales group should be composed of the securities company in charge of the consignment sale as well as other securities companies participating in the consignment sale. Securities Law, art. 25. The principal underwriter in a group sale is required to meet certain standards and conditions. *See* Notice on Issuing the Interim Measure on the Appraisal of Main Underwriter's Professional Qualifications and Quality (issued on September 13, 2002, by the CSRC).

79. Regulations Regarding the Issuing and Trading of Stock, art. 24. The Securities Law provides that the period of a commission sale or exclusive sale should not exceed 90 days. During the period of the commission sale or exclusive sale, the securities company should ensure that subscribers have priority to buy the securities sold on commission or sold exclusively, and the securities company should not retain for itself in advance the securities to be sold on commission, or purchase in advance and retain for itself the securities that are the subject of exclusive sale. Securities Law, art. 26.

80. Securities Law, art. 27; Regulations Regarding the Issuing and Trading of Stock, art. 26.

81. Securities Law, art. 29; Regulations Regarding the Issuing and Trading of Stock, art. 29.

82. Regulations Regarding the Issuing and Trading of Stock, art. 31.

A company applying for listing of its stock is required to provide the listing committee of the stock exchange with its financial records, its latest prospectus, company registration documents, and a letter of recommendation from a member of the stock exchange.[83] The listing committee is required to make a determination within twenty working days.[84] A company that is approved for listing is required to publish a stock listing announcement that provides for the date of approval of listing, the conditions of the issue and structure of stock rights, information concerning the directors, supervisors, and key management personnel, and the financial performance of the company.[85] To protect investors, the CSRC has adopted a number of regulations outlining the standards and procedures for the de-listing of financially distressed companies from trading on the Shanghai and Shenzhen stock exchanges.[86]

d. Disclosure Requirements

The disclosure requirements in the law mandate that all listed firms are required to prepare and submit midterm and annual reports to the CSRC.[87]

83. When applying to the CSRC for listed trading of its shares, a company should lodge the following documents: (1) the listing report; (2) the resolution of the shareholders' general meeting applying for listing; (3) the company's articles of association; (4) the company's business license; (5) company financial accounts reports for the last three years or for the period since the establishment of the company; (6) legal opinions and a letter of recommendation from the securities company; and (7) the most recent prospectus. Securities Law, art. 45. *See also* Standards for Examination and Verification of Share Issues Memorandum (No. 16): Examination and Verification Requirements for Special Item Review of Companies Initially Offering Shares to the Public (issued on February 28, 2003, by the CSRC) (provides that the CSRC may require an applicant to engage a second accounting firm to do follow-up reviews); Notice Regarding Examination Standards on Reduction, Exemption and Reimbursement of Taxes; Government Subsidies and Appropriations (issued on September 6, 2002, by the CSRC) (to increase corporate transparency, these rules require applicants for IPOs or new shares to disclose information on all government subsidies and tax reductions or rebates). *See generally CSRC Ups Information Disclosure Ante for New Share Issuance,* China Market Intelligence, The U.S.-China Business Council (September 11, 2002). *See also* Guidelines Re Contents and Formats for Information Disclosures by Companies That Offer Securities to the Public (issued on March 24, 2003, by the CSRC) (outline the standards for prospectuses and provides that the valid period of a prospectus is extended from three to six months).

84. *See* Notice on Matters Regarding Further Regulation of the Initial Public Offers and Listing of Shares (issued on September 19, 2003, by the CSRC) (standards that further control new listings); Regulations Regarding the Administration of the Listing Approval Committee (issued on December 11, 2003, by the CSRC) (rules mandate public distribution of information about domestic listing hearings such as meeting dates, committee member attendance, and voting results); Supplementary Notification Concerning Guidelines on Implementation of Working Procedures of CSRC's Issuance Examination Committee (issued on July 18, 2002, by the CSRC). For the conditions for issuing new shares by listed companies, *see* Notification of the Relevant Requirements on Listed Companies' Issuance of New Shares (issued on July 24, 2002, by the CSRC).

85. Regulations Regarding the Issuing and Trading of Stock, art. 34.

86. Implementing Procedures for the Suspension and Termination of Listing of Loss-Making Listed Companies (issued on November 30, 2001, by the CSRC); Supplementary Provisions to the Implementing Procedures for the Suspension and Termination of Listing of Loss-Making Listed Companies (issued on November 30, 2001, by the CSRC). *See generally* M. Baigen & R. Sun, *Supplementary Rules for Listing Suspension and Termination,* China L. & Prac. (May 2003).

87. Securities Law, arts. 58, 60; Regulations Regarding the Issuing and Trading of Stock, art. 57. The midterm report is due within two months after the end of the first 180 days of the accounting year

All documents published by a company relating to the issuance or listing of shares or bonds must be authentic, accurate, and complete and must not contain any false or misleading information or omissions.[88] The midterm report is required to contain a financial statement of the company, an analysis of the company's operations and objectives, a review of major litigation involving the company, and other issues that affect the financial position of the company.[89] The company's annual report is required to be more detailed than the midterm report and include the following information and documentation:

(1) Information concerning the company, its products, and services
(2) Information concerning the company's industry sector and business climate
(3) Information concerning the company's assets
(4) Information concerning the total number of shareholders, outstanding capital stock of the company, and major shareholders
(5) Information concerning the directors, supervisors, and senior management personnel
(6) Information concerning the financial status of the company, including a comparative financial report
(7) Information concerning major litigation and other matters that may affect the company's financial performance[90]

In addition to the midterm and annual reports, a company is also required to file a report with the stock exchange and the CSRC in situations involving "major" events that have a relatively significant impact on the market value of a listed company's shares. Major events include, but are not

---

and an audited annual report is due within four months of the end of the accounting year. *See also* Notice on Disclosure of Information Required by Listed and Pre-IPO Companies According to the New Accounting Principles and Systems (issued by the CSRC on June 26, 2001) (provides that, starting in 2001, listed companies are required to prepare their interim reports using new accounting rules).

88. Securities Law, art. 59. Directors or officers of the issuer or personnel from Securities companies that are responsible for misleading or false information are personally liable for losses sustained. Securities Law, art. 63.

89. Regulations Regarding the Issuing and Trading of Stock, art. 58.

90. Securities Law, art. 61; Regulations Regarding the Issuing and Trading of Stock, art. 59. *See* Contents and Format for Information Disclosures by Companies that Offer Securities to the Public Guidelines (No. 2): Contents and Format of Annual Reports (issued on January 6, 2003, by the China Securities Regulatory Commission); Notice on Amendment of "Guideline No. 2 of the Content and Format of Information Disclosure of Companies that Publicly Issue Securities: Content and Format of Annual Report" (issued on December 22, 2003, by the CSRC). The CSRC Disclosure Guidelines regulate the content and timing of public companies' annual reports and require the responsible person of a company, the responsible person in charge of accounting work, and the responsible person of an accounting entity to guarantee the veracity and completeness of the financial statements set forth in an annual report. Further, the guidelines require the board of directors to evaluate in its report the overall business of the company during the reporting period.

limited to, large contracts, changes to company business policy or operations, investments requiring large sums of funds, large debts incurred by the company or defaults of debt, large operational losses, laws and government regulations affecting the company's operation, significant changes to the board of directors, increase or reduction in shares by a majority shareholder, and significant litigation or claims against the company.[91] A company is required to publicly disclose information concerning any major event affecting the company. However, with the permission of the stock exchange, a listed company can refrain from full disclosure if release of the information will damage the company's interests.

A company is required to make public disclosures through national newspapers or magazines designated by the CSRC, or through local publications approved by the stock exchange.[92] All information submitted to, or received by, the CSRC is public information except for commercial secrets and information concerning investigations of violations of law.[93] A listed company has an affirmative duty to publicly correct any misleading report that may affect the market price of the company's shares.[94]

e. Limitations on Share Ownership/Transfer

The Company Law provides that the shares held by its promoters may not be sold or assigned for a period of three years commencing from the date of establishment of the company.[95] A company limited by shares is prohibited from purchasing its own shares except for purposes of cancellation of stock to reduce its capital or by merging with another company that holds its

---

91. Securities Law, art. 62; Regulations Regarding the Issuing and Trading of Stock, art. 60. The Securities Law provides that the following situations are considered to be significant incidents requiring reporting to the CSRC and public disclosure: (1) a significant change in the business direction by the company or a change in the company's scope of business; (2) a significant investment undertaken by the company and any significant decisions on the purchase of assets; (3) the conclusion of a significant contract by the company, which is likely to impact the company's assets, liabilities, rights and interests, or the company's operational results; (4) the incurrence of a significant debt by the company or default on a contractual obligation and inability to pay off a significant debt as it comes due; (5) the sustaining of significant losses by the company or other major loss that are in excess of 10 percent of the company's net assets; (6) any significant changes to the company's production operations; (7) a change in the chairman of the board of directors, or in over one-third of its directors or managers; (8) a significant change in the ownership interest of a shareholder holding greater than 5 percent of the company's shares; (9) a decision by the company to reduce its capital, merge, sell off into smaller entities, dissolve, or apply for bankruptcy; (10) the involvement of the company in significant litigation; or (11) other matters provided for in laws or administrative regulations. Securities Law, art. 62. *See also* Notice of Issuance of "Questions and Answers on the Standards Regarding Disclosure of Information for Companies with Publicly Issued Securities (No. 1)" (issued on January 15, 2004, by the CSRC).

92. Securities Law, art. 64; Regulations Regarding the Issuing and Trading of Stock, art. 63.

93. Securities Law, art. 65; Regulations Regarding the Issuing and Trading of Stock, art. 64. The CSRC is required to issue a public notice if a listed company is delisted. Securities Law, art. 66.

94. Regulations Regarding the Issuing and Trading of Stock, art. 61.

95. Company Law, art. 147.

shares.[96] The stock purchased by the company must be cancelled within ten days of purchase.

The regulations require that directors, supervisors, and senior management personnel disclose to the CSRC and the stock exchange their personal trading activities concerning the company's stock. If there are any changes to the percentage of shares held, directors, supervisors, and officers are required to report to the CSRC within ten days of the purchase, sale, or transfer of shares.[97]

The Regulations Regarding the Issuing and Trading of Stock prohibit short swing profits. The regulations provide that the company owns any profit derived from the purchase or sale of shares by a director, supervisor, or shareholder that holds a 5 percent or greater interest in a company within six months after purchase or sale.[98]

Professional service providers who have access to confidential information concerning the public offering such as accountants, lawyers, and asset appraisal firms are prohibited from buying or holding shares during the distribution period or six months thereafter.[99] In addition, the Regulations Regarding the Issuing and Trading of Stock provide that professionals involved in the preparation of reports for listed companies are prohibited from purchasing or holding shares in listed companies for a period of five

96. Company Law, art. 149.

97. Securities Law, art. 41; Regulations Regarding the Issuing and Trading of Stock, art. 62. The CSRC issued rules in January 1999 providing that companies making an initial public offering may not issue shares to staff members. Under prior rules, companies making an IPO were required to set aside 10 percent of the shares for staff. This rule led to speculative practices sparked by staff share offers. *Ban on Staff Shares,* China Economic Review (Jan. 23, 1999), available on Lexis, News Library. *See also* Administration of Disclosure of Information on the Change of Shareholdings in Listed Companies Procedures (issued on September 28, 2002, by the China Securities Regulatory Commission) (hereinafter the "Change of Shareholder Disclosure Procedures"). The CSRC Change of Shareholder Disclosure Procedures require public disclosure of certain shareholding activities. The new regulations cover any purchase of listed company shares with the intent of gaining "control" and other listed transactions. The CSRC Change of Shareholder Disclosure Procedures impose disclosure obligations on defined persons, including share controllers (such as proxy holders) and shareholders in listed Chinese companies. The procedures require covered persons to submit a report to the CSRC and the stock exchange in response to specified events, to notify the issuer, and to make a public announcement. If the transaction will result in a controlling stake (30 percent or more), the purchaser is to submit an acquisition report to the CSRC. Covered persons are to file the above-mentioned report when (i) their holdings cross (either up or down) the 5 percent threshold (holder-initiated transactions of such shares may be restricted); or (ii) for existing 5 percent holders, when its holdings vary by 5 percent of the company's total shares (with resale prohibitions provided in the Procedures). The covered person is prohibited from transacting in the company's issued shares within three or two working days after the required public announcement, respectively. In either event, the covered person is to make a public announcement regarding the transaction within two working days of transaction consummation. Such announcement is to be made within three working days for transfers involving state-owned shares. If a covered person's share varies by 1 percent of the company's total shares by virtue of transactions on a stock market, the covered person is required to publicly announce such a transaction.

98. Securities Law, art. 42; Regulations Regarding the Issuing and Trading of Stock, art. 38.

99. Securities Law, art. 39; Regulations Regarding the Issuing and Trading of Stock, art. 40.

working days before publication of the audit report, asset valuation report, or legal opinions that they prepare.[100]

The China Securities Regulatory Commission has adopted regulations concerning the standards and procedures for public company takeovers.[101]

f. Corporate Governance Standards

The government has adopted corporate governance standards for listed companies in the PRC.[102] The Listed Company Governance Guidelines provide that listed companies are required to be wholly independent from their controlling shareholders in terms of personnel, assets, finance, organization, and business activities. The Guidelines allow for cumulative voting in most corporate actions, including the election of directors. They require cumulative voting for directors in listed companies with a controlling shareholder. The Guidelines also allow members of the board of directors, independent directors, and certain shareholders to hold voting proxies. However, the Guidelines are not clear whether such proxies are irrevocable or revocable.

The CSRC requires that listed companies have at least two "independent" directors on the company's board of directors.[103] An independent director is a person who has no employment or management position in the listed company other than that of a director, and who has no relationship to the listed company or its shareholders. The purpose of this rule is to reduce the potential for undue influence by the company upon the director and to ensure that the independence and objectivity of the director is preserved. A listed company must also include at least one professional accountant as a

---

100. Regulations Regarding the Issuing and Trading of Stock, art. 40.

101. *See* Chapter 19, Mergers, Acquisitions, and Divisions § C. Administration of the Takeover of Listed Companies Procedures (promulgated on September 28, 2002, by the China Securities Regulatory Commission) (hereinafter the "CSRC Takeover Provisions"). *See also* Notice on Relevant Issues in Transferring the State-owned Shares and Legal Person Shares of Listed Companies to Foreign Investors (issued on November 1, 2002, by the CSRC and the Ministry of Finance) (hereinafter the "State Shares Notice"). The State Shares Notice allows for the transfer of Chinese non-listed shares to foreign investors. Any transfer of state-owned shares is to be approved by MOF. Full payment of the purchase price is required before such transfer can be legally registered. Non-listed shares acquired by foreign investors may not be resold within 12 months after the transfer. Foreign investors may not acquire a Chinese listed company through purchase of shares on China's stock exchanges. *See also* Securities Law, arts. 78–94.

102. Listed Company Governance Guidelines (issued on January 7, 2002, by the China Securities Regulatory Commission and the State Economic and Trade Commission). Effective after May 2004, party members and government officials are prohibited from holding a post in an enterprise, and those officials that currently hold concurrent posts are required to resign. The purpose of this rule is to prevent officials from obtaining corrupt economic benefits from enterprises. *See Officials Banned from Company Posts,* Xinhua News Agency (March 25, 2004) (in support of the new rule, the article quotes Liu Suhua, of the CCP Party School stating that "[i]f one government official has a post in an enterprise, it is very likely that the enterprise will enjoy some preferential policies and benefits from him.")

103. Guidelines for Independent Directors in Listed Companies (issued on August 16, 2001, by the CSRC) (outline qualifications for independent directors and procedures for nomination, appointment, and replacement of independent directors).

member of its board of directors. Independent directors have some special rights, including the right to review and approve substantial transactions before submission to the entire board of directors for approval. Independent directors may also suggest that the board appoint or remove the company's accounting firm, convene a special shareholders' meeting, to convene a board of directors meeting, or appoint an outside auditor or consultant. Consistent with the 2001 CSRC rules on independent directors, the 2003 Listed Company Governance Guidelines also state that independent directors have fiduciary duties to the company and its shareholders, and that independent directors are to comprise the majority of any auditing, nomination, or compensation committees established by the board of directors. Furthermore, the Guidelines provide that at least one independent director on the auditing committee is to be a professional accountant.

The CSRC has issued regulations outlining standards to regulate cash flow between listed companies and their controlling shareholders or affiliates.[104] Pursuant to the CSRC Notice Re Cash Flow, controlling shareholders and affiliates of listed companies are prohibited from requiring a listed company to pay the shareholder/affiliates salaries, welfare and pension payments, insurance premiums, and similar costs and expenses. The Notice further prohibits the flow of cash between listed companies and controlling shareholders, including the issuance of loans, assumption of debt obligations, or provision of loan guarantees. For appropriated funds in violation of the Notice, listed companies and their shareholders/affiliates are required to return at least 30 percent of the appropriated funds annually until the funds are fully returned. The CSRC Notice also imposes liability on responsible management personnel and controlling shareholders of the listed company for activities in violation of the Notice.

g. Penalties and Investigations

The CSRC is the government agency responsible for investigating violations of the Regulations Regarding the Issuing and Trading of Stock. The stock exchanges are allowed to police and enforce their members independently of the CSRC.[105] The following activities may subject an individual or entity to

104. Several Issues Concerning the Regulation of Cash Flows between Listed Companies and Their Affiliates and Security Provided to Outside Parties by Listed Companies (issued on August 28, 2003, by the China Securities Regulatory Commission) (hereinafter the "CSRC Notice Re Cash Flow"). *See generally* M. Baigen & R. Sun, *Cash Flows and External Security: The CSRC Addresses Some Old Issues,* China L. & Prac. (November 2003).

105. Securities Law, arts. 166–174 (authorizing the CSRC to investigate violations of the law); Regulations Regarding the Issuing and Trading of Stock, art. 76.

fines, administrative penalties, civil liability, or criminal liability by the CSRC or the stock exchanges:

(1) Engaging in stock trading outside the approved stock exchanges
(2) Making false or misleading statements or omissions concerning information that is material to the sale of stock
(3) Monopolizing stock market prices by collaboration or by influencing stock prices by releasing false information
(4) Engaging in manipulation of stock prices by collaborating with other persons to withhold transfer of ownership in stock
(5) Disrupting the operation of the stock market by selling or issuing offers to sell shares that the party has no authorization to sell
(6) Failing to obtain approval to make a public offer or for listing shares
(7) Failing to submit the required disclosure reports
(8) Forging, altering, or destroying the operational records or accounting books of the company in order to affect the issuance or trading of the company's stock[106]

A company that issues shares without approval, by means of deception, or in a method and manner inconsistent with the law is subject to monetary penalties, disqualification for issuing shares, and forfeiture of proceeds.[107] The directors, supervisors, and senior management personnel are also subject to penalties and civil liability for violations of the Regulations Regarding the Issuing and Trading of Stock.[108] An underwriter is subject to fines and the revocation of its business license for violations of the Regulations Regarding the Issuing and Trading of Stock, including a failure to follow sales procedures, using a company's shares as collateral, collecting unreasonable commissions, trading stocks for clients, providing clients with loss guarantees, or providing financing for stock trading.[109]

106. Securities Law, art. 71; Regulations Regarding the Issuing and Trading of Stock, art. 74.

107. Securities Law, arts. 175–210; Regulations Regarding the Issuing and Trading of Stock, art. 70.

108. Regulations Regarding the Issuing and Trading of Stock, arts. 17, 70.

109. Securities Law, art. 73; Regulations Regarding the Issuing and Trading of Stock, art. 71. Article 43 of the Regulations Regarding the Issuing and Trading of Stock prohibits a financial organization from lending monies to purchase stock, and Article 44 prohibits securities institutions from lending stock of customers for collateral purposes. The CSRC issued warnings to the Haitong Securities Co., Ltd., and the securities operation department of the Shenzhen Development Bank for illegal stock trading on behalf of clients using credit. *See Record of Events* (October–December 1996), CHINA LAW 104 (1997). The Securities Law prohibits securities companies and their employees from engaging in the following types of fraudulent behavior detrimental to their clients' interests: (1) acting contrary to a client's authorization with respect to the purchasing and selling of securities; (2) failing to supply the client, within the stipulated period of time, with written documentation confirming a transaction; (3) embezzling securities authorized to be bought or sold for a client, or embezzling funds in a client's account; (4) privately purchasing or selling the securities in a client's account, or purchasing or selling securities in the name of the client; (5) inducing the client to engage in unnecessary purchasing and selling of securities, with the aim

The Regulations Regarding the Issuing and Trading of Stock provide that accountants, asset appraisal firms, and attorneys are subject to monetary penalties and the suspension or revocation of their licenses if they produce false and seriously misleading documents or documents with major omissions.[110] A violation of the law by professional service providers may result in a monetary fine of between RMB30,000 and RMB300,000.

The law prohibits insiders and other individuals who have obtained inside information from trading in the shares of a company.[111] The Securities Law provides that the following persons are deemed to be persons with inside information relating to securities trading:

(1) Company directors, supervisors, managers, deputy managers, and relevant high-level administrative officials involved in the issue of shares or company bonds
(2) A shareholder who holds more than 5% of the shares in a company
(3) High-level administrative officials in a company that holds a controlling interest in a second company that issues shares
(4) Officials who are able to obtain information relating to securities trading due to their positions held in the company
(5) Employees of the securities supervision and administration body as well as other officials engaged in the regulation of securities trading pursuant to their legal duties
(6) Relevant officials of social intermediary organizations, securities registration and account settlement organizations, and securities trading service organizations who participate in securities trading pursuant to their legal duties
(7) Other persons as stipulated by the CSRC[112]

The Law defines "inside information" to include information that, in the course of securities trading activities, relates to the operations or finances of a company or will have a significant effect on the market price of a company's securities and has not yet been made public.[113] The following types of information are considered inside information:

(1) Significant incidents as defined in Article 62 of the Securities Law[114]

of obtaining commissions; or (6) other conduct that is contrary to the client's true intentions and is detrimental to the client's interests. Securities Law, art. 73.

110. Regulations Regarding the Issuing and Trading of Stock, art. 73.

111. Securities Law, art. 67; Regulations Regarding the Issuing and Trading of Stock, art. 72. *See* Chapter 23, Criminal Liability for FIE Activities § A.3.a.

112. Securities Law, art. 68.

113. Securities Law, art. 69.

114. Securities Law, art. 62. For text of Article 62, *see supra* footnote 91.

(2) Company plans to distribute dividends or increase capital
(3) Significant changes in the structure of company share ownership
(4) Significant alterations in company liabilities and guarantees
(5) Mortgage and sale of a significant asset used by the company in its business activities or a disposal in excess of 30% of said asset
(6) Any conduct of company directors, supervisors, managers, deputy managers, and relevant high-level administrative officials that is likely to lead to liability to provide compensation for significant losses
(7) Any planned acquisitions of a listed company
(8) Other important information that the CSRC confirms will have a noticeable effect on the trading price of securities[115]

The Law prohibits any persons with inside information, or persons who have illegally obtained inside information, from purchasing or selling any securities involving the company that is the subject of the inside information, or to encourage another person to purchase or sell the said securities based on the inside information.[116]

2. Overseas Listing of Domestic Shares

Pursuant to the Company Law, the State Council issued regulations governing the issuance and listing of stock of Chinese companies outside of China.[117] A Chinese company that is interested in listing its shares overseas (i.e., H-Shares for Hong Kong and N-Shares for New York) is required to secure the approval of the SCSC by filing an application and submitting financial and operational information, including an offering plan, prospectus, and accounting records.[118] The Overseas Share Regulations do not apply to B-Shares, even though foreigners hold such shares, albeit overseas. Nor do the regulations apply to listings by foreign companies with joint venture interests in China. The shares that are issued to overseas investors and that are listed overseas by companies limited by shares are in the form of

115. Securities Law, art. 69.

116. Securities Law, art. 70.

117. Securities Law, art. 29; Company Law, arts. 85, 155; Special Regulations of the State Council Concerning Floating and Listing of Shares Overseas by Companies Limited by Shares (adopted July 4, 1994, by the 22nd Sess. of the Standing Comm. of the State Council), *reprinted in* CHINA LAWS FOR FOREIGN BUSINESS (CCH), Business Regulation ¶ 13-552 (hereinafter referred to as "Overseas Share Regulations"); Notice on the Implementation of Essential Clauses in Articles of Association of Companies Listed Overseas (promulgated on August 27, 1994, by the SCSC), *reprinted in* CHINA LAWS FOR FOREIGN BUSINESS (CCH), Business Regulation ¶ 13-410 (hereinafter the "SCSC Notice, Essential Clauses").

118. Overseas Shares Regulations, arts. 2, 5, & 12. A company is required to implement its overseas offering plan within fifteen days of approval by the SCSC.

registered capital share certificates, with the face value denominated in renminbi and purchased in foreign exchange.[119]

Under the Company Law and the Regulations Regarding the Issuing and Trading of Stock, a company is required to wait at least twelve months before it can issue a subsequent share offering.[120] Under the Overseas Share Regulations, a company is expressly allowed to make an offering overseas in less than twelve months after the completion of a previous offering.[121]

The Overseas Shares Regulations provide that the company is required to provide the shareholders with forty-five days' prior written notice of a meeting of the shareholders.[122] The notice is required to specify the agenda of the meeting, the date, and place of the meeting. Shareholders that intend to attend the meeting are required to provide twenty-one days' written notice to the company. A meeting of the shareholders may be convened only if written replies representing 50 percent of the voting rights of the company have been received. If less than a 50 percent quorum of the shareholders reply to a notice of meeting, the company is required to reschedule the meeting date and resend notice of the meeting.[123] Shareholders that hold 5 percent or more of the company's stock may introduce resolutions to be addressed at the shareholders' meeting.[124]

The company is required to pay all dividends to shareholders of the company's foreign capital shares listed overseas in foreign currency but calculated based upon renminbi.[125] A company is required to follow all foreign exchange rules and regulations with respect to the use of foreign exchange for payment of dividends to shareholders.[126]

Companies listed overseas must adopt a set of articles of association approved by the SCSC.[127] The SCSC Notice sets forth 166 required provisions for articles of association for PRC companies, which are limited by shares and listed overseas in any jurisdiction. A company is required to specify the term of its business operations in the articles of association, which may be indefinite.[128] The articles of association of a company are binding

119. Overseas Shares Regulations, art. 3. *See* Issues Relevant to Further Improving the Foreign Exchange Control for Overseas Listing Circular (issued on Aug. 5, 2002, by the CSRC and SAFE). *See generally* M. Baigen & R. Sun, Foreign Exchange Controls and Overseas Listings, CHINA L. & PRAC. (April 2003).

120. Company Law, art. 137 (1); Regulations Regarding the Issuing and Trading of Stock, art. 11 (2).

121. Overseas Shares Regulations, art. 10.

122. Overseas Shares Regulations, art. 20. In contrast, the Company Law requires only thirty days' written notice to registered shareholders.

123. Overseas Shares Regulations, art. 22.

124. Overseas Shares Regulations, art. 21.

125. Overseas Shares Regulations, art. 27.

126. Overseas Shares Regulations, art. 27.

127. SCSC Notice, Essential Articles, preamble.

128. Overseas Shares Regulations, art. 14.

upon the company, its shareholders, directors, supervisors, managers, and senior management personnel.[129]

A company is authorized to modify the language and numbering of the Essential Clauses so long as the objectives of the provisions are maintained. However, a company that desires to alter or delete the content of the Essential Clauses is required to obtain authorization from the SCSC. A company may include additional articles on issues to reflect the specific circumstances of its operation. A number of the Essential Clauses are specifically designed for listings in Hong Kong and need not be included in the articles of association of a company listed in another jurisdiction.

The Essential Clauses set forth in the SCSC Notice cover a wide range of issues concerning corporate governance and organization, and are consistent with a number of key PRC laws, including the Company Law. The Essential Clauses include, but are not limited to, the following topics:

(1) Purpose and business scope of the company
(2) Shares and registered capital of the company
(3) Reduction in capital and share buy-out provisions
(4) Restrictions on the financial support for the purchase of company shares
(5) Procedures for share certificates and share ledgers
(6) Rights and obligations of shareholders, including the right of inspection, supervision, and to receive dividends
(7) Procedures for and matters to be addressed at shareholders' meetings
(8) Procedures for voting categories of shareholders
(9) Procedures for, and authority of, the board of directors, and the supervisory committee
(10) Qualifications and obligations of company directors, supervisors, managers, and other senior management personnel[130]
(11) Financial and accounting system of the company, publication of financial reports, and the issuance of dividends[131]
(12) Procedures concerning company merger, division, dissolution, and liquidation
(13) Procedures for dispute resolution

129. Overseas Shares Regulations, art. 15.

130. Under Chapter 14 of the Essential Clauses, directors and officers have stringent fiduciary duties. *See generally* Nikkel, *"Chinese Characteristics" in Corporate Clothing: Questions of Fiduciary Duty in China's Company Law,* 80 MINN. L. REV. 503 (1995).

131. A company is required to publish two financial reports each fiscal year, including a midterm and annual report. These reports are required to be audited by an independent PRC qualified accounting firm and prepared in accordance with Chinese and international accounting standards. SCSC Notice, Essential Clauses, Chap. 15.

The articles, when adopted by the company, are binding on the company, directors, shareholders, supervisors, managers, and other senior management personnel.[132]

3. Foreign Capital Shares Listed in China Regulations: B-Shares

In 1995, the State Council adopted regulations that supplement the Company Law and specifically address the issuance and public offering of foreign capital shares listed in China. The purpose of the B-Share Regulations is to standardize the issuing and trading of foreign capital shares listed in China by companies and to protect investors. Subject to approval by the SCSC and the CSRC, a company limited by shares may issue foreign capital shares listed in China. If the total face value of the foreign capital shares exceeds $30,000,000, the SCSC is required to obtain the approval of the State Council.[133] The individuals and entities allowed to invest in B-shares are limited to the following:

(1) Foreign entities or organizations
(2) Entities and organizations from the HKSAR, Macao, or Taiwan
(3) Overseas Chinese citizens[134]

An investor in B-shares is required to present proof of identity and subscriber qualifications when investing.[135] Investors in B-shares have the same rights and obligations as investors in domestic capital shares.[136] A company may specify in its articles of association any special matters concerning the rights and obligations as its shareholders of foreign capital shares. As required under the Company Law, the B-Share Regulations also provide that the articles and association of a company are binding on the company, its shareholders, directors, supervisors, managers, and senior management personnel.[137] The directors, supervisors, and management personnel of the company have fiduciary duties to the company.

A company may obtain approval to issue B-Shares if it has been previously established by a public offering. In order to obtain approval to issue B-Shares, a company must first demonstrate that it is in compliance with state industrial policies relating to the use of raised funds, fixed asset investments, and foreign investment.[138] For B-Shares issued by a public offering,

132. SCSC Notice, Essential Clauses, art. 7.
133. B-Share Regulations, art. 2.
134. B-Share Regulations, art. 4.
135. B-Share Regulations, art. 4.
136. B-Share Regulations, art. 5.
137. B-Share Regulations, art. 6.
138. B-Share Regulations, art. 8. *See also* Announcement on Issues Concerning the Listing and Flotation on the B-Share Market of Non-Tradable Foreign Stakes in Foreign-Invested B-Share Companies

the promoters must subscribe for no less than 35 percent of the total share capital issued by the company, contribute no less than RMB150 million, and issue for public purchase no less than 25 percent of the company's total stock.[139] The primary promoter of the issue must not have committed any serious violations of the law within three years of the proposed issue and must demonstrate profitability for the prior three years.[140]

A company may apply to issue B-Shares to increase its capital. To obtain approval to issue foreign capital shares listed in China to increase capital, a company is required to abide by state regulations and, in particular, to meet the following conditions:

(1) The previous share offering must have been fully subscribed and the funds generated from that issue are required to have been used in a manner consistent with the purpose of the prior offering
(2) The net value of the company's total assets must be no less than RMB150 million
(3) The company must have recorded profits the previous three years
(4) The company has not committed any serious violations of the law since the previous public offering[141]

An application to issue B-Shares requires the company to be selected by the SCSC in consultation with the State Council and government officials.[142] A selected company is required to submit an application and supporting documentation to the CSRC. If the CSRC approves of the application, it will submit the applicant's documents to the SCSC for final approval. If the issue is over $30,000,000, the SCSC is required to report the application to the State Council.[143] The documentation and information to apply for issuance of B-Shares in a public offering or to raise capital include the following:

(1) An application request
(2) A resolution adopted by the promoters supporting the decision to issue B-Shares

(issued on August 16, 2002, by the CSRC) (outlines the conditions and approval procedures for the listing of nontradable foreign shares in B-Share companies).

139. B-Share Regulations, art. 8. If the total share capital that the company intends to issue is valued in excess of RMB400 million, the proportion of shares earmarked for purchase by the public may be as little as 15 percent of the company's total stock.

140. B-Share Regulations, art. 8, §§ (7) & (8).

141. B-Share Regulations, art. 9.

142. B-Share Regulations, art. 10; The SCSC B-Share Rules, Articles 4–6, outline in detail the selection process for companies that wish to issue B-Shares for the first time. The rules also outline the selection process for companies that are seeking approval to offer additional B-Share issues. SCSC B-Share Rules, art. 7.

143. B-Share Regulations, art. 2; SCSC B-Share Rules, art. 10.

(3) Documents demonstrating the establishment of the company including business license or certification
(4) Letter of recommendation to issue B-Shares provided to the company by the local administration of industry and commerce or the State Council
(5) The company's draft articles of association
(6) The company's prospectus[144]
(7) A feasibility study that addresses the proposed use of the funds to be raised by the issuance of the B-Shares
(8) Approval document authorizing the use of the raised funds in a fixed asset investment project, if applicable
(9) Financial statements of the company for the previous three years
(10) Asset valuation report
(11) Legal opinion concerning the company[145]
(12) The underwriting agreement and description of the underwriting strategy
(13) Other documents required by the CSRC[146]

In addition to the above documents, a company that applies to issue B-Shares in an initial public offering is required to submit to the CSRC the following documents:

(1) Information concerning the promoters, including the shares to be subscribed to by the promoters, the capital contribution of the promoters, and capital verification certificate demonstrating the promoter's source of purchase funds
(2) Approval notice concerning the use of the name of the company by the administration of industry and commerce[147]

The interval between the issue of B-Shares listed in China and a prior issue of domestic capital shares may be less than twelve months.[148] The period for underwriting B-Shares cannot exceed ninety days.[149] A company that issues B-Shares is required to employ an underwriter who is approved by the PBOC and the CSRC. The principal underwriter of the B-Share issue is required to submit an underwriting report, including an analysis of the

144. SCSC B-Share Rules, arts. 11–12.
145. For more information concerning the format of legal opinions *see supra* note 67.
146. B-Share Regulations, art. 11, 12; SCSC B-Share Rules, art. 4.
147. B-Share Regulations, art. 11, 12.
148. B-Share Regulations, art. 13. Under the Company Law and Regulations Regarding the Issuing and Trading of Stock, purely domestic listings may be issued only after the passage of a minimum of twelve months. Company Law, art. 137, § (1).
149. SCSC B-Share Rules, art. 16.

underwriting process and the details concerning the ten largest shareholders and their respective share amounts, within fifteen days of the end of the underwriting period.[150] The company is also required to submit to the CSRC a number of reports, including:

(1) A capital verification report on the funds collected through the B-Share issue
(2) The company's business license
(3) The company's resolutions and articles of association adopted at the company's organizational meeting or at a general meeting of the shareholders[151]

The underwriter is required to use a foreign exchange account for the funds tendered to purchase the B-Shares.[152] Dividends paid by a company to a shareholder of foreign capital shares listed in China must be calculated in renminbi and paid in foreign currency. The management of the foreign exchange for purposes of payment of dividends must be consistent with foreign exchange regulations.[153] Dividends and other income derived from B-Shares may be remitted overseas after the payment of all relevant taxes in accordance with the taxation laws.[154]

A company that issues B-Shares is required to release a midterm and annual report as required under the Regulations Regarding the Issuing and Trading of Stock, as well as a report concerning any major event concerning matters that may affect the market price of the company's stock.[155] Information released by the company must be disclosed to both Chinese and foreign investors simultaneously. The content of the disclosure domestically and overseas is required to be identical. The disclosure information is required to be in the Chinese language and, in the event that the company publishes the information in a foreign language, the Chinese language is controlling in the event of a dispute in interpretation.[156] A shareholder who directly or indirectly holds 5 percent or more of the company's total shares must disclose its interest to the CSRC, the stock exchange, and the public within three working days of the acquisition.[157]

150. SCSC B-Share Rules, art. 17.
151. SCSC B-Share Rules, art. 20. These reports must be submitted to the CSRC within seven days of completion or adoption by the company.
152. B-Share Regulations, art. 19.
153. B-Share Regulations, art. 25.
154. B-Share Regulations, art. 26. *See generally* Chapter 9, Taxation Law.
155. SCSC B-Share Rules, art. 36.
156. B-Share Regulations, art. 17; SCSC B-Share Rules, art. 35.
157. SCSC B-Share Rules, art. 38. The SCSC B-Share Rules have a vague disclosure requirement mandating that the investor "explain its intentions" to the CSRC.

The law allows for the conversion of nonlisted foreign investment shares into B-Shares, with the approval of the Ministry of Commerce and the China Securities Regulatory Commission.[158]

4. Foreign-Invested Enterprise Limited by Shares

Foreign-invested enterprises (FIEs) may be established as companies limited by shares, also referred to as an FIE joint stock company.[159] This structure allows foreign investors the opportunity to acquire shares in a Chinese company without taking a direct equity stake as in a joint venture, and permits investors the option of listing on the PRC stock exchanges to raise funds or exit the market. An FIE limited by shares refers to an enterprise consisting of both Chinese and foreign shareholders with corporate status established pursuant to the FIE Limited by Shares Regulations and with total capital that is equivalent to the value of the stock. In such a company, the shareholders assume an amount of liability equal to the percentage of shares purchased. The FIE Limited by Shares Regulations outline the standards and procedures for either establishing an FIE limited by shares as a new entity or by converting an existing FIE, SOE, LLC, or other enterprise into an FIE limited by shares. Although not an express requirement for approval, the FIE Limited by Shares Regulations provide that the Chinese government "shall encourage the establishment of technologically advanced production-type companies."[160] An FIE limited by shares must have a minimum registered capital of RMB30 million ($3.62 million), of which the

158. *See* Questions Relevant to the Conversion of Non-Listed Foreign Investment Shares of Foreign-Invested Companies Limited by Shares into B Shares for Circulation Supplementary Circular (issued on August 16, 2002, by the Ministry of Foreign Trade & Economic Cooperation). Under the Circular, foreign-invested companies limited by shares that are established with proper approval are permitted to apply to MOFCOM to sell their non-listed investment shares. Conversion of the foreign investment shares into B-Shares requires MOFCOM approval. Within one year of such MOFCOM approval, investors may then seek CSRC approval to publicly list the B-Shares. Upon obtaining approval of both MOFCOM and the CSRC, the applicant is to required to apply to amend its Foreign-invested Enterprise Approval Certificate and its company registration. The B-Shares Circular states that holders of covered investment shares are required to have held such shares for one year prior to conversion into a foreign-invested company limited by shares. They are also required to hold the related B-Shares for one year after conversion. *See generally* C. Han, *Conversion of Non-Listed Foreign Investment Shares into B Shares*, China L. & Prac. (October 2002).

159. Provisional Regulations on Several Issues Concerning the Establishment of Foreign Investment Companies Limited by Shares (promulgated on January 10, 1995, by MOFTEC), *reprinted in* China Laws for Foreign Business (CCH), Business Regulation 13-405 (hereinafter "FIE Limited by Shares Regulations"); Notice on Relevant Issues Concerning Foreign-Invested Shareholding Companies (promulgated in 2001 by the Ministry of Foreign Trade and Economic Cooperation). For a bullet-point analysis of the laws and regulations governing FIEs limited by shares, *see* Fact Sheet: Foreign-Invested Company Limited by Shares, The U.S.-China Business Council (last updated July 18, 2003), available online for members at http://www.uschina.org (the U.S.-China Business Council estimates that less than 5 percent of all foreign direct investment in China uses the FIE limited by shares structure).

160. FIE Limited by Shares Regulations, art. 4.

number of shares purchased by the foreign parties must not be less than 25 percent).[161]

A new FIE limited by shares may be established by promotion or by the offering of shares. If the FIE is established through promotional methods, it must comply with the conditions applicable to promoters set forth in the Company Law and at least one of the promoters is required to be a foreign shareholder.[162] In the event that the FIE is established by a share offering, at least one of the promoters, either a Chinese or foreign shareholder, must have a record of profitability for a period of at least three years.

After the promoters have reached an agreement on the establishment of an FIE limited by shares, the applicants are required to submit an application for establishing a company, feasibility study, asset evaluation report, and a prospectus if the company is to be established by a public offering.[163] The application and supporting documents are submitted to MOFCOM for approval.[164] An existing FIE may convert to a company limited by shares but must demonstrate a record of profitability for a period of three years.[165] An FIE will not lose its tax deductions and exemptions by converting to an FIE limited by shares.[166] However, the laws and policies of China concerning foreign investment (namely, whether an investment area is permitted, restricted, or prohibited) continue to apply even after conversion to an FIE joint stock company.[167]

A state-owned enterprise (SOE) may become an FIE limited by shares. In such a situation, the Chinese SOE and foreign shareholders act as promoters

161. FIE Limited by Shares Regulations, art. 7. Contributions to registered capital may be in cash, intellectual property, land-use rights, or in-kind contributions.

162. FIE Limited by Shares Regulations, art. 6.

163. The CSRC has adopted disclosure standards for prospectuses prepared for foreign-invested companies limited by shares (FICLS). *See* Contents and Format of Prospectuses of Foreign-funded Companies Limited by Shares Special Provisions (issued on March 19, 2002, by the CSRC) (hereinafter the "FICLS Disclosure Provisions"). The FICLS Disclosure Provisions require enhanced disclosure in prospectuses issued by FICLS, including those established by Hong Kong, Macao, or Taiwan investors. The FICLS Disclosure Provisions impose a higher disclosure standard on foreign-invested issuers than on domestic PRC issuers, and mandate that a FICLS prospectus disclose (i) risks arising from possible changes in PRC laws, regulations, and policies granting preferential tax treatment to foreign investment enterprises; (ii) foreign exchange risk; (iii) connected transactions with foreign investors; and (iv) personal details of the FICLS's foreign directors and senior management personnel. The FICLS Disclosure Provisions do not contain a "materiality" threshold for disclosure and, arguably, all items, material and nonmaterial, should be disclosed to ensure compliance. Specifically, an issuer must detail all (not limited to material) connected transactions between the issuer and foreign investor for the three years prior to the prospectus's publication. The prospectus is to contain a fairness opinion from issuer's auditors reviewing related transactions and an estimate of the volume of related transactions in the upcoming year.

164. FIE Limited by Shares Regulations, art. 9. There is no statutory limitation of time for the duration of an FIE limited by shares, and the parties, by agreement, may set the duration.

165. FIE Limited by Shares Regulations, art. 15.

166. An FIE limited by shares is subject to the 30 percent national income tax and 3 percent local income tax.

167. FIE Limited by Shares Regulations, arts. 3, 4.

and enter into a promoter's agreement and articles of association for the new enterprise.[168] In order for an SOE to convert to an FIE limited by shares, the SOE is required to have been operating for a minimum period of five years and have a profit for three years. The shares of the FIE limited by shares must be purchased by the foreign shareholders in freely convertible foreign currency and constitute at least 25 percent of the FIE's registered capital. The scope and purpose of the FIE limited by shares must be consistent with state policy concerning foreign investment enterprises.

There are additional requirements for companies seeking to convert to a company limited by shares that issues B-Shares, N-Shares, or H-Shares.[169] The regulations require documentation concerning the original company's trading activities and proof of authorization from securities regulators to issue and list shares domestically or overseas. The applicant is required to submit a number of documents to the MOFCOM in order to obtain approval to become a company limited by shares. The documents to be submitted include the following:

(1) The joint venture contract and articles of association of the original foreign investment enterprise
(2) A resolution of the board of directors of the original foreign investment enterprise concerning the decision to transform the entity to a company limited by shares
(3) A resolution of the board of directors of the original foreign investment enterprise concerning the termination of the original contract and articles of association
(4) A capital verification report concerning the original foreign investment enterprise
(5) The agreement of the promoters, which may include the investors to the original FIE
(6) The proposed company's articles of association
(7) The business license and certificate of approval of the original FIE
(8) A certified financial report for the last three years of the original FIE
(9) An application for the establishment of a company limited by shares
(10) Certificates of creditworthiness for the promoters
(11) The feasibility study for the company[170]

After approval is received from MOFCOM, the company must then file for company registration with the SAIC. Within 30 days of paying the total value

168. FIE Limited by Shares Regulations, art. 18.
169. FIE Limited by Shares Regulations, arts. 21–24.
170. FIE Limited by Shares Regulations, art. 15.

of their subscriptions, the promoters must establish a board of supervisors and a board of directors.[171] Within ninety days of receiving approval, the promoters are required to invest their funds for the purchase of the shares. All documents submitted for approval are required to be in Chinese, and the Chinese version is controlling if there are any translations.[172]

5. Regulation of Brokerage and Trading Firms

Chinese and foreign securities institutions that trade or underwrite foreign capital shares listed in China and overseas (i.e., B-Shares, H-Shares, and N-Shares) are required to obtain approval from the CSRC.[173] Effective July 1, 2002, qualified foreign financial groups are allowed to take stakes in Chinese securities firms, which is expected to attact funds to China from overseas institutional investors, as well as to introduce investment management expertise and know-how from overseas firms.[174]

---

171. The unanimous approval of shareholders and directors is not required on corporate actions, and a two-thirds majority of votes held by shareholders present at a general shareholders' meeting is sufficient for passing resolutions. Shareholder approval of share transfers is not required by law. The elimination of minority shareholder veto power is a key advantage of the FICLS corporate structure.

172. FIE Limited by Shares Regulations, art. 10.

173. Securities Law, arts. 117–145 (outlining the standards, conditions, and approval procedures for securities companies). The Securities Law also outlines the conditions and approval procedures for Securities Registration and Account Settlement Organizations (Securities Law, arts. 146–156), securities trading service organizations (Securities Law, arts. 157–161), and securities industry associations (Securities Law, arts. 162–165), Provisional Administrative Regulations on the Qualification of Domestic and Overseas Securities Institutions Which Deal in Foreign Capital Shares (promulgated November 12, 1996, by the CSRC), *reprinted in* CHINA LAWS FOR FOREIGN BUSINESS (CCH), Business Regulation ¶ 13-594 (hereinafter referred to as "Securities Institutions Regulations"). *See also* Notice on the Adjustment of Standard Charges for the Trading of Special Renminbi-Denominated Shares (B-Shares) (promulgated on August 16, 1994, by the Shenzhen Municipal Securities Administration Office), *reprinted in* CHINA LAWS FOR FOREIGN BUSINESS (CCH), Special Zones & Cities ¶ 120-030 (sets the maximum fees collected by stockbrokers for B-Shares listed on the Shenzhen Stock Exchange); Provisional Regulations of Shenzhen Municipality for the Administration of Securities Institutions (promulgated on June 15, 1991, by the Shenzhen Special Economic Zone Branch of the People's Bank of China), *reprinted in* CHINA LAWS FOR FOREIGN BUSINESS (CCH), Special Zones & Cities ¶ 73-556 (addresses approval procedures for trading companies and other securities institutions). The CSRC issued a set of rules in January 1999 requiring that senior management personnel of securities firms have at least three years' experience in the industry. The rules also bar management personnel from engaging in any activities outside their own firm's business. A violation of the rules is grounds for suspension for up to two years. Further, a person with a criminal record may not be appointed as a senior manager; or if he or she has been dismissed from a financial institution for causing losses, he or she may not be appointed for a period of five years from the time of dismissal. *China: Securities Executives Controlled,* China Business Information Network (Jan. 25, 1999), available on Lexis, News Library. *See* Administrative Measures on Representative Offices of Foreign Securities Organizations Stationed in China (promulgated on April 22, 1999, by the China Securities Regulatory Commission), *reprinted in* CHINA LAWS FOR FOREIGN BUSINESS (CCH), Business Regulation ¶ 7-550 (outlining the application procedures for securities representative offices, documentation required for applications, penalty provisions, etc.).

174. *Foreigners Prepare to Take Stakes in China Brokerages,* WALL ST. J. (July 8, 2002). In addition to allowing foreign firms to invest in domestic brokerage firms, in June of 2002 the CSRC expanded the scope of activities by authorizing domestic securities companies to register to engage in the retail sale of PRC mutual funds to individual investors. Previously, only commercial banks were allowed to sell mutual funds in China. *CSRC Allows Brokerages to Sell Mutual Funds,* CHINA MARKET INTELLIGENCE,

In order to obtain approval, foreign institutions are required to meet a number of conditions to engage in brokerage or underwriting services of foreign capital shares. Although many of the conditions are clear and unambiguous, a number of the requirements are subject to interpretation, including the need to have an "extensive business network." The list of conditions includes the following:

(1) The institution must be approved to engage in brokerage services under the laws of the institution's principal place of business
(2) The institution is required to have net assets of not less than RMB50 million or is bonded by an institution licensed to provide security and is approved by the CSRC
(3) The institution has two years of trading or underwriting experience in international securities
(4) The institution has an extensive business network
(5) The institution's executive directors and senior management personnel must have five years of experience in securities operations and have sound professional reputations
(6) The institution has not been penalized by the securities regulatory authorities of its home country
(7) The institution is required to abide by the laws of the PRC
(8) The institution is required to have at least two individuals who are familiar with China's securities market and the relevant policies and laws[175]

THE U.S.-CHINA BUSINESS COUNCIL (July 24, 2002), available to members online at http://www.uschina.org. *But see* Notice on Relevant Issues Concerning Securities Companies Performing Mutual Investment Management Services (issued on May 15, 2003, by the CSRC). The CSRC notice states that the agency is drafting administrative measures to standardize the performance by securities companies of mutual investment management services. In the interim, securities companies are prohibited from offering mutual investment management services and requires them to cease the implementation of all existing mutual investment plans. Securities companies already providing mutual investment management services are required to submit relevant contracts, product descriptions, and marketing materials to the CSRC. The CSRC also granted securities firms the right to issue corporate bonds upon approval. *See* Interim Measures on the Administration of Bonds of Securities Companies (issued on August 29, 2003, by the CSRC and effective October 8, 2003) (provisions grant Chinese securities companies the authority to issue bonds upon approval by the CSRC. The company must be profitable in the most recent fiscal year and have assets of at least RMB500 million for private issues and at least RMB1 billion for public issues. The value of the newly issued bonds may not exceed 40 percent of a company's net assets, and bond interest is limited to an amount equal to the average annual profit distributed by the company for the most recent three years.)

175. Securities Institutions Regulations, art. 6. Domestic institutions that desire to engage in brokerage activities for foreign capital shares have a different set of conditions, including the authority to operate in foreign exchange, adequate technical facilities, and five professional personnel with the capability to handle foreign related securities operations. Securities Institutions Regulations, art. 5.

In addition to the conditions listed above, a foreign securities institution that is interested in acting as the principal underwriter must also meet the following conditions:

(1) The institution is approved to engage in stock underwriting under the laws of its home country
(2) The institution must have net assets of not less than RMB120 million or have been issued a bond in an equivalent sum by a security institution approved by the CSRC
(3) The institution must not have suspended its stock underwriting in the international market within the last two years
(4) The institution must have at least three professional employees who are familiar with China's securities laws and regulations[176]

An application for qualification submitted by a foreign institution is required to include the company's business license, articles of association, academic and industry credentials of the professional employees, financial information, and information concerning the company's brokerage or underwriting experience.[177] A qualification certificate is valid for a period of two years, and any extension must be filed within three months of expiration. Renewal applications require the submission of financial documents and information concerning the institution's activities during the term of the qualification certificate.[178] The activities of the institution must conform to the qualification certificate. An institution is prohibited from engaging in brokerage or underwriting activities that are outside the scope of the qualification certificate.[179]

An approved institution is required to file with the CSRC a report before January 31st of each year with respect to the brokerage and underwriting activities of the prior year. If an approved overseas underwriter is involved with overseas listings (i.e., H-Shares and N-Shares), the CSRC requires that the institution file a report within thirty days of the conclusion of the underwriting transaction.[180] An institution that engages in either brokerage or underwriting activities is required to maintain its original underwriting documents, trading records, account books, and other reports for a period of seven

176. Securities Institutions Regulations, art. 9. A domestic firm interested in acting as the chief underwriter must meet additional stringent requirements, including experience with underwriting foreign capital shares and a minimum of twenty employees with stock underwriting experience. Securities Institutions Regulations, art. 8.
177. Securities Institutions Regulations, art. 12.
178. Securities Institutions Regulations, arts. 13, 14.
179. Securities Institutions Regulations, art. 15.
180. Securities Institutions Regulations, art. 16.

years.[181] The CSRC is authorized to make periodic and random inspections of institutions involved with brokerage or underwriting activities concerning foreign capital shares.[182] A failure to comply with the regulations may result in suspension of activities or revocation of a qualification certificate.

The CSRC has established standards for the management of client assets by securities institutions.[183] The CSRC requires securities companies that manage client assets to establish a separate department, employ qualified personnel, and implement risk control standards and procedures. Approved securities companies may engage in limited activities; including asset management accounts for individual clients, restricted portfolio asset management plans and unrestricted portfolio asset management plans for multiple clients, and special purpose asset management accounts for clients with special projects.

6. Own-Account Securities Trading

The trading activities of securities firms and investment companies that trade in listed securities for their own accounts are regulated by the CSRC.[184] Listed securities are defined as securities listed on the Chinese stock exchanges, including ordinary renminbi shares, fund certificates, subscription warrants, government bonds, and corporate or enterprise bonds. In order to engage in trading on its own account, an institution must meet certain qualifications and conditions, including the following:

(1) Capital requirements[185]

(2) Two-thirds of senior management personnel and principal business personnel are required to obtain qualification certificates from the CSRC and demonstrate knowledge of securities, financial, and legal issues relevant to securities trading[186]

181. Securities Institutions Regulations, art. 17.

182. Securities Institutions Regulations, art. 18.

183. Trial Measures on the Management of Client Assets by Securities Companies (issued on December 18, 2003, by the CSRC).

184. Administrative Measures on Own-Account Securities Business Conducted by Securities Institutions (promulgated on October 24, 1996, by the China Securities Regulatory Commission), *reprinted in* CHINA LAWS FOR FOREIGN BUSINESS (CCH), Business Regulation ¶ 13-590 (hereinafter the "Own-Account Trading Measures"). Institutions that engage in own-account trading are subject to the FIE Securities Companies Rules, *infra* note 222 and accompanying text.

185. A securities institution that specializes in own-account trading must have net assets of not less than RMB20 million. An institution that engages in securities trading concurrently with other business operations must have securities working funds of not less than RMB20 million. A securities institution that specializes in own-account trading must have net capital of not less than RMB10 million. An institution that engages in securities trading concurrently with other business operations must have net securities working funds of not less than RMB10 million. The term "net securities working funds" refers to liquid funds used specifically for securities business operations by an institution that engages in securities business concurrently with other business operations. Own-Account Trading Measures, art. 7, §§ (1) & (2).

186. Own-Account Trading Measures, art. 7, § (3). The management personnel and principals must not have criminal records and are required to be experienced in the securities industry.

(3) The institution must not have committed any serious violation of the laws or regulations during the previous year or had its qualification to engage in trading revoked in the prior two years[187]
(4) The institution must have been established and officially operating for more than six months
(5) The institution is required to separate the securities trading operation from its other business operations, if applicable
(6) The institution is required to have computer terminals and other "necessary facilities" required for own-account trading activities[188]

A securities institution that meets the basic qualifications is required to apply for approval to the CSRC. The following documents and information are required to accompany the application:

(1) Financial business license and corporate business license
(2) Articles of association
(3) A memorandum describing the internal control system for the company's own-account business[189]
(4) A capital verification certificate on the net assets or securities working funds
(5) Financial statements
(6) Qualification certificates for the institution's employees
(7) A statement on the institution's securities business transactions of the previous year[190]

After the CSRC receives the application and documentation, it has thirty days to examine and respond to the applicant. If an applicant is rejected, the CSRC is prohibited from accepting any further applications from the applicant for six months. If the applicant meets the requirements, a qualification certificate will be issued by the CSRC, and such certificate is valid for a period of one year. An institution that desires to renew its certificate of qualification is required to submit an application and supporting documentation within three months before the end of the validity period.[191]

---

187. Own-Account Trading Measures, art. 7, § (4).
188. Own-Account Trading Measures, art. 7, § (6).
189. An institution is required to "establish a sound internal supervision and control system, conscientiously implement relevant State policies and statutes, always observe the law and regulations, and prevent any activities in the company which involve insider trading, market rigging and deception of clients." Own-Account Trading Measures, art. 17.
190. Own-Account Trading Measures, art. 8.
191. Own-Account Trading Measures, art. 11. The documents that are required to be submitted with the renewal application include the financial statements, qualification certificates for personnel, and the statement of the institution's securities business over the past twelve months.

The CSRC prohibits a securities institution from engaging in insider trading and market manipulation activities.[192] In addition to criminal penalties under the Criminal Law, such violations may result in confiscation of profits, fines ranging from RMB50,000 to RMB500,000, suspension from engaging in own-account trading for periods ranging from six months to one year, or cancellation of qualification certificates to engage in own-account trading with a two-year bar on filing an application for requalification.[193] Institutions are also prohibited from commingling own-account securities transactions with other company business, trading in securities using its own bank account for other companies or individuals, or commissioning other securities institutions to trade in securities on its own behalf.[194] In addition, if a listed company or affiliate holds more than 10 percent of the shares of a securities institution, that institution is prohibited from trading in the shares of the listed company on its own account. Such violations may result in penalties, including suspension, monetary sanctions of between RMB30,000 and RMB300,000, and confiscation of profits.[195] The CSRC is empowered to conduct regular and random audits of securities institutions engaged in own-account trading, and may demand information and documentation from institutions at any time.[196] Original records, including account books, reports, statements, and other business documents, are required to be maintained for a period of seven years.[197] A failure to obtain approval to engage in own-account trading or to engage in trading after approval has been withdrawn is grounds for monetary penalties and future disbarment.[198]

D. Foreign Investment in State Shares and A-Shares

Two policy decisions unveiled by the Chinese government in 2002 mark another step toward opening up China's $500 billion capitalized financial market to the outside world. The first set of rules allows foreign investors to

192. Own-Account Trading Measures, arts. 12, 13. Such activities are also illegal under the Criminal Law, Article 182. *See* Chapter 23, Criminal Liability for FIE Activities § A.3.a.

193. Own Account Trading Measures, art. 36.

194. *See also* Administrative Measures on Settlement Accounts of Clients' Transactions (issued on May 16, 2001, by the CSRC) (outlines detailed guidelines and rules on misuse of investor funds by securities companies, and standards for administration of accounts, transfer of funds, banks' escrow services, reporting requirements to the CSRC, penalty provisions, etc.).

195. Own-Account Trading Measures, art. 34.

196. Own-Account Trading Measures, arts. 28, 29.

197. Own-Account Trading Measures, art. 31. A failure to cooperate with the CSRC is grounds for penalties and suspension.

198. Own-Account Trading Measures, art. 32.

buy nontradable state-owned shares and legal-person shares of listed domestic Chinese companies. The second set of rules sets up a system to allow Qualified Foreign Institutional Investors (QFII), including fund management companies, insurers, securities companies, and other asset management firms, to invest in A-shares, government and convertible bonds, and corporate debt. Prior to the new policies, foreign investors were restricted to buying shares in the illiquid and limited foreign currency–denominated B-shares market.

Notwithstanding the opening of the market, the rules leave many questions unanswered and will most likely take years to be effective without further policy fine-tuning.

1. Foreign Investment in State Shares

On November 1, 2002, the China Securities Regulatory Commission ("CSRC"), the Ministry of Finance ("MOF"), and the State Economic and Trade Commission ("SETC") jointly promulgated a circular that formally allows foreign investors to purchase state-owned and legal-person shares of listed companies in China.[199] This State Shares Notice supersedes a 1995 notice issued by the State Council that suspended trading in such shares. According to the State Shares Notice, foreign investors are now allowed to buy State-owned shares and legal-person shares of listed companies in China.

The State Shares Notice stipulates that the transfer must comply with the requirements in the Foreign Investment Industrial Guidance Catalogue ("Industrial Guidance Catalogue"), which prohibits foreign investment in certain industries.[200]

The State Shares Notice provides that where industrial policies and corporate restructuring are involved, approval from the SETC (now part of MOFCOM) is required. Where the management of State-owned shares is involved, approval from the MOF is required. The State Shares Notice

199. Notice on Relevant Issues in Transferring the State-owned Shares and Legal Person Shares of Listed Companies to Foreign Investors (issued on November 1, 2002, by the CSRC and the Ministry of Finance) (hereinafter the "State Shares Notice"). There have been cases in which nontransferable shares of listed companies were purchased by foreign investors. In 1995, Isuzu Motors and Itochu of Japan bought 40 million "legal person shares," which amounted to 25 percent of Beijing Light Bus, which was listed on the Shanghai Stock Exchange with A-shares. Isuzu took a 15-percent stake, and Itochu holds 10-percent stake in the Chinese company. *See* He Jinsong, "New Hotspot on Securities Market—Acquisition of Domestic Listed Companies by Foreign Investors" at http://www.cctv.com/special/477/1/40096.html. Another case concerned the acquisition of nontransferable shares in listed companies involving Shenzhen Seg Samsung Glass Co., Ltd., and Shenzhen Baoheng (Group) Co., Ltd., where two companies listed with A-shares on the Shenzhen Stock Exchange are reported to have signed share transfer agreements with foreign investors regarding purchase of nontransferable shares of their companies respectively. *See New Waves of Reorganization of Listed Companies Rushing to Face,* SECURITIES TIMES—FINANCE WEEKLY, August 22, 2002; J. Zhou, *State Council Reform and Acquisition of Non-Floating Shares in Listed Companies*, CHINA L. & PRAC. (October 2003).

200. State Shares Notice, art. 2.

further provides that "major issues" shall be reported to the State Council. The rules also provide that the CSRC shall adopt additional standards concerning the acquisition of shares of a listed company and information disclosure.[201]

The general principles guiding share transfers include the obligations to protect the public interest and national economic security, to avoid loss of State-owned assets, to maintain social stability, to introduce advanced management, technology, and funds to accelerate change in the economic structure, to improve competitiveness, to protect the lawful rights of investors, and to assist the development of the stock market in China.[202]

Under the State Shares Notice, foreign investors are required to meet certain standards in order to acquire shares in listed companies. The standards include management capabilities, a strong financial position, and the ability to improve the corporate governance of the listed company and promote its developments.[203] The State Shares Notice further provides that a share transfer shall, in general, be conducted through open competition.

The share transfer agreement is required to be registered with the foreign exchange control authorities prior to the transfer, and the acceptance of foreign exchange by the transferor in the share transfer is required to be approved, in advance, by the foreign exchange control authorities.[204]

After the transfer of the State-owned shares and legal-person shares in listed companies, the subject listed company may receive, or continue to receive, preferential treatment offered to foreign-invested enterprises.[205]

Although the State Shares Notice allows foreign investors to acquire the State-owned shares and legal-person shares in listed companies, the actual procedures are not clearly set forth, and further guidance from the CSRC is required. For example, the "open competition" contemplated in the State Shares Notice is undefined and as a result, the rules are vague and ambiguous. Since State-owned shares and legal-person shares are not publicly listed or available on the stock exchanges, it is uncertain as to how open competition will be effectively accomplished. The State Shares Notice also does not specify the documents needed for approval, the time limits for government review and approval, and a process for appealing any adverse government decision.

201. State Shares Notice, art. 4.
202. State Shares Notice, art. 1.
203. State Shares Notice, art. 3.
204. State Shares Notice, arts. 6, 8.
205. State Shares Notice, art. 9.

2. Investment in A-Shares by Qualified Foreign Institutional Investors (QFII)

On November 5, 2002, the CSRC and the People's Bank of China ("PBOC") promulgated regulations allowing foreign investors to purchase A-Shares.[206] The QFII Measures allow foreign qualified institutions to purchase A-shares and state and corporate bonds traded on the Shanghai and Shenzhen stock exchanges.[207]

The general qualifications for the foreign institutions include sound financial status, good credit, sufficient assets per CSRC standards, and risk control procedures that meet the standards of the laws and securities regulatory requirements in the investor's home country. The QFII Measures further provide that the investor establish policies and procedures for its employees, establish a system of corporate governance and internal control, and have a record without any major penalty imposed by the securities regulatory authorities in the investor's home country.[208]

The assets required by the CSRC differ depending on the type of the foreign institution involved. In order to meet the QFII standards, a fund management institution must have a minimum of five years' industry experience and $10 billion in assets under management in the latest financial year. An insurance company and a brokerage firm must have thirty years' experience or longer, minimum paid-up capital of $1 billion, and securities assets of $10 billion or more in the latest financial year. A commercial bank is required to be among the top 100 globally by assets in the latest financial year and have managed securities assets of at least $10 billion.[209]

---

206. Provisional Administrative Measures on Securities Investment inside China by Qualified Foreign Institutional Investors (promulgated on November 5, 2002, Order No. 12 of China Securities Regulatory Commission and the People's Bank of China), *reprinted in* CHINA LAWS FOR FOREIGN BUSINESS (CCH), Business Regulation ¶13-595 (hereinafter referred to as the "QFII Measures"). As of the third quarter of 2003, the China Securities Regulatory Commission has approved nine QFIIs, including Morgan Stanley, UBS AG, Nomura Securities Co., Ltd., Citigroup Inc., Goldman Sachs Group, Inc., HSBC Holdings plc, Deutsche Bank AG, ING Bank NV, and JP Morgan Chase & Co. Two other investors, Credit Suisse First Boston and Daiwa Securities SMBC, have applied and their applications are pending as of the third quarter of 2003. *See* U.S.-CHINA BUSINESS COUNCIL, CHINA OPERATIONS 2003, ANALYSIS: FOREIGN INVESTMENT IN CHINA, FIRST HALF 2003, p. 20. *See generally* A. McGinty & A. Godwin, *The Missing Piece of the Puzzle: New QFII Rules Open a Share Market,* CHINA L. & PRAC. (Dec. 2002).

207. Shanghai Stock Exchange Detailed Implementing Regulations for Qualified Foreign Institutional Investors (issued on December 1, 2002, by the Shanghai Stock Exchange); Shenzhen Stock Exchange Detailed Implementing Regulations for Qualified Foreign Institutional Investors (issued on December 1, 2002, by the Shenzhen Stock Exchange). The regulations impose a ten percent (10%) maximum limit on the percentage of listed shares of a "A" listed company that a single QFII can acquire, and a maximum of twenty percent (20%) for one or more QFIIs. The regulations also set forth the reporting requirements to the respective stock exchanges and outline the penalties for violations.

208. QFII Measures, art. 6. CSRC will only recognize a QFII that comes from a country that has entered into a Memorandum of Understanding with the CSRC and the regulatory authorities of the home country of a foreign institution.

209. QFII Measures, art. 7.

A foreign institution is required to apply for the domestic securities investment qualification through a custodian bank, which is authorized as a custodian bank by the CSRC, the PBOC, and the State Administration of Foreign Exchange (SAFE). Only commercial banks, including branches of foreign commercial banks in China, may be authorized as a custodian bank.[210] A draft custodian agreement and a power of attorney must be executed between the foreign institution and the custodian bank.

The custodian bank is required to submit application documents to the CSRC and the SAFE on behalf of the foreign institution.[211] Upon receipt of the QFII application, the CSRC will either approve or deny an application and is required to issue a Securities Investment Business License to a QFII within 15 business days of receiving the complete application and supporting documents.[212]

Thereafter, the custodian bank is required to apply for an Investment Quota from the SAFE on behalf of the QFII. In response, SAFE will issue a written notice containing the allowed Investment Quota and a Foreign Exchange Registration Certificate within fifteen business days of receiving the complete application and supporting documents.[213]

Upon obtaining the domestic securities investment qualification, the foreign institution entrusts the custodian bank to apply for a Securities Account and an RMB Settlement Fund Account at a securities registration and settlement unit. Such account information shall be filed by the custodian bank with the CSRC and the SAFE within five business days of opening the accounts.[214]

Upon SAFE's approval, the foreign institution is required to open an RMB Special Account at the custodian bank. The custodian bank will then file such information with the CSRC and the SAFE within five business days of opening the account.[215] The foreign institution shall remit the principal

210. QFII Measures, arts. 13–14. *See* Notice on Commercial Bank Applications for Custodianship with Qualified Foreign Institutional Investors (issued on December 17, 2002, by the PBOC) (outlines the application procedures for commercial banks that wish to be approved to serve as a custodian for a QFII); Notice Concerning Operational Problems with QFII Foreign Exchange (issued on September 9, 2003, by the State Administration of Foreign Exchange) (SAFE rules that tighten control over QFII capital accounts and require that QFIIs open one RMB-denominated account for payment of local expenses). *See generally* D. Liu & N. Zhou, *New Rules on QFII Custodian Banks,* China L. & Prac. (November 2003); M. Gaigen & R. Sun, *How to Set Up a QFII Custodian Business,* China L. & Prac. (Feb. 2003). The SAFE Notice provides that custodian banks are not allowed to establish sub-accounts of the special renminbi account for the different portfolios of a single QFII licensee. Renminbi accounts for QFII investment purposes are also prohibited from being used for other purposes by QFII licensees. *See also* Statement by a CSRC Spokesperson on Issues Relevant to the Administration of Securities Investments in China by Qualified Foreign Institutional Investors (issued on March 19, 2003, by the CSRC) (details the application documents required for QFII status).

211. QFII Measures, art. 8.

212. QFII Measures, art. 9.

213. QFII Measures, art. 10.

214. QFII Measures, art. 17.

215. QFII Measures, art. 23.

fund in a foreign currency approved by the SAFE to the RMB Special Account after settling the foreign exchange within three months of issuance of the Securities Investment Business License by the CSRC.[216]

After completing the application process and opening the required accounts, a QFII is allowed to invest in A-shares, state debts, convertible bonds, and enterprise bonds, all of which are listed on the domestic exchanges in China, or other financial instruments approved by the CSRC.[217] The qualified foreign institutions may entrust only one brokerage firm established in China to manage its securities investment.[218]

All investment by the QFII is required to be consistent with the government's FIE investment policies in accordance with the Foreign Investment Industrial Guidance Catalogue. Therefore, where foreign investment is prohibited, no foreign institution may purchase any shares or bonds of a listed company engaging in the prohibited industry. Where foreign investment is restricted, a foreign institution may only invest in a listed company in accordance with such restriction subject to the QFII Measures. Furthermore, the QFII Measures do not allow a single qualified foreign institution to hold over 10 percent of listed shares of any particular company; and total investment by QFIIs shall not exceed 20 percent of listed shares of a company.[219]

A qualified foreign institution may remit its after-tax profits outside of China upon submitting an application to the SAFE. The recipient of such profits shall be the qualified foreign institution itself.[220]

A closed-end China fund management institution may remit its principal investment only after three years of maintaining the principal in China in installments of no more than 20 percent of the total principal each time and with at least a one-month interval between two transfers. Other qualified foreign institutions may remit their principal only after one year of maintaining the principal in China in installments of no more than 20 percent of the total principal each time and with at least a three-month interval between two transfers.[221]

It is anticipated that only a limited number of institutional investors will have the financial capabilities to participate in the QFII scheme given that the QFII Measures impose strict or even excessive qualifications and fund remittance restrictions. While this is indicative that the Chinese government

216. QFII Measures, art. 25.
217. QFII Measures, art. 18.
218. QFII Measures, art. 19.
219. QFII Measures, art. 21.
220. QFII Measures, art. 29.
221. QFII Measures, art. 26.

intends to attract only large and ostensibly stable investors, many other capable niche companies will be left out of the market for the immediate future. Another obstacle is that the large amount of nontradable shares held by state-owned enterprises may be a disincentive to QFIIs from getting into the market. However, activities should increase when greater emphasis is placed on transparency in financial accounting and corporate governance standards.

E. FIE Securities Companies, FIE Fund Management Companies, and Securities Investment Funds

In June 2002, the China Securities Regulatory Commission adopted rules for the establishment, supervision, and management of FIE Securities Companies.[222] The FIE Securities Company Rules set forth the procedures for establishing

222. Establishment of Securities Companies with Foreign Equity Participation Rules (promulgated on June 1, 2002, by the CSRC) (hereinafter the "FIE Securities Company Rules"). *See also* Securities Company and Senior Executive Personnel and Branch Manager Administration Provisions (issued on October 23, 2003, by the CSRC) (outline standards for qualifications and penalty provisions for management personnel). *See generally* T. Hui, *New Rules for Fund Management and Securities Firms,* South China Morning Post (July 8, 2002); W. Hutchens, *Promises Kept: The CSRC Opens the Door to Foreign Investment in Fund Management Companies,* CHINA L. & PRAC. (July 2002); B. Shouyun, *New Rules on JV Securities Companies: A Limited Opening of China's Securities Industry,* CHINA L. & PRAC. (July 2002). The Securities Law, Chapter VI, outlines the general standards, conditions, and approval procedures for securities companies operating in China, including domestic and FIE securities companies. Securities Law, arts. 117–145. The Securities Law provides that only a securities company that is a member of a particular stock exchange may participate in exchange activities. Securities Law, art. 103. A securities company is a limited liability company or a company limited by shares that has been established in accordance with the provisions of the Company Law and is approved to engage in securities business. Securities Law, art. 118. The State implements a system of administering securities companies based on two categories: comprehensive securities companies and brokerage securities companies. Securities Law, art. 119. A securities company is required to insert the language "limited liability securities company" or "securities company limited by shares" in the name of the company. The words "brokerage" must appear clearly in the name of any brokerage securities company. Securities Law, art. 120. A comprehensive securities company is required to meet the following conditions: (1) the company must have registered capital of at least RMB500 million; (2) senior managers and officials must possess the professional qualifications for employment in the securities industry; (3) the company must have established business premises and satisfactory trading facilities; and (4) the company must have a sound management system and standardized separate administrative systems to deal with operations on its own behalf and in its brokerage operations. Securities Law, art. 121. A brokerage securities company must meet the following conditions: (1) the company must have a minimum registered capital of RMB50 million; (2) senior managers and officials must possess qualifications to work in the securities industry; (3) the company must have established business premises and satisfactory trading facilities; and (4) the company must have a sound management system. Securities Law, art. 122. Approval by the CSRC is required if a securities company establishes or dissolves a branch organization; changes its scope of business, registered capital, or its articles of association; goes through a merger or acquisition; alters its corporate form; or is liquidated or dissolved. Securities Law, art. 123. A comprehensive securities company may engage in the following business activities: (1) securities brokerage business; (2) securities operations on its own behalf; (3) securities consignment sales; and (4) other securities businesses verified and approved by the CSRC. Securities Law, art. 129.

Sino-foreign joint venture securities companies and provide that the scope of business for Chinese-foreign joint venture securities companies may (i) underwrite A-shares, B-shares (within certain limitations), government bonds, and corporate bonds;[223] (ii) broker B-shares; (iii) engage in the sale of government and corporate bonds as a broker and for its own account; and (iv) engage in other activities approved by the CSRC. The CSRC rules prohibit an FIE Securities Company from engaging in the trading of A-shares, whether for itself or on behalf of its clientele, and may not provide asset management services or domestic private placement financing services to clients.

The FIE Securities Company Rules provide that the foreign party in the venture (i) be a licensed securities firm in its home country; (ii) have ten years of operational experience in securities; (iii) have no disciplinary record for violations of the law in its home country; (iv) have implemented risk control and internal control procedures; and (v) demonstrate compliance with other CSRC mandatory conditions. At least one of the venture's Chinese shareholders is to be a domestically funded securities company. The FIE Securities Company Rules provide that the venture's minimum registered capital is required to be in excess of RMB500 million, and the foreign investors' equity position may not be greater than 33 percent of the company's total equity. Furthermore, a single Chinese securities company is required to hold at least 33 percent of the venture's equity. An application for an FIE Securities Company is required to be approved by the CSRC.

Also in June 2002, the China Securities Regulatory Commission adopted rules outlining the standards and procedures for the establishment of a fund management company with foreign investment.[224] The FIE Fund Management Company Rules provide that foreign ownership in an FIE fund management company is restricted to 33 percent, which rises to 49 percent in December 2004. The FIE Fund Management Company Rules require that the foreign investor be licensed as a financial institution in its home jurisdiction, have paid-in capital of at least RMB300 million, and have an exemplary record. The FIE fund management company is required to have paid-in capital of

223. *See* Administration of Securities Company Bonds Tentative Procedures (issued on August 29, 2003, by the CSRC); Guidelines on the Content and Format for Information Disclosure by Companies that Offer Shares to the Public (No. 20): Application Documents for Issuing Bonds by Securities Companies (issued on August 29, 2003, by the CSRC) (Guidelines require securities companies to file application to the CSRC to issue bonds); Guidelines on the Content and Format for Information Disclosure by Companies that Offer Shares to the Public (No. 21): Prospectuses for Public Issue of Bonds by Securities Companies (issued on August 29, 2003, by the CSRC) (outlines the content for prospectus in bond sales). *See generally* M. Baigen & T. Wang, *Bond Issuance by Securities Companies: A New Beginning,* CHINA L. & PRAC. (October 2003).

224. Establishment of Fund Management Companies with Foreign Equity Participation Rules (promulgated on June 1, 2002, by the CSRC). *See generally* T. Hui, *New Rules for Fund Management and Securities Firms,* South China Morning Post (July 8, 2002).

RMB10 million, and may be created by joint promotion or through a QFII's acquisition of a fund management company's equity shares. In the QFII context, the Chinese partner is required to be a trust and investment company or a securities company. The FIE Fund Management Company Rules state that CSRC approval is the only government approval required, and that no role for the Ministry of Commerce is indicated. FIE Fund Management Company accounts are to have an 80:20 portfolio split between corporate securities and government bonds, and CSRC regulations prohibit fund directors from directly or indirectly trading stocks.

Subsequent to the adoption of the FIE Fund Management Company Rules, the National People's Congress passed the Investment Fund Law in October 2003 (effective June 1, 2004), which regulates closed- and open-end funds that are publicly offered.[225] Under the Investment Fund Law, a fund management company must be approved by the CSRC in order to establish and manage investment funds. Under the law, an investment fund management company is required to have a registered capital that exceeds RMB100 million and principal shareholder(s) that are active in the securities management, securities investment consulting, trust asset management, or other financial asset management business. Each principal shareholder of the investment fund management company is required to have registered capital exceeding RMB300 million.

To achieve a valid public offering for a closed-end fund, a fund management company is required to sell more than 80 percent of the total amount of units approved by the CSRC. For an open-end fund, the fund management company must sell more than the minimum amount of approved units to a minimum number of buyers (as stipulated by the CSRC). Investment funds may invest only in publicly listed stocks, bonds, and other securities products designated and approved by the CSRC. The law prohibits the use of investment fund assets for underwriting securities, extending loans, or buying other funds; making equity investments in the fund management company or custodian; and buying securities issued or underwritten by the fund manager's or fund custodian's controlling shareholder.

225. Securities Investment Funds Law of the People's Republic of China (promulgated on October 28, 2003, by the National People's Congress, and effective on June 1, 2004) (hereinafter the "Investment Fund Law"). The Investment Fund Law sets forth 103 articles addressing a variety of issues such as standards and liability of fund managers, guidelines for raising funds, standards for trading of shares of funds, standards for the purchase and redemption of shares of funds, guidelines for operational and disclosure standards, standards for changes to and termination of fund contracts and liquidation of fund property, rights of fund shareholders and exercise thereof, and supervision and legal liability. *See also* Issues Relevant to Standardization of the Transfer of Contributed Capital by Fund Management Companies Shareholders Circular (issued on December 26, 2002, by the CSRC). *See generally* M. Baigen, *Changing of Shareholders of Fund Management Companies,* CHINA L. & PRAC. (March 2003).

F. Arbitration and Litigation of Securities-Related Disputes

The Regulations Regarding the Issuing and Trading of Stock provide that disputes concerning issuing and trading of stock, including disputes between shareholders and the company, may be resolved by mediation or arbitration as specified in the parties' contracts or articles of association.[226] In the absence of a contractual obligation to arbitrate a dispute, an injured party has the right to seek judicial relief in the people's court.[227] Under the SCSC B-Share Rules, the laws of the PRC apply to any dispute between the holders of B-Shares and the company, the company's shareholders of A-Shares, or the company's directors, supervisors, managers, or other senior management personnel.[228]

The Overseas Share Regulations provide for arbitration of disputes between shareholders, the company, the directors, the supervisors, or management personnel, if the articles of association require arbitration. Any Chinese company that desires to list its shares overseas is required to adopt the Essential Clauses required by the SCSC, which provide that all disputes are to be submitted to arbitration with the China International Economic and Trade Arbitration Commission (CIETAC) or the Hong Kong International Arbitration Center.[229] The law applicable to any dispute under the Essential Clauses is the law of the PRC.

Disputes between underwriters or between underwriters and stock exchanges require resolution by mediation or arbitration.[230] In this regard, the SCSC has designated CIETAC to resolve disputes involving securities issues. The types of disputes subject to mandatory arbitration are limited to issues between institutions and stock exchanges.

In September of 2001, the Supreme People's Court issued an order prohibiting the lower people's courts from accepting any securities-related litigation based upon fraud, insider trading, and manipulation of securities markets. The order was premised on the argument that the courts were ill equipped to fairly handle complex securities fraud litigation. On January 15, 2002, the SPC partially lifted the suspension and now permits the courts to

226. Regulations Regarding the Issuing and Trading of Stock, art. 79.

227. Claims by shareholders are limited to breach of contract and for compensatory or liquidated damages (if allowed per contract). Civil Law, arts. 111, 112. *See generally* Latimer, *Gilding the Iron Rice Bowl: The Illusion of Shareholder Rights in China,* 69 WASH. L. REV. 1097 (1994).

228. SCSC B-Share Rules, art. 45.

229. Overseas Share Regulations, arts. 15, 29; SCSC Notice, Essential Clauses, art. 163.

230. Regulations Regarding the Issuing and Trading of Stock, art. 80. For a discussion of CIETAC and China's arbitration laws and regulations, *see* Chapter 21, Mediation and Arbitration § B.

accept civil cases based upon theory of "false statement."[231] According to the circular, a false statement case refers to a civil tort claim involving a false statement or information released in disclosure documents submitted or announced in the securities market. A plaintiff must file the suit within two years following the date of a valid penalty decision made by the China Securities Regulatory Commission ("CSRC") with respect to such a false statement. The suit can be filed by one litigant individually or together with other litigants, but cannot be a class action.

G. Securities-Related Criminal Liability

Under the Criminal Law and its predecessor rules, insider trading, stock manipulation, fraudulent conduct in the registration of a company under the company law, and fraudulent conduct in the issuance of shares are crimes.[232]

231. In January 2002, the Supreme People's Court issued an order that allows for the higher-level people's courts to accept civil claims based upon false statements in the securities market. Notice of the Supreme People's Court on the Relevant Issues Concerning the Acceptance of Civil Tort Dispute Cases Caused by False Statements in the Securities Markets, promulgated on January 15, 2002, by the Supreme People's Court. The order provides that the cases must meet the requirements of the Civil Procedure Code. The SPC Securities Cases Order provides that "compensation cases caused by false statements" means the cases of indemnity claim based on the civil tort in which the obligors for the disclosure of securities information in the securities markets, in violation of the information disclosure obligations set out by the Securities Law of the People's Republic of China, make statements or records contrary to the true facts in the information disclosure documentation submitted or announced, and violate the lawful rights and interests of investors accordingly. SPC Securities Cases Order, art. I. The false statements the subject of the litigation are required to be investigated by China Securities Regulatory Commission, which have made effective punishment decisions. According to the law, a people's court shall not accept a case unless the party concerned files a civil legal proceeding based on the investigation and handling results. The limitations period for such cases is two years, commencing as of the date on which China Securities Regulatory Commission imposes its decision concerning its investigation. *See* Trial of Civil Damages Cases Arising from Misrepresentation in the Securities Market Several Provisions (issued on January 9, 2003, by the Supreme People's Court and effective February 1, 2003). The SPC Securities Market Litigation Provisions are designed to provide the Chinese courts with more tools to work with in managing securities fraud cases. The Provisions define and expand the definition of "misrepresentation" to include fraudulent records, misleading statements, material omissions, and improper disclosure, and provide clear definitions for each. The Provisions also expand the scope of potential defendants that may be held liable for securities fraud to include sponsors, promoters and controlling shareholders of the issuer, the intermediary agencies and service providers (such as accounting firms, law firms, and asset appraisal firms) involved in fraudulent activities, and persons directly responsible for misrepresentation in the intermediary agencies. The SPC Securities Market Litigation Provisions also provide that promoters, issuers, or listing companies shall be strictly liable for misrepresentation, and other persons are assumed to be liable for misrepresentation unless they can prove that they did not engage in fraudulent activities. The burden of proof on a plaintiff includes the following elements: (1) it has invested securities that are directly related to the misrepresentation; (2) it has purchased such securities on or after the misrepresentation date but before such misrepresentation is publicly disclosed or corrected; and (3) it has suffered losses when reselling the securities or while holding such securities after the public disclosure or correction date. The Provisions set forth clear additional guidelines with respect to the calculation of damages.

232. Criminal Law of the People's Republic of China (promulgated March 14, 1997, by the NPC), *reprinted in* 11 CHINA L. & PRAC. 41 (June 1997) (hereinafter the "Criminal Law"); Decision of the Standing Committee of the NPC Concerning Punishment of the Crime Constituting Violation of the Company Law (adopted February 28, 1995, by the 12th Sess. of the Standing Comm. of the 8th NPC), *reprinted in* CHINA LAWS FOR FOREIGN BUSINESS (CCH), Business Regulation ¶ 13-520.

The law makes it a crime for "a well-informed person with inside information" to buy or sell securities before such information is made public. Trading on inside information is punishable by fines of up to five times the illegal gain or prison terms in the maximum of ten years. The Criminal Law also prohibits the dissemination of false information for the purpose of manipulating the prices of traded securities. It is also a crime for an employee of a securities exchange, securities brokerage company, or securities industry association to willfully supply false information, destroy or alter transaction records, or engage in any conduct intending to deceive investors into buying or selling securities.[233] The law further prohibits anyone from engaging in any conduct that manipulates the price of securities. Stock manipulation is subject to fines of not less than one time and not more than five times the illegal income gained in the scheme, and may result in imprisonment of up to five years.[234]

Key Laws and Regulations

Securities Law (promulgated on December 29, 1998, by the 6th Sess. of the Standing Comm. of the 9th NPC, and effective July 1, 1999)

Company Law of the PRC (adopted December 29, 1993, by the 5th Sess. of the Standing Comm. of the 8th NPC, revised and repromulgated on December 25, 1999, by the 13th Sess of the Standing Comm. of the 9th NPC)

Foreign Investment Issues Relating to Listed Companies Several Opinions (issued on November 8, 2001, by the Ministry of Foreign Trade & Economic Cooperation and the China Securities Regulatory Commission)

Provisional Regulations on the Administration of the Issuing and Trading of Stocks (promulgated on April 22, 1993, by the State Council)

Provisional Measures on the Administration of the Registration of Companies Dealing in Futures (promulgated on April 28, 1993, by the SAIC)

Provisional Regulations on the Administration of Futures Trading (Order No. 267, promulgated on June 2, 1999, by the State Council)

Circular Concerning Issues Relevant to Capital Contributions to Futures Brokerages (issued on January 14, 2003, by the China Securities Regulatory Commission)

(Continued)

233. Criminal Law, art. 181.
234. Criminal Law, art. 182. *See* Chapter 23, Criminal Liability for FIE Activities § A.3.

(Continued from previous page)

Circular Concerning the Criteria, Procedure and Submission of Materials for Approving the Qualifications of Shareholders of Futures Brokerages (issued on July 2, 2002, by the China Securities Regulatory Commission)

Regulations of the State Council on Foreign Capital Shares Listed in China by Companies Limited by Shares (promulgated on December 25, 1995, by the State Council)

Detailed Rules for the Implementation of the Regulations of the State Council on Foreign Capital Shares Listed in China by Companies Limited by Shares (promulgated on May 3, 1996, by the State Council Securities Commission)

Notice on the Further Standardization of Work Related to Initial Public Offerings (issued on September 19, 2003, by the China Securities Regulatory Commission and effective October 1, 2003)

Guidelines of the CSRC Issue Examination Board on the Examination and Approval of Initial Public Offerings (issued on May 11, 2001, by the CSRC)

Guidelines on the CSRC Issue Examination Board on Examination and Approval of New Issues by Listed Companies (issued on May 11, 2001, by the CSRC)

Notice on Issuing the Interim Measure on the Appraisal of Main Underwriter's Professional Qualifications and Quality (issued on September 13, 2002, by the CSRC)

Standards for Examination and Verification of Share Issues Memorandum (No. 16): Examination and Verification Requirements for Special Item Review of Companies Initially Offering Shares to the Public (issued on February 28, 2003, by the CSRC)

Notice Regarding Examination Standards on Reduction, Exemption and Reimbursement of Taxes; Government Subsidies and Appropriations (issued on September 6, 2002, by the CSRC)

Guidelines Re Contents and Formats for Information Disclosures by Companies that Offer Securities to the Public (issued on March 24, 2003, by the CSRC)

Notice on Matters Regarding Further Regulation of the Initial Public Offers and Listing of Shares (issued on September 19, 2003, by the CSRC)

Regulations Regarding the Administration of the Listing Approval Committee (issued on December 11, 2003, by the CSRC)

Supplementary Notification Concerning Guidelines on Implementation of Working Procedures of CSRC's Issuance Examination Committee (issued on July 18, 2002, by the CSRC)

Notification of the Relevant Requirements on Listed Companies' Issuance of New Shares (issued on July 24, 2002, by the CSRC)

Implementing Procedures for the Suspension and Termination of Listing of Loss-Making Listed Companies (issued on November 30, 2001, by the CSRC)

(Continued)

(Continued from previous page)

Supplementary Provisions to the Implementing Procedures for the Suspension and Termination of Listing of Loss-Making Listed Companies (issued on November 30, 2001, by the CSRC)

Notice on Disclosure of Information Required by Listed and Pre-IPO Companies According to the New Accounting Principles and Systems (issued by the CSRC on June 26, 2001)

Contents and Format for Information Disclosures by Companies that Offer Securities to the Public Guidelines (No. 2): Contents and Format of Annual Reports (issued on January 6, 2003, by the China Securities Regulatory Commission)

Notice on Amendment of "Guideline No. 2 of the Content and Format of Information Disclosure of Companies that Publicly Issue Securities: Content and Format of Annual Report" (issued on December 22, 2003, by the CSRC)

Administration of Disclosure of Information on the Change of Shareholdings in Listed Companies Procedures (issued on September 28, 2002, by the China Securities Regulatory Commission)

Administration of the Takeover of Listed Companies Procedures (promulgated on September 28, 2002, by the China Securities Regulatory Commission)

Notice on Relevant Issues in Transferring the State-owned Shares and Legal Person Shares of Listed Companies to Foreign Investors (issued on November 1, 2002, by the CSRC and the Ministry of Finance)

Listed Company Governance Guidelines (issued on January 7, 2002, by the China Securities Regulatory Commission and the State Economic and Trade Commission)

Guidelines for Independent Directors in Listed Companies (issued on August 16, 2001, by the CSRC)

Several Issues Concerning the Regulation of Cash Flows between Listed Companies and Their Affiliates and Security Provided to Outside Parties by Listed Companies (issued on August 28, 2003, by the China Securities Regulatory Commission)

Special Regulations of the State Council concerning Floating and Listing of Shares Overseas by Companies Limited by Shares (adopted July 4, 1994, by the 22nd Sess. of the Standing Comm. of the State Council)

Notice on the Implementation of Essential Clauses in Articles of Association of Companies Listed Overseas (promulgated on August 27, 1994, by the SCSC)

Issues Relevant to Further Improving the Foreign Exchange Control for Overseas Listing Circular (issued on August 5, 2002, by the CSRC and SAFE)

Announcement on Issues Concerning the Listing and Flotation on the B-Share Market of Non-Tradable Foreign Stakes in Foreign Invested B-Share Companies (issued on August 16, 2002, by the CSRC)

(Continued)

(*Continued from previous page*)

Questions Relevant to the Conversion of Non-Listed Foreign Investment Shares of Foreign-invested Companies Limited by Shares into B Shares for Circulation Supplementary Circular (issued on August 16, 2002, by the Ministry of Foreign Trade & Economic Cooperation)

Provisional Regulations on Several Issues Concerning the Establishment of Foreign Investment Companies Limited by Shares (promulgated on January 10, 1995, by the MOFTEC)

Notice on Relevant Issues Concerning Foreign Invested Shareholding Companies (promulgated in 2001, by the Ministry of Foreign Trade and Economic Cooperation)

Contents and Format of Prospectuses of Foreign-Funded Companies Limited by Shares Special Provisions (issued on March 19, 2002, by the China Securities Regulatory Commission)

Notice on Relevant Issues Concerning Securities Companies Performing Mutual Investment Management Services (issued on May 15, 2003, by the China Securities Regulatory Commission)

Interim Measures on the Administration of Bonds of Securities Companies (issued on August 29, 2003, by the China Securities Regulatory Commission and effective October 8, 2003)

Trial Measures on the Management of Client Assets by Securities Companies (issued on December 18, 2003, by the China Securities Regulatory Commission)

Administrative Measures on Own-Account Securities Business Conducted by Securities Institutions (promulgated on October 24, 1996, by the China Securities Regulatory Commission)

Administrative Measures on Settlement Accounts of Clients' Transactions (issued on May 16, 2001, by the CSRC)

Notice on Relevant Issues in Transferring the State-Owned Shares and Legal Person Shares of Listed Companies to Foreign Investors (issued on November 1, 2002, by the CSRC and the Ministry of Finance)

Provisional Administrative Measures on Securities Investment inside China by Qualified Foreign Institutional Investors (promulgated on November 5, 2002, Order No. 12 of China Securities Regulatory Commission and the People's Bank of China)

Shanghai Stock Exchange Detailed Implementing Regulations for Qualified Foreign Institutional Investors (issued on December 1, 2002, by the Shanghai Stock Exchange)

Shenzhen Stock Exchange Detailed Implementing Regulations for Qualified Foreign Institutional Investors (issued on December 1, 2002, by the Shenzhen Stock Exchange)

(*Continued*)

(Continued from previous page)

Notice on Commercial Bank Applications for Custodianship with Qualified Foreign Institutional Investors (issued on December 17, 2002, by the PBOC)

Notice Concerning Operational Problems with QFII Foreign Exchange (issued on September 9, 2003, by the State Administration of Foreign Exchange)

Statement by a CSRC Spokesperson on Issues Relevant to the Administration of Securities Investments in China by Qualified Foreign Institutional Investors (issued on March 19, 2003, by the CSRC) (details the application documents required for QFII status)

Establishment of Securities Companies with Foreign Equity Participation Rules (promulgated on June 1, 2002, by the China Securities Regulatory Commission)

Securities Company and Senior Executive Personnel and Branch Manager Administration Provisions (issued on October 23, 2003, by the China Securities Regulatory Commission)

Administration of Securities Company Bonds Tentative Procedures (issued on August 29, 2003, by the CSRC)

Guidelines on the Content and Format for Information Disclosure by Companies that Offer Shares to the Public (No. 20): Application Documents for Issuing Bonds by Securities Companies (issued on August 29, 2003, by the CSRC)

Guidelines on the Content and Format for Information Disclosure by Companies that Offer Shares to the Public (No. 21): Prospectuses for Public Issue of Bonds by Securities Companies (issued on August 29, 2003, by the CSRC)

Establishment of Fund Management Companies with Foreign Equity Participation Rules (promulgated on June 1, 2002, by the China Securities Regulatory Commission)

Securities Investment Funds Law of the People's Republic of China (promulgated on October 28, 2003, by the National People's Congress, and effective on June 1, 2004)

Issues Relevant to Standardization of the Transfer of Contributed Capital by Fund Management Companies Shareholders Circular (issued on December 26, 2002, by the CSRC)

Trial of Civil Damages Cases Arising from Misrepresentation in the Securities Market Several Provisions (issued on January 9, 2003, by the Supreme People's Court and effect on February 1, 2003)

Provisions Regarding Several Issues on the Adjudication of Cases Involving Company Disputes (issued on November 4, 2003, by the Supreme People's Court)

Several Issues Concerning the Trial of Futures Dispute Cases Provisions (issued on May 16, 2003, by the Supreme People's Court)

Chapter 17

Land Use, Real Estate Development, and Natural Resources

While the private ownership of land is not permissible in China, private land-use rights are obtainable for a finite period of time and are generally transferable for a fee. Similarly, the natural resources found within the territory of China are not subject to private ownership, but, as with the use of land, a party may obtain exploitation rights to mineral, petroleum, water, timber, and other natural resources. This chapter addresses the laws regulating the use and exploitation of China's land and natural resources.

A. Land-Use Rights

1. General Land-Use Principles

In the People's Republic of China, all land is owned by the State or, in the rural areas, by the local collectives.[1] Generally, the State holds title to land

1. Law of the People's Republic of China on Land Management (adopted on June 25, 1986, at the 16th Sess. of the Standing Comm. of the NPC and amended on December 29, 1988, by the 5th Sess. of the Standing Comm. of the NPC, revised and repromulgated on August 29, 1998, by the 4th Sess. of the Standing Comm. of the 9th NPC, and as Order No. 8 of the President of the PRC), *reprinted in* China Laws for Foreign Business (CCH), Business Regulation ¶ 14-701 (hereinafter the "Land Management Law"). *See* Sun, *Lawmakers Scrutinize Amendment to Draft Law,* China Daily (June 24, 1998), available on Lexis, News Library, or on the Web site of the China Daily at http://www.chinadaily.com.cn; Sun, *Experts and Public React to Land Law Reform Plan,* China Daily (June 13, 1998), available on Lexis, News Library, or on the Web site of the China Daily at http://www.chinadaily.com.cn; *Land Law to Better Protect Farmland,* China Daily (Jan. 11, 1999), available on Lexis, News Library, or on the Web site of the China Daily at http://www.chinadaily.com.cn. The 1998 amendments impose environmental impact standards on projects concerning the use of land, impose tighter land use zoning requirements, and provide protection for agricultural land. The Ministry of Land and Natural Resources

in urban areas,[2] while the collectives hold title to land in rural areas.[3] Any individual, enterprise, or government agency using land is responsible for the protection, management, and rational utilization of that land.[4] A party may obtain a land-use certificate, which confirms the right of usage, from the Ministry of Land and Natural Resources (MLNR) or its local branch office.[5] To obtain this certificate, a party must submit a land registration application and supporting documentation.[6] Chinese law protects ownership of the right to use land.[7]

2. Utilization and Protection of Land

a. Utilization of Land

Chinese law allows any company, enterprise, organization, or individual in or outside the People's Republic of China to acquire the right to use land and develop, utilize, and engage in business relating to the land, except where the law provides otherwise.[8] An enterprise or individual may obtain land-use rights in one of three ways:[9]

(1) By agreement

(MLNR) is authorized to manage land use resources and to investigate illegal land use schemes. *See* Liu, *3.8 Million Illegal Land Cases Found Nationwide,* China Daily (June 24, 1998), available on Lexis, News Library, or on the Web site of the China Daily at http://www.chinadaily.com.cn. The publication of the draft land administration law is unique in that it was the first time that the NPC sought public comment during the law-making process. *See* Chapter 3, Legislating, the Judiciary, and Lawyers in China § A.1, fn. 16 and accompanying text.

2. Rules for the Implementation of the Law of the People's Republic of China on Land Management (promulgated on Dec. 27, 1998, by the State Council), *reprinted in* China Laws for Foreign Business (CCH), Business Regulation ¶ 14-702 (hereinafter the "Land Management Rules").

3. Land Management Rules, art. 6.

4. Land Management Law, art. 7.

5. Land Management Rules, art. 4. The MLNR has developed a recording system to determine land grants and ownership rights, and whether land is subject to a leasehold interest or mortgage. Land Management Rules, arts. 9, 11.

6. Under the government reorganization plan of 1998, the MLNR has taken over the functions of the State Land Administration, the Ministry of Geology and Mineral Resources, the State Oceanography Bureau, and the State Bureau of Surveying and Mapping. The MLNR is responsible for implementing a national land utilization plan, subject to approval of the State Council. The People's Government in the locality of the land in question is also responsible for settling disputes over the ownership of land. Land Management Rules, art. 8. If a party to the dispute disagrees with a decision, a complaint may be filed in the people's court within thirty days of receiving notice of the decision. Land Management Rules, art. 13. However, a party to the dispute cannot alter the existing condition of the land before the dispute is settled.

7. Land Management Law, art. 11.

8. Provisional Regulations of the People's Republic of China Concerning the Grant and Assignment of the Right to Use State Land in Urban Areas (promulgated on May 24, 1990, by the State Council), *reprinted in* China Laws for Foreign Business (CCH), Business Regulation ¶ 14-716 (hereinafter the "Land-Use Grant and Assignment Regulations").

9. Land-Use Grant and Assignment Regulations, art. 13.

(2) By invitation of tenders
(3) By auction[10]

In consideration for the right to use land, a party is required to enter into a land grant contract and pay the required land grant fees to the State.[11] The collection of land-use fees is governed by the Land Registration Fee Measures, which provide that all users of State land are required to pay land registration fees.[12] The fees vary depending upon the size, purpose, and location of the property.[13] The municipal or local land administration authorities, if authorized by the Ministry of Finance, may collect land registration fees.[14] The fees must be paid within sixty days after execution of the grant contract. If the land user fails to make full payment within such time, the grantor may rescind the contract and claim liquidated or compensatory damages.[15] Upon payment in full, the land user is provided a land-use certificate, which confirms the user's rights to the property.[16]

The grantee may use the land only in accordance with the terms of the contract. However, with the consent of the grantor, and subject to the approval of the land administration department, the land user may change

---

10. *See generally* Regulations of the Shenzhen Special Economic Zone on the Tendering and Auction of Land-Use Rights (promulgated on February 6, 1998, as Order No. 68 of the Shenzhen Municipal People's Government), *reprinted in* CHINA LAWS FOR FOREIGN BUSINESS (CCH), Special Zones & Cities ¶ 120-095 (outlines the types of residential and commercial land subject to auction, invitation and tender process, selection of tenders, auction procedures, and legal liability). An enterprise may also receive property as "allocated land use rights" pursuant to government policy. *See* Provisional Measures on Administration of Allocated Land-Use Rights (promulgated on March 8, 1992, by the State Land Administration), *reprinted in* CHINA LAWS FOR FOREIGN BUSINESS (CCH), Business Regulation ¶ 14-713 (hereinafter the "Allocated Land-Use Rights"). The Ministry of Land and Natural Resources promulgated the updated Land Rights Transfer Law on June 11, 2003, which provides that state-owned land transfer can be accomplished through negotiated agreement if public bidding fails to produce a buyer. However, the transfer of land in certain sectors, including trade and retail, tourism, entertainment, and commercial residential projects, may not be transferred through a process of negotiation. Provisions on the Grant of Use Rights for State-Owned Land by Agreement (issued on June 5, 2003, by the Ministry of Land Resources, and effective August 1, 2003). *See also* Grant of State-Owned Leaseholds by Invitation for Bids, Auction, and Listing Provisions (issued by the Ministry of Land and Natural Resources in May 2002); Beijing Municipality Procedures for Granting, Transferring and Leasing Land-Use Rights (Trial Implementation) (promulgated on September 28, 2002, by the Beijing State-Owned Land Resources and Housing Administrative Bureau). *See generally China Regulates Transfer of Land-Use Rights,* CHINA MARKET INTELLIGENCE, THE U.S.-CHINA BUSINESS COUNCIL (July 9, 2003); F. Li, *Opening the System: Granting Land-Use Rights by Public Notices,* CHINA L. & PRAC. (July 2003).

11. Land-Use Grant and Assignment Regulations, art. 8.

12. Land Management Law; Land Management Rules; Measures of the State Land Administration, the State Bureau of Surveying and Cartography, the State Commodity Pricing Bureau, and the Ministry of Finance on Land Registration Fees and Related Administration (issued on July 21, 1990), art. 2, *reprinted in* CHINA LAWS FOR FOREIGN BUSINESS (CCH), Business Regulation ¶ 14-718 (hereinafter the "Land Registration Fee Measures").

13. Land Registration Fee Measures, art. 3.

14. Land Registration Fee Measures, art. 4.

15. Land-Use Grant and Assignment Regulations, art. 14.

16. Land-Use Grant and Assignment Regulations, art. 15.

the designated use of the land.[17] The grantor also has an obligation to follow the terms of the contract. If the grantor fails to abide by the terms, the grantee has the right to rescind the contract and may claim damages.[18]

If the land user fails to comply with the terms of the contract, the land administration department may impose administrative penalties ranging from the issuance of a warning and imposition of a fine, to the recovery of the land-use rights without compensation.[19] The grantee's right of use may also be withdrawn if:

(1) The land user terminates its business operations
(2) The land remains unused for two successive years without authorization
(3) Highways, railways, airports, and mining sites, the subject of the land-use rights, are effectively abandoned[20]

The right of land use may exist only for a finite period of time. The maximum terms of use are determined in light of the land's purpose, as follows:

(1) Seventy years: residential
(2) Fifty years: industrial
(3) Fifty years: educational, scientific, technological, cultural, public health, or sports
(4) Forty years: commercial, tourism, or recreational
(5) Fifty years: comprehensive use or other purposes[21]

When the grant term expires, the right of use and the title to the structures and attachments on the land pass to the State without compensation.[22] To counter the effect of reversion, the land user may apply for an extension of the term of use and, if an extension is granted, the user is required to follow registration formalities and pay the required fees.[23]

The law requires specific approval for many types of land developments prior to commencement of the intended use. For example, development of State-owned land involving undeveloped property, wetlands, or coastal areas is subject to approval by the local land management departments.[24] If a party

17. Land-Use Grant and Assignment Regulations, art. 18.
18. Land-Use Grant and Assignment Regulations, art. 16.
19. Land-Use Grant and Assignment Regulations, art. 17.
20. Land Management Law, art. 19.
21. Land-Use Grant and Assignment Regulations, art. 12.
22. Land-Use Grant and Assignment Regulations, art. 40.
23. Land-Use Grant and Assignment Regulations, art. 41.
24. Land Management Rules, art. 13.

intends to modify agricultural land into noncultivated land, approval is also required from the local people's government.[25] Activities such as mining, exploration, and excavation are also subject to special government approval.[26]

b. Transfers of Land-Use Rights

A land user who has acquired the right to use land may assign, lease, or mortgage its land-use rights.[27] A transfer must be registered with the MLNR or local land administration.[28] The term "assignment" refers to the act by which a land user passes on the right to use land, and includes a sale, exchange, or gift.[29] When the right to use land is assigned, the rights and obligations specified in the contract for use and the registration documents shall pass to the assignee.[30] The structures and attachments to the property, and the right to use the land beneath them, also pass to the assignee.[31] For an assignment to be valid, a written contract must be executed and registered.[32] If the assignment price is substantially lower than the market price, the government has a pre-emptive right to purchase the rights.[33]

Under the Urban Real Estate Law,[34] the conditions for a valid assignment include the following requirements:

(1) Payment in full of the fee for transfer and possession of the certificate of the right to use the land
(2) Fulfillment of 25 percent of the total investment in a housing construction development project or the availability of land for commercial land development

25. Land Management Rules, art. 14.
26. Land Management Rules, art. 15.
27. Land-Use Grant and Assignment Regulations, art. 4; Law of the People's Republic of China on the Administration of Urban Real Estate (adopted on July 5, 1994, at the 8th Sess. of the Standing Comm. of the NPC), art. 2, *reprinted in* China Laws for Foreign Business (CCH), Business Regulation ¶ 19-593 (hereinafter the "Urban Real Estate Law"). The parties involved must disclose the transaction price to the People's Government at county level or above and carry out the title registration procedures. Urban Real Estate Law, arts. 34–35. The Supreme People's Court has issued a circular that interprets various issues concerning the sale and transfer of commercial real property, including standards for advertisements and promotional materials, liability for punitive damages in situations involving seller fraud, liability for issuance of ownership certificates, standards for purchase deposits, and standards for delivery of premises. *See* Several Issues Concerning the Application of the Law to Trial of Disputes over Commercial Premises Sales and Purchase Contracts Interpretation (issued on April 28, 2003, by the Supreme People's Court) (hereinafter the "SPC Real Property Dispute Interpretation"). *See generally* J. Jiang & Z. Li, *Clearing Up the Law: China's New Judicial Interpretation on the Sale of Commercial Premises,* China L. & Prac. (June 2003); P. Randolph & L. Jianbo, Chinese Real Estate Law (2002).
28. Land-Use Grant and Assignment Regulations, art. 7.
29. Land-Use Grant and Assignment Regulations, art. 19.
30. Land-Use Grant and Assignment Regulations, art. 21.
31. Land-Use Grant and Assignment Regulations, art. 23.
32. Land-Use Grant and Assignment Regulations, art. 20.
33. Land-Use Grant and Assignment Regulations, art. 26.
34. Law of the People's Republic of China on the Administration of Urban Real Estate (adopted on July 5, 1994, at the 8th Sess. of the Standing Comm. of the NPC), art. 2, *reprinted in* China Laws for Foreign Business (CCH), Business Regulation ¶ 19-593 (hereinafter the "Urban Real Estate Law").

(3) A written contract of assignment that specifies the means by which the right to use land was obtained[35]

The Urban Real Estate Law prohibits the assignment of real estate in a number of instances, including the following:

(1) Where the right to use land was obtained through means of transfer that does not meet the conditions for proper assignment
(2) Where a court or administrative agency rules or decides to freeze real estate or to restrict the title to real estate in other ways in accordance with the law
(3) Where the right to use land is recovered in accordance with the law
(4) Where the assignment was made without the written consent of the co-owners
(5) Where an assignment is made pending a dispute over ownership rights
(6) Where there is a failure to carry out registration and obtain a business license in accordance with the law
(7) In other circumstances under which assignment is prohibited by laws and regulations[36]

A "lease" refers to the act by which a land user, acting as lessor, leases his right to use land together with the structures and other attachments thereon to a lessee for its use, with the lessee paying rent to the lessor.[37] When leasing residential property, the lessee and the lessor must enter into a written lease contract that prescribes such provisions as the term of the lease, the purpose of the lease, and repair and maintenance liability, as well as other rights and obligations of the parties concerned.[38] The lessor remains responsible for continued performance of the original land grant contract.[39] Additionally, the lessor is responsible for completing the registration formalities.[40]

(1) Registration of Real Estate Transfers. The Urban Real Estate Transfer Regulations provide that parties to a real estate transfer must enter into a written contract outlining the terms and conditions of the transaction, and approval of the transfer must be obtained by the Ministry of Construction or

35. Urban Real Estate Law, arts. 38, 40.
36. Urban Real Estate Law, art. 37.
37. Land-Use Grant and Assignment Regulations, art. 28; Urban Real Estate Law, art. 52.
38. Urban Real Estate Law, art. 53; Land-Use Grant and Assignment Regulations, art. 29.
39. Land-Use Grant and Assignment Regulations, art. 30.
40. Land-Use Grant and Assignment Regulations, art. 31. The lease contract is required to be reported to the real estate management department of the local government.

local branch.[41] The Regulations provide that "urban real estate transfer" refers to the sale, donation, or transfer by any other lawful means of real estate by its owner to another party. "Transfer by any other lawful means" under the regulations specifically refers to the following activities:

(1) The real estate is valued and used as an investment share or to establish an enterprise legal person with another party
(2) The ownership of real estate is changed when one party provides land use rights while the other party or parties provide capital to develop and manage the real estate by way of a joint venture
(3) The ownership of real estate is transferred as a result of the enterprise being sold, acquired, or merged with another enterprise
(4) The real estate is transferred to satisfy a debt obligation
(5) Any other circumstances prescribed by applicable laws and regulations[42]

When real estate is being transferred, the housing ownership rights (i.e., the rights to the building, structures, and improvements) and the land use rights are transferred simultaneously.[43] Real estate may not be transferred if the ownership certificates have not been obtained by the seller, or if the property rights are subject to court order, have been revoked, are disputed, or if a consent is not obtained from joint owners.[44] The transfer of a real estate interest is required to follow the following procedures:

(1) The parties involved in the real estate transfer are required to execute a written transfer contract
(2) The parties involved in the real estate transfer shall, within 90 days of signing the real estate transfer contract, submit an application to the local real estate administrative department where the real estate is situated, with the real estate ownership certification, legal identification

41. Regulations on the Administration of Urban Real Estate Transfer (promulgated August 7, 1995, by Order No. 45 of the Ministry of Construction; amended August 15, 2001, in accordance with the Decision of the Ministry of Construction on the Amendment of the Regulations on the Administration of Urban Real Estate Transfer), *reprinted in* CHINA LAWS FOR FOREIGN BUSINESS (CCH), Business Regulation ¶ 19-597 (hereinafter the "Urban Real Estate Transfer Regulations"). A real estate transfer contract must contain language addressing the following: (1) the full names, or the names of organizations, and addresses of both parties; (2) the name and certificate/registration number of the real estate ownership certificate; (3) the location, area, and boundaries of the real estate; (4) the land block number, and the method by which the land use rights were acquired and the term of the land use rights; (5) the purpose or nature of the use of the real estate; (6) the transaction price and the method of payment; (7) the time the real estate shall be delivered for use; (8) the liability for breach of contract; and (9) any other matters agreed on by both parties. Urban Real Estate Transfer Regulations, art. 8.

42. Urban Real Estate Transfer Regulations, art. 3.

43. Urban Real Estate Transfer Regulations, art. 5.

44. Urban Real Estate Transfer Regulations, art. 6.

for the transferring parties, the transfer contract, and other relevant documentation, and shall report the price of the transaction

(3) The real estate administrative department shall examine the relevant documentation that has been submitted, and shall issue a written reply as to whether or not the application is accepted within 7 days (if a reply is not issued within 7 days, the application shall be deemed to have been accepted)

(4) The real estate administrative department shall verify the reported transaction price and, where necessary, conduct an on-site assessment of the real estate being transferred[45]

(5) The seller shall pay the relevant taxes and fees in accordance with the regulations

(6) The real estate administrative department shall handle the registration formalities for the ownership of housing and approve and issue the real estate ownership certification[46]

A failure to follow the registration procedures or to pay the required fees and taxes may result in penalties.[47]

(2) Mortgage of Property. The right to use land may also be mortgaged.[48] A "mortgage" refers to the act whereby a mortgagor provides its land-use rights as security for a debt. When the right to use the land is mortgaged, the structures and attachments to the land are also subject to the mortgage.[49] If the debtor fails to pay its debts, the mortgagee is entitled to priority compensation from the proceeds derived from the auction of the mortgaged real estate in accordance with the law.[50] The mortgagor and mortgagee must enter

45. When transferring real estate, the seller is required to accurately report the transaction price, specifically with respect to the payment of fees and taxes. If the reported transaction price is substantially lower than the normal market price, the government may conduct its own assessment and survey, and impose fees and taxes based upon the assessed price. Urban Real Estate Transfer Regulations, art. 14.

46. Urban Real Estate Transfer Regulations, art. 7.

47. Urban Real Estate Transfer Regulations, art. 17.

48. Land-Use Grant and Assignment Regulations, art. 32; Urban Real Estate Law, arts. 2, 46, 49. *See* Notice on Further Strengthening Administration of Real Estate Loan Services (issues on June 5, 2003, by the People's Bank of China) (hereinafter the "Real Estate Loan Notice"). The Real Estate Loan Notice limits lending to luxury and commercial real estate developments. The Notice sets forth the maximum loan ceiling as 70 percent of the property value and requires the registration of real estate loans. Under the Notice, mortgages can be issued only for structures that are completed and not under construction. *See generally* M. Adler & C. Dafei, *China's Central Bank Tightens Real Estate Lending,* China L. & Prac. (Sept. 2003); *PBOC Tightens Real Estate Loan Restrictions,* China Market Intelligence, The U.S.-China Business Council (June 25, 2003), available online to members at http://www.uschina.org.

49. Land-Use Grant and Assignment Regulations, art. 33.

50. Urban Real Estate Law, art. 46; Administrative Measures on Urban Real Estate Mortgages (promulgated on May 9, 1997, and revised on August 15, 2001, by the Ministry of Construction), *reprinted in* China Laws for Foreign Business (CCH), Business Regulation ¶ 19-594 (hereinafter the "Administrative Measures on Urban Real Estate Mortgages").

into a written mortgage contract for the mortgage to be valid.[51] A real estate contract is only effective from the date of registration of mortgage with the applicable government authorities.[52] The mortgage contract is required to include the following terms and conditions:

(1) Name(s) of the mortgagor
(2) Type and amount of the principal debt
(3) Location, description, condition, and building area of the mortgaged real estate
(4) Value of the mortgaged real estate
(5) Occupant and administrator of the mortgaged real estate, form of occupation and administration, occupancy and administrative obligations, and liability for accidental damage or loss
(6) Terms of the mortgage[53]
(7) Conditions governing the loss of mortgage
(8) Liability for breach of contract
(9) Forms of dispute resolution
(10) Date and place of the signing of the mortgage contract
(11) Other matters agreed to by both parties[54]

The registration of a mortgage must be effected within thirty days of execution of the mortgage contract.[55] When registering a real estate mortgage, the following documents must be submitted to the registration authority for examination:

(1) Identification documents of the parties to the mortgage or the qualification certificates of the legal persons
(2) Application for mortgage registration
(3) Mortgage contract
(4) Land-use rights certificate
(5) Evidence that proves the mortgagor has the right to enter into the mortgage
(6) Material which can prove the value of the mortgaged real estate
(7) Other documents required by the registration authority[56]

---

51. Land-Use Grant and Assignment Regulations, art. 34. The Secured Interests Law establishes the standards for mortgages and other forms of collateral. *See* Chapter 7, Contract Law § C.2.

52. Administrative Measures on Urban Real Estate Mortgages, art. 31.

53. The mortgage period must not exceed the amount of time remaining under the land-use term stipulated in the land-use rights contract. Administrative Measures on Urban Real Estate Mortgages, art. 18. The mortgage period must not exceed the operational life of an enterprise. Administrative Measures on Urban Real Estate Mortgages, art. 17.

54. Urban Real Estate Law, art. 49; Administrative Measures on Urban Real Estate Mortgages, art. 26.

55. Administrative Measures on Urban Real Estate Mortgages, art. 30.

56. Administrative Measures on Urban Real Estate Mortgages, art. 32.

The registration authorities are required to examine and verify the application for registration of mortgage rights. If the title of ownership is clear and the documentary materials submitted by the parties to the transaction is complete, the registration authorities are required to render a decision to approve or reject the application for registration within seven days of filing of the application. If rejected, the registration authorities are required to provide written notice to the applicants.[57] If a mortgage contract is amended or terminated, the parties to the mortgage are required to register the amendment or cancellation of contract with the applicable registration authorities within 15 days of the amendment or termination. If mortgaged real estate is disposed of in accordance with the law and land use rights and title to ownership of buildings and other improvements on the land are obtained as a result of the disposition, the parties to the mortgage contract must apply to the local real estate administration department for registration of the transfer of the property ownership within 30 days of the act of disposal.[58]

A mortgagee (lender) has the right to request the disposal of mortgaged real estate—namely through auction or other legal method—in any of the following circumstances:

(1) The mortgagee has not been paid in full on the expiration of the debt repayment period, and the debtor has been unable to conclude a debt repayment agreement with the mortgagee
(2) When the mortgagor dies or is declared dead and there is no one to act for the mortgagor in the repayment of debts on maturity, or the mortgagor's legal heir or beneficiary refuses to repay debts on maturity
(3) The mortgagor is declared dissolved or bankrupt in accordance with the law
(4) The mortgagor violates the law by disposing of mortgaged real estate without authorization
(5) Other circumstances provided for in the mortgage contract[59]

After consultation, the parties to a mortgage contract may agree on the method of disposing of mortgaged property, namely, by auction or sale. If the parties to the mortgage are unable to reach an agreement on disposition of the property, the mortgagee may initiate legal proceedings with the people's court for a disposition order.[60] Before taking any action to enforce a mortgage contract, the mortgagee is required to notify, in writing, both the

57. Administrative Measures on Urban Real Estate Mortgages, art. 33.
58. Administrative Measures on Urban Real Estate Mortgages, art. 35.
59. Administrative Measures on Urban Real Estate Mortgages, art. 40.
60. Administrative Measures on Urban Real Estate Mortgages, arts. 41, 50.

mortgagor (debtor) and any co-owner or lessee of the property. The Regulations provide that a co-owner(s) or lessee(s) is entitled to a priority right of purchase with respect to the subject property in accordance with the law.[61]

When two or more mortgages are registered for the same real property, priority rights for repayments from auction proceeds are based on the order of mortgage registration.[62] Proceeds from the disposal of mortgaged real estate will be distributed in the following order:

(1) Payment of expenses incurred in disposing of the mortgaged real estate
(2) Deduction of taxes payable in relation to the mortgaged real estate
(3) Repayment of the principal and interest payable on the debt owed to the mortgagee and payment of the penalty for breach of contract
(4) Payment of compensation to the mortgagee for losses incurred as a result of the debtor's violation of the contract
(5) Transfer of the balance to the mortgagor, if any

When proceeds from the disposal of mortgaged real estate are insufficient to repay the debt and pay the penalty for breach of contract and relevant compensation, the mortgagee is entitled to seek a deficiency judgment for the shortfall from the debtor.[63]

A mortgagee (lender) may stop the disposal process of mortgaged real estate in any of the following circumstances:

(1) The mortgagee requests the suspension
(2) The mortgagor agrees to repay the debt, and the mortgagee consents to the payment plan
(3) A dispute arises over ownership of the auctioned mortgaged property
(4) The mortgaged real estate is the subject of court proceedings or arbitration
(5) Other circumstances that require the suspension of disposal procedures[64]

Mortgage rights may be transferred or leased only after approval of the mortgagee.[65] Where leased real estate is to be mortgaged, the mortgagor must notify the mortgagee of the circumstances of the lease and notify the lessee of the circumstances of the mortgage.[66] The original lease contract usually remains in force.

61. Administrative Measures on Urban Real Estate Mortgages, art. 42.
62. Administrative Measures on Urban Real Estate Mortgages, art. 43.
63. Administrative Measures on Urban Real Estate Mortgages, art. 47.
64. Administrative Measures on Urban Real Estate Mortgages, art. 46.
65. Administrative Measures on Urban Real Estate Mortgages, art. 37.
66. Administrative Measures on Urban Real Estate Mortgages, art. 21.

If the parties to the mortgage agree to insure the mortgaged real estate, the mortgagor is responsible for insuring the property and is liable for payment of the insurance premium.[67] After insuring the mortgaged real estate, the mortgagor must transfer the insurance policy to the mortgagee for safekeeping. The mortgagee is required to be named the first beneficiary under the insurance policy during the mortgage period.

The mortgage of real estate of a Sino-foreign equity joint venture enterprise, cooperative joint venture enterprise, or wholly foreign-owned enterprise must be approved by its board of directors, except if the enterprise's articles of association stipulate otherwise.[68] When an enterprise or public institution is the subject of a division or merger, any existing mortgage contract remains in effect.[69]

Some types of real estate may not be mortgaged, such as:

(1) Real estate of which the ownership is in dispute
(2) Real estate used for public welfare undertakings in the areas of education, medicine, municipal administration, etc.
(3) Buildings and structures listed for protection as cultural relics and other buildings and structures of important commemorative significance
(4) Real estate that is already publicly listed for demolition and removal in accordance with the law
(5) Real estate that is legally sealed up, confiscated, supervised, and controlled or placed under any other form of restriction
(6) Other real estate that is not permitted to be mortgaged in accordance with the law[70]

3. Eminent Domain

Prior to the expiration of the term of a land grant contract, the State may recover land use rights if the land is required for the public interest.[71] The "public interest" includes State construction for economic, cultural, and national defense as well as public welfare undertakings.[72] In such a case, the State is required to compensate the land user in an amount commensurate with the number of years of use, the time remaining in the land grant contract, the capital invested in improvements and structures, and resettlement

67. Administrative Measures on Urban Real Estate Mortgages, art. 23.
68. Administrative Measures on Urban Real Estate Mortgages, art. 15.
69. Administrative Measures on Urban Real Estate Mortgages, art. 24.
70. Administrative Measures on Urban Real Estate Mortgages, art. 8.
71. Land-Use Grant and Assignment Regulations, art. 42.
72. Land Management Law, art. 21.

costs.[73] The State may also expropriate land that is under collective ownership if doing so is in the public interest.[74] The MNLR has established an administrative review procedure for eminent domain cases.[75]

B. Real Estate Development and Real Estate Transactions

Real estate development, commercial and residential, is subject to urban development plans prepared by national, provincial, and other local governments. Development plans are required by law to be formulated to increase supervision of urban real estate, to maintain order in the real estate market, to safeguard the legal rights and interests of real estate title holders, and to promote the healthy development of the real estate industry.[76] Developers are required to use land consistent with government development plans, and according to the purpose of land grant contracts and within the time limits for commencement of projects.[77] In the event a party fails to commence a project more than one year after the time prescribed in the contract, an idle

73. Land Management Law, art. 28. The 2004 amendments to the PRC Constitution provide that compensation shall be paid to property owners for any expropriation of land by the State. *NPC Concludes: Enacts 14 Amendments, Approves Work Report,* CHINA MARKET INTELLIGENCE, THE U.S.-CHINA BUSINESS COUNCIL (March 18, 2004). Article 13 of the Constitution was amended to provide that the "lawful private property of citizens shall not be violated. The state shall protect private property rights and inheritance rights of citizens in accordance with the law. The state may, in the public interest, expropriate or requisition private property of citizens in accordance with the law and shall provide compensation therefore."

74. Land Management Law, art. 2.

75. Land Management Law, art. 23.

76. Urban Real Estate Law, art. 1. *See also* Administrative Rules on Urban Real Estate Development Operations (promulgated on July 20, 1998, by the State Council), *reprinted in* CHINA LAWS FOR FOREIGN BUSINESS (CCH), Business Regulation ¶ 19-595.

77. Urban Real Estate Law, art. 25. *See also* Several Regulations on the Establishment of Construction Industry Enterprises with Foreign Investment (promulgated on September 18, 1995, by the Ministry of Construction and MOFTEC), *reprinted in* CHINA LAWS FOR FOREIGN BUSINESS (CCH), Business Regulation ¶ 13-596 (hereinafter the "FIE Construction Regulations"). The regulations require minimum capital requirements and other conditions for the establishment of a Foreign-Invested Construction Enterprise (FICE). *See also* Provisional Regulations on Sino-Foreign Cooperative Design of Engineering and Construction Projects (approved on March 27, 1986, by the State Council and issued on June 5, 1986, by MOFTEC and the State Planning Commission), *reprinted in* CHINA LAWS FOR FOREIGN BUSINESS (CCH), Business Regulation ¶ 19-516; Rules for the Trial Implementation of the Economic Responsibility System in Undertaking Contract Projects of Capital Construction (promulgated on March 3, 1983, by the State Council), *reprinted in* CHINA LAWS FOR FOREIGN BUSINESS (CCH), Business Regulation ¶ 12-580. *See* Notice of the State Council on Issues Concerning the Levying and Collection of Taxes on Materials and Goods Imported for Real Estate Construction (promulgated on April 23, 1995, by the State Council), *reprinted in* CHINA LAWS FOR FOREIGN BUSINESS (CCH), Customs ¶ 50-615 (provisions concerning preferential duty treatment for construction materials and equipment). The NPC has adopted a Construction Law designed to improve the supervision and administration of construction activities, to promote the construction industry, and to ensure that construction projects are undertaken in a safe manner. *See* Construction Law of the People's Republic of China (adopted on November 1, 1997, by the 28th Sess. of the Standing Comm. of the 8th NPC), *reprinted in* CHINA LAWS FOR FOREIGN BUSINESS (CCH), Business Regulation ¶ 19-565 (outlines the qualifications for contractors, construction project building permits, construction contracts, tender process, construction project supervision, construction work safety management, construction project quality control, and legal liability). The Construction Law

land fee of up to 20 percent of the land-use fee may be imposed.[78] If the party fails to commence development after two years, the right to use the land may be recovered without compensation.

1. Commercial Land Development FIE

The State Council has adopted specific regulations governing commercial land development by foreign parties.[79] The purpose of the regulations is to attract foreign investment in commercial property development and management, and to ensure that land development is governed in accordance with approved national, provincial, and local plans.[80]

Foreign investors in commercial land development are required to establish either a joint venture enterprise or a WFOE to manage the development project.[81] Additional requirements for the establishment of a Commercial Land Development FIE include the following:

(1) Its own name and organization
(2) Fixed premises
(3) Registered capital in compliance with State Council regulations
(4) Sufficient professional and technical personnel
(5) Business license issued by the SAIC or local branch
(6) Other requirements as stipulated by laws and regulations[82]

A Commercial Land Development FIE is required to obtain rights to use State land in accordance with the land management and urban real estate laws and regulations, which includes registration and approval for all development projects.[83] The development enterprise is required to prepare a feasibility study

was effective March 1, 1998, and applies to all parties engaged in construction activities in China, including the construction of the various types of structures and their auxiliary facilities, as well as the installation activities involving related wiring circuits, pipelines, and equipment. *Id.* art. 2. The Shanghai Municipal government has also developed a set of guidelines for the construction industry, which is effective December 1, 1997. *See* Administrative Rules of the Shanghai Municipality on the Construction Market (adopted on October 21, 1997, by the 39th Sess. of the Standing Comm. of the 10th Shanghai Municipal People's Congress, and amended on October 31, 1999), *reprinted in* CHINA LAWS FOR FOREIGN BUSINESS (CCH), Special Zones & Cities ¶ 240-100 (outlines the qualifications for persons engaged in building activities, general contractor and subcontract activities, role of supervisory agencies, project contracts and building cost calculations, project quality and safety, and penalties and legal liability).

78. Urban Real Estate Law, art. 25.

79. Provisional Administrative Measures Governing Commercial Land Development and Management by Foreign Investors (promulgated on May 19, 1990, by the State Council), *reprinted in* CHINA LAWS FOR FOREIGN BUSINESS (CCH), Business Regulation ¶ 14-723 (hereinafter the "FIE Land Development Measures").

80. FIE Land Development Measures, arts. 1–3.

81. FIE Land Development Measures, art. 4. Development enterprises comprised of Hong Kong, Macao, or Taiwanese companies are considered to be foreign investment enterprises under Chinese law. FIE Land Development Measures, art. 17.

82. Urban Real Estate Law, art. 29.

83. FIE Land Development Measures, art. 5.

that outlines each stage of development and construction, and the overall objectives of the project.[84] Additionally, if the development zone is within an urban planning area, all development and construction projects are required to comply with urban planning regulations and be in accord with local development plans.[85]

A Commercial Land Development FIE may assign its rights of land use only after fulfilling the conditions of the commercial land development plan as determined by the MLNR and local land administration departments, and satisfying the conditions of the land-use rights contract.[86]

2. Real Estate Brokers, Property Managers, and Consultants

Real estate brokers and consultants fall under the definition of "Intermediate Service Agencies" under Chinese law and are required to meet the following conditions:

(1) Possess its own name and organization
(2) Possess fixed business premises
(3) Possess the requisite assets and funds
(4) Possess a sufficient number of professional personnel
(5) Meet other requirements stipulated by laws and statutory regulations[87]

To establish an intermediate real estate service agency and obtain a business license, an application must be submitted to the SAIC or local branch.

The State Council has adopted regulations governing the standards for property management companies employed by property owners to manage the common areas, facilities, and interests of the owners.[88] The Property Management Regulations encourage the use of public tender and bidding to engage a qualified management firm, and stipulate that the functions of property developers be kept separate for property management functions. Pursuant to the Regulations, the consent of the property owners is required

84. FIE Land Development Measures, art. 7.
85. FIE Land Development Measures, art. 8.
86. FIE Land Development Measures, art. 9.
87. Urban Real Estate Law, art. 57.
88. Property Management Regulations (promulgated by the State Council on June 8, 2003). *See also* Administrative Measures on Qualifications for Property Management Enterprises (issued on May 1, 2004, by the Ministry of Construction). The MOC Measures categorize foreign and domestic property management enterprises into three levels: Level 1 has registered capital of RMB5 million and 30 qualified professionals; Level 2 has registered capital of RMB3 million and at least 20 professionals on staff; and Level 3 has registered capital of RMB500,000 and 10 professionals. Level 1 enterprises may accept all types of property management contracts; Level 2 companies may accept residential projects of less than 300,000 sqm and nonresidential projects up to 80,000 sqm; and Level 3 companies may provide property management services for residential projects that are less than 200,000 sqm and commercial projects that are less than 50,000 sqm. A newly established company may only apply as a Level 3 enterprise, and applicants may apply after one year to change their tier level.

for the use and disposal of common areas and facilities. Property management companies are also required to manage the funds of the property owners with due care, and any revenue generated from the facilities must be used for the benefit of the property owners.

C. Petroleum and Mineral Resources

China has promulgated a number of laws and regulations with respect to oil and gas exploration and exploitation.[89] The laws provide registration requirements for exploration and exploitation operations, and regulations outlining the requirements for contracts, operational issues, and obligations of the parties to an offshore petroleum project. China has also developed rules with respect to royalty payments for offshore and inland oil operations.[90]

China has also adopted laws and regulations concerning the exploration and mining of mineral resources.[91] The Mineral Resources Law outlines the

89. *See* Provisional Measures Governing Control of Registration of Oil and Natural Gas Exploration and Exploitation (approved on December 16, 1987, by the State Council and promulgated on December 24, 1987, by the Ministry of Petroleum Industry), *reprinted* in CHINA LAWS FOR FOREIGN BUSINESS (CCH), Business Regulation ¶ 14-661 (outlining registration requirements for exploration/exploitation operations); Regulations of the People's Republic of China on the Exploitation of Offshore Petroleum Resources in Cooperation with Foreign Enterprises (adopted on January 12, 1982, by the State Council), *reprinted* in CHINA LAWS FOR FOREIGN BUSINESS (CCH), Business Regulation ¶ 14-560 (regulations outlining the requirement of exploration/exploitation contracts, operational issues, and obligations of the parties to an offshore petroleum contract); Regulations Regarding the Exploitation of Onshore Oil Resources in Cooperation with Foreign Parties (promulgated on September 23, 2001, by the State Council). China has also adopted special environmental protection rules for offshore oil producers, which require the preparation of a marine environmental impact report. *See* Regulations of the People's Republic of China Concerning Environmental Protection in Offshore Oil Exploration and Exploitation (promulgated on December 29, 1983, by the State Council), *reprinted* in CHINA LAWS FOR FOREIGN BUSINESS (CCH), Business Regulation ¶ 14-660. All petroleum exploration and exploitation contracts are required to be governed by Chinese law. *See* Chapter 7, Contract Law § A.7.

90. Regulations on the Payment of Royalties for the Exploitation of Offshore Petroleum Resources (promulgated on January 1, 1989, by the Ministry of Finance), *reprinted* in CHINA LAWS FOR FOREIGN BUSINESS (CCH), Business Regulation ¶ 14-565; Provisional Regulations on the Payment of Sino-Foreign Co-Operative Ventures of Royalties for the Exploitation of Onshore Oil Resources (promulgated and issued by the Ministry of Finance and approved by the State Council on January 13, 1990), *reprinted* in CHINA LAWS FOR FOREIGN BUSINESS (CCH), Business Regulation ¶ 14-640 (outlining royalty payments for onshore and inland oil exploration operations).

91. *See* Mineral Resources Law of the People's Republic of China (originally adopted on March 19, 1986, and amended on August 29, 1996, by the 21st Sess. of the Standing Comm. of the 8th NPC), *reprinted in* CHINA LAWS FOR FOREIGN BUSINESS (CCH), Business Regulation ¶ 14-711. Under the government reorganization plan of 1998, the Ministry of Land and Natural Resources (MLNR) has taken over the functions of the Ministry of Geology and Mineral Resources, the State Oceanography Bureau, and the State Bureau of Surveying and Mapping. The MLNR is responsible for interpreting and enforcing the Mineral Resources Law. The MLNR has used the Mineral Resources Law to shut down over 50,000 illegal mining operations since 1996. *See generally* Liu, *Conference Emphasizes Regulation of Mining,* CHINA DAILY (Oct. 26, 1998), available on Lexis, News Library, or on the Web site of the CHINA DAILY at http://www.chinadaily.com.cn. *See also* Several Issues Concerning Specific Law Application on Trial of Criminal Cases of Illegal or Prejudicial Mining Interpretation (promulgated on May 29, 2003, by the MLNR); Questions Relevant to Strengthening the Administration of Exploration Rights and Mining Rights Circular (promulgated on January 16, 2003, by the Beijing Municipal People's Government). *See generally* M. Ward & C. Izzard, *Exploration Rights in the PRC: The How To and Where To Guide,* CHINA L. & PRAC. (May 2003).

registration requirements for mining operations, obligations and restrictions on exploration rights, exploration and extraction methods, liability issues, and administrative penalties for violations. The implementing regulations of the Mineral Resources Law sets forth detailed requirements for applications and registration of mining operations, rights and obligations of holders of exploration rights, reporting requirements, fees, and dispute resolution.[92] The State Council has also adopted regulations concerning the royalty payments imposed upon mining operations.[93]

D. Preservation of Cultural Resources

The PRC has adopted standards governing the archaeological excavation of cultural relics, approval procedures for excavation endeavors, registration requirements for museum-stored relics, standards for private collections of cultural relics, standards for exportation of cultural relics, and penalties for violations of regulations governing cultural relics.[94] China has also adopted rules that address the standards for protecting underwater cultural relics in China's territorial and inland waters, standards for archaeological exploration and excavation, approval procedures, and penalties for any violation of the PRC's underwater cultural relics laws.[95]

---

92. Detailed Rules for the Implementation of the Mineral Resources Law of the People's Republic of China (promulgated on March 26, 1994, by the State Council), *reprinted in* CHINA LAWS FOR FOREIGN BUSINESS (CCH), Business Regulation ¶ 14-700; Administrative Measures for Registration of the Mining of Mineral Resources (promulgated on February 12, 1998, by the State Council), *reprinted in* CHINA LAWS FOR FOREIGN BUSINESS (CCH), Business Regulation ¶ 14-704. All contracts involving the exploitation of natural resources are required to be governed by Chinese law. *See* Chapter 7, Contract Law § A.7.

93. Administrative Regulations Governing Collection of Mineral Resource Royalty Fees (promulgated on February 27, 1994, by the State Council), *reprinted in* CHINA LAWS FOR FOREIGN BUSINESS (CCH), Business Regulation ¶ 14-703 (outlines rules for royalty computation for mining operations).

94. Law of the People's Republic of China on the Protection of Cultural Relics (promulgated on October 28, 2002, by the Standing Comm. of the 9th NPC); Detailed Rules for Implementing the Law of the People's Republic of China on the Protection of Cultural Relics (issued May 5, 1992, by the State Bureau of Culture), *reprinted in* CHINA LAWS FOR FOREIGN BUSINESS (CCH), Business Regulation ¶ 14-600. China has had difficulty stemming the flow of cultural relics that are exported and sold on the international market and relies upon international organizations and other governments to assist its efforts in preserving its cultural property. *See* Shao, *UNESCO Offers Aid to Protect Relics,* CHINA DAILY (June 17, 1998), available on Lexis, News Library, or on the Web site of the CHINA DAILY at http://www.chinadaily.com.cn; Z. Huilin, *Relics Protection Given New Zeal*, China Daily (February 23, 2004) (discussion of Shanghai's efforts in 2004 to adopt stricter standards for cultural relics preservation). For a review of China's cultural property protection laws, *see* J. MURPHY, PLUNDER AND PRESERVATION: CULTURAL PROPERTY LAW AND PRACTICE IN THE PEOPLE'S REPUBLIC OF CHINA (1996).

95. Administrative Rules of the People's Republic of China on the Protection of Underwater Cultural Relics (promulgated on October 20, 1989, by the State Council), *reprinted in* CHINA LAWS FOR FOREIGN BUSINESS (CCH), Business Regulation ¶ 14-592.

Key Laws and Regulations

Land Use and Land Transfer Laws

Law of the People's Republic of China on Land Management (adopted on June 25, 1986, at the 16th Sess. of the Standing Comm. of the NPC and amended on December 29, 1988, by the 5th Sess. of the Standing Comm. of the NPC, revised and re-promulgated on August 29, 1998, by the 4th Sess. Of the Standing Comm. Of the 9th NPC, and as Order No. 8 of the President of the PRC)

Rules for the Implementation of the Law of the People's Republic of China on Land Management (promulgated on Dec. 27, 1998, by the State Council)

Provisional Regulations of the People's Republic of China concerning the Grant and Assignment of the Right to Use State Land in Urban Areas (promulgated on May 24, 1990, by the State Council)

Provisions on the Grant of Use Rights for State-Owned Land by Agreement (issued on June 5, 2003, by the Ministry of Land Resources, and effective August 1, 2003)

Grant of State-Owned Leaseholds by Invitation for Bids, Auction, and Listing Provisions (issued by the Ministry of Land and Natural Resources in May 2002)

Beijing Municipality Procedures for Granting, Transferring and Leasing Land-Use Rights (Trial Implementation) (promulgated on September 28, 2002, by the Beijing State-Owned Land Resources and Housing Administrative Bureau)

Law of the People's Republic of China on the Administration of Urban Real Estate (adopted on July 5, 1994, at the 8th Sess. of the Standing Comm. of the NPC)

Several Issues Concerning the Application of the Law to Trial of Disputes Over Commercial Premises Sales and Purchase Contracts Interpretation (issued on April 28, 2003, by the Supreme People's Court)

Regulations on the Administration of Urban Real Estate Transfer (promulgated August 7, 1995, by Order No 45 of the Ministry of Construction, amended August 15, 2001, in accordance with the Decision of the Ministry of Construction on the Amendment of the Regulations on the Administration of Urban Real Estate Transfer)

Notice on Further Strengthening Administration of Real Estate Loan Services (issued on June 5, 2003, by the People's Bank of China)

Administrative Measures on Administrative Measures on Urban Real Estate Mortgages (promulgated on May 9, 1997, and revised on August 15, 2001, by the Ministry of Construction)

Administrative Rules on Urban Real Estate Development Operations (promulgated on July 20, 1998, by the State Council)

Construction Law and Regulations

Construction Law of the People's Republic of China (adopted on November 1, 1997, by the 28th Sess. of the Standing Comm. of the 8th NPC)

(*Continued*)

(*Continued from previous page*)

Several Regulations on the Establishment of Construction Industry Enterprises with Foreign Investment (promulgated on September 18, 1995, by the Ministry of Construction and MOFTEC)

Provisional Regulations on Sino-Foreign Cooperative Design of Engineering and Construction Projects (approved on March 27, 1986, by the State Council and issued on June 5, 1986, by MOFTEC and the State Planning Commission)

Rules for the Trial Implementation of the Economic Responsibility System in Undertaking Contract Projects of Capital Construction (promulgated on March 3, 1983, by the State Council)

Notice of the State Council on Issues concerning the Levying and Collection of Taxes on Materials and Goods Imported for Real Estate Construction (promulgated on April 23, 1995, by the State Council)

Administrative Rules of the Shanghai Municipality on the Construction Market (adopted on October 21, 1997, by the 39th Sess. of the Standing Comm. of the 10th Shanghai Municipal People's Congress, and amended on October 31, 1999)

Provisional Administrative Measures governing Commercial Land Development and Management by Foreign Investors (promulgated on May 19, 1990, by the State Council)

Property Management Regulations (promulgated by the State Council on June 8, 2003)

Administrative Measures on Qualifications for Property Management Enterprises (issued on May 1, 2004, by the Ministry of Construction)

Petroleum Resources

Provisional Measures Governing Control of Registration of Oil and Natural Gas Exploration and Exploitation (approved on December 16, 1987, by the State Council and promulgated on December 24, 1987, by the Ministry of Petroleum Industry)

Regulations of the People's Republic of China on the Exploitation of Offshore Petroleum Resources in Cooperation with Foreign Enterprises (adopted on January 12, 1982, by the State Council)

Regulations of the People's Republic of China Concerning Environmental Protection in Offshore Oil Exploration and Exploitation (promulgated on December 29, 1983, by the State Council)

Regulations on the Payment of Royalties for the Exploitation of Offshore Petroleum Resources (promulgated on January 1, 1989, by the Ministry of Finance)

Provisional Regulations on the Payment of Sino-Foreign Co-Operative Ventures of Royalties for the Exploitation of Onshore Oil Resource (promulgated and issued by the Ministry of Finance and approved by the State Council on January 13, 1990)

(*Continued*)

(*Continued from previous page*)

Mineral Resources

Mineral Resources Law of the People's Republic of China (originally adopted on March 19, 1986, and amended on August 29, 1996, by the 21st Sess. of the Standing Comm. of the 8th NPC)

Several Issues Concerning Specific Law Application on Trial of Criminal Cases of Illegal or Prejudicial Mining Interpretation (promulgated on May 29, 2003, by the MLNR)

Questions Relevant to Strengthening the Administration of Exploration Rights and Mining Rights Circular (promulgated on January 16, 2003, by the Beijing Municipal People's Government)

Detailed Rules for the Implementation of the Mineral Resources Law of the People's Republic of China (promulgated on March 26, 1994, by the State Council)

Administrative Measures for Registration of the Mining of Mineral Resources (promulgated on February 12, 1998, by the State Council)

Administrative Regulations governing Collection of Mineral Resource Royalty Fees (promulgated on February 27, 1994, by the State Council)

Cultural Resources

Law of the People's Republic of China on the Protection of Cultural Relics (promulgated on October 28, 2002, by the Standing Comm. of the 9th NPC)

Detailed Rules for Implementing the Law of the People's Republic of China on the Protection of Cultural Relics (issued May 5, 1992, by the State Bureau of Culture)

Administrative Rules of the People's Republic of China on the Protection of Underwater Cultural Relics (promulgated on October 20, 1989, by the State Council)

Chapter 18

Environmental Protection

Prior to the mid-1980s, China's economic policies emphasized the development of heavy industry rather than the conservation of natural resources or protection of the environment.[1] Although the PRC has adopted a series of environmental laws and regulations, enforcement continues to be secondary to economic and industrial development. In recent years, China has focused more attention on environmental protection and is increasingly investing a greater share of the GDP on pollution control and enforcement measures.[2] The NPC also demonstrates the importance of environmental

1. *See* M. Silks & L. Ross, *Environmental Planning for Investment Projects in China, in* DOING BUSINESS IN CHINA 11-5 (W. Streng & A. Wilcox, eds.) (1996); Wei, Tang & Dörwald, *Insurance, in* BUSINESS LAW IN CHINA: TRADE, INVESTMENT AND FINANCE 405 (D. Laprès & Y. Zhang, eds.) (1998); *China Suffering from Serious Pollution, Report Says,* JAPAN ECON. NEWSWIRE (Jun. 5, 1997), available on Lexis, News Library (discusses China government report concerning environmental woes caused by rapid economic development). *See also* L. RUILAN, HANDBOOK OF REGULATIONS ON ENVIRONMENTAL PROTECTION IN CHINA: RESOURCES FOR THE FUTURE (1995); Dasqupta, Huq, & Wheeler, *Bending the Rules: Discretionary Pollution Control in China,* World Bank Policy Research Working Paper No. 1761, February 1997, available at http://www.worldbank.org/nipr/work_paper/1761/index.htm; Wang & Wheeler, *Pricing Industrial Pollution in China: An Econometric Analysis of the Levy System,* World Bank Research Working Paper No. 1644, September 1996, available at http://www.worldbank.org/nipr/work_paper/1644/index.htm. *See generally* T. Szymanski, *The Clean Development Mechanism in China,* CHINA BUS. REV. Vol. 29, No. 6, November–December 2002 (author addresses the Clean Development Mechanism of the Kyoto Protocol and its potential impact on China).

2. Between 1991 and 1995, China spent an estimated 0.7 percent–0.8 percent of the government budget on improving its environmental condition. In 1997, the national and provincial governments reportedly spent approximately 3 percent on environmental enforcement and remedial efforts. Xiamen, for example, spends close to 3 percent of GDP on environmental protection, up from 1.85 percent in 1996. Shenzhen has invested approximately $93.3 million in environmental protection matters. Local governments are also increasingly adding environmental protection laws. Hainan Island, for example, has adopted over twenty laws and regulations. *See Special Economic Zones Protect Environment,* XINHUA NEWS AGENCY (June 10, 1998), available on Lexis, News Library; *China Laws Support Environmental Protection,* CHINA DAILY (June 5, 1998), available on Lexis, News Library, or on the Web site of

issues by elevating the State Environmental Protection Bureau to a ministry-level "administration" entity in March of 1998. The entity is now known as the State Environmental Protection Administration (SEPA) and has greater powers over enforcement matters.[3] The bureau formerly was under the supervision of the Ministry of Construction, which was guided by principles of economic development and growth in the construction industry, often at odds with environmental policy. The new title and elevation to a higher level reflect the NPC's great concern with environmental affairs and public expectation of environmental protection.[4]

In May of 2002, the State Environmental Protection Administration (SEPA) issued a grim annual report that the environmental situation in China "doesn't encourage optimism."[5] The report states that air quality was heavily polluted in a third of Chinese cities; water pollution remained a chronic problem, with 53 percent of China's 752 rivers and waterways showing high levels of toxins; and 90 percent of pastureland was degraded to various degrees. Rapid economic growth has resulted in many environmental problems, including water and soil pollution resulting from fertilizer and pesticide overuse, excessive discharge of industrial wastes, and the destruction of wetlands and wildlife habitats. In 1997, the Criminal Law was amended to include environmental damage as a crime. Additional laws and regulations are currently being drafted, including a national law to protect and control wetlands.

---

the CHINA DAILY at http://www.chinadaily.com.cn. In 1996, the State Environmental Protection Bureau closed over 70,000 enterprises as a result of violations of the Environmental Protection Law. *See Record of Events (Jan.–Mar. 1997), China Law* 102 (1997). *See Special Economic Zones Protect Environment,* Xinhua News Agency (June 10, 1998), available on Lexis, News Library; *China Laws Support Environmental Protection,* CHINA DAILY (June 5, 1998), available on Lexis, News Library, or on the Web site of the CHINA DAILY at http://www.chinadaily.com.cn. The China Environment Observer (CEO), an unofficial environmental watchdog group in the Henan Province, has openly criticized the national government's environmental protection record. The CEO stated that China has a broad range of environmental laws on the books but "rampant official corruption and lack of political will in a country primarily concerned with economic development have hampered efforts to clean up China's air, soil, and water at every turn." *See China: Unofficial Group Blasts Govt's Enviro Record,* National Journal Group, Greenwire (Jan. 15, 1999), available on Lexis, News Library.

3. *See* the Web site of SEPA at http://www.sepa.gov.cn for more information.

4. *See China Agency Given Greater Powers,* CHINA DAILY (Apr. 1, 1998), available on Lexis, News Library, or on the Web site of the CHINA DAILY at http://www.chinadaily.com.cn.

5. China plans to invest RMB300 billion ($36.6 billion) in environmental development over the next ten years. *See China to Invest Heavily in Environmental Protection,* Xinhua News Service (May 28, 2002) (statement by director of Resource Saving and Comprehensive Utilization Department of SEPA, Zhai Qing); *See* National Tenth Five-Year Plan for Environmental Protection [Huan Fa 2001 No. 193 issued by the State Environmental Protection Agency] and the Official Reply of the State Council on the National Tenth Five-Year Plan for Environmental Protection (promulgated on January 14, 2002, by the State Council). *See also* Notice on Issuing the Tenth Five-Year Plan for Reutilization of Renewable Resources (promulgated on January 10, 2002, by the State Economic and Trade Commission) (outlines the SETC's standards and plan for encouraging Chinese industry to adopt methods for recycling and reuse of resources); Tenth Five-Year Plan for the Development of the Environmental Protection Industry (promulgated on Oct. 12, 2001, by the State Economic and Trade Commission) (outlines the SETC's standards and guidelines for the development of the environmental protection industry in China); Opinions on Accelerating the Development of the Environmental Protection Industry (promulgated on June 12, 2001, by the SETC).

China now realizes the importance of balancing environmental and trade policies, and the need to standardize regulatory practices at a national level. Current policy measures for sustainable development include encouraging the use of clean fuels such as natural gas and electricity, encouraging the use of low-sulfa, high-quality coal, and establishing and enforcing emission standards for vehicles.[6] In addition, the government banned the importation of electronic waste, created a certification and labeling system for environmentally friendly imported products, improved pollutant discharge registration, taken ongoing steps to curb desertification and soil erosion, taken steps to reduce pollution water resources, and introduced tax incentives to encourage investments in environmentally friendly technology.

Since SEPA was created in 1998 and with the promulgation of new laws and regulations, enforcement efforts have improved. SEPA and its local units are charged with supervisory authority and have the right to inspect any enterprise, without a warrant or notice, that is suspected of violating the law or may visit a facility simply to confirm whether the operation is in compliance.

SEPA has issued monetary penalties and ordered facilities to suspend operations that fail or refuse to use pollution control devices, operations that remove pollution control devices without approval, operations that discharge pollutants in excess of standards, or operations that fail or refuse to take remedial measures in a timely manner. The official Chinese press is replete with daily examples of factories shut down or fined for environmental violations.[7] Since the Criminal Law was amended to include environmental crimes, SEPA has obtained prison terms against factory and production managers for damage to the environment. The focus of these investigations has been paper mills, chemical plants, mineral producers, and other pollution-generating facilities. SEPA has also cracked down on local environmental authorities that fail to enforce the law by sheltering polluting enterprises. SEPA has taken steps to end the practice of local protectionism by local government, which is to blame for many environmental problems. The courts, too, are cracking down on pollution by imposing civil damages

---

6. L. Liu, *Sustainability Top of the Agenda,* CHINA DAILY (March 10, 2003) (article quotes Chen Shouping, a deputy to the 10th NPC who states that "Environmental protection is vital in guaranteeing that China's economic development is sustainable in the next twenty years, a key period to achieve the goal of building a *xiaokang* society—one that is well-off in an all-around way.").

7. *See generally* G. Aibing, *Polluting Enterprises Get Punished,* CHINA DAILY (Sept. 26, 2002) (stating that 16,000 enterprises during the first nine months of 2002 were penalized for various environmental law infractions), available on the Web site of the CHINA DAILY; Q. Chuan, *Blitz to Target Polluting Firms,* CHINA DAILY (June 26, 2003) (article states that polluters were "publicly named and shamed" during a national campaign in 2003 to shut down polluting enterprises); G. Zi, *Enforcing Environmental Protection,* CHINA DAILY (August 18, 2003); P. Haixia, *Legislation to Protect Environment Top Priority,* CHINA DAILY (Nov. 6, 2003); P. Wonacott, *Polluters in China Feel No Pain: But Watchdog Seeks Changes by Holding Officials Accountable*, WALL ST. J. (March 24, 2004).

awards against liable parties.[8] In December 2001, an intermediate people's court in the Shaanxi province awarded a township over $1 million in damages resulting from a toxic chemical leak when a tanker truck carrying ten tons of sodium cyanide plunged into a river. This case reflects the public's desire to use the legal system against polluters, and this was one of the first large court-imposed civil damages awards based upon environmental liability.

China's environmental regulatory scheme includes laws or regulations addressing environmental protection,[9] solid waste pollution,[10] water pollution,[11] marine pollution,[12] the prevention of pollution from land-originating

8. *Environmental Matters,* China Daily (Aug. 20, 2002) (article notes that between 1998 and 2001 Chinese courts handled over 21,000 criminal cases involving environmental issues, which was an increase of annual cases by 25 percent).

9. Environmental Protection Law of the People's Republic of China (adopted on December 26, 1989, at the 11th Sess. of the Standing Comm. of the 7th NPC), *reprinted in* China Laws for Foreign Business (CCH), Business Regulation ¶ 14-530 (hereinafter the "Environmental Protection Law"). The NPC's Environmental and Resources Protection Committee intends to revise the Environmental Protection Law. The revision is part of the NPC's goals set forth in the ninth five-year plan. The goal of revision is to draft a basic law that addresses the overlapping provisions in the nine existing environmental protection laws and regulations. *See China NPC Fortifies Legislation Ecology, Resources Top Focus,* China Daily (May 28, 1998), available on Lexis, News Library, or on the Web site of the China Daily at http://www.chinadaily.com.cn. China has also adopted laws concerning the control of noise pollution (1996), conservation of soil and water (1991), coal conservation (1996), forestry (1984 and amended in 1998), water conservation (1988), preservation of grasslands (1985), fisheries (1986), and wildlife protection (1988). *See China List of Environment, Resource Protection, and Related Laws,* China Daily (May 28, 1998), available on Lexis, News Library, or on the Web site of the China Daily at http://www.chinadaily.com.cn. The NPC is developing a law to protect the Yellow River. *See* Guo, *Law to Protect the Yellow River,* China Daily (Oct. 16, 1998), available on Lexis, News Library, or on the Web site of the China Daily at http://www.chinadaily.com.cn.

10. Environmental Protection Law of the People's Republic of China concerning Solid Waste Pollution (promulgated on October 30, 1995, by the 16th Sess. of the Standing Comm. of the 8th NPC), *reprinted in* China Laws for Foreign Business (CCH), Business Regulation ¶ 14-525 (hereinafter the "Solid Waste Pollution Law").

11. Law of the People's Republic of China on Prevention and Control of Water Pollution (promulgated on May 15, 1996, by the Standing Comm. of the NPC); Detailed Rules for the Implementation of the Law of the People's Republic of China on the Prevention and Control of Water Pollution (Order No. 284 of the State Council of the People's Republic of China, promulgated on March 20, 2000, by the State Council), *reprinted in* China Laws for Foreign Business (CCH), Business Regulation ¶ 14-662 (outlines standards for preventing and controlling surface and below-surface water pollution and authorizes SEPA to issue fines up to RMB200,000 for violations). In 2004, the Beijing Municipal Government adopted rules on water resources to better control the exploitation of underground water resources and to encourage the use of recycled water. *See Beijing* to Draft Rules on Water Resources, China Daily (April 1, 2004).

12. Marine Environmental Protection Law of the PRC (adopted on August 23, 1982, at the 24th Sess. of the Standing Committee of the 5th NPC, revised on Dec. 25, 1999, at the 13th Sess. of the Standing Comm. of the 9th NPC, repromulgated on Dec. 25, 1999, by Order No. 26 of the President of the PRC), *reprinted in* China Laws for Foreign Business (CCH), Business Regulation ¶ 14-620 (hereinafter the "Marine Environmental Protection Law"). *See generally China Stresses Marine Environmental Protection,* Xinhua News Agency (May 28, 1998), available on Lexis, News Library; *China Issues White Paper on Marine Development,* Xinhua News Agency (May 28, 1998), available on Lexis, News Library (outlining the China Ocean Agenda 21, which concerns the PRC's development strategy for managing its marine resources); *China Oceans Crying Out for Greater Protection,* China Daily (May 18, 1998), available on Lexis, News Library, or on the Web site of the China Daily at http://www.chinadaily.com.cn. China is a party to the United Nations Convention on the Law of the Sea. *See generally* T. Min, *U.N. Convention Guides China's Ocean Laws,* China Daily (Dec. 5, 2002). China also has adopted various laws and regulations concerning the management and protection of fishery resources. Fishery Law

sources or onshore construction projects,[13] the prevention of discharges by vessels,[14] the prevention of pollution from offshore oil operations,[15] air pollution,[16] the importation of pollutants into China,[17] energy conservation,[18] forestry operations and management,[19] radioactive waste,[20] agricultural

---

of the People's Republic of China (promulgated on Oct. 31, 2000, by the Standing Comm. of the NPC) (replaces 1986 version of the law); Notification on Accomplishing the Work of Control over Fishing Suspension in 2002 (promulgated on April 29, 2002, by the Ministry of Agriculture).

13. Marine Environmental Protection Law, arts. 29–46. *See also* Administrative Regulations of the People's Republic of China to Prevent Land-Originating Pollutants from Damaging the Marine Environment (promulgated on June 22, 1990, by the State Council), *reprinted in* CHINA LAWS FOR FOREIGN BUSINESS (CCH), Business Regulation ¶ 14-622 (hereinafter the "Regulations Concerning the Control of Land-Originating Pollutants"). *See also* Administrative Regulations of the People's Republic of China to Prevent Pollution from Coastal Projects Damaging the Marine Environment (promulgated on June 25, 1990, by the State Council), *reprinted in* CHINA LAWS FOR FOREIGN BUSINESS (CCH), Business Regulation ¶ 14-624 (hereinafter the "Coastal Construction Regulations").

14. Marine Environmental Protection Law, arts. 62–72. *See also* Regulations of the People's Republic of China Controlling the Prevention of Pollution of Sea Areas by Vessels (promulgated on December 29, 1983, by the State Council of the People's Republic of China), *reprinted in* CHINA LAWS FOR FOREIGN BUSINESS (CCH), Business Regulation ¶ 14-663 (hereinafter the "Regulations Concerning Pollution by Vessels"). *See also* Regulations of the People's Republic of China Concerning the Control of the Dumping of Wastes at Sea (promulgated on March 6, 1985, by the State Council of the People's Republic of China), *reprinted in* CHINA LAWS FOR FOREIGN BUSINESS (CCH), Business Regulation ¶ 14-666.

15. Marine Environmental Protection Law, arts. 47–54. *See also* Regulations of the People's Republic of China Concerning Environmental Protection in Offshore Oil Exploration and Exploitation (promulgated on December 29, 1983, by the State Council), *reprinted in* CHINA LAWS FOR FOREIGN BUSINESS (CCH), Business Regulation ¶ 14-660 (hereinafter the "Regulations Concerning Pollution by Offshore Oil Operations").

16. Law of the People's Republic of China on the Prevention and Control of Air Pollution (adopted on September 5, 1987, by the 22nd Sess. of the Standing Comm. of the 6th NPC and amended on August 29, 1995, at the 15th Sess. of the Standing Comm. of the 8th NPC and amended on April 29, 2000, by the Standing Comm. of the NPC), *reprinted in* CHINA LAWS FOR FOREIGN BUSINESS (CCH), Business Regulation ¶ 14-720 (hereinafter the "Law on the Prevention and Control of Air Pollution"). *See Emissions Standards to Clear Air Pollution,* CHINA DAILY (July 26, 2002).

17. Notice on Strict Control of the Transmission of Pollutants into China from Outside Chinese Territory (issued on March 7, 1991, by the State Environmental Protection Bureau and the General Administration of Customs), *reprinted in* CHINA LAWS FOR FOREIGN BUSINESS (CCH), Business Regulation ¶ 14-709 (hereinafter the "Notice on Control of Importation of Pollutants"). China bans the importation of electronic wastes. *See China Develops List of Banned Electronic Waste from Overseas,* Xinhua News Agency (May 31, 2002) (list of banned imports includes television sets, computer displays, copy machines, video cameras, and mobile phones).

18. Energy Conservation Law of the People's Republic of China (promulgated on November 1, 1997, by the 28th Sess. of the Standing Comm. of the 8th NPC), *reprinted in* CHINA LAWS FOR FOREIGN BUSINESS (CCH), Business Regulation ¶ 14-505 (hereinafter the "Energy Conservation Law"). *See also* Certain Regulations of the State Economic Commission and the State Planning Commission for Further Economizing on Electricity Consumption (jointly promulgated on Mar. 12, 1987, by the State Economic Commission and the State Planning Commission), *reprinted in* CHINA LAWS FOR FOREIGN BUSINESS (CCH), Business Regulation ¶ 14-707. Various local governments have adopted their own implementing rules on energy conservation. *See* Implementation of the Energy Conservation Law (promulgated on Oct. 23, 1999, by the Beijing Municipal People's Government).

19. Forestry Law of the People's Republic of China (adopted on Sept. 20, 1984, by the 7th Sess. of the Standing Comm. of the 6th NPC, amended April 29, 1998, by the 2nd Sess. of the Standing Comm. of the 9th NPC), *reprinted in* CHINA LAWS FOR FOREIGN BUSINESS (CCH), Business Regulation ¶ 14-510 (outlines standards for forestry operations and management, forestry protection, timber management, and liability issues).

20. Law on Radioactive Pollution and Control (promulgated on June 28, 2003, by the NPC, and effective Oct. 1, 2003) (law outlines the management and control of radioactive materials, standards for environmental assessments of radioactive materials, registration procedures, prohibitions on importations, and legal liability). *See* Q. Chuan, *Radioactive Law Imminent,* CHINA DAILY (Sept. 29, 2003).

land protection,[21] protection of wildlife,[22] and environmental impact assessment reporting.[23] This chapter also addresses the environmental protection laws of China, including an analysis of the regulatory scheme concerning solid waste, importation of hazardous waste, marine pollution control, and air pollution.

A. Environmental Protection Law

The purpose of the Environmental Protection Law (EPL) is to "protect and improve the human environment and the ecological environment, prevent and control pollution and other environmental hazards, safeguard people's health and promote the development of China's socialist modernization."[24] The EPL applies to the protection of China's environmental resources on land and China's marine resources.[25] This protective law serves as a curative, but also preventative law in that it gives individuals or entities the right to notify the SEPA authorities of the acts of other individuals or entities that have a polluting effect, and it encourages the "development of scientific and educational activities in environmental protection."[26] The EPL grants SEPA and its local branches the power to establish the general environmental quality standards and to develop a monitoring system to ensure that the standards are enforced.[27]

A party that knowingly possesses radioactive waste is required to ensure safety, avoid environmental pollution, and arrange for disposal by the municipal department with the specific responsibility for administration and handling of radioactive waste. Urban Radioactive Waste Administration Measures (issued in 1987 and administered by SEPA). Local regulations add more restrictions in some provinces and cities, and typically restrict or prohibit the transport of radioactive waste from one province to another. *See generally* Tianjin Radioactive Waste Administration Measures, Hebei Radioactive Pollution Prevention and Control Administrative Measures, Jilin Radioactive Waste Disposal Collection and Storage Measures, Henan Radioactive Waste Administration Measures, Guangdong Radioactive Waste Administration Measures, and Sichuan Radioactive Pollution Prevention and Control Administration Measures.

21. The PRC government in 2003 amended several agriculture-related laws to protect the interests of farmers and agricultural resources, including amendments to the Agricultural Law, Law of Rural Land Contract, and Grasslands Law. *See* S. Bin, *New Laws to Safeguard Farmers' Interests,* China Daily (Feb. 18, 2003).

22. Regulations of the People's Republic of China on the Protection of Wild Plants (promulgated on Sept. 30, 1996, by the NPC); Notice of the State Council on the Strict Protection of Precious and Rare Wild Animals (promulgated on April 13, 1983, by the State Council); Implementing Regulations of the People's Republic of China on the Protection of Terrestrial Wildlife (promulgated on March 1, 1992, by the State Bureau of Forestry) (outlines rules for management and protection of wildlife, hunting standards, standards for breeding and domestication of wildlife, standards for business operators that exhibit wildlife, and penalties); Jurisdiction and Case-Registration Criteria for Criminal Cases on Forests and Land Wild Animals (promulgated on May 9, 2001, by the Ministry of Public Security and the State Bureau of Forestry) (outlines the types of criminal matters involving wildlife protection that are handled by the MPS). *See generally Nature Reserves Key to Biodiversity Conservation in China,* Xinhua News Agency (May 22, 2002).

23. Law of the People's Republic of China on Environmental Impact Assessment (promulgated by the Standing Committee of the National People's Congress on October 28, 2002, and effective on September 1, 2003) (hereinafter the "EIA Law"). The EIA Law is similar to the standards and procedures of the National Environmental Policy Act (NEPA) and corresponding state laws in the United States. *See generally New Law to Safeguard Ecosystem,* China Daily (August 27, 2003).

24. Environmental Protection Law, art 1.

25. Environmental Protection Law, art. 3.

26. Environmental Protection Law, arts. 5, 6.

27. Environmental Protection Law, arts. 9, 10, 11.

1. Environmental Protection Responsibility System

The EPL provides that any entity that produces pollutants must initiate an "environmental protection responsibility system," which must effectively assess and control waste gases, waste water, waste residue, dust, noxious gases, radioactive material, noise, vibrations, electromagnetic radiation, or other results of production, construction, or other activities that pollute and harm the environment.[28] The EPL prohibits the construction of industrial or production facilities in regions that require higher protection, such as well-known scenic areas.[29]

The EPL also provides that new industrial operations, or existing operations that intend to install new equipment, are required to install technologically advanced equipment that meets energy efficiency and environmentally safe standards.[30] In new industrial facilities, pollution control equipment is required to be installed and operational at the same time as the primary equipment, and such a facility may not be approved for commencement of production until pollution control equipment is operational.[31] An industrial facility is also prohibited from dismantling or idling pollution control equipment without approval from SEPA. The EPL provides that it is unlawful to transfer pollution-causing production equipment to an enterprise or facility that lacks the capacity to prevent and control pollution emission.[32]

2. Control of Chemicals/Radioactive Materials

The EPL provides that enterprises and individuals that produce, store, transport, sell, or use poisonous chemicals and products containing radioactive properties must guard against environmental contamination.[33] Materials

---

28. Environmental Protection Law, art. 24.

29. Environmental Protection Law, art. 18.

30. Environmental Protection Law, art. 25. The EPL also prohibits the importation of technology and equipment that fail to comply with environmental protection standards. *Id.* art. 30. For a review of the Clean Production Law, *see infra* note 158 and accompanying text.

31. Environmental Protection Law, art. 26.

32. Environmental Protection Law, art. 34.

33. Environmental Protection Law, art. 33. *See also* Administrative Measures on Safety of Hazardous Chemicals (promulgated on January 26, 2002, by the State Council); List of Hazardous Goods, National Standard GB 12268 (promulgated on January 26, 2002, by the State Council) (outlines the use and production of chemicals and safety measures related thereto). At present the local governments of the municipality of Tianjin and Shanghai and the province of Jiangsu have issued their own local regulations specifically addressing the control of hazardous waste. These local regulations are: Tianjin Municipality Prevention and Control of Environmental Pollution by Hazardous Waste Measures; Jiangsu Province Hazardous Waste Administration Measures (Interim); and Shanghai Municipality Prevention and Control of Pollution by Hazardous Waste Measures. China has also adopted environmental regulations governing the registration of "new chemical substances" manufactured or imported into China. *See* Regulations on New Chemical Substances (adopted on Oct. 15, 2003, by the State Environmental Protection Administration). The regulations create a system through which a manufacturer or importer of "new chemical substances," as defined, applies for a registration certificates with the Chemical Registration Center of the State Environmental Protection Administration (CRC-SEPA). Under the regulations, a

constituting "Hazardous Waste" are listed in the National Directory of Hazardous Waste, issued in 1998 and 2002, and administered by the State Administration of Environmental Protection.

3. Control of Construction-Related Pollution

The EPL mandates that developers prepare environmental impact reports (EIR), which are required to assess the amount of pollution likely to be produced by a project and its effect on the environment.[34] The EIR is also required to describe the types of prevention and control measures that will be included in a development project. The land-use and planning authorities may issue project approval only after an EIR has been approved by SEPA.

The EPL also provides that environmental protection policies should be considered when land-use and planning authorities develop urban development and zoning plans.[35] In general, development projects are required to integrate the special characteristics of a local region's natural environment; must take steps to protect the natural vegetation, waterways, and natural scenery; and use designs or architecture in urban areas that includes parks, gardens, and greenbelts.[36]

4. Control of Agricultural-Related Pollution

The EPL mandates that SEPA and local governments take steps to protect and improve agricultural resources, including the prevention of soil contamination and degradation, earth subsidence and erosion, and water loss and contamination. The EPL further requires that government authorities prevent and eliminate plant diseases and insect pests, and manage the appropriate use of chemical fertilizers, pesticides, and plant growth hormones used in agriculture.[37]

"new chemical substance" is any chemical substance that has not yet been manufactured in or imported into China before the date on which the manufacturer or the importer issues the notification, i.e., chemicals that are not in SEPA's existing inventory of chemical substances. The regulations authorize SEPA to establish standards and requirements for the management of new chemical substances. They also mandate SEPA to set up a group of experts to evaluate the environmental impact of new chemical substances. Applicants that falsify information in the application process or engage in one of the prohibited acts enumerated in the regulations are subject to penalties and rejections of their applications by the SEPA for three years.

34. Environmental Protection Law, art. 13. *See also* Administrative Rules on Environmental Protection with Respect to Construction Projects (by Order No. 253 of the State Council of the People's Republic of China and adopted on Nov. 18, 1998, by the 10th Meeting of the Standing Comm. of the State Council, and promulgated on Nov. 29, 1998), *reprinted in* CHINA LAWS FOR FOREIGN BUSINESS (CCH), Business Regulation ¶ 14-523 (outlines standards for environmental impact reviews for construction projects, procedures for construction of environmental protection facilities at construction projects, and liability issues).

35. Environmental Protection Law, art. 22.

36. Environmental Protection Law, art. 23.

37. Environmental Protection Law, art. 20.

5. Inspection, Remedial Action, and Penalties

A pollutant-producing operation is required to register with SEPA.[38] SEPA and its units are charged with supervisory authority and have the right to inspect any enterprise, without a warrant or notice, that is suspected of violating the law.[39] An enterprise that discharges pollutants in amounts in excess of national or local standards is required to pay a discharge fee and is liable to pay the cost of cleanup.[40] SEPA may order an operation that causes serious environmental pollution to take remedial steps to correct the damage within a specific period of time.[41] If environmental damage results or is likely to result from an accident or other unexpected occurrence, the enterprise involved is required to immediately take remedial measures to protect against further damage, to notify authorities and persons in the vicinity of the accident, and to report the incident to SEPA.[42]

SEPA has authority to issue warnings or monetary penalties if the provisions of the EPL are violated by a party that commits any of the following acts:

(1) Refuses to allow SEPA to conduct an inspection of its premises, or deceives environmental authorities during the inspection
(2) Fails to register with SEPA as a pollutant-producing operation, or provides false information to SEPA concerning its operation
(3) Fails to pay the excess discharge fees
(4) Imports technology/equipment that does not comply with the environmental protection requirements
(5) Transfers production equipment that discharges a large amount of pollutants to an installation that does not have a pollution prevention system[43]

SEPA is also authorized to issue monetary penalties and order a facility to suspend its operation if it is in violation of the EPL, including operations that fail or refuse to use pollution control devices, operations that remove

38. Environmental Protection Law, art. 27.

39. Environmental Protection Law, art. 14. In July of 2003, the Shanghai Environmental Protection Bureau launched a new pollution inspection campaign. The campaign focuses on outdated technology, producers of secondary pollution, and discarded electrical equipment and machinery. To review the Shanghai EPB inspection notice and policy statement, *see* http://www.sepb.gov.cn.

40. Environmental Protection Law, art. 28. The pollution discharge fees are exacted for purposes of subsidizing pollution prevention programs and control only. *See* Zhu, *Waste Levy Raised to Cover Treatment Costs,* CHINA DAILY (June 25, 1998), available on Lexis, News Library, or on the Web site of the CHINA DAILY at http://www.chinadaily.com.cn (SEPA to raise discharge fees to cover cost of urban waste treatment plants).

41. Environmental Protection Law, art. 29.

42. Environmental Protection Law, art. 31.

43. Environmental Protection Law, art. 35.

pollution control devices without approval, or operations that fail or refuse to take remedial measures in a timely manner.[44] Criminal penalties may also apply when a violation of the EPL has a significant impact on the loss of personal or public property or causes serious injury or death.[45] SEPA is also authorized to issue incentive rewards to individuals and entities that make significant contributions to protecting and improving the environment.[46]

6. Judicial Remedies

A party that disagrees with an administrative penalty imposed by SEPA or its local branch may, within fifteen days of receiving notice of the penalty decision, file a complaint with the people's court for judicial review.[47] Any person or entity that is injured as a result of a violation of the EPL may petition SEPA to investigate and issue an order for compensation for damages or file an action directly with the people's court.[48] The limitations period for compensation claims, either filed administratively or in court, for environmental damage is three years and is calculated from the date the claimant becomes aware, or should have been aware of, the damage.[49] The EPL provides that a party is not liable for environmental damage due entirely to force majeure or other unavoidable events, so long as the violator takes prompt remedial measures.[50]

B. Control of Solid Waste Pollution

The Solid Waste Pollution Law (SWPL) supplements the EPL and specifically addresses the protection of the environment from solid waste.[51] The objective of the SWPL is to encourage and support the development of clean production

44. Environmental Protection Law, arts. 36, 37, 39.

45. Environmental Protection Law, art. 43. The 1997 Criminal Law provides that it is a crime to seriously damage China's environment and natural resources. An individual that is convicted of an environmental crime may be imprisoned for up to ten years. For a discussion of the Criminal Law, *see* Chapter 23, Criminal Liability for FIE Activities § C. *See generally Amended Criminal Law to Punish Polluters,* Xinhua News Agency (Apr. 10, 1997), available on Lexis, News Library. *See also Tiger-Killing Farmers Imprisoned,* CHINA DAILY (June 15, 1998), available on Lexis, News Library, or on the Web site of the CHINA DAILY at http://www.chinadaily.com.cn (under the Criminal Law and the Law on the Protection of Wildlife, two farmers that killed a protected Siberian Tiger were given prison terms of four years).

46. Environmental Protection Law, art. 8.

47. Environmental Protection Law, art. 40. SEPA may also apply to the court in order to enforce its penalty decision against the errant enterprise or individual. *Id.*

48. Environmental Protection Law, art. 41. A party that elects to petition SEPA may file an action with the people's court if it disagrees with the award or decision of SEPA and is not barred from seeking judicial relief. *Id.*

49. Environmental Protection Law, art. 42.

50. Environmental Protection Law, art. 41.

51. Solid Waste Pollution Law, arts. 1, 2, 3, 5, 6, 7. The Solid Waste Pollution Law does not apply to the marine environment. *Id.* art. 2. The purpose of the Solid Waste Pollution Law is to "reduc[e] production of solid waste, the complete comprehensive and appropriate utilization of solid waste and the harmless disposal of solid waste." *Id.* art. 3.

methods and reduction of solid waste produced in industry.[52] Similar to the EPL, citizens are encouraged to notify the authorities of any individual or entity that violates the law.[53]

1. Product Packaging and Recycling

The SWPL requires business operators to use environmentally safe packaging that can be reused or recycled, or is biodegradable.[54] The law requires that containers or packaging containing dangerous waste materials display symbols identifying the materials.[55]

2. Storage and Transportation of Solid Waste

The SWPL requires enterprises that collect, store, or treat solid waste to register and apply for an operating license.[56] The SWPL requires that individuals and businesses that collect, store, transport, utilize, or treat solid waste adopt measures to prevent solid waste from scattering, washing away, leaking, or in any way polluting the environment. The construction of storage or treatment facilities for industrial solid waste must comply with the SWPL standards and be approved by SEPA.[57] The SWPL prohibits a party from

52. Solid Waste Pollution Law, art. 4. The government in 2003 revised and reformed the pricing and management systems in waste treatment sectors to allow governments to charge issuer fees for treatment in order to attract private debt or equity investors. *See* Opinion Regarding Promoting Development of Industrialization of Urban Sewage and Waste Treatment Sectors (jointly issued on Sept. 10, 2002, by the State Development Planning Commission (SDPC), the Ministry of Construction (MOC), and the State Environmental Protection Agency (SEPA)). All cities throughout China may introduce sewage and waste treatment fee charges by the end of 2003. In both cases, charges are to be approved by municipal governments and after public hearings. The collected fees are required to be used solely for construction, operation, and maintenance of urban sewage and waste treatment facilities. A reasonable return on investment will be determined by reference to long-term loan interest rates, operational costs, and other conditions, depending on individual cases. With the Opinion, the government has promoted a concession system whereby the project developer obtains the right to operate sewage or waste treatment projects for the concession period, through a public tendering process. For new projects, concessions are granted to investors to allow them to build and operate the facility profitably for a certain period of time and subsequently to transfer it to the government for free. *See generally* Y. Wang, *Reforming the Urban Sewage and Waste Treatment Sectors,* CHINA L. & PRAC. (Feb. 2003). *See* Notice Concerning Value-Added Tax Policy Concerning Sewage Processing Charges (promulgated on June 19, 2001, by the Ministry of Finance and the State Administration of Taxation) (outlines VAT exemption for urban sewage processing facilities). *See also* Notification on Implementing the Charging System for Disposal of Urban Domestic Refuse and Promoting the Industrialization of Refuse Disposal (promulgated on July 1, 2002, by the State Development Planning Commission, the Ministry of Finance, the Ministry of Construction, and the State Environmental Protection Administration) (outlines standards and incentives for recycling and disposal of urban refuse). Municipalities are also providing concessions. *See* Beijing Municipality Concessions for Urban Infrastructure Procedures (promulgated by the Beijing Municipal People's Government on August 28, 2003).

53. Solid Waste Pollution Law, art. 9. The government also issues awards to citizens that make contributions to protecting the environment and assist in combating solid waste pollution. *Id.* art 8.

54. Solid Waste Pollution Law, art. 18. The SWPL sets forth additional standards requiring recycling and reuse of household solid waste. *Id.* arts. 35–40.

55. Solid Waste Pollution Law, art. 44.

56. Solid Waste Pollution Law, art. 49. Individuals that are engaged in operations to collect, store, transport, or treat dangerous waste materials must undergo special training and examination. *Id.* art. 54. Such enterprises are required to establish emergency response procedures for addressing accidents involving dangerous solid waste. *Id.* arts. 55–57.

57. Solid Waste Pollution Law, art. 34.

discarding or dumping solid waste during transport to an authorized refuse site.[58] Waste that is transported from one region to another is required to have been approved by SEPA.[59]

The law also provides that it is illegal to transport both passengers and dangerous waste materials together, and also to mix dangerous with non-dangerous waste materials.[60] The SWPL further requires that sites, facilities, containers, equipment, packaging, or other items used to collect, store, transport, or treat dangerous waste materials must be treated to remove any pollutants if they are required to be used for any other purpose.[61]

The key obligation of the producer of hazardous waste under the current laws is that it must contract with a licensed and registered waste disposal company with respect to the handling of "hazardous" waste materials, as defined in Article 49 of the SWPL and set forth in the National Catalogue of Hazardous Waste, which is published by SEPA. Article 64 of the SWPL empowers SEPA to order a party to clean up any polluting activities that may result from entrusting waste materials to an *unlicensed* disposal company. The government can also levy a fine against any party of up to RMB50,000 ($6,097) for using an *unlicensed* disposal company. However, there is no rule at this time that allows the government to pursue cleanup costs from a producer if the waste materials are collected, stored, or transported by a licensed disposal company. At the same time, there is no law or regulation that grants a producer immunity from liability for cleanup costs if the waste is transferred to a licensed disposal company.

A producer of hazardous waste is also required to abide by the *Management Regulation for Hazardous Waste Transfer Manifests*, which took effect on October 1, 1999. The Transfer Manifests Regulations apply to all enterprises that transport dangerous/hazardous waste within China and establish a five-copy transfer manifest that must be completed by and shared among the waste producer and disposal/storage firm. The Transfer Manifests Regulations also provide that the local environmental protection bureaus (EPB) have jurisdiction over the waste producer, the transporter, and the treatment, storage, or disposal (TSD) facility. The Transfer Manifests Regulations also require and create a "cradle-to-grave" approach to hazardous waste management. Producers must apply for approval of Hazardous Waste Transfer Plans and notify the local EPBs prior to the transfer of the hazardous waste.

58. Solid Waste Pollution Law, art. 16.
59. Solid Waste Pollution Law, art. 23.
60. Solid Waste Pollution Law, arts. 50–52. The law defines "dangerous waste materials" as waste with properties that create a health or safety risk to persons or property. *Id.* art. 74 § (4).
61. Solid Waste Pollution Law, art. 53.

The producer's obligations under the Transfer Manifests Regulations are set forth in articles 4–6. Specifically, the Producer is required to report to the local EPB its hazardous waste transfer plan for approval and can obtain original copies of the manifest forms from the EPB at the time its plan is approved. A separate manifest must be prepared for each shipment and/or for each type of waste to be transported. The producer is required to maintain Copy No. 1 (white color) of the manifest for its records and to submit Copy No. 2 (red color) to the local EPB. Fines ranging from RMB10,000 ($1,200) to RMB50,000 ($6,000) may be imposed for violations of the Transfer Manifests Regulations.

Practice Tip: Dealing with PRC Waste Disposal Firms

In addition to working with a qualified and licensed waste disposal company, it is strongly recommend that the waste producer do both its due diligence of its waste disposal services companies and negotiate a contract that spells out the parties' obligations and liabilities. The producer should request that its disposal services companies and any other Chinese party involved with the transportation, storage, and disposal of waste provide a copy of their business license, operator's license, and training certificates prior to engaging in any services.

SEPA confirms that there are no specific requirements for waste disposal services contracts or any rules governing the relationship between the waste producer and the disposal company except with respect to the Transfer Manifests Regulations. There are, however, many requirements for waste disposal companies and a stringent set of licensing rules. If a company meets the requirements, then it is allowed to conduct disposal services business. If a waste producer is currently using a local disposal station, it is probably also using a simple waste services agreement. Most form contracts used by the disposal services companies are simple documents that are very basic and do not address issues that are common in agreements used by most multinational companies operating in more stringent regulatory environments such as the U.S. As China gets tougher with its environmental standards, many companies are negotiating much more detailed waste services agreements that clearly and unequivocally spell out the parties' respective obligations and liabilities.

In sum, the producer needs to (1) understand and follow its obligations under the current laws, including the Transfer Manifests Regulations, (2) conduct a due diligence of the waste services companies that it works with, (3) consider negotiating agreements with its waste services companies that clearly and unambiguously outline the parties' relationship, obligations, and liabilities, and (4) monitor the trends in both the law, including the anticipated Implementing Guidelines, and the enforcement efforts of SEPA and its local EPBs.

The SWPL further provides that the importation of solid waste that cannot be used as a raw material is unlawful, and the importation of solid waste that can be used as raw material is highly regulated.[62] The law further provides that it is strictly prohibited to import dangerous waste materials into China.[63]

3. Control of Solid Waste in Construction Projects

The SWPL requires that construction companies and employees are required to promptly remove and treat all refuse produced during the construction process.[64] If an individual or enterprise intends to engage in a construction project that will produce industrial solid waste, or if a party intends to construct a facility for the storage and treatment of solid waste, the development plans must include an EIR that evaluates the anticipated level of pollution from the solid waste produced by the project and its effect on the environment. The report must also describe pollution prevention and control methods that the development project will implement during the construction process. The EIR must be submitted and approved by SEPA before the planning authorities authorize the commencement of the development project.[65] The SWPL also prohibits developers from constructing waste treatment and storage facilities in proximity to water sources, natural protective zones, scenic and tourist zones, and other areas requiring special protection.[66]

4. Control of Industrial Solid Waste

The SWPL mandates that all levels of government are to encourage the use of production equipment that is capable of reducing the amount of industrial waste. SEPA is required to prepare a list of obsolete production techniques and equipment that produce industrial waste harmful to the environment. The techniques and equipment included in the list are required to be phased out over time and producers, retailers, importers, and consumers are required to cease selling or using the equipment and to cease using production techniques upon demand from SEPA.[67] It is prohibited to sell or transfer equipment that is listed as obsolete by SEPA.

62. Solid Waste Pollution Law, art 25. *See generally* Wingo, *Translation: The Garbage Smuggling Case: Judgment of Division One of the Shanghai Municipal Intermediate Level People's Court January 13, 1997*, 6 PAC. RIM L. & POL'Y 607 (1997) (translated and annotated court decision involving smuggling by U.S. citizen). *See also* Notice on Control of Importation of Pollutants, art. 1.

63. Solid Waste Pollution Law, art. 58.

64. Solid Waste Pollution Law, art. 41.

65. Solid Waste Pollution Law, arts. 12, 13.

66. Solid Waste Pollution Law, art. 22.

67. Solid Waste Pollution Law, art. 27.

A business enterprise that produces industrial solid waste is required to implement a responsibility system for the prevention and control of solid waste pollution in the environment.[68] The SWPL encourages business operators to select and use raw materials and energy sources in a careful manner and to use advanced production equipment and techniques to reduce their solid waste output.[69]

5. Inspection, Remedial Action, and Penalties

SEPA is the PRC agency responsible for enforcing the SWPL and is empowered to conduct inspections and audits of production facilities to ensure compliance with the law.[70] SEPA is required to maintain the confidentiality of all technical and business information received during any audits and investigations under the SWPL.[71] An entity subject to an inspection is required to cooperate with SEPA and its representatives during its investigation. In addition, business enterprises are required to register with SEPA and to provide a detailed annual report concerning the discharge, storage, and treatment of industrial solid waste of the enterprise.[72]

An individual or enterprise that produces solid waste that seriously damages the environment may be ordered by SEPA to take remedial action in a prompt manner.[73] SEPA is also authorized to order remedial measures and to issue monetary penalties if an individual or business enterprise violates any of the provisions of the SWPL.[74] In cases involving bodily injury, loss of life, or serious damage to property, the responsible party may be prosecuted under the Criminal Law.[75]

6. Judicial Remedies

Any individual or enterprise may seek compensation as a result of damages from solid waste pollution. Compensation may be claimed by filing either an administrative petition with SEPA or a complaint directly with the people's

68. Solid Waste Pollution Law, art. 29.
69. Solid Waste Pollution Law, arts. 25, 30.
70. Solid Waste Pollution Law, art. 11.
71. Solid Waste Pollution Law, art. 14. Inspection personnel are required to present their credentials when conducting inspections. *Id.* The trend in the mid-1990s is to require that administrative agencies present their credentials when conducting investigations, inspections, or audits. This requirement ensures that entities are treated with due process and respect, and to protect against abuse by errant authorities.
72. Solid Waste Pollution Law, art. 31.
73. Solid Waste Pollution Law, art. 21.
74. Solid Waste Pollution Law, arts. 59–69. An enterprise that violates the law may be subject to pollution discharge fees. Solid Waste Pollution Law, art. 34. The discharge fees may be used only to prevent and control environmental pollution and not for any other purpose.
75. Solid Waste Pollution Law, art. 72. *See* Chapter 23, Criminal Liability for FIE Activities § C.

court.[76] A party that disputes a decision by SEPA may file an action in the people's court for judicial review within fifteen days of receipt of a decision.[77]

C. Control of Marine Pollution

The Marine Environmental Pollution Law (MEPL) is designed to protect the marine resources of China from the discharge of harmful pollutants and promote sustainable development.[78] The discharge of pollutants from coastal construction, offshore oil exploration and exploitation, vessels, and aircraft is an area of special attention under the MEPL.

1. Control of Land-Originating Pollutants

The MEPL and supplemental regulations regulate activities that result in the introduction of land-based pollutants to the marine environment.[79] The law prohibits the dumping of toxic or harmful liquid waste, medical waste, waste containing high or medium amounts of radioactive substances, petroleum-based substances, aqueous acids, alkalis, poison, or water with an elevated temperature.[80] Enterprises or individuals that discharge land-originating pollutants into the sea must register with the SEPA and submit an EIR that details the nature of the pollutants, the quantity and concentration discharged under normal circumstances, and particulars concerning preventative measures to be employed.[81] For example, before a developer secures approval to commence a construction project in proximity to China's coastal areas, an EIR must be submitted for approval to SEPA.[82] Construction projects may not, by law, destroy seashore shelterbelts, scenic woods, scenic rocks, mangroves, and coral reefs.

It is also prohibited for any individual or business to discharge land-based pollutants in a conservation zone, sightseeing or tourist area, or fishery.[83]

---

76. Solid Waste Pollution Law, art. 71.
77. Solid Waste Pollution Law, art. 71.
78. Marine Environmental Protection Law, art. 1. *See also* Environmental Protection Law, art. 21.
79. Marine Environmental Protection Law, arts. 29–41; Regulations Concerning the Control of Land-Originating Pollutants, art. 1.
80. Regulations Concerning the Control of Land-Originating Pollutants, arts. 13–19.
81. Regulations Concerning the Control of Land-Originating Pollutants, art. 6.
82. Marine Environmental Protection Law, art. 43. The State Council has also developed specific regulations governing construction projects sited near shorelines or other coastal areas. *See* Coastal Construction Regulations, arts. 8, 26 (outlines the requirements for an EIR for a coastal construction project). *See also* Ports Law (adopted at the 3rd Session of the Standing Committee of the 10th National People's Congress, promulgated on June 28, 2003, and effective as of January 1, 2004), arts. 7, 15 (requiring EIR for port construction).
83. Regulations Concerning the Control of Land-Originating Pollutants, art. 8; Coastal Construction Regulations, art. 24.

However, if there is an already existing discharge conduit operating in these areas, the amount of pollutants that may be discharged must comply with national or local standards. In addition, the law permits a party to temporarily store or dispose of solid waste in a coastal area if a written application is submitted to, and approved by, SEPA. The application is required to outline and describe the proposed site, the types of materials to be stored or discharged, the length of time of the storage or discharge, the responsible party, the technology and measures to be employed to prevent damage to the marine environment, and the date of removal.[84]

In the event of an accident involving the contamination of the marine environment by land-based pollutants, the individual or entity involved must notify SEPA within 48 hours of the accident with details of the time and place of the accident, the amount and quality of the discharge, the economic impact, and any injuries sustained by individuals.[85] In addition, the entity or individual involved in the accident must take appropriate remedial action to mitigate the damage.

Violation of the law can include a fine of up to RMB200,000, depending on the seriousness of the offense and the amount of damage caused.[86] In addition, SEPA may order the party to take remedial steps or to pay for the cleanup costs within a specified period of time. If remedial action is not completed promptly, the responsible individuals or enterprise is liable for penalties of twice the amount of the applicable excess discharge fees and a fine of between RMB10,000 and RMB100,000, or the liable party can be ordered to discontinue its operations.[87] A party that disputes an administrative penalty may appeal the decision within fifteen days to the people's court.[88]

2. Control of Pollution by Vessels

The MEPL and supplemental regulations regulate activities that result in the introduction of pollutants to the marine environment by vessels.[89] A vessel is prohibited from discharging its ballast water, tanker washings or bilge,

---

84. Regulations Concerning the Control of Land-Originating Pollutants, art. 11.
85. Regulations Concerning the Control of Land-Originating Pollutants, art. 22.
86. Regulations Concerning the Control of Land-Originating Pollutants, arts. 24–27. If the pollution is due entirely to an act of war, force majeure, or negligence or wrongful act on the part of the government agencies responsible for the maintenance of navigational equipment, liability may not be attributed to the polluting party. Marine Environmental Pollution Law, art. 92; Coastal Construction Regulations, arts. 26–29 (penalties for pollution caused by coastal construction project).
87. Regulations Concerning the Control of Land-Originating Pollutants, art. 28.
88. Regulations Concerning the Control of Land-Originating Pollutants, art. 33; Coastal Construction Regulations, art. 30.
89. Marine Environmental Protection Law, arts. 62–72; Regulations Concerning Pollution by Vessels, arts. 1, 4, 5.

and other oily waters into the ocean or harbor waters.[90] The appropriate pumping facilities must be used when available. If it is necessary for a vessel to discharge its oily water, and there are no pumping facilities available, a written report must be submitted to the applicable harbor authorities, and only after approval is obtained can the vessel discharge the substance. In the event of an illegal discharge of pollutants by a vessel, SEPA or the applicable harbor authorities have jurisdiction to order the responsible parties to take remedial action.[91]

All vessels are required to dispose of their refuse with an authorized disposal agent and are prohibited from dumping waste into China's territorial waters.[92] Vessels with solid waste transported from outside ports where health epidemics are common are required to contact the quarantine authorities for instructions on proper treatment.[93] Precautionary measures must be taken to avoid pollution by oils or other wastes, paint spills, industrial refuse, or scrapings during the construction, repair, or salvage of a vessel.[94] Repairs to a vessel's hull or oil tanks must be conducted in a dry dock and not on or under water, to prevent potential pollution.[95]

The law requires that large vessels maintain pollution control equipment and records of the vessel's activities, and carry adequate insurance to cover against accidental oil spillage.[96] A party in violation of the law is subject to administrative penalties, including fines and confiscation of the vessel, and criminal prosecution where warranted.[97] The law also rewards individuals who report vessels involved in polluting activities and individuals for their efforts to minimize the damages caused by pollution.[98]

3. Control of Pollution by Offshore Oil Operations

The MEPL and supplemental regulations control pollution caused by offshore oil exploration and exploitation.[99] These regulations apply to fixed

90. Regulations Concerning Pollution by Vessels, arts. 14, 19; Marine Environmental Pollution Law, art. 28.

91. Regulations Concerning Pollution by Vessels, art. 7. Chemical dispersing agents may not be used to clean up oil contamination without government approval.

92. Regulations Concerning Pollution by Vessels, art. 28.

93. Regulations Concerning Pollution by Vessels, art. 29.

94. Regulations Concerning Pollution by Vessels, arts. 34, 35, 36.

95. Regulations Concerning Pollution by Vessels, art. 36.

96. Regulations Concerning Pollution by Vessels, art. 15, for a listing of the requirements.

97. Regulations Concerning Pollution by Vessels, arts. 39, 46, 47.

98. Regulations Concerning Pollution by Vessels, art. 50.

99. Marine Environmental Protection Law, arts. 47–54; Regulations Concerning Pollution by Offshore Oil Operations, art. 1. *See also* Administration of Environmental Impact Evaluation of Offshore Oil Exploitation Projects Procedures (promulgated on May 17, 2002, by the State Oceanic Administration) (These procedures require that an oil and gas field operator have an environmental impact report

and mobile oil platforms, oil exploration service vessels, pipelines, oil storage facilities, and other offshore oil-related operations.[100] Before exploration and exploitation are authorized, the interested party must submit an EIR for approval.[101] All parties conducting offshore oil operations are required to carry insurance or other financial guarantee for liability for pollution damage, and to maintain records describing the activities of the operation with respect to pollution control. Pollution control records are required to include the following information:

(1) The operation of anti-pollution equipment and procedures
(2) The treatment and discharge of oily water
(3) The disposal, discharge, and dumping of other wastes
(4) The occurrence of accidents involving oil spills, oil leakage, and blowouts
(5) The remedial efforts employed to correct any accidents
(6) The conducting of explosive operations[102]
(7) Other matters as may be stipulated by the MLNR[103]

In the event of an accidental oil spill, the party involved must attempt to mitigate the damages by employing appropriate remedial measures. In situations involving major oil spills, the responsible party is required to immediately report such an occurrence to the MLNR and SEPA.[104] The regulations do not define a major versus a minor oil spill.

D. Control of Air Pollution

Pursuant to the Law on the Prevention and Control of Air Pollution, SEPA has the power to draft national standards for air pollution control.[105] The

prepared by a qualified evaluation firm. The EIR must be approved by the State Oceanic Administration, and the approved report is thereafter submitted to the State Environmental Protection Administration for recordation); Interim Measures on the Administration of Abandonment of Offshore Oil Platforms (promulgated on July 11, 2002, by the State Oceanic Administration) (outlines registration procedures and standards for abandonment of offshore oil platforms taken out of production).

100. Regulations Concerning Pollution by Offshore Oil Operations, art. 2.

101. Regulations Concerning Pollution by Offshore Oil Operations, arts. 4, 5.

102. The MLNR must be notified if a party intends to use explosives in or near a fishery. Regulations Concerning Pollution by Offshore Oil Operations, art. 13.

103. Regulations Concerning Pollution by Offshore Oil Operations, arts. 9, 10, 18.

104. Regulations Concerning Pollution by Offshore Oil Operations, art. 16.

105. Law on the Prevention and Control of Air Pollution, art. 6. Municipal and local governments may formulate local standards, however, where SEPA has not established a standard on a particular issue or has deferred the matter to the local level. Notice on Controlling Pollution from Raising Dust in Cities (promulgated on April 27, 2001, by the State Environmental Protection Administration and the Ministry of Construction) (outlines standards for control of air pollution caused by construction-related dust). *See also SEPA Tackles Ozone Depletion,* China Market Intelligence, The U.S.-China Business Council

law places a duty on the State to implement economic and technological policies and measures favorable to the prevention and control of air pollution.[106] Business enterprises are obligated to use technology that is more energy efficient and results in less air pollution. To this end, the Chinese government compiles and publishes a list, on a periodic basis, of production technologies that seriously affect air quality and that cannot be sold, purchased, or imported.[107]

1. Control of Construction-Related Air Pollution

The law provides that a developer involved with any construction, improvement, or renovation project is required to prepare and submit to SEPA an EIR that addresses the possible levels of air pollution resulting from the project and the affect of the project on the environment. The EIR is also required to address the pollution prevention methods that the developer intends to adopt during the construction process.[108] A construction project may not commence until SEPA approves the EIR.

2. Control of Air Pollution from Coal Burning

A traditional source of air pollution in China is the burning of coal for energy production and space heating. In response, SEPA has established standards for the levels of smoke and dust discharge from coal-fired boilers.[109] Those boilers that do not meet the specifications are banned from manufacture, sale, or import. Coal washing and other clean-coal technology designed to reduce the sulfur and ash content in coal are strongly encouraged, especially for newly established coal mines, where sulfur levels are relatively higher.[110] The mining of coal containing radioactive, arsenic, or other poisonous substances in excess of the standards is prohibited.

3. Control of Industry-Related Air Pollution

Companies that produce emissions such as those that are foul smelling or comprised of dust particles are required to implement measures to prevent the emissions from affecting the surrounding residential areas by either eliminating or reducing their harmful effects.[111] The law prohibits business operators

(May 2001) (states that SEPA has implemented over forty policies and regulations designed to curb the production, consumption, import, and export of major ozone-depleting substances).

106. Law on the Prevention and Control of Air Pollution, art. 8.

107. Law on the Prevention and Control of Air Pollution, art. 19. For a review of the Clean Production Law, *see infra* note 158 and accompanying text.

108. Law on the Prevention and Control of Air Pollution, art. 11.

109. Law on the Prevention and Control of Air Pollution, arts. 28–31, 38.

110. Law on the Prevention and Control of Air Pollution, arts. 24, 26.

111. Law on the Prevention and Control of Air Pollution, arts. 40, 44.

located in densely populated areas from burning asphalt, rubber, plastics, leather, and other substances that release poisonous and harmful smoke, gases, or dust.[112] When transporting substances that release harmful gases or dust, companies are required to use airtight containers and other preventive measures.[113]

4. Control of Vehicle Emissions

The law establishes air pollution standards for motor vehicles and provides that vehicles that do not comply with emission standards may not be manufactured, sold, or imported.[114] To help reduce the amount of pollutants by motorized vehicles, SEPA encourages the production and use of high-grade unleaded gasoline.[115]

5. Reporting Requirements, Inspection, and Penalties

All companies that release pollutants into the atmosphere are required to report the character and volume of the pollutants and the relevant prevention and control information.[116] A company that releases an excess amount of air pollution, as established by the local or national standards, may be ordered to pay discharge fees as well as to take prompt remedial action.[117] In the case of emissions that are poisonous or hazardous to human health, the company involved must immediately take remedial action to reduce contamination, and must notify the local government authorities and citizens who may be affected by the hazardous emissions.[118] If air pollution results in serious loss of public or private property or injury or loss of life, the responsible party is liable for significant monetary penalties and possible criminal

112. Law on the Prevention and Control of Air Pollution, arts. 41, 57.

113. Law on the Prevention and Control of Air Pollution, art. 42.

114. Law on the Prevention and Control of Air Pollution, art. 32, 33, 34, 53, 55. Measures of Examination and Approval on Criteria of Discharging Atmosphere Pollutants by Local Motor Vehicles (promulgated on February 8, 2001, by the State Council); *See* Shen, *Emission Levels to Be Published,* CHINA DAILY (June 13, 1998), available on Lexis, News Library, or on the Web site of the CHINA DAILY at http://www.chinadaily.com.cn (SEPA announced in June 1998 that vehicles that discharge excessive exhaust fumes are to be banned and that the development of fuel injection devices and catalytic converters is encouraged). *See also* Zhu, *State Tightens Controls on Exhaust Fumes,* CHINA DAILY (June 12, 1998), available on Lexis, News Library, or on the Web site of the CHINA DAILY at http://www.chinadaily.com.cn; Shen, *Use of Lead in Gasoline Restricted in Shenyang,* CHINA DAILY (September 1, 1998), available on Lexis, News Library, or on the Web site of the CHINA DAILY at http://www.chinadaily.com.cn. On July 1, 2003, the National Development and Reform Commission (NDRC) banned the production and sale of "common" unleaded gasoline in China and established the "High Standard Clean Gasoline" benchmark for motor vehicle fuel produced and sold in China. *China Switches Gasoline Standard and Pricing,* CHINA MARKET INTELLIGENCE, THE U.S.-CHINA BUSINESS COUNCIL (July 9, 2003), available online to members at http://www.uschina.org.

115. Law on the Prevention and Control of Air Pollution, art. 34.

116. Law on the Prevention and Control of Air Pollution, art. 12.

117. Law on the Prevention and Control of Air Pollution, arts. 13–15.

118. Law on the Prevention and Control of Air Pollution, art. 61.

prosecution.[119] An injured party has the right to file a complaint in the people's court for compensation for damages resulting from air pollution.[120]

E. Standards for the Importation of Pollutants

Of great concern to China in recent years is the increased importation of harmful pollutants without approval. In response, China adopted the Basel Convention, which is designed to "control the transmission of pollutants between countries and to manage their disposal."[121] The importation of harmful pollutants is strictly controlled, including the following: cyanide-bearing products, asbestos pollutants, waste pesticides, insecticides, herbicides, ether pollutants, waste inorganic fluoride, waste halogens solutions, explosive waste products, household waste, and industrial refuse.[122] A business operator that requires a listed pollutant for use as a raw material must apply to SEPA for approval of any importation.[123] An application for importation of pollutants is required to assess the environmental risk of the importation.[124] Upon arrival at a Chinese port of entry, an authorized shipment of pollutants is required to be inspected by SEPA prior to clearance by China Customs.[125] An unapproved importer of pollutants may be ordered to export the pollutants, and is subject to administrative penalties and criminal prosecution.[126]

F. Energy Conservation

The NPC adopted the Energy Conservation Law in 1997 to promote energy conservation nationwide, to increase the efficient use of energy resources, and to protect the environment.[127] The policy of the PRC is to encourage the

---

119. Law on the Prevention and Control of Air Pollution, art. 61. *See* Chapter 23, Criminal Liability for FIE Activities § C.

120. Law on the Prevention and Control of Air Pollution, arts. 5, 62.

121. Notice on Control of Importation of Pollutants, art. 1. For additional regulations and standards for the control of waste importations, *see* the Web site of MOFCOM at http://www.mofcom.gov.cn. *See also* Solid Waste Pollution Law, art. 24.

122. Notice on Control of Importation of Pollutants, art. 1, appendix 1.

123. For details on the application and the application process, *see* Notice on Control of Importation of Pollutants, art. 4, appendix 2. *See also* Solid Waste Pollution Law, arts. 25, 26.

124. Notice on Control of Importation of Pollutants, art. 3.

125. Notice on Control of Importation of Pollutants, art. 5.

126. Notice on Control of Importation of Pollutants, art. 6. *See* Chapter 23, Criminal Liability for FIE Activities § C. Wingo, *Translation: The Garbage Smuggling Case: Judgment of Division One of the Shanghai Municipal Intermediate Level People's Court January 13, 1997,* 6 PAC. RIM L. & POL'Y 607 (1997) (translated and annotated court decision involving a U.S. citizen who violated the environmental protection laws by smuggling waste paper).

127. Energy Conservation Law, art 1. The law provides that energy resources include coal, crude oil, natural gas, electricity, gas, heating power, and other resources that produce usable energy. *Id.* art. 2. *See*

development and use of new energy resources and renewable energy resources. The law provides that energy conservation is both an economic and environmental policy of the PRC.[128]

The law requires that all feasibility studies for joint ventures, construction projects, and other economic development projects include an assessment of the intended use and management of energy resources.[129] The design and construction of a construction project must comply with standards for the efficient use of energy resources and incorporate energy conservation design standards. Industrial projects that involve obsolete technology, excessive energy consumption, or involve a significant waste of energy resources are prohibited.[130] Projects may not be approved if they do not include a program for energy conservation.

The law requires that business enterprises that produce a large amount of energy-consuming products be encouraged to employ methods of energy conservation or improve their product design to reduce the amount of energy consumed.[131] The Energy Conservation Law requires conservation authorities to institute energy consumption quotas for industrial enterprises.[132] A failure to comply with consumption quotas exposes an enterprise to monetary penalties or a suspension of operations.[133] The Energy Conservation Law also establishes a voluntary certification program that allows a producer to advertise its product as meeting energy conservation quality standards.[134]

---

also Regulations Concerning the Development of Cogeneration (jointly issued in 2001 by the State Development Planning Commission, the State Economic and Trade Commission, the Ministry of Construction, and the State Environmental Protection Administration) (hereinafter the "Cogen Regulations"). The Cogen Regulations encourage local authorities to develop the use of cogeneration—power plants capable of producing both heat and electricity—to increase the efficiency of the electrical supply and to protect the environment. *See generally* T. Mahony, *New Regulations Promote Cogeneration Plants,* CHINA L. & PRAC. (March 2001).

128. Energy conservation is defined as "improved energy use management, the adoption of measures which are technologically viable, economically rational and environmentally and socially acceptable, the reduction of damage and waste created during the various stages between production of energy and its supply to the consumer and a more effective and rational utilization of energy resources." Energy Conservation Law, arts. 3, 4, 5, 6.

129. Energy Conservation Law, art. 12.

130. Energy Conservation Law, art. 13. Existing industrial facilities are also subject to scrutiny for energy conservation. The government may order an operation to upgrade its equipment and machinery or face monetary penalties or suspension of its operations. *Id.* arts. 17, 44. For a review of the Clean Production Law, *see infra* note 158 and accompanying text.

131. Energy Conservation Law, art. 15. Pursuant to the law, the government intends to increase its supervision of industrial operations that are considered key energy users. *Id.* art. 20. Key energy users are required to submit regular reports to energy conservation officials that detail the operation's energy consumption and energy conservation efforts. *Id.* art. 28. Key users are also required to establish a management level position responsible for energy resource management. *Id.* art. 29.

132. Energy Conservation Law, art. 16.

133. Energy Conservation Law, arts. 16, 24, 43.

134. Energy Conservation Law, art. 18. The law prohibits any party from falsely using the energy conservation verification symbol. *See* Energy Conservation Law, art. 27. The misuse of product certification also violates Articles 19 and 26 of the Product Quality Law. *See* Chapter 13, Consumer Protection § A.2.

The law requires that business enterprises develop technical policies and procedures for energy conservation, statistical analysis concerning usage of energy resources, and energy conservation educational and training programs for employees.[135] Employees who have not been trained in energy conservation are prohibited from operating energy-consuming equipment. The law encourages business operators to establish an energy conservation work responsibility system and to reward employees that successfully implement energy conservation policies.[136]

G. Control of Toxics in the Workplace

The government adopted the Law on the Prevention and Control of Occupational Diseases, effective in May 2002.[137] The law sets forth the standards for controlling and supervising occupational injuries and standards for the diagnosis of diseases and employee health care, and provides that employees have a right to advise regulatory authorities of any violations of the law and/or to refuse to work.[138] It is a violation of the law to produce, operate, import, or use equipment and materials that possibly could cause occupational disease hazards.[139] The law further provides that employers are required to notify prospective employees of any possible risks of occupational disease in the workplace, and are required to provide medical care to any injured worker.[140]

The State Council adopted specific regulations governing the protection of workers in operations during which toxic substances are used in the workplace.[141] Under the Toxics in the Workplace Regulations, the employer is required to take effective protective measures to prevent accidental poisoning in the workplace, and to maintain worker compensation insurance according

---

135. Energy Conservation Law, arts. 21, 22.

136. Energy Conservation Law, art. 23.

137. Law on the Prevention and Control of Occupational Diseases, promulgated on May 1, 2002, by the Standing Committee of the National People's Congress. *See also* Notification of the Ministry of Health on the Relevant Issues Concerning the Implementation of the Law on the Prevention and Control of Occupational Diseases, promulgated on May 8, 2002, by the Ministry of Health (outlines tasks and programs to be adopted by the MOH with respect to prevention and control of disease and injury in the workplace). The law sets forth detailed penalty provisions in the event of a violation of the law. Occupational Diseases Law, arts. 62–76. *See generally* J. Kahn, *Foul Water and Air Part of Cost of the Boom in China's Exports,* New York Times, Nov. 4, 2003, § A, Page 1, Column 1 (addressing environmental and health problems in manufacturing sector in China).

138. Occupational Diseases Law, arts. 12, 30.

139. Occupational Diseases Law, art. 27.

140. Occupational Diseases Law, arts. 30, 39–54.

141. Regulations on Labor Protection in the Operational Fields Where Toxic Articles Are Used, adopted by the 57th Executive Meeting of the State Council on April 30, 2002, and effective on May 12, 2002 (hereinafter the "Toxics in the Workplace Regulations"). For more information concerning the regulation of the workplace, see the Web site of the Ministry of Labor and Social Security at http://www.molss.gov.cn.

to the law.[142] In addition to licensing requirements for the use of toxic substances in the workplace, the protective measures outlined in the Regulations provide that the operational areas where toxics are used must be separate from the living quarters, and that no person may reside in the operational areas that are exposed to toxic substances; that the employer install an effective ventilation system if toxics are used in an enclosed area of the workplace; that workers exposed to toxics must be provided with medical care by the employer; and that equipment used with toxic substances be disposed of properly.[143] The Toxics in the Workplace Regulations also grant workers the right to receive training in regard to the handling of toxic substances, and workers are allowed to freely lodge complaints with regulatory authorities and may refuse to work in an environment without proper safeguards from toxic substances.[144] If an employer does not have the required insurance, an injured worker has the right to claim compensation against the employer.[145] The Regulations also restate the prohibition on child labor and the prohibition on exposing minor or pregnant employees to toxic substances.[146] A violation of the law may expose both an employer and management personnel to criminal and administrative penalties including, but not limited to, revocation of business license, fines of up to RMB500,000 per violation, and imprisonment of management personnel.[147]

H. Environmental Impact Assessment Reporting Requirements

The PRC government has adopted a law that now requires developers to prepare comprehensive environmental impact assessment reports of new development projects.[148] Although the assessment report obligation may

142. Toxics in the Workplace Regulations, art. 5.

143. Toxics in the Workplace Regulations, arts. 11, 29, 32–36, 41.

144. Toxics in the Workplace Regulations, art. 38–40. Workers affected by toxic substances have a right to medical expenses, rehabilitation expenses, nursing services, wages and other benefits, disability subsidies, death allowances and funeral expenses, pensions, and other insurance benefits. Art. 41.

145. Toxics in the Workplace Regulations, art. 45.

146. Toxics in the Workplace Regulations, art. 7.

147. Toxics in the Workplace Regulations, arts. 56–69. *See also* Criminal Law, art. 338 (criminal standards for environmental crimes); Chapter 23, Criminal Liability for FIE Activities § C.

148. Law of the People's Republic of China on Environmental Impact Assessment (promulgated by the 30th Sess. of the Standing Committee of the National People's Congress on October 28, 2002, and effective on September 1, 2003) (hereinafter the "EIA Law"), *reprinted in* China Laws for Foreign Business (CCH), Business Regulation ¶ 14-532. The EIA Law is similar to the standards and procedures of the National Environmental Policy Act (NEPA) and corresponding state laws in the United States. *See generally* N. Stender & J. Zhou, *The New EIA Law and Environmental Protection in China,* China L. & Prac. (Dec. 2002) (authors state that the new EIA Law "sends a clear message that environmental protection is viewed as a fundamental goal and a high priority on the government's agenda" and confirms that SEPA "enjoys support at the highest level of government").

principally affect domestic Chinese companies, the law also is relevant to foreign investment enterprises and foreign companies with construction-related investments or activities in China.

The EIA Law requires analysis, forecasting, and assessment of possible environmental impacts caused by new governmental plans and private construction projects. Environmental assessment reports are required to describe measures and countermeasures to prevent or mitigate adverse environmental impacts, as well as methods to follow up and monitor the effectiveness of implementation.[149] Under the law, project developers must retain qualified consultants to prepare the required assessment reports.[150]

The law requires the preparation of comprehensive assessment reports for projects that may have a "substantial environmental impact." Developers also must conduct a public hearing (except when national security is at issue) or otherwise collect comments from the general public and relevant experts before submitting construction applications for government approval.[151] The EIA Law requires that SEPA approve or reject an application within sixty days of receipt. A less comprehensive environmental impact statement may be prepared for projects that cause "light environmental impact." For projects with "very small" environmental impact, it may only be necessary to complete an environmental impact registration form, for which government approval or disapproval can be issued within fifteen days.[152]

The EIA Law provides that an impact report for a construction project shall include the following: (1) detailed profile of the construction project; (2) present situation of surrounding environment of the construction project; (3) analysis, forecast, and assessment of the possible impacts on the environment by the construction project; (4) environmental protection measures anticipated to be taken by the developer and a technical and economic demonstration of the measure; (5) analysis on the economic profits and losses that are anticipated as a result of the environmental impacts of the construction project; (6) recommendations concerning environmental monitoring for the construction project; and (7) overall conclusions concerning the environmental impact assessment. The developers are allowed to proceed with the project only after the various authorities responsible for

149. EIA Law, arts. 2, 10.
150. EIA Law, arts. 19, 20.
151. EIA Law, arts, 11, 21.
152. EIA Law, art. 16.

environmental protection and water and soil conservation approve of the report and remedial measures.[153]

SEPA is responsible for examination and approval of certain major construction projects such as nuclear facilities; top-secret projects; construction projects of cross-province, autonomous regions or municipalities directly under the central government; or construction projects that are examined and approved by the State Council or by the relevant government agencies authorized by the State Council. The provincial and local branches of SEPA may approve local and smaller projects.[154]

If a developer makes any change in the nature, scale, location, production process, or environmental protection methods proposed for a project, the company must apply for new approval of those changes.[155] The law also provides that if the construction project is not commenced within five years after the date of the approval of the construction work, the company is required to apply for a reexamination of the environmental assessment report. The law also requires that competent environmental protection authorities conduct follow-up inspections after the project is put into production or use. They also are authorized to investigate and ascertain causes and liabilities for serious environmental pollution or ecological destruction.[156]

If any company commences a construction project without approval of a required environmental impact assessment, the relevant authorities may issue an order to cease and desist and may impose penalties ranging from RMB50,000 to RMB200,000. In addition, individual managers directly responsible for the construction project may be subject to administrative penalties.[157]

The EIA Law is a positive step in providing the SEPA authorities with the practical tools to review and assess the impact of ongoing construction throughout China. However, while the law provides some guidance on the

153. EIA Law, art. 17. *See also* Administration of Environment-Related Acceptance of Construction Projects Procedures (promulgated December 27, 2001, and effective February 1, 2002, by the State Environmental Protection Administration) (These rules outline the procedures for review and approval of environmental impact reports for construction projects. The rules require that environmental protection facilities commence operations at the same time as the principal structure. *Id.* art. 6. The rules also provide that the construction enterprise is required to apply to the relevant environmental protection department for approval of a trial operation period, and thereafter an inspection of the production and environmental protection facilities will be conducted within thirty days. *Id.* arts. 7, 8, 9, 10. The environmental protection authorities are required to complete the inspection and acceptance process within thirty days of receiving an application for acceptance. *Id.* art. 14. Items to be inspected include the supporting documentation, the completeness and suitability of the environmental facilities, conformity with industry standards, and operating conditions. *Id.* art. 16.).

154. EIA Law, art. 23.

155. EIA Law, art. 24.

156. EIA Law, art. 28.

157. EIA Law, arts. 29–32.

approval of environmental impact assessments, a number of questions will need further clarification, such as the status of the construction projects approved before the effective date of the EIA Law and further clarification on the standards for determining "substantial environmental impact" and other terms in the EIA Law. It is also left for observation as to whether the government will dedicate the administrative resources to properly review and investigate EIA reports, or whether the EIA report requirement only hinders the rights of legitimate developers that conduct their work with an awareness of and sensitivity to environmental protection.

I. Clean Production Law

The government has adopted what is referred to as the Clean Production Law, the objective of which is to promote and encourage state and foreign investments in environmentally friendly production and manufacturing.[158] The Clean Production Law authorizes government agencies to formulate tax and financial policies that encourage the implementation of the use of cleaner production technology.[159] The law also outlines the government policy to phase out the use of outmoded forms of production that result in pollution and contamination.[160] The government is required by the law to promote clean production technology and awareness in schools and organizations, and will also develop symbols and certification marks that encourage energy-savings products, water-saving products, recycling, and environmental protection.[161] The law also requires that companies utilize

158. Law of the People's Republic of China on the Promotion of Cleaner Production (promulgated on June 29, 2002, by the 28th Session of the Standing Committee of the Ninth National People's Congress and effective on January 1, 2003) (hereinafter the "Clean Production Law"). *See* Z. Huanxin, *Congress to Go for Clean Production,* China Daily (March 9, 2002) (states that the NPC policy is to support clean production technology and mentions that 80 percent of the 41 million tons of waste dumped into China's water resources is untreated).

159. Clean Production Law, art. 8.

160. Clean Production Law, art. 12.

161. Clean Production Law, arts. 13–17. *See also* Administration of Recognition of Environmental Protection Products (issued on December 23, 2001, and effective on January 1, 2002, by the State Environmental Protection Administration) (These rules define "environmental protection products" as equipment, instruments, and related chemicals and materials that are used to prevent and treat environmental pollution, improve the ecological environment, and protect natural resources. *Id.* art. 3. These rules outline the procedures for approval of a certification association for environmentally friendly products, and standards for enterprises to have their products listed or certified as environmentally friendly. The rules also note that an Environmental Protection Product Certificate is valid for three years and can be used on the packaging of, and the advertisement for, the products. *Id.* arts. 17, 18. The rules also allow consumers the right to complain to the certification association if the product is improperly granted environmentally friendly status. *Id.* art. 30). *See also* Notification on the Relevant Issues Concerning Certification and Accreditation of the Environmental Management Systems (promulgated on July 22, 2002, by the State Environmental Protection Administration and the Certification and Accreditation Administration).

environmentally friendly packaging and labeling products for consumption in China.[162] The Clean Production Law also mandates that environmental impact assessments be made with respect to the technology and equipment used in the construction, extension, or refurbishment of a manufacturing facility.[163] The law also requires that enterprises shall take the following cleaner production measures in the course of technological transformation:

(1) Adopting nontoxic, harmless, low-toxicity, or low-harm raw materials to substitute for high-toxicity raw materials and raw materials with seriously adverse consequences
(2) Adopting techniques and equipment with high resource-utilization ratio and low output of pollutants to substitute for techniques and equipment with low resource utilization ratio and high output of pollutants
(3) Comprehensively utilizing or recycling waste materials, waste water, and residue heat produced in the course of production
(4) Adopting pollution prevention and control technologies that can make discharge of pollutants reach the national or local standards or make the total amount of discharge of pollutants be controlled within the required quota[164]

162. Clean Production Law, art. 20.
163. Clean Production Law, art. 18.
164. Clean Production Law, art. 19.

Practice Tip: Foreign Investors and Environmental Protection

Environmental issues are playing a more important role in investments in which production equipment is part of the assets either contributed by the Chinese party to a foreign-invested enterprise (FIE) or purchased by the FIE. Many foreign investors quickly realize two dismal facts when investigating potential Chinese partners or acquisition targets: (1) that production equipment fails to meet basic pollution control standards; and (2) that factory sites are significantly contaminated after years of production without regard to environmental standards.

As a prerequisite, a foreign party should conduct a thorough due diligence of technical capabilities and regulatory compliance of a targeted Chinese company. Permits and licenses should be scrutinized to determine if compliance is illusory given that many Chinese companies have enjoyed a cozy relationship with local environmental authorities who may vouch for compliance today but, in the future, may find themselves under the scrutiny of national investigators. A close review of applications may indicate whether the Chinese party procured its permits through corrupt means, misrepresentation, or selective disclosure of factual information.

Foreign investors confronted with acquisitions involving environmental problems are faced with a choice of structuring the investment to include upgrading the facilities with environmental technology to raise the standards of a targeted facility; otherwise, the investor must decide to proceed with an investment with the understanding that the equipment may be outmoded and potentially in violation of the law, or to invest elsewhere. A thorough technical due diligence, conducted in advance, should reveal the technology improvements that are needed.

The foreign party should also include the necessary indemnification language in their agreements to insulate the foreign company from any liability that may arise as a result of activities prior to the acquisition date. An independent environmental assessment report may be used as a reference point for any environmental liability.

Once an FIE operation is under way, foreign investors should establish and monitor a compliance program that takes into consideration China's current laws and regulatory system, as well as international standards. Leaving compliance issues in the hands of the Chinese partner may be a mistake without the proper controls to ensure that practices are more in conformance with corporate and international standards.

In light of SEPA's increased enforcement efforts, it would be a mistake for foreign investors to view China as a destination of relaxed environmental standards, even if past practices reflect the intent to skirt the law. China faces many challenges in its strategy for sustainable development, and foreign investors have the opportunity to be part of the solution and not part of the problem.

(*Continued*)

(*Continued from previous page*)

Environmental Strategies for Foreign Investors

- ✔ Conduct a thorough due diligence review of technical capabilities and regulatory compliance of local partners, contractors, distributors, manufacturers, etc.
- ✔ Conduct a thorough due diligence of any property-related or equipment-related acquisition or business arrangement
- ✔ Conduct environmental site assessments using qualified environmental consultants
- ✔ Review and verify existing permits and licenses
- ✔ Evaluate need for technological improvements
- ✔ Negotiate contractual protections
- ✔ Establish an active post-investment compliance monitoring program
- ✔ Establish compliance team to regularly review, report, and audit an environmental compliance program
- ✔ Monitor changes in the law and policy, as well as monitoring SEPA enforcement efforts.

Key Laws and Regulations

Environmental Protection Law of the People's Republic of China (adopted on December 26, 1989, at the 11th Sess. of the Standing Comm. of the 7th NPC)

Environmental Protection Law of the People's Republic of China concerning Solid Waste Pollution (promulgated on October 30, 1995, by the 16th Sess. of the Standing Comm. of the 8th NPC)

Law of the People's Republic of China on Prevention and Control of Water Pollution (promulgated on May 15, 1996, by the Standing Comm. Of the NPC)

Detailed Rules for the Implementation of the Law of the People's Republic of China on the Prevention and Control of Water Pollution (Order No. 284 of the State Council of the People's Republic of China, promulgated on March 20, 2000, by the State Council)

Marine Environmental Protection Law of the PRC (adopted on August 23, 1982, at the 24th Sess. of the Standing Committee of the 5th NPC, revised on Dec. 25, 1999, at the 13th Sess. Of the Standing Comm. Of the 9th NPC, re-promulgated on Dec. 25, 1999, by Order No. 26 of the President of the PRC)

(*Continued*)

(Continued from previous page)

Fishery Law of the People's Republic of China (promulgated on Oct. 31, 2000, by the Standing Comm. of the NPC)

Notification on Accomplishing the Work of Control Over Fishing Suspension in 2002 (promulgated on April 29, 2002, by the Ministry of Agriculture)

Administrative Regulations of the People's Republic of China to Prevent Land-Originating Pollutants from Damaging the Marine Environment (promulgated on June 22, 1990, by the State Council)

Administrative Regulations of the People's Republic of China to Prevent Pollution from Coastal Projects Damaging the Marine Environment (promulgated on June 25, 1990, by the State Council)

Regulations of the People's Republic of China Controlling the Prevention of Pollution of Sea Areas by Vessels (promulgated on December 29, 1983, by the State Council)

Regulations of the People's Republic of China Concerning the Control of the Dumping of Wastes at Sea (promulgated on March 6, 1985, by the State Council)

Regulations of the People's Republic of China Concerning Environmental Protection in Offshore Oil Exploration and Exploitation (promulgated on December 29, 1983, by the State Council)

Law of the People's Republic of China on the Prevention and Control of Air Pollution (adopted on September 5, 1987, by the 22nd Sess. of the Standing Comm. of the 6th NPC and amended on August 29, 1995, at the 15th Sess. of the Standing Comm. of the 8th NPC and amended on April 29, 2000, by the Standing Comm. of the NPC)

Notice on Strict Control of the Transmission of Pollutants into China from Outside Chinese Territory (issued on March 7, 1991, by the State Environmental Protection Bureau and the General Administration of Customs)

Energy Conservation Law of the People's Republic of China (promulgated on November 1, 1997, by the 28th Sess. of the Standing Comm. of the 8th NPC)

Certain Regulations of the State Economic Commission and the State Planning Commission for Further Economizing on Electricity Consumption (jointly promulgated on Mar. 12, 1987, by the State Economic Commission and the State Planning Commission)

Implementation of the Energy Conservation Law (promulgated on Oct. 23, 1999, by the Beijing Municipal People's Government)

Forestry Law of the People's Republic of China (adopted on Sept. 20, 1984, by the 7th Sess. of the Standing Comm. of the 6th NPC, amended April 29, 1998, by the 2nd Sess. of the Standing Comm. of the 9th NPC)

Law on Radioactive Pollution and Control (promulgated on June 28, 2003, by the NPC, and effective Oct. 1, 2003)

(Continued)

(*Continued from previous page*)

Urban Radioactive Waste Administration Measures (issued in 1987, and administered by SEPA)

Regulations of the People's Republic of China on the Protection of Wild Plants (promulgated on Sept. 30, 1996, by the NPC)

Notice of the State Council on the Strict Protection of Precious and Rare Wild Animals (promulgated on April 13, 1983, by the State Council)

Implementing Regulations of the People's Republic of China on the Protection of Terrestrial Wildlife (promulgated on March 1, 1992, by the State Bureau of Forestry)

Jurisdiction and Case-Registration Criteria for Criminal Cases on Forests and Land Wild Animals (promulgated on May 9, 2001, by the Ministry of Public Security and the State Bureau of Forestry)

Law of the People's Republic of China on Environmental Impact Assessment (promulgated by the Standing Committee of the National People's Congress on October 28, 2002, and effective on September 1, 2003)

Administrative Measures on Safety of Hazardous Chemicals (promulgated on January 26, 2002, by the State Council)

List of Hazardous Goods, National Standard GB 12268 (promulgated on January 26, 2002, by the State Council)

Regulations on New Chemical Substances (adopted on Oct. 15, 2003, by the State Environmental Protection Administration)

Administrative Rules on Environmental Protection with Respect to Construction Projects (by Order No. 253 of the State Council of the People's Republic of China and adopted on Nov. 18, 1998, by the 10th Meeting of the Standing Comm. Of the State Council, and promulgated on Nov. 29, 1998)

Opinion Regarding Promoting Development of Industrialization of Urban Sewage and Waste Treatment Sectors (jointly issued on Sept. 10, 2002, by the State Development Planning Commission, the Ministry of Construction, and the State Environmental Protection Agency)

Notice Concerning Value-Added Tax Policy Concerning Sewage Processing Charges (promulgated on June 19, 2001, by the Ministry of Finance and the State Administration of Taxation)

Notification on Implementing the Charging System for Disposal of Urban Domestic Refuse and Promoting the Industrialization of Refuse Disposal (promulgated on July 1, 2002, by the State Development Planning Commission, the Ministry of Finance, the Ministry of Construction, and the State Environmental Protection Administration)

Beijing Municipality Concessions for Urban Infrastructure Procedures (promulgated by the Beijing Municipal People's Government on August 28, 2003)

(*Continued*)

(*Continued from previous page*)

Administration of Environmental Impact Evaluation of Offshore Oil Exploitation Projects Procedures (promulgated on May 17 2002, by the State Oceanic Administration)

Interim Measures on the Administration of Abandonment of Offshore Oil Platforms (promulgated on July 11, 2002, by the State Oceanic Administration)

Notice on Controlling Pollution from Raising Dust in Cities (promulgated on April 27, 2001, by the State Environmental Protection Administration and the Ministry of Construction)

Measures of Examination and Approval on Criteria of Discharging Atmosphere Pollutants by Local Motor Vehicles (promulgated on February 8, 2001, by the State Council)

Regulations Concerning the Development of Cogeneration (jointly issued in 2001 by the State Development Planning Commission, the State Economic and Trade Commission, the Ministry of Construction, and the State Environmental Protection Administration)

Regulations on Labor Protection in the Operational Fields Where Toxic Articles Are Used, adopted by the 57th Executive Meeting of the State Council on April 30, 2002, and effective on May 12, 2002)

Law of the People's Republic of China on Environmental Impact Assessment (promulgated by the 30th Sess. of the Standing Committee of the National People's Congress on October 28, 2002, and effective on September 1, 2003)

Administration of Environment-Related Acceptance of Construction Projects Procedures (promulgated on December 27, 2001, by the State Environmental Protection Administration)

Law of the People's Republic of China on the Promotion of Cleaner Production (promulgated on June 29, 2002, by the 28th Session of the Standing Committee of the Ninth National People's Congress and effective on January 1, 2003)

Administration of Recognition of Environmental Protection Products (issued on December 23, 2001, and effective on January 1, 2002, by the State Environmental Protection Administration)

Notification on the Relevant Issues Concerning Certification and Accreditation of the Environmental Management Systems (promulgated on July 22, 2002, by the State Environmental Protection Administration and the Certification and Accreditation Administration)

Chapter 19

Mergers, Acquisitions, and Divisions

Until recently, the Chinese government has been reluctant to allow foreign parties the right to purchase State-owned assets or companies. However, the government now realizes that mergers and acquisitions (M&A) of State-owned assets, if monitored and regulated by the State, are an important part of China's development plan. Today, the leadership views M&A activities as a way to better manage underperforming assets, drive growth, and reduce unemployment. To encourage limited M&A activities, the government has adopted regulations that provide some guidance on the process. Nevertheless, certain industries and companies remain off limits to M&A activities for policy and strategic reasons. As China continues to be a prime target for market entry, foreign companies will pursue acquisitions of either an equity interest or the assets of FIEs and SOEs.

This chapter is a summary of the relevant laws and regulations with respect to mergers and acquisitions in China with respect to foreign investors, and specifically the regulations concerning the regulatory requirements involving the acquisition of State-owned enterprises by foreign-investors and the merger/division rules for foreign-invested enterprises in China. This chapter also addresses the takeover procedures adopted by the China Securities Regulatory Commission (CSRC) with respect to the takeover of publicly listed companies. In addition, this chapter addresses the developing anti-monopoly and competition law system in China and potential impact on foreign investors in China.[1]

1. For a bullet-point analysis of the merger and acquisition laws and regulations, *see* FACT SHEET: MERGERS AND ACQUISITIONS, THE U.S.-CHINA BUSINESS COUNCIL (last updated July 23, 2003), available online for members at http://www.uschina.org.

A. Acquisition of Domestic Enterprises by Foreign Investors

Effective April 12, 2003, provisional rules permit a foreign investor to either purchase the outstanding equity of shareholders in a nonforeign- invested domestic enterprise in China (a "domestic company"), or a foreign investor may subscribe to newly issued shares of a domestic company.[2] In either case, the domestic company is converted into a FIE upon completion of the purchase. A foreign investor may also purchase a domestic company's assets and then either operate those assets through an existing FIE or contribute those assets to a newly established FIE.[3]

In acquisitions involving the purchase of an equity interest, the resulting FIE will succeed and assume the obligations to creditors of the prior domestic company. In an asset acquisition, the domestic company that sells the assets will usually retain its obligations to creditors, unless otherwise agreed upon by the parties. The foreign investor, the domestic company, and other parties may enter into agreements regarding the disposition of rights and

---

2. Foreign M&A Regulations Regarding Foreign Investors' Merger with or Acquisition of Domestic Enterprises (hereinafter the "Foreign M&A Regulations") (jointly issued on March 7, 2003, by the Ministry of Foreign Trade and Economic Cooperation (restructured and renamed as the Ministry of Commerce), the State Taxation General Office, the State Administration of Industry and Commerce (SAIC), and the State Administration of Foreign Exchange), *reprinted in* CHINA LAWS FOR FOREIGN BUSINESS (CCH), Business Regulation ¶ 13-625. *See generally* A. Crooke, *China Adds Hurdles to Inbound M&A*, INTERNATIONAL FINANCIAL L. REV. (Sept. 2003); P. Neumann, *Private Acquisitions by Foreign Investors in China: Is the Party Finally Over?*, CHINA L. & PRAC. (April 2003). *See also* Using Foreign Investment to Reorganize State-Owned Enterprises Tentative Provisions (promulgated on Nov. 8, 2002, by the State Economic and Trade Commission, the Ministry of Finance, the State Administration of Industry and Commerce, and the State Administration of Foreign Exchange); Acquisition of Domestic Enterprises by Foreign Investors Tentative Provisions (promulgated on March 7, 2003, by the State Administration of Taxation, the State Administration of Industry and Commerce, and the State Administration of Foreign Exchange). Several municipal governments have adopted their own rules on the acquisition of domestic enterprises. *See* Acquisition of State-Owned Enterprises in the Municipality by Foreign Investors Several Opinions Implementing Rules (promulgated on August 4, 2003, by the Shanghai State-Owned Assets Supervision and Administration Commission, the Shanghai Foreign Investment Commission, and the Shanghai Administration of Industry and Commerce); Acquisition of State-Owned Enterprises in the Municipality by Foreign Investors Several Opinions (promulgated on August 4, 2003, by the Shanghai State-Owned Assets Supervision and Administration Commission, the Shanghai Foreign Investment Commission, and the Shanghai Administration of Industry and Commerce) (outlines the approval procedures for foreign investors to acquire state-owned assets in Shanghai, namely: (i) the submission of an application to the Comprehensive Service Window for Foreign Investment in Merger and Acquisition; (ii) the preparation and submission of an asset valuation report by authorized asset appraisal enterprise; (iii) the negotiation and execution of a property transfer contract by the parties; (iv) the transfer of property and registration of the transfer; (v) the approval of the property transfer by the Shanghai Foreign Investment Commission; and (vi) the registration of changes with the AIC with respect to both the state-owned enterprise and the new foreign-invested enterprise). *See generally* B. Tong & T. Yu, *Acquisition of SOEs in Shanghai: New Rules Open the Market*, CHINA L. & PRAC. (Nov. 2003); Beijing Municipality Interim Rule on Merger and Acquisition of State-Owned Industrial Enterprises by Foreign Investors and Domestic Non-Public Economic Organizations (promulgated on September 30, 2003, by the Beijing Municipal Government), an official translation is available online for members of the U.S.-CHINA BUSINESS COUNCIL at http://www.uschina.org.

3. Foreign M&A Regulations, art. 2.

obligations of the domestic company, provided such arrangements do not harm the interests of creditors, the public, or interested third parties. Agreements on creditors' rights and debts shall be submitted to examination and approval authorities. Domestic companies subject to an asset purchase are required to provide notice to known creditors and to issue a public notice in a provincial or national-level newspaper within ten days from the decision of asset purchase. Creditors shall have the right to demand security or satisfaction of a debt from the domestic company within ten days of receipt of notification or date of public announcement.[4]

Under the Foreign M&A Regulations, mergers and acquisitions of domestic enterprises by foreign investors are referred to as negotiated transfers of shares in domestic-funded enterprises (hereinafter referred to as "domestic companies") to foreign investors or subscription to increased capital of domestic companies by foreign investors and subsequent reestablishment of such domestic companies as foreign investment enterprises (hereinafter referred to as "mergers and acquisitions of shares"). Mergers and acquisitions of shares shall include the establishment of foreign investment enterprises by foreign investors to acquire assets of domestic enterprises for use by the operation of such foreign investment enterprises or acquisition of assets of domestic enterprises for the establishment of foreign investment enterprises and the use of such assets by the operation of such foreign investment enterprises (hereinafter referred to as "mergers and acquisitions of assets").[5]

The regulations provide that all M&A activities shall fully comply with laws, rules, and regulations of China, and conform to principles of "equity and reasonableness, compensation for equal value and honesty and integrity." M&A activity in China shall also not cause excessive consolidation, exclusion or restriction of competition, disruption of social and economic order, and infringement of public interest.[6] Foreign investors engaged in M&A activities should also comply with the laws, rules, and regulations of China on investor qualifications and industrial policies, including the State policies

4. Foreign M&A Regulations, art. 7. *See also* Several Issues Concerning the Trial of Civil Dispute Cases Relating to Enterprise Restructuring Provisions (issued on January 3, 2003, by the Supreme People's Court) (provides that the people's courts have jurisdiction to accept cases involving civil disputes in connection with restructuring, sale, merger, or stock swap of enterprises). *See generally* S. Blayney, *Piercing the Corporate Veil: SPC Provisions Offer Hope for Creditors in Enterprise Restructuring,* CHINA L. & PRAC. (November 2003). In October 2003, the SPC issued a notice stating that the January 2003 notice did not apply to foreign investment enterprises. Supreme People's Court (Ministry of Commerce, Request to Confirm Whether the "Several Issues Concerning the Trial of Civil Disputes Relating to Enterprise Restructuring Provisions" Applies to Foreign Investment) (issued on October 20, 2003, by the Supreme People's Court).

5. Foreign M&A Regulations, art. 2.

6. Foreign M&A Regulations, art. 3.

outlined in the Catalogue of Foreign Investment Industrial Guidelines.[7] The scope of business of the resulting operation postmerger must also comply with the relevant regulations and foreign investment industrial policies.[8]

The law governing both purchase and subscription agreements with domestic companies is required to be Chinese law, and foreign investors engaging in such transactions must comply with the qualification requirements and industrial policies stipulated by other Chinese laws and regulations. Agreements regarding the acquisition of equity in an existing FIE, however, do not need to be governed by Chinese law.

In principle, Chinese law requires that the establishment of an FIE necessitates a minimum foreign investment participation threshold of 25 percent. Consequently, by enabling foreign investors to invest less than 25 percent in a domestic enterprise, the Foreign M&A Regulations effectively operate to create a new breed of FIE. Where the foreign investment participation falls below 25 percent, the approval authority must note on the approval certificate that the "foreign investment proportion is lower than 25 percent." A similar note must be endorsed on the business license issued following registration with the local State Administration for Industry & Commerce (SAIC). However, foreign investment participation rates of less than 25 percent are not encouraged by MOFCOM. Where foreign participation falls below the 25 percent threshold, the enterprise will be precluded from preferential tax treatment and other benefits otherwise available to FIEs.[9]

With regard to capital contributions, the Foreign M&A Regulations provide that where foreign investment participation is less than 25 percent and is denominated in cash, the foreign investor must make the contribution in full to the transferring shareholder or the domestic enterprise within three months of the issuance of the FIE business license. In the event that the foreign investment includes in-kind contribution or the transfer of technology, the foreign investor is required to make the contribution in full within six months of the date of issue of the business license of the FIE. If there is an increase in capital in connection with an equity acquisition, the foreign investor must commit to a schedule for the capital contribution in the

7. Foreign M&A Regulations, art. 4.

8. Foreign M&A Regulations, art. 12.

9. Foreign M&A Regulations, art. 5. *See* Acquisition of Domestic Enterprises by Foreign Investors Tentative Provisions (promulgated on May 28, 2003, by the State Administration of Taxation); Enterprise Tax Treatment Concerning Foreign-Invested Enterprises in Which the Proportion of Foreign Investor Contribution Is Less than 25% (promulgated on April 18, 2003, by the State Administration of Taxation). *See generally* D. Zhang & J. Ding, *Tax Issues in Acquisition of Equity Interest in Domestic Enterprises,* China L. & Prac. (July 2003).

contract and in the articles of association of FIEs. If the schedule provides for a one-time contribution, the foreign investor must complete the contribution within six months after the issuance of the FIE business license.[10]

The Foreign M&A Regulations require that the purchase price be based on an appraisal of the equity interest or the assets to be sold—sale at a price below the appraised value is expressly prohibited. The parties to the transaction are free to select and agree upon a recognized Chinese-based assets valuation institution—all asset valuations must adopt "internationally accepted valuation methods."[11] Where a proposed M&A would affect the State's interest in a domestic enterprise or would result in the transfer of property rights in State-owned assets, then the transaction price or assets valuation must be conducted by a dedicated State-owned assets appraisal institution. However, the extent to which Chinese-based asset valuation institutions are familiar with internationally accepted valuation methods is unclear—while asset appraisal based upon "income generation" is usually preferred in western countries, in China valuation assessment based on the replacement cost of an asset, less depreciation, is preferred.

In M&A transactions involving asset purchases, the total investment amount of the proposed foreign investment enterprise to be established shall be determined on the basis of the consideration for acquired assets and actual scale of production operations.[12] The Foreign M&A Regulations

10. Foreign M&A Regulations, art. 9.

11. Foreign M&A Regulations, art. 8. *See also* Regulations on Several Issues Regarding the Administration of State-Owned Assets Appraisal (promulgated by the Ministry of Finance effective January 1, 2002). *See* Provisional Rules on the Administration of State-Owned Assets and Equity Transactions (promulgated on January 7, 2004, by the State Asset Supervision and Administration Commission and the Ministry of Finance) (The SASAC/MOF Rules outline standards and procedures designed to prevent irregularities and losses in the sale of State assets and to encourage transparency in such transactions. Under the SASAC/MOF Rules, the seller is responsible for resolving all issues concerning personnel, including unpaid salaries and insurance claims before a transaction is approved by the SASAC. All transactions involving State-Owned assets are to take place within an equities market, and after an approved accounting firm has audited the assets that are the subject of the sale. The SASAC will examine transactions in which assets are the subject of sale at below 90 percent of the fair market value price. All information related to the transactions, including property ownership, financial data, and basic information about the parties, is required to be publicly available.) *See also* Supervision and Administration of Enterprise State-Owned Assets Tentative Regulations (issued on May 27, 2003, by the State Council) (establish a legal basis for the administration of State assets, and separate the government's role as a regulator and owner of State assets). Related thereto, on December 31, 2003, the State-Owned Assets Supervision and Administration Commission and the MOF jointly issued the Interim Measures on the Administration of Transfers of State-Owned Property Rights in Enterprises (issued on December 31, 2003, by the State-Owned Assets Supervision and Administration Commission and the Ministry of Finance, and effective February 1, 2004) (define "State-Owned property rights in enterprises" and create a standardized process for the transfers of such rights; require an independent audit and asset appraisal procedures; and provide that the sales/transfer price must be no less than 90 percent of the value of the asset appraisal and must be paid in full within one year of the transaction).

12. Foreign M&A Regulations, art. 14.

provide that the total investment in FIEs established by a merger or acquisition is set at the maximum amounts as set forth below:

(1) Total investment amount of foreign investors shall not exceed 70 percent of the registered capital where the registered capital is below $2.1 million
(2) Total investment amount of foreign investors shall not exceed two times the registered capital where the registered capital is above $2.1 million but below $5 million
(3) Total investment amount of foreign investors shall not exceed 2.5 times the registered capital where the registered capital is above $5 million but below $12 million
(4) Total investment amount of foreign investors shall not exceed three times the registered capital where the registered capital is above $12 million[13]

For purposes of the application and approval process for M&A activities, foreign investors are required to submit the following documents to MOFCOM:

(1) Unanimous resolution passed by shareholders of a domestic limited liability company in respect of share transfer(s) to foreign investor(s) or resolution passed at a general meeting of a domestic company limited by shares in respect of share transfer(s) to foreign investor(s)
(2) Application for reestablishment of the domestic company as a foreign investment enterprise upon the merger and acquisition
(3) Contract and articles of association of the foreign investment enterprise established upon the merger and acquisition
(4) Agreement on transfer(s) of shares in the domestic company to foreign investor(s) or acquisition of increased capital of the domestic company by foreign investor(s)[14]

13. Foreign M&A Regulations, art. 11.

14. The Foreign M&A Regulations provide that M&A-related contracts under the regulations should comply with Chinese law and include the following mandatory language or provisions: (1) detailed description of parties to the agreement, including name and address and name, designation, and nationality of legal representatives of the parties; (2) number of shares and consideration for share transfer or allotment from increased capital; (3) timetable for contributions and method of performance of the agreement; (4) rights and obligations of parties to the agreement; (5) default liability and dispute resolution; and (6) date and venue of execution of the agreement. Foreign M&A Regulations, art. 13.

(5) Financial audit report of the domestic company for the latest financial year
(6) Identification document or business certificate and credit certification of the investor(s)
(7) Description of invested enterprises of the domestic company
(8) Business licenses (duplicate) of the domestic company and its invested enterprises
(9) Employee redeployment plan of the domestic company
(10) Other document required by the regulations[15]

Similar documents are required for the approval of an asset purchase transaction.[16] Investors are not allowed to use assets acquired from a domestic company prior to obtaining approval from the relevant government authorities.[17]

Both equity acquisitions and asset acquisitions are required to be approved by the regulatory authorities—namely, the Ministry of Commerce or local and provincial branch organizations—and must be registered with the local bureau for the State Administration of Industry & Commerce.[18] Under the FIE M&A Foreign M&A Regulations, the parties to the transaction have certain reporting requirements and must obtain the *prior approval* of MOFCOM and the SAIC if an intended merger or acquisition would involve any of the following circumstances:

(1) A party to the intended transaction has annual business revenue in the China market that exceeds RMB1.5 billion

15. Foreign M&A Regulations, art. 12. Other documents required to be submitted include any land-use rights documents relevant to the operation, agreements concerning creditor rights under Article 7 ofthe regulations, copies of public notices under Article 7, and market share report prepared by the foreign investor under Article 19. All documents are required to be submitted in the Chinese language. Foreign M&A Regulations, art. 23.

16. Foreign M&A Regulations, art. 15. Asset purchase agreements under the regulations are required to comply with Chinese law and include the following mandatory language or provisions: (1) description of parties to the agreement, including name (in full) and address and name, designation, and nationality of legal representatives of the parties; (2) list of assets proposed for acquisition and prices; (3) timetable and method of performance of the agreement; (4) rights and obligations of parties to the agreement; (5) default liability and dispute resolution; and (6) date and venue of execution of the agreement. Foreign M&A Regulations, art. 16.

17. Foreign M&A Regulations, art. 15.

18. MOFCOM is required to approve or reject an application within thirty days of filing by the foreign investor. Foreign M&A Regulations, art. 17. Upon approval from MOFCOM, an investor has thirty days to complete the registration procedures with the SAIC and to obtain a business license and an additional thirty days thereafter to complete registration with the tax and customs authorities. Foreign M&A Regulations, art. 18. Domestic companies are thereafter required to have their business licenses and other registration documents amended with the relevant authorities. Foreign M&A Regulations, art. 18.

(2) The aggregate number of mergers and acquisitions of domestic enterprises in the specific industry in China during the past year exceeds ten

(3) A party to the intended transaction holds market share that equals or exceeds 20 percent of the subject market in China; or

(4) The transaction will result in a party to the transaction holding a 25-percent market share in the Chinese market[19]

If the above conditions do not apply, MOFCOM and the SAIC still have the discretion to request that the foreign investor prepare a report if the government is of the opinion that the merger and acquisition by foreign investor(s) will result in major market share held by foreign investor(s) or that there are major factors of significant impact on market competition or national economy and the people's livelihood and national economic security.[20] If the government finds that the proposed acquisition may lead to excessive concentration of market share, which is detrimental to fair competition and consumers' rights and interests, they have the discretion to approve or reject the proposed acquisition. MOFCOM and the SAIC have the discretion to hold public hearings to address the issues raised by the acquisition.[21]

The Foreign M&A Regulations also include a premerger notification requirement for foreign or overseas M&A activities that meet certain criteria. An offshore transaction that involves any one or more of the following circumstances is required to be reported to the regulatory authorities:

(1) A party to an offshore transaction has assets in China with a value in excess of RMB3 billion

(2) A party to the offshore transaction has a business turnover in excess of RMB1.5 billion in the Chinese market in the current year

(3) A party to the offshore transaction and its affiliates collectively hold at least 20 percent of the relevant shares in China

(4) Arising from the proposed offshore transaction, a party to the transaction and its affiliates intend to acquire a Chinese market share of at least 25 percent

19. Foreign M&A Regulations, art. 19.

20. Foreign M&A Regulations, art. 19. The reporting requirement applies if any of the conditions involve a related enterprise.

21. Foreign M&A Regulations, art. 20.

(5) Arising from the offshore transaction, a party thereto will, directly or indirectly, hold equity in more than fifteen FIEs in the subject industry in China[22]

After submitting the filing, MOFCOM/SAIC can determine whether the transaction will harm domestic competition or domestic consumers, and can decide whether or not to approve of the transaction. However, a party to the transaction may apply to the MOFCOM and SAIC for an exemption from investigation in certain limited circumstances; namely, where the proposed transaction would improve the conditions for fair market competition; result in the restructuring of unprofitable enterprises and promote employment; result in the introduction of advanced technology and management talent and improve competitiveness of Chinese domestic enterprises in the international market; or result in the improvement of the environment.[23]

Practice Tip

The new regulations leave much to be desired and, in typical Chinese regulatory fashion, the regulations are vague and ambiguous to give the regulatory authorities as much wiggle room as possible when it comes to implementation. The lack of clarity will give the regulatory authorities time to build their experience in this highly technical area before near-complete standards are carved in stone. Much clarification is needed in order to give foreign investors guidance with respect to their compliance obligations. Pending the adoption of more detailed rules, foreign investors contemplating M&A transactions that directly or indirectly impact market conditions in China should thoroughly evaluate the potential application of the notice requirements of the regulations.[24]

22. Foreign M&A Regulations, art. 21.

23. Foreign M&A Regulations, art. 22.

24. Key issues and unanswered questions left for further clarification by the authorities: How do you determine value of assets (book or fair market value)? How is market share in China determined and on what criteria is it based? What time frame is applicable in determining sales (prior year or preceding twelve months)? Who will be required to file with the government, the target or the acquiring party to the transaction? What documents will be required? How much time will MOFCOM/SAIC take to review the application and what administrative appeals are available for adverse decisions? What are the penalties for noncompliance? What are the standards for an exemption from the examination process? How will the new regulations operate with the proposed Anti-Trust Law that is under development?

B. Merger and Division of Foreign-Invested Enterprises

The government has adopted regulations governing the merger and division of foreign investment enterprises.[25] Under the FIE Merger/Division Regulations, merger activities involving foreign-invested enterprises are categorized as either a merger by *absorption,* or a merger resulting in a *new entity.*[26] A merger by *absorption* refers to a transaction whereby one company completely takes over another company or a group of enterprises. In an *absorption merger,* the acquiring company continues to exist while the targeted company is dissolved and deregistered (after formal completion of the acquisition). A merger that results in a *new entity* refers to a transaction whereby two or more companies merge to establish a new company. In this situation, each party to the merger transaction is formally dissolved and deregistered after formal completion of the merger.[27]

Whether the merger is a result of *absorption* or results in the creation of a *new entity*, the dissolved companies need not go through formal liquidation procedures,[28] and all assets, liabilities, and shareholders' interest will be

25. Merger and Division of Foreign-Invested Enterprises (issued by the Ministry of Foreign Trade and Economic Cooperation and the State Administration of Industry and Commerce on Nov. 22, 2001) (hereinafter the "FIE Merger/Division Regulations"). The 1993 Company Law provides the legal basis for the merger and division of companies and applies to all mergers and acquisitions between any limited liability company and joint stock companies established under Chinese law. *See* Company Law of the People's Republic of China (adopted December 29, 1993, by the 5th Sess. of the Standing Comm. of the 8th NPC), *reprinted in* CHINA LAWS FOR FOREIGN BUSINESS (CCH), Business Regulation ¶ 13-518 (hereinafter the "Company Law"). *See generally Special Feature: In Practice: Realities of Merging FIEs,* CHINA L. & PRAC. (Feb. 2000); *Clear New Guidelines on M&A and Division of FIEs,* CHINA L. & PRAC. (Nov. 1999).

26. The FIE Merger/Division Regulations define "Foreign Investment Enterprises" to include Sino-foreign equity joint enterprises, Sino-foreign cooperative joint ventures that have legal person status, wholly foreign-owned enterprises, or foreign investment joint stock companies. FIEs are collectively referred to as "Companies" in the Regulations. FIE Merger/Division Regulations, art. 2.

27. FIE Merger/Division Regulations, art. 3. The term "merger" refers to two or more companies that join together and become one company in accordance with relevant provisions of the Company Law and through agreement.

28. A company that goes through liquidation and dissolution must follow the Measures on Liquidation Procedures for Foreign Investment Enterprises (approved on June 15, 1996, by the State Council and promulgated on July 9, 1996, by MOFCOM), *reprinted in* CHINA LAWS FOR FOREIGN BUSINESS (CCH), Business Regulation ¶ 13-608 (hereinafter the "FIE Liquidation Procedures"); Company Law of the People's Republic of China (adopted December 29, 1993, by the 5th Sess. of the Standing Comm. of the 8th NPC), arts. 189–198, *reprinted in* CHINA LAWS FOR FOREIGN BUSINESS (CCH), Business Regulation ¶ 13-518 (hereinafter the "Company Law") (discusses bankruptcy and liquidation standards for companies). Prior to the adoption of the FIE Liquidation Procedures, several local governments had formulated their own liquidation standards. *See* Liquidation Measures for Foreign Investment Enterprises in Beijing Municipality (issued as Decree No. 9 by the Beijing Municipal People's Government and effective June 1, 1992), *reprinted in* CHINA LAWS FOR FOREIGN BUSINESS, Special Zones & Cities ¶ 96-324; Rules of the Beijing Municipality on the Dissolution of Foreign Investment Enterprises (adopted on June 8, 1995, by the 17th Sess. of the Standing Comm. of the 10th Beijing Municipal People's Congress), *reprinted in* CHINA LAWS FOR FOREIGN BUSINESS (CCH), Special Zones & Cities ¶ 170-025. *See also* Rules of Shanghai Municipality on Liquidation Procedures for Foreign Investment Enterprises (adopted on August 16,

carried forward through the merger. As a result, the shareholders and creditors, secured and unsecured, of the premerger original companies will become the shareholders and creditors of the postmerger company. Given that the debts and liabilities of the premerger company will be assumed by the postmerger company, careful and comprehensive due diligence should be conducted to better evaluate the level of debt, and scope of obligations, of the premerger companies.

The term *division* refers to one company being divided into two or more companies in accordance with relevant provisions of the Company Law and by a resolution of the company's board of directors. A company *division* may proceed either through the continuous existence method or through dissolution. Division through continuous existence refers to the situation in which one company is divided into two or more companies, whereby the original company continues to exist and one or more new companies are established. Division by dissolution refers to the situation wherein one company is divided into two or more companies, upon which the original company dissolves and two or more new companies are established.[29]

A company merger or division must be carried out in accordance with Chinese laws and regulations, and all merger/division activities must not negatively impact the rights of creditors. A company merger or division must also comply with provisions of the Foreign Investment Guidelines and the Guideline Catalogue of Foreign Investment Industries. A merger or division is not permitted to result in a situation where foreign investors become the sole investor, controlling shareholder, or dominant investor of a company in an industry where control by a foreign investor is prohibited or restricted. The business scope of the operation resulting from a merger or division must also comply with the law and government investment policies.[30] An FIE merger or division is also required to fully comply with the laws and regulations concerning customs, taxation, and foreign exchange administration. After merger or division, the continuous company or the newly established

1991, at the 28th Sess. of the Standing Comm. of the 9th Shanghai Municipal People's Congress), *reprinted in* CHINA LAWS FOR FOREIGN BUSINESS (CCH), Special Zones & Cities ¶ 91-065 (addresses the ordinary and special liquidation procedures, valuation of liquidated assets, and other matters relevant to enterprise dissolution and liquidation). For an analysis of the liquidation procedures *see* Stuken, *Corporate Reorganization: Look Before You Leap,* 11 CHINA L. & PRAC. 60 (Oct. 1997). *See also* Rules of the Tianjin Municipality on the Liquidation of Foreign Investment Enterprises (promulgated on February 13, 1995, by the Standing Comm. of the Tianjin Municipal People's Congress), *reprinted in* CHINA LAWS FOR FOREIGN BUSINESS (CCH), Special Zones & Cities ¶ 200-005.

29. FIE Merger/Division Regulations, art. 4.

30. FIE Merger/Division Regulations, art. 5.

company will, upon approval, continue to enjoy the various foreign investment preferential treatment which the original company was granted.[31]

A company merger/division is required to be approved by the original government agency that approved the company (MOFCOM or local branch). If two or more government agencies have original jurisdiction over the approval process, the examination authority shall be the locality in which the merged company is located. If the total amount of foreign investment of the companies intending to merge is not within the approval power of the companies' original approval authority (e.g., the registered capital exceeds certain threshold amounts), the transaction is required to be examined and approved by the examination authority with appropriate power. If one of the companies intending to merge is a company limited by shares, such a merger is required to be approved by the Ministry of Commerce.[32] If an original company is dissolved or new company is formed in different areas as a result of a merger or division, the authorities in the different areas are required to be advised of the transaction.[33]

The regulations provide that a company is not allowed to proceed with a merger/division transaction before the foreign investors have made their full investments and fulfilled their "cooperation conditions" in accordance with provisions of the contract and Articles of Association of the company. Similarly, a company is not allowed to proceed with merger/division unless it has commenced operations or production as required by the original application approval.[34] These rules appear to be counterproductive given that many merger decisions are designed to resolve problems with a party's failure to pay its required registered capital. Also, the rules may be too restrictive and cumbersome to implement given that some operations are granted the right to make contributions over a period of time, and especially with larger projects.

---

31. FIE Merger/Division Regulations, art. 6. *See* Income Tax Questions Relevant to Enterprise Merger and Division Circular (promulgated on June 21, 2000, by the State Administration of Taxation); Several Questions Concerning Income Tax When Enterprises Are Reorganized or Change Their System Tentative Provisions (promulgated on August 20, 1998, by the State Administration of Taxation); Enterprise Income Tax Tentative Regulations (promulgated on December 13, 1998, by the State Administration of Taxation). *See generally* K. Lu, *Mergers and Tax Treatment of Foreign-Invested Enterprises,* CHINA L. & PRAC. (January 2001).

32. FIE Merger/Division Regulations, art. 7. If there are two or more original approval authorities, the applicant shall submit an application for review by the original authorities. The original authorities have 15 days to respond to the application for review. If no response is given in 15 days, the approval of the original authorities is deemed granted. If the original authorities protest the merger, the applicant may appeal to a higher level administratively. FIE Merger/Division Regulations, art. 22.

33. FIE Merger/Division Regulations, art. 8.

34. FIE Merger/Division Regulations, art. 9.

Postmerger, limited liability companies will continue to be LLCs and companies limited by shares will become a company limited by shares. If a merger occurs between listed companies limited by shares and limited liability companies, the resulting company is a company limited by shares. A non-listed company limited by shares merging with a limited liability company has the option to become either a company limited by shares or a limited liability company postmerger.[35]

When a merger occurs between companies limited by shares or a company limited by shares is established by merger, the registered capital of the merged company is required to be the total sum of the registered capital of the premerger original companies. Where a limited liability company merges with a company limited by shares and becomes a company limited by shares, the registered capital of the resulting company is required to be the sum of the value of shares that are converted from the net capital value of the limited liability company on the basis of the value of each share of the company limited by shares, plus the total value of the shares of the original company limited by shares.[36] The registered capital of a company postdivision is required to be determined by the board of directors of the company in accordance with applicable laws; however, the total sum of the registered capital of the divided companies must be the total amount of the registered capital prior to the division.[37]

The share rights of investors postmerger shall be determined in accordance with the parties' contract or articles of association, and based upon a valuation conducted by an asset valuation organization; however, the ratio of the foreign investors' share rights must not be less than 25 percent of the registered capital of the merged company.[38] The share rights of investing parties in a postdivision company is required to be determined by the investors in the company pursuant to the parties' contract and articles of association; however, the ratio of the foreign investors' share rights shall not be less than 25 percent of the total registered capital of the divided company.[39]

35. FIE Merger/Division Regulations, art. 10. In situations where a merger/division involves a listed company, the transaction must be in conformance with application securities regulations and with the approval of the China Securities Regulatory Commission. FIE Merger/Division Regulations, art. 16. *See generally Trends in Mergers & Acquisitions: the Restructuring of Domestically Listed Chinese Companies*, CHINA L. & PRAC. (June 2001).

36. FIE Merger/Division Regulations, art. 11.

37. FIE Merger/Division Regulations, art. 13.

38. FIE Merger/Division Regulations, art. 12.

39. FIE Merger/Division Regulations, art. 14.

A merger transaction involving Chinese domestic enterprises must comply with Chinese law and regulations on the use of foreign funds and industry policies. Such transactions must also meet the following conditions:

(1) The Chinese domestic enterprise intended to be merged is a limited liability company or a company limited by shares, the existence of which is consistent with the provisions of the Company Law
(2) The investors satisfy the industry qualification standards
(3) The ratio of foreign investors' share rights shall not be less than 25 percent of the registered capital of the merged company
(4) The various parties in the merger agreement shall ensure that the existing staff and workers of the domestic company continue to be employed and/or satisfactory agreements are in place to address the compensation for terminated employees[40]

When an FIE is established after a merger between another FIE company and a domestic enterprise, the total investment amount is required to be the total sum of the investment of the original company and the total enterprise assets of the domestic enterprise as stated in the enterprise financial auditing report. The total registered capital of the new FIE is required to be the sum total of the registered capital of the original FIE company and that of the domestic enterprise combined.[41] The merged company must not hold shares in enterprises in which foreign investment is prohibited.[42]

40. FIE Merger/Division Regulations, art. 17. The requirement set forth in the FIE Merger/Division Regulations that the merger/division agreement include employee settlement standards is consistent with current policies of the Chinese government requiring that all enterprises provide for excess workers in an appropriate manner. Without an employee settlement plan, merger/division transactions will have difficulty obtaining approval.

41. FIE Merger/Division Regulations, art. 18. The regulations require that the ratio between the registered capital and the total investment should comply with the Provisional Regulations Concerning the Ratio of Registered Capital to Total Investment of Joint Ventures Using Chinese and Foreign Investment. In special situations in which these provisional regulations cannot be applied, the postmerger company should obtain the approval of MOFCOM and the SAIC. This rule eliminates the possibility of capital increases or decreases by investors in connection with merger or division transactions. MOFCOM prohibits the practice of the withdrawal of capital in the guise of a merger or division by enterprises that might be seeking to reduce the postmerger/postdivision company's liability to creditors. However, these strict requirements limit the flexibility of investors to inject new capital in connection with any operational reorganization. The requirement that no capital increase or decrease is allowed in the course of any merger or division is also contrary to provisions of the Company Law that contemplate the increase or decrease of capital in connection with a merger or division. Company Law, arts. 186, 187. The Company Law addresses the requirements for matters relating to capital increase/decrease. Given that the entire merger and division process is subject to approval of the government, these restrictions seem unnecessarily strict.

42. FIE Merger/Division Regulations, art. 19.

An applicant for approval of a *merger* is required to submit to the approval authorities the following documents:

(1) An application statement on the company merger signed by the legal representatives of all merging companies and the agreement for a company merger
(2) Resolutions of the board of directors of the merging companies regarding the company merger
(3) Merger agreement and Articles of Association of all merging companies[43]
(4) Approval documents and copies of business licenses of all merging companies
(5) Capital verification reports of all merging companies
(6) Balance sheets and property inventories of all merging companies
(7) The past year's audit reports of all merging companies
(8) The list of creditors of all merging companies
(9) The company contract and Articles of Association of the merged company
(10) The list of members of the board of directors of the merged company
(11) Other documents required by the examination and approval authorities[44]

Where a company is merged with a domestic enterprise, the applicant is also required to file with the authorities a copy of its business licenses of the enterprises.

A company that intends to pursue a *division* of the operation is required to submit the following documents to the approval authorities:

(1) Application for company division signed by the legal representative of the company

43. The regulations provide that a merger agreement is required to set forth certain mandatory language, such as: (1) names, addresses, and legal representatives of various parties to the merger agreement; (2) the name, address, and legal representative of the target company; (3) the total amount of investment capital and the registered capital of the merged company; (4) procedures and timetable of the merger; (5) plans for absorbing accounts receivable and payment of debts and other obligations by various parties of the merger agreement; (6) measures for arrangement of staff and workers; (7) liabilities for breach of agreement; (8) methods for dispute settlement; (9) date and place of the agreement signed; (10) other matters that various parties to the merger agreement deem necessary to be included. FIE Merger/Division Regulations, art. 21.

44. FIE Merger/Division Regulations, art. 20. The applicant in a merger by absorption is the target company. In mergers through the establishment of a new company, both parties will nominate a party to act as the applicant.

(2) The resolution of the board of directors of the company on the company division
(3) The company division agreement signed by the continuing company and the companies to be established resulting from the company division (referred to as various parties to the division agreement)[45]
(4) The company's contract and Articles of Association
(5) The approval document and a copy of business license of the company
(6) The capital verification report of the company
(7) The balance sheet and property inventory of the company
(8) The list of creditors of the company
(9) The company contracts and articles of association of various companies after the division
(10) List of members of the board of directors of the various companies after the division
(11) Other documents required by the examination and approval authorities[46]

If a division results in the establishment of new companies in various regions, the applicant is required to file an application with the authorities in the various regions.

Postmerger the absorbing company or the newly established company is required to assume the debts of the liquidated companies as a result of merger. Companies after division shall assume the debts of the original company according to the division agreement.[47]

When an application is filed for approval of a merger/division, the authorities are required to make a preliminary decision within forty-five days. If the authorities are of the opinion that the merger transaction has the potential for industry monopoly or a possibility of forming a market position dominating certain particular commodities or services and thereby negatively impact fair competition, it may conduct a public hearing and investigation to determine the impact of the proposed merger. In the event

45. A division agreement is required to include the following mandatory language: (1) names, addresses, and legal representatives of various parties to the division agreement; (2) the total amount of investment and the registered capital of the company after the division; (3) method of division; (4) plan for division of company's assets drawn by various parties to the division agreement; (5) plans for absorbing accounts receivable and debts payable drawn by various parties to the merger agreement; (6) measures for staff and workers' arrangements; (7) liabilities for breach of agreement; (8) methods for disputes settlement; (9) date and place of the agreement; (10) other matters that various parties to the division agreement deem necessary to be included. FIE Mergers/Division Regulations, art. 24.
46. FIE Merger/Division Regulations, art. 23.
47. FIE Merger/Division Regulations, art. 25.

that an investigation and/or hearing are conducted, the approval time period may be extended to 180 days.[48] Upon receipt of preliminary approval to proceed with a merger/division transaction, the applicant company shall issue written notice to known creditors and cause to have published a public announcement of the intended transaction in a provincial-level or nationally circulated newspaper at least three times in thirty days. The notice and public announcement shall mention the company's plans for resolving the debts and liabilities of the company.[49]

Within thirty days of receipt of the written notice or ninety days from the date of the public announcement, a creditor has the right to request that a company settle outstanding debt obligations prior to proceeding with a merger/division. If a creditor fails to exercise its rights pursuant to the notice/announcement procedures, the creditor is deemed to have waived its rights to challenge the company's merger/division plans.[50] After the expiration of ninety days after the public announcement was first published, and assuming that no creditor has raised any objection, the applicant of a proposed merger/division transaction is required to submit the following documents to the approval authorities:

(1) Proof of compliance with the public announcement procedures
(2) Proof of compliance with the notice to creditors procedures
(3) Description of the company's plans to settle its debts and liabilities
(4) Other documents that may be required to be submitted by the examination and approval authorities[51]

Upon receipt of the above-referenced materials, the approval authorities have thirty days to approve or reject a company's application to engage in a merger/division transaction.[52] If approved, the applicant is required to complete the various registration formalities to form a new company and/or to

48. FIE Merger/Division Regulations, art. 26.

49. FIE Merger/Division Regulations, art. 27. *See also* Model Notices and Circulars for Merger, Division and Reduction in Registered Capital of Foreign-Invested Enterprises (issued by the State Council on March 14, 2003).

50. FIE Merger/Division Regulations, art. 28.

51. FIE Merger/Division Regulations, art. 29.

52. FIE Merger/Division Regulations, art. 30. The public announcement procedure set forth in the FIE Merger/Division Regulations is similar to the Company Law. However, there is a special requirement that the applicant should not notify the creditors or make any public announcement until the Company or Companies have obtained a preliminary reply from the approval authority favorable to the proposed merger/division transaction. In addition, the regulations provide that after two public announcements, the applicant must reapply to the approval authority in order to obtain final approval for the contemplated merger or division. As a result, there are two approval steps that must be obtained, one before and one after the public announcement, which appears to be unnecessarily duplicative. In practice, the preliminary approval is the most important approval, and the second approval is more a procedural step to ensure that proper notice to creditors and the public was provided as required by law.

cancel an existing company registration.[53] Within thirty days of receiving a new business license, a newly established company or continuing company is required to notify known creditors and to publish a public announcement.[54]

C. Public Company Takeover Procedures

The CSRC has adopted regulations concerning the standards and procedures for public company takeovers.[55] In the private sale takeover context, the purchaser is required to submit a report to the CSRC within two days of the execution of a takeover agreement. At the same time, the purchaser is required to provide notice outlining the details of the transaction to the target company and the public. Upon receipt of the takeover notice, the target company's board of directors is required to prepare an opinion concerning the legality of financial aspects of the takeover, and the target's independent directors are required to issue separate and independent opinions. The board and independent director opinions must be released to the public. In the discharge of these duties, the target's board may retain an independent financial adviser. An independent financial advisor is required to be retained to issue an opinion for management buyouts. A takeover agreement for the transfer of State-owned shares or those shares requiring government approval is effective only on approval.

The Public Company Takeover Procedures allow publicly traded shares to be transferred in a private sale, subject to certain conditions. An authorized securities company is required to handle the transfer and settlement procedures of the takeover, and must apply to the stock exchange and clearinghouse for the suspension of trading in the shares to be transferred. The transferor is required to publicly announce the content of the transfer agreement on the day after the transfer application has been submitted to the applicable stock exchange. The exchange management is required to review the application and issue a decision to approve or reject the takeover within three working days of receipt of the application. Upon receipt of approval by the stock exchange, the securities

53. FIE Merger/Division Regulations, arts. 31–35. The revised articles of association are effective upon the approval date.

54. FIE Merger/Division Regulations, art. 36.

55. Administration of the Takeover of Listed Companies Procedures (promulgated on September 28, 2002, by the CSRC) (hereinafter the "Public Company Takeover Provisions"). *See also* Notice on Relevant Issues in Transferring the State-Owned Shares and Legal Person Shares of Listed Companies to Foreign Investors (issued on November 1, 2002, by the CSRC and the Ministry of Finance) (hereinafter the "State Shares Notice"). The State Shares Notice allows for the transfer of Chinese non-listed shares to foreign investors. Any transfer of State-Owned shares is to be approved by MOF. Full payment of the purchase price is required before such transfer can be legally registered. Non-listed shares acquired by foreign investors may not be resold within 12 months after the transfer. Foreign investors may not acquire a Chinese listed company through purchase of shares on China's stock exchanges. *See also* Securities Law, arts. 78–94.

company thereafter applies to the clearinghouse for the transfer of shares. The transferee is required to publicly announce the transfer within two working days after the transfer is complete. After the shares have been transferred, the securities company is to apply to the stock exchange for the release of the share custody. The transferee is to announce the release within two working days after the release and, thereafter, public trading of such shares may resume. The continued listing or delisting of publicly traded companies acquired by a tender offer is subject to review by the CSRC.[56]

The procedures allow a shareholder to sell shares in a listed company by public solicitation with the approval of the CSRC and applicable stock exchange management. Solicitation to sell shares in a listed company must be made through a securities company. The Procedures contemplate that solicitation transactions are limited to non-listed shares in a listed company.

Consistent with the Securities Law, the Public Company Takeover Procedures require a potential purchaser to make a general offer to all the shareholders of a target company if it intends to control more than 30 percent of the outstanding shares of the target company.[57] A person "controls" a listed company if (i) he or she is the single largest shareholder; (ii) the voting rights being exercised or controlled by him or her are more than those exercised by the largest shareholder of the company; (iii) he or she holds or controls more than 30 percent of the shares or voting rights in the company; (iv) he or she has the right to appoint more than half of the board members by exercising voting rights; and (v) other circumstances determined by the CSRC. A potential purchaser may apply to the CSRC for a waiver of the "general offer" requirement. Pursuant to the Public Company Takeover Procedures, such waiver is appropriate for (i) certain intra-company or related party transactions; (ii) corporate rescues; (iii) where the 30 percent threshold is crossed by virtue of a stock split, capital reductions, inheritance, administrative order or enforcement of a court order; (iv) a shareholder holding more than 50 percent of shares in a listed company intends to increase its holding, and the result of such increase will not cause the shares held by such shareholder to exceed 75 percent of the outstanding shares of such company; (v) underwriters or banks holding more than 30 percent of shares in the ordinary course of their business; and (vi) other circumstances as approved by the CSRC.

An acquiring party that originally held less than 30 percent of the shares in the target company may increase its stake by making a tender offer. The

56. *See* Notice on Relevant Issues Concerning the Conditions for Public Trading of Shares of Acquired Companies Involving Tender Offers (issued on May 20, 2003, by the CSRC) (outlines the conditions under which an acquired company's listed shares may continue to be publicly traded or delisted).

57. Securities Law, arts. 78–94.

shares to be purchased pursuant to a tender offer may not exceed 5 percent of the outstanding shares, and a tender offer shall not result in the acquirer's shares exceeding the 30 percent threshold. Procedurally, at the commencement of a tender offer, the acquirer is required to notify the target and make a public announcement describing the proposed offer. If the Tender Offer Report filed with the CSRC is not rejected within 15 days of receipt, the potential purchaser may publicly release the tender offer documents. If requested by the CSRC within the 15-day period, the potential purchaser is required to amend its tender offer before proceeding with the transaction.

A potential purchaser in a tender offer must obtain an opinion by qualified legal counsel with respect to the veracity, legality, and completeness of the Tender Offer Report. In addition, a potential purchaser is also required to have a financial adviser issue an opinion with respect to the purchaser's financial position. At the same time, the target company's board of directors is required to retain a financial adviser to evaluate the target company's financial condition, and to issue an opinion concerning the fairness of the terms and conditions of the tender offer. In the management buyout context, independent directors are required to retain a financial adviser to review the financial condition of the company and the fairness of the tender offer by management. The target company's board of directors is thereafter required to prepare a Tender Offer Response Report describing the board's recommendation to the shareholders. The Tender Offer Response Report and related opinions must be submitted to the CSRC and released to the public.

If the potential purchaser intends to fund the transaction with cash, 20 percent of the transaction value must be placed in a bank account designated by the securities clearinghouse as performance security. If the takeover transaction is to be funded by transferable securities, such securities must be deposited and held in custody by the securities clearinghouse.

The Public Company Takeover Provisions provide that the term of a tender offer may be in the range of 30 to 60 days, unless there are competing and open tender offers on the table. Once made, a tender offer may not be withdrawn during the designated term. A tender offer may not be revised without the express approval of the CSRC. The Provisions provide that if a potential purchaser unilaterally revokes or withdraws its tender offer prior to the term expiration date, it is prohibited from making any subsequent tender offer with respect to the same target company for one year from the date of withdrawal or revocation.

The Public Company Takeover Provisions regulate the per-share price of a tender offer. Under the Provisions, the offer price for a target company's listed shares is not be lower than the higher of the following: (i) the highest price the acquirer has paid within six months for the target company's securities, or (ii) 90 percent of the average daily-weighted trading price of such listed shares in the past 30 trading days prior to the date of the announcement of the tender offer. Under the Public Company Takeover Procedures, the tender offer price for non-listed shares may not be lower than the higher of the following: (i) the highest price paid by the acquirer within six months of the announcement of the existence of the tender offer; or (ii) the most recent audited book value per share of the target company.

The Public Company Takeover Procedures also prohibit target companies from engaging in certain anti-takeover activities. Specifically, a target company's board may not (i) issue new shares; (ii) issue convertible bonds; (iii) redeem the company's shares; (iv) amend the company's articles of association; or (v) sell all or substantially all of the target's assets with the intent to stall or prevent a takeover.

D. Anti-Monopoly and Competition Law Issues in China M&A

For almost ten years commencing in 1994, China has been drafting an antitrust or anti-monopoly law, which is anticipated to be adopted sometime in 2005.[58] Prior to the creation of the Ministry of Commerce, its predecessors, the State Economic & Trade Commission and the Ministry of Foreign Trade and Economic Cooperation, were both attempting to draft the new antitrust law. After the agencies were combined to form MOFCOM, the responsibility for drafting was delegated to the Division of Domestic Trade Law, Department of Law & Treaty of MOFCOM.

The draft Anti-Monopoly Law would apply to all enterprises in China, as well as non-profit organizations and trade associations.[59] Under the draft

58. Anti-Monopoly Law of the People's Republic of China (draft issued by the Ministry of Commerce on September 10, 2003); a copy of the September 2003 draft is in the files of the author (hereinafter referred to as the "Anti-Monopoly Law"). Given that the draft law contains broad topics, it is anticipated that the relevant authorities will be required to adopt implementing regulations to provide more specificity and guidance on the application of the law. *See generally* P. Neumann & J. Guo, *The Slow Boat to Antitrust Law in China: An Examination of the New Regulations on Monopoly Pricing,* CHINA L. & PRAC. (Sept. 2003).

59. Anti-Monopoly Law, arts. 2, 55. The draft Law also prohibits government agencies from abusing their administrative power to engage in monopolistic activities, such as to force private enterprises to purchase from designated local suppliers, to set up toll roads or customs gates to obstruct the import or local shipment of products, to set discriminatory sales prices for non-local products, to impose discriminatory technical requirements on non-local products, to exclude non-local companies from participating in local bids, or to take other actions to establish regional blockades against non-local products and services. Anti-Monopoly Law, arts. 31–35. A violation on the prohibition of administrative monopolistic conduct may result in administrative or criminal penalties against the responsible government employees. Anti-Monopoly Law, arts. 47, 48.

Anti-Monopoly Law, the term "monopoly" is defined as the following activities that eliminate or restrict competition, damage the interests of other business operators or consumers, or endanger the public interest: (1) agreements, contracts, or other collective actions among business operators; (2) abuse of market power; (3) excessive concentration of enterprises; or (4) abuse of administrative power by government agencies.[60]

1. Prohibition on Monopolistic Agreements

The Law provides that business operators are not allowed to enter into any contract, agreement, or other collective conduct, or do any of the following to exclude or limit competition:

(1) Fix, maintain, or change prices of products
(2) Collude with each other in a tender
(3) Restrict the production or sales quantity of products
(4) Allocate the sales markets or the raw material purchasing markets
(5) Limit the purchase of new technology or new facilities
(6) Jointly boycott transactions
(7) Make other agreements with the effect of limiting fair competition[61]

The Law further provides that certain activities are exempt from the statutory prohibitions on monopoly agreements, such as the following:

(1) Joint action taken by business operators for the purpose of technology improvement, product quality upgrading, efficiency improvement, lower costs, unification of product specifications and models, and R&D
(2) Joint action taken by small- and medium-sized enterprises to improve operational efficiency and to enhance their competitiveness
(3) Joint action taken by business operators to adapt to market changes and to stop seriously decreasing sales volumes or obvious production surplus
(4) Other activities that may eliminate or limit competition but benefit national economic development and the public interest

In situations where a business operator is unsure of whether its agreements may potentially violate the law, it is required to apply to the government for approval.[62] The business operator is required to submit the subject

60. Anti-Monopoly Law, art. 3.
61. Anti-Monopoly Law, art. 8.
62. Anti-Monopoly Law, arts. 9–12. The Law provides that the "Anti-Monopoly Management Body under the State Council" is responsible for reviewing all applications for exemption of agreements

agreement, supporting application, and information concerning the business operators at-issue within 15 days from the date of conclusion of the subject agreement. The Anti-Monopoly Regulatory Commission must review and either approve or reject an agreement within 60 days of submission; thereafter, the agreement is deemed accepted. Following the approval of an agreement, the Anti-Monopoly Regulatory Commission can revoke the approval, modify the terms and conditions of an agreement, or order the termination or correction of the agreement under any of the following circumstances:

(1) Significant change in economic circumstances
(2) Elimination of justification for approval
(3) The business operators fail to observe the additional obligations of the approval
(4) The agreement is approved based on incorrect or misleading information
(5) Abusive use of the exemption[63]

The Law provides that the Anti-Monopoly Regulatory Commission should publish its decisions issued pursuant to Articles 11 and 12 in a national publication. The Law authorizes the Anti-Monopoly Regulatory Commission to impose a fine of up to RMB5 million ($600,000) for any violation under Article 8 of the Law with respect to monopolistic agreements.[64]

2. Prohibition against Abuse of a Dominant Market Position

The Anti-Monopoly Law provides that a business operator is prohibited from abusing its dominant market position, obstructing the activities of other business operators, or engaging in activities designed to eliminate or restrict competition.[65] The Law defines the term "dominant market position" to mean where one or several business operator(s) control(s) a specific market. A business operator will be deemed to have a dominant market position in situations where the operator is the sole business operator in a specific market and it is difficult for new businesses to enter the market; in situations where the business operator is the principal player in the market occupying a "superior status" and it is difficult for other business operators to enter the

---

or arrangements that may fall within the purview of the prohibition. The responsible government agency has not been formed, but it is anticipated that it will be organized shortly after the adoption of the Law (for convenience only, the entity is hereinafter referred to as the "Anti-Monopoly Regulatory Commission").

63. Anti-Monopoly Law, art. 12. If the provisions of Article 12 (3)–(5) are violated, the revocation of approval of an agreement may be retroactive.

64. Anti-Monopoly Law, art. 44.

65. Anti-Monopoly Law, art. 14.

market; or in situations where there are more than two business operators in a specific market but there is no real competition.[66] There is a presumption under the draft Anti-Monopoly Law that business operators in a specific market that have any of the following market shares have a dominant market position: (1) a single business operator with market share over 1/2; (2) two business operators with market share over 2/3; or (3) three business operators with a market share over 3/4.[67]

A company with a dominant market position is prohibited from engaging in certain abusive or unfair practices outlined in the statute. Specifically, a business operator with a dominant market position is prohibited from selling its products at a price higher than the normal price; selling its products at predatory prices to drive out other business, such as to sell product at prices below costs, or to sell below cost in the form of a rebate, subsidy, or gift; discriminating against certain customers that are equally qualified by offering the same products or services at discriminatory prices; refusing to sell products to certain customers; engaging in coercion or force to close transactions, or interfere with fair competition; selling products to customers against their will or under any unreasonable transaction terms; forcing distributors to sell only the business operator's products to the exclusion of other business operators; or controlling the resale price of the products supplied to distributors.[68]

A business operator that abuses its dominant market position is subject to cease and desist orders, civil fines of up to RMB10 million ($1.2 million), or criminal penalties in serious cases.[69]

3. Regulation of Enterprise Concentration

The draft Anti-Monopoly Law prohibits enterprise concentration that eliminates or limits fair market competition, hinders the development of the national economy, or damages the public interest.[70] Enterprise concentration may arise when one or more enterprises merge into an existing enterprise or when more than two enterprises combine to become a new enterprise; when one enterprise gains control over another enterprise through the purchase of shares or assets of the other enterprise; or when two or more enterprises agree to an agency or a joint venture or other arrangement to form a controlling and controlled relationship in the market.[71] If the annual sales of business operators that engage in enterprise concentration exceed the limit set by the

66. Anti-Monopoly Law, art. 15.
67. Anti-Monopoly Law, art. 16.
68. Anti-Monopoly Law, arts. 17–24.
69. Anti-Monopoly Law, art. 45.
70. Anti-Monopoly Law, art. 29.
71. Anti-Monopoly Law, art. 25.

government, the parties to the transaction are required to obtain the approval of the Anti-Monopoly Regulatory Commission.[72] The authorities must approve or reject an application for approval of an enterprise concentration arrangement within 90 business days of receipt of the application and documents in support thereof. An approved application for enterprise concentration may include certain conditions imposed by the government authorities.[73] Special approval may be obtained if an enterprise concentration that eliminates or limits market competition within a specified industry sector is advantageous to the national economy and the public interest.[74]

4. Investigations and Private Rights of Action

The Anti-Monopoly Regulatory Commission has the power to investigate and prosecute violations of the Law.[75] The authorities are authorized to summon concerned persons to supply documentary evidence, and may access the business premises of business operators and the personal residences of management personnel, seal or attach evidence or property, and freeze bank accounts. The Law provides that such searches must be pursuant to the authorization of the people's court, and that at the close of an investigation the authorities are required to issue a public announcement on its decision.[76] However, the Anti-Monopoly Regulatory Commission and its investigative personnel and staff are prohibited from disclosing commercial confidential information obtained during an investigation.[77] A person who refuses to cooperate with an investigation may be subject to civil fines of between RMB100,000 and RMB1 million.[78] The Anti-Monopoly Regulatory Commission is required to petition the people's court to enforce any penalty imposed against a business

72. Anti-Monopoly Law, art. 26. The annual sales limits for market concentration have not been set by the government at the time of publication of the Deskbook. Business operators who fail to obtain approval for enterprise concentration arrangements are subject to orders to cease the concentration and revert back to the original operation(s), and are subject to monetary fines of not more than RMB10 million ($1.2 million). Anti-Monopoly Law, art. 46.

73. Anti-Monopoly Law, art. 28. An application in support of an enterprise concentration arrangement is required to provide the following documents: (1) the status of the business operators, including the names of the enterprises, addresses, the products produced or sold, number of staff, the total assets, the net assets, the annual turnover of the previous year, the tax status, etc; (2) the financial report and sales report of the previous accounting year of the business operators; (3) information on the product production or operation costs, selling prices and quantities produced, etc. of relevant products of the business operators; (4) the effect that the concentration may have on the national economy and public interest; (5) the reasons for the concentration; and (6) other documents required by the Anti-Monopoly Regulatory Commission. Anti-Monopoly Law, art. 27.

74. Anti-Monopoly Law, art. 30.

75. Anti-Monopoly Law, arts. 36, 37. Government personnel that abuse their powers of office or engage in favoritism may be subject to civil and criminal penalties. Anti-Monopoly Law, art. 54.

76. Anti-Monopoly Law, arts. 38, 41.

77. Anti-Monopoly Law, art. 42.

78. Anti-Monopoly Law, art. 51. A person may refuse to cooperate if an investigating officer fails to present documents proving their authority to carry out the investigation. Anti-Monopoly Law, art. 39.

operator in violation of the Law.[79] In addition, any interested party that is dissatisfied with a penalty decision may appeal the decision administratively or by filing a petition with the people's court.[80]

An injured party, including both consumers and business operators, may seek judicial relief before the people's court against any business operator who engages in monopolistic activities.[81] An injured party may obtain compensatory damages, including lost profits. In situations where the court finds it difficult to calculate the losses, the amount of compensation that may be set by the court may be calculated as the profit gained by the perpetrator during the period when the victim's interests are damaged plus the reasonable expenses the victim incurred during the course of investigation and legal proceedings.[82]

Key Laws and Regulations

Foreign M&A Regulations Regarding Foreign Investors' Merger with or Acquisition of Domestic Enterprises (jointly issued on March 7, 2003, by the Ministry of Foreign Trade and Economic Cooperation (restructured and renamed as the Ministry of Commerce), the State Taxation General Office, the State Administration of Industry and Commerce, and the State Administration of Foreign Exchange)

Using Foreign Investment to Reorganize State-Owned Enterprises Tentative Provisions (promulgated on Nov. 8, 2002, by the State Economic and Trade Commission, the Ministry of Finance, the State Administration of Industry and Commerce, and the State Administration of Foreign Exchange)

Acquisition of Domestic Enterprises by Foreign Investors Tentative Provisions (promulgated on March 7, 2003, by the State Administration of Taxation, the State Administration of Industry and Commerce, and the State Administration of Foreign Exchange)

Acquisition of State-Owned Enterprises in the Municipality by Foreign Investors Several Opinions Implementing Rules (promulgated on August 4, 2003, by the Shanghai State-Owned Assets Supervision and Administration Commission, the Shanghai Foreign Investment Commission, and the Shanghai Administration of Industry and Commerce)

(*Continued*)

79. Anti-Monopoly Law, art. 52.
80. Anti-Monopoly Law, art. 53.
81. Anti-Monopoly Law, art. 49.
82. Anti-Monopoly Law, art. 50.

(*Continued from previous page*)

Acquisition of State-Owned Enterprises in the Municipality by Foreign Investors Several Opinions (promulgated on August 4, 2003, by the Shanghai State-Owned Assets Supervision and Administration Commission, the Shanghai Foreign Investment Commission, and the Shanghai Administration of Industry and Commerce)

Beijing Municipality Interim Rule on Merger and Acquisition of State-Owned Industrial Enterprises by Foreign Investors and Domestic Non-Public Economic Organizations (promulgated on September 30, 2003, by the Beijing Municipal Government)

Several Issues Concerning the Trial of Civil Dispute Cases Relating to Enterprise Restructuring Provisions (issued on January 3, 2003, by the Supreme People's Court)

Supreme People's Court (Ministry of Commerce, Request to Confirm Whether the "Several Issues Concerning the Trial of Civil Disputes Relating to Enterprise Restructuring Provisions" Applies to Foreign Investment) (issued on October 20, 2003, by the Supreme People's Court)

Acquisition of Domestic Enterprises by Foreign Investors Tentative Provisions (promulgated on May 28, 2003, by the State Administration of Taxation)

Enterprise Tax Treatment Concerning Foreign-Invested Enterprises in which the Proportion of Foreign Investor Contribution is Less than 25 percent (promulgated on April 18, 2003, by the State Administration of Taxation)

Regulations on Several Issues Regarding the Administration of State-Owned Assets Appraisal (promulgated by the Ministry of Finance effective January 1, 2002)

Provisional Rules on the Administration of State-Owned Assets and Equity Transactions (promulgated on January 7, 2004, by the State Asset Supervision and Administration Commission and the Ministry of Finance)

Supervision and Administration of Enterprise State-Owned Assets Tentative Regulations (issued on May 27, 2003, by the State Council)

Interim Measures on the Administration of Transfers of State-Owned Property Rights in Enterprises (issued on December 31, 2003, by the State-Owned Assets Supervision and Administration Commission and the Ministry of Finance, and effective February 1, 2004)

Merger and Division of Foreign-Invested Enterprises (issued by the Ministry of Foreign Trade and Economic Cooperation and the State Administration of Industry and Commerce on Nov. 22, 2001)

Income Tax Questions Relevant to Enterprise Merger and Division Circular (promulgated on June 21, 2000, by the State Administration of Taxation)

(*Continued*)

(*Continued from previous page*)

Several Questions Concerning Income Tax When Enterprises are Reorganized or Change their System Tentative Provisions (promulgated on August 20, 1998, by the State Administration of Taxation)

Enterprise Income Tax Tentative Regulations (promulgated on December 13, 1998, by the State Administration of Taxation)

Model Notices and Circulars for Merger, Division and Reduction in Registered Capital of Foreign-Invested Enterprises (issued by the State Council on March 14, 2003)

Administration of the Takeover of Listed Companies Procedures (promulgated on September 28, 2002, by the China Securities Regulatory Commission)

Notice on Relevant Issues in Transferring the State-Owned Shares and Legal Person Shares of Listed Companies to Foreign Investors (issued on November 1, 2002, by the CSRC and the Ministry of Finance)

Notice on Relevant Issues Concerning the Conditions for Public Trading of Shares of Acquired Companies Involving Tender Offers (issued on May 20, 2003, by the China Securities Regulatory Commission)

Chapter 20

Enterprise Liquidation, Reorganization, and Bankruptcy

Prior to the initiation of economic reforms in the late 1970s, State enterprises and institutions existed pursuant to central government planning and subsidy. As the NPC and State Council called for financial responsibility of SOEs, the government found a greater need for procedures to allow for the orderly liquidation and dissolution of struggling enterprises to meet the new realities of fiscal independence. At the same time, the government found it necessary to develop procedures to protect the creditors of, and parties to, foreign-invested enterprises. In response, China has developed laws and regulations that address such issues as ordinary liquidation, special liquidation, reorganization of an FIE, creditor remedies during liquidation and bankruptcy proceedings, and the rights of enterprises during bankruptcy proceedings. This chapter addresses a number of issues that may arise for foreign operations under China's laws and regulations governing liquidation, reorganization, and bankruptcy.

A. Liquidation

The process of liquidating an FIE may be initiated for a variety of reasons including the end of the contract term, government intervention, consent of the parties prior to the expiration of the contract, or as a result of difficulties encountered by the parties. The typical problem areas that trigger liquidation include the failure of either party to fulfill its obligations to obtain certain resources, to provide additional capital to the operation, or other obligations required under the parties' contract. In addition, an FIE may choose to liquidate when it has exhausted its tax holidays and preferences, which may be revived if a new operation is formed.

The dissolution and liquidation process is initiated in accordance with the terms of the parties' contract and the FIE Liquidation Procedures adopted by the State Council and MOFTEC.[1] The FIE Liquidation Procedures apply to all FIEs, including joint ventures and wholly foreign-owned enterprises. The FIE Liquidation Procedures recognize two categories of liquidation: ordinary and special liquidation.

1. Ordinary Liquidation Proceedings

In an ordinary liquidation proceeding, the board of directors or management body of the FIE appoints a liquidation committee to manage the dissolution process. A liquidation committee is required to be formed within fifteen days of the commencement of the liquidation proceedings. A liquidation committee is required to consist of at least three members who are selected by the board of directors of the FIE. The board may engage the services of an accountant, attorney, or other professional to serve on a liquidation committee. One member of the committee serves as the chair. Subject to the approval of the board of directors, the liquidation committee may employ administrative personnel to assist with the liquidation process.[2]

---

1. Measures on Liquidation Procedures for Foreign Investment Enterprises (approved on June 15, 1996, by the State Council and promulgated on July 9, 1996, by MOFTEC), *reprinted in* China Laws for Foreign Business (CCH), Business Regulation ¶ 13-608 (hereinafter the "FIE Liquidation Procedures"); Company Law of the People's Republic of China (adopted December 29, 1993, by the 5th Sess. of the Standing Comm. of the 8th NPC, revised and repromulgated on December 25, 1999, by the 13th Sess. of the Standing Comm. of the 9th NPC), arts. 189–198, *reprinted in* China Laws for Foreign Business (CCH), Business Regulation ¶ 13-518 (hereinafter the "Company Law") (discusses bankruptcy and liquidation standards for companies). The FIE Liquidation Procedures are available on the Web site of MOFCOM at http://www.mofcom.gov.cn. Prior to the adoption of the FIE Liquidation Procedures, several local governments had formulated their own liquidation standards. *See* Liquidation Measures for Foreign Investment Enterprises in Beijing Municipality (issued as Decree No. 9 by the Beijing Municipal People's Government and effective June 1, 1992), *reprinted in* China Laws for Foreign Business, Special Zones & Cities ¶ 96-324; Rules of the Beijing Municipality on the Dissolution of Foreign Investment Enterprises (adopted on June 8, 1995, by the 17th Sess. of the Standing Comm. of the 10th Beijing Municipal People's Congress), *reprinted in* China Laws for Foreign Business (CCH), Special Zones & Cities ¶ 170-025. *See also* Rules of Shanghai Municipality on Liquidation Procedures for Foreign Investment Enterprises (adopted on August 16, 1991, at the 28th Sess. of the Standing Comm. of the 9th Shanghai Municipal People's Congress), *reprinted in* China Laws for Foreign Business (CCH), Special Zones & Cities ¶ 91-065 (addresses the ordinary and special liquidation procedures, valuation of liquidated assets, and other matters relevant to enterprise dissolution and liquidation). For an analysis of the liquidation procedures *see* Stuken, *Corporate Reorganization: Look Before You Leap,* 11 China L. & Prac. 60 (Oct. 1997). *See also* Rules of the Tianjin Municipality on the Liquidation of Foreign Investment Enterprises (promulgated on February 13, 1995, by the Standing Comm. of the Tianjin Municipal People's Congress), *reprinted in* China Laws for Foreign Business (CCH), Special Zones & Cities ¶ 200-005.
2. FIE Liquidation Procedures, arts. 5–9; Company Law, art. 191.

A liquidation committee has the following power and authority during the liquidation process:

(1) Perform an inventory of the FIE's property, assets, and equipment;
(2) Compile balance sheets and other financial records of the FIE
(3) Formulate liquidation plans
(4) Notify creditors of the liquidation proceeding
(5) Wind down the business endeavors of the enterprise
(6) Settle claims and pay creditors
(7) Dispose of remaining assets
(8) Collect accounts receivable
(9) Participate in civil proceedings on behalf of the FIE[3]

Upon completion of the FIE's financial records and the plan for liquidation, the liquidation committee is required to report its findings to the SAIC or local branch office. Members of the liquidation committee have a fiduciary obligation to the FIE and are prohibited from misusing their powers to improperly gain control over the FIE's assets.[4] The SAIC has the right to monitor the liquidation proceedings and to send auditors to committee meetings.

The date of commencement of liquidation of an enterprise is the date of expiration of the FIE, the date of approval of dissolution of the FIE by the SAIC, or the date on which the FIE contract is terminated by a ruling of the people's court or an arbitration tribunal. The liquidation period of an FIE may not exceed 180 days from the commencement date of liquidation proceedings to the date the liquidation committee submits a report to the SAIC.[5] If good cause is demonstrated, an extension of the liquidation period may be granted to the liquidation committee for a maximum period of ninety days. During the liquidation period, the FIE is prohibited from engaging in new business operations.

a. Notice of Liquidation: Government Authorities

The board of directors of an FIE is required, within seven days from the date of commencement of its liquidation proceedings, to send written notice of liquidation to the SAIC, China Customs, SAFE, taxation authorities, banking authorities, and other governmental organizations that supervise the FIE. The governmental notice is required to specify the reasons for liquidation.

3. Company Law, art. 193.
4. FIE Liquidation Procedures, arts. 12–15.
5. FIE Liquidation Procedures, arts. 5, 6.

b. Notice of Liquidation: Creditors

Within ten days of its establishment, the liquidation committee is required to provide notice of the proceeding to all known creditors. The liquidation committee is also required to publish notice of the proposed liquidation in a national newspaper and provincial/municipal-level newspaper. The publication must clearly state the name of the FIE, address, reason for liquidation, date of commencement of liquidation, and postal address for the liquidation committee. The notice is required to advise creditors to submit claims within thirty days of receiving the notice or, in the case of a creditor that did not receive written notice, within ninety days of the publication of the first public announcement of the liquidation.[6]

c. Creditors' Claims

Pursuant to the Liquidation Measures, a creditor is required to submit its claim within the statutory time period and to provide documentation substantiating the claim. A failure to declare a claim in a timely manner does not bar a known creditor's rights to be listed in the liquidation report and to be allowed to receive compensation from the FIE. However, an unknown creditor is barred from collecting any monies with respect to claims submitted after the claim bar date.[7]

Upon receipt of a claim from a creditor, the liquidation committee is required to analyze the claim documentation and to either accept or reject the subject claim. A creditor that disagrees with the liquidation committee's decision on a claim has fifteen days to request a reassessment of the decision. If the creditor still disputes the decision of the liquidation committee, the creditor may file a complaint with the people's court within fifteen days of receiving notice of the committee's decision. If the creditor and the FIE are contractually obligated to submit their disputes to an arbitration tribunal, the parties must arbitrate the creditor's claim.[8]

d. Payment of Debts

The Liquidation Measures set forth the priority of payment of debts out of FIE assets. The following is a priority of payments schedule:

(1) Expenses incurred in the administration, sale, and distribution of assets of the FIE during the liquidation process

6. FIE Liquidation Procedures, arts. 16, 17, 18; Company Law, art. 194.
7. FIE Liquidation Procedures, art. 19; Company Law, art. 194.
8. FIE Liquidation Procedures, arts. 20, 21.

(2) Costs incurred during the liquidation, including the publication expenses, defense costs in creditor lawsuits, or arbitration fees
(3) Wages owed to employees and unpaid labor insurance premiums
(4) Taxes owed to the State
(5) Other debts[9]

If a claim is secured by the assets of the FIE and a claim is initiated prior to the commencement of liquidation, the secured creditor has priority over all other creditors, except for wages and taxes, and may collect the debt from the sale of the secured property.[10] If the secured debt exceeds the proceeds from the sale of the secured property, the remaining balance is tendered to the secured creditor after the payment of priority debts (i.e., wages, benefits, and taxes).

After all debts are paid, the liquidation committee is authorized to distribute the assets to the parties to the FIE in the investment contribution ratio set forth in the parties' agreement.[11] If during the liquidation process it is discovered that the assets of the FIE are insufficient to pay its debts, the liquidation committee may apply to the people's court to have the enterprise declared bankrupt. An enterprise that is declared bankrupt will be liquidated in a manner required under China's Bankruptcy Law.

During the sale of FIE assets by the liquidation committee, the various investors in the enterprise have priority right of purchase. However, the sale of the assets must be to the party offering the highest price.[12] The Liquidation Measures provide that certain transactions are invalid if committed within six months of commencement of the liquidation. In particular, the law treats the following activities as invalid:

(1) Assignment or transfer of enterprise property without consideration
(2) Sale of FIE property below the market price
(3) Providing security or collateral in property that previously was unsecured
(4) Premature repayment of debt
(5) Relinquishment of a claim by an FIE[13]

After the tasks in the liquidation plan are completed, the committee is required to prepare and submit a liquidation report to the SAIC and other

9. FIE Liquidation Procedures, arts. 23, 25.
10. FIE Liquidation Procedures, art. 24.
11. FIE Liquidation Procedures, art. 26.
12. FIE Liquidation Procedures, art. 30.
13. FIE Liquidation Procedures, art. 28; Company Law, art. 198.

governmental authorities that exercise supervision over the FIE. The contents of the liquidation report must include:

(1) The reason for, time limit, and process involved in the liquidation
(2) The results of settlement of claims and payment of debts
(3) The results of disposal of liquidation assets

The liquidation committee is required to apply for cancellation of the FIE's registration with the SAIC, customs, and taxation authorities. Upon liquidation and surrender of the business license, the committee is required to provide the Chinese party with all financial and accounting records of the FIE.[14]

2. Special Liquidation Proceedings

In special liquidation proceedings, the liquidation committee is organized by either the SAIC or the government agency responsible for supervising the FIE, and exercises the authority of the members of the board of directors of the enterprise.[15] The liquidation committee in a special liquidation exercises the same authority as a committee in an ordinary liquidation proceeding. The special liquidation committee also has the power to convene meetings of the board of directors.[16]

Under special liquidation proceedings, the liquidation committee is responsible for holding creditors' meetings of all known creditors. The liquidation committee must issue written notice of the creditors' meeting fifteen days prior to convening the meeting. A creditor who is unable to attend may entrust, in writing, a proxy to attend the meeting on his or her behalf. The creditors are entitled to participate as members of a creditors' committee. All members of a creditors' committee have equal voting rights, except those creditors with claims secured by property who have not relinquished their preferential repayment rights.[17] A creditors' meeting will exercise the following powers of office:

(1) Evaluate supporting materials related to claims and claims secured by property
(2) Evaluate the FIE's financial position and assets
(3) Advise the liquidation committee concerning liquidation plans and debt repayment[18]

14. FIE Liquidation Procedures, arts. 33, 34; Company Law, art. 197.
15. FIE Liquidation Procedures, arts. 36, 37; Company Law, art. 192.
16. FIE Liquidation Procedures, art. 38.
17. FIE Liquidation Procedures, arts. 39, 40.
18. FIE Liquidation Procedures, art. 41.

The Liquidation Measures set forth penalties for improper activities during liquidation including the disposal of assets by FIE investors during liquidation proceedings; failure of the liquidation committee to file the liquidation report; concealment of FIE assets; failure to properly notify creditors of the liquidation proceedings; and engaging in new business operations after the commencement of liquidation. The penalties for violations range from fines to confiscation of assets to criminal liability.[19]

3. Alternatives to Liquidation

There are alternatives to liquidation and termination of an operation that should be explored prior to initiating liquidation procedures. On the downside, liquidation can be expensive given the expense of dissolving an enterprise's affairs. Liquidation is also a time-consuming process and may take more time than allowed by the procedures if the parties are in the midst of arbitrating their differences or defending claims and complaints of third parties or creditors. In addition, liquidation is disruptive for employees, customers, and the sponsoring organizations and parent companies. Management personnel are required to either serve as part of the liquidation committee or assist with the winding-up process. Moreover, because the parties are required to give notice of the liquidation process, there is a tremendous loss of face and embarrassment for both parties and especially for the Chinese party that enthusiastically endorsed the venture at the commencement of the parties' relationship. Moreover, the foreign party may find that it may be barred from future opportunities if it has a track record of liquidation. As a result, a foreign party is wise to analyze other options in its evaluation whether to exit the market.

The first alternative to liquidation is for the parties to consider buying out the interest of the other party. A buyout is likely to result in a transformation of the enterprise given that it will no longer be a joint venture between Chinese and foreign parties. If the foreign party purchases the interest of the Chinese party, the enterprise must be converted from a JV to a WFOE. Although a conversion from a JV to a WFOE is not expressly provided for in the law, there are regulations that provide support for converting a JV to a WFOE without the need for full liquidation, dissolution, and, in essence, starting over.[20] Of course, the remaining party will be required to

19. FIE Liquidation Procedures, arts. 44–50. *See* Chapter 23, Criminal Liability for FIE Activities § A.4.

20. *See* Provisional Regulations on the Handling of Income Tax on Reorganizations of Foreign Investment Enterprises such as Mergers, Splits, Reorganization of Equity and Asset Transfer (promulgated April 28, 1997, by the State Administration of Taxation), *reprinted in* CHINA LAWS FOR FOREIGN BUSINESS

obtain the approval of MOFCOM and the SAIC for the conversion. However, the WFOE law and other explanatory notices issued by MOFTEC and the SAIC make it clear that certain industries are off-limits for WFOEs.

In addition to a complete buyout, the foreign party may consider purchasing a portion of the Chinese party's interest in the enterprise as a means to resolving the problems. This alternative usually requires that the foreign party invest additional cash in the operation and, in essence, pay the Chinese party for relinquishing control over the operation. However, before investing monies to purchase the interest of a party, it is important to secure approval given that certain industries prohibit or restrict a foreign party from having a controlling stake.

Similarly, the parties may seek to retain the JV legal entity and simply find a buyer for either the Chinese or the foreign parties' interest. Unless the operation is attractive because of its financial strength, productivity, or assets, finding a potential buyer to assume a parties' obligations may be difficult to locate.

B. Bankruptcy Protection and Creditors' Remedies

The Bankruptcy Law, Company Law, Civil Law, and Code of Civil Procedure address the procedures and standards for bankruptcy in China.[21]

(CCH), Taxation ¶ 32-774. *See generally* Dauchez & Vernay, *Tax Treatment of FIE Reorganizations,* 11 CHINA L. & PRAC. 55 (July/Aug. 1997). *See also* Certain Regulations on Changes to Shareholder's Rights in Foreign Investment Enterprises (promulgated on May 28, 1997, by MOFTEC and the SAIC), *reprinted in* CHINA LAWS FOR FOREIGN BUSINESS (CCH), Business Regulation ¶ 13-512. *See generally* Chapter 4, FIE Organizational Structure and Approval Procedures § G.

21. Law of the People's Republic of China on Enterprise Bankruptcy (Trial Implementation) (adopted December 2, 1986, by the 18th Sess. of the Standing Comm. of the 6th NPC), *reprinted in* CHINA LAWS FOR FOREIGN BUSINESS (CCH), Business Regulation ¶ 13-522 (the "Bankruptcy Law"). An English translation of the Bankruptcy Law is also available on the Web site (Law Digest link) of the PRC Ministry of Commerce at http://www.mofcom.gov.cn. *See also* Civil Law, art. 108 (basic right to petition for bankruptcy); Code of Civil Procedure of the People's Republic of China, arts. 199–206 (bankruptcy procedural issues) (adopted April 9, 1991, by the 4th Session of the Standing Committee of the 7th National People's Congress), *reprinted in* CHINA LAWS FOR FOREIGN BUSINESS (CCH), Business Regulation ¶ 19-201; Company Law, arts. 189–199 (bankruptcy procedure for enterprises). The Guangdong Province has adopted its own bankruptcy law governing limited liability companies and companies limited by shares. *See* Rules of Guangdong Province on Company Bankruptcy (adopted May 14, 1993, by the 2nd Sess. of the Standing Comm. of the 8th Guangdong Provincial People's Congress), *reprinted in* CHINA LAWS FOR FOREIGN BUSINESS (CCH), Special Zones & Cities ¶ 70-915. The Shenzhen SEZ has also adopted its own set of bankruptcy rules. Under the Shenzhen rules, an FIE is allowed to file for protection but only the Shenzhen Municipal Intermediate People's Court has jurisdiction. *See* Rules of the Shenzhen Special Economic Zone on Enterprise Bankruptcy (adopted on November 10, 1993, by the 19th Sess. of the Standing Comm. of the 1st Shenzhen Municipal People's Congress), *reprinted in* CHINA LAWS FOR FOREIGN BUSINESS (CCH), Special Zones & Cities ¶ 73-516. *See generally* Flaxer, *Bankruptcy in China in* American Bankruptcy Institute Journal, 1994 ABI JNL. Lexis 2707 (1994); Seebach, *Bankruptcy Behind the Great Wall: Should U.S. Businesses Seeking to Invest in the Emerging Chinese Market Be Wary?,* 8 TRANSNAT'L L. 351 (1995); Boshkoff & Song, *China's New Bankruptcy Law: A Translation and Brief Introduction,* 61 AM. BANK. L. J. 359 (1987).

Although the Bankruptcy Law applies expressly to State enterprises only, the Liquidation Measures provide that the law applies to FIEs as well.[22] The Bankruptcy Law provides that "[State] enterprises which have incurred serious losses due to poor management and administration and are unable to discharge matured liabilities" are permitted to declare bankruptcy.[23]

Effective September 1, 2002, the Supreme People's Court adopted a set of regulations outlining the procedures and standards for the people's courts with respect to the management of bankruptcy proceedings.[24] The SPC Bankruptcy Case Provisions set forth detailed standards for the submission of bankruptcy petitions, liquidation committees, creditor claims and notice procedures, bankruptcy fraud, and other issues.

1. Application for Bankruptcy

A creditor or debtor may file an application for remedies under the Bankruptcy Law and SPC Bankruptcy Provisions.[25] The local people's court where the debtor resides or has its principal place of business is the court with jurisdiction over a bankruptcy matter.[26]

If a debtor files for bankruptcy, the approval of the governmental department in charge of supervising the debtor must first be obtained.[27] The debtor's petition must provide an explanation of the circumstances for the enterprise's losses and submit accounting information, including a schedule of assets and a detailed list of claims and debts.[28] The debtor is also required

---

22. Bankruptcy Law, art. 2; FIE Liquidation Procedures, art. 27.

23. Bankruptcy Law, art. 3.

24. Several Issues on Trial of Enterprise Bankruptcy Cases Provisions (issued by the Supreme People's Court on July 30, 2002, and effective Sept. 1, 2002), *reprinted in* CHINA L. & PRAC., Oct. 2002, pp. 41–67 (hereinafter referred to as the "SPC Bankruptcy Case Provisions"). The government has struggled to amend the 1986 Bankruptcy Law and, to fill the gaps in the interim, the SPC's rules provide well-needed guidance. *See generally* C. Jin, *The Reform of PRC Corporate Bankruptcy Law: Slowly But Surely,* CHINA L. & PRAC., Oct. 2002, pp. 19–23.

25. Bankruptcy Law, arts. 7, 8.

26. Bankruptcy Law, art. 5; SPC Bankruptcy Case Provisions, art. 1.

27. Bankruptcy Law, arts. 7, 8; SPC Bankruptcy Case Provisions, art. 5. For example, an insurance company is required to obtain the approval of the CIRC prior to filing for bankruptcy relief. *See* Chapter 12, Insurance Law and Regulation §§ A.2.a., A.2.b. The SPC Bankruptcy Case Provisions provide that the consent of shareholders is required to proceed with bankruptcy. SPC Bankruptcy Case Provisions, art. 5.

28. Bankruptcy Law, art. 8; SPC Bankruptcy Case Provisions, art. 6. When a debtor files for voluntary bankruptcy, it is required to submit the following materials to the court: (1) a written bankruptcy petition; (2) proof of the enterprise's qualifications to be the subject of the case; (3) a list containing the names of the legal representative and the main persons in charge of the organization; (4) information on the enterprise's staff and workers and the contingency plan for the settlement thereof; (5) a written explanation of the enterprise's losses accompanied by an audited report; (6) a detailed list of the enterprise's assets as at the bankruptcy petition date, including tangible assets, intangible assets, and the enterprise's investments, etc.; (7) detailed information on the accounts opened by the enterprise with financial institutions, including account opening examination and approval materials, account numbers, funds, etc.; (8) statement of the enterprise's claims listing the names and domiciles of the enterprise's debtors, the amounts of the debts, the times such debts arose and information on reminders and repayment, etc.;

to provide the court with a detailed list of the addresses and contact information for all known creditors. Within seven days of receipt of a petition, the court is required to either accept the petition and place the case on the court docket, or to notify the debtor that additional information and materials be provided.[29] The court will not accept a petition if it finds that the debtor has concealed or transferred assets, and has filed a petition to evade its debts. Similarly, a court will not accept an involuntary petition filed in bad faith by a creditor.[30]

If a creditor files an application against an enterprise, it is required to provide a declaration stating the amount of the claim, whether the claim is secured or unsecured, and information concerning the debtor's failure to discharge the matured liability.[31] The debtor is required to respond to the involuntary application within fifteen days of receiving notification by the people's court.[32]

If a creditor files an involuntary petition against an enterprise, the Bankruptcy Law provides that the application will be denied in situations where the enterprise at issue has "important bearing on the national economy and the people's livelihood."[33] In such cases, the government may provide economic assistance or take other measures to assist in the discharge of liabilities.

2. Notice of Bankruptcy Proceeding and Creditors' Meeting

The court is required to notify the known creditors and to issue a public notice within a period of ten days after accepting a petition for bankruptcy. The written notice to creditors is required to provide the date on which a first creditors' meeting will be convened.[34] The court will also notify all creditors to stay all civil proceedings, if any, against the debtor.[35] The Bankruptcy Law

(9) statement of the enterprise's debts listing the names and domiciles of the enterprise's creditors, the amounts of the claims, the times such claims arose, etc.; (10) information on the secured interests involving the enterprise; (11) information on the legal actions in which the enterprise is already involved; and (12) other materials the submission of which the people's court considers necessary. Information concerning the property of the debtor's branch offices and wholly owned enterprises without independent legal status must be included in the debtor's petition. SPC Bankruptcy Case Provisions, art. 76.

29. SPC Bankruptcy Case Provisions, art. 10.

30. SPC Bankruptcy Case Provisions, art. 12. The court may also dismiss a bankruptcy case after accepting the case if it subsequently learns that the debtor's petition is incomplete or if the whereabouts of assets are unknown. SPC Bankruptcy Case Provisions, art. 14. A debtor may appeal a decision of the court rejecting its petition for bankruptcy protection within ten days after the date of service of the ruling. SPC Bankruptcy Case Provisions, arts. 13, 14.

31. Bankruptcy Law, art. 7; SPC Bankruptcy Case Provisions, art. 8.

32. Bankruptcy Law, art. 10. A debtor may challenge an involuntary petition filed by a creditor. If a debtor's challenge is sustained by the court, the court will not accept the involuntary petition and require the creditor to institute an ordinary civil action against the debtor. SPC Bankruptcy Case Provisions, art. 9.

33. Bankruptcy Law, art. 3.

34. Bankruptcy Law, art. 9; SPC Bankruptcy Case Provisions, arts. 15, 17.

35. Bankruptcy Law, art. 11; SPC Bankruptcy Case Provisions, arts. 19, 20. Any pending civil cases are transferred to the court handling the bankruptcy matter.

further provides that any repayments to select creditors after the application is accepted by the court are invalid except for expenses that are part of the debtor's "normal production operations."[36]

Within thirty days of receiving notice of the bankruptcy petition, a creditor is required to apply to the court for recognition of its claim, to state whether the debt is secured or unsecured, and to provide any other additional information substantiating the claim. A creditor that relies on public notice may file a claim within three months of publication of the notice. A failure to lodge a claim in a timely manner is deemed to be a relinquishment of the claim and may be barred from consideration by the court.[37]

All creditors, without exception, are members of the "creditors' meeting."[38] Members of the creditors' meeting have equal voting rights with the exception of those creditors with secured interests. The chairman of the creditors' meeting is appointed by the court from among the creditors with voting rights. The debtor's legal representative must attend the creditors' meeting and answer questions from the creditors regarding the assets of the debtor. The first creditors' meeting, which shall be scheduled by the court, must be held within fifteen days after expiration of the claims bar date. Additional meetings may be held by the court if necessary, or may also be convened at the request of the liquidation group or by creditors whose combined holdings equal one-quarter or more of the total nonproperty guarantee claims.[39] The functions and powers of the creditors' meeting are, as follows:

(1) To examine the claims and claims documentation presented by creditors
(2) To determine whether claims involving secured property are valid
(3) To evaluate and develop a reorganization plan for the debtor
(4) To evaluate and develop a plan for the distribution of the debtor's property if liquidation is ordered[40]

The Bankruptcy Law provides that resolutions of a creditors' meeting are to be approved by a majority of the creditors with voting rights that represent one-half or more of the total amount of unsecured claims. All resolutions concerning the approval of reorganization plans and conciliation agreements are required to be approved by creditors whose combined holdings equal

36. Bankruptcy Law, art. 12.

37. Bankruptcy Law, art. 9; SPC Bankruptcy Case Provisions, arts. 21–24.

38. Bankruptcy Law, art. 13; SPC Bankruptcy Case Provisions, arts. 39–46. A creditor may appoint a proxy to attend creditors' meetings by power of attorney. SPC Bankruptcy Case Provisions, art. 45.

39. Bankruptcy Law, art. 14. The chairman of the creditors' meeting is also entitled to convene additional meetings.

40. Bankruptcy Law, art. 16; SPC Bankruptcy Case Provisions, arts. 41–42.

two-thirds or more of nonproperty-related claims. Resolutions passed by the creditors' committee are binding on all creditors. A creditor that believes that a decision of the creditors' meeting violates the law or infringes upon the creditor's legitimate rights and interests may request a ruling by the people's court but must do so within seven days of the decision of the creditors' meeting.[41]

3. Secured Claims

The Bankruptcy Law provides that the court is required to "separately register those claims secured by property and those unsecured by property."[42] A creditor with a proven secured claim is entitled to preferential treatment with respect to the secured property.[43] If the amount of the secured claim is in excess of the value of the security, the excess portion of the claim shall become an unsecured bankruptcy claim.

4. Reorganization and Conciliation

A qualified debtor may file an application for reorganization of the enterprise. A draft reorganization plan and conciliation agreement are required to be submitted at the time of the creditors' meeting, and shall outline the time limit for the discharge of the enterprise's liabilities.[44] If a conciliation agreement is acceptable to the creditors' meeting and the court, the court will issue a public announcement and proceedings will be suspended.

The government department in charge of the enterprise at issue is responsible for managing the reorganization process and is required to submit reports at regular intervals to the creditors' meeting concerning the status of the enterprise's efforts. The employees are also entitled to information concerning the status of the reorganization process and are allowed to express their opinions.[45] If an enterprise successfully emerges from reorganization, the court terminates the bankruptcy proceeding and issues a public announcement.[46]

The government also has the discretion to request that the enterprise of "national importance" go through a reorganization process rather than a discharge and liquidation proceeding.[47] A government request for reorganization must be made within three months after the court accepts the application, and the reorganization term may not exceed a period of two years.

41. Bankruptcy Law, art. 16; SPC Bankruptcy Case Provisions, art. 43.
42. Bankruptcy Law, art. 9; SPC Bankruptcy Case Provisions, arts. 55 (2), 71 (2).
43. Bankruptcy Law, art. 32.
44. Bankruptcy Law, arts. 17–19; SPC Bankruptcy Case Provisions, arts. 25–30.
45. Bankruptcy Law, art. 20.
46. Bankruptcy Law, art. 22.
47. Bankruptcy Law, arts. 3, 17.

5. Declaration of Bankruptcy and Liquidation

If reorganization of the enterprise is not successful, the people's court may order the enterprise bankrupt and proceed with liquidation.[48] The court will order an enterprise bankrupt in the event of a failure to implement a conciliation agreement or in the event of a significant decline in the enterprise's financial condition.[49] The court also has the discretion to order a company bankrupt if it finds that the enterprise engage in any acts of concealment, or fraudulent or inappropriate transfers of the bankrupt enterprise's property.[50]

The people's court will establish a liquidation committee within fifteen days of declaration of bankruptcy by the court. The Bankruptcy Law provides that the liquidation committee is responsible for the care, inventory, valuation, and distribution of the bankruptcy estate of the debtor enterprise.[51] The liquidation committee also has the discretion to terminate or fulfill contracts of the bankrupt enterprise, and to offset a creditor's claim based upon the enterprise's counterclaim against the creditor.[52] The court has the discretion to appoint the liquidation committee, which consists of government personnel and professionals.[53] The liquidation committee reports to the court and the creditors' meeting.

The bankruptcy estate consists of the following property:

(1) All property managed and administered by the bankrupt enterprise at the time of the bankruptcy declaration
(2) All property obtained by the bankrupt enterprise between the time of bankruptcy declaration and the end of the proceedings
(3) Other property rights over which the enterprise exercises authority and control[54]

48. Company Law, art. 189; Bankruptcy Law, arts. 21, 22; SPC Bankruptcy Case Provisions, arts. 31–38.

49. Bankruptcy Law, art. 21.

50. Bankruptcy Law, arts. 21, 35.

51. Bankruptcy Law, arts. 17, 24, 25; SPC Bankruptcy Case Provisions, arts. 47–54. Prior to formation of the liquidation committee, the enterprise has a statutory duty to preserve the property, accounting records, seals, and other materials of the enterprise. Bankruptcy Law, art. 27. No individual or unit is allowed to take control over the bankruptcy estate or its files and materials. Bankruptcy Law, art. 25.

52. Bankruptcy Law, arts. 26, 33.

53. Bankruptcy Law, art. 24. The liquidation committee has the discretion to retain professionals to assist with the liquidation process.

54. Bankruptcy Law, art. 28. The definition of the bankruptcy estate is consistent with property "owned" by a State-owned enterprise. The focus is on property that is "managed and administered" rather than property owned by title. SPC Bankruptcy Case Provisions, arts. 64–65. The bankruptcy estate also includes property that was effectively assigned to the debtor, subrogation rights, unmatured claims, and leasehold interests. SPC Bankruptcy Case Provisions, arts. 67, 69, 70. A founder of the debtor is liable for any registered capital that remains unpaid. SPC Bankruptcy Case Provisions, art. 66. Equity interests in third-party entities shall be included in the bankruptcy estate. SPC Bankruptcy Case Provisions, arts. 77–78.

The bankruptcy estate does not include property that is subject to a security interest. If the value of the secured property is in excess of the secured claim, the amount in excess is part of the bankruptcy estate. Property owned by a third party may be recovered by application to the liquidation committee.[55]

The liquidation committee is responsible for developing a distribution plan with the approval of both the creditors' meeting and the court.[56] The liquidation expenses take priority over other claims in the following order:

(1) Expenses incurred in the management, sale, and distribution of bankruptcy estate property, including the expenses for personnel
(2) Legal expenses incurred by the bankrupt enterprise during the bankruptcy proceeding
(3) Other expenses paid during the proceeding for the common benefit of all creditors[57]

The court has the discretion to terminate the bankruptcy proceeding if the bankruptcy estate is insufficient to pay the expenses of the liquidation process. After payment of the liquidation and bankruptcy proceeding expenses, employee wages, employee benefits,[58] and taxes have priority over all other unsecured claimants.[59] The liquidation committee may request that the court terminate the proceedings, after all property and proceeds of property have been distributed.[60] The expenses incurred by a creditor during the bankruptcy proceedings are not recoverable from the bankruptcy estate.[61] At the conclusion of the proceeding, the liquidation committee is required to file an application with the SAIC or local branch to cancel the bankrupt enterprise's registration.[62]

55. Bankruptcy Law, art. 29; SPC Bankruptcy Case Provisions, art. 71. Article 71 of the SPC order provides that the following property is not part of the bankruptcy estate: (1) third-party property in the possession of, or used by, the debtor based on a warehousing, custodial, processing contract, consignment trade, commissioned sale, loan, deposit, lease, or other such legal relationship; (2) property subject to a mortgage, lien, or pledge, except where the rights holder has waived his right of priority; (3) property where title has not passed; (4) property owned by the State; and (5) property owned by the debtor's labor union. Owners of property in the possession of the debtor may repossess the property. SPC Bankruptcy Case Provisions, art. 72.

56. Bankruptcy Law, art. 37; SPC Bankruptcy Case Provisions, arts. 92–95 (outlining standards for distribution plans and procedures).

57. Bankruptcy Law, art. 34; SPC Bankruptcy Case Provisions, arts. 88–91 (standards and procedures for bankruptcy expenses).

58. The Bankruptcy Law provides that the government is required to pay the "basic living requirements" of employees of a bankrupt enterprise pending reemployment, and is required to "make appropriate arrangements" for the reemployment of the personnel of the enterprise. Bankruptcy Law, art. 4; SPC Bankruptcy Case Provisions, art. 90.

59. Bankruptcy Law, art. 37.

60. Bankruptcy Law, art. 38; SPC Bankruptcy Case Provisions, art. 96.

61. Bankruptcy Law, art. 30.

62. Bankruptcy Law, art. 39; SPC Bankruptcy Case Provisions, art. 97.

The court has the discretion to invalidate any of the following activities that occurred within six months prior to the initiation of the bankruptcy proceeding:

(1) Concealment, private distribution, or gratuitous assignment of property
(2) Irregular underselling of enterprise property
(3) Providing security to previously unsecured creditors
(4) Advance discharge of unmatured liabilities[63]

The liquidation committee has the right to petition the court for the return of property transferred or assigned under the above-referenced circumstances. The recovered property becomes part of the bankruptcy estate and subject to auction.[64]

The Bankruptcy Law is vague in a number of areas, including the procedures and standards for reorganization as an option to liquidation. The law also fails to fully explain priority issues with respect to the repayment of creditor claims, although it specifically provides that employee wages, taxes, and legal costs are priority items. The law also fails to specify the standards for the disposition of bankruptcy estate property.

China has rarely used the Bankruptcy Law, notwithstanding that the law has been in effect since 1986. Until 1999, the law was not invoked at all with respect to any major state-owned enterprise since the government began bailing out its financially troubled companies in the late 1980s. In a reverse of prior policy, the government, in January 1999, ordered the Guangdong International Trust and Investment Corporation (GITIC) into bankruptcy to the shock of the international lending community. GITIC's debts totaled RMB36.2 billion ($4.4 billion) against assets of only RMB21.5 billion ($2.6 billion). Foreign lenders—including Citicorp, Merrill Lynch, HSBC, and Sumitomo Trust and Banking—believed that their investments were safe based upon guarantees from provincial officials and the registration and approval of the loans by the State Administration of Foreign Exchange (SAFE). In line with China's new banking policies, the PRC leadership took

63. Bankruptcy Law, arts. 21, 35.

64. Bankruptcy Law, art. 35; SPC Bankruptcy Case Provisions, art. 85. Within one year after the conclusion of the bankruptcy proceeding, the court has the discretion, upon application of an interested party, to set aside any fraudulent or inappropriate transaction. *Id.* art. 40. The Bankruptcy Law provides that "disciplinary sanctions" or criminal liability may be imposed upon the representatives of an enterprise that engages in fraudulent or inappropriate transactions involving the property of a bankrupt enterprise. *Id.* arts. 41, 42. The law further provides that the government audit departments are empowered to conduct an inspection of the enterprise to determine "responsibility" for the bankruptcy. *Id.* art. 42. The Bankruptcy Law provides that if the legal representative of a bankrupt enterprise causes "serious losses to State property," criminal liability will be imposed. *Id.* art. 42.

the position that foreign creditors were accountable for their lending practices with regard to GITIC and that registration with SAFE did not amount to a State guarantee. The foreign creditors were advised that they will not be provided priority over GITIC's employees, GITIC's individual depositors, or the tax authorities.

The GITIC case was a litmus test of the PRC government's use of the Bankruptcy Law, and set the pattern for subsequent insolvency cases involving other SOEs.[65] The GITIC case, and others to follow, exposed the flaws in the current law and have led to the adoption of the SPC Bankruptcy Case Provisions in 2002 which strengthened the petition, repayment, and reorganization procedures.

Key Laws and Regulations

Measures on Liquidation Procedures for Foreign Investment Enterprises (approved on June 15, 1996, by the State Council and promulgated on July 9, 1996, by MOFTEC)

Liquidation Measures for Foreign Investment Enterprises in Beijing Municipality (issued as Decree No. 9 by the Beijing Municipal People's Government and effective June 1, 1992)

Rules of Shanghai Municipality on Liquidation Procedures for Foreign Investment Enterprises (adopted on August 16, 1991, at the 28th Sess. of the Standing Comm. of the 9th Shanghai Municipal People's Congress)

Provisional Regulations on the Handling of Income Tax on Reorganizations of Foreign Investment Enterprises such as Mergers, Splits, Reorganization of Equity and Asset Transfer (promulgated April 28, 1997, by the State Administration of Taxation)

Certain Regulations on Changes to Shareholder's Rights in Foreign Investment Enterprises (promulgated on May 28, 1997, by the MOFTEC and SAIC)

(*Continued*)

65. Landler, *Bankruptcy the Chinese Way: Foreign Bankers Are Shown the End of the Line*, New York Times § C, p. 1, col. 2 (Jan. 22, 1999), available on Lexis, News Library; *China: Silver Linings*, EIU Business China (Jan. 18, 1999), available on Lexis, News Library. In addition to the GITIC matter, the largest bankruptcy in Chinese history involved a sugar factory in the province of Heilongjiang, which had debts of less than $100 million.

(*Continued from previous page*)

Law of the People's Republic of China on Enterprise Bankruptcy (Trial Implementation) (adopted December 2, 1986, by the 18th Sess. of the Standing Comm. of the 6th NPC)

Rules of Guangdong Province on Company Bankruptcy (adopted May 14, 1993, by the 2nd Sess. of the Standing Comm. of the 8th Guangdong Provincial People's Congress)

Rules of the Shenzhen Special Economic Zone on Enterprise Bankruptcy (adopted on November 10, 1993, by the 19th Sess. of the Standing Comm. of the 1st Shenzhen Municipal People's Congress)

Several Issues on Trial of Enterprise Bankruptcy Cases Provisions (issued by the Supreme People's Court on July 30, 2002, and effective Sept. 1, 2002)

Chapter 21

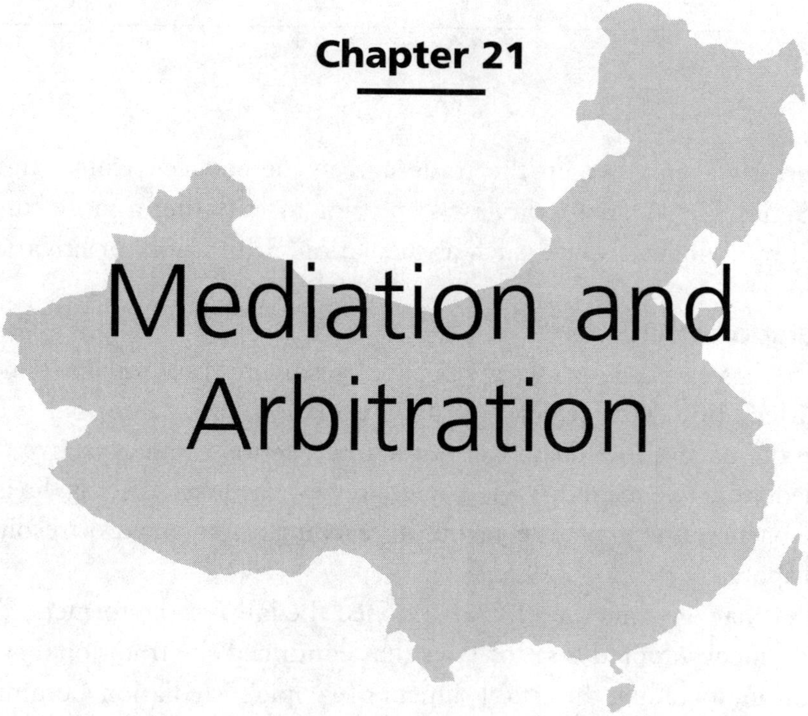

Mediation and Arbitration

The dramatic increase in foreign investment and trade with China results in a rise in the number of disputes between foreign and Chinese parties. China's ability to develop and maintain a predictable dispute resolution system is a critical element for foreign parties in their decisions to invest in China. Foreign investors and traders require reasonable assurances that their interests are adequately protected and that a fair, objective, and effective system of dispute resolution exists. This chapter addresses the various dispute resolution mechanisms in China including consultation, mediation, and arbitration. This chapter also provides recommendations for negotiating an arbitration clause including sample provisions to include in an agreement with a Chinese party.

A. Informal Dispute Resolution: Consultation and Mediation

The Chinese traditionally prefer to resolve disputes in a nonconfrontational manner and, if possible, without the involvement of a third party. Consultation is simply direct negotiation between the disputing parties or their representatives. Consultation is expressly encouraged under Chinese law, and specifically with respect to the Contract Law, Sino-Foreign Co-operative Joint Venture Law, and Sino-Foreign Equity Joint Venture Law.[1] Consultation is

1. For an analysis of the Contract Law, *see* Chapter 7, Contract Law. For a discussion of the Equity Joint Venture Law, *see* Chapter 4, FIE Organizational Structure and Approval Procedures § B.1.

also expressly mentioned in the trade agreement between China and the United States.[2] It is usually the last step prior to initiating a more forceful means of resolving a dispute, such as mediation, arbitration, or litigation.

1. Mediation in China

Mediation has been the primary vehicle of resolving disputes since ancient China. Mediation, also referred to as conciliation, is an informal process whereby the parties to a dispute seek the intervention of an objective third-party mediator. The mediator will usually review the facts, discuss the issues with the parties, and assist the parties in reaching a settlement or resolution of the dispute.

In 1949, at the time the PRC abandoned the laws of the former regime, the government adopted a set of laws that continued the traditional system of mediation, including the establishment of People's Mediation Committees at the neighborhood level and in the workplace.[3] By 1987, China had established over 950,000 People's Mediation Committees nationwide with six million mediators approved to assist with dispute resolution. Annually, the People's Mediation Committees resolve over seven million disputes.[4] Village and neighborhood mediation committees resolve disputes ranging from divorce and separation, maintenance, child support and custody, creditor and debtor disputes, and torts, and are acknowledged as a means to reducing litigation and preventing crime.[5] In addition to committees at the neighborhood level, mediation committees have been established to resolve employment-related disputes in government institutions, enterprises, and schools. Many foreign-funded operations have mediation committees to address workplace issues.[6]

2. The 1979 Trade Agreement between the United States and China highlights the importance of consultation and mediation. Article 8 of the Trade Agreement provides: "(1) The Contracting Parties encourage the prompt and equitable settlement of any disputes arising from or in relation to contracts between their respective firms, companies and corporations, and trading organizations, through friendly consultations, conciliation or other mutually acceptable means." *See* Agreement on Trade Relations between the United States of America and the People's Republic of China, signed July 7, 1979, TIAS 9630, 31 UST 4651, available on Lexis, INTLAW Library, USTRTY File.

3. *See* Jun Ge, *Mediation, Arbitration and Litigation: Dispute Resolution in the People's Republic of China,* 15 UCLA PAC. BASIN L.J. 122, 123–24 (1996) [discussion of the People's Mediation Committees and the Provisional General Rules of China for the Organization of People's Mediation Committees (1954) and the Organic Rules for People's Mediation Committees (1989)] (author notes that the 1989 mediation committee laws allow for improved committee structure and independence from interference and influence).

4. *See Civil Dispute Mediation Committees* (BBC Summary of World Broadcasts and Monitoring Reports, October 19, 1991), available on Lexis, News Library, BBCSWB File.

5. *See* Ren Jianxin, *Mediation, Conciliation, Arbitration and Litigation in the People's Republic of China,* 15 INT'L BUS. LAW. 395 (Oct. 1987).

6. For a discussion of the rules governing labor mediation and labor arbitration, *see* Chapter 10, Labor and Employment Law § A.11.

2. Mediation During Arbitration

The parties to an arbitration proceeding often resolve their disputes prior to the actual selection of the arbitral tribunal, or through mediation with the assistance of the arbitral commission or arbitrators. The China International Economic and Trade Arbitration Commission (CIETAC or the Commission) expressly encourages conciliation and estimates that more than half of the arbitration cases accepted by the Commission are resolved through conciliation.[7] In domestic arbitration matters, approximately 88 percent of cases are resolved through mediation.[8] In practice, CIETAC and the tribunal, both at the outset and during the course of the arbitration proceedings, will request if the parties are interested in resolving their dispute via conciliation. Conciliation and arbitration are not conducted separately but simultaneously. A tribunal has the discretion to engage in mediation in any manner it deems appropriate. Indeed, there is no set format or procedure for mediation.

Conciliation and mediation may only proceed with the consent of the parties and cannot be forced upon the parties by the tribunal or Commission.[9] Should either party request a termination of mediation, the tribunal

---

7. *See generally* Guiguo Wang, *The Unification of the Dispute Resolution System in China: Cultural, Economic and Legal Contributions,* 13 J. INT'L ARB. 5, 28 (1996); Wang Sheng Chang, Resolving Disputes in the PRC: A Practical Guide to Arbitration and Conciliation in China (1996). The 1979 Trade Agreement between the United States and China highlights the importance of conciliation and arbitration. Article 8(2) & (3) provides: "(2) If such disputes cannot be settled promptly by any one of the above-mentioned means, the parties to the dispute may have recourse to arbitration for settlement in accordance with provisions specified in their contract or other agreements to submit to arbitration. Such arbitration may be conducted by an arbitration institution in the People's Republic of China, the United States of America, or a third country. The arbitration rules of procedure of the relevant arbitration institution are applicable, and the arbitration rules of the United Nations Commission on International Trade Law recommended by the United Nations, or other international arbitration rules, may also be used where acceptable to the parties to the dispute and to the arbitration institution. [¶] (3) Each Contracting Party shall seek to ensure that arbitration awards are recognized and enforced by their competent authorities where enforcement is sought, in accordance with applicable laws and regulations." *See* U.S./China Trade Agreement of 1979, *supra* note 2. The U.S. Supreme Court continually emphasizes the federal policy favoring arbitration. *See Dean Witter Reynolds, Inc. v. Byrd,* 470 U.S. 213, 84 L.Ed. 2d 158, 105 S.Ct. 1238 (1985); *Mitsubishi Motors Corp. v. Soler Chrysler-Plymouth, Inc.,* 473 U.S. 614, 87 L.Ed. 2d 444, 105 S.Ct. 3346 (1985). This policy requires U.S. courts to "rigorously enforce agreements to arbitrate" and to resolve "any doubts concerning the scope of arbitrable issues . . . in favor of arbitration." *Dean Witter,* 470 U.S. at 221. The policy favoring enforcement of arbitration agreements "is particularly strong" in cases involving "an international agreement." *Da Hua Non-Ferrous Metals Co., Ltd. v. W.D. Mask Cotton Company,* 1997 U.S. App. Lexis 10644 (6th Cir. 1997).

8. *See* Jun Ge, *supra* note 3, at 127.

9. Arbitration Law of the People's Republic of China (adopted on August 31, 1994, at the 9th Sess. of the Standing Comm. of the 8th NPC) arts. 51, 52, *reprinted in* CHINA LAWS FOR FOREIGN BUSINESS (CCH), Business Regulation ¶ 10-470 (hereinafter the "Arbitration Law"). *See also* Arbitration Rules of the China International Economic and Trade Arbitration Commission (adopted on September 4, 1995, and amended on May 6, 1998, by the China International Chamber of Commerce and as amended by CIETAC on September 5, 2000) arts. 46–50, *reprinted in* CHINA LAWS FOR FOREIGN BUSINESS (CCH), Business Regulation ¶ 10-480 (hereinafter the "CIETAC Rules of Arbitration"). The revised CIETAC Rules expand the scope of CIETAC's jurisdiction over domestic business and commercial disputes, including disputes between FIEs, and specifically excludes jurisdiction over cases involving marriage, adoption, guardianship, inheritance, labor, rural agricultural, or administrative disputes. CIETAC Rules

must discontinue its conciliation efforts and resume the arbitration proceedings.[10] Similarly, the tribunal also has the discretion to terminate conciliation, to avoid a delay in the arbitration proceeding, if it believes its efforts are futile.

The primary barrier to conciliation is initiating the mediation process. A request to mediate can be mistakenly interpreted or viewed, and especially from the perspective of a party that feels strongly about their position, as a sign of weakness or an admission that the initiating party's arguments are baseless. As a result, CIETAC openly encourages the parties to conciliate their disputes to remove the stigma associated with initiating mediation.[11]

It is also advisable to attempt mediation prior to the appointment of an arbitral tribunal or, in the event that the tribunal has been selected, to request that mediation be conducted by an individual separate from the arbitrators that will decide the case in the event that mediation is unsuccessful. Given that the strategy of many mediators is to meet with the parties in private to determine their settlement objectives, members of the tribunal should be excluded as mediators because of the risk of receiving unsubstantiated and potentially damaging ex parte communications.

If a matter is settled through conciliation, the parties may request that the tribunal issue an award based upon the settlement agreement or request that the arbitration proceeding be terminated without the issuance of a formal award.[12] In practice, most settlement agreements are in the form of arbitral awards to ensure implementation by the parties and recognition and enforcement by the courts. If the parties settle a dispute prior to the appointment of the arbitrators, the parties may request that the commission issue an award based upon the settlement agreement.

If mediation fails, the tribunal is required to proceed with the arbitration hearing and render an award. Any information obtained during the mediation process cannot be used as an admission or as evidence to support the parties' claims or defenses during any subsequent arbitration forum or judicial proceeding.[13] The purpose of this rule is to encourage frank discussions

---

of Arbitration, art. 2. The revised Rules outline the methods by which to standardize the handling of domestic cases. CIETAC Rules of Arbitration, arts. 75–84. The revisions also indicate that CIETAC may recognize any reconciliation decided between mediating parties other than CIETAC through the form of an award. CIETAC Rules of Arbitration, art. 44.

10. CIETAC Rules of Arbitration, art. 48.

11. A dispute resolution clause may provide for three levels of dispute resolution procedures with specific time limitations: consultation between the parties, nonbinding mediation and conciliation before an arbitration commission, and binding arbitration before an arbitration commission. The use of standard clauses that are already prepared and accepted by arbitration institutions may reduce uncertainty.

12. Arbitration Law, arts. 49, 50; CIETAC Rules of Arbitration, art. 44.

13. CIETAC Rules of Arbitration, art. 51.

between the mediators and parties to ensure that the parties make genuine efforts to resolve their dispute. This rule is consistent with the ADR practices in the United States and other countries.

3. Mediation During Litigation

In civil litigation matters, the people's courts are authorized to resolve disputes by conciliation with the consent of the parties.[14] Under the Civil Procedure Code, the judge assigned to the case may summon the parties and their witnesses to attend an informal settlement conference.[15] The Civil Procedure Code also authorizes the court to pursue mediation after the close of trial and prior to the issuance of a judgment.[16] If a settlement is reached, the court prepares a settlement statement based upon the parties' agreement that is legally binding upon the parties.[17] If mediation is unsuccessful, the court is required to promptly proceed to trial.

4. Joint Mediation

In January 2004, the China Council for the Promotion of International Trade and the New York–based CPR Institute of Dispute Resolution entered into an agreement to establish a joint mediation center in Beijing for the purpose of creating a forum for the resolution of disputes between Chinese and foreign companies.[18]

CIETAC has also established procedures for joint conciliation with foreign arbitration institutions, including the American Arbitration Association, the Japan International Commercial Arbitration Commission, and other international arbitration organizations.[19] Under the joint conciliation procedures, a foreign party applies to an arbitral organization in its own country. Upon receipt of an application, the arbitral organizations each appoint one or more mediators on an equal basis to mediate the case jointly. As a result of the costs, joint conciliation is usually employed in large, complicated disputes.

---

14. Code of Civil Procedure of the People's Republic of China (adopted April 9, 1991, by the 4th Sess. of the Standing Comm. of the 7th NPC), art. 88, *reprinted in* CHINA LAWS FOR FOREIGN BUSINESS (CCH), Business Regulation ¶ 19-201 (hereinafter the "Civil Procedure Code").
15. Civil Procedure Code, art. 86.
16. Civil Procedure Code, art. 128.
17. Civil Procedure Code, art. 89.
18. For information concerning the CCPIT/CPRI Joint Mediation Center, *see* the Web site of the CPR Institute of Dispute Resolution at http://www.cpradr.org. *See also* P. Kyne, *Chinese, US Companies Get Mediation Center,* WALL ST. J. (January 30, 1994).
19. *See* American Arbitration Association (New York) Conciliation Center/Beijing Conciliation Center: Cooperation Agreement and Beijing/New York Conciliation Rules, 31 I.L.M. 1261 (1992), available on Lexis at INTLAW Library, ILMTY File.

B. China's Arbitration System

If a dispute cannot be resolved by informal means, the disputing parties may proceed to arbitrate provided an arbitration agreement is in place, or alternatively seek judicial relief. If an arbitration agreement exists, the parties are prohibited from instituting legal proceedings in the people's court.[20] Chinese arbitration organizations can be categorized as either domestic or international commissions. Under the Arbitration Law of the PRC, effective September 1, 1995, the government restructured its domestic arbitration system and required that commissions be independent of any administrative organization.[21] This restructuring led to the nationwide dismantling of arbitration commissions having ties to local branches of the State Administration of Industry and Commerce.[22] Currently, there are domestic arbitration commissions in cities throughout China, and each has its own procedural rules, which are required to be consistent with the national Arbitration Law.[23] The Arbitration Law provides that the local chambers of commerce form the commissions at the local and provincial level.

1. Scope of Arbitration and Jurisdiction

The scope of matters that may form the subject matter of the domestic commissions has traditionally been purely "domestic" in character in that the parties were Chinese legal persons and the issues in dispute arose from commercial matters in China.[24] However, domestic commissions are now permitted to accept foreign-related disputes provided the parties have expressly consented to the jurisdiction of the relevant domestic commission.[25] As a

20. Civil Procedure Code, art. 257.

21. Arbitration Law, art. 14.

22. The Arbitration Law provides that the government shall not interfere with any arbitration proceeding or arbitral tribunal. Arbitration Law, art. 8.

23. Domestic arbitration commissions are located in various cities, including but not limited to, Beijing, Shanghai, Tianjin, Guangzhou, Xian, Shenzhen, and Huhehote. Arbitration Law, art. 15.

24. Disputes involving contractual issues and property rights are subject to arbitration. By law, probate matters and family law matters such as divorce, adoption, and child custody are not suitable for arbitration. Administrative disputes involving government ministries and commissions are also not subject to arbitration. Labor mediation and arbitration are required to be resolved under a different set of rules. *See* Chapter 10, Labor and Employment Law § A.11.

25. Notice of the Office of the State Council on Clarification of Several Issues Concerning the Implementation of the Arbitration Law of the People's Republic of China (promulgated on June 8, 1996, by the office of the State Council) art. 3, *reprinted in* CHINA LAWS FOR FOREIGN BUSINESS (CCH), Business Regulation ¶ 10-472 (hereinafter the "Arbitration Law Notice"). A number of domestic arbitration commissions have amended their procedural rules to address the special needs of foreign-related arbitrations including commissions in Beijing, Shanghai, Shenzhen, and Guangzhou. Most of the amendments concern the timing of the submission of documents and notice procedures. *See* Harpole, *State Council Circular Creates a New Forum for Disputants,* 13 CHINA L. & PRAC. 46, 47 (June 1997). China's Arbitration Law fails to provide a definition of the term "foreign related," and we must therefore look

practical matter, few international parties desire to allow the relatively inexperienced domestic commissions to resolve their commercial disputes. The domestic commissions are unattractive as forums for resolving disputes for a number of reasons, including the requirement that Chinese be the official language of the proceedings, and because of the inability to appoint arbitrators to hear cases.[26] Moreover, a domestic arbitration commission is required to submit an application for preservation measures to the basic-level people's court.[27] In contrast, CIETAC is required to submit such an application to the intermediate people's court.[28] Arguably, the intermediate-level court is much more experienced with international-related disputes than the basic level courts.

The commissions traditionally responsible for the resolution of foreign-related commercial disputes are CIETAC and the China Maritime Arbitration Commission (CMAC). CIETAC is headquartered in Beijing and maintains two subcommissions, in Shenzhen and Shanghai.[29] CMAC specializes in maritime disputes.[30]

CIETAC was established in 1954 as the Foreign Trade Arbitration Commission (FTAC) and in 1980 renamed as the Foreign Economic Trade Arbitration Commission (FETAC). The initial purpose of FTAC/FETAC was to provide a forum to resolve disputes arising from contractual obligations in foreign trade matters and specifically between foreign and Chinese parties. In 1989, the Commission was again renamed as CIETAC. Since the early 1990s, the caseload of the CIETAC has increased from 200 disputes

---

to other legislative instruments to gain an understanding of the term. In that regard, Article 304 of the *Several Opinions of the Supreme People's Court Concerning the Implementation of the Civil Procedure Law* (1992) provides that the term "foreign related" includes a case in which either or both parties are of foreign nationality, or a company or organization is located in a foreign country.

26. The Shenzhen Arbitration Commission (a domestic commission) allows for the appointment of foreigners as arbitrators. *See* Arbitration Rules of the Shenzhen Arbitration Commission (promulgated on July 16, 1996, by the Shenzhen Arbitration Commission), *reprinted in* China Laws for Foreign Business (CCH), Special Zones & Cities ¶ 120-080.

27. Arbitration Law Notice, art. 2.

28. Arbitration Law, art. 68.

29. CIETAC Arbitration Rules, art. 11.

30. *See* Arbitration Rules of the China Maritime Arbitration Commission (promulgated September 4, 1995, by the China Maritime Arbitration Commission, revised and adopted on November 22, 2000, by the China International Chamber of Commerce), *reprinted in* China Laws for Foreign Business (CCH), Business Regulation ¶ 10-530. CMAC's rules are similar to CIETAC's rules of arbitration with respect to procedural issues. CMAC has jurisdiction over disputes arising out of a variety of maritime-related matters, including the salvage of vessels, general average, and collisions; disputes concerning the business, work tasks, chartering, mortgage, agency, towage, trading, repair, construction, and demolition of vessels; disputes concerning ocean transport operations under transportation contracts, bills of lading, or other shipping documents; disputes arising out of marine insurance contracts; disputes concerning the development and use of ocean resources, pollution, and damage to the marine environment; disputes involving freight agency contracts, contracts for the supply of shipping materials, labor contracts for foreign crew, and fishing contracts; and other maritime-related disputes that both parties agree require arbitration. CMAC Rules of Arbitration, art. 2.

per year to over 700 applications for arbitration annually.[31] This number has fallen in recent years as a result of the availability of additional arbitral institutions (e.g., Beijing Arbitration Commission, Shanghai Arbitration Commission, etc.) and foreign investors understanding that they are not always required by law to arbitrate before CIETAC. In contrast, the International Chamber of Commerce arbitrates approximately 350 cases a year.

One of the chief advantages of CIETAC over the domestic commissions is that its approved list of arbitrators includes a large number of foreign individuals, including legal professionals from the United States, Hong Kong, Australia, Canada, and various European countries. Prior to 1989, CIETAC's list of arbitrators was exclusively Chinese nationals. Although CIETAC's list of arbitrators includes highly qualified and eminent Chinese jurists, lawyers, and professors, foreign parties prefer to appoint an arbitrator of neutral nationality to ensure that the tribunal will be impartial. Of the approximately 300 approved CIETAC arbitrators, one-third are foreigners or residents of the Hong Kong Special Administrative Region. All approved arbitrators are selected by the Commission and must have professional knowledge and practical experience in such fields as law, economics, trade, and science and technology.[32] Although Chinese is the official language of CIETAC, the Commission permits the parties to select the official language of the proceeding in their arbitration agreement or at the commencement of the proceedings.[33] The parties also have the right to request translation support for hearings and documentation.[34]

CIETAC is also the arbitration organization designated by the Securities Committee of the State Council (SCSC) to resolve disputes involving securities issues. The types of disputes subject to arbitration are limited to issues between institutions and trading centers. Individual investors are excluded from the process.

---

31. See Luming Chen, *Some Reflections on International Commercial Arbitration in China,* 13 J. OF INT'L ARB. 121, 122 (1996). Observers believe that the high number of CIETAC cases is a result of China's insistence that disputes be resolved according to Chinese law and to take place on the mainland. *See Arbitration Disputes Triple in Three Years,* SOUTH CHINA MORNING POST, 4 (December 1, 1994), available on Lexis, News Library, SCHINA File. In 1997, CIETAC accepted 723 cases with over $975 million at issue. The foreign parties in these arbitration cases came from forty-five countries. *China Business Booms for China's Arbitrators,* CHINA DAILY, February 16, 1998, available on Lexis, News Library, or on the Web site of the CHINA DAILY at http://www.chinadaily.com.cn. *See generally* Case Studies of China International Economic and Trade Arbitration: International Trade Disputes (Guo Xiaowen ed. 1996). Since 2000, the caseload of CIETAC has decreased given that more parties have exercised their right to choose alternative dispute resolution forum as allowed under the 1999 Contract Law.

32. CIETAC Rules of Arbitration, art. 10.

33. CIETAC Rules of Arbitration, art. 75.

34. CIETAC Rules of Arbitration, art. 75.

a. Nature of Claims: International Dimension

CIETAC may hear cases involving international and foreign-related disputes between the following categories of parties and matters:

(1) Disputes characterized as foreign-related or international in nature
(2) Disputes related to the Hong Kong Special Administrative Region, the Macao Special Administrative Region, and Taiwan
(3) Disputes between foreign-invested enterprises or between a foreign investment enterprise and a Chinese legal person, physical person, and/or economic organization
(4) Disputes arising from project financing, invitations to tender and bidding submissions, project construction, or other activities conducted by a Chinese legal person, Chinese individual, and /or other economic organization that utilizes capital, technology, or services from foreign countries, international organizations, or from the Hong Kong SAR, the Macao SAR, and the Taiwan region
(5) Disputes that may be taken cognizance of by the Arbitration Commission in accordance with special provisions of, or upon special authorization from, the laws or administrative regulations of the People's Republic of China
(6) Domestic disputes referred to arbitration by the parties through agreement.[35]

Prior to 1998, CIETAC's jurisdiction precluded taking cases involving exclusively Chinese parties. Under the new rules, CIETAC may address disputes involving Chinese entities. The key element for all CIETAC disputes is the requirement that the claims contain an "international" dimension. How broadly CIETAC and the courts define the language "international or foreign economic relations and trade" is left for observation. In the past under CIETAC's former rules, the courts have refused to uphold awards considered

35. CIETAC Rules of Arbitration, art. 2. CIETAC amended its rules in April 1998 to expand its jurisdiction to include disputes between foreign-invested firms and domestic entities. *China Revised Rules Make Arbitration Fairer,* China Daily, April 13, 1998, available on Lexis, News Library; *China CIETAC to Expand Arbitration Scope,* China Daily, April 29, 1998, available on Lexis, News Library, or on the Web site of the China Daily at http://www.chinadaily.com.cn; *Trade Committee to Handle Foreign-Funded Enterprise Disputes,* BBC Summary of World Broadcasts, April 15, 1998, available on Lexis, News Library. For an analysis of the amendments, *see* Harpole, *Revisions to the Arbitration Rules of CIETAC,* 11 China Law News 8 (May 29, 1998); Major Revisions of the Arbitration Rules of China International Economic and Trade Arbitration Commission (issued on April 10, 1998, by the China International Chamber of Commerce), *reprinted in* 131 China International Business (MOFTEC) 56–57 (1998). The 2000 amendments to the CIETAC Rules further expand the jurisdiction of CIETAC to all commercial domestic disputes referred by contract to CIETAC. The amendments prohibit CIETAC from taking jurisdiction over cases involving marriage, adoption, guardianship, maintenance, inheritance, labor, administrative, and rural agricultural contracting. CIETAC Rules of Arbitration, art. 2 (6).

to involve purely domestic transactions, notwithstanding that one of the parties is controlled or owned by foreign interests.[36] In 2000, CIETAC again revised its rules to include "domestic disputes" referred by agreement, which includes any commercial dispute, including disputes between FIEs, provided the parties have contractually agreed to arbitrate the dispute before CIETAC.

It is also uncertain under Chinese law whether the employees, agents, or representatives of parties to an arbitration agreement are subject to arbitration. Under U.S. law, the majority view is that nonsignatories of arbitration agreements may benefit from arbitration clauses under agency principles.[37] Whether CIETAC and the Chinese courts apply this rule is left for observation.

b. Pendant Claims

CIETAC Rules of Arbitration provide that international economic disputes involving both contractual and *non-contractual* issues fall within CIETAC's jurisdiction. Prior to the 1995 rules, several Chinese court cases questioned whether pendant noncontractual claims such as damages for fraud and other torts may be heard by CIETAC as CIETAC's own rules failed to specify whether noncontractual claims could be resolved via arbitration. Today, CIETAC will hear all claims between parties to an arbitration agreement, whether contractual and noncontractual, a position that is consistent with international standards.[38]

2. Arbitration Agreements

A dispute may be submitted to arbitration only if both parties consent by agreement.[39] An arbitration commission has no jurisdiction unless a valid

36. In *China International Engineering Consultation Company v. Beijing Holiday Inn Hotel Company Limited,* the Beijing Intermediate People's Court refused to uphold an award of CIETAC on the grounds that a construction dispute between two Chinese entities was a domestic dispute and outside the jurisdiction of CIETAC. The defendant was a joint venture company partially owned by Hong Kong interests. The court reasoned that the dispute did not involve any foreign-related features and rejected the argument that partial ownership by a foreign party was sufficient to consider the matter an "international" dispute. *See Selected Cases of the People's Courts,* China Legal Application Institution, Supreme People's Court. *See also* CRAWFORD & SALBAING, RESOLVING INTERNATIONAL COMMERCIAL DISPUTES IN CHINA, IN DOING BUSINESS IN CHINA § 21.05 [1](1996). Note, however, that the former Economic Contract Law, which governed domestic contracts prior to 1999, did not prohibit the parties from choosing an international arbitration forum such as CIETAC to hear a dispute. Economic Contract Law, art. 42. *See also* Foreign Economic Contract Law, art. 37.

37. *See Silkworm Screen Printers, Inc. v. Amchi Trading, Ltd., Eastern Commodities, Ltd.*, 1992 U.S. App. Lexis 28843 (4th Circuit).

38. United Nations Convention on the Recognition and Enforcement of Foreign Arbitral Awards, June 10, 1958, art. II, ¶ 1, T.I.A.S. No. 6997, 21 U.S.T. 2517, 330 U.N.T.S. 38 (hereinafter the "New York Convention"), *reprinted at* 9 USC §§ 201–208. The PRC Supreme People's Court acknowledged the principle of supremacy of international conventions over domestic law and that the New York Convention is controlling over China's domestic laws in the event of conflict. *See* Notice of the Supreme People's Court of China on the Implementation of the Convention on the Recognition and Enforcement of Foreign Arbitral Awards (issued on April 10, 1987, by the Supreme People's Court).

39. Arbitration Law, art. 4.

arbitration agreement exists. The parties' express intention to arbitrate a dispute is mandatory for the validity of an arbitration agreement or clause. An agreement to arbitrate a dispute may be set forth in a separate document or included as a clause contained in a commercial contract. An exchange of correspondence, telexes, telegrams, and facsimiles are considered writings sufficient to form an agreement between the exchanging parties.[40] However, the exchange of letters must clearly demonstrate that the parties consent to be bound to the terms and conditions in the documentation. Article 16 of the Arbitration Law requires that an arbitration agreement must be in written form and either be contained in a contract or in an agreement to submit to arbitration. On this point, article 3 of the CIETAC Rules provides that:

> The Arbitration Commission will, upon the written application by one of the parties, accept a case in accordance with the arbitration agreement concluded between the parties, either before or after the occurrence of the dispute, in which it is provided that disputes are to be submitted to the Arbitration Commission for arbitration. An arbitration agreement means an arbitration clause in a contract concluded between the parties or any other form of written agreement providing for settlement of dispute by arbitration.

Several reported non-Chinese courts have addressed the issue of what is considered a "writing" to trigger arbitration before CIETAC. Although such cases are of little precedential value, the court's reasoning is instructive.[41] In the case of *Jiangxi Provincial Metal and Minerals Import and Export Corp. v. Sulanser Company Ltd.*, the Hong Kong Supreme Court found that, although unsigned, the sales contract between the parties was enforceable because the parties attempted to perform under its terms.[42] The Hong Kong court found that defendants admitted the existence of the arbitration clause in a series of letters to a Chinese court, which had been submitted in order to persuade that court to dismiss litigation against the defendant for breach of contract. The Hong Kong court ruled that an exchange of letters between the defendant and the Wuhan Admiralty Court affirmed the existence of a contract, including an agreement to arbitrate.

40. Contract Law, art. 11. This rule is consistent with Article II of the New York Convention, which provides that an agreement in writing shall include an arbitral clause in a contract or "contained in an exchange of letters."

41. There is no case law in the PRC similar to common-law jurisdictions. The courts do not have the power to interpret the law. The authority to interpret is vested in the NPC and its ministries and commissions.

42. *See Hong Kong Supreme Court: Written Agreement Between the Parties Did Exist,* 10 MEALEY'S INT'L ARBITRATION REP. No. 6 (June 1995), available on Lexis at INTLAW Library, MEALEY File.

A similar issue, which frequently arises for foreign parties, involves the incorporation of an arbitration provision in a master contract, which is attached to, and referred in, a purchase order issued to a foreign supplier of goods. Although not parties to the master contract, foreign suppliers have been ordered to arbitrate or to be bound by arbitration awards based upon arbitration provisions in master contracts. In *Polytek Engineering Co., Ltd. v. Jacobson Companies and Jacobson, Inc.*, the United States District Court for the District of Minnesota held that a U.S.-based seller of machinery was bound by an arbitration clause in the master sales agreement between the end user in China and the Hong Kong trading company. The court reasoned that the master sales contract was attached to a purchase order between the seller and the Hong Kong party.[43] The seller claimed that it never agreed to arbitrate any disputes with its Hong Kong customer in China. The court ruled that the principal contract, which was attached to the purchase order, satisfied the New York Convention's definition of an "agreement in writing." As a result, purchase orders, which refer to other contracts or documents, should be fully scrutinized, and any unacceptable provision should be deleted or expressly superseded by different provisions.

a. Validity of an Arbitration Clause

Under Chinese law, a valid arbitration agreement or clause must include the following terms and conditions:

(1) A written expression of the parties' intention to arbitrate any dispute[44]

(2) A written description of the items or issues that are suitable for arbitration[45]

43. *Polytek Engineering Co., Ltd. v. Jacobson Companies and Jacobson, Inc.*, 1997 U.S. Dist. Lexis 19902 (Minnesota DC). A duty to arbitrate can be based upon the doctrine of incorporation. *See Silkworm Screen Printers v. Amchi Trading Ltd., Genco International, Ltd., Eastern Commodities, Ltd.*, 1992 U.S. App. Lexis 28843 (4th Cir. 1992) (court held that the presentation and attachment of a manufacturer's contract containing an arbitration clause was a condition precedent to incorporating the duty to arbitrate before CIETAC into the purchase order).

44. Arbitration Law, art. 16 (1). The agreement should specifically provide that the parties intend to arbitrate all disputes and claims. An arbitration clause should also specifically and clearly state that an award may not be appealed in order to preserve finality of the tribunal's decision. Court relief may be reserved only for obtaining provisional remedies. A number of form contracts (e.g., the standard form of the People's Insurance Company) contain provisions that allow for parties to choose either arbitration or court relief in the event of a dispute. As a result of the choice, the parties are forced to enter into a supplemental agreement before submitting a matter to arbitration or litigation. To correct this problem, Chinese form contracts are now required to contain a forum selection clause, which requires the parties to select arbitration or litigation at the time of executing the original contract. Arbitration Law Notice, art. 4.

45. The parties to a contract may reserve the jurisdiction of the court for issues pertaining to the preservation of property and other provisional remedies. An aggrieved party should have the option to obtain the assistance of the judiciary for injunctive relief, sealing orders, or seizure orders given that the arbitration tribunal does not have coercive powers. This contractual reservation, although not prohibited by the Arbitration Law and CIETAC rules, may conflict with Articles 257 and 258 of the Civil Procedure Code.

(3) A designation of the arbitration tribunal having authority to hear the parties' dispute[46]

Should the arbitration clause or agreement fail to clearly specify the subject matter of dispute capable of resolution via arbitration or the choice of arbitration commission, the parties may enter into a supplementary agreement to clarify the matter. If a supplementary agreement cannot be reached, the arbitration clause or agreement is considered null and void, and therefore unenforceable.[47] An arbitration agreement or clause is also invalid if executed by persons without the necessary civil capacity or legal status to enter into such an agreement or if procured by fraud, economic duress, or other coercive means.[48] Without an enforceable arbitration clause, the only recourse available to the parties is to seek judicial relief.

The selected arbitration commission has the right to determine the existence and validity of an arbitration clause.[49] Under CIETAC rules, it is the Commission, rather than the arbitrators, that is empowered to decide upon the validity or invalidity of the arbitration agreement. In the event that the parties dispute the validity of an arbitration provision, the parties have the right to have the issue resolved by the people's court.[50] The parties are required to raise the validity of the arbitration agreement before the tribunal holds its first hearing.[51]

In June 1996, the State Council issued a notice addressing a number of unresolved issues relating to the Arbitration Law.[52] The Arbitration Law Notice provides that agreements to arbitrate executed before September 1, 1995, the effective date of the Arbitration Law, are valid if they satisfy the requirements applicable at the time the agreement was executed by the parties.

46. Arbitration Law, art. 16.

47. Arbitration Law, art. 18.

48. Arbitration Law, art. 17 (2) and 3. The Hong Kong Supreme Court upheld a CIETAC award in a case in which a defendant's authorized representative signed contracts containing arbitration clauses, notwithstanding that the defendant claimed it ceased to use arbitration clauses months before the signing of the subject contract. *See Arbitration Award Survives Enforcement Challenge,* 9 MEALEY'S INT'L ARBITRATION REP. No. 2 (February 1994), available on Lexis, INTLAW Library, MEALEY File.

49. Arbitration Law, art. 19.

50. Arbitration Law, art. 20; CIETAC Rules of Arbitration, art. 4.

51. Arbitration Law, art. 20; CIETAC Rules of Arbitration, art. 6. The amendment to the CIETAC Rules in 2000 provide that a counterclaim that raises questions concerning jurisdiction over an arbitration agreement and/or arbitration case may not affect the hearing of the case. CIETAC Rules of Arbitration, art. 6. If the parties agree to submit a dispute to CIETAC for mediation, the parties are deemed to consent to CIETAC's jurisdiction of the dispute for purposes of arbitration. Any issues concerning the validity of CIETAC's jurisdiction should be resolved before the parties proceed with either arbitration or mediation. CIETAC Rules of Arbitration, art. 7.

52. Arbitration Law Notice, art. 1.

b. Choice of Law

When a dispute involves Chinese parties only, the applicable law is Chinese law. Chinese law also applies to the resolution of disputes arising from the establishment of equity and contractual joint ventures and cooperation contracts for the exploitation and development of Chinese mineral and natural resources.[53]

In all foreign-related contracts, the parties may choose the law governing the interpretation and enforcement of their agreement.[54] Therefore, while the law applicable to a contract for the formation of a joint venture is Chinese law, where that joint venture enters into commercial contracts with other entities, the parties are free to select the laws of another jurisdiction to govern their contract. In the absence of a choice by the parties, the arbitration tribunal is empowered to determine the applicable law. However, the tribunal is required to apply the law that has the closest connection to the contract such as the law of the place where the contract was concluded, or the law of the place where the contract is/was to be performed.[55] The tribunal may also apply the provisions of relevant international conventions to which China has acceded, or, where applicable, accepted international practices or customs. The tribunal may resort to international practices and customs in situations in which there is no specific Chinese law on an issue in question. The choice of law, however, must not violate Chinese law or the social and public interest.[56]

c. Choice of Forum

Chinese laws permit contracting parties to choose the forum for resolving disputes.[57] Under the U.S./China trade agreement, the parties acknowledge the right to choose the forum for dispute resolution including in the U.S., China, or in third countries.[58] In practice, Chinese parties are insistent on resolving disputes in the Mainland. As China has opened its doors to business, it is gradually accepting dispute resolution before forums in third countries.

In preparing a forum selection clause, the parties should exercise caution. The accurate and current title of the arbitration institution should be clearly specified in the contract. For example, there is a difference between

53. Contract Law, art. 126. For a discussion concerning choice of law provisions, *see* Chapter 7, Contract Law § A.7.
54. Civil Law, art. 145.
55. Contract Law, art. 126.
56. Civil Law, art. 150.
57. Civil Procedure Code, art. 244.
58. U.S./China Trade Agreement, *supra* note 2 art. 8.

the Shenzhen Arbitration Commission, a domestic commission, and the Shenzhen subcommission of CIETAC. A selection clause that is unclear may trigger the jurisdiction of both institutions and, in the absence of written confirmation by the disputing parties, will render the arbitration agreement unenforceable. The Chinese courts have also held that a reference to a set of arbitration rules (e.g., International Chamber of Commerce Rules) is insufficient to designate the arbitration forum. Similarly, a statement that "arbitration is in Singapore" is also considered to be an insufficient designation of forum. To avoid litigating the validity of an arbitration clause, the parties should specifically designate the forum selected, by both name and location.[59]

An arbitration agreement or clause need not contain the specific procedural matters such as the rules governing the proceedings, including the process for the appointment of the tribunal, in order to be valid. A reference to the selected arbitration forum is sufficient to trigger the applicable procedural rules. CIETAC Rules of Arbitration and the Arbitration Law will govern the parties that select CIETAC as the dispute resolution forum.

3. CIETAC Procedures

The various Chinese arbitration commissions each have their own procedural rules with most differences relating to the application forms, the timing of filings, the lists of approved arbitrators and the arbitrator selection process, and the time for issuance of final awards. CIETAC is the forum in which most FIEs will be involved.

a. Arbitration Application

Arbitration proceedings before CIETAC are initiated by the filing of an arbitration application with the Commission. An application is required to state the names and addresses of the applicant(s) and the respondent(s), the arbitration agreement upon which the applicant bases the application, the factual and legal issues in dispute, and the evidence that the applicant offers in support of its claims.[60] The applicant is required to include with the application any documentary and testimonial evidence in support of its claims, and to tender the arbitration application fees to the Commission in accordance with the current fee schedule published by CIETAC.[61]

59. Guiguo Wang, *supra* note 7, at 23–25. *But see* CIETAC Rules of Arbitration, art. 79. Under Article 79 (as amended in 1998), the parties are deemed to have consented to CIETAC if the agreement refers to the "CCPIT Foreign Trade Arbitration Commission," the "Foreign Trade Arbitration Commission of the China Council for the Promotion of International Trade," or the "Foreign Economic Relations and Trade Arbitration Commission."

60. Arbitration Law, arts. 21, 23; CIETAC Rules of Arbitration, art. 14.

61. CIETAC Rules of Arbitration, art. 14, ¶ 2 and 3.

Upon receipt of the application and supporting documentation, CIETAC will serve a notice of arbitration on the defendant(s) and copies of applicant's submissions. CIETAC will also provide both parties with a copy of CIETAC's rules and a list of approved arbitrators. The arbitration proceedings are deemed to have commenced at the time CIETAC issues the arbitration notice.[62] Once the notice is issued, a staff member of CIETAC will be appointed to manage the procedural aspects of the arbitration case.

Within forty-five days of receiving the arbitration notice, the respondents are required to submit to CIETAC a responsive statement in defense of the applicant's claims and in substantiation of its position.[63] A defendant may also file a counterclaim against the applicant in the same proceedings. A counterclaim should be substantiated by legal and factual allegations and supporting documentation[64] and must be filed within sixty days of receipt of the arbitration notice. If justified, CIETAC may extend the time for filing a response. An applicant is required to file a statement in defense to a counterclaim within forty-five days following receipt of the respondent's counterclaim. A party's failure to respond to an arbitration notice or to submit a statement in defense to a claim or counterclaim is not deemed to be in default and does not affect the arbitration proceedings.[65]

All parties to an arbitration proceeding have the right to amend their claims and counterclaims. However, the arbitration panel may refuse to grant a request to amend a claim if the request is untimely made and will affect the normal progress of the proceedings.[66]

CIETAC's rules require that all submissions to the arbitral tribunal or CIETAC include a sufficient number of copies for the entire tribunal (one or three), one copy for the Commission, and one per opposing party.[67] A failure to provide the required number of copies may result in a rejection of the submitted application or document.

---

62. CIETAC Rules of Arbitration, art. 13.

63. CIETAC Rules of Arbitration, art. 17. The defendant's response should raise all objections at the outset and, among other things, the selection of the arbitration forum, the arbitration location, the applicable rules, and the qualifications and partiality of selected and appointed arbitrators. The courts are keen to hindsight objections and usually reject challenges to awards that are raised at the enforcement stage. *See China Agribusiness Development Corporation v. Balli Trading,* Queen's Bench Division (Commercial Court) (January 20, 1997), available on Lexis at INTLAW Library, ENGCAS File.

64. CIETAC Rules of Arbitration, art. 18.

65. Arbitration Law, art. 25; CIETAC Rules of Arbitration, art. 21.

66. CIETAC Rules of Arbitration, art. 19.

67. CIETAC Rules of Arbitration, art. 20.

b. Appointment of Foreign Counsel in Arbitration

Foreign parties have traditionally appointed foreign lawyers to represent them in arbitration proceedings held in China.[68] However, the role of foreign lawyers in arbitration proceedings in China is unclear as a result of certain regulations adopted by the State Council and Ministry of Justice.[69] Article 15 of the Foreign Lawyer Regulations provides a list of permitted activities of foreign law firms and their representatives in China, including entrusting Chinese law firms to handle "Chinese legal affairs." A definition of the term "Chinese legal affairs" is not set forth in the Foreign Law Firm Regulations, but Article 32 of the Foreign Law Firm Implementing Regulations provides a definition that includes *inter alia* (a) providing opinions or certification on specific issues in respect of a contract, agreement, articles of association, or other written documents governed by PRC law; and (b) in the capacity of an agent in arbitration proceedings, issuing opinions or comments on the application of the PRC law and facts involving PRC law. A combined reading of the regulations and the rules indicate that foreign lawyers may be denied the right to represent their clients before arbitration proceedings. The provision is, of course, contrary to one of the fundamental principles of arbitration, namely that it is a strictly private medium of dispute resolution and the parties have a right to choose their agents or legal representatives, if any, during the proceeding.

The Ministry of Justice has sought to clarify the issue—in a recent unpublished reply to CIETAC, the ministry confirmed that foreign lawyers are indeed permitted to serve as legal agents in *international arbitrations* held in China, but are required to consult with a Chinese lawyer in relation to matters pertaining to Chinese law. Moreover, the clarification overtly fails to address the standing of foreign lawyers vis-à-vis domestic or foreign-related arbitration and is considerably at odds with Article 29 of the Arbitration Law, which clearly and unambiguously states: "The parties concerned or legal attorneys may entrust lawyers or other attorneys to handle matters relating to arbitration. In the case where lawyers or other attorneys

68. The Arbitration Law does not require a party to retain a Chinese lawyer in an arbitration before either CIETAC or a domestic commission. Arbitration Law, art. 29; CIETAC Rules of Arbitration, art. 22. In contrast, the Civil Procedure Code, Article 241, requires that foreign litigants in the people's court retain the services of PRC legal counsel.

69. Administrative Regulations on Representative Offices of Foreign Law Firms in China (promulgated by the State Council on December 22, 2001, and effective from January 1, 2002) (hereinafter the "Foreign Law Firm Regulations"); Implementation Regulations of the Administrative Regulations on Representative Offices of Foreign Law Firms in China (promulgated by the Ministry of Justice on June 25, 2002, and effective from September 1, 2002) (hereinafter the "Foreign Law Firm Implementing Regulations"). The foreign legal community in China has reported a number of cases in which Chinese parties have expressly challenged the right of foreign parties to have foreign lawyers and foreign law firms involved in CIETAC proceedings. The author has been advised that the tribunals are refusing to address the petitions without further clarification from the relevant government authorities.

are entrusted with the handling of arbitration matters, the attorneys shall produce a power of attorney to the arbitration commission."

The "informal clarification" of the MOJ also conflicts with Article 22 of the CIETAC rules, which state that "the parties may authorize arbitration agents to deal with the matters relating to arbitration; the authorized arbitration agent must produce a power of attorney to the arbitration commission. Both Chinese and foreign citizens can be authorized to act as arbitration agents." Therefore, unfortunately, the question of a foreign lawyer's ability or otherwise to act in China-based arbitration cases remains unresolved. Unless the matter is settled quickly, foreign law firms are likely to recommend that their clients insist on overseas arbitration for dispute resolution.

c. Arbitrator Appointment

An arbitration case is heard and decided by an arbitration tribunal, and consists of either one arbitrator, if the parties agree, or a tribunal of three arbitrators.[70] All arbitrators must be appointed from CIETAC's approved panel of arbitrators. Within twenty days of receiving the arbitration notice, the parties are required to nominate one arbitrator from the list provided by CIETAC. In the alternative, a party may elect CIETAC to appoint an arbitrator on its behalf.[71] So too, the Commission will appoint an arbitrator when a party fails to make an appointment within the prescribed time.[72] In cases in which there are two or more claimants or respondents in a case, each side, through consultation, will appoint one arbitrator. If either side is unable to jointly appoint an arbitrator, CIETAC will make the appointment. The parties are also required to jointly appoint a third arbitrator within twenty days of receipt of the arbitration notice. If the parties fail to reach a consensus on the third arbitrator, the Commission will select the third arbitrator. The third arbitrator assumes the role of presiding arbitrator or arbitrator-in-chief.[73]

If an appointed arbitrator is an interested party in a proceeding, he or she is required to immediately notify CIETAC and request that he/she be withdrawn from the case.[74] Withdrawal is mandatory in the following situations:

(1) The arbitrator is a party to the dispute or an immediate relative of the parties to the case or their agents

70. Arbitration Law, art. 30; CIETAC Rules of Arbitration, art. 24.
71. CIETAC Rules of Arbitration, art. 16.
72. Arbitration Law, art. 32; CIETAC Rules of Arbitration, art. 26.
73. The importance of the presiding arbitrator cannot be understated. The presiding arbitrator's views are decisive if a majority of the panel is unable to agree on an award. The presiding arbitrator is almost inevitably Chinese. As a result, arbitrating before CIETAC oftentimes gives the Chinese party a home-court advantage. Arbitration Law, art. 53; CIETAC Rules of Arbitration, art. 56.
74. Arbitration Law, art. 34; CIETAC Rules of Arbitration, art. 28.

(2) The arbitrator has a personal interest in the case
(3) The arbitrator has some other relationship with the parties to the case or their agents that may affect the fairness of the award
(4) The arbitrator has had an ex parte meeting with the parties concerned or their agents, or has accepted any gifts or attended banquets provided by the parties concerned or their agents[75]

A party may file an application with the Commission requesting the withdrawal of an arbitrator if the arbitrator's independence and fairness are in question. The challenge seeking withdrawal is required to clearly state the reasons for the request and, if information is known, must be submitted in writing before the commencement of the first hearing of the case. If information is discovered after the commencement of the first hearing, an application seeking withdrawal may be filed with the Commission prior to the end of the final hearing.[76] The chair of CIETAC will rule on any application seeking the withdrawal of an arbitrator.[77]

If an arbitrator is unable to perform his or her duties for any reason, including the result of death, disability, or removal from the approved list of arbitrators, a substitute may be selected via the same manner by which the original arbitrator was selected.[78] Depending upon the stage of the proceeding, the parties may request that the arbitration panel conduct a complete or partial rehearing of the case.

It is advisable for a party involved in an arbitration to specifically request and thoroughly review the biographical information concerning *any* of the arbitrators, especially those appointed by the opposing party or by the Commission. CIETAC has appointed arbitrators that were not on its approved list or whose impartiality was in question.[79]

---

75. Arbitration Law, art. 34.

76. Arbitration Law, art. 35; CIETAC Rules of Arbitration, art. 29.

77. Arbitration Law, art. 36; CIETAC Rules of Arbitration, art. 30. The amendments to the CIETAC Rules in 2000 provide that before the chairperson of the CIETAC decides whether an arbitrator shall be withdrawn, the concerned arbitrator is required to fulfill his or her duties to the tribunal. CIETAC Rules of Arbitration, art. 30. If an arbitrator is removed as a result of accepting gifts from a party to the proceeding, he or she may be found legally responsible for his or her actions, including liability for the costs to reappoint a new arbitrator and the expenses incurred for a rehearing of the arbitration proceeding. An arbitrator found in violation of his or her duties may also be removed from the Commission's list of arbitrators and banned from participating in future matters. Arbitration Law, art. 38.

78. Arbitration Law, art. 37; CIETAC Rules of Arbitration, art. 31.

79. *See, e.g., Logy Enterprises Ltd. v. Haikou City Bonded Area Wansen Products Trading Co.*, 1997-2 HKC 481. In the *Logy Enterprises* case, CIETAC appointed an arbitrator who was a high-ranking official for the China Commodity Inspection Bureau (CCIB). At issue in the case was an inspection certificate issued by CCIB that determined that the foreign party sold a short shipment of steel wire rods. The tribunal, including the CCIB official, ruled in favor of the Chinese buyer of the rods and thereby awarded damages based upon the CCIB inspection certificate. In a bias claim to set aside the tribunal's award, the court rejected a losing party's challenge on the grounds that the court was not in a position

d. Case Hearings

If the parties agree, an arbitration tribunal may render an award based upon written submissions only and without the need of a hearing.[80] Otherwise, the tribunal will set the matter for hearing. The initial hearing date will be set by the tribunal in consultation with the Commission. In practice, the tribunal will work with the parties to set the hearings at mutually convenient times.[81] The parties are granted at least thirty days' notice prior to the initial hearing and may request, for proper reasons, that the hearing date be continued.[82] A request to postpone a hearing date must be filed with the Commission at least twelve days before the scheduled commencement of the hearing. The tribunal has discretion to grant or deny a postponement request.

If a party, after receiving notice, fails or refuses to appear at a hearing, the tribunal may proceed in its absence.[83] Under the Arbitration Law, the failure of a claimant to attend a noticed hearing is deemed to be a withdrawal of the arbitration application. The law does not specifically provide that a respondent, in the absence of the applicant, may proceed to obtain an award in its favor including a decision on the merits of the arbitration application and an award for fees and costs to defend a claim. However, CIETAC's rules provide that the tribunal may issue an award against a party that fails to appear for a noticed hearing. In practice, CIETAC tribunals usually provide the parties with a number of opportunities to be heard before rendering a default decision.[84]

Arbitration hearings are traditionally held privately and the parties, witnesses (experts and percipient), lawyers, commission personnel, and arbitrators are prohibited from discussing the substance or status of the case with third persons.[85] The tribunal, at the request and with the consent of the parties, may open the hearings to the public. If the evidence involves state secrets, the parties are barred from holding public hearings and the

---

to evaluate whether an appointed arbitrator had the potential to improperly influence the outcome of a case. The court reasoned that the Commission was in a better position to evaluate whether an arbitrator was impartial. The challenge was made after the award was issued by the tribunal. *See Award Survives Bias Claim Challenge,* 12 MEALEY'S INT'L ARBITRATION REP. No. 11 (November 1997), available on Lexis at INTLAW Library, MEALEY File.

80. Arbitration Law, art. 39; CIETAC Rules of Arbitration, art. 32.

81. Article 35 (as amended in 1998), allows the parties to choose a site of the arbitration hearing in a location outside of Beijing, Shanghai, or Shenzhen.

82. Arbitration Law, art. 41; CIETAC Rules of Arbitration, art. 33. The thirty-day notice period does not apply to subsequent hearing dates. CIETAC Rules of Arbitration, art. 34.

83. Arbitration Law, art. 42; CIETAC Rules of Arbitration, art. 42.

84. *See generally Polytek Engineering Co., Ltd. v. Jacobson Companies and Jacobson, Inc.,* 1997 U.S. Dist. Lexis 19902 (U.S.-based defendant acknowledged receipt of arbitration notice but refused to attend hearing and refused to provide objections or further responses after the arbitration hearing).

85. CIETAC Rules of Arbitration, art. 37.

proceedings must be held *in camera*.[86] CIETAC arbitrations are held in Beijing, Shenzhen, Shanghai, or at a location jointly agreed upon by the parties, the tribunal, and the Commission.

The tribunal has the discretion to record the hearing in writing, or by audio- or videotape recording.[87] The parties have the right to request that the tribunal modify the record to correct any inaccuracy. Written records of the hearings must be signed and sealed by the arbitrators, court reporters, and parties involved in the arbitration. The record in writing or by tape-recording is available for use and reference only by the arbitration tribunal.

e. Discovery, Investigation, and Presentation of Evidence

Under China's legal system, which follows the civil-law tradition, there is no right to discovery, and court-initiated investigation is the norm. The Chinese system lacks the judicial truth-guarding tools such as requiring witnesses to testify under oath, cross-examination by opposing counsel, and laws that are effective to counter perjury.[88] As a result, and because many parties still arbitrate cases without the assistance of counsel, the tribunal is responsible for conducting an investigation and collecting evidence independently of the parties. Although CIETAC in many ways has divorced itself from the Chinese legal system, it still preserves the judicial tradition in a number of respects.

The parties to an arbitration proceeding are required to produce all evidence, documentary and testimonial, in support of their respective claims, counterclaims, and defenses.[89] However, there are no formal rules for discovery procedures or requirements that evidence be produced in advance of a hearing. In practice, and in the absence of specific discovery procedures set forth in the parties' arbitration agreement, the tribunal and the parties will set a prehearing document exchange schedule to facilitate the orderly production of evidence.

The tribunal is also empowered to conduct its own independent investigations.[90] The tribunal's authority is limited since it does not have the coercive

86. Arbitration Law, art. 40; CIETAC Rules of Arbitration, art. 36.

87. Arbitration Law, art. 48; CIETAC Rules of Arbitration, art. 43.

88. In contrast to CIETAC's evidence rules, the Arbitration Rules of the Shenzhen Arbitration Commission provide in detail the types of evidence that may be submitted and "will only be considered to be factual evidence after it has been subjected to court scrutiny, debate and substantiation and a full and objective examination and verification by the arbitration tribunal." *See* Arbitration Rules of the Shenzhen Arbitration Commission (promulgated on July 16, 1996, by the Shenzhen Arbitration Commission), arts. 42, 43, *reprinted in* CHINA LAWS FOR FOREIGN BUSINESS (CCH), Special Zones & Cities ¶ 120-080. This rule is consistent with the evidentiary standards for administrative litigation. *See* Law of the Administrative Litigation of the People's Republic of China (adopted on April 4, 1989, by the 2nd Sess. of the 7th NPC), art. 31, *reprinted in* CHINA LAWS FOR FOREIGN BUSINESS (CCH), Business Regulation ¶ 19-558.

89. Arbitration Law, art. 43; CIETAC Rules of Arbitration, art. 38.

90. Arbitration Law, art. 43; CIETAC Rules of Arbitration, art. 38.

power to subpoena records, tangible items, or testimonial evidence. In practice, the tribunal will only initiate its own investigation if it finds that the parties are unable or unwilling to cooperate with prehearing document exchanges, or if the tribunal finds that it cannot make an informed decision based upon the materials and evidence provided by the parties. Because the parties bear the cost of the tribunal's independent investigation, the parties should take steps to cooperate in prehearing discovery to avoid triggering the involvement of the tribunal. At the same time, a party that has not secured the cooperation of another party to an arbitration should employ the independent investigatory powers of the tribunal to conduct prehearing discovery.

If the tribunal initiates its own investigation, it is required to inform the parties to allow them to be present.[91] Although there is no bar to ex parte communications, Article 38 of the CIETAC Rules of Arbitration requires the tribunal to notify the parties when it conducts an independent investigation that arguably will result in ex parte communications.

At the time of the hearing, the parties are required to produce all evidence in support of their respective positions. During the hearing, and under the control of the tribunal, the parties may question the witnesses (percipient and experts). The parties also have the right to debate during the hearing process both the facts and the law.[92] At the end of the debate, the presiding arbitrator will request that the parties make concluding arguments.

f. Expert Witnesses and Appraisers

The tribunal may consult with expert witnesses on any technical or special matter, or consult with an appraiser with respect to the value of any property at issue in the arbitration. Such experts may be foreign individuals. The tribunal may demand that a party produce documents, property, or merchandise for examination by an expert or appraiser for the purposes of inspection and appraisal.

Under Article 40 of CIETAC's rules, copies of all expert and appraisal reports are required to be available to the parties. With the approval of the tribunal, any expert or appraiser that renders an opinion may be requested to attend the arbitration hearing. The tribunal also has the right to require an expert or appraiser to explain his or her opinions or findings, and the parties have the right to question the opinions or findings of an expert or appraiser.[93]

91. CIETAC Rules of Arbitration, art. 38.
92. Arbitration Law, art. 47.
93. CIETAC Rules of Arbitration, art. 40.

The right to refute expert testimony under Article 40 has been adopted in response to the *Paklito Investment Ltd. v. Klochner East Asia Ltd.* decision of CIETAC. In *Paklito,* a Hong Kong court refused to enforce an $800,000 CIETAC award in a situation involving a defendant who was prohibited by the tribunal from questioning a technical report obtained from a tribunal-appointed expert. Under the old CIETAC rules, the parties did not have the right to question the technical reports of tribunal-appointed experts. The Hong Kong court found that the old CIETAC rules were inconsistent with China's obligations under the New York Convention and the 1991 Civil Procedure Code of China. Under Article 40 of the 1995 CIETAC Rules, the parties now have the right to question the findings and opinions of experts.[94] The amendments contained in the CIETAC Rules in 2000 include a clause that provides that the tribunal has the discretion of determining whether to accept an experts report or appraisal.[95]

g. Awards

An arbitration award is based upon the decision of a majority of the tribunal members.[96] If the tribunal is unable to agree to a majority decision, the award is based upon the opinion of the presiding arbitrator or arbitrator-in-chief.[97] A dissenting arbitrator has the option to refuse to sign an award and to lodge his or her opinion in a separate file retained by the Commission.[98] Under CIETAC's former rules, the dissenting arbitrator was required to sign the award regardless of his or her opinion. Although a dissenting arbitrator may refuse to sign an award under the current rules, the parties are not allowed access to the dissenter's written opinions, if any.

---

94. For an analysis of the *Paklito* case, *see* Luming Chen, *supra* note 31, at 136–38; *Hong Kong Court Will Not Enforce $800,000 Award,* 8 MEALEY'S INT'L ARBITRATION REP. No. 5 (May 1993), available on Lexis, INTLAW Library, MEALEY File. *But see Apex Tech Investment Ltd. v. Chuang's Development (China) Ltd.*, Hong Kong App. Ct. 231 (1995). In the *Apex Tech* case, the plaintiff argued that a real estate sales contract was invalid because the Chinese developer failed to obtain a land-use certificate that specifically allowed for the right to resell the property to potential buyers in Hong Kong. The CIETAC tribunal conducted its own investigation by contacting the land-use authorities and were advised that the developer was required to obtain consent to amend the use in the land-use certificate. As a result of this investigation and finding, the tribunal found that the sales contract was invalid and rendered an award in favor of the buyer for return of its purchase monies. The developer was not allowed to question the independent investigation of the tribunal or to introduce additional evidence contrary to the tribunal's findings. The Hong Kong court agreed with the CIETAC tribunal's award in that even if the developer were allowed the opportunity to submit additional evidence, it would not have affected the outcome of the award. *See Order Enforcing Award Set Aside by Appeals Court in Hong Kong,* 12 MEALEY'S INT'L ARBITRATION REP. No. 2 (February 1997), available on Lexis at INTLAW Library, MEALEY File.

95. CIETAC Rules of Arbitration, art. 41.

96. Arbitration Law, art. 53.

97. Arbitration Law, art. 53; CIETAC Rules of Arbitration, arts. 54, 56.

98. Arbitration Law, art. 54; CIETAC Rules of Arbitration, arts. 54, 56.

An award must be made independently and without interference from the Commission, or any government institution or individual.[99] CIETAC's rules, however, require the tribunal to submit its draft written award to the Commission for its review. This review is purportedly for the sole purpose of evaluating the written format of the award.[100] In practice, CIETAC will review the award to ensure that it meets the information requirements of the Arbitration Law to avoid any enforcement problems.[101]

In addition to objectivity, an award must be based upon the facts of the case, and in accordance with the applicable laws and regulations and the parties' contract.[102] An arbitration award is required to clearly state information concerning the parties, the arbitration agreement, facts of the dispute, the reasons for the award, the resulting award, the party liable for arbitration costs, and the date of the award.[103] With the approval of the parties, the tribunal may issue a written award without specifying the facts of the case or the reasons for the decision. Usually, the parties will request that a tribunal's written award be issued without the facts if the award is based upon a settlement reached after mediation or independent conciliation. In those instances, the parties may still dispute the facts of a case but will prefer to settle a matter for other reasons such as economics and uncertainty of proceeding with arbitration.

An arbitration tribunal has the discretion to determine the final arbitration fees and expenses payable by the parties in a case, including CIETAC fees, arbitrator fees and expenses, and the cost of experts retained by the tribunal. The tribunal also has discretion to award a sum for "reasonable expenses incurred by the prevailing party in dealing with the arbitration," such as attorney fees. However, the maximum amount of compensation for party expenses cannot exceed 10 percent of the amount awarded to the prevailing party.[104]

The arbitration tribunal may, at the request of a party, issue an interlocutory or partial award at any time during the arbitration proceeding.[105] Generally, partial awards are granted with respect to such items as (1) preliminary issues, including the applicable law governing the parties' transaction, (2) undisputed issues, such as payment for services or merchandise that the recipient does not question, or (3) matters that can be bifurcated, such as liability issues and the determination of the scope of damages. This procedure is designed to facilitate the orderly process of the proceeding. The failure of a

99. Arbitration Law, art. 8.
100. CIETAC Rules of Arbitration, art. 56.
101. Arbitration Law, art. 54.
102. CIETAC Rules of Arbitration, art. 53.
103. Arbitration Law, art. 54; CIETAC Rules of Arbitration, art. 55.
104. CIETAC Rules of Arbitration, art. 59.
105. CIETAC Rules of Arbitration, art. 57.

party to adhere to an interlocutory order will not affect the arbitration proceedings, and the tribunal does not have the coercive powers to enforce such interim awards. However, as a practical matter, the failure of a party to observe and respect the tribunal's authority is likely to be matched with a final award in favor of the opposing party.

The arbitration award is also required to take into consideration "international practices." CIETAC tribunals frequently rely upon international practice and customs in determining the rights and obligations of disputing parties. A recognition of international norms acts to fill the vacuum where Chinese law is nonexistent or ambiguous, and provides the parties with a degree of certainty.[106]

The tribunal is also required to observe the "principles of fairness and reasonableness" in rendering its award.[107] This rule appears to grant the tribunal the powers of equity and, at the same time, the discretion to disregard the applicable law and the parties' express written contract. Although bargained for, a valid and binding agreement may be unfair and unreasonable, but not unconscionable and invalid under the law. Absent a finding of fraud or duress, most jurists would hold a party to its contractual obligations. Yet, in China, arbitrators have the right to assume the role as peacemaker rather than as a decision maker in a manner consistent with international arbitration practices. The requirement that the tribunal observe principles of fairness and reasonableness creates uncertainty in the CIETAC process and constitutes a risk to evaluate in determining whether to select this arbitration institution as a dispute resolution forum.

An arbitration award must be issued by the tribunal within nine months after the formation of the tribunal.[108] Under the former rules, a tribunal was required to issue an award within forty-five days after the closing of the arbitration hearing. This rule caused some confusion since there were questions as to when the case actually closed and, because there was no maximum amount of time between the commencement of the proceeding and the hearing date, cases often lingered for years. The purpose of the current rule is to ensure that the entire process, including the selection of the tribunal, is completed within one year. The arbitration award takes effect on the date that it is issued by CIETAC.[109]

106. For a discussion of CIETAC cases in which the tribunal relied upon international commercial practice, *see* Guiguo Wang, *supra* note 7, at 35–38.

107. Arbitration Law, art. 7; CIETAC Rules of Arbitration, art. 53.

108. CIETAC Rules of Arbitration, art. 52. The time period may be extended by the Commission for justifiable reasons.

109. Arbitration Law, art. 57; CIETAC Rules of Arbitration, art. 56.

An arbitration award is binding and final on the parties, and neither party is permitted to seek judicial review, or request another arbitration institution, to revise or appeal the award.[110] Within thirty days of receiving an arbitration award, any party may submit a written request to the tribunal to correct any written, typographical, or calculation errors set forth in the award.[111] Any written corrections accepted by the panel will form part of the arbitration award.

h. Consent Awards

If a matter is resolved through mediation, the parties may request that the tribunal or the Commission issue an arbitral award based upon the settlement agreement.[112] A consent award is enforceable in a similar fashion as a final award. If either party fails to abide by the terms of the consent award, the other party may apply to the courts for enforcement.

i. Summary Proceedings

CIETAC's rules provide for simplified procedures for disputes with an amount in controversy of less than RMB500,000 ($60,000) or, if both parties agree, for disputes in excess of RMB500,000.[113] Under these summary procedures, the dispute will be resolved by one arbitrator who is either jointly appointed by the parties or, in the event that the parties are unable to agree, appointed by CIETAC.[114] The respondent is required to respond, including the submission of a counterclaim, within thirty days of receipt of the notice of arbitration under these summary procedures. In contrast, the respondent is allowed forty-five days to file a statement in defense and sixty days for a counterclaim in general arbitration matters.[115] The rules do not expressly disallow amendments to claims, but additional claims and counterclaims will not affect the timing of the summary procedure.[116]

---

110. Civil Procedure Code, art. 259; Arbitration Law, art. 9; CIETAC Rules of Arbitration, art. 60.

111. Arbitration Law, art. 56 (fifteen days to correct errors in domestic arbitration awards); CIETAC Rules of Arbitration, art. 61.

112. Arbitration Law, arts. 49, 50; CIETAC Rules of Arbitration, art. 44. The amendments to the CIETAC Rules in 2000 added a provision in Article 44 that provides that settlement agreements reached outside the CIETAC forum may be enforced by CIETAC with the consent of the parties.

113. CIETAC Rules of Arbitration, art. 64. The summary proceeding is consistent with the practices of a number of international arbitration institutions.

114. CIETAC Rules of Arbitration, art. 65. CIETAC will appoint the arbitrator fifteen days after the defendant receives notice of the proceeding.

115. CIETAC Rules of Arbitration, art. 66.

116. CIETAC Rules of Arbitration, art. 72. Article 72 has been amended to provide that in situations where the amount in controversy is revised as a result of the filing of a counterclaim or amended claim, the tribunal has the discretion to determine whether a summary proceeding is appropriate.

Under the summary proceeding rules, the arbitrator has the discretion to hold an oral hearing, or waive the hearing requirement and render a decision based upon the written submissions of the parties.[117] In practice, the tribunal will usually forgo the hearing requirement. If the tribunal intends to hold a hearing, the parties are provided with no less than fifteen days' notice.[118] The summary proceeding rules limit the hearings to a single session, except in situations considered essential by the tribunal.

The summary proceeding rules mandate that awards be issued on an expedited basis. For matters based upon written submissions, the tribunal is required to issue an award within ninety days from the date of the appointment of the arbitrator.[119] If the tribunal has undertaken a hearing, a decision must be rendered within thirty days from the date of the hearing.

j. CIETAC Financial Dispute Arbitration Rules

In April 2003, CIETAC adopted rules designed to provide a summary and prompt forum for resolving disputes related to financial transactions.[120] The CIETAC financial rules gives a broad and sweeping interpretation to the term "financial transactions," which is defined as referring to transactions arising between financial institutions, or arising between financial institutions and other natural or legal persons in the currency, capital, foreign exchange, gold, and insurance markets that relate to financing in both domestic and foreign currencies, and the assignment and sale of any and all types of financial instruments and documents denominated in both domestic and foreign currencies, including but not limited to: (1) loans; (2) deposit certificates; (3) guarantees; (4) letters of credit; (5) negotiable instruments; (6) fund transactions and fund trusts; (7) bonds; (8) collection and remittance of foreign currencies; (9) factoring; and (10) reimbursement agreements between banks.[121] As the above merely comprise examples of the types of financial dispute falling within the remit of the rules, there is ample scope for other financial related disputes to be referred to CIETAC under these rules. In order for the financial arbitration rules to apply, the disputing parties are required to specifically refer to the rules in their arbitration agreement, and a failure to so specify in the arbitration agreement may result in the application of the CIETAC's general rules of arbitration.

117. CIETAC Rules of Arbitration, art. 67.
118. CIETAC Rules of Arbitration, art. 68.
119. CIETAC Rules of Arbitration, art. 73.
120. Financial Dispute Arbitration Rules (adopted on April 4, 2003, by the China Council for the Promotion of International Trade/China Chamber of International Commerce).
121. Financial Dispute Arbitration Rules, art. 2. Securities-related disputes are excluded from the Rules.

Under the Financial Dispute Arbitration Rules, the parties may agree to a venue outside China and a procedure other than that detailed in the financial rules, which said procedure will prevail subject to the approval of the Commission. Arbitrators are required to be selected from CIETAC's dedicated panel of Chinese financial specialists.

The Financial Dispute Arbitration Rules apply a fast-track arbitration procedure. Notification of acceptance, or otherwise, of the Application for Arbitration must be issued by CIETAC within five days of its receipt of the application. A rejection of an application must be accompanied by the reasons therefor. The tribunal may consist of either a sole or three arbitrators—failure on the part of the parties designating the number of arbitrators will result in CIETAC making a determination. Unless otherwise agreed upon by the parties, where a sole arbitrator is to be appointed, such appointment must be jointly made by the parties, or alternatively, they must entrust the appointment to the Chairman of CIETAC, within seven business days of the date of receipt of the Notice of Arbitration. If three arbitrators are to be appointed, each party must effect an appointment within the foregoing seven-business-day period, while the parties are afforded a second seven-business-day period in which to jointly appoint the presiding arbitrator—or entrust such function to CIETAC. In default of the appointment of any arbitrator within prescribed time limits, such appointment will be effected by the CIETAC Chairman.

Consistent with its fast-track theme, the respondent is granted 15 business days to file its defense and counterclaim, in each case with supporting documentation. In turn, the claimant has 15 business days in which to file an answer to the respondent's counterclaim, if any. Considerable flexibility is afforded to the tribunal in the manner of conducting the arbitration—the rules provide that the arbitral tribunal may conduct the arbitration in "such manner as it considers appropriate" but must provide reasonable opportunity to each party to present his case. The parties may jointly agree on a time limit for the presentation of evidence, or, in default of agreement or a determination of such time by the tribunal, the parties must submit all evidence and submission documentation within three days prior to the date of the first oral hearing of the case.[122]

122. Subject to the agreement of the parties, the tribunal will determine whether or not to hold oral hearings. Notification of a hearing must be served on the parties at least ten business days before the scheduled hearing.

Subject to any mandatory rules of law governing the contract underlying the dispute, in determining the applicable substantive law, the tribunal must apply the law that it determines to be appropriate. In all cases, the arbitral tribunal must take into account the terms of the contract, the usages, and standard practices of the trade, and abide by the principles of fairness and reasonableness. An award must be rendered within 45 business days from the date on which the tribunal is formed—considerably faster than the nine-month period afforded under the CIETAC Arbitration Rules. If "necessary and justifiable" the CIETAC Secretary-General may extend the foregoing time limit by up to 15 business days. In respect of any matter not provided for in the financial rules, the CIETAC Arbitration Rules will apply.

4. Pre-Arbitration and Interim Protection of Property and Evidence

The protection of property and evidence pending an award or collection of an award may be a critical concern for an aggrieved party. The arbitration commission and tribunal do not have the coercive powers of judicial officers and are required to apply to the intermediate people's court for provisional protection of property and evidence. The Arbitration Law and the Civil Procedure Code provide remedies that are limited in application and usefulness.

a. Preservation of Property

(1) Pre-Arbitration Application. Although preservation measures are permitted to litigants in a civil proceeding under the Civil Procedure Code, the court is likely to refuse to hear a request for protection of property if the parties to the dispute are bound by a provision that provides that arbitration is the sole method of dispute resolution. If, on the other hand, an arbitration agreement reserves the right to pursue provisional remedies in court, an aggrieved party is required to file an application with the people's court as a separate action under the Civil Procedure Code.

The Civil Procedure Code provides that property preservation measures are heard on an ex parte basis, without the presence of the opposing party, and prior to the initiation of a formal action.[123] An ex parte request must be based upon "urgent circumstances" where the applicant is likely to suffer irreparable injury, and must be ruled on by the court within 48 hours of submission of the application. In such a case, the court is authorized to demand that a bond or other form of security be posted as a prerequisite to

123. Civil Procedure Code, arts. 92–96, 251–56.

issuing a preservation order. The surety is usually set in an amount to cover the value of the property to be preserved. The applicant is required to provide the court with a detailed description of the property and its location. The court may lift the preservation measures if the party in possession posts security in an equivalent amount. The Civil Procedure Code requires an applicant to file a complaint with the court within thirty days for foreign parties (fifteen days for domestic) after the court orders property preservation measures. If a formal complaint is not filed in the required time period, the court may cancel the preservation measures.[124] In practice, the Chinese courts are reluctant to issue preservation measures unless the property is at the risk of destruction or removal from the territory of the PRC.

(2) Pending Arbitration Application. If an agreement provides that all disputes between the parties are subject to arbitration, a party seeking preservation measures is required to file an application with the Commission. The Commission will then apply to the intermediate people's court, or a higher people's court at the provincial level, seeking an order to preserve property that may otherwise be disposed of, destroyed, or sequestered by a party in possession or control.[125] An application by the arbitration commission must be filed in the court where the property is located or where the owner of the property resides.[126] Upon receipt, the court will review the application to determine if it meets the conditions for property preservation and will not evaluate the substantive legal issues between the parties. Consistent with the Civil Procedure Code, the court may request that the applicant tender a guarantee as a condition of a preservation order.

Under the Arbitration Law, the provisional remedy appears to be limited to situations in which an award has been granted, or is likely to be granted, in favor of the party seeking preservation measures.[127] This remedy is also available only after the commencement of the arbitration proceedings, which assumes that all parties are on notice of the proceedings given that the selection of the panel is required before any issues are addressed. As a result, the value of this remedy is questionable given that the party in possession or control of the property is on notice that preservation methods may be sought. The aggrieved party runs the risk that the subject property will be

124. Civil Procedure Code, art. 252.

125. Arbitration Law, art. 28; CIETAC Rules of Arbitration, art. 23. For an analysis of CIETAC's use of the preservation measures, *see China Everbright Foreign Trade Hubei Corporation in an Arbitration for the Conservation of Property under the Letters of Credit Honored but Unpaid by a Bank,* CHINA LAW 85–88 (1996).

126. Arbitration Law Notice, art. 2; CIETAC Rules of Arbitration, art. 23.

127. Arbitration Law, art. 28.

destroyed or sequestered since all parties are on notice of the claims and issues pertaining to the claim.

b. Preservation of Evidence

The Arbitration Law and CIETAC Rules of Arbitration provide measures for the protection of evidence after the commencement of an arbitration proceeding.[128] A party to an arbitration proceeding may request that the Commission apply to the intermediate people's court for an order to preserve or protect evidence that is susceptible to destruction.[129] The application must be filed with the intermediate court in the location where the evidence is purportedly located.[130] Because notice of the application process is known to the party in possession of the evidence in question, the value of this procedure is questionable.

5. Cancellation of Arbitration Awards

A party unhappy with an arbitration award may request that an intermediate level people's court issue an order canceling an arbitration award. An application to cancel an award must be made within six months of receipt of the award.[131] Under Article 58 of the Arbitration Law, a court may set aside an award in the following circumstances:

(1) There is no arbitration agreement between the parties
(2) Items for arbitration were not within the scope of the arbitration agreement or were those upon which the commission had no right to arbitrate
(3) The establishment of the tribunal or arbitration procedures are in contravention of legal proceedings
(4) The evidence upon which the arbitration award is based is forged
(5) The other party has concealed evidence to the degree that fairness has been affected
(6) The arbitrators have engaged in misconduct[132]

The court has two months to render a decision on an application to cancel an award. If the court agrees to cancel the award, the award is void and can no longer be relied upon for enforcement in China or in other countries.

---

128. CIETAC Rules of Arbitration, art. 23. Under the amended 1998 amendments to Article 23 of the CIETAC Rules, an aggrieved party may apply to a lower-level people's court.
129. Arbitration Law, art. 46.
130. Arbitration Law, art. 68; CIETAC Rules of Arbitration, art. 23.
131. Arbitration Law, art. 59.
132. Arbitration Law, art. 58. Note that the cancellation procedures were adopted in the Arbitration Law and are not set forth in the Civil Procedure Code.

6. Award Enforcement Standards and Procedures

The enforcement of arbitration awards in China may be categorized into three distinct types of awards: awards issued in foreign countries, which are enforceable under the New York Convention; foreign-related awards governed by Article 260 of the Civil Procedure Code; and awards issued by domestic arbitration commissions governed by Article 217 of the Civil Procedure Code.

a. New York Convention Awards

An arbitration award issued in a contracting state is enforceable in China under the New York Convention.[133] The purpose of the New York Convention is to facilitate and stabilize international business transactions by promoting the enforcement of foreign arbitration disputes resulting from international commercial transactions and was adopted by China effective April 22, 1987. At the time China acceded to the New York Convention, it issued a "commercial" reservation, which limits the enforcement to awards involving commercial matters rendered in contracting states.[134] China will not enforce noncommercial arbitration awards.

China also made a reservation based upon reciprocity declaring that it will only enforce awards under the New York Convention that are rendered in other contracting states. The recognition of arbitral awards in countries that are not parties to the New York Convention may be enforced under China's Civil Procedure Code.[135]

The Convention directs that "each Contracting State shall recognize arbitral awards as binding and enforce them." A court must "confirm the award unless it finds one of the grounds for refusal or deferral of recognition or enforcement of the award specified in the Convention."[136]

b. Article 260: Foreign-Related Awards

The parties to an arbitration are required by the Arbitration Law to implement the award.[137] In a case in which there is no time limit for the execution

133. *See* Decision on China Joining the Convention on the Recognition and Enforcement of Foreign Arbitral Awards (adopted on December 2, 1986, by the Standing Comm. of the National People's Congress).

134. New York Convention, art. I. The United States has lodged a similar reservation.

135. Civil Procedure Code, art. 268. Article 268 addresses only the enforcement of foreign judgments. In practice, the Civil Procedure Code may be invoked to enforce an arbitration award rendered in a noncontracting country. *See* Guiguo Wang, *supra* note 7, at 42.

136. New York Convention, art. III (V); 9 U.S.C. § 207. The grounds for refusal of recognition are set forth in Article 260 of the Civil Procedure Code.

137. Arbitration Law, art. 62; CIETAC Rules of Arbitration, art. 63; Civil Procedure Code, art. 217 (domestic arbitration), 259 (foreign-related arbitration).

of the award, the parties are required to implement the award immediately.[138] If the losing party refuses to abide by the terms of the award, including the payment of money or delivery of property, the prevailing party may seek to enforce the foreign-related award before an intermediate-level people's court.[139] The prevailing party may also apply to a foreign court having jurisdiction over the defendant or its property for the enforcement of the award.

An arbitration award is final, and the court has no jurisdiction to address a parties' dispute that has been properly addressed in an arbitration proceeding.[140] However, under Article 260 of the Civil Procedure Code, the court will not issue a judgment enforcing a foreign-related arbitral award if it can be demonstrated that

(1) The parties never entered into an agreement for arbitration
(2) The party against whom the award was rendered was not notified of the arbitral proceedings or was unable to state its position to the arbitration tribunal, through no fault of its own[141]
(3) The composition of the arbitration tribunal violates the tribunal's rules or the proceedings do not conform to the tribunal's rules;[142] or

138. CIETAC Rules of Arbitration, art. 63.

139. Arbitration Law, art. 62; Civil Procedure Code, arts. 217, 259. The intermediate people's court is a court at the national level. A higher people's court at the provincial level is equal to the intermediate court at the national level for purposes of enforcement.

140. Arbitration Law, art. 9.

141. This rule is consistent with Article V(1)(b) of the New York Convention. *See Anhui Provincial Import and Export Corp. v. Hart Enterprises International, Inc.*, 1996 U.S. Dist. LEXIS 6041. In the *Hart Enterprises* case, the U.S. District Court for the Southern District of New York held that notice received by facsimile and by express mail from CIETAC to a U.S.-based defendant was sufficient notice to meet the due process requirements under the New York Convention. The District Court upheld a default award against the defendant for failing repeatedly to reply to notices of CIETAC. *See also Party Had Proper Notice of Arbitration: Confirms $1.8 Million Award,* MEALEY'S INT'L ARBITRATION REP. No. 5 (May 1996), available in Lexis, INTLAW Library, MEALEY File.

142. The Hong Kong Supreme Court rejected a defendant's objections to a CIETAC award that was rendered by a tribunal consisting of arbitrators from CIETAC Shenzhen, as opposed to CIETAC Beijing as required by the parties' contract. In the case of *China Nanhai Oil Joint Service Corp. (Shenzhen Branch) v. Gee Tai Holdings Co. Ltd.*, the court ruled that although CIETAC made a technical error, the defendant is estopped from raising the issue given that it never complained or petitioned the Commission or tribunal for relief during the proceeding. The court reasoned that under the New York Convention, the defendant had a duty of good faith to raise its objections to the formation of the arbitral tribunal prior to the enforcement phase of the proceeding. *See Hong Kong Supreme Court Enforces Award Despite Technicality,* 10 MEALEY'S INT'L ARBITRATION REP. No. 8 (August 1995), available on Lexis, INTLAW Library, MEALEY File. The Court of Appeals of Hong Kong in the case of *Logy Enterprises Ltd. v. Haikou City Bonded Area Wansen Products Trading Co.*, 1997-2 HKC 481, rejected a losing party's bias challenge to a CIETAC award on the grounds that the court was not in a position to evaluate whether an appointed arbitrator had the potential to improperly influence the outcome of a case based upon his employment with a Chinese government agency that provided an inspection certificate at issue in the case. The court reasoned that the Commission was in a better position to evaluate whether an arbitrator was impartial. *See Award Survives Bias Claim Challenge,* 12 MEALEY'S INT'L ARBITRATION REP. No. 11 (November 1997), available on Lexis at INTLAW Library, MEALEY File. *See also China Agribusiness Development Corporation v. Balli Trading,* Queen's Bench Division (Commercial Court), January 20, 1997, available on Lexis at INTLAW Library, ENGCAS File (court rejected argument that arbitration clause was invalid because it referred to CIETAC's former rules of arbitration).

(4) The dispute is not covered by the arbitration clause, or the institution had no authority to arbitrate the dispute[143]

A Chinese court may not refuse to enforce an award unless the opposing party can substantiate one of the conditions set forth in Article 260.

A Chinese court will also deny enforcement of an arbitration award if it finds that the award is contrary to the PRC's social and public interest.[144] In the event the court refuses to enforce an arbitral award, the parties have the option to either return to arbitration, if the parties' agreement provides for arbitration, or to initiate an action in the people's court.[145] There is no right to an appeal to a higher court with respect to an order for nonenforcement.

The nonenforcement provisions of Article 260 will not result in an invalidation of the underlying award. The award continues to be legally effective, and enforcement may be attempted in other countries. In contrast, a successful application under the cancellation procedures under Article 58 of the Arbitration Law results in the invalidation of the arbitral award.

c. Article 217: Domestic Awards

Article 217 sets forth the standards for nonenforcement of domestic arbitration awards. Under this section, the Civil Procedure Code adds three additional reasons for the courts to refuse to enforce an award, including circumstances in which the court finds insufficient evidence to support the tribunal's factual determinations, error in the application of the law, or arbitrator misconduct.[146] Pursuant to Article 217, the courts may evaluate the sufficiency of the evidence and the application of the laws by the domestic arbitration tribunals, i.e., the merits of the case. The differences in standards for enforcement of domestic and foreign-related arbitrations has been much criticized by Chinese legal scholars.[147]

---

143. Civil Procedure Code, art. 260.

144. Civil Procedure Code, art. 260; Civil Law, art. 142. Article V (2) of the New York Convention provides that "recognition and enforcement of an arbitral award may also be refused if . . . the recognition or enforcement of the award would be contrary to the public policy of that country."

145. Civil Procedure Code, art. 261.

146. Civil Procedure Code, art. 217. The court in *Huaxing Development Company v. Xianmen Dongfen Rubber Factory, et al.,* held that Article 217 (4) applies to foreign-related arbitrations as well as domestic arbitrations. The court found that Article 237, which is the first provision under the special rules for foreign parties, provides that the other provisions will apply in the absence of specific provisions. This reasoning allowed the court to find that a CIETAC award was based upon insufficient evidence. *See Selected Cases of the People's Courts,* China Legal Application Institution, Supreme People's Court.

147. *See* Guiguo Wang, *supra* note 7, at 41 n. 173.

d. Enforcement Procedures

The time limit for the application for enforcement of an arbitration award under the Civil Procedure Code is one year if the applicant is an individual and six months if the applicant is a legal person or other type of organization.[148] The court of proper jurisdiction for enforcement of an arbitral award is the intermediate people's court at the place where the person against whom enforcement is sought is domiciled or place of residence if his or her domicile is different from his place of residence; or the intermediate people's court where the losing party's assets are located. If the award is a New York Convention award, the intermediate people's court having jurisdiction is where the losing party maintains its domicile, residence, or principal place of business, or at the location of its assets.

The enforcement application must identify the parties, their addresses, and role in the arbitration; the status of the arbitration proceeding, including a brief statement describing the tribunal, the arbitration proceeding, and the award; the subject matter of enforcement, including quantity and location of property, if applicable, and the location of assets, if any; and a statement describing the opposing party's failure to implement the terms of the award and documentary evidence concerning a failure to execute the award. The application should also include a copy of the arbitration award, the arbitration agreement, and a Chinese translation of any document submitted to the court.

In August 1995, in recognition of the adverse consequences of local protectionism and with a view to stamping out the practice of local protectionism, the Supreme People's Court issued its Notice on Several Issues Concerning the Treatment of Certain Aspects of Foreign-Related Arbitration and Foreign Arbitration by the People's Courts[149] (the "1995 SPC Arbitration Enforcement Notice"). The 1995 SPC Arbitration Enforcement Notice established a court reporting system with respect to (a) the invalidity of arbitration agreements in foreign-related commercial and maritime cases, (b) the nonacceptance of foreign-related commercial or maritime cases, (c) the nonenforcement of foreign-related arbitration awards, and (d) the refusal of applications for the recognition and enforcement of international arbitration awards under the New York Convention or reciprocal arrangements. Under the reporting system, in foreign-related commercial or maritime case, if the people's court finds that an arbitration agreement between the disputing parties is invalid or otherwise unenforceable, the court must report its findings

148. Civil Procedure Code, art. 219.
149. Issued by the Supreme People's Court on, and effective from, August 28, 1995.

for approval to the higher people's court before rendering judgment in the case. If the higher people's court concurs with the findings of the lower court, it must in turn report its findings to the Supreme People's Court for approval. In such circumstances, the lower people's court may not give a decision in the case until the Supreme People's Court has issued its approval or directed otherwise. Similarly, where a court finds that an application for the enforcement of a foreign-related award should be refused due to the occurrence of one or more of the events or circumstances detailed at Article 260 of the Civil Procedure Code, or where a court finds that an application for the recognition and enforcement of an international award should be refused under the New York Convention or other international treaty or convention to which China has acceded or under the terms of reciprocal arrangements, the court must not render a decision in the matter but, rather, must report its findings to the higher people's court for approval. Again, if the latter court concurs with the findings of the lower court, the matter must be reported to the Supreme People's Court for a reply. Therefore, in no case may a court reject the validity of an arbitration agreement involving foreign elements, or refuse enforcement of a foreign-related or international award without the prior approval of the Supreme People's Court.

Subsequently, in November 1998, the Supreme People's Court issued its Regulations Concerning the Issue of Fees and Determination Periods in Applications for the Recognition and Enforcement of International Arbitral Awards,[150] which provide, *inter alia*, that applications for the recognition and enforcement of international arbitration awards must be decided within two months following acceptance of the case.[151] The notice also reiterates that where the court determines that an application for recognition and enforcement of an international award ought to be refused, the decision must be referred to the Supreme People's Court in accordance with the 1995 SPC Arbitration Enforcement Notice.

Despite the prolonged delays and difficulties encountered by numerous parties, there are numerous examples in which enforcement has proceeded in a manner envisaged by the New York Convention, i.e., unhindered by judicial incompetence or local protectionism. In *Food Industries' Planning & Servicing Ltd. vs. China Hua Yang Technology and Trade Corporation*,[152]

150. *See* Supreme People's Court Regulations Concerning the Issue of the Fees and the Review Period for the Recognition and Enforcement of Foreign Arbitral Awards (adopted on October 21, 1998, by the Supreme People's Court) (hereinafter the "Court Fees and Review Period Regulations").

151. Court Fees and Review Period Regulations, art. IV.

152. Beijing First Intermediate People's Court, November 17, 1997, (1995) Yi Zhong Zhi Zi No. 31.

a dispute had arisen between the plaintiff and the defendant regarding a turnkey contract for the construction and commissioning of a fruit juice plant. Arising from an arbitration agreement contained in the contract entered into by the parties, in 1995, the Arbitration Institute of the Stockholm Chamber of Commerce rendered an award in favor of the plaintiff; namely, the respondent (the defendant in these proceedings) was ordered to pay substantial sums plus interest to the claimant (the plaintiff herein). The failure of the defendant to comply with the terms of the arbitral award ultimately led to the institution of proceedings for enforcement of the award in China. In its judgment, the court found that the recognition and enforcement of the arbitral award fell within the remit of the New York Convention and that none of the circumstances detailed at Article V(1) and (2) of the New York Convention that could give rise to a refusal to recognize and enforce the award. In consequence, the court ruled to recognize and enforce the award pursuant to Article 140 (first paragraph) and Article 269 of the Civil Procedure Law. The defendant was ordered to comply with the terms of the arbitral award within 15 days from the date of the written ruling of the court and to pay the fees pertaining to the enforcement proceedings.

The Supreme People's Court also prohibits the lower courts from charging a separate fee for the recognition and the enforcement of awards, and that all fees—except for court filing fees not to exceed RMB500 ($61.00)—are to be refunded to an applicant if the court decides not to enforce an award.[153]

e. Obstacles to Enforcement

Although the Chinese courts are bound by the law to recognize arbitration awards, the courts have been slow to enforce awards that may affect local interests and institutions. This is especially true if the award is against a large local enterprise that is important to the community.[154] However, foreign parties are not alone in their problems with local protectionism. Chinese enterprises based outside the nonperformer's territory have also encountered difficulties obtaining the cooperation of the local courts. In addition, Chinese courts in one city have unreasonably resisted assisting the courts in other cities where local interests are at stake.[155]

---

153. Court Fees and Review Period Regulations, arts. I, II, III.

154. *See* M. Bersani, *Enforcement of Arbitration Awards in China,* China Business Review 6 (May-June 1992).

155. *Id.* at 7–8. The author discusses a case involving a Beijing court's efforts to obtain the assistance of a court in the remote Ningxia Province to enforce a CIETAC award against a Ningxia-based company. Beijing court personnel traveled to Ningxia in an effort to secure the local court's assistance, but they continued to refuse to assist in the enforcement efforts.

Another obstacle confronting enforcement is the lack of efficiency with the courts resulting from misunderstanding the law, lack of trained court personnel, and lack of funds for court personnel to accomplish enforcement tasks. Enforcement problems also result from administrative interference by local government officials with judicial proceedings, and overt corruption between the enterprise ignoring the arbitral award and the judiciary.

The Court Fees and Review Period Regulations, noted above, are designed to counter many of the obstacles that confront foreign parties that desire to enforce arbitral awards. Whether the new regulations are effective is left for observation.

7. Drafting an Arbitration Clause in China

CIETAC has made phenomenal strides in its efforts to become a world-class arbitration institution in a short time span and during a period in which China is itself undergoing significant social and economic changes. CIETAC has approved foreign professionals to act as arbitrators, allowed for the use of the English language to be selected as the language of proceedings, and streamlined the time requirements to allow for the prompt and effective resolution of disputes. Nevertheless, foreign parties should first attempt to negotiate an arbitration clause that provides that the selected forum be located outside of China in a third country with a recognized and well-developed arbitration system including, but not limited to, the Arbitration Institute of the Stockholm Chamber of Commerce, the Court of Arbitration of the Zurich Chamber of Commerce, the London Court of International Arbitration, or the International Court of Arbitration for the International Chamber of Commerce in Paris.[156]

This recommendation is based upon a number of institutional problems with CIETAC that make it a less than perfect forum.[157] First, CIETAC has a limited panel of arbitrators from which disputing parties must select

---

156. Other well-respected arbitration institutions include the Hong Kong International Arbitration Center and the Singapore International Arbitration Center. For investment disputes in which the PRC is a party to the agreement, the parties may consider arbitration before the International Center for the Settlement of Investment Disputes of the World Bank in Washington, D.C. If the parties are not nationals of the United States, or if the Chinese party is amenable to arbitration in the U.S., the parties may wish to select the American Arbitration Association as a forum. Prior to the selection of any forum, it is advisable that the party drafting the contract obtain a current copy of the arbitration institution's rules and procedures. In addition, all arbitration institutions provide sample standard clauses to be inserted into agreements.

157. For an interesting case involving one company's experience with CIETAC, *see* E. Iritani, *A Local Firm's Baffling Trip Through China's Arbitration System*, L. A. Times (Dec. 26, 2003), available online at http://www.latimes.com (in a politically sensitive real property matter, a CIETAC tribunal decided "not to decide" after two years of proceeding and delay).

arbitrators. If a person is not on the list, he or she cannot be selected by the parties. In complex matters involving special expertise, this can be problematic, especially in cases involving foreign law questions or matters involving technical expertise. In addition, CIETAC will almost always choose a Chinese national as the presiding arbitrator for a tribunal composed of three arbitrators. The 2-1 balance in favor of the Chinese party is a hometown advantage that many foreigners find unpalatable.

Further, CIETAC rules expressly allow the tribunal to render a decision based upon the principles of "fairness and reasonableness."[158] A "fair" result may not be consistent with the parties' contract or the applicable law. The emphasis on equity versus the law is the historical practice of CIETAC and its predecessor organizations (FTAC and FETAC). Thus, CIETAC arbitrators can act as *amiable compositeurs*. In contrast, both the ICC rules and the AAA International Arbitration Rules provide that a tribunal is not allowed to decide a case as *amiable compositeur* or *ex aequo et bono* unless the parties have expressly authorized it to do so. Because of the uncertainty created by this obligation, and until such time that the rule is abandoned or clarified, a foreign party would be better served by a tribunal that is under no obligation to assess issues on the basis of equity, but rather one that is required to evaluate the dispute based upon the selected substantive law and the terms and conditions of the parties' contract.

In addition, the uncertainty created by the Foreign Law Firm Regulations and Foreign Law Firm Implementing Regulations justifies avoiding arbitration in China altogether, if at all possible. Under the current regulations concerning foreign law firms, a party to an arbitration in China may be denied the right to employ the services of a qualified foreign lawyer or foreign law firm. Whether China will ever amend its arbitration system to be more consistent with international practices is left for observation.

If a party finds that it is necessary to agree to arbitrate a dispute before CIETAC, the following critical points should be included in an arbitration clause:

(1) That the language of the proceedings be in English or the language of the foreign party
(2) That the presiding arbitrator either selected by the parties or appointed by CIETAC be a citizen of a third country[159]

---

158. Arbitration Law, art. 7; CIETAC Rules of Arbitration, art. 53.

159. Neither the Arbitration Law nor the CIETAC Rules of Arbitration preclude the parties from reaching an agreement that the presiding arbitrator be of a neutral nationality. For clarification, the provision should also specify if residents of HKSAR or Macao are deemed to be from a third country.

(3) That an aggrieved party has the right to seek property preservation methods directly before the courts without first filing an application for arbitration[160]

160. Under the Arbitration Law and CIETAC's Rules of Arbitration, a party is not expressly granted or prohibited the right to independently seek measures to protect property or evidence pending a final arbitration award. Under the law and the rules, the parties are required to request that the tribunal seek court relief. The right to seek judicial relief for provisional remedies and conservatory measures is recognized under the United Nations Commission on International Trade Law (UNCITRAL) Model Law on International Commercial Arbitration, art. 9, which provides: "It is not incompatible with an arbitration agreement for a party to request, before or during arbitral proceedings, from a court an interim measure of protection and for a court to grant such a measure." This rule may conflict with articles 257 and 258 of the Civil Procedure Code, which prohibit a party to an arbitration clause from filing an action in the courts. A sample arbitration provision is set forth in Appendix A.

Practice Tips for Arbitration in China

A poorly worded provision and/or a poorly advised client may result in, among other things, the following: invalidation of an arbitration clause resulting in litigation in local courts; a proceeding under an arbitration clause that gives one party an unfair advantage over the other party; dispute resolution procedures that are excessively expensive; and a client that is unhappy with his or her transactional lawyers. Every transactional lawyer should take the time to secure the feedback of a lawyer experienced with arbitration in China before agreeing to a particular arbitration provision. What is it like to arbitrate before a particular institution? What is the availability of qualified arbitrators? What is the practical impact of general and specific language in an arbitration clause? What are the client's options? What factors go into the selection process? An assessment of the following factors should be considered in any decision to select a particular arbitral institution:

- ✔ Location
- ✔ Reputation
- ✔ Facilities
- ✔ Language/translation capabilities
- ✔ Fee structure
- ✔ Case management practices
- ✔ Support from local courts and government
- ✔ Maturity of arbitration rules
- ✔ Availability of qualified counsel in the forum
- ✔ Availability of qualified arbitrators in the forum
- ✔ Availability of summary procedures
- ✔ Experience with complex projects/transactions

In preparing an arbitration clause, the drafting lawyer should keep in mind the following general suggestions:

- ✔ Do not blindly accept the opposing parties' suggestions for an arbitration forum
- ✔ Do review and advise the client on the current rules of arbitration for the proposed arbitral institution
- ✔ Do advise the client on the benefits and burdens of the proposed arbitral institution
- ✔ Do advise the client on the enforcement record for arbitration awards in the opposing parties' jurisdiction(s)
- ✔ Do negotiate the specific terms concerning choice of forum and choice of law

(*Continued*)

(*Continued from previous page*)

- ✔ Depending upon the particular circumstances, do negotiate the terms and conditions that amend or supplement the proposed institution's rules of arbitration in regard to
  - ✔ arbitrator selection procedures, including a requirement of neutrality of nationality for the presiding arbitrator
  - ✔ arbitrator selection from outside an approved list
  - ✔ discovery and evidence gathering (such as consent to the application of the Rules on the Taking of Evidence in International Commercial Arbitration adopted by the International Bar Association)
  - ✔ exchange of lists of witnesses and documents at a time well in advance of hearings
  - ✔ size of tribunal in relationship to size of claim
  - ✔ prohibition on punitive damages
  - ✔ prohibition on the power of the arbitrators to render a decision based upon equity principles
  - ✔ awards of attorney fees and costs
  - ✔ access to the courts for provisional relief
  - ✔ language of the proceedings

In addition to preparing a well-drafted and well-thought-out arbitration provision, many lawyers actively involved with international arbitration will agree that the selection of an arbitrator is the most important step in an arbitration proceeding. In choosing a party arbitrator, counsel should look for an arbitrator that has the following qualities:

- ✔ Working knowledge of applicable evidentiary rules and an appreciation of the concept of burden of proof
- ✔ Working knowledge of the applicable law involved in the transaction
- ✔ Current experience working in the country that is the site of the project or transaction as either a practicing lawyer or arbitrator
- ✔ Proven experience in case management
- ✔ Comparative experience before different arbitral institutions
- ✔ Experience or an understanding of the type of technology involved in the dispute, if a technical issue is in question

The overall lesson to learn is to exercise common sense and foresight in preparing an arbitration clause; otherwise, the parties will end up disputing their dispute resolution procedures before they can resolve their underlying dispute. The next most important lesson is to carefully choose an arbitrator that will play a fair, inquisitive, and decisive role on the panel of arbitrators.

Key Laws and Regulations

Arbitration Law of the People's Republic of China (adopted on August 31, 1994, at the 9th Sess. of the Standing Comm. of the 8th NPC)

Arbitration Rules of the China International Economic and Trade Arbitration Commission (adopted on September 4, 1995, and amended on May 6, 1998, by the China International Chamber of Commerce and as amended by CIETAC on September 5, 2000)

Notice of the Office of the State Council on Clarification of Several Issues Concerning the Implementation of the Arbitration Law of the People's Republic of China (promulgated on June 8, 1996, by the office of the State Council)

Arbitration Rules of the China Maritime Arbitration Commission (promulgated September 4, 1995, by the China Maritime Arbitration Commission, revised and adopted on November 22, 2000, by the China International Chamber of Commerce)

Notice of the Supreme People's Court of China on the Implementation of the Convention on the Recognition and Enforcement of Foreign Arbitral Awards (issued on April 10, 1987, by the Supreme People's Court)

Decision on China Joining the Convention on the Recognition and Enforcement of Foreign Arbitral Awards (adopted on December 2, 1986, by the Standing Comm. of the National People's Congress)

Notice on Several Issues Concerning the Treatment of Certain Aspects of Foreign-Related Arbitration and Foreign Arbitration by the People's Courts (Issued by the Supreme People's Court on, and effective from August 28, 1995)

Supreme People's Court Regulations Concerning the Issue of the Fees and the Review Period for the Recognition and Enforcement of Foreign Arbitral Awards (adopted on October 21, 1998, at the 1029 Session of the Judicial Committee of the Supreme People's Court, Fa Shi [1998] No. 28 with effect from November 21, 1998)

Financial Dispute Arbitration Rules (adopted on April 4, 2003, by the China Council for the Promotion of International Trade/China Chamber of International Commerce)

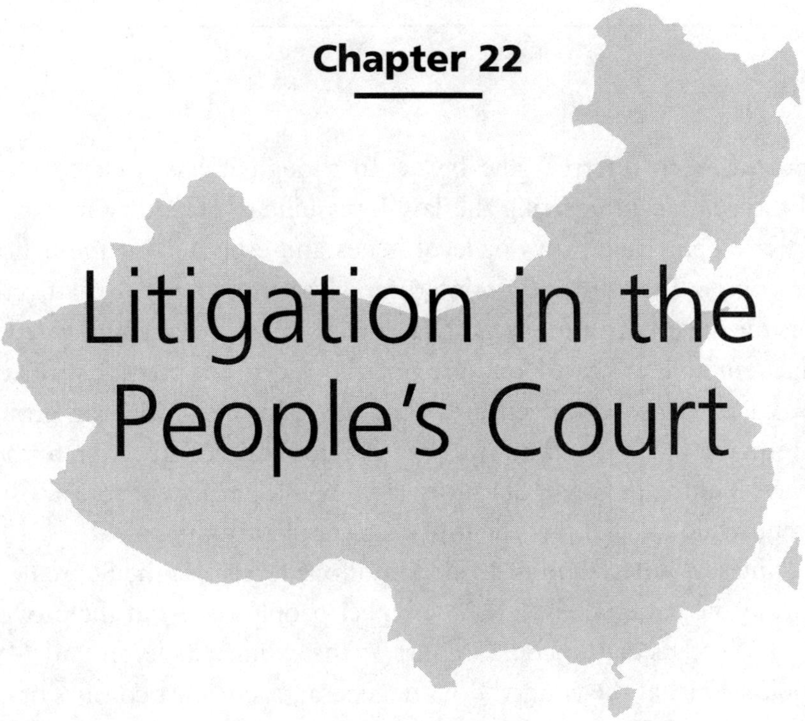

Chapter 22

Litigation in the People's Court

The Chinese court system has gone through dramatic changes in the past few years, and has become more professional and better suited to meet the demands of an economy in transition. However, much work needs to be done in order to give Chinese citizens and foreign investors the comfort level they need to rely on the judicial system in China. As more foreign parties are drawn into local litigation and/or seek remedies in Chinese courts for commercial matters, an understanding of the court structure and procedures is important. This chapter addresses the judicial system of China, and specifically the court and trial procedures.

A. Court Structure: Supreme People's Court

The Supreme People's Court is the highest judicial organ in the PRC and is specifically authorized by the Constitution.[1] The Supreme People's Court supervises the administration of justice by the local people's courts. Although the Supreme People's Court issues directives for the purpose of guiding China's lower courts in applying a particular law or with respect to judicial administration, there is no formal system of judicial precedent.[2] The court does not

1. Const., art. 127.

2. *See* Liu, *"Legal Precedents" with Chinese Characteristics: Published Cases in the Gazette of the Supreme People's Court,* 5 J. Chinese L. 107 (1991) (discussing the role of published decisions in China and the development of the law). The majority of the decisions published by the Supreme People's Court (since commencing in 1985) have focused on providing guidance to the lower courts for purposes of uniformity in sentencing standards in criminal cases. *Id.* 128–129. *See also* A. Chen, An Introduction

have the powers to interpret the law even though it has, in recent years, assumed the role of interpreting the law by issuing explanatory memoranda with respect to particular laws or legal issues and especially at the behest of the lower courts. The authority to interpret is vested with the legislative bodies such as the government ministries. The people's courts are empowered only to adjudicate individual cases, and are not allowed to set precedent for other courts or cases. This system ensures that no individual judge or group of judges can make the law and allows the NPC to retain control and authority over the law-making process.[3] Statutory law plays a prominent role in China's legal system while judicial precedent plays a supplementary role.

The Chinese court system is divided into four levels: (1) the Supreme People's Court at the national level; (2) the higher people's court at the provincial level; (3) the intermediate people's court at the municipal level; and (4) the basic people's court at the county level. In general, each court consists of criminal, civil, economic, and administrative divisions. In addition, specialized courts have been established within the court systems in every major city in China. For example, Intellectual Property Tribunals have been established by the Beijing Municipal Intermediate People's Court and the Beijing Municipal Higher People's Court. There are also special courts established as separate branches, such as the Maritime Court,[4] Military Court, and Railway Transport Court, which are under the supervision of the Supreme People's Court.

In contrast to the U.S. federal-state court distinction, there is one court system in China. Each major city in China has two levels of courts: a basic level and an intermediate level. The provincial high court supervises both. Above the provincial level is the centralized Supreme People's Court located in Beijing, which has appellate jurisdiction over all courts in China. Beijing, Shanghai, Tianjin, and Chongqing are the four municipalities on an administrative level similar to a province that have provincial-level courts as well as two lower-level courts.

In theory, all courts in China exercise judicial autonomy, and are not subject to interference by state administrative agencies, public organizations,

---

TO THE LEGAL SYSTEM OF THE PEOPLE'S REPUBLIC OF CHINA (1992). Chen states: "The typical judgment of a Chinese court is short and does not set out lines or steps of legal reasoning and logical analysis in a way as detailed as in the judgments in common law courts. Relevant statutory provisions may be referred to, but the precise relationship between them in their application to the case will not usually be discussed at length. As there is no established doctrine of precedent, case law will seldom be referred to in the judgment. Lawyers' submissions are not usually responded to in the judgment. Dissenting judgments are not allowed." *Id.* at 114.

3. *See* Baker, *Forgotten Legal China*, 17 HOUSTON J. INT'L L. 363, 367–68 (1995).

4. *See* Detailed Regulations of the Supreme People's Court Governing Maritime Litigation Involving Foreigners (issued on January 31, 1986, by the Supreme People's Court), *reprinted in* CHINA LAWS FOR FOREIGN BUSINESS (CCH), Business Regulation ¶ 19-513.

or individuals.[5] However, the Supreme People's Court, and the judicial system in general, is subject to the supervision of the NPC and the NPC Standing Committee with respect to administrative issues, the political direction of judicial policy, and the general application of the law.[6]

In 1991, the NPC adopted the Code of Civil Procedure governing the court process in civil actions.[7] Prior to 1910, China had no formal civil procedure law and only developed such a law after the Western Powers pressured China to modify and improve its legal system as an incentive to relinquish extraterritorial privileges.[8] In contrast, there is evidence of criminal codes as far back as the Qin Dynasty (221–206 BCE).[9] The 1991 Civil Procedure Code is a by-product of the ongoing legal reform resulting from China's Open Door policy.

A foreign party has the right to file a complaint for relief in the people's court, and a foreign national or foreign entity initiating or responding to legal action in the people's court has the same litigation rights and obligations as Chinese citizens.[10] The Civil Procedure Code has a specific section

5. Const., arts. 126, 128; *See also* Code of Civil Procedure of the People's Republic of China, art. 6 (adopted April 9, 1991, by the 4th Session of the Standing Committee of the 7th National People's Congress), *reprinted in* CHINA LAWS FOR FOREIGN BUSINESS (CCH), Business Regulation ¶ 19-201 (hereinafter "Civil Procedure Code"); Opinions of the Supreme People's Court on Several Questions Concerning the Application of the Civil Procedure Law of the People's Republic of China (issued by the Supreme People's Court on July 14, 1992). One writer noted that the independence of the judiciary "represents a great breakthrough in Chinese legal history, which is replete with examples of court decisions resulting from personal influence." Sang, *China's Civil Procedure Law: A New Guide for Dispute Resolution in China,* 26 INT'L LAW. 413, 416 (1992). A survey of lawyers and judges found that 80 percent believed that "judicial independence" means freedom from interference from administrative organs and not the CCP. P. CORNE, FOREIGN INVESTMENT IN CHINA: THE ADMINISTRATIVE LEGAL SYSTEM 252, fn. 33 (1997).

6. Const., art. 128. The people's courts, including the Supreme People's Court, are not allowed to interpret the Constitution. Only the NPC and its Standing Committee have the power.

7. Adopted April 9, 1991, by the 4th Session of the Standing Committee of the 7th National People's Congress. The Civil Procedure Code replaced the former civil procedure law that was adopted in 1982. For an analysis of the Civil Procedure Code, *see* Sang, *supra* note 5, at 413.

8. A civil procedure law was developed by Shen Jianben, a jurist appointed by Emperor Guangxu in 1902. *See supra* Chapter 2, Development of the Chinese Legal System, § B, fn. 35 and accompanying text. The Nationalist Government enacted a civil procedure law in 1936, which was abolished when the CCP took power. In the 1950s, the NPC drafted a civil procedure law, which was never promulgated. Sang, *supra* note 5 at 414.

9. Sang, *supra* note 5 at 414.

10. Civil Procedure Code, art. 5. One qualification to this rule of equal rights is if the foreign party's country imposes restrictions on Chinese citizens. In such a case, the people's court will exercise reciprocity and place the same restrictions on the foreigner litigant. In addition, foreign party actions will not be decided within any specific period of time. In contrast, in purely domestic actions, the court is required to render a decision within six months of filing. *Id.* at arts. 135, 250. Diplomatic corps may assert immunity under principles of international law. *Id.* at art. 239. Of particular concern for foreigners is the court's right to issue an injunction prohibiting a foreigner from leaving the country in unresolved civil cases. *See* Law of the People's Republic of China on the Control of Foreigners Entering and Leaving the Country (adopted on November 22, 1985, at the 13th Sess. of the Standing Comm. of the NPC), art. 23 (2), *reprinted in* CHINA LAWS FOR FOREIGN BUSINESS (CCH), Business Regulation ¶ 19-510. The fees/costs imposed for cases is addressed in the Measures for the Charging of Court Costs by the People's Court (adopted on June 29, 1989, by the Supreme People's Court), *reprinted at* CHINA LAWS FOR FOREIGN BUSINESS (CCH), Business Regulation ¶ 19-205.

designed for actions involving foreign parties. Whenever this section does not contain a specific provision dealing with a foreign party, all other provisions are deemed to apply.[11]

In addition to the Civil Procedure Code, the Supreme People's Court has adopted a set of interpretive provisions concerning the Code that provides guidance to the courts on the application of the civil procedure standards in China.[12] The SPC CPC Interpretation addresses a number of procedural issues including, *inter alia*, jurisdictional matters, participation of parties, evidence and preservation measures, the detailed procedures for the collection and objective verification of court investigated/collected evidence, the principles of *les ipsa loquitor* in tort cases, court mediation, expenses, procedures at first and second instance, and procedures for presentation of evidence.

1. Procedural Issues in the People's Court

a. Jurisdictional Issues

Under the Civil Procedure Code, the parties to a contract involving foreign interests may include a choice of forum clause in their contract.[13] This provision is applicable only to disputes arising from a contract or property involving foreign relationships and is limited in application. For a dispute involving a Chinese-foreign equity joint venture, a Chinese-foreign cooperative joint venture, or a Chinese-foreign joint venture involving natural resources exploration and development in China, the people's court has mandatory jurisdiction in the absence of an arbitration clause, and the application of Chinese law is mandatory.[14] The forum chosen must also have substantial connections to the dispute.[15]

In the absence of a choice of forum clause, the local people's court has jurisdiction over a dispute in the locality where the following events occur: (1) the contract was signed or to be performed; (2) the objects of the litigation exist; (3) the property of a foreign defendant is located; or (4) any torts occurred.[16] A Chinese court may also exercise jurisdiction over a foreign

11. Civil Procedure Code, arts. 237–269.

12. Supreme People's Court Opinions on the Application of the Civil Procedure Code of the People's Republic of China (promulgated by the Supreme People's Court on, and effective from, July 14, 1992) (hereinafter the "SPC CPC Interpretation").

13. Civil Procedure Code, art. 244; *See also* General Principles of Civil Law of the People's Republic of China, art. 145 (adopted Apr. 12, 1986, at the 4th session of the 6th NPC, effective January 1, 1987), *reprinted in* CHINA LAWS FOR FOREIGN BUSINESS (CCH), Business Regulation ¶ 19-150. For a discussion concerning the development of the Civil Law, *see* J. Chen, From Administrative Authorization to Private Law: A Comparative Perspective of the Developing Civil Law of the People's Republic of China (1995).

14. Civil Procedure Code, art. 246.

15. Civil Procedure Code, art. 244.

16. Civil Procedure Code, art. 243.

party that fails to object to the court's jurisdiction or fails to appear in its defense.[17] Venue is not an issue in China's legal system. However, in the event of a jurisdictional dispute between people's courts, the disputing parties are required to resolve the matter through consultation or apply to a higher-level people's court in order to resolve issues concerning the proper forum.[18]

In general, the basic-level people's court has jurisdiction as a court of first instance of a dispute involving foreign interests.[19] However, an action involving "significant" or "major" issues concerning foreign parties may be filed directly with the intermediate people's court.[20] The intermediate people's court may also exercise jurisdiction as the court of first instance in cases of great importance to the region of the court or in situations where the Supreme People's Court has instructed the intermediate court to assert jurisdiction.[21] The Supreme People's Court has jurisdiction as the court of first instance over cases of great significance to the entire nation.[22]

The SPC CPC Interpretation provides further guidance on jurisdiction issues. Subject to statutory provisions regarding jurisdiction by level and by forum and provisions on exclusive jurisdiction, the parties to a written contract are free to therein identify the court exercising jurisdiction over their contract as being the court sited at (i) the plaintiff's domicile, (ii) the defendant's domicile, (iii) the place of implementation of the contract, (iv) the place of signing the contract, or (v) the location of the object of the lawsuit. Where there is ambiguity regarding the agreement of the parties on the issue of jurisdiction, then the dispute will be tried by the people's court located at the defendant's place of domicile or at the place where the contract is implemented. The following jurisdictional principles apply to specific contract or tort matters:

(1) Where a contractual dispute arises and the place for contractual performance is different from the places of domicile of both contracting parties, the court located in the defendant's place of domicile will exercise jurisdiction

17. Civil Procedure Code, art. 245.
18. Civil Procedure Code, art. 37.
19. Civil Procedure Code, art. 18.
20. Civil Procedure Code, art. 19. The Civil Procedure Code does not define the terms *major* or *significance*. However, the Administrative Litigation Law provides that the Intermediate People's Courts have jurisdiction in the first instance with respect to cases involving the verification of patent rights, customs matters, administrative decisions of the departments of the State Council, and other cases of importance and complexity. *See* Law of Administrative Litigation of the People's Republic of China (adopted on April 4, 1989, by the 2nd Sess. of the 7th NPC), arts. 13–14, *reprinted in* CHINA LAWS FOR FOREIGN BUSINESS (CCH), Business Regulation ¶ 19-558.
21. Civil Procedure Code, art. 19.
22. Civil Procedure Code, art. 21. The Supreme People's Court has exercised original jurisdiction only once in modern history, and that was for the trial of the "Gang of Four" following the Cultural Revolution. Clearly, the circumstances must be truly significant for the Supreme People's Court to step in and take control over a matter.

(2) In a contract for the sale and delivery of goods, the place for the delivery of the goods will be the *loci solutionis*. Where the parties have failed to stipulate the place for delivery, then the *loci solutionis* will be the place of delivery of the goods, i.e., the place where the purchaser must pick up the goods

(3) In an agency agreement, the place of dispatching the goods per the agreed means of dispatch, will be deemed the *loci solutionis*

(4) Where the *loci solutionis* stated in a sales contract differs from the place of delivery stated in the contract, then the *loci solutionis* will be that stated in the contract

(5) In a processing contract, the place for undertaking the processing will be the *loci solutionis*, unless otherwise agreed by the parties in the contract

(6) For leased property, articles, or real estate, the place of use of same is the *loci solutionis* unless otherwise agreed by the parties

(7) If, arising from an insurance contract, a dispute arises relating to insurance coverage of means of transport or goods under transport, jurisdiction will be exercised by the court located at the plaintiff's place of domicile or the place of registration of the agreed means of transport or the port of destination or the place where the insured event occurred

(8) In a dispute over payment under a commercial instrument, jurisdiction will be exercised by the people's court located at the location of disbursement stated in the instrument, or in the defendant's place of domicile. If the instrument fails to state the place of payment, then the place of payment will be deemed the place of domicile or business location of the drawee or his proxy

(9) Where a tort arises, jurisdiction may be exercised by the people's court located either at the defendant's place of domicile or the place where the tortious act occurred

(10) In a tort action arising from damage or personal injury caused by unsuitable or unqualified products, jurisdiction may be exercised by the court located at the place of manufacture, the place where the products are marketed, the place where the tort allegedly occurred, or the place of domicile of the defendant

(11) Jurisdiction over disputes relating to or arising from rail transport or rail transport contracts is exercised by the dedicated railway transportation courts

(12) In an application for a property preservation order, the court sited at the location of the property will have jurisdiction. If, following

> a successful property preservation order, (i) the applicant fails to institute civil proceedings within statutory time limits, and (ii) the party against whom the property reservation order was made suffers loss as a result of the making of the order, then the latter may initiate civil proceedings only before the court that exercised jurisdiction over the property preservation matter[23]

Where the court finds that the parties have entered into a valid written agreement for the resolution of the dispute via arbitration, then the court must refuse acceptance of the proceedings. In such case, the court is obliged to notify the plaintiff that the dispute in question may be resolved only by arbitration. However, if, notwithstanding the existence of an arbitration clause or agreement, the parties fail to identify the appropriate arbitration commission to exercise jurisdiction, or the clause or agreement is ambiguous or otherwise defective thereby rendering it invalid, then the court may accept the complaint and proceed with the litigation. If the defendant objects to the court's acceptance of a lawsuit on the grounds of invalidity of an arbitration clause, the defendant may require the court to issue a written decision on the matter. If both parties to judicial proceedings fail to notify the court of the existence of an agreement for arbitration, but instead prosecute and defend the case, the court will thereafter assert jurisdiction over the case.

To meet its WTO obligations, China adopted special jurisdictional rules governing foreign-related civil and commercial cases.[24] The SPC Foreign Litigation Regulations state that for matters involving foreign-related civil and the commercial disputes, the following courts will exercise jurisdiction as the court of first instance: (a) the people's courts established in economic and technological development zones, (b) the intermediate people's courts located in special economic zones, areas under special planning, municipalities (Beijing, Tianjin, Chongqing, and Shanghai), the capital cities of all provinces and autonomous regions, and (c) the higher people's courts. The decision of the courts in economic and technological development zones may be appealed to the local intermediate people's court. Decisions of the intermediate court at first instance may, of course, be appealed to the higher people's court.

23. SPC CPC Interpretation, arts. 17–31.

24. Regulation on Several Issues on Jurisdiction of Overseas Civil and Commercial Lawsuits, PRC Supreme People's Court Judicial Interpretation [2002] No. 5 (promulgated by the SPC on Feb. 25, 2002, and effective March 1, 2002) (hereinafter the "SPC Foreign Litigation Regulations").

The SPC Foreign Litigation Regulations address jurisdictional issues for five different types of cases, including the following: (a) cases involving the alleged infringement of rights contrary to the terms of a contract governed by foreign law, (b) disputes pertaining to letters of credit, (c) applications for the revocation, or recognition and enforcement of awards rendered by international arbitration, (d) cases relating to the alleged invalidity of clauses or agreements providing for arbitration in civil and commercial cases, and (e) cases for the recognition and enforcement of foreign court judgments or rulings.[25]

b. Participants in Civil Proceedings

Article 49 of the Civil Procedure Code requires that in civil proceedings, a legal person, i.e., a corporation, must be represented by its legal representative, while an unincorporated organization must be represented by its "principal person-in-charge." In that regard, the SPC CPC Interpretation details rules regarding the determination of legal representatives and parties to proceedings.[26] For example, the chief executive of a corporate entity is the legal representative of that corporation. Where a corporation has a board of directors, the chairman of the board is deemed the legal representative; if no chairman has been appointed, then the board must appoint a director to act as legal representative. For organizations without corporate status, the chief director of same will act as legal representative. The SPC CPC Interpretation defines the term "other organization" to include Sino-foreign cooperative joint ventures, partnerships and associations, subsidiaries, sole proprietorships, and all other legally approved entities operating with a business license but without separate corporate status.[27] In the event of any discrepancy between persons actually undertaking a business activity and those persons detailed on the relevant business license, it is proper for all such persons to be collectively included in any proceedings as coparties.

In a dispute involving a partnership, all parties to the partnership are coparties in any proceedings; however, for convenience, the partners may elect a single partner to represent them in procedural matters.[28] In situations involving a merger or acquisition, the merged entity will be the correct litigant in any proceedings arising from the activities of any party prior to the merger.[29]

25. Cases arising from border trade disputes (along China's frontiers), cases involving overseas situated real estate, and cases involving foreign intellectual property rights are not covered by the regulations.
26. SPC CPC Interpretation, arts. 38–64.
27. SPC CPC Interpretation, art. 49.
28. SPC CPC Interpretation, art. 47.
29. SPC CPC Interpretation, art. 50.

In cases where there are many parties, the parties on each side may elect a representative for conducting the case.[30] In this situation, the term "many parties" generally means more than ten parties. While all procedural actions undertaken by the representative during the trial will bind all members that elected him or her any modification to the terms of appointment, any proposed waiver of claims, or proposal to enter into a settlement of the claims is subject to the consent of all the parties that elected the representative.

c. Service of Process

As in the United States, Chinese court rules require, as a condition to establish jurisdiction, that a defendant receive service of process of the action.[31] Adequate service on a party located in China includes personal service, or, in the person's absence, upon an adult family member, legal representative, or, in a case involving a business enterprise, upon the legal representative of the enterprise. If a party or representative refuses to accept service, the court-appointed process server may enlist the assistance of a representative of an individual defendant's employer or request the assistance of the court. If direct service of process is unsuccessful, service may be effected via mail service or by publication.

The people's court is authorized to employ the following methods for service of process on a party to an action that has no presence in China: (1) procedures established by bilateral and international treaties; (2) diplomatic channels; (3) Chinese embassy or consulate in a country where a Chinese citizen is located; (4) the party's legal representative that is specifically authorized to accept service; (5) the party's representative office, branch organization, or business agent in China; (6) mail service, if the law of the country where the party resides permits such delivery (process is deemed

---

30. SPC CPC Interpretation, arts. 58–63. In "class action" cases, it is sometimes difficult to determine the identities of all relevant parties. In such situations, the court has the discretion to issue a public notice setting forth the details of the claims and to call upon all affected persons to file such claim within a specified time period. Thereafter, the court will require the affected parties to elect a representative. All court decisions and rulings will apply equally to all claimants in a class action suit and will additionally apply to persons who filed suit during the period of the class action. The same principles apply in any appeal of a class action claim.

31. *See* Civil Procedure Code, arts. 77–84 (detailing requirements for proper service of process); SPC CPC Interpretation, arts. 79–90. Litigation pleadings to be served on a corporation or an organization must be accepted through the respective signing and sealing of same by the legal representative and the directors of the organization. Service by depositing the pleadings at the place of residence or registered office is effective only where the persons upon whom such pleadings are to be served refuse to sign or seal the pleadings. Pleadings may be served directly on an attorney representing the party being served. Mediation-related documents must be served directly upon the other party—it is not permitted to serve mediation-related pleadings by depositing same at the place of residence or registered office. Service may also be effected through employing the assistance of the local courts in the subject jurisdiction; through a letter of authorization; by serving pleadings at the location of the relevant party's employer; or by adopting service through public notice in a newspaper subject to any special requirements of the court.

received sixty days after the date of dispatch); or (7) publication if all other methods of direct service are unsuccessful (process deemed effected six months after the date of publication).[32] Service of process is the obligation of judicial officers in China and not the responsibility of the litigant.

d. Limitations of Actions

In general, the statutory available time period for initiating an action in the people's court with respect to civil matters is two years.[33] The limitations period is one year for actions involving claims for personal injury, the sale of substandard quality items sold without notice of such defects, the delay or nonpayment of rent, or the loss or damage to a deposited article held in bailment.[34] The limitations period begins to run at the time a breach, infringement, or injury is known, or should have been known.[35] In a claim for personal injury, for example, the limitations period is calculated from the date the injury is sustained or discovered.[36] The people's court is authorized, in special circumstances, to extend the limitations period.[37]

e. Pleading Rules

An action may be initiated by any person or entity with a direct interest in the subject matter of the litigation, and against specific defendants.[38] A plaintiff is required to set forth in its complaint the claim, factual basis, and reasoning for the action, and must also specify the basis for the jurisdiction of the people's court.[39] The complaint must also specify the evidence and sources of evidence supporting the claims, and the names and addresses of witnesses.[40] A plaintiff has the right to amend the complaint, but whether the court will entertain repeated amendments or untimely amendments is not certain from the law.[41]

---

32. Civil Procedure Code, art. 247.

33. Civil Law, art. 135. For a discussion concerning the limitations periods for contract actions, *see* Chapter 7, Contract Law § A.8. For a discussion concerning the limitations period for product liability actions, *see* Chapter 13, Consumer Protection § A.4.

34. Civil Law, art. 136.

35. Civil Law, art. 137.

36. Sang, *supra* note 5, at 422.

37. Civil Law, art. 137. If more than twenty years have passed since the date of the infringement of a civil right, despite the fact that the infringement was recently "discovered," the people's court is prohibited from hearing an action for such stale claims. *Id.* In contrast, the Product Liability Law provides that the right to claim compensation for damages caused by a defective product expires ten years from the date the product was delivered to the first user or consumer. The ten-year period of time is tolled only if there is evidence that the ten-year "period of safe use" has not yet expired. *See* Chapter 13, Consumer Protection § A.3.

38. Civil Procedure Code, art. 108. By implication, the Chinese pleading rules requiring that a specific defendant be named in an action prohibits the use of fictitious or Doe defendants.

39. Civil Procedure Code, art. 108.

40. Civil Procedure Code, art. 110.

41. Civil Procedure Code, art. 52.

A complaint may be either written or oral, in the event that the plaintiff is unable to articulate his or her claim in writing.[42]

A plaintiff may also request provisional remedies such as property preservation measures (i.e., asset seizures) at the time of filing the complaint or on an ex parte basis prior to the initiation of the action.[43] An ex parte request must be based upon "urgent circumstances" where the plaintiff is likely to suffer irreparable injury, and must be ruled on by the court within forty-eight hours of application. In such a case, the court is authorized to demand that a bond or other form of security be posted as a prerequisite to issuing a preservation order.

The court will evaluate the complaint to determine its sufficiency and will determine to accept or reject the case within seven days of filing.[44] If the court accepts the case, the court will serve a copy of the complaint upon the defendant within five days. Thereafter, the defendant must lodge an answer to the complaint, and any counterclaim, within fifteen days after receipt, and the court will then have five days to serve the plaintiff with the defendant's responsive pleading.[45] A responding party may request an extension of time to file an answer if it can demonstrate that additional time is necessary to prepare a responsive pleading.

The Civil Procedure Code authorizes the merging of parties for class actions in situations involving common rights and obligations. Such cases require court approval and the consent of all parties.[46] A third party with an interest in an action may intervene in a proceeding.[47]

f. Discovery and Evidentiary Rules

Consistent with the practice of most civil law countries, but in contrast to the extensive discovery rules in the United States, Chinese law does not provide for formal mechanisms to allow the parties to conduct discovery such as depositions, interrogatories, requests for production of documents, or requests for admission. The people's court is authorized to "collect and examine" the evidence independent of the parties in situations that the court finds necessary or, if a party is unable, as a result of "objective reasons," to obtain the evidence that it needs to prove its case.[48] At trial, evidence is

42. Civil Procedure Code, art. 109. This rule grants access to the courts for persons who are illiterate. If it can be demonstrated that a plaintiff genuinely has difficulty writing the complaint, the court will transcribe the details, type up the complaint, and serve the defendant. *Id.*
43. Civil Procedure Code, arts. 92–96, 251–256.
44. Civil Procedure Code, art. 112.
45. Civil Procedure Code, art. 113.
46. Civil Procedure Code, art. 53.
47. Civil Procedure Code, art. 56.
48. Civil Procedure Code, art. 64.

presented and subjected to cross-examination and verification by the parties with the permission of the court.[49] Civil trials are conducted openly except in situations where the evidence is considered confidential proprietary information, trade secrets, or state secrets, in which cases the evidence is presented in a closed court session.[50]

In December 2001, with a view to modernizing and codifying the rules on the collection, presentation, and interpretation of evidence, the Supreme People's Court issued evidentiary rules to guide the courts with managing cases.[51] The objective of the SPC Rules of Evidence is to guarantee that the courts correctly determine the facts of a case, promptly try cases equitably, and facilitate the disputing parties in exercising their right to seek judicial relief. The provisions reiterate the duty of the parties making claims and counterclaims to present evidence supporting their respective claims before the courts, and the court is required to inform each party of their duties to present supporting evidence and the consequences of failing to do so.[52] In situations where the investigation and collection of evidence is beyond the ability of a party, the affected party may apply to the court for assistance in collecting evidence.[53]

At the time of accepting a case, the court is required to set the deadlines for the exchange and production of evidence.[54] A party that fails or refuses to meet the court-imposed deadline to exchange and produce evidence may waive its right to present evidence at trial. The court has the discretion to

---

49. Civil Procedure Code, arts. 63, 125. *See* Law of Administrative Litigation of the People's Republic of China (adopted on April 4, 1989, by the 2nd Sess. of the 7th NPC), *reprinted in* CHINA LAWS FOR FOREIGN BUSINESS (CCH), Business Regulation ¶ 19-558 (evidentiary standards for administrative litigation require that all evidence is "subject to court examination and verification before it may be used as a basis for judgment," art. 31) (hereinafter the "Administrative Litigation Law").

50. Civil Procedure Code, art. 66. Court hearings involving minors are also closed to the public. In June of 1998, the Beijing No. 1 Intermediate People's Court installed a wide-screen television at the gate of the court that lists on a daily basis the cases set for trial. The purpose of the list is to educate the public that cases are open, and to indirectly pressure the judges to improve their courtroom skills and performance. Open trials are expected to bring more fairness to court proceedings. *See* Shao, *Court Trials Now Open to Public*, CHINA DAILY (June 11, 1998), available on Lexis, News Library, or on the Web site of the CHINA DAILY at http://www.chinadaily.com.cn. The disclosure of "state secrets" is prohibited by law, and the relevant regulations define the terms *secret information* and *illegal disclosure* in broad terms. "State Secrets" are defined as "matters that affect the security and interests of the state," and are illustrated by broad categories of information relating to national defense, "import policy decisions on state affairs," "economic and social development," "science and technology development," "criminal investigations," and "other state secrets that by decision of the state departments on protecting state secrets should be safeguarded." Law on Safeguarding State Security of the People's Republic of China (promulgated by the State Council in 1993); Detailed Rules for the Implementation of the Law on Safeguarding State Security of the People's Republic of China (promulgated by the State Council in 1994).

51. Several Provisions of the Supreme People's Court on the Evidence for Civil Actions (issued on December 21, 2001, by the Supreme People's Court, and effective on April 1, 2002) (hereinafter the "SPC Rules of Evidence").

52. SPC Rules of Evidence, arts. 2, 3.

53. SPC Rules of Evidence, art. 3.

54. SPC Rules of Evidence, arts. 33–43.

extend the evidence exchange dates and, in general, may set two instances of evidence exchange. The exchange of evidence is usually monitored by the court.

The SPC Rules of Evidence outline the standards for *burden of proof* in various tort and contract cases. Article 4 of the Rules details the burden of proof in tort matters as follows:

(1) In a suit for alleged infringement of a patent resulting from a patent for invention of the manufacturing method for new products, the unit or individual that manufactures the identical or similar products will bear the burden of proof for proving that the manufacturing method is different from the patented method
(2) In a tort suit resulting from the personal injury caused by highly dangerous operations, the injured party will bear the burden of proof to prove that the victim intentionally caused and responsible for his/her own injury
(3) In a suit for compensation for damages allegedly caused by environmental pollution, the party alleged to have caused the damage will bear the burden of proving that there exists an exemption recognized by law, and that there is no causation between his act and the harmful consequences thereof
(4) In a tort suit alleging personal injury caused by the breakdown or collapse of a building or any other installation, or the falling of any article from a building or installation, the owner or the manager thereof will bear the burden of proving no fault
(5) In a tort suit alleging personal injury caused by animal breeding, the animal breeder or manager will bear the burden of proving that the victim or a third party was at fault
(6) In a tort suit alleging personal injury caused by a defective product, the manufacturer thereof will bear burden of proving any exemption cause fixed by law
(7) In a tort suit alleging personal injury caused by a common dangerous act, the persons committing such act will bear responsibility for presenting evidence proving that there is no causation between the act and the injury sustained
(8) In a tort suit alleging injury resulting from medical treatment or procedure, the medical institution will bear responsibility for presenting evidence proving that there is no causation between its actions and the harmful consequences; or that there was no medical malpractice[55]

55. SPC Rules of Evidence, art. 4.

In cases involving contractual disputes, the party that claims the existence of the contractual relationship and effectiveness of the contract has the burden of proving such facts. The burden of proving a claim concerning the variation, cancellation, termination, or dissolution of a contractual relationship is on the party that claims such facts.[56] In a dispute involving the alleged nonperformance of a contract, the burden of proof rests with the party claiming nonperformance.

In any particular situation where there are no established rules regarding the burden of proof, the court will determine the burden of proof on the basis of reasonableness, fairness, and good faith. Evidence need not be submitted at trial where a party against whom the evidence is presented admits the alleged facts.[57] However, a party that fails or refuses to admit or deny the allegations in a complaint may be deemed to have admitted the alleged facts after questioning by the court.[58]

In the presentation of evidence, the court will generally accept only original documents and tangible evidence.[59] However, where it is impossible or impractical to present original documents or tangible items, the court may accept verified copies or reproductions. If the evidence is sourced outside of China, the court will require that such evidence be authenticated by a notary public in the source country, or verified as to its authenticity by the relevant Chinese embassy or consulate, or otherwise verified as to its veracity in accordance with the terms and formalities for verification set forth in any treaty entered into by China and the source country.[60] If evidence is in a foreign language, a Chinese translation must also be furnished for the convenience of the court.[61]

A party is entitled to petition the court for assistance with respect to the investigation and collection of evidence in certain limited circumstances,

56. SPC Rules of Evidence, art. 5.

57. SPC Rules of Evidence, art. 8.

58. SPC Rules of Evidence, art. 8. It is not necessary for a party to present evidence as to the following subject matter: (1) well-known and common knowledge facts; (2) the laws of nature and theorem; (3) another fact that may be inferred and judged from the legal rules or known facts and the routine experience and principles; (4) the facts found by the judgments with legal effect of the people's courts; (5) facts determined by the awards with legal effect of an arbitration organization; and (6) facts proved by notarized documents. However, where a party holds evidence against any of the facts enumerated at items (1), (3), (4), (5), or (6) above, that party will be required to present such evidence. SPC Rules of Evidence, art. 9.

59. SPC Rules of Evidence, art. 10.

60. SPC Rules of Evidence, art. 11.

61. SPC Rules of Evidence, art. 12. The provisions also detail rules regarding the manner of presenting and admitting evidence. In particular, a party presenting evidence must classify and number each piece or article of evidence, provide an explanation as to the source of the evidence, and briefly explain the objective or purpose of the evidence to the case. The presenter must also affix his signature and seal to the evidence, state the date of submission, and provide copies for the opposite party. In turn, the people's court will issue a receipt for the evidence indicating the number of copies submitted and the date of submission—the receiving court personnel are required to both sign and seal the receipt.

such as (1) where the evidence under the application for investigation and collection is contained in documentary materials held by a State governmental authority and may be transferred to the people's court only on an ex officio basis; (2) where the evidence is contained in materials relating to State secrets, trade or commercial secrets, or individual privacy; or (3) where the evidence is contained in materials that cannot be collected by the party concerned or his agent ad litem due to reasons outside his or her control.[62] A request to the court for assistance in obtaining evidence is required to detail the nature of the evidence, the content of the evidence to be investigated and collected, the reasons necessary for employing the services of the people's court in investigating and collecting the evidence, and the facts to be proved by the evidence. An application for evidence collection assistance must be filed with the court at least seven days before the date of expiration of time for the production of evidence set by the court.[63] If the court rejects an application for assistance, the affected party has the discretion to file an application for review or reconsideration within three days of the court's decision.[64]

An application to the court for evidence preservation must be made at least seven days prior to the expiration of the time limit for presenting evidence.[65] The court may order the applicant for evidence preservation to post a security.[66] Generally, a court order for the preservation of evidence will involve the sealing up, detention, making of records (such as via audio or visual recordings including photographs), and the making of written statements.[67]

A party to litigation may introduce expert witness testimony with the approval of the court.[68] However, the court must first approve of the request to obtain expert testimony and the parties are required to mutually agree to the appointment of a particular expert, and absent an agreement the court will choose the expert on its own.[69] A party may object to the conclusions of an expert and request that a second expert be retained to provide an analysis or assessment.[70]

The trial court may order an on-site or physical examination of evidence, premises, or tangible items. The court, however, must observe certain procedural safeguards in order to authenticate the examination; namely, it must record the time, venue, and procedures of the examination; the persons

62. SPC Rules of Evidence, art. 17.
63. SPC Rules of Evidence, art. 18.
64. SPC Rules of Evidence, art. 19.
65. SPC Rules of Evidence, art. 23.
66. SPC Rules of Evidence, art. 23.
67. SPC Rules of Evidence, art. 24.
68. SPC Rules of Evidence, arts. 25–29.
69. SPC Rules of Evidence, art. 26.
70. SPC Rules of Evidence, arts. 27–29.

present, and, in particular, the pertinent details of those who carried out the examination; and the results/conclusions of the examination.

(1) Cross-Examination. All evidence submitted by the parties is subject to cross-examination, and cross-examination may be granted only with the permission of the court and may not be conducted in a threatening, humiliating, or inappropriate manner.[71] The SPC Rules of Evidence provide that evidence that has not been cross-examined may not form the legal basis for determining facts. Evidence relating to State secrets, trade or commercial secrets, and individual privacy or other evidence that should not be publicly disclosed according to legal provisions may not be the subject of public cross-examination in court, but may be cross-examined *in camera*.[72] During cross-examination, the parties may question the evidence with the purpose of determining the relevance, authenticity, legality, and probative value of the evidence presented.[73]

If a witness refuses to appear in court or to give evidence, a party relying on such evidence may make application to the court for a subpoena compelling the witness to attend court proceedings.[74] Any witness, including percipient or expert witnesses, are subject to cross-examination by the parties concerned regarding the matters at issue in the case.[75] A witness may be cross-examined by the court, opposing party, or another witness (such as an expert witness).[76] The SPC Rules of Evidence specifically require a witness to provide evidence without inference, commentary, or guessing and to testify to the facts based on personal knowledge.[77] A witness is required to testify outside the presence of other witnesses to avoid unnecessary influence or inadvertent or actual collusion of testimony. These rules apply equally to expert witnesses; however, an expert witness that is unable to attend a court hearing may provide, subject to the permission of the court, a written reply to the court in response to questions of cross-examination.[78]

(2) Examination and Identification of Evidence. In examining evidence, the court must carry out a thorough and comprehensive impartial assessment on the basis of the facts to be proved by such evidence. In determining the probative value of evidence and the degree of probative value, the court

71. SPC Rules of Evidence, arts. 47, 60.
72. SPC Rules of Evidence, art. 48.
73. SPC Rules of Evidence, arts. 50, 51.
74. SPC Rules of Evidence, art. 54. The application for a subpoena must be filed at least ten days before the date of expiration of the time frame for the presenting of evidence.
75. SPC Rules of Evidence, art. 55.
76. SPC Rules of Evidence, art. 58.
77. SPC Rules of Evidence, art. 57.
78. SPC Rules of Evidence, art. 59.

must follow professional ethical guidelines for judicial officers and, in each case, give reasons for its decision.[79] The SPC Rules of Evidence provide that in evaluating evidence, the court is required to take into consideration the following factors: (1) whether the evidence is in original form, i.e., is in the format of an original document, material, or article, and whether the copy or reproduction is consistent with the original documentation, material, or article; (2) the manner in which the evidence is related to the facts of the case; (3) whether the form and source of the evidence accords with the law; (4) whether the content of the evidence is true; and (5) whether any witness or the person providing the evidence has any special or interested relationship with the parties concerned.

The SPC Rules of Evidence provide that certain types of evidence will not be admitted into evidence by the court. For example, any evidence obtained by a party during mediation or conciliation proceedings will not be recognized by the court in any subsequent judicial proceedings following a failed mediation effort.[80] In addition, evidence may not be exclusively relied on to prove any fact that involves the following: (1) testimony given by a minor that fails to correspond to his age and intelligence;[81] (2) testimony given by a witness having a relationship to one party concerned or his agent; (3) audiovisual material with questionable aspects; (4) copies or reproductions, the veracity of which cannot be determined against the original documentation or articles; and (5) testimony of a witness who fails to appear in court to testify without justifiable reasons.[82]

The court is required to accept the following categories of evidence in situations where a party fails to provide rebuttal or contradictory evidence: (1) original documentary evidence, or true copies, photographs, counterparts, or extracts thereof through verification; (2) original material evidence, or true copies, photographs, or video material thereof through verification; (3) unquestionable audiovisual reference material obtained by legal means, or true reproductions thereof through verification; and (4) records of on-site examination of material evidence undertaken by the people's court in accordance with legal procedures following the application of a party concerned.[83] Similarly, expert witness testimony that is not contradicted by rebuttal evidence

79. SPC Rules of Evidence, art. 64.
80. SPC Rules of Evidence, art. 67.
81. SPC Rules of Evidence, art. 69. A person without mental capacity shall not be allowed to testify as a witness. A person without the required civil capacity or a person with limited civil capacity may give evidence as a witness provided that the court takes into account the age, intelligence, or mental health of the witness.
82. SPC Rules of Evidence, art. 70.
83. SPC Rules of Evidence, art. 70.

will be admitted by the court.[84] Where the evidence provided by the parties is contradictory or inconsistent, the court, having regard to all the surrounding facts, will weigh the evidence and determine which evidence has stronger probative value.[85] However, where it is difficult or impossible for the court to determine the evidence of stronger probative value, the court will affirm the evidence based on the rules for the allocation of burden of proof.[86] In situations where it is proven that a party holds evidence that is significant to the opposing party and withholds such evidence without justification, the claim of the other party may be duly inferred from such failure to present the evidence.[87]

The people's court is required to determine the probative value of conflicting evidence presented to support the same fact on the basis of the following principles:

(1) The probative value of public documentary evidence made by State or agencies and social organizations ex officio is, in general, stronger than that of other documentary evidence
(2) The probative value of material evidence, archives, experts' conclusions, examination records, or documentary evidence notarized or registered is, in general, stronger than that of other documentary evidence, audiovisual reference material, and witnesses' testimony
(3) The probative value of original evidence is, in general, stronger than that of the derivative evidence
(4) The probative value of direct evidence is, in general, stronger than that of the indirect evidence
(5) The probative value of evidence provided by witnesses in favor of the parties concerned having a kinship relationship or other close relations is, in general, weaker than that of other witness testimony[88]

Moreover, when assessing evidence presented by witnesses, in determining the probative value of such evidence, the court must have due regard to the witnesses' "intelligence, moral character, knowledge, experience, legal consciousness, and professional techniques."[89] While the court must forward reasons for accepting or refusing to accept the testimony of any witness, the court is not required to give reasons for accepting or rejecting evidence that is undisputed by the parties.[90]

84. SPC Rules of Evidence, arts. 71, 72.
85. SPC Rules of Evidence, art. 73.
86. SPC Rules of Evidence, art. 73.
87. SPC Rules of Evidence, art. 75.
88. SPC Rules of Evidence, art. 77.
89. SPC Rules of Evidence, art. 78.
90. SPC Rules of Evidence, art. 79.

g. Trial Procedure and Supervision

As in most civil law court systems, court proceedings in China are less formal than in common law countries, and the judges are active participants. Chinese judges frequently question and examine witnesses and order evidence to be produced directly to the court as opposed to the parties. The Chinese jurist's role includes both an investigatory function and that of a "trier of fact." As a result, in practice the question of burden of proof is often unclear, although the complainant appears to have the burden of presenting sufficient evidence to trigger and justify the court's involvement. In practice, there is no uniform standard for the application of the rules on burden of proof or the scope and extent of the court's independent investigation of the facts of a particular case.[91]

The trial commences with the court evaluating the evidence after each party makes a presentation or opening statement.[92] After the introduction of evidence at trial, the parties to an action have the right to debate the issues at hand and present arguments in support of their respective positions.[93] At the end of debate, the court will request closing arguments from both parties.[94] A failure by either party to attend a trial is grounds for entry of a default judgment.[95]

The jury system does not exist in China, but one or more judges may act as a panel, or appoint assessors to assist with cases.[96] The membership of the panel must be an odd number, and decisions must be reached by a majority vote.[97] Deliberations on a case are required to be recorded and transcribed, and the decision of the majority must be signed by the panel. Dissenting opinions are also required to be recorded and transcribed.

The PRC recognizes a two-tier final appellate system, and a party may file an appeal with a higher level court if it disputes the trial court's

---

91. Sang, *supra* note 5, at 426. The SPC Rules of Evidence attempt to bring some uniformity with respect to evidentiary standards and the burdern of proof in Chinese courts. *See supra* note 55 and accompanying text.

92. During court proceedings in China, the recognized minority nationalities have the constitutional right to have a translator present. The courts have the duty to supply the translators, and all indictments, judgments, or court notices are required to be translated by the court. These rules apply only to recognized minority nationalities in China, and a foreigner does not have the right to an interpreter during a court proceeding but may request a translator at his or her own expense.

93. Civil Procedure Code, art. 12.

94. Civil Procedure Code, art. 127.

95. Civil Procedure Code, arts. 129–131.

96. Civil Procedure Code, art. 40.

97. Civil Procedure Code, art. 43.

decision.[98] The court of first instance has a statutory duty to inform each of the parties to the case of their respective rights to appeal its decision, or ruling, as the case may be. An appeal may be filed by a party to the proceedings of first instance, by his agent *ad litem* acting on his behalf, or by a statutory agent so appointed where a litigant lacks civil capacity. The decision of the appellate court is final.

The Civil Procedure Code and the SPC CPC Interpretation outline a comprehensive procedure for the orderly supervision of trials, and in particular, supervision over the decisions rendered by the courts. The primary responsibility for supervision rests with the presidents of each court level. Where, for example, the president of each court level determines that a judgment or ruling of its court is incorrect, the president must rule to suspend that judgment or ruling, and, following consultation with a judicial committee, determine if a retrial or review is appropriate.[99] So, too, the Supreme People's Court may order the suspension of any judgment or ruling of the lower courts that it determines to be incorrect and may order a retrial or review, as appropriate.[100] The higher people's court has similar supervisory jurisdiction over the lower courts. In emergencies, the court may orally issue an order for suspension of a judgment or ruling, but must thereafter issue a written order within ten days. A court that has been ordered to review or retry a case must decide whether to reverse, maintain, or amend its ruling or judgment.

In addition, a party may also request a new trial after the effective date of a judgment, in certain limited situations, where:

(1) New evidence is discovered that is sufficient to repudiate the original decision
(2) The primary evidence introduced at trial is demonstrated to be insufficient
(3) The court of first instance made a definite error in the application of the law
(4) The court of first instance failed to follow procedures that affected the validity of the judgment; or

98. Civil Procedure Code, arts. 147–159. For a party domiciled in China, an appeal must be filed within fifteen days of receiving the trial court's decision. A party residing outside of China has thirty days to file an appeal. An extension of time may be granted by the appellate court in special circumstances. A decision of the appellate court is generally final, with limited rights to further appeal. The appellate court will review both the law and the facts of a case. The appellate panel consists only of judges and a decision is usually rendered within three months for domestic actions. Foreign party actions are not limited by the three-month rule. *Id.* art. 250.

99. SPC CPC Interpretation, art. 199.

100. SPC CPC Interpretation, art. 200.

(5) A member of the court or judicial personnel committed misconduct that affected his or her impartiality[101]

A litigant may apply for a retrial either to the court that originally tried the case, or to the higher people's court.[102] Where an application for retrial is submitted to the higher people's court, the court may reject the application (if not in line with the foregoing criteria), return the case to the original court for retrial, or review the case itself and render a decision.

A request for a new trial must be made within two years after a decision becomes effective.[103] Moreover, the SPC CPC Interpretation provides that where, after the effective date of its judgment, the people's court of first instance discovers an error in such judgment and a litigant has proceeded with an appeal within the statutory time frame for so doing, then the court of first instance is obliged to inform the court of second instance of the error. Where the adversely affected party has not appealed, the court of second instance may handle the error through the exercise of its trial supervisory function. Where the court of second instance determines that there occurred a violation of legal proceedings that resulted in an error in the judgment of the court of first instance, then the court is obliged to reverse the original judgment and remand the case over for a new trial before the court of first instance. If the plaintiff files an appeal that includes further claims, or, on appeal, the defendant files a counterclaim, the court of second instance may encourage the parties to mediate the additional claims of the respective parties. If mediation fails, the court must instruct the relevant parties to file their new claims under a new suit.[104]

In certain cases, the court of second instance may directly impose judgment, in the following circumstances: (1) cases that were incorrectly accepted by the court of first instance; (2) cases where the appeal claim is patently unacceptable; (3) cases where the facts of the case have clearly been determined but the trial court incorrectly applied the applicable law; and (4) cases that must be remanded for retrial because the original judgment violates legal proceedings that may affect the outcome of the trial.

Under the Civil Procedure Code, the judicial officers are personally liable, civilly and criminally, for any judicial misconduct, including bribery, favoritism, or other irregularities when handling cases.[105] A judge must also withdraw from a case in situations where he or she (1) is a party to the action or is related to a party or legal counsel; (2) has a personal interest in

101. Civil Procedure Code, art. 179; SPC CPC Interpretation, art. 206.
102. SPC CPC Interpretation, art. 205.
103. SPC CPC Interpretation, art. 204.
104. SPC CPC Interpretation, art. 211.
105. Civil Procedure Code, art. 45.

the action; or (3) has some other relationship that could possibly influence his or her impartial handling of the matter.[106] This rule applies to all court personnel, expert witnesses, and investigators.

The Chinese court rules encourage the use of mediation to resolve disputes but will do so only if the parties, including foreign persons and entities, voluntarily participate.[107] The court is authorized to encourage the parties to mediate a dispute up to the time of rendering a decision.[108] Civil disputes in China traditionally are resolved through mediation. The Civil Procedure Code provides that the people's courts have jurisdiction to resolve any dispute that cannot be resolved through mediation and, in the event that a party reneges on his or her settlement agreement, the people's court has jurisdiction to interpret and enforce the terms of the agreement.[109] Mediation is traditionally favored because of the distrust of the court process and, based upon the Confucian tradition that a virtuous person is one who is willing to compromise and one who strives for peace, harmony, and conciliation.[110]

B. Enforcement of Judgments

Each court has its own enforcement division, which employs judges or judicial officers with the authority to seize real and personal property, bank accounts, order auctions of property, and to take other actions to enforce a court judgment. The judges in the court enforcement divisions are the equivalent of a U.S. marshal or sheriff that supports the court's enforcement efforts.

There are special rules concerning the recognition and enforcement of foreign court judgments. The Civil Procedure Code addresses the issue of judicial assistance in the absence of an express judicial assistance treaty.[111]

106. Civil Procedure Code, art. 45. The Civil Procedure Code allows a party to file an application requesting that the court withdraw. The application is required to explain the reasons for the withdrawal request.

107. Civil Procedure Code, art. 9. The respect for voluntary participation in mediation contrasts with the rule under the 1982 civil procedure law, which required the court to mediate a dispute in the first instance. Under the Civil Procedure Code, the court cannot force the parties to mediate. As a practical matter, the court "will render its judgment promptly," if either party refuses to mediate a dispute. *Id.* Clearly, a litigant who refuses to engage in mediation discussions is likely to be on the receiving end of an adverse judgment. Mediation for foreign parties is governed by Articles 9, 85–91, and 155 of the Civil Procedure Code. For a discussion of mediation in China, *see* Chapter 21, Mediation and Arbitration § A. For a discussion of mediation in labor disputes, *see* Chapter 10, Labor and Employment Law § A.11.a.

108. Civil Procedure Code, art. 128.

109. Civil Procedure Code, art. 16. The court also has jurisdiction over the mediation committee or panel if a violation of the law occurs.

110. *See* Tay, *The Struggle for Law in China*, 21 U. Brit. Colum. L. Rev. 561, 561–62 (1987).

111. Civil Procedure Code, art. 268. Article 268 provides in pertinent part: "In the case of an application or request for recognition and enforcement of a legally effective judgment or written order of a foreign court, the people's court shall, after examining it in accordance with the international treaties concluded or acceded to by the People's Republic of China or with the principle of reciprocity [. . .] recognize the validity of the judgment or written order, and, if required, issue a writ of execution to enforce it [. . .]." Notwithstanding, Article 318 of the of the SPC CPC Interpretation provides that in the event

China has not acceded to any multilateral treaty or convention regarding the mutual recognition and enforcement of foreign rendered judgments. Similarly, while China has signed several treaties offering judicial reciprocity, it has not signed any such treaty with the United States. Due to the absence of a dedicated treaty or reciprocal enforcement arrangements with China, any foreign court judgment made against a Chinese entity will not be enforced in China.

C. Administrative Litigation

A person or entity that disputes an administrative decision by a Chinese government entity may file a complaint with the people's court challenging the decision.[112] The right to judicial review of administrative decisions is available to foreign persons or entities.[113] An interested third party or organization may also join an action upon application to the court.[114] A complaint challenging an administrative decision must be filed with the court within three months of notification of the administrative decision.[115] The court is required to evaluate the legality of an administrative organization's actions and to exercise its judgment independently and without interference from the government or special interests groups.[116] The types of administrative decisions and orders subject to judicial review include the following:

(1) Penalties such as detention or fines
(2) Refusal to issue or cancellation of a license or permit
(3) Orders to terminate production or business operations
(4) Confiscation of merchandise or freezing of assets

---

that (i) a litigant applies to the Chinese Intermediate People's Court of competent jurisdiction to recognize and enforce a validated verdict and ruling made by a foreign court and (ii) the country of the foreign court has not entered into or does not participate in an the international treaty, nor has entered into reciprocal arrangements, the litigant may file suit with the People's Court of competent jurisdiction with a view to obtaining judgment.

112. Administrative Litigation Law, art. 1. For a discussion of the administrative litigation process, *see* P. CORNE, FOREIGN INVESTMENT IN CHINA: THE ADMINISTRATIVE LEGAL SYSTEM 243–260 (1997). *See generally* LIN FONG, ADMINISTRATIVE LAW: PROCEDURES AND REMEDIES IN CHINA (1996).

113. Administrative Litigation Law, arts. 70–73. If a foreign party retains counsel to represent them in the proceeding, a PRC lawyer must be appointed. *Id.* art. 73.

114. Administrative Litigation Law, art. 27.

115. Administrative Litigation Law, art. 39. An extension of ten days may be granted by the court. *Id.* art. 40. The three-month period of time to file for judicial review is inconsistent with the time periods set forth in a number of laws. For example, the Product Quality Law provides that a party may seek judicial review of an administrative penalty but must file an action with the people's court within fifteen days of receiving the decision. *See* Chapter 13, Consumer Protection § A.5. A request for judicial review of a decision by the tax authorities must also be filed with the people's court within fifteen days of receipt of the final decision. *See* Chapter 9, Taxation Law § H. Note that the Administrative Litigation Law provides for a fifteen-day period of time to file an appeal of a lower court's decision to a higher-level people's court.

116. Administrative Litigation Law, arts. 3–6.

(5) Restrictions on personal freedom
(6) Infringement on a company's right of autonomy
(7) Other administrative decisions or orders[117]

The court is prohibited from hearing administrative cases involving national defense or diplomatic issues; personnel matters of the administrative organization such as awards, recruitment, or termination of employees; or decisions by administrative organizations that are considered final in accordance with the law. In addition, given that the courts do not have the constitutional right to question the lawmaking authority of the legislative branch, the courts are prohibited from reviewing the laws, regulations, rules, measures, or decrees issued by administrative organizations.[118]

The people's courts have jurisdiction over administrative cases in the first instance. However, the intermediate people's courts have jurisdiction in the first instance with respect to cases involving the verification of patent rights, customs matters, administrative decisions of the departments of the State Council, and cases of importance and complexity.[119] The Supreme People's Court may exercise original jurisdiction over administrative cases of national importance.[120] The court with proper venue is usually the court where the plaintiff resides or the locality of the property.

The defendant-organization is required to produce all evidence relating to an administrative decision including evidence to support the legality of its actions. The defendants, however, are not permitted to collect any evidence from the plaintiff during the course of the proceedings.[121] The court may conduct its own investigation or order the parties to produce additional evidence.[122] Except where State secrets or confidential matters are involved, all administrative litigation cases are open to the public.[123]

The policy of encouraging mediation in civil actions does not apply in administrative cases.[124] The court has the authority to order the administrative

117. Administrative Litigation Law, art. 11.
118. Administrative Litigation Law, art. 12.
119. Administrative Litigation Law, arts. 13–14.
120. Administrative Litigation Law, art. 16.
121. Administrative Litigation Law, art. 33.
122. Administrative Litigation Law, art. 34.
123. The disclosure of "state secrets" is prohibited by law, and the relevant regulations define the terms *secret information* and *illegal disclosure* in broad terms. "State Secrets" are defined as "matters that affect the security and interests of the state," and are illustrated by broad categories of information relating to national defense, "import policy decisions on state affairs," "economic and social development," "science and technology development," "criminal investigations," and "other state secrets that by decision of the state departments on protecting state secrets should be safeguarded." Law on Safeguarding State Security of the People's Republic of China (promulgated by the State Council in 1993); Detailed Rules for the Implementation of the Law on Safeguarding State Security of the People's Republic of China (promulgated by the State Council in 1994).
124. Administrative Litigation Law, art. 50.

agency to reconsider its decision if the court finds the agency acted with insufficient evidence, incorrectly applied the law, violated legal procedure, abused its authority, or acted outside the scope of its authority.[125] If the agency fails to reconsider its position in light of the court's order, the court may enter judgment in favor of the plaintiff.[126] The court may also render judgment in the agency's favor if it finds sufficient evidence exists to support the agency's position, if legal procedures have been followed, and the agency correctly applied the law.[127] Both parties may appeal the decision of the lower court to a higher people's court. An appeal must be filed within fifteen days of receiving notice of judgment.[128]

Key Laws and Regulations

Code of Civil Procedure of the People's Republic of China (adopted April 9, 1991, by the 4th Session of the Standing Committee of the 7th National People's Congress)

Opinions of the Supreme People's Court on Several Questions Concerning the Application of the Civil Procedure Law of the People's Republic of China (issued by the Supreme People's Court on July 14, 1992)

Detailed Regulations of the Supreme People's Court Governing Maritime Litigation Involving Foreigners (issued on January 31, 1986, by the Supreme People's Court)

Measures for the Charging of Court Costs by the People's Court (adopted on June 29, 1989, by the Supreme People's Court)

General Principles of Civil Law of the People's Republic of China (adopted April 12, 1986, at the 4th session of the 6th NPC, effective January 1, 1987)

Law of Administrative Litigation of the People's Republic of China (adopted on April 4, 1989, by the 2nd Sess. of the 7th NPC)

Regulation on Several Issues on Jurisdiction of Overseas Civil and Commercial Lawsuits, PRC Supreme People's Court Judicial Interpretation [2002] No. 5 (promulgated by the SPC on Feb. 25, 2002, and effective on Mar. 1, 2002)

Several Provision of the Supreme People's Court on the Evidence for Civil Actions (issued on December 21, 2001, by the Supreme People's Court, and effective on April 1, 2002)

125. Administrative Litigation Law, art. 54, § (ii).
126. Administrative Litigation Law, art. 54, § (iii).
127. Administrative Litigation Law, art. 54, § (i).
128. Administrative Litigation Law, art. 58.

Chapter 23

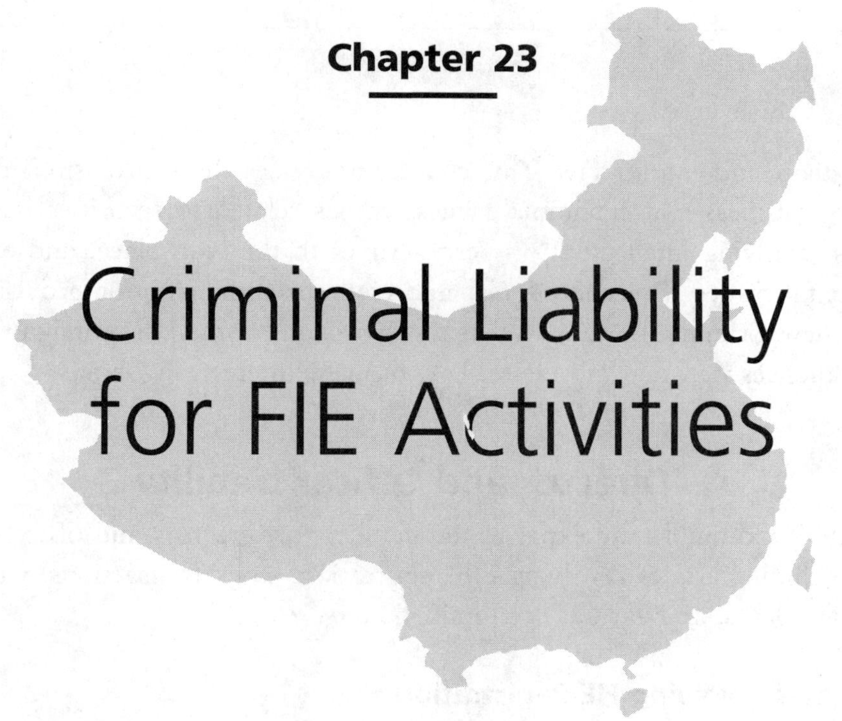

Criminal Liability for FIE Activities

Although China has had criminal codes for over 2,000 years, a comprehensive set of criminal laws and criminal procedure laws was not enacted until 1979. The 1979 Criminal Law reflected the reality of Chinese society in the post–cultural revolution era with little emphasis on private or foreign business activities. With the opening of China to the West, the criminal law and procedure in China have gone through significant change in the past twenty years. While the former criminal laws were rife with political crimes, the current Criminal Law, effective October 1, 1997, devotes considerable attention to business crimes that have become a by-product of China's Open Door policy.[1] The Criminal Law, which incorporates the language of over a dozen different circulars and regulations supplementing the 1979 law, specifically lists punishable crimes and is more predictable, at least in written

---

1. Criminal Law of the People's Republic of China (promulgated March 14, 1997, by the NPC), *reprinted in* 11 CHINA L. & PRAC. 39 (June 1997) (hereinafter the "Criminal Law"). The Criminal Law specifically outlines crimes that, under the former law, were implied only in general terms. The crimes of counterrevolution have been abolished and replaced with crimes against national security including secession (art. 103), subversion (art. 105), treason (art. 108), espionage (art. 110), and unlawful disclosure of state secrets (art. 111). Subversion is no longer a capital punishment. Other crimes, such as hijacking, have been depoliticized and are ordinary crimes under the 1997 law. During its 1999 session, the NPC adopted an amendment to the Constitution to bring the language in line with the Criminal Law. The amendment provides that the term *counter-revolutionary activities* in Article 28 of the Constitution will be replaced by "crimes endangering the national security." Xu, *Amendments Wait for NPC Approval,* CHINA DAILY (Feb. 1, 1999), available on Lexis, News Library, or on the Web site of CHINA DAILY at http://www.chinadaily.com.cn. For a discussion concerning the Criminal Law and the Criminal Procedure Law, *see* WRONGS AND RIGHTS: A HUMAN RIGHTS ANALYSIS OF CHINA'S REVISED CRIMINAL LAW (Lawyers Committee for Human Rights, New York: 1998), and OPENING TO REFORM?: AN ANALYSIS OF CHINA'S REVISED CRIMINAL PROCEDURE LAW (Lawyers Committee for Human Rights, New York: 1996), available via the Web site of the LCHR at http://www.lchr.org.

form, than under prior law. This chapter addresses those provisions concerning business and economic crimes, crimes related to securities issues, crimes involving intellectual property, crimes in the workplace, and environmental crimes. This chapter also addresses the anticorruption provisions of the new Criminal Law, as well as the provisions of the U.S. Foreign Corrupt Practices Act, that may affect U.S. business interests in China.

A. Director and Officer Liability

The 1997 Criminal Law expands the liability for directors and officers of FIEs including crimes involving FIE registration, stock transactions, workplace accidents, and various economic matters.

1. Crimes Involving FIE Registration

Management personnel directly responsible for making false statements at the time of application of an enterprise are subject to criminal fines and imprisonment. Activities subject to criminal penalties include false declaration of registered capital; false information concerning the value of assets contributed to an FIE;[2] false statements concerning creditworthiness of the foreign party; and the submission of other false information designed to mislead the registration and approval authorities.[3] A person who provides false documentation or information for the purpose of obtaining registration may be sentenced to up to three years' imprisonment and penalized in the sum of up to 10 percent of the falsely declared registered capital.[4] A department, division, or work unit of a Chinese enterprise may be fined up to 10 percent of the falsely declared registered capital and the unit management and persons directly responsible for the false statements may be subject to individual penalties and imprisonment.

2. Criminal Liability for Industrial Accidents

Under the 1997 Criminal Law, officers and directors are liable for actions that result in serious industrial accidents, construction site injuries, environmental

2. In 1994, the State Administration of Inspection of Import and Export Commodities introduced an assessment system to address the perceived problem of overvaluation of FIE equipment contributions. Under the assessment system, the inspection agency found that 18 percent of the assets of FIEs were valued significantly higher than actual value. *See Record of Events (January–March 1997),* CHINA LAW 105 (1997).

3. Criminal Law, arts. 158–161; *See also* Decision of the Standing Committee of the National People's Congress Concerning the Punishment of the Crime Constituting Violation of the Company Law (adopted February 28, 1995, by the 12th Sess. of the Standing Comm. of the 8th NPC), arts. 1–3, *reprinted in* CHINA LAWS FOR FOREIGN BUSINESS (CCH), Business Regulation ¶ 13-520 (hereinafter the "Company Law Crimes Decision"). The Criminal Law fully adopts the crimes set forth in the Company Law Crimes Decision.

4. Criminal Law, art. 158.

contamination, and fire damage. Liability will be imposed only if management fails to take steps to correct a problem that results in the damage or injury after receiving notice of the problem area from government inspectors and regulators.[5] An FIE's management should establish a reporting system that promptly and diligently addresses any and all regulatory notices to avoid criminal liability in the event that compliance questions are raised by the relevant authorities.

3. Crimes Involving Stock Transactions

As an underdeveloped stock market, China has experienced disruptive activity that results in erosion of investor confidence in the system. In response, the government has promulgated a number of regulations and circulars setting forth the standards for stock market conduct. Of key importance, the 1997 Criminal Law adds insider trading, market manipulation, and providing false information for the purpose of defrauding investors as crimes.[6]

a. Insider Trading

The insider trading provisions provide that it is a crime for a "well-informed" person with "inside information" concerning a securities transaction to buy or sell securities before the information is released to the public.[7] Inside information is defined as information that will have a major impact on the price of the securities if released to the public. The insider trading prohibition also makes it a crime for a party that obtains inside information through unlawful means to buy or sell securities before the information is made public. Trading securities on inside information is subject to imprisonment of up to

5. Criminal Law, art. 134–139. The government is cracking down on accidents in the construction industry. Jiang, *Ministry Seeks Safer Building Practices,* CHINA DAILY (May 23, 1998), available on Lexis, News Library, or on the Web site of the CHINA DAILY at http://www.chinadaily.com.cn; Jiang, *Bridge Accident Sentencing,* CHINA DAILY (April 5, 1999), available on Lexis, News Library, or on the Web site of the CHINA DAILY at http://www.chinadaily.com.cn (thirty-one government officials received the death sentence or lengthy jail terms for corruption and faulty construction that resulted in the collapse of a bridge killing forty people in Qijiang). The NPC has adopted a Construction Law designed to improve the supervision and administration of construction activities to ensure that construction projects are undertaken in a safe manner. *See* Construction Law of the People's Republic of China (adopted on November 1, 1997, by the 28th Sess. of the Standing Comm. of the 8th NPC), *reprinted in* CHINA LAWS FOR FOREIGN BUSINESS (CCH), Business Regulation ¶19-565 (outlines the qualifications for contractors, construction project building permits, construction contracts, tender process, construction project supervision, construction work safety management, construction project quality control, and legal liability). The Ministry of Public Security is cracking down on businesses and state-owned enterprises that fail to properly maintain stockpiles of legal explosives for construction, mining, or other enterprises that use explosives. Managers that fail to properly maintain explosives or to report lost or illegal issues of explosives are personally liable. *See generally Explosives Urged to be Checked Up,* Xinhua News Agency (May 15, 1998), available on Lexis, News Library.

6. For a discussion of the problems encountered in China's stock market, *see* STUDIES ON THE CHINESE MARKET ECONOMY SERIES, THE CHINESE SECURITIES MARKET (eds. Gao Shangquan & Chi Fulin, Foreign Language Press, Beijing) 115–119 (1996).

7. Criminal Law, art. 180; Securities Law, art. 67. *See* Chapter 16, Securities Regulation § C.1.g.

five years or between five to ten years in "exceptionally serious" cases. The law further provides that if members of a government department, division, or work unit engage in insider trading, the unit is subject to a monetary fine and the management personnel of the unit, in addition to the other directly responsible parties, are subject to imprisonment and monetary fines.

b. Market Manipulation

The 1997 Criminal Law also prohibits the dissemination of false information for the purpose of manipulating the prices of traded securities. This section further makes it a crime for an employee of a securities exchange, securities brokerage company, or securities industry association to willfully supply false information, destroy or alter transaction records, or engage in any conduct intending to deceive investors into buying or selling securities.[8]

The law further prohibits anyone from engaging in any conduct that manipulates the price of securities. Stock manipulation is defined as the following:

(1) Engaging in successive sales or purchases by building a dominant position in terms of funds or shares, or using an individual's dominant position in terms of information, and thereby manipulating securities trading prices
(2) Engaging in collusive activities with another person to mutually trade securities at a prearranged time, price, and method or to mutually buy and sell securities not held by the parties to the transaction, thereby affecting the price and volume of securities traded
(3) Buying or selling securities to or from oneself without transfer of ownership of the securities by means of making oneself the other party to the transaction, thereby affecting the price or volume of securities traded
(4) Manipulating securities trading prices by other methods[9]

Stock manipulation is subject to fines of not less than one and not more than five times the illegal income gained in the scheme, and may result in imprisonment of up to five years.

---

8. Criminal Law, art. 181. In April of 1998, the China Securities Regulatory Commission (CSRC) sanctioned a number of individuals and institutions involved in a market manipulation case related to the Shenzhen-listed Hainan Minyuan Modern Agriculture Development Co. Ltd. Hainan Minyuan made false declarations concerning its profit earnings and capital reserves for 1996. The CSRC issued penalties in the sum of RMB2 million ($241,000). *See* Ren, *Market Manipulators Punished,* CHINA DAILY (April 29, 1998), available on Lexis, News Library, or on the Web site of the CHINA DAILY at http://www.chinadaily.com.cn.

9. Criminal Law, art. 182; Securities Law, art. 71.

c. Issuance of Shares without Approval

The issuance of shares or bonds without the approval of the relevant authorities is a crime and subjects the offending party to a term of imprisonment of up to five years and a fine of between 1 and 5 percent of the illegally raised funds.[10]

d. False Information in Stock Transactions

It is a crime for a person to issue shares or corporate bonds based upon a prospectus or subscription form containing false or misleading information.[11] It is also a crime to provide financial and accounting information to shareholders or the public containing misrepresentations, or to engage in active concealment of accurate information.[12]

In November of 1998, the Beijing No. 1 Intermediate People's Court sentenced the president and bookkeeper of the Hainan Minyuan Modern Agriculture Development Shareholding Co., Ltd., to prison terms for issuing false financial and accounting information concerning the company.[13] The court found that Hainan Minyuan—which was traded on the Shenzhen Stock Exchange—did not have the RMB570 million ($68.7 million) in revenue claimed in the company-issued report. The court further found that the company's report misled investors into believing that it had the required permits for construction of an office tower when it did not.

4. Miscellaneous Economic Crimes

a. Crimes Involving Corporate Decisions in Violation of the Law

The 1997 Criminal Law provides that individual directors are liable for resolutions of the board that violate the law or result in serious losses to the FIE. A director can be protected only if he or she expresses opposition to the proposed action and records such opposition in the minutes of the directors' meeting.[14]

b. Crimes Involving Falsification of Corporate Records and Documents

The Criminal Law makes it a crime to alter or falsify financial instruments including bills of exchange, promissory notes, checks, bank deposit slips,

10. Criminal Law, art. 179.
11. Criminal Law, art. 160.
12. Criminal Law, art. 161.
13. Shao, *Court Rules in Case of Fraudulent Report*, China Daily (Nov. 13, 1998), available on Lexis, News Library, or on the Web site of China Daily at http://www.chinadaily.com.cn.
14. Criminal Law, art. 118.

collection vouchers, letters of credit, or credit card applications.[15] It is also a crime to alter or falsify State treasury bonds or other negotiable instruments issued by the Chinese government, or to alter or falsify share certificates of an enterprise.[16] The Criminal Law further provides that money laundering, misuse of foreign exchange, and tax evasion are crimes.[17] Such crimes may result in lengthy prison terms and monetary penalties.

c. Collusion

Collusion is a poorly defined offense, but it can potentially involve substantial penalties. Liability for collusion arises in the case of contracts entered

15. Criminal Law, art. 177. It is also a crime to misuse foreign currency or to violate the foreign exchange laws and regulations. *See* Chapter 11, Financial Regulation § B.9. An insurance company and its personnel are subject to criminal liability for filing false reports or refusing to file reports. *See* Chapter 12, Insurance Law and Regulation § E. Insurance brokers/agents are also subject to criminal liability if they violate their fiduciary duties. *See* Chapter 12, Insurance Law and Regulation § H. The Criminal Law defines computer crimes for the first time and sets a maximum sentence of five years for conviction. *See* He, *Cyberspace Crimes on the Rise,* CHINA DAILY (Oct. 20, 1998), available on Lexis, News Library, or on the Web site of the CHINA DAILY at http://www.chinadaily.com.cn; He, *Hackers Face Punishment in China,* CHINA DAILY (Oct. 20, 1998), available on Lexis, News Library, or on the Web site of the CHINA DAILY at http://www.chinadaily.com.cn. In 1998, the Public Security Bureau prosecuted over 100 computer hacker cases. The PSB estimates that the cases brought to court amount to only 15 percent of the actual occurrences, the majority of which go undetected. *Agency Reports Computer Hacker Cases,* Xinhua News Agency (Jan. 6, 1999), available on Lexis, News Library.

16. Criminal Law, art. 178.

17. Criminal Law, art. 191. *See* Administrative Law of the PRC on the Levying and Collection of Taxes (adopted on September 4, 1992, at the 27th Sess. of the Standing Comm. of the 7th NPC and amended on February 28, 1995, at the 12th Sess. of the Standing Comm. of the 8th NPC), arts. 37–56, *reprinted in* CHINA LAWS FOR FOREIGN BUSINESS (CCH), Taxation ¶ 39-621 (hereinafter the "Administrative Law on Tax Collection") (outlines the rules for registering with the tax authorities, recordkeeping requirements, tax collection, tax investigations, administrative appeals process, and judicial relief). *See generally* Sommers & Phillips, *Assessing the Tax Administration Law of the People's Republic of China,* 18 LOY. L.A. INT'L & COMP. L. J. 339 (1996). *See also* Supplementary Regulations of the Standing Committee of the NPC on Punishment for Tax Evasion and Refusal to Pay Tax (adopted on September 4, 1992, by the 27th Sess. of the Standing Comm. of the 7th NPC), *reprinted in* CHINA LAWS FOR FOREIGN BUSINESS (CCH), Taxation ¶ 39-610. Since the Administrative Law on Tax Collection was adopted, the people's courts have tried 5,917 cases of tax evasion and sentenced 4,241 individuals to prison terms for violating the tax laws. *See Tax Crimes,* CHINA DAILY (June 13, 1998), available on Lexis, News Library, or on the Web site of the CHINA DAILY at http://www.chinadaily.com.cn. *See also* Provisional Regulations Regarding the Administrative Punishments on Disciplinary Measures on Activities Violating the Foreign Exchange Administrative Regulations, including Arbitrage, Illegal Procurement, Illegal Evasion and Illegal Transactions in Foreign Exchange (issued on January 25, 1999 by the Ministry of Supervision, Ministry of Personnel, People's Bank of China, State General Administration of Customs and the State Administration of Foreign Exchange) (hereinafter the "FOREX Disciplinary Measures"). These Regulations follow the Administrative Regulations on Foreign Exchange, the Provisional Regulations on State Civil Servants, and the Regulations Concerning the Rewards and Disciplinary Sanctions for Enterprise Employees. The FOREX Disciplinary Measures apply to civil servants, employees of financial institutions approved to engage in foreign exchange business activities, and employees of state-owned foreign trade enterprises. The FOREX Disciplinary Measures set forth a list of illegal FOREX-related activities and detail penalties for such activities the severity of which is based upon the amount of money involved. The punishments include, in ascending order of severity, sanction of warning, recorded demerit, special recorded demerit, demotion, dismissal from office, continued employment on probation, and expulsion. In case of regulatory violations, the relevant personnel in charge and other directly responsible personnel may be held responsible, and not the enterprise. If an infraction violates both the PRC Criminal Laws and the FOREX Disciplinary Measures, criminal penalties may be imposed upon the responsible party.

into between Chinese entities and non-Chinese entities when the following elements are present:

(1) Two parties enter into a contract
(2) The parties collaborate maliciously
(3) Actual harm is done to the Chinese government or a third party suffers actual harm (due to such malicious collaboration)

When the foregoing elements are affirmatively established to demonstrate collusion, the scope of liability includes rescission of the contract and the mandatory return to the government of any illegal gains. In addition, in serious cases, other penalties may be imposed, including reprimands, fines, and detention.

Several points should be noted. Firstly, liability does not arise under the relevant regulations unless a contract is executed. Secondly, liability may be imposed even though the parties who collude do not make a profit from their act of collusion, provided the government or a third party is harmed. Thirdly, although "malice" is described as a necessary element to establish liability, there is no definition of what constitutes malice, and it seems likely that the court's finding in relation to this point may well be influenced by the degree of the harm suffered by the government or third party.

d. Interested Party Transactions

A director or manager may not exploit his position and powers of office in the company to seek personal gain. Under Chinese law, a director or manager of a company is not permitted to engage on his own behalf or on behalf of other parties in any business activities that are identical to, or similar to, the type of business of which he is director or manager, or to engage in any activities that would cause damage to the interests of the company of which he is director or manager. If a director or manager engages in any of the foregoing activities, he will be required to relinquish the benefits to the company.

A businessperson who is found to have abused his powers of office or to have used his position to seize a company's property or assets may be sentenced, in the event of a large amount, to a term of imprisonment of up to five years or criminal detention. In cases involving a "*very large amount*" a term of imprisonment in excess of five years may be imposed together with the confiscation of property.

Furthermore, a government official is not permitted to hold a position in a private business enterprise concurrently with his or her public duties.

B. Crimes Involving Intellectual Property Infringement

The Criminal Law makes it unlawful to misuse the copyrights, trademarks, and business secrets of another party.[18] The provisions concerning intellectual property infringement were developed in response to pressure from the international community and in particular from the United States.

1. Criminal Trademark Infringement

The Criminal Law provides that it is a crime to use a trademark identical to a registered trademark on the same type of merchandise without the permission of the registered owner. It is also a crime to sell merchandise with knowledge that it depicts a counterfeit registered trademark on any type of merchandise. The law further provides that it is unlawful to manufacture any representation of a registered trademark without permission of the registered owner. A person who violates the law is subject to imprisonment of up to three years and in serious cases, including repeated incidents of infringement or where the sales volume of infringing goods is relatively large, the term of imprisonment may be from three to seven years.[19] In addition to imprisonment, a violation may also result in the imposition of monetary penalties.

2. Criminal Patent Infringement

With respect to patent infringement, the Criminal Law provides that it is unlawful to intentionally misrepresent ownership of a patent belonging to another party. In such cases, the infringing party is liable for imprisonment of not more than three years and potential monetary penalties.[20]

3. Criminal Copyright Infringement

Copyright infringement is a crime only in limited situations. Criminal infringement will be found only if there is evidence that the infringing party seeks to obtain financial gain from the copying and there is evidence of large income received from the illicit activities. Criminal infringement includes the following activities:

(1) Reproduction and distribution of another person's work, including documents, manuscripts, musical scores, cinematography productions,

18. Criminal Law, § 7.
19. Criminal Law, arts. 213–215.
20. Criminal Law, art. 216.

computer software, and other forms of written media without the permission of the copyright owner

(2) Publication of a book to which another person or entity enjoys the exclusive publishing rights

(3) Reproduction and distribution of an audio or video recording without the permission of the copyright holder

(4) Production and sale of a work of art without the permission of the copyright owner[21]

The penalty for criminal copyright infringement is a prison term of not more than three years and the imposition of a monetary fine.[22]

4. Unlawful Disclosure of Trade Secrets

Under the Criminal Law, the unlawful disclosure and use of a "business secret" is a criminal act and is punishable by imprisonment of up to seven years in serious cases.[23] A "business secret" is defined as nonpublic technical and economic information for which the owner, or party licensed by the owner, has adopted measures to maintain its confidentiality. The illegal activities include the following:

(1) Obtaining a business secret by theft, enticement of promise by profit, coercion, or other improper means

(2) Disclosing, using, or permitting another person to use a business secret of the holder of rights thereto that has been obtained by theft, enticement, coercion, or other improper means

(3) Disclosing, using, or permitting another person to use a business secret in one's possession, where such disclosure, use, or permission is in violation of an agreement or in breach of the confidentiality requirements of the holder of rights in respect to the business secret[24]

Criminal liability is triggered in cases where the party that discloses business secrets is one that knew or should have known that the disclosure or use was inappropriate. The disclosure of business secrets by a particular department, division, or work unit may result in the imposition of monetary penalties assessed against the department, division, or work unit. Management

21. Criminal Law, art. 217.

22. Criminal Law, art. 218.

23. Criminal Law, arts. 219, 220. Under the Company Law, directors, supervisors, and managers have an obligation to maintain confidentiality of company secrets, except if allowed to disclose such confidential information by the board of directors. *See* Company Law, art. 62. *See also Business Secrets*, CHINA ECONOMIC REVIEW, April 23, 1998, available on Lexis, News Library.

24. Criminal Law, art. 219.

personnel who are directly responsible for the unit, in addition to those persons that are responsible for the illegal disclosure, are subject to terms of imprisonment and the imposition of monetary penalties assessed against them individually.[25]

It is recommended that confidentiality and nondisclosure provisions in agreements admonish the parties concerning potential criminal liability for improper disclosure of business secrets. At the same time, expatriate personnel of FIEs must be advised of their duties under the law and to stress that violation of a confidentiality agreement may lead to criminal penalties in China. The improper disclosure of State secrets is also a crime under the Criminal Law.[26]

C. Criminal Liability for Environmental Crimes

The Criminal Law provides that it is a crime to seriously damage China's environment and natural resources.[27] The State Environmental Protection Administration (SEPA) is charged with investigating and enforcing the environmental protection statutes.[28] SEPA applies the Criminal Law provisions to punish individuals and entities that import hazardous waste illegally into China for storage or disposal,[29] or that discharge untreated wastes into waterways.[30] An individual that is convicted of an environmental crime may be imprisoned for up to ten years, and business enterprises may be shut

25. Criminal Law, art. 220.

26. Criminal Law, art. 111. The disclosure of "state secrets" is prohibited by law, and the relevant regulations define the terms *secret information* and *illegal disclosure* in broad terms. "State Secrets" are defined as "matters that affect the security and interests of the state," and are illustrated by broad categories of information relating to national defense, "import policy decisions on state affairs," "economic and social development," "science and technology development," "criminal investigations," and "other state secrets that by decision of the state departments on protecting state secrets should be safeguarded." Law on Safeguarding State Security of the People's Republic of China (promulgated by the State Council in 1993); Detailed Rules for the Implementation of the Law on Safeguarding State Security of the People's Republic of China (promulgated by the State Council in 1994).

27. Criminal Law, art. 338. *See also* Environmental Protection Law, art. 43. For a discussion of the Environmental Protection Law, *see* Chapter 18, Environmental Protection § A.1. *See also* Wingo, *Translation: The Garbage Smuggling Case: Judgment of Division One of the Shanghai Municipal Intermediate Level People's Court January 13, 1997,* 6 PAC. RIM L. & POL'Y 607 (1997) (translated and annotated court decision involving smuggling of waste paper by a U.S. citizen in violation of environmental laws). *See also Criminal Code Amended to Ensure Environmental Enforcement,* CHINA COUNCIL FOR INTERNATIONAL COOPERATION ON ENVIRONMENT AND DEVELOPMENT, Vol. 3, No. 2 (June 1997), available at http://www.iisd1.iisd.ca/trade/cciced/cnjune97.pdf.

28. The State Environmental Protection Bureau changed its name and became a ministry-level "administration" entity in March of 1998. *See China Agency Given Greater Powers,* CHINA DAILY (Apr. 1, 1998), available on Lexis, News Library, or on the Web site of the CHINA DAILY at http://www.chinadaily.com.cn. The new title and elevation to a higher level reflects the NPC's concern with environmental affairs and public expectation of environmental protection.

29. SEPA claims that certain developed countries are using China as a dumping ground for their hazardous waste. *See Amended Criminal Law to Punish Polluters,* Xinhua News Agency (Apr. 10, 1997), available on Lexis, News Library.

30. *See China Laws Support Environmental Protection,* CHINA DAILY (June 5, 1998), available on Lexis, News Library, or on the Web site of the CHINA DAILY at http://www.chinadaily.com.cn.

down and responsible managers of business operations can be arrested and imprisoned.[31]

D. Corruption and Bribery

The act of gift-giving as a means to nurture *guanxi* (personal connections) is an important business activity that has its roots in China's hierarchical society and oftentimes may determine whether a person or enterprise will succeed in China. With a history of constant shortages of goods and services, paying homage to those individuals who can deliver needed items is a means to bypass the Chinese bureaucracy. Those who have valuable connections are able to improve their job and personal situations, obtain a superior apartment, or may secure government approval for a permit or license. Unfortunately, gift-giving can cross the line from incidental gratuities to payments of cash and property that violate both Chinese and U.S. laws.

1. China's Rules on Corruption and Gift Giving

a. General

In China, gift-giving is a very common and widely accepted practice. While monetary contributions to public officials are prohibited, small "incidental" gifts are normally acceptable. Incidental gifts include such items as pens, bottles of wine, dinners, and other types of relatively small gifts. Offering an official a vacation in Hawaii, on the other hand, is not considered incidental under the law. In addition, each individual Chinese agency may have its own internal rules regarding the receipt of gifts by its officials. Such internal rules may require that gifts be reported or that gifts be prohibited. However, these internal regulations would be operative only to agency officials and not to a foreign party.

The issue of improper gift-giving is addressed in the Criminal Law and other provincial and local regulations.[32] Chinese government officials are

---

31. Criminal Law, art. 339.

32. Criminal Law, Chapter 8 (Crimes of Corruption and Bribery); Company Law, art. 214; Company Law Crimes Decision, art. 9. *See also* Regulations on Giving and Accepting Gifts in Foreign Public Activities (promulgated by the State Council); Decision of the Standing Committee of the National People's Congress Regarding the Severe Punishment of Criminals Who Seriously Undermine the Economy (adopted on March 28, 1982, by the 22nd Sess. of the Standing Comm. of the 5th NPC); and the Supplementary Regulations Governing Punishment of Crimes of Embezzlement and Bribery (adopted January 21, 1988, by the 24th Sess. of the Standing Comm. of the 6th NPC). There are more than 2,000 anti-corruption laws and regulations that have been enacted nationwide over the past five years. *Anti-Corruption Legal System to be Set Up*, Xinhua News Agency (November 11, 2003). In 2003, China ranked 66 out of 133 countries in the annual survey conducted by Transparency International, which gave China a Corruption Perception Index (CPI) score of 3.4 A CPI 2003 Score relates to perceptions of the degree of corruption as seen by business people, academics and risk analysts, and ranges between 10 (highly clean) and 0 (highly corrupt). For more information on TI's survey process, *see* www.transparency.org.

required to limit their gifts to foreign guests to Chinese handicrafts or "practical objects of daily use." Under the law, Chinese officials who receive a gift in excess of RMB200 ($24) are required to surrender the gift to their supervising agencies. Moreover, gifts of cash and securities are strictly prohibited. A violation of the anti-corruption laws, including laws prohibiting bribery, concealing illegal gains, tax evasion, and embezzling funds, are capital offenses and are punishable by extensive prison terms or the imposition of the death penalty if large sums are at issue.[33]

In recent years, under pressure from the central, provincial, and municipal governments, the Chinese authorities have increased vigilance in an attempt to uncover and punish corruption and bribery. This campaign has led to a significant number of criminal prosecutions for embezzlement, bribery, and corruption at all government levels nationwide. Most notably, there have been numerous prosecutions of high-level officials for corruption, including highly publicized cases involving the vice-governor of Jiangxi province (1999), the deputy chairman of the National People's Congress standing committee (2000), the mayor of Shenyang (2001), the governor of Yunnan province (2002), the vice-governor of Hebei province (2002), various officials in Xiamen (2002), the governor of the Bank of China (2004), and high-level transportation officials responsible for the construction of the national highway system in the provinces of Henan, Guangdong, Sichuan, and Ningxia (2003–2004).[34]

---

33. *See Record of Events (October–December 1996),* CHINA LAW 103 (1997). On November 14, 1996, the Beijing Municipal People's Court sentence the assistant general manager of Shaougang Capital Iron and Steel Corporation to death for accepting kickbacks of $1.3 million and offering bribes to government officials of $174,000. Between 1993–1996, 158,000 people, mainly Party members, have been punished for corruption, embezzlement, and other economic crimes in China. In 1995, the government launched a massive anti-graft campaign, which netted Beijing Party chief Chen Xitong and 50 other officials. Chen was sentenced to life imprisonment for embezzling public funds and dereliction of duty relating to a $2.2 billion corruption scandal. His son, Chen Xiaotong, and personal secretary, Chen Jian, received prison sentences for 12 and 15 years respectively for their part in the scandal. *See also Chinese Tax Official Given Life Sentence for Graft,* Agence France Presse (Apr. 17, 1998), available on Lexis, News Library; *Take-Bribes Case,* CHINA DAILY (March 19, 1998), available on Lexis, News Library, or on the Web site of the CHINA DAILY http://www.chinadaily.com.cn (death sentence for bribery); *Banker Sentenced to 3 Years,* CHINA DAILY (June 12, 1998), available on Lexis, News Library, or on the Web site of the CHINA DAILY at http://www.chinadaily.com.cn (bank manager received $11,000 in gifts to help a factory obtain financing from the Bank of Communications). The Supreme People's Court established a telephone hotline for persons to complain about any judge or judicial officer who engages in embezzlement, bribery, or other corrupt activities such as abuse of power, concealing or forging evidence, leaking secrets, or unlawful coercion. *See Reporting Center,* CHINA DAILY (May 12, 1998), available on Lexis, News Library, or on the Web site of the CHINA DAILY at http://www.chinadaily.com.cn. *See also* Sun, *State Focuses on Corruption Fight,* CHINA DAILY (Mar. 11, 1998), available on Lexis, News Library, or on the Web site of the CHINA DAILY at http://www.chinadaily.com.cn; Wang, *Courts Clamp Down on Crime,* CHINA DAILY (Mar. 11, 1998), available on Lexis, News Library, or on the Web site of the CHINA DAILY at http://www.chinadaily.com.cn. With respect to the issuance of employment permits to foreign personnel, Chinese law prohibits the collection of inappropriate fees, abuse of authority in the issuing of permits, or the fraudulent issuance of permits. Such activities constitute criminal acts and are subject to imprisonment or fines. Employment of Foreigners Regulations, art. 31.

34. *See generally* R. Zhou, *Corruption's Long and Winding Road,* CHINA DAILY (May 13, 2004); *China Hunts Corrupt Officials Who Abscond Overseas,* CHINA DAILY (March 24, 2004).

In March 2003, a report of the Supreme People's Procuratorate (SPP)[35] issued at the National People's Congress contained statistics on criminal prosecutions for the offenses of bribery and corruption, finding that over the previous five-year period, the SPP prosecuted a total of 207,103 cases for embezzlement, bribery, and derogation from official duty. Of these cases, 5,541 cases treated the offenses of embezzlement, bribery, and misappropriation of public funds in excess of RMB1 million. Arising from the foregoing cases, a total of 12,830 persons holding State positions at or above the county level were found guilty. While the report does not provide any details of the year-by-year increase or decrease in case numbers, it does state that the SPP has enhanced its enforcement activities in the pursuit of offenders.

b. Bribery

The Criminal Law provides that the prohibition on official bribery applies to State functionaries (or personnel of State agencies engaged in public service),[36] as well as to persons that offer bribes.[37] To establish the criminal offense of official bribery, there must be (i) an offer of property (2) to a state functionary, and (3) in return for a benefit, or assistance in obtaining a benefit.[38] The term "property" essentially means anything that has value and generally refers to cash, goods, or other pecuniary benefits. Under the law, criminal penalties may be imposed based on the value of the property received. Under Article 383, the following penalties may be imposed on a government official who receives a bribe:

(1) For bribes received in value of RMB100,000, a mandatory prison term of ten years to life imprisonment may be imposed. In especially "serious cases," which are undefined, the death sentence may be imposed.

(2) For bribes received in value of RMB50,000 to RMB100,000, a mandatory prison term of five years may be imposed. In especially "serious cases," which are undefined, life imprisonment may be imposed.

35. For more information on the SPP, *see* Chapter 3, Legislating, the Judiciary, and Lawyers in China § B.2.

36. Criminal Law, art. 93. "State functionaries" refers to "personnel of State organs who are engaged in public service according to law. Personnel of State-owned companies or enterprises or institutions and people's organizations who are engaged in public service and personnel who are appointed and sent by State organs, State-owned companies or enterprises or institutions to non-State-owned companies or enterprises or institutions or mass organizations to carry out public service, and other personnel who are engaged in public service according to law, shall be treated as State Functionaries." Individuals that work for SOEs or non-State–owned enterprises are not included within the definition of state functionary.

37. Criminal Law, arts. 385 (definition of "offeree"); 389 (definition of "offeror").

38. Criminal Law, art. 389.

(3) For bribes received in value of RMB5,000 to RMB50,000, a prison term ranging from one to seven years may be imposed.
(4) For bribes received in value of less than RMB5,000, a prison term of up to two years may be imposed.[39]

If mitigating circumstances are present and the amount of the bribes is relatively low (less than RMB10,000), the individuals involved may be exempt from a prison term and punished administratively. Mitigating circumstances include cooperation with the authorities, admission of guilt, and return or surrender of any property received by an offeror. If a government official demands or requests a bribe, such demand is considered an aggravating circumstance and subjects the individual to a "heavier punishment."[40]

A person who offers a bribe is subject to a heavier punishment than is the intended recipient and may be sentenced, at a minimum, to a fixed term of imprisonment for five years. As an enhancement, if evidence exists that a person who offers a bribe sought to obtain illegal gain and where the circumstances are "serious" or cause "great damage to State interests," the person may be sentenced to five to ten years imprisonment.[41] An illegal gain would be something that the offeror is not entitled to receive under the law. An offeror who provides property to a state functionary due to extortion but receives no pecuniary gain in return is not guilty of a crime of bribery.[42] In order to commit an act of bribery, the offeror must offer property in order to seek illegitimate gain. If mitigating circumstances exist—such as where the

39. Criminal Law, art. 383. The value of property and character of the property in bribery cases is an important issue. In People's Procuratorate of Henan Province vs. Jie Wen Lin et al., decided by the Zhou Kou Intermediate People's Court of Henan Province on March 7, 2000, the defendant, a bank manager in a State-owned bank, had received two gifts from a customer. These comprised (a) a monetary gift of RMB30,000 ($3,630), and (b) a woolen coat valued at RMB1,500 ($182). At trial, evidence was presented that the defendant had approved certain loan applications of the customer's company. The court determined that the gift of RMB30,000 ($3,630) constituted an offer of property to a State functionary but also ruled that the gift of a coat did not constitute a bribe.

40. Criminal Law, arts. 385, 386. Under Article 383, the level of penalties is greater for "serious cases."

41. Criminal Law, art. 390. The term "serious case" is not defined in the Criminal Law, but the Supreme People's Court issued an explanatory circular detailing certain activities regarded as bribery charges subject to "severe" punishment. Bribery cases considered to be "serious" and subject to "severe penalty" are as follows: (1) bribes in a large amount, multiple offers to bribe, or bribes offered to many State functionaries; (2) bribes offered to Party leaders or judicial staff; (3) bribes offered to customs, FOREX, and tax officials for the purposes of smuggling, evading taxes, tax fraud, foreign-exchange fraud, foreign-exchange evasion, or the purchase and/or sales of foreign-exchange; and (4) bribes offered to the personnel of bank or securities regulatory authorities in order to illegally conduct banking or securities business, and have "seriously" damaged State interests. *See* Notice for Severely Treating Serious Corruption Simultaneously when Severely Treating Serious Bribery Cases (jointly issued on March 4, 1999, by the Supreme People's Court and the Supreme People's Procuratorate). The government also blacklists companies that engage in bribery from participating in construction projects in China. *See China to Blacklist Convicted Bribers in Construction Industry in Five Provincial Areas,* Xinhua News Agency (May 9, 2004).

42. Criminal Law, art. 389.

person offering the bribes admits their crime prior to the initiation of prosecution—he or she may be exempt from or may receive a reduced punishment.[43]

The essential issue in determining a crime of official bribery is that the gift of property—regardless of value—is given to a State functionary in return for a benefit, or assistance in obtaining a benefit. Whether the offeror actually receives the requested benefit is of no consequence. All co-conspirators, or those that facilitate the crime of bribery, may be punished as principal offenders.

c. Gifts to State Functionaries

The giving and acceptance of gifts by Chinese officials are governed by regulations adopted by the State Council, which apply only to the recipient of a gift and do not apply to the gift provider. The State Council has issued regulations on the acceptance of gifts by government officials that participate in functions involving foreign parties.[44] While the regulations apply only to Chinese officials, it is important for a foreign company to be aware of these provisions with a view to fully appreciating the context in which gifts may be exchanged with Chinese officials. Under the Regulations Involving Gifts from Foreigners, the term "gift" is defined to include cash, in-kind, or negotiable securities.[45]

The law requires that a Chinese party decline to receive any gift of cash or negotiable securities from a foreigner, or such gift shall be handed over to the State Treasury if it is impossible to decline the gift.[46] Gifts received at official functions involving foreign guests are required to be declared and disposed of pursuant to the regulations. Specifically, a recipient is required

43. Criminal Law, art. 390.

44. Regulations of the State Council of the People's Republic of China on Giving & Receiving Gifts at Official Functions Involving Foreigners (promulgated on December 5, 1993, by the State Council) (hereinafter the "Regulations Involving Gifts from Foreigners"). The State Council has adopted similar rules with respect to gifts received by domestic enterprises and individuals. The State Council has adopted regulations concerning overseas travel for government officials. Regulations Concerning Overseas Visits by High-Level Officials (issued on August 17, 1989, by the State Council and the Central Committee of the Communist Party). These regulations provide that a high-level government official may not (a) undertake an overseas visit that is not suitable to his position, (b) accept any financial assistance from foreign business, or (c) propose to any foreigner that an invitation to travel overseas be tendered. Officials who travel overseas are required to comply with State reporting and approval procedures. In general, a high-level government official is prohibited from making more than one overseas visit per year, unless otherwise required by his or her job duties. The length of stay in any one country should not exceed 3–5 days. Special approval is required where an official intends to be accompanied by his or her spouse, and approval is not granted for accompanying children. Personnel that come within the purview of the definition of a high-level official varies depending on the particular ministry, commission, department, agency, institution, etc., and each agency has its own internal rules concerning overseas travel. As a matter of practice, any official at the level of departmental head or above would be considered a high-level official.

45. Regulations Involving Gifts from Foreigners, art. 2.

46. Regulations Involving Gifts from Foreigners, art. 7.

to prepare and file a declaration form within one month of receipt of the gift for any item valued in excess of RMB200 ($24), and to surrender such gift to its work unit. A gift valued at less than RMB200 may be retained by the recipient.[47] A failure to properly declare and surrender gifts pursuant to the regulations is grounds for penalties and possible criminal prosecution.[48]

Under the Regulations Involving Gifts from Foreigners, a Chinese party is not allowed to give a visiting foreign guest a gift unless given a gift first, and any such gifts must be made in keeping with international practice.[49] In the selection of gifts—and all such gifts must be approved by supervising authorities—the regulations restrict the types of gifts to be given to include mainly souvenirs with distinctive Chinese characteristics, traditional handicraft items, and items of practical necessity.[50]

d. Commercial Bribery

Under the Criminal Law, commercial bribery is a distinct criminal offence from the crime of official bribery, which refers to bribery by state functionaries in public service.[51] The major statutory provisions governing commercial bribery are set forth in the Criminal Law and the Commercial Bribery Regulations.[52] Under the Criminal Law, the elements of the crime of commercial bribery include the following: (1) an offer of property (2) to a member of the working personnel of a company or enterprise (3) in return for a benefit, or assistance in obtaining a benefit, and (4) the amount of the bribe must be relatively large.[53] The principal distinctions between an act of official bribery and commercial bribery is that the offeree is not required to be a State functionary, and the amount of the bribe must be relatively large, which term is undefined.

Under the Commercial Bribery Regulations, commercial bribery is defined as the offering of bribes in the form of "property or other means"

47. Regulations Involving Gifts from Foreigners, art. 7.

48. Regulations Involving Gifts from Foreigners, art. 12 (outlines administrative penalties for failing to follow rules). The Criminal Law also provides that personnel who fail to surrender gifts to the State may, if the value of the gift is relatively large, be prosecuted for the criminal offense of corruption. Criminal Law, art. 394.

49. Regulations Involving Gifts from Foreigners, arts. 3, 5.

50. Regulations Involving Gifts from Foreigners, arts. 4, 5, 6.

51. Government personnel in China oftentimes have dual or multiple roles that require that they participate in commercial transactions on behalf of the State (where the government is the customer) and SOEs. This overlapping of duties between persons in government agencies and those in the State commercial sector leads to the application of both the official bribery and the commercial bribery rules.

52. Criminal Law, arts. 163 (standards applicable to the offeree of a commercial bribe), 164 (standards applicable to the offeror). *See also* Unfair Competition Law, art. 8, 22; Provisional Regulations for the Prohibition of Commercial Bribery Activities (issued on November 15, 1996, by the State Administration of Industry and Commerce), art. 1 (hereinafter the "Commercial Bribery Provisions"). The Commercial Bribery Regulations expand and clarify the rules under Article 8 of the Unfair Competition Law.

53. Criminal Law, arts. 163, 164.

by a businessperson to a unit (entity) or individual in order to sell or purchase merchandise.[54] The Commercial Bribery Regulations define the term "property" to include cash or material objects, including those that are disguised as fees for promotional advertisements, scientific research, service or consultancy, commissions, financial support, and reimbursements, with the exclusion of small promotional gifts according to business customs.[55] The term "other means" includes other benefits besides "property" and includes domestic or international tours (or entertainment). The Commercial Bribery Regulations also provide that off-the-books (secret) commissions, discounts, and rebates are activities that may be punishable as bribes.[56] The giving of cash or articles as gifts to an enterprise involved in a commercial transaction is deemed to be commercial bribery, unless the gift is categorized as "minimal value promotional gifts" in accordance with commercial practice.[57] Both the offeror and the offeree are criminally liable for activities that amount to commercial bribery.

Under the Criminal Law, acts of commercial bribery by an offeror are punishable by imprisonment of three years or less (less serious cases) or up to ten years (serious cases), and offerers are subject to property forfeiture.[58] Offerees of commercial bribes are subject to imprisonment of less than five years (less serious) and over five years (more serious cases), and are subject to property forfeiture.[59] Both the offeror and offeree are subject to monetary fines as well. Mitigating circumstances—such as the admission of the crime—may be taken into consideration in the imposition of a lesser penalty. Commercial bribery may also constitute a violation of administrative regulations and subject the participants to civil liability under the Unfair Competition Law.[60]

54. Commercial Bribery Regulations, art. 2.

55. Commercial Bribery Regulations, art. 2.

56. Commercial Bribery Regulations, art. 5. Legitimate commercial discounts, rebates, or commissions that are negotiated and recorded in company records or contracts generally will not be subject to scrutiny. However, the failure to disclose discounts, rebates, and commissions may lead to a bribery investigation by the SAIC. It is imperative that all negotiated discounts, rebates, and commissions are properly recorded in company books, transaction documentation, and/or correspondence. The same principle applies with respect to the reimbursement of travel and accommodation expenses—ensure that agreement to settle same is recorded in company books, transaction documentation, and/or correspondence.

57. Commercial Bribery Regulations, art. 8. An advertisement gift that is widely distributed and of *de minimus* value is acceptable. Such gifts usually depict the trademark, trade name, name, and/or logo of the company that has provided such gift. A pen, notebook, coffee mug, or calendar bearing the company's logo would be an appropriate advertisement gift. Cash may never be used as a promotional gift.

58. Criminal Law, art. 164.

59. Criminal Law, art. 163.

60. The Unfair Competition Law employs a broader definition of commercial bribery. Unfair Competition Law, art. 8. Article 8 of the Unfair Competition Law provides that "Business operators shall not resort to bribery with money, materials or by other means in buying or selling commodities. Any undisclosed rebates to units or individuals that have not been entered into the accounts shall be treated

Practice Tips: Proper Gift-Giving in China

- ✔ Entertainment and gifts must always be given purely on the basis of goodwill, and never on the basis of an expected return or benefit that would not have materialized in the absence of such entertainment or gift.
- ✔ In dealing with State Functionaries or individuals, a foreign company should avoid providing extravagant meals, entertainment, or gifts.
- ✔ High-level State Functionaries should never be invited to undertake an overseas visit at the expense of a foreign company.
- ✔ A foreign company should always check the identity of the stated holder of any given bank account with a view to satisfying itself that the intended recipient of transferred funds corresponds to the confirmed account holder.
- ✔ In dealing with agents, the foreign company should ensure that payments to be made to an agent are reasonable and correspond to the value of services rendered by that agent.
- ✔ In dealing with agents, the foreign company must always be satisfied that no part of payments to be made to an agent will be paid, either directly or indirectly, to a State Functionary or government official.

2. U.S. Foreign Corrupt Practices Act

In addition to China's corruption laws, U.S. companies and their employees are subject to the Foreign Corrupt Practices Act, which prohibits U.S. companies from making corrupt payments to foreign officials for the purpose of obtaining or retaining business.[61] Given the frequency that the issue of improper payments arises in countries with nonmarket or developing economies such as China, a discussion herein is instructive.

---

as bribes, and the acceptance by any unit or individual of such rebates shall be treated as the acceptance of a bribe. Business operators may, in an express manner, give discounts to buyers or commissions to middlemen with the amount of such discounts or commissions being entered into the accounts, and business operators may accept discounts or commissions with the amounts being entered into the accounts." The Unfair Competition Law provides that a non-criminal violation of the commercial bribery provisions may be subject to an administrative penalty of between RMB10,000 ($1,210) to RMB200,000 ($24,213). Unfair Competition Law, art. 22.

61. 15 U.S.C. §§ 78m, 78dd-1, 78dd-2, 78ff. The Foreign Corrupt Practices Act (FCPA) was originally enacted in 1977 and has been amended. The FCPA is part of the Securities Exchange Act of 1934. This book does not address every U.S. law that applies to operations in China. The FCPA is specifically addressed given the prevalence of gift-giving in China. Readers are cautioned to evaluate the tax, securities, antitrust, export control, employment, environmental, and other U.S. laws and regulations that have been given extraterritorial effect and apply directly to the activities of U.S. companies in China. For additional information concerning the FCPA, *see generally* Geroe, *Complying with the U.S. Antibribery Laws,* 31 INT'L LAW. 1037 (1997); Pendergast, *Foreign Corrupt Practices Act: An Overview of Almost Twenty Years of Foreign Bribery Prosecutions,* 7 INT'L Q. 187 (1995) (review of FCPA cases); Givant, *The Sword That Shields: The U.S. Foreign Corrupt Practices Act Can Protect U.S. Firms Doing Business in China,* CHINA BUS. REV. 29 (May-June 1994).

Practice Tips: Improper Payments

- ✔ Payments to any political entity in China.
- ✔ Payments made in violation of laws and regulations.
- ✔ Payments that are either not recorded in the books of the company or are incorrectly recorded in the company books.
- ✔ Payments to any government or commercial entity that are made in the expectation of any corresponding return or benefit.
- ✔ Payments made in the understanding, express or implied, that part or all of such payment should or will in turn be paid to a third party as a bribe in return for an expected return or benefit.
- ✔ Payments made to government officials or employees for the purpose of receiving a benefit that would not have materialized in the absence of such payment.
- ✔ Payments to State Functionaries that are related to the performance of their duties.
- ✔ Transactions that fail to disclose the full value (except for discounts given in the ordinary course of business).
- ✔ Payment to a third party for goods or services rendered by another party, unless adequate supporting documentation is furnished.
- ✔ Payment for unvouched expenses, such as travel and accommodation expenses.

The FCPA's legislative history describes that the illegal payments ran the "gamut from bribery of high foreign officials in order to secure some type of favorable action by a foreign government to so-called facilitating payments that allegedly were made to ensure that government functionaries discharged certain ministerial or clerical duties."[62] The FCPA was enacted by Congress to stop the ongoing practice of bribing foreign officials and to restore public confidence in the American business system.

The 1988 amendment to the FCPA expressed the sense of Congress that the executive branch should negotiate an international agreement to bind the members of the organization for Economic Cooperation and Development (OECD) to govern persons from OECD countries concerning prohibited acts

62. H.R. Rep. No. 640, 95th Cong., 1st Sess. 4 (1977). The FCPA has its genesis in the Watergate scandal and resultant investigation by the Watergate Special Prosecutor and Securities Exchange Commission (SEC) of illegal political contributions made to foreign political parties and governments. The SEC revealed that in the mid-1970s over 400 U.S. companies, of which 117 companies were Fortune 500 firms, made questionable or illegal payments in excess of $300 million to foreign government officials.

under the standards of the FCPA. On May 27, 1994, the OECD approved a recommendation in which OECD member states agreed that bribery distorts international competitive conditions; that countries share the responsibility to combat bribery in international business transactions; and that further action is needed on the national and international level. The OECD recommended that member states should "take concrete and meaningful steps" to meet the goal of deterring, preventing, and combating bribery of foreign officials.

In November of 1998, President Clinton signed the International Anti-Bribery and Fair Competition Act of 1998 (the "1998 OECD Amendments"), which amends the FCPA to implement the provisions of the OECD Convention on Combating Bribery of Foreign Officials in International Business Transactions (the "OECD Anti-Bribery Convention" or the "Convention").[63] The OECD Anti-Bribery Convention was adopted by thirty-three countries (twenty-eight OECD members plus Argentina, Brazil, Bulgaria, Chile, and Slovakia) on November 21, 1997, and signed on December 17, 1997.[64] The OECD Anti-Bribery Convention was ratified by the U.S. Senate on July 31, 1998.

The OECD Anti-Bribery Convention requires each of the signatory countries to enact and enforce anti-foreign bribery laws and to impose "effective, proportionate and dissuasive criminal penalties [for foreign corrupt payments] . . . comparable to those applicable to the bribery of the [signatory country's] own public officials."[65] The preamble of the OECD Anti-Bribery Convention provides that "[b]ribery is a widespread phenomenon in international business transactions, including trade and investment, which raises serious moral and political concerns, undermines good governance and economic development, and distorts international competitive conditions."

Although the OECD Anti-Bribery Convention is consistent with the FCPA, there are a number of significant changes to the FCPA, including (1) expanded extraterritorial reach of the FCPA, (2) an increase in the range of individuals and companies subject to the FCPA, and (3) broader scope of

---

63. A copy of the Convention is reprinted on the Web site of the U.S. Department of Justice at the following address: http://www.usdoj.gov. Pursuant to the Convention, the DOJ has submitted a response and supplemental response to questions concerning the FCPA from other signatory countries. These documents provide an excellent summary of information concerning the DOJ's interpretation of the FCPA and the application thereof. *See Response of the United States to the Phase I Questionnaire* (Oct. 30, 1998), available on the Web site of the DOJ; *Supplemental Response of the United States to the Phase I Questionnaire* (undated 1999 report), available on the Web site of the DOJ. The 1998 OECD Amendments are effective February 15, 1999.

64. China, a country considered to be a prime source of violations of the FCPA, has refused to sign the OECD Anti-Bribery Convention.

65. OECD Anti-Bribery Convention, art. 3, ¶ 1. The Council of Europe has adopted its own convention concerning antibribery. A copy of the convention is available at the Web site of the DOJ at http://www.usdoj.gov.

prohibitions. The amendments to the FCPA under the 1998 OECD Amendments are addressed in more detail below.

Compliance under the FCPA for companies with China operations is of particular concern given that underpaid government officials still control a sizable portion of the business that U.S. companies have targeted. The FCPA also has special relevance to Chinese companies that are subject to the U.S. Securities Exchange Act. A brief review of FCPA standards is instructive.

a. FCPA Prohibitions

The FCPA prohibits "issuers" and "domestic concerns" from making unlawful payments. Issuers are defined as

(a) All companies, whether domestic or foreign, that have a class of securities registered pursuant to Section 13 of the Securities Exchange Act, and
(b) All companies that are required to file reports pursuant to Section 15(d) of the Securities Exchange Act[66]

Domestic concerns are defined in the FCPA as

(a) Any individual who is a citizen, national, or resident of the United States, and
(b) Any corporation, partnership, association, joint-stock company, business trust, unincorporated organization, or sole proprietorship that has its principal place of business in the United States or is organized under the laws of a state of the United States or any territory, possession, or commonwealth of the United States[67]

The 1998 OECD Amendments extend coverage of the FCPA to all other persons, natural or juridical, who do any act in furtherance of a corrupt payment while in the territory of the United States.[68]

b. Prohibition on Direct Payments

The FCPA prohibits two types of activities. In particular, the FCPA prohibits bribes directly made by issuers or domestic concerns to foreign officials. The second prohibition is the responsibility of a company for bribes paid by intermediaries.

66. 15 U.S.C. § 78dd-1 (a).
67. 15 U.S.C. § 78dd-2 (h)(1).
68. 15 U.S.C. § 78dd-3. The DOJ takes the position that corporate liability is not predicated upon the participation or authorization by management. A corporate entity is liable for the acts of its employees if they act within the scope of their employment relationship and for the benefit of the corporation. Whether management condemns or approves of the employee's conduct is irrelevant.

The "foreign corrupt practices" prohibited under the FCPA include the making of an offer, gift, promise to give, or authorization of the giving of anything of value to any foreign official for purposes of

(a) Influencing any act or decision of such foreign official in his or her official capacity, or inducing such foreign official to do or omit to do any act in violation of the lawful duty of such official
(b) Inducing such foreign official to use his or her influence with a foreign government or instrumentality thereof to affect or influence any act or decision of such government or instrumentality; or
(c) *Securing any improper advantage,* in order to assist the issuer or domestic concern in obtaining or retaining business for or with, or directing business to, any person[69]

c. Prohibition on Payments by Intermediaries

It is also unlawful to make a payment to any person, while "knowing" that all or a portion of the payment will be offered, given, or promised, directly or indirectly, to any foreign official (or any foreign political party, official, or candidate) for the purposes of influencing any act or decision in order to assist a company in obtaining or retaining business for or with, or directing business to, any person.[70] The "knowledge standard" encompasses the concepts of "conscious disregard" or "willful blindness" of the illegal payment. This standard includes a conscious purpose to avoid learning the truth and deliberate ignorance of known circumstances that reasonably alert one to the high probability of violations of the law.[71]

d. Scope of Application

Prior to the 1998 OECD Amendments, the coverage of the FCPA was limited to U.S. citizens and firms falling within the statutory definition of "issuer" or

69. 15 U.S.C. § 78dd-1(a)(1)(A), (2)(A), & (3)(A); 15 U.S.C. § 78dd-2(a)(1)(A), (2)(A), & (3)(A). The language "securing any improper advantage" was added to the FCPA pursuant to the 1998 OECD Amendments. This amendment is consistent with the DOJ's longstanding position that any improper governmental benefits, including favorable regulatory decisions, are illegal under the FCPA. The DOJ takes a broad view as to what constitutes an improper advantage. In October 1998, the DOJ obtained a conviction against Saybolt, Inc., a petroleum inspection firm that had paid bribes to the Panamanian government to obtain a lease arrangement at the Panama Canal. The jury interpreted the payment to obtain a lease as an unlawful payment designed to assist the defendant corporation in obtaining or retaining business because the lease would improve its competitiveness and profitability. The company officials received four-month prison sentences and $20,000 fines, and the company paid a $4.9 million criminal fine (which included penalties under the FCPA and as a result of EPA reporting requirements). *See Former Saybolt Chief Convicted,* Oil Daily (Oct. 21, 1998), available on Lexis, News Library; *Saybolt, Inc. Agrees to Plead Guilty to Falsifying Reports to the EPA and Violating the Foreign Corrupt Practices Act and to Pay Fine of $4.9 Million,* Business Wire (Aug. 18, 1998), available on Lexis, News Library.

70. *See* 15 U.S.C. §78dd-1(a)(3); 15 U.S.C. §78dd-2(a)(3); 15 U.S.C. §78dd-3(a)(3). *See also* OECD Anti-Bribery Convention, art.1, ¶ 1.

71. H.R. Rep. No. 576, 100th Cong., 2d Sess. 920 (1988).

"domestic concern" and the corrupt activities were required to have a nexus to the territory of the United States. Today, the law provides that "any person," which includes any domestic or foreign company and any U.S. citizen or alien, is subject to liability for any acts that occur *within* the territorial boundaries of the United States.[72] In addition, U.S. persons are liable under the FCPA for their activities "*outside* the United States." For activities outside the United States, the use of a "means or instrumentality of interstate commerce"—such as the mail or telephone communications—is not necessary to trigger application of the FCPA.[73]

The FCPA applies to any company, officer, director, employee, or agent of a company, and any shareholder acting on behalf of the company. Individuals and companies may be liable if they aid, abet, counsel, command, induce, procure, or willfully cause another to violate the antibribery provisions, or if they conspire to violate the provisions.[74] However, the courts have held that a foreign official may not be charged with conspiracy to violate the FCPA.[75] Further, the OECD Anti-Bribery Convention and the 1998 OECD Amendments do not impose liability on domestic companies for illegal payments made outside the United States by their wholly foreign-owned subsidiaries.

e. Element of Corrupt Intent

A key element of the prohibitions requires that the payment be made "corruptly" and "for purposes of" influencing a decision. Although not defined in the statute, the legislative history notes that the payment must be intended to induce the recipient to "misuse his official position" in order to wrongfully direct business to the payor or his client, or to obtain a preferential administrative or regulatory ruling or legislative enactment. The word "corruptly" connotes an "evil motive or purpose" and does not require that the act be "fully consummated, or succeed in producing the desired outcome."[76]

---

72. 15 U.S.C. §78dd-2(g). *See also* OECD Anti-Bribery Convention, art. 4, ¶ 1. Jurisdiction is based upon the principle of territoriality; namely, the United States has the right to control the activities of any person within the sovereign boundaries of the United States.

73. 15 U.S.C. §78dd-1(g); 15 U.S.C. §78dd-2(i). *See also* OECD Anti-Bribery Convention, art. 4, ¶ 2. Jurisdiction is based upon the principle of nationality; namely, the U.S. government has the right to regulate the activities of its citizens and corporations anywhere in the world.

74. 18 U.S.C. §§ 2, 371.

75. *See United States v. Castle*, 925 F.2d 831 (5th Cir. 1991).

76. *See* Senate Report No. 114, 95th Cong., 1st Sess. 10, *reprinted in* 1977 U.S. Code Cong. & Admin. News 4098, 4108. *See United States v. Liebo*, 923 F.2d 1308, 1312 (8th Cir. 1991). In the *Liebo* decision, the court stated that "an act is 'corruptly' done if done voluntarily and intentionally, and with a bad purpose of accomplishing either an unlawful method or means. The term 'corruptly' is intended to connote that the offer, payment, and promise was intended to induce the recipient to misuse his official position." *See also Bryan v. United States*, 118 S. Ct. 1939, 1945 (1998) (approving a similar definition of willfulness).

f. Covered Activities

The FCPA prohibits payments, offers to pay, and promises to pay, or authorizing to pay "anything of value." The FCPA contemplates that "anything of value" includes not only monetary payments but also the transfer and/or misuse of company assets such as aircraft, boats, vehicles, and real property.[77]

g. Recipients

The FCPA prohibits corrupt payments to a foreign official, a foreign political party or party official, or any candidate for political office. The Act defines "foreign official" to mean any officer or employee of a foreign government or any department, agency, or instrumentality thereof, or any person acting in an official capacity for or on behalf of any such government or department, agency, or instrumentality.[78] The United States recognizes that the term "foreign government" includes any government, faction, or body of insurgents within a country, irrespective of recognition by the United States. Thus, the United States maintains that Taiwan is a "foreign government" under the FCPA, although the United States does not formally recognize Taiwan as an independent sovereign state.[79]

Prior to 1988, the term "foreign official" did not include any employee of a foreign government or agency whose duties were essentially ministerial or clerical. The language "ministerial and clerical" led to confusion given that it was difficult to determine a government official's tasks or duties. The FCPA was amended in 1988 to focus on the purpose of the payment rather than the functions and responsibilities of the foreign official.

The 1998 OECD Amendments added *public international organizations* to the definition of "foreign official," which includes the United Nations, the World Bank, the International Monetary Fund, the World Trade Organization, the Organization of American States, the Council of Europe, and the European Union.[80] The International Olympic Committee does not fall within the definition of a *public international organization* at this time.

h. Exception for Routine Governmental Action

The FCPA provides that the prohibitions shall not apply to "any facilitating or expediting payment to a foreign official, political party, or party official the purpose of which is to expedite or to secure the performance of a routine

77. *See* 15 U.S.C. § 78dd-1(a); § 78dd-2(a); § 78dd-3(a).

78. 15 U.S.C. § 78dd-1(f)(1)(A); 15 U.S.C. §78dd-2(h)(2)(A); 15 U.S.C. §78dd-3(f)(2). *See also* OECD Anti-Bribery Convention, art. 1, ¶ 4.

79. 22 U.S.C. § 3303.

80. 15 U.S.C. § 78dd-1(f)(1)(A); 15 U.S.C. §78dd-2(h)(2)(A). *See also* OECD Anti-Bribery Convention, preamble.

governmental action."[81] This exception applies to all payments to secure routine governmental actions by any foreign official, regardless of the official's title, status, or duties.

The term "routine governmental action" means only an action that is ordinarily and commonly performed by a foreign official in

(a) Obtaining permits, licenses, or other official documents to qualify a person to do business in a foreign country
(b) Processing governmental papers, such as visas and work orders
(c) Providing police protection, mail pickup and delivery, or scheduling inspections associated with contract performance or inspections related to transit of goods across country
(d) Providing phone service, power and water supply, loading and unloading cargo, or protecting perishable products or commodities from deterioration; or
(e) Actions of a similar nature

The term "routine governmental action" does not include any decision by a foreign official whether, or on what terms, to award new business to or to continue business with a particular party, or any action taken by a foreign official involved in the decision-making process to encourage a decision to award new business to or continue business with a particular party.[82]

i. Affirmative Defenses

The FCPA provides for two specific defenses to a violation of the antibribery prohibitions. The FCPA provides that it is not a violation of the law if the payment, gift, offer, or promise of anything of value that was made was lawful under the written laws and regulations of the country in question. The foreign compulsion defense applies only where the law is in writing and does not apply to unwritten rules, customs, or practices.[83]

Secondly, the prohibitions under the FCPA do not apply to payments that are considered bona fide expenditures, such as travel and lodging expenses, incurred by or on behalf of a foreign official and directly related to (i) the promotion, demonstration, or explanation of products or services; or (ii) the execution or performance of a contract with a foreign government.[84] These provisions mean that an official's visit to U.S. facilities for technical

81. 15 U.S.C. § 78dd-1(b); 15 U.S.C. § 78dd-2(b). This exception was not affected by the 1998 OECD Amendments.
82. 15 U.S.C. § 78dd-1(f) (3)(B); 15 U.S.C. § 78dd-2(h)(4)(B); 15 U.S.C. § 78dd-3 (f)(4)(B).
83. 15 U.S.C. § 78dd-1(c) (1); 15 U.S.C. § 78dd-2(c)(1).
84. 15 U.S.C. § 78dd-1(c) (2); 15 U.S.C. § 78dd-2(c)(2).

meetings and training sessions are permissible. However, a payment is not a bona fide expenditure if "corruptly" made in return for an official act or omission.[85]

j. Penalties for Violations

The Securities and Exchange Commission (SEC) is responsible for civil enforcement of the accounting provisions and the antibribery provisions with respect to issuers. The Department of Justice (DOJ) is responsible for all criminal enforcement and for civil enforcement of the antibribery provisions with respect to domestic concerns and all other individuals that come under the FCPA's jurisdiction.

The statute of limitations for criminal violations of the FCPA is five years. The statute of limitations for civil violations is also five years. However, the Ninth Circuit Court of Appeals recently ruled that "limitations periods do not bind the United States when it sues to vindicate a public right or interest, absent a clear showing of Congressional intent to the contrary."[86] The court reasoned that imposing the statute of limitations on actions under the securities laws would "conflict with the underlying policies of the securities laws."[87] Whether the SEC may pursue FCPA civil actions after the limitations period is left for observation.

A violation of the FCPA exposes a company to fines of up to $2 million per incident. The amount of the fines can also be more than the amount specified in the FCPA because of the alternative fines provisions.[88] Under this law, individuals may be fined up to $250,000 or up to twice the amount of the gross gain or gross loss if the defendant derives pecuniary gain from the offense or causes a pecuniary loss to another person. The FCPA further provides that the penalty provisions do not override the provisions in other federal statutes such as tax and money laundering laws.

Officers, directors, and shareholders who willfully violate the antibribery provisions are subject to a $100,000 fine or imprisonment of up to five years,

---

85. Although there is little case law on the "reasonable and bona fide expenditure" defense, the Attorney General has issued a number of opinions concerning the DOJ's interpretation. *See* DOJ Release 81-02 (Dec. 11, 1981) (providing product samples permissible so long as the samples are intended for inspection, testing, and sampling and not for personal use); DOJ Release 82-01 (Jan. 27, 1982), DOJ Release 83-03 (Jul. 26, 1983), DOJ Release 85-01 (Jul. 16, 1985) (the payment of reasonable and necessary expenses, including meals, lodging, entertainment, and travel for foreign officials was appropriate for purposes of meetings, site inspections, and product demonstrations); DOJ Release 92-01 (Feb. 1992), DOJ Release 96-01 (Nov. 25, 1996) (training to government officials as part of joint venture agreement is permissible); DOJ Release 83-02 (Jul. 26, 1983) (payment of limited expenses for government official to tour company facilities at the conclusion of the official's vacation in the United States).

86. *SEC v. Rind,* 991 F.2d 1486, 1491 (9th Cir. 1993).

87. *Id.* At 1492.

88. 18 U.S.C. § 3571.

or both. Any employee or agent of a company who is a U.S. citizen, national, or resident, or who is otherwise subject to the jurisdiction of the United States, and who willfully violates the antibribery provisions, is subject to a fine up to $100,000 or imprisonment for up to five years, or both. The 1998 OECD Amendments make both foreign and domestic nationals equally liable for both criminal and civil enforcement penalties.

Monetary penalties imposed upon individuals may not be paid by the domestic concern or issuer. Prior to 1988, the government could not prosecute an individual until his or her company was found in violation of the FCPA. Today, the government may go directly against an individual. The 1988 amendment to the FCPA grants the government a right of action to impose a civil fine of up to $10,000 against any firm or individual that violates the antibribery provisions. The government may also enjoin any act or practice constituting a violation of the antibribery provisions.

A company or individual found to violate the FCPA may not participate in government procurement contracts.[89] The only exception to the rule is where the agency has a "compelling reason" to allow participation, such as in situations where national security is an overriding concern. Further, the Internal Revenue Code (relating to trade or business expenses) provides that no deduction will be allowed for a payment made to a foreign government official if the payment would be unlawful under the FCPA.[90] The burden of proof in a tax action is on the government to prove the illegality of the payment by clear and convincing evidence.

k. Exposure to Private Litigation

A number of court decisions have held that there is no private right of action for a violation of the FCPA.[91] However, a violation of the antibribery provisions of the FCPA may give rise to a private right of action under the Racketeer Influenced and Corrupt Organizations Act (RICO) by a competitor who alleges that the bribery caused the defendant to win a foreign contract.[92] Moreover, under the OECD Anti-Bribery Convention, the DOJ

89. A company may be suspended from participation in public contracts if accused of fraud or "any other offense indicating a lack of business integrity or business honesty that seriously and directly affects the present responsibility of a Government contractor or subcontractor." F.A.R. §9.407-2(a). Upon conviction or civil judgment, the government may bar a company from all public contracts for a period of three years. F.A.R. § 9.406-2(a). Suspension and disbarment are not limited to the specific agency at issue and apply to all government contracting. F.A.R. § 9-401.

90. 26 U.S.C. § 162 (c); 26 U.S.C. § 7454; 26 C.F.R. § 1.162-18.

91. *See Lamb v. Philip Morris, Inc.*, 915 F.2d 1024 (6th Cir. 1990), *cert. denied,* 498 U.S. 1086, 111 S. Ct. 961 (1991).

92. *See* 18 U.S.C. §§ 1962–1968. *See also Dooley v. United Technologies Corp.*, 803 F. Supp. 428 (1992, D.C. Dist. Ct.).

has the power to lodge a complaint with the OECD on behalf of its nationals in the event that a foreign company violates the Convention.

l. Government Guidance

The Attorney General is required to issue an opinion in response to a specific inquiry from a person or firm within thirty days of the request in regard to compliance with the FCPA. An opinion issued by the DOJ may be used in a court proceeding to demonstrate that the subject conduct is presumed to be in conformance with the FCPA.[93]

m. Compliance with the FCPA

The FCPA provides that a company is required to maintain books, records, and accounts, which, in reasonable detail, accurately and fairly reflect the company's transactions. The purpose is to ensure that the company's records conform to generally accepted accounting principles in order to prevent undisclosed transactions such as kickbacks and bribes. The U.S. government also emphasizes the importance of periodically reviewing the effectiveness of a system of internal accounting controls. The key is to develop a program to evaluate the system to determine whether it works within the company in question. The employees need to be warned that compliance programs will be constantly monitored by direct observation, supervision, and testing.

The U.S. government also emphasizes that it is the responsibility of a company to investigate the background, as well as to monitor, the activities of its outside consultants and distributors. To ensure compliance, a company should conduct a due diligence review of its distributors, consultants, and representatives. This includes an investigation of the reputation of the person in question. If he or she has a reputation for demanding illegal payments, knowledge of prior activities may be imputed to a firm. As part of an investigation, it is especially important to be wary of consultants who make suspicious accommodation requests such as payment to a bank account outside of China, "in-kind" payment of fees rather than in currency, or requests for payments to third parties. Information may be obtained through the U.S. Embassy or consulates in China, attorneys, accountants, industry trade associations, and other sources concerning a Chinese consultant's background and reputation.

93. 28 C.F.R. § 80 (procedures for DOJ review). The Department of Commerce also supplies general guidance to exporters who have questions concerning the FCPA. However, the DOC will not guarantee that the information supplied will remain confidential and that the information supplied may be released to interested persons under the Freedom of Information Act. In addition, an interested party may not rely upon the information and advice received from the DOC in an enforcement action.

Key Laws and Regulations

Criminal Law of the People's Republic of China (promulgated March 14, 1997, by the NPC)

Decision of the Standing Committee of the National People's Congress Concerning the Punishment of the Crime Constituting Violation of the Company Law (adopted February 28, 1995, by the 12th Sess. of the Standing Comm. of the 8th NPC)

Supplementary Regulations of the Standing Committee of the NPC on Punishment for Tax Evasion and Refusal to Pay Tax (adopted on September 4, 1992, by the 27th Sess. of the Standing Comm. of the 7th NPC)

Provisional Regulations regarding the Administrative Punishments on Disciplinary Measures on Activities Violating the Foreign Exchange Administrative Regulations, including Arbitrage, Illegal Procurement, Illegal Evasion and Illegal Transactions in Foreign Exchange (issued on January 25, 1999, by the Ministry of Supervision, Ministry of Personnel, People's Bank of China, State General Administration of Customs and the State Administration of Foreign Exchange)

Safeguarding State Security of the People's Republic of China (promulgated by the State Council in 1993)

Detailed Rules for the Implementation of the Law on Safeguarding State Security of the People's Republic of China (promulgated by the State Council in 1994)

Decision of the Standing Committee of the National People's Congress Regarding the Severe Punishment of Criminals Who Seriously Undermine the Economy (adopted on March 28, 1982, by the 22nd Sess. of the Standing Comm. of the 5th NPC)

Supplementary Regulations Governing Punishment of Crimes of Embezzlement and Bribery (adopted January 21, 1988, by the 24th Sess. of the Standing Comm. of the 6th NPC)

Regulations of the State Council of the People's Republic of China on Giving & Receiving Gifts at Official Functions Involving Foreigners (promulgated on December 5, 1993, by the State Council)

Provisional Regulations for the Prohibition of Commercial Bribery Activities (issued on November 15, 1996, by the State Administration of Industry and Commerce)

Chapter 24

Special Zones of the PRC

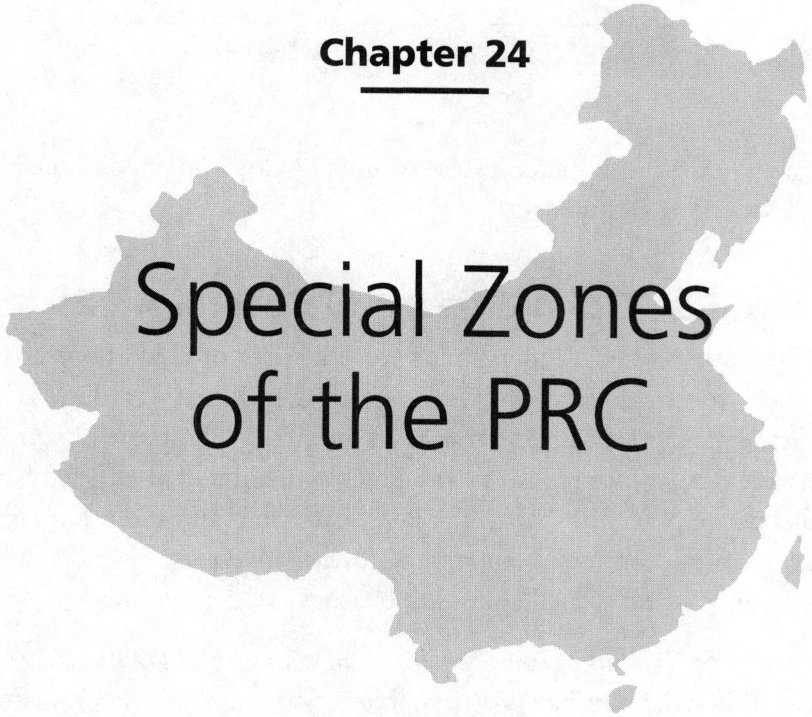

The acknowledged catalyst for China's phenomenal growth over the past twenty years has been the policies of the government with respect to the special economic zones, technology zones, port cities, and other special administrative regions. Any company doing business in the PRC needs to understand and appreciate the rules governing special zones established in different regions and cities throughout China, and the impact of those rules upon an operation established in the zones. A foreign investor should analyze the differences between the zones including an analysis of the variations in tax benefits, land-use requirements, employment rules and restrictions, registration assistance, and other matters. In addition to the rules and regulations affecting an operation in a particular zone, an investor must also analyze the practical aspects of doing business in a zone, including the costs of a particular zone, proximity to transportation and resources, availability of skilled labor, and access to markets. Although a complete analysis of all laws and regulations concerning the various zones is beyond the scope of this book, this chapter analyzes the basic policies of the PRC concerning the zones.

This chapter also analyzes the legal issues relevant to the Hong Kong Special Administrative Region (HKSAR) and Macao Special Administrative Region (MSAR) under the one-country two-systems principle. In this regard, this chapter briefly discusses the Joint Declaration between Great Britain and the PRC concerning the former British colony, and the PRC's Basic Law concerning the HKSAR. This chapter also addresses the provisions of the trade and market access agreements known as the Closer Economic Partnership

Arrangement (CEPA) negotiated by the Mainland Government and the Hong Kong and Macao governments.

A. SEZs, Open Cities, and Coastal Areas

Starting in 1980, the PRC leadership adopted a series of regulations governing incentives to attract foreign investment to the SEZs, coastal areas, and other zones. The first set of regulations was intended to limit the regions that were allowed to offer incentives. As foreign investment increased and resulted in lopsided development in China, the PRC leadership allowed other regions and cities to offer incentives to encourage foreign investors.

In general, China's special zones are characterized as follows:

Economic & Technological Development Zones (ETDZ): ETDZs are areas within cities that have been established to attract foreign investment by granting preferential tax concessions for production operations. Industrial Parks (IP) and Export Processing Zones are planned within the framework of existing ETDZs, and the municipal government in charge of such zones is authorized to grant further reductions in tax exemptions. There are 54 EDTZs in China.

Export Processing Zones (EPZ): The State Council has selected and approved 15 cities to act as EPZs since April 2000. EPZs are designed to be export processing oriented and are under the supervision of China Customs.[1]

Free Trade Zones (FTZ): FTZs are established under the supervision of China Customs, and no tariffs are imposed on importations into the specific FTZs. There are 15 FTZs in China, including zones in Fujian Province (Fuzhou FTZ, Xiamen Xiangyu FTZ); Guangdong Province (Guangdong FTZ, Shantou FTZ); Shenzhen (Futian FTZ, Shantoujiao FTZ, Yantiangang FTZ, and Zhuhai FTZ); Hainan Province (Hainan Haikou FTZ); Jiangsu Province (Zhangjiangang FTZ); Liaoning (Dalian FTZ); Shandong Province (Qingdao FTZ); Shanghai (Waigaoqiao FTZ); Tianjin (Tianjin FTZ); and Zhejiang Province (Ningbo FTZ).[2]

National Border & Economic Cooperation Zones (NBECZ): The NBECZs are open cities along the land borders of China and are designed to encourage border trade with China's neighboring countries. The State Council has approved 14 NBECZs in China since 1992.

1. For regulatory background on EPZs, *see* Chapter 15, Customs and Trade Regulation § B.3.
2. For regulatory background on FTZs, *see* Chapter 15, Customs and Trade Regulation § B.3.

New & High Technology Development Zones (NHTDZ): The NHTDZs are State-level zones established to promote particular industries or technology, and enterprises within the zones may qualify for certain tax and customs benefits. There are 53 NHTDZs in China.

The regulatory history in the development of the above-mentioned zones has its history in legislation adopted since 1980, including as follows:

1. SEZ Regulations

In August of 1980, the PRC adopted regulations for the pilot establishment of special economic zones (SEZs) in certain regions such as Shenzhen (which borders the New Territories of Hong Kong), Zhuhai (which borders Macao), Shantou (Guangdong Province), and Xiamen (Fujian Province).[3] The SEZ Regulations adopted by the NPC granted foreign investors the right to establish joint ventures with Chinese enterprises and provided preferential tax treatment and other incentives. The SEZ Regulations empowered the local governments to work independently and without interference of the Central People's Government in developing policies and laws to encourage economic development and job creation. The SEZs were, in essence, used by the government as a testing ground for economic and legal reform such as preferential taxation policies, reform of government organizations, price reform, and establishment of financial and securities markets.

Under the SEZ Regulations, the income tax rate for enterprises located in the SEZs is 15 percent.[4] Production enterprises with foreign investment that have an operation term of at least ten years are exempt from enterprise income tax in the first two profit-making years and pay tax at half rate for the following three years. After the expiration of the period of exemption and reductions, FIEs that manufacture products for export may, with approval, be subject to a reduced income tax rate of 10 percent. In addition, enterprises with advanced technology are entitled to additional tax reductions of

3. Regulations of the People's Republic of China on Special Economic Zones in Guangdong Province (approved on August 26, 1980, at the 15th Sess. of the Standing Comm. of the 5th NPC), *reprinted in* CHINA LAWS FOR FOREIGN BUSINESS (CCH), Special Zones & Cities ¶ 70-800 (hereinafter the "SEZ Regulations"); Implementing Measures of Guangdong Province for the Encouragement of Foreign Investment (promulgated on April 26, 1987, by the Guangdong Provincial People's Government), *reprinted in* CHINA LAWS FOR FOREIGN BUSINESS (CCH), Special Zones & Cities ¶ 70-810 (hereinafter the "SEZ Implementing Measures"). For a Chinese view of the SEZ development and history, *see* NEW PROGRESS IN CHINA'S SPECIAL ECONOMIC ZONES, STUDIES ON THE CHINESE MARKET ECONOMY SERIES (Gao Shangquan & Chi Fulin, eds.) Foreign Language Press, Beijing (1997).

4. SEZ Regulations, art. 14. The preferential rate contrasts with the national tax rate of 33 percent, of which 30 percent is earmarked for the national government and 3 percent for local government. For more information on taxation laws as applied to FIEs, *see* Chapter 9, Taxation Law.

50 percent for an additional three years beyond the initial periods mentioned above. Service industries with foreign investment exceeding $5 million, and with an operation period of at least ten years, are entitled to tax exemptions in the first profit-making year and pay half tax for the following two years.

In addition to preferential taxation, FIEs in the SEZs are entitled to exemption from customs duties and turnover taxes on products destined for the export market and produced with imported materials.[5] FIEs in SEZs are also entitled to exemption from export duties and turnover taxes on export products manufactured with raw materials from China, with the exclusion of items such as crude oil and petroleum products. The SEZ Regulations further provide for exemptions on import duties on equipment, spare parts, components, and raw materials used for production in the SEZs. However, materials and equipment that are transferred from the SEZs to other parts of China may be subject to customs duties and turnover taxes.

2. Coastal Zone Regulations

In November of 1984, the State Council issued regulations permitting reduction of, or exemption from, enterprise income tax and turnover taxes for FIEs operating in fourteen coastal port cities and the Hainan Island, a special administrative region off the southern coast of China.[6] The Coastal Zone Regulations also provided for the establishment of open economic zones in three river-delta areas of China, including the following:

(1) Changjiang Delta Zone of the Yangtze River, which includes the cities of Suzhou, Wuxi, Changzhou, Jianxing, and Huzhou
(2) Zhujiang Delta of the Pearl River in the Guangdong Province
(3) Southern Fujian Delta Economic Zone in the southeast of the Fujian Province

Similar to SEZs, the open economic zones are authorized to provide incentives to foreign investors to encourage development and job growth.

5. For a discussion concerning taxation issues, *see* Chapter 9, Taxation Law. For a discussion concerning customs issues, *see* Chapter 15, Customs and Trade Regulation.

6. Provisional Regulations on Reduction and Exemption of Enterprise Income Tax and Consolidated Industrial and Commercial Tax for the Fourteen Coastal Cities and the Special Economic Zones (promulgated on November 15, 1984, by the State Council), *reprinted in* CHINA LAWS FOR FOREIGN BUSINESS (CCH), Special Zones & Cities ¶ 70-845 (hereinafter the "Coastal Zone Regulations"). The fourteen cities listed in the Coastal Zone Regulations include Beihai, Dalian, Fuzhou, Guangzhou, Linanyungang, Nantong, Ningbo, Qingdao, Qinhuangdao, Shanghai, Tianjin, Wenzhou, Yantai, and Zhanjiang. Many local governmental authorities advertise or attend trade shows to market their investment laws and policies in order to attract foreign investors. For an example of the preferential policies and investment opportunities in the city of Nantong, *see* http://www.chinadaily.net/adv/nantong/nantong2.htm#policy.

The tax incentives authorized under the Coastal Zone Regulations include the following:

(1) A 15 percent national enterprise income tax rate on income derived from production, business, and other sources of income generated by any joint venture, cooperative enterprise, or wholly foreign-owned enterprise operating in the coastal zones[7]
(2) Reductions or exemptions of local tax as decided by the local authorities[8]
(3) A 10 percent income tax on income derived from dividends, interest, rentals, royalties, and other sources of income from individuals[9]
(4) Exemption from turnover taxes for imported materials and equipment (if transferred to other parts of China, the items are subject to taxation)

3. Regulations Concerning the Encouragement of Foreign Investment

In October of 1986, the State Council adopted regulations authorizing cities, provinces, and autonomous regions throughout China the right to promulgate investment incentives for FIEs engaged in manufacturing for the export market and incentives for technologically advanced enterprises.[10] In particular, the Regulations Concerning the Encouragement of Foreign Investment granted the following types of preferential treatment to export enterprises and technologically advanced enterprises:

(1) Exemption from paying State subsidies to employees, with the exception of labor insurance and welfare expenses[11]
(2) Special treatment on land-use fees[12]
(3) "National" treatment with respect to fees charged for water, power, transportation, and communication facilities[13]
(4) Special access to short-term working capital loans and other credit facilities for use in production and export distribution[14]

---

7. Coastal Zone Regulations, § II, art. 1.
8. Coastal Zone Regulations, § II, art. 2.
9. Coastal Zone Regulations, § II, art. 4.
10. State Council Regulations Concerning Encouragement of Foreign Investment (promulgated on October 11, 1986, by the State Council), *reprinted in* CHINA LAWS FOR FOREIGN BUSINESS (CCH), Business Regulation ¶ 13-509 (hereinafter the "Regulations Concerning the Encouragement of Foreign Investment"). For a discussion concerning preferential tax treatment, *see generally* Chapter 9, Taxation Law.
11. Regulations Concerning the Encouragement of Foreign Investment, art. 3.
12. Regulations Concerning the Encouragement of Foreign Investment, art. 4.
13. Regulations Concerning the Encouragement of Foreign Investment, art. 5.
14. Regulations Concerning the Encouragement of Foreign Investment, art. 6.

(5) Exemption on the payment of income tax on dividends remitted abroad[15]
(6) Income tax holidays and reductions[16]
(7) Exemptions from turnover taxes for exported products[17]

In response, local governments began offering a wide range of investment incentives, including exemptions from local taxation, land-use fees, and other forms of taxation, as well as streamlined approval procedures for FIEs that are attracted to the local areas.

4. Regulations Promulgated by Particular Zones, Cities, and Provinces

In China, there are twenty-three provinces, three municipalities directly under the central government, five autonomous regions inhabited primarily by minority groups (non-Han), and the Hong Kong and Macau special administrative regions.[18] The people's congresses of the provinces, regions, and municipalities and their respective standing committees may adopt regulations that govern local activities. The local congresses are required to report their legislative activities to the NPC's Standing Committee for approval. Although the organizational structure of the local congresses mirrors the NPC structure, it is unclear as to whether the provincial governments will adopt the national reforms initiated by the NPC in March 1998 and 2003.

The local people's congresses have adopted thousands of local laws since 1979, ranging from traffic rules and foreign investment incentives to domestic relations laws.[19] In addition to enacting laws that regulate purely local activities, local people's congresses have also been authorized to enact foreign investment laws for the four special economic zones, the coastal cities and Hainan Island, and technological and special development zones. For example, the cities of Shenzhen and Shanghai have been authorized to enact

15. Regulations Concerning the Encouragement of Foreign Investment, art. 7.
16. Regulations Concerning the Encouragement of Foreign Investment, arts. 8, 9, 10.
17. Regulations Concerning the Encouragement of Foreign Investment, art. 11.
18. For a discussion of the political and judicial structure of the HKSAR, *see infra* Hong Kong Special Administrative Region § B.
19. Although the legislative power of the NPC is paramount over local authorities, local legislation sometimes conflicts with national legislation concerning certain issues. For example, in 1986 the central government issued regulations setting a national standard for usury. This rule was disputed by some local authorities given that interest rates on private loans differed depending upon the development level of a particular region. *See* Ping, *Drafting the Contract Law in China,* 10 COLUM. J. ASIAN LAW, 245, 247 (1996). *See generally* GUANGDONG: SURVEY OF A PROVINCE UNDERGOING RAPID CHANGE (Y. M. Yeung & David Chu, eds. 1996).

laws on an experimental fashion to allow authorities to observe their function and impact prior to nationwide application.

A foreign investor must take into consideration a wide range of laws that may impact a particular operation, including laws developed on a national, provincial, or local level, and those developed specifically for preferential zone authority. A brief review of the types of laws promulgated by two of the most important jurisdictions, Shenzhen and Shanghai, is instructive.

a. Shenzhen

The Shenzhen municipal government and the provincial government of the Guangdong Province have adopted a wide range of rules and regulations affecting FIEs operating in the SEZ including, but not limited to, product quality,[20] environmental protection,[21] land-use rights,[22] foreign economic contracts,[23]

20. *See* Administrative Rules of the Shenzhen Special Economic Zone on Product Quality (adopted on March 30, 1995, by the 29th Sess. of the Standing Comm. of the 1st Shenzhen Municipal People's Congress), *reprinted in* CHINA LAWS FOR FOREIGN BUSINESS (CCH), Special Zones & Cities ¶ 120-015. The Shenzhen SEZ has developed its own rules governing product quality and provides for stringent inspection rules and authority of the government to suspend production or sale of products found in violation of product quality standards.

21. Rules of the Shenzhen Special Economic Zone on Environmental Protection (promulgated on September 16, 1994, by the Standing Comm. of the Shenzhen Municipal People's Congress), *reprinted in* CHINA LAWS FOR FOREIGN BUSINESS (CCH), Special Zones & Cities ¶ 120-010. The Shenzhen environmental rules address the environmental regulatory system and procedures in Shenzhen, environmental management of construction projects, environmental protection standards, preventive measures, and liability issues.

22. Rules of the Shenzhen Special Economic Zone on the Transfer of Land-Use Rights (promulgated on July 8, 1994, by the Standing Committee of the Shenzhen Municipal People's Congress), *reprinted in* CHINA LAWS FOR FOREIGN BUSINESS (CCH), Special Zones & Cities ¶ 73-504; Rules on Land Management of the Special Economic Zones of Guangdong Province (issued on May 22, 1991, by the Standing Committee of the Guangdong Provincial People's Congress), *reprinted in* CHINA LAWS FOR FOREIGN BUSINESS (CCH), Special Zones & Cities ¶ 70-900. The Shenzhen Land-Use Transfer Rules address the mandatory language for transfer contracts, procedures for auction of land-use rights, procedures for transfer by public tender, termination of land-use rights, and liability issues. *See also* Rules of the Shenzhen Special Economic Zone on the Assignment of Real Estate (promulgated on August 21, 1993, by the Standing Comm. of the Shenzhen Municipal People's Congress), *reprinted in* CHINA LAWS FOR FOREIGN BUSINESS (CCH), Special Zones & Cities ¶ 73-539 (addresses the standards for real estate assignments and purchase contracts for real estate); Regulations of the Shenzhen Special Economic Zone on Land-Use Fees and Fee Reductions and Exemptions (promulgated on April 16, 1991, by the Shenzhen Municipal People's Government), *reprinted in* CHINA LAWS FOR FOREIGN BUSINESS (CCH), Special Zones & Cities ¶ 73-520 (standards for land-use fee preferences); Measures of Shenzhen Special Economic Zone on Collection of Land-Use Fees (promulgated on August 3, 1990, by the Shenzhen Municipal People's Government), *reprinted in* CHINA LAWS FOR FOREIGN BUSINESS (CCH), Special Zones & Cities ¶ 73-583 (addresses the collection procedures for land-use fees, exemptions standards from land-use fees, and penalties for failure to pay the required fees).

23. The Guangdong Provincial Government developed a foreign economic contract law that is similar to the national law for the Shenzhen SEZ. *See* Regulations of Shenzhen Special Economic Zone on Economic Contracts Involving Foreigners (promulgated on February 7, 1984, by the Guangdong Provincial People's Government), *reprinted in* CHINA LAWS FOR FOREIGN BUSINESS (CCH), Special Zones & Cities ¶ 73-505 (hereinafter the "Shenzhen FEC Law").

government procurement,[24] renminbi business for foreign-funded financial institutions,[25] and mortgage loan contracts.[26]

The Shenzhen Municipal People's Congress has adopted a number of regulations concerning the employment relationship, including the following:

(1) Nonresident workers employed within the city of Shenzhen[27]
(2) Reduction in employment[28]
(3) Unemployment insurance[29]
(4) Worker compensation insurance[30]
(5) Labor contracts[31]

---

24. Shenzhen has developed it own government purchasing regulations, which require public bidding for large contracts and other standards to ensure against corruption and to preserve fair competition. *See* Zhang & Li, *Congress to Debate Purchasing Law: Regulation Urgently Required to Curb Corruption and Cut Waste in Governmental Spending,* CHINA DAILY Business Weekly (Nov. 15–21, 1998), available on Lexis, News Library, or on the Web site of the CHINA DAILY at http://www.chinadaily.net/cndy.

25. Guiding Principles on the Trial Conduct of Renminbi Business by Foreign-Funded Financial Institutions in Shenzhen (promulgated on August 13, 1998, by the Shenzhen Special Economic Zone Branch of the PBOC), *reprinted in* CHINA LAWS FOR FOREIGN BUSINESS (CCH), Special Zones & Cities ¶ 120-062 (outlines the rules for conducting renminbi business in Shenzhen and the PBOC approval procedures).

26. Regulations of Guangdong Province on Mortgage Loan Administration (promulgated on December 20, 1992, by the Guangdong Provincial People's Government), *reprinted in* CHINA LAWS FOR FOREIGN BUSINESS (CCH), Special Zones & Cities ¶ 70-892 (addresses the standards for mortgage rights, mandatory provisions for mortgage contracts, registration requirements for mortgages, foreclosure and sale of mortgaged property, and liability issues).

27. Rules of the Shenzhen Special Economic Zone on Laborers (adopted on May 28, 1993, by the 16th Sess. of the Standing Comm. of the 1st Shenzhen Municipal People's Congress), *reprinted in* CHINA LAWS FOR FOREIGN BUSINESS (CCH), Special Zones & Cities ¶ 73-541. Employers of nonresident workers are prohibited from discriminating against workers and specifically with respect to compensation, working hours, and other workplace conditions. Nonresident workers have the right to join and organize trade unions.

28. Measures of the Shenzhen Special Economic Zone on Enterprise Staff Reductions for Economic Reasons (promulgated on November 15, 1996, by the Shenzhen Municipal People's Government), *reprinted in* CHINA LAWS FOR FOREIGN BUSINESS (CCH), Special Zones & Cities ¶ 120-070. The measures address the standards for terminating employees as a result of financial considerations, the termination procedures based upon residency (permanent residents have preference), disclosure requirements to trade unions and employee representatives, procedures for rehiring employees subject to layoffs, and penalties for violations of the standards.

29. Rules of the Shenzhen Special Economic Zone on Unemployment Insurance (promulgated on November 28, 1996, by the Shenzhen Municipal People's Government), *reprinted in* CHINA LAWS FOR FOREIGN BUSINESS (CCH), Special Zones & Cities ¶ 120-075. The Shenzhen Unemployment Rules outline the standards for unemployment insurance funds, unemployment benefits, standards for unemployment insurance agencies, and legal obligations and penalties for violations.

30. Rules of the Shenzhen Special Economic Zone on Industrial Injury Insurance (promulgated on February 26, 1994, by the Standing Comm. of the Shenzhen Municipal People's Congress), *reprinted in* CHINA LAWS FOR FOREIGN BUSINESS (CCH), Special Zones & Cities ¶ 73-515 (addresses requirements for worker compensation insurance, insurance fund management, worker compensation benefits, worker compensation administrative system and supervision, procedures for benefits disputes, and liability issues).

31. *See* Rules of the Shenzhen SEZ on Labor Contracts (promulgated on August 4, 1994, by the Standing Comm. of the Shenzhen Municipal People's Congress), *reprinted in* CHINA LAWS FOR FOREIGN BUSINESS (CCH), Special Zones & Cities ¶ 73-502. The Shenzhen Labor Rules outline the mandatory terms for labor contracts, subsidies and benefits, and termination. *See also* Labor Regulations Governing the Special Economic Zones in Guangdong Province (adopted on August 12, 1988, at the 3rd Sess. of the Standing Comm. of the 7th Guangdong Provincial People's Congress), *reprinted in* CHINA LAWS FOR FOREIGN BUSINESS (CCH), Special Zones & Cities ¶ 70-885; Provisional Regulations of the Shenzhen Special Economic Zone on Labor Management for Foreign Investment Enterprises (promulgated on August 1, 1987, by the Shenzhen Municipal People's Government), *reprinted in* CHINA LAWS FOR

Shenzhen has also adopted a system of uniform treatment for both nationals and foreigners with respect to a number of issues affecting business enterprises, including pricing and access to the domestic market.[32] The Shenzhen government requires that foreigners be charged prices that are comparable to those imposed upon Chinese nationals. However, the uniform price standards do not include prices charged by private enterprises and are limited in scope with respect to the following:

(1) Fees imposed for use of the Wutongshan Tunnel
(2) Fees for electricity
(3) Administrative fees for the purchase or lease of commercial real property such as office buildings, factories, and apartment complexes
(4) Fees imposed for medical treatment at municipal hospitals or clinics
(5) Fees imposed at scenic and tourist sites within the Shenzhen Municipality[33]

In addition to uniform prices for the above items, the Shenzhen government allows foreign access to the domestic market with respect to the following:

(1) An FIE that is confirmed by the municipal government as a technologically advanced enterprise may sell all of its production within China
(2) An FIE involved in certain types of food production and high-yield agricultural development may sell its full production within China
(3) An FIE that produces goods in China that are not subject to State restrictions may outline its planned domestic sales directly in its processing trade contracts and, upon approval of the contract, need not obtain further verification to engage in domestic sales
(4) A newly established FIE may set its own ratio for domestic and export sales, provided that its products are not subject to State restrictions[34]

FOREIGN BUSINESS (CCH), Special Zones & Cities ¶ 73-544 (labor regulations of SEZ governing recruitment, termination, and dispute resolution of FIE).

32. The Shenzhen SEZ, effective January 1, 1997, mandates that foreigners receive standard rates for expenses consistent with local enterprises. *See* Notice of the Shenzhen Municipal People's Government on Progressively Implementing Domestic Chinese Treatment for Foreign Investment Enterprises and Foreigners in Shenzhen (promulgated August 15, 1996, by the Shenzhen Municipal People's Government), *reprinted in* CHINA LAWS FOR FOREIGN BUSINESS (CCH), Special Zones & Cities ¶ 120-065 (hereinafter the "Shenzhen FIE Uniform Standards").

33. Shenzhen FIE Uniform Standards, art. 2.

34. Shenzhen FIE Uniform Standards, art. 1. Post-WTO, the market access under the local rules has been superseded by the right to trade and distribute under China's WTO commitments.

b. Shanghai

For foreign investment and commercial activities, Shanghai is considered to be the most open and liberal of all Chinese cities. In the first six months of 2002, Shanghai recorded a 12.5 percent annual increase in utilized foreign direct investment—it also recorded a 30 percent annual increase in contracted investment. By 2015, the municipal government expects that close to 700 multinational companies will establish a presence within Shanghai. The Shanghai government's objective is to become China's top high-technology investment center by 2010. At present, several foreign companies operate research and development centers in Shanghai. Shanghai continues to promote itself as a high-technology investment center especially in light of intense competition from the Beijing-Tianjin cities corridor. As competition increases between the municipalities, it is expected that the Shanghai government will become increasingly flexible in approving new projects and in granting preferential treatment.

The Shanghai government also encourages manufacturing and processing operations and provides the following benefits to companies in Shanghai's FTZ:

(1) No requirements for import or export licensing certificates, or manufacturing and working license certificates for manufacturing in the zone
(2) All materials and machines may be imported tax-free
(3) All manufacturing equipment and office articles for self-use by an enterprise enjoy tax-free treatment
(4) Finished products may be sold in domestic and foreign markets. Where finished goods are sold in Chinese market, raw materials, parts, and components imported into the zone and used in the manufacturing process will be assessed for Customs duties
(5) Processing enterprises can concurrently engage in international trade and tax-free storage business

The Shanghai-based free trade zone of Waigaoqiao was the first to permit Chinese-foreign joint ventures and wholly foreign-owned trading enterprises. The principal benefit of Waigaoqiao is to allow foreign investors to engage in import/export trade without using Chinese intermediaries. Shanghai municipal government has been at the forefront in implementing municipal-level legislative amendments to reflect China's WTO commitments and has completed a review of outstanding laws and regulations that require amendment in order to fully comply with such commitments.

Waigaoqiao is equipped with a deepwater port and is developing plans to improve logistics and distribution practices to become the gateway into China. To improve port efficiency, Shanghai Customs implemented the Asia Pacific Economic Cooperation (APEC) Shanghai Model Port project that has had a direct impact on the movement of goods. Customs has also established a computer network to speed up Customs procedures with the eventual goal of 24-hour customs clearance.

The general preferential policies of Waigaoqiao include:

(1) Products may be freely traded between the FTZ and outside border areas, and are exempt from customs duties and licensing requirements
(2) In the FTZ, bonded processing, warehousing, and displaying may be conducted without time limits; and bonded products may be purchased and sold freely within the FTZ
(3) All facilities, construction materials and various types of utilities and facilities used by enterprises in the FTZ are exempt from taxes and licenses
(4) For manufacturing enterprises, the tax rate is 15 percent. Manufacturing enterprises with a term of at least ten years shall, from the first profitable year, be exempt from tax for the first two years, and a 50 percent reduction in tax will apply for the third, fourth, and fifth years
(5) After-tax profits may be converted into foreign currency and remitted overseas without the imposition of profit tax
(6) All commodities entering the FTZ may be stored without the imposition of tax or supervision fees
(7) Tax-free commodities may be withdrawn from storage as required
(8) For FTZ-invested enterprises, goods, including machinery, mechanical facilities, office equipment (including used equipment) may be imported duty-free (transportation vehicles are excluded)

The Waigaoqiao FTZ also permits the establishment of trading companies with the following particulars:

(1) Overseas-invested businesses may register and establish trading companies in the FTZ as WFOEs and obtain a business license for undertaking import and export trade and acting as trade agents within the Waigaoqiao FTZ. No restrictions will be imposed on the business scope of the operation.
(2) Business within the FTZ are entitled to retain in full their spot foreign exchange and conduct settlement and sale of FOREX with banks with the approval of SAFE. In contrast, domestic foreign

trading companies in non-free-trade zone areas must comply with foreign-exchange settlement and sale regulations and are generally not permitted to keep their spot foreign exchange.

(3) Businesses within the FTZ are exempted from VAT when they engage in trade with other companies in the FTZ.

(4) Trading companies within the FTZ are subject to 15 percent enterprise income tax rate. In situations where the term of operation is greater than ten years, the enterprise is entitled to a tax holiday in the first profit-making year and to a reduced 10 percent income tax rate in the following two years. (Note: In contrast, outside the FTZ the income tax rate for trade-sector businesses is 33 percent and 15 percent in the Pudong area, and without the benefit of a tax holiday or reduction in the initial years of operation.)

(5) Trading companies within the FTZ may have direct trade relations with overseas-invested businesses and businesses with import and export licenses in non-free-trade zones in the country. They may also conduct import and export trade and domestic trade through bonded production factory markets within the FTZ or through domestic businesses that have import and export licenses. VAT incurred in domestic trade may be deferred or reduced.

(6) Goods shipped into the FTZ from outside China are exempted from import duties and no import license is required; goods exported from the FTZ to outside China are exempted from export duties and no export license is required (except for those subject to quotas imposed by importing and exporting countries). Imported equipment, construction materials, and office appliances for the self-use of the businesses in the FTZ (except automobiles) are exempt from import duties and no import license is required.

(7) Goods handled by domestic import and export trading companies and products of Chinese businesses authorized to engage in import and export of their own products, once shipped into the FTZ, are treated as exports.

The Shanghai Municipality has promulgated specific measures concerning a number of issues including, but not limited to, labor relations in FIEs,[35]

35. Rules of Shanghai Municipality on Labor and Personnel Management in Foreign Investment Enterprises (promulgated on December 20, 1994, by the Standing Comm. of the Shanghai Municipal People's Congress), *reprinted in* CHINA LAWS FOR FOREIGN BUSINESS (CCH), Special Zones & Cities ¶ 240-025. *See generally* SHANGHAI: TRANSFORMATION AND MODERNIZATION UNDER CHINA'S OPEN POLICY (Y.M. Yeung & Sung Yun-wing, eds., 1996). *See also Shanghai Raises Minimum Wage,* CHINA MARKET INTELLIGENCE, THE U.S.-CHINA BUSINESS COUNCIL (July 30, 2003) (describes notice issued by the Shanghai

land-use,[36] real property mortgages,[37] construction,[38] chain store operations,[39] agency contracts,[40] approval procedures for companies limited by

---

authorities raising the minimum wage as of July 1, 2003, from RMB535 ($64.71) per month to RMB570 ($68.94) per month). *See* Rules of the Shanghai Municipality on Labor and Personnel Management in Foreign Investment Enterprises (promulgated on December 20, 1994, by the Standing Comm. of the Shanghai Municipal People's Congress), *reprinted in* China Laws for Foreign Business (CCH), Special Zones & Cities ¶ 240-025 (provide for employee recruitment, dismissal, and resignation; compensation and benefits; hours of work; and dispute resolution); Shanghai Employment Contract Rules (issued by the Shanghai Labor and Social Security Bureau on May 1, 2002) (provide that FIE employment contracts are required to be in the Chinese language; provide that contracts set forth working conditions and compensation and that compensation be at least equal to that set forth in an applicable collective labor contract; provide that an employment relationship will be deemed to exist where a person has performed the duties of an employee as required by the employer, even if there is no employment contract; provide that an employee may terminate employment at any time; provide that the employer is to provide 30 days' notice before termination; that a part-time employment relationship may be created if the employee works for not more than 50 percent of the legal working hours of a relevant time period; that an employer shall pay social security on behalf of the part-time employee and the proportional share of workers' compensation obligations where applicable; that the temporary suspension of an employment contract in certain situations is allowed; provide that an employment contract may require an employee knowledgeable of the employer's trade secrets to provide advance notice of not more than six months to terminate the contract; that an employment contract may contain a noncompetition clause for a period not exceeding three years after employment termination and that such noncompetition provision must be supported by consideration; that an employment contract may stipulate damages in case of a breach by the employee of (i) the term of the contract or (ii) the employee's confidentiality obligation as provided in the employment contract; and that employment contracts survive company merger or division). In 2003, the Shanghai Labor and Social Security Bureau launched an inspection of foreign and domestic enterprises to determine compliance with the Shanghai Employment Contract Rules. *See Shanghai to Inspect Implentation of Employment Rules,* China Market Intelligence, The U.S.-China Business Council (July 16, 2003), available online to members at http://www.uschina.org.

36. *See* Measures of Shanghai Municipality on the Transfer of Real Estate (promulgated on April 30, 1997, by Shanghai Municipal People's Congress), *reprinted in* China Laws for Foreign Business (CCH), Special Zones & Cities ¶ 240-075. The Shanghai real estate measures address the sale, purchase, gift, transfer, and exchange of real estate and other land-use rights; requirements for land-use certificates; and mandatory language for real estate contracts. *See* Administrative Measures of Shanghai Municipality on the Use of Land by Foreign Investment Enterprises (promulgated on June 21, 1996, by the Shanghai Municipal People's Government), *reprinted in* China Laws for Foreign Business (CCH), Special Zones & Cities ¶ 240-045 (hereinafter the "Shanghai FIE Land-Use Rules"). The Shanghai FIE Land-Use Rules address the valuation of property used by FIEs and determinations of land-use fees, land-use applications and examination procedures, conditions of land-use, termination of land-use, and penalties for illegal land-use. *See generally* Li Ling-hin, Privatization of Urban Land in Shanghai (1996).

37. Measures of Shanghai Municipality on Real Estate Mortgages (promulgated on August 22, 1994, by the Shanghai Municipal People's Government), *reprinted in* China Laws for Foreign Business (CCH), Special Zones & Cities ¶ 240-015. The mortgage rules outline the types of property rights that are subject to mortgage, including land-use rights and structures, mandatory language for mortgage contracts and authentication procedures, obligations of the mortgagor to maintain the property, inspection rights of the mortgagee, legal liability of the parties to a mortgage contract, and registration procedures for mortgages.

38. The Shanghai city government has developed a set of guidelines for the construction industry, which were effective December 1, 1997. *See* Administrative Rules of the Shanghai Municipality on the Construction Market (adopted on October 21, 1997, by the 39th Sess. of the Standing Comm. of the 10th Shanghai Municipal People's Congress, and amended on October 31, 1999), *reprinted in* China Laws for Foreign Business (CCH), Special Zones & Cities ¶ 240-100 (outlines the qualifications for persons engaged in building activities, general contractor and subcontract activities, role of supervisory agencies, project contracts and building cost calculations, project quality and safety, and penalties and legal liability).

39. *See also* Certain Regulations of Shanghai Municipality on Commercial Chain Enterprises (promulgated on November 25, 1997, by the Shanghai Municipal People's Government), *reprinted in* China Laws for Foreign Business (CCH), Special Zones & Cities ¶ 240-105 (outlining the registration requirements, operational standards for chain store operations, and requirements for chain store and franchise agreements).

40. *See* Administrative Measures of Shanghai Municipality Governing Agents (promulgated on July 11, 1994, by the Shanghai Municipal People's Government), *reprinted in* China Laws for Foreign

shares,[41] special rules allowing renminbi business for foreign-funded financial institutions,[42] and standards for the establishment of cooperative share-formulated enterprises (employee-owned enterprises).[43]

B. Hong Kong Special Administrative Region (HKSAR)

Until 1997, Hong Kong (including Hong Kong Island, Kowloon, Stonecutters Island, and the New Territories) was a colony of Great Britain with its sovereignty based on three nineteenth-century treaties with China. In 1842, the island of Hong Kong was ceded in perpetuity to Great Britain based upon the Treaty of Nanking in 1842 with the Qing government following the First Opium War. Pursuant to the First Convention of Peking in 1860, Kowloon and Stonecutters Island were also ceded in perpetuity to Great Britain. In 1898, Great Britain received a ninety-nine-year lease over the New Territories on mainland China immediately across from Hong Kong Island. Pursuant to the terms of the 1898 treaty, the lease expired on June 30, 1997, and the New Territories reverted to China on July 1, 1997.

When the PRC was established in 1949, the Chinese leadership took the position that the treaties granting territorial rights to Great Britain were invalid because they were improperly obtained through force. The PRC further argued that the treaties were inequitable because, at the time of the original negotiations, the parties were not on equal footing economically or politically. Every leader of modern China has vowed to secure the return of Hong Kong to Mainland rule.

In 1979, Great Britain broached the subject of renewing the lease on the New Territories with the Chinese government. In response, the PRC

BUSINESS (CCH), Special Zones & Cities ¶ 240-005. The Shanghai Agency Measures address the standards for agency relationships, registration requirements, mandatory content for agency contracts, requirements for commissions, liability and breach of contract issues, and dispute resolution matters.

41. Provisional Measures of Shanghai Municipality on the Examination and Approval of Companies Limited by Shares (promulgated on June 26, 1997, by the Shanghai Municipal People's Government), *reprinted in* CHINA LAWS FOR FOREIGN BUSINESS (CCH), Special Zones & Cities ¶ 240-095 (special requirements for approval process for companies limited by shares in Shanghai).

42. Provisional Administrative Measures of Shanghai Pudong on Foreign-Funded Financial Institutions Conducting Trial Renminbi Business Operations (promulgated on December 2, 1996, by the People's Bank of China), *reprinted in* CHINA LAWS FOR FOREIGN BUSINESS (CCH), Special Zones & Cities ¶ 240-065. The measures address the licensing process required of foreign financial institutions doing renminbi business, and sets forth the foreign exchange capital requirements to engage in renminbi transactions.

43. Provisional Measures of Shanghai Municipality on Cooperative Share-Formulated Enterprises (promulgated on May 17, 1997, by the Shanghai Municipal People's Government), *reprinted in* CHINA LAWS FOR FOREIGN BUSINESS (CCH), Special Zones & Cities ¶ 240-085.

government made it clear that it would not renew the lease after 1997 and that the continuation of Britain's administration of Hong Kong or the territories after the lease terms was unacceptable. Although the British government held major portions of Hong Kong (i.e., Hong Kong Island, Kowloon, and Stonecutter's Island) in perpetuity, these areas could not exist separate from the New Territories because of its dependence upon the Mainland for its water and other resources, which consisted of 92 percent of the total land and water resources for the Colony. Great Britain was also concerned that the PRC would react militarily if it continued to occupy the portions of Hong Kong held in perpetuity after the lease on the New Territories expired. The United Kingdom had no choice but to attempt to negotiate a peaceful transition with the Chinese government in order to protect the residents of the colony.

1. Joint Declaration

In 1983–84, Great Britain and the PRC negotiated an agreement determining the status of Hong Kong, which is referred to as the "Joint Declaration."[44] The goal of Great Britain during negotiations was to ensure the stability and prosperity of Hong Kong. However, Great Britain's position was weakened as a result of China's insistence that if no agreement were reached, China would unilaterally determine Hong Kong's fate. On September 26, 1984, the Joint Declaration was signed in Beijing, which stipulated that the sovereignty of Hong Kong would revert to China effective July 1, 1997. The Joint Declaration provides that the former colony is a "special administrative region" of China for a period of fifty years under a formula known as "one country, two systems."[45] The Joint Declaration provides that Beijing controls foreign policy and defense matters; however, Hong Kong continues to independently operate on economic matters. Hong Kong has retained its status as a customs-free port area and world financial center, and is referred to as the Hong Kong Special Administrative Region (HKSAR).[46] HKSAR residents pay no taxes to the PRC, and English remains the official

44. People's Republic of China—United Kingdom: Agreement on the Future of Hong Kong, Sept. 26, 1984, *reprinted in* 23 I.L.M. 1366 (1984) (hereinafter the "Joint Declaration"). A full text of the Joint Declaration may be located at the Web site of the Government of Hong Kong SAR at http://www.info.gov.hk. The Joint Declaration was ratified by the British Parliament in March 1985 and by the Third Session of the Sixth National People's Congress of the PRC on April 10, 1985.

45. The one country, two systems policy was enunciated by the late Deng Xiaoping and reflected in Annex I of the Joint Declaration. Quebec, Scotland, and Louisiana are cited as examples of jurisdictions under the one country, two systems form.

46. Joint Declaration, art. 1. Article 31 of the PRC Constitution supports the policy of one country, two systems and, specifically, authorizes the establishment of special zones and regions.

language (with English and Chinese the official languages of the judiciary). The Joint Declaration provides in pertinent part:

(1) The socialist system and socialist policies shall not be practiced in the HKSAR and that the existing capitalist system and lifestyle shall remain unchanged for fifty years
(2) The HKSAR shall enjoy a high degree of autonomy
(3) The HKSAR shall have executive, legislative, and independent judicial power, including that of final adjudication[47]
(4) The laws currently in force in Hong Kong will remain "basically unchanged"[48]
(5) The courts of HKSAR shall exercise judicial power independently and free from interference
(6) The current social system, lifestyle, and economic system in Hong Kong will remain unchanged[49]
(7) The rights and freedoms of speech, press, assembly, association, strike, travel, movement, correspondence, choice of occupation, academic research, and religious belief are guaranteed by law in the HKSAR[50]
(8) The HKSAR shall use its financial revenues exclusively for its own purposes and shall not be handed over to the PRC
(9) The HKSAR government shall be responsible for maintaining order in the region and Chinese military forces stationed in the region are for defense purposes only

2. Basic Law of the HKSAR

Pursuant to the Joint Declaration, the NPC adopted the Basic Law of the HKSAR in April 1990, which became effective on July 1, 1997.[51] The

47. The HKSAR is allowed to exercise legislative autonomy so long as the laws do not violate the Basic Law. *See infra* note 51 and accompanying text. Judicial independence is preserved except that the power of final judgment that previously rested with the Privy Council in London is now the authority of the newly formed HKSAR Court of Final Appeal.

48. Joint Declaration, art. 3. Many commentators believe that Hong Kong's legal system will erode over time. *See* Dellapenna, *Symposium: Policy Approaches and Human Rights Concerns: The Lesson of the Triple Twisted Pine: Plum Blossoms on Mountain Peaks and the Future of the Rule of Law in Hong Kong,* 30 VANDERBILT J. TRANS. L. 637 (1997) (the author states that "In Hong Kong, a well-functioning system of courts will be under intense pressure to devolve into a system where favoritism and worse problems flourish. The United States . . . needs to be on guard about such developments, to encourage those favorable to the rule of law as well as guard against developments inimical to our own self-interests. If the rule of law is to be retained in Hong Kong and democracy achieved, governments must be willing to speak out forthrightly to the Chinese regarding their violations of the Joint Declaration or the Basic Law." *Id.* at 673). *See also* Jordan, *Lost in the Translation: Two Legal Cultures, the Common Law Judiciary and the Basic Law of the Hong Kong Special Administrative Region,* 30 CORNELL INT'L L. J. 335 (1997); W. VAN KEMENADE, CHINA, HONG KONG, TAIWAN, INC. (1998).

49. Joint Declaration, art. 5.

50. Joint Declaration, art. 13.

51. Basic Law of the Hong Kong Special Administrative Region of the PRC (adopted April 4, 1990, by the 3rd Sess. of the 7th NPC), *reprinted in* CHINA LAWS FOR FOREIGN BUSINESS (CCH), Special Zones &

HKSAR Basic Law consists of 160 articles covering a range of topics on the law and legal system of the HKSAR, and reiterates the principles of the Joint Declaration. Although the drafters of the Basic Law published an English version, the Chinese version approved by the NPC is the controlling instrument. The Standing Committee of the NPC is vested with the power to interpret the HKSAR Basic Law but must consult with the Committee for the Basic Law of the HKSAR, an entity consisting of legal experts from Hong Kong and other regions of the PRC.[52]

a. Political Rights of Hong Kong Residents

The HKSAR Basic Law sets out the fundamental rights and obligations of the Hong Kong citizens, and prescribes the political structure, judiciary, and civil service of the HKSAR. The Basic Law provides for the protection of civil and political rights of Hong Kong residents[53] including the following:

(1) Equality before the law
(2) The right to stand for election and right to vote
(3) Freedom of association, of assembly, of procession, and of demonstrations
(4) Freedom of speech, press, and publication
(5) The right and freedom of collective bargaining and right to strike
(6) The right not to be subjected to arbitrary or unlawful arrest or search

Cities ¶ 100-010 (hereinafter the "HKSAR Basic Law"). A full text of the Basic Law can also be found at the Web site of the HKSAR government at http://www.info.gov.hk. *See also* Decision of the Standing Committee of the National People's Congress on the Handling of Pre-Existing Hong Kong Laws in Accordance with Article 160 of the "Basic Law of the Hong Kong Special Administrative Region of the People's Republic of China" (adopted on February 23, 1997, at the 24th Meeting of the Standing Comm. of the 8th People's Congress), *reprinted in* CHINA LAWS FOR FOREIGN BUSINESS (CCH), Special Zones & Cities ¶ 500-015. The PRC has also adopted the Basic Law of the Macao Special Administrative Region that reverted to Chinese sovereignty on December 20, 1999. The Macao Basic Law embodies the principle of one country, two systems, which provides that the socialist system will not be practiced in Macao. Other aspects of the Macao Basic Law are consistent with the Basic Law of the HKSAR. For a translation of the Macao Basic Law, *see* Basic Law of the Macao Special Administrative Region of the PRC (adopted on March 31, 1993, by the 1st Sess. of the 8th NPC), *reprinted in* CHINA LAWS FOR FOREIGN BUSINESS (CCH), Special Zones & Cities ¶ 105-010.

52. HKSAR Basic Law, art. 158.

53. The HKSAR Basic Law, Article 24, defines a permanent resident as (a) PRC citizens born in Hong Kong; (b) PRC citizens who have resided in Hong Kong for at least seven consecutive years; (c) persons not of PRC citizenship who have validly entered Hong Kong, resided in Hong Kong for at least seven consecutive years, and declared Hong Kong as their permanent place of residence; (d) persons under 21 years of age born in Hong Kong of residents described in (c) above; and (e) other residents who, before the establishment of the HKSAR, had the right of abode in Hong Kong only. Permanent residents have the right of abode in Hong Kong, and the right to vote and to stand for election in the HKSAR. Non-permanent residents are qualified to hold Hong Kong identity cards but have no right of abode in Hong Kong. *See also* Nationality Law of the People's Republic of China (adopted July 1, 1997, by the NPC), *reprinted in* CHINA LAWS FOR FOREIGN BUSINESS (CCH), Special Zones & Cities ¶ 500-020.

(7) Freedom of privacy of communication
(8) Freedom of movement, emigration, and travel
(9) Freedom of religion
(10) Freedom of occupation
(11) Freedom to engage in academic research, literary and artistic creation, and other cultural activities
(12) The right to confidential legal advice, access to courts, choice of attorneys for the protection of legal rights, and the right to institute legal proceedings in courts against the acts of government authorities[54]

Many of the political rights set forth in the Basic Law are also provided in China's Constitution. Article 35 of the PRC Constitution provides that "[c]itizens of the People's Republic of China enjoy freedom of speech, of the press, or assembly, of association, or procession and of demonstration."[55]

b. Economic Rights of Hong Kong Residents

The HKSAR Basic Law provides that the socialist policy of the PRC shall not be imposed upon Hong Kong, and that the previous capitalist system and

54. HKSAR Basic Law, Chap. 3.

55. Critics claim that, although the PRC constitution provides the various rights and freedoms set forth in the Joint Declaration and the Basic Law, as a matter of practice such fundamental rights are suspended by political expediency. *See* J. SPENCE, THE SEARCH FOR MODERN CHINA 710–11 (1990). The introduction of the National Security (Legislative Provisions) Bill by the Hong Kong Government on February 24, 2003, which would have redefined or introduced new standards for the crimes of treason, created an uproar that resulted in the largest public protests in Hong Kong history. Under intense political pressure, the Hong Kong Government withdrew the bill on September 5, 2003. The Hong Kong Government, at the behest of Beijing, is of the opinion that the Basic Law requires some form of legislation similar to the bill and, thus, the Hong Kong government is constitutionally required to enact legislation on issues covered by the bill. As a result, the National Security Bill may be reintroduced in some form. The National Security Bill would amend several criminal ordinances to codify the obligation imposed by the Basic Law that requires Hong Kong to "enact laws on its own to prohibit any act of treason, secession, sedition, subversion against the Central People's Government, or theft of state secrets, to prohibit foreign political organizations or bodies from conducting political activities in the Region, and to prohibit political organizations or bodies of the Region from establishing ties with foreign political organizations or bodies." Basic Law, art. 23. Among other things, the National Security Bill would replace the existing law on treason with a new definition of treason that provides that a Chinese national commits the crime of treason against the Chinese government by (i) joining or being a part of foreign armed forces at war with the PRC; (ii) instigating foreign armed forces to invade the PRC with force; or (iii) assisting any public enemy at war with the PRC. The Bill abolishes the common law offences of misprision of treason and compounding treason. The National Security Bill proposes to create a new offence of "subversion," defined as the use of force or "serious criminal means" or engagement in war that "seriously endangers the stability of the PRC," and is directed against the PRC or its government and seeks to "disestablish" the government. The Bill would also criminalize "secession," defined as withdrawing any part of the PRC from its sovereignty by force or serious criminal means that seriously endangers the territorial integrity of the PRC or by engaging in war. Further, the Bill proposes that a person commits "sedition" by inciting others to commit treason, subversion, secession, or violent disorder that would seriously endanger the stability of the PRC. The Bill would also incorporate the PRC crimes involving the disclosure of State Secrets into Hong Kong law. The National Security Bill would also increase the powers of police officers in investigation of acts of treason, subversion, secession, sedition, or handling seditious publication. *See Generally* J. Baglole, *Protesters Call for Full Elections in Hong Kong,* WALL ST. J. (January 1, 2004).

way of life shall remain unchanged for a period of fifty years.[56] The HKSAR Basic Law, and specifically Chapter 5, provides a number of assurances concerning economic issues. In particular, the law stipulates that the HKSAR shall have independent finances and use its tax revenues for its own purposes, and that the PRC government shall not levy taxes against the residents of the HKSAR. The HKSAR is empowered to enact its own tax laws, continue to operate as a free port, and is not bound by China's foreign exchange policies. The Basic Law also provides that the Hong Kong dollar will continue to circulate as the legal tender of the region and be freely convertible.

With respect to trade issues, the HKSAR will function as a separate customs territory and pursue a policy of free trade. In this regard, Article 116 of the Basic Law provides in full:

> The Hong Kong Special Administrative Region shall be a separate customs territory. The Hong Kong Special Administrative Region may, using the name "Hong Kong, China," participate in relevant international organizations and international trade agreements (including preferential trade arrangements) such as the General Agreement on Tariffs and Trade and the arrangement regarding international trade in textiles. Export quotas, tariff preferences and other similar arrangements, which are obtained or made by the Hong Kong Special Administrative Region or which were obtained or made and remain invalid, shall be enjoyed exclusively by the Region.

Since January 1, 1995, Hong Kong has been a member of the World Trade Organization (WTO),[57] and will continue to be a member in its own right as the HKSAR, notwithstanding China's accession to the WTO in December 2001.[58]

c. Political Structure of the HKSAR

Prior to 1985, the people of Hong Kong were not permitted to govern themselves in a democratic manner. Although Hong Kong had its own legislature, known as the Legislative Council (LegCo), the Governor, who was appointed by Great Britain, appointed all members of LegCo. Elections of LegCo members were first introduced in 1985, and interestingly after the execution of the

56. HKSAR Basic Law, art. 5.

57. The PRC provided the WTO with a pledge that Hong Kong will continue to enjoy full autonomy in its external commercial relations. For more information concerning the World Trade Organization, visit the WTO's Web site at http://www.wto.org.

58. China was a founding member of the GATT in 1948 but left the forum after the formation of the PRC in 1949. *See* Damrosch, *GATT Membership in a Changing World Order: Taiwan, China, and the Former Soviet Republics,* 1992 COLUM. BUS. L. REV. 19.

Joint Declaration. The LegCo was replaced on July 1, 1997, by the Provisional Legislative Council (PLC), which was appointed by a 400-member Selection Committee comprised of Hong Kong citizens appointed by the PRC.

The Basic Law is intended to give legal effect to the Joint Declaration, and defines the relationship between the PRC government and the HKSAR. The Government of the HKSAR is similar to the colonial government and includes a Chief Executive, which previously carried the title "Governor." The Chief Executive is the head of the HKSAR and must be a PRC citizen, a permanent resident of the HKSAR who has lived in Hong Kong for at least twenty consecutive years, and at least forty years of age. The Chief Executive must also not have any right of abode in any other foreign country. Other executive positions require similar qualifications except that only fifteen consecutive years of residency in Hong Kong are required. The Chief Executive has a five-year term of office and may serve a maximum of two consecutive years. The Chief Executive is selected by the PRC government or by election of the Hong Kong people.[59]

The Chief Executive is empowered to nominate the executive authorities of the HKSAR, including the heads of departments, the Commissioner of the Police, Commissioner of Corruption, and other executive positions. The Chief Executive is also authorized to veto legislation passed by the HKSAR Legislative Council if it is not compatible with the overall interests of the region. The Legislative Council may override a veto of the Chief Executive by a two-thirds majority vote.

The Legislative Council is composed of PRC citizens who are permanent residents of the HKSAR and have no right of abode in a foreign country. Nevertheless, permanent residents who are non–PRC citizens or who have foreign rights of abode may comprise up to 20 percent of the total membership of the Legislative Council. Pursuant to Article 68 of the Basic Law, members of the Legislative Council are determined by election. The first term of members is for a two-year period with subsequent terms of four years. The procedures for election of the first, second, and third legislatures are set forth in Annex II of the Basic Law. On July 1, 1997, the Provisional Legislative Council, which was appointed by the PRC, came into power.[60]

59. HKSAR Basic Law, art. 45.

60. On July 29, 1997, the Hong Kong Court of Appeal upheld the establishment and validity of the Provisional Legislative Council of the HKSAR. The court reasoned that the PLC is a legal body and that laws passed by the Council have legally binding status. The PLC was originally established as an interim body, for the purpose of carrying out the necessary legislative functions until elections could be held for a new Legislative Council held in early 1998. *See* Harpole, *HK: Provisional Legislative Council Upheld*, 1 CHINA L. NEWS (CCH) 18 (July 1997).

d. Judicial System of the HKSAR

The Basic Law sets forth the procedures for the continuity of the HKSAR judiciary and provides that the judicial system under Great Britain will be maintained. Section 10 provides that the continuity of legal proceedings, the criminal justice system, and the public justice system shall not be affected by the PRC takeover. After July 1, 1997, all actions brought on behalf of or against the Government of Hong Kong may be brought by or on behalf of the Government of the HKSAR. The key exception is that the Basic Law established a new Court of Final Appeal, which replaced the United Kingdom's Privy Council as the ultimate judicial authority.[61] The previously named Supreme Court is renamed as the High Court and the former High Court is renamed the Court of First Instance.

The courts of the HKSAR are required to adjudicate cases based on HKSAR laws and may refer to precedents of other common law jurisdictions.[62] Article 8 of the Basic Law provides in full:

> The laws previously in force in Hong Kong, that is, the common law, rules of equity, ordinances, subordinate legislation and customary law shall be maintained, except for any that contravene the law, and subject to any amendment by the legislature of the Hong Kong Special Administrative Region.

The courts have no jurisdiction over acts of state such as defense matters and foreign affairs questions. When issues concerning acts of state arise in court cases, the courts are required to obtain authorization to assert jurisdiction from the Chief Executive, which is binding on the courts.[63] In addition, the courts are also required to seek an interpretation of the Basic Law from the Standing Committee of the NPC (through the Court of Final Appeal) on matters concerning the relationship between the PRC and the HKSAR. Any interpretation rendered by the Standing Committee is binding upon the HKSAR courts. Critics claim that the PRC has effectively stripped the HKSAR judiciary of its independence by denying it the right to interpret the Basic Law.[64]

The Basic Law provides that both Chinese and English may be used as the official language by the judiciary of HKSAR.[65] Since 1995, the Hong

61. HKSAR Basic Law, art. 81.
62. HKSAR Basic Law, arts. 8, 84.
63. HKSAR Basic Law, art. 19.
64. *See* Palumbo, *Analysis of the Sino-British Joint Declaration and the Basic Law of Hong Kong: What Do They Guarantee the People of Hong Kong After 1997?*, 6 Conn. J. Int'l L. 667, 708 (1991).
65. HKSAR Basic Law, art. 9.

Kong government, pursuant to the Official Language Ordinance, removed English as the only language in the courts. Since that time, Hong Kong's ordinances have been slowly translated. Problems have arisen given the difficulty in finding Chinese characters that are linguistically similar to common law legal terms.

The judges of the HKSAR court system are appointed by the Chief Executive on the recommendation of an independent commission composed of local judges, members of the legal profession, and other members of the Hong Kong community. Judges are chosen on the basis of judicial and professional qualifications and may be recruited from other common law jurisdictions. Those judges appointed and serving prior to the establishment of the HKSAR may remain employed and retain their seniority. The Chief Judge of the Court of Final Appeal and the Chief Judge of the High Court are required to be PRC citizens who are permanent residents of Hong Kong and who have no right to abode in any foreign country. The Standing Committee of the NPC has the power to appoint or remove a judge from the bench.

In January 1999, the Hong Kong Court of Final Appeal issued a landmark immigration ruling that challenged the authority of the NPC and resulted in the first constitutional crisis between the HKSAR and the Mainland government. In its decision, the court ruled that any Mainland Chinese person with at least one Hong Kong parent has the constitutional right to live in Hong Kong. The ruling states that China violated the rights of immigrants by insisting, in a law that was passed after the July 1997 handover, that they obtain exit visas before moving to Hong Kong. The court went one step further and stated that it had the power to overrule Mainland legislation that conflicts with the Basic Law. The decision ruffled a few feathers in Beijing and led to calls for the HKSAR government to correct the court's decision.

The Hong Kong government, led by Chief Executive Tung Chee-hwa asked the court to explain the ruling in an effort to temper the dispute with Beijing. Specifically, the HKSAR Justice Department requested that the Court of Final Appeal clarify whether Hong Kong courts or Mainland Chinese lawmakers have the ultimate power to interpret the Basic Law.[66] Chief Justice Andrew Li clarified the ruling by stating that the court never meant to question the authority of the NPC, so long as the PRC legislature acts in

66. *See* Crowell, *Battle Over the Law,* ASIAWEEK 18 (Feb. 19, 1999), available on Lexis, News Library; Medina, *Criticism That Hong Kong's Legal System Damaged,* AP WORLDSTREAM (Feb. 27, 1999), available on Lexis, News Library; Cheung, *Hong Kong Court 'Clarifies' Ruling,* AP Online (Feb. 26, 1999), available on Lexis, News Library; Landler, *China Tells Hong Kong It Wants Immigration Ruling 'Rectified',* N. Y. TIMES § 1, pg. 13, col. 1 (Feb. 14, 1999); Rosenthal, *Immigration Ruling by Hong Kong Court Is Generating New Tensions with Beijing,* N. Y. TIMES § A, pg. 14, col. 1 (Feb. 11, 1999); Hajari, TIME 22 (Feb. 22, 1999), available on Lexis, News Library.

accordance with the Basic Law.[67] Li, however, did not specify what the court's reaction would be if they found that Mainland laws were in conflict with the Basic Law. In response to the court's clarification, the Hong Kong legal community claimed that the territory's legal system and autonomy had been compromised. The Hong Kong Bar Association stated that it regretted that the court was persuaded to clarify the decision that "requires no further explanation."[68] Chinese President Jiang Zemin attempted to reassure the Hong Kong public and international observers that the territory's legal system remained "basically unchanged."[69]

By playing the role that they had been trained to play under a British-styled judicial system, the justices of the Court of Final Appeal exposed the "one country, two systems" policy as a farce. Worse, this unnerving affair sent a message to the people of Hong Kong that the HKSAR government would bow to Beijing and place political pressure on the territory's highest court to clarify a controversial ruling, rather than uphold the integrity of the judiciary's independence. Like China, the judicial system of the HKSAR can never be independent until it is given the power to interpret, as well as to enforce the law. The business and public confidence, and hence the stability and growth of Hong Kong, is dependent upon the PRC's willingness to follow and uphold the Basic Law,[70] which includes real recognition that the judiciary remains autonomous and insulated from the influence of politics, from any source.[71]

67. On February 26, 1999, the Court of Final Appeal issued a statement that stated that "the court accepts that it cannot question the authority of the (NPC) or the Standing Committee to do any act which is in accordance with the provision of the Basic Law."

68. *Hong Kong Bar Association Slams Government Over Recent Court Decisions,* AGENCE FRANCE PRESSE (Mar. 5, 1999), available on Lexis, News Library.

69. *Chinese President Says Hong Kong's Legal System Undented,* AGENCE FRANCE PRESSE (Mar. 4, 1999), available on Lexis, News Library; *Abode Row 'Over in Many Ways',* HONG KONG STANDARD (Mar. 3, 1999), available on Lexis, News Library.

70. The Basic Law Drafting Committee (BLDC), which was appointed by the NPC in June of 1985, prepared the HKSAR Basic Law. The BLDC consisted of individuals from both the PRC and Hong Kong. Many commentators believed that the PRC government from the start orchestrated the drafting and consultative processes. *See* Skeen, *Can Capitalism Survive Under Communist Rule? The Effect of Hong Kong's Reversion to the People's Republic of China,* 29 INT'L LAW. 175, 181 n. 62 (1995). In October of 1998, PRC President Jiang Zemin in a meeting with HKSAR Chief Executive Tung Chee-hwa reiterated the central government's policy to "unswervingly implement" the "one country, two systems" principle and would not interfere in the internal affairs of the HKSAR. *See President Reiterates Pledge to HKSAR,* CHINA DAILY (Oct. 19, 1998), available on Lexis, News Library, or on the Web site of the CHINA DAILY at http://www.chinadaily.com.cn. While the Basic Law is akin to a constitutional mandate for the HKSAR, the Reunification Ordinance, adopted by the Provisional Legislative Council on July 1, 1997, provides more practical authority for the continuity of the legal system. Reunification Ordinance of the Hong Kong Special Administrative Region (adopted on July 1, 1997, by the Provisional Legislative Council). For a brief analysis of the Reunification Ordinance, *see* Daw, *The Legal System's First Three Months,* 11 CHINA L. & PRAC. 66–67 (Oct. 1997). The Reunification Ordinance has 32 sections that address such issues as the maintenance and interpretation of laws previously in force; establishment of the courts; continuity of legal proceedings; and continuity of existing legal powers of governmental authorities, government documents, and contracts.

71. *AmCham Warns of Harm to Investment,* HONG KONG STANDARD (Feb. 12, 1999), available on Lexis, News Library. The American Chamber of Commerce in Hong Kong issued a statement that "[a]ny attempt to overturn the CFA's decision, or a period of prolonged uncertainty over the controversy, could potentially undermine international confidence in the Special Administrative Region's legal and judicial independence." The AmCham was the first foreign organization to voice its concern with the controversy.

The precedent, to date, indicates that the judicial systems—HKSAR and the Mainland—are subject to the influence and control of Beijing and that the independence of the judiciary is imaginary at best.

3. China Market Access under CEPA

Preferential China market access opportunities have been granted to Hong Kong companies under the Closer Economic Partnership Agreement (CEPA) signed by Hong Kong and Mainland China on June 29, 2003.[72] CEPA also affords such investment opportunities to U.S. and other foreign services suppliers established in Hong Kong provided such entities engage in substantive business operations.

There are qualifying criteria, and it remains unclear, for example, whether a foreign services provider that has provided substantive services in Hong Kong over many years but is not a *registered Hong Kong company*, will remain outside the remit of CEPA. Of course, for foreign companies operating in Hong Kong that fail to satisfy minimum CEPA qualifying criteria, the option of utilizing CEPA via the acquisition of an existing qualified Hong Kong company can be attractive. In these and in many other respects, the implementation of CEPA is open for observation. CEPA benefits are effective January 1, 2004.

CEPA marked the conclusion of eighteen months of negotiations, and heralded, inter alia, the granting of preferential treatment to Hong Kong companies vis-à-vis access to the China market. In particular, CEPA acts to (a) reduce or eliminate tariffs and nontariff barriers with respect to trade in goods between both territories, (b) serves to liberalize market access for certain Hong Kong services providers by reducing or eliminating discriminatory treatment, and (c) promotes trade and investment facilitation measures.

In relation to trade in goods, CEPA provides that from January 1, 2004, (i) the Mainland will apply zero tariffs on a range of listed imports from Hong Kong meeting CEPA rules of origin requirements across some 270

72. Mainland/Hong Kong Closer Economic Partnership Arrangement (CEPA) (executed by the Mainland and HKSAR on June 29, 2003), available on the Web site of the Hong Kong Trade Development Council at http://www.tdctrade.com. Implementation Annexes were signed on September 29, 2003. A similar arrangement was reached between the Mainland and the Macao SAR. See http://www.economia.gov.mo for more information about the arrangement with Macao. *See generally* M. Pottinger, *Hong Kong Details China Trade Pact*, WALL ST. J. (Sept. 30, 2003), pg. 1; B. Walsh, *Will CEPA Make Any Difference?*, TIME (July 14, 2003), Vol. 1, No. 1; *Hong Kong Wins Greater Access With CEPA Passage*, CHINA MARKET INTELLIGENCE, THE U.S.-CHINA BUSINESS COUNCIL (July 2, 2003), available online to members at http://www.uschina.org; *CEPA Finalized; Telecommunications to Benefit*, CHINA MARKET INTELLIGENCE, THE U.S.-CHINA BUSINESS COUNCIL (October 8, 2003), available online to members at http://www.uschina.org. P. Kuo & J. Ryan, *China Watch: Hong Kong, China Flesh Out CEPA Trade Deal*, WALL ST. J. (Sept. 29, 2003); D. Ryan, *The Impact of CEPA on Hong Kong Transportation and Logistics Companies: A Head Start on the Competition*, CHINA L. & PRAC. (Oct. 2003); *China to Target Smuggling Tied to Trade Pact*, DowJones Newswire (Dec. 30, 2003). The PRC General Administration of Customs has issued its own set of rules of origin applicable to CEPA imports. For a Chinese language version of the rules of origin, *see* http://www.customs.gov.cn.

product codes—not later than January 2006, this preferential rate is to be applied to all other goods imported from Hong Kong that satisfy CEPA rules-of-origin requirements. The provisions concerning tariffs and rules of origin are set forth in the Procedures for Implementing Zero Tariffs (Annex 1) and Certificates of Origin Procedures (Annex 2). The Rules of Origin procedures provide a 30 percent value-added requirement for forty product codes such as some electronic and optical components, watches and clocks, and watch movements in order to qualify as Hong Kong origin goods. Product development costs incurred in Hong Kong shall be considered when calculating the value-added percentage.

In order to be processed for claims of zero tariffs under Annex 1, imported products must be accompanied by a Certificate of Hong Kong Origin-CEPA issued by the Hong Kong Trade & Industry Department or government-approved certificate organization such as the Federation of Hong Kong Industries, the Indian Chamber of Commerce Hong Kong, the Chinese Manufacturers Association of Hong Kong, or the Chinese General Chamber of Commerce.[73]

Both sides have engaged in consultations regarding cooperation in trade and investment promotion; customs clearance facilitation; quarantine and inspection of commodities; food safety and quality assurance; electronic commerce; transparency in law and regulations; and the development of small and medium-sized enterprises.

CEPA also provides for market access preferential treatment afforded to Hong Kong companies across eighteen services sectors. From January 1, 2004, these Hong Kong services sectors will immediately benefit from market access or the removal of specific market access restrictions. The services sectors scheduled to benefit from such liberalization include management consultancy, transportation services, distribution, logistics, freight forwarding, warehousing and storage services, tourism, banking, and insurance services—and CEPA further opens the door by providing that either side may request consultations to *further* liberalize trade in services. Critically, a services supplier of another WTO member that is a juridical person constituted under the laws of one side will be entitled to treatment granted by the other side under CEPA, provided that it engages in *substantive business operations* as stipulated in CEPA. The impact of CEPA on services is most important to Hong Kong given that 87 percent of the domestic economy of Hong Kong is based on the services sector.

73. *See also* Provisions on the Place of Origin Rules for Goods Traded Under CEPA (promulgated on December 30, 2003, by the General Administration of Customs).

CEPA sets forth detailed qualifying criteria for "Hong Kong companies." With respect to convention services, management consulting services, advertising services, transportation services, distribution services, freight forwarding agency services, storage and warehousing services, logistics services, tourism services, audiovisual services, real estate services, and construction and related engineering services, the qualifying criteria for Hong Kong companies are as detailed at (1) to (6) below. CEPA sets forth separate qualifying criteria for Hong Kong companies in the banking, insurance, and legal services sectors.

(1) The Hong Kong applicant must be an enterprise registered and established pursuant to the Hong Kong Companies Ordinance or other relevant Hong Kong ordinance. Therefore, registered overseas companies and their offices in Hong Kong do not fall within the remit of CEPA.

(2) The Hong Kong applicant must conduct substantive business operations in Hong Kong. To determine this, CEPA assesses the nature and scope of the business/commercial activities undertaken by the applicant. Moreover, the business that the applicant enterprise intends to undertake in the Mainland must be the same in nature as the substantive business of the applicant in Hong Kong—the intended business must fall within the scope of actual business operations engaged in by the applicant in Hong Kong.

(3) The Hong Kong applicant must be subject to Hong Kong profits tax jurisdiction. In that regard, in the provision of its substantive services, the applicant must be able to prove its Hong Kong profits tax liability, and it must be in a position to furnish supporting evidence of such liability, i.e., tax returns or receipts. An applicant will not be prevented from the benefits of CEPA where it has suffered corporate losses or is exempt from Hong Kong profits tax liability, provided it can prove that it has engaged in substantive operations in Hong Kong for at least three years.

(4) To provide the foregoing services in the Mainland, the Hong Kong applicant enterprise must be registered and established and have engaged in substantive business operations in Hong Kong for at least three years. However, for construction and related engineering services, the period of substantive operations is five years; for real estate companies, there are no requirements vis-à-vis minimum period of business operations in Hong Kong.

(5) The Hong Kong applicant must either own or rent premises in Hong Kong for conducting its substantive business operations—the scale

of the premises must correspond to the scope and scale of the business operations of the applicant. In that regard, liaison offices, post-office box companies, and enterprises established for the purpose of providing services to parent companies are not eligible to benefit from the preferential treatment afforded under CEPA.

(6) At least 50 percent of the total staff of the Hong Kong applicant must be employed in Hong Kong.

CEPA provides specific market access liberalization commitments with respect to the subject services sectors, including the following.

a. Management Consulting

From January 1, 2004, Hong Kong companies will be permitted to establish wholly owned enterprises in the Mainland for the provision of management consultancy services except legal, accounting, auditing, and certification services, etc. Hong Kong companies seeking to establish such wholly owned enterprises must comply with the registered capital requirements set forth in the Mainland's Company Law.

b. Distribution Services

Hong Kong companies are permitted (i) to establish wholly owned enterprises in the Mainland for the provision of commission agents' services and wholesale trade services, and (ii) to establish wholly owned external trading companies in the Mainland. The market access requirements for Hong Kong services providers have been lowered as follows: to establish an external

CEPA: Services Sectors

- Management consulting services
- Accounting services
- Real estate and construction services
- Distribution services
- Freight forwarding agency services
- Transport services
- Audiovisual services
- Banking services
- Insurance services
- Convention and exhibition services
- Advertising services
- Medical and dental services
- Logistics services
- Storage and warehousing services
- Tourism services
- Legal services
- Securities services
- Telecom services

trading company, the minimum average annual sales volume in the three years prior to application has been reduced from the existing requirement of $30 million to $10 million; the minimum registered capital for establishing an external trading company has been reduced from RMB50 million to RMB20 million. For the establishment of an external trading company in China's central or western regions, the respective corresponding figures have been reduced from $20 million to $5 million and from RMB30 million to RMB10 million.[74] For establishing a wholesale commercial enterprise, the minimum average annual sales volume for the three years prior to application has been reduced from $2.5 billion to $30 million. The minimum assets value requirement in respect of the year prior to application has been reduced from the present requirement of not less than $300 million to $10 million; the minimum registered capital for establishing a wholesale commercial enterprise has been lowered from RMB80 million to RMB50 million. For the establishment of a wholesale commercial enterprise in China's central or western regions, the corresponding figures have been lowered respectively from $2.5 billion to $20 million and from RMB60 million to RMB30 million. For Hong Kong wholly owned enterprises providing commission agents' services or wholesale trade services in the Mainland, there are no geographic restrictions.

c. Retail Trade Services and Distribution

Hong Kong investors are permitted to establish wholly owned retail commercial enterprises in the Mainland under CEPA. The requirements for Hong Kong companies seeking to establish retail commercial enterprises have been lowered; namely, the minimum average annual sales volume of the enterprise in the three years prior to application has been lowered from the present requirement of $2 billion to $100 million; the minimum assets value of the applicant in the year immediately prior to application has been lowered from $200 million to $10 million; the minimum registered capital requirement for establishing a retail commercial enterprise has been lowered from the present requirement of RMB50 million to RMB10 million (in central and western regions of the Mainland, the minimum registered capital requirement has been lowered from RMB30 million to RMB6 million).

74. *See* Supplementary Rules for Provisional Regulation on the Establishment of Sino-Foreign Joint Equity Foreign Trading Company (issued on January 8, 2004, by the Ministry of Commerce). Applicants for a JV under the MOFCOM CEPA Rules must have an average annual trading volume with Mainland China of at least $10 million for the past three years, and $5 million for applicants planning to set up foreign trading companies in central and western China. Applicants must also have minimum registered capital of RMB20 million ($2.4 million) or RMB10 million ($1.2 million) for those operations to be established in central and western China.

Hong Kong enterprises will be permitted to establish retailing enterprises in all prefectural-level cities in the Mainland, and additionally in county-level cities in the province of Guangdong. In the automotive sector, Hong Kong companies are permitted to establish wholly owned retail enterprises for the sale of motor vehicles—up to thirty chain outlets may be established. Where a proposed chain store operator plans to establish more than thirty chain outlets, the provisions set forth in China's WTO accession package will apply.

On December 7, 2003, MOFCOM issued regulations that permit services providers from the special administrative regions of Hong Kong and Macao to establish joint ventures trading enterprises or wholly foreign-owned trading enterprises on the Mainland.[75] The regulations were adopted pursuant to China's treaty obligations under the CEPA. The CEPA Trading Company Measures require that the foreign investor maintain, on average, $10 million in annual trade with the Mainland for three years, and the minimum registered capital required is RMB20 million ($240,000).

d. Franchising

Hong Kong companies are permitted to establish wholly owned enterprises in the Mainland to engage in franchising. Separate dedicated franchising regulations will be issued at a later stage.

CEPA: Trading and Distribution

- WFOEs permitted for commission agents' services and wholesale trade services on Mainland; WFOEs allowed for external trading companies. No geographic restrictions. Under WTO, JVs with majority foreign interest given full rights December 2003, and WFOEs December 2004
- External Trading Companies: Average annual trading values reduced to not less than $10 million in three prior years (from $30 million for JV foreign party); Minimum registered capital reduced to RMB20 million (from RMB50 million)
- Wholesale Commercial Enterprises: Average annual turnover reduced to $30 million in three years prior (from $2.5 billion) and asset value reduced to $10 million in prior year (from $300 million); Minimum capital requirements of RMB50 million ($6.04 million) (from RMB80 million)
- Lower numbers for western regions

75. Supplementary Provisions on the Interim Measures on the Establishment of Sino-Foreign Equity Joint Venture Trading Companies (promulgated on December 7, 2003, by the Ministry of Commerce) (hereinafter the "CEPA Trading Company Measures").

CEPA: Retail Trade Services; Franchising

- WFOEs allowed for retail commercial enterprises; under WTO only JVs allowed
- Average annual turnover is reduced to $100 million in prior three years (from $2 billion) and asset value reduced to $10 million (from $200 million)
- Minimum capital requirement is reduced to RMB10 million (RMB6 million in central/western regions)
- Applies to all prefectural-level cities on Mainland and at county-level cities in Guangdong
- Automotive up to thirty outlets. More than thirty chain outlets subject to WTO accession requirements
- Franchising: WFOEs allowed; one year ahead of WTO timetable

e. Logistics and Freight Forwarding Agency Services

Hong Kong companies are permitted to establish wholly owned logistics services enterprises in the Mainland. The term "logistics services" includes road transportation, storage and warehousing, loading and unloading, value-adding processing, packaging, delivery, and the provision of ancillary information and consultancy services for ordinary road freight; freight transportation agency services in the Mainland; and the management and operation of logistics services via electronic systems. Hong Kong companies will be permitted to provide freight transport agency services in the Mainland on a wholly owned basis. For international freight forwarding agency companies established in the Mainland by Hong Kong companies, the minimum registered capital requirement will be the same as that applicable to Mainland enterprises.

f. Storage and Warehousing Services

Hong Kong companies are permitted to establish wholly owned enterprises in the Mainland to provide storage and warehousing services—the minimum registered capital requirement will be the same as that applicable to Mainland enterprises.

g. Road Transport Services

Hong Kong companies are permitted to establish wholly owned enterprises in the Mainland to provide road freight transportation services and to provide direct nonstop road freight transportation services between Hong Kong and each mainland province. Hong Kong companies will be permitted to establish wholly owned passenger transport enterprises in the western regions of the Mainland for the provision of road passenger transportation services.

h. Films, Audiovisual Products, and Cinema Construction

CEPA specifically addresses market access for the audiovisual products and film industry. Specifically, CEPA provides as follows:

(1) Hong Kong companies are permitted to establish joint ventures on the Mainland with majority ownership (up to 70 percent) to engage in the distribution of audiovisual products (including motion pictures) and sound recording products.

(2) Chinese language motion pictures produced by Hong Kong companies may be imported for distribution in the Mainland on a quota-free basis, subject to censorship authority approval. CEPA exempts Hong Kong motion picture companies from the quota system.

(3) Motion pictures produced jointly by Hong Kong and Mainland companies are treated as Mainland movies for distribution on the Mainland.

(4) For motion pictures produced jointly by Hong Kong and Mainland companies, the ceiling on the number of Mainland actors has been removed, although at least one-third of the leading actors must be from the Mainland; similarly, the restriction that the film story take place on the Mainland is lifted, although the plot or leading characters must be "related" to the Mainland—in this regard, the precise meaning of the term "related" is unclear. The limitation that requires the story take place on the Mainland is still imposed on motion pictures co-produced with enterprises outside of Hong Kong.

(5) Hong Kong companies are permitted to construct and/or renovate cinema theatres on a joint venture or cooperative basis, with majority ownership being permitted for Hong Kong companies. In contrast, foreign investors that do not use a Hong Kong enterprise may not be allowed to hold a majority interest.

CEPA provisions will encourage audiovisual products manufacturers, film producers, and cinema operators to pursue the Hong Kong angle to tap the China market.

i. Banking

For Hong Kong banks and finance companies seeking to establish in the Mainland, the minimum asset requirement has been lowered to $6 billion.

Hong Kong banks are entitled to establish branches or corporate entities, while finance companies will be entitled to establish corporate entities. The minimum asset requirement for establishing branches or corporate entities has also been reduced to $6 billion. Presently, the Mainland requires that a Hong Kong bank seeking to establish a joint venture bank or joint venture finance company (or a Hong Kong finance company seeking to establish a joint venture finance company) in the Mainland, must first establish a representative office—this requirement will no longer apply. For branches of Hong Kong banks operating in the Mainland, the requirements for obtaining the right to conduct renminbi business have been eased: (i) the requirement that the bank must have engaged in business in the Mainland for at least three years has been lowered to two years, and (ii) profitability is to be assessed on the basis of the overall profitability of all branches rather than the profitability of any individual branch.

j. Securities

CEPA provides that Exchanges and Clearing Limited will be permitted to establish a representative office in Beijing, in accordance with the procedures applicable to foreign securities exchanges. Securities professionals from Hong Kong will be permitted to practice in the Mainland in accordance with applicable procedures.

k. Insurance

Hong Kong residents who have Chinese citizenship and who have passed the Mainland's actuarial science examination will be permitted to practice in the Mainland. Hong Kong insurance groups formed as a result of mergers are permitted to enter the Mainland insurance market subject to the following market access conditions; namely, (i) a worldwide assets value of $5 billion, (ii) one or more of the insurance companies within the group must have at least thirty years' insurance market experience, and (iii) at least one of the group members must have established a representative office in the Mainland for at least two years. The present 10 percent capital participation limit for Hong Kong insurance companies investing in a Mainland insurance company is raised to 15 percent, and was again raised in the Annexes to 24.9 percent. Hong Kong residents who have obtained the Mainland's insurance qualifications will be entitled to practice in the Mainland. The Mainland and Hong Kong have agreed that where the above market access provisions have a significant impact on the trade or relevant sectors of either party, the parties will engage in consultations to resolve the issues.

I. Telecom Services

The Mainland and Hong Kong negotiated market access for certain telecom services. The access to Hong Kong telecom companies to five areas of business, including Internet data services, call centers, Internet access centers, content services, and storage/forwarding services, commenced on October 1, 2003, which is a three-month head start over the WTO timetable. The agreement provides that access is limited in the form of a 50/50 joint venture, and Hong Kong telecom companies would not be subject to geographic restrictions.

CEPA will benefit those companies that are either based in, or have a subsidiary based in, Hong Kong. For companies without a presence in Hong Kong, CEPA will encourage foreign parties to pursue acquisition targets in Hong Kong. There are many unanswered questions that require clarification from both the Chinese and Hong Kong governments. There is also much guesswork on how the respective governments will implement the agreement, especially in light of China's current WTO obligations. Overall, the CEPA agreement appears to afford Hong Kong–based enterprises an edge over other foreign investors. Any enterprise that seeks to enter or expand its operations in China should evaluate the potential opportunities available under CEPA.

Key Laws and Regulations

Regulations of the People's Republic of China on Special Economic Zones in Guangdong Province (approved on August 26, 1980, at the 15th Sess. of the Standing Comm. of the 5th NPC)

Implementing Measures of Guangdong Province for the Encouragement of Foreign Investment (promulgated on April 26, 1987, by the Guangdong Provincial People's Government)

Provisional Regulations on Reduction and Exemption of Enterprise Income Tax and Consolidated Industrial and Commercial Tax for the Fourteen Coastal Cities and the Special Economic Zones (promulgated on November 15, 1984, by the State Council)

State Council Regulations Concerning Encouragement of Foreign Investment (promulgated on October 11, 1986, by the State Council)

People's Republic of China—United Kingdom: Agreement on the Future of Hong Kong, Sept. 26, 1984

Basic Law of the Hong Kong Special Administrative Region of the PRC (adopted April 4, 1990, by the 3rd Sess. of the 7th NPC)

Decision of the Standing Committee of the National People's Congress on the Handling of Pre-Existing Hong Kong Laws in Accordance with Article 160 of

(Continued)

(*Continued from previous page*)

the "Basic Law of the Hong Kong Special Administrative Region of the People's Republic of China" (adopted on February 23, 1997, at the 24th Meeting of the Standing Comm. of the 8th People's Congress)

Basic Law of the Macau Special Administrative Region of the PRC (adopted on March 31, 1993, by the 1st Sess. of the 8th NPC)

Mainland/Hong Kong Closer Economic Partnership Arrangement (CEPA) (executed by the Mainland and HKSAR on June 29, 2003)

Provisions on the Place of Origin Rules for Goods Traded Under CEPA (promulgated on December 30, 2003, by the General Administration of Customs)

Supplementary Rules for Provisional Regulation on the Establishment of Sino-Foreign Joint Equity Foreign Trading Company (issued on January 8, 2004, by the Ministry of Commerce)

Appendix A

Sample Contracts

MANUFACTURING AGREEMENT

This MANUFACTURING AGREEMENT is entered into by and between ________________ (the "Company") and ________________ ("Manufacturer"), in accordance with the "Law of the People's Republic of China on Economic Contracts Involving Foreign Interests" and other relevant laws.

1. *Manufacturing Process:* Manufacturer shall produce, manufacture, and package a ______ (referred to herein as the "Products") by employing the latest technology and equipment (hereinafter referred to as "Manufacturing Process"). Said Manufacturing Process shall be conducted at Manufacturer's facilities located at ________________. The Products shall meet all specifications as set forth in Exhibit "A" of this Agreement. Manufacturer acknowledges and understands that the specifications and drawings set forth in Exhibit A are in the English language, and agrees that it fully understands said specifications and drawings. Manufacturer further agrees that the English version of Exhibit A shall be controlling and that no other version of the specifications or drawings will control or influence the quality and results of the manufacturing process of the Products. The Company expressly reserves the right to reject any Products which do not meet the standards set forth in Exhibit "A", or if the Products are inconsistent with the samples provided by Manufacturers to the Company. Manufacturer agrees to allow a representative of the Company to be on-site at any time during the Manufacturing Process.

2. *Production Schedule:* Manufacturer shall produce a test quantity of product based upon the following schedule:

________, 19/20	[x] Units
________, 19/20	[y] Units

After the initial [x + y] units are produced, shipped, and delivered to the Company's customer, the parties will thereafter mutually agree upon the quantity and scheduling for the production of additional units.

3. *Scope of Agreement:* Manufacturer acknowledges that it is acting solely as a contract-manufacturer and this Agreement does not form a joint venture or association of any type. Manufacturer, and its affiliates or subsidiaries, agree not to sell or market the Products which are the subject of this Agreement at any time during and after the termination of this Agreement in the United States, the People's Republic of China, and any other country.

4. *Subcontracting:* No other production facility shall be used without the advance written approval of the Company. Manufacturer agrees to provide the Company thirty (30) days advanced written notice of any change in the production facility location. If the consent of the Company is obtained for purposes of subcontracting, any and all subcontractors shall be bound by the terms of this Agreement.

5. *Packaging:* Manufacturer shall package the Products in accordance with the specifications as shown in Exhibit "B" of this Agreement. All packaging materials shall be provided by and at the sole cost and expense of Manufacturer. Manufacturer shall maintain a supply of packaging materials in a quantity of not less than an amount required for one full month's supply of the Products.

6. *Materials:* The Company shall supply [______________] components used in the Manufacturing Process. Manufacturer shall train its personnel to avoid damaging the [___________] components. However, the Company shall allow a damage rate for the subject zippers used in the Manufacturing Process to the sum of [z] percent ([z]%), and the Company shall bear the cost of this percentage. If the damage rate exceeds the [z] percent ([z]%) allocation, Manufacturer shall reimburse or credit the Company for the damaged [______________]. Manufacturer will assist the Company with the import of the [__________] components or any and all other raw materials, component parts, ingredients, and other necessary materials supplied by the Company. Manufacturer shall handle all export formalities in connection with this Agreement.

Manufacturer agrees to only use materials meeting international and the Company's customer's standards in the Manufacturing Process. Specifically,

Manufacturer shall require its suppliers, including [________________], and other suppliers of parts and materials, to abide by international quality standards and restrictions, and shall reject any parts or materials which do not meet international and the Company's customer's standards. Manufacturer shall require its suppliers to use [________________] materials that are consistent with the product specifications attached hereto as Exhibit "C" of this Agreement. The Company expressly reserves the right to reject any Products that fail to meet international standards for [________________] materials and production.

The Company agrees to assist Manufacturer in obtaining a reliable, prompt, and cost-effective supply of raw materials, such as [__________], to be used in the Manufacturing Process.

7. *Warehousing and Security:* Manufacturer shall provide the Company with ample storage space, without cost, for the materials, parts, and finished Products. The Parties agree that the packaging materials, parts, and finished Products shall be stored at Manufacturer's premises, unless written permission is granted from the Company.

Manufacturer agrees to provide storage for the packaging materials, ingredients, and packaged Products which is secure from theft, shrinkage, moisture, or vermin. Manufacturer shall also purchase a loss and damage insurance policy sufficient to cover the total value of the materials, parts, and finished products. Manufacturer further agrees to reimburse the Company for any and all damage to the materials, parts, and finished Products which is not compensated for under the insurance policy or by the insurance company while such materials, parts, and finished products are in the possession of, or under the custody or control of, Manufacturer.

8. *Pricing and Terms:* The Company shall pay to manufacturer the sum of US $ FOB Shanghai per unit for the first [x + y] units produced under this Agreement. The pricing terms may be renegotiated after the completion of the test quantity set forth in section 2 of this Agreement.

The Company agrees to pay Manufacturer for the manufacturing of the Products by Letter of Credit (L/C) under the terms and conditions set forth in the Letter of Credit, a copy of which is attached to as Exhibit "D" of this Agreement.

9. *Term and Termination:* The term of this Agreement is for a period of one year and may be renewed by the Parties by written stipulation. Either party may, however, terminate this Agreement, without cause, upon not less than one hundred twenty (120) days of written notice to the other party. Either party shall have the right to terminate the Agreement, prior to the expiration of the term hereof, upon the occurrence of any of the following events:

a. Breach or default by any party of any of the terms, obligations, covenants, representations or warranties under this Agreement which are not waived in writing by the non-defaulting party. In such case, the non-defaulting party shall notify the other of such alleged breach or default and the other party shall have a period of thirty (30) days to cure the same.

b. The other party is declared insolvent or bankrupt, or makes an assignment for the benefit of creditors, or a receiver is appointed.

c. Either party is unable to continue its operation due to causes of force majeure as defined in Paragraph 19 of this Agreement.

d. Either party engages in any activity that is considered a conflict of interest with the other party, or directly or indirectly competes with the products or business activities of the other party.

10. *Warranties of Manufacturer:* Manufacturer warrants that the Products shall be free from all defects and shall meet all written specifications and drawings as set forth in Exhibit A. Should there be any defects in the products manufactured by Manufacturer and such defects are caused by Manufacturer during the manufacturing process or the period in which Manufacturer has control of the products, Manufacturer shall be responsible for curing such defects and for any and all direct or consequential damages as a result of such defects.

11. *Proprietary Information and Intellectual Property:* Manufacturer expressly agrees that all rights, title, and interest to all trademarks, service marks, patents, copyrights, technology, formulas, know-how, non-patented technology, trade secrets, designs, technical documentation, applications literature, sales information, customer lists, and other technology (hereinafter referred to as "Proprietary Information and Intellectual Property") owned by the Company or its customers shall at all times remain the sole property of the Company and its customers. Manufacturer expressly acknowledges and agrees that the Products, specifications and drawings, and source(s) of materials and parts, are Proprietary Information and Intellectual Property of the Company and its customers. Manufacturer further expressly acknowledges and agrees that any other information revealed by the Company to Manufacturer in the future is Proprietary Information and Intellectual Property and entitled to full protection under this Agreement.

Manufacturer shall not use, duplicate, or transfer the Proprietary Information and Intellectual Property of the Company for any purpose except to accomplish the production objectives of this Agreement. Manufacturer shall not make any modifications to the Products and/or components owned and/or contributed by the Company, without the prior written consent of the Company.

Manufacturer shall treat all of the Company's Proprietary Information and Intellectual Property in confidence and shall protect the same with the same degree of care as that with which it protects its own confidential or proprietary information. In the absence of a the Company's prior written consent, Manufacturer shall not disclose the Company's Proprietary Information and Intellectual Property to any person except authorized representatives of the Manufacturer or duplicate, transfer, or use the same for any purpose other than in connection with the performance of this Agreement. Manufacturer further agrees that its employees, agents, affiliates, related organizations, and representatives shall be bound by the terms of this section prohibiting the unauthorized disclosure, duplication, transfer, and use of the Company's Proprietary Information and Intellectual Property. This Article shall be effective for the duration of this Agreement and for an additional period of fifteen (15) years after expiration or premature termination of this Agreement.

Manufacturer further agrees that it shall not, under any circumstances, contact the Company's customers or suppliers of materials or parts, except where specifically authorized in writing by the Company.

12. *Indemnification by the Company:* the Company agrees to defend, indemnify and hold Manufacturer harmless from all actions, claims, liabilities, costs, damages and expenses, including attorneys' fees, arising from or asserted against Manufacturer or which Manufacturer shall be compelled to pay, sustain or incur by reason of the use of the Proprietary Information and Intellectual Property defined in section 11, provided that Manufacturer shall give prompt notice to the Company of any claim or pending action so that the Company may have the opportunity to defend its interests.

13. *Indemnification by Manufacturer:* Manufacturer agrees to defend, indemnify and hold the Company harmless from all actions, claims, lawsuits, liabilities, costs, damages, fines, penalties and expenses, including attorneys' fees, resulting from claims arising from, or relating to, any acts or omissions of Manufacturer or from the Products or any component thereof, or packaging, excluding, however, claims which might be filed or asserted concerning the transportation and/or storage of the Products to the extent that such transportation and/or storage is provided by the Company.

14. *Notice of Claims:* Manufacturer and the Company shall provide prompt, written notice to each other in the event that either party receives any information or notice that a claim has been, or has substantial likelihood of being, made against such party, and which entitles or would entitle

such party to indemnification, insurance or warranty rights, protection or benefits pursuant to the terms of this Agreement.

15. *Inspection:* During the term hereof, the Company shall have the right, upon reasonable notice to Manufacturer, to observe and monitor Manufacturer's Quality Control program testing techniques as applied to the Products.

16. *Production Disruption:* If Manufacturer is unable to perform under the terms of this Agreement because of any form of casualty to its premises or equipment or by reason of any work stoppage of its employees or any other cause beyond its control, Manufacturer will cooperate with the Company to arrange for the transfer of the responsibility for the production of the Product to a qualified contractor at the expense of the Manufacturer.

17. *Assignment:* This Agreement shall not be assignable by either party without the prior written consent of the other party.

18. *Entire Agreement:* This Agreement constitutes the entire agreement of the Parties with respect to the subject matter herein and supersedes any and all other agreements, understandings, statements or representations, either oral or in writing.

19. *Force Majeure:* Should either of the parties hereto be directly affected in or prevented from the execution of this Agreement by force majeure events such as earthquake, typhoon, flood, fire, war and any other unforeseeable events whose occurrence and consequence cannot be prevented or avoided, the party encountering the force majeure shall, without delay, inform the other party by certified mail of the event, and within fifteen (15) days thereafter provide detailed information regarding the circumstance of the force majeure event and a valid certificate certifying the reasons by which this Agreement or any part hereof cannot be performed or the performance hereof may be delayed. By taking into account the extent of the impact of the force majeure event on the performance of the Agreement, the parties hereto shall consult with each other to decide whether this Agreement shall be terminated or if part of the obligations hereof shall be released or the performance thereof should be delayed.

20. *Governing Law:* The execution and performance of this Agreement is governed by the laws of the ____________________________.

21. *Time of the Essence:* Time is expressly declared to be of the essence of this Agreement.

22. *Waiver and Amendment:* No breach of any provisions hereof can be waived unless in writing. Waiver of any one breach shall not be deemed to be a waiver of any other breach of the same or any other provision. This Agreement may be amended only by written agreement executed by the Parties.

23. *Severability:* If any part of this Agreement shall be determined to be invalid or unenforceable by any court of competent jurisdiction, such determination shall not affect the remainder of the Agreement.

24. *Settlement of Dispute:* Any disputes arising from the execution of, or in connection with, this Contract shall be settled through amicable consultation between the Parties. In the event that a settlement cannot be reached through consultation, the disputes shall be submitted to the ____________________________. The arbitration shall be conducted in accordance with the arbitration procedures of the arbitration commission. The award rendered by the arbitration commission shall be final and legally binding on both parties hereto. The prevailing party shall be entitled to the payment of the arbitration fees.

25. *Language:* This Agreement shall be executed in Chinese and English versions and there shall be two copies of each of the two original versions. Each party thereto shall have a copy of the original versions. The Chinese version is provided to Manufacturer for references only and the text in English language shall be the legally binding document.

26. *Commencement of Agreement:* This Agreement and accompanying documents are required to be formally signed by the legal representatives of both parties hereto and approved by the relevant government authorities if such approval is required. This Agreement shall become effective from the date of such approval by the relevant government authorities if such approval is required; if no government approval is required, the Agreement shall be effective immediately after it is signed by both parties.

27. *Notice:* Any notice in connection with this Agreement shall be in writing and addressed as follows:

The Company: ____________________

____

____

Tel: ________________

Fax: ________________

Manufacturer: ____________________

____

____

Tel: ________________

Fax: ________________

Where any notice or communication between the parties hereto if served by cable, telex or facsimile, relating to the rights and obligations of either party, a written letter thereof shall follow.

28. *Other Matters:* Any matter not covered in this Contract shall be decided upon consultation of both parties hereto and the result of such consultation shall become a supplement to this Contract. The supplement shall have the same legal effect as the Agreement.

29. *Authorization:* This Agreement is signed by the respective legal representatives of Manufacturer and the Company in Shanghai, People's Republic of China, on _________ and the representatives hereunder signed warrant that they have the full authority to execute this Agreement and bind the parties on whose behalf they are executing the Agreement.

Dated: ___________ [The Company]

By: ___________________________
Name: ___________________________
Title: ___________________________

Dated: ___________ [The Manufacturer]

By: ___________________________
Name: ___________________________
Title: ___________________________

Exhibit A
Product Specifications

Exhibit B
Packaging Specifications

Exhibit C
Material Specifications

Exhibit D
Letter of Credit

DISTRIBUTION AND MARKETING AGREEMENT

THIS AGREEMENT made and entered into this _____ day of ________, _________ by and between ____________________ (the "Company") and ___________________ (the "Marketer")

WHEREAS, Company is a manufacturer and seller of _______ products (hereinafter referred to as the "Products"); and

WHEREAS, Marketer is a trading company with the resources and expertise to distribute and sell Company's Products in the People's Republic of China; and

WHEREAS, Company desires to appoint Marketer as the distributor and marketer for the Products in the geographical territory defined herein and on the terms and conditions hereinafter set forth; and

NOW THEREFORE, in consideration of the mutual undertakings of the parties, IT IS AGREED AS FOLLOWS:

1. *Appointment as Marketer*

a) *Territory of Marketer.* Company hereby appoints Marketer, and Marketer hereby accepts such appointment, as Company's sole and exclusive Marketer for the distribution of its Products in the Territory defined as the People's Republic of China but excluding [____________] and any zone, sub-zone, region, or area within its jurisdiction or territorial boundaries including, but not limited to, [_______________] (hereinafter referred to as the "Territory").

b) *Alteration of Territory.* No alteration in the Territory and no agreement between Marketer and any third party purporting to alter the Territory shall be effective without the prior written approval of Company.

c) *Appointment of Others by Marketer.* Marketer shall be permitted to appoint sub-marketers, resellers, and sales representatives within the Territory for the sale of the Products. Any and all sub-marketers, resellers, and representatives appointed by Marketer are required to abide by the terms of this Agreement and specifically with respect to compliance with all laws and regulations concerning the sale of the subject Products. Marketer shall be fully responsible for the activities of all appointed sub-marketers, resellers, and representatives and shall indemnify the Company for any claim made with respect to the actions or omissions of any and all individuals or organizations appointed under this subsection.

d) *Modification of Product Line.* Company reserves the right at any time, in its sole and exclusive discretion and without recourse on

Marketer's part, (i) to modify or alter any of the Products and/or (ii) to add or to delete any Products from its product line, on the condition of not affecting confirmed orders.

e) *Grant of License.* Company hereby grants to Marketer a license to use Company's trademarks, trade names and trade secrets in the course of performing its obligations under this Agreement. Company's labels shall only be used for Company's Products. Company's trademarks, trade names and trade secrets can only be used in such a manner that their protective status is not jeopardized.

2. *Minimum Quota Requirement.* In order to maintain the exclusive territorial rights under this Agreement, Marketer is required to purchase a minimum volume of Products per quarter in an amount to be decided by Company on a quarterly basis (hereinafter referred to as the "Minimum Quota Requirement"). The Minimum Quota Requirement shall be set forth in an addendum to this Agreement and attached hereto as Exhibit 1.

3. *Sales and Marketer*

a) *Sale of Products.* Company agrees to sell to Marketer the Products requested, subject to availability, subject to the credit terms specifically described in Section 4 hereunder, and subject to Marketer being in compliance with all of the terms and conditions of this Agreement. No order from Marketer for the Products shall be binding upon Company until accepted by Company, and nothing in this Agreement shall impose on Company the obligation to produce any Products or prevent Company from making such changes in any of its Products as Company in its sole judgment may decide.

b) *Prices of Products.* The prices to be paid by Marketer and discounts to be granted, if any, shall be established by both parties in good faith negotiation. Company shall endeavor to maintain reasonable prices for each of the Products.

4. *Terms of Sale*

a) *Expenses Paid by Marketer.* Unless otherwise agreed in writing between the parties, all Products shall be sold Ex Factory and Marketer shall pay all freight, sales taxes, insurance and duties on the Products. Specifically, Marketer is responsible for all taxes, tariffs, and fees imposed by the People's Republic of China including consumption tax, business tax, value added tax, customs duties, handling fees, and any other fee or levy imposed by governmental authorities. The Company, in its sole discretion, may require marketer to pay for the Products by wire transfer, irrevocable letter of credit (L/C), or on credit terms.

b) *Credit Terms*

(i) The Company may provide Marketer with credit for the purchase of the Products in an amount to be solely determined by the Company. The credit terms shall be for a maximum period of forty-five *(45)* days from the date of shipment from Company's place of business. If payment is not received on any Products within forty-five *(45)* days of shipment of the Products, Marketer agrees to pay interest on the balance due per shipment at a rate of ten percent (10%) per annum.

(ii) The Marketer shall provide the Company with a secured interest in the Products, its equipment, and other assets of Marketer as collateral for the credit provided to Marketer under this section. The secured interest shall be evidenced by a Security Contract, a copy of which shall be attached hereto as Exhibit 2, and registered with the relevant authorities.

c) *Letter of Credit Terms*

(i) The Company may also require Marketer to pay for the Products with an irrevocable letter of credit (hereinafter referred to as "L/C"). All L/C's shall be issued by an international, national, or regional bank in favor of Company. Reimbursement for the aforementioned sight draft shall be through a bank located within the United States of America, and the Negotiating Bank must be authorized to claim and receive reimbursement telegraphically.

(ii) All L/C's shall show the Company as beneficiary and payable in U.S. Dollars within 30 days of shipment of Products. Any and all charges incurred inside the People's Republic of China for the L/C shall be paid for by Marketer.

(iii) All L/C's shall be subject to International Chamber of Commerce (ICC) rules (Brochure 400) unless otherwise agreed upon by Company and Marketer.

(iv) All L/C's allow partial shipments and partial payments. All L/C's shall show that all charges for amendments to the credit, including related communications expenses, which are the responsibility of the Marketer are for the account of the Marketer. All L/C's shall have an expiry date of no less than 30 days after the date of initiation to allow for order processing.

5. *Obligations of Marketer*

a) *Best Efforts to Sell.* Marketer shall use its best efforts to promote, sell and expend the sale of Products within the Territory through the use of an active and effective sales organization.

b) *Maintenance of Inventory.* Marketer shall maintain an inventory of the Products sufficient to meet the demand of customers throughout the territory in a timely manner.

c) *Governmental Approvals.* Marketer shall obtain and maintain all necessary government approval, licenses, permits, registration certificates, and other forms of approval which are necessary or advisable for the sale of the Products and the implementation of this Agreement within the Territory.

d) *Notification of Certain Facts.* Marketer shall promptly inform Company of any facts or opinions likely to be relevant in relation to the manufacture, sale, use or development of the Products within the Territory, including (but not limited to) those concerning safety and labeling requirements and the activities of Company's competitors.

e) *Limited to Territory.* Marketer shall not, directly or through any third person or entity (whether or not controlled by Marketer), establish a sales office, a warehouse, or a distribution center outside the Territory, or solicit orders for the Products from customers outside the Territory. Any such order obtained by Marketer shall be forwarded promptly by Marketer to Company without any other action on the part of the Marketer. This includes any and all sales or inquiries from customers located in the Municipality of Shanghai or its regions, zones, or subzones as defined in section 1(a).

f) *Costs and Commissions.* Marketer shall bear all costs of, and all liabilities related to its performance of this Agreement, including (but not limited to) the payment of commission or other compensation to its sales representatives.

g) *Advertising Expenses.* Marketer is responsible for all advertising and promotional expenses incurred in marketing the Products pursuant to this Agreement. Marketer shall provide the Company with a courtesy copy of all advertising for its records.

h) *No Unauthorized Representations.* Marketer is not authorized to make, and shall not make, any representations or warranties with respect to the Products except those representations and warranties authorized in writing by Company. Marketer is fully responsible for compliance under the Advertising Law of the People's Republic of China (adopted October 27, 1994), Law of the People's Republic of China on the Protection of the Rights and Interests of Consumers (adopted October 31, 1993), and the Law of the People's Republic of China Against Unfair Competition (adopted September 2, 1993). Marketer shall indemnify and hold Company harmless from all claims, demands, administrative or governmental penalties or fines, actions, causes of action, fees, costs, attorneys' fees and expenses arising from any and all promotional sales or marketing activities, representations, warranties, and statements (written or verbal) made by Marketer or any of its agents, employees, representatives and/or assigns in relation to the Products, this Agreement or the Company.

i) *Compliance with Law.* In addition to the laws and regulations set forth in section 5(h), Marketer shall comply with any and all other laws and government regulations of the People's Republic of China concerning customs, taxation, price controls, trade involving items containing ____________________, and any and all laws which may in any way affect the sale of the Products.

j) *Preservation of Goodwill.* Marketer shall at all times conduct itself in an appropriate manner, so as not to injure the business, goodwill, reputation or good standing of Company.

k) *Quarterly Report and Business Plan.* Marketer shall provide Company with a quarterly report and business plan which outlines (1) the sales of Company's Products during the preceding quarter; (2) the promotional activities of Marketer during the preceding quarter including the names and addresses of actual and potential customers; (3) the business environment in the Territory including a discussion of the activities of Company's competitors, the laws and governmental policies affecting the sale of the Products, and the economic conditions in the Territory affecting the sale of the Products; and (4) anticipated sales for the current quarter. This report shall be provided to Company by the end of each quarterly month of the calendar year (i.e., March, June, September, and December).

l) *Compliance with Corruption Laws.* Marketer shall comply with he U.S. Foreign Corrupt Practices Act and China's anti-corruption laws and shall require any sub-marketer, reseller, or representative to comply with said laws as well.

6. *Obligations of Company*

a) *Provide Information.* Company shall furnish to Marketer such information and instructions as may be reasonably required by Marketer to promote the sale of the Products. The quantities so provided shall be determined by Company and shall be provided with or without charge at the Company's sole discretion.

b) *Exclusive Right to Distribute within Territory.* Company shall not during the term of this Agreement either directly or indirectly, sell or distribute any of the Products within the Territory except through Marketer.

c) *No Engagement of Another within Territory.* Company shall not commission or engage any other agent, representative or distributor engaged in a business similar to that of Marketer for the purposes of selling the Products during the term of this Agreement within the Territory.

d) *No Providing Products to be Sold in Territory to Another.* Company shall not provide its Products to any other agent, representative or distributor directly or indirectly under any other label to be sold in the Territory.

e) *Invoice in Dollars.* Company shall invoice all orders directly to Marketer in U.S. Dollars at prices in effect at the time the order is placed.

f) *Provision of Documents.* All essential documents for each order shall be sent by the Company to Marketer.

g) *Domestic Facility.* Company shall maintain at its Los Angeles facilities, or other location designated by Company, a sufficient level of inventory to meet the demand of customers of Marketer.

7. *Intellectual Property, Trade Secrets and Non-Competition*

a) *Prohibition on Other Similar Products.* Marketer agrees that, during the term of the Agreement, and any renewal hereof, neither Marketer nor any of its representatives, agents, or employees acting under Marketer's direction or within the scope of authority conferred upon such representative, agent, or employee of Marketer, shall sell, offer for sale, or act as a representative or agent within the Territory with respect to the sale of any merchandise of the same nature as existing Products.

b) *Prohibition on Other Similar Businesses.* Marketer agrees that it shall not, directly or indirectly, own, control, operate, manage, participate in any sole proprietorship, corporation, partnership or entity whose primary business is of the same nature as the business of Company.

c) *Acknowledgment of Intellectual Property Rights.* Marketer acknowledges and agrees that all trademarks, trade names, service marks, copyrights, patents, trade secrets, trade dress, designs, artwork, specifications, and other intellectual property are exclusively owned, on a worldwide basis, by Company (hereinafter referred to as "Intellectual Property").

(i) Marketer agrees that none of the Intellectual Property will be used for its benefit outside of its work for the Company either during the period of this Agreement or thereafter.

(ii) If Marketer is required to register the Intellectual Property with the governmental authorities in the Territory, such registration shall be in the name of the Company only.

(iii) Marketer shall actively police the marketplace and shall immediately contact the Company if it suspects any person or entity is misusing Company's Intellectual Property. Marketer shall assist Company in enforcing Company's rights to the Intellectual Property in the Territory.

8. *Term, Termination and Conditions for Extension of Term*

a) *Term.* The term of this Agreement is for a period of three (3) years commencing on the date of execution of this Agreement.

b) *Termination Upon Notice.* Company may terminate this Agreement, effective upon thirty (30) days prior written notice, under the following circumstances:

(i) *Material Breach.* In the event Marketer fails to remedy a material breach of a covenant or commitment under this Agreement, which failure shall continue for thirty (30) days after receipt of written notice to Marketer from Company of such breach; provided, however, that if such breach is not willful and is of a nature such that it can be cured, but not within such thirty (30) days, then the commencement by Marketer of the prompt and diligent curing of such default within said thirty (30) days shall constitute the "remedy" of any such breach if the breach is cured within sixty (60) days of such written notice. Marketer shall also reimburse Company for any actual damages suffered by Company in connection with such breach within a reasonable time after its commitment of same.

(ii) *Death or Cessation of Participation by Majority Owners.* In the event of; (i) the death of principals and/or majority owners of Marketer, or their incapacitation for a period of ninety (90) or more substantially consecutive days, such that said principals or majority owners are unable to perform their normal day-to-day functions for Marketer during such ninety (90)-day period; or (ii) the principals for majority owners of Marketer cease for any reason whatsoever (other than for normal vacation periods) to participate actively in the day-to-day management and affairs of Marketer for a period of thirty (30) substantially consecutive days.

c) *Termination—Failure to Meet Quota.* If Marketer fails to meet any quota set forth in this Agreement or addendum hereof, the Company may, at its option, immediately terminate the Agreement. In addition, if Marketer fails to pay for the Products in accordance with the terms and conditions set forth in Section 4 herein, Company may, at its option, immediately terminate this Agreement.

d) *Termination—Bankruptcy.* This Agreement shall terminate automatically if Marketer has a receiver and/or manager appointed for, or execution levied upon, all or any part of its business or assets; proceedings are commenced for the voluntary or involuntary bankruptcy or liquidation of Marketer; or Marketer becomes unable to pay its debts as they fall due.

e) *Renewal.* This Agreement may be renewed, at the option of the Company, for additional one (1) year periods, provided that a Quota Schedule for each such renewal period is determined on or before the expiration date of the initial term hereof and any succeeding renewal hereof.

f) *Definition of Material Breach.* For the purposes of this Section 8, the term "material breach" shall include, without limitation, a specific action or omission or a series of related actions or omissions which result in actual damages to the other party in excess of [Ten Thousand U.S. Dollars (US$10,000)] for a single action or the series of actions taken as a whole. "Material breach" shall also include fraud, any willful failure on the part of the Marketer to deliver the Products to customers, and any violation of Sections 4 (payment), 5 (obligations), or 7 (intellectual property) hereof.

g) *Cooperation.* In the event that Company terminates this Agreement pursuant to this Section 8, the parties agree to cooperate in good faith to facilitate the transition of the business for the Products in the Territory to Company or any third person or entity designated by Company, and the post-termination non-competition obligation under Section 7.2 shall commence as of the effective date of such termination.

9. *Effects of Termination*

a) Upon the expiration or early termination of this Agreement for any reason whatsoever, the following shall take effect;

(i) All licenses, interest or rights granted to Marketer under or pursuant to this Agreement shall immediately cease and Marketer shall make no further sales of Products.

(ii) All Intellectual Property and promotional materials shall be returned to the Company.

(iii) All Products that have not been paid for shall be returned to the Company.

b) Without prejudice to a party's right to claim any actual damages or other claims for breach of this Agreement, the early termination or expiration of, or the failure to renew this Agreement shall not, in and of itself, entitle a party to any compensation or damages of any kind or character whatsoever, whether on account of the loss by Company or Marketer of present or prospective profits or discounts on sales or anticipated sales, or expenditures, investments or commitments made in connection with the distribution of the Products or in connection with the establishment, development, or maintenance of Marketer's business, or on account of any other cause or reason whatsoever.

10. *Personal and Corporate Guarantee.* The principal of Marketer, ___________, shall provide the Company with a guarantee with respect to the obligations under this Agreement and specifically with respect to the repayment of monies under this section. The guarantee shall be evidenced by a written Guarantee Contract, a copy of which shall be attached hereto as Exhibit 4.

11. *Exhibits.* This Agreement shall have the following Exhibits, each of which forms an integral part of this Agreement:

EXHIBIT	*MATTER*
1	Minimum Quota Requirement
2	Security Contract
3	Guarantee Contract

12. *General Terms and Conditions*

a) *Assignment.* This Agreement is not assignable by either party without the prior written consent of the other party hereto except that Company may assign the Agreement to any subsidiary, affiliate, or commonly controlled company or as part of a sale of substantially all of its assets.

b) *Entire Agreement; Modification.* As of the date of the parties' execution hereof, this Agreement, the Security Contract, and the Guarantee Contract contain the entire and only agreement between the parties with respect to the subject matter hereof and any representation, promise, or condition not incorporated herein shall not be binding upon either party. No change, modification or waiver of this Agreement or any provision hereof or right to act hereunder shall be binding unless made in writing and signed by both parties hereto.

c) *Independent Contractor.* Marketer shall act only as an independent contractor of Company, and not as an agent or employee of Company. It is not the intent of the parties to create under this Agreement any joint venture, partnership, business association, or other form of business entity. Except as otherwise provided herein, in no event shall Company be liable in any manner for the acts and omissions of Marketer to compensate its employees, representatives, and agents. Marketer shall have no right to legally bind Company in any manner whatsoever.

d) *Governing Language.* This Agreement, the Security Contract, and the Guarantee Contract shall have an English version and Chinese version, both being equally valid and enforceable.

e) *Cooperation of Marketer.* Marketer shall sign and deliver all instruments and other documents necessary or useful to carry out or confirm the intentions of the parties as expressed herein and shall assist and fully cooperate with Company and its designees and agents in all matters relating to this Agreement.

f) *Disputes.* The parties hereto shall attempt to settle any dispute arising out of or relating to this Agreement in an amicable manner. In the event that such attempts should fail, then the parties hereto agree that any dispute or claim arising out of this Agreement, directly or indirectly, or arising out of the relationship of the parties hereto, shall be resolved before the International Arbitration Court of the International Chamber of Commerce (Paris), pursuant to the ICC's arbitration rules existing at the time of the application. This agreement shall be governed by the laws of the State of California, United States of America. Arbitration shall be held in Paris, France, or at another mutually agreed upon location. The prevailing party shall be entitled to an award of arbitration expenses including an award of attorneys' fees.

IN WITNESS WHEREOF, the parties have executed this Agreement on the date and year first hereinabove written.

MARKETER		COMPANY	
By:	____________________	By:	____________________
Name:	____________________	Name:	____________________
Title:	____________________	Title:	____________________

SECURITY AGREEMENT

This SECURITY AGREEMENT is made on ______, ______ between ____________ (the "Mortgagee") and ____________ (the "Mortgagor")

WHEREAS:

1. Simultaneously with the execution and delivery of this Security Agreement, Mortgagor, as distributor and marketer, and Mortgagee, as manufacturer and seller, are entering into that certain Distribution and Marketing Agreement (the "Distribution Agreement") pursuant to which Mortgagee agrees to sell to Mortgagor, and Mortgagor agrees to purchase, ____________ products ("Products") in the geographical territory defined in such Distribution Agreement.

2. As security for payment under the Distribution Agreement, the Mortgagor desires to grant to Mortgagee, and Mortgagee agrees to accept such grant, a security interest in form of mortgage (the "Security Interest") on the Collateral described in Section 2(a).

NOW THEREFORE, Mortgagee and Mortgagor have agreed through consultation to enter into this Security Agreement on the terms and conditions set forth below:

1. *Definitions*. Unless otherwise defined in this Security Agreement, certain terms are defined as follows:

a) "Collateral" is defined in Section 2(a).

b) "Distribution Agreement" is defined in Recitals.

c) "Event of Default" means any of the events listed in Section 9(a).

d) "Law" means all laws, decrees, regulations, rules, announcements, notices, opinions, replies, and explanations, etc. promulgated or circulated by China's National People's Congress or the Chinese government and its subordinate ministries, commissions, provincial departments, bureaus and other agencies, or China's People's Supreme Court. People's Congress shall include all levels of people's congress including national, provincial, municipal, prefectural, county and district; government agencies shall cover government agencies at all levels including the State Council, ministries, provinces, municipalities, prefectures, counties and districts.

e) "Mortgage Duration" means the valid duration of this Security Agreement stipulated in Section 12(a).

f) "Mortgage Ratio" means the ratio between the amount of the debt secured by mortgage and the value of the Collateral, as stipulated in Section 3(e) of this Security Agreement.

g) "Notice of Default" means a written notice of an Event of Default to the Mortgagor issued by the Mortgagee pursuant to Section 9(b) of this Security Agreement.

h) "Obligations" means the obligations secured hereunder, whether now existing or hereafter arising, including without limitation the principal of the credit, interest and all other fees payable by the Mortgagor under the Distribution Agreement, liquidated damage or default interest, indemnity payment for damage suffered and expenses incurred in connection with the exercise of the mortgages (including without limitation any agent fees, evaluation costs, processing fees, accounting fees, court fees and attorney fees).

i) "Other Documents" means any other documents executed by the Mortgagor in connection with the Distribution Agreement and this Security Agreement, including without limitation the Guarantee Contract and any insurance policies naming the Mortgagor as the beneficiary.

j) "PRC" of "China" means People's Republic of China. For purpose of this Security Agreement, the definition of PRC shall exclude Hong Kong Special Administrative Zone, Macao and Taiwan.

k) "Products" is defined in Recitals.

l) "Registration Authorities" means any government authorities in charge of mortgage registration in ________________ Municipality.

m) "Security" means mortgage, pledge, lien and/or any other third party security.

n) "Security Interest(s)" is defined in Recitals.

o) "USA" means the United States of America.

2. *Security Interests.*

a) As collateral security for the timely and full payment for any amount due under the Distribution Agreement, the Mortgagor hereby grants, for the Mortgage Duration, to the Mortgagee for its benefit a Security Interest in, all of the Mortgagor's right, title and interest in and to the following, whether now or hereafter existing or acquired (the "Collateral"):

(i) all inventory in all of its forms, wherever located, including without limitation Products delivered by the Mortgagee and held by the Mortgagor for sale from time to time in accordance with Section 4(c) of the Distribution Agreement, packaging materials and work in process, materials used and consumed in the Mortgagor's business and all accessions thereto (collectively as "Inventory"), and

(ii) all other assets in all of its forms, wherever located, including all machinery, furnishings, vehicles and all parts thereof and accessions, additions, attachments, improvements, substitutions and replacements thereto and therefor (collectively as "Assets").

b) This Security Agreement shall create a continuing security interest in the Collateral and shall

(i) remain in full force and effect until termination of the Distribution Agreement and the payment in full thereunder;

(ii) be binding upon the Mortgagor and its successors, transferees and assigns, and

(iii) inure, together with the rights and remedies of the Mortgagee hereunder, to the benefit of the Mortgagee and its successors and assigns.

3. *Mortgage Registration.*

a) *Registration of Mortgaged Collateral.* In order to perfect the Security Interests created herein, within five (5) working days after the first and each of the following deliveries of the Products, the Mortgagor shall (or if so requested by the Mortgagee, the Mortgagor shall entrust the Mortgagee or any third party designated by the Mortgagee to) register the mortgaged Collateral with the following Registration Authorities, as the case may be, with all expenses in connection therewith to be borne by the Mortgagor:

(i) [__________ Municipal Administration of Industry and Commerce for mortgage on Inventory, machinery, furnishings];

(ii) [__________ Municipal Public Security Bureau, Vehicle Administration Division, for mortgage on vehicles].

b) *Foreign Exchange Security Registration.* When required by Law, within five (5) working days after execution of this Security Agreement, the Mortgagor shall (or if so requested by the Mortgagee, the Mortgagor shall entrust the Mortgagee or any third party designated by the Mortgagee to) register this Security Agreement, which is a foreign exchange security agreement, with the State Administration of Foreign Exchange, ______________ Branch, and obtain a certificate in connection therewith.

c) *Delivery of Original Certificate.* Within five (5) days after completion of each of the aforementioned mortgage registration and corresponding foreign exchange security registration, the Mortgagor shall deliver the original registration certificates to the Mortgagee (or its designated agent) for possession and safekeeping. Except as otherwise provided in Section 3(d), the Mortgagee shall possess and keep such original registration certificates for the valid duration of this Security Agreement.

d) *Possession of Documents by Mortgagor.* If, due to government inspection, renewal of certificates or other necessities in the ordinary course of business, the Mortgagor requires temporary possession of the documents in the Mortgagee's (or its designated agent's) possession and safekeeping, the Mortgagor may at any time make its request in writing to the Mortgagee (or its designated agent) three (3) days prior to the date it requires such documents. The Mortgagor shall specify the purpose and duration of such temporary possession and the Mortgagee shall have absolute discretion whether or not to agree to the Mortgagor's request.

4. *Value of the Collateral and Mortgage Ratio.*

a) *Value of Inventory.* Unless otherwise provided by the Law, for the purpose of mortgage registration, the value of the Inventory shall be determined in the following way, whichever amount is larger:

(i) at any given time, the sum of the book value of all accumulated Inventory in stock plus all outstanding account receivables at such time; or

(ii) at any given time, the accumulated amount of the contractual value of the delivered Products minus the accumulated amount of the payment made by the Mortgagor to the Mortgagee up to such time; or

(iii) the annual estimated average amount of the contractual value of the Products delivered in every three months.

b) *Value of Assets.* For the purpose of mortgage registration, the Mortgagor and the Mortgagee agree that the total value of the Assets shall be US $_________.

c) *Asset Appraisal Report.* In the event that the parties disagree on the value of the Collateral, the Mortgagor shall, at its cost, engage an asset appraisal agency to issue an asset appraisal report on the value of the Collateral. Such asset appraisal agency shall commence appraisal on each of the Collateral only after receiving written confirmation from the Mortgagee. In the event the Mortgagee disputes any appraisal report or result thereof, the Mortgagor shall reappoint another asset appraisal agency under the instruction of the Mortgagee to conduct another value appraisal.

d) *Effect of Valuation.* The Mortgagee and the Mortgagor hereby agree that the value of the Collateral under Section 4(a) and the appraised value of the Assets for the purpose of mortgage registration under Section 4(b) shall not affect the value of the Collateral determined in accordance with the Law and this Security Agreement at any time when the Mortgagee exercises its rights hereunder.

e) *Mortgage Ratio.* The Mortgage Ratio of the Collateral hereunder is 100%, except as otherwise provided by the Law.

5. *Possession and Management of the Collateral.*

a) *Mortgagor's Possession of Collateral.* Except as otherwise provided in this Security Agreement, the Collateral shall be held by the Mortgagor for the Mortgage Duration. The Mortgagor may sell or otherwise dispose of the Products in accordance with the Distribution Agreement. While holding the Collateral, the Mortgagor shall use its best efforts to maintain the well-being and integrity of the Collateral. The Mortgagee shall be entitled to enter and inspect the premises of any of the Collateral at any time. The Mortgagor shall not refuse or delay in responding to any reasonable demand by the Mortgagee for entry and inspection and shall provide all possible assistance.

b) *Damage to Collateral.* In the event the Collateral are damaged or destroyed in accidents, the Mortgagor shall promptly notify the Mortgagee of the circumstances and take measures to prevent any further damage. If, due to such damage or destruction or otherwise, the Collateral are no longer adequate to secure the Obligations, the Mortgagor shall, from time to time, and at the request of the Mortgage, provide a new Security to make up for the shortfall.

c) *Inadequate Security.* In the event the value of the Collateral shall decrease and cease to be adequate to secure the Obligations due to the acts of government, the Mortgagor shall promptly notify the Mortgagee and shall, from time to time, and at the request of the Mortgagee, provide a new Security to make up for the shortfall.

6. *Insurance.*

a) *Coverage for Collateral.* The Mortgagor shall, within five (5) days after delivery of the first batch of Products and obtaining titles to any Assets, or otherwise within the time required by the Mortgagee, purchase or cause to be purchased insurance coverage for all the Collateral.

b) *Amount.* The amount of insurance coverage shall not be less than the value of the Collateral as stipulated in Section 4(a) or any other value as determined by the Mortgagee from time to time, which amount may be higher or lower than the value of the Collateral;

c) *Assignment to Assignee.* The Mortgagor, as assignor, shall assign to the Mortgagee, as assignee, all of its rights, interests, and benefits under such insurance policies so that the Mortgagee will enjoy all rights of the insured under such insurance policies.

d) *Delivery of Policy.* Within five (5) days of the date of issuance of each insurance policy, the Mortgagor shall deliver the original policy to the Mortgagee (or its designated agent) for possession and safekeeping. Except as otherwise provided in Section 3(d), the Mortgagee shall possess and keep such insurance policies for the valid duration of this Security Agreement.

e) *Expiration of Policy.* The Mortgagor shall not withdraw or suspend any insurance policy during the Mortgage Duration. Upon the expiration of any insurance policy prior to the expiration of the valid duration of this Security Agreement, the Mortgagor shall renew and maintain or cause to be renewed and maintained such insurance policy one month in advance in accordance with the provisions of this Section.

f) *Mortgagor's Obligations.* The Mortgagor shall perform all its obligations under the insurance policies (including without limitation timely payment of insurance premiums of itself or causing the others to make timely payment thereof) to maintain valid insurance coverage on the Collateral during the entire Mortgage Duration.

g) *Mortgagor's Payment of Premiums.* Insurance premiums and all related expenses shall be borne by the Mortgagor.

h) *Mortgagee's Rights to Proceeds.* Upon the occurrence of any insured event under any such insurance policy, the Mortgagee shall have the right at any time to pursue claims with the insurance company as the first named beneficiary and to possess, accept and control all insurance proceeds. The Mortgagee shall have absolute discretion over the use of insurance proceeds, which uses may include, without limitation, payment or prepayment of all or part of the Obligations, and repair or replacement of any damaged Collateral. The Mortgagor shall not be entitled to raise any objection to the Mortgagee's decision over this issue.

i) *Mortgagor's Failure to Perform.* In the event the Mortgagor fails to perform its obligations under Section 6(a), 6(c) and 6(d) above, the Mortgagee shall be entitled to insure the Collateral in its own name or in the name of the Mortgagor or to continue payment of insurance premiums on existing insurance policies. Any insurance premium shall be borne by the Mortgagor, and any premium or fees paid by the Mortgagee shall be reimbursed in full by the Mortgagor. Any loss (including any loss of interest calculated in accordance with the interest calculation formula under the Distribution Agreement) suffered by the Mortgagor resulting therefrom shall also be borne by the Mortgagor.

7. *Mortgagor's Representations and Warranties.* Mortgagor hereby represents and warrants as follows:

a) *Duly Organized.* The Mortgagor is a [limited liability company] organized under Chinese Law. All formalities of approval and registration for its establishment have been completed and certificates for such approval and registration have been issued by the approval and registration authorities empowered for such approval and registration. The Mortgagor has the right to possess, make use of, dispose of its property and assets and engage in all business activities permitted by its business license.

b) *Authority.* The Mortgagor has full power and authority for the execution and performance of this Security Agreement, the Distribution Agreement and Other Documents. Except as otherwise provided in Section 3(a) and 3(b), all formalities for authorization, approval, consent, license, registration and filing necessary for the Mortgagor's execution and performance of this Security Agreement, the Distribution Agreement and Other Documents have been completed.

c) *Genuineness.* All documents and information provided and produced by the Mortgagor to the Mortgagee in connection with, or required by, this Security Agreement, the Distribution Agreement and Other Documents are genuine and reliable and without any forgery or concealment of truth.

d) *Full Rights in Collateral.* Subject to this Security Agreement, the Mortgagor has the full right, title and interests in the Collateral. There is no Security on the Collateral other than the Security Interest created under this Security Agreement. No individual, legal person, organization, or non-legal person entity has any claim over the Collateral. The Collateral have not been adversely affected by any Law, court judgment or ruling, or government policy.

e) *Mortgagee's Right to Possession.* Within the valid duration of this Security Agreement, in the event the Mortgagee is entitled to exercise its rights in connection with the Security under this Security Agreement, the Mortgagee may at any time enter, take possession and use the Collateral.

f) *No Pending Litigation.* The Mortgagor and/or the Collateral are not involved in any litigation, arbitration or administrative sanctions.

8. *Mortgagor's Covenants.*

a) *Covenants.* The Mortgagor covenants with the Mortgagee that, during the Mortgage Duration, it will:

(i) continue to perform the obligations under all Security Agreements and agreements (including without limitation the obligations under this Security Agreement, the Distribution Agreement and the Other Documents) to which it is signatory;

(ii) Unless permitted by the Distribution Agreement or otherwise with a prior written consent of the Mortgagee, not dispose of or lease out or create or permit any other Security that may affect the rights and interests of the Mortgagee on all or any part of the Collateral;

(iii) abide by and carry out all Laws related to the Collateral and present to the Mortgagee within three (3) days of receipt of any notice, directive or suggestion issued or promulgated by any relevant authority regarding the Collateral, and at the same time abide by such notice, directive or suggestion, or raise objections thereto or file appeal or petition therefor or express an opinion thereon in accordance with the Mortgagee's instructions or with the consent of the Mortgagee;

(iv) in the event a third party illegally encroaches upon or attempts to encroach upon any of the Collateral, take all measures necessary to prevent such illegal encroachment or to repossess from such third party such Collateral;

(v) timely pay all taxes and fees levied in connection with the Collateral by relevant departments of the government and the municipal administrative department;

(vi) notify the Mortgagee promptly of any event that may affect the Mortgagor's ownership of all or any portion of the Collateral or that may affect any guarantee, obligation or mortgage created under this Security Agreement.

b) *No Interruption of Rights.* The Mortgagor agrees that the Mortgagee's exercise of its rights in connection with the Security over the Collateral pursuant to the terms of this Security Agreement (including without limitation, the possession, use, or disposal of and the enjoyment of benefits from the Collateral) shall not be interrupted or obstructed by the Mortgagor or any successor or agent or receiver of the Mortgagor or any other person through legal or non-legal procedures. In the event of any such interruption or obstruction, the Mortgagor and any successor or agent or receiver of the Mortgagor shall take all measures necessary to thwart such interruption or obstruction.

c) *Mortgagor's Protection of Security Interest.* The Mortgagor warrants to the Mortgagee that, in order to protect or perfect the Security under this Security Agreement, the Mortgagor will honestly execute, and cause any other party with an interest in the Collateral to execute, all rights certificates, Security Agreements, and/or perform and cause such other interested party to perform actions required by the Mortgagee, and facilitate the exercise of rights and authorized actions by the Mortgagee under this Security Agreement, execute with the Mortgagee or parties designated by the Mortgagee all documents and registration related to assignment or any amendment to ownership certificates, and provide to the Mortgagee, within a reasonable period of time, all notices, orders and decisions in connection with the Collateral that the Mortgagee may deem necessary.

d) *Notification of Litigation.* In the event the Mortgagor and/or the Collateral are, or are likely to be, involved in any litigation, arbitration or administrative punishment, the Mortgagor will immediately notify the Mortgagee in writing and at all times deal with such litigation, arbitration or administrative punishment in accordance with written instructions from the Mortgagee (or in the absence of written instructions, in the most reasonable method or way with a view toward protecting the Collateral and their value).

e) *Performance of Representations; Indemnity.* The Mortgagor warrants to the Mortgagee that, in the interest of the Mortgagee, the Mortgagor will abide by and perform all warranties, undertakings, agreements, representations and conditions. In the event the Mortgagor fails to perform, or fails to perform completely, such warranties, undertakings, agreements, representations and conditions, it will indemnify the Mortgagee for all losses suffered as a result thereof.

9. *Events of Default.*

a) *Definition.* Any one of the following shall constitute an Event of Default under this Security Agreement:

(i) The Mortgagor fails to pay in full when due any amounts required by the Distribution Agreement;

(ii) Any representation or warranty made by the Mortgagor in Section 7 of this Security Agreement is untrue or contains falsehood or errors, and/or the Mortgagor is in breach of any warranty set forth in Section 7 of this Security Agreement;

(iii) The Mortgagor is in breach of any covenant set forth in Section 8 of this Security Agreement;

(iv) The Mortgagor fails to follow any instruction given by the Mortgagee pursuant to any provision of this Security Agreement, or the Mortgagee is unable to exercise any of its rights under this Security Agreement;

(v) The Mortgagor abandons the Collateral or, without the prior written consent of the Mortgagee, mortgages, pledges, permits liens on, donates, lends, entrusts, or otherwise disposes of the Collateral;

(vi) The Mortgagor fails to timely pay any taxes or fees (including without limitation any insurance premium, land use fees, and registration fees) related to the Collateral;

(vii) Any loan, guarantee, indemnity, undertaking or other repayment obligation of the Mortgagor in favor of any other party (i) is accelerated due to default or any other reason; or (ii) is due but cannot be repaid or performed by the Mortgagor, such that the Mortgagee believes that the Mortgagor's ability to perform its Obligations under the Distribution Agreement and this Security Agreement has been affected;

(viii) Any dissolution, liquidation, bankruptcy, or closure of the Mortgagor due to any merger, restructuring, acquisition, court judgment or ruling, award by arbitration tribunal or administrative order of government department, or any assignment of a receiver or trustee to handle all or part of the Mortgagor's assets, or all or any portion of the Mortgagor's assets have become subject to custodial control pursuant to any court judgment or ruling, award by arbitration tribunal or administrative order of government department;

(ix) The Mortgagor is unable to pay any other debts in excess of [US $__________] or its equivalent in other currencies;

(x) As a result of any new Law, this Security Agreement or one or more of its main provisions becomes unlawful or the

Mortgagor becomes unable to continue to perform any one or more of its Obligations under this Security Agreement;

(xi) Any consent, license, approval, registration or authorization from any government department that is necessary to make this Security Agreement enforceable, lawful or valid is withdrawn, suspended, invalidated or substantially revised;

(xii) Any material adverse change occurs with respect to the business prospect or all or any portion of the assets owned by the Mortgagor, such that the Mortgagee believes that the Mortgagor's ability to perform its Obligations under the Distribution Agreement and this Security Agreement has been affected;

(xiii) All or any portion of the Mortgagor's assets are, or are likely to be, confiscated, seized, forcefully acquired (whether with compensation or not) or damaged or destroyed, and for any reason such situation is not resolved within ten days, such that the Mortgagee believes that the Mortgagor's ability to perform its Obligations under the Distribution Agreement and this Security Agreement has been affected;

(xiv) The Mortgagor (or its investors) changes the Mortgagor's equity structure, asset structure, method and scope of production and operation without the prior written consent of the Mortgagee;

(xv) The successor, trustee or receiver of the Mortgagor refuses to perform any of its Obligations under the Distribution Agreement and this Security Agreement;

(xvi) Any of the mortgage registrations for the Collateral with the Registration Authorities or any other registration including those without limitation the foreign exchange registration set forth in Section 3(b) hereunder (including registration for any modifications) cannot be completed for any reason; or the Registration Authorities and any other government agency is unable to provide the Mortgagee with certification of any registration of the mortgage (including registration for any modifications) under this Security Agreement;

(xvii) The Mortgagor breaches any other provision of this Security Agreement due to its action or inaction;

(xviii) Any other situation which affects the Mortgagee's rights under the Law to exercise its rights in connection with the Security under this Security Agreement.

b) *Notification of Event of Default.* Upon becoming aware of, or discovering the occurrence of, any Event of Default listed in Section 9(a) or any event that may lead to an Event of Default, the Mortgagor shall immediately notify the Mortgagee both orally and in writing.

c) *Mortgagee's Demand of Repayment.* The Mortgagor agrees that, unless any Event of Default listed in Section 9(a) that has already occurred has been resolved to the satisfaction of the Mortgagee or the Mortgagee for any reason temporarily waives all or part of any of its rights under this Security Agreement, the Mortgagee may, at any time during or after the occurrence of any Event of Default under Section 9(a) of this Security Agreement, notify the Mortgagor in writing demanding immediate repayment of all of the principal, interest, fees and any other due amounts under the Distribution Agreement and/or issue a Notice of Default to the Mortgagor and dispose of the Collateral pursuant to Section 10 of this Security Agreement.

d) *No Waiver.* Within the Mortgage Duration, any inaction, grace or delay in exercising any of its rights and interests under this Security Agreement by the Mortgagee with respect to any Event of Default by the Mortgagor shall not damage, affect or limit any rights and interests of the Mortgagee under the Law or this Security Agreement, or any rights and interests of the Mortgagee under the Distribution Agreement. Any inaction, grace or delay in exercising any of the Mortgagee's rights and interests shall not be regarded as an explicit or implicit authorization by the Mortgagee for any Event of Default of the Mortgagor, nor shall it be regarded as evidence of the Mortgagee's position with respect to the Mortgagor in connection with the Event of Default under the Law or this Security Agreement.

10. *Disposition of Collateral; Notice of Default.*

a) *Mortgagee's Rights in Collateral.* The Mortgagee shall be entitled to exercise its rights in connection with the Collateral under this Security Agreement upon determination at its sole discretion that one or more Event of Default identified in Section 9(a) of this Security Agreement has occurred or is occurring. When exercising such rights the Mortgagee shall issue a Notice of Default to the Mortgagor and notify the Registration Authorities concurrently.

b) *Disposition of Collateral.* The Mortgagee shall be entitled to dispose of all or any part of the Collateral within the stipulations of the Law and this Security Agreement. The Mortgagor and the Mortgagee both agree that after issuance of a Notice of Default by the Mortgagee, unless the Mortgagor objects thereto in writing within five (5) days of the delivery of the Notice of Default, the Mortgagor and the Mortgagee shall be deemed to have agreed that the Mortgagee shall have discretion to dispose of such Collateral in any of the following ways:

(i) Commission any legally registered independent intermediary to sell all or any portion of the Collateral hereunder with reference to market prices in either a public or a private sale; and/or

(ii) Commission any legally registered independent auctioneer to conduct an auction of all or any portion of the Collateral hereunder in accordance with the Law; and/or

(iii) Commission any legally registered independent asset appraisal agency to evaluate part or all of the Collateral hereunder, and set off the Obligations of the Mortgagor in favor of the Mortgagee with all or a portion of such Mortgaged Equipment based on such valuation; and

(iv) Use any other lawful method to dispose of all or any portion of the Collateral hereunder, whereupon the Mortgagee may transfer to others all title and interest to Collateral free and clear of any rights of the Mortgagor.

c) *Agreement Regarding Disposition, Value and Payment; No Liability of Mortgagee.* The Mortgagee and the Mortgagor may, from time to time by agreement, (i) determine the manner of disposition of the Collateral, or (ii) determine the value of the Collateral; and the Collateral shall be taken as the payment of all or any part of the Obligations of the Mortgagor to the Mortgagee. The Mortgagee shall have no liability for exercising any of its rights hereunder, and shall have no obligation to protect against diminution in value of the Collateral or any liability for injury to such Collateral.

d) *Appointed Successor.* The Mortgagee may appoint any natural person, legal person, institution, organization or non-legal person entity as its appointed successor to exercise its right to dispose of the Collateral.

e) *Disputes Regarding Disposition.* If the Mortgagor and the Mortgagee fail to reach agreement on the disposition of the Collateral hereunder as stipulated in Section 10(b) hereunder or by any other method, the Mortgagee may at any time enforce Security in accordance with Section 14 under this Security Agreement.

f) *First Priority Mortgage.* The Mortgagee shall have first priority mortgage rights to receive all proceeds of any disposed Collateral until all Obligations have been paid in full.

g) *Cooperation of Mortgagor.* In the event that the Mortgagee exercises its rights to possess, use, or dispose of the Collateral hereunder, the Mortgagor (or its successor or agent) shall not raise any objections, defenses or create any obstacles and shall use its best efforts to assist the Mortgagee in exercising its rights in connection with the mortgage under this Agreement. In connection with the exercise of such rights, the Mortgagee may (i) require the Mortgagor to assemble the Collateral, (ii) enter onto the Mortgagor's premises and remove such Collateral, (iii) move and store such Collateral using the Mortgagor's equipment, and (iv) see and inspect the Mortgagor's books and records regarding such Collateral.

11. *Assignment.*

a) *No Assignment by Mortgagor.* Except with the prior written consent of the Mortgagee, the Mortgagor shall not assign its rights and obligations under this Security Agreement (including without limitation any assignment, gift, mortgage, pledge, lien or trust).

b) *Assignment by Mortgagee.* The Mortgagor hereby agrees that, without limiting the generality of Section 2(b)(iii), the Mortgagee may, at any time and without further consent from the Mortgagor, assign all or any of its rights and interests under this Security Agreement to any one or more natural persons, legal persons, agencies, organizations or nonlegal person entities. In such event, the assignee or re-assignee of the Mortgagee shall enjoy all rights and undertake all obligations of the Mortgagee under this Security Agreement. In the event that the Mortgagee so assigns its rights and obligations under this Security Agreement, the Mortgagor, at the request of Mortgagee, shall execute all necessary agreements and/or documents to effect such assignment.

c) *Registration of Change of Mortgagee.* Should an assignment result in a change of the Mortgagee, the Mortgagor shall (or at the request of the Mortgagee, shall entrust the Mortgagee or a third party designated by the Mortgagee to) complete the formalities of registration for such change within three (3) working days of receipt of notification of such change at the Registration Authorities and bear all expenses in connection therewith.

d) *Creditor's Rights.* Any assignment of the Security under this Security Agreement shall be concurrent with an assignment of the creditor's rights enjoyed by the Mortgagee under the Distribution Agreement. The security rights under this Security Agreement shall not be assigned to become security for any other creditor's rights.

e) *Binding on Successors.* Unless otherwise agreed, this Security Agreement shall be equally effective on the Mortgagor, the Mortgagee and each and every one of their successors and assignees.

12. *Termination.*

a) This valid duration of this Security Agreement shall end and this Security Agreement shall terminate six (6) months after all amounts in connection with the Obligations have been fully repaid and the Mortgagor has no outstanding Obligations under the Distribution Agreement. Within thirty (30) days after the termination of this Security Agreement, the Mortgagor shall arrange for cancellation of mortgage registration under this Security Agreement pursuant to the applicable laws and regulations. All fees and disbursements incurred by the Mortgagee in connection with the termination of this Security Agreement shall be borne or reimbursed by the Mortgagor.

b) The termination of this Security Agreement shall not affect the exercise of any rights under this Security Agreement by the Mortgagee or any designated successor of the Mortgagee.

13. *Fees and Taxes.*

a) All fees, taxes and actual expenses, including without limitation, attorney's fee, accountant's fee, valuation fee, production costs, advanced tax payments, stamp duties and any other fees and taxes related to this Security Agreement shall be borne by the Mortgagor. If the Mortgagee is required by Law to pay any taxes and fees on any income under this Security Agreement, the Mortgagor shall pay such taxes and fees on behalf of the Mortgagee or fully reimburse the Mortgagee for sums already paid.

b) If, as a result of the Mortgagor failing to pay any taxes and fees when due, as stipulated in this Security Agreement, or for any other reason, the Mortgagee is required to pay any such taxes or fees in connection with this Security Agreement, or is subject to any claims from any third party, the Mortgagor shall bear all expenses and fees resulting therefrom, including without limitation all taxes, penalties, processing fees, administrative fees, litigation costs, attorneys' fees and any insurance premiums related to the handling of the Collateral. In addition, the Mortgagor shall pay interest on such expenses and fees to the Mortgagee, at a reasonable rate determined at the sole discretion of the Mortgagee, calculated from the date the Mortgagee actually paid such expenses and fees to the date the Mortgagee actually receives reimbursement for such payments, along with payment of all interest accrued thereon.

c) The Mortgagor shall be responsible for paying all taxes and fees levied by relevant government departments on the Collateral. If the Mortgagor fails to pay such taxes and fees when due, thus causing the Mortgagee to pay such taxes and fees in order to protect its interests under this Security Agreement, the Mortgagee shall be entitled to seek reimbursement for such payments with interest from the Mortgagor in accordance with Section 13(b).

14. *Settlement of Disputes.*

a) The execution, interpretation, enforcement and settlement of disputes in connection with this Security Agreement shall be governed by the law of [______________].

b) In the event of a dispute, both parties to this Security Agreement shall attempt to resolve such dispute through friendly consultation. If the dispute cannot be resolved through such consultation, the Mortgagee shall have the right to choose mediation, arbitration, litigation or other settlement methods permitted by the law of [________________]. However, the option to choose arbitration for settling a dispute under this Security Agreement is subject to the Mortgagee and the Mortgagor reaching a separate agreement for arbitration. Prior to the resolution of any dispute, the Mortgagor shall unconditionally continue to perform its obligations under other provisions of this Security Agreement.

c) If a legal proceeding is taken to settle the disputes, the Mortgagee shall have the right to choose a forum at the defendant's place of abode, the place of performance of this Security Agreement, the place of execution of this Security Agreement, the plaintiff's place of abode, the location of the subject of dispute, or any other court with jurisdiction. If the Mortgagee brings the case to any of the abovementioned courts, the Mortgagor shall accept and not object to the choice of such court on jurisdictional grounds.

15. *Notice.* All notices (including without limitation Notice of Default) by either party to this Security Agreement for the exercise of rights and performance of obligations under this Security Agreement shall be made in writing, via registered airmail, express delivery (or courier), telegram, telex and fax. Any notice by registered airmail shall be deemed received on the fifth day after posting. Any notice by express

delivery (or courier) shall be deemed received on the date of the signed acknowledgment of receipt. Any notice by telegram, telex, or fax shall be deemed received on the date sent (proof of transmission shall be required as evidence). Any notice by telegram, telex or fax shall be confirmed immediately in letter form by registered airmail or express delivery (or courier). If the date of receipt is not a business day or delivery takes place after business hours, the immediately following business day shall be deemed the date of receipt. The delivery addresses, telex and fax numbers shall be the following (or such other addresses, telex and fax numbers that may be provided to the other party in writing from time to time):

Secured Party: ____________________
Address: ____________________
Legal Representative: ____________________
Position: ____________________
Telephone: ____________________
Telefacsimile: ____________________

Debtor: ____________________
Address: ____________________
Legal Representative: ____________________
Position: ____________________
Telephone: ____________________
Telefacsimile: ____________________

16. *Effectiveness of this Security Agreement.*

a) This Security Agreement shall take effect upon registration with the Registration Authorities after its execution by the Mortgagee and the Mortgagor.

b) Any amendment, supplement or alteration to this Security Agreement shall be in writing and shall only take effect after execution by authorized representatives of both parties and filing with the Registration Authorities.

17. *Miscellaneous.*

a) *Headings.* The headings for the sections of this Security Agreement are for the convenience of reference and cross reference and shall not affect the framework or interpretation of this Security Agreement.

b) *Entire Agreement.* This Security Agreement (including the attachments) constitutes the complete agreement by both parties over the subject of this Security Agreement and supersedes all previous agreements, project proposals, feasibility studies, understandings and negotiations (whether oral or written, or between the parties or by either party, or for submission to any relevant government department) related to the subject. Neither party has made or relied upon any representations, descriptions, expositions, undertakings, understandings, conditions, warranties that are not contained in this Security Agreement.

c) *Severability.* If any of the provisions in this Security Agreement is deemed invalid or unenforceable by any court or arbitration tribunal, the other articles of this Security Agreement shall remain valid and enforceable. In such event, the parties to this Security Agreement shall formulate new provisions to replace the invalid or unenforceable provisions in accordance with the spirit of this Security Agreement.

d) *Governing Language*. This Security Agreement shall be written in both Chinese and English and both versions shall have equal legal effect.

e) *Number of Originals.* This Security Agreement shall be signed in _____ originals and each of the Mortgagor, the Mortgagee and the mortgage registration authorities shall hold one original.

f) *Date and Place of Execution.* This Security Agreement is made and signed by authorized representatives of the parties on __________, 20__ in ____________.

SIGNED BY AND BETWEEN
[The Mortgagor]

By: ____________________
Name: ____________________
Title: ____________________

[The Mortgagee]

By: ____________________
Name: ____________________
Title: ____________________

CONTRACT FOR THE EMPLOYMENT OF CHINESE EMPLOYEES

____________ ("Party A") and ____________ ("Party B") have concluded this Contract with respect to the employment of Chinese Employees, with terms and conditions as follows:

1. *Obligations of Party B.* Party B shall have the following obligations:

a) *Recommendation of Employees.* Party B shall recommend Chinese Employees for employment by Party A (the "Employees") according to the requirements of Party A. The exact number of Employees and the Service Fees to be paid to each (the "Service Fees") are set forth in the Appendix (1) of this Contract.

b) *No Violation of Laws.* Party B shall be responsible for ensuring that all Employees abide by the laws, regulations, and decrees of the People's Republic of China and they observe the office rules and regulations of Party A and keep Party A's business confidential.

c) *Services to Be Provided.* Party B shall provide supplementary services to the Employee and use the Service Fees to be paid by Party A to Party B as payment of wages to Employees and expenses for personnel management, social insurance and other services to the Employees. These other services will include services relating to (1) legal proceedings, (2) preservation of organizational affiliations, (3) administrative duties (including maintaining personnel files), (4) evaluations of Employees and assignment of professional titles according to relevant regulations, (5) negotiation of contracts with former employers whose Employee has been appointed by Party A to fill a vacancy, (5) formalities pertaining to passport applications and exit permits for the Employees when Party A so requires for business purposes, and (6) obtaining information and consulting services.

d) *Insurance.* Party B shall pay a premium of no less than _______ RMB personal accident insurance plus no less than ___________ RMB additional medical insurance for Employees to the People's Insurance Company of China or China Social Insurance Mutual-Aid Society. In case an Employee who has been insured is injured, disabled or killed while on duty, Party B must pay compensation according to the relevant regulations as set forth by the People's Insurance Company of China; at the same time, Party A shall pay the full Service Fee to the Employee for the entire period of medical treatment. Party B shall buy from the China Social Insurance Mutual-Aid Society or the People's Insurance Company of China medical treatment and hospitalization insurance policies of no more than __________ RMB for each Employee. (Details are set forth in Appendix (2) of this Contract.)

e) *Diligent Work Efforts.* Party B shall encourage Employees to work diligently for Party A and award those who have demonstrated outstanding performance and who have worked with Party A for a full five years.

f) *Disciplinary Procedures.* Party B shall be responsible for the discipline of those Employees who do not perform their duties satisfactorily for Party A.

g) *Personal Support.* Party B shall assist Employees with social and personal difficulties.

h) *Opportunities and Subsidies for Terminated Employees.* For any Employee whose employment has been terminated, through no fault of his or her own, and who is still qualified for recommendation pursuant to Party B's policy, Party B shall offer new employment opportunities and certain unemployment subsidies for a period of time.

i) *Cooperation with Party A.* Party B shall take the initiative to listen to the opinions and proposals of Party A, in order to achieve high quality and efficient services.

2. *Withdrawal of Employee by Party A.* Under ____________ circumstances, if the two parties fail to reach an agreement, Party B shall retain the right to withdraw an Employee from his or her employment with Party A with a thirty-day advance notice to Party A and the Employee. Party B's right to withdraw an Employee shall apply only to those Employees that were actually recommended and/or recruited by Party B. The compensation to Party A due to the withdrawal shall be calculated as set forth in Section 3(c) of this Contract. If the service of the Employee is terminated because he or she violates the laws, regulations or decrees of the People's Republic of China, neither Party A nor Party B shall pay or receive compensation. If the above-mentioned violations cause losses to Party A, Party A may seek recovery through legal proceedings, and Party B has the duty to assist the judicial department.

3. *Obligations of Party A.* Party A shall have the following obligations:

a) *Respect Chinese Customs.* Party A shall respect Chinese morals, customs and lifestyles and provide Employees with suitable working conditions and labor protection for carrying out their tasks.

b) *Limitation of Termination; Pregnant and Ill Employees.* Party A shall not terminate the employment of female Employees who are pregnant or on maternity leave for a period not to exceed three (3) months, or of Employees who are injured on duty or who are ill, during the period of medical treatment in a hospital not to exceed thirty (30) days.

c) *Service [and Management] Fees.* Party A shall pay the Employee's monthly Service Fee [and the Employment Management Fee] as set forth in Appendix (3).

d) *Limitation on Hours; Missed Meal Allowance.* Employees shall work for no more than eight hours a day and no more than 40 hours a week. If the Employees are asked to work extra hours, or to work on days off or legal holidays, their salaries for such will be calculated in accordance with Sections 41 and 44 of "The Labor Law of The People's Republic of China." Whenever a customary meal is missed because of work, Party A shall pay the Employees a missed meal allowance. If overtime work extends after 9:30 p.m., Party A shall pay Employees a night meal allowance. The amount of a missed meal allowance or night meal allowance shall be decided by Party A.

e) *Lunch Subsidy.* Party A shall pay Employees a certain amount of lunch subsidy, which shall be decided by Party A.

f) *Vacation.* Party A shall allow their Employees an annual vacation of fifteen (15) consecutive days (or fifteen (15) accumulated working days) with full pay. For those who have been employed by Party A for five years or more, Party A shall add more vacation days according to Party A's actual business conditions. Employees who have been employed by Party A less than one year are entitled to one day of vacation for each month of service. Party A shall pay certain subsidies for Employees whose vacation is terminated by Party A because of work. The subsidy shall be the same as the salary that would be paid to Employees who have been asked to work by Party A on holidays.

g) *Extra Month's Service Fee.* Party A shall pay, at the end of each calendar year, an extra month's Service Fee to any Employee who has been engaged for half a year or more. For those who have been engaged for less than half a year, the annual extra pay should be 1/12 of his or her monthly Service Fee times the number of months he or she has worked for Party A.

h) *Limitation on Monthly Service Fee.* Party A shall continue to pay the monthly Service Fee for Employees whose accumulated sick leave does not exceed thirty days (30) and/or maternity leave does not exceed ninety days (90) in one calendar year.

i) *Business Expenses within China.* Party A shall pay, besides board, lodging and travel expenses, a sum of not less than ____ RMB as pocket money per person, per day, to Employees who are on business trips within China but outside Beijing.

j) *Business Expenses outside of China.* Party A shall pay, besides board, lodging and travel expenses, a sum of not less than ________ US dollars (US $________) subsidy per person, per day, to Employees who go on trips outside China, and shall assume responsibility for the Employees' security while they are outside China.

k) *Automobile Insurance.* Party A shall insure its vehicles, driven by its Chinese Employees, against damage to the vehicles and for liability to its passengers and third parties. If Party A has not covered the above-mentioned insurance, in the event of traffic accidents which fall within the scope of employment for which the Employee is responsible, Party A should bear responsibility for the damages arising therefrom.

3. *Rights of Party A.* Party A shall enjoy the following rights:

a) *Probation Period.* Party A may impose a maximum period of three months' probation on the Employees. During the period of probation, Party A has the right to terminate the probation of the Employee if it finds that the candidate is not suitable for the job. On completion of the probation period, the probationer will be accepted as a regular Employee; the period of his or her employment shall be calculated from the first day of the probation period.

b) *Choosing Employees.* Party A may choose its own Employees with the approval of Party B, who will handle the formalities related to the lawful employment. The probation period and relevant severance pay for the Employee hired under this provision are the same as for Employees recommended by Party B.

c) *Termination of Employee; Severance.* Party A shall have the right to dismiss an Employee upon consultation with Party B upon a thirty-days' notice in writing to Party B. The notice shall state the cause of the dismissal.

For an Employee who has been employed by Party A for more than half a year, but less than one and a half years, the severance pay shall be one month's Service Fee.

For an Employee who has been employed by Party A for more than one and a half years, but less than two and a half years, the severance pay shall be two months' Service Fee.

For each additional year of employment thereafter, an additional one month's Service Fee shall be paid. The maximum severance pay, however, shall not exceed six months' Service Fee. When an Employee is dismissed due to serious violations of Chinese laws and regulations or Party A's regulations (which regulations shall be made available to Party B),

Party A may be relieved of payment of severance fees, as per an agreement with Party B after consultation.

d) *Resignation of Employee.* If the Employee intends to resign, he or she will have to submit the resignation to Party A thirty days in advance. If any other agreements are in existence, both parties shall abide by such agreements. Upon receiving the resignation notice from the Employee, Party A should notify Party B in written form ten days in advance of the resignation, otherwise the Service Fee will continue to be charged until the date on which Party B receives the notification from Party A.

e) *Separate Agreement.* Party A may enter into separate agreements with the Employees. Such agreements may not violate the laws, regulations and rules of the People's Republic of China and the provisions of this Contract.

5. *Settlement of Payment.*

a) The Service Fee mentioned in this Contract shall be fixed as set forth in Appendix (1) of this Contract and shall be paid as set forth in Appendix (3) of this Contract.

b) An Employee's Service Fee shall be decided through consultations between Party A and Party B in the form set forth in Appendix (3). On completion of each service year, Party A shall increase the Service Fee for its Employees. The amount of increase shall be decided through consultations between the two parties.

c) Party A shall pay the Employees' monthly Service Fee at the end of each month. If the severance pay and/or annual Extra Month's Service Fee is applicable, Party A will pay them to Party B at the first of that month. If the payment is not made until the period of the 15th to 20th, 21st to 30th, 1st of the next month and thereafter into the next month, a surcharge of 1%, 3%, and 5% for arrearage shall be levied respectively.

d) All accounts made by Party A to Party B shall be calculated in RMB.

6. *Dispute Resolution.* Any dispute arising between Party A and Party B shall be settled through consultations. Should such consultations fail, the case shall be submitted to the China International Economic & Trade Arbitration Commission (CIETAC) in Beijing for arbitration with the expenses to be borne by the losing party. This contract shall be interpreted under Chinese law

7. *Miscellaneous.*

a) *Appendix.* For matters not covered in this Contract, the two parties shall negotiate and work out an appendix to be included into this Contract. The appendix shall be equally binding.

b) *Modification.* If this contract must be amended or modified during the course of its performance as a result of new laws, regulations and rules enacted by the Chinese government, Party A and Party B shall negotiate to amend or modify this contract based on the new laws, regulations and rules.

c) *Term.* This Contract shall be valid for a period of one year from ________________, and its validity shall be automatically extended for another one year if no objection is raised by either party one month prior to its expiration.

d) *Governing Language.* This contract has been prepared in both Chinese and English in duplicate. Each party holds a copy and it is agreed by both parties that the Chinese version and the English version shall be equally binding.

IN WITNESS WHEREOF, this Contract has been executed by each of the parties effective as of the day and year written below.

SIGNATURES:

For Party A:	For Party B:
By: ______________________	By: ______________________
Name: ______________________	Name: ______________________
Title: ______________________	Title: ______________________
Date:	Date:

APPENDIX (1) TO THE CONTRACT FOR THE EMPLOYMENT OF CHINESE EMPLOYEES REGARDING EMPLOYMENT SERVICE FEES

__________________ ("Party A") and __________________ ("Party B") have concluded "The Contract for the Employment of Chinese Employees" (hereinafter referred to as the Contract). The collection and payment of the employment Service Fees as agreed to in the Contract shall be made in the following manner:

1. Party B shall issue a collection certificate pursuant to the Contract through its working bank by the 1st of each month. Party A shall make the payment accordingly.

2. The payments for the employment of the Chinese Employees are as follows:

Number	Name	Title	Employment Service Fee	Employment Management Fee	Remarks

The contract period for the above named Employee(s) is one year. From ____________, Party A agrees to pay the agreed amount to Party B's nominated account.

Name of Party B: ____________________

RMB Bank:

Bank Name
Branch
Account No

Foreign Exchange Bank:

Bank Name
Account No

SIGNATURES:

For Party A:		For Party B:	
By:	______________________	By:	______________________
Name:	______________________	Name:	______________________
Title:	______________________	Title:	______________________
Date:		Date:	

APPENDIX (2) TO THE CONTRACT FOR THE EMPLOYMENT OF CHINESE EMPLOYEES REGARDING MEDICAL EXPENSES

______________ ("Party A") and ______________ ("Party B") have concluded this agreement with respect to Party B bearing the medical expenses of Chinese Employees, as Appendix (3) of the CONTRACT FOR THE EMPLOYMENT OF CHINESE EMPLOYEES; the terms and conditions are as follows:

1. *Payment of Medical Expenses.* Party B shall pay a premium for the medical treatment and hospitalization insurance of the Employees to China Social Insurance Mutual-Aid Society or the People's Insurance Company of China, as follows:

a) For Employees between the age of [18-60] years, if they are proven to be healthy through examination by the appointed hospital, Party B will pay [80%–95%] of medical expenses and hospitalization for the Employee, not to exceed [20,000] RMB per year, provided that they maintain such healthy status during a 30-day observation period immediately following the examination. (Those who renew their employment agreement one month prior to its expiration will not be subject to the 30 day observation period.) In addition, Party B shall implement a system for the medical and hospitalization expenses, that is, Party B shall provide full payment of the qualified amount of submitted medical and/or hospitalization expenses totaling less than [300] RMB per year, at the end of each calendar year.

Party B shall pay for [80%–95%] of the medical and/or hospitalization expenses according to the following system:

[300-5,000 RMB	pay 80%
5,001-10,000 RMB	pay 90%
10,001-20,000 RMB	pay 95%]

b) Party B shall reimburse for hospital expenses according to the above system, when Employees seek medical advice at the appointed hospital; Party B shall reimburse the following:

(i) expenses for medicine (the public health service has stipulated certain medicines which are at one's own expense and which will not be included here).

(ii) expenses for treatment: expenses for oxygen therapy, blood transfusions, surgery, and/or any related handling charges.

(iii) expenses for a hospital bed: maximum 10 RMB per day, maximum 60 days per hospital stay.

(iv) expenses for examination: clinic exams are limited to [300] RMB (each time), hospitalization is limited to [1000] RMB (each time).

c) Party B will not have a duty to pay for the following expenses by Employees:

(i) Routine health examinations, convalescent care, recovery treatment and parturition.

(ii) Purchase of transplant organs; installation of artificial limbs, ocular prostheses, dental prostheses; purchase of wheelchairs and makers.

(iii) Cosmetology and orthopedic expenses.

(iv) Consultations with doctors at any non-appointed hospitals.

(v) Accidents and accidents for which third parties are liable.

(vi) Expenses that occur as a result of war and/or military movement.

(vii) Expenses as a result of pre-existing physiological deficiencies and/or congenital diseases.

(viii) Expenses which are related to an Employee's medical case history which was intentionally withheld or not disclosed by the Employee.

d) If an Employee has any of the following diseases before the Contract is signed, Party B shall not be responsible for any related medical and hospitalization expenses:

[Malignant tumor, aplastic anemia, infectious diseases, psychosis, epilepsy, cerebral blood vessel disease, myocardial infarction, high blood pressure (higher than phase 2), heart disease (heart functioning at a level higher than phase 2), bronchitis, chronic blocked pulmonary emphysema, tuberculosis, liver sclerosis, chronic nephritis, kidney tuberculosis, complex kidney disease, diabetes, lupus erythematosus, congenital disease.]

e) Employees shall submit medical and hospitalization expenses to Party B on a quarterly basis starting from the date this Appendix is signed, and shall submit all expenses for a given year within fifteen days after the end of that year. Otherwise, Party B shall treat any unsubmitted expenses as an automatic waiver by the Employee of Party B's responsibility for such expenses. An expense claim shall be accompanied by the following documents:

(i) original evidence of medical treatment charges and hospitalization expenses (including receipts and prescriptions), and diagnoses and medical treatment records.

(ii) receipts which Party B thinks are necessary.

f) When an Employee's accumulated medical treatment and hospitalization expenses exceed [1000] RMB and [5000] RMB, he or she should notify Party B within 10 days.

g) If an Employee experiences serious illness during the Contract's period of validity and he or she does not recover prior to its expiration, Party B will renew the Contract.

h) Party B's appointed hospitals are:

(i) ____________________________

(ii) ____________________________

i) Under special circumstances, where Party A and Party B reach an express agreement by which Party B shall withdraw an Employee, Party B will continue to be responsible for the Employee's medical expenses as set forth in this Appendix.

Where Party B withdraws an Employee during the period of this contract, Party B shall reimburse [70%–90%] of the Employee's outstanding medical expenses, not to exceed [20,000] RMB. The payment standards are as follows:

[300–5000 RMB	pay for 70%
5,001–10,000 RMB	pay for 80%
10,000–20,000 RMB	pay for 90%]

If an Employee quits work because of violations of the laws, regulations and/or decrees of the People's Republic of China, Party B will not pay for any of his or her medical expenses from the date the Employee quits work.

j) Where an Employee obtains the payment of medical or hospitalization expenses through means of deception or intentional concealment of information, once discovered, Party B shall impose a penalty on the Employee of [5] times the medical and/or hospitalization expenses, in addition to any recovery of paid expenses. Party B reserves the right to recover all economic losses, from Employees or their beneficiaries, as a result of investigation and verification of such fraud or deception. If necessary, Party B will report any serious violations or acts of fraud or deception to the court for enforcement of the law.

k) ____________________ shall be responsible for the above medical expenses. ____________________ shall receive from Party B accident insurance for the sum of not less than RMB [40,000], additional medical insurance in the sum of RMB [10,000], and household property insurance in the sum of not less than RMB [20,000].

2. *Term.* This appendix shall be valid for a period of one year from ____________________ and its validity shall be automatically extended for another one year if no objection is raised by either Party one month prior to its expiration.

SIGNATURES:

For Party A:	For Party B:
By: ____________________	By: ____________________
Name: ____________________	Name: ____________________
Title: ____________________	Title: ____________________
Date:	Date:

APPENDIX (3) TO THE CONTRACT FOR THE EMPLOYMENT OF CHINESE EMPLOYEES REGARDING THE EMPLOYMENT SERVICE FEE PAID

1. *Payments in Connection With Employee A.* After amicable discussions between Party A and Party B, both parties reach the following agreement for the salary of Employee A:

a) *Employment Fees.* [Party A shall pay a Employment Management Fee to Party B in the monthly sum of RMB ________. The entire monthly Employment Management Fee is to be paid by Party A to Party B before the end of each month. Party B should issue a receipt against such payment. Party A shall pay the balance of Employee's compensation to Employee A (RMB ________).] or [The salary of the Employee should be calculated as follows, and paid directly from Party B to the Employee: Employee's salary = monthly employment Service Fee multiplied by [x]%. The entire monthly Service Fee is to be paid by Party A to Party B before the end of each month. Party B should issue a receipt against such payment. Party B shall pay the Employee's salary.]

b) *Rights and Obligations.* Both parties will still have all rights and obligations stipulated in THE CONTRACT FOR THE EMPLOYMENT OF CHINESE EMPLOYEES.

c) *Other Charges.* The following charges are to be paid by Party A according to item (1) above:

(i) [the increase in the monthly Employment Management for each additional year] or [the increase in the monthly employment Service Fee for each additional year and the extra month's Service Fee to be paid at the end of each year.]

(ii) severance fee, if applicable.

d) Lunch subsidy, missed meal allowance, night meal allowance, traveling compensation and overtime payments are to be paid to the Employee directly by Party A.

e) Party A shall encourage the Employee to pay tax for all the income the Employee receives directly from Party A. However, payment of any and all individual income tax applicable to the Employee shall be his sole responsibility.

2. *Term.* This Appendix shall be valid for a period of one year from ________________, and its validity shall be automatically extended for another one year if no objection is raised by either Party one month prior to its expiration.

SIGNATURES:

For Party A:

By: ______________________________
Name: ______________________________
Title: ______________________________

Date:

For Party B:

By: ______________________________
Name: ______________________________
Title: ______________________________

Date:

TECHNOLOGY LICENSE AGREEMENT

THIS AGREEMENT is made by and between ______________________ ("Licensor"), __________________ (the "Company"), __________________ ("Licensee") and __________________ (the "Sales Company").

WITNESSETH

WHEREAS, Licensor owns certain technology know-how, non-patented technology, trade secrets, designs, technical documentation, applications literature, sales information, customer lists and sales leads, and other technology with respect to the design, fabrication, finishing, and sale of ____________ products (hereinafter referred to as "Licensed Technology");

WHEREAS, Licensor is prepared to grant to Licensee an exclusive license to use, manufacture, market, and exploit any and all rights which Licensor owns in the Licensed Technology;

WHEREAS, Licensee desires to license and obtain such rights from Licensor;

NOW, THEREFORE, in consideration of the mutual covenants and promises set forth herein, the parties agree as follows:

1. *License.* Licensor hereby grants an exclusive fifteen (15) year license to Licensee to use, manufacture, market, and exploit the Licensed Technology subject to the Limitations on Territory and Minimum Quota provisions of this Agreement.

2. *Limitations on Territory.*

   a) This exclusive license is limited to the following territories, countries, or regions: ______________________ (hereinafter referred to as the "Authorized Territory").

   b) Licensee agrees and acknowledges that it shall not manufacture, market, or sell, either directly or indirectly, any product using the Licensed Technology to any other territory, country, or region except for the Authorized Territory expressly described in subsection 2(a).

   c) Licensee acknowledges and agrees that Licensor, or any other party designated by Licensor, has the option to become the exclusive distributor of Licensee's products which use the Licensed Technology for the territory of [the United States of America, Canada, and Latin America]. Said option may be exercised at any time during the term of this Agreement.

3. *Exclusivity.* This Agreement is an "exclusive license" which means that Licensor and the Company shall not grant the rights granted herein to any other individual or entity with respect to the Authorized Territory, and

that Licensor and the Company shall be excluded from using, marketing, selling, or exploiting such rights in the Authorized Territory. This Agreement applies to Licensor and the Company, and their employees, agents, principals, related organizations, and/or subsidiaries.

4. *Interim Sales Period/the Company Production.*

a) Notwithstanding the restrictions set forth in 3(a) and 3(b) above, the parties agree and acknowledge that customer inquiries and sales within the Authorized Territory may be made directly to the Company prior to the establishment of satisfactory production by Licensee (hereinafter referred to as "Interim Sales Period").

b) During the Interim Sales Period, the Company shall not be under any obligation to fill any orders for customers located within the Authorized Territory except if in the Company's sole discretion it determines that such orders can be met with the Company's current production capacity and in an economically feasible manner. All customer inquiries during the Interim Sales Period shall be referred directly to the Company. Licensee, in its discretion, has the right to declare an end to the Interim Sales Period and to advise the parties that it is prepared to accept orders for production from the Sales Company.

c) Licensee and the Sales Company shall not, during the Interim Sales Period or at any time during the term of this Agreement, provide any quote, bid, or sales confirmation on behalf of, or in the name of, the Company or Licensor.

d) Licensee and the Sales Company shall not be entitled to any commission, royalty, or other compensation for sales made by the Company during the Interim Sales Period.

5. *Licensed Technology.*

a) The Licensed Technology constitutes the latest technology and proprietary information in the ________________, and employs techniques and methods which are innovative and unique to the industry.

b) The Licensed Technology shall include the following technology:

(i) Design and production technology including ___________.

(ii) Catalogs and sales materials. A true and correct copy of Licensor's product catalogs and sales materials is attached to this Agreement as Addendum 1.

(iii) List of customers and sales leads in the Authorized Territory, and pricing information specific as to the type of product, customer, and location.

c) If Licensor develops any future improvements to the Licensed Technology, Licensor shall give Licensee the opportunity to purchase any and all future improvements and technology advancements as it may relate to the Licensed Technology during the term of this Agreement that have been developed by Licensor or the Company. The purchase price of said improvements and advancements shall be based upon the development costs incurred by Licensor or the Company.

d) Notwithstanding subsection 5(c), in the event that the sales of the Sales Company exceed the quota amounts set forth in Section 13, Licensor shall provide Licensee with the know-how and information to implement the improvements and advancements to the License Technology free of charge. Licensor, in its discretion, has the right to stop providing Licensee with the improvements and advancements if the Sales Company fails to continue to meet its quota obligations under Section 13. Licensee acknowledges that the improvements and advancements provided free of charge under this subsection only include techniques, information, methods, and know-how. If an improvement or advancement requires the purchase of additional Processing Equipment, Licensee shall be responsible for purchasing said equipment or machinery. Licensor will assist Licensee with the purchase of any additional Processing Equipment.

e) The Licensed Technology excludes all proprietary information and technology as it relates to aluminum finishes. Licensee acknowledges and agrees that it shall not, at any time, manufacture, market, or sell, directly or indirectly, any ________________. A violation of this covenant is grounds for immediate termination of this Agreement and return of all Licensed Technology.

6. *Procurement of Processing Equipment.*

a) Licensor shall assist Licensee in the procurement of processing equipment and machinery to enable Licensee to exploit the Licensed Technology (hereinafter referred to as "Processing Equipment"). Specifically, Licensor shall facilitate the selection, purchase, shipment and delivery, installation, and testing of the Processing Equipment on behalf of Licensee.

b) Licensor has advised Licensee that the Processing Equipment may be purchased for a budgeted amount in the approximate sum of US $________. Licensee acknowledges and agrees that the US $________ budget for the purchase of the Processing Equipment is wholly separate from, and not included in, the License Fee or Royalties as described in Sections 10 and 11 of this Agreement. Attached hereto as Addendum 2 is a Project Budget and Payment Schedule which outlines the License Fee and funds required to purchase the Processing Equipment. Licensor shall commence the procurement of the Processing Equipment within thirty (30) days of receipt of the initial License Fee as required under Section 10 of this Agreement. At the direction of Licensor, Licensee shall secure the necessary letters of credit or other financial instruments required by the original equipment manufacturer(s) of the Processing Equipment.

c) Licensee recognizes that any and all warranties or guarantees concerning the Processing Equipment shall be provided by the original manufacturer and not Licensor or the Company, or their employees, officers, agents, subsidiaries, or related organizations. All servicing and maintenance of the Processing Equipment shall be the responsibility of the original manufacturer of the Processing Equipment. Licensor and the Company shall not be responsible for service and maintenance of the Processing Equipment at any time. The original equipment manufacturer, and not Licensor or the Company, shall provide all information and documentation necessary to maintain the Processing Equipment.

d) A list of all Processing Equipment to be purchased pursuant to this Agreement shall be supplied with the Licensed Technology upon receipt of the initial License Fee.

7. *Training and Processing Equipment Set-Up.*

a) Licensor shall provide training at the facilities of the Company in ___________, for four (4) qualified employees of Licensee. The Training Period may commence at any time upon receipt of the initial License Fee set forth in Section 10. The training for all four Licensee employees shall be held concurrently, and shall be for a period of not less than three (3) months and until the employees master the techniques and methods of the Licensed Technology but no longer than a maximum period of one (1) year. The cost of training Licensee's employees, including the cost of materials, books, manuals, and instructor time, is included in the License Fee.

b) Licensee shall be responsible for all personal expenses of its employees to attend the training at the Company including, but not limited to, travel, lodging, food, transportation, security, wages, medical care and other benefits, and any other expense incurred by Licensee's employees during the training period. Licensee shall also be responsible for obtaining the necessary immigration approval for its employees to attend the training at the Company, and shall comply with all U.S. labor laws and other regulations concerning the presence of the employees in the United States. Licensor shall assist Licensee in obtaining the necessary immigration approval for the employees and shall assist Licensee with respect to obtaining the necessary government approval under U.S. labor regulations.

c) All Licensee employees that participate in the training at the Company shall be required to sign a confidentiality agreement in order to protect all parties to this Agreement. Licensee acknowledges and agrees that it is in its best interest to allow only trusted and loyal employees to attend the training at the Company.

d) Licensor will provide additional training at the time the Processing Equipment is set-up at Licensee's factory in ________________. The training to be provided at Licensee's factory shall be limited to a thirty (30) day period of time during the initial installation of the Processing Equipment.

8. *Technical Assistance.*

a) Licensor shall provide Licensee with technical assistance and support during the initial installation of the Processing Equipment and for a period of six (6) months after production begins. The technical assistance provided by Licensor under this Agreement shall include assistance, advice, counseling, and information with respect to the Licensed Technology (hereinafter "Licensor Technical Assistance"). The Licensor Technical Assistance provided under this Section, in Licensor's option, may be limited to telephonic communications, facsimile communications, or electronic mail communications. If Licensee desires that Licensor provide Licensor Technical Assistance after the six (6) month period described herein, Licensee shall reimburse Licensor for any and all expenses and costs including all labor costs, materials, and travel expenses.

b) The original equipment manufacturer that supplies the Processing Equipment shall provide Licensee with the technical assistance and support concerning the operation and maintenance of the Processing Equipment (hereinafter "OEM Technical Assistance"). Licensor, in its efforts to assist Licensee in procuring the Processing Equipment as required under Section 6 of this Agreement, shall require that the original equipment manufacturer contractually agree to fully provide Licensee with accessible and reliable OEM Technical Assistance. Based upon Licensor's prior experience with the equipment suppliers, Licensor assures Licensee that the original equipment manufacturers will provide prompt and competent technical assistance and support to meet the needs of Licensee.

9. *Sales and Marketing.*

a) Licensor and the Company shall provide Licensee with the names, addresses, and telephone numbers of all customers, contacts, and sales leads located in the Authorized Territory.

b) Licensee shall be responsible for marketing, sales, and distribution of all products using the Licensed Technology in [the People's Republic of China, Macau, and Hong Kong.]

c) For all Authorized Territory not listed in subsection 9(b), the parties to this Agreement shall operate a sales organization to be located in ___________. The sales organization shall be entitled ____________ (hereinafter referred to as the Sales Company), and shall be wholly owned by Licensee. The President of Sales Company shall be ____________, and the Vice President of sales of Sales Company shall be ______________. The Vice President's term of employment by Sales Company shall be ______________. The Vice President's duties shall include, but not be limited to, organizing and establishing a marketing network for Sales Company in the Authorized Territory and assisting Sales Company in meeting its minimum sales quota under Section 13 of this Agreement.

d) Licensee agrees that all sales in the Authorized Territory, except for the [People's Republic of China, Macau, or Hong Kong,] shall be made by and through the Sales Company. Licensee expressly agrees that it shall not make any direct sales to any party located outside of the [People's Republic of China, Macau, and Hong Kong]. If Licensee makes any sales outside of the [People's Republic of China, Macau, and Hong Kong] independently of the Sales Company, Licensee shall pay a royalty to Licensor pursuant to Section 11 as if the sale was made directly by the Sales Company.

e) The Sales Company shall be established and operating within one (1) year from the date of execution of this Agreement. After the Sales Company is established, it shall operate continuously throughout the term of this Agreement.

f) Licensee and Sales Company shall not at any time or for any reason use the trademarks, service marks, and trade names of Licensor or the Company, including the language and letters "___________."

10. *License Fee.*

a) In consideration of the exclusive license hereunder and services provided by Licensor, Licensee shall pay to Licensor a License Fee in the sum of US$________, payable as follows:

(i) A single payment of US$________ directly to Licensor at the time of executing this Agreement.

(ii) The sum of US$________ payable in four equal installments of US$________ to be paid to Licensor every six (6) months commencing six (6) months after the installation of the Processing Equipment or no later than twelve (12) months after the execution of this Agreement. All installments under this subsection shall be paid in full within three (3) years after execution of this Agreement. Attached hereto as Addendum 2 is a Project Budget and Payment Schedule which outlines a payment schedule for the License Fee.

(iii) The installment payments set forth herein shall be secured and guaranteed by an irrevocable and confirmed commercial letter of credit issued by a financial institution approved by Licensor (hereinafter referred to as "Letters of Credit"). The Letters of Credit are an integral part of this Agreement and are attached hereto, and incorporated herein, as Addendum 3.

b) Licensee shall pay a Commission to the Vice President of the Sales Company on the terms and conditions set forth in the Commission Agreement attached hereto as Addendum 4. Attached hereto as Addendum 2 is a Project Budget and Payment Schedule which outlines a payment schedule for the Commission.

c) Licensee shall be responsible and pay for any and all taxes which Licensee is required to pay under the laws of the People's Republic of China that may apply to the License Fee or Commission described in this Section including all income taxes, transaction tax, stamp tax, or other similar taxes or fees imposed by the government of the People's Republic of China.

11. *Royalties.*

a) In consideration of the exclusive license hereunder, Sales Company shall pay to Licensor the following royalties during the term of this Agreement for all sales in the Authorized Territory:

(i) __________ percent (____%) for annual net sales of less than US$_____________; _____________ (____%) for all annual net sales ranging from US$___________ to US$___________; ___________ percent (____%) for all annual net sales over US$_____________.

(ii) The term "net sales" as used in this Agreement is defined as the monies actually received from the customer and does not include the cost of shipping, insurance, or taxes.

b) The royalty payments herein shall be paid within thirty (30) days from the end of each calendar quarter after the establishment of the Sales Company. Such royalty payments shall be made by wire transfer remittance to the bank account designated by Licensor in U.S. dollars. The royalties shall be calculated on a quarterly basis at an average rate of ____________ percent (____%) of the net sales. The total royalty due under subsection 11(a)(i) shall be adjusted at the end of the fiscal year to reflect the actual annual net sales made by the Sales Company.

c) No royalty shall be due Licensor for any sales made by Licensee in [People's Republic of China, Macau, or Hong Kong,]. However, if Licensee makes any sales outside of [People's Republic of China, Macau, or Hong Kong,] independently of the Sales Company, Licensee shall pay a royalty to Licensor pursuant to subsection 11(a) as if the sale was made directly by the Sales Company.

d) Licensee shall guarantee the payment of all royalties to be paid to Licensor by the Sales Company. If for any reason the Sales Company dissolves, discontinues its operations, or is unable to conduct its business, Licensee shall guarantee the payment of all royalties to be paid Licensor by Sales Company. In the event that Sales Company ceases to do business as a result of an unforeseeable cause such as a natural disaster, Licensee shall not be responsible for the payment of royalties to Licensor; however, Licensee shall pay a royalty to Licensor pursuant to subsection 11(a) for all monies received by Licensee on items produced by Licensee and ordered by customers through the Sales Company prior to unforeseeable event.

e) On a quarterly basis, Sales Company shall furnish Licensor with complete and accurate statements, including copies of all purchase orders and invoices of the products sold by Sales Company showing the relevant calculations and amount due to Licensor as royalty payments; such statements shall be certified as accurate by a Sales Company executive officer, and provided to Licensor.

12. *Audit.*

a) Licensor, or any party it may delegate, shall have the right, upon reasonable notice, to audit at its cost all records of Sales Company for the previous twelve (12) months relevant to the sales which are the subject of this Agreement, in order to ascertain the sales of Sales Company and the royalty thereon. Licensor, or any party it may delegate, shall have the right, upon reasonable notice, to obtain copies of all shipping records concerning sales made by Sales Company of products produced with the Licensed Technology.

b) Should any material deficiency of royalty payment be revealed as a result of such audit, Sales Company and/or Licensee shall immediately pay all reasonable costs of such audit and all the deficient royalty together with interest thereon at the rate of _______ percent (___%) per annum computed from the next day on which the deficient royalty should have been paid. A "material deficiency" under this provision is any amount in excess of US$__________.

13. *Minimum Quota.*

a) The parties agree that in order to retain the exclusive license with respect to the Authorized Territory (except for the People's Republic of China and Hong Kong), Sales Company shall meet the following minimum quota for the sale of all products using the Licensed Technology (hereinafter referred to as "Minimum Quota") commencing from the date of establishment of Sales Company, and no later than twelve (12) months after production begins:

YEAR 1:	US $__________
YEAR 2:	US $__________
YEARS 3-15:	US $__________

b) In the event that Sales Company fails to meet the Minimum Quota, Licensor, at its option, may terminate the exclusive license as it relates to the Authorized Territory, except for [People's Republic of China, Macau, or Hong Kong].

14. *Term and Termination.*

a) The term of this agreement is for a period of fifteen (15) years commencing from the date of execution of this Agreement. This Agreement may be extended for an additional term with the consent of the parties based upon the same terms and conditions.

b) Either party shall have the right to terminate this Agreement, prior to the expiration of its terms, under any one of the following circumstances:

(i) bankruptcy of either party;

(ii) insolvency of either party;

(iii) assignment by either party, for the benefit of its creditors;

(iv) appointment of a receiver for either party's property, in whole or in part; or

(v) a change of ownership or control which results in a party becoming, directly or indirectly, owned or controlled by a competitor.

c) If either party commits any substantial breach of this Agreement, the non-breaching party shall give written notice of such breach, and if such breach is not remedied by the breaching party within sixty (60) days of such notice, the non-breaching party shall be entitled to terminate this Agreement forthwith.

15. *Confidentiality.*

a) During the term of this Agreement, Licensee and Sales Company may have access to confidential information of Licensor. Licensee and

Sales Company shall protect such information in the same manner in which it would protect its own confidential information of like importance and to maintain the confidentiality of such information. Licensee and Sales Company agree that they shall not disclose or use confidential information of Licensor for its own benefit or the benefit of any other person or entity. Licensee and Sales Company further agree that they shall not, at any time, disclose the Licensed Technology to any person or entity, that is not subject to a confidentiality agreement, including any partner, customer, distributor, joint venture partner, supplier, or other similar person or entity, without the prior written consent of Licensor.

b) During the term of this Agreement, Licensor may have access to confidential information of Licensee and shall protect such information in the same manner in which it would protect its own confidential information of like importance and to maintain the confidentiality of such information. Licensor agrees that it shall not disclose or use confidential information of Licensee for its own benefit or the benefit of any other person or entity.

c) Licensee and Sales Company agree and acknowledge that only trusted and loyal employees shall have access to the Licensed Technology and that they shall require that those employees with access to enter into a confidentiality agreement prohibiting the disclosure and misuse of the Licensed Technology.

d) The parties hereto both agree that the terms and conditions of this Agreement are to remain confidential at all times.

16. *Prohibition on Disposition of Rights to or Misuse of Licensed Technology.*

a) Licensee agrees that it shall not sell, assign, sublicense, lease, or otherwise transfer the Licensed Technology to any other person or entity, including any partner, customer, distributor, joint venture partner, supplier, or other similar person or entity, at any time. Licensee further agrees that it shall not allow any person or entity, including any partner, customer, distributor, joint venture partner, supplier, or other similar person or entity, to use, test, improve, manipulate, or otherwise exploit the Licensed Technology in any manner without the written consent of Licensor.

b) Licensor shall have the right to obtain injunctive relief to prohibit Licensee from violating the terms of this provision or subsection 9(f).

17. *Indemnification.*

a) Each party (the "indemnitor") agrees to indemnify and hold harmless the other party (the "indemnitee"), its agents, employees, successors and assigns from and against any and all liabilities, losses, damages, claims, suits and expenses, including reasonable attorney's fees, of whatsoever kind and nature imposed upon, incurred by, or asserted against the indemnitee, its agents, employees, successors and assigns for bodily injuries (including death) or damage to property relating to or arising out of the indemnitor's negligent acts or omissions, provided that the maximum liability of the indemnitor under this provision shall be [$1,000,000] per occurrence.

b) Licensor represents and warrants that the Licensed Technology shall in no way infringe any U.S. or foreign patents, copyrights or proprietary rights owned or controlled by any third party.

18. *Limitation of Liability.* Except for a breach of a party's confidentiality and nondisclosure obligations pursuant to Section 15, and except for obligations arising under a party's third party indemnification obligations pursuant to Section 17, neither party will be liable to the other for incidental, consequential or special damages even if advised of the possibility of such damages.

19. *General Provisions.*

a) Time is of the essence of this Agreement.

b) This Agreement contains all of the agreements, understandings, representations and conditions made between the parties hereto.

c) No provision of this Agreement may be amended or added to except by an agreement in writing signed by the parties hereto or their respective successors in interest.

d) This Agreement shall inure to the benefit of and be binding upon the successors, heirs and assigns of the parties.

e) In the event that a dispute arises under this Agreement, the parties hereby agree to submit the disputed issues to arbitration before the Singapore International Arbitration Center and that the rules of arbitration of the Center shall control.

f) If any party should institute any action or arbitration proceeding under this Agreement, the prevailing party in such action or arbitration shall be entitled to reasonable attorneys' fees and costs.

g) This Agreement shall be governed by the laws of the People's Republic of China, and any questions arising hereunder shall be construed or determined according to such laws.

h) It is not the intent of the parties to create under this Agreement any joint venture, partnership, business association, or other form of business entity. Except as otherwise provided herein, in no event shall either party be liable in any manner for the acts and omissions of the other party to compensate its employees, representatives, and agents. Neither party shall have the right to legally bind the other party in any manner whatsoever.

i) This Agreement has been prepared in both the English and Chinese languages and both versions are equally binding.

j) The persons executing this Agreement warrant that they have the authority to bind their respective entities. Licensee further warrants that it has full right, power and authority to enter into the Agreement.

k) The Company shall guarantee the performance of Licensor under the terms and conditions of this Agreement.

l) If this Agreement is required to be approved by the relevant government authorities, it shall not be effective until such authority is obtained.

IN WITNESS WHEREOF, the parties hereto have executed this Agreement as noted below.

Dated:___________, [LICENSOR]

By: ____________________
Name: ____________________
Title: ____________________

Dated:___________, [THE COMPANY]

By: ____________________
Name: ____________________
Title: ____________________

Dated:___________, [LICENSEE]

By: ____________________
Name: ____________________
Title: ____________________

Dated:___________, [SALES COMPANY]

By: ____________________
Name: ____________________
Title: ____________________

JOINT VENTURE CONTRACT
TO ESTABLISH
AN EQUITY JOINT VENTURE USING CHINESE
AND FOREIGN INVESTMENT
AMONG
[PARTY A AND PARTY B]

____
(date)

Table of Contents

JOINT VENTURE CONTRACT, dated __________, is entered into in [place], People's Republic of China (the "PRC" or "China"), between ____________ ("Party A") and ________________ ("Party B").

PRELIMINARY STATEMENTS

(1) Party A is a joint stock company organized under the laws of the PRC.
(3) Party B is a corporation organized under the laws of [__________] and is a manufacturer of certain products described on *Exhibit A*.
(4) Party A and Party B jointly have conducted and completed a feasibility study for the operation of an enterprise to manufacture those products described on *Exhibit A*.
(5) After friendly consultations conducted in accordance with the principles of equality and mutual benefit, Party A and Party B have agreed to establish an equity joint venture enterprise in accordance with the Law of the People's Republic of China on Joint Ventures Using Chinese and Foreign Investment (the "Joint Venture Law"), the implementing regulations issued thereunder, other relevant laws and regulations of China, and the provisions of this Joint Venture Contract.

NOW THEREFORE, the parties hereby agree as follows:

CHAPTER 1.

GENERAL PROVISIONS

Article 1.1. *Definitions.*
The following terms as used in this Contract shall have the meanings set forth below:
(1) "Approval Authority" shall mean _______________ Municipal Foreign Economics and Trade Commission, its authorized agent or its successor authority.
(2) "Articles of Association" shall mean the Articles of Association of the Company in the form agreed to by the Parties.
(3) "Associated Company" shall mean with respect to a Person, any other Person, which, directly or indirectly, is in control of, is controlled by, or is under common control with, such Person. For purposes of this definition, "control" of a Person shall mean the power, directly or indirectly, either to (i) vote 50% or more of the securities having ordinary voting power for the election of directors of such Person or (ii) direct or cause the direction of the management and policies of such Person whether by contract or otherwise.

(4) "Board of Directors" shall mean the board of directors of the Company.
(5) "Company" shall mean the joint venture company to be established pursuant to the terms of this Contract.
(6) "Contract" means this Joint Venture Contract and the Exhibits hereto.
(7) "Effective Date" shall mean the date on which the approval document of this Contract is issued by the Approval Authority.
(8) "Establishment Date" shall mean the date on which the business license of the Company is issued by the ________ Municipal Administration for Industry and Commerce.
(9) "Feasibility Study" shall mean the completed feasibility study report dated [ ], jointly prepared by the Parties.
(10) "Going Concern Value of the Company" shall mean the value of the Company as a going concern determined based on a valuation methodology acceptable to internationally-recognized certified public accounting firms and based on the sum of (i) a multiple of projected earnings for all then projected periods and (ii) the Company's terminal value at the end of such projected periods.
(11) "Governmental Authority" shall mean any foreign or domestic national, provincial, territorial or local governmental authority, quasigovernmental authority, court, governmental organization, governmental commission, governmental board, bureau or instrumentality, regulatory, administrative or other agency, or any political or other subdivision, department or branch of any of the foregoing.
(12) "Lease" shall mean a lease executed, or to be executed, by the Company and [________________________] for the occupancy by the Company of that certain premises commonly known as [________________] located [____________________].
(13) "Officials" shall mean the Chairman of Party B and the Chairman of Party A.
(14) "Operating Agreements" shall have the meaning set forth in Section 13.1(3).
(15) "Party" shall mean each of Party A and Party B, which are sometimes collectively referred to as the "Parties," and their respective successors and permitted assigns.
(16) "Percentage" with respect to Party A shall mean [x]% and with respect to Party B shall mean [y]%.
(17) "Person" shall mean and include an individual, a partnership, a joint venture, a corporation, a limited liability company, a trust, an unincorporated organization and any Governmental Authority.

(18) "Products" shall mean those products listed on Exhibit A.
(19) "Representative" shall mean with respect to a Person, any and all directors, officers, employees, representatives or agents of such Person.
(20) "RMB" or "Renminbi" shall mean the lawful currency issued by The People's Bank of China.
(22) "Senior Officers" shall mean the General Manager, the two (2) Deputy General Managers, [the Managers of Finance, Marketing, Engineering and Quality] and such other senior officers as are designated as such from time to time by the Board of Directors.
(22) "Territory" shall mean the PRC, excluding, solely for the purposes of this Contract, Taiwan and Macau.
(23) "US$" or "United States Dollars" shall mean the lawful currency of the United States of America.

CHAPTER 2.

PARTIES TO THE JOINT VENTURE

Article 2.1. *Joint Venture Parties.* The Parties to this Contract are:

a) Party A:
Legal Address: ____________________
____
____
Legal Representative: ____________________
Position: ____________________
Nationality: ____________________
Fax: ____________________
Telephone: ____________________

a) Party B:
Legal Address: ____________________
____
____
Legal Representative: ____________________
Position: ____________________
Nationality: ____________________
Fax: ____________________
Telephone: ____________________

CHAPTER 3.

REPRESENTATIONS

Article 3.1. *By Party A.* Party A hereby represents as of the date hereof as follows:

(1) *Duly Organized.* Party A is a joint stock company duly organized and validly existing with the status of a legal person under the laws of China.

(2) *Duly Authorized.* The execution and performance by Party A of this Contract (i) are within its corporate power and business scope; (ii) have been duly authorized by all necessary corporate action; (iii) do not contravene its Articles of Association; and (iv) do not contravene any law or contractual restriction binding on or affecting it.

(3) *No Governmental Consents Required.* No authorization, consent or approval or other action by, and no notice to or filing with, any Governmental Authority is required for the due execution, delivery and performance by Party A of this Contract, except for the approval of this Contract by the Approval Authority.

(4) *Enforceability.* Subject to the approval of this Contract by the Approval Authority, this Contract is the legal, valid and binding obligation of Party A, enforceable against Party A in accordance with its terms.

(5) *No Violation of Law.* Party A is not in violation of any statute, law, rule or regulation that materially affects or might materially affect Party A's ability to perform its obligations under this Contract or the consummation of the transactions contemplated hereby. Party A is not subject to any judgment, order, writ, injunction, decree or award issued by any Governmental Authority or arbitral body relating to it, or to its property, business or operations, that affects or might affect Party A's ability to perform its obligations under this Contract or the consummation of the transactions contemplated hereby in any materially adverse manner.

(6) *No Pending Claims.* There are no claims, actions, suits, investigations or proceedings pending or, to the best of Party A's knowledge, threatened against Party A, at law or in equity, or before or by any Governmental Authority or arbitral body which, if determined adversely, would have a material adverse effect on Party A's ability to perform its obligations under this Contract or the consummation of the transactions contemplated hereby. Party A is not in default with respect to, and the execution, delivery and performance by Party A of this Contract and the consummation of the transactions contemplated hereby will not conflict with or result in a breach or violation of, any judgment, order, writ, injunction

or decree of any Governmental Authority or arbitral body applicable to Party A.

(7) *No Brokerage Commission.* No Person is entitled to any brokerage commission, finder's fee, advisory fee or like payment from Party A in connection with the transactions contemplated by this Contract.

Artilce 3.2. *Party B.*

Party B hereby represents as of the date hereof as follows:

(1) *Duly Organized.* Party B is a corporation duly incorporated [, and] validly existing [and in good standing] under the laws of ___________.

(2) *Duly Authorized.* The execution and performance by Party B of this Contract (i) are within its corporate power and business scope; (ii) have been duly authorized by all necessary corporate action; (iii) do not contravene its constituent documents; and (iv) do not contravene any law or contractual restriction binding on or affecting it.

(3) *No Governmental Consents Required.* No authorization, consent or approval or other action by, and no notice to or filing with, any Governmental Authority is required for the due execution, delivery and performance by Party B of this Contract, except for the approval of this Contract by the Approval Authority.

(4) *Enforceability.* Subject to the approval of this Contract by the Approval Authority, this Contract is the legal, valid and binding obligation of Party B, enforceable against Party B in accordance with its terms.

(5) *No Violation of Law.* Party B is not in violation of any statute, law, rule or regulation that materially affects or might materially affect Party B's ability to perform its obligations under this Contract or the consummation of the transactions contemplated hereby. Party B is not subject to any judgment, order, writ, injunction, decree or award issued by any Governmental Authority or arbitral body relating to it, or to its property, business or operations, that affects or might affect Party B's ability to perform its obligations under this Contract or the consummation of the transactions contemplated hereby in any materially adverse manner.

(6) *No Pending Claims.* There are no claims, actions, suits, investigations or proceedings pending or, to the best of Party B's knowledge, threatened against Party B, at law or in equity, or before or by any Governmental Authority or arbitral body which, if determined adversely, would have a material adverse effect on Party B's ability to perform its obligations under this Contract or the consummation of the transactions contemplated hereby. Party B is not in default with respect to, and the execution of, delivery and performance by Party B of this Contract and the

consummation of the transactions contemplated hereby will not conflict with or result in a breach or violation of, any judgment, order, writ, injunction or decree of any Governmental Authority or arbitral body applicable to Party B.

(7) *No Brokerage Commission.* No Person is entitled to any brokerage commission, finder's fee, advisory fee or like payment from Party B in connection with the transactions contemplated by this Contract.

CHAPTER 4.
ESTABLISHMENT OF THE COMPANY

Article 4.1. *Establishment of the Company.*
The Parties agree to establish the Company in accordance with the Joint Venture Law, other relevant PRC laws and regulations and the terms of this Contract as a limited liability equity joint venture company.

Article 4.2. *Name.*
The name of the Company in Chinese is: ______________________
The name of the Company in English is: ______________________
The legal address of the Company shall be at: ______________________
____
____
PRC

Article 4.3. *PRC Law.*
The Company shall be a legal person under the laws of the PRC, it shall observe the laws and regulations of China, and its legal rights and operational autonomy shall be fully protected in accordance with the laws and regulations of the PRC.

Article 4.4. *Limited Liability.*
The Company shall be a limited liability company. The liability of each Party under any and all circumstances shall be limited to the amount of the registered capital expressly subscribed to by it and no Party shall have any further liability to contribute money or other property to, or in respect of, the registered capital, losses, debts, liabilities or other obligations of the Company. The profits of the Company shall be shared by the Parties as set forth in Article 15.7. The Parties shall have no liability for any losses, debts, liabilities or other obligations of the Company beyond the amount of their respective investments in the registered capital of the Company subscribed to by them.

Article 4.5. *Branches.*
With the approval of the local administration bureau for industry and commerce, the Company can establish branches, offices or similar establishments at any location within China.

CHAPTER 5.

PURPOSE, SCOPE, AND SCALE OF BUSINESS

Article 5.1. *Purpose.*
The purpose of the Company is to combine the knowledge and experience of the Parties into a jointly-managed organization to engage in the manufacture, sourcing, production, marketing, sale and servicing of the Products in the Territory and to perform such other acts as the Board of Directors directs consistent with this Contract. The initial Products shall include ______________________. Future production by the Company of models sourced will be considered and determined by the Board of Directors based upon sales volume/economics.

Article 5.2. *Scope.*
The business scope of the Company shall include the manufacture, sourcing, production, marketing, sale and servicing of ____________________.

Article 5.3. *Estimated Scale of Production.*
According to the Feasibility Study, the Parties estimate that the Company will achieve the following rates of production of the following Products within the following time periods:

Years After Establishment Date	*Product*	*Quantity*
1		______________
2		______________
3		______________
4		______________

The Parties agree that there is no assurance that such production may be achieved by such target dates or at any subsequent date. The actual production figures may be either increased or decreased by the Board of Directors during actual production based on the market situation, improvements in productive capacity and other appropriate factors. The Company may add additional products and production lines as economic and market conditions warrant upon the approval of the Board of Directors.

CHAPTER 6.

TOTAL AMOUNT OF INVESTMENT AND REGISTERED CAPITAL

Article 6.1. *Total Investment.*

(1) The total amount of investment in the Company shall be US $[ ], including: (i) Registered Capital of US $[ ], and (ii) loans of up to US $[ ] by ______________ to the Company for ____________________.

(2) The unit of currency for measuring, among other things, the total investment, registered capital and contributions thereof for purposes of this Contract shall be the United States Dollar. The exchange rate to convert Renminbi contributed by Party A to United States Dollars shall be the average exchange rate between United States Dollars and Renminbi promulgated by the People's Bank of China on the date on which the capital is contributed.

(3) All capital contributions in foreign exchange shall be made to the foreign exchange account of the Company at the office of an authorized bank in ____________, China.

(4) All capital contributions of the Parties to the Company shall be for the exclusive use of the Company.

Article 6.2. *Registered Capital.*

The total registered capital of the Company shall be US $[_________].

Article 6.3. *Capital Contributions.*

The respective capital contributions of the Parties shall be as follows:

(1) Party A:

Cash An amount of RMB equal to US $[ ]

The Parties agree that the contribution of an amount of RMB equal to US $[_________] in cash by Party A to the registered capital of the Company shall equal [x]% of the registered capital of the Company.

(1) Party B:

Cash US $[_________]

The Parties agree that the contribution of US $[_________] in cash by Party B to the registered capital of the Company shall equal [y]% of the registered capital of the Company.

Article 6.4. *Schedule of Investment Contributions.*

Subject to the conditions set forth in Article 6.5, Party A shall make its capital contributions to the Company in the following installments and no later than the dates set forth below:

	Amount	*Date*
Cash	An amount of RMB equal to US $[________]	Within [ninety (90)] days after the Establishment Date
Cash	An amount of RMB equal to US $[________]	Within [__________] days after the Establishment Date

(2) Subject to the conditions set forth in Article 6.5, Party B shall make its capital contributions to the Company in the following installments and no later than the dates set forth below:

	Amount	*Date*
Cash	US $[________]	Within [ninety (90)] days after the Establishment Date
Cash	US $[________]	Within [__________] days after the Establishment Date

Article 6.5. *Conditions Precedent to Capital Contribution.*
The obligation of each Party to make its respective capital contribution to the Company is subject to the condition precedent that the following documents shall have been duly executed by the relevant parties thereto and delivered to the Parties:

(1) this Contract and the Articles of Association shall have been approved together by the Approval Authority; and
(2) the Company shall have obtained its business license.

Each of the above documents must be satisfactory in form and substance to each Party. If within [__________] (___) days after the Effective Date any of the above documents has not been executed and delivered to the Parties in form and substance satisfactory to each Party (or the execution and delivery thereof has not been waived), this Contract may be terminated by any Party by written notice given to the other Parties. If this Contract is terminated pursuant to this Article 6.5, no Party shall have any right whatsoever to require the other Parties to make its capital contribution to the Company or to claim any damages from the other party.

Article 6.6. *Loans.*
The difference, if any, between the amount of total investment required and the amount of registered capital of the Company may be raised by the Company by way of loans or other means. The Company may apply for loans in its own name.

Article 6.7. *Verification of Capital Contributions.*
An accounting firm registered in China shall be engaged by the Company to verify the capital contributions of each Party and provide a certificate of ver-

ification after the Parties have paid up capital contributions. The Company, upon the receipt of a satisfactory certificate of verification, shall issue a Certificate of Capital Contribution to each Party. The Certificate of Capital Contribution shall include the following items: name of the Company; the Establishment Date; the names of the Parties and their respective capital contributions to date; the date on which the capital contributions were made; and the date of issuance of the Certificate of Capital Contribution. The Certificate of Capital Contribution shall be conclusive evidence of the respective Party's capital contribution to the Company to date. The Certificate of Capital Contribution shall be effective when jointly signed by the Chairman and Vice Chairman and the seal of the Company is affixed thereon.

Article 6.8. *Increase of Registered Capital.*
The registered capital of the Company may be increased from US $[______], provided that any such increase is unanimously approved by the Board of Directors and approved by the Approval Authority. After any such increase in the registered capital, the Parties shall amend the Contract to reflect any change in the relative proportion of the investment of the Parties in the registered capital of the Company.

Article 6.9. *Transfer of Equity Interests.*

(1) *Prohibition of Transfer.* Except as provided in Article 20.2 and subject to the procedures and limitations set forth below in this Article 6.9, no Party may transfer all or any part of its equity interest in the Company in any manner whatsoever without the prior consent of the other Parties, the unanimous approval of the Board of Directors, and approval from the Approval Authority.

(2) *Offer Notice.* If any Party shall desire to transfer some or all of its equity interest (the "Transferring Party's Interest") in the Company to any third party other than, in the case of Party B, an Associated Company of Party B, such Party (the "Transferring Party") shall secure a binding written offer (the "Third Party Offer") to purchase the Transferring Party's Interest and shall promptly provide to the other Parties (the "Offerees") written notice (the "Offer Notice") of the Third Party Offer, attached to which shall be a true and complete copy of the Third Party Offer. The price (the "Offer Price") set forth in the Third Party Offer must be payable entirely in cash.

(3) *Irrevocable and Exclusive Offer.* The Offer Notice shall constitute, for a period of sixty (60) days from the date on which it shall have been deemed to be given, an irrevocable and exclusive offer to sell to each Offeree (or any Associated Company designated by an Offeree), at the

Offer Price, a portion of the Transferring Party's Interest equal to the proportion that the equity interest in the Company owned by such Offeree bears to the total of the equity interests in the Company owned by all of the Offerees or such lesser portion of the Transferring Party's Interest as such Offeree chooses in its discretion.

(4) *Acceptance of Offer.* Each Offeree may accept the offer set forth in an Offer Notice by giving notice to the Transferring Party, prior to the expiration of such offer, specifying the maximum portion of the Transferring Party's Interest that the Offeree wishes to purchase.

(5) *Notice to Antidilutive Offeree.* If any Offeree does not agree to purchase all of the Transferring Party's Interest to which it is entitled, the Transferring Party shall promptly so notify each Offeree that has so agreed (an "Antidilutive Offeree"), such notice to constitute an offer to sell, irrevocable for fifteen (15) days, to each such Antidilutive Offeree the portion of the remaining Transferring Party's Interest (the "Remaining Interest") equal to the proportion that the equity interest in the Company owned by such Antidilutive Offeree bears to the total of the equity interests in the Company owned by all such Antidilutive Offerees. Each Antidilutive Offeree shall notify the Transferring Party within such fifteen (15) day period, specifying the portion of Remaining Interest which such Antidilutive Offeree agrees to purchase. To the extent that any such Antidilutive Offeree does not fully agree to purchase its proportionate share of the Remaining Interest, the procedures set forth in the two immediately preceding sentences shall be repeated, *mutatis mutandis,* until all the Remaining Interest is sold or until no Party agrees to purchase any more Remaining Interest.

(6) *Payment.* If the Offerees collectively agree to purchase all of the Transferring Party's Interest pursuant to paragraphs (2) through 6.9(5) of this Article 6.9, they shall pay for such Transferring Party's Interest within fortyfive (45) days following completion of the procedures set forth in paragraphs (3) and (5) of this Article 6.9.

(7) *Transfer After Expiration of Offer.* If the offers made by the Transferring Party to the Offerees pursuant to paragraphs (3) and (5) of this Article 6.9 expire without an agreement by one or more Offerees to purchase all of the Transferring Party's Interest, the Transferring Party may transfer the Transferring Party's Interest to the third party within ninety (90) days after the expiration date, subject to (i) obtaining the prior written consent of the Offerees (which consent shall not be unreasonably withheld) and the unanimous approval of the Board of Directors (each Offeree hereby agrees to cause the members of the Board of Directors

designated by such Party to approve such transfer) and (ii) the execution and delivery by such third party of an assignment and assumption agreement, in form and substance satisfactory to the Offerees, pursuant to which such third party shall assume all of the rights and obligations of a Party pursuant to or under this Contract. In the event that such transfer is not consummated within such 90-day period, the Transferring Party shall not be permitted to sell its equity interest in the Company without re-complying with the requirements set forth in paragraphs (2) through (7) of this Article 6.9; *provided, however,* that such transfer may be made without so recomplying with such requirements if the transfer was delayed by factors beyond the reasonable control of the Transferring Party and such transfer is consummated within sixty (60) days following the end of such 90-day period.

(8) *Transfer to Associated Company.* Notwithstanding the foregoing but subject to any required approval from the Approval Authority, each of the Party B may transfer all or any part of its respective equity interest in the Company to any Associated Company of either such Party upon notification to the other Parties. With respect to any such transfer, Party A hereby agrees to any such transfer and waives any right of first refusal with respect to such transfer. Party A also hereby agrees to cooperate with Party B to effect such transfer, including causing members of the Board of Directors designated by it to approve such transfer and executing any required documents in connection with such transfer. To the extent that Party B transfers a part, but not all of its equity interest in the Company to any such Associated Companies, the Parties agree to take such steps as may be advisable to reflect appropriately the addition of such Associated Company as a new Party, including the amendment of this Contract.

Article 6.10. *Additional Equity Transfer Provisions.*

(1) *Effectiveness of Transfer.* Any transfer of a Party's equity interest in the Company under Article 6.9 shall not become effective until all necessary governmental approvals have been obtained. Upon the receipt of such governmental approvals, the Parties shall cause the Company to cancel the then outstanding Certificates of Capital Contribution and to issue new Certificates of Capital Contribution to reflect the new ownership interests. The Parties shall also amend this Contract, if required, to reflect the admission of a new party to this Contract.

(2) *Release of Liability.* If all of the equity interests in the Company owned by any Party are transferred pursuant to and in compliance with Article 6.9,

then such Party shall be released from all liabilities under this Contract, except for such liabilities as may have arisen prior to the first date on which such Party ceases to own any equity interest in the Company. The other Parties, as well as any other Person or Persons that may become party to this Contract pursuant to any transfer of any equity interest in the Company, shall execute and deliver an agreement giving effect to the foregoing, in form and substance acceptable to the Party being released.

CHAPTER 7.

RESPONSIBILITIES OF EACH PARTY TO THE JOINT VENTURE

Article 7.1. *Responsibilities of the Parties.*
The Parties shall be responsible for performing their following respective obligations contained in Articles 7.2, 7.3, and 7.4 in a timely and effective manner. The Parties agree that the cost involved in performing the following respective obligations shall be borne by the respective Party except to the extent otherwise agreed by the Parties and the Company or as set forth in any of the Operating Agreements.

Article 7.2. *By Party A.*
Party A shall be responsible for the following:

(1) Upon request from the Company, prior to the Establishment Date, the organizational and preparatory work for the Company;

(2) Upon request from the Company, provide assistance to the Company and the other Parties in liaison activities with all appropriate national and/or local governmental agencies and authorities (including but not limited to those authorities in ________________ Municipality and ___________ Province) to cause complete and timely implementation of this Agreement and the transactions contemplated thereby;

(3) Upon request from the Company, provide assistance to the Company and the other Parties in completion of all import formalities, including the obtaining of any required PRC import licenses (if any) for, and assisting the Company to arrange the transportation to the Company's facilities from the designated port of entry in China of all machinery, materials and equipment to be imported by the Company;

(4) Upon request from the Company, provide assistance to the Company in the arrangement of all export affairs, including the obtaining of any required PRC export licenses (if any) for, and assisting the Company to transport from the Company's facilities to the designated shipping port in China of, all Products to be exported by the Company;

(5) Upon request from the Company, provide assistance to the Company with respect to the expatriate personnel of the Company in connection with the arrangement of PRC entrance and exit formalities, work permit certificates, residence approvals and providing assistance in finding accommodations compatible with the style and standard of living of such personnel in their respective home countries and the making of all PRC domestic travel arrangements;

(6) Upon request from the Company, provide assistance to the Company with respect to Chinese personnel of the Company, selected by the General Manager for training in the United States or elsewhere overseas, in connection with the arrangement of PRC entrance and exit affairs and the making of international travel arrangements from China the United States or such other overseas locations;

(7) Upon request from the Company, provide assistance to the Company and the other Parties in applying for and obtaining the maximum benefit of all permitted reductions in, or exemptions from, PRC, provincial or local income taxes (including withholding taxes), import duties, value added, business and consumption taxes, local surcharges, real estate taxes, vehicle taxes or any other tax reductions or exemptions to which the Company and the other Parties are currently or may in the future become entitled;

(8) Upon request from the Company, provide assistance to the Company in recruiting local personnel;

(9) Upon request from the Company, provide assistance to the Company in procuring machinery, equipment and materials in the PRC;

(10) Upon request from the Company, provide assistance to the other Parties and the Company to obtain from the appropriate PRC Governmental Authorities all necessary licenses and foreign exchange approvals (if any) to permit the repatriation out of the PRC of all profits, dividends, return of capital, proceeds of liquidation and sale of the Company, and payment of interest and principal of any foreign exchange loans provided by foreign banks and entities in foreign exchange, after the payment of applicable PRC taxes;

(11) Upon request from the Company, provide assistance to the Company and the other Parties and the expatriate personnel of the other Parties and the Company to obtain from the appropriate PRC authorities all necessary licenses and foreign exchange approvals (if any) to permit the repatriation of such personnel's salaries and benefit payments in foreign exchange, after payment of applicable PRC taxes;

(12) Contribute capital in accordance with the time schedule set forth in Article 6.4; and

(13) Upon request from the Company, provide assistance to the Company on other matters referred to it by the Company for which Party A agrees to provide assistance.

Article 7.3. *Responsibilities of Party B.*

Party B shall be responsible for the following:

(1) Provide assistance to the Company with respect to the design of the factory and the installation of equipment;

(2) Provide assistance to the Company in the selection of equipment and materials to be used in the manufacture of the Products;

(3) Provide the Company with advanced and appropriate technology for the manufacture of the Products;

(4) Assist the Company in handling the training of the Company's workers, including overseas training and study if necessary;

(5) Provide assistance to the Company in developing advanced management techniques;

(6) Provide assistance to the Company in recruiting management, finance, technology, engineering and other staff;

(7) Provide assistance to the Company with respect to Chinese personnel of the Company, selected by the General Manager for training in the United States or elsewhere overseas, in connection with the arrangement of overseas entrance and exit affairs (including visa applications), work permits, providing assistance in finding accommodations appropriate for such personnel and the making of international travel arrangements from the United States or such other overseas location to China;

(8) Provide assistance to the Company in liaison activities with relevant foreign businesses;

(9) Prior to the Establishment Date, the organizational and preparatory work for the Company;

(10) Contribute capital in accordance with the time schedule set forth in Article 6.4; and

(11) Such other matters referred to it by the Company for which Party B agrees to provide assistance.

Article 7.4. *Responsibilities of All Parties.*

Each Party shall be responsible for the following:

(1) To make their respective capital contributions in the registered capital of the Company pursuant to Article 6.4;

(2) To ensure that a set of proper books and records of the Company are kept in accordance with "The Accounting System of the People's Republic of China for Foreign Investment Enterprises" and the "Regulations of the People's Republic of China for the Financial Administration of Foreign Investment Enterprises" in the Chinese and English languages;
(3) To refrain from mortgaging, pledging or permitting any liens on any property of the Company and each Party's respective equity interests in the Company without the prior written approval of the Board of Directors;
(4) To cooperate to achieve the purpose and goals of the Company as set forth in this Contract and the Operating Agreements by executing any and all documents and taking all actions necessary or advisable to effect the foregoing;
(5) To prevent any borrowing or lending of money in the name of the Company or establishment of any subsidiary of the Company without the approval of the Board of Directors; and
(6) As soon as practical after the Establishment Date, to cause the Company to enter into the Operating Agreements.

CHAPTER 8.

MARKETING

Article 8.1. *General Principles*
In accordance with relevant PRC laws and regulations, the Company shall have the right to price and sell its products and services at its own discretion in both the PRC and abroad and may develop other sales-related services. [The Parties intend that initially one hundred percent (100%) of the Products will be exported pursuant to the Distribution Agreement described in Article 13.1(3) for sales of the Products by Party C.] The Company's products and services may be sold for RMB or foreign exchange, as permitted by applicable law. [Joint branding in the PRC of the Products (other than name-branded Products) shall be phased in over a three (3) year period.]

Article 8.2. *Design and Development of New Products.*
Where the Board of Directors has decided that the Company will manufacture and sell any new product in the PRC or a portion thereof, the design and development of such new product shall be conducted primarily by Party B.

Article 8.3. *Trademarks; Technology Licensing.*
(1) The Company shall, within [thirty (30)] days after the Establishment Date, enter into the Trademark License Agreements described in Article

13.1(3) pursuant to which Party B and Party D grant to the Company certain licenses to use in the Territory the names ["________________"] and trademarks and service marks of Party B and Party D in connection with the manufacture of the Products. The Company shall not obtain licenses to other foreign trademarks without the approval of the Board of Directors.

(2) The Company shall, within [thirty (30)] days after the Establishment Date, enter into the Technology License Agreement described in Article 13.1(3) pursuant to which Party B grants to the Company a license to use in the Territory certain technology in connection with the manufacture of the Products.

CHAPTER 9.

FOREIGN EXCHANGE

Article 9.1. *Use of Foreign Exchange.*

Foreign exchange held by the Company shall be used in accordance with applicable laws and regulations and shall be allocated for use in the following priority:

(1) Payment for imported equipment and materials, the purchase price of which is denominated in foreign currency;

(2) Repayment of principal and payment of interest on loans to the Company denominated in foreign currency;

(3) Payment of the salary and other benefits of expatriate employees and payment of travel and other expenses of Directors in connection with their attendance at meetings of the Board of Directors;

(4) Distributions of profit to the Parties; and

(5) Such other payments as the Board of Directors may determine.

CHAPTER 10.

BOARD OF DIRECTORS

Article 10.1. *Formation of the Board of Directors.*

The Board of Directors of the Company shall come into existence on the Establishment Date and shall convene its first meeting within [ninety (90)] days after the Establishment Date. The Board of Directors shall be the highest organ of authority of the Company. The name list of the initial Directors as designated by the Parties is set forth in *Exhibit B* hereto. The Board of Directors shall have all the authority conferred by law in the conduct of the business of the Company and shall have the responsibility for making significant decisions concerning the management of the business and affairs of the Company.

Article 10.2. *Directors.*

The Board of Directors will be comprised of six (6) Directors. Of these, five (5) shall be appointed by Party B and one (1) shall be appointed by Party A. The Chairman shall be designated by Party B, and the Vice Chairman shall be appointed by Party A. The term of office for the Chairman, Vice Chairman and the Directors is for a period of [four (4)] years and may be renewed with the approval of the Party which appointed such Director. The Party that appoints a Director shall have the power to remove such Director from the Board of Directors without cause at any time and to replace the removed Director with another individual designated by such Party. The Directors of the Company shall serve without compensation except as otherwise stipulated in Article 10.4.

Article 10.3. *Chairman of the Board.*

The Chairman of the Board of Directors is the legal representative of the Company and may perform such activities as are authorized in the Articles of Association, or such activities as may be expressly authorized in writing by the Board of Directors. The Chairman shall preside at all meetings of the Board.

Article 10.4. *Meetings of the Board of Directors.*

Regular meetings of the Board of Directors shall be held semiannually in March and September of each year, or such other times as the Parties may agree. At any meeting, a quorum shall consist of at least four (4) Directors attending in person, by proxy or participating by telephone. A meeting shall be duly called if called by the Chairman or by any two (2) Directors in the case of special meetings. All Board of Director meetings shall be called upon seven (7) days' prior written notice (or upon such lesser period of time as the Directors shall unanimously agree in writing from time to time) to all Directors, to be held at the headquarters of the Company, or any other location approved by the Board of Directors. Directors may be present and vote in person, by proxy or by telephone, provided that adequate facilities are available for telephonic participation. The Chairman and the Vice Chairman shall each have the same right of one vote accorded to each of the other Directors. The Board of Directors may take any action within its powers by unanimous written consent of all Directors without necessity of a meeting. Notice of any meeting may be waived in writing at any time before or after the meeting and will be waived by any Director by his or her attendance at such meeting. [All reasonable travel and lodging costs incurred by Directors in connection with their attendance at meetings of the Board of Directors shall be borne by the Company unless the Parties agree otherwise.] All additional requirements and procedures applicable to meetings of the Board of Directors shall be detailed in the Articles of Association.

Article 10.5. *Board Approval Requirements.*
The Board of Directors shall have and exercise all of the powers belonging or pertaining to the Company. Except as otherwise set forth in Article 10.6 or in the Articles of Association, all actions taken by the Board of Directors shall require the vote of a majority of the Directors present or represented at a duly constituted meeting of the Board of Directors.

Article 10.6. *Action Requiring Unanimous Approval.*
Any action taken with respect to any of the following matters shall require the unanimous vote of all Directors:
(1) Any amendments to this Contract or the Articles of Association;
(2) Any termination, winding up, liquidation or other dissolution of the Company;
(3) Increasing the registered capital of the Company, the transfer thereof or the adjustment of the Parties' capital contribution ratio; and
(4) Any merger of the Company with any other economic organization.

CHAPTER 11.

BUSINESS MANAGEMENT

Article 11.1. *Business Management.*
The management of the Company shall consist of a General Manager, two Deputy General Managers, and Managers of Marketing and Plant which shall be appointed by the Board of Directors. Such Senior Officers shall be nominated by Party B. The day-to-day operation of the Company shall be under the sole direction of the General Manager, and the Deputy General Managers and Managers of Marketing and Plant ("the Functional Managers") shall report directly to the General Manager. A Deputy General Manager shall act on behalf of the General Manager in carrying out the business of the Company when the General Manager is unavailable. The Functional Managers shall mark the Deputy General Managers for copies of all correspondence from them to the General Manager concerning the business of the Company objectively considered necessary to ensure the Deputy General

Managers have access to the same information as the General Manager concerning the business of the Company and likewise the Functional Managers shall mark the General Manager for copies of all correspondence from them to the Deputy General Managers concerning the business of the Company objectively considered necessary to ensure the General Manager has access to the same information as the Deputy General Managers concerning the business of the Company.

Article 11.2. *Term of Office.*
The General Manager and the Deputy General Managers shall, unless they become incapacitated, retire or are removed from office earlier by the Board of Directors pursuant to Article 11.3, hold office for a term of [four (4)] years each, or such lesser term as is determined by the Board of Directors. The other Senior Officers of the Company shall, unless they become incapacitated, retire or are removed from office earlier by the Board of Directors pursuant to Article 11.3, hold office for a term of [one (1)] year each, or such other term as is determined by the Board. The General Manager and the other Senior Officers may serve consecutive terms if reappointed by the Board of Directors.

Article 11.3. *Power of Board to Dismiss Senior Officers.*
The General Manager and other Senior Officers of the Company shall not hold posts concurrently as general manager or other senior officers in any other economic organizations nor shall they participate in any economic activity which may compete with the interests of the Company. The Board of Directors may, by a resolution adopted by a simple majority of the Board of Directors, remove the General Manager or any other Senior Officer of the Company at any time without cause. Any management personnel engaging in any graft or other illegal activity may be immediately terminated by the Board of Directors by a resolution adopted by a simple majority of the Board of Directors. If it becomes necessary due to dismissal or resignation to replace the General Manager or any other Senior Officer, the Board of Directors shall determine his replacement; *provided, however,* that the Party that nominated the Senior Officer to be replaced shall nominate the replacement Senior Officer.

Article 11.4. *Monthly Reports.*
The General Manager shall prepare monthly operational reports [and financial statements] of the Company which shall be in [Chinese and English] unless the Board of Directors waives or modifies such requirement.

Article 11.5. *Other Voting Agreements.*

Each Party agrees to vote and take all other possible action necessary (including, without limitation, reaffirming or renewing any and all voting agreements set forth in this Contract to the extent required by applicable law) to ensure that the provisions of this Contract and any Operating Agreements are carried out in all respects, and to execute and deliver such additional documents and instruments, and to perform such additional acts, as may be reasonably necessary or appropriate to effectuate, carry out and perform all of the terms, provisions and conditions of this Contract and all Operating Agreements.

CHAPTER 12.

PURCHASE OF MATERIALS, EQUIPMENT, AND SPARE PARTS

Article 12.1. *Principles of Procurement.*

The Company may at any time in accordance with its requirements purchase machinery, equipment, spare parts or materials from PRC or foreign suppliers. In purchasing machinery, equipment, spare parts or raw materials required for the Company's activities, the Company shall give priority to PRC suppliers whenever items from such suppliers are competitive with like imported items with respect to quality, specifications, performance, and other materials terms. Party B shall use its best efforts to assist the Company with the procurement of any equipment, materials and supplies which the Company must import.

Article 12.2. *Sourcing from Party C.*

The Company shall enter into the Sourcing Agreement described in Article 13.1(3) within [thirty (30)] days after the Establishment Date.

CHAPTER 13.

RELATIONSHIP BETWEEN THE COMPANY AND THE PARTIES

Article 13.1. *Independence, Transition and Cooperation.*

(1) Commencing with the Establishment Date, the Company will be an independent economic and legal entity, separate and distinct from each of the Parties, and will be responsible for the management and control of its assets and the management and operation of its business.

(2) Each Party agrees that it will respect the Company's operational autonomy. Unless approved by the Board of Directors at a meeting in accordance with the provisions of this Contract and the Articles of Association, none of the Parties or their employees will directly or indirectly interfere with the Company's plans, production, management, products, marketing, use of funds, personnel, financial, insurance or in any other matters.

(3) After the Establishment Date, the Parties shall enter into, or cause their Associated Companies to enter into, ancillary agreements (each, an "Operating Agreement") with the Company as follows:

(a) Party B will enter into a Technology License Agreement with the Company substantially in the form of *Exhibit C*;

(b) Party B will cause Party C to enter into a Sourcing Agreement with the Company substantially in the form of *Exhibit D*;

(c) Each of Party B and Party D will enter into a separate Trademark License Agreement with the Company, which in the case of Party B will be substantially in the form of *Exhibit E-1* and in the case of Party D will be substantially in the form of *Exhibit E2*;

(d) Each of Party A, Party B and Party D will enter into a separate Service and Information Providing Agreement with the Company, which in the case of Party A will be in the form of *Exhibit F-1*, in the case of Party B will be substantially in the form of *Exhibit F-2* and in the case of Party D will be substantially in the form of *Exhibit F-3*; and

(e) Party B will cause Party C to enter into a Distribution Agreement with the Company for the sales of the Products substantially in the form of *Exhibit G*.

Article 13.2. *Personnel.*
The Parties agree that the Company may seek to recruit personnel (including technical personnel) from the labor market.

Article 13.3. *Competition with the Company.*
A covenant not to compete in the form of *Exhibit H* is incorporated into this Contract.

CHAPTER 14.

LABOR MANAGEMENT

Article 14.1. *Staff and Workers.*
Labor plans and contracts covering the recruitment, qualifications and testing, employment, dismissal and resignation, wages, labor insurance, welfare,

bonuses, labor discipline, retirement insurance and other matters concerning the staff and workers of the Company shall be handled in accordance with the "Labor Law of the People's Republic of China" the "Regulations on Labor Management in Foreign Investment Enterprises" and other relevant laws and regulations of the PRC and local government.

Article 14.2. *Administrative Personnel.*
The appointment of Senior Officers, their salaries, subsidies, social insurance, welfare and standard of travel expenses shall be decided by the Board of Directors.

Article 14.3. *Employee Qualifications.*
The total number of people employed by the Company, their compensation and work shift hours shall be determined by the General Manager in accordance with the "Regulations on Labor Management in Foreign Investment Enterprises" and related laws and regulations and can be changed by the General Manager from time to time to achieve the purposes of the Company.

Article 14.4. *Labor Discipline.*
The Company shall have the widest authority consistent with relevant laws and regulations to implement modern methods for advanced, scientific management and quality control, including the power, which shall be exercised autonomously, to take disciplinary action against any of the workers and personnel by giving warnings, recording demerits, reducing salaries and/or wages and by dismissal. Any dismissal shall be reported to the local labor bureau for the record.

Article 14.5. *Training.*
In order to promote the technical and managerial skills of the Company's employees, both short and long term training programs shall be implemented by the Company. All training costs, including travel, lodging, meals and insurance shall be paid for by the account of the Company.

Article 14.6. *Compensation.*
(1) The Company shall pay salaries to its expatriate employees in foreign exchange pursuant to the terms of the relevant employment contract to be entered into by the Company and the respective expatriate employee. Expatriate employees shall be permitted, after payment of all PRC income taxes due, to remit such foreign exchange earnings to a designated bank abroad. If requested by the Company or Party B, Party A shall assist expatriate employees in facilitating such transfers.

(2) The expatriate General Manager or any other expatriate Senior Officers who are hired with the approval of the General Manager shall receive salaries and welfare and other benefits from the Company as decided upon by the Board of Directors, including a foreign living allowance which is fair and reasonable by international standards. With respect to expatriate employees, technical experts and staff and their families and foreign consultants to the Company, Party A shall, if requested by the Company, assist such persons in applying for and obtaining PRC entry visas, exit permits and work permits, tax and public security registrations and in facilitating their travel and living arrangements within the PRC, and arranging for appropriate accommodations, communications and medical care and satisfactory meals for such expatriate personnel and their families.

(3) The salaries of the Chinese personnel shall be paid in RMB pursuant to the terms of their employment contract with the Company (including any trade union contract applicable to such personnel).

Article 14.7. *Trade Union.*
The staff and the workers of Company shall have the right to establish a trade union in accordance with the relevant laws of China and actively support the work of the trade union. Meetings of the trade union shall be held only after ordinary working hours. The Company shall pay an amount equal to two percent (2%) of the total wages received by the staff and employees of the Company (or such lesser amount as may be permitted by applicable law from time to time) to the Company's trade union for such trade union's use in accordance with the applicable laws of China on the management of trade unions.

CHAPTER 15.

TAXES, FINANCE, AND AUDIT

Article 15.1. *Tax Treatment.*
The Company shall pay income, business, value added and other taxes, and shall enjoy such exemptions from taxation and other tax benefits as may be available to it, in accordance with the relevant laws and regulations of China. The Company shall seek to be treated as a "product export enterprise" and/or "technologically advanced enterprise" so as to enjoy the tax benefits of such status. The Company shall inform the Parties annually as to whether it has qualified for such tax benefits or other tax benefits available to it based upon the nature of its business.

Article 15.2. *Accounting System.*

(1) The [Manager of Finance] of the Company, under the supervision of the General Manager, shall be responsible for the financial management of the Company.

(2) The financial affairs and accounting of the Company shall be handled in accordance with "The Accounting System of the People's Republic of China for Foreign Investment Enterprises" and the "Regulations of the People's Republic of China for the Financial Administration of Foreign Investment Enterprises" promulgated by the Ministry of Finance of the PRC. The accounting system and procedure to be adopted by the Company shall be submitted to the Board of Directors for approval. Once approved by the Board of Directors, the accounting system and procedures shall be filed with the government department in charge of the Company and with the relevant local department of finance and the tax authorities for the record. The accounting system of the Company shall adopt the methods and principles of the accrual method and debit and credit accounting systems used internationally. All accounting records, vouchers, books and statements of the Company shall be prepared and kept in Chinese and English. The annual, quarterly, and monthly financial statements and reports shall be prepared by the [Manager of Finance] and shall be approved by the General Manager and jointly signed by the General Manager and the [Manager of Finance] and shall be prepared and kept in Chinese and English and furnished to the Parties and to the Board of Directors.

(3) The Company adopts the [RMB] [US$] as its standard bookkeeping currency. When the currency of a bank deposit, other cash receipt or expenditure, receipt from a claim or expense for a debt is different from the standard bookkeeping currency, the currency of receipt or expenditure shall also be recorded in addition to the standard bookkeeping currency. Actual exchange gains or losses will be recorded in accordance with the relevant regulations.

(4) The fiscal year of the Company shall run from January 1 to December 31 of the same year. All important financial and accounting records and statements shall require the approval and signature of the General Manager [and the Manager of Finance].

(5) [The Company shall deliver to each Party as soon as practicable and in any event within thirty (30) days after the end of each month in each fiscal year, a Profit and Loss Statement and Cash Flow Statement for such month and a Balance Sheet as at the end of such month, setting forth in each case in comparative form figures for the corresponding period in the preceding financial year, all in reasonable detail.]

(6) The Company shall deliver to each Party as soon as practicable and in any event within sixty (60) days after the end of each quarterly period in each fiscal year, a Profit and Loss Statement and Cash Flow Statement for such period, and a Balance Sheet as at the end of such period, setting forth in each case in comparative form figures for the corresponding period in the preceding fiscal year, all in reasonable detail.
(7) At the end of each financial year, the [Manager of Finance] shall prepare the annual accounts ("Annual Accounts") including the Balance Sheet as at the end of such period, and the Profit and Loss Statement and Cash Flow Statement, setting out all details required by the accounting system and such additional information as will be required to produce financial statements conforming to generally accepted accounting principles in the PRC and to International Accounting Standards.
(8) At the end of each fiscal year, the [Manager of Finance] shall prepare such information as shall be necessary for the preparation of any tax returns and statements as may be required by each Party. This shall include furnishing each Party with certified copies of government receipts for income taxes paid within China.
(9) The Board of Directors and the Parties or their Representatives shall have access to the financial books and records of the Company at all reasonable times.

Article 15.3. *Annual Audit and Annual Accounts.*
An internationally recognized accounting firm registered in China and approved by the Board of Directors shall be engaged by the Company, as its independent auditor, to examine and verify the Annual Accounts, and such accounting firm shall submit its report to the General Manager and the [Manager of Finance]. After approval of the Annual Accounts by such Senior Officers, the Company shall submit to the Parties and to each member of the Board of Directors the Annual Accounts as soon as practicable and in any event within one hundred twenty (120) days after the end of the relevant fiscal year, together with the audit report of the independent auditor.

Article 15.4. *Foreign Exchange and Renminbi Bank Accounts.*
The Company shall separately open foreign exchange accounts and RMB accounts at banks located in China approved by the People's Bank of China. The Company may open accounts at banks located abroad upon approval of the State Administration of Foreign Exchange. The Company's foreign exchange transactions shall be handled in accordance with the relevant laws and regulations of the PRC relating to foreign exchange control. In the event that the Company opens foreign exchange accounts at banks located abroad, deposits of payments received by the Company from any international

transactions may be made directly to such accounts. Any conversion of foreign exchange into Renminbi must be approved by the Board of Directors; provided that the Board of Directors may delegate such approval authority to the General Manager.

Article 15.5. *Settlement of Expenses.*
Except where payment in foreign exchange is required pursuant to this Contract or other contracts entered into by the Company, or pursuant to any provisions of relevant PRC laws and regulations, all payments to be made by the Company in the PRC (including but not limited to expenses and compensation for labor other than expatriate personnel) shall, unless the Company decides otherwise, be settled and paid by the Company in RMB.

Article 15.6. *Funds.*
The Company shall establish and contribute annually from its after-tax profits to a reserve fund, a development fund and a staff and workers welfare and benefit fund. The amount to be contributed to said funds will be determined by the Board of Directors, subject to applicable laws.

Article 15.7. *Profit Distribution.*
The Company shall distribute to the Parties, pro rata in accordance with their respective registered capital in the Company, as regularly as practicable, the Company's profits distributable as dividends consistent with maintaining the funds described in Article 15.6 and the Company's best interest. The Board of Directors will fully consider Party B's goal of having the Company distribute as dividends the maximum amount of profits possible. In order to facilitate such distribution, each Party shall cause the Directors nominated by it to vote in favor of any approval of the Board of Directors for the distribution of such amounts, including, without limitation, attending or causing the Directors nominated by such Party to attend any meeting of the Board of Directors, called for the purpose of approving such distribution.

Article 15.8. *Carry Over.*
Before a previous fiscal year's losses of the Company have been made good, no profits may be distributed to a Party by the Company. Undistributed profits from a previous fiscal year may be distributed with a current fiscal year's profits or, in cases of losses, to the extent of the accumulated amount in excess of the current fiscal year's losses.

Article 15.9. *Personal Income Tax.*
Staff and workers of the Company shall pay personal income taxes according to the "Individual Income Tax Law of The People's Republic of China" and the implementing regulations therefor. The Company will arrange to

withhold from the salary paid to each expatriate employee, and pay over to the tax authorities in accordance with applicable law, the anticipated amount of personal income taxes estimated (in accordance with applicable law and regulations) to be payable in China by such expatriate employee, and shall generally assist each expatriate employee in complying with the requirements of Chinese law concerning such personal income taxes.

Article 15.10. *Appropriation of Foreign Exchange Available.*
Subject to Article 9.3, Party B shall have priority in the distribution of funds from the Company's foreign exchange account(s) for, upon liquidation, its share of the assets of the Company.

CHAPTER 16.

DURATION OF THE JOINT VENTURE

Article 16.1. *Duration.*
The duration of the Company shall be twenty (20) years from the Establishment Date. The duration of the Company may be extended at the end of its term if an application for the extension of the duration, proposed by one Party, and approved by the Board of Directors, shall be submitted to the Approval Authority six (6) months prior to the expiry date of the Company.

CHAPTER 17.

INSURANCE

Article 17.1. *Insurance.*
The Parties shall cause the Company to be covered by appropriate insurance policies underwritten by the People's Insurance Company of China or such other insurance company that is permitted to underwrite insurance policies in the PRC.

CHAPTER 18.

AMENDMENT, ALTERATION, AND DISCHARGE OF THE CONTRACT

Article 18.1. *Amendments: Waivers.*
During the term of this Contract the Parties shall have the right to make amendments and supplements after consultations between the Parties. Neither this Contract nor any subsequent agreement the effect of which is to amend this Contract shall be binding on any Party to this Contract unless

and until it has been signed on such Party's behalf by a duly authorized representative and approved by the Approval Authority and commencement of performance hereunder or under any such subsequent agreement shall not constitute a waiver of this requirement.

Article 18.2. *Improvement in Terms.*
If, after the date hereof, the issuance, amendment, supplement or rescission by the PRC, _______ Municipality or any subdivision or agency thereof, of any tax, foreign exchange, customs or any other laws, rules, regulations or decrees, or the interpretation thereof permits terms and conditions more favorable to the Company or any Party than the terms of this Contract or the laws, rules, regulations and decrees applicable to the Company as of the date of this Contract, the Company or such Party or both shall receive the benefits of such new conditions, and Party A shall exercise its best efforts to assist the Company to obtain the appropriate PRC approvals, if any, required to qualify for the benefit of such new laws, rules, regulations, decrees or interpretation thereof. If only one Party is entitled to the benefits of any such favorable treatment and such treatment has an unfavorable effect on the other Party, the Parties shall immediately consult to determine if there is a result that is acceptable to both Parties. During the pendency of any such consultations, the Parties shall temporarily not implement any such favorable treatment.

Article 18.3. *Amendment By Reason of Adverse Changes in Law.*
If a Party's economic benefits under this Contract are directly or indirectly (through its interest in the Company) adversely affected because of any change in PRC tax, foreign exchange, customs or other laws, rules, regulations or decrees, or the interpretation thereof, or any amendment or supplement to or rescission thereof, including, without limitation, any adverse variation from the Company's preferential PRC tax treatment, the Company's ability to import materials for export products free of PRC customs duties and the Company's ability to maintain a foreign exchange account in China, retain its foreign exchange earnings and exchange currency at foreign exchange swap centers and/or designated foreign exchange banks, by the PRC or any subdivision or agency thereof, the affected Party or Parties shall promptly give notice of such occurrence and the Parties shall, upon receipt of such notice, immediately consult and make the necessary amendments to the relevant provisions of this Contract in order to maintain each Party's respective economic benefits hereunder. Party A shall exercise its best efforts to assist the Company to procure approval for such amendments from the Approval Authority.

CHAPTER 19.

LIABILITIES FOR BREACH OF OBLIGATION TO MAKE CAPITAL CONTRIBUTIONS

Article 19.1. *Failure to Make Capital Contributions When Due.*
Should any Party fail to pay on schedule its respective capital contribution in accordance with the provisions of Chapter 6, the breaching Party shall pay to the other Parties (the "Non-Defaulting Parties"), pro rata in proportion to the equity interest in the Company owned by a Non-Defaulting Party to the total of the equity interests in the Company owned by all of the Non-Defaulting Parties, in cash as a penalty an amount equal to [0.05]% per day of the value of the capital contribution which was not made when due for each day following the date when such capital contribution was due but not made. If such capital contribution is not paid within three (3) months of the date when it is due, the provisions of Article 20.1 shall apply.

CHAPTER 20.

TERMINATION

Article 20.1. *Termination Events.*
If any of the following conditions or events (each a "Termination Event") shall occur and be continuing:

(1) *By Agreement.* The Parties shall agree to terminate this Contract and liquidate the Company voluntarily prior to the expiration of the term of the Company; or
(2) *Heavy Losses; Bankruptcy.* If the Company suffers heavy losses of more than [fifty percent (50%)] of the registered capital of the Company from which it cannot financially recover or the Company is declared bankrupt, or any action by or against the Company is commenced to wind up or liquidate the Company and such action is not dismissed within [sixty (60)] days; or
(3) *Inability of Board to Resolve Matters.* The Board of Directors is unable for a period of [forty-five (45)] days to make a determination on any matter material to the operation of the Company and such matter fails to be resolved to the satisfaction of all parties by the Officials, or their Representatives, through friendly consultation within sixty (60) days after its submission by the Board of Directors (the Officials, or their Representatives, shall use their best efforts to make such determination amicably through friendly consultation) and the issue has not been submitted for resolution pursuant to Article 25.2; *provided, however,* that the

continued failure or inability to resolve or otherwise determine any such matter shall be of such a nature as could materially adversely affect the business operations of the Company; or

(4) *Force Majeure*. The Company is unable to continue operations for [six (6)] consecutive months or more because of force majeure as described in Chapter 22; or

(5) *Failure to Obtain Approvals*. The Company fails to obtain the approvals required under Article 18.2 or Article 18.3; or

(6) *Material Breach*. A Party shall commit a material breach of this Contract or any of the Operating Agreements to which it is a party, the effect of which would have a material adverse effect on the business operations of the Company, and such Party fails to remedy same within ninety (90) days after delivery of notice by any other Party of the occurrence or existence of such breach or such longer period as may be agreed by the non-defaulting Parties; or

(7) *Appointment of Receiver*. A Party shall apply for or consent to the appointment of a receiver, trustee or liquidator for substantially all of its assets or such a receiver, trustee or liquidator shall be appointed, or such Party shall have filed against it an involuntary petition of bankruptcy which has not been dismissed within thirty (30) days, or shall file a voluntary petition of bankruptcy, or a petition or answer seeking reorganization, or an arrangement with creditors, or shall seek to take advantage of any other law relating to relief of debtors, or shall make an assignment for the benefit of creditors; or

(8) *Merger*. Without limiting the generality of Article 20.1(10), a Party shall consolidate with or merge with or into another entity, whether or not such Party is the surviving entity of such transaction, unless immediately after such consolidation or merger, the owners of the equity interests in such Party prior to the transaction continue to own directly or indirectly more than fifty percent (50%) of the new or surviving entity; or

(9) *Sale of Substantially All Assets*. Without limiting the generality of Article 20.1(10), a Party shall sell or otherwise dispose of, or enter into an understanding, agreement or commitment to sell or otherwise dispose of, (i) all or substantially all of its assets or (ii) all or substantially all of the assets of such Party's business component which is primarily responsible for carrying out the obligations of this Contract, to a third party (other than, in the case of Party B, to its Associated Companies); or

(10) *Acquisition by Third Party.* If a third party (other than, in the case of Party B, to its Associated Companies) acquires twenty percent (20%) or more of the outstanding equity interests in such Party, and any other Party determines, in its reasonable judgment, that (i) such third party is a competitor of the Company or (ii) such acquisition of the equity interests by the third party is detrimental to the business of such other Party, the Company or any Associated Company of such other Party; or

(11) *Transfer of Equity Interest in Violation of Agreement.* A Party shall transfer any of its equity interest in the Company to a third party in violation of the provisions of Article 6.9 and, upon application by any other Party to invalidate such transfer, the Approval Authority refuses to invalidate the transfer or fails to respond to such application within three (3) months following the date on which such application is made; *provided,* that such circumstances shall constitute a Termination Event only upon the declaration of any non-transferring Party; or

(12) *Expropriation of Assets.* All or any material portion of the assets of the Company are nationalized, expropriated or otherwise confiscated by any PRC national, provincial or local authority; or

(13) *Failure to Agree Regarding Amendments.* The Parties shall fail to agree upon the amendments required by Article 18.3;

then, in any such event, the provisions of Articles 20.2 and 20.3 shall apply.

Article 20.2. *Sale Upon Termination.*

If a Termination Event as set forth in Article 20.1 occurs and is continuing and one of the Parties has notified the other Parties thereof, Party B may purchase the equity interest of Party A in the Company and continue to operate the Company in accordance with the following terms:

(1) *Appraisals; Determination of Going Concern Value.* Each of Party A and Party B shall, within forty-five (45) days after delivery of notice of such Termination Event, appoint one (1) internationally-recognized certified public accounting firm (other than any firm that is then acting or in the past has acted as the primary accounting firm of the Company or as the primary accounting firm of any of the Parties) which shall have passed the qualification verification by the relevant Governmental Authorities, to calculate the Going Concern Value of the Company. Each accounting firm shall issue a written appraisal report setting forth the Going Concern Value of the Company within forty-five (45) days after the date on which such accounting firm was appointed. If the two

appraisals differ by ten percent ([x]%) or less, the average of the two appraisals shall be adopted as the Going Concern Value of the Company. If the two appraisals differ by a margin of more than ten percent ([x]%), then the two accounting firms shall jointly select a third internationally-recognized certified public accounting firm (other than any firm that is then acting as the primary accounting firm of the Company or as the primary accounting firm of any of the Parties) to calculate the Going Concern Value of the Company (which appraisal shall be within the range of valuations established by the first two appraisals), and the calculation by such accounting firm of the Going Concern Value of the Company shall be final and binding for all purposes. The third accounting firm shall complete its appraisal report within thirty (30) days of its appointment. The expense of the valuation proceedings shall be borne by the Parties pro rata in the proportion that the equity interest in the Company owned by a Party bears to the total of the equity interests in the Company owned by all of the Parties. If either Party A or Party B fails to appoint an independent and competent accounting firm within the time limit set forth above, the appraisal prepared by the accounting firm appointed by the other Party in accordance with the foregoing provisions shall be deemed to be final and conclusive and shall be adopted as the Going Concern Value.

(2) *Option of Party A to Transfer Equity Interest—Termination Under Certain Provisions.* If a Termination Event described in paragraphs (6), (8), (9), (10) or (11) of Article 20.1 exists with respect to Party B, commencing on the date Party A receives notice of the Going Concern Value of the Company, Party A shall have the option to transfer its equity interest in the Company to Party B at a price equal to the product of (x) one hundred ten percent (1[x]%) of the Going Concern Value of the Company as determined pursuant to paragraph 1.1(1) above *multiplied* by (y) Party A's Percentage of the registered capital of the Company at the time of the purchase. Party A's ability to exercise this option shall lapse [forty-five (45)] days after the receipt of such notice. Party A shall exercise such option by sending written notice thereof to Party B.

(3) *Option of Party B to Purchase Equity Interest—Termination Under Certain Provisions.* If a Termination Event described in paragraphs of (6), (8), (9), (10) or (11) of Article 20.1 exists with respect to Party A, commencing on the date Party B receives notice of the Going Concern Value of the Company, Party B shall have the option to purchase Party A's equity interest in the Company at a price equal to the product of (x)

ninety percent (90%) of the Going Concern Value of the Company as determined pursuant to paragraph 1.1(1) above *multiplied* by (y) Party A's Percentage of the registered capital of the Company at the time of the purchase. Party B's ability to exercise this option shall lapse [forty-five (45)] days after the receipt of such notice. Party B shall exercise such option by sending written notice thereof to Party A.

(4) *Option of Party B to Purchase Equity Interest—Other Provisions.* If a Termination Event that is not covered by paragraphs (2) and (3) of this Article 20.2 exists, commencing on the date Party B receives notice of the Going Concern Value of the Company, Party B shall have an option to purchase Party A's equity interest in the registered capital of the Company at a price equal to the product of (x) the Going Concern Value of the Company as determined pursuant to paragraph (1) above *multiplied* by (y) Party A's Percentage of the registered capital of the Company at the time of such purchase. Party B's ability to exercise this option shall lapse [forty-five (45)] days after the receipt of such notice. Party B shall exercise such option by sending written notice thereof to Party A.

(5) *Contract Evidencing Transfer Under Option.* If either of Party A or Party B chooses to exercise its option as set forth in this Article 20.2, then they shall forthwith enter into a contract setting forth the transfer of such equity interests in the Company and the purchase price as determined pursuant to paragraph (2), (3) or (4), as the case may be, of this Article 20.2. Payment of the purchase price pursuant to such option shall be made by Party B not later than [sixty (60)] days after the date on which such contract has obtained all required government approvals. If such government approvals cannot be obtained within [sixty (60)] days after the date on which such option is exercised (or such later date as may be determined by the Party exercising the option in its sole discretion), such contract, at the option of the Party exercising the option, shall be null and void, and the provisions of Article 20.3 shall apply.

(6) *Form of Purchase Price.* The payment of the purchase price shall be in United States Dollars.

Article 20.3. *Termination.*

Upon:

(1) the failure of the Parties or the Company, as set forth in paragraph 1.1(5) of Article 20.2, to obtain government approval for the purchase contract in respect of either Party's exercise of the options set forth in such Article 20.2, or

(2) the failure of both Party B and Party A to exercise their options pursuant to Article 20.2 within the time periods set forth therein, or
(3) the failure by both Party B and Party A to appoint accountants pursuant to paragraph (1) of Article 20.2 within [thirty (30)] days after delivery by any Party to the other of notice of the occurrence of a Termination Event [(except in the case of a Termination Event as described in paragraph (5) of Article 20.1)], or
(4) written notice by a Party to the other Parties that a Termination Event as described in paragraph (5) of Article 20.1 has occurred, or
(5) the expiration of the Company's original term (if not extended) or any extension thereof,

then the Company shall be dissolved and the Contract terminated in accordance with the Joint Venture Law, the implementing regulations issued thereunder and the Articles of Association, and it shall be deemed as if the Board of Directors has made a unanimous approval for the Company to be dissolved.

CHAPTER 21.

DISPOSAL OF THE ASSETS ON DISSOLUTION

Article 21.1. *Liquidation Committee.*
Upon the expiry of the Company's term or upon earlier termination of this Contract, the Board of Directors shall establish a Liquidation Committee in accordance with the "Implementation Regulations of the PRC on Joint Ventures Using Chinese and Foreign Investment," "Provisions on Liquidation of Foreign Investment Enterprises," and other relevant laws and governmental regulations. The Liquidation Committee shall establish procedures for liquidation of the assets of the Company and settling the liabilities thereof as described below. The Liquidation Committee shall consist of one (1) member appointed by Party A and six (6) members appointed by Party B. One of the members appointed by Party B shall be the Chairman of the Liquidation Committee and the member appointed by Party A shall be the Vice Chairman of the Liquidation Committee. Such members may be, but are not required to be, members of the Board of Directors.

Article 21.2. *Liquidation Procedure.*
The Liquidation Committee shall render a full and complete accounting of the Company's property and assets, and liabilities; prepare detailed schedules of liabilities and assets; propose a settlement scheme; and supervise the implementation thereof after approval by the Board of Directors.

Article 21.3. *Legal Actions.*
The Liquidation Committee may represent the Company in bringing or defending any legal actions on behalf of the Company.

Article 21.4. *Priority Disbursements.*
Liquidation expenses and expenses of the Liquidation Committee and the wages of the members of the liquidation working group shall be paid out of the remaining assets of the Company by according such expenses a first priority in the distribution of such assets. Liquidation costs include:
(1) fees required for the management, sale and distribution of the Company's assets;
(2) public announcement and litigation and arbitration fees; and
(3) other fees incurred in the course of liquidation.

Article 21.5. *Residual Assets.*
After the Liquidation Committee has settled all the legitimate debts of the Company (including tax) (including, if applicable, the expenses of the Liquidation Committee in accordance with Article 21.4), the remaining assets, shall be distributed to the Parties in accordance with their respective Percentage of the registered capital. As between the Parties, Party B shall have first priority with respect to any remaining foreign exchange assets of the Company provided that in all events the remaining assets will be distributed to the Parties in accordance with their respective interests.

Article 21.6. *Publication.*
After all accounts have been settled, the Company shall present a report approved by the Liquidation Committee and the Board of Directors to the Approval Authority (a copy of which shall be delivered to each Party) and shall complete formalities with the ____________ Municipal Administration Bureau for Industry and Commerce to cancel the Company's business registration, return the business license, and at the same time make a public announcement.

CHAPTER 22.
FORCE MAJEURE

Article 22.1. *Force Majeure.*
Any party to this Contract shall be excused from its obligations hereunder when and to the extent that performance is delayed or prevented by any event of Force Majeure. "Force Majeure" shall mean any event beyond the reasonable control of a Party, and which is unavoidable notwithstanding the

reasonable care of the Party or Parties affected, and shall include force of nature, fire, explosion, geological change, storm, flood, earthquake, lightning, act of war, or total or partial failure of the sources of supply of materials or energy or of means of transportation. The Party or Parties affected by Force Majeure which seeks to excuse its performance under this Contract or under any of the provisions hereunder shall promptly notify the other Party to this Contract advising of the excuse and the steps it will take to complete such performance. Each Party seeking the excuse will be excused from such performance to the extent such performance is delayed or prevented provided that the Party or Parties so affected shall use the utmost reasonable practicable efforts to complete such performance. The Parties agree to resume performance hereunder with the utmost dispatch whenever the causes of such excuse are cured or remedied.

CHAPTER 23.

CONFIDENTIALITY

Article 23.1. *Disclosure Limitation.*
Each Party shall maintain in confidence all confidential information (oral or written) identified as such received from the Company or the other Parties, whether of a commercial or technical nature ("Confidential Information"), shall use such Confidential Information only for the benefit of the Company and shall not disclose any such Confidential Information to a third party or make any unauthorized use thereof. Each Party shall treat such Confidential Information with the same degree of care against disclosure or unauthorized use which it affords to its own confidential information of a similar nature or a reasonable degree of care, whichever is greater. The obligation of confidential treatment shall not apply to any Confidential Information that (i) has become generally available in the public domain, (ii) was in the receiving Party's possession prior to disclosure as evidenced by documentary records, (iii) was independently developed by the receiving Party, provided that the Person(s) developing the same did not have prior access to Confidential Information received from the Company or the other Parties or (iv) was received from a third party who had a right to disclose such information. Notwithstanding the foregoing obligations, any Party may use, disclose or have an interest in any technology or know-how belonging to the Company pursuant to a valid license from or agreement with the Company.

Article 23.2. *Required Actions.*
In furtherance, and not in limitation, of the foregoing, each Party agrees to do the following with respect to all such Confidential Information of the other Parties or the Company: (i) instruct and require all of its Representatives to maintain the confidentiality of such Confidential Information and not to use such Confidential Information except as expressly permitted herein; and (ii) restrict disclosure of such Confidential Information to those of its Representatives who have a "need to know" consistent with the purposes for which such Confidential Information was disclosed. Each Party further agrees not to remove or destroy any proprietary or confidential legends or markings placed upon any documentation or other materials.

Article 23.3. *Permitted Disclosures.*
In the event that a Party or any of its Representatives is requested pursuant to or required by the disclosure requirements of any rule, regulation or form of any Governmental Authority or by oral questions, interrogatories, requests for information or documents by any Governmental Authority or other Person in legal proceedings, subpoenas, civil investigative demands or other similar processes to disclose any of the Confidential Information received from a disclosing Party or the Company, the recipient Party so requested or required or whose Representative has been so requested or required shall provide the disclosing Party or the Company, as the case may be, with prompt written notice of any such request or requirement so that the disclosing Party or the Company, as the case may be, may object to production, seek a protective order or other appropriate remedy and/or waive compliance with the provisions of this Contract. The recipient Party or representative shall exercise its best efforts (at the sole expense of the disclosing Party) to preserve the confidentiality of such Confidential Information, including, without limitation, by cooperating with the disclosing Party or the Company, as the case may be, to obtain an appropriate protective order or other reliable assurance that confidential treatment will be accorded such Confidential Information. If, in the absence of a protective order or other remedy or the receipt of a waiver of the disclosing Party, such recipient Party or any of its representatives is nonetheless legally compelled to disclose such Confidential Information to any tribunal or else stand liable for contempt or suffer other censure or significant penalty, such recipient Party or representative may, without liability hereunder, disclose to such tribunal only that portion of the Confidential Information which is legally required to be disclosed.

CHAPTER 24.

APPLICABLE LAW

Article 24.1. *Applicable Law.*
The formation of this Contract, its validity, interpretation, execution and settlement of any disputes arising hereunder shall be governed by and construed in accordance with the laws of the PRC.

CHAPTER 25.

SETTLEMENT OF DISPUTES

Article 25.1. *Consultation.*
In the event of any dispute, controversy, or claim arising out of or relating to any provision of this Contract or the interpretation, enforceability, performance, breach, termination, or validity hereof, including, without limitation, this Chapter 25 (a "Dispute"), the Parties shall attempt, in good faith, to amicably resolve the Dispute. Any Party may give the other Parties written notice of any Dispute not resolved in the normal course of business. Within twenty (20) days after receipt of said notice, the General Manager and the Deputy General Managers shall negotiate in good faith to resolve the Dispute. If such individuals are not successful, the matter shall be referred to the Officials who shall confer in an attempt to agree on a resolution of the Dispute. If either the relevant individuals or the Officials are successful, the Parties shall take all action necessary to ensure that their resolution of the Dispute is implemented in a manner consistent with all requirements of applicable law. If the Dispute has not been resolved within one hundred twenty (120) days of the receipt of the disputing Party's notice by the other Parties, or if the other Parties will not meet within twenty (20) days of its receipt of such notice, any Party may submit the Dispute to arbitration as provided in Article 25.2. If an executive of a Party intends to be accompanied at a meeting by an attorney, the executives of the other Parties shall be given at least five (5) business days notice of such intention and may also be accompanied by attorneys.

Article 25.2. *Arbitration.*

(1) Any Dispute that is not resolved pursuant to Article 25.1 within one hundred twenty (120) days of the receipt of the disputing Party's notice by the other Parties, or that may otherwise be referred to arbitration pursuant to Article 25.1, shall be referred to and finally resolved by

arbitration under the Rules of Conciliation and Arbitration of the International Chamber of Commerce in force at that time which rules are deemed to be incorporated by reference into this Article 25.2, by three arbitrators appointed by ________________________. The language of arbitration shall be English and the place of arbitration shall be ________________.

(2) The award of the arbitrator(s) shall be the sole and exclusive remedy between the Parties regarding any and all claims and counterclaims with respect to the subject matter of the Dispute and shall be binding and conclusive upon the Parties, their successors and assigns, and each shall comply in good faith with any and all rulings of the arbitrator(s).
(3) Judgment upon the award of the arbitrators may be entered in any court of competent jurisdiction.
(4) Notwithstanding the foregoing, where such a Dispute exists, either Party A or Party B is also a party to an arbitral proceeding arising out of the same transaction or series of related transactions, and there is a possibility of conflicting rulings on a common issue of law or fact, the parties shall, if the other parties to such arbitral proceeding agree, consolidate such proceeding and the arbitration hereunder.

Article 25.3. *Operation of the Company.*
Throughout the pendency of any dispute or difference submitted to the Officials or their representatives for resolution pursuant to Article 25.1 or to arbitration pursuant to Article 25.2, the Company shall continue to conduct its business activities in accordance with the business plans for the Company then in effect.

CHAPTER 26.

LANGUAGE

Article 26.1. *Language of the Contract.*
This Contract is written both in the Chinese and English languages. Both versions shall have equal validity.

CHAPTER 27.

EFFECTIVENESS OF THE CONTRACT AND MISCELLANEOUS

Article 27.1. *Effective Date.*
The Contract shall become effective on the Effective Date.

Article 27.2. *Prior Agreements.*
This Contract and its Exhibits, which are hereby incorporated by reference as inseparable and integral parts of this Contract, constitute the whole and entire agreement between the Parties and shall supersede any other previous oral or written agreements or communications among the Parties relating to the Company or the joint venture among the Parties.

Article 27.3. *Waiver.*
Waiver by any Party of a breach of or right under this Contract must be in writing and will not constitute a waiver of any other or subsequent breach or right.

Article 27.4. *Notice.*
In any case where any notice or other communication is required or permitted to be given hereunder, such notice or communication shall be in writing and (i) personally delivered, (ii) sent by international air courier service with confirmation of delivery requested or (iii) transmitted by fax as follows:

If to Party A: ______________________________
____
____
Fax: ________________________
Tel: ________________________

If to Party B: ______________________________
____
____
Fax: ________________________
Tel: ________________________

All such notices or other communications shall be deemed to have been given and received (i) upon receipt if personally delivered, (ii) when delivery is confirmed if sent by international air courier service and (iii) when confirmed (either orally or in writing) if by fax.

Article 27.5. *Table of Contents; Headings.*
The table of contents and chapter, article and other headings of this Contract are for convenience of reference only and still not be deemed or construed as in any way limiting or extending the language of the provisions to which the table of contents and such chapters, articles and other headings may refer. Unless otherwise stated, references to Chapters, Articles and Exhibits herein are references to Chapters, Articles and Exhibits hereof.

Article 27.6. *Severability.*
If any provision of this Contract should be or become fully or partly invalid, illegal or unenforceable in any respect for any reason whatsoever, the validity, legality and enforceability of the remaining provisions of this Contract shall not in any way be affected or impaired thereby.

Article 27.7. *Original Copies.*
This Contact is executed in three (3) original counterparts each of which shall have equal effect in law.

IN WITNESS WHEREOF, the Parties hereto have signed this Contract as of [ ], ___________.

PARTY A:

By: ________________________________
Name:
Title:

PARTY B:

By: ________________________________
Name:
Title:

EQUITY TRANSFER AGREEMENT

This EQUITY TRANSFER AGREEMENT (this "Agreement") is entered into on the _____ day of ________, by the following four parties:

1. Name: ______________________________
   (the "Transferor")
   Address: ______________________________
   ____
   ____
   ____
   Legal Representative:
   Title:
   Nationality:
2. Name: ______________________________
   (the "Chinese Partner")
   Address: ______________________________
   ____
   ____
   ____
   Legal Representative:
   Title:
   Nationality:
3. Name: ______________________________
   (the "Company")
   Address: ______________________________
   ____
   ____
   ____
   Legal Representative:
   Title:
   Nationality:
4. Name: ______________________________
   (the "Transferee")
   Address: ______________________________
   ____
   ____
   ____
   Legal Representative:
   Title:
   Nationality:

WHEREAS:

1. The Company was originally organized under the Joint Venture Agreement for the Company between the Transferor and the Chinese Partner on [__________, _______] (the "Original Agreement") and the Articles of Association for the Company (the "Original Articles"). The Original Agreement and the Original Articles became effective on [__________, _______] with the approval of the [______________] (hereinafter referred to as the "Original Approval Authority") (approval document no. ___________).

2. According to the Capital Payment Verification Report issued by [the CPA firm] on [__________, _______] (the "Capital Payment Verification Report"), as of the date of verification, the Transferor had invested USD________________ in the Company, and the Chinese Partner had invested USD__________ in the Company; giving the Transferor [x]% and the Chinese Partner [y]% of the paid-up registered capital of the Company.

3. On [__________, _______], the Transferor, the Transferee and [XYZ] Bank (hereinafter referred to as the "Lender") entered into and executed a loan agreement (hereinafter referred to as the "Loan Agreement"), pursuant to which [XYZ] Bank provided to the Transferor a [US$________] credit facility with the Transferee acting as the Loan Agent.

4. In order to induce the Lender to make Loans under the Loan Agreement, the Transferor and the Transferee proposed and are to sign a pledge agreement (the "Pledge Agreement"), pursuant to which the Transferor is to pledge and assign, to the Transferee as the Security Agent thereunder, for the ratable benefit of the Lender, the Lender and/or the Loan Agent, the [x]% equity interest it holds in the Company as a continuing security for the due and punctual payment of its obligations under the Loan Agreement.

5. It is a condition precedent to, among other things, the execution and effectuation of the Pledge Agreement that the Chinese Partner agrees to the equity transfer contemplated by this Agreement upon the occurrence of any Event of Default listed in Article [____] of such proposed Pledge Agreement (an "Event of Default"); and the Transferee and the Lender are relying on the undertakings of the Chinese Partner and the undertakings of the Transferor herein;

NOW, THEREFORE, the Chinese Partner, the Transferor and the Company hereby agree with the Transferee for the ratable benefit of the Transferee, the Lender and/or the Loan Agent as follows:

1. *Equity Transfer.*
   a) *Transfer of Equity Interest.* The Transferor hereby agrees to transfer all of its [x]% equity interest in the Company to the Transferee, or at its direction, to any third party or parties, to satisfy its obligations, for the ratable benefit of the Transferee, the Lender and/or the Loan Agent, under the Loan Agreement and the proposed Pledge Agreement, upon the occurrence of any Event of Default.
   b) *Acceptance of Equity Interest.* The Transferee hereby agrees to accept such [x]% equity interest in the Company from the Transferor to set off all or any part of the Transferor's obligations under the Loan Agreement and the proposed Pledge Agreement upon the occurrence of any Event of Default.
   c) *Waiver of Right of First Refusal.* The Chinese Partner hereby agrees to the aforementioned equity transfer from the Transferor to the Transferee and further waives its right of first refusal with respect to such equity transfer.
   d) *Valuation of Equity Interest.* Both the Transferor and the Transferee agree that, for purposes of satisfying the Transferor's obligations under the Loan Agreement and the proposed Pledge Agreement, the value of the Transferor's equity in the Company to be transferred shall equal to (i) USD____________ as stated in the aforementioned Capital Payment Verification Report or (ii) [x]% of the amount of the book value of the Company's total assets at the time of delivery of a notice of default minus the Company's total liabilities at such times, whichever is less. Such book value of the Company's total assets and total liabilities shall be determined by an independent certified public accountant registered in China and acceptable to both the Transferor and the Transferee, within five (5) days after delivery of a notice of default by the Transferee to the Transferor upon the occurrence of any Event of Default. The expenses and fees in connection therewith shall be borne by the Transferor.
   e) *New Capital Payment Verification Report.* Following the aforementioned equity transfer, the Chinese Partner and the Transferee shall cause the Company to immediately engage a China-registered accountant to verify the capital contributions of both parties after such equity transfer and issue a new Capital Payment Verification Report to reflect the replacement

of the Transferor by the Transferee as the holder of 80% of the equity in the Company.

f) *Cessation of Transferor's Participation and Rights in Company.* Following such transfer, the Transferor shall cease to have any direct or indirect, formal or informal, participation in the business and financial affairs and operations of the Company and, shall cease to have any rights over any tangible or intangible capital assets of the Company.

2. *Transferor's Representations and Warranties.*
   a) *Representations and Warranties.* The Transferor represents and warrants as to itself that:
      (i) *Duly Organized.* It is duly incorporated, validly existing and in good standing under the laws of the country of its incorporation;
      (ii) *Duly Executed.* The execution, delivery and performance of this Agreement by it:
         (1) are within its corporate power and business scope;
         (2) have been duly authorized by all necessary corporate action for proper authorization;
         (3) do not contravene any law or contractual restriction binding on or affecting it;
      (iii) *Enforceability.* Subject to the approval of the Original Approval Authority, this Agreement constitutes its legal, valid and binding obligations enforceable in accordance with its terms;
      (iv) *Ownership.* The Transferor holds complete and valid ownership and disposition rights in and to the equity to be transferred to the Transferee pursuant to Section 1;
      (v) *Governmental Approval.* The equity transfer to the Transferee hereunder requires no approval from any governmental authority other than the Original Approval Authority;
      (vi) *No Liens.* There exists no mortgage, pledge, lien, other security interest, preferential right or trust right whatsoever over the equity to be transferred to Transferee hereunder.
   b) *Indemnity for Breach.* The Transferor undertakes to indemnify the Transferee against any losses that may result from untruthful representations and warranties in Section 2(a) above.

3. *Transferee's Representations and Warranties.* The Transferee represents and warrants as follows:

a) *Duly Organized.* It is a corporation duly incorporated, validly existing and in good standing under the laws of the country of its incorporation.

b) *Duly Executed.* The execution, delivery and performance of this Agreement by the Transferee:

(i) are within its corporate power and business scope;

(ii) have been duly authorized by all necessary corporate action for proper authorization;

(iii) do not contravene any law or contractual restriction binding on or affecting the Transferee.

c) *Enforceability.* Subject to the approval from the Original Approval Authority, this Agreement constitutes its legal, valid and binding obligations enforceable in accordance with its terms.

4. *Chinese Partner's Representations and Warranties.* The Chinese Partner represents and warrants as follows:

a) *Duly Organized.* It is a corporation duly incorporated and validly existing under the laws of the People's Republic of China.

b) *Duly Executed.* The execution, delivery and performance of this Agreement by the Chinese Partner:

(i) are within its corporate power and business scope;

(ii) have been duly authorized by all necessary corporate action for proper authorization;

(iii) do not contravene any law or contractual restriction binding on or affecting the Chinese Partner.

c) *Enforceability.* Subject to the approval from the Original Approval Authority, this Agreement constitutes its legal, valid and binding obligations enforceable in accordance with its terms.

5. *Company's Representations and Warranties.* The Company represents and warrants as follows:

a) *Duly Organized.* It is a corporation duly incorporated, validly existing and in good standing under the laws of the People's Republic of China.

b) *Duly Executed.* The execution, delivery and performance of this Agreement by the Company:

(i) are within its corporate power and business scope;

(ii) have been duly authorized by all necessary corporate action for proper authorization;

(iii) do not contravene any law or contractual restriction binding on or affecting the Company.

c) *Enforceability.* Subject to the approval from the Original Approval Authority, this Agreement constitutes its legal, valid and binding obligations enforceable in accordance with its terms.

6. *Representations and Warranties of the Transferor, the Chinese Partner and the Company.*

a) *Representations and Warranties.* The Transferor, the Chinese Partner and the Company jointly and severally represent and warrant as follows:

(i) *Financial Statements.* The Transferor, the Chinese Partner and the Company have, to the best of their ability, caused the Company to submit to Transferee and its designated representative the Company's financial statements as of ________________, __________ and all necessary documents and information (the "Financial Statements"). The Transferor, the Chinese Partner and the Company hereby confirm that the Financial Statements correctly reflect the Company's financial status as of ____________________, __________. The Financial Statements have been provided by the Company and confirmed with signatures by the Transferor and the Chinese Partner and are attached hereto as Attachment 1;

(ii) *No Unfavorable Changes.* The Company has undergone no unfavorable changes in its operation, effectiveness, finances and assets since ____________, ________;

(iii) *No Liens.* There exists no mortgage, pledge, lien, other security interest, preferential right or trust right whatsoever over any property owned by the Company;

(iv) *No Violation of Law.* The Company, the Transferor and the Chinese Partner have not engaged or participated in any violation of China's laws and regulations such that the Company would be subject, now or in the future, to revocation of its business license, fines or other legal or administrative punishment that would materially adversely affect the operation of the Company;

(v) *No Legal Action.* The Company, the Transferor and the Chinese Partner are not involved in any Company-related legal action, arbitration, investigation or administrative procedure that is either ongoing or likely to start;

(vi) *No Other Debts.* The Financial Statements list all debts, overdue payments and unpaid taxes of the Company as of ___________, _______. No debts, overdue payments or unpaid taxes other than those listed in the Financial Statements has resulted or will result from operational activities of the Company prior to ___________, _______. The Company has not incurred any debts, overdue payments or unpaid taxes other than in the ordinary course of business since ___________, _______, and the Company is required to keep its expenditures within the ordinary course of business until the date on which the equity transfer provided by Section 1 of this Agreement is completed.

(vii) *Duly Organized.* The Company is duly incorporated, validly existing and in good standing under the laws of the People's Republic of China. The Company possesses all required and necessary licenses and registrations to conduct its business as currently conducted;

(viii) *No Employee-Related Fees.* As of the effective date of this Agreement pursuant to Section 17 below, the Company has no outstanding payment obligations in respect of employee pension funds, unemployment insurance, labor welfare funds, or any other employee-related fees and reserves.

b) *Liability for Breach.* The Transferor and the Chinese Partner shall jointly and severally bear all economic and legal liabilities resulting from any breach of the representations and warranties under Section 6(a) above and shall indemnify the Transferee against any losses that may result from such breach.

7. *Conditions Precedent to Effectuation of this Agreement.* The effectuation of this Agreement is subject to (a) all the representations and warranties of the Transferor and the Chinese Partner contained herein being true and accurate in all material respects as of the date made and as of the date of execution, and (b) the Transferee's receipt of evidence

that the Original Approval Authority has approved this Agreement and the equity transfer hereunder;

8. *Post-transfer Proportions of Equity Holdings and Profit and Risk Sharing.*

a) *Equity Holdings.* Following completion of the equity transfer hereunder, the Transferee shall hold [x]% of the equity in the Company and the Chinese Partner shall hold [y]% of the equity in the Company. The Transferee and the Chinese Partner shall both facilitate the issuance by the Company of a Certificate of Capital Contribution to the Transferee and the Chinese Partner respectively based on the Capital Payment Verification Report pursuant to Section 1(e) above and the Capital Payment Verification Certificates issued by the Company based upon such Capital Payment Verification Report.

b) *Profit and Risk Sharing.* The Transferee and the Chinese Partner agree that from the day of issuance of the new business license for the Company following the equity transfers hereunder, the Transferee and the Chinese Partner shall apportion any profits of the Company such that the Transferee receives [x]% thereof and the Chinese Partner receives [y]% thereof. All related risks shall be apportioned likewise.

9. *Apportionment of Relevant Expenses.* All relevant expenses incurred in connection with the equity transfers hereunder (including but not limited to the accountants' fees and amendment fees for the industry and commerce registration) shall be borne by the Transferor; provided that all attorneys' fees and other consultants' fees shall be borne by the party incurring the same.

10. *New Contract of the Company.* The Transferee and the Chinese Partner shall through consultation sign a new or amended Contract to replace the current Contract. Such new or amended Contract shall be written in both Chinese and English and shall become effective following approval by the Original Approval Authority. Upon completion of the equity transfer, the Transferee shall have the right to rename the Company after consultation with the Chinese Partner.

11. *Confidentiality of the Transaction.* Any information received by any party from any other party in connection with the transfer contemplated by this Agreement shall be deemed to be confidential. The parties hereto agree that any such information shall be used solely for the purpose of evaluating and consummating the transfer contemplated hereby, and that no party shall publish through the news media or leak

or disclose to any person who is not a party to this Agreement any such information.

12. *Agreement to Perform Necessary Acts.* Each party hereto agrees to do any and all things, take any and all the actions, perform any further acts and execute and deliver any further documents that are reasonably necessary to carry out and effect the provisions of this Agreement.

13. *Resolution of Disputes.*

a) *Arbitration.* All disputes in connection with this Agreement shall be settled by friendly consultations among the relevant parties. In the event no agreement can be reached within sixty days after one party proposes friendly consultations to settle such dispute, any relevant party may bring such dispute to the [Shenzhen Branch of the Chinese International Economic and Trade Arbitration Commission in Shenzhen, China] for arbitration under the then current rules of such commission.

b) *Language.* The language used in arbitration shall be Chinese and English. Any document used in arbitration may be written in Chinese and/or English.

c) *Expenses.* Any arbitration decision shall be final and all expenses for arbitration shall be borne by the losing party.

14. *Governing Laws.* This Agreement shall be governed by the laws of the People's Republic of China.

15. *Languages.* This Agreement is written in both Chinese and English. Both versions shall have equal legal validity.

16. *Entire Agreement.* This Agreement represents the entire agreement among the parties hereto regarding the equity transfers contemplated hereby and replaces and supersedes any other written or oral agreements among such parties on the same subject.

17. *Terms of Validity.* This Agreement shall be submitted for approval to the Original Approval Authority after due execution by authorized representatives from the Chinese Partner, the Transferor, the Transferee and the Company and shall become effective on the day the approval document is issued by the Original Approval Authority.

The agreement is signed on the ______ day of __________, ______ in ________, China by the representatives of the parties.

THE TRANSFEROR

Representative: ________________________
Name:
Title:

THE CHINESE PARTNER

Representative: ________________________
Name:
Title:

THE COMPANY

Representative: ________________________
Name:
Title:

THE TRANSFEREE

Representative: ________________________
Name:
Title:

SAMPLE ARBITRATION CLAUSE

1. *Arbitration.* Any and all dispute, disagreement, controversy, or claim arising out of or relating to this contract, or the breach, termination, or invalidity thereof, shall be settled through consultation between the parties. [In the event that the parties are unable to resolve their differences through consultation, the matter shall be submitted to the China International Economic and Trade Arbitration Commission (CIETAC) for mediation and conciliation.][1] In the event that the parties are unable to settle this matter through consultation [or mediation] within a period of thirty (30) days, either party has a right to submit this matter for binding and final arbitration before CIETAC.

2. *Location of Proceedings.* The arbitration proceeding, including all hearings or meetings, shall be in [__________].

3. *Provisional Remedies.* Either party to this contract may request any judicial or other authority to order any provisional or conservatory measure, including attachment, seizure, garnishment, or sealing, prior to the institution of the arbitration proceeding, or during the proceeding, for the preservation of its rights and interests.

4. *Governing Arbitration Rules.* Any arbitration proceeding pursuant to this contract shall be conducted in accordance with the arbitration rules of CIETAC in effect on the date on which the proceeding is instituted. If the terms and provisions of this contract differ from CIETAC's arbitration rules, the language of this contract shall be controlling and supersede the arbitration rules.

5. *Selection of Arbitrators.* The arbitral tribunal shall consist of three (3) arbitrators. Each party shall have the right to choose one (1) arbitrator from CIETAC's approved list of arbitrators. The third arbitrator, who shall be the presiding arbitrator, shall be selected by mutual consent of the parties from CIETAC's list of arbitrators, or by CIETAC in the event that the parties are unable to agree. The presiding arbitrator shall be a national of a country other than the People's Republic of China or [the United States of America].

6. *Governing Law.* This contract shall be governed by and construed in accordance with the laws of the People's Republic of China.[2]

---

1. If the parties wish to forego mediation as a formal second step in the dispute resolution process, this sentence may be omitted. Under CIETAC rules, the subject of mediation will be broached by the arbitrators and the commission before and during an arbitration proceeding.

2. The parties have the right to choose the applicable law in contracts other than joint ventures and those involving the exploitation and exploration of natural resources.

7. *Governing Language.* This contract shall be executed in both [English] and Chinese, and [English] shall be the governing language. The mediation and arbitration proceedings shall be conducted in [English], and documents in the [English] language shall be accepted by the tribunal.

8. *Attorneys' Fees.* The prevailing party shall be entitled to an award of arbitration expenses including an award for reasonable attorneys' fees, expert witnesses fees, arbitrator fees, and all other reasonable costs and expenses incurred with respect to the arbitration proceeding.

SAMPLE LETTER OF CREDITWORTHINESS

(Bank Letterhead)

Date________________

Ministry of Foreign Trade and
Economic Cooperation
Commission of Foreign Trade and
Economic Cooperation
Beijing Municipal People's Government
190 Chao Yang Men Nei Da Jie
Beijing, China

Dear Sir/Madam:

We confirm that ____________ (the "Corporation"), has been a valued deposit and credit customer of this bank since 19/20___. The Corporation maintains a combined average deposit balance in the low ten (10) figure range and XYZ Bank has total credit commitments in the low ten (10) figure range for the Corporation. To date, all deposit and credit facilities have been handled as agreed and the Corporation's management has maintained a satisfactory working relationship with XYZ Bank.

We consider the Corporation to be highly respectable and undoubted for their normal business engagements and that it is able to fulfill contractual obligations it enters into.

The above information is provided in strict confidence and without any responsibility on the part of the bank or its officers.

____
Vice President/Credit Executive

Appendix B

Bibliography and Electronic Research Guide

A. Selected Bibliography

1. Laws and Regulations: English/Chinese Translations and Services

China's Foreign Economic Legislation, vol. I–IV (China Foreign Language Press, 1979–85)

China Hand, vol. 1–2 (The Economist Intelligence Unit)

China Laws for Foreign Business, Business Regulation, vol. 1–4 (CCH International)

China Laws for Foreign Business, Special Zones and Cities, vol. 1–3 (CCH International)

China Laws for Foreign Business, Customs (CCH International)

China Laws for Foreign Business, Taxation (CCH International)

China Law and Practice, 10 issues per year (Asia Law & Practice)

China Law Reference Service, vol. 1–8 (CCH International)

Laws of the People's Republic of China, vol. 1–5 (Lubrecht & Cramer, 1996) (Legislative Affairs Commission of the Standing Committee of the National People's Congress of the People's Republic of China)

2. Treatises/Law Review and Business Review Articles

a. Arbitration and Mediation

B. BEAUMONT, D. CHOI, AND J. LUK, COMMENTARY ON THE CHINESE ARBITRATION ACT (Simmonds & Hill Publishing, Ltd., 1995)

B. BEAUMONT AND H. MARCUS, CHINESE INTERNATIONAL COMMERCIAL ARBITRATION (Simmonds & Hill Publishing, Ltd., 1994)

Bersani, *Enforcement of Arbitration Awards in China: Foreigners Find the System Sorely Lacking,* CHIN. BUS. REV., May–June 1992, at 6

C. DEJUN, M. MOSER, AND W. SHENGCHANG, INTERNATIONAL ARBITRATION IN THE PEOPLE'S REPUBLIC OF CHINA: COMMENTARY, CASES AND MATERIALS, SECOND EDITION (Butterworths, 2000)

N. KAPLAN, J. SPRUCE, AND M. MOSER, HONG KONG AND CHINA ARBITRATION: CASES AND MATERIALS (Michie, 1994)

M. MOSER, INTERNATIONAL ARBITRATION IN THE PEOPLE'S REPUBLIC OF CHINA (Michie, 1995)

Note, *Playing by a New Set of Rules: Will China's New Arbitration Laws and Recent Membership in the ICC Improve Trade with China?,* 12 J. INT'L ARB. 51 (1995)

Perkovich, *A Comparative Analysis of Community Mediation in the United States and the People's Republic of China,* 10 TEMP. INT'L & COMP. L.J. 313 (1996)

b. Bankruptcy and Reorganization

David, *A Review and Analysis of Enterprise Bankruptcy Laws in China,* 2 INSOLVENCY L.J. 164 (1994)

Harmer, *Insolvency Law and Reform in the People's Republic of China,* 64 FORDHAM L. REV. 2563 (1996)

Note, *Bankruptcy Behind the Great Wall: Should U.S. Businesses Seeking to Invest in the Emerging Chinese Market Be Wary?,* 8 TRANSNAT'L L. 351 (1995)

Minor and Stevens-Minor, *China's Emerging Bankruptcy Law,* 22 INT'L LAW. 1217 (1988)

c. Banking Regulations and Financial Management

ACCOUNTING STANDARDS FOR BUSINESS ENTERPRISES (China Publishing House of Law, 1993)

L. BRAHM, BANKING AND FINANCE IN CHINA (Michie, 1997)

COMMERCIAL BANKING LAW IN THE PRC (Asia Law & Practice, 1995)

Deutsch, *Legislation Profiles: Letter of Credit Legislation,* 4 CHINA LAW NEWS 9–10 (Oct. 1997)

FOREX MANAGEMENT FOR FIEs IN THE PRC (Asia Law & Practice, 1996)

GENERAL RULES ON FINANCIAL AFFAIRS FOR THE ENTERPRISES (China Publishing House of Law, 1993)

P. GRUB AND J. LIN, FOREIGN DIRECT INVESTMENT IN CHINA (Quorum Books, 1991)

G. JAN, HOW TO DO BUSINESS WITH CHINA (American Institute of Technology, 1997)

Lange and Ross, *New Project Finance Measures Further Limit Lenders' Room for Maneuver, in* CHINA LAW & PRACTICE 51–54 (June 1997)

Lam and Kan, *Impact of Recent Changes in China's Foreign Security Measures in China Lending,* 12 J. INT'L BANKING L. 367 (1997)

F. LEES AND K. LIAW, FOREIGN PARTICIPATION IN CHINA'S BANKING AND SECURITIES MARKET (Quorum Books, 1996)

Li, Walker, Fox, Lau, and Leung, *Foreign Exchange Reform in the PRC: Impact on Foreign Direct Investment and State-Owned Enterprises,* 11 J. INT'L BANKING L. 228 (1996)

Y. LUO, INTERNATIONAL INVESTMENT STRATEGIES IN THE PEOPLE'S REPUBLIC OF CHINA (Ashgate, 1998)

Tokley and Ravn, *Banking Law in China,* 2 Asian Com. L. Rev. 163 (July/Aug. 1997)

d. Bibliography Materials and China Law Research

C. JOHNSON, CHINESE LAW: A BIBLIOGRAPHY OF SELECTED ENGLISH-LANGUAGE MATERIALS (Diane Publications, 1995)

Fu, *Select Bibliography on Chinese Business Law: Companies, Joint Venture, Banking, Insurance and Consumer Laws,* 4 CANBERRA L. REV. 257 (1997/1998)

Hom, *Legal Education in the People's Republic of China: A Select Annotated Bibliography of English-Language Materials,* 6 CHINA L. REP. 73 (1989)

Khu, *Selected Bibliography of English-Language Materials on the Law of the People's Republic of China,* 28 COLUM. J. TRANSNAT'L L. 531 (1990)

F. LIN, CHINESE LAW PAST AND PRESENT (Columbia Univ. 1966)

Lung, *Annotated Bibliography of Selected English-Language Literature on Chinese Law,* 6 LEGAL REFERENCE SERVICES Q. 95 (1986)

Luo, *How to Find the Law of the People's Republic of China: A Research Guide and Selective Annotated Bibliography,* 88 LAW LIBR. J. 402 (1996)

Note, *Selected Bibliography: the Reintegration of Hong Kong into China,* 30 VAND. J. TRANSNAT'L L. 793 (1997)

Pinard, *The People's Republic of China: A Bibliography of Selected English-Language Legal Materials,* 3 CHINA L. REP. 46 (1985)

Pinard, *The People's Republic of China: A Bibliography of Selected Annotated English Language Legal Materials,* 6 CHINA L. REP. 11 (1989)

e. Company Law, Securities, and Privatization

Art and Gu, *China Incorporated: The First Corporation Law of the People's Republic of China,* 20 YALE J. INT'L L. 273 (1995)

CHINESE SECURITIES MARKET, STUDIES ON THE CHINESE MARKET ECONOMY SERIES (Gao Shangquan and Chi Fulin, eds.) (Foreign Language Press, 1996)

Han, *China's Company Law: Practicing Capitalism in a Transitional Economy,* 5 PAC. RIM L. & POL'Y J. 457 (1996)

INVESTING IN CHINA B SHARES (W. Zee, ed.) (American Educational Systems, 1991)

Note, *The Company Law of the People's Republic of China,* 13 UCLA PAC. BASIN L.J. 373 (1995)

Note, *"Chinese Characteristics" in Corporate Clothing: Questions of Fiduciary Duty in China's Company Law,* 80 MINN. L. REV. 503 (1995)

Symposium, *Focus on Privatization in China,* 5 DUKE J. COMP. & INT'L L. 145 (1995)

Tomasic, *Company Law and the Limits of the Rule of Law in China,* 4 AUSTL. J. CORP. L. 470 (1995)

G. WANG AND R. TOMASIC, CHINA'S COMPANY LAW (Michie, 1994)

Yu, *The Emerging Framework of China's Business Organizations Law,* 10 TRANSNAT'L LAW. 39 (1997)

f. Contracts and Secured Interests

Cheng and Rosett, *Contract with a Chinese Face: Socially Embedded Factors in the Transformation from Hierarchy to Market, 1978–1989,* 5 J. CHINESE LL. 143 (1991)

Chu, *The New Partnership Enterprise Law of China,* 2 ASIAN COM. L. REV. 154 (July/Aug. 1997)

CREATING AND ENFORCING SECURITY IN THE PRC (Asia Law & Practice, 1997)

R. FOLSOM, INTERNATIONAL BUSINESS AGREEMENTS IN THE PEOPLE'S REPUBLIC OF CHINA (Kluwer Law Tax Publications, 1997)

Grow, *Resolving Commercial Disputes in China: Foreign Firms and the Role of Contract Law,* 14 NW. J. INT'L L. & BUS. 161 (1993)

INVESTING IN CHINESE SECURITIES: STRATEGIES FOR THE FOREIGN INVESTOR (Asia Law & Practice, 1995)

Johnson and Barale, *China's New Security Law,* 11 J. INT'L BANKING L. 31 (1996)

Note, *Taking Mortgage Interests in Real Property under the Guarantee Law of the People's Republic of China,* 21 HASTINGS INT'L & COMP. L. REV. 539 (1998)

Note, *Contract Law in the People's Republic of China: Rule or Tool: Can the PRC's Foreign Economic Contract Law Be Administered According to the Rule of Law?,* 30 VAND. J. TRANSNAT'L L. 495 (1997)

P. POTTER, THE ECONOMIC CONTRACT LAW OF CHINA: LEGITIMATION AND CONTRACT AUTONOMY IN THE PRC (University of Washington Press, 1992)

Webb, *Towards a Contract Law of China: Some Salient Features,* 1996 LLOYD'S MAR. & COM. L.Q. 245 (May 1996)

g. Consumer Protection, Unfair Competition, and Regulatory Issues

D. KING AND G. TONG, CONSUMER PROTECTION IN CHINA: TRANSLATIONS, DEVELOPMENTS AND RECOMMENDATIONS (Rothman, 1991)

L. SAADAT, THE LAWYER'S GUIDE TO CHINA'S TECHNICAL REGULATIONS FOR IMPORTED PRODUCTS (American Bar Association, 2001)

Snell, *The Development of Competition Policy in the People's Republic of China,* 28 N.Y.U. J. INT'L L. & POL. 575 (1996)

Song, *Competition Policy in a Transitional Economy: The Case of China,* 31 STAN. J. INT'L L. 387 (1995)

Wang, *Celebrations Turn to Sorrow: Where Is China's Consumer Protection Law?,* 4 CANBERRA L. REV. 151 (1997/98)

Weiguo, *Fraudulent Conduct and Punitive Damages in the Consumer Protection Law of China,* 4 CANBERRA L. REV. 111 (1997/98)

Yu, *An Unfair Competition Law Without a Core: An Introductory Comparison between U.S. Antitrust Law and the New Law of the People's Republic of China,* 4 IND. INT'L & COMP. L. REV. 315 (1994)

h. Courts, the Judiciary, and Legal Profession

Bai, *Chinese Constitutional Law,* 26 BRACTON L.J. 77 (1994)

Bing, *Assessing China's Legal System of Judicial Review of Administrative Actions,* 8 CHINA L. REP. 1 (1994)

R. BROWN, UNDERSTANDING CHINESE COURTS AND LEGAL PROCESS: LAW WITH CHINESE CHARACTERS (Kluwer Law Tax Publications, 1997)

A. CHEN, AN INTRODUCTION TO THE LEGAL SYSTEM OF THE PEOPLE'S REPUBLIC OF CHINA (Michie, 1992)

Dellapenna, *The Role of Legal Rhetoric in the Failure of Democratic Change in China,* 2 BUFF. J. INT'L L. 231 (1995/96)

Finder, *The Supreme People's Court of the People's Republic of China,* 7 J. CHIN. L. 145 (1993)

Gelatt, *Lawyers in China: The Past Decade and Beyond,* 23 N.Y.U. J. INT'L L. & POL. 751 (1991)

Li, *Teaching, Research, and the Dissemination of International Law in China: The Contribution of Wang Tieya,* 31 CAN. Y.B. INT'L L. 189 (1993)

Nanpinq, *An Ignored Source of Chinese Law: The Gazette of the Supreme People's Court,* 5 CONN. J. INT'L L. 271 (1990)

Note, *Class Action Litigation in China,* 6 HARV. L. REV. 1523 (1998)

Ping, *Chinese Legal Reform: Achievements, Problems and Prospects,* 9 J. CHIN. L. 67 (1995)

R. Reyes, *The Enforcement of Foreign Court Judgments in the People's Republic of China: What the American Lawyer Needs to Know,* 23 BROOK. J. INT'L L. 241 (1997)

Sang, *China's Civil Procedure Law: A New Guide for Dispute Resolution in China,* 26 INT'L LAW. 413 (1992)

Zongling, *The Role of Lawyers in Social Change: China,* 25 CASE W. RES. J. INT'L L. 163 (1993)

i. Criminal Law and Procedure

Chen, *The Criminal Justice System in China: Present Position and Development Trends,* 1 CHINA L.Q. 42 (1996)

J. COHEN, THE CRIMINAL PROCESS IN THE PEOPLE'S REPUBLIC OF CHINA: 1949–1963 (Harvard Univ. Press 1968)

Chen, *The Chinese Criminal Legal System and Its Impact on the Foreign Investor,* 10 CHIN. L. NEWS 1 (1998)

J. HECHT, OPENING TO REFORM?: AN ANALYSIS OF CHINA'S REVISED CRIMINAL PROCEDURE LAW (Lawyers Committee on Human Rights, 1996)

G. MACCORMACK, TRADITIONAL CHINESE PENAL LAW (Edinburgh University Press, 1991)

Wang, *The Judicial Explanation in Chinese Criminal Law,* 43 AM. J. COMP. L. 569 (1995)

C. WING-HUNG LO, CHINA'S LEGAL AWAKENING: LEGAL THEORY AND CRIMINAL JUSTICE IN DENG'S ERA (Hong Kong University Press, 1995)

R. XIN, TRADITION OF THE LAW AND LAW OF THE TRADITION: LAW, STATE AND SOCIAL CONTROL IN CHINA (Greenwood Press, 1997)

THE 1997 CRIMINAL CODE OF THE PEOPLE'S REPUBLIC OF CHINA (W. S. Hein, 1998)

j. Environmental Law

Bachner, *Regulating Pollution in the People's Republic of China: An Analysis of the Enforcement of Environmental Law,* 7 COLO. J. INT'L ENVTL. L. & POL'Y 373 (1996)

Nagle, *The Missing Chinese Environmental Law Statutory Interpretation Cases,* 5 N.Y.U. ENVTL. L.J. 517 (1996)

Ross, *The Next Wave of Environmental Legislation: Tougher Rules Could Have a Significant Impact on Key Chinese Sectors,* Chin. Bus. Rev., July/Aug. 1994, at 30

L. ROSS, ENVIRONMENTAL POLICY IN CHINA (Indiana University Press, 1988)

L. RUILAN, HANDBOOK OF REGULATIONS ON ENVIRONMENTAL PROTECTION IN CHINA (Resources Future, 1995)

V. SMIL, CHINA'S ENVIRONMENTAL CRISIS: AN INQUIRY INTO THE LIMITS OF NATIONAL DEVELOPMENT (East Gate Books, 1993)

Stewart, *Environmental Statutory Interpretation in China and the United States,* 5 N.Y.U. ENVTL. L.J. 556 (1996)

k. Foreign Investment

A COMING OF AGE: DEVELOPMENTS IN SINO-FOREIGN JOINT VENTURES, (N. Campbell, ed.) Advances in Chinese Industrial Studies, Vol. 5, (Jai Press, 1997)

AN INVESTOR'S GUIDE TO CHINA'S PROVINCES AND CITIES, U.S.-China Business Council, Second Edition (R. Gates, ed.) (2003)

BEIJING INVESTMENT GUIDE (jointly published by the Beijing Municipal Foreign Economic and Trade Commission, Beijing Municipal Planning Commission, and the Information Office of Beijing Municipal Government, 1995)

B. BRACHNER AND H. FU, COMMERCIAL LAWS IN THE PEOPLE'S REPUBLIC OF CHINA: REGULATION AND REFORM (Michie, 1995)

Brink and Li, *A Legal and Practical Overview of Direct Investment and Joint Ventures in the "New" China,* 28 J. MARSHALL L. REV. 567 (1995)

BUSINESS LAW IN CHINA: TRADE INVESTMENT AND FINANCE (Daniel A. Lapres and Zhang Yuejiao, eds.) (International Chamber of Commerce, 1997)

D. CHANG, AMERICAN BUSINESS IN CHINA, 1998–1999 (Caravel, 1998)

CHINA INVESTMENT GUIDE (China International Economic Consultants, Inc., CITIC Publishing House, and Longman, 1989)

CHINA INVESTMENT MANUAL (Asia Law & Practice, 1994)

CHINA: PERSPECTIVES (Arthur Anderson & Co., 1993)

CHINESE FOREIGN ECONOMIC LAW: ANALYSIS AND COMMENTARY (R. Mu and W. Guiguo, eds.) (International Law Institute, 1994)

P. CORNE, FOREIGN INVESTMENT IN CHINA: THE ADMINISTRATIVE LEGAL SYSTEM (Transnational Publishers, Inc., 1997)

K. CUTSHAW AND J. ZHANG, CORPORATE COUNSEL'S GUIDE TO DOING BUSINESS IN CHINA (Business Laws, Inc., 1995)

DOING BUSINESS IN CHINA (W. Streng and A. Wilcox, eds.) (Juris Publishing, Inc., 1990)

ESTABLISHING REPRESENTATIVE AND BRANCH OFFICES IN THE PRC (Asia Law & Practice, 1996)

GUIDE TO TRADING AND INVESTING IN SHANGHAI (Gongshang Publishing House, 1994)

Huang, *An Introduction to Foreign Investment Laws in the People's Republic of China,* 28 J. MARSHALL L. REV. 593 (1995)

INVESTMENT IN CHINA (compiled jointly by the Foreign Investment Administration, the China Economic and Trade Consultant Corporation, and the Ministry of Foreign Trade and Economic Cooperation, 1993)

W. JIA, METAMORPHOSIS OF CHINESE FOREIGN INVESTMENT LAWS AND POLICIES: IMPLICATIONS FOR ECONOMIC DEVELOPMENT IN THE 1990S AND BEYOND (Quorum Books, 1994)

LIFE AND DEATH OF A JOINT VENTURE (Asia Law & Practice, 1996)

OBTAINING PRC APPROVALS FOR FIEs AND INFRASTRUCTURE PROJECTS (Asia Law & Practice, 1996)

Z. KHAN, PATTERNS OF DIRECT FOREIGN INVESTMENT IN CHINA (World Bank, 1991)

R. POMFRET, INVESTING IN CHINA: TEN YEARS OF THE OPEN DOOR POLICY (Iowa State University Press, 1991)

PRC JOINT VENTURES: DRAFTING AND NEGOTIATING CONTRACTS (Asia Law & Practice, 1997)

PROCEDURES FOR THE ESTABLISHMENT OF REPRESENTATIVE OFFICES OF FOREIGN ENTERPRISES (Foreign Enterprise Services Corporation, 1996)

THE PROFILE OF AN OPPORTUNITY: THE RISKS AND REWARDS OF INVESTING IN CHINA (D. Bloodworth, ed.) (Times Academic Press, 1995)

Reinganum, *Negotiating Direct Investment in the People's Republic of China,* 1995 PRIV. INV. ABROAD 24:1

J. REUVID, DOING BUSINESS WITH CHINA (Kogan Page Ltd., 1997)

M. ROEHRIG, FOREIGN JOINT VENTURES IN CONTEMPORARY CHINA (St. Martin's Press, 1994)

J. SHAPIRO, DIRECT INVESTMENT AND JOINT VENTURES IN CHINA: A HANDBOOK FOR CORPORATE NEGOTIATIONS (Quorum Books, 1991)

R. STRANGE, J. SLATER, AND L. WANG, TRADE AND INVESTMENT IN CHINA: THE EUROPEAN EXPERIENCE (Routledge, 1998)

H. SUN, FOREIGN INVESTMENT AND ECONOMIC DEVELOPMENT IN CHINA, 1979–1996 (Ashgate, 1998)

Symposium, *Doing Business in China,* 14 NW. J. INT'L L. & BUS. 15 (1993)

G. WANG, BUSINESS LAW OF CHINA: CASES, TEXTS, AND COMMENTARY (Michie, 1993)

H. WATERS, CHINA'S ECONOMIC DEVELOPMENT STRATEGIES FOR THE 21ST CENTURY (Quorum Books, 1997)

Wu, *Joint Venture Law of the People's Republic of China,* 7 CORP. & BUS. L.J. 15 (1994)

Xu and Chew, *Foreign Investment Enterprises in China,* 17 EAST ASIAN EXECUTIVE REP. 9, Dec. 15, 1995

H. ZHENG, CHINA'S CIVIL AND COMMERCIAL LAW (1988)

l. Hong Kong Special Administrative Region

J. DELLAPENNA AND P. NORTON, CHINA AND HONG KONG IN LEGAL TRANSITION: COMMERCIAL AND HUMANITARIAN ISSUES (ABA 2000)

Fung, *The Future Shape of Hong Kong's Legal System,* 1 CHINA L.Q. 48 (1996)

Jordan, *Lost in the Translation: Two Legal Cultures, the Common Law Judiciary and the Basic Law of the Hong Kong Special Administrative Region,* 30 CORNELL INT'L L.J. 335 (1997)

Y. GHAI, HONG KONG: THE CHANGE OF SOVEREIGNTY AND THE BASIC LAW (Hong Kong University Press, 1997)

Symposium, *Hong Kong's Reintegration into the People's Republic of China: Constitutional Issues, Policy Approaches and Human Rights Concerns, and Economic and Legal Implications,* 30 VAND. J. TRANSNAT'L L. 417 (1997)

m. Industry-Specific Articles/Publications

Jianduan, *A Milestone of Air Legislation in China: Some Thoughts on the Civil Aviation Law of the People's Republic of China,* 62 J. AIR L. & COM. 823 (Feb./March 1997)

THE REGULATIONS FOR UTILIZATION OF FOREIGN CAPITAL IN CHINA'S POWER INDUSTRY (PRC Ministry of Power, ed.) (Songbin Systems Press, 1997)

M. RYAN, WORLD-WIDE PHARMACEUTICAL IN CHINA: INVESTING IN AND BARGAINING WITH A SOCIALIST STATE IN TRANSITION (Georgetown University, 1995)

Wolf, *The Legal Framework for Joint Development of China's Onshore Oil Resources: Negotiation Strategies and Future Prospects,* 9 J. CHIN. L. 141 (1995)

n. Insurance Regulations

Chaput, *An Introduction to Insurance Law and Coverage in the People's Republic of China,* 30 TORT & INS. L.J. 871 (1995)

Qinhuo, *The Legal Protection of the Insured's Rights and Interests under the Insurance Law of China,* 4 CANBERRA L. REV. 189 (1997/98)

Simms, *China's Insurance Law,* CHIN. BUS. REV., Sept./Oct. 1996, at 30

o. Intellectual Property Law

Berkman, *Intellectual Property Rights in the PRC: Impediments to Protection and the Need for the Rule of Law,* 15 UCLA PAC. BASIN L.J. 1 (1996)

Birden, *Technology Transfers to China: An Outline of Chinese Law,* 16 LOY. L.A. INT'L & COMP. L.J. 413 (1994)

Fei, *Copyright Practice in the Two Regimes of One Country: A Prospective Harmonization Process in Hong Kong and the PRC,* 19 EUR. INTELL. PROP. REV. 360 (1997)

Hayward, *China: Registration and Enforcement Procedures: Practical Steps for Doing Business in the PRC,* 76 TRADEMARK WORLD 29 (1995)

Hill and Evans, *Chinese Patent Law: Recent Changes Align China More Closely with Modern International Practice,* 27 GW. J. INT'L L. & ECON. 359 (1993–94)

Lugang, *Customs Protection in the PRC,* 82 TRADEMARK WORLD 12 (1995)

Note, *Protecting Ideas and Ideals: Copyright Law in the People's Republic of China,* 27 LAW & POL'Y INT'L BUS. 1185 (1996)

Note, *The Sleeping Giant Awakens: The Development of Intellectual Property Law in China,* 9 J. CHINA L. 93 (1995)

Note, *China's Copyright Law and the TRIPS Agreement,* 5 J. TRANSNAT'L L. & POL'Y 431 (1996)

Note, *Copyright Law and the People's Courts in the People's Republic of China: A Review and Critique of China's Intellectual Property Courts,* 17 U. PA. J. INT'L ECON. L. 415 (1996)

Ou, *The Practice of Patent Law in China: Some Firsthand Observations,* 15 WIS. INT'L L.J. 313 (1997)

PRACTICAL HANDBOOK OF LAWS OF PEOPLE'S REPUBLIC OF CHINA GOVERNING INTELLECTUAL PROPERTY (J. Min, L. Qin, C. Tian, eds.) (PRC Publishing House of Law 1994)

Ramjerdi and D'Amato, *The Intellectual Property Rights Laws of the People's Republic of China,* 21 N.C. J. INT'L L. & COM. REG. 169 (1995)

Ren, *Copyright Law of China: Can It Effectively Protect U.S. Works?,* 16 LOY. L.A. ENT. L.J. 67 (1995)

Simone, *A Stronger Front Line: New Customs Regulations May Help Enforce Intellectual Property Rights,* CHIN. BUS. REV., Mar./April 1996, at 36

Symposium, *Intellectual Property Protection of Software: International Perspectives,* 14 J. MARSHALL J. COMPUTER & INFO. L. 657 (1996)

Thurston, *Country Risk Management: China and Intellectual Property Protection,* 27 INT'L LAW. 51 (1993)

Wang, *The Chinese Traditions Inimical to the Patent Law,* 14 J. INT'L L. BUS. 15 (1993)

Willard, *The Protection of Computer Software in the People's Republic of China: Current Law and Case Develpments in the "One-Copy" Country,* 14 J. MARSHALL J. COMPUTER & INFO. L. 695 (1996)

p. Labor and Employment

CHINA LABOR AND SOCIAL SECURITY LAW: ESSENTIAL FACTS EXPLAINED (CCH Asia Pacific, 1998)

H. JOSEPHS, LABOR LAW IN CHINA: CHOICE AND RESPONSIBILITY (Michie, 1990)

Josephs, *Labor Law in a "Socialist Market Economy": The Case of China,* 33 COLUM. J. TRANSNAT'L L. 559 (1995)

Li, *Legal Aspects of Labor Relations in China: Critical Issues for International Investors,* 33 COLUM. J. TRANSNAT'L L. 522 (1995)

Lo, *Labor and Employment in the People's Republic of China: From a Non-Market-Driven to a Market-Driven Economy,* 6 IND. INT'L & COMP. L. REV. 337 (1996)

Williams and Woo, *The "Worthy" Unemployed: Societal Stratification and Unemployment Insurance Programs in China and the United States,* 33 COLUM. J. TRANSNAT'L L. 457 (1995)

q. Land Use and Real Property Law

Huang and Hua, *An Overview of China's Real Estate Law,* 28 J. MARSHALL L. REV. 593 (1995)

Kerzner, *The Commercial Real Estate Laws of the People's Republic of China and Shenzhen: An Overview,* 26 VAND. J. TRANSNAT'L L. 581 (1993)

r. Legal History, Theory, and Reform

BASIC CONCEPTS OF CHINESE LAW (T. Lee, ed.) (Garland, 1996)

BASIC PRINCIPLES OF CIVIL LAW IN CHINA (W. Jones, ed.) (M. E. Sharpe, 1989)

G. CHANG, THE COMING COLLAPSE OF CHINA (Random House, 2001)

J. CHEN, FROM ADMINISTRATIVE AUTHORIZATION TO PRIVATE LAW: A COMPARATIVE PERSPECTIVE OF THE DEVELOPING CIVIL LAW IN THE PEOPLE'S REPUBLIC OF CHINA (Martinus-Nijhoff Publishers, 1994)

CHINA'S LEGAL REFORM (S. Lubman, ed.) (Oxford University Press, 1996)

CHINESE LAW AND LEGAL THEORY (M. Palmer, ed.) (NYU Press, 1996)

D. BODDE AND C. MORRIS, LAW AND IMPERIAL CHINA (Harvard Univ. Press, 1967)

E. FARMER, ZHU YUANZHANG, AND, EARLY MING LEGISLATION: THE REORDERING OF CHINESE SOCIETY FOLLOWING THE ERA OF MONGOL RULE (Brill Academic Publications, 1995)

R. FOLSOM, J. MINAN, AND L. OTTO, LAW AND POLITICS IN THE PEOPLE'S REPUBLIC OF CHINA IN A NUTSHELL (West Publishing, 1992)

B. HSU, THE COMMON LAW IN CHINESE CONTEXT (Hong Kong University Press, 1992)

P. HUANG, CIVIL JUSTICE IN CHINA: REPRESENTATION AND PRACTICE IN THE QING (Stanford University Press, 1996)

W. JONES, THE GREAT QING CODE: A NEW TRANSLATION (Oxford University Press, 1994)

Josephs, *Defamation, Invasion of Privacy, and the Press in the People's Republic of China,* 11 UCLA PAC. BASIN L.J. 191 (1993)

R. KEITH, CHINA'S STRUGGLE FOR THE RULE OF LAW (St. Martin's Press, 1994)

Ma, *The Chinese Concept of the Individual and the Reception of Foreign Law,* 9 J. CHIN. L. 207 (1995)

G. MACCORMACK, THE SPIRIT OF TRADITIONAL CHINESE LAW (University of Georgia Press, 1995)

B. MCKNIGHT, LAW AND ORDER IN SUNG CHINA (Cambridge University Press, 1995)

Peerenboom, *Law and Morality in Ancient China: The Silk Manuscripts of Huang-Lao,* 106 YALE L.J. 1885 (1997)

R. SEIDMAN, A. SEIDMAN, AND J. PAYNE, LEGISLATIVE DRAFTING FOR MARKET REFORM: SOME LESSONS FROM CHINA (St. Martin's Press, 1997)

T. STEPHENS, ORDER AND DISCIPLINE IN CHINA: THE SHANGHAI MIXED COURT, 1911–1927 (University of Washington Press, 1991)

R. THOMPSON, CHINA'S LOCAL COUNCILS IN THE AGE OF CONSTITUTIONAL REFORM, 1898–1911 (Harvard University Press, 1995)

S. VAN DER SPRINKEL, LEGAL INSTITUTIONS IN MANCHU CHINA (Athlome Press, 1962)

s. Special Economic Zones

J. PARK, THE SPECIAL ECONOMIC ZONES OF CHINA AND THEIR IMPACT ON ITS ECONOMIC DEVELOPMENT (Praeger Publishers, 1996)

NEW PROGRESS IN CHINA'S SPECIAL ECONOMIC ZONES (G. Shangquan and Chi Fulin, eds.) (Foreign Language Press, 1997)

t. Taxation

A COLLECTION OF TAX LAWS AND REGULATIONS OF THE PEOPLE'S REPUBLIC OF CHINA (China Publishing House of Law, 1994)

THE CHINA TAX AND ACCOUNTING MANUAL (Asia Law & Practice, 1996)

Chui and Yang, *The Value-Added Tax in China: Identifying Important Issues,* 23 INT'L TAX J. 71 (1997)

Curley and Fortunato, *Tax Considerations for Investors in China: A Preliminary Look,* 20 N.C.J. INT'L L. & COM. REG. 531 (1995)

Dauchez and Vernay, *Tax Treatment of FIE Reorganizations,* 11 CHINA L. & PRAC. 55 (July/Aug. 1997)

Gensler, *The 1994 Individual Income Tax Law of the People's Republic of China,* 26 CAL. W. INT'L L.J. 115 (1995)

Gensler, *The 1994 Consumption Tax of the People's Republic of China,* 13 UCLA PAC. BASIN L.J. 293 (1995)

Gensler, *The People's Republic of China Business Tax of 1994,* 8 TRANSNAT'L LAW. 103 (1995)

LU AND TANG, STATE INTERVENTION AND BUSINESS IN CHINA: THE ROLE OF PREFERENTIAL POLICIES (Elgar, 1997)

Mak, *The Historical Development of Income Tax Law for Domestic and Foreign Enterprises in China,* 22 INT'L TAX J. 51 (1996)

Maugue, *Tax Incentives in the People's Republic of China: Who Benefits?,* 5 TUL. J. INT'L & COMP. L. 155 (1997)

Ng, *An Overview of the Turnover Tax System in China and the Tax-Planning Opportunities for Foreign Investors,* 23 INT'L TAX J. 25 (1997)

Note, *China's Choice: Tax Incentives to Fund Economic Development,* 9 TEMP. INT'L & COMP. L.J. 413 (1995)

Peck, Kung, and Ho, *Enter the VAT,* The China Business Review 40–43 (Mar./Apr. 1994)

Sommers and Phillips, *Assessing the Tax Administration Law of the People's Republic of China,* 18 LOY. L.A. INT'L & COMP. L.J. 339 (1996)

Thomson, *Liability to Tax and Transfer Pricing in the People's Republic of China: A Comparative Analysis,* 4 PAC. RIM L. & POL'Y 327 (1995)

Xiangyuan and Huang, *China on the Horizon: Exploring Current Legal Issues: China's New VAT System,* 28 J. MARSHALL L. REV. 619 (1995)

u. Trade Law

Y. CHEN, CHANGING PATTERNS IN CHINESE FOREIGN TRADE LAW AND INSTITUTIONS (Oceana, 1992)

COLLECTION OF LAWS AND REGULATIONS OF CHINA CONCERNING IMPORT/EXPORT COMMODITY INSPECTION (American Overseas Book Company, 1994)

Shen, *Anti-Dumping and Countervailing Laws: An Emerging System in China,* 2 ASIAN COM. L. REV. 135 (July/Aug. 1997)

Wang, *China's New Foreign Trade Law: Analysis and Implications for China's GATT Bid,* 28 J. MARSHALL L. REV. 495 (1995)

B. Electronic Research Guide

Electronic research on the Internet has grown dramatically worldwide. For China-related research, Web sites inside and outside of China provide a variety of information concerning China's laws and regulations, business opportunities, culture, travel, and other matters of interest to foreign investors. Some sites improve over time, some are not maintained, and others contain blatantly incorrect information. Readers that conduct research on the Internet must do so with caution, given that the reliability of information may vary depending upon the objectives and intentions of the Web site sponsor.

1. China-Related and General News Media Sites

The following Web sites are sponsored by China-based media companies:

Business Beijing (http://www.cbw.com): *Business Beijing* is a magazine published monthly by the Information Office of the Beijing Municipal Government, the Beijing Municipal Foreign Economic and Trade Commission, and the Beijing Municipal Planning Commission. The online version of the magazine reprints articles concerning business and legal issues.

Beijing Guide (http://www.beijing-guide.com): *Beijing Guide* is a site co-sponsored by the Beijing Foreign Economic Relations and Trade Commission and the Nengyuan Corporation of Beijing. The site includes information concerning the approval procedures for joint ventures and wholly foreign-owned enterprises.

China Daily (http://www.chinadaily.com.cn): Site sponsored by *China Daily*, China's official English newspaper. Fee-base for access to some information.

People's Daily (http://www.people.com.cn, OR: "english.peopledaily.com .cn" *for English readers*): Fee-based online version in Chinese and English of the government-run newspaper.

Shanghai Daily (http://www.shanghaidaily.com): Fee-based online version of newspaper based in Shanghai that includes regional information.

Other general media sites have articles and stories concerning China business and legal issues, including, but not limited to:

Journal of Commerce (http://www.joc.com): *Washington Post* (http://www.washingtonpost.com), *New York Times* (http://www.nytimes.com), *Los Angeles Times* (http://www.latimes.com), CNN (http://www.cnn.com), *South China Morning Post, Hong Kong* (http://www.scmp.com), and *Hong Kong Standard* (http://www.thestandard.com.hk).

2. Sites Sponsored by Private Companies and Enterprises

Beijing Now (http://www.beijingnow.com): Privately sponsored Web site that includes up-to-date information for business and travelers to the City of Beijing.

China Entrepreneurs Information Services Network (CEISnet) (http://www .ceis.gov.cn): Private Web site providing information about China companies.

Great China Telecom Ltd. (http://www.great-china.net): Information in English and Chinese concerning China trading companies and other information.

Longchuan's Chinese Collections (http://www.ee.tut.fi/~niu/chinese.html): Comprehensive list of links to Chinese publications published worldwide.

Technology Catalyst International (http://www.technology-catalysts.com/strategic_analysis/conchina.htm): Site sponsored by Virginia based Technology Catalysts International, which is a consulting service specializing in the China chemical and food industries.

3. Government Sponsored (P. R. China)

a. Sites Sponsored by Chinese Governmental Organizations

China Council for the Promotion of International Trade (CCPIT) (http://www.ccpit.org): Information concerning trade delegations, trade shows and exhibitions, and procedures for establishing representative offices and sample application forms.

China Law Database (http://www.chinalaw.net): Fee-based site of the State Information Center sponsored by the State Development and Planning Commission, providing all the archives of Chinese laws and regulations issued by the Chinese ministries and each local people's government at municipal and city level.

Chinese Embassy, Washington D.C. (http://www.china-embassy.org): Site sponsored by the PRC government that contains information regarding China visas and passports, travel, politics and diplomacy, and general information about China. *See also* the Web site of the PRC Consulate in Los Angeles (http://www.china.consulatela.org), the PRC Consulate in New York (http://www.nyconsulate.prchina.org), or the PRC Embassy in the United Kingdom (http://www.chinese-embassy.org.uk).

China National Technical Import & Export Corporation (CNTIC) (http://www.cntic.com.cn): This Web site is sponsored CNTIC, which is one of China's largest foreign trading companies specializing in technology trade. The site allows users to search and retrieve information including product name, specifications, usage, company contacts, catalogue information, product photos, and other product data.

Shanghai Environmental Online (http://www.envir.online.sh.cn): Site sponsored by the Shanghai Environment Education Center, which outlines the local environmental protection regulations and provides information on environmental issues.

Wuhan HongDun Industry & Commerce Consultancy Network (en.whhd.gov.cn/intro/aboutweb.htm): English language site sponsored by Wuhan Municipal Administration of Industry and Commerce, which includes economic and commercial information, preferential policies for foreign investment, and translations of the local regulations for development zones.

XinJiang Environmental Protection Bureau (http://www.xjepb.gov.cn): Web site of the XinJiang Environmental Protection Bureau, which has translations of the environmental laws and regulations of China.

Chinese Society of Human Rights Studies (http://www.humanrights-china.org): The Web site contains documents concerning human rights in China including the Chinese government's white paper on human rights.

b. Sites Sponsored by Chinese Government agencies of the State Council

1. Sites of China Judicial Organs

The Supreme People's Court (http://www.court.gov.cn): Chinese Web site of The Supreme People's Court of the People's Republic of China.

The Supreme People's Procuratorate (http://www.spp.gov.cn): Chinese Web site of The Supreme People's Procuratorate of the People's Republic of China.

2. Sites Sponsored by Ministries and Commissions under Direct Control of the State Council

Ministry of Agriculture (http://www.agri.gov.cn): Web site sponsored by the MOA, in Chinese only.

Ministry of Civil Affairs (http://www.mca.gov.cn): Web site of the MCA, in Chinese only.

Ministry of Commerce (MOFCOM) (http://www.mofcom.gov.cn): Comprehensive site of MOFCOM that includes English translations of customs, foreign investment, environmental protection, and taxation laws. The site also provides information concerning trade shows, the top Chinese enterprises, and trade statistics. MOFCOM was established from the recent merger of the former Ministry of Foreign Trade and Economic Cooperation (known as MOFTEC) and the State Economic and Trade Commission (known as SETC).

Ministry of Communications (http://www.moc.gov.cn): Web site of MOC, in Chinese only.

Ministry of Construction (http://www.cin.gov.cn): Web site of the Ministy of Construction, in Chinese only.

Ministry of Culture (http://www.ccnt.gov.cn): English and (simplified and traditional) Chinese Web site of CCNT, with special edition of information for overseas Chinese.

Ministry of Education (http://www.moe.edu.cn): Chinese Web site of MOE.

Ministry of Foreign Affairs (http://www.fmprc.gov.cn): Web site of the MOFA in English, simplified and traditional Chinese, French, and three other languages.

Ministry of Finance (http://www.mof.gov.cn): English and Chinese Web site of MOF with information concerning policies and regulations.

Ministry of Health (http://www.moh.gov.cn): Chinese Web site of MOH.

Ministry of Information Industry (http://www.mii.gov.cn): Chinese Web site of MII.

Ministry of Justice (http://www.legalinfo.gov.cn): Chinese Web site of MOJ.

Ministry of Labour and Social Security (http://www.molss.gov.cn): Chinese Web site of MOLSS.

Ministry of Land and Resources (http://www.mlr.gov.cn): English and Chinese Web site of MLR.

Ministry of Personnel (http://www.mop.gov.cn): Chinese Web site of MOP.

Ministry of Public Security (http://www.mps.gov.cn): Chinese Web site of MPS.

Ministry of Railway (http://www.chinamor.cn.net): Chinese Web site of MOR.

Ministry of Science and Technology (http://www.most.gov.cn): English and Chinese Web site of MOST.

Ministry of Water Resources (http://www.mwr.gov.cn): Chinese Web site of MWR.

National Audit Office (http://www.audit.gov.cn): English and Chinese Web site of the National Audit Office.

National Development and Reform Commission (http://www.sdpc.gov.cn): Chinese Web site of NDRC (formerly known as the State Development and Planning Commission, i.e. "SDPC").

National Population and Family Planning Commission (http://www.sfpc.gov.cn): English and Chinese Web site of SFPC.

People's Bank of China (http://www.pbc.gov.cn): English and Chinese Web site of PBOC.

State Commission of Science, Technology and Industry for National Defense (http://www.costind.gov.cn): Web site of COSTIND, in Chinese only.

State Ethnic Affairs Commission (http://www.seac.gov.cn): Web site of SEAC, accession by public restricted.

[Note: No Web site is available to the Ministry of National Defense, the Ministry of Supervision, and the Ministry of State Security of the People's Republic of China.]

3. Special Organ under the Direct Control of the State Council

State Assets Regulatory and Management Commission of State Council (http://www.sasac.gov.cn): English and Chinese Web site of SASAC.

4. Sites Sponsored by Bureaus and Administrations of the State Council

Counselor's Office of the State Council (http://www.counsellor.gov.cn): Chinese Web site of the Counselor's Office of the State Council, which mainly consists of democratic members and patriotic nonpartisans and is responsible for the united front work.

General Administation of Civil Aviation of China (http://www.caac.gov.cn): Chinese Web site of CAAC.

General Administration of Customs (http://www.customs.gov.cn): Chinese Web site sponsored by GAC.

General Administration of Quality Supervision, Inspection and Quarantine (http://www.aqsiq.gov.cn): Chinese Web site sponsored by GAQSIQ.

Government Offices Administration of State Council (http://www.ggj.gov.cn): Chinese Web site of the Government Offices Administration of State Council.

National Bureau of Statistics (http://www.stats.gov.cn): Web site of NBS in English and simplified and traditional Chinese.

National Copyright Administration (http://www.ncac.gov.cn): Chinese Web site of NCAC providing information mainly regarding administration over copyrights in China.

National Tourism Admnistration (http://www.cnta.gov.cn): Web site sponsored by NTA providing information in English, Chinese, and Japanese.

State Administration of Industry and Commerce (http://www.saic.gov.cn): Chinese Web site of SAIC providing information regarding administration, laws, and regulations on fair trade, consumer rights protection, market regulation, domestic and foreign enterprises registration, advertisement supervision, individual and private company supervision, and trademark registration, prosecution, and adjudication.

State Administration of Radio, Film and Television (http://www.sarft.gov.cn): Chinese Web site of SARFT.

State Administration of Religious Affairs (http://www.sara.gov.cn): Web site of SARA, public access restricted.

State Administration of Safe Production Supervision (http://www.chinasafety.gov.cn): Chinese Web site of SASPS, it is also known as State Administration of Coal Mining Safety (SACMS) with regard to supervision and administration of coal mining work safety.

State Food and Drug Administration (http://www.sda.gov.cn): Chinese Web site of SFDA.

State Environment Protection Administration (http://www.zhb.gov.cn): Chinese Web site of SEPA.

State Forestry Bureau (http://www.forestry.gov.cn): Chinese Web site of SFB.

State General Administration of Sports (http://www.sport.gov.cn): Chinese Web site of SGAS with links to over 40 other national and local sites relating to sports.

State Intellectual Property Office (http://www.sipo.gov.cn): formerly known as China Patent Office, the Web site is sponsored by SIPO, which is responsible for evaluating patent applications. The site includes information regarding Chinese laws and regulations on patent.

State Administration of Taxation (http://www.chinatax.gov.cn): Chinese Web site of the SAT.

c. Sites Sponsored by Offices of State Council

Legislative Affairs Office (http://www.chinalaw.gov.cn): Web site sponsored by the State Council Legislative Affairs Office providing information regarding legislation in China in English and simplified and traditional Chinese.

Taiwan Affairs Office (http://www.gwytb.gov.cn): Simplified and traditional Chinese Web site of the State Council Taiwan Affairs Office.

[Note: The State Council also has some other offices known as the Foreign Affairs Office, Overseas Chinese Affairs Office, Hong Kong and Macao Affairs Office, Economic Restructuring Office, Information Office, and Research Office; they either do not have any Web sites or restrict public access to their sites.]

d. Sites Sponsored by Institutions under Direct Control of State Council

China Banking Regulatory Commission (http://www.cbrc.gov.cn): English and Chinese Web sites of CBRC.

China Seismological Bureau (http://www.csb.gov.cn): Chinese Web site of CSB.

China Insurance Regulatory Commission (http://www.circ.gov.cn): Chinese Web sites of CIRC.

China Meteorological Administration (http://www.cma.gov.cn): English and Chinese Web sites of CMA.

China Securities Regulatory Commission (http://www.csrc.gov.cn): English and Chinese Web sites of CSRC.

Chinese Academy of Science (http://www.cashq.ac.cn): English and Chinese Web sites of CAS.

Chinese Academy of Social Science (http://www.cass.net.cn): English and Chinese Web sites of CASS.

Chinese Academy of Engineering (http://www.cae.cn): Chinese Web sites of CAE.

Development Research Center of State Council (http://www.drc.gov.cn): English and Chinese Web sites of DRC.

National Natural Science Foundation (http://www.nsfc.gov.cn): Web site of NSFC providing information in both English and Chinese (simplified and traditional).

National School of Administration (http://www.nsa.gov.cn): Chinese Web sites of NSA.

State Electricity Regulatory Commission (http://www.serc.gov.cn): Chinese Web sites of SERC.

Xinhua News Agency (http://www.xinhua.org): Site sponsored by the PRC's state-run news agency.

[Note: The National Council of Social Security Fund is also a governmental organ under the direct control of the State Council; it hasn't established its own Web site yet.]

e. Sites Sponsored by Bureaus Supervised by Commissions and Ministries

State Administration of Cultural Heritage (http://www.sach.gov.cn): Chinese Web site of SACH, which is supervised by the Ministry of Culture.

State Administration of Foreign Exchange (http://www.safe.gov.cn): English and Chinese Web site of SAFE, which is supervised by the People's Bank of China.

State Administration of Foreign Experts Affairs (http://www.safea.gov.cn): Chinese Web site of SAFEA, which is supervised by the Ministry of Personnel.

State Administration of Traditional Chinese Medicine (http://www.satcm.gov.cn): English and Chinese Web site of SATCM, which is supervised by the Ministry of Health.

State Archives Administration (http://www.saac.gov.cn): Chinese Web site of SAAC.

State Bureau of Surveying and Mapping (http://www.sbsm.gov.cn): Chinese Web site of SBSM, which is supervised by the Ministry of Land and Resources.

State Grain Administration (http://www.chinagrain.gov.cn): English and Chinese Web site of SGA, which is supervised by the State Development and Reform Commission.

State Oceanic Administration (http://www.soa.gov.cn): Chinese Web site of SOA, which is supervised by the Ministry of Land and Resources.

State Post Bureau (http://www.chinapost.gov.cn): Chinese Web site of SPB, which is supervised by the Ministry of Information Industry.

State Tobacco Monopoly Administration (http://www.tobacco.gov.cn): Chinese Web site of STMA, which is supervised by the Ministry of Commerce.

[Note: The State Bureau for Letters and Calls and the National Administration for the Protection of State Secrets are also bureaus supervised by commissions and ministries; however, no Web site was found for direct online information for either of the two.]

4. Government Sponsored (United States)

U.S. Embassy, Beijing (http://www.usembassy-china.org.cn): Contains U.S. publications prepared by Embassy staff concerning political, commercial, and consular affairs. The site also includes useful links to other China-related sites.

United States Trade Representative (http://www.ustr.gov): Information concerning trade relations between the U.S. and China, trade barrier information, including China's customs rules, export licensing, and tariff policies, and the U.S. position concerning China's entry to the WTO.

Department of Commerce, International Trade Administration (http://www.ita.doc.gov): ITA site consists of industry-specific information for China.

5. Other China-Related Sites

a. China Business and Economy Sites

Business Weekly on the Web (http://www.chinadaily.com.cn/en/bw/index.html): Weekly report prepared by the *China Daily* on news, investment, trade, finance, etc.

China and Taiwan Exporter Directory (manufacture.com.tw): Taiwan Products Online.

China Online (http://www.chinaonline.com): ChinaOnline is a business information service that offers information on the business climate in China.

Chinabiz.org (http://www.chinabiz.org): ChinaBiz provides online information about China business.

ChinaWeb (http://www.sd.cninfo.net/song/chinaweb.htm): ChinaWeb is a bilingual, online financial service dedicated to news, information, and insights on the Greater China market.

b. China News and Media

CCC News (http://www.cccnews.com): Online news for worldwide Chinese. In English and Chinese.

China.com (http://www.welcome-to-china.com): Tourist/business e-magazine.

Asian Studies (http://www.asianstudies.com): News on China and Hong Kong.

China News (http://www.chinanews.com): News on the Chinese Central Government.

China News Digest (http://www.cnd.org): Online news about China.

China Online (http://www.chinaonline.com): Business news and analysis service for the Chinese marketplace.

China Regional News (http://www.chinapages.com): News about China.

China Reporters (http://www.chinareporter.com): Web site featuring business news about China.

Chinese Daily Digest (http://www.digest.demon.co.uk): Web site covers Greater China.

China Economy (ce.cei.gov.cn): English Web site covers economic news in China.

China Business Monitor Newsletter (http://www.friedlnet.com/c/friedlnet_newsletter.html): A free weekly e-mail alert from FriedlNet.com, which provides China business and economic news and analysis (English only).

c. Non-Ministerial National Web Sites

APEC (211.99.196.218/apec/english/Eindex.htm).

Beijing Olympics 2008 (http://www.beijing-olympic.org).

China Human Resources Market (http://www.chrm.gov.cn).

China Internet Information Center (http://www.china.org.cn).

China Light Industry Information (http://www.clii.com.cn).

China National Tourism Association (http://www.cnta.com).

China Non-Ferrous Metal Information Network (http://www.atk.com.cn).

Institute of Software (http://www.ios.ac.cn).

d. Local Governmental Sites

Shanghai (http://www.shanghai.gov.cn).

Shanghai Foreign Investment Service Center (http://www.sfisc.com).

Great Britain-China Center (http://www.gbcc.org.uk): Site is sponsored by the UK's Foreign and Commonwealth Office and includes general business information concerning China.

University of Maryland School of Law, Chinalaw Web (http://www.qis.net/chinalaw): University-sponsored site that includes translations of certain China laws and regulations, summaries concerning legal issues, and other helpful information.

6. Fee-Based Research Services

China Infobank (http://www.chinainfobank.com): Fee-based online version providing analysis, articles, reports regarding China's economic information.

China Law and Practice (http://www.chinalawandpractice.com): Fee-based online version in both Chinese and English published by Asia Law & Practice, providing analysis, articles, and digests regarding China's legislation, and full-text translation of Chinese laws and regulations.

Economist Intelligence Unit (http://www.eiu.com): Fee-based site that includes legal and business information for China.

Isinolaw (http://www.isinolaw.com): Fee-based online version in both Chinese and English providing analysis, articles, and summaries regarding China's legislation, and full-text translation of Chinese laws and regulations.

Lexis-Nexis (http://www.lexis.com): Online legal research service with extensive international law and international trade law libraries. Select laws and regulations are available at INTLAW Library, CHINA File.

7. Trade Associations

American Chamber of Commerce in China (www.amcham-china.org.cn) and Hong Kong (http://www.amcham.org.hk): Sites include information about business and legal issues affecting Hong Kong and China.

Hong Kong Trade Development Council (http://www.tdctrade.com): Site sponsored by the Hong Kong Trade Development Council that includes China-related business information.

U.S.-China Business Council (http://www.uschina.org): Site sponsored by the U.S.-China Business Council that contains information regarding general business in China. Some materials are accessible for members only.

8. International Organizations

Asian Development Bank (http://www.adb.org): Information concerning the activities of the Asian Development Bank with some documents specifically relating to China.

International Monetary Fund (http://www.imf.org): The site contains information concerning the work of the IMF. Some reports are available concerning the economic stability and growth of China and Hong Kong.

World Bank (http://www.worldbank.org): Information concerning World Bank activities, including information involving China's World Bank Projects, environmental projects and cooperation, and economic information concerning China.

World Trade Organization (http://www.wto.org): Contains publications and information concerning the activities of the WTO. Some China-related information can be found on the site.

Appendix C

Contact Information

A. Chinese Government Organizations

All-China Federation of Industry and Commerce
Huang Mengfu, Chairman
93 Beiheyan Dajie, Dongcheng
Beijing 100006, China
Tel: (86-10) 6513 6677
Fax: (86-10) 6513 1769

State Administration for Entry-Exit Inspection and Quarantine of P.R. China
9 Ma Dian Dong Lu, Haidian
Beijing 100088, China
Tel: (86-10) 8226 1600
Fax: (86-10) 8226 0011

China Council for the Promotion of International Trade
Zhong Min, Chairman
1 Fuxingmenwai Street
Beijing 100860, China
Tel: (86-10) 6801 3344 ext. 8210
Fax: (86-10) 6801 1370

China National Automotive Industry Corporation
Gu Raotian, President
Mao Junmen, Director of Foreign Affairs
No 46 Fu Cheng Road
Beijing 100036, China
Tel: (86-10) 8812 3968
Fax: (86-10) 8812 5556

China National Cereals, Oils, & Foodstuffs Import & Export Corporation (COFCO) Zhou, Mingchen, President Lu Jianyi, President's Office Tower A, COFCO Plaza, No. 8 Jianguo Men Nei Da Jie Beijing 100005, China	Tel: (86-10) 6527 1818 Fax: (86-10) 6527 8612
China National Offshore Oil Corp. Fu Chengyu, President 6 Dong Wai Xia Jie Beijing 100027, China	Tel: (86-10) 8452 1010 Fax: (86-10) 6460 2600
China Patent Office No. 6 Xituchenglu, Haidian Beijing 100088, China	Tel: (86-10) 6208 3114 Fax: (86-10) 6201 9307
Civil Aviation Administration of China 155 Dongsixidajie Beijing 100710, China	Tel: (86-10) 6401 5931 Fax: (86-10) 6513 5959
General Administration of Customs Mou Xinsheng, Director Liu Yulin, Director of Foreign Affairs 6 Jianguomennei Dajie, Beijing 100730, China	Tel: (86-10) 6519 5008 Fax: (86-10) 6519 5394, 6519 4004
Ministry of Agriculture Du Qinglin, Minister 11 Nongzhanguang Nanli, Chanyang District Beijing 100026, China	Tel: (86-10) 6419 1114 Fax: (86-10) 6419 2468
Ministry of Communications Zhang Chunxian, Minister Hu Jinlu, Foreign Affairs Office 11 Jianguomennei Dajie, Dongcheng District Beijing 100736, China	Tel: (86-10) 6529 2114 Fax: (86-10) 6529 2345
Ministry of Construction Wang Guangtao, Minister 9 Rd. San Li He, Haidian Beijing 100835, China	Tel: (86-10) 6839 4114

Ministry of Information Industry Wang Xudong, Minister Yang Shilian, International Cooperation 13 Xicnang'anjie Beijing 100804, China	Tel: (86-10) 6601 4249 Fax: (86-10) 6201 6362
Ministry of Commerce Lu Fuyuan, Minister U.S. Affairs Division American & Oceanian Affairs Department 2 Dong Chang'anjie Dongcheng District Beijing 100731, China	Tel: (86-10) 6519 8114 Foreign Trade Division: 6519 7420 Foreign Investment Division: 6519 7304; 6519 7332 Foreign Affairs Office: 6519 8577; 6519 8203 Law Treaty Division: 6519 8723 Bureau of Fair Trade for Import and Export Tel: (86-10) 6519 8477/8969
Ministry of Justice (MOJ) Zhang Fusen, Minister 10 Chaoyangmen Nandajie Beijing 100020, China	Tel: (86-10) 6520 5114 Department of Lawyers: (86-10) 6520 5908 Foreign Affairs Division: (86-10) 6520 6239
Ministry of Labor and Social Security Zheng Silin, Minister Lin Maizhu, Director of Foreign Affairs 12 Hepinglizhongjie, Dongcheng District Beijing 100716, China	Tel: (86-10) 8420 1114
Ministry of Land and Natural Resources Sun Wensheng, Minister 64 Funeidajie, Xicheng District Beijing 100812, China	Tel: (86-10) 6655 8001 Fax: (86-10) 6655 8004
Ministry of National Defense Cao Gangchuan, Minister 20 Jingshanqianjie Beijing 100009, China	Tel: (86-10) 6673 0000 Fax: (86-10) 6201 8356

Ministry of Health — Tel: (86-10) 6879 2114
Wu Yi, Minister
1 Rd. Xi Zhi Men Wai Nan
Beijing 100044, China

Ministry of Public Security — Tel: (86-10) 6520 2114
Zhou Yongkang, Minister
14 Dongchangan Jie
Beijing 100741, China

Ministry of Railways — Tel: (86-10) 5184 0114
Liu Zhijun, Minister
10 Fuxingjie, Haidian District
Beijing 100844, China

Ministry of Water Resources — Tel: (86-10) 6320-2114
Wang Shu Cheng, Minister
2 Beiguanglu Ertiao, Xuanwu District
Beijing 100053, China

People's Bank of China — Tel: (86-10) 6619 4114; Fax: (86-10) 6601 5346
Zhou Xiaochuan, Governor
Jin Qi, Director of Foreign Affairs
32 Chengfangjie, Xicheng District
Beijing 100800, China

China Insurance Regulatory Commission — Tel: (86-10) 6601 6688; Fax: (86-10) 6601 1869, 6602 5862
Wu Dingfu, President
Ran Haiquong, Division Chief
410 Fuchengmen Dajie
Beijing 100034, China

Petrochemical Industry Bureau (formerly the Ministry of Chemical Industry) — Tel: (86-10) 6492 0183; Fax: (86-10) 6492 0162
Li Yong Wu, Minister
Shen Wei, International Cooperation
Building 16, Section 4
An Hui Li, Chaoyao District
Beijing 100723, China

State Administration for Industry and Commerce — Tel: (86-10) 6803 2233; Fax: (86-10) 6803 3403
Wang Zhongfu, Director
8 Sanlihe Donglu, Xichengqu
Beijing 100820, China

State Administration for Commodity Inspection
Li Changjiang, Director
9 Ma Dian Dong Lu, Haidian District
Beijing 100088, China
Tel: (86-10) 8226 0114

State Administration of Foreign Exchange (SAFE)
Guo Shuqing, Director
Fl. 4, Ping An Plaza, Finance Avenue
Beijing, 100032, China
Tel: (86-10) 6621 8899
Fax: (86-10) 6840 2277
Beijing Bureau: 6519 9562; 6519 9557

State Administration of Taxation
5 Yang Fang Dian Xi Lu, Haidian District
Beijing 100053, China
Tel: (86-10) 6341 7114

State Council Intellectual Property Office
Wang Jingchuan, Director-General
6 Xi Tu Cheng Lu, Ji Men Qiao
Xicheng District
Beijing 100088, China
Tel: (86-10) 6209 3114

State Development Planning Commission
Ma Kai, Minister
Xun Tongmao, Director of Foreign Affairs
38 Yuetan Nanjie, Xicheng District
Beijing 100824, China
Tel: (86-10) 6850 1240
Fax: (86-10) 6850 1090

State Drug Administration
Zheng Xiao Yu, Director
Huang Jiye, Director of Foreign Affairs
38A Beilishilu
Beijing 100810, China
Tel: (86-10) 6831 3344
Fax: (86-10) 6831 5648

State Environmental Protection Agency Administration
Xie Zhenghua, Director
Tang Dingding, Directer of Bilateral Cooperation
115 Xizhimennei Nanxiaojie, Xicheng District
Beijing 100035, China
Tel: (86-10) 6615 3366
Fax: (86-10) 6615 1789

State Forestry Bureau
Wang Zhi Bao, Minister
Yang Yuchou, Director of Foreign Affairs
18 Hepingli Dongjie, Dongcheng District
Beijing 100714, China
Tel: (86-10) 8423 8800
Fax: (86-10) 8423 8751

1. Beijing Government Contacts (City Code: 10)

Beijing Customs
10 Guang Hua Lu
Beijing 100026, China
Duty & Tariff Division: 6539 6400
General Office: 6539 6789

Beijing Foreign Enterprise Service Corporation (FESCO)
No. 18 Chaoyangmen Nan Dajie
Beijing 106020, China
Tel: (86-10) 8541 8888

Beijing Municipal Administration for Industry and Commerce
36 Su Zhou Jie, Haidian District
Beijing 100080, China
Tel: (86-10) 8269 0999

Beijing Municipal Foreign Economic Relations and Trade Commission
190 Chaoyangmennei Dajie
Dong Cheng District
Beijing 100010, China
Tel: (86-10) 6523 6688
Fax: (86-10) 6513 5946

Beijing Local Taxation
8 Che Gong Zhuang Ave, Xicheng District
Beijing 100044, China
Tel: (86-10) 8837 1766

Beijing Development and Planning Commission
D 2 South Street, Fuxingmen,
Beijing 100031, China
Tel: (86-10) 6641 5588
Fax: (86-10) 6641 0891

China International Economics and Trade Arbitration Commission (CIETAC)
6 Fl. Gaolan Plaza, No. 32 Liangmaqiao
Chaoyang District
Beijing 100016, China
Tel: (86-10) 6464 6688
Fax: (86-10) 6464 3500

China Council for the Promotion of International Trade (CCPIT) — Tel: (86-10) 6801 3344; Fax: (86-10) 6801 1370
China Chamber of International Commerce (CCOIC)
1 Fuxingmenwai Street
Beijing 100860, China

China International Talent Development Center (CITDC) — Tel: (86-10) 6561 6688
East Wing 3/F A301 Hanwei Plaza
No. 7 Guanghua Road
Chao Yang District
Beijing 100004, China

2. Shanghai Government Contacts (City Code: 21)

CCPIT Shanghai Pudong Sub-Council — Tel: (86-21) 5081 2626; Fax: (86-21) 5840 5423
No. 135 Dongfang Road
Shanghai 200120, China

CCPIT Shanghai Sub-Council — Tel: (86-21) 5306 0228; Fax: (86-21) 6386 9915
No. 28 Jin Ling Xi Lu
Shanghai 200021, China

Foreign Investment Commission (FIC) — Tel: (86-21) 6236 8800; Fax: (86-21) 6236 8024, (86-21) 6236 8026
Cosmos Tower, 15 Fl.
83 Loushanguan Road
Shanghai 200336, China

Labor Bureau Foreign Employment Administration Office — Tel: (86-21) 6253 1522; Fax (86-10) 6256 2238
215 Jiangxi Road
Shanghai 200000, China

Shanghai Administration for Industry and Commerce — Tel: (86-21) 6422 0000
301 Zhao Jia Bin Street
Shanghai 200032, China

Shanghai Customs — Tel: (86-21) 6323 2410; Fax: (86-21) 6323 2095
13 Zhongshan Dong Yi Lu
Shanghai 200002, China

Shanghai Foreign Economic Service Corporation (FESCO) Rm. 604, No. 227 Huang Pi Rd.(N) Huang Pu District Shanghai 200003, China	Tel: (86-21) 5117 5118 Fax: (86-21) 6375 8929
Shanghai Foreign Investment Center 55 Loushanguan Road Shanghai 200335, China	Tel: (86-21) 6275 5191 Fax: (86-21) 6275 8166
Shanghai Municipal People's Government Foreign Economic Relations and Trade Commission 55 Loushanguan Road Shanghai 200335, China	Tel: (86-21) 6275 2200 Fax: (86-21) 6275 1778
Shanghai Public Security Bureau—Aliens Exit/Entry Administration Division 1 Kuan Shan Lu Shanghai 200080, China	Tel: (86-21) 6357 7097
Shanghai Taxation Bureau, Foreign Taxation Sub-Bureau 31 Jian Guo Zhong Lu Shanghai 200025, China	Tel: (86-21) 6445 9814

3. Shenzhen Government Contacts (City Code: 755)

CCPIT Shenzhen Sub-Council 3009 Xin Zhou Lu, Shenzhen Guangdong 518048, China	Tel: (86-755) 8356 1569; 8356 1519 Fax: (86-755) 8330 1702
Shenzhen Customs 64 Heping Road Shenzhen 518017, China	Tel: (86-755) 8439 8110
Shenzhen Trade Promotion Council (STPC) 6th Fl., No. 3009 Xin Zhou Lu Shenzhen J18048, China	Tel: (86-755) 8356 1658 Fax: (86-755) 8330 1702

4. Chinese Overseas Contacts

China Chamber of Commerce USA Office 100 Lighting Way, 4th Fl. Secaucus, NJ 07094-5611	Tel: (201) 422-8572 Fax: (201) 422-8558

China Council for Promotion of International Trade (CCPIT) 2001 Jefferson Davis Highway, Suite 608 Arlington, VA 22202	Tel: (703) 412-9889 Fax: (703) 412-5889
Chinese Consulate General in Los Angeles 443 Shatto Place Los Angeles, CA 90020	Tel: (213) 380-3104; (213) 380-2602 Fax: (213) 380-1961
Chinese Embassy in Washington, DC 2300 Connecticut Ave., NW Washington, DC 20008	Tel: (202) 328-2500; (202) 328-2523 TLX: 440673 PRCC Ul Fax: (202) 232-7855

B. U.S. Government Offices in China

U.S. Embassy Beijing
No. 3 Xiu Shui Beijie
Beijing 100600, China

Ambassador's Office	Tel: (86-10) 6532 3831 x400
Visa Section	Tel: (86-10) 6532 3431 x253 Fax: (86-10) 6532 3178
American Citizen Services	Tel: (86-10) 6532 3431 x252 Fax: (86-10) 6532 2483
Defense Attache Office	Tel: (86-10) 6532 3831, x600 Fax: (86-10) 6532 2160
Economic Section	Tel: (86-10) 6532 3831 x432 Fax: (86-10) 6532 6422
Foreign Agricultural Service Agricultural Affairs Office	Tel: (86-10) 6532 3431 x275 Fax: (86-10) 6532 2962
Foreign Commercial Service	Tel: (86-10) 6532 6924 x332 Fax: (86-10) 6532 3297

Non-Im Visas, Dennis Halpin	Tel: (86-10) 6532 3431 x240 Fax: (86-10) 6532 2483
Political Section	Tel: (86-10) 6532 3831 x560 Fax: (86-10) 6532 6423
Shanghai Agricultural Trade Office	Tel: (86-21) 6279 8622 Fax: (86-21) 6279 8336
Mailing Address from U.S.: U.S. Embassy Beijing Department of State Washington, DC 20521-7300	
American Consulate Guangzhou No. 1 South Shamian Street Guangzhou 510133, China	Tel: (86-20) 8121 8000 Fax: (86-20) 8121 9001 Tel: (86-20) 8667 4011 Fax: (86-20) 8666 0705
American Consulate Shanghai 1469 Huaihai Zhong Lu Shanghai 200031, China	Tel: (86-21) 6433 6880 Fax: (86-21) 6433 4122 Tel: (86-21) 6279 7630 Fax: (86-21) 6279 7639
American Consulate, Chengdu No. 4 Lilingshiguan Road, Section 4 Renmin Nanlu Chengdu 610041, China	Tel: (86-28) 555 3119; 558 3520 Tel: (86-28) 558 3992 Fax: (86-28) 558 3520
American Consulate, Shenyang No. 52, 14th Wei Road Heping District Shenyang 110003, China	Tel: (86-24) 2322 1198 Fax: (86-24) 2322 2206

C. China-Related U.S. Government Offices in Washington, DC

Office of U.S. Trade Representative China Desk 600 17th Street, NW Washington, DC 20506	Tel: (202) 395-3900 Fax: (202) 395-3911

TPCC Trade Information Center	Tel: 800 USA-TRADE
U.S. Department of Agriculture AgExport Services Division Foreign Agricultural Service Ag Box 1052 14th and Independence Streets, SW Washington, DC 20250-1080	Tel: (202) 720-6343 Fax: (202) 690-4374 Tel: (202) 720-7420
U.S. Department of Agriculture Asia, Africa, and Eastern Europe Division Foreign Agricultural Service Stop 1080 14th and Independence Streets, SW Washington, DC 20250-1080	Tel: (202) 720-1289 Fax: (202) 690-1093
U.S. Department of Commerce International Trade Administration Office of China Economic Area Room 1229 14th Street and Constitution Avenue Washington, DC 20230	Tel: (202) 482-3583 Fax: (202) 482-1576
U.S. Department of State Office of China and Mongolia Bureau of East Asia and Pacific Affairs Room 4318 2201 C Street, NW Washington, DC 20520	Tel: (202) 647-6796 Fax: (202) 647-6820

D. Trade Associations

1. Chinese Trade Associations

China Association of Enterprises with Foreign Investment 8 Yong An Dong Li, Jian Wai Da Jie Beijing 100022, China	Tel: (86-10) 8528 8917 Fax: (86-10) 8528 8906
China Chamber of Commerce for Import and Export of Foodstuffs, Native Produce and Animal By-Products 21 Xitangzi Lane, Dongcheng District Beijing 100006, China	Tel: (86-10) 6513 2567; (86-10) 6513 6677 Fax: (86-10) 6513 9064

China Chamber of Commerce for Import and Export of Light Industrial Products and Arts and Crafts 11 Xinghua Road Hepingli Beijing 100013, China	Tel: (86-10) 6773 2686 Fax: (86-10) 6773 2689
China Chamber of Commerce for Import and Export of Machinery and Electronic Products 14th Floor, North Office Tower New World Centre No. 3B, Chongwenmenwai Street Chongwen District Beijing 100062, China	Tel: (86-10) 6709 2712; 6709 2711 Fax: (86-10) 6709 2613; 6709 2615
China Chamber of Commerce for Import and Export of Textile 7 Fl., No. 12 Nanli, Pan Jia Yuan Chaoyang District Beijing 100021, China	Tel: (86-10) 6773 9291 Fax: (86-10) 6513 6202
China Chamber of Commerce of Medicines and Health Products Import and Export 8 Fl., No. 12 Nanli, Pan Jia Yuan Chaoyang District Beijing 100021, China	Tel: (86-10) 6773 4761 Fax: (86-10) 6773 4768
China Chamber of Commerce of Metals, Minerals and Chemicals Import and Export 5 Fl., Langang Building, A1, Nanshoupokou Guanganmemwai Beijing 100055, China	Tel: (86-10) 6725 3441 Fax: (86-10) 6348 8940
China International Contractors Association Fl. 10, A, 15, San Li He Street Beijing 100037, China	Tel: (86-10) 8808 3099

2. Foreign Trade Associations

American Chamber of Commerce in Beijing Charles M. Martin, Chairman China Resources Building, #1903 8 Jianguomenbei Dajie Beijing 100005, China	Tel: (86-10) 8519 1920 Fax: (86-10) 8519 1910

Australian Chamber of Commerce
8th Fl., Office Tower Beijing Hong Kong
Macau Centre (Swissotel)
2 Chaoyangmenbei Dajie
Beijing 100027, China
Tel: (86-10) 6595 9252
Fax: (86-10) 6595 9253

British Chamber of Commerce
The British Centre, Room 1001
China Life Tower
No. 16 Chaoyangmenwai Avenue
Beijing 100020, China
Tel: (86-10) 8525 1111
Fax: (86-10) 8525 1100

Canada–China Business Council
CITIC Tower, Room 18-2
19 Jianguomenwai Dajie
Beijing 100004, China
Tel: (86-10) 6512 6120;
(86-10) 6500 2255
ext. 1820 or 1821
Fax: (86-10) 6512 6125

China Office:
CITIC Building
Room 260
Beijing 100004, China
Tel: (86-10) 6500 2255
ext. 2664 or 2670
Fax: (86-10) 6512 5854;
6592 0727

French Chamber of Commerce and Industry
S123 Office Building, Lufthansa Center
50 Liangmaqiao Road
Chaoyang District
Beijing 100016, China
Tel: (86-10) 8451 2071
Fax: (86-10) 8451 2068

U.S.–China Business Council
Robert Kapp, President
1818 N Street, NW, Suite 500
Washington, DC 20036-5559
Tel: (202) 429-0340
Fax: (202) 775-2476

CITIC Building, Suite 902
19 Jianguomenwai Ave.
Beijing 100004, China
Tel: (86-10) 6592 0727;
(86-10) 6500-2255
ext. 3920/3921
Fax: (86-10) 6512 5854

E. Bar Associations

All China Lawyers Association
5th Fl., Qing Lan Mansion
24 Dong Si Shi Tiao
Beijing 100007, China
Tel. (86-10) 6406 0213

Index